MW00760294

To the Student:

This text was created to provide you with a high-quality educational resource. As a publisher specializing in college texts for business and economics, our goal is to provide you with learning materials that will serve you well in your college studies and throughout your career.

The educational process involves learning, retention, and the application of concepts and principles. You can accelerate your learning efforts utilizing the supplements accompanying this text:

- Study Guide for use with Corporate, Partnership, Estate and Gift Taxation, 1992 Edition; and
- 1990 Tax Return Practice Problems for Corporations, S Corporations, and Partnerships.

These learning aids are designed to improve your performance in the course by highlighting key points in the text and providing you with assistance in mastering basic concepts.

Check your local bookstore, or ask the manager to place an order for you today.

We at Irwin sincerely hope this text package will assist you in reaching your goals, both now and in the future.

CORPORATE, PARTNERSHIP, ESTATE AND GIFT TAXATION

1992 Edition

CORPORATE, PARTNERSHIP, ESTATE AND GIFT TAXATION

1992 Edition

GENERAL EDITORS

James W. Pratt, D.B.A., C.P.A.
Jane O. Burns, Ph.D., C.P.A.
William N. Kulsrud, Ph.D., C.P.A.

CONTRIBUTING AUTHORS:

Jane O. Burns, Ph.D., C.P.A.
Texas Tech University

Edward J. Schnee, Ph.D., C.P.A.
University of Alabama

Marguerite R. Hutton, Ph.D., C.P.A.
Western Washington University

Jerrold J. Stern, Ph.D.
Indiana University

Sally M. Jones, Ph.D., C.P.A.
University of Texas at Austin

Steven C. Thompson, Ph.D., C.P.A.
University of Houston

William N. Kulsrud, Ph.D., C.P.A.
Indiana University

John C. Tripp, Ph.D., C.P.A.
University of Denver

Michael A. O'Dell, Ph.D., C.P.A.
Arizona State University

Michael J. Tucker, J.D., Ph.D., C.P.A.
George Mason University

Nathan Oestreich, Ph.D., C.P.A.
San Diego State University

James L. Wittenbach, D.B.A., C.P.A
University of Notre Dame

James W. Pratt, D.B.A., C.P.A.
University of Houston

TAXATION SERIES

Homewood, IL 60430
Boston, MA 02116

Sponsoring editor: Ron M. Regis
Project editor: Margaret S. Haywood
Production manager: Irene H. Sotiroff
Compositor: Publication Services, Inc.
Typeface: 11/13 Times Roman
Printer: R.R. Donnelley & Sons Company

ISBN 0-256-10043-8
ISSN 0742-7824

Printed in the United States of America

1 2 3 4 5 6 7 8 9 0 DO-W 8 7 6 5 4 3 2 1

PREFACE

This text is designed for use by undergraduate or graduate accounting, business, or law students in their study of advanced topics in Federal taxation. The text emphasizes those areas of taxation generally accepted as essential to the education of those pursuing careers in taxation or tax-related fields. The first eight chapters are devoted to the tax problems of regular corporations and their shareholders. These chapters are followed by a separate chapter examining the special problems of international taxation, an area of growing importance. Two chapters consider the taxation of partnerships and partners while one chapter examines S corporations. Federal estate and gift taxation is discussed in one chapter. Two additional chapters contain the related topics of the income taxation of estates, trusts, and beneficiaries and the major aspects of family tax planning.

For those students who have not had previous exposure to tax research, a separate chapter provides an introduction to this important topic. The skills explained in this chapter may be applied to the research questions contained at the end of most chapters. In addition, a chapter is devoted to the procedural aspects of taxation, including the special concerns for those involved in tax practice.

The scope of this text is intentionally broad to accommodate a variety of uses and to provide flexibility for instructors in designing advanced tax courses. It is neither our intention nor our belief that all of the contents can or should be covered in a single three-semester-hour course. The sheer technical detail of the material presented is obviously more than can be covered in one course without selective pruning. Our hope is that instructors can adapt the text to satisfy their varying needs. In this regard, the ample coverage of what we believe are the most relevant topics—filled with examples and exhibits—should meet the desires of the most demanding users.

A typical use for this text is in a second course in taxation which emphasizes research while concentrating on taxation of business enterprises: corporations and partnerships. Chapter 16 contains the material concerning tax research. Although this material appears later in the text, the chapter is a self-contained unit that may be assigned at any point during the course. Several users who emphasize tax research have reported that this chapter is assigned and research projects are required even though the topic is not explicitly covered in the classroom.

Chapter 1 introduces the subject of business taxation by providing an overview of the various forms of business organization (e.g., corporations—regular and S—partnerships, and trusts). After this review, the chapter proceeds to examine the fundamentals of corporate income taxation by contrasting the taxation of corporations with that of individuals. Consideration of corporate taxation is continued in Chapter 2 as the problems of forming a corporation, including the design of the corporation's capital structure, are addressed. Chapters 3 and 4 examine the tax consequences relating to nonliquidating corporate distributions.

These chapters consider cash and property dividends, stock redemptions, and partial liquidations. To manage the numerous topics covered in these two chapters, instructors may wish to emphasize some subjects to the exclusion of others. Chapter 5 completes the discussion of corporate distributions with coverage of complete liquidations and collapsible corporations. The special penalty taxes applying to corporations—the personal holding company tax and the accumulated earnings tax—are the subject of Chapter 6. Many instructors may choose to teach this chapter following Chapter 2 (concerning organization) to illustrate some of the risks of incorporation and to provide the rationale for many of the distribution problems considered in Chapters 3, 4, and 5. The following two chapters, Chapter 7 on corporate reorganizations and Chapter 8 on consolidated returns, delve into special aspects of corporate taxation. Many instructors may wish to omit these chapters in order to give greater coverage to other topics. Chapter 9 contains an overview of the problems of international taxation. This chapter provides an excellent vehicle for those wishing an introduction to this subject. Chapter 10 explores the basic problems of partnership taxation—primarily formation and operation—while Chapter 11 examines special considerations in partnership taxation such as the sale of a partnership interest, liquidating distributions, family partnerships, and tax shelter limited partnerships. Chapter 12 completes the sequence of chapters on business taxation by discussing the taxation of S corporations.

For those who enviably have a third course in taxation, this text contains sufficient material for such an offering. The course might focus solely on family financial planning, including such topics as the estate and gift tax as well as the income taxation of fiduciaries. On the other hand, other advanced topics omitted in a previous course might be considered for coverage in the third course.

The *1992 Edition* has been revised to reflect the changes introduced by the Revenue Reconciliation Act of 1990 as well as other significant judicial and administrative developments during the past year. In the event that other significant changes in the tax law occur during the year, we will continue our policy of providing users with timely update supplements.

A comprehensive package of instructional aids is available with this text.

- *Solutions Manual:* containing solutions to the discussion questions and computational problems at the end of each chapter. These solutions are referenced to specific pages and examples from the text, and where appropriate, to supporting statutory or administrative authorities.

- *Instructor's Guide:* containing solutions to the tax research problems, tax return problems, and a test bank containing over 750 objective questions (true-false and multiple choice), with answers referenced back to specific pages and examples in the text.

- *Chapter Lecture Outlines:* containing a summary of the key points of each chapter.

- *CompuTest III:* a microcomputer testing system for use with an IBM-PC or IBM-compatible, along with data disks containing all of the questions from the test bank included in the Instructor's Guide. This software package can be used to create quizzes or exams in a minimum amount of time.

- *CompuGrade:* a microcomputer software program designed to maintain test scores for several different classes on a floppy disk. This program disk comes in the package with CompuTest III.

- A *Student Study Guide*, written by Professor Steven C. Thompson (University of Houston). It provides students with chapter highlights and self-review exams and answers.

- *Tax Return Practice Problems for Corporations, S Corporations, and Part-nerships*, written by Professor Marguerite R. Hutton (Western Washington University). It contains one practice problem for each of these tax entities and blank copies of the 1990 tax return forms required to be completed by students.

We are greatly indebted to those who have made many useful suggestions regarding the prior editions of this text. We specifically thank Professors Ronald F. Flinn (Creighton University), Karen A. Fortin (University of Miami), Carolyn Jarmon (Empire State University), and Mary Yates (Central Missouri State University) for their excellent suggestions; their comments greatly aided our editorial efforts. In this regard, we continue to invite all readers—students and instructors—to call errors and omissions to our attention. As with any work of this magnitude, it is extremely difficult to identify all errors and shortcomings without help, particularly in the dynamic area of Federal taxation. Because this text is revised annually, errors can be *quickly* corrected and constructive criticism will be incorporated on a *continuing* basis.

Finally, we are most appreciative of the professional and technical services received from the staff at Publication Services. This *1992 Edition* would not have been possible without their help.

January, 1991

James W. Pratt
Jane O. Burns
William N. Kulsrud

CONTENTS IN BRIEF

PART V

TAX RESEARCH AND TAX PRACTICE

CONTENTS

3

CORPORATE DISTRIBUTIONS: CASH, PROPERTY, AND STOCK DIVIDENDS

4

CORPORATE DISTRIBUTIONS: STOCK REDEMPTIONS AND PARTIAL LIQUIDATIONS

5   COMPLETE LIQUIDATIONS

6   PENALTY TAXES ON CORPORATE ACCUMULATIONS

PART II

ADVANCED CORPORATE TAX TOPICS

7 CORPORATE REORGANIZATIONS

8   CONSOLIDATED TAX RETURNS

9 INTERNATIONAL TAXATION

PART III

FLOW-THROUGH ENTITIES

10 TAXATION OF PARTNERSHIPS AND PARTNERS

11 SPECIAL PARTNERSHIPS, ASSET DISTRIBUTIONS, AND DISPOSITIONS OF PARTNERSHIP INTERESTS

12   S CORPORATIONS

PART IV

FAMILY TAX PLANNING

13 ESTATE AND GIFT TAXATION

14   INCOME TAXATION OF ESTATES AND TRUSTS

15 FAMILY TAX PLANNING

PART V

TAX RESEARCH AND TAX PRACTICE

16 SOURCES AND APPLICATIONS OF FEDERAL TAX LAW

17 TAX PRACTICE AND PROCEDURE

Appendices and Index

CORPORATE, PARTNERSHIP, ESTATE AND GIFT TAXATION

1992 Edition

PART I

CORPORATE TAXATION

CONTENTS

Upon completion of this chapter, you will be able to:

- Identify the alternative forms of doing business

- Define a corporation for Federal income tax purposes

- Compare and contrast corporate and individual taxation

- Compute the corporate income tax, including the tax for personal service corporations and controlled corporations

- Identify important features of the corporate alternative minimum tax (AMT)

- Describe the corporate tax forms and filing requirements

CHAPTER OUTLINE

Chapter 1

INCOME TAXATION OF CORPORATIONS

Every business organized and operated within the United States is classified for Federal income tax purposes as *one* of the following four business forms:

1. Sole proprietorship

2. Partnership

3. Regular corporation

4. S corporation

Usually a taxpayer has a choice of which of these tax forms his or her business will take. The choice may be based on *tax* or *nontax* factors, or some combination of both. For example, the dominant tax reason for not operating a business in the regular corporate form is the avoidance of *double taxation* of the same source of income. If the business is operated as a regular corporation, its income is taxed once at the corporate level *and* again (as dividends) when the income is distributed to the shareholder(s). Conversely, the most significant nontax reason for selecting the corporate form is the *limited liability* that this form offers to its owner or owners. Unfortunately, this nontax benefit may be of little value to small business owners who must personally guarantee repayment of corporate debt, or to professional corporations of physicians, CPAs, and attorneys who cannot avoid personal liability for their professional services under state law. For these corporations, insurance provides the greatest protection against liability just as it does for the unincorporated business.

Although there are many other tax and nontax factors that should be considered in selecting a particular business form, the purpose of this chapter is to examine the Federal income taxation of regular corporations. One logical way to do this is to compare and contrast corporate taxation with the taxation of income earned by the other business forms. Thus, a brief overview of these business forms is presented below.

OVERVIEW OF BUSINESS FORMS

As stated above, a business can be operated as a *sole proprietorship*, a *partnership*, or a *corporation*. If the corporate form is selected, and certain requirements are met, the owner or owners may *elect* to be treated as an S corporation for Federal income tax purposes. Each of these business forms is discussed below.

SOLE PROPRIETORSHIPS

More businesses are operated as proprietorships than any other form. This is partially a reflection of our entrepreneurial society. It is also the simplest form available—personally, legally, and for tax purposes. A proprietorship's net income or net loss is computed much the same as for any other business. The major difference is that in taxation the proprietorship is *not* separated from its owner. As a result, the owner cannot enter into taxable transactions with the proprietorship as a creditor, an employee, a customer, or in any other role.

For information purposes, proprietorship *ordinary income* and *deductions* are reported on *Schedule C* (or Schedule F if a farming operation) which is a supporting document for the owner's Form 1040.[1] Proprietorship net ordinary income also is the basis for calculating any *self-employment* tax liability.[2] All items subject to special tax treatment, such as capital gains and losses, charitable contributions, and dividend income, are reported on the appropriate tax return schedules as though incurred by the owner rather than the proprietorship. In essence, the sole proprietorship serves as a *conduit*—that is, all items of income, gain, loss, deduction, or credit it possesses flow through to the individual.

> **Example 1.** T is employed as an accounting professor at State University where he earns a salary of $48,000. T also operates a consulting practice as a sole proprietorship which earned $15,000 during the year. In connection with his consulting practice, T generated a $400 general business tax credit. The sole proprietorship does not file a separate return and pay a tax (net of the general business credit) on its income. Instead, T reports the sole proprietorship income on Schedule C and includes this income along with his salary on his personal tax return (Form 1040). In addition to the regular income tax imposed on T, he must add his self-employment tax (computed on Schedule SE, Form 1040) and subtract the $400 general business credit (computed on Form 3800).

---

[1] Code §§ 61(a) and 162. Please note that this and all future references to the Code are to the *Internal Revenue Code of 1986*. The section symbol (§) will be used throughout the text to indicate the particular section of the Code referred to. See Chapter 16 for an in-depth discussion of tax citations.

[2] See § 6017.

PARTNERSHIPS

Like the sole proprietorship, the partnership is a conduit for Federal income tax purposes. This means that the partnership itself is never subject to the Federal income tax and that all items of partnership income, expense, gain, or loss *pass through* to the partners and are given their tax effect at the partner level.[3] The partnership is required to file a return, however. This return (Form 1065) is merely an information return reporting the results of the partnership's transactions and how those results are divided among the partners. Using this information, the partners each report their respective share of the various items on their own tax return.[4] Because the partner pays taxes on his or her share of the partnership income, distributions made by the partnership to the partner generally are not taxable to the partner.[5]

> **Example 2.** For calendar year 1991, AB Partnership had net income subject to tax of $18,000. During the year, each of its two equal partners received distributions of $4,000. The partnership is not subject to tax, and each partner must include $9,000 in her annual income tax return despite the fact that each partner actually received less than this amount. The partnership must file an annual income tax return reporting its transactions and the ways in which those transactions affect each partner.

In some respects, the partnership is treated as a separate entity for tax purposes. For example, many tax elections are made by the partnership,[6] and a partnership interest is generally treated as a single asset when sold.[7] In transactions between the partners and the partnership, the parties are generally treated like unrelated parties.[8] These and other controlling provisions related to the Federal income tax treatment of partnerships are discussed in Chapters 10 and 11.

---

[3] § 701.

[4] § 702(a).

[5] § 731(a).

[6] § 703(b).

[7] § 741 states that the sale or exchange of an interest in a partnership shall generally be treated as the sale of a capital asset.

[8] § 707(a).

S CORPORATIONS

The Internal Revenue Code provides the possibility for certain closely held corporations to elect to be treated as conduits (like partnerships) for Federal income tax purposes. This election is made pursuant to the rules contained in Subchapter S of the Code.[9] For this reason, such corporations are referred to as S corporations. If the corporation elects S status, it is taxed in virtually the same fashion as a partnership. Like a partnership, the S corporation's items of income, expense, gain, or loss pass through to the shareholders to be taxed at the shareholder level. The S corporation files an information return (Form 1120S), similar to that for a partnership, reporting the results of the corporation's transactions and how those results are allocated among the shareholders. The individual shareholders report their respective shares of the various items on their own tax returns. Chapter 12 contains a discussion of the taxation of S corporations and their shareholders.

CORPORATE TAXPAYERS

Section 11 of the Code imposes a tax on all corporations. The tax applies to both domestic and foreign corporations and their foreign and domestic source income.[10] Although § 11 requires all corporations to pay tax, other provisions in the law specifically exempt certain types of corporations from taxation. For example, a corporation organized not for profit but for religious, charitable, scientific, literary, educational, or certain other purposes is generally not taxable.[11] However, if a nonprofit organization conducts a business which is not related to the purpose for which its exemption was granted, any resulting taxable income would be subject to tax.[12] In addition to the special provisions governing taxation of nonprofit corporations, the rules applying to S corporations vary from those applying to "regular" corporations as mentioned above.

While the overall taxation of corporations is similar to the taxation of individuals, several important differences exist. For example, the basic formula for computing the corporate tax varies from that used for individuals. Also, the treatment of dividend income received by a corporation is not the same as that imposed on dividends received by an individual.[13] These and other differences are discussed later in this chapter.

---

[9] §§ 1361 through 1379.

[10] § 882(a). See Chapter 9 for more details.

[11] § 501(a).

[12] § 501(b).

[13] See §§ 243 through 246.

WHAT IS A CORPORATION?

A corporation is an artificial "person" created by state law. The state may impose restrictions on the issuance of shares and the type of business conducted. The state also specifies the requirements for incorporation, such as the filing of articles of incorporation, the issuance of a corporate charter, and the payment of various fees (e.g., franchise taxes).

However, whether or not an entity meets the state's requirements as a corporation does not always govern its tax treatment. Congress stated in the Internal Revenue Code that "the term *corporation* includes associations, joint-stock companies, and insurance companies."[14] This broad definition has resulted in entities being taxed as corporations even though they are not considered corporations under applicable state law. It is also possible that an entity classified as a corporation under state law might not be taxed as a corporation for Federal income tax purposes.

ASSOCIATIONS

As mentioned above, an *association* is considered to be a corporation for Federal tax purposes. The Regulations define associations in terms of their corporate characteristics,[15] which are common to most corporations:

1. Associates

2. A profit motive

3. Continuity of life

4. Centralized management

5. Limited liability

6. Free transferability of interests

In testing an entity to see if it is an association (and is therefore taxed as a corporation), the presence or absence of the above characteristics is considered. Because all business forms possess a profit motive, and all business organizations other than sole proprietorships have more than one owner (associates), an organization will be treated as an association if it possesses a *majority* of the remaining four corporate characteristics. If it does not possess a majority of these characteristics, it is taxed as either a partnership or a trust.

---

[14] § 7701(a)(3).   [15] Reg. § 301.7701-2.

Example 3. Twenty persons form an organization to invest in real estate (associates). Their agreement states that the organization has a life of 24 years and that no member can dissolve the organization before that time (continuity of life). The organization is to be managed by five members elected by all the members (centralized management). Under local law, each member is personally liable for the organization's debts (there is *no* limited liability). The members may sell their interests in the organization (there is free transferability of interests). This organization has the following corporate characteristics not common to all business organizations:

1. Continuity of life
2. Centralized management
3. Free transferability of interests

Since the organization has a majority of the four corporate characteristics not common to all business forms (3 out of 4), it may be treated as a corporation for Federal tax purposes *even though it is not a corporation under state law.*

It is important to note what could happen to any anticipated tax benefits if an organization, such as the one in *Example 3* above, was unexpectedly classified as an association. For example, if the owners of the real estate business referred to in this example expect excess losses in the early years of operations, the corporate tax entity would not be the best choice of business form unless the organization qualified for and elected S corporation status. If the business is treated as a partnership or an S corporation, the excess losses flow through to the owners and may be deductible on their personal tax returns, subject to the passive activity loss rules. However, if the entity is classified as an association and is thereby taxable as a regular corporation, the excess losses simply accumulate at the corporate level in the form of net operating loss carryovers, the tax benefit of which expires at the end of 15 years.[16] Obviously, if the organization's owners do not think that the business is a corporation, they certainly will not file the required election to be treated as an S corporation for Federal income tax purposes. Thus, unless the organization qualifies as a partnership for tax purposes, any anticipated tax benefits will *either* be lost or, at best, unduly delayed.

For many years, taxpayers and the IRS engaged in heated arguments over the classification of a noncorporate business organization as an association. This controversy developed on two different fronts. *First,* to take advantage of the favorable tax benefits of corporate pension plans, taxpayers who were prohibited under state law from operating in the corporate form would arrange the organization of their noncorporate professional service businesses so that they possessed a majority of the corporate characteristics, and would thereby be classified as associations taxable under Federal income tax law as corporations. Associations

---

[16]   See § 172(b)(1)(B).

of doctors, dentists, attorneys, and other professionals became commonplace as a result of this obvious "tax-motivated" effort. After many court battles,[17] this side of the controversy was settled when every state adopted a *professional corporation act* allowing physicians, attorneys, CPAs, and others to incorporate their business practices. Unfortunately, recent changes in the Federal income taxation of such professional service corporations have eliminated many of the tax benefits originally sought by the "incorporated" professionals. For example, the once favorable treatment of corporate pension plans for such professionals has been offset by restrictions imposed on the maximum tax deductible contributions the corporation can use to fund its employee-owner's plan. These restrictions, coupled with an allowed increase in the maximum tax deductible funding of pension plans by unincorporated professionals (e.g., Keogh plans), have significantly decreased incorporation of professional service businesses motivated by the desire for more favorable treatment of pension plans. In addition, the Revenue Act of 1987 eliminated the benefits of a graduated corporate tax rate structure for such corporations. As a result, the taxable income of these corporations will be taxed at the highest corporate rate—currently 34 percent—which is greater than the maximum tax rate of the individual owner (currently 31 percent). These changes are discussed in greater detail later in this chapter.

On the *second* front of this controversy were the organizations, such as the one described in *Example 3* above, seeking to be treated as partnerships for Federal income tax purposes. The key issue of this side of the controversy was the organizations' desire to be allowed to have the deductible business losses flow through and at the same time to be allowed to provide most of the owner-investors with limited liability. These organizations were formed as *limited partnerships,* managed by one or more general partners (centralized management), provided limited liability to the investor-limited partners, and often allowed free transferability of partnership interests. Unlike the professional association issue, the IRS tended to classify these business arrangements *as* associations, thereby denying the taxpayers partnership treatment. After much litigation,[18] most states adopted *uniform laws*[19] providing for the organization, operation, and termination of both general and limited partnerships. As a result, for most cases today a business formed and operated as a partnership (either general or limited) under the appropriate state's law will be treated as such for Federal income tax purposes.

An important exception, however, is the so-called *publicly traded partnership* (PTP). The Revenue Act of 1987 mandates that a partnership meeting the definition of a PTP be treated *and* taxed as a regular corporation. Basically, a partnership is a PTP if it (1) is a limited partnership, (2) was organized after

---

[17] For examples, see *U.S. v. Kintner,* 54-2 USTC ¶9626, 47 AFTR 995, 216 F.2d 418 (CA-9, 1954); *Jerome J. Roubik,* 53 T.C. 365 (1969); and *Kurzner v. U.S., 23 AFTR2d 1482, 413 F.2d 97 (CA-5, 1969).*

[18] As examples, see *P.G. Larson,* 66 T.C. 159 (1976), and *Zuckman v. U.S.,* 75-2 USTC ¶9778, 36 AFTR2d 6193, 524 F.2d 729 (Ct. Cls., 1975).

[19] Both the *Uniform Partnership Act* and the *Uniform Limited Partnership Act* have been adopted by most states.

December 17, 1987 and (3) has interests that are traded on an established securities market or are readily tradeable on a secondary market. Certain exceptions exist for PTPs in existence on December 17, 1987 and for those with income consisting primarily of interest, dividends, rental income from real property and gains from the sale of such property, gains from the sale of capital or § 1231 assets, and income and gains from development, mining or production, refining, transportation, or marketing of any mineral or natural resource. These rules are discussed in Chapter 11.

SHAM CORPORATIONS

In some instances the IRS will ignore the fact that an entity is considered a corporation as defined by its state law. This may happen when a corporation's only purpose is to reduce taxes of its owners or to hold title to property. If the corporation has no real business or economic function, or if it conducts no activities, it may be a "sham" or "dummy" corporation.[20] Generally, as long as there is a business activity carried on, a corporation will be considered a separate taxable entity.[21]

> **Example 4.** M owns a piece of real estate. To protect it from his creditors, M forms X Corporation and transfers the land to it in exchange for all of X Corporation's stock. The only purpose of X Corporation is to hold title to the real estate, and X Corporation conducts no other business activities. It is properly incorporated under state law. The IRS is likely to designate X Corporation as a sham corporation and to disregard its corporate status. Any income and expenses of X Corporation will be considered as belonging to M.
>
> If X Corporation had conducted some business activities (such as leasing the property and collecting rents), it is likely that it will not be considered a sham corporation.

Generally the IRS, but not the taxpayer, is allowed to disregard the status of a corporation. The courts have frequently agreed that if a taxpayer has created a corporation, he or she should not be allowed to ignore its status (i.e., in order to reduce taxes). However, the Supreme Court has ruled that a taxpayer could use a corporate entity as the taxpayer's agent in securing financing.[22] Thus, under certain conditions, taxpayers may use a corporation for a business purpose and not have it treated as a corporation for Federal tax purposes.

---

[20] See *Higgins vs. Smith*, 40-1 USTC ¶9160, 23 AFTR 800, 308 U.S. 473 (USSC, 1940).

[21] *Moline Properties, Inc.*, 43-1 USTC ¶9464, 30 AFTR 1291, 319 U.S. 436 (USSC, 1943).

[22] *Jesse C. Bollinger*, 88-1 USTC ¶9233, 61 AFTR2d 88-793, 108 S.CT. 1173 (USSC, 1988)

COMPARISON OF CORPORATE AND INDIVIDUAL INCOME TAXATION

A corporation's taxable income is computed by subtracting various deductions from its gross income.[23] Although this appears to be the same basic computation as for individual taxpayers, there are numerous important differences. In order to highlight these differences, Exhibits 1-1 and 1-2 contain the tax formulas for corporate and individual taxpayers.

GROSS INCOME

The definition of gross income is the same for both corporations and individuals.[24] However, there are some differences in the exclusions from gross income. For example, capital contributions to a corporation (i.e., purchase of corporate stock by shareholders) are excluded from gross income.[25]

DEDUCTIONS

Corporations have no "Adjusted Gross Income." Thus for corporations, there are no "deductions for A.G.I." or "deductions from A.G.I." All corporate expenditures are either deductible or not deductible. All allowable deductions are subtracted from gross income in arriving at taxable income.

Corporations are considered to be "persons" only in a legal sense, and are *not* entitled to the following "personal" deductions that are available for individuals:

1. Personal and dependency exemptions

2. Standard deduction

3. Itemized deductions

All activities of a corporation are considered to be business activities. Therefore, corporations usually deduct all their losses since such losses are considered business losses.[26] In addition, corporations do not have to reduce their casualty losses by either the $100 statutory floor or by 10 percent of adjusted gross income. (Corporations have no A.G.I., as mentioned.)

Corporations do not have "nonbusiness" bad debts, since all activities are considered business activities. All bad debts of a corporation are business bad debts.[27]

---

[23] § 63(a).

[24] § 61(a).

[25] § 118(a).

[26] § 165(a). Like individuals, certain corporations are subject to the passive loss rules discussed in Chapter 10.

[27] § 166.

Exhibit 1-1
Tax Formula for Corporate Taxpayers

Income (from whatever source)	$xxx,xxx
Less: Exclusions from gross income	− xx,xxx
Gross Income	$xxx,xxx
Less: Deductions	− xx,xxx
Taxable Income	$xx,xxx
Applicable tax rates	xx%
Gross tax	$xx,xxx
Less: Tax credits and prepayments	− x,xxx
Tax due (or refund)	$xx,xxx

Exhibit 1-2
Tax Formula for Individual Taxpayers

Total Income (from whatever source)		$xxx,xxx
Less: Exclusions from gross income		− xx,xxx
Gross Income		$xxx,xxx
Less: Deductions for adjusted gross income		− xx,xxx
Adjusted gross income		$xxx,xxx
Less 1. The larger of		
a. Standard deduction	$x,xxx	
or	*or*	− x,xxx
b. Total itemized deductions	$x,xxx	
2. Number of personal and dependency exemptions × exemption amount		− x,xxx
Taxable Income		$xxx,xxx
Applicable tax rates (from Tables or Schedules X,Y, or Z)		xx%
Gross tax		$ xx,xxx
Less: Tax credits and prepayments		− x,xxx
Tax due (or refund)		$ xx,xxx

There are several deductions that are available only for corporations.[28] These are deductible in addition to the other business deductions and include the dividends-received deduction and the amortization of organizational expenditures.

DIVIDENDS-RECEIVED DEDUCTION

As mentioned earlier, double taxation occurs when corporate profits are distributed in the form of dividends to the shareholders. The corporation is not allowed a deduction for the dividends paid, and an individual shareholder is not entitled to an exclusion. Therefore, when one corporation is a shareholder in another corporation, *triple* taxation might occur. To prevent this, Congress provided corporations with a deduction for dividends received.[29]

General Rule. The dividends-received deduction (DRD) generally is 70 percent of the dividends received from taxable domestic (U.S.) corporations.[30] However, a corporation that owns at least 20 percent—but less than 80 percent—of the dividend-paying corporation's stock is allowed to deduct *80* percent of the dividends received.[31] In addition, members of an *affiliated group* are allowed to deduct 100 percent of the dividends that are received from another member of the same group. A group of corporations is considered affiliated when at least 80 percent of the stock of each corporation is owned by other members of the group.[32]

Taxable Income Limitation. The 70 percent dividends-received deduction may not exceed 70 percent of the corporation's taxable income computed without the deduction for dividends-received, net operating loss carryovers or carrybacks, and capital loss carrybacks.[33] However, if the dividends-received deduction adds to *or* creates a net operating loss for the current year, the 70 percent of taxable income limitation *does not* apply.

Like the dividends-received deduction percentage, the taxable income limitation percentage becomes *80* percent rather than 70 percent if the dividend-paying corporation is at least 20 percent owned by the recipient corporation. In the unlikely event a corporation receives dividends subject to *both* the 70 percent and

[28] § 241.

[29] §§ 243 through 246.

[30] § 243(a)(1).

[31] § 243(c).

[32] §§ 243(a)(3), 243(b)(5), and 1504.

[33] § 246(b).

80 percent rules, a special procedure must be followed. First, the 80 percent limitation is applied by treating the "70 percent dividends" as other income. The 70 percent limitation is then applied by treating the "80 percent dividends" as if they had not been received.[34]

Exhibit 1-3 contains a format for the computation of the 70 percent dividends-received deduction, and *Examples 5, 6,* and *7* illustrate this computational procedure.[35]

Exhibit 1-3
*Computation of Corporate
Dividends-Received Deduction*

Step 1:   Multiply the dividends-received from taxable domestic (U.S.) cor-
          porations by 70 percent. This is the *tentative* dividends-received
          deduction (DRD).

Step 2:   Compute the tentative taxable income for the current year, using
          the *tentative* DRD (from Step 1):
          Total revenues (including dividend income)
                Less: Total expenses
                Equals: Taxable income (before DRD)
                Less: Tentative DRD (Step 1)
                Equals: Tentative taxable income (loss)
          If the tentative taxable income is *positive*, the taxable income
          limitation may apply. Go to step 3.
          If the tentative taxable income is *negative*, there is no taxable
          income limitation. The dividends-received deduction is the amount
          computed in Step 1.

Step 3:   Compute the taxable income limitation:
          Taxable income (before DRD) (Step 2)
                Add: Any net operating loss carryovers or carrybacks from
                          other years that are reflected in the taxable income.
                Add: Any capital loss carrybacks from later years that
                          are reflected in taxable income.
                Equals: Taxable income (before DRD), as adjusted
                Multiply by 70 percent
                Equals: Taxable income limitation

Step 4:   Compare the tentative DRD (Step 1) to the taxable income limi-
          tation (Step 3). Choose the *smaller* amount. This is the corporate
          dividends-received deduction.

---

[34]   § 246(b)(3).

[35]   To apply the 80 percent rules, simply substi-
       tute 80 percent for 70 percent in this exhibit
       and accompanying examples.

Example 5. R Corporation has the following items of revenue and expense for the year:

Dividends received from domestic corporations.............	$40,000
Revenue from sales.......................................	60,000
Cost of goods sold and operating expenses................	$54,000

The dividends-received deduction is computed as follows:

Step 1:

$40,000   dividends received

$\times$ 70%

$28,000   *tentative* dividends-received deduction (DRD)

Step 2:

Dividend income.................................	$ 40,000
Revenue from sales	+ 60,000
Total revenues..................................	$100,000
Less: Total expenses.........................	− 54,000
Taxable income (before DRD)....................	$ 46,000
Less: Tentative DRD..........................	− 28,000
Tentative taxable income........................	$ 18,000

Since the tentative taxable income is *positive,* the taxable income limitation may apply. Go to Step 3.

Step 3:

Compute the taxable income limitation:

Taxable income (before DRD)...................	$ 46,000
Multiply by 70%	$\times$ 70%
Taxable income limitation	$ 32,200

Step 4:

Compare the tentative DRD ($28,000) to the taxable income limitation ($32,000). Choose the *smaller* amount ($28,000). In this case, R Corporation's dividends-received deduction is $28,000 (not subject to limitation).

Example 6. Assume the same facts as in *Example 5* except that the revenue from sales is $50,000. The dividends-received deduction is computed as follows:

Step 1:

$40,000   dividends received

$\times$ 70%

$28,000   *tentative* (DRD)

Step 2:

Dividend income.................................	$ 40,000
Revenue from sales	+ 50,000
Total revenues..................................	$ 90,000
Less: Total expenses.........................	− 54,000
Taxable income (before DRD)....................	$ 36,000
Less: Tentative DRD..........................	− 28,000
Tentative taxable income........................	$ 8,000

Since the tentative taxable income is *positive,* the taxable income limitation may apply. Go to Step 3.

Step 3:   Compute the taxable income limitation:

Taxable income (before DRD)....................	$ 36,000
Multiply by 70%	× 70%
Taxable income limitation	$ 25,200

Step 4:   Compare the tentative DRD ($28,000) to the taxable income limitation ($25,200). Choose the *smaller* amount ($25,200). In this case, R Corporation's dividends-received deduction is $25,200 (limited to 70% of taxable income).

Example 7.   Assume the same facts as in *Example 5* except that the revenue from sales is $41,000. The dividends-received deduction is computed as follows:

Step 1: $40,000   dividends received
× 70%

$28,000   *tentative* (DRD)

Step 2:

Dividend income.............................	$ 40,000
Revenue from sales	+ 41,000
Total revenues...............................	$ 81,000
Less: Total expenses.......................	− 54,000
Taxable income (before DRD)................	$ 27,000
Less: Tentative DRD.......................	− 28,000
Tentative taxable income (loss)	($ 1,000)

Because the tentative taxable income (loss) is *negative,* there is no taxable income limitation. The dividends-received deduction is $28,000.

The taxable income limitation discussed above *does not* apply to dividends received from affiliated corporations that are entitled to the 100 percent dividends-received deduction.[36]

Other Restrictions on Dividends-Received Deduction.   There are three additional limitations or restrictions that may be imposed on the dividends-received deduction. First, unless a corporation has held the stock for more than 45 days before its sale or other disposition, any dividends-received on such stock will not be eligible for the dividends-received deduction.[37] This restriction was created to stop the perceived abuse of corporate taxpayers purchasing dividend-paying stock shortly before dividends were declared and selling such stock immediately after the right to receive the dividends became fixed (i.e., the date of record or ex-dividend date).

Example 8.   The treasurer of R Inc. temporarily invested $1,000 of R's working capital by purchasing stock in D Corporation. Shortly thereafter, R received a dividend of $100 from D, causing the value of R's stock to drop to $900. R then sold the stock and realized a short-term capital loss of $100 ($900−$1,000). Economically, R is no better off than before

---

[36]   § 246(b)(1).   [37]   § 246(c)(1).

the dividend because it spent $1,000 and received $1,000 ($900 + $100). From a tax view, however, the corporation effectively reports a loss from the transaction of $70 ($30 dividend income − $100 capital loss), assuming the capital loss can be used[38] and the dividends-received deduction is allowed. The 45-day rule attempts to prevent such schemes by requiring the taxpayer to accept the risk of holding the stock for a period of time.

Note that the plan revealed in *Example 8* succeeds if the taxpayer is willing to accept the risk of holding the stock for more than 45 days. Another rule aimed at such plans attacks so-called *extraordinary dividends*.[39] If a corporation receives an extraordinary dividend within the first two years that the stock is owned, the basis of the stock must be reduced by the nontaxable portion of the dividend. An extraordinary dividend is generally any dividend that equals or exceeds 10 percent of the taxpayer's basis of common stock, or 5 percent of the basis of preferred stock. If the taxpayer can prove the value of the stock, the taxpayer can use such value instead of basis to determine if the dividend is extraordinary.

> **Example 9.**   Assume the same facts as in *Example 8*, except that the stock was sold three months after it was purchased. In this case, the dividends-received deduction is allowed. However, the dividend is an extraordinary dividend because the amount is at least 10% of the cost of the stock [$100 = (10% × $1,000)]. Thus, R must reduce the basis of the stock by the nontaxable portion of the dividend, $70. Therefore, on the sale of the stock R recognizes a loss of only $30 ($900−$930). Observe that the required reduction in basis produces the right economic result; that is, R is now unaffected from a tax view ($30 dividend income − $30 capital loss = $0).

A third restriction on a corporation's dividends-received deduction prohibits corporations from taking advantage of this deduction by borrowing funds and using them to purchase dividend-paying stock.

> **Example 10.**   This year, X Corporation borrowed money and purchased dividend-paying stock. During the year, X received $1,000 of dividend income but paid $1,000 of interest expense. Although the income and expense wash from an economic view, without a special rule, X would be taxed on only $300 of income because of the dividends-received deduction.

To prohibit arbitrage transactions such as that described in *Example 10* above, the Code denies corporations the dividends-received deduction to the extent the purchase price of the stock was financed with borrowed funds.

---

[38]   The tax treatment of a corporation's capital gains and losses is discussed later in this chapter.

[39]   § 1059(a).

The restriction on the dividends-received deduction applies to so-called *debt-financed portfolio stock*. Generally, the term applies to any stock that was either acquired by debt-financing or refinanced by the taxpayer, *and* where all or a portion of the indebtedness remained unpaid prior to the receipt of dividends on the stock. In such cases, the deduction for these dividends is limited to the product of

1. 70 percent,[40] and

2. 100 percent minus the *average indebtedness percentage*

For this purpose, the average indebtedness percentage is calculated by dividing the average unpaid indebtedness for the period by the stock's adjusted basis.[41]

> **Example 11.**   On September 1, 1991, T Corporation received dividends of $10,000 from General Motors Corporation. T had purchased the General Motors stock with $100,000 of borrowed funds in 1990. Assuming the average unpaid balance of the debt between dividend dates was $60,000, T Corporation's average indebtedness percentage is 60%, and the dividends-received deduction for this stock is limited to $2,800.
>
> | | |
> |---|---|
> | Dividends received on debt-financed portfolio stock .... | $10,000 |
> | Times: 70% × (100% − 60%) .... | ×   28% |
> | Dividends-received deduction .... | $ 2,800 |

ORGANIZATIONAL EXPENDITURES

When a corporation is formed, various expenses directly related to the organization process are incurred, such as attorneys' fees, accountants' fees, and state filing charges. Although some of the attorneys' and accountants' fees may be ordinary and necessary business expenses that do not benefit future periods (and are therefore deductible), most of these expenditures will benefit future periods and are therefore capitalized as *organizational expenditures*. These organizational expenditures are intangible assets that have value for the life of the corporation.

Generally, assets with indefinite lives may not be amortized for Federal income tax purposes. However, Congress has given corporations the option of electing to *amortize* organizational expenditures.[42] If they so elect, corporations may amortize (deduct) the costs ratably over a period of not less than 60 months (i.e., 60 months or longer). The 60-month period starts in the month in which the corporation begins business.

---

[40]   § 246A(a)(1); 80 percent in the case of any dividend from a 20 percent or more owned corporation.

[41]   See §§ 246A(a)(2) and 246A(d).

[42]   § 248.

The Regulations give the following examples of organizational expenditures:[43]

1. Legal services incident to the organization of the corporation, such as drafting the corporate charter, by-laws, minutes of organizational meetings, and terms of original stock certificates

2. Necessary accounting services

3. Expenses of temporary directors and of organizational meetings of directors or stockholders

4. Fees paid to the state of incorporation

The Regulations also give several examples of items that are *not* considered organizational expenditures, such as costs of issuing stock.[44] The costs of issuing stock are considered selling expenses, and therefore are a reduction in the proceeds from selling the stock. They reduce stockholders' equity and do not create any tax deduction.

It is important to note that only those organizational expenditures *incurred* before the end of the corporation's first taxable year will qualify for deduction.[45] Neither the taxable year of actual payment nor the corporation's method of accounting (i.e., cash or accrual) affect this requirement. However, any subsequent expenditures for such items as corporate charter or by-laws revisions are not eligible for amortization.

> **Example 12.** N Corporation was formed on July 1, 1991 and incurred and paid qualifying organizational expenditures of $3,000. N Corporation has chosen to use the calendar year for tax purposes. It has also elected to amortize the organizational expenditures over 60 months. On its first tax return (1991), N Corporation's amortization deduction will be $300, computed as follows:
>
> $$\frac{\text{Organizational expenditures}}{60 \text{ months}} = \text{Amortization per month}$$
>
> $$\frac{\$3,000}{60 \text{ months}} = \$50 \text{ Amortization per month}$$
>
> $$\$50 \times 6 \text{ months in 1991 (July} - \text{December)} = \underline{\$300}$$
>
> The amortization deduction for organizational expenditures for 1992 will be $600 ($50 per month $\times$ 12 months).

An election to amortize organizational expenditures is made by attaching a statement to the corporation's first tax return.[46] If the election is not made, the organizational expenditures may not be amortized.

---

[43] Reg. § 1.248-1(b)(2).

[44] Reg. § 1.248-1(b)(3).

[45] Reg. § 1.248-1(a).

[46] Reg. § 1.248-1(c).

A similar election is available for the organizational costs of partnerships.[47] This is discussed in Chapter 10.

NET OPERATING LOSS

Corporations, like individuals, are entitled to deduct net operating loss carryovers in arriving at taxable income. Numerous modifications are required in computing an individual's net operating loss.[48] However, only two modifications are considered in computing a corporation's net operating loss. These two modifications are the net operating loss deductions[49] and the dividends-received deduction.[50] Net operating loss deductions for each year are considered separately. Therefore, the net operating loss deductions for other years are omitted from the computation of the current year's net operating loss. The modification relating to the dividends-received deduction is that the 70 percent (or 80%) taxable income limitation is ignored (i.e., the dividends-received deduction is allowed in full).

A corporate net operating loss may be carried back three years and carried forward 15 years.[51] The loss is first carried back to the earliest year. Any unabsorbed loss is carried to the second prior year, then the first prior year (the first year after the loss was created), and then forward until the loss is completely used or the 15-year period expires.

A corporation may elect not to carry the loss back.[52] If a corporation makes this election, the loss would be carried forward for 15 years. No loss would be carried back. This election is irrevocable.

> **Example 13.** T Corporation had the following items of revenue and expense for 1991:
>
> | | |
> |---|---:|
> | Revenue from operations . . . . | $42,000 |
> | Dividends from less than 20% owned corporation . . . . | 40,000 |
> | Expenses of operations . . . . | 63,000 |
>
> T Corporation's net operating loss for 1991 is computed as follows:
>
> | | |
> |---|---:|
> | Revenue from operations . . . . | $42,000 |
> | Dividend income . . . . | 40,000 |
> | Total revenue . . . . | $82,000 |
> | Less: Total expenses . . . . | − 63,000 |
> | Less: Dividends-received deduction (ignore the taxable income limitation) . . . . | − 28,000 |
> | Net operating loss (negative taxable income) . . . . | ($ 9,000) |

---

[47]   § 709.

[48]   § 172(d).

[49]   § 172(d)(1).

[50]   § 172(d)(5).

[51]   § 172(b)(1).

[52]   § 172(b)(3)(C).

The 1991 net operating loss is carried back three years to 1988. If T Corporation's taxable income for 1988 is $3,000, the 1991 net operating loss is treated as follows:

1988 taxable income..................................	$3,000
Less: NOL carryback..............................	− 9,000
NOL carryover to 1989..............................	($ 6,000)

A corporate net operating loss is carried back by filing either Form 1120X (Amended U.S. Corporation Income Tax Return) or Form 1139 (Corporation Application for Tentative Refund). T Corporation should receive a refund of its 1988 income tax paid.

CHARITABLE CONTRIBUTIONS

A corporation's charitable contribution deduction is much more limited than the charitable contribution deductions of individuals. As with individuals, the charitable contributions must be made to qualified organizations.[53] The amount that can be deducted in any year is the amount actually donated during the year and, *if the corporation is on the accrual basis*, any amounts that are authorized during the year by the board of directors may be added as well, provided the amounts are actually paid to the charity by the 15th day of the third month following the close of the tax year.[54]

> **Example 14.** C Corporation donated $2,000 cash to United Charities (a qualified charitable organization) on June 3, 1991. On December 20, 1991 the board of directors of C Corporation authorized a $2,500 cash donation to United Charities. This $2,500 was actually paid to United Charities on March 12, 1992. C Corporation uses the calendar year as its accounting period.
>   If C Corporation is a *cash basis* corporation,
>
>> Only the $2,000 contribution to United Charities made in 1991 may be deducted in 1991. The additional $2,500 authorized contribution may not be deducted until 1992.
>
>   If C Corporation is an *accrual basis* corporation,
>
>> Then $4,500 ($2,000 + $2,500) may be deducted in 1991.
>
>> **Note:** If the $2,500 donation authorized on December 20, 1991 had been paid after March 15, 1992, the $2,500 contribution deduction would not be allowed until 1992.

---

[53] § 170(c).   [54] §§ 170(a)(1) and (2).

Contributions of Ordinary Income Property.   When property is contributed, the fair market value of the property at the time it is donated may generally be deducted. There are, however, several exceptions to this general rule. One exception involves donations of *ordinary income property.*[55] The Regulations define ordinary income property as property that would produce a gain *other than* long-term capital gain if sold by the contributing corporation for its fair market value. The charitable contribution deduction for ordinary income property generally may not exceed the corporation's basis in the property.

> **Example 15.**   G Corporation donates some of its inventory to a church. The inventory donated is worth $5,000 and has an adjusted basis to G Corporation of $2,000. G Corporation's deduction for this contribution is $2,000, its adjusted basis in the inventory.

Two exceptions permit corporate taxpayers to claim contribution deductions in excess of the basis of the ordinary income property. First, a corporation is allowed to deduct its basis *plus* one-half of the unrealized appreciation in value (not to exceed twice the basis) of any inventory item donated to a qualifying charity and used solely for the care of the ill, the needy, or infants.[56] This rule also applies to a gift to a college or university of a corporation's newly manufactured scientific equipment if the recipient is the original user of the property and at least 80 percent of its use will be for research or experimentation.[57] In either case, the corporation is required to obtain a written statement from the charity indicating that the use requirement has been met.

Contributions of Capital Gain Property.   In *two* situations a corporation also is limited in the amount of deduction it may take when appreciated long-term capital gain property is contributed.[58] The *first* situation occurs when tangible personal property donated to a charity is put to a use that is not related to the charity's exempt purpose. The *second* situation in which a limitation will apply is the donation of appreciated property to certain private foundations. The limitation applied in these cases is that the fair market value of the property must be reduced by the unrealized appreciation (i.e., the deduction is limited to the property's adjusted basis). For other types of capital gain property, the contributions deduction is the fair market value of the property.

---

[55]   Reg. § 1.170A-4(b)(1).

[56]   § 170(e)(3).

[57]   § 170(e)(4).

[58]   § 170(e)(1).

Example 16. L Corporation donated a painting to a university. The painting was worth $10,000 and had an adjusted basis to L Corporation of $9,000. If the painting is placed in the university for display and study by art students, this is considered a use related to the university's exempt purpose.[59] The limitation mentioned above would not apply, and L Corporation's charitable contribution deduction would be $10,000, the fair market value of the painting.

If, however, the painting is immediately sold by the university, this is considered to be a use that is not related to the university's exempt purpose L Corporation's contribution deduction would be limited to $9,000, its basis of the painting ($10,000 fair market value–$1,000 unrealized appreciation).

Annual Deduction Limitations. In addition to the limitations based on the type of property contributed, there is a maximum annual limitation. The limitation is 10 percent of the corporation's taxable income before certain deductions.[60] The 10 percent limitation is based on taxable income without reduction for charitable contributions, the dividends-received deduction, net operating loss carrybacks, or capital loss carrybacks. Amounts contributed in excess of this limitation may be carried forward and deducted in any of the five succeeding years.[61] In no year may the total charitable contribution deduction exceed the 10 percent limitation. In years in which there is *both* a current contribution and a carryover, the current contribution is deductible first. At the end of the five-year period, any carryover not deducted expires.

Example 17. M Corporation has the following for tax year 1991:

Net income from operations	$100,000
Dividends received (subject to 70% rules)	10,000
Charitable contributions made in 1991	8,000
Charitable contribution carryforward from 1990	5,000

M Corporation's contribution deduction for 1991 is limited to $11,000, computed as follows:

Net income from operations	$100,000
Dividends received	+ 10,000
Taxable income without the charitable contribution deduction and the dividends-received deduction	$110,000
Multiply by 10% limitation	× 10%
Maximum contribution deduction for 1991	$ 11,000

---

[59] Reg. § 1.170A-4(b)(3).

[60] § 170(b)(2).

[61] § 170(d)(2).

Taxable income for the year will be $92,000, computed as follows:

Net income from operations.....................		$100,000
Dividends received.............................		10,000
		$110,000
Less: Special corporate deductions:		
Charitable contributions................	$11,000	
Dividends received		
(70% of $10,000).....................	+ 7,000	
Total special deductions................		− 18,000
M Corporation's 1991 taxable income............		$ 92,000

Example 18. Based on the facts in *Example 17*, M Corporation has a $2,000 charitable contribution carryover remaining from 1990. The first $8,000 of the $11,000 allowed deduction for 1991 is considered to be from the current year's contributions, and the $3,000 balance is from the 1990 carryover. Thus, the remaining (unused) $2,000 of the 1990 contributions must be carried over to 1992.

CAPITAL GAINS AND LOSSES

The definition of a capital asset, the determination of holding period, and the capital gain and loss *netting process* are the same for corporations as they are for individuals. Under the first step of the netting process, each taxpayer combines short-term capital gains and losses, and the result is either a *net* short-term capital gain or a *net* short-term capital loss. Likewise, the taxpayer combines long-term capital gains and losses with a result of either a *net* long-term capital gain or a *net* long-term capital loss. If the taxpayer has *both* a net short-term capital gain and a net long-term capital gain—or a net short-term capital loss and a net long-term capital loss—*no* further netting is allowed. If the taxpayer has *either* a net short-term capital gain and a net long-term capital loss, or a net short-term capital loss and a net long-term capital gain, these results are combined in the second stage of the netting process. The *three* possible results of the netting process are[62]

1. *Capital gain net income*—either a net short-term capital gain with no further netting allowed, or the *excess* of a net short-term capital gain over a net long-term capital loss

2. *Net capital gain*—either a net long-term capital gain with no further netting allowed, or the *excess* of a net long-term capital gain over a net short-term capital loss

---

[62] See § 1222(9), (10), and (11).

3. *Net capital loss*—either a net short-term capital loss or a net long-term capital loss with no further netting allowed, the *sum* of both net short-term and net long-term capital losses, the *excess* of a net short-term capital loss over a net long-term capital gain, or the *excess* of a net long-term capital loss over a net short-term capital gain

Capital Gains. Historically, the tax law has treated short-term capital gains (i.e., capital gain net income) of both individuals and corporations as ordinary income while providing favorable treatment for long-term capital gains (i.e., net capital gains). In 1986, this tradition ended when the special treatment for long-term capital gains was eliminated. However, the 1986 changes proved only temporary, at least for individuals. Beginning in 1991, an individual's long-term capital gains may again enjoy favorable treatment as they are taxed at the lesser of the taxpayer's marginal rate or 28 percent. A special tax calculation ensures that an individual's long-term capital gains are not taxed at the top rate of 31 percent. Congress did not extend equivalent treatment to corporate taxpayers. Corporations include both net long-term capital gains and net short-term capital gains along with other income and compute the tax liability at the prevailing rates.[63] Thus, a corporation's long-term and short-term capital gains are effectively treated as ordinary income and can be taxed at a rate as high as 39 percent (34 percent plus a 5 percent surcharge).

Capital Losses. Individuals and corporations treat capital losses quite differently. As a general rule, individuals are allowed to offset capital losses against capital gains and up to $3,000 of ordinary income annually. If both a net short-term capital loss and a net long-term capital loss exist, the taxpayer first offsets the net short-term capital loss against ordinary income. Any short-term or long-term capital loss not absorbed is carried forward until it is exhausted. Capital losses retain their character as either short-term or long-term when they are carried forward.

Capital losses of a corporation offset only capital gains.[64] A corporation is never permitted to reduce ordinary income by a capital loss. As a result, corporations cannot deduct their excess capital losses for the year. Instead, a corporation must carry the excess capital losses back for three years and forward for five years,[65] to use them to offset capital gains in those years. The losses are first carried back three years. They will reduce the amount of capital gains reported in the earliest year. Any amount not used to offset gain in the third previous year can offset gain in the second previous year and then the first previous year. If the sum of the capital gains reported in the three previous years is less than the capital loss, the excess is carried forward. Losses carried forward may be used to offset capital gains recognized in the succeeding five tax years. Losses unused at the end of the five-year carryforward period expire.

---

[63] § 1201(a).

[64] § 1211(a).

[65] § 1212(a).

Example 19. B Corporation has income, gains, and losses as follows:

	1988	1989	1990	1991
Ordinary income...............	$100,000	$100,000	$100,000	$100,000
Net capital gain or (loss)........	4,000	3,000	2,000	(10,000)
Total income.................	$104,000	$103,000	$102,000	$ 90,000

B reported taxable income in years 1988, 1989, and 1990 of $104,000, $103,000, and $102,000, respectively, since net capital gains are added into taxable income. In 1991, B must report $100,000 taxable income because capital losses are nondeductible. However, B Corporation is entitled to carry the net capital loss back to years 1988, 1989, and 1990 and file a claim for refund for the taxes paid on the capital gains for each year. Because the 1991 capital loss carryback ($10,000) exceeds the sum of the capital gains in the prior three years ($9,000), B has a $1,000 capital loss carryforward. This loss carryforward can be used to offset the first $1,000 of capital gains recognized in years 1992 through 1996.

Corporations treat all capital loss carrybacks and carryovers as short-term losses. At the present, this has no effect on the tax due and it is often immaterial whether the carryover is considered long-term or short-term. However, if Congress ever reinstates special treatment for long-term capital gains, keeping short-term and long-term carryovers separate will once again have meaning.

SALES OF DEPRECIABLE PROPERTY

Corporations generally compute the amount of § 1245 and § 1250 ordinary income recapture on the sales of depreciable assets in the same manner as do individuals. However, Congress added Code § 291 to the tax law in 1982 with the intent of reducing the tax benefits of the accelerated cost recovery of depreciable § 1250 property available to corporate taxpayers. As a result, corporations must treat as ordinary income 20 percent of any § 1231 gain *that would have been* ordinary income if Code § 1245 rather than § 1250 had applied to the transaction.[66] Similar rules apply to amortization of pollution control facilities and intangible drilling costs incurred by corporate taxpayers. The amount that is treated as ordinary income under § 291 is computed in the following manner:

Amount that would be treated as ordinary income under Code § 1245....................	$xx,xxx
Less: Amount that would be treated as ordinary income under § 1250..........	(x,xxx)
Equals: Difference between recapture amounts.	$xx,xxx
Times: Rate specified in § 291...............	× 20%
Equals: Amount that is treated as ordinary income.......................	$xx,xxx

---

[66] See Appendix H for the current ACRS depreciation tables, including the straight-line recovery percentages.

Example 20. D Corporation sells residential rental property for $500,000 in 1991. The property was purchased for $400,000 in 1986, and D claimed ACRS depreciation of $120,000. Straight-line depreciation would have been $65,000. D Corporation's depreciation recapture and § 1231 gain arc computed as follows:

Step 1:	Compute realized gain:		
	Sales price............................		$500,000
	Less: Adjusted basis		
	Cost............................	$400,000	
	ACRS depreciation.............	− 120,000	− 280,000
	Realized gain.........................		$220,000
Step 2:	Compute excess depreciation:		
	Actual depreciation		$120,000
	Straight-line depreciation............		− 65,000
	Excess depreciation...................		$ 55,000
Step 3:	Compute § 1250 depreciation recapture:		
	Lesser of realized gain of $220,000 or		
	Excess depreciation of $55,000		
	§ 1250 depreciation recapture.........		$ 55,000
Step 4:	Compute depreciation recapture if § 1245 applied:		
	Lesser of realized gain of $220,000 or		
	Actual depreciation of $120,000		
	Depreciation recapture if § 1245 applied......................		$120,000
Step 5:	Compute § 291 ordinary income:		
	Depreciation recapture if § 1245 applied......................		$120,000
	§ 1250 depreciation recapture.........		− 55,000
	Excess recapture potential............		$ 65,000
	Times: § 291 rate...................		× 20%
	§ 291 ordinary income		$ 13,000
Step 6:	Characterize recognized gain:		
	§ 1250 depreciation recapture.........		$ 55,000
	Plus: § 291 ordinary income		+ 13,000
	Ordinary income		$ 68,000
	Realized gain.........................		$220,000
	Less: Ordinary income..............		− 68,000
	§ 1231 gain...........................		$152,000

TRANSACTIONS BETWEEN CORPORATIONS AND THEIR SHAREHOLDERS

Like noncorporate taxpayers, corporations are not allowed to deduct a loss incurred in a transaction between related parties.[67] For example, a loss on the sale of the property from a corporation to a shareholder who owns more than 50 percent of the corporation is nondeductible. In such case, the unrecognized loss must be suspended and may be used by the shareholder to offset gain when the property is sold. A corporation also may be denied deductions for *accrued* but *unpaid* expenses incurred in transactions between related parties. For example, an accrual basis corporation may not deduct accrued expenses payable to related parties on a cash basis *until* the amount actually is paid.[68] For this purpose, a related party is any person owning directly or constructively more than 50 percent of the corporation's outstanding stock. In calculating constructive ownership, stock owned by family members and other entities owned by the taxpayer are included.[69] With respect to the matching of income and deduction provision only, the Tax Reform Act of 1986 expanded the definition of a related party in the case of a *personal service corporation* to include any employee-owner that owns any of the corporation's stock. For this purpose, a personal service corporation is one where the principal activity of the corporation is the performance of personal services *and* where such services are substantially performed by employee-owners. This rule applies to firms engaged in the performance of services in the fields of health, law, engineering, architecture, accounting, actuarial science, performing arts, or consulting.

The sale of property at a *gain* between a corporation and its controlling shareholders is not affected by the disallowance rules. Instead, the gain is *reclassified* as ordinary income rather than capital or § 1231 gain if the property is *depreciable* by the purchaser.[70] For purposes of this rule, a controlling shareholder is defined the same as under the disallowed loss rule (i.e., more than 50% ownership).[71] In calculating ownership, stock owned by other entities and the taxpayer's spouse must be included with the taxpayer's direct ownership.[72] In addition, sales of depreciable property between a corporation and a more than 50 percent shareholder are ineligible for the installment method.[73]

---

[67] § 267(a)(1).

[68] § 267(a)(2).

[69] §§ 267(b) and (c).

[70] § 1239(a).

[71] § 1239(c)(1).

[72] § 1239(c)(2).

[73] § 453(g).

COMPUTATION OF CORPORATE INCOME TAX

The corporate income tax rates in effect for 1991 are as follows:[74]

Taxable Income	Tax Rate
$ 1 - $50,000	15%
50,001 - 75,000	25
Over $75,000	34

Example 21.   Z Corporation has taxable income of $100,000 for its calendar year 1991. Its tax liability is computed as follows:

$$15\% \times \$\ 50{,}000\ =\ \$\ 7{,}500$$
$$25\% \times\ \ \ 25{,}000\ =\ \ \ 6{,}250$$
$$34\% \times\ \ \ 25{,}000\ =\ \ \ 8{,}500$$

Taxable income . . . . $100,000 $22,250 Tax

Z Corporation's tax liability before credits is $22,250.

In an effort to restrict the tax benefit of the lower graduated rates to small corporate businesses with taxable incomes of $100,000 or less, a 5 percent *surtax* is imposed on corporate taxable income in excess of $100,000, up to a maximum surtax of $11,750—the net "savings" of having the first $100,000 of corporate income taxed at the lower rates rather than at 34 percent.[75]

Example 22.   L Corporation has taxable income of $120,000 for its 1991 calendar year. Its tax liability is computed as follows:

$$15\% \times \$50{,}000\ =\ \ \ \$\ 7{,}500$$
$$25\% \times\ \ 25{,}000\ =\ \ \ \ 6{,}250$$
$$34\% \times\ \ 45{,}000\ =\ \ \ 15{,}300$$

Tax liability before surtax. $29,050
   Plus: 5% surtax on $20,000 . . . . +   1,000

Total tax liability for 1991 . . . . $30,050

Example 23.   P Corporation has taxable income of $335,000 for its 1991 tax year. Its tax liability is computed as follows:

$$15\% \times \$\ 50{,}000\ =\ \ \ \$\ \ \ 7{,}500$$
$$25\% \times\ \ \ 25{,}000\ =\ \ \ \ \ 6{,}250$$
$$34\% \times\ \ 260{,}000\ =\ \ \ 88{,}400$$

Tax liability before surtax $102,150
   Plus: 5% sutax on $235,000 . . . . +   11,750

Total tax liability for 1991 . . . . $113,900

Note that the 5% surtax on the $235,000 income in excess of $100,000 completely offsets the benefit of the lower graduated tax rates of 15% and 25%. Thus, corporations with taxable income of $335,000 or more will have a flat tax rate of 34% ($335,000 × 34% = $113,900).

---

[74]   § 11(b).   [75]   *Ibid.*

Taking the 5 percent surtax into account, Exhibit 1-4 presents a corporate tax rate schedule applicable to *most* corporations. The rate structure contained in Exhibit 1-4 is not available to so-called personal service corporations or to certain related corporations. The specific rules applicable to these corporations are discussed below.

PERSONAL SERVICE CORPORATIONS

As described earlier, a personal service corporation (PSC) is a corporation where the principal activity is the performance of services in the fields of health, law, engineering, architecture, accounting, actuarial science, the performing arts, or consulting, *and* substantially all of the stock is owned by employees, retired employees, or their estates.[76] Apparently concerned that PSCs were being used to shield income from the employee-owners' higher individual tax rates, Congress denied the benefits of the lower tax rates to such corporations for taxable years after 1987. As a result, the taxable income of a PSC is subject to a flat rate of 34 percent.[77]

CONTROLLED CORPORATIONS

Certain related corporations must share the tax benefits of the lower graduated tax rates. That is, corporations that are members of a *controlled group* are allowed only *one* layer of income to qualify for *each* of the tax rates below the top marginal rate. Without such a rule, the owner(s) of a corporation that earns more than $75,000 in 1991 could obtain substantial tax savings simply by creating another corporation to which sales or services and the resulting income could be diverted. Such income would then be taxed at marginal rates lower than the top marginal rate plus the surtax imposed on the original corporation.

Exhibit 1-4
Corporate Tax Rate Schedule

Taxable Income (T.I.)	Tax
$ 0 – $ 50,000	15% on T.I. > $ 0 + $ 0
50,000 – 75,000	25% on T.I. > 50,000 + 7,500
75,000 – 100,000	34% on T.I. > 75,000 + 13,750
100,000 – 335,000	39% on T.I. > 100,000 + 22,250
Over $335,000	34% on all T.I.

---

[76] § 448(d)(2).

[77] § 11(b)(2). Note that a PSC is not subject to the 5 percent surtax since it does not benefit from the lower corporate tax rates.

Example 24.   Quik-Fix Inc. operates a very successful auto repair business at a single location in Los Angeles. Projected income and the resulting tax liability for 1991 are $150,000 and $41,750 [$22,250 + ($150,000 − $100,000 = $50,000 × 39%)] , respectively. Absent a related corporation rule, the shareholder(s) of Quik-Fix Inc. could create another separately owned corporation, or have Quik-Fix Inc. create a subsidiary corporation to which enough repair work could be directed, in order to split the anticipated $150,000 taxable income. By splitting the income between two corporations, a $14,250 [$41,750 − $27,500 ($13,750 tax per corporation × 2)] tax savings could be achieved.

The members of the controlled group are permitted to allocate the use of the lower tax rates in any manner they so *elect,* provided every corporate member of the group agrees to the allocation. If the members of the group do not elect a particular apportionment, however, they will be required to share each lower tax rate bracket *equally.*[78] This requirement could result in a loss of some of the tax benefit of the lower corporate tax rates.

Example 25.   In 1991, M Corporation reported taxable income of $75,000 while N Corporation suffered a loss of $25,000. If M and N are members of a controlled group, they are allowed only one benefit of the lower tax rate schedule. If they do not elect to apportion this benefit, their respective tax liabilities will be $19,625 and zero. M Corporation's tax is computed as follows:

15% × $25,000	=	$ 3,750
25% × 12,500	=	3,125
34% × 37,500	=	12,750
Taxable income $75,000		
Tax liability		$19,625

Note that the failure to elect a particular apportionment of the lower tax rate schedule results in an equal division of the $50,000 and $25,000 income (i.e., $25,000 and $12,500 each) subject to the 15 and 25% rates, even though none of N Corporation's income is subject to these rates. If an election is made to apportion the full amount of the rate brackets to M Corporation, the tax liability of M is reduced to $13,750 [(15% × $50,000 = $7,500) + (25% × $25,000) = $6,250)], the same tax liability due if M were unrelated to N.

In addition to the rate bracket limitation described above, a controlled group of corporations is also subject to one accumulated earnings credit, one $40,000 exemption amount for purposes of the corporate alternative minimum tax, and one use of the $10,000 election to expense business property. Therefore, it is

---

[78]   § 1561(a).

important to properly determine whether a group of corporations is a "controlled group" for these purposes. If it is, additional information must be recorded on the corporate tax return (see Schedule J, Line 1 on the Form 1120 located at the end of this chapter).

Code § 1563(a) defines controlled groups as

1. Parent corporations and their 80 percent owned subsidiaries (referred to as a *parent-subsidiary* controlled group)

2. Two or more corporations at least 80 percent owned by five or fewer noncorporate shareholders, who collectively own more than 50 percent of the stock of each corporation (referred to as a *brother-sister* controlled group)

3. Three or more corporations, each of which is a member of either a parent-subsidiary controlled group *or* a brother-sister controlled group, *and* at least one of which is both the common parent corporation of a parent-subsidiary controlled group and a member of a brother-sister controlled group (referred to as a *combined* controlled group)

Parent-Subsidiary Controlled Group. A parent-subsidiary controlled group consists of one or more chains of corporations connected through stock ownership with a common parent corporation.[79] Such a group exists if one corporation—the parent—*directly* owns 80 percent or more of the total combined voting power of all classes of stock entitled to vote or 80 percent of the total value of all classes of stock of another corporation—a subsidiary.[80] Additional corporations are included in the group if at least 80 percent of their voting stock or 80 percent of the value of their stock is directly owned by a parent and/or subsidiary corporation.

> **Example 26.** P Corporation is the sole shareholder of Q Corporation. Because of this stock ownership, P and Q Corporations are members of a parent-subsidiary controlled group. If P Corporation acquires all of the stock of T Corporation, the parent-subsidiary controlled group expands to include P, Q, and T Corporations. Assuming Q Corporation and T Corporation each own 45% of the outstanding stock of U Corporation, the parent-subsidiary controlled group is expanded to include U Corporation. Note that P Corporation (the common parent) need not own any of U Corporation's stock for U to be included as a member of the controlled group. It is sufficient that other members of the group (Q and T) own at least 80% (in value or voting power) of another corporation for such corporation to be included in the group. (See Exhibit 1-5 for an illustration of this parent-subsidiary controlled group.)

---

[79] § 1563(a)(1).

[80] A parent-subsidiary controlled group is essentially the same type of group that is eligible to file a consolidated tax return. See Chapter 8 for a discussion of consolidated tax returns.

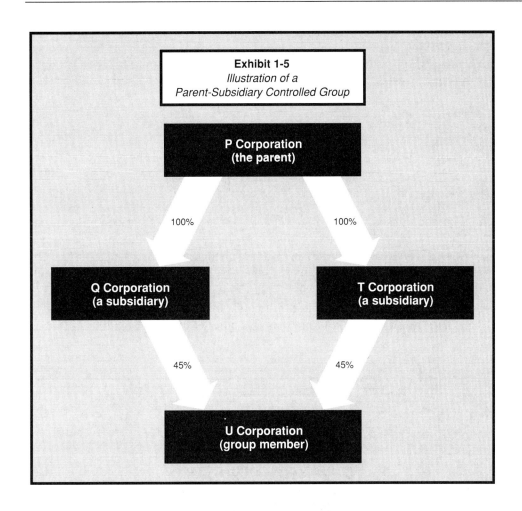

Exhibit 1-5
*Illustration of a
Parent-Subsidiary Controlled Group*

P Corporation
(the parent)

100%   100%

Q Corporation
(a subsidiary)

T Corporation
(a subsidiary)

45%   45%

U Corporation
(group member)

Brother-Sister Controlled Group. A brother-sister controlled group consists of two or more corporations connected through the stock ownership of certain noncorporate shareholders. Such a group exists if five or fewer individuals, estates, or trusts own (1) at least 80 percent of the total combined voting power of all classes of stock entitled to vote or at least 80 percent of the total value of all classes of the stock of *each* corporation, and (2) more than 50 percent of the total combined voting power of all classes of stock entitled to vote or more than 50 percent of the total value of shares of all classes of stock of each corporation, taking into account only the *lowest* stock ownership percentage of each shareholder that is identical with respect to each corporation.[81]

---

[81] § 1563(a)(2).

Example 27. The stock of Corporations X, Y, and Z is owned by the following unrelated shareholders:

Individuals	Corporations			Lowest Identical Ownership
	X	Y	Z	
A	40%	20%	30%	20%
B	30	40	20	20
C	30	40	50	30
Total	100%	100%	100%	70%

(handwritten annotation: over 50%)

Corporations X, Y, and Z are members of a brother-sister controlled group because (1) at least 80% of the stock of each corporation is owned by a group of five or fewer persons who own stock in *each* corporation (thereby meeting the 80% ownership test), and (2) each of the members of this same shareholder group (A, B, and C) have identical ownership interest of 70% in each corporation (satisfying the 50% ownership test). (See Exhibit 1-6 for an illustration of a brother-sister controlled group.)

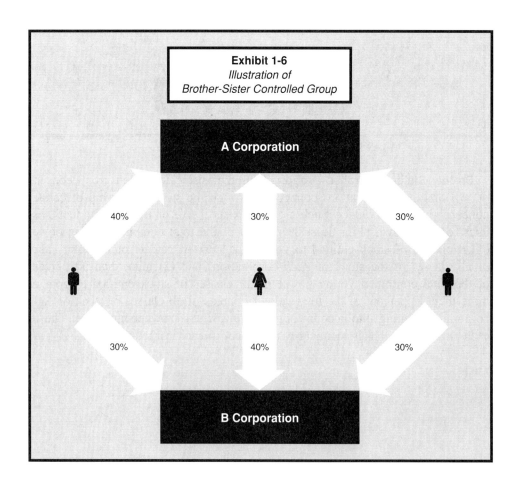

Exhibit 1-6
Illustration of
Brother-Sister Controlled Group

Example 28. Changing the facts in *Example 27*, the stock ownership of X, Y, and Z Corporations appears as follows:

	Corporations			Lowest Identical Ownership
Individuals	X	Y	Z	
A	70%	10%	20%	10%
B	20	70	10	10
C	10	20	70	10
Total	100%	100%	100%	30%

Does not apply

Although the 80% ownership test is met for each of the corporations, the lowest identical stock ownership does not exceed 50%. Thus X, Y, and Z are not members of a brother-sister controlled group.

For purposes of the 80 percent test, a shareholder's stock ownership is counted only if stock in each of the potential group members is owned.[82]

Example 29. Individuals R and S own the stock of X and Y Corporations as follows:

	Corporations		Lowest Identical Ownership
Individuals	X	Y	
R	100%	60%	60%
S	–	40	
Total	100%	100%	60%

Although it would initially appear that X and Y are a controlled group, they are not. S's ownership in Y is not counted towards the 80% test because S does not own any of the stock in X. If S's 40% is eliminated, only 60% of X and Y is owned.

Exhibit 1-7 contains an illustration of a combined controlled group.

ALTERNATIVE MINIMUM TAX

Like individuals, corporations are subject to the alternative minimum tax. The tax is computed at a 20 percent rate (in contrast to the 24% rate for individuals) on alternative minimum taxable income (AMTI) in excess of $40,000.[83] The $40,000 exemption is reduced by 25 percent of the amount of AMTI in excess of $150,000.[84] Consequently, the exemption is completely eliminated for AMTI in excess of $310,000.

---

[82] See *U.S. v. Vogel Fertilizer Co.*, 82-1 USTC ¶9134, 49 AFTR2d 82-491, 455 U.S. 16 (USSC, 1982).

[83] See §§ 56(a) and (b).

[84] § 55(d)(3)(A).

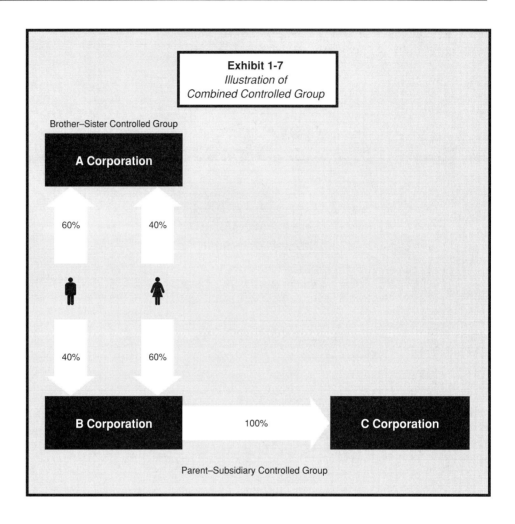

Exhibit 1-7
Illustration of Combined Controlled Group

Brother–Sister Controlled Group

A Corporation

60%   40%

40%   60%

B Corporation   100%   **C Corporation**

Parent–Subsidiary Controlled Group

The computation of a corporation's alternative minimum tax (AMT) liability is illustrated in Exhibit 1-8. Note that like an individual taxpayer, a corporation will have an AMT liability *only* if its tentative AMT (reduced by allowable credits) *exceeds* its regular tax liability for the year.

AMT Adjustments.   Creations of the Tax Reform Act of 1986 (TRA 86), these adjustments simply reflect timing differences. Relative to the regular tax treatment, the AMT provisions normally postpone deductions and accelerate income. Several of these adjustments are identified in Exhibit 1-9. For the items shown in Exhibit 1-9, the adjustments are positive initially (i.e., added back to regular taxable income in computing AMTI) but are reversed in later years (i.e., subtracted from taxable income to arrive at AMTI). Perhaps the best example of this phenomenon is depreciation. Regular tax depreciation for personal property

---

Exhibit 1-8
Calculation of the
Corporate Alternative Minimum Tax

Start with:	Regular taxable income	$xxx,xxx
Plus/Minus:	AMT adjustments (see Exhibit 1-9)	± xx,xxx
Equals:	AMT adjusted taxable income	$xxx,xxx
Plus:	Sum of tax preference items (see Exhibit 1-11)	+ xx,xxx
Equals:	Alternative minimum taxable income(AMTI)	$xxx,xxx
Less:	Exemption [$40,000 − 25% of (AMTI − $150,000)]	− xx,xxx
Equals:	AMTI base	$xxx,xxx
Times:	AMT rate	× xx%
Equals:	Gross alternative minimum tax	$xxx,xxx
Less:	AMT foreign tax credit	− xx,xxx
Equals:	Tentative AMT	$xxx,xxx
Less:	Regular tax liability	− xx,xxx
Equals:	Alternative miminum tax	$ xx,xxx

(MACRS) is computed using a 200 percent declining balance method, a specified cost recovery, and the appropriate convention. Regular tax depreciation for real property is computed using the straight-line method, the half-year convention, and a life of 31.5 years for nonresidential realty and 28.5 years for residential realty. In contrast, depreciation for AMTI is generally computed under ADS, the alternative depreciation system. ADS requires the calculation to be made using the straight-line method, the appropriate convention, and the class life of the property for personal property and 40 years for real property. However, for AMT purposes the Code normally requires depreciation of personal property to be computed using the 150 percent declining balance method rather than straight-line.[85] Due to differences in the rates and lives that are used to compute regular and AMT depreciation, positive or negative adjustments are required in computing AMTI.[86]

---

[85] § 56 (a)(1)(A)(ii).

[86] The taxpayer may elect to use AMT depreciation (life and method) for regular tax purposes to avoid separate depreciation schedules.

Exhibit 1-9
Selected AMT Adjustments

1. Regular tax cost recovery deductions on property placed in service after 1986 in excess of amount allowed for AMT purposes*

2. Regular tax deductions for pollution control facilities and mining, exploration, and development costs in excess of required AMT amortization*

3. Excess of AMT gain reported from long-term contracts on the percentage completion method over amount reported as regular tax gain under the completed contract method*

4. Regular tax NOLs in excess of AMT NOL deduction*

5. Seventy-five percent (75%) of the adjusted current earnings (ACE) in excess of AMTI (computed before this adjustment item)*

*Each of these items represents a timing difference. As such, they are *positive adjustments* (i.e., additions to regular taxable income in arriving at AMTI) in the early years; when reversed, they become *negative adjustments*.

Example 30. T Corporation placed an asset costing $100,000 in service on February 15, 1991. Assuming the asset is "3-year property," the effect on alternative minimum taxable income (AMTI) is computed as follows:

	1991	1992	1993	1994
Regular tax deduction (200%)	$33,330	$44,450	$14,810	$ 7,410
AMT deduction (150%)	(25,000)	(37,500)	(25,000)	(12,500)
Effect of adjustment on AMTI	$ 8,330 Increase	$ 6,950 Increase	($10,190) Decrease	($5,090) Decrease

Note that the above example illustrates the need to maintain one set of depreciation records for each tax system in order to compute the basis of assets for gain or loss determination. It is also important to note that this depreciation adjustment applies *only* to assets placed in service after 1986. The excess depreciation on assets placed in service before 1987 will give rise to a tax preference item *rather* than an AMT adjustment.

The most significant aspect of the corporate AMT enacted by TRA 86 is the adjustment for "adjusted current earnings" (ACE). Congress was concerned that certain corporations were reporting income for financial accounting purposes yet reporting little or no taxable income. To address this problem, Congress created the ACE adjustment to ensure that all corporations would pay some minimum tax on book income. In theory, the ACE adjustment simply requires taxpayers to compare book income to taxable income to determine the amount of financial accounting income that somehow escaped tax. The computation of AMTI requires that a portion of this amount be added to taxable income. Technically, the ACE adjustment is equal to 75 percent of the difference between *adjusted current earnings* and AMTI.[87] In this calculation, adjusted current earnings serves as a proxy for book income.

> **Example 31.** Z Corporation has adjusted current earnings (ACE) of $80,000 and alternative minimum taxable income (without regard to the ACE adjustment) of $50,000. Because ACE exceeds AMTI by $30,000, 75% of this amount must be added to Z Corporation's AMTI. As a result, the corporation's AMTI for the year is $72,500 [$50,000 + ($30,000 × 75%)].

The computation of adjusted current earnings begins with alternative minimum taxable income (AMTI) calculated before the adjustments for ACE or the AMT NOL. To determine the ACE amount, positive or negative adjustments are made to AMTI for special items that have not already been included in the calculation of AMTI. The formula for computing the ACE adjustment is shown in Exhibit 1-10.

As shown in Exhibit 1-10, a host of adjustments must be made to AMTI to reach ACE. Perhaps the most important of these is the adjustment for depreciation. Depreciation for ACE is generally computed under ADS as it is for AMTI. However, as noted above, the Code requires AMTI depreciation for most personal property to be computed using a 150 percent declining balance rate. This rule does not exist for ACE. Thus ACE and AMTI depreciation for personalty will differ and require an adjustment. Due to these differences, taxpayers not only must maintain depreciation schedules for regular tax and AMT purposes, but they also will be required to keep a third set of ACE depreciation records for personalty.[88]

One final observation should be made about the ACE adjustment. The ACE adjustment can be positive or negative. However, any negative adjustment cannot exceed prior net positive adjustments. For this reason, the corporation may want to keep track of its ACE adjustments each year even if it is not subject to the AMT.

> **Example 32.** In 1991, X Corporation had an AMTI of 100,000 and an ACE amount of $300,000. The positive ACE adjustment that is added to AMTI is $150,000 [75% × ($300,000 − $100,000)]. In 1992, X had an AMTI of $400,000 and an ACE amount of $100,000. In this case, the negative ACE amount is $225,000 [75% × ($100,000 − $400,000)]. The negative adjustment to AMTI is limited to $150,000, the positive adjustment in prior years.

---

[87] § 56(g).

[88] Depreciation for ACE will normally be identical to that computed for earnings and prof-

its purposes discussed in Chapter 3; differences may arise, however.

Exhibit 1-10
Calculation of the ACE Adjustment

AMTI

Plus: Income excluded from AMTI but included for ACE
            State and municipal bond interest income
            Life insurance proceeds > cash surrender value (e.g., key person
              life insurance)
            Income element included in cash surrender value of life insurance
            Entire gain on installment sale (except when interest is charged)
            Certain other adjustments

        Deductions not allowed for ACE
            70% dividends-received deduction (80% and 100% generally are
              allowed for ACE)
            Amortization of organization expenses incurred after 1989
            Excess of FIFO over LIFO
            AMTI depreciation in excess of that allowed for ACE

Less: Expenses attributable to income excluded above
            Life insurance expenses
            Interest incurred on debt to acquire tax-exempt bonds
        ACE depreciation in excess of that allowed for AMTI

Equals: Adjusted current earnings (ACE)

        Less: AMTI

Equals: Base

        Times: 75%

Equals: ACE adjustment (positive or negative)

Tax Preference Items.   Corporations are required to use many of the tax preferences that individuals use in arriving at AMTI. These items are presented in Exhibit 1–11.

Minimum Tax Credit.   To alleviate the possibility of double taxation under the two tax systems, Congress introduced an alternative minimum tax credit in 1986. Basically, the alternative minimum tax paid in one year may be used as a credit against the taxpayer's future regular tax liability. The credit may be carried

Exhibit 1-11
Tax Preference Items[89]

1. Depletion in excess of basis with respect to natural resources

2. Excess intangible drilling and development costs

3. Excess reserves for losses on bad debts of financial institutions

4. Tax-exempt interest income (net of expenses related to its production) from private activity bonds

5. Untaxed appreciation on charitable contributions of capital gain property (except for contributions of tangible personal property made during taxable years beginning in 1991)

6. Excess accelerated depreciation (over straight-line amount) on nonrecovery real property placed in service before 1981

7. Excess accelerated cost recovery deductions (over straight-line alternative) on 19, 18, and 15-year real property placed in service before 1987

forward indefinitely until used—however, the credit cannot be carried back *nor* can it be used to offset any future minimum tax liability.[90]

> **Example 33.** K Corporation's total AMT liability for 1991 is $70,000. This amount is carried forward to 1992 to reduce the regular tax (but not the minimum tax) in that year. If the 1992 regular tax is $130,000 (the minimum tax liability would be $70,000), the $70,000 credit carryover may be used to offset only $60,000 of the regular tax ($130,000 regular tax − $70,000 minimum tax). The remaining $10,000 credit may be carried over to 1993.

TAX CREDITS

Most of the same tax credits available to individuals also are available to corporations. However, corporations are not entitled to the earned income credit, the child care credit, or the credit for the elderly.[91]

---

[89] § 57 sets forth all the tax preference items and the specifics of each calculation.

[90] § 53(a).

[91] See §§ 32, 21, and 22.

ACCOUNTING PERIODS AND METHODS

Accounting Periods. A corporation generally is allowed to choose either a calendar year or fiscal year for its reporting period.[92] However, a personal service corporation (PSC) must use a calendar year for tax purposes unless it can satisfy IRS requirements that there is a business purpose for a fiscal year or a special election is made.[93] If a PSC elects to use a fiscal year, it is subject to special rules governing the deductions for payments to employee-owners during the year.[94] Like PSCs, S corporations generally must use a calendar year for tax purposes.[95] Exceptions to this rule are discussed in Chapter 12.

Accounting Methods. Unlike individuals, most corporations are denied the use of the cash method of accounting for tax purposes. There are three basic exceptions, however. The cash method may be used by the following:

1. Corporations with average annual gross receipts of $5 million or less in all prior taxable years

2. S corporations

3. Personal service corporations[96]

CORPORATE TAX FORMS AND FILING REQUIREMENTS

Corporations are required to report their income and tax liability on Form 1120 (or on Form 1120-A for those corporations with gross receipts, total income, and total assets *all* under $250,000). Page 1 of this form contains the summary of taxable income and tax due the Federal government or the refund due the corporation. There are separate schedules for the computation of cost of goods sold, compensation of officers, dividends-received deduction, and tax computation.

In addition to the computational schedules, Form 1120 also has several schedules which contain additional information, such as financial balance sheets for the beginning and end of the year. Form 1120 also contains *two* schedules of reconciliation, Schedules M-1 and M-2.

Form 1120-A is a much shorter form than Form 1120. Although page 1 of this form is very similar to Form 1120, there are fewer supporting schedules, a simplified balance sheet, and no Schedule M-2 (see pages 1-50 and 1-51 for a copy of Form 1120-A).

---

[92]   § 441.

[93]   §§ 441(i) and 444.

[94]   § 280H.

[95]   § 1378(b). But see § 444 for an exception, and Chapter 12 for further discussion.

[96]   § 448.

Schedule M-1 is a reconciliation of income per books and income per tax returns. Both permanent and timing differences will appear in this schedule.

Example 34. Z Corporation reports the following data for 1991:

Net income per books	$44,500
Federal income tax liability	7,500
Officer's life insurance premiums	5,000
Excess accelerated cost recovery	6,000
Excess charitable contributions	1,000
Municipal bond interest	2,000

A completed Schedule M-1 is shown below.

Schedule M-1	Reconciliation of Income per Books With Income per Return (This schedule does not have to be completed if the total assets on line 15, column (d), of Schedule L are less than $25,000.)		
1 Net income per books	44,500	**7** Income recorded on books this year not included on this return (itemize):	
2 Federal income tax	7,500	**a** Tax-exempt interest $ 2,000	
3 Excess of capital losses over capital gains			
4 Income subject to tax not recorded on books this year (itemize):			2,000
		8 Deductions on this return not charged against book income this year (itemize):	
5 Expenses recorded on books this year not deducted on this return (itemize):		**a** Depreciation $ 6,000	
a Depreciation $		**b** Contributions carryover $	
b Contributions carryover $			
c Travel and entertainment $			6,000
	6,000	**9** Total of lines 7 and 8	8,000
6 Total of lines 1 through 5	59,000	**10** Income (line 28, page 1)—line 6 less line 9	50,000

The starting point in completing the M-1 is the net income per books of $44,500. Added to this amount are items that are deducted in computing net income per books but that are not allowed in computing taxable income. These are the federal income tax, charitable contributions in excess of the 10% taxable income limitation, and premiums on "key-person" life insurance. Next, the net income per books is decreased by income included in book income but not included in taxable income (i.e., municipal bond interest). And finally, there is an adjustment for accelerated cost recovery in excess of straight-line depreciation allowed for income tax purposes but not allowed for book income determination.

A problem sometimes arises with respect to the Federal income tax (FIT) adjustment on the Schedule M-1. If the actual FIT amount is entered in Line 2, this amount may differ from the FIT expense accrued by the corporation. In this case, an over or under accrual amount must be determined so that the net effect is to adjust the book income by the accrued expense. Thus, in *Example 34*, if the actual FIT was entered on Line 2 in the amount of $7,500 but the corporation accrued FIT expense of $9,000, there would be an overaccrual amount of $1,500 that must be shown on the Schedule M-1. This adjustment may be made on Line 5. An underaccrual amount may also be shown on Line 5 as a negative entry.

Schedule M-2 reconciles opening and closing retained earnings. This schedule uses *accounting* rather than tax data. Corporations without any special transactions will show an increase in retained earnings for net income and a decrease for distributions (i.e., dividends) as the major items in Schedule M-2.

> **Example 35.** This is a continuation of *Example 34*. Additional information with respect to Z Corporation includes
>
> | | |
> |---|---:|
> | Retained Earnings balance at beginning of year .... | 150,000 |
> | Cash dividends paid .... | 10,000 |
>
> A completed Schedule M-2 is shown below.

Schedule M-2	Analysis of Unappropriated Retained Earnings per Books (line 25, Schedule L) (This schedule does not have to be completed if the total assets on line 15, column (d), of Schedule L are less than $25,000.)			
1 Balance at beginning of year	150,000	5 Distributions: a Cash	10,000
2 Net income per books	44,500	b Stock	
3 Other increases (itemize): _____		c Property	
		6 Other decreases (itemize): _____	
		7 Total of lines 5 and 6	10,000
4 Total of lines 1, 2, and 3	194,500	8 Balance at end of year (line 4 less line 7)	184,500

The use of these schedules is further illustrated in an example of a corporate tax return presented later in this chapter.

FILING REQUIREMENTS

Form 1120 must be filed by the 15th day of the third month following the close of the corporation's tax year.[97] As mentioned previously, a regular corporation is permitted to elect either a calendar or fiscal year. The decision generally is unaffected by the tax years of its shareholders.[98] The selection is made by filing the first return by the appropriate due date; for calendar year corporations, the due date is March 15. The return must be signed by an officer or other authorized person.[99]

Corporations may obtain an automatic six-month extension of time to file the tax return.[100] The extension only covers the return—not the tax due. The request for extension (Form 7004) must be accompanied by the full amount of estimated tax due. The extension can be terminated by the government on ten days' notice. With permission of the IRS, corporations may be granted an additional three-month extension of time to file.

---

[97] § 6072(b).

[98] Although a regular corporation's selection of a calendar or fiscal year is not affected by the tax years of its shareholders, a corporation electing to be treated as a conduit (flow-through) entity under Subchapter S of the Code generally is required to adopt the same tax year as its shareholders. See Chapter 12 for greater details.

[99] § 6062.

[100] § 6081(b).

ESTIMATED TAX PAYMENTS

Corporations are required to file and pay estimated tax (including any estimated AMT liability).[101] The estimates are due the 15th day of the 4th, 6th, 9th, and 12th months of the tax year. For a calendar year corporation, the payment dates for estimated taxes are as follows:

> April 15
> June 15
> September 15
> December 15

One-fourth of the estimated tax due is to be paid on each payment date.

To avoid a penalty for underpayment of the estimated tax, at least 90 percent of the corporation's tax due for the year must be paid as estimated taxes.[102] Specifically, the corporation must pay *one-fourth* of this amount—22.5 percent (90% ÷ 4) of the tax shown on its return—by the due date of each installment.[103] However, the underpayment penalty is not normally imposed where the installment for any period is

1. At least 25 percent of the tax shown on the prior year's return (if such a return was for 12 months and showed a tax liability); or

2. Equal to or in excess of 90 percent of the tax due for each quarter based on annualized taxable income.[104]

> **Example 36.** B Corporation, a calendar year corporation, made timely 1991 estimated tax payments of $20,000 each quarter. The actual tax liability for 1991 is $120,000; the 1990 tax liability was $98,000. Income was earned evenly throughout the year.
>
> B could have avoided the underpayment penalty by paying installments of $24,500, the lesser of $27,000 or $24,500, as computed below.

$$90\% \text{ of current year's tax:} \quad \frac{90\% \times \$120,000}{4} = \$27,000$$

$$100\% \text{ of last year's tax:} \quad \frac{100\% \times \$98,000}{4} = \$24,500$$

> Because the estimated payments were insufficient, B must pay a penalty based on the underpayment that occurred with each installment, $4,500 ($24,500 − $20,000). Note that the annualized income exception is not available because income is earned ratably throughout the year.

---

[101] § 6154.

[102] § 6655.

[103] § 6655(b).

[104] See §§ 6655(d) and (e) for these exceptions, and Chapter 17 for a discussion of underpayment penalties.

A so-called *large* corporation—one with taxable income of $1 million or more in any of its three preceding taxable years—is not allowed to use exception 1 above *except* for its first estimated tax payment of the year.[105] If a large corporation uses the first quarter exception, any deficiency between the normal required amount (i.e., 90% of the current year's tax) and the amount paid under the first quarter exception (100% of last year's tax) must be made up with the second installment.

Example 37. Assume the same facts as in *Example 36*, except that the corporation's taxable income for the last three years was as follows:

Year	Taxable Income
1988	$ 900,000
1989	1,200,000
1990	800,000

Because the corporation has taxable income in one of its last three taxable years that is $1 million or more (i.e., 1989), it is considered a large corporation. Consequently, unlike other corporations, it is allowed to base its installment payments on last year's tax *only* for the first payment. Therefore, its first installment would be $24,500. Its second installment payment amount would be $29,500, computed as follows:

Normal installment for large corporation.............	$27,000	$27,000
Installment based on last year's tax................	(24,500)	
Deficiency...	$ 2,500	2,500
Second installment................................		$29,500

Note that the third and fourth installments would drop to the normal 90 percent amount of $27,000.

Finally, a corporation whose tax liability for the year is less than $500 is not subject to the underpayment penalty.[106] If a corporation does not qualify for any of the exceptions, its underpayment penalty is computed on Form 2220.

---

[105]   § 6655(d)(2).   [106]   § 6655(f).

EXAMPLE OF CORPORATE TAX RETURN

The next few pages contain an illustration of a corporation's annual Federal income tax return (Form 1120). This return is based on the following information:

R Corporation is a calendar year, cash method taxpayer that operates a men's clothing store. John Beyond owns 100% of R Corporation's stock and is employed as the company's only officer. The corporation had the following items of income and expense for the current year:

Gross sales	$390,000
Sales returns	2,000
Inventory at beginning of year	12,000
Purchases	110,000
Inventory at end of year	14,000
Salaries and wages	
Officers	40,000
Other	15,000
Rent expenses	12,000
Interest expense	5,000
Interest income	
Municipal bonds	700
Other	1,000
Charitable contributions	7,900
Depreciation	11,000
Dividend income	3,000
Advertising expenses	5,000
Professional fees paid	2,000
Taxes paid (state income and payroll taxes)	4,000
Premiums paid on key-man life insurance policy	4,550

R Corporation timely paid $60,000 in estimated income tax payments based on its prior year's tax liability of $59,520. All dividends received by the corporation qualify for the 70% dividends-received deduction. The corporation declared and paid dividends of $6,500 to its sole shareholder. Additional information is provided in the balance sheets in Schedule L.

R Corporation's 1990 tax liability is computed as follows:

15% ×	$ 50,000	=	$ 7,500		
25% ×	25,000	=	6,250		
34% ×	25,000	=	8,500		
39% ×	80,000	=	31,200		
Taxable income	$180,000		$53,450	Tax	

Note: The sample corporate tax return is on 1990 tax forms because the 1991 forms were not available at the publication date of this text. Also, a blank Form 1120-A follows this sample completed tax return for comparative purposes.

Form **1120**	**U.S. Corporation Income Tax Return**		OMB No. 1545-0123

Department of the Treasury
Internal Revenue Service

For calendar year 1990 or tax year beginning _____ 1990, ending _____, 19 ____

1990

▶ Instructions are separate. See page 1 for Paperwork Reduction Act Notice.

Check if a—

A Consolidated return ☐
B Personal holding co. ☐
C Personal service corp.(as defined in Temp. Regs. sec. 1.441-4T—see Instructions) ☐

Use IRS label. Otherwise, please print or type.

Name **R CORPORATION**

Number, street, and room or suite no. (If a P.O. box, see page 2 of Instructions.) **123 JONES AVENUE**

City or town, state, and ZIP code **ANYWHERE, USA 98765**

D Employer identification number **74-0987650**

E Date incorporated **1-1-81**

F Total assets (see Specific Instructions) $ **212,300**

G Check applicable boxes: (1) ☐ Initial return (2) ☐ Final return (3) ☐ Change in address

Income

1a	Gross receipts or sales **390,000** b Less returns and allowances **2,000** c Bal ▶	1c	**388,000**
2	Cost of goods sold (Schedule A, line 7)	2	**108,000**
3	Gross profit (line 1c less line 2)	3	**280,000**
4	Dividends (Schedule C, line 19)	4	**3,000**
5	Interest	5	**1,000**
6	Gross rents	6	
7	Gross royalties	7	
8	Capital gain net income (attach Schedule D (Form 1120))	8	
9	Net gain or (loss) from Form 4797, Part II, line 18 (attach Form 4797)	9	
10	Other income (see Instructions—attach schedule)	10	
11	**Total income**—Add lines 3 through 10 ▶	11	**284,000**

Deductions (See Instructions for limitations on deductions.)

12	Compensation of officers (Schedule E, line 4)	12	**40,000**
13a	Salaries and wages **15,000** b Less jobs credit **-0-** c Balance ▶	13c	**15,000**
14	Repairs	14	
15	Bad debts	15	
16	Rents	16	**12,000**
17	Taxes	17	**4,000**
18	Interest	18	**5,000**
19	Contributions (**see Instructions for 10% limitation**)	19	**7,900**
20	Depreciation (attach Form 4562) 20 **11,000**		
21	Less depreciation claimed on Schedule A and elsewhere on return 21a **-0-**	21b	**11,000**
22	Depletion	22	
23	Advertising	23	**5,000**
24	Pension, profit-sharing, etc., plans	24	
25	Employee benefit programs	25	
26	Other deductions (attach schedule) ▶	26	**2,000**
27	**Total deductions**—Add lines 12 through 26. ▶	27	**101,900**
28	Taxable income before net operating loss deduction and special deductions (line 11 less line 27)	28	**182,100**
29	**Less: a** Net operating loss deduction (see Instructions) 29a		
	b Special deductions (Schedule C, line 20) 29b **2,100**	29c	**2,100**
30	**Taxable income**—Line 28 less line 29c	30	**180,000**
31	Total tax (Schedule J, line 10)	31	**53,450**

Tax and Payments

32	**Payments: a** 1989 overpayment credited to 1990 32a		
	b 1990 estimated tax payments 32b **60,000**		
	c Less 1990 refund applied for on Form 4466 32c ( ) d Bal ▶ 32d		
	e Tax deposited with Form 7004 32e		
	f Credit from regulated investment companies (attach Form 2439) 32f		
	g Credit for Federal tax on fuels (attach Form 4136). See Instructions 32g	32h	**60,000**
33	Enter any **penalty** for underpayment of estimated tax—Check ▶ ☐ if Form 2220 is attached	33	
34	**Tax due**—If the total of lines 31 and 33 is larger than line 32h, enter amount owed	34	
35	**Overpayment**—If line 32h is larger than the total of lines 31 and 33, enter amount overpaid	35	**6,550**
36	Enter amount of line 35 you want: **Credited to 1991 estimated tax** ▶ **6,550** **Refunded** ▶	36	**NONE**

Please Sign Here

Under penalties of perjury, I declare that I have examined this return, including accompanying schedules and statements, and to the best of my knowledge and belief, it is true, correct, and complete. Declaration of preparer (other than taxpayer) is based on all information of which preparer has any knowledge.

▶ *John Beyond*   Signature of officer   Date **3/14/91**   ▶ Title **PRESIDENT**

Paid Preparer's Use Only

Preparer's signature ▶ *Sherry L. Hartman*   Date **3/10/91**   Check if self-employed ☐   Preparer's social security number

Firm's name (or yours if self-employed) and address ▶ **ROY W. HARTMAN & DAUGHTERS   11318 KINGSLAND BLVD. SEALY, TX**   E.I. No. ▶ **74-2735841**   ZIP code ▶ **77540**

Form 1120 (1990) Page **2**

Schedule A **Cost of Goods Sold** (See Instructions for line 2, page 1.)

1 Inventory at beginning of year	1	12,000
2 Purchases	2	110,000
3 Cost of labor	3	
4a Additional section 263A costs (see Instructions—attach schedule)	4a	
b Other costs (attach schedule)	4b	
5 Total—Add lines 1 through 4b	5	122,000
6 Inventory at end of year	6	14,000
7 Cost of goods sold—Line 5 less line 6. Enter here and on line 2, page 1.	7	108,000

8a Check all methods used for valuing closing inventory:
    (i) ☐ Cost   **(ii)** ☑ Lower of cost or market as described in Regulations section 1.471-4 (see Instructions)
    (iii) ☐ Writedown of "subnormal" goods as described in Regulations section 1.471-2(c) (see Instructions)
    (iv) ☐ Other (Specify method used and attach explanation.) ▶ -
  b Check if the LIFO inventory method was adopted this tax year for any goods (if checked, attach Form 970) . . . . . . ☐
  c If the LIFO inventory method was used for this tax year, enter percentage (or amounts) of
    closing inventory computed under LIFO . . . . | 8c |
  d Do the rules of section 263A (with respect to property produced or acquired for resale) apply to the corporation? . . ☐ Yes ☑ No
  e Was there any change in determining quantities, cost, or valuations between opening and closing inventory? If "Yes,"
    attach explanation . . . . ☐ Yes ☑ No

Schedule C **Dividends and Special Deductions** (See Instructions.)

	(a) Dividends received	(b) %	(c) Special deductions: (a) × (b)
1 Dividends from less-than-20%-owned domestic corporations that are subject to the 70% deduction (other than debt-financed stock)	3,000	70	2,100
2 Dividends from 20%-or-more-owned domestic corporations that are subject to the 80% deduction (other than debt-financed stock)		80	
3 Dividends on debt-financed stock of domestic and foreign corporations (section 246A)		see Instructions	
4 Dividends on certain preferred stock of less-than-20%-owned public utilities		41.176	
5 Dividends on certain preferred stock of 20%-or-more-owned public utilities		47.059	
6 Dividends from less-than-20%-owned foreign corporations and certain FSCs that are subject to the 70% deduction		70	
7 Dividends from 20%-or-more-owned foreign corporations and certain FSCs that are subject to the 80% deduction		80	
8 Dividends from wholly owned foreign subsidiaries subject to the 100% deduction (section 245(b))		100	
9 Total—Add lines 1 through 8. See Instructions for limitation			2,100
10 Dividends from domestic corporations received by a small business investment company operating under the Small Business Investment Act of 1958		100	
11 Dividends from certain FSCs that are subject to the 100% deduction (section 245(c)(1))		100	
12 Dividends from affiliated group members subject to the 100% deduction (section 243(a)(3))		100	
13 Other dividends from foreign corporations not included on lines 3, 6, 7, 8, or 11			
14 Income from controlled foreign corporations under subpart F (attach Forms 5471)			
15 Foreign dividend gross-up (section 78)			
16 IC-DISC and former DISC dividends not included on lines 1, 2, or 3 (section 246(d))			
17 Other dividends			
18 Deduction for dividends paid on certain preferred stock of public utilities (see Instructions)			
19 Total dividends—Add lines 1 through 17. Enter here and on line 4, page 1. ▶	3,000		
20 Total deductions—Add lines 9, 10, 11, 12, and 18. Enter here and on line 29b, page 1 . . . . ▶			2,100

Schedule E **Compensation of Officers** (See Instructions for line 12, page 1.)
Complete Schedule E only if total receipts (line 1a, plus lines 4 through 10, of page 1, Form 1120) are $500,000 or more.

(a) Name of officer	(b) Social security number	(c) Percent of time devoted to business	Percent of corporation stock owned		(f) Amount of compensation
			(d) Common	(e) Preferred	
1		%	%	%	
		%	%	%	
		%	%	%	
		%	%	%	
		%	%	%	

2 Total compensation of officers . . . .
3 **Less:** Compensation of officers claimed on Schedule A and elsewhere on return . . . . (   )
4 Compensation of officers deducted on line 12, page 1 . . . .

Form 1120 (1990)   Page **3**

Schedule J   **Tax Computation**

1   Check if you are a member of a controlled group (see sections 1561 and 1563) . . . . ▶ ☐

2   If the box on line 1 is checked:

   a Enter your share of the $50,000 and $25,000 taxable income bracket amounts (in that order):

     (i) |$_____| (ii) |$_____|

   b Enter your share of the additional 5% tax (not to exceed $11,750) ▶ |$_____|

3   Income tax (see Instructions to figure the tax). Check this box if the corporation is a qualified personal service corporation (see Instructions on page 12). ▶ ☐ . . . . | **3** | 53,450 |

4a Foreign tax credit (attach Form 1118)	**4a**	
b Possessions tax credit (attach Form 5735)	**4b**	
c Orphan drug credit (attach Form 6765)	**4c**	
d Credit for fuel produced from a nonconventional source (see Instructions)	**4d**	

  e General business credit. Enter here and check which forms are attached:

     ☐ Form 3800   ☐ Form 3468   ☐ Form 5884

     ☐ Form 6478   ☐ Form 6765   ☐ Form 8586 . . . . . . | **4e** |

  f Credit for prior year minimum tax (attach Form 8801) . . . . . . | **4f** |

5   **Total**—Add lines 4a through 4f . . . . | **5** | –0– |

6   Line 3 less line 5 . . . . | **6** | 53,450 |

7   Personal holding company tax (attach Schedule PH (Form 1120)) . . . . . . | **7** | |

8   Recapture taxes. Check if from: ☐ Form 4255 ☐ Form 8611 . . . . | **8** | |

9a Alternative minimum tax (attach Form 4626). See Instructions . . . . | **9a** | |

  b Environmental tax (attach Form 4626) . . . . | **9b** | |

10 **Total tax**—Add lines 6 through 9b. Enter here and on line 31, page 1 . . . . | **10** | 53,450 |

Additional Information (See General Instruction F.) | Yes | No |

H Refer to the list in the Instructions and state the principal:

  (1) Business activity code no. ▶ _____

  (2) Business activity ▶ _____

  (3) Product or service ▶ _____

I (1) Did the corporation at the end of the tax year own, directly or indirectly, 50% or more of the voting stock of a domestic corporation? (For rules of attribution, see section 267(c).) . | | ✕ |

    If "Yes," attach a schedule showing: (a) name, address, and identifying number; (b) percentage owned; and (c) taxable income or (loss) before NOL and special deductions of such corporation for the tax year ending with or within your tax year.

  (2) Did any individual, partnership, corporation, estate, or trust at the end of the tax year own, directly or indirectly, 50% or more of the corporation's voting stock? (For rules of attribution, see section 267(c).) If "Yes," complete (a) through (c) . . . . | ✕ | |

    (a) Attach a schedule showing name, address, and identifying number.

    (b) Enter percentage owned ▶ __100%_____

    (c) Was the owner of such voting stock a foreign person? (See Instructions.) **Note:** If "Yes," the corporation may have to file Form 5472 . . . . | | ✕ |

    If "Yes," enter owner's country ▶ _____

J Was the corporation a U.S. shareholder of any controlled foreign corporation? (See sections 951 and 957.). . . . . | | ✕ |

  If "Yes," attach Form 5471 for each such corporation.

K At any time during the tax year, did the corporation have an interest in or a signature or other authority over a financial account in a foreign country (such as a bank account, securities account, or other financial account)? . . . . | | ✕ |

  (See General Instruction F and filing requirements for form TD F 90-22.1.)

  If "Yes," enter name of foreign country ▶ _____

L Was the corporation the grantor of, or transferor to, a foreign trust that existed during the current tax year, whether or not the corporation has any beneficial interest in it? . . . . . | | ✕ |

  If "Yes," the corporation may have to file Forms 3520, 3520-A, or 926.

M During this tax year, did the corporation pay dividends (other than stock dividends and distributions in exchange for stock) in excess of the corporation's current and accumulated earnings and profits? (See sections 301 and 316.) . . . . | | ✕ |

  If "Yes," file Form 5452. If this is a consolidated return, answer here for parent corporation and on **Form 851**, Affiliations Schedule, for each subsidiary.

N During this tax year, did the corporation maintain any part of its accounting/tax records on a computerized system? . . . . | | ✕ |

O Check method of accounting:

  (1) ☐ Cash

  (2) ☐ Accrual

  (3) ☐ Other (specify) ▶ _____

P Check this box if the corporation issued publicly offered debt instruments with original issue discount . . . . . ☐

  If so, the corporation may have to file Form 8281.

Q Enter the amount of tax-exempt interest received or accrued during the tax year ▶ |$_____|

R Enter the number of shareholders at the end of the tax year if there were 35 or fewer shareholders ▶

Form 1120 (1990)

Schedule L — Balance Sheets

Assets	Beginning of tax year (a)	Beginning of tax year (b)	End of tax year (c)	End of tax year (d)
1 Cash		3,000		32,000
2a Trade notes and accounts receivable	18,000		21,000	
b Less allowance for bad debts	(—)	18,000	(—)	21,000
3 Inventories		12,000		14,000
4 U.S. government obligations				6,500
5 Tax-exempt securities (see Instructions)				
6 Other current assets (attach schedule)				
7 Loans to stockholders				
8 Mortgage and real estate loans				
9 Other investments (attach schedule)		20,000		104,800
10a Buildings and other depreciable assets	42,000		42,000	
b Less accumulated depreciation	(5,000)	37,000	(8,000)	34,000
11a Depletable assets				
b Less accumulated depletion	( )		( )	
12 Land (net of any amortization)				
13a Intangible assets (amortizable only)				
b Less accumulated amortization	( )		( )	
14 Other assets (attach schedule)				
15 Total assets		90,000		212,300
Liabilities and Stockholders' Equity				
16 Accounts payable		15,000		11,000
17 Mortgages, notes, bonds payable in less than 1 year				
18 Other current liabilities (attach schedule)				
19 Loans from stockholders				
20 Mortgages, notes, bonds payable in 1 year or more				
21 Other liabilities (attach schedule)				
22 Capital stock: a Preferred stock				
b Common stock	1,000	1,000	1,000	1,000
23 Paid-in or capital surplus		9,000		9,000
24 Retained earnings—Appropriated (attach schedule)				
25 Retained earnings—Unappropriated		65,000		191,300
26 Less cost of treasury stock		( )		( )
27 Total liabilities and stockholders' equity		90,000		212,300

Schedule M-1 — Reconciliation of Income per Books With Income per Return (This schedule does not have to be completed if the total assets on line 15, column (d), of Schedule L are less than $25,000.)

1 Net income per books	132,800	7 Income recorded on books this year not included on this return (itemize):	
2 Federal income tax	53,450	a Tax-exempt interest $ 700 MUNICIPAL BONDS	
3 Excess of capital losses over capital gains			700
4 Income subject to tax not recorded on books this year (itemize):			
		8 Deductions on this return not charged against book income this year (itemize):	
5 Expenses recorded on books this year not deducted on this return (itemize):		a Depreciation . . . $ 8,000	
a Depreciation . . . $		b Contributions carryover $	
b Contributions carryover $			
c Travel and entertainment . $			8,000
PREMIUMS PAID ON KEY-MAN LIFE INSURANCE POLICY	4,550	9 Total of lines 7 and 8	8,700
6 Total of lines 1 through 5	190,800	10 Income (line 28, page 1)—line 6 less line 9	182,100

Schedule M-2 — Analysis of Unappropriated Retained Earnings per Books (line 25, Schedule L) (This schedule does not have to be completed if the total assets on line 15, column (d), of Schedule L are less than $25,000.)

1 Balance at beginning of year	65,000	5 Distributions: a Cash	6,500
2 Net income per books	132,800	b Stock	
3 Other increases (itemize):		c Property	
		6 Other decreases (itemize):	
		7 Total of lines 5 and 6	6,500
4 Total of lines 1, 2, and 3	197,800	8 Balance at end of year (line 4 less line 7)	191,300

Form 1120-A

Department of the Treasury
Internal Revenue Service

U.S. Corporation Short-Form Income Tax Return

Instructions are separate. See them to make sure you qualify to file Form 1120-A.

For calendar year 1990 or tax year beginning .... , 1990, ending .... , 19 .....

OMB No. 1545-0890

1990

A Check this box if corp. is a personal service corp. (as defined in Temp. Regs. sec. 1.441-4T— see Instructions) ▶ ☐

Use IRS label. Otherwise, please print or type.

Name

Number, street, and room or suite no. (If a P.O. box, see page 2 of Instructions.)

City or town, state, and ZIP code

B Employer identification number

C Date incorporated

D Total assets (see Specific Instructions)

$

E Check applicable boxes: (1) ☐ Initial return (2) ☐ Change in address

F Check method of accounting: (1) ☐ Cash (2) ☐ Accrual (3) ☐ Other (specify) . . ▶

Income

1a	Gross receipts or sales	**b** Less returns and allowances	**c** Balance ▶ 1c
2	Cost of goods sold (see Instructions)		2
3	Gross profit (line 1c less line 2)		3
4	Domestic corporation dividends subject to the 70% deduction		4
5	Interest		5
6	Gross rents		6
7	Gross royalties		7
8	Capital gain net income (attach Schedule D (Form 1120))		8
9	Net gain or (loss) from Form 4797, Part II, line 18 (attach Form 4797)		9
10	Other income (see Instructions)		10
11	**Total income**—Add lines 3 through 10 . . . . ▶		11

Deductions

(See Instructions for limitations on deductions.)

12	Compensation of officers (see Instructions)		12
13a	Salaries and wages	**b** Less jobs credit	**c** Balance ▶ 13c
14	Repairs		14
15	Bad debts		15
16	Rents		16
17	Taxes		17
18	Interest		18
19	Contributions (**see Instructions for 10% limitation**)		19
20	Depreciation (attach Form 4562) 20		
21	Less depreciation claimed elsewhere on return 21a		21b
22	Other deductions (attach schedule)		22
23	**Total deductions**—Add lines 12 through 22. . . . . ▶		23
24	Taxable income before net operating loss deduction and special deductions (line 11 less line 23) . .		24
25	**Less: a** Net operating loss deduction (see Instructions) 25a		
	b Special deductions (see Instructions) 25b		25c
26	**Taxable income**—Line 24 less line 25c		26
27	**Total tax** (Part I, line 7)		27

Tax and Payments

28	**Payments:**	
a	1989 overpayment credited to 1990.	28a
b	1990 estimated tax payments . .	28b
c	Less 1990 refund applied for on Form 4466	28c ( ) Bal ▶ 28d
e	Tax deposited with Form 7004	28e
f	Credit from regulated investment companies (attach Form 2439) . .	28f
g	Credit for Federal tax on fuels (attach Form 4136). See Instructions .	28g
h	**Total payments**—Add lines 28d through 28g . . . . Check ▶	28h
29	Enter any **penalty** for underpayment of estimated tax—Check ▶ ☐ if Form 2220 is attached	29
30	**Tax due**—If the total of lines 27 and 29 is larger than line 28h, enter amount owed	30
31	**Overpayment**—If line 28h is larger than the total of lines 27 and 29, enter amount overpaid	31
32	Enter amount of line 31 you want: **Credited to 1991 estimated tax** ▶ Refunded ▶	32

Please Sign Here

Under penalties of perjury, I declare that I have examined this return, including accompanying schedules and statements, and to the best of my knowledge and belief, it is true, correct, and complete. Declaration of preparer (other than taxpayer) is based on all information of which preparer has any knowledge.

▶ Signature of officer   Date   ▶ Title

Paid Preparer's Use Only

Preparer's signature ▶	Date	Check if self-employed ▶ ☐	Preparer's social security number
Firm's name (or yours if self-employed) and address		E.I. No. ▶	
		ZIP code ▶	

For Paperwork Reduction Act Notice, see page 1 of the Instructions.

Form **1120-A** (1990)

Form 1120-A (1990) Page **2**

Part I   Tax Computation

1	Income tax (see Instructions to figure the tax). Check this box if the corp. is a qualified personal service corp. (see Instructions). ▶ ☐	**1**
2a	General business credit. Check if from: ☐ Form 3800 ☐ Form 3468 ☐ Form 5884	
	☐ Form 6478 ☐ Form 6765 ☐ Form 8586 **2a**	
b	Credit for prior year minimum tax (attach Form 8801) **2b**	
3	**Total credits**—Add lines 2a and 2b	**3**
4	Line 1 less line 3	**4**
5	Recapture taxes. Check if from: ☐ Form 4255 ☐ Form 8611	**5**
6	Alternative minimum tax (attach Form 4626). See Instructions	**6**
7	**Total tax**—Add lines 4 through 6. Enter here and on line 27, page 1.	**7**

Additional Information (See General Instruction F.)

G Refer to the list in the Instructions and state the principal:

   (1) Business activity code no. ▶ ....

   (2) Business activity ▶ ....

   (3) Product or service ▶ ....

H Did any individual, partnership, estate, or trust at the end of the tax year own, directly or indirectly, 50% or more of the corporation's voting stock? (For rules of attribution, see section 267(c).)   Yes ☐ No ☐
If "Yes," attach schedule showing name, address, and identifying number.

I Enter the amount of tax-exempt interest received or accrued during the tax year . . . . ▶ |$

J (1) If an amount for cost of goods sold is entered on line 2, page 1, complete (a) through (c):

   (a) Purchases (see Instructions) . . .

   (b) Additional sec. 263A costs (see Instructions —attach schedule) . .

   (c) Other costs (attach schedule) . .

(2) Do the rules of section 263A (with respect to property produced or acquired for resale) apply to the corporation?   . . . Yes ☐ · No ☐

K At any time during the tax year, did you have an interest in or a signature or other authority over a financial account in a foreign country (such as a bank account, securities account, or other financial account)? (See General Instruction F for filing requirements for form TD F 90-22.1.) . . . . . . Yes ☐   No ☐
If "Yes," enter the name of the foreign country ▶ ....
....

L Enter amount of cash distributions and the book value of property (other than cash) distributions made in this tax year ▶ |$

Part II   Balance Sheets

		(a) Beginning of tax year		(b) End of tax year	
Assets	1	Cash			
	2a	Trade notes and accounts receivable			
	b	Less allowance for bad debts	(	)	(	)
	3	Inventories			
	4	U.S. government obligations			
	5	Tax-exempt securities (see Instructions)			
	6	Other current assets (attach schedule)			
	7	Loans to stockholders			
	8	Mortgage and real estate loans			
	9a	Depreciable, depletable, and intangible assets			
	b	Less accumulated depreciation, depletion, and amortization . .	(	)	(	)
	10	Land (net of any amortization)			
	11	Other assets (attach schedule)			
	12	Total assets			
Liabilities and Stockholders' Equity	13	Accounts payable.			
	14	Other current liabilities (attach schedule)			
	15	Loans from stockholders			
	16	Mortgages, notes, bonds payable.			
	17	Other liabilities (attach schedule)			
	18	Capital stock (preferred and common stock)			
	19	Paid-in or capital surplus			
	20	Retained earnings			
	21	Less cost of treasury stock	(	)	(	)
	22	Total liabilities and stockholders' equity			

Part III   Reconciliation of Income per Books With Income per Return (Must be completed by all filers.)

1	Net income per books	
2	Federal income tax	
3	Excess of capital losses over capital gains	
4	Income subject to tax not recorded on books this year (itemize)	
5	Expenses recorded on books this year not deducted on this return (itemize)	

6 Income recorded on books this year not included on this return (itemize) ....

7 Deductions on this return not charged against book income this year (itemize) ....

8 Income (line 24, page 1). Enter the sum of lines 1 through 5 less the sum of lines 6 and 7 . . . .

☆U.S.GPO: 1990-265-254 E.I.43-1410168

PROBLEM MATERIALS

DISCUSSION QUESTIONS

1-1 *What Is a Corporation?*   Although an entity may be a corporation under state law, what characteristics must the entity possess to be treated as a corporation for Federal tax purposes? What difference will it make on the Federal tax classification if the entity possesses *all* or only a few of these characteristics?

1-2 *Disregard of Corporate Form.*   Why might the IRS try to disregard an entity which meets the state law requirements of a corporation? Under what circumstances might shareholders try to use the corporate form but attempt to disregard it for Federal tax purposes?

1-3 *Corporate vs. Individual Taxation.*   What are the differences in income tax treatment of corporations and individuals for the items below?

    a.   Dividends received
    b.   Classification of deductions
    c.   Casualty losses
    d.   Charitable contribution limitations
    e.   Net capital gain treatment
    f.   Capital loss deduction
    g.   Capital loss carryovers and carrybacks
    h.   Gain on sale of depreciable realty

1-4 *Dividends-Received Deduction.*   Why is a corporation allowed a dividends-received deduction? Under what circumstances is the recipient corporation allowed an 80 percent rather than the usual 70 percent dividends-received deduction?

1-5 *Limitations on Dividends-Received Deduction.*   What are the limitations imposed on a corporation's dividends-received deduction? Under what circumstances can one of these limitations be disregarded?

1-6 *Charitable Contribution Carryovers.*   Under what circumstances must a corporation carry over to subsequent years its qualifying contributions? If contributions are made in the current year and the corporation has a contribution carryover from a prior year, which contributions are deducted first? Why do you suppose Congress imposes this ordering of contribution deductions?

1-7 *Controlled Corporate Groups.*   What types of related corporations are subject to the limitation of one graduated tax rate structure? Describe each group of related corporations subject to this restriction.

1-8 *Five Percent Surtax.*   Which corporations are subject to the 5 percent surtax? What is the marginal tax rate on the last dollar of taxable income of a corporation with 1990 taxable income of $170,000? What is the flat tax rate imposed on a corporation with 1990 taxable income of $335,000?

1-9   *Alternative Minimum Tax.*   Some taxpayers believe that the alternative minimum tax is an amount of tax paid in lieu of the regular income tax. Are these taxpayers correct? Explain.

1-10   *Adjusted Current Earnings Adjustment.*   The Tax Reform Act of 1986 added an adjustment to the corporate alternative minimum tax calculation for adjusted current earnings (ACE). Notice that alternative minimum taxable income must be adjusted upward by nontaxable income (e.g., tax-exempt interest, key-person life insurance proceeds), a depreciation adjustment, and the dividends-received deduction. What was Congress trying to accomplish with this ACE adjustment?

PROBLEMS

1-11   *Comparison of Corporate vs. Individual Taxation.*   In each of the situations below, explain the tax consequences if taxpayer T were either a corporation or a single individual.

   a.   For the current year, T has gross income of $60,000, including $10,000 dividends from Ford Motor Company. Without regard to taxable income, how much of the dividend income will be subject to tax?

   b.   During the current year, T sustains a total loss of an asset. The asset was valued at $2,000 shortly before the loss and had an adjusted basis of $2,700. If the casualty loss was incurred by T as an individual, it would be a personal rather than a business loss. Without regard to any taxable income limitation, what is the measure of the casualty loss deduction?

   c.   For the calendar year 1991, T has long-term capital gains of $10,000 and short-term capital losses of $4,000. What is the maximum amount of Federal income tax T will be required to pay as a result of these capital asset transactions?

   d.   During 1991, T had $8,000 of long-term capital gains and $3,000 of short-term capital gains. During 1990, the only prior year with capital asset transactions, T had a short-term capital loss of $6,000. How much of T's 1991 gross income will consist of capital gains?

   e.   T's taxable income for 1991, before any deduction for charitable contributions, is $50,000. If T were an individual, adjusted gross income would be $60,000. If T made cash contributions of $40,000 during the year, what is the maximum amount that could be claimed as a deduction for 1991?

   f.   T sells residential rental property for $250,000 in 1991. The property was purchased for $200,000 in 1986, and T claimed ACRS depreciation of $60,000. Straight-line depreciation would have been $38,000. Calculate T's depreciation recapture and § 1231 gain on the sale.

1-12 *Capital Gains and Losses.* Y Corporation incurred the following items of capital gain and loss in 1991:

Net STCG	$ 20,000
Net STCL	(10,000)
Net LTCG	5,000
Net LTCL	(28,000)

A review of Y's past tax returns shows that Y Corporation reported the following net capital gain/(loss) in prior years: 1987—$6,000; 1988—$8,000; 1989—($3,000); and 1990—$1,000.

a.   Calculate Y's net capital gain (loss) for 1991. How is this reported on the 1991 Form 1120?

b.   Calculate the amount of capital loss carryback to 1987, 1988, 1989, and 1990.

c.   Calculate the amount of capital loss carryforward to 1992. How will this loss be treated in 1991 (i.e., as a short-term or long-term capital loss)?

1-13 *Dividends-Received Deduction.* K Corporation has the following items of revenue and expense for the current year:

Sales revenue, net of returns	$100,000
Cost of sales	30,000
Operating expenses	40,000
Dividends (from less than 20% owned corporation)	20,000

a.   What is K Corporation's dividends-received deduction for the current year?

b.   Assuming that K Corporation's operating expenses were $72,000 instead of $40,000, compute its dividends-received deduction for the current year.

1-14 *Dividends-Received Deduction.* During 1991, R Corporation (a cash method, calendar year taxpayer) has the following income and expenses:

Revenues from operations	$170,000
Operating expenses	178,000
Dividends (from less than 20% owned corporation)	40,000

a.   What is R Corporation's 1991 dividends-received deduction?

b.   Assuming R Corporation's 1991 tax year has not yet closed, compute the effect on its dividends-received deduction if R accelerated $5,000 of operating expenses to 1991 that were planned for 1992.

1-15 *Organizational Expenditures.* G Corporation incurred and paid $4,800 of qualifying organizational expenditures in 1991. Assuming G Corporation makes an election under § 248 to amortize these costs, compute the maximum amount that may be deducted for each of the following years if G Corporation adopts a calendar tax year.

a.   For 1991, during which G Corporation began business on September 1?

b.   Calendar year 1992?

c.   Calendar year 1996?

1-16 *Organizational Expenditures.* Which of the following expenditures qualify under § 248 to be amortized over a period of not less than 60 months?

a.   Expenses of a market survey to determine the feasibility of starting a new business.

b.   Expenses of temporary directors.

c.   Legal services incident to the organization of the corporation.

d.   Fees paid to the state of incorporation.

e.   Expenses incident to the issuance of stock.

f.   Accounting services incident to the organization of the corporation.

1-17 *Charitable Contribution Deductions.* T Corporation has the following for tax year 1991:

Net income from operations......................	$600,000
Dividends (from less than 20% owned corporation)............................	100,000

a.   What is T Corporation's maximum charitable contribution deduction for 1991?

b.   Assuming T Corporation made charitable contributions of $68,000 during 1991 and had a $10,000 charitable contribution carryover from 1990, compute how much of its 1990 contributions will be carried over to 1992.

1-18 *Charitable Contribution Pledges.* All of the board members of Z Corporation were invited to a gala New Year's Eve party hosted by the American Theatrical Society (a qualified charitable organization). About an hour before midnight on December 31, 1991, representatives of the charity asked the invited guests to make generous charitable contributions. Z's board members held an impromptu meeting and decided to pledge $10,000 (well within the statutory limits for corporate charitable contributions). Z is a calendar year, accrual basis corporation. Assuming Z Corporation made actual payments of the pledged amount on February 28, 1992, will Z be entitled to a charitable contribution deduction for 1991? Would your answer change if the payment was made on March 29, 1992?

1-19 *Sale of Depreciable Realty.* Z Corporation purchased a mini-warehouse unit in December 1986 for $400,000. Using the tables under ACRS, Z Corporation deducted depreciation of $104,000 prior to the sale. The unit was sold in January 1991 for $410,000. Assuming that straight-line depreciation for the period would have been $66,000, answer the questions below.

a.   What is the amount and character of Z Corporation's gain?

b.   Same as (a) except the property was a 30-unit apartment complex.

1-20 *Computation of Corporate Tax Liability.* L Corporation had taxable income of $150,000 for 1991. What is L Corporation's 1991 income tax liability before credits or prepayments?

1-21 *Surtax Computation.* F Corporation had taxable income of $250,000 for 1991. What is F Corporation's 1991 income tax liability before credits or prepayments? If F Corporation is a personal service corporation, what is its 1991 income tax liability before credits or prepayments?

1-22 *Members of Controlled Groups.*   R, U, S, and T Corporations each have only one class of outstanding stock. Given the stock ownership of these corporations by the four unrelated individuals indicated below, indicate which of the corporations are members of controlled groups.

	Corporations			
Individuals	R	U	S	T
A	30%	5%	40%	50%
B	10	10	10	20
C	40	5	10	10
D	20	80	0	20

1-23 *Alternative Minimum Tax Computation.*   V Corporation has regular taxable income of $100,000 for 1991. The following items were taken into consideration in arriving at this number:

1.   A building acquired in 1986 was depreciated using ACRS. The depreciation claimed was $90,000, and straight-line depreciation would have been $60,000.

2.   Key-person life insurance proceeds of $80,000 were received but were not included in taxable income.

In light of these facts, perform the following computations.

a.   Compute V Corporation's alternative minimum taxable income (AMTI).

b.   Assuming V has no tax credits for 1991, compute the corporation's alternative minimum tax liability for 1991.

1-24 *Corporate Tax Computation.*   T Corporation had the following items of income for its 1991 calendar year:

Net income from operations......................	$150,000
Dividends received (from less than 20% owned corporations)......................	10,000
Charitable contributions..........................	30,000
Net operating loss carryover from 1990...........	30,000
Long-term capital gains..........................	8,000
Long-term capital losses.........................	6,000
Short-term capital gains..........................	3,000
Capital loss carryover from 1990.................	9,000

a.   Compute T Corporation's 1991 income tax liability before credits or prepayments.

b.   What are the nature and amount of any carryovers to 1992?

1-25 *Schedules M-1 and M-2.* The P Corporation reports the following information for 1991:

Net income per books............................	$125,730
Federal income taxes (actual).....................	10,500
Net capital loss	3,600
Travel and entertainment	
(20% portion disallowed for FIT)................	300
Proceeds of life insurance on president............	75,000
Insurance premlums on llfe of president...........	1,250
Tax-exempt interest	3,500
ACRS deductions in excess of straight-line	
depreciation used for book purposes............	1,400
Excess charitable contributions....................	520
Unappropriated retained earnings	
(beginnning of 1991)...........................	$200,000
Dividends paid during the year....................	23,500

Complete the following Schedules M-1 and M-2 below.

Schedule M-1	Reconciliation of Income per Books With Income per Return (This schedule does not have to be completed if the total assets on line 15, column (d), of Schedule L are less than $25,000.)		
1 Net income per books		7 Income recorded on books this year not included on this return (itemize):	
2 Federal income tax		a Tax-exempt interest $_____	
3 Excess of capital losses over capital gains . .		-------------------------------------	
4 Income subject to tax not recorded on books this year (itemize): -----------------------		-------------------------------------	
-----------------------------------		8 Deductions on this return not charged against book income this year (itemize)·	
5 Expenses recorded on books this year not deducted on this return (itemize):		a Depreciation . . . $_____	
a Depreciation . . . $_____		b Contributions carryover $_____	
b Contributions carryover $_____		-------------------------------------	
c Travel and entertainment . $_____		-------------------------------------	
-----------------------------------		-------------------------------------	
-----------------------------------		9 Total of lines 7 and 8	
6 Total of lines 1 through 5		10 Income (line 28, page 1)—line 6 less line 9 .	
Schedule M-2	Analysis of Unappropriated Retained Earnings per Books (line 25, Schedule L) (This schedule does not have to be completed if the total assets on line 15, column (d), of Schedule L are less than $25,000.)		
1 Balance at beginning of year		5 Distributions: a Cash	
2 Net income per books		b Stock	
3 Other increases (itemize): _____		c Property	
-------------------------------------		6 Other decreases (itemize): _____	
-------------------------------------		-------------------------------------	
-------------------------------------		7 Total of lines 5 and 6	
4 Total of lines 1, 2, and 3		8 Balance at end of year (line 4 less line 7)	

1-26 *Reconciliation of Book and Taxable Income.* D Corporation, a calendar year, accrual basis corporation, reported net income per books of $300,000 for the tax year ended December 31, 1991. Included in the calculation of net book income were the following items:

Accrued federal income tax......................	$ 90,000
Life insurance proceeds on officer who died during 1991	120,000
Insurance premiums on key-people life insurance..................................	6,000
Net loss on sale of securities held for investment.................................	4,000
Depreciation.....................................	50,000

Depreciation claimed on the tax return was $86,000. The actual tax calculated on the tax return was $80,000 (i.e., D Corporation had an overaccrual of federal income tax of $10,000).

What is D Corporation's taxable income for 1990?

1-27 *Corporate Estimated Tax.* F Corporation, a calendar year corporation, reported the following information with respect to its tax liabilities for 1990 and 1991:

Actual 1991 tax liability (regular tax)..............	$120,000
Actual 1991 alternative minimum tax..............	15,000
Actual 1990 tax liability (regular tax)..............	100,000

F made timely quarterly estimated tax payments of $26,000 during 1991. F Corporation is *not* a "large" corporation (i.e., it did *not* have taxable income of $1 million or more in any of the three preceding taxable years). The 1990 tax liability was for a full 12-month period.

Compute the amount of quarterly underpayment for F Corporation, if any.

1-28 *Corporate Estimated Tax.* Refer to Problem 1-27. Assume that F Corporation is a "large" corporation.

Compute the amount of quarterly underpayment for F Corporation, if any.

TAX RETURN PROBLEM

1-29   Paul Schroeder is the owner of ABC Manufacturing Corporation in Denver, Colorado. Paul is in the process of preparing the 1990 income tax return for ABC and needs guidance on how to depreciate recently acquired assets (personalty) for regular tax purposes. His problem is that, because of a substantial amount of alternative minimum tax (AMT) adjustments, ABC is exposed to the AMT for 1990. Of course, he wants to choose a depreciation method that will minimize ABC's negative tax consequences from application of the AMT. Paul has heard that he can avoid creating an AMT adjustment [including the "adjusted current earnings" (ACE) adjustment] by electing to depreciate ABC's assets acquired in 1990 by using the straight-line method under the Alternative Depreciation System (ADS). Paul thinks it might be a good idea to elect ADS so that exposure to the AMT in 1990 is not exaggerated. The facts of this case are:

1.   Paul estimates that ABC Corporation will have net income of $300,000 without regard to depreciation of the assets acquired in 1990.
2.   ABC Corporation has other AMT adjustments of $200,000.
3.   If Paul uses MACRS (modified ACRS) to depreciate the personalty acquired, the depreciation amount will be $50,000. If he elects to use the straight-line method under ADS to avoid creation of an AMT or ACE adjustment, the first-year depreciation will amount to $14,600.

Prepare tax Form 4626 assuming that Paul elects to use MACRS to depreciate ABC's personalty acquired in 1990. Prepare a second Form 4626 assuming that Paul elects to use the straight-line method under ADS. Which depreciation method should Paul use for ABC Corporation?

TAX RESEARCH PROBLEM

1-30   Linda Smith is a single investor living in Phoenix, Arizona who wants to buy an apartment building for $240,000 in Houston, Texas. Because real estate prices are currently attractive, Linda plans to acquire the property at a good price and hold it until the real estate market improves (hopefully, within the next five years).

By agreeing to make a $40,000 down payment on the apartment building, Linda has obtained a loan commitment from National Mortgage Company for $200,000 on a nonrecourse note with a 17 percent interest rate (the interest rate is high because of the speculative nature of the investment). However, because Texas usury law limits the interest rate to 15 percent when a loan is made to a noncorporate entity, the lender requires that the loan be made to a corporate entity.

Linda is concerned about the negative tax implications of holding the investment in the corporate form. She wants to receive the tax benefits from the investment (e.g., loss pass-throughs) for use on her personal return (she will qualify for the $25,000 actively-managed rental realty exception to the passive activity loss rules). Linda knows that losses generated by a regular corporation will not pass-through to her and they may be used only to offset future corporate income.

Linda has considered forming a corporation under state law and making the S corporation election for Federal income tax purposes. Although this looks like a good alternative, she is concerned that her pass-through losses will soon exceed her $40,000 direct investment in the corporation and the remaining losses will be suspended just as they would be with a regular corporation.

Linda has also considered forming a regular corporation under state law and having the corporation treated as her agent (i.e., a nontaxable entity). This would be a great alternative if it works, because she could obtain her loan and still have the investment losses pass-through for use on her personal return. Can this be done? What specific steps must she take to ensure that the IRS will not treat the corporation as a taxable entity?

Research aid:

Jesse C. Bollinger, 88-1 USTC ¶9233, 61 AFTR2d 88-793, 108 S.Ct. 1173 (USSC, 1988).

LEARNING OBJECTIVES

Upon completion of this chapter you will be able to:

- Explain the basic tax consequences of forming a new corporation, including

    - Determination of the gain or loss recognized by the shareholders and the corporation

    - Determination of the basis of the shareholder's stock in the corporation and the corporation's basis in the property received

- Describe the requirements for qualifying a transfer to a corporation for tax-free treatment

- Recognize the tax consequences of transferring property to an existing corporation

- Understand the effects of transferring liabilities to a corporation

- Describe special problems involved in computing depreciation of assets transferred to the corporation

- Explain the effect of contributions to capital by shareholders and nonshareholders

- Identify the tax considerations in determining whether the corporation's capital structure should consist of stock or debt

CHAPTER OUTLINE

Chapter 2

CORPORATE FORMATION AND CAPITAL STRUCTURE

The previous chapter examined the fundamental rules of corporate income taxation. Beginning with this chapter and extending through Chapter 7, attention is directed to a variety of special tax problems that often arise in organizing and operating a corporation. For example, this chapter focuses on the tax consequences of forming a corporation. In addition, this chapter considers how the tax law affects a corporation's decision to use debt or stock to raise capital. Subsequent chapters look at the tax problems associated with distributions by the corporation to its shareholders and the tax aspects of corporate mergers and other types of reorganizations.

The technical discussion contained in this and the next several chapters concerning corporations and their shareholders ultimately seeks to answer two basic questions:

1. What is the tax effect of the transaction on the corporation?

2. What is the tax effect of the transaction on the shareholder?

The pages that follow all concern the rules and the rationale necessary for answering these two seemingly straightforward inquiries.

INCORPORATION IN GENERAL

Prior to examining the tax aspects of forming and transferring property to a corporation, a few comments reviewing the incorporation process may be helpful. Forming a corporation is generally a very simple procedure. In most states, the law requires an application, entitled the "Articles of Incorporation," to be filed with the appropriate state agency for the privilege of operating as a corporation. The information typically required in the articles of incorporation includes (1) the name and address of the corporation, (2) the period for which it will exist, (3) the purpose for which the corporation is organized, (4) the number and type of shares of stock that the corporation will have authority to issue, (5) the provisions relating to the regulation of the internal affairs of the business, and

(6) the number and names of the initial board of directors of the corporation. Once drafted, the articles of incorporation are submitted along with any funds necessary for payment of fees charged by the state. The representative of the state subsequently reviews the articles, and approval is routinely given. Upon approval, the state grants the corporation the right to operate within its boundaries pursuant to state law.

Once the decision to incorporate has been made, an important question concerns the selection of the state of incorporation. Two factors are generally considered: (1) the various advantages and disadvantages of the substantive corporation laws of the alternative states, and (2) the costs of incorporating in the state where the corporation will be operating versus the costs of qualifying as a foreign corporation authorized to do business in the state of operations. With respect to this latter factor, state and local taxes are often extremely important.

The final step in the incorporation process requires the transfer of assets by the investors to the corporation. In the simple case, investors merely contribute cash and other assets to the corporation in exchange for stock. As a practical matter, however, even simple transfers require numerous considerations.

> **Example 1.**   Several years ago, R and S started making dolls in R's basement and selling them primarily during the Christmas season. Business grew at such a rate that they were forced to acquire additional equipment and to move their operation from R's home to a small building that S owned. They were so successful that in their third year of operations they were unable to fill all of their Christmas orders. To attract the capital necessary to expand and meet demand, they decided to incorporate their business. The two contacted numerous people who indicated they would be interested in investing in the corporation. Accordingly, they met with their attorney and accountant who provided the services related to incorporation.

Examination of the situation in the example above suggests numerous concerns that should be addressed. For instance, R and S must initially determine which assets and liabilities of their existing business they should transfer to the corporation. In addition, they must determine the method of transfer: should the property be contributed in exchange for stock and/or debt, or perhaps leased or sold to the corporation? With respect to the other investors, some may wish to contribute cash for stock while others may desire debt in exchange for their investment. Another consideration relates to the method of compensating the attorney and the accountant. When a cash shortage exists, it is not unusual for these individuals to receive stock as payment for their services. As analysis of this example indicates, there are many decisions confronting those forming a corporation. Interestingly, tax factors play an important role in determining how these decisions should be made.

IDENTIFYING THE TAX CONSEQUENCES

The tax consequences related to incorporating a new business *or* making transfers to an existing corporation are a direct result of the form of the transaction. In the typical situation, the taxpayer transfers property to the corporation in exchange for stock. It is the exchange feature of this transaction which has tax implications. Under the general rule of Code § 1001, an exchange is treated as a taxable disposition, and the taxpayer must recognize gain or loss to the extent that the value of the property received exceeds or is less than the adjusted basis of the property transferred.

> **Example 2.** G is contemplating the incorporation of his restaurant business. Under the arrangement proposed by his accountant, G would transfer the following assets to the corporation.
>
> | Asset | Adjusted Basis | Fair Market Value |
> |---|---|---|
> | Equipment.................. | $12,000 | $10,000 |
> | Building.................... | 30,000 | 50,000 |
> | Total..................... | $42,000 | $60,000 |
>
> In exchange for the assets, G would receive stock worth $60,000. As a result, G would realize a gain of $18,000, representing the difference between his amount realized, stock valued at $60,000, and the adjusted basis in his assets of $42,000. Note that under the general rule, G would be required to recognize the gain and pay tax—a cost that may cause him to change his mind about the virtues of incorporating.

The problems of applying the general rule requiring recognition of gain or loss on transfers to a corporation are twofold. First, when gain is recognized, the tax cost incurred may prohibit the taxpayer from using the corporate form where otherwise it is entirely appropriate. Second, since losses are also recognized, taxpayers could arbitrarily create artificial losses even though they continue to own the asset, albeit indirectly through the corporation.

> **Example 3.** Consider the facts in *Example 2* above. Without any special provision, G could transfer the equipment to the corporation and recognize a $2,000 loss ($10,000 − $12,000) even though he still maintained control of the asset through ownership of the corporation.

In 1921, Congress recognized these difficulties and enacted an exception generally providing that no gain or loss is recognized on most transfers to controlled corporations. This treatment was based on the so-called *continuity of interest* principle. According to this principle, when the transferor exchanges property for stock in a corporation controlled by that transferor, there is merely a change of ownership and nothing more. In essence, the transferor's economic position is unaffected since investment in the asset is continued through investment in the corporation.[1] Congress believed that as long as this "continuity of interest" was maintained, it was inappropriate to treat the exchange as a taxable event. This is not to say, however, that any gain or loss realized goes permanently unrecognized. Rather, similar to the treatment of a like-kind exchange, any gain or loss realized on the transaction is postponed until that time when the transferor liquidates the investment or "cashes in"—usually when the stock is sold.[2]

A rather intricate set of statutory provisions exists to ensure that the policy objectives underlying nonrecognition are achieved yet not abused. Due to these provisions, several questions must be addressed whenever a transfer is made to a corporation.

1. Has the transferor or the corporation realized any gain, loss, income, or deduction on the transfer that must be recognized? If so, what is its character?

2. What is the basis and holding period of any property received by the transferor and the corporation?

Although the answers to these questions can be elusive at times, the general rules—which are mandatory if the requirements are satisfied—may be summarized as follows:

3. No gain or loss is recognized by the transferor or the corporation on the exchange.[3]

4. The transferor assigns or substitutes the basis of the property transferred to the corporation as the basis of the stock received (substituted basis).[4]

5. The corporation uses the transferor's basis as its basis for the property received (carryover basis).[5]

> **Example 4.** During the year, R decided to incorporate her copying business. She transferred her only asset, a copying machine (value $25,000, adjusted basis $15,000), to the corporation in exchange for stock worth $25,000. Although R realized a $10,000 gain on the exchange ($25,000 − $15,000), no gain is recognized. R's basis for her stock is the same as her basis for the asset she transferred, $15,000. In other words, she substituted the basis of the old property for the new. The basis assigned to the machine by the corporation is the same as that used by R, $15,000— in effect, the shareholder's basis carries over to the corporation. Note that

---

[1] Reg. § 1.1002-1(c).

[2] *Portland Oil Co. v. Comm.,* 40-1 USTC ¶9234, 24 AFTR 225, 109 F.2d 479 (CA-1, 1940).

[3] §§ 351(a) and 1032.

[4] § 358.

[5] § 362.

these basis rules preserve future recognition of the gain originally realized. For example, if R immediately sells her stock for its $25,000 value, she would recognize the $10,000 gain that was postponed on the transfer to the corporation. Similarly, if the corporation were to sell the copying machine for $25,000, it would recognize the $10,000 gain previously deferred.

Unfortunately, these rules can serve only as guidelines. The specific provisions of the Code that contain various exceptions are discussed below.

SECTION 351: TRANSFERS TO CONTROLLED CORPORATIONS

Section 351 provides the general rule governing transfers to controlled corporations. It should be emphasized that this rule governs not only transfers to newly organized corporations but to existing corporations as well. For example, after a corporation has been formed and operated for a time, an infusion of capital to the business might be necessary, requiring either a new or an old shareholder, or both, to make a transfer to the corporation. If the transfer falls within the scope of § 351, that provision's rules apply. Section 351(a) reads as follows:

> **General Rule.** No gain or loss shall be recognized if property is transferred to a corporation by one or more persons solely in exchange for stock in such corporation and immediately after the exchange such person or persons are in control of the corporation.

A close examination of this rule reveals three basic requirements which must be satisfied before the deferral privilege is granted:

1. Only transferors of *property* are eligible.
2. Transferors of property qualify only if they *control* the corporation after the exchange.
3. Transferors of property who are in control receive nonrecognition only to the extent that they receive *solely stock*.

These three aspects of § 351 are analyzed below.

THE PROPERTY CONDITION

Only those persons who transfer *property* to the corporation are eligible for nonrecognition. Although the Code does not define property, the term has been broadly construed to encompass virtually all of those items that one would normally believe to constitute property. For example, the term property includes money, all real property such as land and buildings, and all personal property such as inventory and equipment. In addition, such items as accounts receivable (including the unrealized receivables of a cash basis taxpayer), notes receivable, installment receivables, patents, and other intangibles are considered property.

Property versus Services. Despite the lack of a definition of property, § 351 provides specifically that property does *not* include services.[6] Apparently, Congress believed that an exchange of *services for stock* was not the economic equivalent of an exchange of *property for stock*. When property is exchanged, the form of ownership merely changes from direct to indirect. When services are exchanged, however, the transaction is more akin to a cash payment for the services, followed by a purchase of stock. Section 351 adopts this view and, therefore, does not treat services as property. Instead, stock received for services is considered compensation for such services, and the shareholder must recognize ordinary income equal to the value of the stock received for the services rendered.[7] Consistent with the recognition of income, the service shareholder assigns a basis to the stock received equal to the amount of income recognized— in effect, the cost of the stock. The corporation is allowed to treat the issuance of stock for the services just as if it had paid cash.[8] Accordingly, the corporation may deduct or capitalize the costs, depending on the nature of the services.

> **Example 5.** This year, R decided to incorporate his taxi business. R's attorney drafted the articles of incorporation and handled all other legal aspects of forming the corporation. Upon approval by the state, R transferred the assets to the corporation in exchange for 90 shares of stock. In addition, his attorney received 10 shares valued at $10,000 as compensation for his legal services. The attorney is not entitled to defer recognition of the compensation since he transferred services to the corporation and not property. Therefore, he recognizes $10,000 of ordinary income, and his basis in the stock is $10,000, reflecting the fact that he was required to report income on the exchange. The corporation treats the issuance of stock as payment for an organization expense which must be capitalized and amortized over a period not less than 60 months.

THE CONTROL CONDITION

As indicated above, the purpose of § 351 is to grant deferral to those exchanges where there has been no substantive change in the transferor's economic position. This policy is reflected in the statute by the presence of a requirement concerning *control*. According to § 351, deferral is permitted only if those who transferred property (rather than services) control the corporation. Control is defined as ownership of at least 80 percent of the total combined voting power of all classes of stock entitled to vote *and* 80 percent of the total number of shares of all other classes of stock of the corporation immediately after the exchange.[9] For this purpose, stock does not include stock rights or stock warrants.[10]

---

[6]   § 351(d).

[7]   Reg. § 1.351-1(a)(2) ex. 3.

[8]   Rev. Rul. 217, 1962-2 C.B. 59.

[9]   § 368 (c).

[10]   Reg. § 1.351-1(a)(1)(ii).

Example 6.   This year, H, I, and J formed a new corporation. H exchanged equipment for 50% of the stock, I exchanged land for 40% of the stock, and J exchanged cash for the remaining 10% of the stock. Section 351 applies to all of the exchanges because the transferors of property—H, I, and J, *as a group*—own at least 80% of the stock immediately after the exchange.

It is not necessary that the transferors of property acquire control on the exchange. It is sufficient if the transferors own 80 percent of the stock after the exchange, taking into account the stock received on the exchange as well as any stock already owned by the transferors.

Example 7.   For the last several years, X Corporation has had 100 shares of stock outstanding: 60 shares owned by J and 40 shares owned by K. This year, J transferred property to X in exchange for an additional 100 shares. Although J received stock representing only 50% of the shares outstanding (100 ÷ 200), the control test is satisfied because *both* the stock received *and* the stock owned by the transferor prior to the exchange is counted towards control. Since after the exchange J owns 160 of the 200 shares outstanding, the 80% control test is satisfied, and § 351 applies to his exchange.

Example 8.   Assume the same facts as above, except that K made the transfer and received the 100 shares. In this case, K owns only 140 shares of the 200 shares outstanding, or 70%. Thus, the 80% test is not satisfied, and K's transfer is taxable.

Stock Received for Services.   In determining whether the control test is satisfied, only the stock of those who transfer *property* is counted. Since property, by definition, does not include services, stock received in exchange for services is not counted towards control.

Example 9.   During the year, B and C formed T Corporation with the help of A, an attorney, who agreed to be compensated in stock. The three individuals contributed the following in exchange for stock:

Transferor	Transfer	Shares Received
A	Services	20
B	Machine	20
C	Land	60
		100

Since the transferors of property, B and C, own 80% of T's outstanding stock after the transfers, their exchanges are nontaxable under § 351. Because A's only contribution to T was services, his ownership is not included in determining whether control exists, and his exchange is not governed by § 351. Instead, A is treated as simply receiving compensation in the form of property, and must report income equal to the value of the stock. In addition, A's basis in the stock will be equal to the value reported as income.

Example 10.   Assume the same facts as above, except that A received 40 shares of stock for his services. In this case, § 351 does not apply to any of the exchanges since the transferors of property, B and C, own only 67% (80 ÷ 120) of the stock after the exchange. Thus, the exchanges of property by B and C, as well as A's contribution of services, are taxable. Note that if those who exchange *only* services receive *more than* 20% of the stock, application of § 351 is denied for all transferors.

Transfers of Both Property and Services.   In situations where some persons transfer property to the corporation while others provide services, it is clear that the stock ownership of the service shareholder is disregarded for purposes of the control test. A question arises, however, as to the treatment of the transferor who contributes both property and services in exchange for stock. The Regulations address this problem by generally providing that all of the stock received by a transferor of both property and services is considered in determining whether control is achieved.[11]

Example 11.   E, F, and G have decided to form a corporation. According to their plan, E will transfer equipment worth $40,000 (basis $25,000) to the corporation for 40 shares of stock while F will transfer land worth $10,000 (basis $2,000) for 10 shares. G is still contemplating what his contribution to the corporation will be. If G contributes solely services worth $50,000 to the corporation for 50 shares of stock, neither E nor F will qualify for nonrecognition since the transferors of property, E and F, would own only 50% of the stock outstanding [(40 + 10) ÷ (40 + 10 + 50)].

Example 12.   Assume the same facts as above, except that G contributes property worth $20,000 and services worth $30,000 for 50 shares of stock. In this case, all of the stock received—not just that portion received for the property—is considered in applying the control test. Therefore, G is treated as a transferor of property, and all of his ownership is counted toward meeting the 80% standard. Thus the transferors of property own 100% of the stock [(40 + 10 + 50) ÷ (40 + 10 + 50)]. Although § 351 grants nonrecognition to this transaction, G still recognizes income equal to the value of the services rendered, $30,000. In all cases, an individual who is compensated for services must recognize income.

Nominal Property Transfers.   Certain situations exist when a small contribution of property by a transferor could produce very favorable results. For instance, consider a transaction that does not qualify for § 351 treatment because the service shareholder receives more than 20 percent of the stock. Given the general rule of the Regulations, the service shareholder could enable his or her stock to be counted toward control by simply transferring $1 of cash or other property along

---

[11]   Supra Footnote 7.

with the services. To discourage this practice, the Regulations indicate that nominal transfers of property for the purpose of qualifying the service shareholder's stock are ignored.[12] The IRS has elaborated further on this rule specifying that for advance ruling purposes, the value of the property transferred must not be less than 10 percent of the value of the services rendered (value of property ÷ value of service ≥ 10%).[13]

> **Example 13.** As part of an incorporation transaction, B provides services worth $30,000 and transfers property worth $20,000 (basis $8,000) for 50% of the stock. C transfers equipment for the other 50% of the stock. In this case, all of B's stock (not just those shares received for property) is counted in determining control because the property transferred is not relatively small in value compared to the value of the services provided. In fact, the property's value exceeds the 10% threshold prescribed by the IRS for advance ruling purposes ($20,000 ÷ $30,000, or 67%, exceeds 10%). Since B's ownership is considered toward control, the transferors of property own 100% of the stock, and thus the exchanges of property qualify for nonrecognition. As noted above, however, even though the property transfers qualify under § 351, B's transfer of services does not, and therefore he would recognize income of $30,000 on the exchange.

A second situation when the nominal transfer issue arises involves the admission of a new shareholder to the corporation. A prospective shareholder may be unwilling to be the sole transferor of property because receipt of less than an 80 percent interest causes any gain or loss realized to be recognized. In such case, existing shareholders may transfer property along with the new shareholder so that the existing shareholders' stock could also be counted toward control. By counting both the old and the new shareholders' ownership, the 80 percent test would be satisfied and the new shareholder would not recognize any gain or loss on the transaction. To prevent abuses (e.g., the transfer of $1 of property by the existing shareholders) the Regulations provide that nominal transfers of property are ignored. In this regard, the IRS also has indicated that for advance ruling purposes, a property transfer is counted toward control if the value of the property transferred is equal to 10 percent or more of the value of the stock and securities already owned by the transferor (value of property ÷ value of preexisting ownership ≥ 10%).[14]

> **Example 14.** T owns all 80 shares of X Corporation, which has a value of $200,000. She wishes to admit N as a new shareholder. N would contribute property worth $50,000 (basis $5,000) for 20 shares of stock. As structured, N would recognize a gain on the exchange since he would own only 20% of the stock after the exchange. However, if T also contributes at least

---

$20,000 (the IRS benchmark: 10% of her $200,000 share value), her stock ownership would be counted along with that of N in determining control. In such case, the transferors would own 100% of the stock after the exchange, and thus N's gain would be deferred.

Control "Immediately after the Exchange." The statute provides that the point in time when control is measured is immediately after the exchange. Read literally, this condition suggests that all transfers must be made precisely at the same time if nonrecognition is to be obtained. However, according to the Regulations, simultaneous transfers are unnecessary. It is sufficient if all of the transfers are made pursuant to a prearranged plan which is carried out expeditiously.[15] Thus, if the transfers satisfying the 80 percent test are made in a timely manner, nonrecognition is permitted.

Example 15. Four individuals, A, B, C, and D, decided to form a corporation with each owning 25% of the stock. A, B, and C make their transfers in January while D makes her transfer in March. If control is measured after A, B, and C have contributed their property, their transfers would be tax free under § 351 since they own 100% of the shares outstanding immediately after the exchange. In contrast, D's contribution may be considered an isolated transfer. Therefore, her transfer would be taxable since she was the only transferor and she owned only 25% of the stock after the exchange. If D desires nonrecognition, her transfer must be considered part of a prearranged plan that calls for her contribution.

In certain circumstances, a transferor may find nonrecognition undesirable. For example, if the transferor would realize a loss on the transfer, recognition may be the preferred treatment. In such case, a transferor may deliberately attempt to separate his or her transfer from other qualifying transfers. It should be emphasized, however, that the transfer may be treated as part of the plan unless it is sufficiently delayed so as to be completely disassociated from the other transfers.

Another problem associated with the "control-immediately-after-the-exchange" requirement involves so-called "momentary control." The issue is whether the 80 percent test is satisfied when the transferors have control for a brief moment after the exchange only to lose it because they dispose of sufficient shares to reduce their ownership below the necessary 80 percent. Note that the same difficulty could arise if the corporation subsequently issues additional shares.

Example 16. W has decided to incorporate his business. He anticipates transferring all of the assets to the corporation for 100% of its stock. Immediately after the exchange, W plans to give 15% of the stock to his son and sell another 20% to an interested investor. If control is measured prior to W's gift and sale of shares, § 351 applies since the 80% test is met. However, if control is measured after the gift and sale, W would own only 65% and § 351 would not allow nonrecognition.

---

[15]   Reg. § 1.351-1(a)(1).

As a general rule, "momentary control" normally is sufficient if the transferor does indeed have control. Control is evidenced by the fact that the transferor has—upon the receipt of the stock—the freedom to retain or dispose of the stock as desired.[16] As long as the subsequent transfers are not a part of a prearranged plan which inevitably leads to the transferors' loss of control, the statute should be satisfied. In any event, transfers immediately after the exchange should be considered carefully so that the dramatic effect of decontrol can be avoided.

SOLELY FOR STOCK AND THE "BOOT" EXCEPTION

The general rule of § 351 indicates that a transfer qualifies only if the transferor receives *solely* stock in exchange for the property transferred. The solely-for-stock requirement ensures that nonrecognition is granted when the transferor has not used the exchange to effectively liquidate or "cash in" on the investment in the property transferred.[17] However, receipt of property other than stock (e.g., cash) does not completely disqualify an exchange. Instead, § 351(b) requires that the transferor recognize gain to the extent that other property—so-called "boot"—is received.

Several aspects of the "boot" exception require clarification.[18] First, the amount of the gain recognized—as determined by the amount of the boot received—can never exceed the gain actually realized on the exchange.[19] Second, receipt of boot never triggers recognition of losses. Losses realized are never recognized.[20] This latter rule can be traced to one of the original purposes of § 351: a transferor should not be able to obtain losses when control of the asset is maintained. The final aspect of the boot rule warranting emphasis concerns liabilities and is discussed in detail below. Suffice it to say at this juncture that the transfer of liabilities by the transferor is generally not considered boot for purposes of determining recognized gain or loss.[21]

> **Example 17.** AAA Corporation has been in business several years. This year the original shareholders, Q and R, decided to contribute additional assets. Q transferred land worth $10,000 (basis $8,000) which was subject to a mortgage of $1,000 in exchange for stock worth $6,000 and cash of $3,000. R transferred equipment valued at $15,000 (basis $20,000) for

---

[16] See, for example, *Intermountain Lumber Co.,* 65 T.C. 1025 (1976).

[17] Prior to October 3, 1989, an exchange for stock *or securities* qualified for nonrecognition. As discussed below, the Revenue Reconciliation Act of 1989 eliminated this treatment for exchanges after October 2, 1989.

[18] § 351(b)(1).

[19] If more than one asset is transferred, Rev. Rul. 68-55 1968-1 C.B. 140 adopts a sepa-rate property approach for computing gain or loss. The gain or loss realized and recognized is separately computed for each property transferred assuming that a proportionate share of the stock, securities, and boot is received for each property (e.g., an asset representing 10% of the value of all properties transferred is allocated 10% of the stock and boot).

[20] § 351(b)(2).

[21] § 357(a).

stock worth $9,000 and cash of $6,000. Since Q and R own 100% of the stock after the exchange, nonrecognition under § 351 is permitted but only to the extent that stock is received. The tax consequences of the exchange are determined as follows:

	Q	R
Amount realized:		
Stock	$ 6,000	$ 9,000
Cash	3,000	6,000
Liability	1,000	0
Total amount realized	$10,000	$ 15,000
Adjusted basis of property transferred	(8,000)	(20,000)
Gain (loss) realized	$ 2,000	$ (5,000)
Gain recognized:		
Lesser of		
Boot received	$ 3,000	$ 6,000
or		
Gain realized	$ 2,000	0
Gain recognized	$ 2,000	
Loss recognized		0

Q recognizes a gain of $2,000. Note that Q's gain recognized is limited to the gain realized even though the boot exceeded the realized gain. Also observe that the liability transferred was not treated as boot. In contrast, R recognizes none of his realized loss even though he receives boot.

Securities as Boot. For many years, an exchange qualified for nonrecognition under § 351 if the transferor received stock *or securities* (e.g., long-term notes). Apparently, the original draftsmen of § 351 believed that the long-term creditor interest that a transferor obtained with the receipt of securities was sufficiently equivalent to the equity interest obtained with stock to warrant tax-free treatment. In effect, the authors of § 351 felt that the use of long-term debt satisfied the continuity of interest principle. In 1989, however, this approach was rejected, and § 351 was altered to allow nonrecognition only where stock is received.[22] In revising § 351, Congress presumably felt that an exchange for securities was more akin to a sale than a continuation of the transferor's investment. As a result, securities or debt of any type received as part of the exchange is now treated as boot. Thus, any gain realized on the exchange must be recognized to the extent of any securities received. However, Proposed Regulations provide that such gain may be recognized as the debt is repaid (i.e., using the installment method).[23] Loss is not recognized. The impact of this new treatment of securities on the corporation's capital structure is discussed later in this chapter.

---

[22] § 351(a) as revised by the Revenue Reconciliation Act of 1989.

[23] Prop. Reg. § 1.453-1(f)(3).

Character of Gain. Once it is known that gain must be recognized on the exchange, the character of that gain must be determined. The character of the gain depends on the nature of the asset in the hands of the transferor. If the asset is a capital asset, the gain is short or long-term capital gain depending on the transferor's holding period. If the asset is § 1231 property—generally real or depreciable property used in a trade or business held for more than six months—the gain is a § 1231 gain except to the extent that the recapture provisions such as §§ 1245 and 1250 require gain to be treated as ordinary income due to depreciation allowed on the property.

A provision that may trap the unwary taxpayer is § 1239. Under § 1239, gain recognized on a sale or exchange of depreciable property (including patents) between certain "related" persons is considered ordinary. Among the relationships considered tainted for this provision is one commonly existing in exchanges qualifying for § 351 treatment: an individual and his or her more than 50 percent owned corporation. Moreover, in measuring ownership, an individual is treated as owning stock of certain related persons as provided by the constructive ownership rules contained in § 267(c). Section 1239 was designed in part to prevent taxpayers from selling property to their controlled corporation to obtain a step-up in basis at the cost of a capital gains tax. A discussion of such plans is contained in the tax planning section at the end of this chapter.

LIABILITIES ASSUMED BY THE CORPORATION

Many incorporation transactions involve the transfer of property encumbered by debt or the assumption of the transferor's liabilities by the corporation. For example, when a sole proprietor incorporates his or her business, it would not be unusual to find a transfer of mortgaged real estate as well as the transfer of routine accounts payable to the corporation. Normally, when a taxpayer is relieved of a liability, it is treated as if the taxpayer received cash and then paid off the liability. If such treatment were extended to § 351 transfers, the transferor would be deemed to have received boot for any liabilities transferred and, therefore, required to recognize any gain realized. This approach was in fact made acceptable by virtue of the Supreme Court's decision in *U.S. v. Hendler*.[24]

Shortly after the *Hendler* decision, however, Congress recognized that the practical effect of treating liabilities as boot was to make many incorporation transactions taxable. This in turn interfered with the taxpayer's choice of business form, a result that is inconsistent with the underlying policy of § 351. As a result, Congress enacted a special provision governing the treatment of liabilities.

Currently, § 357(a) provides that when a corporation assumes the liabilities of a transferor or receives property subject to a liability as part of a § 351 transaction, the liability is not treated as boot for purposes of computing gain or loss recognized.

---

[24] 38-1 USTC ¶9215, 20 AFTR 1041, 303
U.S. 564 (USSC 1938).

Example 18.   This year, T transferred land worth $20,000 (basis $15,000) to his wholly owned corporation. The land was subject to a mortgage of $10,000. Normally, T would be treated as having received a cash payment equal to the liability from which he was relieved, $10,000. Under § 357(a), however, relief of a liability is not treated as boot and thus no gain is recognized.

Although immunizing the transferor from gain when liabilities are transferred was warranted, it created an additional problem: the potential for tax avoidance. Sections 357(b) and (c) address these difficulties.

Section 357(b): Curbing Tax Avoidance.   To understand the abuse that could occur without any special provisions, consider the following examples:

Example 19.   B, a taxpayer in the 15% bracket, owns land worth $100,000 (basis $25,000) which he plans to contribute to his wholly owned corporation. He also is in need of cash of $20,000. B could contribute the land to the corporation for 80 shares of stock worth $80,000 and cash of $20,000. In such case, he would be required to recognize $20,000 of his realized gain because of the boot received. Consequently, B would pay tax of $3,000 ($20,000 × 15%) on the gain. After the transaction, B would have 80 additional shares of stock and cash of $17,000.

Example 20.   Assume the same facts as above, except that immediately before the exchange, B mortgages the land and receives $20,000 in cash. Subsequently, B transfers the land now subject to the $20,000 mortgage to the corporation for 80 shares of stock worth $80,000. Since the liabilities transferred by B are not treated as boot, B recognizes no gain. After the transaction, B has 80 additional shares of stock and cash of $20,000.

A comparison of the result in *Example 19* to that in *Example 20* quickly reveals that by capitalizing on the general rule of § 357(a), B is able to cash in on the appreciation of his investment without paying any tax. Because liabilities are not treated as boot, B was able to avoid $3,000 in tax. Moreover, he has been completely relieved of his obligation to pay the debt. Although B would be required to reduce the basis of the stock received for the liability, the reduction might be a small price to pay for the deferral of the gain. Congress recognized that the purpose of § 351 could be undermined in this fashion and addressed the problem in § 357(b).

Section 357(b) requires that the principal purpose of the liability transfer be scrutinized. If, after taking all of the circumstances into consideration, it appears that the principal purpose of the liability transfer is to avoid tax or alternatively there is no bona fide business reason for the transfer, all liabilities are treated as boot.[25] Note that *all* liabilities are treated as boot and not just those which had an improper purpose.[26] It should be noted that the IRS requires that the corporate purpose for any liability assumption must be stated on the tax return for the year the assumption occurs.[27]

As suggested above, whether liabilities must be treated as boot can be determined only in light of the surrounding circumstances. Since most liabilities arise from routine business operations, the bona fide business purpose test normally insulates the taxpayer from application of § 357(b). Perhaps the liabilities on which the transferor is most vulnerable are those incurred shortly before they are transferred. Nevertheless even these should withstand attack if the transferor can support them with a good business purpose. However, any personal obligations of the transferor that might be assumed by the corporation are unlikely candidates for satisfying the business purpose test and most probably would be treated as boot. In this regard it should be remembered that if one tainted liability is transferred (e.g., a personal obligation) it could be disastrous since all liabilities would be treated as boot—even those incurred for business reasons.

Section 357(c): Liabilities in Excess of Basis. Section 357(c) was enacted to eliminate a technical flaw in the law which arises when liabilities on property transferred exceed the property's basis. The following example illustrates the problem.

> **Example 21.** Z transferred an office building subject to a mortgage to her wholly owned corporation. The office building is worth $100,000 and has a low basis of $45,000 due to accelerated depreciation deductions. The mortgage has a balance of $70,000. Upon the transfer, Z received stock valued at $30,000 (the difference between the property's value and the mortgage) and thus realized a gain of $55,000 ($30,000 + $70,000 − $45,000). Under the general rule of § 357(a), Z recognizes no gain on the transfer since the liabilities are not treated as boot. Given that the purpose of § 351 is to defer the gain, Z's basis should be set equal to an amount which would result in a $55,000 gain if she were to sell her stock for its $30,000 value. In order to do this, the basis of the stock must be a negative $25,000. Alternatively, the basis could be reduced only to zero, in which case Z would effectively escape tax on $25,000—a subsequent sale for $30,000 would yield a $30,000 gain ($30,000 − $0) when the theoretically correct gain should be $55,000. Note that the $25,000 which would escape tax is the amount by which the liability exceeds the property's basis.

---

[25] For an illustration, see *R.A. Bryan v. Comm.*, 60-2 USTC ¶9603, 6 AFTR2d 5191, 281 F.2d 233 (CA-4, 1960).

[26] Reg. § 1.357-1(c).

[27] Rev. Proc. 83-59, 1983-2 C.B. 575.

As the above example reveals, the problem faced by the courts was which method of dealing with the problem was more acceptable: (1) allow a negative basis—a concept that would be unprecedented in the Code but would ensure that the proper gain would be preserved; (2) allow a zero basis and enable a portion of the gain to escape tax; or (3) require the taxpayer to recognize gain to the extent the liability exceeded basis—an approach consistent with the view that the transferor is, in fact, better off to that extent (i.e., the transferor has in effect received a cash payment that exceeds the transferor's investment in the property as reflected by its basis). After the courts struggled with the issue, Congress provided a solution in 1954 with the enactment of § 357(c).[28] This provision requires that the taxpayer recognize gain to the extent that the total liabilities transferred on the exchange exceed the total basis of all property transferred.[29] Note that this is an *aggregate* rather than an asset-by-asset test.

> **Example 22.**   Assume the same facts as in *Example 21*. Under Code § 357(c), Z must recognize gain to the extent that the $70,000 mortgage on the property exceeds its $45,000 basis. Thus, Z recognizes $25,000 ($70,000 − $45,000) of the total $55,000 gain realized on the exchange. As discussed below, Z's basis will become zero, and a later sale of the stock for $30,000 would cause him to recognize the remaining portion of the $55,000 gain realized, $30,000.

According to Regulation § 1.357-2(b), the character of the gain is determined by allocating the total recognized gain among all assets except cash based on their relative fair market values. The type of asset and its holding period are used to determine the character of the gain allocated to it.

Liabilities of the Cash Basis Taxpayer.   Prior to 1978, requiring a transferor to recognize gain when liabilities exceeded basis posed difficulties when the transferor used the cash method of accounting. The following example demonstrates the dilemma.

---

[28]   See, for example, *Woodsam Associates, Inc. v. Comm.,* 52-2 USTC ¶9396, 42 AFTR 505, 198 F.2d 357 (CA-2, 1952).

[29]   If both § 357(b) (liability bailouts) and § 357 (c) (liabilities in excess of basis) apply, § 357(b) controls, causing all liabilities to be treated as boot. See § 357(c)(2)(A).

Example 23. D, an accountant, uses the cash method of accounting. This year he decided to incorporate his practice, transferring the following assets and liabilities to the corporation:

	Fair Market Value	Adjusted Basis
Cash......................................	$ 3,000	$3,000
Accounts receivable........................	40,000	0
Furniture and equipment	5,000	5,000
	$48,000	
Accounts payable..........................	$35,000	0
Notes payable.............................	7,000	7,000
Net worth.................................	6,000	0
	$48,000	

When determining whether gain should be recognized, liabilities transferred must be compared to the basis of the assets transferred. The difficulty confronting the cash basis taxpayer stems from the fact that some of the assets transferred have a zero basis—in this case, the accounts receivable have no basis. Thus, if the term *liability* is construed literally, the taxpayer has transferred liabilities of $42,000 which exceed the $8,000 ($5,000 + $3,000) basis of his assets by $34,000. Under a strict interpretation of the rule, D would be required to recognize gain of $34,000. Note that if D were an accrual basis taxpayer, the receivables would have a basis thus preventing recognition of gain.

As suggested in the example, the problem confronting the courts was the definition of liabilities. Some courts believed that accounts payable of a cash basis taxpayer should be ignored while others did not.[30] After much conflict, § 357 was amended to clarify what liabilities were to be considered. As now defined, liabilities do not include those which would give rise to a deduction when paid or those to which § 736(a) apply (amounts payable to a retiring partner or in liquidation of a deceased partner's interest).[31] However, a liability incurred for an expense that must be capitalized is considered a liability.[32]

Example 24. Assume the same facts as in *Example 23*, except that one of the accounts payable represents a bill of $500 for architectural drawings of D's planned office building. The remaining accounts payable are for routine deductible expenses. Upon the transfer of assets and liabilities to the corporation, D is considered as having transferred liabilities of $7,500.

---

[30] See *John P. Bongiovanni v. Comm.*, 73-1 USTC ¶9133, 31 AFTR2d 73-409, 470 F.2d 921 (CA-2, 1972); *Peter Raich*, 46 T.C. 604 (1966); and *Donald D . Focht*, 68 T.C. 223 (1977).

[31] § 357(c)(3). As discussed within, these liabilities are also ignored for basis purposes [see § 357(d)(2)].

[32] § 357(c)(3)(B).

The $7,500 is the sum of the $7,000 note payable which when paid would not be deductible and the $500 account payable for the drawings which when paid must be capitalized. The remaining accounts payable are not treated as liabilities since the corporation may deduct their payment when made. Because the $7,500 of liabilities does not exceed the $8,000 basis of the assets transferred ($3,000 + $5,000), D recognizes no gain on the exchange under § 357(c).

BASIS OF TRANSFEROR'S STOCK

The rules for computing the transferor's basis for any stock received reflects Congressional desire to defer rather than eliminate recognition on the exchange. As indicated above, the purpose of § 351 is to allow nonrecognition only as long as the transferor maintains an interest in the property transferred. Thus, any gains and losses not recognized on the original exchange should be recognized when the transferor or the corporation effectively severs its interest in the property. This policy is achieved in the provisions governing the basis assigned to the transferor's stock and the basis computed for the property transferred to the corporation.

> **Example 25.** T transfers property with a value of $100 and a basis of $40 to a corporation in exchange for stock worth $100. Under § 351, none of the $60 gain realized is recognized. This gain does not escape tax, but is preserved by assigning a basis to the stock equal to the basis of the property transferred, $40. If the stock is later sold for its $100 value, the taxpayer would recognize the $60 gain initially postponed.

The transferor's basis for the stock received is often referred to as a *substituted* basis since the basis of the property transferred is generally substituted as the basis for the stock received.

If a shareholder recognizes gain due to the receipt of boot, only the portion of the gain that is not recognized needs to be built into the basis of the stock. This approach is reflected in the formula for the computation of the transferor's basis in Exhibit 2-1.[33] As seen in the formula, the transferor's basis is initially the same as the property transferred, but is increased for the gain recognized on the exchange so that this amount will not be taxed twice. The combination of these two amounts represents the transferor's basis for the stock and boot received. A portion of this total is then allocated to the boot by subtracting the *value* of the boot. In effect, the basis assigned to the boot is its value, while the remaining basis is assigned to the stock. This arithmetic ensures that the deferred gain is built into the transferor's basis for the stock.

---

[33]   § 358.

Exhibit 2-1
Transferor's Basis of Stock Received

Adjusted basis of property transferred................... $xx,xxx
+ Gain recognized.. x,xxx
− Boot received.. (xxx)
− Liabilities transferred.................................. (xxx)

= Basis of stock received................................. $xx,xxx

---

Example 26. T transfers property with a value of $120 and a basis of $40 to C Corporation in exchange for stock worth $90 and $30 cash. T realizes an $80 ($90 + $30 − $40) gain, $30 of which is recognized due to the boot received. As determined below, T's basis in the stock is $40, while his basis in the cash is its value of $30.

> Basis of property transferred.............. $40
> + Gain recognized.......................... 30
> − Boot received............................ (30)
> = Basis of stock........................... $40

Note how a subsequent sale of the stock for its $90 value would cause T to recognize the previously postponed gain of $50 ($90 − $40).

Effect of Liabilities. Although liabilities transferred by the transferor are not considered boot for purposes of computing gain or loss on the exchange, they normally are treated as boot in determining the transferor's basis.[34] This treatment ensures eventual recognition of the gain or loss deferred on the exchange.

Example 27. K, a cash basis taxpayer, transferred land to her corporation. The land was valued at $50,000 (basis $35,000) and was subject to a $30,000 mortgage. In exchange for the land, K received stock worth $20,000. Although K realizes a $15,000 gain ($30,000 + $20,000 − $35,000), none of the gain is recognized because the corporation's acquisition of the property subject to the debt is not considered boot for purposes

---

[34] § 358(d).

of gain or loss recognition. In contrast, K's basis for the stock received is computed treating the liability as boot as follows:

Adjusted basis of property transferred	$ 35,000
+ Gain recognized	0
− Boot received (including liabilities transferred)	(30,000)
Basis of stock	$ 5,000

K's basis in the stock is $5,000. Should K subsequently sell the stock for its $20,000 value, the $15,000 gain postponed on the exchange would be recognized. Note that the effect of this approach is the equivalent of treating the shareholder as receiving a cash payment, which is considered a nontaxable return of capital.

It should be noted that not all liabilities are treated as boot for purposes of determining basis. As explained earlier, Code § 357(c)(3) provides that those liabilities relating to routine deductible expenditures are not considered liabilities in determining whether liabilities exceed basis. Similarly, when computing the shareholder's basis, such liabilities are also ignored.[35]

Example 28. Assume the same facts as in *Example 27* above, except that the corporation also assumed $20,000 of K's routine accounts payable that would be deductible when paid. K still recognizes no gain on the transaction since the payables are ignored because the corporation could deduct the payments when made. Similarly, these liabilities are ignored in computing basis. Thus, K's basis also remains the same.

Holding Period. The transferor's holding period may affect the tax treatment if the property received in the exchange is disposed of in the future. In determining the holding period of the stock and boot received, the rules of § 1223 apply. This provision allows a transferor to add the time that the property transferred was held to the actual holding period of the property received if both of the following conditions are satisfied:[36]

1. The property transferred was a capital asset or § 1231 property (generally real or depreciable business property) in the hands of the transferor.

2. The basis of the property received was determined in reference to the basis of the property transferred to the corporation.

Since the basis of the stock is determined by using the basis of the property transferred as a starting point, the transferor's holding period for the stock includes the holding period of the transferred property, but only if the property transferred is a capital asset or § 1231 property. The holding period of any boot received begins on the date of the exchange since its basis is not determined in reference to the property transferred but is its value.

---

[35] § 357(d)(2).   [36] § 1223(1).

CORPORATION'S GAIN OR LOSS

The treatment of the corporation on the exchange is very straightforward relative to that of the transferor shareholder. The corporation recognizes no gain or loss when it receives money, property, or services in exchange for its stock.[37] This rule applies whether the stock exchanged is previously unissued stock or treasury stock.[38] As stated earlier, however, the corporation treats the issuance of stock for services just as if a cash payment had been made. In such case, the corporation may capitalize or deduct the amount depending on the type of services rendered.[39]

CORPORATION'S BASIS FOR PROPERTY RECEIVED

Like the basis rules for the transferor, those for the corporation ensure that any gain or loss deferred on the exchange is properly recognized if the corporation subsequently disposes of the property. The basis assigned to the property received by the corporation is sometimes referred to as a *carryover* basis. This term is used because the transferor's basis is "carried over" and generally serves as the corporation's basis as well. However, if the transferor recognizes any gain on the exchange, the amount of gain is added to the corporation's basis to prevent the gain from being recognized twice. The formula for computing the corporation's basis is shown in Exhibit 2-2.[40]

Exhibit 2-2
Basis of Assets Received by the Corporation

Adjusted basis of the property to the transferor..	$x,xxx
+ Gain recognized on the exchange........................	xxx
= Aggregate basis of property received..................	$x,xxx

---

[37] § 1032.

[38] Supra Footnote 37.

[39] Supra Footnote 8.

[40] § 362.

> **Example 29.** During the current year, Y transferred land worth $50,000 (basis $10,000) to her wholly owned corporation for 40 shares of stock worth $47,000 and cash of $3,000. Y realizes a $40,000 gain ($47,000 + $3,000 − $10,000). She recognizes $3,000 of the gain since she received boot of $3,000. The corporation's basis in the land is $13,000 (transferor's $10,000 basis + transferor's $3,000 gain recognized).

The basis calculation for the corporation is not troublesome when the transferor recognizes no gain on the exchange. In such case, the corporation merely "steps into the shoes" of the transferor and its basis for each asset received is identical to the transferor's basis. However, if the transferor contributes more than one asset and recognizes gain, it is unclear how the aggregate basis should be allocated among the various assets. Since it is generally assumed that each asset transferred should have a basis at least equal to that of the transferor, the crucial question concerns the allocation of the gain recognized. Perhaps the most logical method would be to allocate the gain to the asset(s) responsible for it. Unfortunately, several other methods have been suggested and the acceptable one has yet to be identified.

Holding Period. The rule governing the corporation's holding period for property received is consistent with the notion that the corporation essentially "steps into the shoes" of the transferor in a § 351 exchange. Accordingly, the corporation's holding period for all assests received includes that of the transferor.[41]

SPECIAL CONSIDERATIONS

Several additional concerns arise when property is transferred to a controlled corporation. For example, the possibility of recapture of depreciation or the investment credit must be considered. Similarly, the method of applying the Modified Accelerated Cost Recovery System (MACRS) to determine the proper amount of depreciation requires attention. These and other problems are addressed below.

Recapture of Depreciation. The depreciation recapture provisions of §§ 1245 and 1250 often require the taxpayer to recognize gain on what otherwise would be a nontaxable transaction. This treatment makes certain that the potential recapture is not avoided. When property is transferred to a controlled corporation, however, recapture is not triggered.[42] Instead the recapture potential shifts to the corporation. Therefore, if the corporation subsequently disposes of the property, it must recapture not only amounts related to the depreciation it has claimed, but also the appropriate amount of any depreciation claimed by the transferor.

---

[41] § 1223(2).   [42] §§ 1245(b)(3) and 1250(d)(3).

Recapture of Investment Tax Credit. Although the investment credit was repealed beginning in 1986, the possibility of recapturing unearned credits continues to exist. The recapture rules for the investment credit generally provide that the credit must be recaptured upon a disposition prior to the time when the credit has been fully earned (e.g., later sale of the property by the corporation or a sale or other disposition of the transferor's stock).[43] If recapture is necessary, it is the obligation of the transferor-shareholder and *not* the corporation as is the case with depreciation recapture. In other words, potential depreciation recapture is shifted to the corporation while investment credit recapture remains with the shareholder.

Depreciation Computations. Often times depreciable property is placed in service prior to its transfer to a corporation. When such property is transferred, certain rules must be adhered to in computing the depreciation deduction and in allocating it between the transferor and the corporation. When the property transferred qualifies for depreciation using MACRS, depreciation for the year of the transfer and subsequent years generally is computed using the transferor's period and method.[44] For the year of transfer, the depreciation must be allocated between the transferor and the corporation according to the number of months held by each.[45] In determining the number of months that each holds the property, the corporation is assumed to hold the property for the entire month in which the property is transferred.

> **Example 30.** In 1986, S retired from the military and started his own copying business. After being in business for several years, he decided to incorporate. On September 23, 1991, he transferred assets of the business to a corporation in exchange for all of its stock. Among the assets transferred was an automobile purchased for $10,000 in June 1990. In 1990, S's depreciation deduction using the optional MACRS tables (contained in Appendix H) for five-year property was $2,000 (20% × $10,000). For the year of the transfer, 1991, depreciation of the automobile is computed using the same method used by the transferor S. Thus, depreciation for the year is $3,200 (32% of $10,000). The $3,200 depreciation deduction must be allocated between S and the corporation based on the number of months held by each. S is treated as having held the property for eight months (January–August) while the corporation is given credit for holding the asset for the remaining four months of the year (the month of the transfer, September, through December). S may deduct $2,134 ($3,200 × 8 ÷ 12) while the corporation may deduct the remaining depreciation ($3,200 × 4 ÷ 12).

---

[43] See § 47 (a); Reg. §§ 1.47-3(f)(1) and 1.47-3(f)(5); Rev. Rul. 76-514, 1976-2 C.B. 11; and *James Soares*, 50 T.C. 909 (1968) for examples of when unearned investment tax credit must be recaptured.

[44] § 168(i)(7) and Prop. Reg. 1.168-5(b)(2)(B). Special rules apply for depreciating any gain element in the corporation's basis. See Prop. Reg § 1.168-5(b)(7).

[45] Prop. Reg. 1.168-5(b)(4)(i).

It should be emphasized that any computations made with respect to S, such as computing his basis in the stock received or his gain or loss on the transfer, must reflect the depreciation allocated to him. Therefore the basis of the property transferred (which generally is substituted for the basis of the stock received) is $5,866 ($10,000 − $2,000 − $2,134). Note that the corporation's basis is also $5,866 on the day of the transfer, but it uses the full $10,000 cost to compute its future depreciation deductions just as S would have—had he retained the property.

Example 31.   Assume the same facts as above. In 1992 the corporation continues to compute depreciation on the automobile using S's period and method. Therefore, the corporation's depreciation for 1992 is $1,920 ($10,000 × 19.2%).

The MACRS operating rules also require a modification in the normal depreciation calculation for property *other than real property* when a corporation has a short taxable year—a taxable year of less than 12 months. For purposes of determining whether the corporation has a short taxable year, the taxable year does not include any month prior to the month in which the business begins. For example, if two individuals form a calendar year corporation which starts business on September 14, it is treated as having a short taxable year beginning in September and ending on December 31. When property is placed in service during a short taxable year, standard depreciation conventions (i.e., half-year, mid-month, and mid-quarter) must be followed in computing the depreciation deduction. For example, personal property placed in service during a short taxable year of four months is treated as having been in service for half the number of months in that year (i.e., two months).[46]   As a result, the corporation would be entitled to $2/12$ of the annual depreciation amount. If depreciation is calculated using the optional tables, however, the deduction would be $4/12$ of the amount normally computed using the table. This fraction, $4/12$, is used instead of $2/12$ since the rate prescribed in the table for the first year already reflects the half-year convention. Consequently, if the tables are used for calculating the deduction, depreciation is computed by multiplying the amount determined in the normal manner by the fraction of the year—expressed in months—during which the corporation was in business.[47]

Example 32.   After many years of wanting to have her own company, B finally decided in 1992 to test her fortunes in the limousine business. On May 17, 1992, she transferred $50,000 in cash to a corporation in exchange for all of its stock. On the same day, the corporation purchased a limousine (5-year property) for $30,000. The corporation adopted the calendar

---

[46]   Conference Agreement, Conference Report H.R. 3838 (9/18/86), U.S. Government Printing Office: 1986, 99th Congress, 2d Session, Report 99-841, p. II-46.

[47]   Prop. Reg. 1.168-2(f)(1).

year for reporting. Since the corporation was not in business prior to May, it has a short taxable year of eight months. Consequently, the depreciation deduction is $4,000 computed as follows:

Cost of equipment.....................................	$30,000
Rate per depreciation tables (Appendix H-3).........	$\times$ 20%
Short taxable year fraction...........................	$\times$ $8/12$
Depreciation...	$ 4,000

CONTRIBUTIONS TO CAPITAL

The previous section examined transfers to controlled corporations when the transferor received stock and other property in exchange. From time to time, transfers may be made to a corporation when the transferor receives nothing in exchange. Such transfers are termed *contributions to capital* and are subject to special tax treatment. As discussed below, the tax treatment of capital contributions generally depends on the source of the contribution: shareholders or nonshareholders.

SHAREHOLDER CONTRIBUTIONS

The tax treatment of a *cash* contribution to capital made by a shareholder normally presents little difficulty. A corporation may exclude the contribution from its gross income as long as it is truly a contribution and not merely disguised compensation for something the corporation has provided or will provide to the shareholder.[48] If the facts suggest the latter, the corporation recognizes income on the transfer. Assuming the transfer is a contribution and not compensation, the shareholder treats the contribution as an additional cost of the stock previously owned and increases the basis in the stock.[49]

If a contribution of *property* is made by a shareholder, the treatment varies only with respect to the basis computations. Assuming the contribution is voluntary, the shareholder's basis in his or her stock is increased by the basis of the property transferred plus any gain recognized—which usually does not arise. The corporation's basis for the property is the same as the transferor's, increased by any gain recognized.

A question that arises frequently in this area concerns the treatment of a loan, or some other debt made by the shareholder to the corporation, which the shareholder subsequently forgives. It is not uncommon, particularly in small closely held corporations, for shareholders to make advances to their corporations which as a practical matter are never repaid and ultimately are forgiven by the shareholder. As a general rule, when a debt is canceled, the debtor must recognize

---

[48] § 118.   [49] Reg. § 1.118-1.

income. When the debtor-creditor relationship is between a corporation and its shareholders, however, the courts have normally characterized the transaction as a nontaxable contribution to capital as long as the facts suggested that the shareholder intended to make a contribution.[50]

NONSHAREHOLDER CONTRIBUTIONS

Capital contributions are not limited to those made by shareholders. Nonshareholders also make contributions to businesses notwithstanding their lack of a proprietary interest. These contributions are usually prompted by the hope of deriving some indirect benefit. For example, in their drive to create jobs, governmental units and other types of nonshareholders often provide attractive financial packages to lure corporations to locate in their area. When the economic incentives include capital contributions, special tax considerations arise.

A nonshareholder contribution may be excluded by the corporation from gross income if the transfer is an inducement rather than payment for corporate goods or services.[51] If the corporation receives a contribution of property, the basis of the property is considered zero so that normal tax benefits associated with basis (e.g., depreciation) cannot be obtained.[52] Note that a corporation could circumvent this result by requesting a cash contribution and using it to acquire property which would then have a basis equal to its cost. To preclude such action, the corporation must reduce the basis of any property acquired with the money during the next 12-month period.[53] If all or a part of the money has not been used at the end of this period to acquire property, the basis of other property must be reduced by the amount not spent. The basis of property subject to depreciation, depletion, or amortization is reduced first.[54] Any further reductions required are applied to other property.

> **Example 33.** To attract a professional football team to locate in its area, the city government contributed a practice facility worth $4 million to the corporation owning the team. The corporation recognizes no income from the contribution, and the basis of the facility is zero. Had the city contributed $4 million in cash to the corporation which subsequently acquired an office building for $3 million, the corporation would have a basis in the office building of zero. In addition, if the remaining $1 million had not been spent at the end of the 12-month period, the basis of other corporate property must be reduced by $1 million.

---

[50] Reg. § 1.61-12(a); See, for example, *Hartland Assocs.*, 54 T.C. 1580 (1970).

[51] § 118.

[52] § 362(c)(1).

[53] § 362(c)(2).

[54] Reg. § 1.362-2(b).

THE CORPORATION'S CAPITAL STRUCTURE

In financing corporate operations, management primarily relies on the issuance of stock or debt or some combination thereof to secure necessary capital. The ultimate configuration of stock and debt used—normally referred to as the corporation's *capital structure*—is shaped by many factors, including the tax law. Various tax provisions have significant implications for whether a corporation's capital should be acquired by issuing stock or by creating debt. The principal considerations in deciding between stock or debt are discussed in the following sections.[55]

STOCK VERSUS DEBT: A COMPARISON

Appreciated Property. Prior to the revisions of § 351 in 1989, a corporation could issue stock *or debt* in exchange for property without tax consequences. Consequently, a corporation had the flexibility to issue stock or debt as otherwise suited its needs. Normally, this meant a heavy dosage of debt was used in the capital structure because of its many advantages, discussed below. However, the Revenue Reconciliation Act of 1989 altered the traditional playing field. As explained earlier, Congress revised § 351 so that the receipt of securities is treated as boot. Therefore, if debt is issued in exchange for property that has appreciated, the transferor must recognize gain. This may serve as an important limitation on the use of debt. However, the Proposed Regulations do allow any gain attributable to receipt of the debt to be reported as the debt is collected using the installment sales method; this may reduce the impact of the change.[56]

It should be observed that the treatment of securities as boot has no effect if the transferor does not realize any gain on the exchange. For example, contributions of cash or loss property in exchange for securities can be made without tax consequences. Thus, the 1989 Act did not kill the corporation's use of securities to raise capital but only imposed an important limitation that must be considered when planning the formation of the corporation and subsequent exchanges.

Interest versus Dividends. No doubt the most obvious distinction between stock and debt concerns the tax treatment of interest and dividends. Quite simply, the corporation can deduct interest payments but not dividend payments. The implications of this distinction are twofold. First, since interest payments reduce taxable income while dividend payments do not, the corporation's cost of using debt to raise capital may be less than the cost for stock. Assuming a corporation paid Federal and state taxes at about a 40 percent rate, that corporation would be required to earn $100 to pay a $60 dividend while only $60 of income is needed

---

[55] For an excellent analysis of the relationship between debt and the tax law, see Plumb, "The Federal Income Tax Significance of Corporate Debt: A Critical Analysis and a Proposal," 26 *Tax Law Review,* 369 (1971).

This is an in-depth treatise devoting almost 300 pages to the topic.

[56] Supra, Footnote 23.

to pay the same amount in interest. This difference looms as such a powerful incentive that commentators have criticized this apparent advantage for leading to excessive debt financing.[57]   Second, since interest payments are deductible, debt enables the avoidance of double taxation. Consequently, debt serves as an excellent vehicle for shareholders of a closely held corporation to bail out the earnings and profits of a corporation.

> **Example 34.**   J and B each received $500,000 from their father to start their own businesses. J transferred his $500,000 to his corporation for shares of stock worth $200,000 and a note bearing 10% interest, payable in annual installments of $20,000 for 15 years. B invested his $500,000 in exchange solely for stock. Both corporations are equally successful. Ignoring salary payments, J and B both desire $30,000 from their corporations. By designing his capital structure to include debt, J's corporation distributes the $30,000 to J in the form of a deductible interest payment, thus avoiding the double tax penalty. In contrast, the distribution from B's corporation represents a nondeductible dividend. Consequently, B's $30,000 has been taxed twice—once when the corporation earns the income and again when the income is distributed as dividends to B.

Debt Repayment versus Stock Redemption.   A second distinction between stock and debt concerns the tax consequences resulting from repayment of debt as compared to redemption of stock. When the investor in a publicly held corporation needs funds, a sale of a portion of the investment (stock or debt) enables a tax free recovery of the investment's cost and a capital gains tax on any excess. For an investor in a closely held corporation, however, the situation changes dramatically. In this case, there probably is little market for the investment, and even if there were, a transfer to an outsider is probably not acceptable. For the investor whose investment is in stock, the alternative is a sale of the stock to the corporation (i.e., a redemption). Notwithstanding the fact that a "sale" may occur in form, the Code generally provides that such sales are treated as dividends.[58] On the other hand, if the investor's investment takes the form of debt, repayments of the debt generally are treated as a tax-free return of the debt's principal. Although a redemption can result in sale and capital gain treatment under some circumstances, this outcome still falls short of the nontaxable treatment available with debt. Like the interest-dividend distinction, the difference between repayments of debt and redemptions of stock affords shareholders of a closely held corporation an excellent opportunity to bail out corporate earnings.

---

[57]   See, for example, U.S. Department of the Treasury, *Blueprints for Basic Tax Reform*, p. 69.

[58]   § 302. The redemption provisions are discussed in Chapter 4.

Example 35.   Assume the same facts as in *Example 34* above. In addition to receiving an annual interest payment of $30,000, J also receives an annual principal payment of $20,000 that is tax free. If B desires to receive a similar payment of $20,000, he could sell stock to his corporation worth $20,000 (note that a sale to an outside third party is normally an unacceptable alternative when the corporation is closely held). Although the transaction may be structured as a sale, the redemption provisions of the Code require that this amount be treated as a dividend since the distribution has all the characteristics of a dividend (i.e., B's interest has not been reduced, the distribution is pro rata). Consequently, B acquires the $20,000 at the cost of two taxes.

As the above examples suggest, shareholders of closely held corporations have long preferred debt to stock when exchanging their assets with the corporation. Consequently, the closely held corporation's capital structure usually is heavily tipped in favor of debt. When this condition exists—the capital structure consists primarily of debt and little stock—the corporation is said to be *thinly capitalized*. If a corporation is too thinly capitalized, all or a portion of its debt may be treated as stock. Of course, if debt is reclassified as stock, all of the advantages of debt are lost. The possible characterization of debt as stock is considered in more detail below.

Accumulated Earnings Tax Considerations. Another difference between stock and debt involves application of the accumulated earnings tax provisions. These provisions impose a penalty tax in addition to the regular corporate tax to dissuade taxpayers from shifting income to the corporation where it has traditionally been taxed at lower corporate rates. Although the top corporate rate currently exceeds the top individual rate, income could still be shifted to the corporation and taxes saved if the actual corporate rate paid (e.g., 15% on the first $50,000) was less than the rate paid by the individual (e.g., 28% or 31%). To foil attempts by individuals who wish to take advantage of shifting income, the accumulated earnings tax levies a penalty when corporations accumulate earnings beyond the reasonable needs of the business. Herein lies the importance of debt. The repayment of debt is considered a reasonable need.[59] Thus the corporation is allowed to accumulate the funds necessary to discharge the debt. In contrast, the redemption of stock is not considered a reasonable need and hence accumulations for such purpose are not permitted. As a result, the presence of debt in the capital structure serves as a justification for accumulations, whereas the presence of stock does not.

---

[59]   Reg. § 1.537-2(b)(3). The accumulated earnings tax is discussed in Chapter 6.

Worthless Debt versus Worthless Stock. Since not all businesses prosper, an investor must consider the tax result if his or her investment in the corporation goes sour. The tax consequences attributable to worthless stock and debt can vary widely depending on the circumstances. For this reason, the subject of worthless investments is considered in detail later in this chapter. Basically, however, if stock or debt becomes worthless, a capital loss is usually recognized. Thus, deductions for worthlessness are normally restricted to the extent of capital gains *plus* $3,000. The major exception to this rule is contained in § 1244, which generally provides special treatment for the first million dollars of stock issued. Investors who own this stock are entitled to ordinary loss treatment if the stock is disposed of at a loss or if it becomes worthless. Since many businesses do not succeed, this distinction must be carefully weighed before using a substantial amount of debt in the capital structure.

DEBT TREATED AS STOCK

In view of the favorable tax treatment given to debt, corporations, particularly those that are closely held, have often tried to exploit their advantages by using a high proportion of debt in their capital structures. The lack of taxpayer restraint in this area was well illustrated in one case where the shareholders had advances outstanding to the corporation exceeding 100 times the value of the stock.[60] In these circumstances, the government is apt to ignore the fact that the instrument is debt on its face (i.e., it contains all the formal characteristics of debt), and focus instead on its substance. If it is determined that the alleged debt instrument is simply a disguised equity interest, it may be reclassified and treated as stock.

A recharacterization of debt as stock can be disastrous. For example, all interest previously paid becomes taxable as dividends. Similarly, repayments of debt principal are treated as payments in redemption of stock and are likely to be treated as dividends. In short, the favorable tax treatment is lost and unfavorable treatment is imposed.

Whether a purported debt instrument is debt or stock has been a subject of scores of cases. In fact, the problem so plagues the government that in 1969 Congress enacted the now infamous § 385. The primary thrust of § 385 is to authorize the Treasury to draft Regulations clarifying the circumstances that would warrant a recharacterization of debt as stock. To this date, however, Treasury has been unable to write Regulations that are both acceptable to the financial community and at the same time not easily circumvented or abused. Consequently, over 20 years after the enactment of § 385, Regulations do not exist.

---

[60] In *Glenmore Distilleries Co.*, 47 B.T.A. 213 (1942), capital stock was $1,000 while shareholder advances were $131,458.

Section 385 does identify certain factors that should be considered in determining whether a true debtor-creditor relationship has been established. The factors to be considered are

1. Whether there is a written unconditional promise to pay on demand or on a specified date a sum certain in money in return for an adequate consideration in money or money's worth, and to pay a fixed rate of interest

2. Whether there is subordination to or preference over any indebtedness of the corporation

3. The ratio of debt to equity of the corporation

4. Whether there is convertibility into the stock of the corporation

5. The relationship between holdings of stock in the corporation and holdings of the interest in question

Unfortunately, this list is simply a distillation of factors already identified by the courts. Consequently, in absence of Regulations, the courts continue their struggle to distinguish debt from equity. Whether an instrument is stock or debt seems to be a question of risk. An early court case captured the definitional problem well, stating:

> [the] vital difference between the shareholder and the creditor [is that the] shareholder is an adventurer in the corporate business; he takes the risk, and profits from success. The creditor, in compensation for not sharing the profits, is to be paid independently of the risk of success, and gets a right to dip into capital when the payment date arrives.[61]

Unfortunately, the threshold of risk at which an investor transcends creditor status and becomes a shareholder has not been clearly identified. The various cases suggest that the issue must ultimately be resolved in light of the taxpayers intent: Did the investor intend to provide risk capital susceptible to the fortunes of the business or to establish a debtor-creditor relationship? Consequently, most of the court cases involve an examination of various factors that may be indicative of the investor's true intention.

The reclassification controversy takes place on two fronts. The first involves instruments that have all the formal characteristics of debt. These instruments, normally considered *straight debt*, contain an unqualified promise to pay a sum certain at a maturity date along with a fixed percentage in interest. Straight debt normally has a maturity date that is reasonably close in time, and interest that is payable regardless of the corporation's income. In addition, the debt is not

---

[61] *Commissioner v. O.P.P. Holding Corp.*, 35-1 USTC ¶9179, 15 AFTR 379, 76 F.2d 11, 12 (CA-2, 1935).

subordinated to those of general creditors but has similar rights, and the debt also gives the holder the right to enforce payment upon maturity or default. The second type of debt involves *hybrid* securities, so-called because they are really neither stock nor debt but a blend. A hybrid security is often convertible to stock or contains some feature normally associated with stock. For example, the security may entitle the holder to vote on corporate affairs much like a shareholder, or the security's interest payments may be contingent on earnings much like dividends.

A review of the various court decisions indicates that hybrid securities usually have more difficulty in qualifying as debt than does straight debt. Courts apparently are somewhat reluctant to grant debt status to instruments that are obviously not debt on their face (e.g., instruments structured with conversion or participation features). On the other hand, straight debt is not above suspicion. An instrument that meets the classical definition of debt may still be characterized as stock depending on the surrounding circumstances. For example, straight debt is particularly vulnerable where there is an excessive debt-to-equity ratio or the debt is held in the same proportion as stock.

As suggested earlier, the clearest signal that debt is not what it is purported to be is a high debt-to-equity ratio. Although no particular ratio is conclusive, a ratio exceeding 4:1 suggests that things are not what they might seem.[62] Where the ratio of debt to equity is high—such as in an extreme case when all of the capital is in the form of debt—all or virtually all of the risk is borne by creditors. In such situations, repayment of the debt is so linked with the fortunes of the business—since there are no other sources for payment—that it must be said that it represents risk capital and warrants recharacterization as stock.

The fact that shareholders hold debt in the same proportion as they hold stock (e.g., a 60% shareholder holds 60% of the debt) normally raises a strong inference that the shareholders never intended to act like creditors. Accordingly, the courts have been willing to reclassify the instrument. This inference stems from the theory that a shareholder-creditor who holds debt in a greater proportion than stock (e.g., 70% debt, 30% stock) is more likely to act like a creditor and exercise his or her legal right to recover the excess should circumstances warrant.

---

[62] Prior to the Supreme Court's decision in *John Kelley Co. v. Comm.*, 46-1 USTC ¶9133, 34 AFTR 314, 326 U.S. 521 (USSC, 1946), the Tax Court bestowed debt status notwithstanding ratios that were far greater than 4:1. In Kelley's companion case, *Talbot Mills*, the Court, in stating that a 4:1 ratio was not "obviously excessive," provided a benchmark of sorts for about a decade. Later decisions, however, indicated that there was no "magic" ratio and consequently no discernible pattern developed. The Regulations that were proposed contained certain safe harbor ratios. For example, straight debt was classified as debt where the ratio is less than 3:1.

Example 36. When J and K incorporated their business, J contributed 60% of the funds while K contributed the other 40%. For his contribution J received 30 shares of stock worth $30,000 and a $24,000 demand note while K received 20 shares of stock worth $20,000 and a $16,000 demand note. Thus, J received 60% of the stock (30 ÷ 50) and 60% of the debt [$24,000 ÷ ($24,000 + $16,000)] while K received 40% of the stock (20 ÷ 50) and 40% of the debt [$16,000 ÷ ($24,000 + $16,000)]. After several years of operations, it became evident that the business could fail. At that time, the corporation had $20,000 in cash and some equipment that had no value if the business ceased. Its only liabilities included the two notes to J and K. In this situation, neither J nor K has an incentive to act like a creditor since their holdings in stock are identical to those in debt. J and K would share the remaining assets in the same 60–40 split regardless of whether they exercised their legal rights as creditors. On the other hand, if their holdings were disproportionate, (e.g., J owned 80% of the debt and 20% of the stock while K owned 20% of the debt and 80% of the stock), it is unlikely that J would abandon his creditor rights since to do so would severely reduce his recovery.

The conclusion to be drawn from the previous example is merely this: disproportionate holdings support a debtor-creditor relationship while proportionate holdings do not.[63] The converse is not necessarily true, however. Proportionate holdings are not conclusive evidence that the debt is equity since considering them as such would deny the principle that an investor can be both a shareholder and a creditor. For example, if debt were always treated as stock when proportional holdings existed, a one-person corporation could never make a "loan" to his or her corporation since shareholder debt and equity would always be held in the same proportion. Therefore, proportional holdings normally must be coupled with some other factor such as an unreasonably high interest rate before the instrument is reclassified.[64] The high interest rate would simply add further credence to the need for reclassification since it suggests the shareholder was using the debt to bail earnings out of the corporation.

LOSSES ON STOCK AND DEBT INVESTMENTS

As most individuals who form corporations know, not all businesses succeed. When a corporation is unprofitable, the failure ultimately must be borne by those who provided the capital (i.e., the holders of the corporation's debt or stock). For this reason, an investor must understand the tax consequences resulting from losses on stock or debt and use this knowledge in choosing between them.

An investor's losses may be classified into four categories: (1) worthless securities (i.e., stock and certain types of debt), (2) business and nonbusiness bad

---

[63] See, for example, *Wachovia Bank & Trust Co. v. U.S.*, 61-1 USTC ¶9362, 7 AFTR2d 1071, 288 F.2d 750 (CA-4, 1961).

[64] *Piedmont Corp. v. Comm.*, 68-1 USTC ¶9189, 21 AFTR2d 534, 388 F.2d 886 (CA-4, 1968).

debts, (3) losses on sale of stock and debt, and (4) losses on § 1244 stock. Each of these is discussed below.

Worthless Securities.   When a security becomes worthless, special rules govern the loss.[65]   These rules apply only to those items satisfying the definition of security. The term *security* means stock, stock rights, bonds, debentures, or any other evidence of indebtedness issued by a corporation or the government with interest coupons or in registered form.[66]   In addition, the security must be considered a capital asset before the special rules apply. If a qualifying security becomes worthless at any time during the year, the resulting loss is treated as arising from the sale or exchange of a capital asset on the *last day* of the taxable year. Therefore, losses from worthlessness are treated as either short- or long-term capital losses.

> **Example 37.**   M incorporated her business on November 1, 1991, receiving 100 shares of stock. The stock had a basis of $25,000. On July 1, 1992, seven months after M acquired her stock, the corporation declared bankruptcy. Since the stock is worthless, M has a capital loss of $25,000. In addition, the loss is considered long-term since the holding period exceeds one year—November 1, 1991 to December 31, 1992, the day on which the hypothetical sale is deemed to occur. Due to the limitations on deductions of capital losses, M may deduct a maximum of $3,000 (assuming she has no capital gains) and the unused loss of $22,000 could be carried over until it is exhausted.

As noted within, however, if stock qualifies as § 1244 stock the loss on worthlessness may be ordinary. Another variation in the general treatment permits ordinary loss treatment for a corporation where the securities are in certain affiliated corporations—generally an 80 percent owned subsidiary that has less than 10 percent of its receipts from passive sources.

Bad Debts.   If a debt does not meet the definition of a security (e.g., a bond), a loss due to worthlessness is governed by the rules for bad debts.[67]   The tax treatment depends on whether it is a business or a nonbusiness bad debt. Business bad debts that are totally or partially worthless may be deducted as ordinary losses. In contrast, a nonbusiness bad debt can only be deducted when it is totally worthless and is always treated as a short-term capital loss.

Given the significantly different treatments accorded business and nonbusiness bad debts, the distinction between the two is very important. According to the Code, a debt is considered a business bad debt only if it is incurred by a corporation or is created or acquired in connection with the taxpayer's trade or business.[68]   The imprecision of this definition has led to a great deal of litigation.

---

[65]   § 165(g).

[66]   § 165(g)(2).

[67]   § 166.

[68]   § 166(d)(2).

The most perplexing problem in this area concerns shareholder advances. It is very common in a closely held corporation where business is suffering for shareholders to periodically lend the corporation funds on open account. If the loans subsequently become worthless, the shareholder attempts to characterize the loans as arising from a trade or business so that an ordinary loss can be claimed. To the dismay of many shareholders, the Supreme Court has held that a shareholder who is merely an investor is not considered as being in a trade or business.[69] Thus the loan is considered a nonbusiness bad debt and treated as a short-term capital loss.

Although the Supreme Court's ruling settled the turmoil when the shareholder is only an investor, controversy still exists when a shareholder is also an employee or has some other type of business relationship with the corporation. For example, numerous cases have held that when the dominant motive for the loan by the shareholder-employee is to protect his or her employment with the corporation and thus maintain a salary, the debt is considered as arising from the taxpayer's trade or business.[70]

SECTION 1244 STOCK

Absent special rules, the $3,000 limitation on deductions for capital losses would discourage investment in new corporations. For example, if an individual invested $30,000 in a new corporation's stock and the stock became worthless, it could take as long as ten years to deduct the loss. In contrast, a sole proprietor or partner is able to directly recover the worthless investment without limitation. In 1958 Congress addressed these problems by enacting § 1244. Under § 1244, losses on "Section 1244 stock" generally are treated as ordinary rather than capital losses.

Eligible Shareholders. Ordinary loss treatment is available only to *individuals* who are the *original* holders of the stock, including individuals who were partners in a partnership when the partnership originally purchased the stock.[71] If these persons transfer the stock (e.g., sell, give, devise, or in the case of a partnership, distribute the stock to its partners), the § 1244 advantage does not transfer to the subsequent holder.

Ordinary Loss Limitation. If § 1244 stock is sold at a loss or the stock becomes worthless, the taxpayer may deduct up to $50,000 annually as an ordinary loss.[72] Taxpayers who file a joint return may deduct up to $100,000 regardless of whether the stock is owned jointly or separately. When the loss in any one year exceeds the $50,000 or $100,000 limitation, the excess is considered a capital loss subject to normal restrictions. Note that gains on the sale of § 1244 stock are treated in the normal fashion.

---

[69] *A.J. Whipple v. Comm.*, 63-1 USTC ¶9466, 11 AFTR2d 1454, 373 U.S. 193 (USSC, 1963).

[70] See, for example, *John M. Trent v. Comm.* 61-2 USTC ¶9506, AFTR2d 1599, 291 F.2d 669 (CA-2, 1961). See *U.S. v. Edna Generes*, 72-1 USTC ¶9259, 29 AFTR2d 72-609, 405 U.S. 93 (USSC, 1972) where the Supreme Court held that job protection must be the dominant motivation for the loan.

[71] Reg. § 1.1244(a)-1(b).

[72] § 1244(b)(1).

Example 38.   K, married, is one of the original purchasers of WNK Corporation's stock, which qualifies for special treatment under § 1244. She separately purchased the stock two years ago for $150,000. During the year, she sold all of the stock for $30,000 resulting in a $120,000 loss. On her joint return for the current year, she may deduct $100,000 as an ordinary loss. The portion of the loss exceeding the limitation, $20,000 ($120,000 − $100,000), is treated as a long-term capital loss. Assuming K has no capital gains, she may deduct $3,000 of the remaining loss and carry over $17,000 ($20,000 − $3,000) as a long-term capital loss to the following year.

Without some special provision, § 1244 would enable a taxpayer to convert a capital loss into an ordinary loss. For example, assume a taxpayer owns a capital asset that has a basis of $30,000 and a value of $20,000. If the individual shareholder sold the asset, he or she would recognize a $10,000 capital loss. Assume instead that the shareholder transferred the property to a corporation in exchange for § 1244 stock. The basis of the stock would be $30,000. If the taxpayer subsequently sold the stock for $5,000, an ordinary loss of $25,000 would be recognized under § 1244, and the taxpayer would have successfully converted the $10,000 capital loss into an ordinary loss. To prohibit this scheme, the taxpayer is required to reduce the basis of the § 1244 stock to the value of the property at the time of the transfer.[73] If this principle had been applied in the illustration above, the taxpayer would have a § 1244 loss of $15,000 ($5,000 − $20,000), and the remaining $10,000 loss would be a capital loss. Note that the capital loss has been preserved.

Section 1244 Stock Defined.   Stock issued by a corporation qualifies as § 1244 stock only if certain requirements are satisfied. As a practical matter, these conditions are easily met and § 1244 treatment is automatic for a limited amount of stock issued. As a general rule, § 1244 treatment applies when a domestic corporation issues stock for money or property and the corporation is (1) a "small business corporation" when the stock is issued, and (2) an "operating company" when the shareholder's loss is sustained.[74]

The rule cited above is effective for all stock issued after November 6, 1978. For previously issued stock, the conditions are similar, but important differences exist. For example, a written plan had to be in effect concerning certain aspects of the stock offering. When losses on "old" stock are realized, special attention should be given to the applicable rules.

Stock for Money and Property.   Section 1244 treatment is available only for stock that is issued for money and property other than stock or securities. For this purpose, stock includes common stock and preferred stock issued after July 18, 1984. It should be emphasized that this rule precludes favorable treatment for stock issued for services, preferred stock, or convertible securities. In addition, further contributions to capital that increase a shareholder's stock are not treated as allocable to the § 1244 stock.

---

[73]   § 1244(d)(1).   [74]   § 1244(c).

Small Business Corporation. The corporation must qualify as a small business corporation (SBC) at the time the stock was issued for § 1244 to apply.[75] A corporation is an SBC if its total capitalization (amounts received for stock issued, contributions to capital, and paid-in surplus) does not exceed $1 million. In determining the corporation's capitalization, the amount of stock issued for property is determined by using the property's adjusted basis reduced by any liability to which the property is subject or which is assumed by the corporation. This requirement effectively limits § 1244 treatment to those individuals who originally invest the first $1 million in money and property in the corporation.

> **Example 39.** In 1991 R and S provided the initial capitalization for CBT Corporation. R purchased 600 shares at a cost of $1,000 a share for a total cost of $600,000. S transferred property worth $200,000 (basis of $125,000) that was subject to a mortgage of $50,000 in exchange for 150 shares of stock worth $150,000. In 1992, R and S convinced their good friend T to purchase 500 shares of stock at a cost of $1,000 per share or a total of $500,000. All of the shares of both R and S qualify since the amount received for stock by the corporation, $675,000 ($600,000 cash + property with an adjusted basis of $125,000 − the liability of $50,000), did not exceed $1 million. Only 325 of T's shares qualify for § 1244 treatment, however, since 175 of the 500 purchased were issued when the corporation's total capitalization exceeded $1 million.

It should be emphasized that the corporation need not be an SBC at the time the shareholder incurs the loss. SBC status is required only when the shareholder receives the stock.

Operating Company. Another condition that must be satisfied before § 1244 applies concerns the nature of the corporation's activities. The corporation must be considered an *operating company* at the time the shareholder incurs the loss.[76] A corporation is treated as an operating company if at least 50 percent of its gross receipts for the five most recent taxable years (or the years it has been in existence if less) ending before the date of the loss are derived from sources *other than* royalties, rents, dividends, interest, annuities, and gains from sales or exchanges of stocks or securities. Without this rule, a taxpayer could convert a loss, which normally would be a capital loss if suffered in an individual capacity, into an ordinary loss. This requirement is ignored when a corporation's deductions for the test period—other than the dividends-received deduction and the deduction for net operating losses—exceed its gross income.[77]

---

[75] § 1244(c)(3).

[76] § 1244(c)(1)(C).

[77] § 1244(c)(2)(C).

TAX PLANNING

TAXABLE VERSUS NONTAXABLE TRANSFERS
TO CONTROLLED CORPORATIONS

At the beginning of this chapter, it was noted that there were various ways to transfer property to a corporation. This chapter went to great lengths exploring § 351 which generally enables a taxpayer to transfer property without consequences. In certain situations, however, the taxpayer may find that greater benefits can be obtained by avoiding § 351 and making the transfer a taxable transaction. For example, a taxpayer may desire to recognize a loss on property which is to be transferred to a corporation.

> **Example 40.**   J has decided to transfer assets to a new corporation. Among the assets he plans to transfer is equipment which has a basis of $10,000 but is only worth $3,000. If J transfers the equipment in a wholly nontaxable transaction under § 351, the potential loss on the equipment will not be recognized currently but will be depreciated over the next few years. On the other hand, if the transaction were taxable, J could recognize the loss immediately.

Another situation where the taxpayer historically has reaped rewards by avoiding § 351 involves appreciated property. In the typical scenario, the taxpayer traded recognition of gain—minimized through use of the capital gain and installment sales provisions—for a step-up in the basis of property. Moreover, assuming the taxpayer received debt on the exchange, all of the advantages of debt were also secured.

> **Example 41.**   In 1980 R purchased land for $10,000. Over the years the land has continued to appreciate and R now estimates that the land, with some development (roads, sewers, etc.), could be subdivided and sold for a total of $510,000. Although the land currently constitutes a capital asset in R's hands, if he were to subdivide it and sell the lots, any income would most probably be ordinary income. R might convert the ordinary income into favorable capital gain by establishing a corporation that would purchase and develop the land. R, along with other investors, could organize a corporation to which he would then sell the property for $510,000. In payment, the corporation would give R a note payable for the entire sales price. The note would be payable in installments over four years. The corporation would develop, subdivide, and sell the land. By following these steps, R achieves substantial tax savings. Although he sold the land to the corporation and must recognize gain, the entire gain is capital gain. Prior to 1987, instead of reporting $500,000 of income, R effectively reported $200,000 ($500,000 − 60% of $500,000). In addition, assuming the installment sales method is used, the gain will be reported ratably over the four years that

he receives the note payments. If the corporation sells the land for what it is worth, $510,000, it recognizes no gain since its basis in the land is its cost, $510,000. Lastly, by selling the land for debt R has created a vehicle for obtaining cash out of his corporation via deductible interest payments and tax-free payments of principal. These interest payments essentially replace dividends that otherwise might have been necessary to obtain the cash from the corporation. Even though the favorable capital gain treatment has been reduced, the other benefits remain.

Example 42. Assume the same facts as above, except that the property transferred is an apartment complex which currently generates substantial taxable income. In this case, R increased his basis of depreciable property at the cost of a capital gains tax which—like that in the situation above—is reduced by deferring it over the installment period. By so doing, R may benefit through increased depreciation deductions which reduce the taxable income produced by the property. R has also maintained his ownership of the property so that he can further benefit if it continues to appreciate.

As the above examples illustrate, a taxable transfer may pay handsomely. Taxpayers usually avert nonrecognition in one of three ways: (1) selling the property to the corporation—usually for debt, (2) exchanging the property in a § 351 transaction in which boot received (e.g., securities) causes recognition, and (3) exchanging the property with the corporation when § 351 does not apply [e.g., the transferor(s) do not have the requisite 80% control]. These plans are far from failsafe, however. Before examining the tax risks of each of the three taxable transfers, two preliminary considerations must be addressed.

Transfers to Related Parties. When the taxpayer attempts to recognize gain or loss on the transfer of property to a corporation, the initial hurdles are §§ 1239 and 267—the former applying where appreciated property is sold to the corporation and the latter where the property has declined in value. As previously discussed, § 1239 causes the gain on the sale of depreciable property (including patents) between a taxpayer and his or her more than 50 percent owned corporation to be treated as ordinary income. In addition, § 453(g) provides that the installment sales method cannot be used when the sale is between "related parties" as defined in § 1239 (i.e., a taxpayer and his or her more than 50% owned corporation). But notice that §§ 1239 and 453(g) are ineffective as long as the taxpayer is not treated as owning more than 50 percent of the stock.

Example 43. Assume the same facts as in *Example 42* above. R could collaborate with another unrelated individual, say S, to develop the land. S might contribute sufficient cash or other property to the newly formed corporation for 50% or more of the stock. If he does, R receives 50% or less of the stock and § 1239 does not apply to his sale—thus capital gain and an installment sale are assured.

Further, the installment sales method can be used when it can be established that none of the principal purposes of the sale was tax avoidance. Thus, if the taxpayer can show a good business reason for the sale, the installment sales technique is still available.

When the taxpayer sells property hoping to recognize a loss, § 267 may cause difficulty. It might be remembered that this provision in part prohibits the taxpayer from deducting any losses on sales between the taxpayer and his or her more than 50 percent owned corporation. Like § 1239, however, this provision is defeated when the taxpayer does not own actually or constructively more than 50 percent of the corporation.

The Code provides yet another pitfall that clearly reduces the advantage of an installment sale in this and other situations. Section 453(i) requires that gain must be recognized on the installment sale in the year of the sale to the extent of any recapture income under §§ 1245, 1250, and 291. This can occur if the debt was considered stock. Such treatment applies *regardless* of the amount that is received during the year of sale. This rule effectively accelerates to the sale year the recognition of gain that otherwise would be deferred. As a result, the cost of obtaining a step-up in basis may be substantially increased in the case of an installment sale of depreciable property.

Sales to a Controlled Corporation.   Since a sale is normally structured so that the transferor-seller receives debt on the exchange—enabling installment recognition of gain—the transaction risks being treated as tax-free under § 351. This can occur if the debt is considered stock. Such treatment spells disaster for the taxpayer. Under § 351, the basis of the property carries over to the corporation and, without the step-up in basis, potential capital gain benefits and higher depreciation deductions are lost.

Notwithstanding the fact that the transaction is structured as a sale, § 351 may apply because in effect the seller is exchanging property for what may be considered stock of the corporation. Recall that § 351 requires nonrecognition when stock is received by the transferor. Whether § 351 is ultimately applied, however, normally depends on whether the debt received by the seller can be considered stock.

> **Example 44.**   In *Aqualane Shores*, three individuals transferred $600 to a corporation in exchange for all of its stock.[78]   Immediately thereafter, the three sold appreciated land to the corporation for notes of about $192,000 which were to be paid by the corporation in five equal installments. The corporation developed, subdivided, and sold the land as residential property. Upon audit of the corporation, the IRS challenged the amount of income reported, asserting that the basis of the land should have been the lower basis of the individuals since the "purported sale" was truly a nontaxable

---

[78]   59-2 USTC ¶9632, 4 AFTR2d 5346; 269 F.2d 116 (CA-5, 1959); also see *Burr Oaks Corp. v. Comm.*, 66-2 USTC ¶9506, 18 AFTR2d 5018, 365 F.2d 24 (CA-4, 1966); for cases where the taxpayer was victorious in this area see *Sun Properties, Inc.*, 55-1 USTC ¶9261, 47 AFTR 273, 220 F.2d 171 (CA-5, 1955).

exchange under § 351. The court agreed with the IRS, suggesting that the debt of the corporation was truly stock. In so doing, it emphasized that the corporation was undercapitalized and had failed to pay the installments on the notes when due.

Transfers for Boot. The above technique relied on sale treatment to make the transaction taxable. In using that method, the taxpayer attempts to avoid § 351. Another technique, however, generally achieves the same result within the confines of § 351. According to this plan, the transferor simply exchanges his or her property under § 351 for boot—usually short-term notes.[79] Short-term notes are used because there is less likelihood that they might be considered stock. This method does not achieve the desired result when loss property is transferred to the corporation since losses are not recognized under § 351.

Transfers Not Qualifying under § 351. Still another technique involves not satisfying the requirements of § 351. For example, if property is transferred and those who made the transfer do not own 80 percent of the stock of the corporation immediately after the exchange, the transaction is taxable since § 351's control test is not met.[80] In this situation, the transfer is taxable just as if the taxpayer had sold the property to the corporation.

LEASING VERSUS TRANSFERRING

Leasing property to a corporation may be an attractive alternative to transferring it by sale or exchange. Although the step-up in basis is not obtained, other advantages exist. Leasing provides one of the same benefits of debt: it gives the taxpayer a technique for withdrawing capital from the corporation. Rental payments on the lease may be deducted by the corporation; hence, double taxation is avoided. Although the rental payments would be taxed as ordinary income, the taxpayer might mitigate the ordinary income tax by giving the property to a lower-bracket family member and thus shifting the income as well. Of course, the taxpayer must be mindful of the kiddie tax whenever shifting income to a child. Also note that depreciation and perhaps other deductions are also transferred so loss of these benefits must be considered. Tax-saving techniques that involve shifting income to other taxpayers through the creation of trusts and other means are discussed in Chapter 15.

---

[79] The taxpayer was successful in using this approach recently in *Jolana S. Bradshaw v. U.S.*, 82-2 USTC ¶9454, 50 AFTR2d, 82-5238, 683 F.2d 365 (Ct. Cls., 1982).

[80] See *Granite Trust Co. v. U.S.*, 57-1 USTC ¶9201, 50 AFTR 763, 238 F.2d 670 (CA-1, 1957).

SHIFTING INCOME BY GIVING DEBT

Shifting the corporation's income to another taxpayer is not limited to gifts of property followed by a lease. The same result can be achieved by giving the corporation's debt to a lower-bracket family member. Unlike leasing techniques, using debt to shift income allows the taxpayer to ignore the problems of shifting depreciation and other expenses of leased property. In addition, when debt is transferred, control of the corporation is not lost since it is maintained by those holding the corporation's stock.

PRECONTRIBUTION ALLOCATIONS

Taxpayers must also give attention to any difference between the basis of the property that they transfer to the corporation and its fair market value. Most individuals who contribute properties that have a value equivalent to properties from their fellow contributors are satisfied if they receive an equivalent value of stock. For example, if K transfers $10,000 cash to a corporation while L transfers property worth $10,000 (basis $3,000), it would not be unlikely for both to receive 50 percent of the corporation's stock. However, this would be an inequitable allocation of the stock. In effect, K has purchased a 50 percent interest in the property transferred to the corporation by L and consequently should enjoy the tax benefits from that property (e.g., depreciation) *as if* it had a basis of $10,000 [or $5,000 with respect to him (50% of $10,000)]. Since the tax basis of the property carries over to the corporation, K effectively benefits from a basis of $1,500 rather than $5,000. Consequently, some adjustment should be made to take into account the inequity which results from the difference between the transferor's basis in the property and its fair market value.[81]

---

[81] For an interesting approach to this problem, see Enrico Petri and John P. Seagle, "Determining an Equitable Allocation of Tax Benefits under § 351," *Journal of Accountancy* (January, 1984), pp. 86–94.

PROBLEM MATERIALS

DISCUSSION QUESTIONS

2-1 *Considerations when Incorporating.* During the year, J decided to incorporate her boutique, which she has operated as a sole proprietorship for several years. The business has various assets including a building, office equipment, accounts receivable, and inventory. Prepare a list of tax-related issues that should be discussed with J concerning the incorporation of her business.

2-2 *Rationale for § 351.* Discuss briefly the theory underlying the nonrecognition treatment provided for transfers to controlled corporations.

2-3 *Section 351: Requirements.* Identify the general conditions that must be satisfied before nonrecognition is permitted on an exchange of assets for stock of a corporation.

2-4 *Service Shareholders.* During the year, R and S formed C Corporation. For each of the following independent situations, indicate whether § 351 applies to the exchange.

  a. R contributed property worth $70,000 in exchange for 70 shares of stock and S contributed services worth $30,000 in exchange for 30 shares of stock.

  b. R contributed property worth $70,000 in exchange for 70 shares of stock and S contributed services worth $25,000 for 25 shares of stock in addition to property worth $5,000 for 5 shares of stock.

  c. R contributed property worth $70,000 in exchange for 70 shares of stock and S contributed services worth $29,000 for 29 shares in addition to property worth $1,000 for 1 share.

2-5 *Contributions of Services in Exchange for Stock.* P and Q formed a new corporation this year. P contributed property and Q contributed services.

  a. What is the maximum percentage of the outstanding stock that Q may receive if P's exchange of property is to qualify for nonrecognition under § 351?

  b. Under what circumstances could Q receive a greater percentage of stock for services than specified above?

2-6 *Control Test: General Rules.* Indicate whether § 351 applies to the following exchanges.

  a. This year, M, N, and O formed R Corporation. Each contributed property in exchange for 60, 30, and 10 shares of R, respectively.

  b. Two years after the formation of R Corporation, M transferred additional property in exchange for 100 more shares of stock.

2-7   *Solely Stock.* S transferred appreciated property to a newly created corporation for 60 percent of its stock while T transferred appreciated property for 40 percent of the stock and the corporation's 20-year note, payable in equal installments with 10 percent interest.

    a.   Does § 351 apply to either of these exchanges?

    b.   How may T report any gain to be recognized from this exchange?

2-8   *Immediately after the Exchange.* R, S, and T all transferred property to JOB Corp. In exchange, each individual received 50 shares of stock. R and S contributed their assets in early January of the current year, and T transferred her assets near the end of March.

    a.   Does § 351 apply to any of these exchanges?

    b.   Why might T have waited to make her transfer?

2-9   *Property Requirement.* Which of the following items do not qualify as property under § 351?

    a.   Building

    b.   Machinery

    c.   Inventory

    d.   Services

    e.   Patent

    f.   Note receivable

2-10   *Exchange for Stock.* Below is a list of items that a corporation may transfer to a prospective shareholder. Indicate which items would cause recognition to the transferor, assuming the exchange otherwise qualifies under § 351?

    a.   Preferred stock of the transferee corporation

    b.   Rights to purchase stock of the transferee corporation

    c.   Twenty-year note of the transferee corporation, payable in equal installments with 10 percent interest

    d.   Convertible bonds of the transferee corporation

    e.   Money

2-11   *Avoiding § 351.* Under what circumstances might a transferor deliberately violate the provisions of § 351?

2-12   *Transfer of Liabilities.* Indicate whether the following statements are true or false, assuming a transferor contributes liabilities to a corporation as part of a § 351 exchange. If the statement is false, explain why.

    a.   The transfer of liabilities normally is not treated as boot received for purposes of computing gain or loss on the transfer.

    b.   The transfer of liabilities normally is not treated as boot received for purposes of computing basis of property received.

    c.   The transfer of liabilities causes any gain realized to be recognized to the extent total liabilities exceed the total basis of the assets transferred.

    d.   The transfer of any liabilities incurred without business purpose or for the purpose of avoiding taxes causes all liabilities to be treated as boot for purposes of gain recognition.

e.   If the liabilities transferred exceeded the aggregate basis of the assets transferred and were incurred for the purpose of avoiding taxes, the liabilities are treated as boot.

f.   Liabilities of a cash basis taxpayer do not include accounts payable which when paid would give rise to a deduction.

2-13   *Accommodation Exchange.*   S's father, F, has agreed to admit him as a shareholder of the business for his contribution of appreciated property. S would receive 9 percent of the stock. However, S is unwilling to contribute the property if gain must be recognized. What steps might be taken to ensure that S does not recognize gain?

2-14   *Post-Transfer Dispositions.*   G has decided to incorporate her sole proprietorship. She plans to give 25 percent of the stock to her daughter and sell 30 percent of the stock to an interested investor immediately after the business is incorporated. What tax risks might G encounter under this arrangement?

2-15   *Depreciation Recapture.* D incorporated his accounting practice this year receiving only stock on the exchange. As part of the incorporation transaction, he transferred a computer worth $5,000. Depreciation claimed by him prior to the transfer was $1,000. Two months after the transfer the corporation sold the computer realizing a $2,500 gain. Briefly explain how the depreciation recapture provisions operate in this situation.

2-16   *Section 351 and Corporate Gain or Loss.* Indicate the effect, if any, on the corporation's taxable income as a result of the following:

a.   Corporation issues its own previously unissued stock to A in exchange for property in a transaction qualifying under § 351.

b.   Corporation issues its own previously unissued stock to A in exchange for property in a transaction not qualifying under § 351.

c.   Corporation issues its treasury stock to A in exchange for property in a transaction qualifying under § 351.

d.   Corporation issues its own previously unissued stock to A in exchange for legal services that A provided in conjunction with the incorporation transaction.

2-17   *Corporation's and Transferor's Bases and Holding Periods.*   Briefly indicate how a transferor and a corporation determine bases and holding periods for property received in the following exchanges qualifying under § 351.

a.   Machine purchased December 3, 1988 is transferred to a corporation in exchange for stock on March 7, 1991.

b.   Legal services are provided to a corporation on May 5, 1991 in connection with the articles of incorporation. The transferor receives stock for the services on May 30, 1991.

c.   Inventory purchased June 6, 1991 is transferred to a corporation on December 20, 1991 in exchange for stock and a note payable in one year with 10 percent interest.

2-18 *Sale to an S Corporation.* J owns and operates a small delicatessen in down-town Chicago. The business is located in a 12-story building that J inherited in 1952. The building is located two blocks from a major convention center currently under construction. J's basis in the land and building is $25,000 but the property is currently worth $500,000. D is a real estate developer interested in renovating the building and converting it to a 600-room hotel. Recently he approached J about a joint venture where J would contribute the land and building and D would contribute his development expertise. D expects operating losses in the first two years of business but profits thereafter. J and D have asked your advice on whether J should sell the property to a newly formed S corporation or exchange the property for the corporation's stock. Briefly discuss these two alternatives.

2-19 *Contributions to Capital.* JEL Inc., one of the new "high-tech" firms, relocated their headquarters to Metropolis this year because the city contributed $250,000 of seed money to the corporation for research. In addition, the city gave the corporation an office building.

   a.   Discuss the tax consequences of the contributions to JEL.

   b.   How would your answer in (a) above change if a group of JEL shareholders currently living in Metropolis had made the contributions?

2-20 *Comparison of Stock and Debt.* Prepare a list containing the advantages and disadvantages of using stock and debt in the capital structure of a corporation.

2-21 *Debt Recharacterization.* Answer the following questions:

   a.   Outline the circumstances when debt is highly suspect and likely to be reclassified as stock.

   b.   Explain what is meant when a corporation is said to be "thinly capitalized."

   c.   Briefly discuss the tax consequences if the corporation's debt is reclassified as stock.

2-22 *Losses: Stock versus Debt.* Q and R incorporated their partnership two years ago, each receiving 50 shares of stock and a 10-year note which is payable in equal installments with 13 percent interest. To the dismay of Q and R, the economy slowed and the business crumbled. Both the stock and debt became worthless this year.

   a.   Discuss the tax consequences resulting from the losses on the debt and stock.

   b.   Assume that Q advanced the corporation money on open account during the last six months of operations. His aim was to keep the business afloat. How should Q treat the worthless advances?

2-23   *Section 1244 Stock.*

    a.   Explain the significance of owning "§ 1244" stock.

    b.   G owns 100 shares of DSA Corp. stock that she received from sources described below. In each case indicate whether the shares received constitute § 1244 stock, assuming the stock qualified as § 1244 stock in the hands of the person from whom she received it.

        1.   20 shares inherited from her uncle
        2.   35 shares given to her by her father
        3.   15 shares purchased from C
        4.   20 shares issued to G for a contribution of cash when the corporation's total capital was $300,000
        5.   10 shares issued to G for a contribution of services to the corporation when the corporation's total capital was $300,000

PROBLEMS

2-24   *Control Test.* Individuals M, N, and O quit their jobs this year and started a business selling and servicing lawn mowers and garden equipment.

    a.   M contributed machinery worth $10,000 (basis $12,000) for 10 shares of stock and N contributed equipment worth $20,000 (basis $15,000) for 20 shares of stock. O agreed to be in charge of the service department and received 20 shares for services to be performed during the first year of business. Does the exchange qualify for special tax treatment provided by § 351?

    b.   Same as (a), except that O received five shares.

2-25   *Corporate Formation—Services.* This year, L and P decided to organize LP, Inc. They received stock in exchange for the following asset contributions to the corporation:

Transferor	Contributed	Market Value	Transferor's Basis	Shares Received
L	Equipment	$50,000	$33,000	50
P	Cash	20,000	20,000	20

In addition, services were performed in exchange for 30 shares of stock worth $30,000.

    Compute (1) each transferor's recognized gain or income, (2) each transferor's basis in the stock, and (3) LP's basis in the assets for each of the following situations.

    a.   Y performed the services involved in the incorporation of LP.

    b.   Y performed the services two years after L and P made their contribution.

    c.   L performed the services involved in the incorporation of LP.

    d.   P performed the services involved in the incorporation of LP.

2-26 *Transfers to Controlled Corporations: Fundamentals.* During the year, A and B formed a new corporation. Each received 100 shares of stock for contributing the following assets:

Transferor	Property Transferred	Transferor's Basis	Fair Market Value
A	Cash	$100,000	$100,000
B	Land and building	20,000	70,000
	Equipment	40,000	30,000

  a.   Compute the gain or loss realized and recognized by A and B.
  b.   Compute the basis of the stock received by A and B.
  c.   Compute the gain or loss recognized by the corporation.
  d.   Compute the bases of the assets received by the corporation.

2-27 *Control—Additional Contributions.* Q owns 550 shares and Z owns 150 shares of QZ, Inc. Six years after QZ's formation, X contributes land ($60,000 market value and $20,000 basis) for 200 shares of QZ. At the same time, Q contributes $30,000 cash for an additional 100 shares of QZ. Determine the likely tax effects of these additional contributions.

2-28 *Corporate Formation.* F and V, retired carpenters, decided to organize the SWS Corporation which would build wooden swing sets for children. The items transferred and received were as follows:

Transferor	Asset Transferred	Market Value	Transferor's Basis	Shares Received
F	Equipment	$20,000	$18,000	50
V	Warehouse	25,000	10,000	50
	Mortgage on warehouse	5,000		

  a.   Compute the gain or loss recognized by F and V.
  b.   Compute the gain or loss recognized by SWS Inc.
  c.   Compute the bases of the stock received by F and V.
  d.   Compute the bases of the assets received by SWS Inc.

2-29   *Section 351 and Boot.* X Corporation was formed several years ago by Q and R to operate a custom T-shirt shop in Dayton. Each received 50 shares of stock. This year, Q and R decided to expand and bring in S, T, and U, who operated a similar shop in Toledo. To this end, the following investments were made by the new and existing shareholders.

Transferor	Property Transferred	Transferor's Basis	Fair Market Value	Received
S	Shirt Inventory	$60,000	$110,000	100 shares, $10,000 cash
T	Land and building	74,000	80,000	70 shares, $10,000 cash
U	Embroidery equipment Cost $75,000 Depreciation $ 9,000	66,000	40,000	30 shares, $10,000 cash
R	Cash	100,000	100,000	100 shares

a.   Does the transaction qualify for § 351 treatment?

For the remaining questions, assume the transaction is eligible for § 351 treatment.

b.   Compute the gain or loss recognized by S, T, and U.
c.   Compute the bases of the stock received by S, T, and U.
d.   Compute the bases of the assets received by the corporation.

2-30   *Corporate Formation—Boot.* This year, E, H, and K decided to organize EHK, Inc. They received stock in exchange for the following asset contributions to the corporation:

Transferor	Property Contributed	Market Value	Transferor's Basis	Shares Received
E	Land	$70,000	$68,000	35
H	Patent	70,000	15,000	35
K	Equipment	60,000	80,000	30

Compute (1) each transferor's recognized gain or loss, (2) each transferor's basis in the stock, and (3) EHK's basis in the assets for each for the following situations.

a.   All three exchanges were made simultaneously.
b.   All three exchanges were made simultaneously and each shareholder received a four-year note from EHK for $10,000. Equal note payments are to be made plus 10 percent interest each December 31.
c.   K's exchange occurred by an agreement made two years after the exchanges by E and H.

2-31   *Comprehensive Corporate Formation.* M's Diner Inc. (MDI) was formed by M, A, F, and V on April 1, 1991 to operate a restaurant. M transferred restaurant equipment worth $13,000 purchased by him on October 3, 1987 for $12,000. He had deducted $4,000 of depreciation. For her interest, A contributed a building (and the land on which it sat) in which the restaurant would be housed. The building was worth $25,000 (basis $13,000) and was subject to a $15,000 mortgage which was assumed by the corporation. No depreciation had been claimed on the building. F contributed tables and chairs that she had used in another venture. The furniture was worth $11,000 (basis $16,000). V provided legal services incident to the incorporation worth $10,000. Each individual received 100 shares of MDI stock worth $100 per share. In addition, M and F received notes payable in one year with 10 percent interest in the amount of $3,000 and $1,000, respectively.

a.   Does the transaction qualify as a nontaxable exchange? Explain.

For the remaining questions, *assume* that the transfer qualifies for treatment under § 351 and all parties use the calendar year for tax purposes.

b.   Compute the gain or loss realized and recognized by each of the shareholders.

c.   Compute the basis of the stock and other property received by each of the shareholders.

d.   What effect does the exchange have on MDI's taxable income?

e.   Compute the basis of the property received by MDI.

f.   On what date does M's holding period begin for the stock he received?

g.   On what date does MDI's holding period begin for the restaurant equipment?

h.   Comment on the application of the depreciation recapture provisions to this transaction.

i.   Does either § 1239 or § 267 apply to this transaction?

2-32   *Sections 357(b) and (c) Calculations.* M owns all of the stock of RCC Inc., a land development company. Two years ago M contributed land worth $150,000 (basis of $90,000 and subject to a $100,000 mortgage) to the corporation in exchange for stock worth $50,000. Upon audit this year, the IRS determined that M had mortgaged the property shortly before transferring it to the corporation. For this reason, the IRS asserted that the liability was incurred to avoid taxes and has proposed an adjustment to M's tax liability for the year of the transfer. Assuming M is in the 50 percent bracket, how much additional tax would be imposed if the IRS adjustment is ultimately upheld?

2-33   *Liabilities of Cash Basis Taxpayer.* Dr. Q has operated his medical practice as a sole proprietorship for the last two years. Like most individuals he uses the cash method of accounting. This year, he decided to incorporate his practice to take advantage of certain employee fringe benefits. He transferred the following assets and liabilities in exchange for all of the stock.

	Value
Cash	$1,000
Unrealized accounts receivable	8,000
Equipment	6,800
Accounts payable	4,000
Note payable on equipment	1,500

The equipment had a basis of $2,000. In addition, the accounts payable are all for routine deductible expenditures except a $200 bill from his attorney for services relating to the incorporation of his business.

   a.   Is Dr. Q required to recognize any gain on the transfer?
   b.   Compute Dr. Q's basis for his stock.

2-34   *Section 357(c) Liabilities.* During the year, D transferred the following assets and liabilities to his wholly owned corporation in exchange for stock worth $50,000.

Asset	Adjusted Basis	Fair Market Value
Land	$90,000	$150,000
Mortgage on warehouse	–	(100,000)
Total	$90,000	$ 50,000

   a.   Compute D's gain or loss realized.
   b.   Compute D's gain or loss recognized.
   c.   Compute the basis of the stock received by D.
   d.   Compute the bases of the assets to the corporation.
   e.   After being apprised of the tax consequences of the transfer described above, D is having second thoughts. How might any gain recognition above be avoided, assuming D still wants to contribute the land to the corporation?

2-35 *Section 357: Treatment of Liabilities.* Each of the transfers below qualifies as a § 351 transaction. In addition, the transferor is a cash basis taxpayer and the corporation assumes the liabilities involved in the transfer. For each transfer, compute the following:

1. Transferor's recognized gain.
2. Transferor's basis in the stock received.
3. Corporation's basis in each asset received.

a. R transfers land with a basis of $60,000 and subject to a mortgage of $20,000 in exchange for stock worth $100,000.

b. S transfers a crane with a basis of $40,000 and a $50,000 note payable secured by the crane in exchange for stock worth $70,000.

c. Same facts as (b) above, except that the note was created two weeks before the transfer and S used the proceeds to take his wife on a vacation to the Virgin Islands.

d. T transfers accounts receivable worth $12,000, dental equipment with a basis of $15,000, a $10,000 note payable secured by the equipment, and routine accounts payable for lab bills of $7,000 for stock worth $50,000.

2-36 *Section 351 and Depreciation Recapture.* Several years ago, B transferred all of the assets of his sole proprietorship to a newly formed corporation in exchange for all of its stock. Among the assets contributed was equipment that B had purchased for $10,000 and for which he had claimed $2,000 of depreciation. Since the transfer, the corporation has claimed $1,500 of depreciation. This year, the corporation sold the asset for $14,000. Compute the corporation's gain recognized on the sale and its character.

2-37 *Contributions to Capital: Calculations.* MND Corp. recently announced its plan to close a fabrication plant in Terraville and build a new facility in another city. The plant closing would eliminate over 1,000 jobs. Since the economy of Terraville was closely tied to the plant's operations, the city government voted to give land worth $30,000 to MND that could be used as a site for a new structure. In addition, the Chamber of Commerce agreed to raise $200,000 which it would contribute to the corporation to apply to the construction cost of a new plant. Due to these actions by the city and the Chamber, MND decided to remain in Terraville. Assuming MND received the land and cash and constructed a plant for $900,000, what are the tax consequences?

2-38 *Depreciation of Contributed Property.* On October 1, 1990 K incorporated his rug cleaning business which he has operated for several years. As part of the incorporation, he transferred a truck which he had purchased for $500 in 1989 and for which he had claimed depreciation using MACRS percentages for five-year property of $100. On October 15, 1990 the corporation purchased a new van for $10,000. Both K and his corporation use the calendar year for tax purposes.

    a.   Using the tables in Appendix H-3, compute the corporation's depreciation on the truck and the van for 1990.

    b.   Assume that prior to October, 1990 K had never been in business and the corporation acquired the truck for $500 and the van for $10,000 on October 15, 1990. Compute the depreciation on the two items for 1990.

2-39 *Section 1244 Stock: Calculations.* In January, 1986, S, single, contributed $210,000 cash to HJI, Inc. for 80 shares of § 1244 stock. This year, S sold the stock for $40,000. S's taxable income is $70,000, including a short-term capital gain of $1,000 but excluding the sale of HJI stock. What is S's taxable income after accounting for the HJI stock sale?

2-40 *Section 1244: Basis Problems.* M, who is single, transferred property worth $120,000 and a basis of $300,000 to Z Corporation in exchange for § 1244 stock. Two years later, M sold all of his stock for $90,000. Assuming M has no other property transactions during the year, compute the effect on M's A.G.I.

2-41 *Worthless Stock, Debt, and Advances.* P formed WRE Corp. in 1980 receiving stock and a 15-year note on the exchange. This year the stock (basis $50,000) and debt (basis $10,000) became worthless when the corporation declared bankruptcy. During the demise of WRE, P advanced the business $20,000 on open account and now these loans are also uncollectible. Assuming the purpose of P's advances were to protect her employment and $75,000 a year salary, how will the losses affect her taxable income?

2-42 *Stock versus Debt.* Compare the tax implications of situations A and B.

	Situation A	Situation B
Stock issued	$120,000	$80,000
Debt owed to shareholders	0	40,000

The debt was issued as a 10-year note with 10 percent annual interest. Each year's interest and one-fifth of the note are payable each December 31. Shareholders will receive $30,000 from the corporation each year, which is considered first as payment of any debt obligations, and second as dividends. Assume marginal tax rates are 34 percent for the corporation and 28 percent for the shareholders. Compute the tax savings and costs for (1) the corporation and (2) the shareholders for Situations A and B in the first year when $30,000 is distributed. (Assume interest for the year is $4,000.)

2-43   *Worthless Stock versus Debt.* Refer to Problem 2-42. At the end of year 2, before distributions to shareholders, the corporation declares bankruptcy, and shareholders will receive nothing from the corporation for their stock or debt. Assume a 28 percent marginal tax rate for two individuals, X and Y, each filing as head of household and on the cash basis. X and Y own the stock and debt as follows:

	Situation A	*Situation B*
Stock issued to X	$84,000	$56,000
Y	36,000	24,000
Debt owed to X		10,000
Y		20,000
Interest owed to X		1,000
Y		2,000

Compute the tax savings for X and Y as a result of reporting the losses for Situations A and B in the current year.

TAX RETURN PROBLEM

2-44   During 1990, Lisa Cutter and Jeff McMullen decided they would like to start their own gourmet hamburger business. Lisa and Jeff believed that the public would love the recipes used by Lisa's mom, Tina Woodbrook. They also thought that they had the necessary experience to enter this business, as Jeff currently owned a fast-food franchise business while Lisa had experience operating a small bakery. After doing their own market research, they established Slattery's Inc., which was incorporated on February 1, 1991. The company's address is 5432 Partridge Pl., Tulsa, Oklahoma 74105 and its employer identification number is 88-7654321.

The company started modestly. After refurbishing an old gas station that it had purchased, the company opened for business on February 25, 1991. Shortly after business began, however, business boomed. By the close of 1991, the company had established two other locations. Slattery's has three shareholders who own stock as follows:

Shareholder	*Shares*
Lisa Cutter...............	500
Jeff McMullen.............	200
Tina Woodbrook...........	300
Total outstanding........	1,000

Slattery's was formed on February 1, 1991. On that date, shareholders made contributions as follows:

> Lisa Cutter contributed $30,000 in cash and 200 shares of MND stock, a publicly held company, which had a fair market value of $20,000. Lisa had purchased the MND stock on October 3, 1987 for $8,000.
>
> Jeff McMullen contributed equipment worth $20,000 which he had used in his own business until he contributed it. The equipment's basis was $48,000 (original cost in February 1989, $100,000; depreciation using MACRS accelerated percentages for five-year property, $52,000).
>
> Tina Woodbrook contributed $30,000 in cash.

The company is on the accrual basis and has chosen to use the calendar year for tax purposes. The corporation's adjusted trial balance for financial accounting purposes reveals the following information:

	Debit	Credit
Cash.....................................	$242,800	
Ending inventory...........................	16,000	
Equipment................................	35,000	
Land.....................................	10,000	
Building..................................	15,000	
Improvements to building..................	55,000	
Accumulated depreciation..................		$ 9,000
Notes payable............................		93,000
Accounts payable.........................		40,000
Taxes payable............................		8,000
Salaries payable..........................		20,000
Capital stock.............................		100,000
Sales....................................		400,000
Gain on sale of MND stock.................		18,000
Dividend from MND Corporation............		2,000
Legal expenses...........................	500	
Accounting expenses......................	400	
Miscellaneous expenses...................	2,100	
Premium on key-man life insurance policy	800	
Advertising...............................	8,600	
Purchases...............................	100,000	
State income taxes........................	8,000	
Federal income taxes.....................	37,000	
Payroll taxes.............................	12,500	
Salary expenses..........................	120,000	
Insurance................................	9,000	
Repairs..................................	6,500	
Contributions.............................	17,600	
Depreciation per books....................	9,000	
Interest expense..........................	200	

The company has provided additional information below.

- The company took a physical count of inventory on December 31, 1991. On that date, it was determined that ending inventory was $16,000.
- On February 9, 1991, the corporation purchased an old gas station for $25,000 to house the restaurant. Of the $25,000 purchase price, $10,000 was allocated to the land while $15,000 was allocated to the building. Prior to opening, the old gas station was renovated. Improvements to the structure were made during February at a cost of $55,000.
- The legal costs were for work done by Slattery's attorney in February for drafting the articles of incorporation and by-laws. Accounting fees that were paid in May were for setting up the books and the accounting system. Miscellaneous expenses included a $100 fee paid in February to the State of Oklahoma to incorporate.
- The MND stock was sold for $38,000 on April 3, 1991. Shortly before the sale, MND had declared and paid a dividend. Slattery's received $2,000 on April 1, 1991. MND was incorporated in Delaware.
- The corporation purchased refrigeration equipment (7-year property) on February 15, 1991 for $15,000.
- Slattery's has elected not to use the limited expensing provisions of Code § 179. In addition, it claimed the maximum depreciation with respect to all other assets. Any other elections required to minimize the corporation's tax liability were made.
- Lisa Cutter (Social Security No. 447-52-7943) is president of the corporation and spends 90 percent of her working time in the business. Salary expense includes her salary of $60,000. No other officers received compensation. The key-man life insurance policy covers Lisa's life and the corporation is the beneficiary.
- The company paid estimated income taxes during the year of $37,000. For simplicity's sake, in completing the tax return do not adjust the books to reflect the actual tax due.

Required: Prepare Form 1120 and other appropriate forms and schedules for Slattery's. On separate schedule(s), show all calculations used to determine all reported amounts except those for which the source is obvious or which are shown on a formal schedule to be filed with the return.

TAX RESEARCH PROBLEMS

2-45   JLK Inc. is a rapidly growing development and construction company operating in Denver. Several years ago it decided to expand its business to the mountains so it could take advantage of the lucrative condominium market. To this end, the corporation persuaded M, N, and O, all of whom had built several projects in mountain communities to become a part of JKL. M, N, O, and JKL contributed assets to a new corporation, X, in a transaction qualifying under § 351. M contributed the following assets for 25 percent of the stock, worth $450,000, and $50,000 cash: land worth $300,000 (basis $25,000); office building worth $70,000 (basis $90,000); and a crane worth $130,000 (basis $100,000). This year the corporation subdivided the land and began selling the unimproved property. What basis should X corporation assign to the land for purposes of computing gain and loss on the lot sales?

2-46   Q and R formed SLI Inc. in 1987 and opened a small amusement park. The park's main attraction was a waterslide, five stories high. Pursuant to the incorporation agreement, Q and R both contributed cash of $400,000. In exchange they each received 100 shares of the stock worth $100,000 and a six-year note for $300,000 payable in equal installments with 10 percent interest annually. During 1991, business became sluggish.

    a.   Q and R believe the business is going to fail. Can Q and R obtain ordinary loss treatment for their investment should it become worthless? Answer this question independent of the facts in (b).

    b.   After much deliberation, Q and R decided that the business could still succeed. The pair decided they needed something to spur profits, such as a stand-up roller coaster. On March 7, 1991 Q and R both contributed an additional $500,000 for 500 shares of stock. In August it was determined that the corporation required additional capital and S was admitted as a shareholder. S received 500 shares for a $500,000 contribution on August 15, 1991. In June 1992 SLI was adjudged bankrupt and the stock of SLI became worthless. How will Q, R, and S treat their stock losses? How will Q and R treat their loss on the unpaid note?

2-47   T, an individual taxpayer, plans to incorporate his farming and ranching activities, currently operated as a sole proprietorship. His primary purpose of incorporating is to transfer a portion of his ownership in land to his son and daughter. T believes that gifts of stock rather than land will keep his business intact. Included in the property he plans to transfer is machinery purchased two years earlier. T's current thought is to incorporate and immediately transfer 40 percent of the corporate stock to his two children. What potential tax problems might result if T pursues his current plans? Would it make any difference if T received all voting stock and had the new corporation transfer nonvoting stock to the children?

Partial list of research aids:

> Rev. Rul. 59-259, 1959-2 C.B. 115.
> Reg. § 1.47-3(f)(5).
> *W.F. Blevins*, 61 T.C. 547 (1974).

2-48   RST Corporation is currently owned by three individuals: R, S, and T. The corporation has a net worth of $300,000 and has 500 shares (1,000 shares authorized) of common stock outstanding. R owns 200 shares (40%), and S and T each own 150 shares (30%). Individual E owns land worth $90,000, which the corporation could use as a new plant site. However, E is not interested in selling the land now because it would result in a large capital gain tax. E is willing to transfer the land to the corporation in exchange for 60 shares of its common stock or securities of equivalent value, but only if the transfer will be nontaxable. How would you advise the parties to structure the transaction?

Research aids:

> Rev. Rul. 73-472, 1973-2 C.B. 115.
> Rev. Proc. 76-22, 1976-1 C.B. 562.
> Reg. § 1.351-1(a)(1)(ii).

LEARNING OBJECTIVES

Upon completion of this chapter you will be able to:

- Explain the tax effect of a corporate distribution on the shareholders and the distributing corporation

- Define a dividend for tax purposes

- Compare the concept of retained earnings with the concept of earnings and profits

- Explain how earnings and profits are calculated, and the function of earnings and profits in measuring dividend income

- Identify the special problems related to distributions of property (other than cash), including how to:

  - Determine the amount of the dividend to the shareholder

  - Determine the shareholder's basis of the property distributed

  - Determine the amount of gain or loss recognized by the distributing corporation

  - Determine the effect of a distribution of property on the corporation's earnings and profits

- Identify a constructive distribution

- Explain the tax consequences of a stock dividend

CHAPTER OUTLINE

Chapter 3

CORPORATE DISTRIBUTIONS
Cash, Property, and Stock Dividends

After shareholders have formed a corporation and operations are underway, one of their primary concerns is getting money out of the corporation. Unfortunately, this area, *corporate distributions*, is what one noted expert described as a "wonderfully complex subject."[1] The complexity stems from the vastly differing treatments accorded to distributions whose forms differ ever so slightly. For example, if a corporate distribution is considered a dividend, it is not deductible by the corporation, so double taxation results. In contrast, if the distribution to the shareholder is considered a type of payment that is deductible by the corporation (e.g., salary for services performed), double taxation does not occur. As one might expect, this dichotomy—deductible versus nondeductible treatment— causes many shareholders to go to great lengths to avoid dividend treatment.

Beyond this threshold question lurk still other important considerations. Assuming the distribution is made *with respect to the shareholder's stock* (e.g., it is not in fact some type of deductible payment), a determination must be made as to whether the distribution represents a return *on* the shareholder's investment (i.e., a distribution of corporate earnings or a dividend) or a return *of* the shareholder's capital. The distinction is critical because dividends are generally taxable as ordinary income whereas distributions of capital are tax-free to the extent of the shareholder's investment (i.e., stock basis) and taxable as favorable capital gain to the extent they exceed basis.

The rules governing corporate distributions are further complicated because they may take a variety of forms. A corporation may distribute cash or property including its own stock and obligations. Upon receipt of a corporate distribution, a shareholder may or may not surrender stock. After the distribution, the corporation may continue in the same or some modified form, or may completely terminate its operations. To determine whether a distribution under these various circumstances is a return on capital or a return of capital, the Code provides a virtual labyrinth of rules. These rules are the subject of this and the following chapter.

---

[1] Boris I. Bittker and James S. Eustice, *Federal Taxation of Corporations and Shareholders* (Boston: Warren, Gorham and Lamont), p. 7–1.

Corporate distributions generally fall into one of the following categories:

1. Section 301 distributions: distributions of property including cash where the shareholder normally does not surrender stock and which may be treated as a dividend or a return of capital, depending on whether the distributions are made from earnings and profits of the corporation

2. Distributions of stock and stock rights of the distributing corporation

3. Redemptions: distributions to a shareholder in exchange for stock and the corporation continues to operate

4. Redemptions in partial liquidation: distributions to a shareholder in exchange for stock and the corporation terminates a portion of its business

5. Redemptions in complete liquidation: distributions to a shareholder in exchange for stock and the corporation ceases to conduct business

6. Spin-offs, split-offs, and split-ups: distributions of stock of one or more subsidiaries as part of a corporate division

This chapter focuses on the first two categories of distributions, or what are commonly known as cash, property, and stock dividends. The other types of corporate distributions are considered in subsequent chapters.

SECTION 301:
DISTRIBUTIONS IN GENERAL

As a practical matter, virtually all distributions consist of cash and constitute ordinary dividend income to the shareholders. However, the Code contains a somewhat elaborate system to accommodate distributions of property and to ensure that returns of capital are nontaxable. Section 301 contains the general rule governing the tax treatment of distributions of property to a shareholder. For this purpose, property is defined broadly to include money, securities, and other property except stock (or rights to purchase stock) of the distributing corporation.[2] The following material considers the basic rules governing distributions. This discussion is followed by an examination of the special problems arising when a corporation distributes property other than money. The treatment of stock distributions is considered later in this chapter.

---

[2] § 317(a).

TAXATION OF DISTRIBUTIONS TO SHAREHOLDERS: STATUTORY SCHEME

When a corporation distributes property, § 301 requires that the amount of the distribution be included in the shareholder's gross income to the extent that it constitutes a *dividend*.[3] The term *dividend*, a precisely defined word as explained below, generally means any distribution of property that is out of the corporation's earnings and profits.[4] The critical presumption contained within the distribution provisions is that any distribution made by the corporation with respect to its stock is deemed first to be a distribution out of earnings and profits to the extent thereof. Therefore, as long as the corporation has sufficient earnings and profits, distributions are treated as taxable dividends. Amounts that are not considered dividends because of inadequate earnings and profits are treated as nontaxable returns of capital to the extent of the shareholder's basis for the stock.[5] In effect, the nondividend portion of the distribution is applied to and reduces the basis of the stock. Should the return of capital distribution exceed the shareholder's basis, the excess is treated as gain from the sale of the stock, normally capital gain if the stock is a capital asset.[6]

> **Example 1.** On December 1, JKL Inc. distributed $10,000 to its sole share-holder, T. At the close of the year, the corporation had earnings and profits of $6,000 before taking into account the distribution. Assuming T's basis in her stock is $3,000, the $10,000 distribution is treated as follows: a taxable dividend to the extent of the corporation's earnings and profits, $6,000; a tax-free return of capital to the extent of her basis in the stock, $3,000; and a capital gain to the extent the return of capital distribution exceeds her basis, $1,000 ($4,000 − $3,000). Note that in this case, the return of capital distribution reduces T's basis in her stock to zero.

As this example suggests, the treatment of property distributions is closely tied to the notion of earnings and profits.

EARNINGS AND PROFITS

Under the statutory scheme, a dividend can be distributed only if the corporation has earnings and profits—or as it is usually called, E&P.[7] Interestingly, the Code, which normally goes to great lengths to define its words, fails to define the term *earnings and profits*. Although the statute offers some guidance concerning how certain transactions affect E&P, the meaning of E&P is conspicuously absent.[8]

---

[3] § 301(c).

[4] § 316(a).

[5] § 301(c)(2).

[6] § 301(c)(3).

[7] § 316(a).

[8] § 312 describes the effect of certain transactions *on* E&P.

As a result, the Treasury and the courts have had to fashion a definition of E&P in light of its purpose. The primary function of E&P is to provide a measure of the amount a corporation can distribute without "dipping" into its capital. In so doing, it provides a standard for determining whether a distribution represents a taxable dividend or a tax-free return of capital.

Given the definition of E&P—an amount that can be distributed without impairing the corporation's capital—E&P generally represents the corporation's economic income that can be distributed. In this regard, E&P actually consists of two parts: *current E&P*, which represents current economic income computed on an annual basis; and *accumulated E&P*, which is simply the sum of each year's current E&P reduced by distributions. Generally, current taxable income, as adjusted for certain items, serves as a proxy for the corporation's current economic income (i.e., current E&P).

> **Example 2.**   X and Y Corporation were both formed this year. For the year, X Corporation reported a loss while Y reported $20,000 of income after taxes. If X makes a distribution, the distribution is a return of the shareholders' capital since X has no current or accumulated E&P. In contrast, any distribution made by Y—up to $20,000—is treated as having been paid out of its current earnings (i.e., current E&P) and is, therefore, a taxable dividend.

E&P is somewhat similar to the legal concept of "earned surplus" and the accounting concept of "retained earnings," neither of which include paid-in-capital or subsequent contributions to capital. This is not to say, however, that E&P is equivalent to either retained earnings or earned surplus. Indeed, in many cases E&P may bear little resemblance to either. For example, when a corporation issues a stock dividend, generally accepted accounting principles require the capitalization of part of the retained earnings balance (i.e., the transfer of an amount equal to the market value of the stock from the retained earnings account to the capital stock account). If this were allowed for tax purposes, corporations could avoid paying dividends simply by declaring stock dividends that would eliminate their E&P. For tax purposes, however, a nontaxable stock dividend has no effect on the corporation's ability to pay dividends, and consequently the E&P balance is unaffected.

Current E&P is not the same as current taxable income. Nor is accumulated E&P simply the sum of each year's taxable income. Taxable income, fraught with special provisions designed to achieve some objective or furnish some relief, is not necessarily representative of the corporation's economic income. For the most part, taxable income provides only a blurred picture of the corporation's capacity to pay dividends. Nevertheless, taxable income has traditionally been used as the starting point in the computation of E&P.

Since E&P represents the corporation's economic income, numerous adjustments to taxable income must be made to arrive at the corporation's E&P. For example, tax-exempt interest must be added to taxable income because it represents economic income that the corporation could distribute without violating its capital account. A general formula for computing E&P is presented in Exhibit 3-1. Each of these adjustments to taxable income is considered in detail below.

The calculation of E&P is normally made using the same accounting methods used to compute taxable income.[9] For example, a corporation that adopts the cash receipts and disbursements method of accounting uses the same method for determining E&P. Over the years, however, Congress has required corporate taxpayers to adopt accounting methods for computing E&P that vary from those they use for computing taxable income. The objective of many of these modifications is to conform E&P more closely to the economic concept of income. For example, when calculating E&P, taxpayers are not allowed to use the Accelerated Cost Recovery System (ACRS) to compute depreciation. Instead, they must use the slower-paced Alternative Depreciation System (ADS) with its straight-line method and longer class lives. A partial list of the special adjustments that must be made in computing E&P appears in Exhibit 3-2.

Modifications for E&P: Excluded and Deferred Income. Under the Regulations, all income normally excluded in computing taxable income must be included in determining E&P. Accordingly, E&P must be increased for items such as tax-exempt interest on state and local bonds[10] and life insurance proceeds. Several items that are technically excluded from income by the Code are not added back to taxable income to determine E&P since they do not represent income. For example, contributions to capital, gifts, and bequests would be ignored in making the computation.

Exhibit 3-1
Calculation of Current Earnings and Profits

```
        Current taxable income (or net operating loss)
    +   Exempt and nondeferrable income
    −   Items not deductible in computing taxable income
    +   Deductions not permitted in computing E&P

    =   Current earnings and profits (or deficit)
```

---

[9] Reg. § 1.312-6(a).   [10] Reg. § 1.312-6(b).

Exhibit 3-2
*Partial List of Adjustments Used
in Computing Current Earnings and Profits*

Taxable Income:

Plus:

Tax-exempt interest income
Deferred gain on installment sales
Dividends-received deduction
Excess of accelerated depreciation over straight-line depreciation
Excess of ACRS depreciation over ADS straight-line depreciation [§ 312(k)(3)]
Excess of LIFO cost of goods sold over FIFO cost of goods sold
Four-fifths (⅘) of deduction for immediate expensing of assets under § 179 taken
   during the current year [§ 312(k)(3)(B)]
Excess of deductions for construction period interest and taxes over the amorti-
   zation of such costs
Excess of depletion taken over cost depletion
Increases in cash surrender value of life insurance when the corporation is the
   beneficiary (directly or indirectly)
Proceeds of life insurance when the corporation is the beneficiary (directly or
   indirectly)
Amortization of organization and circulation expenditures
Net operating loss deductions carried over from other years
Federal income tax refunds
Recoveries of bad debts and other deductions, but only if they are *not* included
   in taxable income under the tax benefit doctrine
Income based on the percentage-of-completion method rather than the
   completed-contract method
In the year they are reflected in taxable income: charitable contribution carryovers,
   capital loss carryovers, and other timing differences (since they reduced E&P
   in the year they originated)

Exhibit 3-2 Continued:

Minus:

Federal income taxes
Nondeductible expenses:
    Penalties and fines
    Payments to public officials not reflected in taxable income
    Expenses between related parties not deductible under § 267
    Interest expense related to the production of tax-exempt income
    Life insurance premiums when the corporation is the beneficiary (directly or
        indirectly)
    Travel, entertainment, and gift expenses that do not meet the substantiation
        requirements of § 274(d)
    Twenty percent of meals and entertainment disallowed as a deduction under
        § 274(n)
Other expenses that are disallowed to the corporation as the result of an IRS
    audit
Nondeductible losses between related parties under § 267
Charitable contributions in excess of the 10 percent limitation
Excess capital losses for the year that are not deductible
Gains on sales of depreciable property to the extent that accelerated depreciation
    or ACRS exceeds the straight-line depreciation method used for computing
    increases in E&P
Gains on sales of depletable property to the extent that depletion taken exceeds
    cost depletion
One-fifth ($\frac{1}{5}$) of any immediate expensing deduction under § 179 taken during the
    previous four years [§ 312(k)(3)(B)]
Foreign taxes paid that have been treated as credits on the corporation's tax return

Equals: ***Current Earnings and Profits***

Note: The above exhibit does not include the effect of corporate distributions and
dividends on E&P—this is discussed later in the chapter.

Income items are generally included in E&P in the year in which they are *recognized*. Consistent with this principle, gain postponed under the like-kind exchange provisions or the rules permitting nonrecognition on certain involuntary conversions is not reflected in E&P in the year realized but in the year recognized.[11] In contrast, the installment sales method may not be used for computing E&P. As a result, the entire amount of any gain realized on an installment sale must be included in E&P in the year of the sale.[12] Similarly, income and deductions of a corporation using the completed contract method of accounting must be accounted for using the percentage of completion method.[13]

As explained below, distributions of appreciated property cause the distributing corporation to recognize gain. These gains must be included in the computation of E&P prior to any reduction to E&P caused by the distribution.[14]

Items Nondeductible for E&P. The Code provides a lengthy list of items which, although deductible in computing taxable income, cannot be deducted currently in calculating E&P. In this category of required adjustments is one affecting all corporations that account for inventory using the LIFO method. Effective for taxable years beginning after September 30, 1984, these corporations must generally use the FIFO method in computing cost of goods sold for determining E&P.[15]

Several other modifications in this group involve the methods used to account for capital expenditures. No doubt the most important of these concerns depreciation. As mentioned above, depreciation deductions for E&P generally must be calculated using a straight-line method.[16] For property subject to pre-1987 ACRS, the straight-line method must be followed using the recovery periods shown in Exhibit 3-3. For property subject to post-1986 ACRS (often called modified ACRS or simply MACRS), the Alternative Depreciation System (ADS) straight-line method must be used. The recovery periods for ADS are summarized in Exhibit 3-4, while the ADS depreciation percentages are shown in Exhibits 3-5 and 3-6. Assets expensed under the limited expensing provision of § 179 must be depreciated using the straight-line method over a five-year period.

> **Example 3.** On January 15 of this year, T Corporation purchased a warehouse for $110,000, $10,000 of which was allocable to the land. Under ACRS, T claims a depreciation deduction of $3,042 ($100,000 × 3.042% per Appendix H) in computing taxable income. Under ADS, which must

---

[11] § 312(f)(1).

[12] § 312(n)(5).

[13] § 312(n)(6).

[14] § 312(b). As explained within, E&P is increased for any gain recognized on the distribution. The increase by itself may create

sufficient E&P to cause taxation of the distribution to the shareholder. Following the distribution, E&P is reduced by the property's value.

[15] § 312(n)(5).

[16] § 312(k)(1) is applicable only for taxable years beginning after June 30, 1972.

Exhibit 3-3
*Earnings and Profits and ACRS:
Depreciable Lives*

Pre-1987 ACRS Property	Earnings and Profits Straight-Line Extended Life in Years
3-year	5
5-year	12
10-year	25
15-year public utility	35
15-year real	35
19-year real	40

be used in computing E&P, depreciation is $2,396 ($100,000 × 2.396% per Exhibit 3-6). Consequently, in computing E&P, taxable income must be increased by $646 ($3,042 − $2,396), the excess of ACRS depreciation over ADS depreciation.

Similar to the modifications for depreciation, adjustments must be made for the following:

1. *Depletion*. Only cost depletion may be used in computing E&P.[17]

2. *Intangible drilling costs*. These costs must be capitalized and amortized over 60 months.[18]

3. *Mineral exploration and development costs*. These costs must be capitalized and amortized over 120 months.[19]

4. *Construction period interest, taxes, and other carrying charges*. These costs must be capitalized and amortized over the life of the related property.[20]

5. *Organization and circulation expenditures*. Amortization of these costs is not permitted in computing E&P. These costs must be capitalized.[21]

---

[17] Reg. § 1.312-6(c)(1).

[18] § 312(n)(2)(A).

[19] § 312(n)(2)(B).

[20] § 312(n)(1).

[21] § 312(n)(3).

Exhibit 3-4
Alternative Depreciation System
Recovery Periods

General Rule: Recovery period is the property's class life unless:

    1.   There is no class life (see below), or
    2.   A special class life has been designated (see below).

Type of Property	*Recovery Period*
Personal property with no class life	12 years
Nonresidential real property with no class life	40 years
Residential real property with no class life	40 years
Cars, light general purpose trucks, certain technological equipment, and semiconductor manufacturing equipment	5 years
Computer-based telephone central office switching equipment	9.5 years
Railroad track	10 years
Single-purpose agricultural or horticultural structures	15 years
Municipal waste water treatment plants, telephone distribution plants	24 years
Low-income housing financed by tax-exempt bonds	27.5 years
Municipal sewers	50 years

Another adjustment required in computing E&P involves the dividends-received deduction. Since this deduction does not affect the corporation's ability to pay dividends, it must be added back to taxable income when computing E&P.

> **Example 4.** During the year, C Corporation received dividends of $100,000. Because of the dividends-received deduction, only $30,000 of the $100,000 is included in the corporation's taxable income [$100,000 − (70% × $100,000)]. In computing E&P, the corporation must include the full $100,000. Consequently, a positive adjustment of $70,000 must be made to the corporation's taxable income to arrive at the proper balance of E&P.

The net operating loss deduction must also be added back, since this deduction simply represents a carryover or carryback of a loss incurred in another year. Losses reduce E&P in the year they are incurred.

Items Nondeductible for Taxable Income. Various items that cannot be deducted in computing taxable income may be deducted in computing E&P since they reduce the amount that could be paid out to shareholders. Several of the more important expenses and losses which may be subtracted include the following:

Exhibit 3-5
ADS Straight-Line Depreciation Percentages
Using the Half-Year Convention
for Property with Certain Recovery Periods

Recovery Year	Recovery Period (Class Life)	
	5 Years	12 Years
1	10.00%	4.17%
2	20.00	8.33
3	20.00	8.33
4	20.00	8.33
5	20.00	8.33
6	10.00	8.33
7		8.34
8		8.33
9		8.34
10		8.33
11		8.34
12		8.33
13		4.17

Source: Rev. Proc. 87-57, 1987-2 C.B. 687, Table 8.

1. *Federal income taxes.* An accrual basis taxpayer reduces current E&P for the taxes imposed on current taxable income, while a cash basis taxpayer reduces current E&P only for those taxes paid.

2. *Charitable contributions.* Those in excess of the 10 percent limitation are also deductible in computing E&P (i.e., contributions are deductible in full in the year paid).

3. *Expenses related to tax-exempt income.*

4. *Premiums paid on key-man life insurance policies.* These amounts may be deducted to the extent they exceed any increase in the policy's cash surrender value.

5. *Excess of capital losses over capital gains.* Since net capital losses are not deductible in computing current year taxable income, they must be deducted in computing current E&P.

6. *Related party losses and expenses.* Losses and expenses disallowed under the related party rules of § 267 are subtracted in computing current E&P.

Although the above list identifies numerous nondeductible items that must be considered in computing E&P, it is by no means exhaustive. Any outlay that

Exhibit 3-6
ADS Straight-Line Depreciation Percentages
Real Property
Using the Mid-Month Convention

Residential Property and Nonresidential Real Property

Month Placed in Service	Recovery Year		
	1	2–40	41
1	2.396%	2.500%	0.104%
2	2.188	2.500	0.312
3	1.979	2.500	0.521
4	1.771	2.500	0.729
5	1.563	2.500	0.937
6	1.354	2.500	1.146
7	1.146	2.500	1.354
8	0.938	2.500	1.562
9	0.729	2.500	1.771
10	0.521	2.500	1.979
11	0.313	2.500	2.187
12	0.104	2.500	2.396

Source: Rev. Proc. 87-57, 1987-2 C.B. 687, Table 13.

reduces the amount available to distribute, yet is not a capital expenditure, may represent a potential adjustment for E&P (e.g., nondeductible political contributions, lobbying expenses, and penalties).

Example 5. This year, D Corporation sold securities yielding a short-term capital loss of $25,000. The corporation had no capital gains during the year. As a result, none of the loss is deductible in computing current taxable income. Nevertheless, E&P must be reduced by $25,000 since the loss reduces the corporation's ability to pay dividends.

Example 6. E Corporation maintains a life insurance policy of $500,000 on its president, T. During the year, the corporation paid the annual premium of $5,000. In addition, the cash surrender value of the policy increased by $2,000. Although the annual premium payments are not deductible, they do reduce E&P. Similarly, increases in the cash surrender value of the policy that are nontaxable are included in E&P.

In 1991, T died when the cash surrender value was $60,000. The corporation received the face amount of the policy, $500,000. Although the $500,000 is nontaxable, E&P must be adjusted. Since the corporation has adjusted E&P previously for increases in the cash surrender value and because part of the $500,000 represents a return of that value, only $440,000 ($500,000 − $60,000) is added to E&P.[22]

CURRENT VERSUS ACCUMULATED E&P

As noted above, E&P consists of two basic parts: current E&P and accumulated E&P. The distinction between current and accumulated E&P is very important for, as explained below, the two are often viewed as two separate pools of earnings from which distributions can be made. As a result, under the current approach a corporation can make taxable dividend distributions if it has current E&P, notwithstanding the fact that it may have a deficit in accumulated E&P.

DIVIDEND DISTRIBUTIONS

Under the statutory approach described above, only that portion of a distribution which is a dividend is included in the shareholder's gross income.[23] A *dividend* is defined as a distribution paid *out of either current or accumulated E&P.*[24] In this regard, any distribution made during the year is deemed to come first from any *current E&P* that may exist.[25] If the distribution exceeds current E&P, then the distribution is considered as having been paid from any *accumulated E&P* of prior years.[26] The presumption that every distribution is first out of current E&P and then from accumulated E&P results in the following rules that must be applied in determining the source of the distribution:[27]

1. Current E&P is allocated among *all* distributions made during the year on a pro rata basis, as follows:

$$\frac{\text{Amount of distribution}}{\text{Total current distributions}} \times \frac{\text{Current}}{\text{E\&P}} = \frac{\text{Distribution's}}{\text{share of current E\&P}}$$

   For this purpose, current E&P is computed on the last day of the taxable year *without* reduction for any distributions made during the year.

2. Accumulated E&P is allocated among distributions made during the year in *chronological* order.

---

[22] Rev. Rul. 54-230, 1954-1 C.B. 114.

[23] § 301(c)(1) and 316.

[24] § 316(a).

[25] § 316(a)(2).

[26] § 316(a)(1).

[27] Reg. § 1.316-2.

3. If there is a deficit in current E&P (e.g., a current operating loss), it is prorated on a daily basis against any accumulated E&P existing on the date of the distribution. For example, if there is a distribution on February 1, the amount of the deficit that occurs through January 31 is determined and netted against accumulated E&P. If the actual deficit suffered prior to the date of distribution can be determined, that amount is used rather than the amount determined under the proration method.

4. If a deficit in accumulated E&P exists, it is ignored and all distributions are dividends to the extent of their share of current E&P.

These operating rules are illustrated in the following examples.

> **Example 7.** At the beginning of the taxable year, K Inc. had accumulated E&P of $40,000. Current E&P for the year was $27,000. During the year, K made cash distributions to its sole shareholder, J, of $30,000 on April 1 and $60,000 on October 1. The treatment of these distributions is shown below.
>
> | Distribution | | Current | Remaining | Accumulated | Return | *capital gain* |
> | Date | Amount | E&P* | Distribution | E&P | of Capital | Sale |
> |---|---|---|---|---|---|---|
> | 4/1 | $30,000 | $ 9,000 | $21,000 | $21,000 | 0 | 0 |
> | 10/1 | 60,000 | 18,000 | 42,000 | 19,000 | $15,000 | $8,000 |
>
> $$* \quad \frac{\$30,000}{\$30,000 + \$60,000} \times \$27,000 = \$\,9,000$$
>
> $$* \quad \frac{\$60,000}{\$30,000 + \$60,000} \times \$27,000 = \$18,000$$
>
> As shown above, both distributions are deemed to consist of their allocable share of current E&P. The April 1 distribution represents a $9,000 distribution from current E&P while the October 1 distribution represents $18,000 of current E&P. Accumulated E&P is allocated on a chronological basis; thus, $21,000 of the $40,000 balance is allocated to the remaining portion of the April 1 distribution (i.e., the distribution not out of current E&P, $30,000 − $9,000) and the remaining accumulated E&P of $19,000 is allocated to the October 1 distribution. As a result, the entire $30,000 distribution on April 1 is treated as a dividend while only $37,000 ($18,000 + $19,000) of the October 1 distribution of $60,000 is a dividend. The remaining $23,000 balance ($60,000 − $37,000) of the October 1 distribution is considered a return of the shareholder's basis. Assuming J has a $15,000 basis in his stock, the $23,000 is applied to and reduces J's basis to zero, while the $8,000 ($23,000 − $15,000) excess over his basis is considered capital gain from the sale of his stock.

Note that in the example above the allocation process had no effect on the amount of dividend income that J reports (i.e., J's dividend after the allocation is $67,000, the same as the sum of current and accumulated E&P) because he was the corporation's only shareholder. However, if there are changes in ownership during the year, the allocation process can affect the amount of dividend income that the shareholder must include in income.

Example 8. On June 30, 1991 M sold 100% of the stock of L Inc. to B for $12,000. L had accumulated E&P at the beginning of the year of $20,000, while current E&P for the year was $40,000. The corporation made distributions of $40,000 on April 1 and $40,000 on October 1. As computed below, all of the $40,000 distribution to M on April 1 is a dividend while only $20,000 of the $40,000 distribution to B is a dividend. Although both M and B owned 100% of the corporation for six months of the year and both received equal distributions, M must report twice as much dividend income because accumulated E&P is allocated chronologically.

Distribution		Current	Remaining	Accumulated	Return	*capital gain*
Date	Amount	E&P*	Distribution	E&P	of Capital	Sale
4/1	$40,000	$20,000	$20,000	$20,000	0	0
10/1	40,000	20,000	20,000	0	$12,000	$8,000

$$* \frac{\$40,000}{\$40,000 + \$40,000} \times \$40,000 = \$20,000$$

taxable inc. = 28000 + 20,000 = 48,000

Example 9. At the beginning of the year, K Corporation had accumulated E&P of $60,000. Unprofitable operations for the year resulted in a $36,500 deficit in K Corporation's current E&P. During the year, the corporation made cash distributions of $30,000 on April 1 and $60,000 on October 1. The deficit is prorated on a daily basis (excluding the date of distribution) and reduces any accumulated E&P otherwise available on the date of distribution. Accordingly, in determining accumulated E&P as of the date of the first distribution, April 1, the beginning balance of accumulated E&P is reduced by $9,000 of the current deficit ($36,500 ÷ 365 × 90), leaving $51,000 ($60,000 − $9,000) available for distribution. Since accumulated E&P exceeds the April 1 distribution, all $30,000 of the distribution is a dividend. Accumulated E&P available for the October distribution is $2,700 [$60,000 − deficit to October 1 of $27,300 (273 ÷ 365 × $36,500) − previous distribution of $30,000], reflecting both the deficit through September 30 and the previous distribution of $30,000.

Example 10. At the beginning of the year, D Corporation had a deficit in accumulated E&P of $100,000 resulting from unprofitable operations in prior years. This year, the corporation had an excellent year, with current E&P of $60,000. On November 30 of this year, the corporation distributed $70,000 to its sole shareholder, M, who had a basis in her stock of $16,000. M must report a dividend of $60,000, representing a distribution of current E&P—notwithstanding the fact that the corporation had a deficit in accumulated E&P. Note that a deficit in accumulated E&P is *not* netted with current E&P. The remaining distribution of $10,000 reduces M's basis in her stock to $6,000 ($16,000 − $10,000).

DISTRIBUTIONS OF PROPERTY

In the previous section, it was assumed that all distributions made by a corporation to its shareholders were cash distributions. Although the vast majority of corporations distribute only cash, in certain cases the corporation may distribute land, inventory, or other property in lieu of or in addition to cash. As a general rule, property distributions are treated in the same manner as cash distributions. Indeed, when the basis of the distributed property is equal to its fair market value, the treatment is virtually identical with that accorded cash distributions. In theory, the *result* is the same as if the corporation had sold the property and distributed the cash proceeds from the sale. In such case, there would be no concern with gain or loss at the corporate level and any resulting adjustment to E&P, since the property's value and basis are equivalent. Unfortunately, the basis and value of the property are rarely equal, leading one to ask how far the "as if sold" approach is taken. In short, the distribution of property raises several additional questions that are not present with cash distributions:

1. Does the corporation *recognize gain or loss* on the distribution?
2. What is the effect of the distribution on the corporation's *E&P*?
3. What is the *amount* of the distribution to the shareholder?
4. What is the *basis* of the distributed property in the hands of the shareholder?

These and other considerations related to property distributions are addressed below. Before proceeding, it should be mentioned that the following rules apply to distributions of virtually all types of property, including the corporation's own securities (e.g., bonds and notes).[28] However, distributions of the corporation's own stock (e.g., stock dividends), as well as rights to acquire such stock, are subject to a special set of provisions discussed later in this chapter.

EFFECT OF PROPERTY DISTRIBUTION ON THE SHAREHOLDER: AMOUNT AND BASIS OF PROPERTY DISTRIBUTION

The effect of a distribution of property on a shareholder is determined using the same basic rules that apply to cash distributions. Like cash distributions, property distributions generally are treated as dividends to the extent they are out of E&P and otherwise are treated as nontaxable returns of capital to the extent of the shareholder's basis. The only pitfall presented by property distributions in this regard concerns the unique problems of appreciated property. As the discussion below warns, a distribution of appreciated property could increase E&P, which in turn could affect the amount of the dividend to the shareholder.

---

[28]   §§ 301 and 317(a).

When a distribution of property is made, two issues uncommon to cash distributions arise: (1) what is the amount of the distribution; and (2) what is the shareholder's basis of the property distributed? When cash distributions are made, the amount of the distributions is simply the value of the cash received, and of course the basis of the cash is also its value. When a property distribution is made, however, the Code sets forth special rules for determining its amount and basis to the shareholder.

Amount.   The amount of the distribution is the property's fair market value as of the date of distribution. This amount properly reflects the value of the benefit received by the shareholder.[29] If, in connection with the distribution, the shareholder assumes a liability of the distributing corporation or takes the distributed property subject to a liability, the amount of the distribution must be reduced by the liability (but not below zero).[30] This modification is necessary because the shareholder's wealth has increased only by the net amount of the distribution (fair market value − liability). In short, the shareholder's income includes as a dividend the fair market value of any property received (adjusted for liabilities) to the extent the distribution is out of E&P.

Basis.   The shareholder's basis for the property received is the property's fair market value.[31] This basis reflects the fact that the shareholder has been taxed on such value and any future gain or loss is properly measured from this point. In contrast to the computation of the amount of the distribution, the shareholder's basis in the property is *not* affected—neither decreased nor increased—by any liabilities assumed in connection with the distribution. Note that this approach is in essence the same as that used for any other basis computations. For example, if property is purchased for $10,000, the taxpayer's basis for the property is its cost, regardless of whether $10,000 in cash is paid or a $10,000 note is given. In effect, the liability assumed is included in the basis because it represents part of the taxpayer's cost of the property.

> **Example 11.**   During the year, G Inc. distributed land worth $150,000 to its sole shareholder, B. The corporation acquired the land for $60,000. B took the property subject to a mortgage of $20,000. The amount of the distribution is $130,000 ($150,000 − $20,000) and is treated as a dividend, assuming the corporation has that much E&P. B's basis in the land is its fair market value of $150,000. Note that if B immediately sold the land for $150,000 and paid the $20,000 liability, no gain or loss would be recognized and B would be better off by $130,000, the amount of the distribution included in income.

---

[29]   § 301(b)(1)(A).   [31]   § 301(d)(1).

[30]   § 301(b)(2).

CORPORATE GAIN OR LOSS
ON PROPERTY DISTRIBUTIONS

General Rule.   Section 311 provides that a corporation must recognize gain—*but not loss*—upon the distribution of property other than its own obligations.[32] The gain to be recognized is computed as if the corporation had sold the property to the distributee shareholder for the property's fair market value.

> **Example 12.**   P Corporation distributed land worth $100,000 (basis $20,000) and equipment worth $30,000 (basis $45,000) to its sole share-holder, Q. P must recognize the $80,000 ($100,000 − $20,000) gain re-alized on the distribution of the land. Although P also realizes a loss on the distribution of the equipment, the loss is not recognized. Note that gain and loss are computed on an asset by asset basis.

Observe that the gain recognition rule of § 311 ensures that the appreciation on distributed property does not escape tax. This would otherwise occur because the shareholder's basis in the property is its fair market value. For instance, in *Example 12* above, the shareholder's basis in the land would be $100,000. Therefore, a subsequent sale of the land for $100,000 would result in no gain at the shareholder level. For this reason, the corporation is required to recognize the gain just as if it had sold the property. This treatment ensures that—at least in the case of appreciated property—there is no distinction between sales of property followed by a distribution and distributions of property. In both cases, two taxes occur: one at the corporate level upon the sale or distribution, and one at the shareholder level upon receipt of the sales proceeds or property.

Losses.   The restriction against loss recognition was enacted to prohibit tax-payers from circumventing the basic rule requiring gain recognition. For example, assume a wholly owned corporation holds appreciated land worth $1,000, which its sole shareholder wishes to extract for his own use. Assume for the sake of simplicity that the land has a basis of zero. Also assume the owner of the corpo-ration holds equipment that has a fair market value of zero but a basis of $1,000. Absent a prohibition against losses, the owner could take the following steps to avoid the tax on the gain recognized by the corporation when the property is distributed. First, the owner would contribute the equipment (with the built-in loss) to the corporation, for which the corporation would take a $1,000 carry-over basis. Second, the corporation would distribute *both* the property and the equipment. If the $1,000 loss on the equipment (value $0, basis $1,000) were allowed, it would offset the $1,000 gain on the land that must be recognized (value $1,000, basis $0). Moreover, the taxpayer would not pay any tax on the distribution of the equipment since it has a value of zero, and the taxpayer would still hold the equipment after the series of transactions is complete.[33] The rule against loss recognition prevents such possibilities.

---

[32]   §§ 311 (a) and (b).

[33]   Note that the shareholder would have a zero basis in the equipment, so no further loss would result.

The no-loss rule also bars taxpayers from creating artificial losses when the property is still under the taxpayer's control. For example, consider a wholly owned corporation that desires losses to reduce its income. Absent the loss prohibition rule, it could distribute loss property to its sole shareholder and recognize the loss even though the property was still controlled by the shareholder. Section 311 foils this scheme by disallowing the loss.

Property Subject to a Liability. When property subject to a liability is distributed, the corporation is relieved of an obligation. In such case, the effect to the corporation is the same as if it had sold the property for cash equal to the liability and paid off the debt. Consistent with this approach, § 311 provides that the fair market value of the property is deemed to be *no less* than the amount of the liability.[34] Thus, when the liability exceeds both the fair market value and the basis of the property, the corporation must recognize gain equal to the excess of the liability over the basis. If the liability does not exceed the property's fair market value, it is ignored for gain recognition purposes and the fair market value is used.

> **Example 13.** T Corporation owns land with a basis of $10,000 and which is subject to a liability of $40,000. Due to recent rezoning, the property has declined in value to $25,000. During the year, T distributed the land as a dividend to its sole shareholder, R. Since the liability exceeds the value of the property, the corporation has essentially received cash equal to the liability. Thus, the corporation must recognize a gain of $30,000 ($40,000 liability − $10,000 basis). Had the liability been $3,000, T Corporation would have recognized a gain of $15,000 ($25,000 value − $10,000 basis) because the liability is ignored in this instance.

EFFECT OF PROPERTY DISTRIBUTIONS ON THE CORPORATION'S E&P

Like distributions of cash, distributions of property require the corporation to make appropriate adjustments to its E&P. The general rule of Code § 312 demands that the corporation reduce E&P by the *adjusted basis* of the distributed property—in effect, the unrecovered amount of E&P tied up in the asset.[35]

> **Example 14.** K Corporation purchased equipment several years ago for $10,000. After claiming $2,000 of depreciation on the asset, the corporation distributed it to its shareholder when it had a value of $5,000. The corporation must reduce E&P by the adjusted basis of the equipment, $8,000 ($10,000 − $2,000).

Although the general rule applies in most cases, special adjustments must be considered in three instances: (1) distributions of appreciated property; (2) distributions of property subject to a liability; and (3) distributions of the corporation's own obligations (e.g., bonds).

---

[34] § 311(b)(2).   [35] § 312(a).

Distributions of Appreciated Property. When a corporation calculates its E&P, special care must be taken in determining the effect of distributions of appreciated property. These distributions present unique problems because the corporation is required to recognize gain.

Due to the gain recognition requirement, the impact of appreciated property distributions on E&P is twofold.[36] First, E&P must be increased by the gain recognized on the distribution. Second, E&P must be decreased by the fair market value of the property.[37] The effect of these adjustments is equivalent to what would have occurred had the corporation sold the property (thereby increasing E&P by the gain on the sale) and distributed the cash proceeds from the sale. Generally, the *net* effect is to reduce E&P by the original basis of the distributed property. However, E&P would decrease for any taxes resulting from the gain recognized.

> **Example 15.**   During the year, D Inc. distributed land worth $50,000 (basis $10,000). Since the distributed property is appreciated, the corporation must recognize a gain of $40,000 ($50,000 − $10,000). The gain increases D's current E&P by $40,000. D's E&P is then reduced by the fair market value of the property, $50,000. Thus, the net effect of the distribution on the corporation's E&P—ignoring any taxes paid on the gain—is to decrease E&P by $10,000, as follows:
>
> | | |
> |---|---:|
> | Increase E&P by gain recognized.................. | $40,000 |
> | Decrease E&P by value of property............... | (50,000) |
> | Net decrease in E&P .... | ($10,000) |

As suggested above, the effect of the distribution is the same as if the corporation had sold the property for $50,000 (thereby increasing E&P by the $40,000 gain) and distributed the $50,000 proceeds (thereby decreasing E&P by $50,000). Note also that the net decrease in E&P is equal to the original basis of the distributed property, $10,000.

Corporations sometimes overlook the nuances in property distributions only to be surprised that what they originally thought would be a nontaxable return of capital distribution is in fact a dividend.

> **Example 16.**   Near year end, T, the accountant for Z Inc., examined the corporation's financial position to determine the possible consequences of a property distribution. Upon inspection, he determined that the corporation had neither accumulated E&P nor current taxable income. Based on this assessment, T believed that the time was right for distributing land

---

[36]   § 312(b).

[37]   It may be useful to think of the basis to the distributing corporation as being increased by the gain recognized. By so doing, the general rule would still apply.

worth $100,000 (basis $20,000) since the distribution apparently would be a nontaxable distribution to the shareholder. On the distribution, however, the corporation is required to recognize a gain of $80,000 ($100,000 − $20,000). The gain in turn increases E&P, causing the distribution to be treated as a dividend to the extent of any E&P created on the distribution itself.

Property Subject to a Liability. When property subject to a liability is distributed, or when the shareholder assumes liabilities in connection with the distribution, the corporation benefits from the relief of the liability. To reflect this benefit, the normal charge to E&P must be reduced by the amount of the liability.[38]

Example 17. During the year, C Corporation, which has substantial E&P, distributed land worth $60,000 (basis $80,000) to its sole shareholder. The land is subject to a $30,000 mortgage. Under the general rule, C reduces E&P by the basis of the property, $80,000. This charge must be reduced, however, by the amount of the mortgage, $30,000. Thus, C's E&P is reduced by $50,000 ($80,000 − $30,000).

Example 18. D Corporation distributed a building worth $100,000 (basis $70,000) to its sole shareholder. The building is subject to a mortgage of $40,000. In contrast to the previous example, the property has appreciated, thus requiring an additional adjustment to E&P. The net effect of the distribution is to reduce E&P by $30,000, determined as follows:

Increase E&P by the gain recognized..............	$ 30,000
Decrease E&P by the value of property............	(100,000)
Normal charge to E&P..........................	($ 70,000)
Reduction for liability	40,000
Net decrease in E&P	($ 30,000)

Example 19. E Corporation distributed a warehouse worth $50,000 (basis $40,000) to its sole shareholder. The warehouse is subject to a mortgage of $75,000. The net effect of the distribution is to *increase* E&P by $35,000, determined as follows:

Increase E&P by gain recognized ($75,000 − $40,000)...........................	$35,000
Decrease E&P by value (not less than the liability)	($75,000)
Normal charge to E&P..........................	($40,000)
Reduction for liability	75,000
Net increase in E&P.............................	$35,000

---

[38] § 312(c).

Note that reducing the normal charge to E&P by the liability effectively increases E&P. This properly reflects the fact that the corporation is better off without the liability.

Obligations of the Distributing Corporation. When a corporation distributes its own obligation (e.g., a bond), E&P is normally reduced by the principal amount of the obligation.[39] Without some modification, corporations could use this general rule essentially to eliminate E&P at little or no cost to the shareholder.

> **Example 20.** K Corporation has $500,000 of E&P, which it would like to eliminate to make return of capital distributions. To this end, it issued bonds with a principal amount of $500,000 to its shareholders. Since the bonds bear interest at a rate of only 3%, they are worth only $100,000. As a result, the noncorporate shareholders report dividend income of only $100,000, but the corporation, in the absence of a special rule, could reduce its E&P account by the principal amount of the bonds, $500,000. In effect, the corporation could wipe out $500,000 of E&P at the cost of a tax on $100,000.

To end the discrepancy between the amount of the dividend reported and the amount of the E&P reduction, Congress modified the general rule. Where the corporation distributes its own obligations that have original issue discount, E&P is reduced by the "issue price" of the obligation.[40] The issue price is normally the same as the obligation's value.

> **Example 21.** Same facts as in *Example 20*. The reduction to E&P is limited to the issue price of the securities, which normally approximates the securities' fair market value. Accordingly, K would reduce E&P by $100,000, leaving it with a balance of $400,000.

CONSTRUCTIVE DISTRIBUTIONS

The rules governing corporate distributions apply solely to distributions paid with respect to the shareholder's stock and only if paid to the shareholder while in a shareholder capacity.[41] Consequently, when a shareholder receives payments as an employee for services rendered or as a creditor in satisfaction of a debt, the distribution rules are inapplicable. Similarly, the distribution rules do not apply when the corporation's payments are for property (e.g., a purchase) or for the use of property (e.g., rent), since the shareholder is not receiving these payments as a shareholder.

---

[39] § 312(a)(2).

[40] *Ibid.*

[41] § 301(a).

This is not to say, however, that the distribution rules are reserved solely for those distributions that have been formally authorized by the corporation's board of directors. For tax purposes, the failure to officially "declare a dividend" in the manner required by state law does not absolve the distribution from dividend treatment. If a corporation informally provides a benefit to a shareholder, it may be construed as a *constructive* or *disguised* distribution. The finding of a constructive distribution can be disastrous because the shareholder must report the distribution as a dividend and the corporation is not permitted to deduct the payment. Consequently, double taxation occurs.

The likelihood of discovering constructive distributions is greatest when the corporation is closely held. Constructive dividends are normally found in this setting because the dealings between the corporation and the shareholders are usually unstructured and informal. The fact that the corporation is an entity distinct from its owners is frequently overlooked because the corporation often is merely the alter ego of the shareholder. In effect, the shareholder who is also the chief executive officer and chairman of the board is likely to treat the corporate checkbook as his or her own. As a result, transactions often occur that are not made at arm's length. Some of these transactions may represent a deliberate attempt on the part of the shareholders to secure the use of corporate earnings without suffering the double tax penalty that arises upon a formal dividend distribution. For example, the corporation may try to disguise a nondeductible dividend simply by classifying the payment as a deductible bonus. Other transactions, however, may be recast as dividend distributions even though their effect was unintentional. Suffice it to say here that dealings between closely held corporations and their shareholders are quite vulnerable to dividend treatment.

Constructive dividends can take many forms. In all cases, however, a dividend is not imputed unless the transaction is deemed to be for the personal benefit of the shareholder rather than the corporation—often a difficult determination. The transactions most commonly recast as a dividend are summarized below.

Excessive Compensation. When a corporation pays a shareholder-employee compensation that is deemed excessive for the services provided, that portion considered unreasonable is treated as a constructive dividend to the shareholder and is not deductible by the corporation. Similarly, excessive payments for the corporate use of shareholder property (i.e., excessive rents, interest, and royalties) may also give rise to a constructive dividend. Constructive distributions may also be found when the corporation purchases property from a shareholder at an excessive price. Unfortunately, what is considered excessive in these situations is a question that has plagued taxpayers and the government for many years. One need only review the countless number of cases to realize that reasonableness can only be determined on a case by case basis.[42]

---

[42] For examples, see *Mayson Manufacturing Co. v. Comm.,* 49-2 USTC ¶9467, 38 AFTR 1028, 178 F.2d 115 (CA-6, 1949) concerning excessive compensation; and *Fairmount Park Raceway Inc. v. Comm.,* 64-1 USTC ¶9183, 13 AFTR2d 416-B, 327 F.2d 780 (CA-7, 1964) concerning excessive rents.

Loans.   One method of avoiding any type of taxable distribution to the shareholder (e.g., salary, dividend, or rent) is to loan the shareholder funds as may be required. Because taxation can be completely avoided, corporate advances to shareholders are highly vulnerable for recharacterization as dividends. To avoid recharacterization, the advance must represent a *bona fide loan*. A bona fide debtor-creditor relationship is generally suggested by the following: the advance is recorded on the books of the corporation and is evidenced by a note; the shareholder has made payments on the note according to a fixed schedule; the note bears a reasonable charge for interest; the note is secured by collateral; the due dates for payments have been enforced. Advances on open account, demand loans, loans that do not bear adequate interest, and loans that have no fixed maturity date are likely to be treated as disguised dividends.

In 1984, Congress ended the controversy concerning low-interest or no-interest loans to shareholders and employees. Section 7872 imputes a daily interest payment, at the applicable Federal rate, compounded semiannually, from the borrower (e.g., the shareholder or employee) to the corporation, which the corporation is deemed to have paid back to the borrower. The borrower generally is permitted to deduct the hypothetical interest payment made to the corporation. In addition, the borrower treats the transfer from the corporation as a dividend or compensation, depending on the borrower's status. On the other hand, the corporation may deduct the payment if it is considered compensation. The corporation is denied a deduction if the payment is treated as a dividend. Recently proposed regulations provide guidelines to be used in determining whether the hypothetical payment to a shareholder-employee is compensation or a dividend.[43] When the corporation is publicly held, the payment is treated as a dividend if the shareholder-employee owns more than 0.05 percent of the stock. In contrast, if the corporation is not publicly held, the payment is treated as a dividend if the shareholder-employee owns more than five percent of the stock. These guidelines are to be followed unless there exists convincing evidence to the contrary.

Although these rules can be quite onerous, § 7872 provides limited relief. The provision does not apply for any day that the loan between the corporation and the shareholder and/or employee does not exceed $10,000. For this purpose, loans to a husband and wife are aggregated and treated as a single loan.

> **Example 22.**   On January 1, 1991 Z Corp. loaned R, a 40% shareholder, $100,000, payable on demand without interest. At the end of the year, the loan was still outstanding. Assuming the applicable Federal rate of interest is 10% for the entire year, R is treated as having made an interest payment of $10,250 (10% compounded semiannually = 10.25% × $100,000) to the corporation. In addition, he is deemed to have received a dividend of

---

[43]   Prop. Reg. § 1.7872-9.

$10,250. Whether this deemed transaction is merely a wash for R (i.e., the imputed income is offset by a deduction for the imputed payment) depends on whether R may deduct the interest. On the other hand, the corporation is not entitled to a deduction for the $10,250 payment because it is considered a dividend.

Payments for the Shareholder's Benefit. If the corporation pays the personal obligation of a shareholder, the payment may be treated as a constructive distribution. Whether the payment is ultimately treated as a distribution depends on the purpose of the expenditure. When it can be shown that the expenditure is incurred primarily for the benefit of the corporation, distribution treatment is avoided. Conversely, a constructive distribution ordinarily results when the expenditure is primarily for the benefit of the shareholder. As one might expect, it is usually difficult to ascertain the primary purpose for the outlay. Constructive distributions arising from a payment for the shareholder's benefit have been found to exist when the corporation paid the following: the shareholder's debt; charitable contributions where shareholders or their relatives receive benefits from the charity; the shareholder's expenses for financial and accounting services; and the payment of the shareholder's travel and entertainment expenses.

Shareholder Use of Corporate Property. Constructive distributions can also occur when a shareholder uses corporate property for personal purposes at no cost. The most common distribution in this category is use of the company car. Of course, use of other company-owned property such as boats, airplanes, and entertainment facilities, including hunting lodges, also risks distribution treatment. Distributions of this type are typically avoided by having the shareholder reimburse the corporation for any personal use of the property or by including the value of such benefits in the shareholder's income as compensation.

Bargain Purchases. Corporations often allow shareholders to purchase corporate property at a price less than the property's fair market value. These so-called bargain purchases (to be distinguished from qualified employee discounts) are treated as constructive distributions to the extent the fair market value of the property exceeds the amount paid for the property by the shareholder.

DISTRIBUTIONS OF STOCK AND STOCK RIGHTS

As previously mentioned, corporate distributions of its own stock—commonly referred to as stock dividends—are not governed by the property distribution rules discussed above. Due to the unique characteristics of stock dividends, Congress has created a special set of rules prescribing their treatment. These provisions, currently found in § 305, are the product of many controversies over stock dividends that began early in tax history.

STOCK DIVIDENDS:
A HISTORICAL PERSPECTIVE

The Revenue Act of 1913, the first tax statute, provided no information on whether stock dividends were taxable. As a result, the government attempted to tax stock dividends under the all-inclusive definition of income. Although they succeeded in the lower courts, the Supreme Court ruled in *Towne v. Eisner* that a stock dividend was not income under the 1913 Act.[44] Congress attempted to address the problem in the Revenue Act of 1916 by requiring the taxation of all dividends. Shortly thereafter, however, the Supreme Court, in the landmark case of *Eisner v. Macomber*, ruled that the provisions of the 1916 Act were unconstitutional where a corporation made a distribution of common on common.[45] Congress responded to this decision by providing in the Revenue Act of 1921 that stock dividends were nontaxable. This general rule still exists today in § 305.

The general rule, as originally authored by the Supreme Court, was based on the theory that "a stock dividend really take[s] nothing from the property of the corporation and add[s] nothing to that of the shareholder."[46] This rationale still represents the guiding principle for determining the taxability of a stock dividend. When a corporation distributes its own stock, it is not distributing an asset of the business; indeed, the corporation's assets remain completely intact. On the shareholder side, assuming all shareholders receive their proportionate share of the stock distributed, they have essentially received nothing because their interest in corporate assets remains unchanged. Since the net effect is to leave both the corporation and the shareholder in the same economic position as they held prior to the distribution, the stock dividend—a misnomer in this case—is nontaxable. Note, however, that when the distribution is not pro rata (i.e., not all shareholders received their proportionate share of the distribution), the shareholders' interests have been altered, thus suggesting an alternative tax treatment.

Over the years, the general rule excluding all stock dividends from tax has been modified to prohibit sophisticated schemes designed by management to satisfy the desires of their shareholders. For example, absent a special rule, the corporation could distribute cash to some shareholders and stock to others and the stock distribution would escape tax even though the interests of the shareholders have changed dramatically. In this case, the shareholders who received stock have exchanged immediate returns of ordinary income for possible capital gain. To prohibit this and other possibilities, Congress has provided that certain types of stock dividends are taxable. The specific provisions applying to stock dividends are discussed below.

---

[44] *Henry R. Towne v. Eisner*, 1 USTC ¶14, 3 AFTR 2959, 245 U.S. 418 (USSC, 1918).

[45] 1 USTC ¶32, 3 AFTR 3020, 252 U.S. 189 (USSC, 1920).

[46] *Ibid.*

NONTAXABLE DISTRIBUTIONS
OF STOCK AND RIGHTS

Subject to five exceptions considered below, § 305 provides that gross income does not include distributions of stock of the distributing corporation. Similarly, when a corporation distributes rights to acquire its own shares, the distribution is nontaxable. The sole effect of a nontaxable distribution of stock or rights concerns the shareholder's basis.

Basis of Distributed Stock: Nontaxable Distribution. If the distribution of stock is nontaxable, only the shareholder's basis *per share* is altered. Specifically, the shareholder must allocate a portion of the basis of the original stock to the distributed stock. Technically, the basis is allocated between the "old" and "new" stock in proportion to the relative fair market values of the old and new stock on the date of distribution, as illustrated in Exhibit 3-7.[47] When the old shares are identical to the new shares, however, the basis for each share is simply determined by dividing the basis of the old stock by the total number of shares held by the shareholder after the distribution. Since the cost basis of the old shares effectively carries over to the new shares, the holding period of the old shares also carries over to the new shares.[48] Thus, the shareholder is treated as holding the new stock for the same period as the old stock.

> **Example 23.** B owns 30 shares of XYZ Corporation common stock which she acquired on December 4, 1984 for $900. On May 1, 1991, the corporation declared a 3 for 2 stock split for common shareholders. [Note that this split is the equivalent of a 50% stock dividend ([3 − 2] ÷ 2)]. As a result, B received 15 additional shares of common stock. The common shares had a value of $40 on the date of distribution. Each of the 45 shares held after the distribution has a basis of $20 per share, determined as follows:
>
> $$\frac{\text{Basis in old stock}}{\substack{\text{Number of shares} \\ \text{after distribution}}} = \frac{\$900}{45} = \$20 \text{ per share}$$

The holding period for both the old and new shares begins on December 4, 1984, the acquisition date of the original stock.

If the nontaxable stock distribution consists of shares that are not identical to the original shares, the basis allocation using relative values as shown in Exhibit 3-7 must be used.

---

[47] § 307.   [48] § 1223(b).

Exhibit 3-7
Basis of Stock and Rights Received
in Nontaxable Distribution

Basis of Stock:

Step 1:   Determine total fair market value (FMV) of old and new stock.

FMV of old stock.......................... $xx,xxx
+ FMV of new stock received .... xx,xxx

Total FMV of stock........................ $xx,xxx

Step 2:   Allocate original basis of old stock between old and new stock according to relative FMVs.

$$\frac{\text{FMV of old stock}}{\text{Total FMV of stock}} \times \begin{array}{c}\text{Original basis} \\ \text{of old stock}\end{array} = \begin{array}{c}\text{New basis} \\ \text{of old stock}\end{array}$$

$$\frac{\text{FMV of new stock}}{\text{Total FMV of stock}} \times \begin{array}{c}\text{Original basis} \\ \text{of old stock}\end{array} = \begin{array}{c}\text{Basis of new} \\ \text{stock received}\end{array}$$

Basis of Rights:

Step 1:   Determine total fair market value (FMV) of old stock and the rights received.

FMV of old stock.......................... $xx,xxx
+ FMV of rights received .... xx,xxx

Total FMV of stock and rights .... $xx,xxx

Step 2:   If FMV of rights ≥ (15% of value of stock), allocation of basis between old stock and rights required; otherwise elective.

Step 3:   Allocate original basis of old stock between old and new rights received according to relative FMVs.

$$\frac{\text{FMV of old stock}}{\begin{array}{c}\text{FMV of stock} \\ \text{and rights}\end{array}} \times \begin{array}{c}\text{Original basis} \\ \text{of old stock}\end{array} = \begin{array}{c}\text{New basis} \\ \text{of old stock}\end{array}$$

$$\frac{\text{FMV of rights}}{\begin{array}{c}\text{FMV of stock} \\ \text{and rights}\end{array}} \times \begin{array}{c}\text{Original basis} \\ \text{of old stock}\end{array} = \begin{array}{c}\text{Basis of new} \\ \text{rights received}\end{array}$$

Example 24. Assume the same facts as in *Example 23*, except that the 15 shares received were preferred stock worth $160 per share. The basis allocation is computed as follows:

Step 1: Determine total fair market value (FMV) of old and new stock.

FMV of old stock (30 shares × $40)	$1,200
+ FMV of new stock received	
(15 shares × $160)	2,400
Total FMV of stock	$3,600

Step 2: Allocate original basis of old stock between old and new stock according to relative FMVs.

$$\frac{\text{FMV of old stock}}{\text{Total FMV of stock}} \times \begin{array}{c}\text{Original basis}\\ \text{of old stock}\end{array} = \begin{array}{c}\text{New basis}\\ \text{of old stock}\end{array}$$

$$\frac{\$1,200}{\$3,600} \times \$900 = \$300$$

$$\frac{\text{FMV of new stock}}{\text{Total FMV of stock}} \times \begin{array}{c}\text{Original basis}\\ \text{of old stock}\end{array} = \begin{array}{c}\text{Basis of new}\\ \text{stock received}\end{array}$$

$$\frac{\$2,400}{\$3,600} \times \$900 = \$600$$

The revised basis of the common stock is $300 while the basis of the preferred stock is $600. The holding periods of both the common stock and the preferred stock begin on December 4, 1984.

Stock Rights. The treatment of nontaxable distributions of rights follows the pattern designed for nontaxable distributions of stock. As a general rule, the shareholder must allocate the basis of the original stock between the stock and the rights in proportion to their relative fair market values. The formula for allocating the basis of the original stock is shown in Exhibit 3-7. As indicated there (Step 2), however, if the fair market value of the rights is less than 15 percent of the fair market value of the stock as of the date of distribution, the basis of the rights is zero *unless* the shareholder elects to make the normal allocation.[49] The election must be filed with the shareholder's return for the year in which the rights are received.[50] Failure to properly make the election results in a zero basis for the rights. If the basis allocation is made, the holding period of the original stock carries over to the rights. If the rights are subsequently exercised to purchase stock, the holding period of the acquired stock begins on the date of acquisition.

---

[49] § 307(b)(1).   [50] Reg. § 1.307-2.

A shareholder who receives stock rights has three alternatives with respect to their use: (1) the rights may be sold, in which case the gain or loss is measured using the basis that was assigned to the rights; (2) the rights may be exercised, in which case any basis assigned to the rights is added to the basis of the stock acquired with the rights; or (3) the rights may lapse, in which case any basis that may have been assigned to the rights reverts back to the original stock—in other words, a loss cannot be created by allocating basis to the rights and then allowing them to lapse.[51]

> **Example 25.**   T Corporation distributed nontaxable stock rights to its shareholders on January 3. C received 100 rights on the 100 shares of common stock he purchased three years ago for $1,000. On the date of distribution, T Corporation's common stock had a value of $15 per share and the rights had a value of $5 each. On March 1, C sold the rights for $7 each. The stock had a value of $17 per share on March 1. C is required to allocate his stock basis between the stock and the rights because the value of the rights is at least 15% of the value of the stock ($500 ÷ $1,500 = 33%). The allocation is based on the relative fair market values of the stock and the rights as of January 3, the date of the distribution. The March 1 value of the stock is irrelevant. The basis allocation is computed as follows:

Step 1:	FMV of C's common stock (100 × $15)...............	$1,500
	FMV of C's stock rights (100 × $5)...................	500
	Total FMV of stock and stock rights..................	$2,000

$$(a) \quad \frac{\text{FMV of C's common stock}}{\text{Total FMV of stock and stock rights}} \times \text{Old basis}$$

$$\frac{\$1,500}{\$2,000} \times \$1,000 = \underline{\$750} \text{ ($7.50 per share)}$$

$$(b) \quad \frac{\text{FMV of C's stock rights}}{\text{Total FMV of stock and stock rights}} \times \text{Old basis}$$

$$\frac{\$500}{\$2,000} \times \$1,000 = \underline{\$250} \text{ ($2.50 per stock right)}$$

C's gain on the sale of his stock rights is computed as follows:

Selling price of stock rights (100 × $7).............	$700
Less: Basis in stock rights.......................	250
Gain on sale of stock rights.......................	$450

---

[51]   Reg. § 1.307-1(a).

Example 26. Assume the same facts as in *Example 25*, except that C does not sell the stock rights, but allows them to lapse on June 1. Since the stock rights lapsed, rather than being exercised or sold, there is no basis allocated to them. C has no recognized loss (since the rights have no basis) and the basis of the old shares remains $1,000.

Example 27. Assume the same facts as in *Example 25*, except that the fair market values of the stock and rights on January 3 were $19 and $1, respectively. Since the total value of the rights ($100) is less than 15% of the value of the stock (15% of $1,900 = $285), no allocation is required. C would have a $700 gain on the sale of the stock rights since their basis was zero. The gain would be long-term because the holding period of the rights includes the holding period of the stock.

Example 28. Assume the facts from *Example 27*, except that C elected to allocate basis between the stock and the stock rights. The basis of the rights is computed as follows:

$$\frac{\text{FMV of stock rights}}{\text{FMV of stock and stock rights}} \times \text{Old basis}$$

$$\frac{(100 \text{ rights} \times \$1)}{(100 \text{ rights} \times \$1) + (100 \text{ shares} \times \$19)} \times \$1,000 \text{ Old basis}$$

$$\frac{\$100}{\$2,000} \times \$1,000 = \underline{\underline{\$50}} \text{ basis in stock rights}$$

In this situation, the sale of the rights for $700 would result in a $650 gain ($700 − $50).

Effect on Distributing Corporation. Nontaxable stock or right distributions have no effect on the distributing corporation. The corporation recognizes no gain or loss.[52] In addition, in contrast to the capitalization of earnings required for financial accounting purposes, E&P of the distributing corporation is unchanged.[53]

---

[52] § 311(a)(1). [53] § 312(d).

TAXABLE STOCK DIVIDENDS

As noted above, five exceptions contained in § 305 require the taxation of certain stock dividends. When these exceptions apply, the stock or right distributions become subject to the special rules governing property distributions discussed above.[54] With respect to the shareholder's treatment of the distribution, the *amount* of the distribution is the fair market value, regardless of whether the shareholder is a corporation or an individual.[55] Of course, the amount of the distribution is treated as a dividend to the extent it is considered out of E&P. The shareholder's basis of the stock is its fair market value and the holding period begins on the date of distribution. With respect to the effect of the taxable distribution on the corporation, the corporation recognizes no gain or loss.[56] However, the corporation does reduce E&P by the fair market value of the taxable stock or rights distributed at the time of distribution.

The distributions selected for taxation reflect the basic principle first announced in *Eisner v. Macomber*: distributions that do not alter the proportionate interests of the shareholders are tax-free, while those that do are taxable. The taxable stock and right distributions are[57]

1. *Distributions in Lieu of Money:* Distributions in which the shareholder may elect to receive the corporation's stock or other corporate property

2. *Disproportionate Distributions:* Distributions in which some shareholders receive property and the other shareholders receive an increase in their proportionate share of corporate assets or E&P

3. *Distributions of Common and Preferred Stock:* Distributions in which some common shareholders receive common stock while other common shareholders receive preferred stock

4. *Distributions on Preferred Stock:* Any distribution *on* preferred stock, *other than* an increase in the conversion ratio of convertible preferred stock made solely to take into account a stock dividend or stock split with respect to the stock to which the convertible may be converted

5. *Distributions of Convertible Preferred Stock:* Distributions of convertible preferred stock unless it is established that they are not substantially disproportionate

In addition to these taxable distributions, dividend income may arise from a variety of other events (e.g., a change in the redemption or conversion price) affecting the corporation's outstanding stock.[58] A complete discussion of these rules is beyond the scope of this book.

---

[54]   § 305(b).

[55]   Reg. § 1.305-1(b).

[56]   § 311(a).

[57]   § 305(b)(1) through (5).

[58]   § 305(c).

TAX PLANNING

As may be apparent from previous reading, the corporate entity offers many tax advantages. For example, corporate tax rates historically have been substantially lower than individual tax rates. Indeed, the difference between corporate and individual tax rates has ranged as high as 64 percentage points in the short history of our income tax (see Exhibit 3-8). This disparity alone has caused many taxpayers to operate their businesses in the corporate form to avoid high individual tax rates. Although this trend was reversed in 1987, there is some question as to how long the new relationship will endure. In any event, the corporation, as a separate taxable entity, still serves as a means to split income. By splitting income between the taxpayer and one or more corporations, the taxpayer can minimize the tax rate that applies to such income.

Exhibit 3-8
Individual and Corporate Tax Rates:
A Comparison of the Top Marginal Rates

Year	Individual Rate (%)	Corporate Rate (%)	Difference
1934–35	63	13.75	49.25
1936–37	79	15	64
1938–39	79	19	60
1940	79	22.1	56.9
1941	81	31	50
1942–43	88	40	48
1944–45	90	40	50
1946–47	85.5	38	47.5
1948–49	77	38	39
1950	80	42	38
1951	87.2	50.75	36.45
1952–53	88	52	36
1954–63	87	52	35
1964	77	50	27
1965–78	70	48	22
1979–81	70	46	24
1982–86	50	46	4
1987	38.5	40	(1.5)
1988–90	28	34	(6.0)
1991	31	34	(3.0)

Example 29.   J is married and files a joint return. This year, J's sole proprietorship had net income of $100,000 before taxes. Ignoring the availability of any deductions or exemptions, J's personal tax liability based on a joint return for 1990 is $25,234. If J incorporates the business and draws a salary of $50,000, he will pay an individual tax of only $9,976. The balance of the income, $50,000 ($100,000 − $50,000) is taxed to the corporation. The 1990 corporate tax on such income is $7,500. As a result, the total tax paid on the $100,000 income is $17,476 ($7,500 + $9,976). By splitting the income between the corporation and himself, J has saved taxes of $7,758 ($25,234 − $17,476).

In addition to the potential for income splitting, other advantages are obtained by incorporation. For instance, the dividends-received deduction and certain nontaxable fringe benefits (including health and life insurance) are available only through use of the corporate form. Whenever the corporate form is used, however, the potential for double taxation exists. Thus, much of the planning related to corporate taxation involves capitalizing on the attractions of the corporate entity while at the same time avoiding or at least reducing the double tax penalty. In short, the obvious aim of most planning concerned with distributions has been to devise ways of extracting earnings from the corporation without suffering the double taxation penalty resulting from dividend treatment. It should be emphasized, however, that when the *shareholder* is a corporation, dividend treatment is generally preferable because of the dividends-received deduction.

AVOIDING DISTRIBUTIONS OUT OF EARNINGS AND PROFITS

Since a distribution is taxable as a dividend only to the extent it is made out of earnings and profits, dividend treatment can be avoided simply by making the distribution when the corporation does not have E&P.

Example 30.   Z Corporation has a deficit in both accumulated and current E&P for the current year. Despite recent losses, it expects operations to become profitable next year. Assuming the corporation plans to make a distribution, timing is critical. Given its projections, a distribution in the current year would be a return of capital, while a distribution in the following year would be taxable as a dividend to the extent of the corporation's current E&P for that year.

As the above example illustrates, dividend treatment was avoided by making the distribution when the corporation did not have E&P. Similar results can be obtained if the corporation eliminates E&P prior to the distribution. One way E&P can be eliminated at little or no cost is by distributing property that has a high basis but a low market value.

Example 31. T Corporation has no current E&P but has accumulated E&P of $40,000. If T distributes property with a market value of $1,000 and a basis of $40,000, the E&P would be totally eliminated at the cost of a tax on a dividend of only $1,000. This advantage is secured because E&P is reduced by the basis of any property distributed, while the amount of the dividend is the property's market value. Note that a subsequent cash distribution would not be a dividend because the property distribution wiped out E&P. Although this technique eliminates E&P, its cost may be prohibitive because the $39,000 loss realized on the property distribution is not recognized and would forever be lost.

The IRS has provided yet another method for eliminating E&P. As previously explained, current E&P is normally allocated pro rata to all distributions during the year. In Revenue Ruling 69-440, however, the Service carved out an exception when there are different classes of stock, such as common and preferred.[59] In this Ruling, the IRS held that current E&P is allocated first to distributions on stock on which dividends must be paid before dividends can be paid on other classes of stock. This Ruling can be used to obtain significant savings when the preferred shareholders are corporations and the common shareholders are noncorporate taxpayers.

Example 32. X Corporation has common and preferred stock outstanding. According to the terms of the preferred stock, it is entitled to its rightful share of dividends before any dividends may be paid on the common. Y Corporation owns all of the preferred stock. The common stock is held by H, an individual. X has current E&P of $100,000 and a deficit in accumulated E&P. X distributes $150,000 during the year, $100,000 to Y as required and $50,000 to H. Because Y has priority regarding distributions, the entire $100,000 is a dividend. However, because Y is a corporation, it is entitled to use the dividends-received deduction in computing the tax on the dividend. On the other hand, the distribution to H is a nontaxable return of capital since all of the E&P has been allocated to the distribution on preferred. In effect, Y Corporation has been used to siphon off the E&P of X at virtually no cost because of the dividends-received deduction.

NONDIVIDEND DISTRIBUTIONS

Double taxation also can be avoided to the extent the corporation makes deductible payments either directly or indirectly to its shareholders. The best examples of such payments—which in effect are distributions—are those that are nontaxable to the shareholder-employee but are immediately deductible by the corporation. For example, the corporation can establish a medical reimbursement plan that pays the medical expenses of its shareholders. In the context of a one-person corporation, this is an extremely valuable benefit because the payment is

---

[59]   1969-2 C.B. 46.

nontaxable to the shareholder-employee. Moreover, the corporation is entitled to deduct all of the payment, which, if made by the shareholder-employee, could be deducted only to the extent it exceeded 7.5 percent of adjusted gross income. Similar advantages can be obtained for group-term life insurance, group legal services, meals and lodging, employee death benefits, and other employee fringe benefits.

In addition, the corporation could pay expenses that benefit the shareholder personally. For example, travel and entertainment may be primarily for the benefit of the corporation but also indirectly benefit the shareholder-employee. In effect, the ability to deduct the costs of country club memberships, tickets for sporting events and the theater, sumptuous dining, travel, and other perquisites for the shareholder-employee provides a means to extract earnings from the corporation at no tax cost. Clearly, combining business with pleasure has its rewards. In making such payments, however, the parties must be concerned with the possibility that the IRS may prescribe dividend treatment for the transaction. In the case of nonstatutory fringe benefits that the shareholder-employee *indirectly* receives, dividend treatment is usually avoided if it can be shown that the expenditure was undertaken primarily for the benefit of the corporation rather than for the shareholder.

Charitable contributions by closely held corporations illustrate the dilemma the IRS faces in determining whether the payments primarily benefit the corporation or the shareholders. It seems that charitable contributions made by a closely held corporation, which is effectively the alter ego of its shareholders, clearly benefit the shareholder rather than the corporation. Nevertheless, in a private letter ruling, the IRS has held that no benefit inures to the shareholder—and thus no dividend—unless the contribution by the corporation satisfies the shareholder's charitable pledge.[60] Given this interpretation, for the charitably minded owner, earnings are easily obtained from the corporation without penalty as long as the taxpayer has no obligation to make a charitable contribution.

The second category of corporate payments that avoid dividend treatment are those that are deductible but tax deferred. This next best alternative consists primarily of payments to qualified pension and profit sharing plans. Contributions to these plans on behalf of the shareholder-employee are immediately deductible by the corporation but not taxable until the shareholder-employee receives the benefits. More importantly, the earnings on the contributions are not taxed until distributed. Contributions to qualified plans essentially provide another means to secure the earnings of the corporation without double taxation, since the contributions are working for the shareholder-employee's benefit. Moreover, subject to limitations, the shareholder-employee can borrow from these plans. In so doing, the shareholder is paying interest to himself or herself, thus compounding interest tax-free for later distribution.

---

[60]   See Letter Rul. 8152094 and *Henry J.*
       Knott, 67 T.C. 681 (1977).

The third technique for avoiding dividend treatment is making deductible payments that are taxable to the shareholder-employee. For example, the corporation may make salary payments to compensate the shareholder for services to the corporation, interest payments on loans made by the shareholders to the corporation, or payments of rent for property leased from the shareholder. In this regard, however, the parties must take care that the distributions not be considered as excessive and hence as dividends.

In the previous paragraphs, methods for obtaining corporate earnings by completely avoiding double taxation have been considered. An alternative approach is to accept double taxation but attempt to reduce the cost of the second tax. Historically, the shareholder could effectively obtain the corporation's earnings at favorable capital gains rates if the stock was sold. Unfortunately, the repeal of the capital gain deduction in 1987 appears to have eliminated this alternative.

PROBLEM MATERIALS

DISCUSSION QUESTIONS

3-1 *Distributions in General.* The Code contains an intricate scheme governing the tax consequences of a distribution by a corporation to its shareholders. This system is attributable, at least in part, to the fact that corporate distributions can assume a variety of forms.

    a.   Briefly outline the various forms or types of distributions, indicating the characteristic (or characteristics) distinguishing one from the other.

    b.   What are the principal objectives underlying the rules prescribing the treatment of corporate distributions?

3-2 *Earnings and Profits Concept.* The concept of earnings and profits serves an important role in the taxation of corporate distributions. Address each of the following:

    a.   What does E&P represent (i.e., conceptually) and what is its function?

    b.   Explain the relationship between E&P, "retained earnings," and "earned surplus."

3-3 *Sections 301 and 316: Statutory Framework.* Assuming a shareholder receives a cash distribution from a corporation, briefly explain the general rules governing the tax consequences to the shareholder.

3-4 *Reporting Corporate Distributions.* Schedule B of Form 1040 is used by individual taxpayers to report dividend and interest income. Two lines in that form require the reporting of "capital gain distributions" and "nontaxable distributions," respectively. To what does each of these lines refer?

3-5 *E&P Computation in General.* Briefly explain the following:

    a.   How is current E&P computed (i.e., the general formula)?

    b.   How is accumulated E&P computed?

    c.   Why is there a need to distinguish between current and accumulated E&P?

3-6 *Distributions: Operating Rules.* Indicate whether the following statements are true or false. If the statement is false, explain why.

    a.   Since most corporations make distributions only when they are profitable and then only to the extent of their current earnings, there generally is no need to compute accumulated E&P.

    b.   A distribution made during a year when the corporation has neither accumulated E&P nor current E&P cannot be a dividend.

    c.   Assuming R Corporation has $50,000 of accumulated E&P at the beginning of its second year of operations, a distribution of $10,000 will have the same effect to the shareholder whether it is made in the first year or second year of operations.

d.   A corporation with a deficit in accumulated E&P that substantially exceeds current E&P cannot make a dividend distribution.

e.   If a corporation makes four equal distributions, each of which exceeds current E&P of $10,000 and accumulated E&P of $0, the amount of the first distribution that constitutes a dividend will exceed the amount of the last distribution that constitutes a dividend. Assume all distributions are made during one taxable year.

f.   If a corporation makes four equal distributions, each of which exceeds current E&P of $10,000 and accumulated E&P of $5,000, the amount of the first distribution that constitutes a dividend will exceed the amount of the last distribution that constitutes a dividend. Assume all distributions are made during one taxable year.

3-7   *Property Distribution: "Amount."*   When a corporation makes a distribution of property, the "amount" of the distribution must be determined to ascertain the distribution's effect on the shareholder. Briefly explain the rules for determining the "amount" of a property distribution.

3-8   *Property Distributions: Effect on Corporate Taxable Income.* Code § 311 contains the general rule governing the tax consequences to corporations on distributions of property. According to this rule, does a corporation usually recognize gain or loss on distributions of property? Explain.

3-9   *Property Distributions and Liabilities.*   Corporations sometimes distribute property encumbered by a liability. Indicate whether the following are true or false, and if false, explain why.

a.   The liability has no effect on the amount of the dividend to be reported by the shareholder.

b.   The liability has no effect on the shareholder's basis for the property.

c.   Distributing the liability increases the corporation's E&P.

3-10   *Property Distributions: Effect on E&P.*   When a corporation makes a distribution of property, a series of adjustments may be required.

a.   Is E&P ever increased as a result of a property distribution? If so, explain why.

b.   As a general rule, by what amount is E&P reduced when property is distributed?

c.   As a practical matter, when can this general rule be relied upon? Explain.

3-11   *Constructive Distributions.*   The rules governing corporate distributions apply only to distributions paid *with respect to the shareholder's stock*. Can the distribution rules cause dividend treatment in the absence of a formal corporate resolution declaring a dividend? Explain.

3-12   *Stock Dividends.*   As a general rule, stock dividends are nontaxable. However, like so many general rules in the Code, this one is also subject to exceptions.

a.   Why are stock dividends usually nontaxable?

b.   Under what circumstances will stock dividends be taxable? Include in your answer the reason why taxation results.

c.   Are distributions of rights to purchase stock of the distributing corporation treated in the same manner as stock dividends?

PROBLEMS

3-13   *E&P Computation.*   For its current taxable year, K Corporation, a manufacturer of nuts and bolts, reported the following information using the accrual method of accounting:

Income:	
Sales..	$575,000
Cost of goods sold (LIFO)............................	(175,000)
Gross profit from operations..........................	$400,000
Interest income:	
Municipal bonds....................................	9,000
Corporate bonds...................................	20,000
Dividends received...................................	10,000
Ordinary income on installment sale..................	14,000
Life insurance proceeds..............................	50,000
Expense:	
Selling and administrative expenses...................	90,000
Amortization of organization expense.................	500
Fines for overweight trucks...........................	1,000
Depreciation..	50,000
Long-term capital loss................................	3,000
Net operating loss from prior year.....................	60,000

In addition to the information above, the company's records reveal:

1.   Cost of goods sold using FIFO would have been $150,000.
2.   The installment sale income arose from the sale of land for $100,000 (basis $30,000); $20,000 cash was received this year. The income was ordinary due to previous reporting of net § 1231 losses.
3.   The dividends were received from a 30 percent owned domestic corporation.
4.   Depreciation was computed using accelerated methods; straight-line depreciation using the appropriate recovery periods would have been $37,000.
5.   Cash distributions to shareholders during the year were $12,000.
6.   Organization expense represented amortization of total organization expense of $2,500.
7.   Life insurance proceeds arose from the death of the company's chief executive officer; K Corporation had paid the premiums on a term insurance policy covering the officer.

Required:

a.   Compute K Corporation's taxable income.
b.   Compute K's current E&P.

3-14 *E&P Computation.* USC Corp. reported $600,000 of taxable income during the year. A review of the corporation's financial records revealed this additional information:

1. Taxable income included $50,000 of accelerated depreciation in excess of straight-line depreciation.
2. A short-term capital loss of $30,000 was incurred this year.
3. Gross income of the corporation included $100,000 dividends received from a 50 percent owned domestic corporation.
4. Interest income of $13,000 from bonds issued by the city of Chicago was included in the company's income reported for financial accounting purposes.
5. The corporation made contributions of $9,000 in excess of the amount currently deductible.
6. Cash distributions to shareholders during the year were $20,000.

Compute the corporation's current E&P.

3-15 *Single Cash Distributions—Deficit E&P.* The books of P Inc. and Q Inc. reveal the following information at year-end *before* each corporation makes a $25,000 cash distribution on the last day of the taxable year:

	P Inc.	Q Inc.
Capital stock	$150,000	$200,000
Current E&P (deficit)......................	30,000	(30,000)
Accumulated E&P (deficit).................	(40,000)	40,000

Compute the tax effects of each distribution for P Inc., P's shareholders, Q Inc., and Q's shareholders.

3-16 *Operating Rules: Single Cash Distribution.* F Inc. made a $50,000 distribution on February 1 of this year to its sole shareholder, H. H has a basis in her stock of $12,000. Determine the tax consequences of the distribution to H for each of the following situations:

	Accumulated E&P	Current E&P
a.	$ 6,000	$30,000
b.	(20,000)	15,000
c.	60,000	(25,550)
d.	(8,000)	(4,550)

3-17 *Operating Rules: Multiple Cash Distributions.* W Corporation was owned by C prior to a sale of all of his stock (basis at the beginning of the year, $5,000) to D in June for $10,000. During the year, W Corporation distributed $60,000 on May 1 and $40,000 on September 1. Indicate how the distributions would be treated by individual shareholders C and D in the following situations:

	Accumulated E&P	Current E&P
a.	$10,000	$50,000
b.	(70,000)	50,000
c.	95,000	(18,250)

3-18 *Multiple Cash Distributions—Positive E&P.* Z Corporation's books reveal the following information at year-end *before* cash distributions are considered:

Capital stock.............................	$100,000
Current E&P..............................	22,000
Accumulated E&P........................	32,000

M is a 10 percent shareholder whose basis for 1,000 shares is $8 per share, or $8,000 total. Compute the tax consequences to Z and M if corporate cash distributions during the year were

a. $30,000 on December 31.
b. $12,000 for each of the first two quarters and $18,000 for each of the last two quarters.

3-19 *Distribution of Appreciated Property: General Concepts.* During the year, XYZ Sand and Gravel Corporation distributed a parcel of land to its sole shareholder, A. The land (value $20,000, cost $3,000) had been used in the corporation's quarry operations.

a.   What is the effect of the distribution on the shareholder's taxable income?
b.   What is A's basis in the land?
c.   What is the effect of the distribution on XYZ's taxable income?
d.   What is the effect of the distribution on XYZ's E&P?
e.   How would your answers to (a), (b), (c), and (d) change if A were a corporation?

3-20 *Distribution of Property Subject to a Liability.* Answer Problem 3-19, assuming the property was subject to a mortgage of $7,000.

3-21 *Property Distributions: Comprehensive Problem.*   MDI Corporation is owned equally by M, an individual, and FGH Corp. MDI has $100,000 of E&P. During the year, MDI made the distributions described below. Assume that there are two of each item; thus, each shareholder received one of the items. For each distribution indicate the following:

1.   The effect of the distribution on the shareholder's taxable income;
2.   The shareholder's basis for the property received;
3.   The effect of the distribution on MDI's taxable income; and
4.   The effect of the distribution on MDI's E&P.

  a.   Land actively used by the corporation in its business since its purchase in 1982, value $5,000 (cost $1,000).
  b.   Same as (a), except the land was subject to a mortgage of $3,500.
  c.   Business equipment worth $3,000 (1981 cost, $8,000; depreciation claimed, $1,000).
  d.   MDI 10-year, 4 percent, $10,000 bond (value $8,500).

3-22 *Property Distributions: Effect on Noncorporate Shareholder.*   During the year, WRK Corp. distributed the items listed below to its sole shareholder, F, an individual. WRK has substantial E&P. For each of the distributed items, answer the following:

1.   What is the effect of the distribution on the shareholder's taxable income?
2.   What is the shareholder's basis of the property received?

  a.   A small acreage of land used in the corporation's farming business was distributed, having a value of $70,000 (basis $20,000).
  b.   Same as (a), except the acreage was subject to a mortgage of $30,000, which F assumed.
  c.   A warehouse worth $60,000 (adjusted basis $90,000). Straight-line depreciation of $10,000 had been deducted since the property's acquisition in 1981.

3-23 *Effect of Distributions: Corporate Shareholder.*   Answer Problem 3-22, assuming that F is a corporate shareholder.

3-24 *Effect of Distributions on Corporate Taxable Income.*   Indicate the effect of the distributions identified in Problem 3-22 on the corporation's taxable income, assuming that shareholder F is an individual.

3-25 *Effect of Distributions on Corporate E&P.*   Indicate the effect of the distributions identified in Problem 3-22 on the corporation's E&P, assuming that shareholder F is an individual.

3-26 *Property Distributions.* L Corporation has the following information at year-end *before* year-end property distributions are made.

Capital stock............................	$440,000
Current E&P..............................	90,000
Accumulated E&P........................	110,000

Assume L's marginal tax rate is 34 percent and its shareholders' marginal tax rate is 28 percent. The property distributed is

a. T Inc. preferred stock held as an investment by L with a $40,000 market value and a $50,000 basis;

b. Depreciable equipment with a $30,000 market value, a $45,000 cost, $20,000 accumulated depreciation, and a $25,000 basis (ignore ITC recapture); and

c. Land with a $32,000 market value, $28,000 basis, and a mortgage of $34,000.

Compute L's gain or loss and E&P *after* the distributions.

3-27 *Disguised Distributions.* SDF Corporation, a home developer, is owned equally by F and S, father and son. Briefly discuss the tax consequences arising from the following situations:

a. A review of the corporation's books reveals an account entitled "F Suspense." Closer examination discloses that the corporation debits this account for checks made payable to F. Most of these checks are cash advances to F made during the current year. The average balance of this account during the current year exceeded $20,000.

b. One of the checks charged to a suspense account maintained for S was for $6,000. The payment was for a garage that was added on to S's home to house the company car that he drives.

c. S drives a car that was purchased by the corporation and is titled in the corporation's name. S uses a credit card issued to the corporation (also in the corporation's name) by a major oil producer to purchase all of his gas and pay for miscellaneous repairs on the company car. The corporation routinely pays the credit card bill, which for this year was $3,000.

d. During the year, the corporation paid S's daughter, D, $12,000 to empty the trash and vacuum the corporate offices (about 2,000 square feet of office space) once a week.

e. The corporation added a screened-in porch to F's home at a cost of $3,500. The corporation normally charges cost plus 30 percent on projects of this type but charged F only $3,500.

f. F sold land to the corporation for $100,000. The corporation plans to develop a subdivision on the property. Similar land was available for $75,000.

3-28 *Stock Dividends: Computations.*   R owns 50 shares of A Corporation common stock, which he purchased in 1975 for $100 per share. On January 1 of the current year, A Corporation declared a dividend of one share of new preferred stock for each share of common. The shares were distributed on March 1. On that date, the common stock was selling for $150 per share and the preferred stock for $50 per share.

    a.   How much income must R recognize on the receipt of the preferred stock?

    b.   What is R's basis in the preferred stock?

    c.   On June 1, R sells 25 shares of common stock for $175 per share and 25 shares of preferred stock for $75 per share. What is R's recognized gain or loss? Is it long-term or short-term?

3-29 *Stock Dividends: Computations.*   E, an individual, has the following stock dividend information:

	Purchase Date	Stock Purchase Price	Stock Dividend	Market Price per Share at Distribution	
				Common	Preferred
a.	5/13/86	1,000 shares in S Inc., $5,000	100 shares common	$ 6	
b.	10/3/89	100 shares common in T Inc., $1,000	50 shares preferred	$15	$10
c.	11/2/90	20 shares preferred in U Inc., $1,200	2 shares preferred		$75

All stock dividends were distributed in the current year from the corporations' E&P, and all shareholders were required to receive the shares. Compute the tax effects to E for each of the three stock dividends.

3-30 *Stock Rights: Computations.*   Y Corporation's profits had taken a deep dive in recent years. To encourage purchase of its stock, the corporation issued one stock right for each share of outstanding common stock. The rights allow the holder to purchase a share of stock for $1. The common stock was selling for $1.50 when the rights were issued (June 1). The value of the stock rights on June 1 was $0.50 each. A owns 1,000 shares of common stock for which he paid $20 per share 10 years ago, and therefore received 1,000 stock rights. A sold 100 rights on July 1 for $175. He exercised 100 rights on August 1 when the stock was selling for $1.80 per share. The remaining rights lapsed on December 30.

    a.   How much dividend income must A recognize?

    b.   How much gain or loss must A recognize on the July 1 sale of the stock rights? Is it long-term or short-term?

    c.   What is A's recognized loss when the remaining rights lapse?

    d.   What is the basis of the original 1,000 shares on December 31?

3-31 *Stock Rights: Computations.* K, an individual, received 100 stock rights with a $300 (100 × $3) market value on 1,000 shares of common stock with a value of $25,000 (1,000 × $25) and a basis of $18,000. Compute the tax effects for the following situations.

    a.   K makes no special elections. He sells 25 rights for $3.50 each ($3.50 × 25 = $87.50), exercises 50 rights when the per share price is $25 plus one right (50 × $25 = $1, 250 paid), and forgot to exercise or sell the remaining 25 rights.

    b.   Same as (a) except K makes the election to allocate basis to the rights.

3-32 *Transactions Affecting E&P.* For each of the following transactions, indicate whether a special adjustment must be made in computing R Corporation's current E&P. Answer assuming that E&P has already been adjusted for current taxable income.

    a.   During the year, the corporation paid estimated Federal income taxes of $25,000 and estimated state income taxes of $10,000.

    b.   The corporation received $5,000 of interest income from its investment in tax-exempt bonds.

    c.   The corporation received a $10,000 dividend from General Motors Corporation.

    d.   The corporation purchased machinery for $9,000 and expensed the entire amount in accordance with Code § 179.

    e.   The corporation reported a § 1245 gain of $20,000.

    f.   The corporation had a capital loss carryover of $7,000 from the previous year. This year the corporation had capital gains before consideration of the loss of $10,000.

3-33 *Transactions Affecting E&P.* For each of the following transactions, indicate whether a special adjustment must be made in computing K Corporation's current E&P. Answer assuming that E&P has already been adjusted for current taxable income.

    a.   Negligence penalty of $5,000 for failure to issue Form 1099 to independent contractors.

    b.   Realized gain of $10,000 on like-kind exchange, $4,000 of which was recognized.

    c.   Distribution of formally declared dividend of $10,000 to shareholders.

    d.   Income from long-term contract completed this year as reported on completed contract basis was $70,000. Twenty percent of the work was done this year.

    e.   Charitable contribution of $12,000 in cash, of which $10,000 was deducted.

3-34 *Depreciation and E&P.* During 1991, D Corporation purchased a new light duty truck for $10,000. D computed depreciation using MACRS and deducted $2,000 of depreciation. What adjustment, if any, must be made in computing D's E&P for 1991?

3-35   *Gain for E&P.*   Using the same facts as in Problem 3-34, assume D Corporation sold the truck for $9,000 on June 30, 1992. Depreciation for 1992, using MACRS, was $1,600 ($10,000 × 32% × ½). What adjustment, if any, must be made in computing D's E&P for 1992? Assume E&P has been properly adjusted for all previous years.

RESEARCH PROBLEM

3-36   P Inc. owns all of the stock of T Corporation, which operates a chain of ice cream shops throughout the southwest. B Corp., a food conglomerate, wishes to expand into the ice cream business and is planning to acquire T. T currently has substantial cash balances. B's controller has suggested the following proposal for consummating the acquisition. Under the proposal, T distributes all of its cash to P, followed by a sale of the stock of T to B. The price of the T stock would reflect the shrinkage in T's value due to the cash distribution to P. Evaluate the proposal from the perspectives of both P and B.

Research Aid:

Rev. Rul. 75-493, 1975-2, C.B. 108.

LEARNING OBJECTIVES

Upon completion of this chapter you will be able to:

- Define a redemption and distinguish it from other types of nonliquidating distributions
- Recognize when a redemption is treated as a sale rather than a dividend
- Apply the constructive stock ownership rules to determine the effect of a redemption
- Identify the tax consequences of a redemption to shareholders, including how to:
  - Calculate the effect on shareholder taxable income
  - Calculate the shareholder's basis in any property received
  - Determine the effect on the basis of any stock held by the shareholder that was not redeemed
- Identify the tax consequences of a redemption to the distributing corporation, including how to:
  - Calculate the effect on the corporation's taxable income
  - Calculate the effect on the corporation's earnings and profits
- Identify when sales of stock to a related corporation are treated as a redemption by such corporation of its own stock
- Describe when redemptions related to paying death taxes are given sale treatment
- Define a partial liquidation and explain its tax treatment
- Explain a preferred stock bailout and the tax consequences relating to a sale or redemption of § 306 stock

CHAPTER OUTLINE

Chapter 4

CORPORATE DISTRIBUTIONS
Stock Redemptions and Partial Liquidations

In this chapter, the emphasis switches from distributions with respect to the shareholder's stock—dividend distributions—to distributions in redemption of the shareholder's stock. In form, a redemption is not complicated. A *redemption* is defined as the acquisition by a corporation of its own stock from a shareholder in exchange for property. From the shareholder's point of view, the transaction appears to be identical to a sale to a third party, warranting favorable capital gain treatment.[1] However, appearances may be deceiving. Under certain circumstances, what in form may look like a sale may in effect be no different from a dividend. Because of the significantly different tax treatment of sales and dividends (capital gain vs. ordinary income), shareholders often prefer to structure distributions from their corporations as redemptions. As one might expect, the Code does not sit idly by letting shareholders select dividend or capital gain treatment as they please. As wil be seen in this chapter, redemptions that are essentially equivalent to a dividend are treated as such. This chapter examines the problems inherent in determining how redemption distributions are taxed.

STOCK REDEMPTIONS

Before examining the tax problems associated with redemption transactions, it may be helpful to consider why shareholders redeem rather than sell their stock to a third party. Redemptions often occur for the same reasons that other sales occur. For example, the shareholder may simply desire to withdraw from the business. This situation might arise when a shareholder wishes to make an investment elsewhere or wants to retire from the business. In contrast, sale of the shareholder's interest might be prompted by his or her death. In such case, the corporation may be obligated under some type of buy-sell agreement with the shareholders to purchase the decedent's interest from the estate.

---

[1]   § 317(b).

Regardless of the circumstances, for some shareholders who wish to sell their stock, the only prospective buyer may be the corporation itself. Such a limited market typically exists when the corporation is closely held. In this setting, the other shareholders often do not have the resources to purchase the stock, yet all parties concerned do not want the stock to be sold to an outsider. When this situation arises, the corporation may have funds available to purchase all or a portion of the shareholder's stock. Similarly, if a shareholder wants to sell to a third party, the prospective buyer may have insufficient cash or other assets to make the purchase. In this case, the corporation may in effect finance the transaction in a "bootstrap acquisition," so-called because the buyer's lack of funds is supplemented by those from the corporation. In an acquisition of this type, the corporation purchases some of the shareholder's stock and the remaining shares are purchased by the outsider.

Redemption of the corporation's own stock may also be appropriate from a corporate viewpoint. From time to time, management may decide that the best use of corporate resources is to invest in itself. Redemptions of this type normally occur when management believes that the current selling price of its stock is low. Such corporate "buy backs" were common after the market crash in 1987.

Perhaps the greatest use of redemptions, at least historically, has been to extract E&P out of the corporation at a cost significantly lower than that incurred with dividends. The cost is lower because the redemption transaction is treated as a sale. Over the years, sale treatment usually has produced substantial savings since any gain would be considered favorable capital gain. In effect, the shareholder paid a cheap second tax and avoided the harsh double tax penalty normally associated with dividends. It is this possibility—that is, the potential for bailing out E&P at the cost of a capital gains tax—that necessitates a set of complex rules to distinguish whether the redemption was a true sale or merely a disguised dividend. With the elimination of the capital gains deduction in 1987, the stakes were lowered substantially. However, the reinstatement of favorable capital gain treatment in 1991 has once again placed a premium on sale treatment. In addition, sale treatment enables a shareholder to recover any basis in the stock before having to report income. Of course, capital gain treatment also is beneficial for those taxpayers with capital losses in excess of $3,000. Finally, sale treatment enables the taxpayer to use the installment sales method to lengthen the period over which any gain is reported.

In contending with the redemption provisions, it is important to remember the traditional role of dividends and capital gains in the tax arena. Tax practitioners generally equate dividends with the most undesirable tax result—*double* taxation of the same income! On the other hand, capital gain treatment has long been the taxpayer's proverbial pot of gold at the end of the tax rainbow, worthy of whatever steps are necessary to obtain it. For this reason, the area of redemptions has always been quite fertile for controversy: is the distribution a dividend or is it capital gain? In digesting the redemption rules, understand that these rules were designed when the stakes were high, and the government wanted to ensure that only deserving taxpayers were rewarded.

TREATMENT OF STOCK REDEMPTIONS:
GENERAL CONSIDERATIONS

As defined, a redemption has the same characteristics as an ordinary sale: the stock of the shareholder is *exchanged* for property of the corporation. In such case, the transaction normally would receive capital gain treatment. Upon closer scrutiny, however, the transaction may have an effect that more closely resembles a dividend than a sale. That this may be true is easily seen in the classic example in which a corporation redeems a portion of its sole shareholder's stock. Although the shareholder surrenders stock as part of the exchange, like a dividend distribution, the interest of the shareholder in corporate assets as well as the shareholder's control over corporate affairs is completely unaffected.

> **Example 1.** K Corporation has 100 shares of outstanding stock, all of which are owned by B. If K Corporation redeems 30 of B's shares, B still owns 100% of the stock outstanding. Since the redemption has not substantially affected B's interest in the corporation, the redemption distribution does not qualify for exchange treatment. Rather, it is treated as a dividend to the extent of K's E&P.

In the case of the one owner corporation as illustrated above, it is somewhat obvious that the transaction more closely resembles a dividend than a sale. Dividend treatment is not limited to this situation alone, however. The effect is similar whenever the redemption is pro rata among all shareholders (e.g., a redemption of 10% of the stock held by each shareholder) since each shareholder's interest after the transaction is the same as before. In other situations, however, it may be unclear whether the redemption should be treated as a dividend or as a sale. For example, a distribution which technically is not pro rata—and thus deserving of sale treatment—may still warrant dividend treatment if the relationships among shareholders are considered.

> **Example 2.** H and W each own 50% of the stock of KIN Corporation. If, in a non–pro rata redemption, the corporation redeems all of H's shares and none of W's shares, it is clear that H's interest has been significantly altered and that sale treatment would be appropriate. However, if H and W were husband and wife, it is easy to conclude that the redemption has had no effect on the *family's* interest in or control over the corporation.

As early as 1921, Congress recognized that the effect of a redemption may be indistinguishable from that of a dividend; consequently, Congress took action. From that time until 1954, sale treatment was granted only to redemptions which were *not essentially equivalent to a dividend*. If dividend equivalency was found, the amount paid by the corporation for the stock was taxed as a dividend to the extent that the corporation had E&P. To the dismay of all concerned, however, Congress provided no clues as to when a redemption was equivalent to a dividend.

Lacking guidance, the courts generally found dividend equivalency only when the redemption was pro rata; yet in some cases, pro rata redemptions received sale treatment when a valid business purpose for the transaction was found. As a result, the courts were barraged by redeeming shareholders hoping to establish a satisfactory purpose or to find another road to capital gain treatment.

With the enactment of the 1954 Code, Congress attempted to clarify those situations in which redemptions would qualify for sale treatment. Current law, contained in § 302, provides sale treatment for the following redemptions:

1. The redemption is not essentially equivalent to a dividend.[2]

2. The redemption is substantially disproportionate.[3]

3. The redemption is in complete termination of the shareholder's interest.[4]

4. The redemption is in partial liquidation of the distributing corporation.[5]

5. The redemption is made in order to pay death taxes.[6]

In addition, special rules exist to police so-called redemptions through related corporations:[7] sales of stock of one corporation which the shareholder controls to another corporation which the shareholder also controls. In designing all of these rules, Congress took into account the problems presented where shareholders of the corporation are related (see *Example 2* above) by enacting § 318. This provision contains "constructive ownership" rules which must be considered in determining how the shareholder's interest has been affected by the redemption.

Before proceeding with a discussion of the constructive ownership rules and each of the redemption provisions, it should be emphasized that the critical question in all cases is whether the distribution is treated as a payment in exchange for the shareholder's stock (i.e., as a sale) or a distribution of property to which § 301 applies (i.e., as a possible dividend).[8] This question is critical since other tax consequences flow from this initial determination. For example, if the redemption is treated as a distribution of property rather than as a sale, all of the rules discussed in Chapter 3 concerning property distributions under § 301 come into play.

---

[2] § 302(b)(1).

[3] § 302(b)(2).

[4] § 302(b)(3).

[5] § 302(b)(4).

[6] § 303.

[7] § 304.

[8] §§ 302(a) and (d). In the following discussion, the term "sale" is used for "distribution as payment in exchange for stock," and it is normally assumed that the sale results in capital gain rather than ordinary income treatment. Similarly, the term "dividend" is generally used to imply a distribution of property subject to § 301 even though the distribution is only a dividend to the extent it is out of E&P.

Whether the redemption is treated as a sale or a dividend, consideration must be given to the following questions in each case:

1. Is the redemption treated as a sale or as a distribution of property?

2. If the redemption qualifies as a sale, what is the gain or loss realized and recognized, and what is its character? If the redemption is treated as a distribution of property, what amount is considered dividend income and/or return of capital?

3. How is the basis of the shareholder affected?

4. What is the shareholder's basis in any property received?

5. Does the corporation recognize any gain or loss on the redemption?

6. What is the effect of redemption on the corporation's E&P?

TREATMENT OF THE SHAREHOLDER: SALE VERSUS DIVIDEND

In the following sections, the rules that must be applied to determine whether the redemption is treated as a sale or a dividend distribution are considered. Prior to exploring these rules, however, the effect on the shareholder that flows from this determination should be fully understood.

Sale or Exchange Treatment. If the redemption qualifies as a sale, the transaction is treated like any other sale of stock. The shareholder's gain or loss realized is the difference between the amount realized as paid by the corporation and the adjusted basis of the stock. The realized gain or loss normally is recognized and treated as a capital gain or loss, assuming the stock is a capital asset. However, § 267 disallows recognition of the loss if the shareholder owns more than 50 percent of the stock. When the corporation redeems the stock with property, the shareholder's basis in the property is its fair market value.

Dividend Treatment. If the redemption does not qualify for sale or exchange treatment, the *entire* amount received by the shareholder for the stock (*not* just the amount in excess of the stock's basis) is considered a property distribution and thus a dividend to the extent that it is out of E&P. In addition, all other rules related to property distributions discussed previously apply.

A somewhat confusing issue arising when the redemption is treated as a dividend concerns the basis of the stock that the shareholder has surrendered. The Regulations permit the shareholder to add the basis of the surrendered stock to the basis of the remaining shares owned by the shareholder.[9]

---

[9] When the shareholder owns no other shares in the corporation (e.g., when the interest is completely terminated), the basis is added to the shares owned by related parties whose ownership is attributed to the shareholder. See Reg. § 1.302-2(c).

Example 3. Z Corporation has 100 shares of outstanding stock, all of which are owned by R. R's basis for the shares is $10,000 or $100 per share. During the year, the corporation redeemed 20 shares of R's stock for a $25,000 note, payable in equal installments with interest over the next 10 years. If this transaction were treated as a sale, R would report a long-term capital gain of $23,000 ($25,000 − $2,000), deferred over the next 10 years using the installment method. However, since the effect of this distribution is the same as a dividend, R must report the entire amount of the note, $25,000, as dividend income this year, assuming that Z Corporation has adequate E&P. Note that R has not only lost any benefit to be derived from capital gain treatment but also the right to offset his basis against the distribution. Accordingly, R's total basis for his remaining 80 shares is $10,000. Because the distribution is treated as a dividend, R's basis in his remaining shares has increased from $100 per share to $125 per share. It should also be emphasized that without sale treatment, R cannot defer the gain over the next 10 years. Instead, he must report the entire $25,000 of dividend income this year because the distribution of the note is a distribution of property subject to all the normal distrubution rules. This treatment could produce a significant hardship for R because he has not received any cash from the transaction that could be used to pay the tax.

Although sale treatment is typically favored by noncorporate shareholders, corporate shareholders have traditionally found dividend treatment more to their liking. This preference, of course, is attributable to the dividends-received deduction available only to corporate taxpayers. For many years, ingenious corporations were able to parlay this deduction and the basis rules for redemptions to their advantage.

Example 4. As director of corporate finance of LAR Corporation, D recently learned that BIG Inc., a publicly held corporation, would be redeeming 200,000 shares of its 1 million shares outstanding for $100 per share, if tendered to BIG within the next 60 days. LAR immediately purchased 10,000 shares of BIG for $100 a share or $1 million. LAR then tendered 2,000 of the shares to BIG for exactly what it paid, receiving $200,000. Assuming the sale to BIG were treated as a *dividend*, LAR would report $60,000 [$200,000 − dividends-received deduction of $140,000 (70% × $200,000)] as income and its basis in the remaining 8,000 shares would remain at $1 million. The value of the stock immediately after the redemption was still worth $100 per share since both the assets and the number of shares outstanding declined proportionately. LAR later sold its remaining 8,000 shares for $100 per share or $800,000 and reported a capital loss of $200,000 ($800,000 − $1 million). As a result of these transactions,

LAR reported $60,000 of income and a capital loss of $200,000—in effect a $140,000 loss (assuming the short-term capital loss can be used against short-term capital gains). Note that this loss and the resulting tax savings were obtained without any real economic loss. LAR's cash outlay was $1 million—but it was totally recovered through the redemption and the sale ($200,000 + $800,000).

In 1986 Congress moved to ensure that corporations could not obtain the advantages illustrated above. For corporate taxpayers, any amount received in a redemption that is non–pro rata—yet is treated as a dividend—is treated as an *extraordinary dividend*. Similarly, any distribution a corporation receives that is in partial liquidation and is considered a dividend, is treated as an extraordinary dividend. Both of these rules operate without regard to the amount of the dividend or the period for which the stock was held.[10] As a result, the corporation must reduce its basis in its remaining stock by the untaxed portion of the dividend. To the extent that the untaxed portion of the dividend exceeds the basis of the stock, the corporate shareholder must recognize gain as if it had sold the stock. These rules are intended to prohibit corporations from engaging in arbitrage transactions similar to those discussed in Chapter 1.

> **Example 5.** Assume the same facts as in *Example 4*. Beginning in 1987, the redemption distribution received by LAR would be treated as an extraordinary dividend since it is treated as a dividend and is non–pro rata (i.e., the same proportion of stock, say 10%, was not redeemed from all shareholders). Consequently, LAR must reduce the basis of its remaining stock by the untaxed portion of the dividend, $140,000. Due to this adjustment, on the subsequent sale by LAR of the stock for $800,000, the corporation's loss is reduced to $60,000 determined as follows:
>
> | | | |
> |---|---:|---:|
> | Amount realized............................. | | $800,000 |
> | Adjusted basis: | | |
> | Original basis........................... | $1,000,000 | |
> | − Untaxed portion of the dividend...... | (140,000) | |
> | = Revised basis....................... | | (860,000) |
> | Loss recognized on sale.................... | | ($60,000) |

Note that the $60,000 loss exactly offsets the $60,000 gain reported earlier on receipt of the dividend. This treatment ensures that the tax rules reflect the economic reality that no gain or loss was actually incurred on the series of transactions.

---

[10] § 1059(e).

CONSTRUCTIVE OWNERSHIP RULES

The tests for dividend equivalency contained in the various redemption provisions generally focus on the shareholder's ownership interest in the corporation before and after the redemption to determine how that interest has been affected. As a general rule, if after the redemption the shareholder does not have control of the corporation and has had a substantial reduction in ownership, the redemption qualifies for sale treatment. As illustrated above, the relationships existing among the shareholders of the corporation must be considered in determining whether a shareholder's interest truly has been altered. Section 318 provides that in applying the ownership tests, the shareholder is treated as not only owning the shares that are actually or directly owned but also those shares of certain related parties. In other words, stock owned by one party is attributed to another party. As noted below, however, the constructive ownership rules do not apply to redemptions made in order to pay death taxes. In addition, the *family* attribution rules may be waived under certain circumstances. The attribution rules are summarized below.[11]

Attribution to Family Members. An individual is considered as owning the stock owned by his or her spouse and other family members, including children, grandchildren, and parents.[12] Note that an individual does not own the stock owned by his or her brothers, sisters, or grandparents. Stock that is attributed to one family member cannot be reattributed from that family member to another family member.[13]

> **Example 6.** H and W are married and have one son, S. These individuals, S, H, W, and W's father, F, each own 25% of D Corporation's outstanding stock. Under the attribution rules, H is considered as owning 75% of the stock [25% directly, 25% indirectly through his wife, and 25% indirectly through his son—note that H does not own the stock of his father-in-law, F, since stock attributed to one family member (W) is not reattributed to another family member]. W owns 100% of the stock (25% directly, and the other 75% indirectly through her husband, son, and father). S is considered as owning 75% of the stock (25% directly, 25% indirectly through his mother, and 25% indirectly through his father—note that S does not own the stock of his grandfather, F). F is considered as owning 75% of the stock (25% directly, 25% indirectly through his daughter W, and 25% indirectly through his grandson, S).

Entity-to-Owner Attribution. Stock owned either directly or indirectly (i.e., stock owned constructively) by an entity is generally considered as owned proportionately by those having an interest in the entity.[14]

---

[11] § 318.

[12] § 318(a)(1).

[13] § 318(a)(5)(B).

[14] § 318(a)(2).

1. *Partnerships*. Stock owned by a partnership is considered as owned proportionately by its partners (e.g., if a partner owns a 30 percent interest in the partnership, the partner owns 30 percent of whatever stock the partnership owns).[15]

2. *Estates and Trusts*. Stock owned by an estate is considered as owned proportionately by the beneficiaries of the estate.[16] A similar rule applies to trusts.[17]

3. *Corporations*. Stock owned by a corporation is considered as owned proportionately *only* by shareholders owning either directly or indirectly at least 50 percent of the corporation's stock.[18]

Example 7. R owns 60% of the stock of X Corporation and 30% of the stock of Y Corporation. The remaining 70% of Y's stock is owned by X. This ownership pattern is diagrammed below.

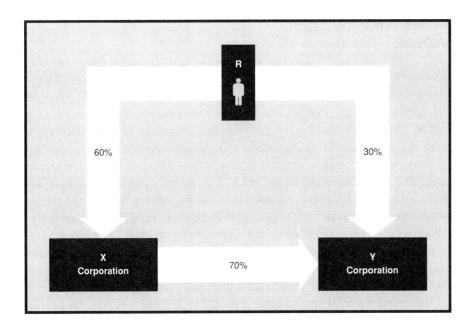

R is considered as owning 72% of Y [30% directly and 42% (60% × 70%) indirectly through X]. If R's ownership in X had been less than 50%, none of X's ownership in Y would be attributed to R, and thus R would own only 30% of Y.

---

[15] § 318(a)(2)(A). Whether stock indirectly owned by the partnership is reattributed to the partners is clarified in § 318(a)(5).

[16] *Ibid.*

[17] § 318(a)(2)(B).

[18] § 318(a)(2)(C).

Owner-to-Entity Attribution. Stock owned by those having an interest in an entity is generally attributed in *full* to the entity.[19] Thus, stock owned by a partner is considered as owned by the partnership, while stock owned by the beneficiaries of an estate is considered as owned by the estate. Stock owned by a shareholder is attributed to the corporation only if the shareholder owns either directly or indirectly at least 50 percent of the corporation. Similar rules apply to trusts.

> **Example 8.**   Same as *Example 7* above. X Corporation is considered as owning 100% of the stock of Y (70% directly and 30% indirectly through R). If R had owned less than 50% of the stock of X, X would be treated as owning only 70% of Y.

Section 318 contains several other rules clarifying problems concerning reattribution and options that must be considered when applying the constructive ownership rules in practice.[20]

REDEMPTIONS NOT EQUIVALENT TO A DIVIDEND: § 302(b)(1)

Although the 1954 Code made substantial changes in the redemption provisions, as in prior law, a subjective dividend equivalency test was maintained. Section 302(b)(1) currently grants sale treatment if the redemption is "not essentially equivalent to a dividend." Although the language contained in this provision is identical to that contained in its predecessor, it quickly became apparent that the two provisions were to be interpreted differently. The thrust of the new rule was initially clarified in the landmark case of *U.S. v. Maclin P. Davis*.[21] In *Davis*, the Supreme Court modified the rule of prior law, holding that a redemption would not be considered equivalent to a dividend if there is a *meaningful reduction in the shareholder's interest*. Moreover, the Court indicated that whether a valid business purpose exists for the redemption is irrelevant in determining whether the transaction should be classified as a sale or a dividend. In addition, the Court stated that the constructive ownership rules generally must be taken into account when applying the dividend equivalency test of § 302(b)(1).

---

[19]   § 318(a)(3).

[20]   §§ 318(a)(4) and (5).

[21]   70-1 USTC ¶9289, 25 AFTR2d 70-287, 397 U.S. 301 (USSC, 1970).

Because of the uncertainty of the "meaningful reduction" principle, the usefulness of § 302(b)(1) is limited. It generally serves as a last resort where shareholders seeking sale treatment cannot satisfy the other objective tests discussed below. In determining whether the meaningful reduction requirement is satisfied, the critical factor to be considered is the effect of the redemption on the shareholder's right to vote and exercise control over the corporation. For example, in one case, a taxpayer's interest dropped from 85 percent to 61.7 percent and was considered meaningfully reduced because a two-thirds majority (66⅔%) was required to authorize a merger or consolidation or to alter the articles of incorporation.[22] In another situation, where the shareholder's ownership dropped from 57 percent to 50 percent, the Service ruled that the redemption resulted in a meaningful reduction since the shareholder was no longer in control but was merely equal to the other shareholder.[23] The meaningful reduction principle has also been applied in several other situations where the shareholder failed the objective tests of §§ 302(b)(2) and (3).

SUBSTANTIALLY DISPROPORTIONATE REDEMPTIONS: § 302(b)(2)

Dissatisfaction with the subjective dividend equivalency test of Code § 302(b)(1) caused Congress to establish several situations where sale treatment is assured if certain requirements are satisfied. The first safe harbor is contained in § 302(b)(2) concerning substantially disproportionate redemptions. Under this provision, a redemption is considered substantially disproportionate and qualifies for sale treatment if each of the following conditions are met:

1. Immediately after the redemption, the shareholder owns *less than 50 percent* of the total combined voting power of all classes of stock entitled to vote.

2. Immediately after the redemption, the shareholder's *percentage* ownership of *voting* stock is *less than 80 percent* of the shareholder's *percentage* ownership immediately before the redemption.

3. Immediately after the redemption the shareholder's percentage ownership of *common* stock is *less than 80 percent* of the shareholder's percentage ownership immediately before the redemption.

Note that if the corporation has only one class of voting common stock outstanding, conditions 2 and 3 above effectively merge to become a single requirement since satisfaction of 2 also satisfies 3 and vice versa. To simplify subsequent discussion, it is assumed that the corporation's only stock outstanding is voting common.

---

[22] *William F. Wright v. U.S.,* 73-2 USTC ¶9583, 32 AFTR2d 73-5490, 482 F.2d 600 (CA-8, 1973).

[23] Rev. Rul. 75-502, 1975-2 C.B. 111.

The thrust of the substantially disproportionate test is twofold: if the shareholder is no longer in control after the redemption (50% test) and has what amounts to a 20 percent loss in ownership (80% test), the redemption has significantly altered the shareholder's interest and the transaction should receive sale treatment. Two operational aspects of this test should be emphasized. First, when applying the 80 percent test, note that it is the shareholder's *percentage* ownership that must drop below 80 percent of what it was prior to the redemption and *not* the shareholder's number of shares. Second, when applying both the 50 and 80 percent tests, the constructive ownership rules must be used.

Example 9. TNT Corp. has 100 shares of outstanding stock which are owned by three unrelated individuals as follows: A owns 60 shares, B 30 shares, and C 10 shares. During the year, TNT redeemed 15 of A's shares for $20,000. A's basis for all 60 shares was $12,000 or $200 per share. Examination of A's ownership before and after the redemption reveals the following:

	Shares Owned	
	Pre-redemption	Post-redemption
Directly.....................................	60	45
Indirectly...................................	0	0
Total owned...............................	60	45
Percentage owned.........................	60%(60÷100)	53%(45÷85)

In order for the redemption to be substantially disproportionate, A's percentage ownership after the redemption must be (1) less than 50%, and (2) less than 80% of his percentage ownership before the redemption or 48% (60% × 80%). Since his post-redemption ownership of 53% exceeds the 50% threshold, the redemption does not qualify for sale treatment. Even if A's post-redemption percentage had fallen to 49%, the redemption would not be substantially disproportionate because the post-redemption percentage must drop below 48%. In this regard, note that A's stock ownership after the redemption, 45 shares, is less than 80% of the *number of shares* that he owned before the redemption, 48 shares (60 × 80%). This is irrelevant, however; it is his *percentage ownership* in TNT that must be considered.

Since the redemption does not qualify for sale treatment, the entire $20,000 distribution is treated as a dividend assuming TNT had adequate E&P. The basis of the 15 shares redeemed is added to the basis of the 45 shares A continues to hold. Thus his total basis remains as $12,000 but his per-share basis has increased from $200 per share to $267 per share ($12,000 ÷ 45).

Example 10.   Assume the same facts as in *Example 9* above, except that TNT redeems 30 shares. A's post-redemption percentage ownership is now 43% [30 ÷ (100 − 30)]. Since the post-redemption percentage is less than 50% *and* less than 80% of what he owned before (48%), the redemption qualifies for sale treatment. Thus, A recognizes a capital gain of $14,000 ($20,000 amount realized − $6,000 basis in the 30 shares redeemed). The basis in the remaining 30 shares is still $200 per share or $6,000 in total.

Example 11.   Assume the same facts as in *Example 10* above, except that C is A's 70% owned corporation. A's ownership must be recomputed to give effect to the constructive ownership rule as follows:

	Shares Owned	
	Pre-redemption	Post-redemption
Directly......................................	60	30
Indirectly	7(70%×10)	7(70%×10)
Total owned..............................	67	37
Percentage owned.........................	67%(67÷100)	53%(37÷70)

Since A's post-redemption ownership has not fallen below 50%, the redemption does not qualify for sale treatment. Thus, the result is the same as in *Example 9* above. Had A owned only 40% of the stock in C Corporation, none of C's ownership would have been attributed to A. In such case, the redemption would qualify for sale treatment and the result would be identical to that in *Example 10* above.

REDEMPTIONS IN COMPLETE TERMINATION OF THE SHAREHOLDER'S INTEREST: § 302(b)(3)

Section 302(b)(3) provides sale treatment for redemptions that are "in complete termination of a shareholder's interest." At first glance, it appears that this provision is unnecessary since any redemption that terminates the shareholder's interest would qualify for sale treatment as a substantially disproportionate redemption. The important distinction between the two provisions concerns application of the family attribution rules. If the shareholder's *direct* interest is completely terminated, the *family* attribution rules may be waived.[24]   Thus, the termination of interest rule permits sale treatment even though the shareholder's family continues ownership of the corporation.

---

[24]   § 302(c)(2).

Example 12.   M and her daughter, D, started a corporation 15 years ago. M and D each own 50 shares of the 100 shares of stock outstanding. M now wants to retire. D wants to continue to operate the corporation by herself but has insufficient funds to purchase her mother's stock. To meet M's desires, the corporation redeems all 50 shares of M's stock. This redemption does not qualify as a substantially disproportionate distribution since M is deemed to own 100% of the stock both before and after the redemption. However, because the redemption completely terminates M's direct interest, she may elect to waive the family attribution rules. If the election is made, none of D's stock is attributed to M and the redemption qualifies for sale treatment.

The family attribution rules may generally be waived only if the redeeming shareholder is willing to totally sever his or her interest in the corporation. In order to waive the attribution rules the following conditions must be satisfied:[25]

1.   The shareholder must not retain any interest in the corporation except as a creditor. The statute expressly prohibits the shareholder from continuing as an officer, director, or employee.

2.   The shareholder cannot acquire any interest in the corporation for at least 10 years from the date of the redemption. The sole exception to this prohibition is stock that is acquired by bequest or inheritance.

3.   The shareholder must file an agreement with the IRS which indicates that the shareholder will notify the Service if a prohibited interest is acquired within the 10-year period. The agreement must be attached to the return for the year in which the redemption occurs.

Whether the redeeming shareholder is considered to have acquired the so-called prohibited interest may be unclear in some instances. The IRS generally considers the performance of any type of service to be an acquisition of an interest notwithstanding the fact that the shareholder is not compensated.[26] As a result, a former shareholder may be at risk whenever he or she is asked for counsel.

Entities are also permitted to waive the family attribution rules that might otherwise prohibit a complete termination of their interest in the corporation. Waiver is authorized if *both* the entity and the individuals whose ownership is attributed to the entity do not have a prohibited interest.

Example 13.   H, his wife, W, and their son S, each own 25 of the 100 shares of outstanding stock of KIN Corp. The remaining 25 shares are owned by a trust established for the benefit of S. Prior to the redemption of any of the trust's shares, the trust is considered as owning all 100 shares (25 directly and 75 through S, the beneficiary of the trust; note that the stock of H and W attributed to S may be reattributed to the trust). Any redemption

---

[25]   *Ibid.*   [26]   Rev. Rul. 70-104, 1970-1 C.B. 66.

of the trust's shares would not affect the ownership of the trust, because it would still be treated as owning all of the remaining shares outstanding through S. In order to waive family attribution and thus avoid attribution of the shares of H and W to S, and reattribution to the trust, all of the shares of both S and the trust must be redeemed since neither the trust nor the beneficiary may retain an interest.

REDEMPTIONS QUALIFYING
AS PARTIAL LIQUIDATIONS

The Code also extends sale treatment to certain redemptions that occur due to a termination or a contraction of a portion of the corporation's business—a so-called partial liquidation. Sale treatment is apparently justified in this case on the theory that the redemption proceeds represent a portion *of* the shareholder's capital which was formerly employed in the business rather than a return *on* capital. Technically, Section 302(b)(4) grants sale treatment only when the redemption distribution is to a *noncorporate shareholder* and is in *partial liquidation* of the distributing corporation. A distribution is considered in partial liquidation only if[27]

1. The distribution is not essentially equivalent to a dividend; or

2. The distribution is attributable to the termination of one of two or more "qualified" businesses.

In addition to satisfying either of the above requirements, the distribution must be made pursuant to a plan and must be made within the taxable year that the plan is adopted or in the following taxable year.

Dividend Equivalency Test for Partial Liquidations. As noted above, a distribution qualifies for partial liquidation treatment if it is *not essentially equivalent to a dividend*. Although identical language appears in § 302(b)(1), as discussed previously, the Code makes it clear that the phrase is to be interpreted differently in the partial liquidation area. In determining dividend equivalency for a distribution in partial liquidation, the focus is on the distribution's effect on the distributing corporation. This is in contrast to the dividend equivalency test of § 302(b)(1) where the concern was the effect of the redemption on the shareholder.

A distribution in partial liquidation is not considered equivalent to a dividend if it is attributable to a genuine contraction of the corporation's business. The "corporate contraction theory" is illustrated in the Regulations, which use an example based on the Tax Court's decision in *Joseph W. Imler* in 1948.[28] In this case, a fire destroyed the upper two stories of a seven-story building that the corporation owned. The upper two stories had been rented in part to another company. Upon receipt of the insurance proceeds, the corporation decided it was too costly to rebuild and distributed the cash to its shareholders, one of whom

---

[27] § 302(e).

[28] 11 T.C. 836 (1948); Reg. § 1.346-1(a)(2).

was Mr. Imler. Although the government argued that the distribution to Mr. Imler should be treated as an ordinary dividend, the Tax Court held that there had been a "bona fide contraction in the business" and granted partial liquidation treatment. Unfortunately, in other situations it is often difficult to determine whether a contraction has occurred. The Service has allowed partial liquidation treatment where a full line department store was converted to a discount apparel store and there was a reduction in inventory, employees, and related items.[29] On the other hand, the Regulations indicate that the distribution of funds attributable to a reserve for an expansion program that has been abandoned does not qualify as a partial liquidation.[30]

Termination of Business.   In 1954, Congress recognized the uncertainty inherent in the dividend equivalency test and created a safe harbor where the taxpayer can be assured of sale treatment. To qualify as a partial liquidation under the safe harbor rules, a distribution must satisfy the following:

1.   The distribution must be attributable to either the corporation's ceasing to conduct a "qualified business" or must consist of the assets of a "qualified business."

2.   Immediately after the distribution, the corporation must be actively engaged in a qualified business.

Note that these two rules require the corporation to have at least *two* qualified businesses, one that is retained and another that is sold or distributed. For these purposes, a *qualified business* is a business that satisfies the following conditions:

1.   The activities in which the corporation engage constitute a business (rather than an investment).

2.   The business was conducted throughout the five-year period ending on the date of the distribution.

3.   The business was not acquired in a taxable transaction in the five-year period ending on the date of distribution.

These requirements were designed to prevent the bailout of the corporation's E&P as capital gain.

> **Example 14.**   C Inc. is owned and operated by J. Over the past several years, the corporation has accumulated cash which J would now like to obtain without suffering the double tax penalty associated with dividends. He plans to use the cash to acquire a small apartment complex which is currently under construction by T Corp. A normal redemption is unavailable since none of the standards of §§ 302(b)(1), (2), or (3) (meaningful reduction, substantially disproportionate, termination of interest) could be

---

[29]   Rev. Rul. 74-296, 1974-1 C.B. 80.   [30]   Reg. § 1.346-1(a)(2).

satisfied. As an alternative, J has suggested that he could cause the corporation to purchase the apartment building, operate it for a short time, then distribute the building in partial liquidation of some of his shares. This transaction, however, would not meet the safe harbor tests for partial liquidations for several reasons: the apartment project would be acquired in a taxable transaction within five years of the distribution; the project may not be considered a business but rather investment property; and the project activities will have been conducted for less than five years prior to the distribution.

As the above example illustrates, the safe harbor tests prevent the corporation from purchasing assets desired by the shareholder and subsequently distributing them with the hope that such distributions would be considered in partial liquidation and thus qualify for capital gain treatment. The rules do enable legitimate contractions to qualify for capital gain treatment, however.

Example 15. C Corporation was organized in 1982 to manufacture video games. The corporation was immediately successful and diversified by purchasing from Q Corporation a small computer company in 1984. By 1991, the profitability in the video game market had become nominal, and C sold the entire business to a competitor who continued to market games under C's name. C distributed the proceeds from the sale to its shareholders in redemption of 5% of their stock. The distributions qualify for partial liquidation treatment since all of the conditions are satisfied; that is, the distribution was attributable to the termination of an active business (video business) that had not been acquired in a taxable transaction in the five years prior to the distribution and that had been conducted for at least five years. In addition, the corporation retained an active computer business which had not been acquired in a taxable transaction in the five years prior to the distribution and which had been conducted for at least five years.

Example 16. Same facts as in *Example 15* above, except assume that C had acquired the computer company from Q in 1988 in an exchange qualifying for nonrecognition under § 351 concerning transfers to controlled corporations. In addition, assume Q had operated the computer business since 1979. The distribution still satisfies all of the conditions for partial liquidation treatment. The acquisition of the computer company within five years of the distribution is permissible since it was acquired in a nontaxable transaction. Note that the distributed business must qualify *and* that the corporation must have at least one retained business that qualifies. Also note that the distributing corporation need not operate the business for five years. It is sufficient if it was conducted by anyone for five years.

The tests for determining whether a group of activities constitutes a qualified trade or business are virtually identical to those pertaining to the active business requirement, contained in § 355, relating to corporate divisions discussed in Chapter 7. Additional aspects of these tests are considered in that discussion.

Effect of Partial Liquidation on Shareholders. As noted above, if the distribution qualifies as a partial liquidation, a noncorporate shareholder is entitled to sale treatment. Corporate shareholders, however, are not eligible for partial liquidation treatment. Thus, such a redemption distribution to a corporate shareholder is subject to the other tests of § 302(b). Similarly, if the distribution does not qualify as a partial liquidation for a noncorporate shareholder, the distribution is also governed by the other redemption provisions of §§ 302(b) or 303. Note that in the case of a corporate shareholder, if the distribution is treated as a dividend, it is treated as an extraordinary dividend.[31]

> **Example 17.** S, an individual, and LJK Inc. each own 50 of the 100 outstanding shares of PLQ Corporation stock. Both S and LJK have a basis of $5,000 ($100 per share) for their stock, which they have held for 15 years. PLQ has manufactured shirts and ties for 25 years. This year it sold the tie portion of the business. In a transaction qualifying as a partial liquidation, PLQ redeemed 20 shares of stock from both S and LJK for $20,000. PLQ has substantial E&P. Since the redemption qualifies as a partial liquidation, S, the noncorporate shareholder, is treated as having sold her stock. Thus, she reports capital gain of $18,000 [$20,000 − ($100 × 20)]. On the other hand, LJK does not receive sale treatment since it is not a noncorporate shareholder. Thus the treatment of LJK's distribution must be determined under the other tests of § 302. Since LJK's ownership after the distribution is not less than 50% (30 ÷ 60), the redemption is not substantially disproportionate and thus it is treated as a dividend. Consequently, LJK reports a dividend of $20,000 which is eligible for the 80% dividends-received deduction. However, the dividend is also treated as an extraordinary dividend. As such, LJK is required to reduce its basis in the stock by the untaxed portion of the dividend, $16,000 (80% × $20,000). Since the basis reduction of $16,000 exceeds LJK's original basis of $5,000, LJK is required to report—in addition to the dividend income—gain from the sale of stock of $11,000 ($16,000 − $5,000).

---

[31]   § 1059(e).

REDEMPTIONS TO PAY DEATH TAXES: §303

In § 303, Congress carves out yet another situation where sale treatment is guaranteed. Under § 303, a redemption of stock that has been included in the decedent's gross estate generally qualifies for sale treatment if the stock's value represents a substantial portion of the value of the estate. Sale treatment is granted under § 303 notwithstanding the fact that the redemption may not meet the tests established in § 302 discussed above.

The special rules of § 303 evolved from Congressional concern that the financial burden of paying death taxes may force the sale of family businesses. When the estate is comprised primarily of stock of a corporation, the only source of funds for payment of the estate tax may be from the corporation itself since the market for the corporation's shares may be limited. Absent a special rule, a redemption of the shares of the estate or beneficiary may be treated as a dividend and consequently represents a costly method to finance the estate tax. The only reasonable alternative that may exist is sale to an outside party. To lessen the need for such sales, § 303 was designed to reduce the cost of a redemption by granting it sale treatment. The benefits of sale treatment in this context are particularly favorable since the basis of the shares is normally equivalent to their fair market value due to the step-up permitted for inherited property. As a result, the family not only avoids a dividend tax, but usually escapes tax entirely.

To secure sale treatment under § 303, the following conditions must be satisfied.

1. *Thirty-Five Percent Test.* The value of the redeeming corporation's stock must be more than 35 percent of the *adjusted gross estate*.[32] The adjusted gross estate is the total gross estate—generally the fair market value of all of the property owned by the decedent at date of death—reduced by deductions permitted by §§ 2053 and 2054 for funeral and administrative expenses, claims against the estate, debts, and casualty losses. In determining whether the 35 percent test is met, stock in two or more corporations may be combined if at least 20 percent of the total value of each outstanding stock is included in the gross estate.[33]

2. *Qualifying Amount.* The maximum amount of the redemption distribution that can qualify for sale treatment is limited to the sum of all taxes imposed on account of the shareholder's death (both Federal and state taxes such as estate and inheritance taxes) and the deductions allowed on the estate tax return for funeral and administrative expenses.[34]

3. *Shareholder Restrictions.* Section 303 applies to a redemption distribution only to the extent that the recipient shareholder's interest in the decedent's estate is directly reduced because of the payment of those items noted above: death taxes and funeral and administrative expenses.[35]

---

[32] § 302(b)(2)(A).

[33] § 303(b)(2)(B).

[34] § 303(a)(1).

[35] § 303(b)(3).

4. *Time Limits*.   Section 303 generally applies only to distributions made within 90 days after the statute of limitations for assessment of the estate tax expires. Since the limitations period expires three years after the due date for filing of the estate tax return—which is nine months after the date of death—the distribution normally must be made within approximately four years after the date of death (3 years + 9 months + 90 days = 4 years). This period may be extended under certain conditions.[36]

Example 18.   R died owning $1,120,000 of property, including a 15% interest in X Corporation valued at $400,000 (10,000 shares at $40 per share) and a 30% interest in Y Corporation worth $165,000. R's funeral and administrative expenses were $30,000, while claims against the estate totaled $90,000. R's adjusted gross estate is $1 million ($1,120,000 − $90,000 − $30,000). Since the $400,000 value of the X stock exceeds 35% of the adjusted gross estate of $350,000 (35% of $1 million), a redemption of the X stock qualifies for sale treatment subject to the other limitations of § 303. The Y stock cannot be redeemed pursuant to § 303, because its $165,000 value does not exceed the 35% benchmark of $350,000 nor can it take advantage of the aggregation rule. Although Y stock is eligible to be combined with other stocks for this test—since at least 20% of its value is included in the estate—it can only be combined with other 20% stocks. Because only 15% of the value of the X stock is included in the gross estate, no other stock can be combined with it. Had at least 20% of X been included in the gross estate, the stock of both X and Y could have been combined, thus enabling Y to qualify.

Example 19.   Same facts as in *Example 18* above but assume the following additional facts. The Federal estate tax and state inheritance tax imposed on account of R's death totaled $170,000. According to R's will, his estate, after payment of expenses and claims, would be shared equally by his son, S, and daughter, D. The total amount qualifying for § 303 treatment is limited to $200,000, the sum of the death taxes of $170,000 and the funeral and administrative expenses of $30,000. In addition, since S's share of the estate bears $1/2$ of the burden of all of these expenses, a subsequent redemption of his shares qualifies for § 303 treatment but not to exceed $100,000. A similar conclusion is reached for D.

Example 20.   Same facts as in *Example 18* above. Two years after the death of R, all of the estate's assets are distributed to S and D. At that time, S's basis in his 5,000 shares of X stock is $200,000 (5,000 × $40 per share, the stock's fair market value at R's death) and the stock is worth $500,000 or $100 per share. During the year, X distributed $300,000 in redemption of 3,000 shares of S's X stock. Of the $300,000 distributed, $100,000

---

[36]   §§ 303(b)(1)(A), (B), and (C).

qualifies as payment in *exchange* for S's stock under § 303. S reports long-term capital gain on this deemed sale of $60,000 [$100,000 sales price − $40,000 basis of the shares that could be purchased for $100,000 ($100,000 ÷ $100 × $40 basis per share)]. The remaining distribution of $200,000 would qualify for sale treatment only if it satisfies the requirements of § 302.

TREATMENT OF THE REDEEMING CORPORATION

An analysis of basic redemption rules would be incomplete without considering the effect of the redemption distribution on the redeeming corporation. Two questions must be considered:

1. Does the corporation recognize gain or loss on the distribution of property?

2. What is the effect of the distribution on the redeeming corporation's E&P?

Gain or Loss. Code § 311—which was discussed in conjunction with property distributions in Chapter 3—provides the rule applying to all nonliquidating distributions. Recall that under § 311, the distributing corporation must recognize gain—*but not loss*—upon the distribution of property other than its own obligations. Thus, when the corporation distributes property in redemption of stock, it must recognize any gain inherent in the property while any loss goes unrecognized.

When property subject to a liability is distributed, the fair market value of the property is deemed to be *no less* than the amount of the liability.[37] Thus, when the liability exceeds the property's fair market value and the basis of the property, the corporation must recognize gain equal to the excess of the liability over the basis. If the liability does not exceed the property's fair market value, it is ignored for gain recognition purposes and the fair market value is used.

> **Example 21.** T contributed land to a corporation many years ago which the corporation uses as a parking lot. This year T has decided to retire from the business and is willing to take the land in payment for his 20% interest in the business. The basis of his interest is $15,000. The land is worth $50,000 and has a basis of $10,000. If the corporation accepts T's proposal and redeems the stock by distributing the land, the corporation must recognize gain of $40,000 ($50,000 − $10,000). Gain must be recognized regardless of whether the distribution receives sale or dividend treatment. Note that if the property's value had been only $3,000, the corporation would not have recognized any loss. Moreover, such loss would be permanently lost since the basis of the property to the distributee would have been its value of $3,000!

---

[37] § 311(b)(2).

Example 22. V Corporation operates a hat and glove business. This year V liquidated the hat business and—as part of a transaction qualifying as a partial liquidation—distributed the following assets to its sole shareholder, M: cash of $5,000; furniture worth $10,000 (cost, $18,000 and depreciation, $5,000); and a small warehouse worth $30,000 which had a basis of $20,000 and which was subject to a mortgage of $45,000. Although the corporation realizes a $3,000 loss [$10,000 − ($18,000 − $5,000)] on the distribution of the furniture, none of the loss is recognized. In contrast, the corporation must recognize a gain on the distribution of the warehouse of $25,000 ($45,000 liability − $20,000 basis).

Earnings and Profits. The E&P of a corporation must be adjusted to reflect any redemption distributions. First, if the corporation must recognize gain on the distribution under § 311, E&P must be increased for the gain.[38]

The amount of the reduction of E&P on account of the distribution depends on whether the distribution qualifies for sale treatment. If the distribution does not qualify for sale treatment, E&P is reduced according to the rules applying to property distributions.

If the redemption qualifies for sale treatment under §§ 302 or 303, only a portion of the distribution is charged against E&P. E&P is reduced by the redeemed stock's proportionate share of E&P but not more than the amount of the redemption distribution.[39]

Example 23. K Corporation has 100 shares outstanding, 40 of which are owned by B. K has $100,000 of E&P. During the year, K redeemed all of B's shares for $50,000. If the redemption qualifies as a sale, E&P must be reduced by the amount of E&P attributable to the stock. Since 40% of the stock was redeemed (40 ÷ 100), 40% of E&P or $40,000 is eliminated, leaving a $60,000 balance. Had K redeemed the 40 shares for $25,000, the reduction in E&P would have been limited to $25,000, the lesser of 40% of E&P or the amount of the redemption distribution.

The various rules applying to redemption are summarized in Exhibit 4-1.

---

[38]   § 312(b)(1).   [39]   § 312(n)(7).

Exhibit 4-1
Section 302 Redemptions: Summary

Type	Sections 302(b)(1),(2), and (3)	Section 302(b)(4) Partial Liquidation
Comments	**Sale if**	**Noncorporate S/H Only** **Sale if**
	1. Not essentially equivalent to a dividend (shareholder level)	1. Not essentially equivalent to a dividend (corporate contraction)
	2. Substantially disproportionate: post-redemption percentage ownership less than a. 50 percent overall; and b. 80 percent of preredemption ownership	2. Attributable to termination of qualified business a. Business, not investment b. Conducted five years preredemption c. Not acquired in taxable transaction in five years preredemption
	3. Complete termination of interest: family attribution waived if prohibited interest not acquired for 10 years	
	Otherwise: Section 301 Distribution	**Otherwise:** Section 301 Distribution unless Section 302(b)(1), (2), or (3) applicable
Effect on Shareholder	**Sale:** Gain/loss realized = FMV − AB **Section 301:** Dividend to extent of E&P	**Sale:** Gain/loss realized = FMV − AB **Section 301:** Dividend to the extent of E&P
Shareholder's Adjusted Basis	**In Remaining Stock:** **Sale:** Unchanged **Section 301:** Increase by AB of stock surrendered	**In Remaining Stock:** **Sale:** Unchanged **Section 301:** Increase by AB of stock surrendered
	In Property Received: **Sale:** FMV **Section 301:** FMV	**In Property Received:** **Sale:** FMV **Section 301:** FMV
Effect on Distributing Corporation's Taxable Income	**Gain:** Recognized **Loss:** Not Recognized	**Gain:** Recognized **Loss:** Not Recognized
Effect on Distributing Corporation's E&P	**Reduction** **Sale:** By redeemed stock's share of E&P not > amount distributed **Section 301:** By money, AB of property	**Reduction** **Sale:** By redeemed stock's share of E&P not > amount distributed **Section 301:** By money, AB of property

STOCK REDEMPTION BY RELATED CORPORATIONS

As seen in the previous sections, Congress has devised an intricate scheme to prohibit shareholders from bailing out E&P from their corporations by using carefully planned redemptions. Absent special provisions, however, the rules discussed thus far could be easily defeated when a shareholder controls two or more corporations through a brother-sister or parent-subsidiary arrangement (see Exhibit 4-2).[40]

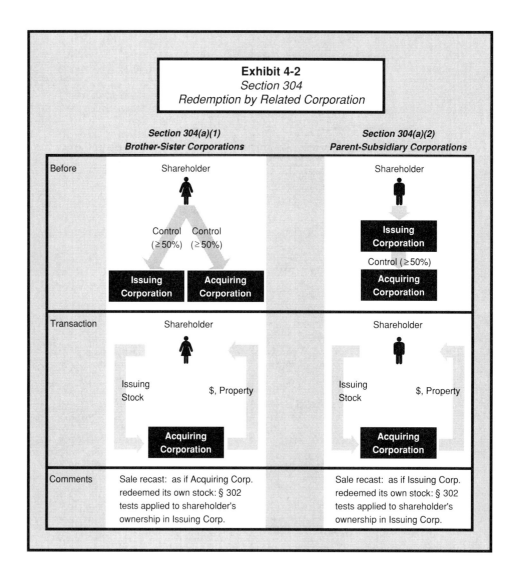

Exhibit 4-2
Section 304
Redemption by Related Corporation

Section 304(a)(1)
Brother-Sister Corporations

Section 304(a)(2)
Parent-Subsidiary Corporations

Before

Shareholder

Control   Control
($\geq 50\%$)   ($\geq 50\%$)

Issuing Corporation   Acquiring Corporation

Shareholder

Issuing Corporation

Control ($\geq 50\%$)

Acquiring Corporation

Transaction

Shareholder

Issuing Stock $, Property

Acquiring Corporation

Shareholder

Issuing Stock $, Property

Acquiring Corporation

Comments

Sale recast: as if Acquiring Corp. redeemed its own stock: § 302 tests applied to shareholder's ownership in Issuing Corp.

Sale recast: as if Issuing Corp. redeemed its own stock: § 302 tests applied to shareholder's ownership in Issuing Corp.

---

[40]   See for example, *John Wanamaker, Trustee,*
49-2 USTC ¶9486, 38 AFTR 1014, 178 F.2d
10 (CA-3, 1949).

Example 24. A owns 100% of the stock of both X and Y. [Note: when a shareholder(s) controls two or more corporations in this manner, the corporations are referred to as brother-sister corporations]. If X redeems some of its stock from A, dividend treatment results under § 302 since A's interest is not changed by the redemption. A similar result would occur if Y were to redeem some of its shares from A. Alternatively, A might sell some of his X stock to Y for $10,000. In effect, A has received a dividend distribution of $10,000 since he still controls both corporations after the sale. However, the normal redemption provisions of § 302 would not apply to the sale since neither corporation acquired *its own stock*. Thus, without additional rules, a shareholder could obtain cash at will from his or her controlled corporations at the cost of a capital gains tax.

Example 25. Assume the same facts as in *Example 24* above, except that X owns 100% of Y. (Note here that the relationship between the corporations is parent-subsidiary.) A sale of A's X stock to Y for $10,000 has the same effect as described above: a dividend distribution of $10,000 since A's interest in X is unaffected by the transaction because X controls Y.

To prevent shareholders from effectively redeeming stock through sales to related corporations, Congress enacted § 304. This provision recasts the "sale" to the related corporation as a redemption and applies the tests of § 302 to determine the tax treatment. The rules apply only when control is present (see Exhibit 4-2).[41] For this purpose, control generally means ownership of at least 50 percent of each corporation's stock. In determining whether control exists, the constructive ownership rules of § 318 are applied with a slight modification. Attribution of stock to and from a corporation occurs as long as the shareholder constructively owns at least 5 percent of the corporation.[42] If control is found, a special set of rules applies, depending on whether the brother-sister or parent-subsidiary relationship exists between the corporations.

Brother-Sister Redemptions. As noted above and illustrated in Exhibit 4-2, a brother-sister relationship exists where one or more shareholders are in control in each of two corporations and neither corporation controls the other (as is the case with a parent-subsidiary relationship). In this situation, if the controlling shareholder (or shareholders) sells stock of one corporation (referred to as the issuing corporation) to the other corporation (referred to as the acquiring corporation), the brother-sister redemption rules apply. According to these rules,

---

[41] Note that § 303 might also be applied.

[42] § 304(c)(3)(B). Note also that downward attribution from a shareholder to a corpora-

tion is proportional if less than 50 percent is owned [Code § 304(c)(3)(B)(ii)(II)].

the sale by the shareholder to the acquiring corporation is recast as a redemption by the acquiring corporation of its own stock. The stock of the issuing corporation that is actually obtained by the acquiring corporation is treated as a contribution to the acquiring corporation's capital in exchange for some of the acquiring corporation's stock.

Section 304(a)(1) creates a hypothetical (and clearly bewildering) two-step transaction. First, the stock of the issuing corporation actually obtained by the acquiring corporation is deemed to have been contributed to the acquiring corporation's capital in exchange for some of the acquiring corporation's stock. The acquiring corporation is then treated as having redeemed its own stock that it just issued, for the price it actually paid. The basis assigned to the acquiring corporation's stock that is considered redeemed is the same as the stock of the issuing corporation that was actually sold (or deemed contributed to the acquiring corporation's capital). The critical ownership tests of § 302 are applied to the shareholder's interest in the issuing corporation.[43]

If the distribution does not qualify for sale treatment, the distribution is treated as having been made by the acquiring corporation to the extent of its E&P and then by the issuing corporation to the extent of its E&P.[44] In addition, since the distribution is treated as a dividend, the basis of the issuing corporation's stock that was actually sold is added to the shareholder's basis for the acquiring corporation's stock. The basis of the issuing corporation's stock in the hands of the acquiring corporation is the shareholder's basis.[45]

Example 26. S owns all of the 100 shares of outstanding stock of I Corp. and 70 of the 100 shares of outstanding stock of A Corp. He purchased the I shares for $500 per share (total $50,000) and the A shares for $300 per share (total $21,000) several years ago. A has $10,000 of E&P while I has $70,000 of E&P. S sold 40 shares of I (basis $20,000) to A (acquiring corporation) for $60,000. Since S controls (owns at least 50%) both I and A, the brother-sister redemption rules apply to the sale. S is treated as having contributed the I (issuing corporation) stock to the capital of A in exchange for A shares. S assigns a basis of $20,000 to these A shares, the same as the basis of the I stock contributed to A's capital. A is then treated as having redeemed the A shares just issued for the amount which was actually paid, $60,000. The hypothetical redemption is tested by examining S's ownership in the issuing corporation, I, before and after the hypothetical redemption. Before the redemption, S owned 100% of I. After the redemption, he owns

---

[43] For this purpose, attribution from a corporation to its shareholder or from a shareholder to a corporation occurs without regard to the 50% threshold normally required [§ 304(b)(1)].

[44] § 304(b)(2).

[45] Although the basis as determined under § 362 is technically the shareholder's basis increased by any gain recognized, any dividend income recognized on the transaction is not considered gain. See Reg. § 1.304-2(c) Ex. (1).

88% of I [(60 shares directly + 28 shares [70% of 40] indirectly through A) ÷ 100]. Since the redemption is not substantially disproportionate (S owns neither less than 50% after the redemption nor less than 80% of what he owned before), is not a complete termination of his interest, or is not made to pay death taxes, it is treated as a $10,000 dividend out of A's E&P and as a $50,000 dividend out of I's E&P. S increases his basis in his A stock by the basis of the I stock redeemed, $20,000. Thus, his total basis in A stock is $41,000 ($20,000 + $21,000). A's basis in the I stock, hypothetically acquired by a contribution to capital, is $20,000, which is the basis of the I stock in the hands of S.

Example 27. Assume the same facts as *Example 26* above, except that A had a deficit in E&P of $9,000 attributable to several years of losses. The amount of the dividend in this case is still $60,000 attributable to the E&P of I Corp.

If the redemption is treated as a sale, it is considered a sale of the acquiring corporation's stock that was deemed issued in exchange for the issuing corporation's stock. For purposes of computing gain or loss on the sale, as noted above, the basis assigned to the acquiring corporation's shares is that of the issuing corporation's stock that was actually sold. The sale has no effect on the shareholder's basis in the remaining stock of either the issuing corporation or the acquiring corporation. In other words, the basis of the shares that the shareholder has not transferred remains the same.[46] The acquiring corporation's basis in the issuing corporation's stock that it purchased is the cost of that stock.[47]

Example 28. Assume the same facts as in *Example 26* above, except that before the redemption S owned 50 shares of I Corp. Before the sale, S owned 50% of I directly, and after the sale he owned 38% [10 shares directly and 28 (70% of 40) indirectly through A Corp.]. Since S's percentage ownership after the redemption is less than 50% and less than 80% of his ownership prior to the redemption [38% is less than 40% (80% of 50%)], the redemption qualifies for sale treatment under the substantially disproportionate rules of § 302(b)(2). Thus, S is treated as having sold A shares with a basis of $20,000 (the same as his basis in the I shares actually sold) for $60,000 resulting in a long-term capital gain of $40,000. S's basis in the remaining 10 shares of I is unaffected by the sale and remains as $5,000 ($500 × 10). S's basis in his A Corp. stock is also unaffected by the sale and remains as $21,000. A's basis in the stock it has purchased from S is the cost of that stock, $60,000.

---

[46] Reg. § 1.304-2(a).

[47] See the Tax Reform Act of 1986, Act § 1875(c), and the House Committee Report.

Parent-Subsidiary Redemptions.   Section 304(a)(2) is designed to address the problems arising when a shareholder sells stock of a parent corporation to the parent's subsidiary (see Exhibit 4-2). For this purpose, the required parent subsidiary relationship exists when the parent owns 50 percent of the stock of the subsidiary. Note that the shareholder need not control either corporation as is required in the brother-sister context. Rather, the question is whether one corporation controls the other.

In the parent-subsidiary situation, if a shareholder sells stock of the parent (issuing corporation) to the subsidiary (acquiring corporation), the exchange is recast as a redemption by the issuing parent of its own stock. This approach differs from that for brother-sister redemptions where the acquiring corporation is considered as having redeemed its own stock. As in the brother-sister redemption rules, however, the § 302 tests pertaining to ownership are applied to the shareholder's interest in the issuing parent corporation. Also, as in the brother-sister redemption rules, if the redemption does not qualify for sale treatment, the distribution is treated as having been made by the acquiring subsidiary corporation to the extent of its E&P and then by the issuing parent corporation to the extent of its E&P.[48] In addition, the shareholder's basis in any remaining stock held in the issuing parent corporation is increased by the basis of the stock surrendered to the acquiring subsidiary.[49] Note that the basis adjustment is made to the issuing parent corporation's stock in this case while it was made to the acquiring corporation's stock in the brother-sister situation. The basis of the stock acquired by the subsidiary is its cost.[50]

> **Example 29.**   K owns 60 of the 100 shares of outstanding stock of P Corp. She acquired the shares several years ago for $60,000. In addition, P owns 80% of the outstanding stock of its subsidiary, S Corp. P Corp. has $100,000 of E&P while S has $30,000 of E&P. During the year, K sold 10 shares of her P stock to S for $70,000 (basis $10,000). The ownership tests of § 302 are applied to the shareholder's interest in the issuing parent corporation P. Before the redemption, K owned 60% of P and after the redemption she owned 54% [50 shares directly and four shares indirectly through P (her new ownership in P, 50% × P's ownership in S, 80% × S's ownership of P, 10%)]. Since K's ownership in P Corp. after the redemption is not less than 50%, the redemption does not qualify as a

---

[48]   § 304(b)(2).

[49]   Reg. § 1.304-3(a).

[50]   With respect to the basis of the stock in the hands of the acquiring subsidiary, in absence of any provisions contained in the Code or Regulations, the basis of the stock should be its cost under § 1012.

substantially disproportionate redemption under § 302(b)(2) and thus does not qualify for sale treatment. Accordingly, the distribution is treated as a $70,000 dividend, $30,000 out of the E&P of S Corp. and $40,000 out of the E&P of P Corp. K's basis in her remaining stock of the issuing parent corporation P is increased by $10,000, the basis of the P shares sold. Thus, her total basis in the P Corp. stock is still $60,000; however, this is the basis for 50 shares of stock rather than 60 shares, as was the case before the redemption. The basis of the P stock acquired by S Corp. is $70,000, its cost.

If the parent-subsidiary redemption qualifies for sale treatment, the shareholder computes gain or loss in the normal fashion using the basis of the issuing parent's stock in the calculation. In this case, the shareholder's bases in the remaining stock of both the issuing parent and acquiring subsidiary corporations are unaffected and thus remain the same.

> **Example 30.**   Assume the same facts as *Example 29* above, except that the sale qualifies as a redemption made in order to pay death taxes under § 303. In this case, the shareholder has a $60,000 long-term capital gain ($70,000 − $10,000). The basis in her remaining 50 shares of P Corp. stock is $50,000 while the basis in her S Corp. stock is not affected.

PREFERRED STOCK BAILOUTS: § 306

As may be apparent from the previous discussion, shareholders have devised various schemes over the years to extract E&P out of the corporation without suffering the double tax penalty incurred with dividend distributions. A popular technique that achieved this objective prior to 1954 was the so-called *preferred stock bailout*. According to this plan, the corporation declared a dividend of nonvoting preferred stock to be distributed to holders of the corporation's common stock. Notwithstanding efforts by the government to treat this as a taxable stock dividend, the distribution of preferred stock on common is considered nontaxable since it has no effect on the interest of the common stock shareholders. Upon receipt of the nontaxable stock dividend, a portion of the shareholder's basis in the common stock was allocated to the preferred stock. The next step in the plan was a prearranged sale of the preferred stock by the shareholder to a friendly third party. The sale normally resulted in favorable long-term capital gain to the shareholder. The corporation subsequently redeemed the third party's stock with the cash that would have been distributed as a dividend to the shareholder. The third party was willing to participate in the scheme since the corporation redeemed the stock at a price which exceeded its cost to the third party as a reward for facilitating the bailout. By following these steps, the shareholder was able to obtain cash out of the corporation—albeit indirectly through an accommodating third party—at the cost of a capital gains tax. The courts approved this scheme, as illustrated below.[51]

> **Example 31.** T owns all 100 shares of the outstanding common stock of P Corporation. T had acquired these shares for $20,000 several years ago. During the year, T caused the corporation to distribute a nontaxable preferred stock dividend of 10 shares. At the time of the dividend, the common stock was worth $40,000 and the preferred stock was worth $10,000. T assigned a basis of $4,000 to the shares [$10,000 ÷ ($10,000 + $40,000) × $20,000] and sold them to his friend F for $10,000, realizing a long-term capital gain of $6,000 ($10,000 − $4,000). P Corporation subsequently redeemed the 10 shares from F for $10,500. After the transactions have been completed, T reports a long-term capital gain of $6,000 that should have been characterized as a dividend of $10,000 assuming the corporation had adequate E&P at the time the preferred stock was distributed.

In 1954, Congress enacted § 306 to prohibit taxpayers from using the preferred stock bailout to avoid taxes. The thrust of this provision is to assign the § 306 "taint" to the preferred stock received as a nontaxable stock dividend and cause a subsequent sale or redemption of such "tainted" stock to result in ordinary or dividend income.

SECTION 306 STOCK DEFINED

As suggested above, if "§ 306 stock" is sold or redeemed, the provisions of § 306 generally operate to deny the benefits of sale treatment. Section 306 stock is defined as follows:[52]

1. *Stock Received as a Dividend.* Stock (other than common stock distributed with respect to common) that is received as a nontaxable dividend.

   > **Example 32.** Same facts as in *Example 31* above. The nontaxable distribution of preferred stock is § 306 stock.

2. *Stock Received in a Corporate Reorganization or Division.* Stock (other than common stock) that is received tax-free in a corporate reorganization or division where the effect of the transaction was substantially the same as the receipt of a stock dividend, or where the stock was received in exchange for § 306 stock.

---

[51] *C.P. Chamberlain v. Comm.,* 53-2 USTC ¶9576, 44 AFTR 494, 207 F.2d 462 (CA-6, 1953).

[52] § 306(c)(1).

Example 33.   T owns all of the outstanding common stock of X Corporation Y Corporation and X agree to a merger where Y will absorb X. Pursuant to the merger transaction, T receives common and preferred stock in Y, and T's stock in X is cancelled. The preferred stock is § 306 stock since this is a nontaxable reorganization and the receipt of the preferred stock by T has the same effect as a nontaxable stock dividend.

3.   *Stock with a Substituted or Carryover Basis.* Stock that has a basis determined in reference to the basis of § 306 stock.

Example 34.   B gave 100 shares of § 306 stock worth $50,000 (basis $10,000) to her son Z. Since the basis of the stock in Z's hands is the donor's basis of $10,000, the stock is § 306 stock.

Note that stock inherited from a decedent loses the § 306 taint since the basis of the stock is its fair market value (i.e., it is not determined by reference to the basis of the decedent).

4.   *Stock Received in § 351 Exchange.*   Stock, other than common stock, acquired in a § 351 exchange if the receipt of money (in lieu of the stock) would have been treated as a dividend to any extent.[53]

Even though stock may satisfy one of the definitions above, it is not considered § 306 stock if the corporation had no current or accumulated E&P at the time the stock was distributed.[54] Stock escapes the § 306 taint in this case because a distribution at such time would not have been taxable as a dividend.

Example 35.   Same facts as *Example 31* above. If the corporation had no E&P at the time that the preferred stock was distributed, the stock would not be § 306 stock.

DISPOSITIONS OF § 306 STOCK

The provisions of § 306 apply whenever there is a disposition of § 306 stock. However, the effect of § 306 differs somewhat depending on whether the stock is sold to a third party or redeemed by the distributing corporation.

Sales of § 306 Stock. If a shareholder sells or disposes of § 306 stock other than by redemption, potential bailout is prohibited by effectively dividing the amount realized into two components: an ordinary income component and a return of capital component. The amount realized is treated as ordinary income

---

[53] In making this determination, rules similar to those contained in Code § 304(b)(2) must be considered.

[54] § 306(c)(2).

to the extent that the shareholder would have had a dividend if *at the time of distribution* cash had been distributed (in lieu of stock) in an amount equal to the fair market value of the stock.[55] Thus, the ordinary income component is measured by E&P at the date the § 306 stock is distributed. Even though the taxable amount is determined with respect to E&P, it is treated as ordinary income and not dividend income; accordingly, the corporation makes no adjustment to its E&P account. The remainder of the amount realized is treated as a return of the shareholder's basis. To the extent that the return of capital component exceeds the shareholder's basis, the shareholder recognizes gain from the sale of stock, usually capital gain. If the shareholder's basis is not fully recovered, no loss is recognized for the unrecovered basis. Rather, the shareholder adds the unrecovered basis of the preferred stock to the basis of the common stock with respect to which the preferred stock was distributed.

Example 36.   T owns all 100 shares of the outstanding common stock of PSB Corp. T had acquired these shares for $20,000 several years ago. On May 1, 1988, when the corporation had E&P of $7,000, it distributed to T a nontaxable preferred stock dividend of 10 shares worth $15,000. T assigned a basis of $4,000 to the preferred shares. On June 7, 1991 T sold the preferred shares to his friend F for $12,000. At the time of the sale, the corporation had E&P of $30,000. Absent § 306, T would report a long-term capital gain of $8,000 ($12,000 − $4,000). Pursuant to § 306, however, T reports ordinary income of $7,000 and long-term capital gain of $1,000 determined as follows:

Amount realized......................	$12,000
Ordinary income:	
Amount that would have been a	
dividend had cash been distributed	
in lieu of stock....................	− 7,000
Return of capital......................	$ 5,000
Adjusted basis:........................	− 4,000
Gain on sale	$ 1,000

Note that the amount of the $15,000 distribution that would have been a dividend had cash been distributed in lieu of stock is measured by the corporation's E&P at the time of distribution, $7,000.

Example 37.   Assume the same facts as above, except that E&P at the time of the distribution, May 1, 1988, was $11,000. In this case, $11,000 is ordinary income. No loss is recognized for the unrecovered basis

---

[55]   § 306(a)(1).

of $3,000; rather, the basis of the common stock on which the stock was distributed is increased by $3,000 to $19,000 ($16,000 + $3,000). These results are summarized below.

Amount realized......................	$12,000
Ordinary income:	
Amount that would have been a	
dividend had cash been distributed	
in lieu of stock....................	− 11,000
Return of capital......................	$ 1,000
Adjusted basis	− 4,000
Loss not recognized..................	$ 3,000

Redemptions of § 306 Stock. If a shareholder redeems § 306 stock, the amount realized is considered a distribution of property subject to the normal rules of § 301. As a result, the amount realized in this case is treated as a *dividend* to the extent of the corporation's E&P *at the time of the redemption*. To the extent the distribution exceeds E&P, it is treated as a return of the shareholder's basis with any excess considered gain from the sale of stock. Any basis which is not recovered is added to the basis of the common shares with respect to which the § 306 stock was distributed. Since the distribution is treated as a normal property distribution, the corporation must make an adjustment to its E&P.

> **Example 38.** Assume the same facts as in *Example 36* above, except that instead of selling the stock to F, the corporation redeemed the shares. In this case, the entire amount realized of $12,000 is treated as a dividend since E&P at the date of the redemption is $30,000. The $4,000 basis of the shares is added to the shareholder's basis for the common stock, resulting in a total basis for the common stock of $20,000 ($4,000 + $16,000). Note that this result is very harsh since only $7,000 of ordinary income would have been recognized had a cash distribution been made in lieu of stock at the date of distribution.

EXCEPTIONS TO § 306

The special rules governing redemptions and other dispositions of § 306 stock are disregarded for certain dispositions where the shareholder's interest is terminated or where the § 306 taint is retained by the transferor, transferee, or both. The exception granted for transactions that completely terminate the shareholder's interest is justified on the theory that the series of transactions no longer resembles an ordinary dividend distribution since the shareholder's interest has substantially changed. The other exception is not truly an exception because the § 306 taint remains. Section 306 provides several other exceptions as well.[56]

---

[56] See § 306(b).

TAX PLANNING

EXTRACTING CORPORATE EARNINGS AT CAPITAL GAINS RATES

Notwithstanding the gauntlet of requirements that redemptions must run, they provide opportunities for withdrawing corporate earnings at a cost lower than that incurred with a dividend distribution. For this reason, the taxpayer should always consider the possibility of structuring a distribution as a redemption rather than as a dividend. In planning, however, it should be remembered that a *corporate* shareholder no longer obtains a benefit from structuring the redemption as a dividend due to the extraordinary dividend rules.

REDEMPTIONS OF GIFTED STOCK

When planning for the owner of an interest in a closely held business, gifts of stock are often made to shift income to family members in a lower bracket (e.g., children). This technique is particularly useful when the corporation has elected to be taxed as an S corporation since the income of the entity flows through to the lower-bracket family member. Whether the corporation is an S corporation or a regular corporation, the stock given to the children can later be redeemed by the corporation to provide funds as their own needs arise. For example, corporate stock could be transferred in trust to a child who is seven years old, and the stock could be redeemed during his or her college age years to provide funds for tuition and other expenses. In order to secure sale treatment, however, the redemption must be postponed for more than 10 years from the date the stock was gifted. The conclusion derives from several special rules regarding the family attribution waiver under Code § 302(b)(3). According to this provision, the family attribution rules cannot be waived if any of the redeemed stock was acquired from a related person within 10 years of the redemption.[57] This rule prohibits a father from giving his son or another related party some of his stock, immediately followed by a redemption of the son's stock with favorable sale treatment. Thus, in order for this technique to be successful, stock must be gifted more than 10 years before the anticipated redemption. Alternatively, the child could acquire the stock directly from the corporation for a contribution (e.g., when the value of the stock was low when the corporation was formed) and the restriction would be avoided.

---

[57]   § 302(c)(2)(B)(i).

BOOTSTRAP ACQUISITIONS

As suggested earlier in this chapter, redemptions are often used as a means to finance the sale of a shareholder's stock. Often times, a prospective buyer has insufficient cash to make the purchase. However, if the corporation has cash, or perhaps desirable property, the buyer can purchase some of the shareholder's stock while the corporation redeems the remaining shares. This technique is referred to as a "bootstrap acquisition."

> **Example 39.** R owns all 100 shares of X Corporation's outstanding stock, worth $100,000. S wishes to buy the corporation from R but can secure only $20,000 for the purchase. Assuming X has sufficient assets, S could purchase 20 of the shares from R while X redeemed the other 80 shares. In this case, the redemption would qualify as a complete termination of R's interest, and sale treatment would be secured.

The IRS initially disputed the results achieved in bootstrap acquisitions, arguing the distribution would have been treated as a dividend to the seller if the redemption had occurred prior to the sale. Currently, however, favorable results can be achieved if the redemption is carefully planned.[58]

REDEMPTIONS TO PAY DEATH TAXES

The provisions pertaining to redemptions to pay death taxes provide an excellent vehicle for extracting earnings from the corporation at favorable rates. As explained earlier, because the basis of the redeemed stock is stepped up to its value at the decedent's death, there may be little if any tax to pay on the redemption. Because of these favorable aspects, owners of a closely held corporation should consider arranging for a redemption after death to provide their estate with assets to pay the death taxes. This may entail gifts of property prior to the death of the shareholder to ensure that the stock ultimately represents more than 35 percent of the decedent's adjusted gross estate. In this regard, it should be mentioned that gifts within three years of the decedent's death are included in the adjusted gross estate. Thus, any gifting to qualify the stock under § 303 should be planned far in advance.

In planning a § 303 redemption, the timing of the redemption is very important. The Regulations indicate that the limitation of § 303 treatment to the amount of death taxes and funeral and administrative expenses is allocated on a chronological basis.[59] This rule must be followed even if one of the redemptions would qualify for sale treatment under the general rules of § 302.

[58] *Fern R. Zenz v. Quinlivan,* 54-2 USTC ¶9445, 45 AFTR 1672, 213 F.2d 914 (CA-6, 1954).

[59] Reg. § 1.303-2(g)(2).

> **Example 40.** When R died, total funeral and administrative expenses were $25,000, while death taxes were $275,000 As a result, § 303 treatment is limited to $300,000 ($275,000 + $25,000). In the year following R's death, T—one of R's heirs—redeemed all of her inherited stock, receiving $250,000. During the second year, the estate redeemed $100,000. Only $50,000 of the estate's redemption qualifies under § 303 since the first $250,000 allowable was allocated to T's redemption. This would be true even if T's redemption qualified for capital gain treatment under § 302.

As the above example illustrates, steps should be taken to ensure that § 303 treatment is not wasted on a redemption that otherwise would qualify for capital gains under § 302.

Another attractive feature of the § 303 redemption is that accumulations to redeem stock once the shareholder has died are exempt from the accumulated earnings tax. Thus, if the redemption is to take place over a period of years, accumulations by the corporation would be justified.

REDEMPTIONS AND CHARITABLE CONTRIBUTIONS

For owners of a closely held corporation, redemptions can serve as an attractive means to obtain charitable contributions. As discussed in Chapter 3, the corporation may make the contribution for the owner directly as a means to avoid double taxation. Another technique for charitable giving involves redemptions. This method enables the shareholder to obtain a charitable deduction without having to part with the cash immediately.

> **Example 41.** K is the sole shareholder of X Corporation. During the year, she decided to contribute $100,000 to her alma mater, Indiana University. Initially she planned to give a small amount each year. On the advice of her accountant, she transferred all of her nonvoting preferred stock (not § 306 stock), worth $100,000, to the school. Subsequently, the corporation redeems the stock, giving the school a note for $100,000 payable over 20 years. In this situation, K is entitled to a charitable contribution deduction of $100,000 in the year she transfers the stock. Note that this is true even though the cash is actually paid to the charity in installments. Moreover, K has no dividend income and has not lost any control over X. In addition, the corporation is entitled to reduce its E&P account for the E&P attributable to the shares redeemed.

The favorable treatment obtained in this example is secure as long as the charity is not required to surrender the shares for redemption.[60]

---

[60] *Daniel D. Palmer,* 75-2 USTC ¶9726, 36 AFTR2d 75-5942, 523 F.2d 1308 (CA-8, 1975).

PROBLEM MATERIALS

DISCUSSION QUESTIONS

4-1 *Redemptions in General.* When a shareholder sells stock in a corporation, the transaction normally results in capital gain or loss. The Code may alter this result, however, when the sale of the stock is made to the corporation that issued the stock.

    a.   What term is used to describe a corporation's acquisition of its own stock?

    b.   Why might a corporation acquire its own stock? Answer from the point of view of both the shareholder and the corporation.

    c.   Indicate the alternative treatment accorded such exchanges and explain why a different treatment might be necessary.

4-2 *Redemptions: Tax Consequences to Shareholders.* R Corporation, which has substantial E&P, redeems 50 of T's 70 shares (basis of $100 per share) for $60,000.

    a.   What effect does the redemption have on T's taxable income and the basis for his stock, assuming the transaction qualifies as a sale?

    b.   What effect does the redemption have on T's taxable income and the basis for his stock, assuming the distribution does not qualify for sale treatment?

4-3 *Redemptions: Dividend Equivalency.* A redemption is treated as payment in exchange for the shareholder's stock when it is not essentially equivalent to a dividend. When is a redemption distribution not equivalent to a dividend? Include in your answer comments concerning all tests used to determine dividend equivalency, as well as comments on how the following factors affect the dividend equivalency determination: valid business purpose, pro rata distributions, and relationships among the shareholders.

4-4 *Attribution Rules.* Answer the following:

    a.   What is the purpose of the constructive ownership rules of § 318?

    b.   Give an example of (1) family attribution, (2) entity-to-owner attribution, and (3) owner-to-entity attribution.

    c.   Are the constructive ownership rules applicable to all situations where stock ownership must be considered? If not, indicate those situations where they are not applicable.

4-5 *Redemptions to Pay Death Taxes.* In § 303, Congress has provided special treatment for redemptions of stock included in the gross estate of the decedent. In light of this general rule, address the following questions.

    a.   What is the significant difference between § 303 and § 302, the general provision governing redemptions? Why is the treatment of § 303 particularly favorable?

    b.   In general, when are the benefits of § 303 available?

    c.   As a practical matter, the benefits of § 303 have become quite limited over the years. What prompts such a conclusion?

4-6   *Partial Liquidations in General.*   Under § 302(b)(4), sale treatment is granted to a redemption distribution qualifying as a partial liquidation if it is "not essentially equivalent to a dividend." This same language appears in the general redemption rule of § 302(b)(1).

     a.   Is this phrase interpreted in the same fashion for both provisions? Explain.

     b.   The partial liquidation provisions contain a safe harbor test, which a shareholder can utilize to secure sale treatment without concern for the vague dividend equivalency test mentioned above. Outline the requirements of this test and explain their purpose.

4-7   *Redemptions: Effect on Corporate Taxable Income.*   Do the rules governing the tax consequences to the corporation on the distribution of property in a redemption differ from those applying to § 301 distributions of property? Explain.

4-8   *Redemptions: Effect on Corporate E&P.*   Z Corporation, which had $100,000 of E&P at the end of the year, redeemed 60 shares of its 100 shares outstanding for $70,000. Briefly explain the series of adjustments to Z's E&P that must be made if

     a.   The redemption is treated as a dividend.

     b.   The redemption is treated as a sale or exchange.

4-9   *Redemptions by Related Corporations.*   By definition, a corporation cannot "redeem" the stock of another corporation, yet the title of § 304 clearly suggests otherwise.

     a.   Explain the purpose of § 304 (concerning sales of stock by a shareholder to a related corporation). Include in your answer an explanation of why this provision not only looms as a trap for the unwary but also serves as a device to police possible abuse of the corporate redemption provisions.

     b.   How are the ownership tests of § 302 applied to a brother-sister redemption? a parent-subsidiary redemption?

     c.   If one of the related corporations in a brother-sister or parent-subsidiary redemption has a deficit of $10,000 in E&P, while the other has positive E&P of $10,000, sale treatment effectively results regardless of how the transaction is characterized. Is this statement true or false? Explain.

4-10   *Preferred Stock Bailouts.*   Section 306 provides special treatment on the sales of certain stock.

     a.   Explain the abuse that § 306 is designed to curb.

     b.   How does § 306 eliminate the loophole described above?

     c.   The treatment under § 306 varies depending on whether stock is sold or redeemed. What is the critical difference?

PROBLEMS

4-11   *Redemptions: § 302(b)(2).* Z Corporation has 1,000 shares of stock outstanding owned as follows:

Shareholder	Shares Owned
A	100
B	100
C	200
D	600
	1,000

All shareholders paid $100 per share for their stock. Z has substantial earnings and profits.

a.   During the year, the corporation redeemed 400 shares of D's stock for $400,000. What is the effect of the redemption on D?

b.   Same as (a) except the corporation redeemed 200 shares of D's stock for $200,000.

4-12   *Redemptions: § 302(b)(3).* X Corporation has 1,000 shares of stock outstanding owned as follows:

Shareholder	Shares Owned
E	100
F	100
H	200
W	600
	1,000

H and W are husband and wife. For each of the following *independent* situations, indicate whether the redemption would qualify for sale treatment. Assume the transaction qualifies unless otherwise implied.

a.   X redeemed all of H's stock. H received cash of $50,000 and a $100,000 note payable in annual installments with interest over the next five years.

b.   X redeemed all of E's stock. E will continue his employment with X as vice president.

c.   Several years ago, X redeemed all of the stock of F's father, G. At that time, G filed the appropriate agreement with his tax return, indicating he would notify the IRS if he acquired any stock in X within 10 years of the redemption. This year F died, leaving all of his stock to his father.

4-13   *Redemptions: Basics.*   B owns 60 shares of X Corporation while his wife and son own 30 and 10 shares, respectively. Each of the shareholders has a basis in his or her stock of $1,000 per share. X has substantial E&P. What are the consequences to B if the corporation redeems 30 shares of his stock for $150,000?

4-14 *Family Attribution.* Ms. B owns 30 percent of the stock of F Corporation. The remaining 70 percent of the stock is owned by the members of her family. Indicate whether Ms. B would be treated as constructively owning the stock owned by the following individuals under the family attribution rules of § 318.

a. Her father
b. Her daughter
c. Her sister
d. Her grandfather
e. Her grandson
f. Her father-in-law
g. Her son-in-law
h. Her uncle

4-15 *Entity to Owner Attribution.*   C Corporation has 100 shares outstanding, owned as shown below.

Shareholder	Shares
L..	20
Partnership A (L is a 10% partner).........	20
Partnership B (L is a 60% partner).........	20
Corporation X (L is a 10% shareholder).....	20
Corporation Y (L is a 60% shareholder).....	20
	100

Under the constructive ownership rules of § 318, how many shares of stock is L deemed to own?

4-16 *Entity to Owner Attribution.*   C Corporation has 100 shares outstanding, 90 percent of which are owned by the A&B Partnership. Mr. A owns a 70 percent interest in the partnership and Mr. B owns a 30 percent interest in the partnership. Answer the following questions in light of the constructive rules of § 318.

a. How many shares do A and B each own in C?
b. Same as (a) except A&B is a corporation.

4-17 *Owner to Entity Attribution.*   D Corporation has 100 shares outstanding, owned as shown below. For each situation, determine how many shares the named entity owns in D Corporation under the constructive ownership rules of § 318.

a. How many shares does Partnership X own in D?

Shareholder	Shares in D
Mr. J.......................................	60
Partnership X (J is a 20% partner)..........	40
	100

b. How many shares does Corporation X own in D?

Shareholder	Shares in D
Mr. J.......................................	60
Corporation X (J is a 20% shareholder).....	40
	100

c. Same as (b) except J owns 80 percent of X.

4-18 *Constructive Ownership Rules.* M, Inc.'s 1,000 shares of stock are owned as follows:

Shareholder	Shares Owned
B	300
D, B's wife	190
F, B's brother	80
H, D's mother	70
J, Inc.	110
L, a partnership	120
N, a trust	130
Total	1,000

Both J, Inc. and L are owned 60 percent by B and 40 percent by F. N was established by H for the benefit of B's and D's children, ages 7 and 10. Determine the direct and indirect ownership interest in M, Inc. attributable to each of M's shareholders.

4-19 *Redemptions and Constructive Ownership Rules.* Z Corporation has 200 shares of common stock outstanding, 100 owned by A and 100 owned by B. Z plans to redeem all 100 shares owned by A. Indicate the number of shares owned by A after the redemption in each of the following cases.

a. B is A's wife.
b. B is A's estranged wife. They continue to be married only for political reasons.
c. B is a corporation. A owns 50 percent of B's stock.
d. B is a corporation. A owns 40 percent of B's stock.
e. A is a corporation. B owns 50 percent of A's stock.
f. B is the wife of A's son, R.
g. A is a trust whose sole beneficiary is B's son.

4-20 *Multiple Shareholder Redemption.* T Corporation has 100 shares of stock outstanding owned, as indicated below. Buck Smith is married to Tina Smith, while John Brown is the father of Lucy Brown. The Smiths and the Browns are not related. During the year, the corporation redeemed 33 shares from the shareholders as shown below, paying $2,000 for each share redeemed. Each shareholder had a $200 basis in each share of stock owned prior to the redemption.

Name	Shares Before	Shares Redeemed
Buck Smith	40	23
Tina Smith	10	2
John Brown	45	4
Lucy Brown	5	4
	100	33

a. What are the tax consequences of the redemption to Buck Smith? Indicate the income, its character, and the basis of his remaining stock.
b. What are the tax consequences of the redemption to John Brown? Indicate the income, its character, and the basis of his remaining stock.

4-21   Section *311 and Redemption Distributions.*   This year, C Corporation redeemed all of the stock of two of its shareholders, A and B. The corporation distributed land worth $75,000 (basis $10,000) to A and equipment worth $30,000 (basis $40,000) to B. What are the effects of the distributions, if any, on C's taxable income?

4-22   *Earnings and Profits.*   A distribution is made when D, Inc. has assets valued at $500,000 (basis of $300,000), E&P of $80,000, and 10,000 shares of stock outstanding. T receives assets valued at $100,000 (basis of $60,000) for all his D stock (2,000 shares with a basis of $25,000). Compute the corporation's E&P balance after the exchange if it is treated as (a) a dividend, or as (b) a sale.

4-23   *Section 302 Redemptions.*   H and D (unrelated), F and S (father and son), and PAC Corporation own the outstanding shares of stock of CEL Corporation, as follows:

Shareholder	Adjusted Basis for Stock	Pre-redemption Ownership
H	$5,000	40
D	10,000	10
F	15,000	25
S	1,000	5
PAC	25,000	20
Total		100

In addition, H owns 80 percent of PAC, while F owns the remaining 20 percent. CEL Corporation has $100,000 of E&P. Each individual is an employee of CEL.

a.   What are the tax consequences to H and CEL if CEL redeems 20 shares of H's stock for $15,000? Include in your answer the effect on (1) H's taxable income, (2) H's basis of his stock in CEL, (3) CEL's taxable income, and (4) CEL's E&P.

b.   Same as (a) except H owns 45 percent of PAC.

c.   S wishes to redeem his shares only if he can obtain sale treatment. Can S's desires be accommodated? Explain.

d.   What amount of gain or loss, if any, must CEL recognize if it distributes a crane worth $50,000 (cost $40,000, depreciation $10,000) to PAC for five of its shares?

e.   Same as (d) except the property's basis to CEL was $75,000.

4-24 *Partial Liquidations: Qualification.* HPI Corp. has 500 shares outstanding, 400 owned by B and 100 owned by R. HPI operates the following:

1. A tavern which it purchased for $100,000 cash from its prior owners in 1977.

2. A sporting goods store it obtained in March 1989 from B in exchange for 300 shares of HPI stock. B had operated the store as a sole proprietor since 1970. Prior to this acquisition, HPI had 200 shares outstanding, 100 owned by both B and R.

3. An apartment building which it purchased three years ago. The building was new when it was acquired.

Each of the activities described above are equivalent in value. HPI desires to distribute one of these to B in exchange for 167 shares of stock on December 1, 1991. Of those listed, which may B receive and be assured of sale treatment? Explain your answer.

4-25 *Partial Liquidation: Shareholder Treatment.* C, an individual, owns all 100 of the outstanding shares of Y Corporation. She had acquired the stock for $100 per share several years ago. In a transaction qualifying as a partial liquidation, Y redeemed 20 shares of C for $30,000.

a. What are the tax consequences to C?

b. Same as (a) except assume that C is a corporation.

4-26 *Partial Liquidation: Computations.* DSA Corp., which is in the printing business, is owned equally by the following parties: individuals Q, R, S, and corporation TUV. Each shareholder has a $10,000 basis in the 25 shares of stock owned, which they acquired 10 years ago when they formed the corporation. During the year, DSA redeemed 10 shares from Q for $15,000. Assuming the redemption qualifies as a partial liquidation, answer the following:

a. What is the effect of the redemption on the taxable income of Q?

b. Assume DSA obtained Q's shares in exchange for photocopying equipment worth $15,000 (cost $8,000 in 1981, depreciation $6,000). What amount of gain or loss, if any, must DSA recognize on the transfer?

c. Same as (a) except DSA redeemed 10 shares from TUV for $15,000.

4-27 *Partial Liquidation: Computations.* CRS Corp. is owned and operated by J, K, L, and UGH, Inc. J owns 40 shares (basis $20,000), which he acquired when the corporation was organized in 1982. K owns 15 shares (basis $7,500), which she also acquired upon organization. L owns 20 shares, which he acquired from K in 1989 for $12,000. UGH owns the remaining 25 shares (basis $9,000). CRS has E&P of $200,000. As part of a transaction qualifying as a partial liquidation, CRS redeemed the following in 1991: 20 shares from J for $20,000; 10 shares from K in exchange for a warehouse used in CRS's business worth $10,000 (cost in 1984 was $7,000, depreciation claimed using the straight-line method was $3,000); 15 shares from L in exchange for land used in the business worth $15,000 (basis $25,000).

For each of the shareholders identified in (a–d) below, indicate (1) the effect of the redemption on taxable income; and (2) the basis of any property received.

a. J

b. K

c. L

d. What is the effect of the redemption on the taxable income of CRS?

4-28   *Death Tax Redemptions: Qualification/Computations.*   On January 1, 1991 K died. His gross estate of $2 million included a 10 percent interest (10,000) shares in XYZ Corporation worth $800,000 and a 25 percent interest in ABC Inc. worth $100,000. Funeral and administrative expenses deductible under §§ 2053 and 2054 were $60,000. Deductible debts were $240,000. Estate and state inheritance taxes were $90,000. The entire estate after payment of claims and taxes was payable to K's sole heir Z.

    a.   Would a redemption of either XYZ or ABC stock qualify for sale treatment under § 303?

    b.   On August 1, 1991, XYZ redeemed 1,000 shares of its stock for $80,000 from the estate. What are the tax consequences to the estate?

    c.   Refer to (b). Would additional redemptions of XYZ stock qualify for § 303 treatment? If so, in what amount?

4-29   *Brother-Sister Redemptions.*   T owns 50 of the 100 outstanding shares of ISC Corp. stock and 80 of the 100 outstanding shares of ACC Corp. stock. The remaining shares of each corporation are held by a party unrelated to T. T has a basis in the ISC stock of $5,000 ($100 per share) and a basis in the ACC Corp. stock of $4,000 ($50 per share). The E&P of ISC and ACC are $10,000 and $15,000, respectively. During the year, T sold 30 shares of ISC to ACC for $20,000.

    a.   Compute T's gain or loss on the sale and state its character.

    b.   What is T's basis in her remaining shares of ISC?

    c.   What is T's basis in her shares of ACC?

    d.   What is ACC's basis in the ISC shares purchased?

    e.   Answer (a–d) assuming T owns 60 of ACC's shares.

4-30   *Parent-Subsidiary Redemptions.*   T owns 120 of the 200 outstanding shares of P Corporation stock. His basis in the shares is $6,000 ($50 per share). P owns 90 of the 100 outstanding shares of S Corporation stock. The E&P of P and S are $25,000 and $30,000, respectively. During the year, T sold 80 shares of P stock to S for $40,000.

    a.   Compute T's gain or loss on the sale and state its character.

    b.   What is T's basis in his remaining shares of P?

    c.   What is S's basis in the P shares purchased?

    d.   Answer (a–c) assuming T sells 20 shares.

4-31   *Preferred Stock Bailouts: Computations.*   T owns 100 shares of the outstanding common stock of WIC Corp. On June 3, 1987, the corporation distributed 20 shares of preferred stock as a nontaxable dividend to T. The preferred stock was worth $50,000. Accumulated E&P on June 3, 1987 was $40,000. The basis allocated to the preferred stock was $8,000.

    a.   Assume T sells the preferred stock to a third party for $42,000 on July 15, 1991 when WIC's E&P is $65,000. What are the tax consequences to T and WIC?

    b.   Same as (a) except WIC redeems the preferred stock.

4-32 *Application of § 306.* For each of the following situations, indicate whether § 306 applies, and if so, how?

    a.   T received a nontaxable distribution of preferred stock with respect to her common stock on May 2, 1991, when the corporation had a deficit in E&P of $50,000.

    b.   R received a nontaxable distribution of common stock (value $40,000) with respect to his common stock on June 1, 1991, when the corporation had E&P of $70,000.

    c.   X Corporation decided to reshuffle its capital structure. Consequently, it issued one share of common stock and one share of preferred stock to each common shareholder in exchange for all of the outstanding shares of common stock. The transaction qualified as a tax-free recapitalization under the reorganization provisions.

    d.   G inherited 50 shares of § 306 stock from his uncle.

    e.   H gave 30 shares of § 306 stock to her nephew.

    f.   E sold 50 shares of TYX common and 30 shares of TYX preferred that was § 306 stock to her father. This completely terminated her direct interest in TYX.

RESEARCH PROBLEMS

4-33 D Corporation has 100 shares outstanding owned as shown below.

Shareholder	Shares
Ms. J.	60
Partnership X (J is a 20% partner)	20
Partnership Y (J is a 70% partner)	20
	100

Under the constructive ownership rules of §318, determine the number of shares owned by each of D's shareholders.

Research source:

§ 318 (a)(5)

4-34 C Corporation has 100 shares outstanding, owned as shown below.

Shareholder	Shares
Mr. R.	60
Corporation X (R is a 20% shareholder)	20
Corporation Y (R is a 70% shareholder)	20
	100

Under the constructive ownership rules of §318, determine the number of shares owned by each of C's shareholders.

Research Source:

§318 (a)(5)

4-35   Bennie and his son, Ted, formerly owned Aluminum Tennis Frames Incorporated (ATF) equally. The corporation has manufactured and sold aluminum tennis frames to the leading sellers of tennis racquets in the United States for the past 10 years. In 1984 Bennie decided to turn his entire business over to his son and retire to the good life. To this end, ATF redeemed all of Bennie's shares to completely terminate his interest. ATF redeemed the shares by giving Bennie a note payable with 10 percent interest in 10 annual installments. Bennie filed the appropriate agreement necessary to waive the family attribution rules and hence, reported the gain on the redemption as a capital gain as each installment payment was received.

In 1991 Bennie, yearning for the excitement of business, decided he wanted to go back into business. During his absence from ATF, the business had grown and prospered primarily due to the tennis boom in the late seventies. Consequently, ATF had more orders than it could handle properly. Knowing this, Bennie approached his son about supplying ATF with racquet frames. Bennie and his son are considering signing an agreement whereby Bennie's company will provide racquet frames to ATF. It is anticipated that in 1991 all of Bennie's business will consist of sales to ATF. During 1992 and 1993, the percentage of Bennie's business attributable to the agreement with ATF is expected to drop slightly as the company plans to produce racquets for other companies, as well as a unique "elephant size" racquet (the Dumbo), which it will sell directly to tennis retailers and via mail order.

Bennie and his son have come to you to ask whether there are any tax ramifications related to the planned agreement.

4-36   In 1968 Perry and his wife, Della, incorporated his construction business. The business was quite successful, allowing the couple to enjoy the finer things in life. Over the years, however, Perry and Della became disenchanted with each other and decided to go their separate ways. Nevertheless, Della would not divorce Perry, fearing that it would have a negative impact on her political career.

Recently, Della decided to run for the state legislature. Needing money for her campaign, she is considering selling some of her stock back to the corporation. Can she obtain sale treatment if the corporation redeems a portion of her shares?

Upon completion of this chapter you will be able to:

- Define a liquidation and distinguish liquidating from nonliquidating distributions

- Explain some of the reasons for liquidating a corporation

- Determine the tax consequences of a liquidation to a shareholder and the liquidating corporation

- Discuss the special rules that apply when a parent corporation liquidates a subsidiary

- Explain the special election available to an acquiring corporation allowing it to treat the purchase of a target corporation's stock as a purchase of its assets

- Identify a collapsible corporation and explain the related tax consequences

Chapter 5

COMPLETE LIQUIDATIONS

Chapters 3 and 4 considered several types of corporate distributions: distributions of property and stock as well as those relating to redemptions and partial liquidations. In all of these situations, the corporation continues to operate all or part of its business. At some time during the corporation's life, however, it may be appropriate to terminate the corporation's existence. In such case, the corporation must wind up its business affairs and proceed with a *complete liquidation*.

A liquidation may be desirable for a number of reasons. Many liquidations occur because the business's profitability, or lack thereof, no longer justifies continuing the corporation. Liquidation also may be desirable where shareholders simply seek the corporation's cash and other assets to meet other needs.

A liquidation often occurs in conjunction with a sale of the corporation's business. For example, a party interested in acquiring a target corporation's business might purchase the target's assets—rather than its stock. In such case, the corporation may sell the assets and subsequently distribute the sale proceeds to its shareholders in complete liquidation. Alternatively, the corporation may distribute its assets to its shareholders in complete liquidation whereupon the shareholders sell the assets to the interested buyer. On the other hand, the buyer may purchase the target's stock and subsequently liquidate its new subsidiary to obtain the subsidiary's assets. Regardless of how the sale is consummated, knowledge of the tax provisions governing liquidations is mandatory.

Still other tax factors may provide the motive for liquidation. Shareholders and management may wish to discard the corporate form to avoid such tax problems as double taxation or the risk of incurring the accumulated earnings tax or the personal holding company tax—special penalty taxes imposed on corporations that have improperly accumulated their earnings. If the corporation is suffering losses, another form of business such as a partnership would enable deduction of the losses by the owners.

Regardless of the reason for the corporate liquidation, the transaction should not be planned without a full awareness of the tax consequences. This chapter examines various tax aspects of complete liquidations as well as the related problems of so-called *collapsible corporations*.

COMPLETE LIQUIDATIONS IN GENERAL

The various liquidation rules do not operate unless the distribution is considered a distribution in complete liquidation. According to the Code, a distribution is treated "as in complete liquidation of a corporation if the distribution is one of a series of distributions in redemption of all of the stock of the corporation pursuant to a plan."[1] The Regulations elaborate, providing that liquidation treatment applies only if the corporation is in a "status of liquidation."[2] This status exists when a corporation ceases to be a going concern and is engaged in activities whose sole function is the winding up of its business affairs. Interestingly, a formal written plan indicating the intention to liquidate is not required; factors merely suggesting the intention to liquidate may be sufficient to warrant liquidation treatment. In addition, it is not necessary for the corporation to dissolve for the liquidation to be complete.[3] In fact, the corporation may retain a nominal amount of assets provided the reason for the retention is to preserve the corporation's legal existence.[4] Because of the imprecision in the definition of a corporate liquidation, it is sometimes difficult to determine whether the corporation is in a status of liquidation and thus whether the liquidation provisions apply.

Since a complete liquidation results in the termination of the corporation, its treatment differs somewhat from that accorded stock redemptions and other corporate distributions. Nevertheless, the basic tax question that must be addressed in both situations is the same: what is the effect of the liquidation on the liquidating corporation and its shareholders?

The tax treatment of the shareholders of the liquidating corporation is normally governed by Code § 331. This rule provides that a shareholder treats the property received in liquidation of a corporation as proceeds obtained from the *sale* of stock. Therefore, the shareholder must recognize gain or loss. The gain or loss is typically capital gain or loss since the shareholder's stock is usually a capital asset. The basis of any property received by the shareholder is its fair market value.[5]

The tax treatment of the liquidating corporation is normally governed by Code § 336. Section 336 generally provides that the corporation must recognize gain and loss on the distribution of property to its shareholders as part of a complete liquidation. As part of the liquidation, the corporation's earnings and profits are usually eliminated as is the corporation's basis in any property it distributes.

---

[1]   § 346(a).

[2]   Reg. § 1.332-2(c).

[3]   Ibid.

[4]   Ibid.

[5]   § 334(a).

Example 1.   Corporation X owns one asset, land, with a basis of $1,000 and a fair market value of $10,000. According to a plan of complete liquidation of X, the corporation distributes the asset to its sole shareholder, Y, who purchased his stock for $500. Section 331 requires Y to recognize a gain of $9,500 ($10,000 − $500) as if he had sold the stock. Y's basis in the property is its fair market value of $10,000. Pursuant to § 336, the corporation must recognize a gain on the distribution of the land of $9,000 ($10,000 − $1,000).

In addition to these general provisions governing complete liquidations, special rules exist that apply when a parent corporation causes a subsidiary to liquidate. These rules are contained primarily in Code §§ 332 and 337. A special set of rules contained in §338 may come into play as part of an acquisition when a parent corporation purchases the stock of another corporation and continues to operate it as a subsidiary.

The remainder of this chapter discusses the detailed tax treatment of corporate liquidations. It is normally assumed that the corporation is in the process of liquidating and fulfills the requirements evidencing a "status of liquidation" as discussed previously. If a "status of liquidation" does not exist, the following rules do not apply. Instead, the corporation and the shareholders are considered as having made and received a dividend distribution or distribution in redemption of part of the corporation's stock and are treated accordingly.

COMPLETE LIQUIDATIONS: EFFECT ON SHAREHOLDERS

When a shareholder receives a distribution in complete liquidation of a corporation, two questions must be addressed:

1.   What is the amount of gain or loss recognized and what is its character?

2.   What is the basis of any property received?

The answers to these questions depend on whether the rules generally covering all liquidations apply—those contained in § 331—or the special rules of § 332 concerning liquidations of a subsidiary. In this section, the general rules governing all liquidations other than those of an 80-percent-owned subsidiary are considered.

THE GENERAL RULE: § 331

Gain or Loss.   Under the general liquidation rules prescribed by § 331, amounts received by shareholders in complete liquidation of a corporation are considered as in full payment for their stock. Each shareholder recognizes gain or loss equal to the difference between the *net* fair market value of the property received (fair market value of the assets received less any liabilities assumed or taken subject to by the shareholder) and the basis of the stock surrendered.[6] If the stock was purchased at different times and for different amounts, the gain or loss is computed on each separate lot.[7] The liquidating distribution is allocated according to the number of shares in each lot.

> **Example 2.** C purchased 200 shares of ABC Corporation stock for $8,000 on January 1, 1986. On June 1, 1991 C purchased an additional 100 shares for $15,000. On October 7, 1991 C received $30,000 in complete liquidation of ABC. The allocation of the $30,000 between the two lots of stock and C's gain and loss on the deemed sale is computed below.

	1986 Lot	1991 Lot
Number of shares	200	100
Fraction of total	200/300	100/300
× Total received	× $30,000	× $30,000
Amount realized	$20,000	$10,000
Adjusted basis	(8,000)	(15,000)
Gain (loss) recognized	$12,000	($5,000)

Generally, corporate stock is a capital asset. Therefore, the gains and losses recognized under § 331 are capital gains and losses. Since each stock acquisition is treated separately, it is possible for a shareholder to have a long-term gain or loss on one block of stock and a short-term gain or loss on another block.

> **Example 3.** Same facts as *Example 2*. The gain on the stock acquired in 1986 is long-term, while the loss on the stock acquired in 1991 is short-term.

Time of Recognition. Shareholders could receive liquidating distributions all in one year or in a series over several years. When the shareholder receives all of the distributions in one taxable year, the exact amount of the gain or loss is reported in the year of receipt. If the payments are received in two or more taxable years, the shareholder must use the *cost recovery method* for recognition of gain or loss.[8] Under this method, each payment received is first applied against the basis of the stock.[9] After reducing the stock's basis to zero, all subsequent receipts are recognized as gain when received. In no case is loss recognized until all distributions are received.

---

[6] § 1001.

[7] Reg. § 1.331-1(e).

[8] Rev. Rul. 68-348, 68-2 C.B. 141.

[9] When a shareholder receives a distribution of property of indeterminable value, income may be reported under the open transaction doctrine causing a different result in some instances. See, for example, *Stephen H. Dorsey*, 49 T.C. 606 (1968).

Example 4. J owns 100 shares of M Corporation with a basis of $10,000. From 1991 to 1994, J received the following series of liquidating distributions from M Corporation.

Date of Distribution	Amount of Distribution
December 31, 1991	$7,000
January 7, 1992	2,000
January 12, 1993	3,000
January 21, 1994	4,000

Since she is receiving installments over several years, she uses the cost recovery method to report her gain. As shown below, the first $7,000 is nontaxable and reduces her basis from $10,000 to $3,000. The 1992 distribution of $2,000 is also nontaxable but further reduces her basis to $1,000. The first $1,000 received in 1993 is nontaxable. The remaining amounts are taxable when received. Therefore, J has a $2,000 gain in 1993 and a $4,000 gain in 1994.

	1991	1992	1993	1994
Remaining Basis	$10,000	$3,000	$1,000	$ 0
Distribution	(7,000)	(2,000)	(3,000)	(4,000)
Remaining basis	$3,000	$1,000	$ 0	$ 0
Gain recognized	$ 0	$ 0	$2,000	$4,000

Example 5. Assume the same facts as in *Example 4*, except that J receives only the 1991 and 1992 distributions. Again J uses the cost recovery method. She recognizes a $1,000 loss in 1992 following the final distribution—$10,000 (basis) − [$7,000 + $2,000 (1991 and 1992 distributions)].

Installment Notes. Absent special rules, the distribution of an installment note by a liquidating corporation to its shareholders would create a hardship for the shareholder. Under the general liquidation rules, shareholders must compute their gain on the "sale" of the stock using the full fair market value of the note. For example, consider a corporation that distributes a note to its sole shareholder worth $100,000 that is payable over the next five years in annual installments of $20,000. Under § 331, gain on the distribution must be computed as if the shareholder had received the entire $100,000 when the note was received— even though cash is actually collected over the next five years! Such treatment obviously could create a cash flow problem since the tax would be due currently but note payments would not be received until later. To eliminate this problem, a special exception has been created.

If a shareholder receives an installment note attributable to a sale of property by the liquidating corporation, the cash collections on the note (rather than the receipt of the note itself) may be treated as payment for the *stock*.[10] This special treatment is available only if the sale by the liquidating corporation that produces the installment note occurs within the 12-month period beginning on the date the plan of liquidation is adopted, and the liquidation is completed by the close of this 12-month period. If the liquidation takes more than 12 months (i.e., more than 12 months have elapsed from the time the plan is adopted to the time the final distribution to shareholders is made), the rule does not apply. Similarly, the rule does not apply to installment notes arising from sales *prior* to the adoption of the plan of liquidation. In addition, the special rule does not apply to installment obligations arising from the sales of inventory unless all the inventory of a trade or business is sold to one person in one transaction—a so-called *bulk sale*.[11] If the corporation is engaged in two or more businesses, a sale of the inventory of each business can qualify as a bulk sale. The effect of these rules is to reserve this special treatment for installment obligations attributable to sales of property— other than routine sales of inventory—occurring during the 12-month liquidation period.

> **Example 6.**   Z Corporation opened its first discount fur coat store in 1982 and was immediately successful. Over the next seven years, it expanded rapidly, establishing over 50 stores in 20 states. To obtain additional cash for expansion, it sold a warehouse on June 1, 1989, receiving $100,000 cash and a note for $500,000 payable in 10 annual installments. In 1991 the corporation was no longer able to compete and adopted a plan of liquidation on May 1, 1991. It had "going out of business" sales during the month of June at all of its locations. All of the inventory not sold at the end of June was sold on July 12, 1991 to its biggest competitor, E Corporation, for a $900,000 note payable over the next five years. Z distributed all of its assets, including the two notes, to its sole shareholder, D, on December 15, 1991. The sequence of events and their treatment are shown below.

6-1-89	5-1-91	12-Month Qualification Period		
		7-12-91	12-15-91	4-30-92
Sale of warehouse (nonqualified)	Adoption of plan	Sale of inventory (qualified)	Liquidation complete	

In reporting her gain on the liquidation, D is entitled to special treatment on the note received from E Corporation since it arose from a sale occurring after the plan of liquidation was adopted, and the liquidation was completed within 12 months. Although the property sold to E was inventory, special

---

[10]   § 453(h)(1)(A). Note that the corporation must recognize gain on the distribution of the installment note under § 336.

[11]   § 453(h)(1)(B).

treatment is still allowed since the sale qualifies as a bulk sale (i.e., substantially all of its inventory was sold to one person in one transaction). The note arising from the sale of the warehouse does not qualify for special treatment since it arose prior to the time the plan of liquidation was adopted.

When a shareholder receives an installment note that satisfies each of the requirements, a special calculation is made. The shareholder is effectively treated as having sold part of the stock for the note and the remaining part for any other property received. To determine the gain on each of the sales, the shareholder's basis in the stock is allocated between the note and the other property received based on their relative values. The gain or loss on the sale of the stock for the other property received is reported currently while the gain on the note is reported as payments are received.

Example 7. At the time N Corporation adopts a plan of liquidation, it owns the following assets:

	Basis	Fair Market Value
Cash.............................	$10,000	$10,000
Land..............................	10,000	25,000

Following adoption of the plan, N sells the land for $25,000 and receives the purchaser's installment note. N distributes the cash and installment note to its stockholder, B, whose basis in the stock is $3,500. B must allocate his basis between the assets received as follows:

$$\frac{\text{Cash}}{\text{Total receipts}} = \frac{\$10,000}{\$35,000} \times \$3,500 = \$1,000 \text{ basis allocated to cash}$$

$$\frac{\text{Note}}{\text{Total receipts}} = \frac{\$25,000}{\$35,000} \times \$3,500 = \$2,500 \text{ basis allocated to installment note}$$

B recognizes $9,000 gain on the cash received ($10,000 received − $1,000 basis). B's basis in the installment note becomes $2,500. Therefore, B will recognize gain equal to 90% of each dollar received on the note [($25,000 face amount − $2,500 basis = $22,500 gain) ÷ $25,000 face amount].

Basis to Shareholder. When a shareholder uses the general rule of § 331 to determine gain or loss on the liquidation, the shareholder's basis in the property received in the liquidation is its fair market value on the date of distribution.[12] In effect, the shareholders are treated as if they had purchased the assets using stock as the consideration.

---

[12]　§ 334 (a).

Example 8. K owned 100 shares of stock in L Corporation. K's adjusted basis in the stock was $400. L Corporation completely liquidated and distributed to K $200 cash and office equipment worth $700 in exchange for his stock. K's recognized gain is computed as follows:

Cash received by K	$200
Fair market value of property distributed to K	700
Amount realized	$900
Less: K's adjusted basis in his stock	(400)
Realized gain	$500

K's entire realized gain of $500 is recognized. K's basis in the cash received is $200. K's basis in the office equipment received is $700, its fair market value on the date of distribution.

COMPLETE LIQUIDATION: EFFECT ON THE CORPORATION

The previous discussion examined the effect of a complete liquidation on the shareholder. In this section, the effects of the liquidation on the liquidating corporation are considered. The primary concern is whether the corporation recognizes gain or loss on the distribution.

GAIN OR LOSS TO THE LIQUIDATING CORPORATION

Section 336 provides that a corporation generally must recognize gain *and* loss on the distribution of property as part of a complete liquidation. The gain and loss are computed as if such property were sold to the shareholder at its fair market value.

Example 9. Sleepwaves Corporation, a waterbed retailer, fell on hard times and decided to dissolve the business. During the year, the corporation adopted a plan of liquidation and completely liquidated. The furniture that the corporation was unable to move in their going-out-of-business sale was distributed to its sole shareholder. This inventory was worth $5,000 (basis $1,000). In addition, the corporation distributed land held for investment worth $8,000 (basis $10,000). The corporation must recognize $4,000 of ordinary income ($5,000 − $1,000) on the distribution of inventory, and a $2,000 capital loss ($8,000 − $10,000) on the distribution of the land.

Note that the gain and loss recognition rule of § 336 ensures that the appreciation on distributed property does not escape tax. This avoidance would otherwise occur because the shareholder's basis in the property is its fair market value. For instance, in *Example 9* above, the shareholder's basis in the inventory would be

$5,000. Therefore, a subsequent sale for $5,000 would result in no gain at the shareholder level. For this reason, the corporation is required to recognize the gain just as if it had sold the property.[13]

Liabilities. If the shareholder assumes a corporate liability or takes the property subject to a liability, the fair market value of the property is treated as being no less than the liability.[14] Therefore, where the liability exceeds the value of the property, gain must be recognized to the extent the liability exceeds the basis of the property.

> **Example 10.** T Corporation's only asset is a building with a basis of $100,000 that is subject to a liability of $400,000. The low basis is attributable to accelerated depreciation. The property is currently worth $250,000. Pursuant to a liquidation, T distributed the building to its sole shareholder, R. T Corporation must recognize a gain of $300,000 ($400,000 liability − $100,000 basis). Had the liability been $200,000, T would have ignored the liability and recognized a gain of $150,000 ($250,000 value − $100,000 basis).

Loss Recognition. The treatment of distributions in liquidation differs from that in nonliquidating distributions in that the corporation is normally allowed to recognize loss on a liquidating distribution.[15] This is not true for all liquidating distributions, however. As with nonliquidating distributions, Congress was concerned that taxpayers may utilize the loss recognition privilege to circumvent the gain recognition rule. To prohibit possible abuse, § 336(d) provides two exceptions concerning the treatment of losses.

Distributions to Related Parties. Section 336(d)(1) prohibits the liquidating corporation from recognizing losses on distributions to *related parties* if the distribution is either:

1. Non–pro rata (i.e., each shareholder did not receive his or her pro rata share of each type of property); or

2. The distributed property was acquired by the corporation during the five-year period prior to the distribution in either a nontaxable transfer under § 351 (relating to transfers to controlled corporations) or a contribution to capital.

For this purpose, a related party is the same as that defined in Code § 267 (e.g., an individual who owns either directly or constructively more than 50 percent of the distributing corporation's stock).

---

[13] Prior to 1987, corporations recognized gain only under limited circumstances and never recognized loss on the distribution or sale of property in connection with a liquidation.

[14] § 336(b).

[15] Note that § 267 concerning sales between related parties does not apply to a corporate distribution in complete liquidation. See § 267(a)(1).

Example 11. J is the sole shareholder of Z Corporation. In anticipation of the corporation's liquidation, J contributed a dilapidated warehouse to the corporation with a built-in loss of $100,000 (value $200,000, basis $300,000). Shortly thereafter, Z distributed the warehouse along with land worth $90,000 (basis $20,000). Absent a special rule, the corporation would recognize a loss of $100,000 which would offset the gain on the land that it must recognize of $70,000 ($90,000 − $20,000). Under the loss prohibition exception, however, no loss is recognized since the distribution is to a related party, J, and the property was acquired as a contribution to capital within five years of the liquidation.

Example 12. B and C own 70 and 30% of the stock of X Corporation, respectively. Pursuant to a plan of liquidation, X disposed of most of its assets, having only cash and two parcels of undeveloped land remaining:

Assets	Adjusted Basis	Fair Market Value
Cash.............................	$400,000	$ 400,000
Goodland.........................	100,000	300,000
Badland..........................	450,000	300,000
		$1,000,000

During the year, X distributed 70% of the assets to B and 30% of the assets to C. B received Badland and the cash while C received Goodland. X must recognize a $200,000 ($300,000 − $100,000) gain on the distribution of Goodland. However, none of the $150,000 loss on the distribution of Badland is recognized since the distribution of the loss property was to a related party (i.e., B owned more than 50% of the stock) *and* the distribution was disproportionate (i.e., B did not receive his 70% share of the property but rather 100%).

Example 13. Same facts as above except B received Goodland while C received Badland. In this case, X recognizes both the gain and loss. The loss is recognized since the loss property was not distributed to a related party but rather a minority shareholder. Even if the loss property had been contributed four years ago, the loss would be recognized since it is not distributed to a related party (but see discussion below concerning tax-motivated contributions of loss property).

Tax Avoidance Exception. The loss limitation rule of § 336(d)(1) applies only when loss property is distributed to a related party. Absent an additional rule, the loss prohibition could be avoided by distributing recently contributed loss property to a minority shareholder. To prevent this possibility, a second limitation on losses is imposed. Under § 336(d)(2), the amount of loss recognized by a liquidating corporation on the sale, exchange, or distribution of any property acquired in a § 351 transaction or as a contribution of capital is reduced. However, this rule applies only if the principal purpose for the acquisition was the recognition of a loss by the corporation in connection with the liquidation. It is generally presumed that any property acquired in the above manner during the two-year period prior to the date on which a plan of liquidation is adopted was acquired for the purpose of recognizing a loss. When the tax-avoidance motive is found, the rule effectively limits the loss deduction to the decline in value that occurs while the property is in the hands of the corporation. In other words, any built-in loss existing at the time of contribution is not deductible.

To ensure that any built-in loss is not deducted, the Code provides a special computation. For purposes of determining the *loss* on the disposition of the tainted property, the basis of such property is reduced (but not below zero) by the amount of the built-in loss (i.e., the excess of the property's basis over its value at the time the corporation acquired it). By reducing the basis, any subsequent loss recognized is reduced.

> **Example 14.** R, S, T, and U own the stock of Q Corporation. Knowing that the corporation planned to liquidate, R contributed land to the corporation with a built-in loss of $100,000 (value $200,000, basis $300,000) in exchange for shares of Q stock, which qualified for nonrecognition under Code § 351. During the course of liquidation, the corporation sold the property for $160,000. Under the general rule, the corporation would recognize a loss of $140,000 ($160,000 amount realized − $300,000 carryover basis). However, since the property was acquired in a § 351 exchange and the principal purpose of the transaction was to recognize loss on the property in liquidation, the special rule applies. The loss recognized is limited to that which occurred in the hands of the corporation, $40,000 ($200,000 value at contribution − $160,000 amount realized). In other words, the loss computed in the normal manner, $140,000, must be reduced by the built-in loss of $100,000. Technically, Q Corporation would compute the loss by reducing its basis in the property by the amount of built-in loss as follows:

Amount realized............................			$160,000
Adjusted Basis:			
Carryover basis........................		$300,000	
− Basis reduction:			
Carryover basis.....................	$300,000		
− Value at contribution................	− 200,000		
Built-in loss.........................		−100,000	
Adjusted basis.............................			(200,000)
Loss recognized............................			($40,000)

As noted above, loss property transferred more than two years before the plan of liquidation is adopted is generally exempt from the loss prohibition rule. In many cases, however, this rule may provide little relief for those situations where abuse clearly was not intended. For this reason, Congress instructed the IRS to write regulations creating at least two additional exceptions. First, the basis-reduction rule generally does not apply to property acquired during the first two years of a corporation's existence. Thus, persons who form a new corporation by transferring assets to it are not penalized if they are later forced to liquidate the venture. Second, the basis reduction rule applies only if there is no "clear and substantial relationship" between the contributed property and the corporation's current or anticipated business. For example, if the shareholders contribute raw land in New Mexico to a corporation that conducts all of its business in the Northeast and that does not expect to expand, there is not a clear and substantial relationship between the property and the corporation's business; thus, the basis reduction rule would apply.

BASIS AND EFFECT ON EARNINGS AND PROFITS

When a corporation liquidates, it normally distributes all its assets and dissolves. As a result, the corporation has no property remaining for which to compute basis. Similarly, the liquidating distributions effectively eliminate all the corporation's earnings and profits.

LIQUIDATION OF A SUBSIDIARY

EFFECT ON THE PARENT: CODE § 332

General Rule. Although a shareholder generally recognizes gain or loss on the receipt of a liquidating distribution, Code § 332 provides an important exception when the shareholder is a parent corporation and it causes its subsidiary to liquidate. Under § 332, a parent corporation generally recognizes no gain or loss on property it receives from the liquidation of a subsidiary corporation. This provision was originally designed to permit corporations to simplify complex corporate structures tax-free. In such case, any gain or loss not recognized is deferred through the basis provisions. The bases of the assets generally carry over from the subsidiary to the parent, ensuring that any unrecognized gain is recognized on a subsequent sale of the assets.

> **Example 15.**   S Corporation is a wholly owned subsidiary of P Corporation. S Corporation's only asset is land, which is leased to P. The land has a basis of $100,000 and a fair market value of $500,000. P liquidates S and receives the land. Under the normal liquidation rules, P would recognize a gain of $400,000. However, under the parent-subsidiary liquidation rules of § 332, P does not recognize any gain. P's basis for land is $100,000, the same as S's basis. Also, note that P's basis in its S Corporation stock is ignored.

Section 332 applies only if *three* requirements are satisfied:

1. *Ownership.* The parent corporation must own at least 80 percent of the voting power *and* at least 80 percent of the total value of the stock (except nonvoting, nonparticipating preferred stock) on the date of adoption of a plan of liquidation and at all times thereafter until the liquidation is completed.[16] Section 332 and the related provisions apply only to the parent. Minority shareholders—those owning less than 80 percent of the stock—are subject to the general liquidation rules of § 331 discussed earlier in this chapter.

2. *Cancellation of stock.* All of the subsidiary's property must be distributed in complete cancellation or redemption of the subsidiary's stock pursuant to a plan. The timing of the distributions depends on the nature of the corporation's plan of liquidation.

3. *Plan and time limits.* The liquidating distributions must be made pursuant to a plan of liquidation and within certain time limits. If all distributions occur within one taxable year of the subsidiary, no *formal* plan is necessary.[17] In such case, a shareholder's resolution authorizing the liquidating distributions constitutes a plan. Where the distributions do not take place within one taxable year, a formal plan must exist and the distributions must be made within three years of the close of the year in which the first distribution is made.[18] For example, assuming the subsidiary is a calendar year taxpayer and the first distribution is made during 1991, the final distribution can occur no later than December 31, 1994. In effect, the liquidation can occur over a four-year period.

If any of the above requirements are not satisfied (e.g., distributions are not made in a timely manner), the special liquidation-of-a-subsidiary rules of § 332 do not apply to any of the distributions. Instead, the general rule of § 331 applies. On the other hand, it is important to note that § 332 is *not elective.* If the above conditions are met, § 332 and the related provisions must be followed.

Insolvent Subsidiary. Section 332 does not apply if the subsidiary is insolvent since the parent corporation would not receive any assets in exchange for its *stock,* which is a requirement of a liquidation. Instead, § 165(g), concerning worthless securities (e.g., the subsidiary's stock), applies. This provision states that the corporation has a capital loss on a deemed exchange on the last day of the year. The loss is ordinary if the subsidiary is an affiliated corporation under § 165(g)(3). The subsidiary is considered an affiliated corporation if two conditions are satisfied. First, the parent corporation must own at least 80 percent of the voting power and at least 80 percent of each class of nonvoting stock (except nonvoting, nonparticipating preferred stock). Second, the subsidiary must have

---

[16] § 332(b)(1).

[17] § 332(b)(2).

[18] § 332(b)(3).

more than 90 percent of its gross receipts for all taxable years from sources other than rents, royalties, dividends, interest, and gains from sales or exchanges of stock and securities.

> **Example 16.** As part of a plan of expansion into the fast-food business, P Corporation purchased all of the stock of T Corporation for $100,000. This year, T became insolvent, having liabilities of $400,000 and assets of $250,000. As a result, P liquidated T, receiving all of its assets and assuming all of its liabilities. The liquidation rules do not apply since T is insolvent. P Corporation may deduct $100,000 as an ordinary loss since T is an affiliated corporation *and* it is an operating company (i.e., more than 90% of its gross receipts are not from passive sources).

EFFECT ON SUBSIDIARY: CODE § 337

Under the general rules governing liquidations, a liquidating corporation normally must recognize gain or loss on the distribution of property in complete liquidation. However, gain or loss recognition is not theoretically necessary when the gain or loss inherent in the distributed property is preserved for later recognition by the distributee. Preservation normally is accomplished by requiring the distributee shareholder to assume the liquidating corporation's basis. Under the normal liquidation rules of § 331, however, the shareholder recognizes gain or loss and takes a basis in the distributed property equal to its fair market value. In such case, recognition by the liquidating corporation is consistent since the gain or loss is not preserved.

Pursuant to the parent-subsidiary liquidation rules of § 332, the parent corporation does not recognize gain on the receipt of property from its subsidiary since the property is still held in the corporate form. In addition, under § 334(b) discussed below, the subsidiary's basis of the property carries over to the parent. As a result, any gain or loss attributable to the subsidiary is preserved for later recognition when the property is disposed of by the parent. Since the gain or loss is preserved, it is inappropriate to require a subsidiary to recognize gain or loss on a distribution of property when § 332 applies. Consequently, a special exception exists, exempting liquidating subsidiaries from gain or loss recognition. (See Exhibit 5-1 for a comparison of the general liquidation rules to the parent-subsidiary rules.)

Section 337. Under § 337, a subsidiary does not recognize gain or loss on the distribution of property to its *parent* corporation. The nonrecognition provision applies only to distributions of property *actually* transferred to the parent. Property distributed to any minority shareholder is generally governed by § 336, which requires gain or loss recognition. But as explained below, loss on distributions of property to minority shareholders is not recognized.

> **Example 17.** P Corporation owns 90% of the outstanding stock of S Corporation while the remaining 10% is owned by unrelated parties. In a liquidation pursuant to § 332, S distributed property to P with a fair market value of $90,000 (basis $40,000). In addition, S distributed property to

the minority shareholders worth $10,000 (basis $8,000). S recognizes no gain on the distribution to P since § 337 exempts a subsidiary from gain or loss recognition on distributions of property to its parent. However, S must recognize a gain of $2,000 ($10,000 − $8,000) on the distribution to the minority shareholders.

Gain and loss recognition is based on how the property is actually distributed, rather than on some hypothetical pro rata distribution to all shareholders.

Example 18. P Corporation owns 80% of the stock of S Corporation while the remaining 20% is owned by a monority shareholder, M. S Corporation owns assets valued at $200,000, consisting of land worth $160,000 (basis $60,000) and $40,000 cash. During the year, S liquidated under § 332, distributing the land to P and the cash to M. S recognizes no gain on the distribution of the property since it was distributed in its entirety to the parent corporation. Absent the rule discussed above, it may have been argued that S would be required to recognize 20% of the gain on the land as if 20% of the land had been distributed to M.

Absent any limitation, the above rule would allow the subsidiary to distribute gain assets to the parent to avoid gain recognition and loss assets to the minority shareholders to obtain loss recognition. To prohibit this scheme, § 336(d)(3) provides that no loss is recognized on distributions to minority shareholders under § 332.

Indebtedness of Subsidiary to Parent. Ordinarily when one taxpayer is indebted to another and the debt is satisfied using property, the indebted taxpayer realizes gain or loss as if it had sold the property and used the proceeds to pay the debt. Section 337(b) contains an exception to this general rule. The exception states that when a subsidiary corporation is indebted to its parent corporation and the subsidiary liquidates under § 332, no gain or loss is recognized by the subsidiary when it transfers property to the parent to satisfy the debt.

Example 19. S Corporation is a wholly owned subsidiary of P Corporation. S owes P $100,000 on account. As part of a complete liquidation, S transfers appreciated property worth $100,000 (basis $25,000) to P in settlement of the debt. Since S is being liquidated under § 332, it does not recognize any of the $75,000 gain realized on the transfer of property in payment of the debt. Note that P's basis in the property would be the same as S's, $25,000.

SECTION 334: BASIS OF ASSETS

Section 334(b)(1): The General Rule. When a subsidiary is liquidated by its parent corporation, the basis of the assets transferred from the subsidiary to the parent must be determined. Generally, the basis of each of the assets transferred is the same for the parent corporation as it had been for the subsidiary—a so-called *carryover basis*.[19] This rule applies not only to property transferred in cancellation of the subsidiary's stock, but also to property transferred in order to satisfy the subsidiary's debt to the parent. The amount of the parent's investment in the subsidiary's stock is ignored. The parent's basis is determined solely by the subsidiary's basis.

> **Example 20.**   S Corporation had assets with a basis of $1 million and no liabilities. P Corporation bought all of the stock of S Corporation for $1.2 million. Several years after the purchase, when S Corporation's assets have a basis of $800,000, P Corporation liquidates S Corporation in a tax-free liquidation under § 332. P Corporation's basis in the assets received from S Corporation is $800,000, the same basis as S Corporation had in the assets. The $400,000 difference between the basis of the assets and P Corporation's basis in the stock of S Corporation is lost.

> **Example 21.**   Assume the same facts as in *Example 20*, except that P Corporation had paid $700,000 (instead of $1.2 million) for S Corporation's stock. P Corporation's basis in the assets received from S Corporation is still $800,000, the same as S Corporation's basis in the assets. In this example, rather than losing a $400,000 investment, P Corporation received a $100,000 tax-free increase in its basis in S Corporation and its assets ($800,000 basis in S Corporation's assets − $700,000 basis that P Corporation had in S Corporation's stock).

As demonstrated above, this carryover of the basis of assets from a subsidiary to its parent can be either beneficial (*Example 21*) or detrimental (*Example 20*) to the parent corporation. For this reason, a parent corporation that plans to sell the business of its subsidiary must carefully evaluate whether a sale of stock or a sale of assets is preferable.

When the parent corporation in a § 332 liquidation uses the carryover basis of the subsidiary as its basis in the assets received [§ 334(b)(1)], the subsidiary recognizes no gain or loss on the distribution. This approach—nonrecognition with a carryover basis—ensures that any gain or loss inherent in the subsidiary's assets is preserved for later recognition. Note, also, that when the carryover basis rules of § 334(b)(1) are used, the depreciation recapture rules are not triggered. [20] Any recapture potential shifts to the parent corporation. In addition, the holding periods of the assets received by the parent corporation in the liquidation include their holding period while the assets were owned by the subsidiary.[21]

---

[19]   § 334(b)(1).

[20]   §§ 1245(b)(3) and 1250(d)(3).

[21]   § 1223(2).

When § 332 and the carryover basis provisions of § 334(b)(1) apply, the parent corporation inherits the tax attributes of the subsidiary under § 381. The E&P of the subsidiary is added to the E&P of the parent. (However, a deficit in the subsidiary's E&P cannot reduce a positive balance in the parent's E&P.) If the subsidiary has any net operating loss carryovers, § 381 generally entitles the parent to use such losses.[22] This rule in effect provides corporations with the opportunity to shop for other corporations that have net operating losses that they are unable to use for immediate benefit. To prevent so-called *trafficking in NOLs*, Congress enacted § 269, which authorizes the government to disallow the deduction where the principal purpose of the acquisition was to evade or avoid tax. The limitations applying to use of NOLs obtained through acquisitions are discussed in greater detail in Chapter 7.

The *Kimbell-Diamond* Problem. The general requirement calling for the subsidiary's basis to be carried over to the parent was the subject of dispute in *Kimbell-Diamond Milling Co. v. Comm.*[23] In this case, Kimbell-Diamond's plant was destroyed by fire and the corporation wished to purchase replacement property to avoid recognizing gain on the involuntary conversion. The only desirable plant was owned by another corporation that would not sell. To acquire the asset, Kimbell-Diamond purchased the corporation's stock and then liquidated the corporation. Kimbell-Diamond then used the basis of the assets of the liquidated corporation as its basis for the assets pursuant to §§ 332 and 334(b)(1). The amount that Kimbell-Diamond had paid for the stock of the corporation was much less than the liquidated corporation's basis in the assets. Thus, by using the carryover basis, Kimbell-Diamond received much larger depreciation deductions (and therefore had much smaller taxable income) than if it had actually purchased the plant. Upon audit, the IRS reclassified the transaction as a *purchase of assets* rather than a purchase of stock followed by a separate liquidation. As a result, the basis of the plant and other assets of the acquired corporation was their cost (i.e., their value) rather than a higher carryover basis. Upon further review, the Tax Court as well as the Fifth Circuit Court of Appeals agreed with the IRS that the two transactions should be treated as a "single transaction," thus creating the now infamous *Kimbell-Diamond* exception.

Under the *Kimbell-Diamond* rule, if the original purpose of the stock acquisition was to acquire assets, the acquiring corporation was required to use as its basis for the subsidiary's assets the cost of the subsidiary's stock rather than a carryover basis. Unfortunately, application of this principle was extremely troublesome since the basis of the liquidated subsidiary's assets ultimately depended on ascertaining the intent of the acquiring corporation—a subjective determination that all too often led to litigation. To make matters worse, the IRS found that corporate taxpayers could use the *Kimbell-Diamond* exception to their advantage. For example, consider a target corporation that has assets with a low basis but a high value. In this situation, the acquiring corporation would attempt

---

[22] The amount of NOL usable in any year may be limited if there has been an ownership change. See Chapter 7 for a discussion of this rule.

[23] 14 T.C. 74 (1950), *aff'd.*, 51-1 USTC ¶9201, 40 AFTR 328, 187 F2.d 718 (CA-5, 1951).

to avoid the carryover basis rules and obtain a cost basis in the subsidiary's assets by relying on the *Kimbell-Diamond* decision. Of course, in this case, the IRS found itself on the other side of the fence, arguing that the *Kimbell-Diamond* rule did not apply.

> **Example 22.**   S Corporation had a single asset worth $800,000 and a basis of $500,000. During the year, P Corporation purchased all of the stock of S for $800,000 and promptly liquidated it. Under the normal parent-subsidiary liquidation rules, P's basis would be $500,000. However, if P could successfully argue that the *Kimbell-Diamond* approach applied, its basis would be a cost basis of $800,000, that is, the price that P paid for S's stock.

The effect of the *Kimbell-Diamond* decision was to create a great deal of controversy. In some cases, a parent corporation would argue that the *Kimbell-Diamond* exception applied, and, therefore, its basis in the liquidated subsidiary's assets would be essentially the fair market value (i.e., the purchase price of the subsidiary's stock). In other cases, a parent would argue that the normal carryover basis rules applied. As a practical matter, a parent was often unsure what its basis ultimately would be.

Beginning in 1954, Congress tried several times to eliminate the problems with corrective legislation. However, a truly palatable solution was not found until the enactment of Code § 338 in 1982. Section 338 provides a rather unique solution in that it allows the parent corporation to select the basis that it would prefer (i.e., a carryover basis or a basis equal to the asset's fair market value). As explained below, however, this choice does not come without a price.

SECTION 338: STOCK PURCHASES TREATED AS ASSET PURCHASES

Under § 338, if the parent corporation purchases the stock of a subsidiary, it may *elect* to treat the *stock* purchase as a purchase of assets. This election essentially enables the parent to obtain the same basis that it would have obtained had it purchased the assets directly (i.e., a basis equal to fair market value rather than a carryover basis). If the election is made, the Code creates an interesting fiction to reach this result: the subsidiary is treated as having sold all of its assets to itself for the assets' fair market value. As a result, gain or loss is generally recognized and the subsidiary's basis for its assets is equal to the price paid by the parent corporation for the subsidiary's stock. In short, § 338 enables the corporation to choose between a carryover or purchase basis for the subsidiary's assets.

Although § 338 treats the stock acquisition as if it were an acquisition of the assets, there is no requirement in the statute that the subsidiary be acquired with the intent to obtain its assets. If the formal requirements of § 338 are met, the rules apply. Therefore, the acquisition of stock need not be for any particular purpose. In addition, there is no requirement that the subsidiary *actually* be liquidated.

Qualified Stock Purchase. To qualify under § 338, the parent corporation must make a *qualified stock purchase*: a *purchase* of stock of the target corporation possessing at least 80 percent of the voting power and representing at least 80 percent of the value of all the stock (except non-voting, nonparticipating, preferred stock).[24] To qualify as a *purchase*, the stock may not be acquired from a related party, in a transaction that qualifies under Code § 351 (relating to non-taxable corporate formations), or in any transaction that results in the purchaser using a carryover basis (e.g., gift or tax-free reorganizations).[25] As suggested above, the acquisition of control may occur in a series of transactions; however, the parent must obtain at least 80 percent control within any 12-month period.[26]

Example 23. S Corporation has 100 shares of stock outstanding. P Corporation purchases stock from unrelated parties as follows:

January 2, 1991	5 shares
May 5, 1991	50 shares
November 6, 1991	20 shares
February 12, 1992	15 shares

P Corporation acquires control of S on February 12, 1992, the first date that P owns at least 80% of S. Although the purchases extended over more than 12 months, since 80% of the stock was obtained in a 12-month period (May 5, 1991 through February 12, 1992), the acquisitions constitute a qualified stock purchase. The fact that P purchased five shares of S stock on January 2, 1991 is immaterial.

If the parent corporation meets the purchase requirement, it must elect to treat the acquisition as an asset purchase by the fifteenth day of the ninth month following the month of acquisition.[27] After the election, the subsidiary generally increases or decreases the basis of its assets to the price paid for the stock. The election, once made, is irrevocable. Failure to make the election results in the parent being treated as purchasing stock and thus prohibits the subsidiary from adjusting the basis of its assets.

Technical Effect of § 338. As mentioned above, § 338 does not require a liquidation. As a result, both the parent and the subsidiary may continue to exist. To accomplish its objective, § 338 effectively treats the target subsidiary as two distinctly different corporations: *old target* and *new target*. Under § 338, old target is treated as having sold all of its assets to new target for their fair market value as of the close of the acquisition date. The results of this fantasy are twofold. First, the subsidiary (i.e., old target) must recognize gain and loss on the hypothetical sale—a fully taxable transaction. Any gain or loss

---

[24] § 338(d)(3).

[25] § 338(h)(3). Stock acquired from a related corporation (including that where the basis of the stock carries over) may be treated as *purchased* if at least 50 percent of the

stock of the related corporation was purchased. § 338(h)(3)(C).

[26] §§ 338(d) and (h).

[27] § 338(g).

recognized on the hypothetical sale is reported on the *final* return of the old target for the period ending on the acquisition date. Second, the basis of the assets to the subsidiary (i.e., new target) is their cost, generally the price paid by the acquiring corporation for the subsidiary's stock as adjusted for certain items discussed below.

> **Example 24.**   P Corp. purchased 100% of the outstanding stock of S Corp. for $1 million. S had only one asset, land with a basis of $600,000 and a fair market value of $1 million. Assuming a § 338 election is made, S must recognize a $400,000 gain on the deemed sale of the land. Its basis in the land then becomes $1 million.

For purposes of determining the subsidiary's new basis in its assets, the deemed purchase price is generally equal to the price that the parent corporation paid for the subsidiary's stock. This price must be adjusted for ownership of less than 100 percent (i.e., the portion not owned by the parent) as well as liabilities of the subsidiary and other relevant items.[28] Note that in increasing the purchase price of the stock for liabilities of the subsidiary, such liabilities include the tax liability attributable to income arising from the deemed sale.

> **Example 25.**   During the year, P Corporation purchased all of the stock of S Corporation for $1 million. S's only asset is land with a basis of $200,000. It has no liabilities. Assuming P makes the appropriate election under § 338, S is deemed to have sold its assets, in this case the land, for its fair market value, $1 million. Thus, S must recognize a gain of $800,000 ($1,000,000 − $200,000). The tax liability arising from the deemed sale is $272,000 ($800,000 × 34%). After the hypothetical sale and repurchase, P's basis in the land is $1,272,000, its purchase price of the stock, $1 million, increased by the liability arising on the deemed sale of $272,000. Note that P, as the new owner of S, bears the economic burden of the tax liability. Consequently, assuming the value of the land is truly $1 million, P would no doubt desire to reduce the purchase price of the stock by the liability that arises with a § 338 election; that is, it probably would try to buy the stock for $728,000 ($1,000,000 − $272,000). If P did buy the stock for $728,000, the gain on the deemed sale would still be $800,000 since the land is considered sold for its value of $1 million. In such case, the tax liability would still be $272,000 and the basis of the land under § 338 would be $1 million ($728,000 purchase price of the stock + $272,000 tax liability). Note that the effect of these rules is to reduce the value of the target subsidiary by an amount equal to the tax liability that would arise if § 338 were elected.

---

[28]   § 338(a). Section 338(b) provides that the basis is the sum of the grossed-up basis of stock purchased during the 12-month ac-quisition and the basis of stock not pur-chased during that period, adjusted as nec-essary.

If the parent corporation owns less than 100 percent of the subsidiary, the deemed price must be "grossed up" to take into account the minority interest. The adjustment for a minority interest results in a deemed purchase price called the *grossed-up basis*. This grossed-up basis is obtained by multiplying the actual purchase price of the stock by a ratio, the numerator being 100 percent and the denominator equal to the percentage of the subsidiary stock owned by the parent.[29] This computation can be expressed as follows:

$$\text{Grossed-up basis} = \frac{\text{Parent corporation's basis in the subsidiary's stock on the acquisition date}}{} \times \frac{100 \text{ percent}}{\text{Pecentage of subsidiary's stock held by parent on the acquisition date}}$$

Example 26. P Corporation purchased 90% of the outstanding stock of S Corporation for $900,000. S Corporation had only one asset, land with a basis of $600,000. Assume that there are no liabilities or other relevant items that affect the deemed purchase price. Since P owns less than 100% of S, a grossed-up basis must be calculated. The result is $1 million [$900,000 purchase price × (100 ÷ 90, the percentage of S owned by P)]. If P elects § 338, S's basis for the land is $1 million. Note that the grossed-up purchase price will be increased by the liabilities of S Corporation.

Allocation of Deemed Purchase Price. The temporary regulations under Code § 338 provide that the deemed purchase price of the stock is to be allocated to the subsidiary's assets using the *residual value* approach.[30] Under this technique, assets must be grouped into four classes for purposes of making the allocation:

1. *Class I:* Cash, demand deposits, and other cash equivalents

2. *Class II:* Certificates of deposit, U.S. government securities, readily marketable securities, and other similar items

3. *Class III:* All assets other than those in Classes I, II, or IV, such as accounts receivable, inventory, plant, property, and equipment

4. *Class IV:* Intangible assets in the nature of goodwill and going concern value

---

[29] § 338(b)(4). Note that this approach must be modified when the parent holds stock not acquired during the 12-month period.

[30] Temp. Reg. § 1.338(b)-2T.

According to the system, the purchase price is first allocated to Class I assets in proportion to their relative fair market values as determined on the date following the acquisition. Because Class I assets are either cash or cash equivalents, the basis assigned to them is their face value. Once this allocation is made, any excess of the purchase price over the amount allocated to Class I assets is allocated to Class II assets, again based on relative fair market values. Any excess purchase price remaining after making the allocation to Class II assets is allocated to Class III assets based on relative fair market values. In allocating such excess to Class II and Class III assets, the amount allocated *cannot exceed the fair market value* of the asset. Thus, any purchase price that remains after the allocation to the Class I, II, and III assets is assigned to Class IV assets—hence, the reason for calling this method the *residual* value approach. By limiting the allocation to Class I, II, and III assets to the assets' fair market values, the rules generally seek to ensure that corporate taxpayers allocate the proper amount to goodwill.

For purpose of these allocation rules, the temporary regulations provide that the fair market value of the asset is its gross value computed without regard to any mortgages, liens, or other liabilities related to the property. These rules are illustrated in the following example.

> **Example 27.** P Corporation purchases from an unrelated person 100% of the stock of S Corporation on June 1, 1991. Assume the purchase price adjusted for all relevant items is $100,000. S's assets at acquisition date are
>
> | | Basis | Fair Market Value |
> | --- | --- | --- |
> | Cash | $10,000 | $10,000 |
> | Accounts receivable | 20,000 | 20,000 |
> | Inventory | 25,000 | 55,000 |
> | Total | $55,000 | $85,000 |
>
> The purchase price is first allocated to cash in the amount of $10,000. This leaves $90,000 to be allocated. Since there are no Class II assets, the allocation is to Class III. If the residual approach were not required, the taxpayer might allocate all of the remaining $90,000 to the receivables and inventory despite the fact that their value is only $75,000. If this were allowed, income from the sale of the inventory would be reduced and a loss would result when the receivables were collected. However, since the remaining purchase price ($90,000) exceeds the fair market value of the Class III assets, the basis of the assets in this class is their fair market value, $20,000 for the receivables and $55,000 for the inventory. This leaves $15,000 of the purchase price that has not been allocated. It is all assigned to goodwill.

Other Consequences of § 338 Election. Section 338 not only entitles the subsidiary to a stepped-up basis for its assets, it also treats the subsidiary as a new corporation in every respect. As a result, the subsidiary may adopt any tax year it chooses, unless it files a consolidated return with the parent corporation, in which case it must adopt the parent's tax year. It may adopt new accounting methods if it desires. MACRS depreciation may be used for all of the hypothetically purchased property—the anti-churning rules being inapplicable since the old and new subsidiary are considered unrelated. The new subsidiary acquires none of the other attributes of the old subsidiary. The earnings and profits of the old subsidiary are eliminated and any net operating loss carryovers of the old subsidiary are unavailable to the new subsidiary.

Consistency Provisions. In most situations, the target subsidiary has some assets that have appreciated in value (i.e., fair market value exceeds the asset's basis) and other assets whose value is less than the basis. In such case, the acquiring corporation, desiring the highest basis possible for the assets, might first purchase the appreciated property, then purchase the subsidiary's stock, and then liquidate the subsidiary under § 332. By so doing, the acquiring corporation would obtain the best of both worlds: a basis for the appreciated property equal to its fair market value and a carryover basis for the other assets. In the latter case, the basis is higher than it would have been had the assets themselves been purchased or had the stock been purchased followed by an election under § 338. To prohibit the acquiring corporation from effectively selecting the basis that is most desirable for each separate asset, the Code contains the so-called *consistency* provisions. According to these rules, an acquiring corporation is deemed to have made an election under § 338 to treat the stock purchase as an acquisition of assets—thus precluding a carryover basis—if it purchased any of the target subsidiary's assets during the consistency period. This period begins one year before the date of the first acquisition that comes within § 338 and ends one year after the acquisition date (i.e., the date on which the corporation obtains 80% control).

> **Example 28.** P Inc. purchased 60% of S Corporation's stock on March 7, 1991 and the remaining 40% on December 4, 1991. The consistency period runs from March 7, 1990 through December 4, 1992. If P acquires any assets of S during this period, it is deemed to have made a § 338 election, in effect causing all of the subsidiary's assets to reflect the purchase price of the stock.[31]

Similar rules exist requiring consistency for acquisitions where affiliated members of either the parent or subsidiary's group are involved.

---

[31] It is possible for P to file a protective carryover basis election. If it had, the purchase would not cause an automatic §338 election. Instead, P's basis in the asset would be the same as S's basis (i.e., a carryover basis).

Exhibit 5-1
Summary of Corporate Liquidation Provisions

Type	§ 331: *General Liquidation*	§ 332: *Subsidiary Liquidation*
Comments	Shareholders surrender all stock in exchange for property and liquidating corporation ceases to exist.	Parent recognizes no gain or loss and can elect purchase or carryover basis if 1. 80% control 2. Plan of liquidation 3. Distributions within one taxable year or three years after close of year plan adopted
Effect on Shareholder	***Sale Treatment*** Gain or loss realized = FMV − AB; Exception: Gain reported on installment obligation as payments received	***Sale Treatment*** Gain or loss: Parent recognizes no gain or loss
Shareholder's Adjusted Basis	***In Assets Received*** FMV [§ 334(a)]	***In Assets Received*** 1. Carryover, or 2. Stock price + liabilities if 80% control acquired in 12 months by purchase
Effect on Distributing Corporation's Taxable Income	***Sale Treatment*** Gains and losses recognized	***Gain or loss*** Carryover Basis: No gain or loss on liquidation Purchase Basis: Deemed sale, gain and loss recognized
Effect on Distributing Corporation's E&P and Tax Attributes	E&P eliminated; other tax attributes disappear	***Carryover Basis:*** Parent inherits subsidiary's attributes ***Purchase Basis:*** All attributes eliminated

COLLAPSIBLE CORPORATIONS

Section 341 states that the gain from sale or exchange of stock of a *collapsible corporation*, or a distribution in partial or complete liquidation of a collapsible corporation, is ordinary income (rather than dividend income or capital gain) to the shareholder.[32] This provision was enacted by Congress in order to prevent shareholders from receiving favorable capital gains treatment upon liquidation of their interest in a company that has not yet realized a substantial portion of its income.

> **Example 29.** G forms M Corporation to produce a movie. She invests $1,000. After the movie is completed, but before it is sold, M liquidates. If the film is worth $10,000, G has a capital gain of $9,000. A subsequent sale of the film by G for $10,000 results in *no* realized gain since G's basis in the film is $10,000. If the corporation had sold the film instead of liquidating, the corporation would have reported ordinary income of $9,000 ($10,000 − $1,000 cost to produce the film). On a subsequent liquidation, G would still report a capital gain based on the distribution of cash. Section 341 is designed to convert G's capital gain into ordinary income where M is liquidated before it recognizes a substantial portion of its income.

Due to the recognition of gain by M in liquidation, however, the usefulness of schemes such as that described above (as well as the significance of § 341) is severely diminished.

A *collapsible corporation* is defined as a corporation formed or availed of principally for the manufacture, production, or purchase of § 341 property with the *view* to a sale of the stock or a liquidation of the corporation before the corporation realizes two-thirds of the income from the property. Section 341 property includes inventory, items held for sale in the ordinary course of business, unrealized receivables, and § 1231 assets.[33] In order to qualify as § 341 property, the above items must be held by the corporation for less than three years. If the fair market value of the § 341 assets is at least equal to 50 percent of the fair market value of all the assets owned and 120 percent of the adjusted basis of the § 341 assets, § 341(c) creates a rebuttable presumption that the corporation is a collapsible corporation.[34] In applying this test, cash, stock in other corporations, and obligations that are capital assets are not considered.

---

[32] § 341(a).

[33] § 341(b)(3).

[34] § 341(c).

Example 30.   T Corporation, which was formed in 1990, owns the following on December 31, 1991:

	Basis	Fair Market Value
Cash	$10,000	$10,000
Inventory	20,000	30,000
Machinery and equipment	400,000	450,000
Land	400,000	500,000
	$830,000	$990,000

The § 341 properties are the inventory and the land. The machinery and equipment are excluded since they were used in the production of the inventory.[35] The fair market value of the § 341 property, $530,000, exceeds 50% of the total fair market value of assets, $490,000 [50% × ($990,000 − $10,000 cash)] and also exceeds 120% of its basis, $504,000 (120% × $420,000). Therefore, T Corporation meets the mathematical tests for a collapsible corporation.

A review of the definition of a collapsible corporation—a corporation formed for the manufacture or production of § 341 property including inventory—reveals that most corporations meet the initial test of collapsibility. Consequently, the crucial aspect of the collapsible corporation definition concerns the *view to collapse* the corporation. The definition of the term *view* is much broader than the term *intent*. The Regulations state that the requisite *view* exists if the sale or liquidation was merely contemplated as a recognized possibility.[36] The *view* does not have to be held by all the shareholders; rather, the *view* must be held by those persons in control of the corporation either through stock ownership or otherwise.[37] The corporation is collapsible if the view exists at any time *during* the manufacture, construction, or purchase of property. Thus, if the view arises after these activities are completed, collapsibility is avoided. Unfortunately, it is virtually impossible to determine when either the view arises or the activities are truly complete.

In addition to the requisite *view*, the sale or liquidation must occur before two-thirds of the income from the § 341 property is realized.[38] The two-thirds threshold represents a clarification made in 1984. Prior to this revision, collapsibility was avoided by recognizing a substantial portion of the income from § 341 property.

---

[35]   § 341(b)(3)(D).

[36]   Reg. § 1.341-2(a)(2).

[37]   *Ibid.*

[38]   Rev. Rul 72-48, 72-1 C.B. 102.

Only certain shareholders of corporations that have met the above conditions receive ordinary income treatment rather than capital gain treatment on dispositions or liquidation. The shareholders affected are those who own more than 5 percent of the value of the stock.[39] However, no shareholder will have ordinary income if the gain occurs more than three years after the completion of the production of the assets because the corporation would not then meet the definition of a collapsible corporation. In addition, a shareholder may escape collapsible treatment under the relief provisions of §§ 341(e) and (f).

---

[39] § 341(d).

TAX PLANNING

BUYING AND SELLING BUSINESSES

Although the term *liquidation* usually carries negative connotations, such is not always the case. Liquidations often arise in conjunction with a sale of a business. For this reason, knowledge of the tax rules governing liquidation is imperative whenever a business is being sold or purchased.

There are numerous methods that can be used for buying and selling the business of a corporation. Interestingly, the liquidation provisions play an important role in determining how the transaction is structured. Assuming the disposition of the business is to be taxable, the transfer normally takes one of two forms: a sale of assets, or a sale of stock. In most transactions, the parties must first determine whether the buyer will purchase stock or assets. Once this initial decision is made, most stock and assets sales follow a similar pattern.

When the buyer and seller agree upon a sale of assets, the transfer can be consummated in one of two ways. The target corporation may sell the assets desired by the buyer and distribute the sales proceeds and any unwanted assets to the shareholders in complete liquidation. Alternatively, the shareholders could sell the assets of the target. This could be accomplished by causing the target to distribute the assets to the shareholders in complete liquidation, followed by a sale of the assets by the shareholders.

A stock acquisition is far more straightforward. The selling shareholder simply sells the stock to the buyer. The buyer may decide to operate the corporation or, alternatively, liquidate the business.

Nontax Considerations.   Several nontax factors may dictate the form of the transaction (i.e., a sale of stock or assets). For example, stock sales are far easier to carry out than asset sales. When assets are sold, titles must be changed—perhaps for hundreds of assets—and creditors must be notified in conformance with the applicable bulk sales laws. Stock sales are much simpler in this regard since the seller merely sells the stock to the buyer.

Another important factor that may control the form of the sale, if present, is the existence of some nonassignable right such as a license, lease, trademark, or other favorable contractual arrangement. If such contracts cannot be assigned, only a sale of stock can preserve such rights.

Perhaps the most important factor to consider is the possibility of unknown or contingent liabilities. In a risky business, the seller wants to absolve himself from all liability—both known and unknown. Consequently, a sale of stock is desirable since the purchaser obtains not only all of the assets but all of the liabilities. Of course, the purchaser in this case wants to limit any exposure and may be unwilling to accept responsibility for the unknown (e.g., product liability or adjustments in prior taxes). When a stock sale is otherwise desirable, this problem may be alleviated by having the seller indemnify the buyer for any undisclosed liabilities.

Still other considerations may determine the form of the transaction. A sale of assets may be desirable where minority shareholders may be unwilling to sell their stock and the buyer does not want to share the business with outsiders. Similarly, the corporation may have undesirable assets that the buyer does not want to pay for. In such case, an asset sale would be favored.

Tax Considerations. Tax factors must also be considered when buying or selling a business. In this regard, a thorough understanding of the rules governing liquidations is indispensable.

From the seller's perspective, a sale of stock is often desirable. This derives from the fact that the sale of stock results in only a *single tax* at what historically have been favorable capital gains rates. On the other hand, a sale of assets normally results in *two taxes*: one at the corporate level on the sale or distribution of the business's assets, and one at the shareholder level upon liquidation. Obviously, the seller normally would prefer to sell stock to avoid the additional tax. Unfortunately, buyers may be willing to purchase the stock only at a substantial discount in light of the unfavorable consequences of *buying* stock.

On the buyer's side, the most important consideration is the basis in the assets acquired. In a purchase of stock, the basis of the acquired assets remains unchanged and does not reflect the purchase price of the stock. The buyer can obtain a basis equal to the asset's value only if the corporation is liquidated, or in the case of a corporate purchaser, an election is made pursuant to § 338. In such case, the buyer would bear the burden of the second tax. On the other hand, if the buyer purchases assets, the basis of such assets is their cost and the burden of the corporate-level tax is shifted to the seller. For this reason, the buyer is unwilling to purchase the stock at a price equal to the value of the corporation's assets.

Example 31. Target Corporation is 100% owned by Seller, who has a basis in his stock of $10,000. Target's sole asset is a steel mill worth $100,000 (basis $30,000). If Buyer purchases the stock of Target for $100,000, the results are twofold. Seller would pay a single tax on a gain of $90,000 ($100,000 − $10,000) while Buyer would own a corporation that holds a steel mill with a basis in the mill of $30,000. In effect, Buyer's basis in the assets acquired is far less than cost. Buyer could obtain a step-up in basis, however, but only at the cost of a second tax. If Buyer is a corporation, the § 338 election could be made, resulting in a deemed sale of the mill and a tax on a gain of $70,000 ($100,000 − $30,000). If Buyer is a noncorporate purchaser, a liquidation under the general rules would have the same result: the corporation would recognize a gain of $70,000 on the distribution of the property in liquidation. (Note that in such case, Buyer would have no gain on the liquidation since the basis in the stock, $100,000, is equivalent to the value of the assets received.) In each case, Buyer would incur a tax in order to obtain a cost basis in the assets. For this reason, a tax-wise Buyer would only be willing to purchase the stock at a price reflecting the tax inherent in the appreciated assets. From Seller's view, the value of his business is diminished by the corporate level tax which must be paid either directly in a sale of assets or indirectly in the form of a reduced sales price for the stock.

It should be emphasized that the above discussion deals with the typical situation where the assets have a value exceeding their basis. Other facts may suggest a different approach to disposing of the business.

> **Example 32.** Just last year, P Corporation purchased all of the stock of S Corporation for $1 million. S has a basis in its assets of $1.5 million. This year, Buyer Corporation has indicated that it would like to purchase the business of S for $1.2 million. In this case, P should liquidate S Corporation under § 332 and then sell the assets received from S. In so doing, it would recognize a loss of $300,000 ($1.2 million sales proceeds − $1.5 million carryover basis in S Corporation's assets), whereas a sale of stock would have produced a gain of $500,000 ($1.5 million − $1 million basis in S Corporation stock). Of course, the Buyer would prefer to buy stock in this instance so that it could enjoy a $1.5 million basis which exceeds its cost.

SECTION 338 ELECTION

When a corporate purchaser acquires another corporation, perhaps the most important tax consideration to be addressed is whether the § 338 election should be made. The § 338 election normally results in a step-up in the target corporation's assets equal to the assets' fair market value, with any additional basis assigned to goodwill. (See *Example 27.*) This step-up, however, can only be obtained at a tax cost arising on the deemed sale that results when the § 338 election is made. Therefore, the propriety of making the § 338 election can only be determined by evaluating whether the tax benefits to be obtained from the step-up in basis are worth the immediate tax cost.

Normally, the tax benefits to be secured from the step-up in basis enabled by a § 338 election (e.g., increased depreciation) are deferred. In some instances, such as where part of the basis is assigned to goodwill, no benefit is obtained from the basis step-up until the acquired business is sold. Consequently, a proper assessment of whether a § 338 election is worthwhile would involve discounting the future tax savings to determine their present value and comparing such benefits to their cost.

SHAREHOLDER CONSIDERATIONS

When the general liquidation provisions of § 331 apply, consideration should be given to the possibility of spreading the gain to be recognized by the shareholder over more than one year. By arranging for a series of liquidating distributions that spans several years, the gain is recognized in smaller increments thus reducing the marginal tax rate which otherwise would apply if the shareholder received the distribution in lump sum or all in one year.

Taxes might also be saved by making gifts of the stock prior to the liquidation to family members who are in low tax brackets. Gifts in trusts, or where the donor retains a reversionary interest in the trust, must be avoided, however, since a sale of the stock or property recently transferred to a trust is normally attributed to the donor under § 644.

LIQUIDATING A SUBSIDIARY

Any time a corporation purchases control of another corporation, consideration should be given to a § 338 election. The analysis should compare the future tax benefit of the basis step-up (e.g., increased depreciation and cost of goods sold) with the current tax liability resulting from the deemed sale.

Occasionally, a subsidiary is formed to enter a new business or to expand to a new geographical location. These new businesses often are unprofitable to the extent of bordering on insolvency. In these cases (especially if the subsidiary is insolvent), the parent should compare the tax treatment afforded by § 165(g) concerning worthless securities to that resulting from liquidating the subsidiary. Section 165(g) provides for an ordinary loss on the worthlessness of a subsidiary's stock. This treatment is more favorable than the nonrecognition, carryover basis rules of subsidiary liquidations contained in § 332. To receive the favored treatment, the stock must be worthless. Therefore, all the assets must be transferred to creditors. If any asset is distributed to the parent in exchange for the stock, the security is obviously not worthless and a liquidation is deemed to occur. Therefore, it may be more beneficial to allow the creditors to take all of the subsidiary's assets rather than receiving a nominal amount that will preclude a loss deduction.

PROBLEM MATERIALS

DISCUSSION QUESTIONS

5-1   *Complete Liquidations in General.*   ABC Inc., a furniture store, is owned and operated by two brothers, F and G. While at dinner one evening they decided that they should no longer continue the business. As a result, they advertised a going-out-of-business sale to begin on June 1. Prior to that date the corporation began distributing cash and other assets of the business. As the assets of the business were sold, other distributions were made and creditors were paid off. At the close of the year, all of the assets had been distributed and the corporation was a mere shell. No stock was ever actually surrendered and cancelled. Will the distributions be treated as being made in complete liquidation? Explain and include the reasons why the determination is important.

5-2   *Section 331: Effect on Shareholder.*   K Corporation was no longer profitable. As a result, J, an individual and the sole shareholder of the corporation, decided to completely liquidate under the general liquidation provisions of § 331. The corporation distributed assets worth $100,000 to J in exchange for his stock which he had acquired several years earlier for $20,000. How will J treat the liquidating distribution?

5-3   *Section 334(a): Shareholder Basis.*   JCT Corp., a publishing firm, was owned by M. The corporation had published only one successful book in its 10-year history and consequently M decided to terminate its existence. JCT distributed cash of $15,000, equipment worth $40,000 (basis $8,000), and land worth $60,000 (basis $12,000) to M for all of her stock which had a basis of $3,000. What is the basis of the assets to M assuming the general rules applying to liquidations are followed?

5-4   *Section 336: Treatment of the Distributing Corporation.*   P Corp. adopted a plan of complete liquidation on June 1 of this year and subsequently distributed its only two assets, a patent worth $20,000 (basis $25,000) and land worth $50,000 (basis $10,000). What are the tax consequences to the corporation assuming the general rules applying to liquidations are followed?

5-5 *General Rules: §§ 331, 334(a), 336.* The balance sheet for M Corporation immediately prior to its liquidation appears below:

Cash.....................	$10,000	Accounts payable........	$8,000
Machinery...............	30,000	Earnings and profits......	52,000
Land....................	25,000	Common stock...........	5,000
Total..................	$65,000	Total..................	$65,000

The fair market values of all the assets were equivalent to their bases except for the land, which was worth $40,000. M Corporation distributed all of its assets to its sole shareholder, Q, for all of her stock which she had acquired two years earlier for $30,000. Assuming the general rules applying to liquidations are followed, answer the questions below:

a. What amount of gain or loss must Q recognize?

b. What is the basis of the assets received by Q?

c. What amount of gain or loss must M Corporation recognize?

5-6 *Liquidation of a Subsidiary: §§ 332 and 334(b)(1).* E Corp., a manufacturer of components for computers, has decided that a logical expansion of its operations would be in the robotics industry. T Inc. is presently building robots to be used in the automotive industry but is not profitable. E believes that with their expertise they can make T a profitable firm in three years. T's principal asset is worth $100,000 but has a basis of $150,000. E desires to acquire T and liquidate it to take advantage of T's losses and the high basis in its asset. What steps must E take to achieve their objective?

5-7 Kimbell-Diamond *Exception.* Consider the facts in Problem 5-6 above and answer the following questions:

a. How might the *Kimbell-Diamond* exception frustrate the objective of E?

b. Is the *Kimbell-Diamond* exception still applicable under the current statutory scheme?

5-8 *Section 338: Stock vs. Asset Purchases.* L Inc. is contemplating expansion by acquiring M Corporation. The principal asset of M is a manufacturing plant that is worth $500,000 and has a basis of $200,000, net of depreciation of $100,000. Assuming that L desires to buy the stock of M for $500,000, answer the following:

a. What steps can be taken, if any, by L to obtain a stepped-up basis for the plant?

b. Can L obtain the step-up in basis in a nontaxable transaction?

5-9 *Consistency Provisions.* J Corporation has decided to expand by acquiring M Inc. M Inc. owns land worth $100,000 (basis $25,000) and equipment worth $200,000 (basis $500,000). In order to obtain the highest basis for M's assets, J's advisor has suggested that it should initially purchase the land for $100,000. Subsequent to the land acquisition, the corporation was advised to purchase all of the stock of M for $200,000 and liquidate the company under § 332 and utilize the carryover basis provisions of § 334(b)(1). Comment on the validity of the advisor's plan.

5-10 *Collapsible Corporations.*   W has developed many real estate projects through-out the city. Ten years ago, he created a corporation that built an apartment project. The apartment project has not been successful and now W is convert-ing the apartments to condominiums for sale. Sales have been slow so W has decided that he would like to unload the whole business by selling his stock to H. Would the collapsible corporation provisions apply in this situation? Explain why or why not and state why the determination is important.

PROBLEMS

5-11 *Liquidations—General Rules (§§ 331 and 336).*   S, an individual, owns all of the stock of B Corporation. S purchased the stock 10 years ago for $300,000. S decided to completely liquidate B Corporation, and all of the assets of B Corpo-ration were distributed to S. The balance sheet for B Corporation immediately prior to the liquidation is as follows:

		Basis	Fair Market Value
Cash		$ 40,000	$ 40,000
Marketable securities (acquired after 1953)		90,000	80,000
Equipment	$300,000		
Less: Accumulated depreciation	(150,000)	150,000	200,000
Land		520,000	880,000
Total assets		$800,000	$1,200,000
Retained earnings		$500,000	$ 0
Common stock		300,000	1,200,000
Total equity		$800,000	$1,200,000

Assume earnings and profits prior to the liquidation were equivalent to retained earnings.

a.   What is S's recognized gain or loss?
b.   What is S's basis in the assets received?
c.   How much, if any, gain or loss will B Corporation recognize as a result of the liquidation?

5-12 *Loss Considerations.*   Assume the same facts as in Problem 5-11 except the marketable securities were contributed in anticipation of the liquidation. How much gain or loss will B Corporation recognize on the liquidation?

5-13 *Liquidations (§ 332).*   Assume the same facts as in Problem 5-11 except that the stock is owned by S Inc. and the liquidation is pursuant to § 332.

a.   How much, if any, gain or loss must S Inc. recognize?
b.   What is the basis of the assets received by S Inc.?
c.   How much gain or loss, if any, must B Corporation recognize as a result of the liquidation?
d.   Assuming B Corporation has a deficit in earnings and profits and an NOL carryover, will these facts affect S Inc.?

5-14 *Section 338 Election.* Same facts as in Problem 5-11 except all the stock was purchased by Z Corporation during the last 12 months for $1 million. Assume Z makes a § 338 election.

   a. What is Z Corporation's recognized gain or loss?
   b. What, if any, income must B Corporation recognize?
   c. Assuming a 50 percent tax rate, what is the basis of the assets to B Corporation after the election?

5-15 *Section 331: Gain on Series of Distributions.* MAV Corporation decided to liquidate in 1991. In December 1991, the corporation distributed $30,000 to its sole shareholder, Y. The corporation also made liquidating distributions of $50,000 and $60,000 in 1992 and 1993, respectively. Y purchased all of her stock in 1986 for $35,000.

   a. Compute the amount of the gain or loss that must be recognized by Y on each of the distributions.
   b. Same as (a) except Y's basis in her stock is $200,000.

5-16 *Section 336: Gain or Loss on Distributions.* MOD Inc. operated a restaurant in downtown Phoenix. The business prospered for eight months, until several customers became stricken with food poisoning. Fearing the impact of this event on business, the company liquidated, distributing the items noted below to its sole shareholder. Indicate the effect on the distributing corporation for each of the following distributions, assuming the liquidation is a general liquidation under § 331.

   a. Land adjacent to the restaurant used as a parking lot worth $100,000 (basis $40,000).
   b. Land and building in which the restaurant was housed worth $200,000 (basis $90,000). Straight-line depreciation of $30,000 had been claimed and deducted.
   c. Restaurant supplies such as paper napkins, towels, etc., for which the corporation had claimed a deduction of $5,000.
   d. Oven equipment worth $10,000 (basis $15,000). Accelerated depreciation of $5,000 had been claimed. Straight-line depreciation would have been $3,000.
   e. One hundred cases of XXX wine, the house wine worth $12,000 (basis $7,000). The wine was accounted for using the LIFO method. Basis using the FIFO method would have been $9,000.
   f. A note receivable arising from the sale of land which occurred prior to the adoption of the plan of liquidation. The note had a face and fair market value of $100,000 (basis $35,000).
   g. Same as (f) except the sale occurred after the plan of liquidation was adopted.

5-17 *Section 336: Liabilities.* K Corporation purchased land with a building for $1 million, paying $200,000 cash and an $800,000 note payable at the end of five years. To date, the corporation has claimed depreciation of $600,000. As a result of a zoning change to adjacent land, the property has a fair market value of $725,000. K decides to liquidate and distributes the land and building to its sole shareholder, S. How much gain or loss must K recognize?

5-18   *Section 338 Election.*   P Corp. purchased 100 percent of S Corp. stock on January 15, 1991 for $500,000. At that time, S Corp. had two assets: appreciated land and equipment. The land was worth $400,000 (basis $15,000) and was subject to a $100,000 mortgage. The equipment was worth $200,000 (basis $70,000, net of $25,000 of depreciation). Assuming P makes an election under § 338 concerning the basis of the assets, indicate whether the following statements are true or false. If false, indicate why.

a.   The basis allocated to the assets of S will exceed $500,000.

b.   Assuming the basis allocated to the land and equipment is $612,000 ($500,000 cost + liability + tax), the basis for the land will be $408,000 while the basis for the equipment will be $204,000.

c.   S Corp. recognizes gain of $25,000 as a result of the election.

d.   Assuming P purchased only 80 percent of S's stock for $440,000, the basis of the assets would not differ from that which would result had P purchased 100 percent of S's stock.

e.   S Corp. may use MACRS in depreciating the equipment even if it was not doing so prior to the acquisition.

f.   S Corp.'s E&P will not be affected by the election.

5-19   *Collapsible Corporations.*   JKL Inc. is owned and operated by G. The corporation was formed to develop a nursing home, its sole asset. In 1991, the project was completed at a cost of $400,000. G intends to sell his stock in the corporation. For each of the following situations indicate whether the collapsible corporation provisions would apply to the sale. Assume that all tests for collapsibility are met unless otherwise stated.

a.   The sale will occur in 1992 for $500,000.

b.   G had planned on retiring from the rentals of the nursing home units, but financial difficulties arising during the construction of the project required the sale of the property.

c.   G owns 4 percent of the corporation's stock.

d.   G will liquidate the corporation rather than sell his stock to a third party.

e.   The nursing home units are sold as condominiums. Assume that G contemplated selling his stock before construction was completed, but did not actually sell until one-half of the units were sold.

5-20 *Distribution of Installment Obligation.* As of June 1, 1991, Z Corporation owns only two assets when a plan of liquidation is adopted.

	Basis	Fair Market Value
Marketable securities...........................	$10,000	$20,000
Undeveloped real estate.......................	30,000	80,000

On July 5, 1991, Z sells the land for $80,000 in exchange for the purchaser's installment note. Z Corporation distributes the securities and note to its sole shareholder, K. K's basis in Z's stock is $10,000.

a. What is K's gain recognized in 1991?
b. Assume that in 1992 K receives the first installment payment on the note of $20,000. How much gain must K recognize?
c. What is K's basis in the assets received?
d. Does Z Corporation recognize any gain? If so, how much?

5-21 *Section 338: Basis Calculation.* On January 1, 1991 P Corporation purchases from an unrelated person all the outstanding stock of S Corporation for $90,000. S's balance sheet on the purchase date is as follows:

Assets	Basis	Fair Market Value
Cash......................................	$ 5,000	$ 5,000
Accounts receivable	20,000	20,000
Inventory(LIFO)............................	20,000	40,000
Equipment (accumulated depreciation of $10,000)..................	30,000	45,000
Total assets	$75,000	$110,000
Liabilities		
Accounts payable..........................	$20,000	$ 20,000
Equity....................................	55,000	90,000
Total liabilities and equity................	$75,000	$110,000

P properly elects § 338. S's tax rate is 34 percent.

a. What is the aggregate basis of S's assets after this transaction?
b. What is the basis for each individual asset?

5-22   *Selling a Business: § 332 vs. § 338.*   On June 1 of this year, Big Corporation acquired all of the stock of Little Corporation from Seller for $1 million. Seller's basis for his stock was $100,000. Little's balance sheet on June 1 revealed the following information:

Assets	Adjusted Basis	Fair Market Value
Cash..	$ 50,000	$ 50,000
Accounts receivable	450,000	450,000
Inventory	300,000	400,000
Equipment.....................................	70,000	200,000
Land..	30,000	100,000
	$900,000	$1,200,000

Liabilities and Equity		
Accounts payable............................	$200,000	$ 200,000
Retained earnings...........................	600,000	
Common stock	100,000	1,000,000
	$900,000	$1,200,000

In addition to the information above, an inspection of Little's prior tax returns indicated that it had investment credit recapture potential of $40,000. Little also had accumulated earnings and profits of $800,000 and a capital loss carryover of $60,00. Little is in the 34 percent marginal tax bracket.

a.   What are the tax consequences to Seller on the sale of the stock to Big?

b.   What are the tax consequences to Big and Little if Big liquidates Little shortly after the purchase and the § 338 election *is not* made? Indicate the gain or loss realized and recognized for each corporation, the basis of Little's assets to Big, and the treatment of Little's earnings and profits and capital loss carryover.

c.   What are the tax consequences to Big and Little if Big liquidates Little shortly after the purchase and the § 338 election *is* properly made? Indicate the gain or loss realized and recognized for each corporation, the basis of Little's assets to Big, and the treatment of Little's earnings and profits and capital loss carryover.

d.   Should the § 338 election be made? Explain why or why not.

5-23   *Sale of Subsidiary's Business.*   On May 1 of this year, P Corporation, a bank, acquired all of the stock of S Corporation, an insurance company, for $4 million. Shortly thereafter, state law was altered such that banks could no longer hold the stock of insurance companies. Consequently, P liquidated S under § 332 and sold all of S's assets for their fair market value of $4 million.

a.   Compute P's gain or loss assuming S's basis for its assets is $3 million.

b.   Compute P's gain or loss assuming S's basis for its assets is $5 million.

c.   Compute P's gain or loss assuming it sold the stock of S.

d.   Based on the results obtained above, what advice can you give P?

5-24 *Code § 336 Limitations on Losses.* R, S, and T own 60, 30, and 10 percent of the stock of Dynamic Developer Inc., respectively. Pursuant to a plan of liquidation, Dynamic sold all of its assets except for the following:

Assets	Adjusted Basis	Fair Market Value
Cash..	$300,000	$300,000
Land..	10,000	80,000
Warehouse................................	220,000	120,000
		$500,000

Indicate the amount of gain or loss that Dynamic must recognize in the following situations.

a. The corporation distributed the warehouse and $180,000 of cash to R, land and $70,000 of cash to S, and $50,000 of cash to T.

b. The corporation distributed the land and $220,000 of cash to R, the warehouse and $30,000 of cash to S, and $50,000 to T.

c. The corporation distributed the cash to the shareholders in their respective shares and distributed the land and warehouse, having each retitled such that each shareholder would own his or her respective shares.

d. Same as (c) except the warehouse had been contributed by R to the corporation four years ago in a nontaxable transaction at which time the property was worth $300,000 (basis $250,000).

e. Same as (b) except the warehouse had been contributed by R to the corporation one year ago in a nontaxable transaction at which time the property was worth $200,000 (basis $250,000).

RESEARCH PROBLEMS

5-25 S, an individual, manufactures and sells high-speed, high-quality portable printers to be used with personal computers. A major computer manufacturer agrees to buy all of S's output and to sell the printer with its computer provided S will guarantee to double production by the end of the year. The only way S can fulfill the contract is to acquire additional machines to manufacture laser printers. After unsuccessfully trying to buy the machines, S buys all the outstanding stock of M Corporation which owns the machines that S needs. S paid $600,000 for the stock. The basis of the machines (M's only assets) is $200,000. S immediately liquidates M and uses the machines in her business. What is the basis of the machines to S?

Research aids:

Kimbell-Diamond Milling Co., 14 T.C. 74 (1950) *aff'd.* 51-1 USTC ¶9201, 40 AFTR 328, 187 F2d. 715 (CA-5), 1955.

H.B. Snivley, 19 T.C. 850, *aff'd.* 55-1 USTC 9221, 46 AFTR 1703, 219 F2d. 266 (CA-5, 1955).

Chrome Plate, Inc., 78-1 USTC ¶9104, 40 AFTR2d 77-6122, *aff'd.* 80-1 USTC ¶9332, 45 AFTR2d 80-1241.

5-26   Data Corporation is interested in acquiring Sales Corporation. Since Data will pay a premium over book value for the stock, it will only make the purchase if it can make a valid § 338 election. Data has insufficient cash to buy all the stock whereas Sales has an excess of working capital. Therefore, Data plans the following:

1.   Purchase 40 percent of Sales stock on the open market in September, 1991.
2.   At the next shareholders meeting, convince the remaining shareholders of Sales Corporation to sell 30 percent of their stock to Data and have the corporation redeem the remaining 30 percent. The purchases will occur between March and August 1992. The redemptions will occur in November and December 1992.

If the transactions occur as planned, will Data be able to make a § 338 election?

5-27   Average Corporation is wholly owned by J, an individual. Although Average has not been very profitable, its assets have been appreciated in value. J wants to liquidate Average. However, he does not want to pay the tax on the appreciation at the corporate level. Therefore, he plans to contribute depreciated porperty to the corporation, which will sell it to an unrelated third party. J then plans to wait two years and one month and adopt a plan of liquidation. The corporation will distribute the appreciated property to J. J expects to use the capital loss carryover from the property he contributed to offset the gain on the distribution. Will J's plan succeed?

Upon completion of this chapter you will be able to:

■ Understand the rationale for the two corporate penalty taxes: the accumulated earnings tax and the personal holding company tax

■ Identify the circumstances that must exist before the accumulated earnings tax will apply

■ Recognize when earnings have accumulated beyond the reasonable needs of the business

■ Explain how the accumulated earnings tax is computed

■ Indicate when the personal holding company tax applies

■ Apply the stock ownership and income tests to determine if a corporation is a personal holding company

■ Explain how the personal holding company tax is computed and how it might be avoided

CHAPTER OUTLINE

Chapter 6

PENALTY TAXES ON CORPORATE ACCUMULATIONS

INTRODUCTION

In addition to the regular tax, a corporation may be subject to two penalty taxes—the *accumulated earnings tax* and the *personal holding company tax*. As the label "penalty" suggests, the primary goal of these taxes is not to raise revenues but rather to prohibit certain activities. The objective of the accumulated earnings tax and the personal holding company tax is to discourage individual taxpayers from using the corporate entity solely for tax avoidance. These taxes contend with potential abuse by imposing limitations on the amount of earnings a corporation may retain without penalty. The rationale for these taxes is readily apparent when some of the opportunities for tax avoidance using the corporate structure are considered.

Perhaps the best illustration of how the corporate entity could be used to avoid taxes involves the 70 percent dividends-received deduction. As discussed in Chapter 1, this deduction is available only to corporate taxpayers. Nevertheless, individuals could take advantage of the deduction by establishing a corporation and transferring their dividend-paying stocks to it. By so doing, all dividend income would be taxable to the corporation instead of the individual. Using this arrangement, the corporation would pay tax on dividends at an effective rate of 10.2 percent or lower [34% × (100% − 70%)] in 1991. Most individual taxpayers with taxable dividend income would reap substantial tax savings from this arrangement since all individual marginal rates are 15 percent or higher. This is but one of the alluring features of the corporate entity.

Another corporate advantage that individuals may use to avoid taxes concerns the difference between individual and corporate tax rates. Prior to the enactment of the Tax Reform Act of 1986, the top individual tax rate had perennially exceeded the top corporate tax rate—at one time by as much as 64 percentage points (see Exhibit 3-8 in Chapter 3). Individuals could capitalize on this disparity by shifting their ordinary income to a corporate entity. By so doing, they could obtain substantial tax savings. Although the 1986 Act reversed this longstanding relationship between corporate and individual tax rates, an individual can still obtain savings at lower levels of taxable income by splitting income between the individual and his or her corporation. For example, in 1991 the average corporate tax rate applying to $50,000 of taxable income is 15 percent while that for an individual is 20.4 percent. The savings obtained by utilizing this disparity, the dividends-received deduction, and other advantages of the corporate entity, illustrate that individuals could achieve wholesale tax avoidance if not for some provision denying or discouraging such plans.

The two penalty taxes battle avoidance schemes such as those above by attacking their critical component: the accumulation. This can be seen by examining the two previous examples. The fate of both tax savings schemes rests on whether the shareholder can reduce or totally escape the second tax normally incurred when the income is ultimately received. In other words, the success of these arrangements depends on the extent to which double taxation is avoided. Herein lies the role of corporate accumulations. As long as the earnings are retained in the corporation, the second tax is avoided and the taxpayer is well on the way to obtaining tax savings. To foil such schemes, Congress enacted the accumulated earnings tax and the personal holding company tax. Both taxes are imposed on unwarranted accumulations of income—income that normally would have been taxable to the individual at individual tax rates if it had been distributed. By imposing these taxes on unreasonable accumulations, Congress hoped to compel distributions from the corporation and thus prevent taxpayers from using the corporate entity for tax avoidance.

Although these penalty taxes are rarely incurred, each serves as a strong deterrent against possible taxpayer abuse. This chapter examines the operation of both the accumulated earnings tax and the personal holding company tax.

Mitigation of the double tax penalty and any resulting tax savings are not achieved solely through corporate accumulations. The effect of double taxation can be reduced or avoided in other ways. The most common method used to avoid double taxation is by making distributions that are deductible. Typical deductible payments include compensation for services rendered to the corporation, rent for property leased to the corporation by the shareholder, and interest on funds loaned to the corporation. All of these payments are normally deductible by the corporation (thus effectively eliminating the corporate tax) and taxable to the shareholder. Avoidance of the double tax penalty does not ensure tax savings, however. All of these payments are taxable to the shareholder; thus, savings through use of the corporate entity may or may not result. For example, savings could occur if the payments are made to shareholders after they have dropped to a tax bracket lower than the one in which they were when the earnings were initially realized by the corporation. In addition, even if the shareholder's tax bracket remains unchanged, deferral of the tax could be beneficial.

> **Example 1.** L operates a home improvement company, specializing in kitchen renovations. He is in the 28% bracket in 1991. Assume that he incorporates his business in 1991 and it earns $100,000, of which $50,000 is paid to him as a salary and $50,000 is accumulated. In 1991 L saves $6,500 [(28% − 15%) × $50,000] in taxes on the $50,000 not distributed. However, if the $50,000 accumulated is distributed to L as a salary in 1996 when he is still in the 28% bracket, the $6,500 of taxes originally saved is lost. Although no taxes have been saved, L continues to benefit because he has been able to postpone the $6,500 in tax for five years. Assuming

his after tax rate of return is 10%, the present value of the $6,500 tax is reduced to $4,035—a savings of $2,465, or almost 38%. Note that the savings would have increased if the distribution had been made to L when his tax bracket dropped below 28%.

ACCUMULATED EARNINGS TAX

The accumulated earnings tax, unlike most taxes previously discussed, is not computed by a corporation when filing its annual income tax return. There is no form to file to determine the tax. Normally, the issue arises during an audit of the corporation. Consequently, the actual tax computation is made only after it has been determined that the penalty must be imposed.

AN OVERVIEW

The accumulated earnings tax applies whenever a corporation is "formed or availed of" for what is generally referred to as the *forbidden purpose*, that is, "for the purpose of avoiding the income tax with respect to its shareholders ... by permitting earnings and profits to accumulate instead of being ... distributed."[1] Whether a corporation is in fact being used for the forbidden purpose and thus subject to penalty is an elusive question requiring a determination of the taxpayer's *intent*. Without guidance from the law, ascertaining the taxpayer's intent might prove impossible. However, the Code states that the required intent is deemed present whenever a corporation accumulates earnings beyond its reasonable needs unless the corporation can prove to the contrary by a preponderance of evidence.[2] The problems concerning intent are considered in detail below.

Not all corporations risk the accumulated earnings tax. The Code specifically exempts tax-exempt corporations, personal holding companies, and passive foreign investment companies.[3] In addition, the tax normally does not apply to an S corporation since it does not shield shareholders from tax. An S corporation's earnings are taxed to its shareholders annually.

If it applies, the accumulated earnings tax is imposed on the annual increment to the corporation's total accumulated earnings, *not* on the total accumulated earnings balance. This annual addition is referred to as *accumulated taxable income*. The tax is 28 percent of the corporation's accumulated taxable income.[4] This tax does not replace any other taxes (e.g., the corporate income tax or the alternative minimum tax) but is imposed in addition to these taxes.

---

[1] § 532(a).

[2] § 533(a).

[3] § 532.

[4] § 531. The Revenue Reconciliation Act of 1990 did not change this rate to conform with the top marginal tax rate imposed on individuals.

Example 2.   In an audit of P Corporation, it was determined that the company had accumulated earnings beyond the reasonable needs of its business. In addition, the corporation's accumulated taxable income was $150,000. Since evidence of the forbidden purpose is present and the corporation has accumulated taxable income, the accumulated earnings tax must be paid. P Corporation's accumulated earnings tax is $42,000 ($150,000 × 28%).

In short, the corporation actually pays the accumulated earnings tax only if the forbidden purpose is found and it has accumulated taxable income. The following sections examine the determination of the taxpayer's intent and the computation of accumulated taxable income.

INTENT

The accumulated earnings tax is imposed only if the corporation is formed or used for the purpose of avoiding income tax on its shareholders by accumulating earnings.[5]   Unfortunately, the Code provides no objective, mechanical test for determining whether a corporation is in fact being used for the forbidden purpose. As a result, application of the accumulated earnings tax rests on a subjective assessment of the shareholders' intent. The Code and regulations offer certain guidelines for making this assessment. Section 533 provides that a corporation is deemed to have been formed or used for the purpose of avoiding tax on its shareholders in two situations:

1.   If the corporation has accumulated earnings beyond the reasonable needs of the business

2.   If the corporation is a mere holding or investment company

The first situation is the most common cause of an accumulated earnings tax penalty. Consequently, avoidance of the accumulated earnings tax normally rests on whether the corporation can prove that its balance (i.e., that in excess of the $250,000 or $150,000 threshold) in accumulated earnings and profits is required by the reasonable needs of the business. Before discussing what constitutes a "reasonable need" of the business, it should be noted that other circumstances may indicate that the forbidden purpose does or does not exist.

According to the Regulations, the following factors are to be considered in determining whether the corporation has been used to avoid tax:[6]

1.   Loans to shareholders or expenditures that benefit shareholders personally

2.   Investments in assets having no reasonable connection with the corporation's business

3.   Poor dividend history

---

[5]   § 532(a).   [6]   Reg. § 1.533-1(a)(2).

Although these factors are not conclusive evidence, their presence no doubt suggests improper accumulations.

In determining whether the requisite intent exists, the courts have considered not only the criteria mentioned above but also whether the corporation's stock is widely held. As a general rule, the accumulated earnings tax does not apply to publicly held corporations. Publicly held corporations normally are protected since the number and variety of their shareholders usually preclude the formation of a dividend policy to minimize shareholder taxes. Nevertheless, the tax has been applied to publicly held corporations in which management was dominated by a small group of shareholders who were able to control dividend policy for their benefit.[7] Moreover, in 1984, Congress eliminated any doubts as to whether publicly held corporations are automatically exempt from the penalty tax. Section 532(c) currently provides that the tax be applied without regard to the number of shareholders of the corporation. Thus, the tax may be imposed on a publicly held corporation if the situation warrants.

While publicly held corporations usually are immune from the penalty tax, closely held corporations are particularly vulnerable since dividend policy is easily manipulated to meet shareholders' desires. Indeed, it may be a formidable task to prove that the corporation was not used for tax avoidance in light of the *Donruss* decision.[8] In that case, the Supreme Court held that the tax avoidance motive need not be the primary or dominant motive for the accumulation of earnings before the penalty tax is imposed. Rather, if tax avoidance is but one of the motives, the tax may apply.

As a practical matter, it is difficult, if not impossible, to determine the actual intent of the corporation and its shareholders. For this reason, the presumption created by § 533(a) looms large in virtually all accumulated earnings tax cases. Under this provision, a tax avoidance purpose is deemed to exist if earnings were accumulated beyond the reasonable needs of the business.[9] As might be expected, most of the litigation in this area has concerned what constitutes a reasonable need of the business. In fact, many cases do not even mention intent, implying that the accumulated earnings tax will be applied in all cases in which the accumulation exceeds business needs. Except in the unusual case in which a corporation's intent can be demonstrated, a corporation should be prepared to justify the accumulations based on the needs of the business.

---

[7] See *Trico Products*, 42-2 USTC ¶9540, 31 AFTR 394, 137 F.2d 424 (CA-2, 1943). In *Golconda Mining Corp.*, 58 T.C. 139 (1972), the Tax Court held that the tax applied where management controlled 17 percent of the outstanding stock of a publicly held corporation but the Ninth Circuit reversed, suggesting the tax should be applied solely to closely held corporations, 74-2 USTC ¶9845, 35 AFTR2d 75-336, 507 F.2d 594 (CA-9, 1974). Tax applied to publicly held corporation in *Alphatype Corporation v. U.S.* 76-2 USTC ¶9730, 38 AFTR2d 76-6019 (Ct. Cls., 1976). In Rev. Rul. 73-305, 1975-2 C.B. 228 the IRS confirmed its position that it will apply the tax to publicly held corporations.

[8] *U.S. v. Donruss*, 69-1 USTC ¶9167, 23 AFTR2d 69-418, 393 U.S. 297 (USSC, 1969).

[9] § 533(a).

REASONABLE NEEDS OF THE BUSINESS

The Code does not define the term "reasonable needs of the business." Instead it states that the reasonable needs of the business include the *reasonably anticipated needs* of the business.[10] The Regulations clarify the term reasonably anticipated needs.[11] First, the corporation must have specific, definite, and feasible plans for the use of the accumulation. The funds do not have to be expended in a short period of time after the close of the year. In fact, the plans need only require that the accumulations be expended within a *reasonable* time in the future. However, if the plans are postponed indefinitely, the needs will not be considered reasonable. As a general rule, the plans must not be vague and uncertain. If the plans are based on specific studies containing dollar estimates and are approved by the board of directors, the corporation is in a better position to prove that the plans qualify as reasonable business needs.

In addition to reasonably anticipated needs, the Code and Regulations identify certain specific reasons for accumulations that are considered to be reasonable needs of the business.[12] Several of these are discussed below.

Stock Redemptions from an Estate. A corporation is allowed to temporarily accumulate earnings in order to redeem the stock of a deceased shareholder in conjunction with Code § 303 (discussed in Chapter 4).[13] The accumulations may commence *only after* the death of a shareholder. The fact that a shareholder dies after accumulations have been made and the corporation redeems his or her stock under § 303 is ignored in evaluating pre-death accumulations.[14] If the shareholder owned stock in two or more corporations, each corporation is entitled to accumulate only a portion of the total redeemable amount unless the estate's executor or administrator has indicated that more shares of one of the corporations will be offered for redemption than will those of another corporation.[15] The requirements of § 303 (relating to redemption of stock to pay death taxes) must be met in order for this provision to apply.

Product Liability Loss Reserves. The Code also allows accumulations to cover product liability losses.[16] Product liability is defined as damages for physical or emotional harm as well as damages and loss to property as a result of the use of a product sold, leased, or manufactured by taxpayer.[17] The amount accumulated can cover *both* actual and reasonably anticipated losses.

Business Expansion or Plant Replacement. Perhaps the most common reason for accumulating earnings that the Regulations specifically authorize is for

---

[10] § 537(a)(1).

[11] Reg. § 1.537-1(b).

[12] See § 537(a) and (b), and Reg. § 1.537-2.

[13] § 537(b)(1).

[14] § 537(b)(5).

[15] Reg. § 1.537-1(c)(3).

[16] § 537(b)(4).

[17] § 172(j).

bona fide expansion of business or replacement of plant.[18]   This provision includes the purchase or construction of a building.[19]   It also includes the modernization, rehabilitation, or replacement of assets.[20]   However, this provision does not shield a corporation which has not adequately specified and documented its expansion needs.[21]

Acquisition of a Business Enterprise.   A second reason offered in the Regulations for accumulating earnings is for the acquisition of a business enterprise through the purchase of stock or assets.[22]   This appears to encourage business expansion, since the Regulations state that the business for which earnings can be accumulated includes any line of business the corporation wishes to undertake, and not just the line of business previously carried on.[23]   However, this provision for accumulation is limited by the statement in the Regulations that investments in properties or securities that are *unrelated* to the activities of the business of the corporation are unacceptable reasons for accumulations.[24]   The statements in the Regulations raise a question as to the validity of accumulations for diversification. On one hand the corporation can acquire an enterprise or expand its business into any field. On the other hand the acquisition should be related to the corporation's activities. This apparent conflict in the Regulations is reflected in court decisions. A corporation that manufactured automobile clutches was permitted to accumulate income to acquire a business that would make use of the corporation's metal-working expertise, whereas a corporation in the printing business was not permitted to accumulate income to acquire real estate.[25]   The extent to which a corporation can diversify is uncertain. It appears that diversification into passive investments is unacceptable whereas diversification into an operating business, no matter how far removed from the original line of business, is acceptable.

Retirement of Indebtedness.   The Regulations also provide for the accumulation of earnings to retire business indebtedness.[26]   The debt can be to either a third party or a shareholder as long as it is a *bona fide* business debt.

---

[18]   Reg. § 1.537-2(b)(1).

[19]   *Sorgel v. U.S.*, 72-1 USTC ¶9427, 29 AFTR2d 72-1035, 341 F. Supp. 1 (D. Ct. Wisc., 1972).

[20]   *Knoxville Iron*, 18 TCM 251, T.C. Memo 1959-54.

[21]   *I.A. Dress Co.*, 60-1 USTC ¶9204, 5 AFTR2d 429, 273 F.2d 543 (CA-2, 1960), *affg.* 32 T.C. 93; *Herzog Miniature Lamp Works, Inc.*, 73-2 USTC ¶9593, 32 AFTR2d 73-5282, 273 F.2d 543, (CA-2, 1973).

[22]   Reg. § 1.537-2(b)(2).

[23]   Reg. § 1.537-3(a).

[24]   Reg. § 1.537-2(c)(4).

[25]   *Alma Piston Co.*, 22 TCM 948, T.C. Memo 1963-195; *Union Offset*, 79-2 USTC ¶9550, 44 AFTR2d 79-5652, 603 F.2d 90 (CA-9, 1979).

[26]   Reg. § 1.537-2(b)(3).

Investments or Loans to Suppliers or Customers. The Regulations state that earnings may be accumulated to provide for investments or loans to suppliers or customers.[27] However, loans to shareholders, friends and relatives of shareholders, and corporations controlled by shareholders of the corporation making the loan indicate that earnings are possibly being accumulated beyond reasonable business needs.[28]

Contingencies. Although the Regulations do not specifically allow accumulations for contingencies, they do imply approval of such accumulations as long as the contingencies are not unrealistic.[29] Unfortunately, the distinction between realistic and unrealistic contingencies is difficult to define. However, the more specific the need, the more detailed the cash estimate, and the more likely the occurrence, the easier it will be to prove the accumulation is reasonable.

Redemption of Stock. As noted above, accumulations to redeem stock from a decedent's estate under § 303 constitute a reasonable need of the business. This provision does not cover any other stock redemption. Several cases have held that a redemption may be a reasonable need provided the redemption is for the benefit of the corporation and not the shareholder.[30] For example, the redemption of a dissenting minority shareholder's stock can be for the corporation's benefit whereas the redemption of a majority shareholder's stock would be for the shareholder's benefit. It might also be possible to prove that the redemption was necessary to reduce or eliminate disputes over management or conduct of the business.

Working Capital. Another reason mentioned in the Regulations for a reasonable accumulation of earnings and profits is the need for working capital.[31] This is one of the primary justifications corporations use for the accumulation of earnings. A corporation is permitted to retain earnings to provide necessary working capital. Initially, the courts tried to measure working capital sufficiency by using rules of thumb. A current ratio of 2.5 to 1 generally meant that the corporation had not accumulated income unreasonably.[32] The courts considered a current ratio more than 2.5 to 1 an indication of unreasonable accumulation.

In the 1965 case of *Bardahl Mfg. Corp.*, the Tax Court utilized a formula to compute the working capital needs of a corporation.[33] Under this approach (called the *Bardahl* formula), the working capital needed for one operating cycle is computed. This amount in essence represents the cash *needed* to meet expenses incurred during the operating cycle—the period required for a business to convert

---

[27] Reg. § 1.537-2(b)(5).

[28] Reg. §§ 1.537-2(c)(1), (2), and (3).

[29] Reg. § 1.537-2(c)(5).

[30] See *John B. Lambert & Assoc. v. U.S.*, 38 AFTR2d 6207 (Ct. Cls., 1976); *C.E. Hooper, Inc. v. U.S.*, 38 AFTR2d 5417, 539 F.2d 1276 (Ct. Cls., 1976); *Mountain State Steel Foundries, Inc. v. Comm.*, 6 AFTR2d 5910, 284 F.2d 737 (CA-4, 1960); and *Koma, Inc. v. Comm.*, 40 AFTR 712, 189 F.2d 390 (CA-10, 1951).

[31] Reg. § 1.537-2(b)(4).

[32] *J. Scripps Newspaper*, 44 T.C. 453 (1965).

[33] *Bardahl Mfg. Corp.*, 24 TCM 1030, T.C. Memo 1965-200.

cash into inventory, sell the merchandise, convert the customer's accounts receivable into cash, and pay its accounts payable. This necessary working capital is then compared to actual working capital. If necessary working capital is greater than actual working capital, an accumulation of earnings to meet the necessary working capital requirements is justified. If actual working capital is greater than the working capital needed, the corporation must show other reasons for the accumulation of earnings in order to avoid the accumulated earnings tax.

The initial step of the *Bardahl* formula is to calculate the inventory, accounts receivable, and accounts payable cycle ratios. These ratios are computed as follows:

$$1.\ \textit{Inventory cycle ratio} \quad = \quad \frac{\text{Average inventory}}{\text{Cost of goods sold}}$$

$$2.\ \textit{Accounts receivable cycle ratio} \quad = \quad \frac{\text{Average accounts receivable}}{\text{Net sales}}$$

$$3.\ \textit{Accounts payable cycle ratio} \quad = \quad \frac{\text{Average accounts payable}}{\text{Purchases}}$$

The ratios resulting from these calculations represent the cycle expressed as a percentage of the year. In other words, if the accounts receivable cycle ratio is 10 percent, then it normally takes about 36 days ($10\% \times 365$) to collect a receivable once it has been generated by a sale.

Instead of using the *average* inventory and the *average* receivables, a corporation can use *peak values* if it is in a seasonal business. If the corporation uses peak values for the other ratios, it may be required to use peak payables.

Once computed, the three ratios are combined. The result represents the number of days—expressed as a fraction of the year—during which the corporation needs working capital to meet its operating expenses. The operating cycle ratio is computed as follows:

$$
\begin{array}{l}
 \text{Inventory cycle ratio} \\
+\ \text{Accounts receivable cycle ratio} \\
\underline{-\ \text{Accounts payable cycle ratio}} \\
=\ \text{Operating cycle ratio}
\end{array}
$$

The operating cycle ratio is multiplied by the *annual operating expenses* to compute the necessary working capital. Operating expenses are defined as the cost of goods sold plus other annual expenses (i.e., general, administrative, and selling expenses). The operating expense category does not include depreciation since depreciation does not require the use of cash. However, the category can include income taxes if the corporation pays estimated taxes and will make a tax payment during the next operating cycle.[34] Other expenses should be included if they will require the expenditure of cash during the next operating cycle.

---

[34] *Empire Steel*, 33 TCM 155, T.C. Memo 1974-34.

The required working capital computed by the *Bardahl* formula is compared to actual working capital to determine if there have been excess accumulations. Since the computed working capital is based on accounting data, it is normally compared to actual working capital (current assets − current liabilities) computed from the corporation's financial statements. There are exceptions to this rule. Financial statements are not used if they do not clearly reflect the company's working capital. The Supreme Court authorized the use of fair market value instead of historical cost to value a firm's current assets in *Ivan Allen Co.*[35] The assets in question were marketable securities that had appreciated. The decision is broad enough to permit the Internal Revenue Service to determine actual working capital based on current value anytime there is a significant difference between cost and market.

Any corporation whose actual working capital does not exceed required working capital (per the *Bardahl* formula) should be exempt from the accumulated earnings tax. If the actual working capital exceeds required working capital, the excess is considered an indication of unreasonable accumulations. This excess is compared to the reasonable needs of the business (other than working capital) to determine if the accumulations are unreasonable. To the extent that the corporation has needs, it may accumulate funds. If all of the excess working capital is not needed, the tax is imposed. The tax is based on the accumulated taxable income and not the excess working capital.

> **Example 3.**   K owns and operates K's Apparel, Inc. (KAI). After hearing that a friend's corporation was recently slapped with an accumulated earnings tax penalty, she asked her accountant to determine the vulnerability of her own business. The following is a balance sheet and income statement for 1990 and 1991 for KAI.

---

[35]   *Ivan Allen Co. v. U.S.*, 75-2 USTC ¶9557, 36 AFTR2d 75-5200, 422 U.S. 617 (USSC, 1975).

Balance Sheet

	1990	1991
Current Assets:		
Cash	$ 55,000	$ 67,000
Marketable securities	10,000	8,000
Accounts receivable (net)	45,000	55,000
Inventory	30,000	20,000
Total Current Assets	$140,000	$150,000
Property, plant, and equipment (net)	300,000	425,000
Total Assets	$440,000	$575,000
Current Liabilities:		
Notes payable	$ 5,000	$ 4,000
Accounts payable	50,000	30,000
Accrued expenses	8,000	16,000
Total Current Liabilities	$ 63,000	$ 50,000
Long-term debt	37,000	40,000
Total Liabilities	$100,000	$ 90,000
Stockholders' Equity:		
Common stock	10,000	10,000
Earnings and profits	330,000	475,000
Total Liabilities and Stockholders' Equity	$440,000	$575,000

Income Statement

	1990	1991
Sales	$400,000	$500,000
Cost of goods sold:		
Beginning inventory	$ 40,000	$ 30,000
Purchases	300,000	320,000
Ending inventory	(30,000)	(20,000)
Total	$310,000	$330,000
Gross profit	$ 90,000	$170,000
Other expenses:		
Depreciation	$ 40,000	$ 55,000
Selling expenses	10,000	15,000
Administrative	20,000	50,000
Total	$ 70,000	$120,000
Net income before taxes	$ 20,000	$ 50,000
Income tax expense	(2,000)	(5,000)
Net income	$ 18,000	$ 45,000

In addition to this information, K indicated that at the end of 1991 the securities were worth $15,000 more than their book value, or $23,000. K also estimates that her reasonable needs for the current year 1991 amount to $20,000.

Under the *Bardahl* formula, her working capital needs are determined as follows:

Step 1:   Operating cycle expressed as a fraction of the year (in thousands):

$$\text{Inventory cycle} = \frac{\text{Average inventory}}{\text{Cost of goods sold}} = [(30 + 20) \div 2] \div 330 = 0.0758$$

$$+ \; \text{Receivable cycle} = \frac{\text{Average receivables}}{\text{Sales}} = [(45 + 55) \div 2] \div 500 = 0.1000$$

$$- \; \text{Payables cycle} = \frac{\text{Average payables}}{\text{Purchases}} = [(50 + 30) \div 2] \div 320 = (0.1250)$$

$$= \text{Operating cycle expressed as percentage of the year} \qquad = 0.0508$$

Step 2:   Computation of operating expenses:

Operating expenses:	
Cost of goods sold................................	$330,000
Selling expenses..................................	15,000
Administrative expenses..........................	50,000
Taxes	5,000
Total operating expenses..........................	$400,000

Step 3:   Working capital needs:

Operating expenses (Step 2).......................	$400,000
× Operating cycle (Step 1)..........................	× 0.0508
= Working capital needs.............................	$ 20,320

K's working capital needs, $20,320, must be compared to actual working capital using the assets' fair market value. Any excess of actual working capital over required working capital must be compared to the current year's needs to determine if unwarranted accumulations exist. Assuming the marketable securities are actually worth $23,000, the comparison is made as follows:

Actual working capital:		
Current assets		
($150,000 + $15,000)..........	$165,000	
− Current liabilities................	(50,000)	
= Actual working capital................................		$115,000
− Required working capital (Step 3)....................		(20,320)
= Excess working capital...............................		$ 94,680
− Reasonable needs....................................		(20,000)
= Accumulations beyond current needs................		$ 74,680

The accumulated earnings tax focuses on whether the corporation has accumulated liquid assets beyond its reasonable needs that could be distributed to shareholders. In this case, actual working capital exceeds required working capital and other needs of the business by \$74,680, implying that the accumulated earnings tax applies. If so, the actual penalty tax is computed using accumulated taxable income, as explained below.

COMPUTATION OF THE ACCUMULATED EARNINGS TAX

The purpose of the accumulated earnings tax is to penalize taxpayers with unwarranted accumulations. To accomplish this, a 28 percent tax is imposed on what the Code refers to as *accumulated taxable income*. Accumulated taxable income is designed to represent the amount that the corporation could have distributed after funding its reasonable needs. In essence, the computation attempts to determine the corporation's dividend-paying capacity. Exhibit 6-1 shows the formula for computing accumulated taxable income.[36]

Exhibit 6-1
Accumulated Taxable Income[37]

Taxable income:

Plus:
1. The dividends-received deduction
2. Any net operating loss deduction that is reflected in taxable income
3. Any capital-loss carryovers from other years that are reflected in taxable income

Minus:
1. Federal income taxes for the year, but not the accumulated earnings tax or the personal holding company tax
2. The charitable contributions for the year in excess of the 10 percent limitation
3. Any net capital loss incurred during the year reduced by net capital gain deductions of prior years that have not previously reduced any net capital loss deduction
4. Any net capital gain (net long-term capital gain − the net short-term capital loss) for the year minus the taxes attributable to the gain and any net capital losses of prior years that have not reduced a net capital gain deduction in determining the accumulated earnings tax

Equals: **Adjusted taxable income**

Minus:
1. Accumulated earnings credit (see Exhibit 6-2)
2. Dividends paid deduction (see Exhibit 6-3)

Equals: **Accumulated taxable income**

---

[36] § 535.

[37] § 535. Several additional adjustments are required for computing taxable income of a holding or investment company.

The computation of accumulated taxable income begins with an imperfect measure of the corporation's ability to pay dividends—taxable income. To obtain a more representative measure of the corporation's dividend-paying capacity, taxable income is modified to arrive at what is often referred to as *adjusted taxable income*.[38] For example, the deduction allowed for dividends received is added back to taxable income since it has no effect on the corporation's ability to pay dividends. The same rationale can be given for the net operating loss deduction. In contrast, charitable contributions in excess of the 10 percent limitation may be deducted in determining adjusted taxable income since the corporation does not have the nondeductible amount available to pay dividends. For the same reason, Federal income taxes may be deducted in computing adjusted taxable income.

The deduction for capital gains stems from the assumption that these earnings are used to fund the corporation's needs and consequently may be accumulated with impunity. Capital losses are deductible since these amounts are unavailable for payment of dividends and are not reflected in taxable income. As shown in Exhibit 6-1, however, the deductions for capital gains as well as capital losses must be modified.

Prior to 1984, corporations were entitled to reduce taxable income not only by the amount of their net capital gains (reduced by related taxes) but also by the full amount of their net capital losses, depending on whether a net capital gain or loss occurred. Consequently, there was an advantage in recognizing capital gains in one year and capital losses in another year in order to avoid netting and thus permit both gains and losses to be deductible in full. For example, if the corporation had a capital loss of $1,000 this year and a capital gain of $5,000 next year (ignoring taxes), both could be deducted in full each year in computing adjusted taxable income. However, if they occurred in the same year, the deduction would be limited to $4,000. To eliminate this planning opportunity, corporations are now required to reduce their net capital losses by any net capital gain deductions that have been used to arrive at adjusted taxable income in prior years. Under these rules, it is immaterial in what order or in what year gains and losses are recognized. In effect, taxable income is reduced only by the overall net gain or loss that the corporation has recognized to date.

---

[38]   This term is not found in the Code; it is used here solely for purposes of exposition.

Example 4. T Corporation has the following income and deductions for 1991:

Income from operations............................	$150,000
Dividend income (from less than 20% owned corporations)......................................	40,000
Charitable contributions............................	25,000

T Corporation computes its taxable income as follows:

Income from operations......................		$150,000
Dividend income............................		40,000
Income before special deductions............		$190,000
Special deductions:		
Charitable contribution (limited)..........	$19,000	
Dividend-received deduction.............	28,000	
Total special deductions.................		(47,000)
Taxable income.............................		$143,000

T Corporation's Federal income taxes for 1991 are $39,020. T Corporation's adjusted taxable income is computed as follows:

Taxable income............................		$143,000
Plus: Dividend-received deduction		28,000
		$171,000
Minus the sum of		
Federal income taxes....................	$39,020	
Actual charitable contributions for the year minus the charitable contribution deduction reflected in taxable income ($25,000 − $19,000)..................	6,000	(45,020)
Equals: Adjusted taxable income...........		$125,980

Two additional deductions are permitted in computing accumulated taxable income: the dividends-paid deduction and the accumulated earnings credit. The deduction allowed for dividends is consistent with the theory that the tax should be imposed only on income that has not been distributed. The accumulated earnings credit allows the taxpayer to accumulate without penalty $250,000 or an amount equal to the reasonable needs of the business, whichever is greater.

ACCUMULATED EARNINGS CREDIT

In creating the accumulated earnings tax, Congress realized that a corporation should not be penalized for keeping enough of its earnings to meet legitimate business needs. For this reason, in computing accumulated taxable income, a corporation is allowed—in effect—a reduction for the amount out of current year's earnings necessary to meet such needs. This reduction is the *accumulated earnings credit*.[39] Note that despite its name, the credit actually operates as a deduction. As a practical matter, it is this credit that insulates most corporations from the accumulated earnings tax.

Specifically, the credit is the greater of two amounts as described in Exhibit 6-2 and discussed further below. Generally, however, the credit for the current year may be determined as follows:

Reasonable business needs (or $250,000 if larger)	$xxx,xxx
Less: Beginning Accumulated E&P	(xx,xxx)
Accumulated earnings credit.	$xxx,xxx

Part 1 of Exhibit 6-2 contains the general rule authorizing accumulations. It permits corporations to accumulate earnings to the extent of their reasonable needs without penalty.[40] In determining the amount of the earnings and profits for the taxable year that have been retained to meet the reasonable needs of the business, it is necessary to consider to what extent the accumulated earnings and profits are available to cover these needs.[41] In effect, prior accumulations reduce the amount that can be retained in the current year. If the corporation's accumulated earnings and profits are sufficient to meet the reasonable needs of the business, *none* of the current earnings and profits will be considered to be retained to meet the reasonable needs of the business.

Exhibit 6-2
Accumulated Earnings Credit[42]

The accumulated earnings credit is the greater of

1. *General Rule:* Earnings and profits for the taxable year that are retained to meet the reasonable needs of the business, minus the net capital gain for the year (reduced by the taxes attributable to the gain),

   or

2. *Minimum Credit:* $250,000 ($150,000 for personal service corporations) minus the accumulated earnings and profits of the corporation at the close of the *preceding* taxable year, adjusted for dividends paid in the current year *deemed* paid in the prior year.

---

[39] § 535(c).

[40] § 535(c)(1).

[41] Reg. § 1.535-3(b)(1)(ii).

[42] § 535(c)(1).

Part 2 of Exhibit 6-2 is the so-called *minimum credit*.[43] For most corporations the amount of the minimum credit is $250,000. For personal service corporations, the minimum credit is $150,000. Personal service corporations are corporations that provide services in the area of health, law, engineering, architecture, accounting, actuarial science, performing arts, or consulting. The lower credit for personal service corporations reflects the fact that their capital needs are relatively small when compared to retail or manufacturing businesses.

To determine the amount of the minimum credit available for the current year, the base amount, $250,000 ($150,000), must be reduced by the accumulated earnings and profits at the close of the preceding tax year. For purposes of this computation, the accumulated earnings and profits at the close of the preceding year are reduced by the dividends that were paid by the corporation within $2\frac{1}{2}$ months after the close of the preceding year.[44]

> **Example 5.** X Corporation, a calendar year retail department store, had current earnings and profits for 1991 of $75,000. Its accumulated earnings and profits at the close of 1990 were $200,000. X Corporation has paid no dividends for five years. X Corporation's taxable income for 1991 included a net capital gain of $20,000. [The taxes related to this net capital gain were $6,800 (34% × $20,000).] The reasonable needs of X Corporation are estimated to be $240,000. The amount of X Corporation's current earnings and profits that are retained to meet reasonable business needs is computed as follows:
>
> | | |
> |---|---:|
> | Estimated reasonable needs of X Corporation | $240,000 |
> | Less: Accumulated earnings and profits as of 12/31/90 | (200,000) |
> | Extent to which current earnings and profits are needed to cover the reasonable needs of the business | $ 40,000 |

Even though the current earnings and profits are $75,000, only $40,000 of the current earnings and profits are needed to meet the reasonable needs of the business.

---

[43] § 535(c)(2).　　　　[44] § 535(c)(4).

The accumulated earnings credit is the greater of

1.	Current earnings and profits to meet the reasonable needs of the business..............................		$ 40,000
	Minus: Net capital gain.............	$20,000	
	Reduced by the taxes attributable to the gain...	(6,800)	(13,200)
	General rule credit......................		$ 26,800

or

2.	$250,000...............................		$250,000
	Minus: Accumulated earnings and profits as of 12/31/90..........		(200,000)
	Minimum credit........................		$ 50,000

X Corporation's accumulated earnings credit is $50,000, the greater of the general rule credit ($26,800) or the minimum credit ($50,000).

Example 6. Assume the same facts as in *Example 5*, except that X Corporation is an engineering firm. The general rule credit would still be $26,800, but the minimum credit would be computed as follows:

$150,000..	$150,000
Minus: Accumulated earnings and profits as of 12/31/90..................	(200,000)
Minimum credit (the minimum credit cannot be a negative number)..................	$ 0

In this situation the accumulated earnings credit is $26,800, the greater of the general rule credit ($26,800) or the minimum credit ($0).

Two aspects of the accumulated earnings credit deserve special mention. First, the minimum credit has a very limited role. Since the $250,000 (or $150,000 for service corporations) is reduced by the prior accumulations, the minimum credit will always be zero for firms that have greater than $250,000 of accumulated earnings. In other words, accumulations in excess of $250,000 must be justified by business needs.

The second aspect involves capital gains. As discussed previously, capital gains (net of related taxes) are subtracted from taxable income in arriving at adjusted taxable income. Therefore, a corporation can accumulate all of its capital gains without the imposition of the accumulated earnings tax. At the same time, however, capital gains are subtracted from business needs in arriving at the general credit (see Exhibit 6-2). As a result, a capital gain may cause accumulations of ordinary income to be subject to the special tax even though the capital gain itself escapes penalty. In effect, the computations are based on the assumption that business needs are funded first from capital gains and then from income from operations.

DIVIDENDS-PAID DEDUCTION

Exhibit 6-1 indicated that both the accumulated earnings credit and the dividends-paid deduction are adjustments in computing accumulated taxable income. Exhibit 6-3 lists the types of dividends that constitute the dividends-paid deduction.

To qualify for the dividend deduction, the distribution must constitute a "dividend" as defined in § 316.[45] As previously discussed, § 316 limits dividends to distributions out of current earnings and profits and accumulated earnings and profits since 1913. Property distributions qualify only to the extent of their adjusted basis.[46]

Throwback Dividends. The dividends-paid deduction includes not only dividends paid during the year, but also so-called *throwback dividends*, dividends paid during the 2 1/2 months following the close of the tax year.[47] Amounts paid during the 2 1/2 month period *must* be treated as if paid in the previous year.[48] This treatment is mandatory and not elective by the shareholders or the corporation.

Consent Dividends. In addition to actual dividends paid, the corporation is entitled to a deduction for consent dividends.[49] Sometimes a corporation may have a large amount of accumulated earnings, but insufficient cash or property to make a dividend distribution. In order to avoid the accumulated earnings tax, the

---

Exhibit 6-3
Dividends-Paid Deduction[50]

1. Dividends paid during the taxable year,[51]

2. Dividends paid within 2 1/2 months after the close of the taxable year,[52]

3. Consent dividends,[53] plus

4. Liquidating distributions.[54]

Equals: **Dividends-Paid Deduction**

---

[45] § 562(a).

[46] Reg. § 1.562-1(a).

[47] § 563.

[48] Reg. § 1.563-1.

[49] § 565.

[50] §§ 561 through 565.

[51] § 561(a)(1).

[52] § 563(a).

[53] § 565.

[54] § 562(b)(1).

corporation may obtain a dividends-paid deduction by using consent dividends—so called because the shareholders consent to treat a certain amount as a taxable dividend on their tax returns even though there is no distribution of cash or property. Not only are the shareholders deemed to receive the amount to which they consent, but they also are treated as having reinvested the amount received as a contribution to the corporation's capital.

To qualify a dividend as a consent dividend, the shareholders must file a consent form (Form 972) with the corporate income tax return. The consents must be filed by the due date (including extensions) of the corporate tax return for the year in which the dividend deduction is requested. Only shareholders who own stock on the last day of the tax year need file consent forms. On the forms, each shareholder must specify the amount of the consent dividend and then include this amount as a cash distribution by the corporation on his or her individual income tax return. Consent dividends are limited to the amount that would have qualified as a dividend under Code § 316 had the dividend been distributed in cash.[55] Only shareholders of common and participating preferred stock may consent to dividends.[56]

Liquidating Distributions.   If the distribution is in liquidation, partial liquidation, or redemption of stock, the portion of the distribution chargeable to earnings and profits is included in the dividend deduction.[57] For partial liquidations and redemptions, this is the redeemed stock's proportionate share of accumulated E&P. For complete liquidations, any amount distributed within the two years following the adoption of a plan of liquidation and that is pursuant to the plan is included in the dividends-paid deduction, but not to exceed the corporation's current earnings and profits for the year of distribution.[58]

PERSONAL HOLDING COMPANY TAX

As mentioned earlier in this chapter, the accumulated earnings tax is not the only penalty tax applicable to corporations. Congress has also enacted the personal holding company tax. This tax evolved in 1934 from the need to stop the growing number of individuals who were misusing the corporate entity despite the existence of the accumulated earnings tax. The personal holding company tax was designed to thwart three particular schemes prevalent during that period.

The first two schemes specifically aimed to take advantage of the disparity between individual and corporate tax rates. At that time, the maximum individual tax rates were approximately 45 percentage points higher than the maximum corporate rates. A typical plan used to take advantage of this differential involved the formation of a corporation to hold an individual's investment portfolio. This

---

[55]   Reg. § 1.565-2(a).

[56]   § 565(f).

[57]   § 562(b)(1).

[58]   § 562(b)(1)(B).

plan allowed an individual's interest and dividends to become taxable to the corporation rather than to the individual and consequently to be taxed at the lower corporate rates. Another, somewhat more sophisticated, technique enabled the transfer of an individual's service income to a corporation. The blueprint for this plan required the formation of a corporation by an individual (e.g., movie star) who subsequently became an employee of the corporation. With the corporation in place, parties seeking the individual's services were forced to contract with the corporation rather than with the individual. The individual would then perform the services, but the corporation would receive the revenue. Finally, the corporation would pay the individual a salary which was less than the revenue earned. Through this plan, the individual succeeded in transferring at least some of the revenue to the corporation, where it would be taxed at the lower corporate rates.

The final scheme was not specifically designed to take advantage of the lower corporate rates. Instead, its attraction grew from the practical presumption that all corporate activities are business activities. Given this presumption, an individual would transfer his or her personal assets (e.g., a yacht, race car, or vacation home) along with other investments to the corporation. Under the veil of the corporation, the expenses relating to the personal assets, such as maintenance of a yacht, would be magically transformed from nondeductible personal expenses to deductible business expenses which could offset the income produced by the investments. In short, by using the corporate form, individuals were able to disguise their personal expenses as business expenses and deduct them.

Although the Internal Revenue Service tried to curb these abuses using the accumulated earnings tax, attempts often failed. These failures normally could be attributed to the problem of proving that the individuals actually intended to avoid taxes. Aware of this problem, Congress formulated the personal holding company tax, which could be applied without having to prove that the forbidden purpose existed. In contrast to the accumulated earnings tax, which is imposed only after a subjective assessment of the individual's intentions, the personal holding company tax automatically applies whenever the corporation satisfies two objective tests.

Not all corporations that meet the applicable tests are subject to the penalty tax, however. The Code specifically exempts certain corporations. These include S corporations, tax-exempt corporations, banks, life insurance companies, surety companies, foreign personal holding companies, lending and finance companies, and several other types of corporations.[59]

If the personal holding company tax applies, the tax is 28 percent of undistributed personal holding company income.[60] Like the accumulated earnings tax, the personal holding company tax is levied in addition to the regular tax.[61] The personal holding company tax differs from the accumulated earnings tax,

---

[59] § 542(c).

[60] § 541.

[61] *Ibid.*

however, in that the corporation is required to compute and remit any personal holding tax due at the time it files its annual return. Form 1120-PH is used to compute the tax and must be filed with the corporation's annual Form 1120. In those cases where both the accumulated earnings tax and the personal holding company tax are applicable, only the personal holding company tax is imposed.[62]

PERSONAL HOLDING COMPANY DEFINED

The personal holding company tax applies only if the corporation is considered a personal holding company (PHC). As might be expected in light of the schemes prevalent at the time the tax was enacted, a corporation generally qualifies as a personal holding company if it is closely held and a substantial portion of its income is derived from passive sources or services. Specifically, the Code provides that a corporation is deemed to be a personal holding company if it satisfies both of the following tests.[63]

1 *Ownership*—At any time during the last half of the taxable year, more than 50 percent of the value of the corporation's outstanding stock is owned by five or fewer individuals.[64]

2 *Passive income*—At least 60 percent of the corporation's adjusted ordinary gross income consists of personal holding company income (PHCI).[65]

Before each of these tests is examined in detail, the distinction between the personal holding company tax and the accumulated earnings tax should be emphasized. The accumulated earnings tax applies only when it is proven that it was the shareholder's intention to use the corporation to shield income from individual tax rates. In contrast, application of the personal holding company tax requires only that two mechanical tests be satisfied. As a result, a corporation may fall victim to the personal holding company tax where there was no intention to avoid tax by misusing the corporation. For example, consider a closely held corporation in the process of liquidating. During liquidation, the corporation may have income from operations and passive income from temporary investments (investments made pending final distributions). If the passive income is substantial—60 percent or more of the corporation's total income—the corporation will be treated as a personal holding company subject to the penalty tax even though there was no intention by the shareholders to shelter the passive income. As this example illustrates, the mechanical nature of the personal holding company tax, unlike the subjective nature of the accumulated earnings tax, presents a trap for those with the noblest of intentions.

---

[62] § 532(b)(1).

[63] § 542.

[64] § 542(a)(2).

[65] § 542(a)(1).

PHC OWNERSHIP TEST

As indicated above, the first part of the two-part test for personal holding company status concerns ownership. Apparently it was Congressional belief that the tax-saving schemes described above succeeded primarily in those cases where there was a concentration of ownership. For this reason, the ownership test is satisfied only if five or fewer individuals own more than 50 percent of the value of the corporation's outstanding shares of stock at any time during the last half of the taxable year.[66] As a quick study of this test reveals, a corporation having less than ten shareholders always meets the ownership test since there will always be a combination of five or fewer shareholders owning more than 50 percent of the stock (e.g., $100\% \div 9 = 11\%$; $11\% \times 5 > 50\%$). Thus, it becomes apparent that closely held corporations are extremely vulnerable to the tax.

In performing the stock ownership test, the shareholder's *direct* and *indirect* ownership must be taken into account.[67] Indirect ownership is determined using a set of constructive ownership rules designed specifically for the personal holding company area.[68] According to these rules, a taxpayer is considered owning indirectly the following:

1. Stock owned directly or indirectly by his or her family, including his or her brothers, sisters, spouse, ancestors, and lineal descendents[69]

2. His or her proportionate share of any stock owned by a corporation, partnership, estate, or trust in which he or she has ownership (or of which he or she is a beneficiary in the case of an estate or trust)[70] and

3. Stock owned indirectly or directly by his or her partner in a partnership[71]

In using these rules, the following guidelines must be observed: (1) stock attributed from one family member to another cannot be reattributed to yet another member of the family,[72] (2) stock attributed from a partner to the taxpayer cannot be reattributed to a member of his or her family or to yet another partner,[73] (3) stock on which the taxpayer has an option is treated as being actually owned,[74] and (4) convertible securities are treated as outstanding stock.[75] In addition, Code § 544 contains other rules that may affect an individual's stock ownership.

---

[66] § 542(a)(2).

[67] *Ibid.*

[68] § 544.

[69] § 544(a)(2).

[70] § 544(a)(1).

[71] § 544(a)(2).

[72] § 544(a)(5).

[73] *Ibid.*

[74] § 544(a)(3).

[75] § 544(b).

INCOME TEST

Although the stock ownership test may be satisfied, a corporation is not considered a personal holding company unless it also passes an income test. In general terms, this test is straightforward: at least 60 percent of the corporation's income must be derived from either passive sources or certain types of services. Unfortunately, the technical translation of this requirement is somewhat more complicated. According to the Code, at least 60 percent of the corporation's *adjusted ordinary gross income* must be *personal holding company income*.[76] This relationship may be expressed numerically as follows:

$$\frac{\text{Personal holding company income}}{\text{Adjusted ordinary gross income}} \geq 60\%$$

As will be seen below, the definition of each of these terms can be baffling. However, the general theme of each term and the thrust of the test should not be lost in the complexity. Personal holding company income is generally passive income, while adjusted ordinary gross income is just that, ordinary gross income with a few modifications. Performing the income test is, in essence, a matter of determining whether too much of the corporation's income (adjusted ordinary gross income) is passive income (personal holding company income).

> **Example 7.**   K, a high-bracket taxpayer, wished to reduce her taxes. Upon the advice of an old friend, she transferred all of her stocks and bonds to a newly formed corporation of which she is the sole owner. During the year, the corporation had dividend income of $40,000 and interest income of $35,000. In this case, the corporation is treated as a personal holding company because *both* the stock ownership test and the income test are satisfied. The stock ownership test is met since K owned 100% of the stock in the last half of the year. The income test is also met since all of the corporation's income is passive income—or more specifically, its personal holding company income, $75,000 ($40,000 dividends + $35,000 interest) exceeds 60% of its adjusted ordinary gross income, $45,000 (60% of $75,000).

The technical definitions of adjusted ordinary gross income and personal holding income are explored below.

ADJUSTED ORDINARY GROSS INCOME

The first quantity that must be determined is adjusted ordinary gross income (AOGI).[77] As suggested above, the label given to this quantity is very appropriate since the amount which must be computed is just what the phrase implies; that

---

[76]   § 542(a)(1).

[77]   § 543(b)(2).

is, it includes only the ordinary gross income of the corporation with certain adjustments. In determining AOGI, the following amounts must be computed: (1) gross income, (2) ordinary gross income, and (3) the adjustments to ordinary gross income to arrive at AOGI. Therefore, the starting point for the calculation of AOGI is gross income.

Gross Income. The definition of gross income for purposes of the personal holding company provisions varies little from the definition found in § 61. Accordingly, gross income includes all income from whatever source except those items specifically excluded. In addition, gross income is computed taking into consideration cost of goods sold. The only departure from the normal definition of gross income concerns property transactions. Only the net gains from the sale or exchange of stocks, securities, and commodities are included in gross income.[78] Net losses involving these assets do not reduce gross income. Similarly, any loss arising from the sale or exchange of § 1231 property is ignored and does not offset any § 1231 gains.

Ordinary Gross Income. In applying the income test, capital-gain type items are ignored and consequently have no effect on whether the corporation is treated as a personal holding company. Therefore, since the quantity desired is adjusted "ordinary" gross income, the second step of the calculation requires the removal of capital-gain type items from gross income. As seen in Exhibit 6-4, all capital gains and § 1231 gains are subtracted from gross income to arrive at ordinary gross income.[79] It should be noted that this amount, "ordinary gross income," is not simply a subtotal in arriving at AOGI. As discussed below, ordinary gross income (OGI) is an important figure in determining whether certain types of income are treated as personal holding company income.

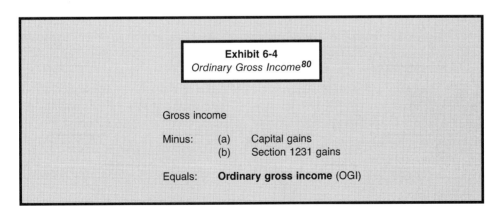

Exhibit 6-4
Ordinary Gross Income[80]

Gross income

Minus: (a)   Capital gains
          (b)   Section 1231 gains

Equals: **Ordinary gross income** (OGI)

---

[78] Prop. Reg. § 1.543-12(a). Also see Reg.
§§ 1.542-2 and 1.543-2.

[79] § 543(b)(1).

[80] *Ibid.*

Adjustments to OGI. For many years, OGI generally served as the denominator in the income-test fraction shown above. In 1964, however, modifications were necessary to discourage the use of certain methods taxpayers and their advisors had forged to undermine the income test. The popular schemes capitalized on the fact that $1 of gross rental income could shelter 60 cents of passive personal holding company income. This particular advantage could be obtained even though the rental activity itself was merely a break-even operation. Consequently, a taxpayer could easily thwart the income test and reap the benefits of the corporate entity by investing in activities that produced substantial gross rents or royalties, notwithstanding the fact that these activities were not economically sound investments.

> **Example 8.** Refer to the facts in *Example 7*. Absent special rules, K could circumvent the income test by purchasing a coin-operated laundry which generated gross rents of more than $50,000 (e.g., $51,000) and transferring it to the corporation. In such case, assuming the rents would not be treated as personal holding income, the personal holding company income would still be $75,000 (dividends of $40,000 + interest of $35,000). However, when the laundry rents are combined with the personal holding company income to form the new AOGI, personal holding company income would be less than 60% of this new AOGI [$75,000 < 60% × ($40,000 + $35,000 + $51,000) = $75,600]. Although the laundry business might not show a profit, this would be irrelevant to K since she would have gained the advantage of the dividend received deduction and avoided personal holding company status.

To deter the type of scheme illustrated above, the calculation now requires rental and royalty income to be reduced by the bulk of the expenses typically related to this type of income: depreciation, interest, and taxes. This requirement reduces the ability of the activities to shelter income. For instance, in *Example 8* above, K would be required to reduce the gross rental income by depreciation, interest, and taxes—which would severely curtail the utility of purchasing the leasing business.[81] The specific modifications that reduce ordinary gross income to arrive at adjusted ordinary gross income are shown in Exhibit 6-5.[82] Exhibits 6-6 and 6-7 illustrate the adjustments required to be made to gross income from rents and mineral, oil, and gas royalties for purposes of computing adjusted ordinary gross income.

---

[81] Under current law, it is also likely that the rents would be treated as PHCI, thus further spoiling the plan.

[82] § 543(b)(2).

Exhibit 6-5
Adjusted Ordinary Gross Income[83]

Ordinary gross income (OGI)

Minus: (a) Depreciation, property taxes, interest expense, and rents paid related to gross rental income. These deductions may not exceed gross rental income. (Gross rental income is income for the use of corporate property and interest received on the sales price of real property held as inventory.)

(b) Depreciation and depletion, property and severance taxes, interest expense, and rents paid related to gross income from mineral, oil, and gas royalties. These deductions may not exceed the gross income from the royalties.

(c) Interest on tax refunds, on judgments, on condemnation awards, and on U.S. obligations (only for a dealer in the obligations).

Equals: ***Adjusted ordinary gross income*** (AOGI)

Exhibit 6-6
Adjusted Income from Rents[84]

Gross rental income

Minus: (a) Depreciation
(b) Property taxes
(c) Interest expense
(d) Rents paid

Equals: ***Adjusted income from rents***

[83]   *Ibid.*   [84]   *Ibid.*

Exhibit 6-7
*Adjusted Income from Mineral,
Oil, and Gas Royalties*[85]

Gross income from mineral, oil, and gas royalties (including production payments and overriding royalties)

Minus: (a) Depreciation and depletion
(b) Property and severance taxes
(c) Interest expense
(d) Rents paid

Equals: **Adjusted income from mineral, oil, and gas royalties**

PERSONAL HOLDING COMPANY INCOME (PHCI)

Following the computation of AOGI, the corporation's personal holding company income must be measured to determine whether it meets the 60 percent threshold. Although personal holding company income can be generally characterized as passive income and certain income from services, the Code identifies eight specific types of income which carry the personal holding company taint.[86] These are listed in Exhibit 6-8. Selected items of PHCI are discussed below.

Dividends, Interest, Royalties, and Annuities. The most obvious forms of PHCI are those usually considered passive in nature: dividends, interest, royalties, and annuities.[87] Generally, identification and classification of these items present little problem. The most noteworthy exception concerns royalties. Mineral, oil, gas, copyright, and computer software royalties generally are included in this category of PHCI. However, as seen in Exhibit 6-8, items b, c, and d, these royalties are not treated as PHCI if certain additional tests are satisfied.

Example 9.   B Corporation has three stockholders. Its income consisted of

Gross income from a grocery	$52,000
Interest income	38,000
Capital gain	6,000

B Corporation's OGI (see Exhibit 6-4) is $90,000, computed as follows:

Gross income ($52,000 + $38,000 + $6,000)	$96,000
Minus: Capital gains	(6,000)
OGI	90,000

---

[85]   § 543(b)(4).

[86]   § 543.

[87]   § 543(a)(1).

Exhibit 6-8
Personal Holding Company Income (PHCI)

Dividends, interest, royalties (except mineral, oil, or gas royalties, copyright royalties, and certain software royalties), and annuities.

Plus: (a) Adjusted income from rents, *but* the adjusted income from rents is not added to PHCI *if*

    1. The adjusted income from rents is 50 percent or more of AOGI, and
    2. The dividends paid, the dividends considered paid, and the consent dividends equal or exceed

        (i) PHCI computed without the adjusted income from rents
        (ii) Minus 10 percent of OGI.

(b) Adjusted income from mineral, oil, and gas royalties, *but* the adjusted income from these royalties is *not* added to PHCI *if*

    1. The adjusted income from the royalties is 50 percent or more of AOGI,
    2. PHCI computed without the adjusted income from these royalties does not exceed 10 percent of OGI, and
    3. The § 162 trade or business deductions equal or exceed 15 percent of AOGI.

(c) Copyright royalties, *but* the copyright royalties are *not* added to PHCI *if*

    1. The copyright royalties are 50 percent or more of OGI,
    2. PHCI computed without the copyright royalties does not exceed 10 percent of OGI, and
    3. The § 162 trade or business deductions related to the copyright royalties equal or exceed 25 percent of

        (i) The OGI minus the royalties paid, plus
        (ii) The depreciation related to the copyright royalties.

In this example, AOGI is the same as OGI since the amounts which are subtracted from OGI to arrive at AOGI are zero (see Exhibit 6-5).

B Corporation's PHCI is $38,000, the amount of the interest income (see Exhibit 6-8). Since the corporation's PHCI ($38,000) is not 60 percent or more of its $90,000 AOGI ($90,000 × 60% = $54,000), it does not meet the income requirement.

Although B Corporation meets the stock ownership requirement since it has only three shareholders, it does not meet *both* the ownership requirement and the income requirement. As a result, it is not a personal holding company and is not subject to the personal holding company tax.

Exhibit 6-8 Continued

(d) Software royalties, but these are *not* added to PHCI *if*

1. The royalties are received in connection with the licensing of computer software by a corporation which is actively engaged in the business of developing, manufacturing, or production of such software,
2. The software royalties are 50 percent or more of OGI,
3. Research and experimental expenditures, § 162 business expenses, and § 195 start-up expenditures allocable to the software business are generally 25 percent or more of OGI computed with certain adjustments, and
4. Dividends paid, considered paid, and the consent dividends equal or exceed

   (i) PHCI computed without the software royalties and certain interest income
   (ii) Minus 10 percent of OGI.

(e) Produced film rents, *but* the produced film rents are *not* added to PHCI *if* the produced film rents equal or exceed 50 percent of OGI.

(f) Rent (for the use of tangible property) received by the corporation from a shareholder owning 25 percent or more of the value of the corporation's stock. This rent is only included in PHCI if PHCI computed without this rent and without the adjusted income from rents exceeds 10 percent of OGI.

(g) Income from personal service contracts *but only if*

1. Someone other than the corporation has the right to designate who is to perform the services or if the person who is to perform the services is named in the contract, and
2. At some time during the taxable year, 25 percent or more of the value of the corporation's outstanding stock is owned by the person performing the services.

(h) Income of estates and trusts taxable to the corporation.

Equals: ***Personal holding company income (PHCI)***

Example 10. Assume the same facts as in *Example 9* except that B Corporation had received $88,000 of interest income.

B Corporation's OGI and AOGI would be computed as follows:

88,000

Gross income ($52,000 + $88,000 + $6,000)	$146,000
Minus: Capital gains	(6,000)
OGI (also AOGI)	$140,000

B Corporation's PHCI is now $88,000, the amount of the interest income. Since the corporation's $88,000 of PHCI is more than 60% of the $140,000 AOGI ($140,000 × 60% = $84,000), it meets the income requirement.

Since B Corporation meets both the ownership requirement and the income requirement, *it is* a personal holding company.

Adjusted Income from Rents. Rental income presents a special problem for the personal holding company provisions. Normally, rents—generally defined as compensation for the use of property—represent a passive type of income. However, for many corporations, most notably those involved in renting real estate and equipment, rental operations are not merely a passive investment but represent a true business activity. If all rental income were considered personal holding income, closely held corporations involved in the rental business could not escape PHC status. To provide these corporations with some relief, rental income is not treated as PHCI under certain circumstances.

The amount of rental income potentially qualifying as PHCI is referred to as the *adjusted income from rents*.[88] As seen in Exhibit 6-6, adjusted income from rents consists of the corporation's gross rental income reduced by the adjustments required for determining AOGI—depreciation, property taxes, interest expense, and rental payments related to such income (e.g., ground lease payments). The corporation's adjusted income from rents is treated as PHCI unless it can utilize the relief measure suggested above. Specifically, adjusted income from rents is PHCI unless: (1) it is 50 percent or more of the corporation's AOGI, and (2) the corporation's dividends during the taxable year as well as dividends paid within the first 2½ months of the following year *and* consent dividends are not less than the amount by which nonrental PHCI (e.g., dividends and interest) exceeds 10 percent of OGI.[89]

These relationships may be expressed as follows:

1. Adjusted income from rents $\geq$ (50% × AOGI); *and*

2. Dividends $\geq$ [nonrental PHCI − (10% × OGI)].

As the latter expression indicates, when rents represent a substantial portion of OGI relative to nonrental PHCI (as typically would be the case where a corporation is truly in the rental "business"), no dividends are required. In other words, as long as nonrental income is not a major portion of the corporation's total income—does not exceed 10 percent of the corporation's OGI—dividends are unnecessary. Otherwise, a corporation in the rental business is forced to make dividend distributions to avoid penalty.

---

[88] § 543(b)(3).   [89] *Ibid.*

Example 11. D Corporation had four shareholders in 1991 and therefore met the stock ownership requirement. The following information is available for D corporation for 1991:

Interest income	$10,000
Gross rental income	25,000
Depreciation, property taxes, and interest expense related to rental income	24,000
Maintenance and utilities related to rental income	3,000
Dividends paid during 1991	8,000

OGI (Exhibit 6-4) is $35,000 ($10,000 + $25,000). AOGI (see Exhibit 6-5) is computed as follows:

OGI	$35,000
Minus: Depreciation, property taxes, and interest expense related to rental income	(24,000)
AOGI	$11,000

D Corporation's adjusted income from rents is computed as follows (see Exhibit 6-6):

Gross rental income	$25,000
Minus: Depreciation, property taxes, and expense related to rental income	(24,000)
Adjusted income from rents	$ 1,000

Note that in determining AOGI and adjusted income from rents, the maintenance and utility expenses are ignored. Such expenses are also not taken into account in determining gross income or OGI. The next step is to determine if the adjusted income from rents is to be added to PHCI. It is *not* added to PHCI if *both* of the following tests are met.

Test 1 (50% test): Is the adjusted income from rents 50% or more of AOGI?

The adjusted income from rents ($1,000) is *not* 50% or more of AOGI ($11,000), so Test 1 is *not* met.

The adjusted income from rents is excluded from PHCI only if *both* Test 1 and Test 2 are met. Since Test 1 is not met, the adjusted income from rents *is* included in PHCI, and there is no need to go on to Test 2. However, Test 2 is done here for illustrative purposes.

Test 2 (10% test): Does the total of the dividends paid, the dividends considered paid, and the consent dividends equal or exceed PHCI (computed without the adjusted income from rents) reduced by 10% of OGI? This can also be expressed as:

Dividends $\geq$ [nonrental PHCI $-$ (OGI $\times$ 10%)]. Nonrental PHCI is $10,000 (interest income). OGI $\times$ 10% = $35,000 $\times$ 10% = $3,500. Therefore, nonrent PHCI ($10,000) minus OGI $\times$ 10% ($3,500) is $6,500. Since the total dividends ($8,000) were more than $6,500, Test 2 *is* met.

However, as mentioned above, *both* Test 1 and Test 2 must be met if the adjusted income from rents is to be excluded from PHCI. Therefore, the adjusted income from rents *is part of PHCI.*

D Corporation's PHCI is computed as follows (see Exhibit 6-8):

Interest income	$10,000
Adjusted income from rents	1,000
PHCI	$11,000

D Corporation's $11,000 PHCI is more than 60% of the $11,000 AOGI. In this example, in fact, PHCI is 100% of AOGI since all of the income is personal holding company income. D Corporation, therefore, meets *both* the ownership requirement and the income requirement, and thus is a personal holding company.

The rules relating to mineral, oil, gas, copyright, and software royalties are very similar to those discussed above for rents. See Exhibits 6-7 and 6-8, items b, c, and d.

Income from Personal Service Contracts.   The shifting of service income to a corporation by highly compensated individuals, such as actors and athletes, is sharply curtailed by the personal holding company provisions. The PHC provisions attack the problem by treating service income as PHCI under certain conditions. Generally, amounts received by a corporation for services provided are treated as PHCI if the party desiring the services can designate the person who will perform the services and that person owns 25 percent of the corporation's stock[90]   (see Exhibit 6-8, item g).

Example 12.   T Corp., a producer of motion pictures, wanted RK to act in a new movie it was producing. Assume that RK's services could be obtained only by contracting with his wholly owned corporation, RK Inc. Accordingly, a contract is drafted providing that RK Inc. will provide the services of RK to T Corp. for $500,000. All of the income is PHCI to RK Inc. since RK owns at least 25% of the corporation *and* he is actually designated in the contract to perform the services.

---

[90]   § 543(a)(7).

Given the general rule, it would appear that virtually all service corporations are likely candidates for the PHC tax. This problem was considered in Revenue Ruling 75-67.[91] According to the facts of the ruling, a corporation's primary source of income was attributable to the services of its only employee, a doctor, who also owned 80 percent of the corporation's stock. In this case, all the facts suggested that the income would be PHCI. The only question was whether the doctor's patients formally designated him as the one to perform the services. Although a formal designation was lacking, it was implicit since the doctor was the only employee of the corporation and the patients never expected someone other than the doctor to perform the services. Despite evidence to the contrary, the IRS ruled that the income was not PHCI on the theory that there was no indication that the corporation was obligated to provide the services of the doctor in question. In addition, the ruling emphasized that the services to be performed were not so unique as to prohibit the corporation from substituting someone else to perform them. The Service also relied on the uniqueness rationale in situations involving a CPA who had incorporated his or her practice and a musical composer who had incorporated his or her song-writing activities.[92] Apparently, as long as the services are not so unique as to preclude substitution and there is no formal designation of the individual who will perform the services, a service business can escape PHC status.

COMPUTATION OF THE PHC TAX

The personal holding company penalty tax is 28 percent of the *undistributed personal holding company income*. Undistributed personal holding company income is defined as adjusted taxable income minus the dividends-paid deduction.[93] The computation of adjusted taxable income and undistributed PHCI is shown in Exhibit 6-9.

Like the computation of accumulated taxable income, the calculation attempts to determine the corporation's dividend-paying capacity. As a practical matter, the tax is rarely paid because of a deduction allowed for "deficiency dividends" which can be made once it has been determined the PHC tax applies.

---

[91] Rev. Rul. 75-67, 1975-1 C.B. 169.

[92] Rev. Rul. 75-290, 1975-1 C.B. 172; Rev. Rul. 75-249, 1975-1 C.B. 171; and Rev. Rul. 75-250, 1975-1 C.B. 179.

[93] § 545(a). The term "adjusted taxable income" is not found in the Code.

Exhibit 6-9
Undistributed Personal Holding Company Income [94]

Taxable income

Plus: (a) Dividends-received deduction.

(b) Net operating loss deduction (but not a net operating loss of the preceding year computed without the dividends received deduction).

(c) The amount by which the § 162 (trade or business) deductions and the § 167 (depreciation) deductions related to rental property exceed the income produced by the rental property, unless it can be shown that the rent received was the highest possible and that the rental activity was carried on as a bona fide business activity.

Minus: (a) Federal income taxes (but not the accumulated earnings tax or the personal holding company tax).

(b) The amount by which actual charitable contributions exceeds the charitable contributions deduction reflected in net income.

(c) Net capital gain reduced by the taxes attributable to the net capital gain.

Equals: ***Adjusted taxable income***

Minus: Dividends-Paid Deduction

Equals: ***Undistributed Personal Holding Company Income***

Dividends-Paid Deduction. The dividends-paid deduction for personal holding companies is similar to the one for the accumulated earnings tax. It includes the following types of distributions:

1. Dividends paid during the taxable year

2. Throwback dividends: dividends paid within 2 $1/2$ months after the close of the taxable year (but subject to limitation as discussed below)

3. Consent dividends

4. Liquidating distributions and

5. Deficiency dividends

Note that this list of qualifying distributions is identical to that provided in Exhibit 6-3 for the accumulated earnings tax, except for the special deficiency dividend. In addition, personal holding companies are entitled to a dividend carryover, which is not available for accumulated earnings tax purposes. [95]

---

[94] § 545.

[95] § 561(a)(3).

Throwback dividends. As in the accumulated earnings tax computation, a personal holding company is allowed a deduction for throwback dividends (i.e., dividends paid within $2\frac{1}{2}$ months after the close of the taxable year).[96] However, the PHC throwback dividend differs from that for the accumulated earnings tax in two ways. First, it is included in the dividends-paid deduction only if the corporation makes an *election* at the time the corporate tax return is filed to treat them as applying to the previous year.[97] Second, the amount treated as a throwback dividend is limited to the smaller of the following:[98]

1. Twenty percent of the dividends actually paid during the taxable year in question

2. Undistributed PHCI (computed without the dividends paid during the $2\frac{1}{2}$-month period)

Consent dividends. The rules for consent dividends are the same for personal holding companies as for the accumulated earnings tax.[99] As mentioned previously, a consent dividend is an amount that a shareholder agrees to consider as having been received as a dividend even though never actually distributed by the corporation. Consent dividends are limited to shareholders who own stock on the last day of the tax year. Their shares must be either common stock or *participating* preferred stock. Consent dividends do not include preferential dividends. A shareholder who consents to a dividend is treated as having received the amount as a cash dividend and contributing the same amount to the corporation's capital on the last day of the year.

Dividend carryover. A personal holding company is also entitled to a *dividend carryover* as part of its dividends-paid deduction.[100] If the dividends paid in the two prior years exceed the adjusted taxable incomes (see Exhibit 6-9) for those years, the excess may be used as a dividend carryover (and therefore as part of the dividends-paid deduction) for the year in question.

Deficiency dividends. Once a determination has been made that a corporation is subject to the personal holding company tax, the tax can still be abated by the use of a *deficiency dividend*.[101] Following the determination of the personal holding company tax, the corporation is given 90 days to pay a deficiency dividend. This must be an *actual cash dividend* which the corporation elects to treat as a distribution of the personal holding company income for the year at issue, and it is taxable to the shareholders. It does not reduce the personal holding company income of any year other than the year at issue. A deficiency dividend effectively reduces the amount of the penalty tax. However, interest and penalties are still imposed as if the deduction were not allowed. Thus, the corporation may be able

---

[96] § 563.

[97] § 563(b).

[98] *Ibid.*

[99] § 565.

[100] § 564.

[101] § 547.

to escape the tax itself—but not any interest or penalties related to such tax. It should also be noted that the deficiency dividend is available *only* to reduce the personal holding company tax. This escape is not available to those subject to the accumulated earnings tax.

Example 13. C Corporation determined that it was a personal holding company and had to file Form 1120-PH. Its records for 1991 reveal the following:

Gross profit from operations	$150,000
Dividend income	400,000
Interest income	350,000
Long-term capital gain	30,000
Gross income	$930,000
Compensation	(30,000)
Selling and administrative	(100,000)
	$800,000
Dividends-received deduction	(280,000)
Charitable contributions	(80,000)
Taxable income	$440,000
Federal income tax @ 34%	$149,600

Charitable contributions actually made during the year were $90,000, but are limited to $80,000 (10% × $800,000 taxable income before the deductions for contributions and dividends received). C paid dividends of $20,000 in 1991 and $10,000 during the first $2\frac{1}{2}$ months of 1992, which it *elects* to throw back to 1991 in computing the dividends-paid deduction. The personal holding company tax is computed as follows:

Taxable income	$440,000
+ Dividends-received deduction	280,000
− Excess charitable contributions	(10,000)
− Federal income taxes	(149,600)
− Long-term capital gain net of tax [$30,000 − (34% × $30,000)]	(19,800)
Adjustable taxable income	$540,600
− Dividends paid deduction:	
1991	(20,000)
1992 Throwback (Limited to 20% of 1990 dividends)	(4,000)
UPHCI	$516,600
Times: PHC tax rate	× 28%
PHC tax	$144,648

C Corporation's tax liability for 1991 is $294,248 ($149,600 regular tax + $144,648 PHC tax). The PHC tax could be avoided by paying a deficiency dividend equal to UPHCI ($516,600). However, the payment of the dividend would not eliminate any penalties or interest that might be assessed on the $144,648 PHC tax due if Form 1120-PH is not filed in a timely manner.

TAX PLANNING

ACCUMULATED EARNINGS TAX

For taxpayers wanting to use the corporate form to shield their income from individual taxes, the accumulated earnings tax represents a formidable obstacle. Although there is an obvious cost if the tax is incurred, that cost may be far more than expected. This often occurs because the imposition of the tax for one year triggers an audit for all open years. In addition, the IRS usually takes the position that the negligence penalty of Code § 6653 should be imposed whenever the accumulated earnings tax is applicable. Moreover, in contrast to the personal holding company tax which can normally be averted using the deficiency dividend procedure, the accumulated earnings tax, once levied, cannot be avoided. At the time of the audit, it is too late for dividend payments or consent dividends!

Despite the potential cost of the tax, the rewards from avoidance—or at least the deferral—of double taxation are often so great that the shareholders are willing to assume the risk of penalty. Moreover, many practitioners believe that with proper planning the risk of incurring the accumulated earnings tax is minimal, particularly since the tax is not self-assessed but dependent on the audit lottery. In addition, it is possible to shift the burden of proof to the IRS. The discussion below examines some of the means for reducing the taxpayer's exposure to the accumulated earnings tax.

LIQUID ASSETS AND WORKING CAPITAL

Normally, the accumulated earnings tax is not raised as an issue unless the corporation's balance sheet shows cash, marketable securities, or other liquid assets that could be distributed easily to shareholders. The absence of liquid assets indicates that any earnings that have been retained have been reinvested in the business rather than accumulated for the forbidden purpose. It is a rare occasion, however, when such assets do not exist. Consequently, most IRS agents routinely assess whether the level of the corporation's working capital is appropriate by applying the *Bardahl* formula.

The courts have made it clear that the *Bardahl* formula serves merely as a guideline for determining the proper amount of working capital. In *Delaware Trucking Co., Inc.*, the court held that the amount needed using the *Bardahl* formula could be increased by 75 percent due to the possibility of increased labor and other operating costs due to inflation.[102] Nevertheless, in those in-

---

[102]   32 TCM 104, T.C. Memo 1973-29.

stances where working capital appears excessive, the Internal Revenue Manual directs agents to require justification of such excess. Therefore, the corporation should closely control its working capital to ensure that it does not exceed the corporation's reasonable needs.

One way to reduce working capital is to increase shareholder salaries, bonuses, and other compensation. Since these payments are deductible, double taxation is avoided. This technique also has the benefit of reducing taxable income, which in turn reduces the accumulated earnings tax should it apply. However, this method of reducing working capital may not be feasible if the compensation paid exceeds a reasonable amount. To the extent that the compensation is unreasonable, the payments are treated as dividends and double taxation results. In addition, if the unreasonable compensation is not pro rata among all shareholders, the dividend will be considered preferential and no deduction will be allowed for the dividend in computing adjusted taxable income.

Another method for reducing working capital is for the corporation to invest in additional assets. However, the taxpayer must be careful to avoid investments that are of a passive nature or that could be considered unrelated to the corporation's existing or projected business. With respect to the latter, the courts have rules that the business of a controlled subsidiary is the business of the parent while the business of a sister corporation normally is not the business of its brother.[103]

REASONABLE NEEDS

The courts have accepted a variety of reasons as sufficient justification for the accumulation of earnings. On the one hand, the needs deemed reasonable have been both certain and well-defined, such as the repayment of corporate debt. On the other hand, the courts have approved needs as contingent and unknown as those arising from possible damage from future floods.

One contingency that seemingly could be asserted by all corporations as a basis for accumulating funds is the possibility of a business reversal, depression, or loss of major customer. Interestingly, the courts have often respected this justification for accumulations, notwithstanding the fact that it is a risk assumed by virtually all business entities. Acceptance of this need, however, appears to be dependent on the taxpayer's ability to establish that there is at least some chance that a business reversal could occur that would affect the taxpayer. For example, in *Ted Bates & Co.*, the corporation was in the advertising business and received 70 percent of its fees from only five clients.[104] In ruling for the taxpayer, the court held that the corporation was allowed to accumulate amounts necessary to cover its fixed costs for a period following the loss of a major client. Much of the court's opinion was based on its view that the advertising business was extremely competitive and the possibility of losing a client was not unrealistic. A similar decision was reached where a manufacturer sold all its products to

[103] For example, see *Latchis Theatres of Keene, Inc. v. Comm.*, 54-2 USTC ¶9544, 45 AFTR 1836, 214 F.2d 834 (CA-1, 1954).

[104] 24 TCM 1346, T.C. Memo 1965-251.

one customer and had to compete with others for that customer's business. The court believed that accumulations were necessary to enable the corporation to develop new markets if it lost its only customer. Relying on a possible downturn in business as a basis for accumulations has not always sufficed. In *Goodall*, the company accumulated earnings in light of the prospect that military orders would be lost.[105] The court upheld the penalty tax, indicating that even if the loss occurred, it would not have a significant effect because the corporation's business was expanding.

Although the courts have sustained various reasons for accumulations, a review of the cases indicates that the taxpayer must demonstrate that the need is realistic. This was made clear in *Colonial Amusement Corp.*[106] In this case, the corporation's accumulations were not justified when it wanted to construct a building on adjacent land and building restrictions existed that prohibited construction.

In establishing that a need is realistic, a taxpayer's self-serving statement normally is not convincing. Proper documentation of the need is critical. This is true even when the need is obvious and acceptable. In *Union Offset*, the corporation stated at trial that its accumulations were necessary to retire outstanding corporate debt, a legitimate business need.[107] To the taxpayer's dismay, however, the Tax Court still imposed the tax because the corporation had failed to document in any type of written record its plan to use the accumulations in the alleged manner. In this case, a simple statement in the Board of Directors' minutes concerning the proposed use of the funds would no doubt have saved the taxpayer from penalty.

S CORPORATION ELECTION

In those cases where it is difficult to justify accumulations, the shareholders may wish to elect to be treated as an S corporation. Since the earnings of an S corporation are taxed to the individual shareholders rather than the corporation, S corporations cannot be used to shelter income and thus are immune to the accumulated earnings tax. However, the election insulates the corporation only prospectively (i.e., only for that period for which it is an S corporation). Prior years open to audit are still vulnerable. In addition, the S election may raise other problems. The shareholders will be required to report and pay taxes on the income of the corporation even though it may not be distributed to them. As a result, cash flow problems may occur. Further, because the corporation has accumulated earnings and profits, the excess passive income tax specifically designed for C corporations that have elected S status may apply.[108] For these reasons, an S election should be carefully considered.

[105] *Robert A. Goodall Estate v. Comm.*, 68-1 USTC ¶9245, 21 AFTR2d 813, 391 F.2d 775, (CA-8, 1968).

[106] 7 TCM 546.

[107] 79-2 USTC ¶9550, 603 F.2d 90 (CA-9, 1979).

[108] See Chapter 12 for a discussion of this special tax imposed on S corporations with excessive passive income.

PERSONAL HOLDING COMPANY TAX

The personal holding company tax, like the accumulated earnings tax, is clearly a tax to be avoided. Unfortunately, the personal holding company tax differs from the accumulated earnings tax in that it is not reserved solely for those whose intent is to avoid taxes. Rather, it is applied on a mechanical basis, regardless of motive, to all corporations that fall within its purview. For this reason, it is important to closely monitor the corporation's activities to ensure that it does not inadvertently become a PHC.

One important responsibility of a practitioner is to recognize potential personal holding company problems so that steps can be taken to avoid the tax or the need to distribute dividends. This responsibility not only concerns routine operations but extends to advice concerning planned transactions that could cause the corporation to be converted from an operating company to an investment company. For example, a corporation may plan to sell one or all of its businesses and invest the proceeds in passive type assets. Similarly, a planned reorganization (discussed in Chapter 7) may leave the corporation holding stock of the acquiring corporation. Failure to identify the possible personal holding company difficulty which these and other transactions may cause can lead to serious embarrassment.

Although the thrust of most tax planning for personal holding companies concerns how to avoid the tax, there are certain instances when a planned PHC can provide benefits. Both varieties of personal holding companies, the planned and the unplanned, are discussed below.

PHC CANDIDATES

All corporations could fall victim to the PHC tax. However, some corporations are more likely candidates than others. For this reason, their activities and anticipated transactions should be scrutinized more carefully than others.

Potential difficulties often concern corporations that are involved in rental activities and those that have some passive income. In this regard, it should be noted that the term "rent" is defined as payments received for the use of property. As a result, "rental companies" include not only those that lease such items as apartments, offices, warehouses, stadiums, equipment, vending machines, automobiles, trucks, and the like, but also those that operate bowling alleys, roller and ice skating rinks, billiards parlors, golf courses, and any other activity for which a payment is received for use of the corporation's property. All of these corporations are at risk since each has rental income which could be considered passive personal holding company income unless it satisfies the special two-prong test for rental companies.

There are several other types of corporations that must be concerned with PHC problems. Investment companies—corporations formed primarily to acquire income producing assets such as stock, bonds, rental properties, partnership interests, and similar investments—clearly have difficulties. Corporations that derive most of their income from the services of one or more of their shareholders also are vulnerable. In recent years, however, the Service has taken a liberal view toward the professional corporations of doctors, accountants, and several others. Another group of corporations that are probable targets of the PHC tax includes those that collect royalty income. The royalty income might arise from the corporation's development and licensing of a product (e.g., patent on a food processor or franchises to operate a restaurant). Other logical candidates for the PHC tax are banks, savings and loans, and finance companies since the majority of their income is interest income from making loans and purchasing or discounting accounts receivables and installment obligations. Banks and savings and loans need not worry, however, since they are specifically excluded from PHC status. Finance companies are also exempt from the penalty tax, but only if certain tests—not discussed here—are met. Consequently, those involved with finance companies should review their situation closely to ensure such tests are satisfied.

AVOIDING PHC STATUS

In general, if a corporation is closely held *and* 60 percent of its income is derived from passive sources or specified personal services, the PHC tax applies. Thus, to avoid the PHC tax *either* the stock ownership test or the income test must be failed.

STOCK OWNERSHIP TEST

The stock ownership test is satisfied if five or fewer persons own more than 50 percent of the stock. This test is the most difficult to fail since it requires dilution of the current shareholders' ownership. Moreover, dilution is very difficult to implement in practice due to the constructive ownership rules. The rules make it virtually impossible to maintain ownership in the family since stock owned by one family member or an entity in which the family member has an interest is considered owned by other family members. Therefore, to fail the ownership test, sufficient stock must be owned by unrelated parties to reduce the ownership of the five largest shareholders to 50 percent or less. Unfortunately, it is often impossible to design an arrangement that meets these conditions yet is still desirable from an economic viewpoint.

PASSIVE INCOME TEST

The corporation is deemed to satisfy the passive income test if 60 percent of its adjusted ordinary gross income (AOGI) is personal holding company income (PHCI)—income from dividends, interest, annuities, rents, royalties, or specified shareholder services. The potential for failing this test is perhaps more easily seen when this test is expressed mathematically:

$$\frac{\text{PHCI}}{\text{AOGI}} \geq 60\%$$

The steps that can be taken to fail this test fall into three categories: (1) increasing operating income or AOGI, (2) reducing PHCI, and (3) satisfying the exceptions to remove the PHC taint from the income.

Increasing Operating Income.   One way to fail the 60 percent test is to increase the denominator in the income test fraction, AOGI, without increasing the numerator. This requires the corporation to increase its operating income without any corresponding increase in its passive income. Obtaining such an increase is not easy since it is essentially asking that the corporation generate more gross income. This does not necessarily mean that sales must increase, however. The corporation might consider increasing its profit margin. Although this could reduce sales, the resulting increase in gross income could be sufficient to fail the test. Alternatively, the corporation might consider expanding the operating portion of the business. Expansion not only increases AOGI but also may have the effect of reducing PHCI if the investments generating the PHCI are sold to invest in the expansion.

Reducing Personal Holding Income.   Failing the income test normally is accomplished by reducing personal holding company income. It is sometimes asserted that merely reducing PHCI is not sufficient since both the numerator and the denominator in the test fraction are reduced by the same amounts. (This occurs because AOGI includes PHCI.) A mathematical check of this statement shows that it is incorrect and that a simple elimination of PHCI aids the taxpayer.

> **Example 14.**   Z Corporation has $100,000 of AOGI, including $70,000 of interest income which is PHCI. Substituting these values into the test fraction reveals that the corporation has excessive passive income.
>
> $$\frac{\text{PHCI}}{\text{AOGI}} = \frac{\$70,000}{\$100,000} = 70\%$$
>
> If Z Corporation simply reduces its interest income by $30,000, the corporation would fail the income test despite the fact that both the numerator and the denominator are reduced by the same amounts.
>
> $$\frac{\text{PHCI}}{\text{AOGI}} = \frac{\$40,000}{\$70,000} = 57.1\%$$

One way a corporation could eliminate part of its PHCI is by paying out as shareholder compensation the amounts that otherwise would be invested to generate PHCI. Alternatively, the corporation could eliminate PHCI by switching its investments into growth stocks where the return is generated from capital appreciation rather than dividends. Of course, the taxpayer would not necessarily want to switch completely out of dividend-paying stocks since the advantage of the dividends-received deduction would be lost.

The corporation could also reduce its PHCI by replacing it with tax-exempt income, capital gains, or § 1231 gains. This would have the same effect as simply eliminating the PHCI altogether.

Example 15. Same as *Example 14* above except the corporation invests in tax-exempt bonds which generate $20,000 of tax-exempt, rather than taxable, interest. In addition, the corporation realizes a $10,000 capital gain instead of taxable interest. The effect of replacing the taxable interest of $30,000 with capital gains of $10,000 and tax-exempt income of $20,000 would produce results identical to those above. This derives from the fact that the tax-exempt interest and capital gains are excluded from both the numerator, PHCI, and the denominator, AOGI, creating fractions identical to those shown above.

REMOVING THE PHC TAINT

In some situations, income which is normally considered PHCI (e.g., rental income) is not considered tainted if certain tests are met. For example, the Code provides escape hatches for rental income; mineral, oil, and gas royalties; copyright royalties; and rents from the distribution and exhibition of produced films. Although additional tests must be met to obtain exclusion for these types of income, there is one requirement common to each. *Generally*, if a corporation's income consists predominantly (50% or more) of only one of these income types, exclusion is available. More importantly, this condition can normally be obtained without great difficulty. To satisfy the 50 percent test, the taxpayer should take steps to ensure that a particular corporation receives only a single type of income. This may require forming an additional corporation that receives only one type of income, but by so doing the 50 percent test is met and the PHC tax may be avoided.

With proper control of their income, these corporations will have no difficulty in satisfying the income test since at least 50 percent of their AOGI is from one source. For corporations with rental income, however, dividends equal to the amount that their nonrental PHC income exceeds 10 percent of their OGI still must be paid. Note, however, that if a corporation has little or no nonrental PHC income, no dividends are necessary to meet the test. Also note that each additional dollar of gross rents, unreduced by expenses, decreases the amount of dividend that must be paid.

Example 16. G Corporation has $60,000 of OGI, including $53,000 of rental income and $7,000 of dividend income. In this case, dividends of only $1,000 are necessary since nonrental PHCI exceeds the 10% threshold by only $1,000 [$7,000 − (10% of OGI of $60,000)]. If the taxpayer wants to avoid distributing dividends, consideration should be given to increasing gross rents. Note how an increase of $10,000 in gross rents to $63,000 would increase OGI and concomitantly eliminate the need for a dividend. This increase in gross rents would be effective even if the typical adjustments for depreciation, interest, and taxes reduce the taxpayer's net profit to zero or a loss. This is true because such adjustments are not included in determining OGI, but only AOGI. Thus, an incentive exists for the corporation to invest in breakeven or unprofitable activities as a means to eliminate the dividend.

REDUCING THE PHC TAX WITH DIVIDENDS

If the tests for PHC status cannot be avoided, the penalty can be eliminated or minimized by the payment of dividends. Although a similar opportunity exists for the accumulated earnings tax, the treatment of dividends differs in several important respects.

On the one hand, the PHC tax requires quicker action than the accumulated earnings tax. For accumulated earnings tax purposes, all dividends paid within the $2^1/_2$-month period after the close of the taxable year are counted as paid for the previous year. However, for purposes of the PHC tax, the after-year-end dividends are limited to 20 percent of the amount actually paid during the year. Thus, if no dividends are paid during the year, then none can be paid during the $2^1/_2$-month period. On the other hand, the PHC tax can almost always be avoided through payment of a deficiency dividend, which is not available for the accumulated earnings tax. The deficiency dividend may come at a high price, however. As previously mentioned, any interest and penalties that would have been imposed had the penalty tax applied must be computed and paid as if the PHC tax were still due.

PLANNED PERSONAL HOLDING COMPANIES

Treatment of a corporation as a personal holding company is normally considered a dire consequence. Yet, in certain cases, PHC status may not be detrimental and at times can be beneficial. Two of these situations are outlined below.

Certain taxpayers seeking the benefits of the corporate form are unable to avoid characterization as a personal holding company. For example, an athlete or movie celebrity may seek the benefits reserved solely for employees, such as group-term life insurance, health and accident insurance, medical reimbursement plans, and better pension and profit-sharing plans. In these situations, if the individual incorporates his or her talents, the corporation will be considered a PHC since all of the income for services will be PHCI. This does not mean that the PHC tax must be paid, however. The PHC tax is levied only upon undistributed PHCI. In most cases, all of the undistributed PHCI can be eliminated through the payments of deductible compensation directly to the individual or deductible contributions to his or her pension plan. As a result, the individual can obtain the benefits of incorporation without concern for the PHC tax. This technique was extremely popular prior to 1982, when the benefits of corporate pension plans were significantly better than those available to the self-employed (i.e., Keogh plans).

Over the years, personal holding companies have been used quite successfully in estate planning in reducing the value of the taxpayer's estate and obtaining other estate tax benefits. Under a typical plan, a taxpayer with a portfolio of securities would transfer them to a PHC in exchange for preferred stock equal to their current value and common stock of no value. The exchange would be tax free under Code § 351. The taxpayer would then proceed to give the common stock to his or her children at no gift tax cost since its value at the time is zero. The taxpayer would also begin a gift program, transferring $10,000 of preferred stock annually to heirs which would also escape gift tax due to the annual gift tax exclusion. There were several benefits arising from this arrangement.

First and probably foremost, any appreciation in the value of the taxpayer's portfolio would accrue to the owners of the common stock and thus be successfully removed from the taxpayer's estate, avoiding both gift and estate taxes. Second, the corporation's declaration of dividends on the common stock would shift the income to the lower-bracket family members. Dividends on the preferred stock would also be shifted to the extent that the taxpayer has transferred the preferred stock. The dividends paid would in part aid in eliminating any PHC tax. Third, the taxpayer's preferred stock in the PHC would probably be valued at less than the value of the underlying assets for estate and gift tax purposes. Although the IRS takes the position that the value of the stock in the PHC is the same as the value of the corporation's assets, the courts have consistently held otherwise. The courts have normally allowed a substantial *discount* for estate and gift tax valuation, holding that an investment in a closely held business is less desirable than in the underlying shares since the underlying securities can easily be traded in the market while the PHC shares cannot.[109]

[109]　For example, see *Estate of Maurice Gustane Heckscher*, 63 T.C. 485 (1974). Also, see Chapter 13 for possible limitations on this estate planning technique.

PROBLEM MATERIALS

DISCUSSION QUESTIONS

6-1   *Double Taxation.* List four approaches that corporations use to avoid the effects of double taxation.

6-2   *Accumulated Earnings Tax.* What is the purpose of the accumulated earnings tax?

6-3   *Accumulated Earnings Tax.* What is the accumulated earnings tax rate? Why do you suppose Congress chose this particular tax rate?

6-4   *Accumulated Taxable Income.* What is the difference between accumulated taxable income and taxable income?

6-5   *Accumulated Earnings Credit.* What is the accumulated earnings credit? How does it affect the accumulated earnings tax?

6-6   *Dividends-Paid Deduction.* What constitutes the dividends-paid deduction for purposes of the accumulated earnings tax?

6-7   *Throwback Dividend.* What is a throwback dividend?

6-8   *Consent Dividends.* What is a consent dividend? What is its purpose?

6-9   *Intent of Accumulations.* What situations are considered to indicate the intent of a corporation to unreasonably accumulate earnings?

6-10   *Reasonable Needs.* List six possible reasons for accumulating earnings that might be considered reasonable needs of the business.

6-11   *Reasonable Needs—The* Bardahl *Formula.* What is the *Bardahl* formula? How is it used?

6-12   *Personal Holding Company Tax.* What is the purpose of the personal holding company tax?

6-13   *Personal Holding Company.* What requirements must be met by a corporation in order for it to be a personal holding company?

6-14   *Ownership Requirement.* What is the ownership requirement for personal holding companies? What constructive ownership rules apply?

6-15   *Income Requirement.* What is the income requirement for personal holding companies? What terms must be defined in order to determine if a corporation meets the income requirement?

6-16   *Income Requirement.* What tests must be met in order to determine whether the adjusted income from rents is included in personal holding company income?

6-17   *Computing the Personal Holding Company Tax.* How is the personal holding company penalty tax computed?

6-18 *Adjusted Taxable Income*. How does adjusted taxable income differ from taxable income?

6-19 *Dividends-Paid Deduction*. How does the dividends-paid deduction for personal holding company tax purposes differ from the dividends-paid deduction for accumulated earnings tax purposes?

6-20 *Deficiency Dividends*. What is a deficiency dividend? What is its purpose? What effect does it have on the personal holding company tax?

PROBLEMS

6-21 *Computing the Accumulated Earnings Tax*. Z Corporation had accumulated taxable income of $180,000 for the current year. Calculate Z Corporation's accumulated earnings tax liability.

6-22 *Computing Adjusted Taxable Income*. R Corporation has the following income and deductions for the current year:

Income from operations	$200,000
Dividend income	60,000
Charitable contributions	40,000

Compute R Corporation's adjusted taxable income.

6-23 *Minimum Accumulated Earnings Tax Credit*. B Corporation, a calendar year manufacturing company, had accumulated earnings and profits at the beginning of the current year of $60,000. If the corporation's earnings and profits for the current year are $270,000, what is B Corporation's minimum accumulated earnings tax credit?

6-24 *Accumulated Earnings Tax Credit*. Assume the same facts in Problem 6-23 above, except that B Corporation has estimated reasonable business needs of $300,000 at the end of the current year.

a. Compute B Corporation's accumulated earnings tax credit for the current year.
b. Would your answer differ if B Corporation was an incorporated law practice owned and operated by one person? If so, by how much?

6-25   *Computing the Accumulated Earnings Tax.* T Corporation had accumulated earnings and profits at the beginning of 1991 of $300,000. It has never paid dividends to its shareholders and does not intend to do so in the near future. The following facts relate to T Corporation's 1990 tax year:

Taxable income..................................	$200,000
Federal income tax..............................	61,250
Dividends received (from less than	
20% owned corporations)...................	40,000
Reasonable business needs as of 12/31/91	356,850

    a.   What is T Corporation's accumulated earnings tax?

    b.   If T Corporation's sole shareholder wanted to avoid the accumulated earnings tax, what amount of consent dividends would be required?

6-26   *Dividends-Paid Deduction.* J Corporation, a small oil tool manufacturer, projects adjusted taxable income for the current year of $200,000. Its estimated reasonable business needs are $500,000; and the corporation has $380,000 of prior years' accumulated earnings and profits as of the beginning of the current year. Using this information, answer the following:

    a.   Assuming no dividends-paid deduction, what is J Corporation's accumulated earnings tax for the current year?

    b.   If J Corporation paid $50,000 of dividends during the year, what is J Corporation's accumulated earnings tax liability?

    c.   If J Corporation's shareholders are willing to report more dividends than the $50,000 actually received during the year, what amount of consent dividends is necessary to avoid the accumulated earnings tax?

    d.   If the corporation's shareholders are not interested in paying taxes on hypothetical dividends, what other possibility is available to increase the dividends-paid deduction?

6-27   *Working Capital Needs—The* Bardahl *Formula.* X Corporation wishes to use the *Bardahl* formula to determine the amount of working capital it can justify if the IRS agent currently auditing the company's records raises the accumulated earnings tax issue. For the year under audit, X Corporation had the following:

Annual operating expenses......................	$285,000
Inventory cycle ratio............................	.41
Accounts receivable cycle ratio..................	.61
Accounts payable cycle ratio	.82

    a.   How much working capital can X Corporation justify based on the above facts?

    b.   If X Corporation's turnover ratios are based on annual averages, what additional information would you request before computing working capital needs based on the *Bardahl* formula?

6-28   *Working Capital Needs*—Bardahl *Formula.* B owns and operates BKA Inc., which is a retail toy store. One Wednesday morning in January, 1992, she noticed in the *Wall Street Journal*'s tax column an anecdote about a small corporation that was required to pay the accumulated earnings tax. Concerned, B presented the following information to her tax advisor to evaluate her exposure as of the end of 1991.

Balance Sheet

	1990	1991
Current Assets:		
Cash	$ 15,000	$ 30,000
Marketable securities (cost)	10,000	23,000
Accounts receivable (net)	55,000	45,000
Inventory	30,000	50,000
Property, plant, and equipment (net)	500,000	552,000
Total Assets	$610,000	$700,000
Current Liabilities:		
Accounts payable	$ 13,000	$ 31,000
Long-term debt	147,000	119,000
Common stock	50,000	50,000
Earnings and profits	400,000	500,000
	$610,000	$700,000

Income Statement

Sales		$400,000
Cost of goods sold:		
Beginning inventory	$ 30,000	
Purchases	220,000	
Ending inventory	(50,000)	
Total		(200,000)
Gross profit		$200,000
Other Expenses:		
Depreciation	$ 70,000	
Selling expenses and administrative	25,000	
Interest	5,000	
Total		(100,000)
Net income before taxes		$100,000
Income taxes		(25,750)
Net income		$ 74,250

B noted that the market value of the securities was $40,000 as of December 31, 1991. In addition, B estimates the future expansion of the business (excluding working capital) will require $25,000. Determine whether the accumulated earnings tax will apply to B.

6-29 *Personal Holding Company—Income Requirement.* K Corporation is equally owned and operated by three brothers. K Corporation's gross income for the current year is $80,000, which consists of $10,000 of dividend income, interest income of $40,000, and a long-term capital gain of $30,000.

    a.   Calculate ordinary gross income.
    b.   Calculate adjusted ordinary gross income.
    c.   Is K Corporation a personal holding company?

6-30 *Personal Holding Company—Rent Exclusion.* T Corporation has gross income of $116,000, which consists of gross rental income of $86,000, interest income of $20,000, and dividends of $10,000. Depreciation, property taxes, and interest expense related to the rental property totaled $16,000. Assuming T Corporation has seven shareholders and has no dividends-paid deduction, answer the following:

    a.   What is T Corporation's ordinary gross income?
    b.   Adjusted ordinary gross income?
    c.   Does the rental income constitute personal holding company income?
    d.   Is T Corporation a personal holding company?

6-31 *Personal Holding Company Income.* V Corporation is equally owned by two shareholders. The corporation reports the following income and deductions for the current year.

Dividend income	$30,000
Interest income	15,000
Long-term capital gain	10,000
Rental income (gross)	80,000
Rental expenses:	
Depreciation	10,000
Interest on mortgage	9,000
Property taxes	3,000
Real estate management fees	8,000

    a.   Calculate ordinary gross income.
    b.   Calculate adjusted ordinary gross income.
    c.   Calculate adjusted income from rentals.
    d.   Calculate personal holding company income.
    e.   Is V Corporation a personal holding company?
    f.   If V Corporation paid $3,000 of dividends to each of its two shareholders during the current year, how would this affect your answers to (d) and (e) above?

6-32   *Items of PHC Income.* Indicate whether the following would be considered personal holding company income.

    a.   Income from the sales of inventory
    b.   Interest income from AT&T bond
    c.   Interest income from State of Texas bond
    d.   Dividend income from IBM stock
    e.   Long-term capital gain
    f.   Short-term capital gain
    g.   Rental income from lease of office building (100% of the corporation's income is from rents)
    h.   Fees paid to the corporation for the services of Jose Greatfoot, internationally known soccer player.

6-33   *PHC Income Test.* All of the stock of C Corporation is owned by B. Next year, the corporation expects the following results from operations:

Sales	$500,000
Costs of goods sold	200,000
Other operating expenses	40,000
Interest income	10,000

What is the maximum amount of dividend income that the corporation can have without being classified as a personal holding company?

6-34   *Computing the Personal Holding Company Tax.* P Corporation is owned by five individuals. For the current year P had the following:

Taxable income	$200,000
Federal income tax	60,750
Dividends received	40,000
Long-term capital gain	10,000

Compute P Corporation's personal holding company tax assuming P meets the income test and that the long-term capital gain was taxed at 34 percent.

6-35   *Personal Holding Company—Dividend Deduction.* H, a personal holding company, anticipates having undistributed personal holding company income of $120,000 before any dividend deduction for 1991. The company wishes to distribute all of its income to avoid the penalty. Because of cash flow problems, it wishes to pay as much of this dividend as it can in the $2\,1/2$ months after the close of the tax year.

    a.   What is the *maximum* amount that H can distribute during 1992 to accomplish its task if dividends of $50,000 were paid during 1991?
    b.   What is the *minimum* amount that H must distribute during 1991 and still be able to defer until 1992 the payment of any additional dividends?

6-36   *Personal Holding Company—Service Income.* J, an orthopedic surgeon, is the sole owner of J Inc. The corporation employs surgical nurses and physical therapists in addition to J. The nurses assist Dr. J on all operations, and the therapists provide all follow-up treatment. J Inc. bills all clients for all services rendered and pays the employees a stated salary. Will any of J Inc.'s fee be personal holding company income?

6-37 *PHC Dividends-Paid Deduction.* Indicate whether the following distributions would qualify for the personal holding company dividends-paid deduction for 1991.

    a.   Cash dividends paid on common stock in 1991.

    b.   Dividend distribution of land (value $20,000, basis $5,000) paid on common stock in 1991.

    c.   Cash dividends paid on common stock March 3, 1992.

    d.   Cash dividends paid on common stock in 1990.

    e.   Consent dividend; the 1991 corporate tax return was filed on March 3, 1992; the consents were filed on May 15, 1992.

    f.   Cash dividend paid in 1994 shortly after it was determined that the corporation was a personal holding company.

    g.   The corporation adopted a plan of liquidation in 1989 and the final liquidating distribution was made during 1991.

6-38 *Accumulated Earnings Tax Dividends-Paid Deduction.* Indicate whether the distributions identified in problem 6-37 would qualify for the accumulated earnings tax dividends-paid deduction for 1991.

6-39 *Understanding the PHC Tax.* Indicate whether the following statements regarding the personal holding company tax are true or false.

    a.   The PHC tax is self-assessed and, if applicable, must be paid in addition to the regular income tax.

    b.   An S corporation or partnership may be subject to the PHC tax.

    c.   A corporation that can prove that its shareholders did not intend to use it as a tax shelter is not subject to the PHC tax.

    d.   A publicly traded corporation normally would not be subject to the PHC tax.

    e.   A corporation that derives virtually all of its income from leasing operations does not risk the PHC tax, even though such income is normally considered passive.

    f.   Federal income taxes reduce the base on which the PHC tax is assessed.

    g.   Long-term capital gains are not subject to the PHC tax.

    h.   A corporation that consistently pays dividends normally would not be subject to the PHC tax.

    i.   Throwback dividends are available to reduce the corporation's potential liability without limitation.

    j.   Corporations without cash or property that they can distribute cannot benefit from the dividends-paid deduction.

    k.   The PHC tax is not truly a risk because of the deficiency dividend procedure.

    l.   A corporation may be required to pay both the accumulated earnings tax and the personal holding company tax in the same year.

6-40 *Understanding the Accumulated Earnings Tax.* Indicate whether the statements in problem 6-39 are true or false regarding the accumulated earnings tax.

RESEARCH PROBLEMS

6-41   H Corporation is owned and operated by William and Wilma Holt. The corporation's principal source of income for the past few years has been net rentals from five adjacent rent houses located in an area that the city has condemned in order to expand its freeway system. The Holts anticipate a condemnation award of approximately $400,000, and a resulting gain of $325,000. Although convinced that they will have the corporation reinvest the proceeds in other rental units, the Holts would like to invest the corporation's condemnation proceeds in a high-yield certificate of deposit for at least three years. They have come to you for advice.

   a.   What advice would you give concerning the reinvestment requirements of Code § 1033?

   b.   If H Corporation will have substantial interest income in the next few years, could the § 541 tax be a possibility?

   c.   If the Holts have considered liquidating the corporation and reinvesting the proceeds in rental units, what additional information would you need in order to advise them?

6-42   Stacey Caniff is the controlling shareholder of Cotton, Inc., a textile manufacturer. She inherited the business from her father. In recent years earnings have fluctuated between $0.50 and $3.00 per share. Dividends have remained at $0.10 per share for the last ten years with a resulting increase in cash. On audit, the IRS agent has raised the accumulated earnings tax issue. In your discussion with Stacey, she has indicated that the dividends are so low because she is afraid of losing the business (as almost happened to her father during the depression), of decreased profitability from foreign competition, and of the need to modernize if OSHA were to enforce the rules concerning cotton dust. Evaluate the possibility of overcoming an accumulated earnings tax assessment.

PART II

ADVANCED CORPORATE TAX TOPICS

CONTENTS

LEARNING OBJECTIVES

Upon completion of this chapter you will be able to:

- Understand the basic tax consequences arising from corporate reorganizations, including corporate mergers, acquisitions, and divisions

- Describe the seven different types of reorganizations and what requirements must be met for nontaxable treatment

- Discuss the tax treatment of the acquiring corporation, the target corporation, and the target's shareholders

- Explain the rules governing the carryover of the tax attributes from one corporation to another

CHAPTER OUTLINE

Chapter 7

CORPORATE REORGANIZATIONS

INTRODUCTION

During its life, circumstances may arise that cause a corporation to alter the form in which it conducts its business. For instance, a corporation may want to combine its business operations with another corporation, or conversely, split its operations into several parts. Over the past 20 years, corporations have often found that restructuring is necessary for economic survival and growth. As a result, business combinations—mergers and acquisitions—and divisions have been rampant. Perhaps the most striking example of a corporate restructuring was the breakup of American Telephone and Telegraph Corporation in 1983 into eight separate companies. This divestiture can be contrasted with the merger of General Electric and RCA. Since these corporate divisions and combinations usually involve exchanges of stock and property, they normally would be taxable transactions without special treatment. To ensure that the tax laws would not impede corporate realignments, Congress enacted certain provisions that allow for nonrecognition of gain or loss in various types of corporate reorganizations.

The reorganization provisions contained in the tax law are not confined to situations involving corporate giants such as AT&T. Rather, they exist to enable corporations of any size to restructure to meet business needs without the interference of taxes. The following example illustrates a typical situation in which the reorganization rules apply.

> **Example 1.** A highly successful cable television company, CTV, desires to expand by acquiring FM, a corporation owning a radio station in Chicago. CTV's management is convinced that their expertise can be used to make FM a very profitable operation. The acquisition of the radio station could be made in several ways. CTV could purchase the stock of FM from its shareholders and operate the newly acquired corporation as a subsidiary. This method would result in tax to the FM shareholders—perhaps an undesirable result—and may require CTV to use its cash which it may be unwilling to do. Alternatively, CTV and FM could agree to a merger where

CTV would acquire FM using its own stock rather than using cash or other consideration. If a merger occurred, CTV would issue CTV stock to the FM shareholders in *exchange* for their stock. As a result, FM would be absorbed into CTV and the FM shareholders would become CTV shareholders. Since a merger generally qualifies as a reorganization, the exchange of FM stock for CTV stock by FM's shareholders is nontaxable.

If CTV desired not to absorb FM in a merger transaction—perhaps because the license granted to FM to operate the radio station cannot be assigned to CTV under government regulations—it could simply issue CTV stock to the FM shareholders in *exchange* for their FM stock and operate FM as a subsidiary. As above, the FM shareholders would become CTV shareholders instead of FM shareholders, and everyone would enjoy tax-free treatment since a stock for stock exchange normally qualifies as a reorganization.

Note that in both situations described above, CTV is able to restructure its operations generally unaffected by tax considerations. However, any gain or loss realized on the transactions does not go permanently unrecognized. The basis rules applying to reorganizations ensure that recognition occurs if and when there is a subsequent disposition of the stock or property.

Reorganizations are normally nontaxable because the shareholders have not liquidated their investment but merely have continued it in a modified form. In other words, they remain shareholders, albeit in a reorganized corporation. Since the shareholders have not converted their equity interests into cash, they have not realized (in an accounting sense) any of the appreciation in their investment, nor have they received the equivalent of a corporate distribution. Moreover, the shareholders lack the ability to pay any tax since they have not "cashed in" but rather still own property. In light of these circumstances, Congress has permitted properly structured reorganizations to be carried out without the imposition of tax.

The reorganization provisions are very similar to the like-kind exchange rules which enable taxpayers to exchange properties held for productive use or investment tax-free. As with like-kind exchanges, however, if the shareholders involved in a reorganization receive boot or terminate their interest in the property, there may be tax consequences. In addition, the unrecognized gains and losses are preserved through the basis assigned to the various properties.

This chapter discusses the various types of reorganizations and the requirements that must be satisfied if a reorganization is to be considered a nontaxable transaction.

TAX-FREE REORGANIZATIONS: GENERAL REQUIREMENTS

In order for a transaction to be given nonrecognition treatment under the reorganization provisions, it must meet several general requirements.

1. The reorganization must meet certain tests in the Regulations regarding "continuity of interest" and "continuity of business enterprise."

2. The reorganization must be conducted according to one of several acceptable patterns—there are seven qualifying forms or types of reorganizations eligible for nonrecognition.

3. The reorganization must meet the judicially imposed condition requiring a "business purpose" for the transaction.

4. A plan of reorganization must exist and such plan must be adopted by each corporation involved in the transaction.

Before examining these requirements, the general context in which they are applied as well as some terminology must be understood. The important characteristics of a reorganization can be readily seen in a merger transaction that qualifies as a so-called "A" reorganization. In a merger, one corporation, E, referred to as the *transferee*, acquires the assets of another corporation, T, called the *transferor*, in exchange for E stock, securities, and other consideration. The shareholders of the transferor, T, exchange their stock of the transferor for the package of consideration provided by the transferee and the T stock is cancelled. This somewhat confusing set of transactions is illustrated in Exhibit 7-2 and is examined in detail later in this chapter. In considering the tax treatment of these exchange transactions, the somewhat more descriptive term, *acquiring corporation*, is normally used in lieu of *transferee corporation*. Similarly, the transferor corporation is typically referred to as the *target*, or *acquired corporation*. References to prior or former shareholders are to the shareholders of the target (transferor) corporation since they are no longer shareholders in the target but rather shareholders in the acquiring corporation.

CONTINUITY OF INTEREST

As previously suggested, nonrecognition of gains on exchanges related to a reorganization is premised on the theory that the shareholders have a *continuity of interest*; that is, they retain a substantial proprietary interest in the continuing business. This concept was first developed by the court in *Cortland Specialty Co.*[1] and is now contained in the Regulations. The Regulations state:

---

[1] *Cortland Specialty Co. v. Comm.*, 3 USTC ¶980, 11 AFTR 857, 60 F.2d 937 (CA-2, 1932).

> the term [reorganization] does not embrace the mere purchase by one corporation of the properties of another, for it imports a continuity of interest on the part of the transferor or its shareholders in the properties transferred. If the properties are transferred for cash and deferred payment obligations…the transaction is a sale and not an exchange in which gain is not recognized.[2]

To prevent taxpayers from disguising what are essentially sales as nontaxable reorganizations, the continuity-of-interest doctrine requires that transferors maintain their stake in the continuing business as shareholders in the reorganized corporation.[3] For example, in *LeTulle v. Scofield*,[4] the Supreme Court denied tax-free treatment to a reorganization where the target corporation and its shareholders received only cash and bonds in exchange for all of its assets. The Court indicated that the status of the shareholders had changed. They were no longer shareholders but rather creditors of the restructured entity. The effect of this and other decisions is to require transferors to continue their interest through stock ownership in the reorganized corporation.

The thrust of the continuity-of-interest doctrine is to limit the types of consideration items that an acquiring corporation can offer to the target's shareholders. If the exchange is to qualify for favorable treatment, it is clear that the consideration package must contain stock of the acquiring corporation in order that the target's shareholders have an equity interest in the acquiring corporation. The percentage of consideration that is stock has never been precisely specified by the Regulations or the Courts. The IRS has indicated its position, however. For ruling purposes, the Service requires at least 50 percent of the consideration to be stock of the acquiring corporation.[5] This is not to say that at least half of what each shareholder receives must be stock. Instead, the test is applied to the target's shareholders as a group—not individually. As a result, an acquiring corporation has great flexibility in designing the package of consideration that the target's owners will receive.

> **Example 2.**　B Corporation wishes to merge with Target Corporation. Most of Target's shareholders are in favor of the merger; however, a minority of Target's shareholders have threatened a lawsuit if the merger is consummated. If B Corporation restructures the transaction so that the shareholders of Target who oppose the merger receive cash and the majority of Target's shareholders receive stock, the transaction should meet the continuity of interest requirement.

---

[2]　Reg. § 1.368-2(a).

[3]　Rev. Rul. 77-415, 1977-2 C.B. 311 and Rev. Rul. 77-479, 1977 C.B. 119.

[4]　*LeTulle v. Scofield*, 40-1 USTC ¶9150, 23 AFTR 789, 308 U.S. 415 (USSC, 1940).

[5]　Rev. Proc. 77-37, 1977-2 C.B. 568.

Another aspect of the continuity-of-interest requirement concerns the length of time the former owners must maintain their interest in the new entity. Normally it is sufficient if the prior owners have the requisite interest immediately after the transaction. However, if there is a prearranged plan to dispose of the ownership, the Service is likely to apply the step transaction doctrine, arguing that the reorganization was just one step in a plan to bail out the earnings of the target corporation, and deny nonrecognition.[6]

> **Example 3.** G incorporated his business, T Inc., many years ago with a capital contribution of $10,000. The stock of the corporation is now worth $500,000 representing substantial cash balances. G wishes to cash in on the appreciation. In the past, G has always shunned offers for his business but now plans to accept 300 shares of stock of ACQ Inc., a publicly traded corporation, for all of his shares as part of a merger of ACQ and T. The exchange will qualify as a nontaxable reorganization assuming G maintains his ownership in ACQ Inc. However, if G sells the ACQ shares shortly after the merger for $500,000—thus effectively bailing the earnings out of his formerly owned corporation as capital gain rather than dividend income—the Service may object. No doubt the government might argue that the reorganization was simply one step in a plan to avoid taxes and treat the exchange as a taxable transaction.

CONTINUITY OF BUSINESS ENTERPRISE

A reorganization is classified as a nontaxable transaction because it results in a continuation of the *business* in modified form. To ensure that the business is continued, the Regulations contain a *continuity of business* enterprise requirement.[7] To meet this requirement, the acquiring corporation must either continue the target corporation's historic business or use a significant portion of the target corporation's assets in a business.[8]

> **Example 4.** Target Corporation, which contains substantially appreciated assets, has been only marginally profitable the last few years. Its shareholders would like to liquidate the corporation and invest in another business. C Corporation has a large capital loss carryforward and needs additional cash for expansion. Target is merged into C with Target's shareholders receiving C stock. C immediately sells Target's assets and invests the cash in its existing business. This transaction does not meet the continuity of business enterprise requirement. Note that Target's shareholders do not end up owning stock in a corporation that will continue Target's old business but rather have sold the old corporation and invested in C.

---

[6] For example, see *McDonald's Restaurant of Illinois*, 82-2 USTC ¶9581, 50 AFTR2d 82-5750, 688 F.2d 520 (CA-7, 1982).

[7] Reg. § 1.368-1(d).

[8] Reg. § 1.368-1(d)(2).

Continuing the target corporation's historic business generally requires continuing the target's most recently conducted line of business.[9] It does not require continuing all of the acquired corporation's lines of business nor does it require continuing the business in the exact same manner. If the target corporation has more than one line of business, the test is satisfied where the most significant line is continued. In addition, reasonable changes can be made in the management of the business, and duplicative or unnecessary assets can be sold. The extent of the changes will be viewed in context of all the facts and circumstances.

Using a significant portion of the acquired corporation's assets means using a significant portion of the assets used by the target (or acquired) corporation in its historic business.[10] It does not mean using all the assets nor does it mean using the assets in the same manner.

> **Example 5.** P Corporation manufactures computers and Target Corporation manufactures components for computers. Target sells all of its output to P. On January 1, 1991, P decides to buy imported components only. On March 1, 1991, Target merges into P. P retains Target's assets as a backup source of supply. P is considered to be using a significant part of Target's assets even though they are kept as a backup.[11]

CONTROL

In addition to imposing the continuity requirement, the reorganization provisions frequently require the acquiring corporation to obtain control of the target corporation or for the shareholders of the acquiring corporation to be in control of the corporation immediately after the transaction. For these purposes, control is defined as at least 80 percent of the total voting power and at least 80 percent of all other classes of stock.[12] To meet the latter test, the shareholders must own at least 80 percent of the total number of shares of each class of nonvoting stock.[13] This is the same definition of control that is applied for purposes of corporate formations under § 351.

---

[9] Reg. § 1.368-1(d)(3)(iii).

[10] Reg. § 1.368-1(d)(4).

[11] Reg. § 1.368-1(d)(5), *Example 2*.

[12] § 368(c).

[13] Rev. Rul. 59-259, 59-2 C.B. 115.

ACCEPTABLE PATTERNS OF REORGANIZATION: TYPES A–G

There are seven qualifying patterns of reorganization. The descriptions, which are contained in §§ 368(a)(1)(A) through (G), are as follows:

Type A— a statutory merger or consolidation;

Type B— the acquisition by one corporation, in exchange solely for all or a part of its voting stock (or in exchange solely for all or a part of the voting stock of a corporation which is in control of the acquiring corporation), of stock of another corporation if, immediately after the acquisition, the acquiring corporation has control of such other corporation (whether or not such acquiring corporation had control immediately before the acquisition);

Type C— the acquisition by one corporation, in exchange solely for all or a part of its voting stock (or in exchange solely for all or a part of the voting stock of a corporation which is in control of the acquiring corporation), of substantially all of the properties of another corporation, but in determining whether the exchange is solely for stock the assumption by the acquiring corporation of a liability of the other, or the fact that property acquired is subject to a liability, shall be disregarded.

Type D— a transfer by a corporation of all or a part of its assets to another corporation if immediately after the transfer the transferor, or one or more of its shareholders (including persons who were shareholders immediately before the transfer), or any combination thereof, is in control of the corporation to which the assets are transferred; but only if, in pursuance of the plan, stock or securities of the corporation to which the assets transferred are distributed in a transaction which qualifies under §§ 354, 355, or 356;

Type E— a recapitalization;

Type F— a mere change in identity, form, or place of organization of one corporation, however effected; or

Type G— a transfer by a corporation of all or part of its assets to another corporation in a Title 11 or similar case, but only if, in pursuance of the plan, stock or securities of the corporation to which the assets are transferred are distributed in a transaction which qualifies under Code §§ 354, 355, or 356.

In referring to the different types of reorganizations, tax practitioners generally shorten the reference and simply call each by the subparagraph in which it is described. Therefore, the seven transactions are usually referred to as "A," "B," "C," "D," "E," "F," or "G" reorganizations.

The seven acceptable patterns of reorganization may be classified into two categories: divisive and nondivisive. As the name suggests, a *divisive reorganization* is one where a single corporation is divided into two or more corporations. After the division the original corporation may or may not survive. The "D" reorganization is the sole divisive reorganization. All other reorganizations are *nondivisive*.

The nondivisive reorganizations can be further subdivided into two groups: those that are acquisitive reorganizations and those that are not. In the *acquisitive reorganizations*—the "A," "B," "C," and acquisitive "D" reorganizations—one corporation acquires another corporation's stock, assets, or some combination thereof. Note while studying these reorganizations that one of the distinctions between them is what is acquired (e.g., stock or assets). Another distinction is the type of consideration that may be used by the acquiring corporation. Although the rules concerning consideration that may be used reflects the continuity-of-interest requirement (i.e., stock of the acquiring corporation must be exchanged), variations in the consideration packages exist.

The other nondivisive reorganizations are the "E," "F," and "G" reorganizations. In the "E" reorganization, a single corporation reconfigures its capital structure (e.g., issues stock to its shareholders in exchange for their bonds). The "F" reorganization rules govern the tax consequences when the corporation merely changes its name or place of incorporation, or makes some other alteration in its form. The "G" reorganization concerns bankrupt corporations.

As this brief overview indicates, reorganizations come in various shapes and sizes. They vary in the number of corporations involved, the type of consideration that may be used, the properties transferred, and other subtle ways. Exhibit 7-1 summarizes the general characteristics of the various reorganizations. Each of the reorganizations is explored in detail below.

"A" REORGANIZATION

The "A" reorganization is defined as a statutory merger or consolidation.[14] "Statutory" means that the reorganization qualifies as a merger or consolidation under the appropriate state law.[15] In a merger, one corporation (the acquiring corporation) absorbs another corporation (target corporation). There are basically two steps in a merger. First, the target corporation transfers all of its assets and liabilities to the acquiring corporation in return for stock and securities (and possibly other property) of the acquiring corporation. Then the target corporation, which now contains solely the stock and securities (and other property) of the acquiring corporation, dissolves by exchanging the acquiring corporation's stock for its own stock. As a result, the former shareholders of the target corporation become shareholders in the acquiring corporation; and the acquiring corporation is the sole corporation that survives. This is illustrated in Exhibit 7-2.

---

[14] § 368(a)(1)(A).   [15] Reg. § 1.368-2(b)(1).

> **Example 6.** J owns all the stock of Target Corporation. B owns all the stock of Acquiring Corporation. J and B agree to merge Target and Acquiring in an "A" reorganization. Target Corporation transfers its assets and liabilities to Acquiring Corporation in return for Acquiring Corporation stock. Target Corporation then dissolves by transferring the Acquiring stock to J in exchange for its (Target's) stock. Acquiring is the sole surviving corporation. J and B are the shareholders of Acquiring Corporation.

A consolidation is a statutory combination of two or more corporations in a *new* corporation. It involves the same two steps as a merger. First, the target corporations transfer their assets to the new consolidated corporation in return for stock and securities of the new corporation. Then the target corporations dissolve by distributing the new corporation's stock to their shareholders in return for their own stock. This is illustrated in Exhibit 7-3.

> **Example 7.** J owns all the stock of T1 Corporation, whose assets have a fair market value of $500,000. B owns all the stock of T2 Corporation, whose assets have a fair market value of $300,000. C owns all the stock of T3 Corporation, whose assets have a fair market value of $200,000. J, B, and C agree to consolidate their corporations in an "A" reorganization. T1, T2, and T3 transfer their assets to A Corporation, a new entity, in return for shares of stock. Assuming A Corporation issues 1,000 shares of stock, T1 receives 500 shares, T2 receives 300 shares and T3 receives 200 shares. T1, T2, and T3 then dissolve by transferring the A stock to its shareholder in return for its outstanding stock. J, B, and C become the shareholders of A Corporation.

The "A" reorganization requires that the merger or consolidation qualifies as such under state law. Although state laws differ, they generally require that the merger be approved by the board of directors and the shareholders of each corporation involved in the reorganization. This can be a time-consuming and expensive requirement. It is usually considered one of the major disadvantages of the "A" reorganization. The other major disadvantage of the "A" reorganization is that the acquiring corporation will be responsible for all the liabilities of the target corporation, including contingent liabilities.

The "A" reorganization, unlike the "B" and "C" reorganizations, does not contain any statutory limitations on the consideration that the acquiring corporation can issue to the target corporation in return for its assets. As long as state law permits, the acquiring corporation can issue its common stock (voting and nonvoting), preferred stock (voting, nonvoting, participating and nonparticipating) and securities. The exact percentages of each are dictated by the business considerations and the desires of the shareholders of the target corporation. This ability to issue a variety of considerations makes the "A" reorganization very flexible. Yet, this flexibility is not unlimited. The transaction must meet the continuity-

<table>
<tr><td colspan="6" align="center">Exhibit 7-1
Reorganization Characteristics</td></tr>
<tr>
<th rowspan="2">Reorg.</th>
<th rowspan="2">Shortened Title</th>
<th colspan="2">Acquiring Corporation</th>
<th colspan="2">Target Corporation</th>
</tr>
<tr>
<th>Transfers</th>
<th>Receives</th>
<th>Transfers</th>
<th>Receives</th>
</tr>
<tr>
<td rowspan="2">A</td>
<td>Merger</td>
<td>Stock, securities and/or other property</td>
<td>Target's assets and liabilities</td>
<td>All property and liabilities</td>
<td>Goes out of existence</td>
</tr>
<tr>
<td>Consolidation</td>
<td>All property and liabilities</td>
<td>Goes out of existence</td>
<td>All property and liabilities</td>
<td>Goes out of existence</td>
</tr>
<tr>
<td>B</td>
<td>Stock acquisition</td>
<td>Soley voting stock</td>
<td>Controlling stock of target</td>
<td>– – –</td>
<td>– – –</td>
</tr>
<tr>
<td>C</td>
<td>Asset acquisition</td>
<td>Soley voting stock and possibly other property</td>
<td>Substantially all the assets of target</td>
<td>Substantially all its assets</td>
<td>Voting stock of acquiring corporation</td>
</tr>
<tr>
<td rowspan="2">D</td>
<td>Acquisitive</td>
<td>Substantially all its assets</td>
<td>Goes out of existence</td>
<td>Controlling stock</td>
<td>Assets of acquiring corporation</td>
</tr>
<tr>
<td>Divisive</td>
<td>Some of its assets</td>
<td>Controlling stock and securities of target (distributes to share-holders)</td>
<td>Controlling stock and securities</td>
<td>Assets of acquiring corporation</td>
</tr>
<tr>
<td>E</td>
<td>Recapitalization</td>
<td>New stock and securities</td>
<td>Its old stock and securities</td>
<td>– – –</td>
<td>– – –</td>
</tr>
<tr>
<td>F</td>
<td>Change in identity</td>
<td>New stock and securities</td>
<td>Its old stock and securities</td>
<td>– – –</td>
<td>– – –</td>
</tr>
<tr>
<td>G</td>
<td>Bankruptcy</td>
<td>Some or all of its assets</td>
<td>Stock and securities of target (distributes to share-holder)</td>
<td>Stock and securities</td>
<td>Assets from acquiring corporation</td>
</tr>
</table>

| | Acquiring Corporation's Shareholders | | | Target Corporation's Shareholders | |
	Transfers	Receives	Realized Gain recognized	Transfers	Receives
	– – –	– – –	To extent boot is received	Exchange stock and securities	Stock and securities of new corp.
	Exchange stock and securities	Stock and securities of new corp.	To extent boot is received	Exchange stock and securities	Stock and securities of new corp.
	– – –	– – –	None	Controlling stock	Voting stock of acquiring corporation
	– – –	– – –	To extent boot is received	– – –	– – –
	Stock and securities	Controlling stock and securities of target	To extent boot is received	– – –	– – –
	May transfer stock and securities	Controlling stock and securities of target	To extent boot is received	– – –	– – –
	Old stock and securities	New stock and securities	To extent boot is received	– – –	– – –
	Old stock and securities	New stock and securities	To extent boot is received	– – –	– – –
	May transfer stock and securities	Controlling stock and securities of target	To extent boot is received	– – –	– – –

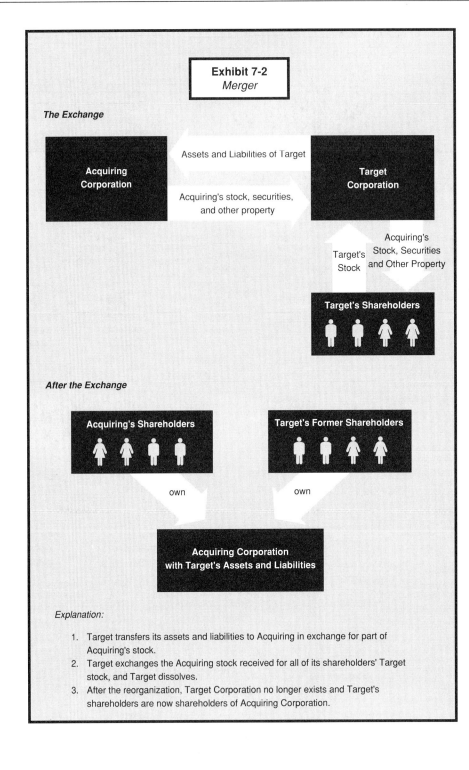

Exhibit 7-2
Merger

The Exchange

Acquiring Corporation

Assets and Liabilities of Target

Acquiring's stock, securities, and other property

Target Corporation

Target's Stock

Acquiring's Stock, Securities and Other Property

Target's Shareholders

After the Exchange

Acquiring's Shareholders

Target's Former Shareholders

own

own

Acquiring Corporation with Target's Assets and Liabilities

Explanation:

1. Target transfers its assets and liabilities to Acquiring in exchange for part of Acquiring's stock.
2. Target exchanges the Acquiring stock received for all of its shareholders' Target stock, and Target dissolves.
3. After the reorganization, Target Corporation no longer exists and Target's shareholders are now shareholders of Acquiring Corporation.

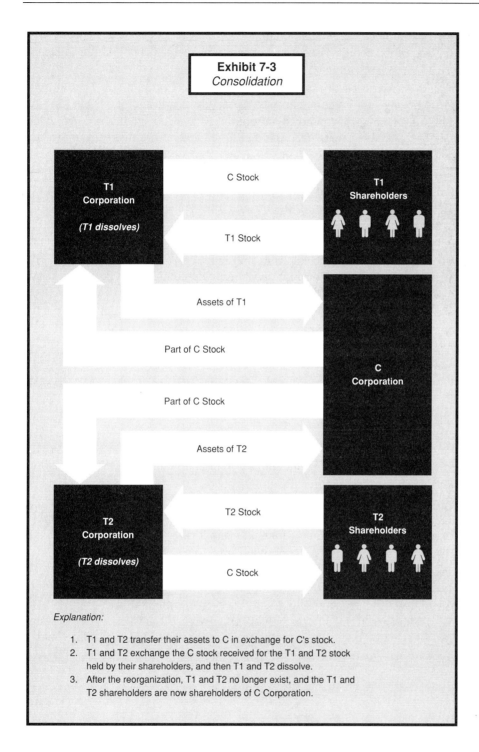

Exhibit 7-3
Consolidation

Explanation:

1. T1 and T2 transfer their assets to C in exchange for C's stock.
2. T1 and T2 exchange the C stock received for the T1 and T2 stock held by their shareholders, and then T1 and T2 dissolve.
3. After the reorganization, T1 and T2 no longer exist, and the T1 and T2 shareholders are now shareholders of C Corporation.

of-interest requirement. The shareholders of the target corporation must receive enough stock of the acquiring corporation so that they have a continuing financial interest in the reorganized firm. There is no minimum percent of the total consideration paid that must be in the stock of the acquiring corporation. As indicated previously, however, it is the government's position for issuing advanced rulings that at least 50 percent of the consideration used must be stock of the acquiring corporation.[16] The computation is made in the aggregate for all the shareholders of the target corporation, not on an individual shareholder basis.

> **Example 8.** Individuals J and B each own 50% of Target Corporation. The fair market value of all the outstanding shares of Target Corporation is $10,000. On March 1, Target is merged into Acquiring Corporation. Acquiring Corporation transfers to Target Corporation shares of its common stock with a fair market value of $6,000 and bonds worth $4,000. On the dissolution of Target Corporation, J receives common stock of Acquiring Corporation worth $5,000, and B receives stock of $1,000 and bonds of $4,000. This transaction meets the continuity-of-interest requirement because the stock of Acquiring Corporation received by J and B had a fair market value of $6,000, which exceeds 50% of the value of the outstanding stock of Target Corporation prior to the merger. The fact that B received all the bonds and that the Acquiring Corporation's stock she received is less than 50% of the value of the Target stock she surrendered is immaterial for qualification as an "A" reorganization.

Transfers to a Subsidiary (Drop-Downs). The end result of an "A" reorganization, whether merger or consolidation, is one surviving corporation. This may not be the most useful form.

> **Example 9.** The ABC Insurance Company wishes to expand into the brokerage business and mutual funds. It has located T Corporation, which it desires to acquire. The shareholders of T are interested in a nontaxable merger. However, combining the two corporations could cause ABC problems. First, it might violate state insurance rules against diversification. Second, it might change the asset reserves that the state requires ABC to maintain since the total assets that ABC owns will have increased. Finally, the management of T receives bonuses based on profitability that would be difficult to maintain if the corporations are merged.

---

[16]   Rev. Proc. 77-37, 1977-2 C.B. 568.

As the above example illustrates, a merger may be undesirable where management of the acquiring corporation does not want to combine the assets of its corporation with those of the target. A possible solution to the one-corporation problem of the "A" reorganization would be for the acquiring corporation to create a new subsidiary following the reorganization. The acquiring corporation would transfer the assets of the target company to the newly formed (or existing) subsidiary in a nontaxable § 351 exchange. The two steps would solve the problem. Normally when a transaction consists of two related steps, the government applies the step-transaction doctrine and denies independent tax treatment to the "independent" steps. If the step transaction doctrine were applied to the suggested solution, the transaction could not be an "A" reorganization because the acquiring corporation does not end up with the assets of the target. Since 1954, however, the Code has permitted the transfer of all or part of the assets received from the target corporation to a subsidiary of the acquiring corporation without disqualifying the "A" reorganization.[17]

> **Example 10.**   Same facts as *Example 9*. ABC could acquire the target corporation and still maintain separate corporations in a nontaxable transaction. First, T Corporation would be merged into ABC. The shareholders of T would receive ABC stock and thereby satisfy their needs. ABC would then create Newco and transfer the assets acquired from T to Newco in a § 351 transaction. The merger followed by the drop-down of the target's assets to a subsidiary qualifies as an "A" reorganization.

The drop-down of assets illustrated in *Example 10* results in the creation of a parent-subsidiary group. In that example, Newco is a subsidiary of ABC. If the acquiring corporation is not in control of the corporation receiving the assets immediately after the exchange, the special rule allowing transfers does not apply, resulting in probable disqualification of the reorganization.

Triangular Mergers.   The "A" reorganization and the "A" reorganization followed by a drop-down of assets to a controlled subsidiary can be used in many but not all situations. The stumbling block often confronting the parties is the approval of the transaction by the acquiring corporation's shareholders. It may not be feasible to obtain their approval either because of time, cost, or disagreement. There are also situations, because of state laws, in which the target may not be merged into the acquiring corporation even if it is only temporary before a drop-down. In addition, the acquiring corporation may be unwilling to assume the

---

[17]   § 368(a)(2)(C).

target's liabilities. The acquiring corporation can avoid these difficulties by having an existing or newly created subsidiary merge with the target. In such case, the target's shareholders become minority shareholders in the subsidiary—a result they may find undesirable. A *triangular merger* can overcome this problem.[18] In a triangular merger, the target corporation is merged directly into an existing or newly created subsidiary. Instead of using its own stock as consideration, however, the subsidiary transfers stock of its parent corporation to the target in exchange for the assets. The target dissolves by distributing the stock of the parent to its shareholders in return for its own stock. A triangular merger starts with a parent and subsidiary corporation and ends up with a parent and an enlarged subsidiary. The shareholders of the parent corporation are the former owners of the parent plus the former owners of the target. The transaction is illustrated in Exhibit 7-4.

There are three requirements for a triangular merger.[19] First, a controlled subsidiary (at least 80% owned by the parent) must receive substantially all the assets of the target corporation in the merger. It is the government's position that *substantially all* means at least 90 percent of the fair market value of the net assets *and* at least 70 percent of the fair market value of the gross assets.[20] Second, the transaction must have satisfied the requirements of an "A" reorganization if the target had been merged into the parent corporation instead of the subsidiary. Third, no stock of the controlled subsidiary can be used.

> **Example 11.** Bank Company owns all the stock of Savings Corp. Bank Company desires to acquire First Federal Inc. as part of its subsidiary Savings Corp. To this end, First Federal is merged into Savings Corp. First Federal transferred all of its assets, except land acquired for expansion, to Savings in return for 1,000 shares of Bank Company stock. The assets transferred to Savings have a fair market value of $10 million. First Federal dissolves by transferring the stock of Bank Company, with a fair market value of $10 million, and the land, with a fair market value of $1 million, to its shareholders in return for its stock. The transaction is a valid triangular merger since all three requirements are satisfied. Savings received more than 90% of First Federal's assets; therefore it received substantially all the assets of the target corporation. In addition, if First Federal had been merged directly into Bank Company, it would have been a valid "A" reorganization. Finally, the only stock transferred to First Savings was stock of the parent company (i.e., Bank Company).

---

[18]   § 368(a)(2)(D).

[19]   *Ibid.*

[20]   Rev. Proc. 77-37, 1977-2 C.B. 568.

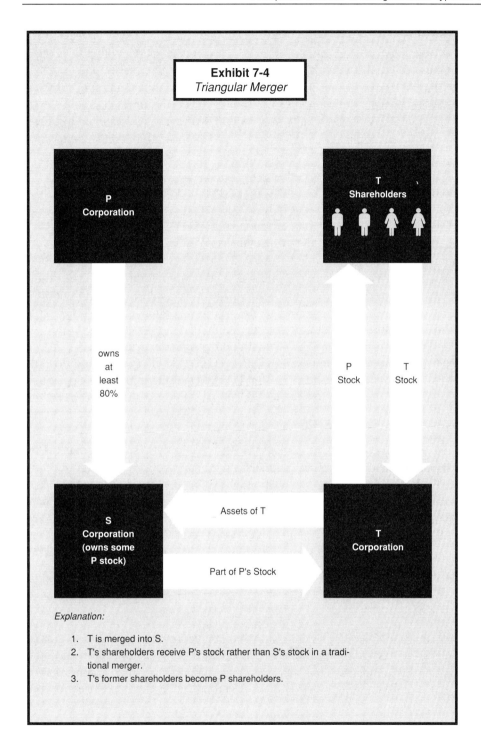

Exhibit 7-4
Triangular Merger

P Corporation

T Shareholders

owns
at
least
80%

P
Stock

T
Stock

Assets of T

S Corporation (owns some P stock)

T Corporation

Part of P's Stock

Explanation:

1. T is merged into S.
2. T's shareholders receive P's stock rather than S's stock in a traditional merger.
3. T's former shareholders become P shareholders.

Example 12.   Same facts as *Example 11* except First Federal transferred all of its assets to Savings and received Bank Company stock with a fair market value of $1 million and long-term bonds with a fair market value of $10 million. This would probably not be a valid triangular merger. Although Savings received substantially all the assets and the only stock transferred was stock of Bank Company, less than 10% of the total consideration given to First Federal shareholders was stock. Such a small a percentage of stock would probably not pass the continuity-of-interest requirement.

Reverse Triangular Merger.   There is a variation of the triangular merger called the *reverse triangular merger.*[21] This variation is used whenever there is a business purpose for maintaining the target corporation's identity. For example, if the target corporation owned licenses that could not be conveniently transferred, the target corporation would have to be the surviving corporation.

In the reverse triangular merger, the subsidiary corporation is merged into the target corporation; that is, the corporation that is to be acquired. Voting stock of the parent of the merged subsidiary is given to the shareholders of the target corporation in return for the target's stock. The law requires that the target corporation end up with "substantially all" the property it owned before the merger and "substantially all the property" of the merged subsidiary.[22] In addition, the parent corporation must obtain control (at least 80% of the voting and 80% of the other stock) of the target corporation.[23] This transaction is illustrated in Exhibit 7-5.

Example 13.   CTV is a highly successful cable television company. It desires to expand into the radio broadcasting business by acquiring FM. However, FM's FCC license cannot be transferred to another corporation. CTV creates a wholly owned subsidiary R. R is merged into FM. FM's shareholders receive voting stock of CTV in return for all their shares of FM. This is a valid reverse triangular merger. R, CTV's initial subsidiary, goes out of existence. FM becomes a wholly owned subsidiary of CTV and FM's original shareholders become shareholders in CTV.

"B" REORGANIZATION

In contrast to the "A" reorganization in which one corporation acquires the assets of another, the "B" reorganization is defined as the acquisition of *stock* of one corporation by another.[24] Thus, the target corporation becomes a subsidiary of the acquiring corporation. There are two requirements of a "B" reorganization.

---

[21]   § 368(a)(2)(E).

[22]   § 368(a)(2)(E)(i).

[23]   § 368(a)(2)(E)(ii).

[24]   § 368(a)(1)(B).

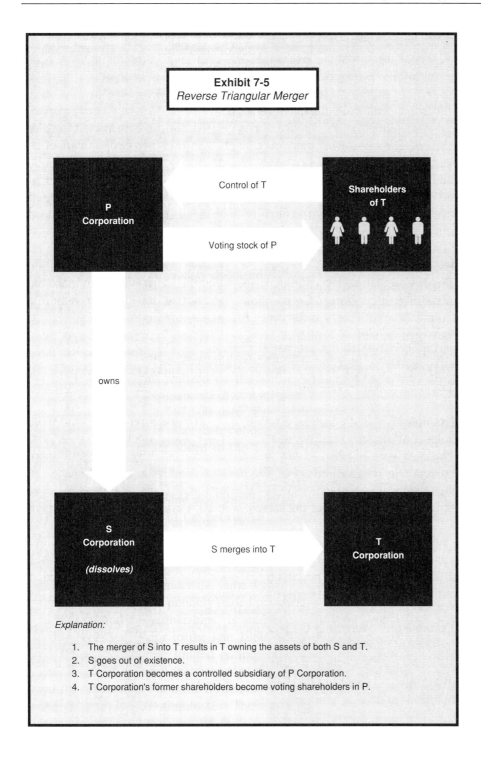

Exhibit 7-5
Reverse Triangular Merger

P Corporation

Control of T

Voting stock of P

Shareholders of T

owns

S Corporation

(dissolves)

S merges into T

T Corporation

Explanation:

1. The merger of S into T results in T owning the assets of both S and T.
2. S goes out of existence.
3. T Corporation becomes a controlled subsidiary of P Corporation.
4. T Corporation's former shareholders become voting shareholders in P.

1. The target's stock must be acquired using solely voting stock.

2. Immediately after the exchange, the acquiring corporation must be in control of the target corporation.

The "B" reorganization is illustrated in Exhibit 7-6.

The consideration that the acquiring corporation can use is restricted to *solely voting stock*. The transfer of nonvoting stock, securities, or cash as part of the consideration for the target's stock violates this solely-for-voting-stock requirement and invalidates the "B" reorganization. The voting stock can be either the stock of the acquiring corporation or of a corporation that controls the acquiring corporation (i.e., its parent). Stock of both the acquiring corporation and its parent may not be used.

> **Example 14.** Acquiring Corporation desires to acquire Target Corporation. Target Corporation's shareholders insist that the transaction be nontaxable. Acquiring offers Target Corporation shareholders one share of Acquiring Corporation voting stock for every five shares of Target Corporation stock they own as part of a plan of reorganization. All of Target Corporation's shareholders accept the offer. The exchange of Acquiring stock for Target stock qualifies as a "B" reorganization since Acquiring obtained control of Target for solely voting stock.

> **Example 15.** Same facts as *Example 14* except the offer permits the shareholders of Target to receive one share of Acquiring stock or cash of $100. The cash was included to buy out a dissident minority of Target's shareholders. Ninety-five percent of Target's shareholders accept the stock, and the remainder accept the cash. The transaction does not qualify as a "B" reorganization since it does not meet the solely-for-voting-stock requirement.

As indicated above, the second condition of the "B" reorganization requires the acquiring corporation to be in control of the target corporation immediately after the acquisition. It is not necessary that control be acquired in the transaction. It is sufficient if control exists after the exchange.

> **Example 16.** Acquiring Corporation owns 90% of Target Corporation (and thus already has the requisite control). Acquiring can acquire the remaining 10% of Target's stock in a nontaxable "B" reorganization provided it only uses voting stock in the transaction.

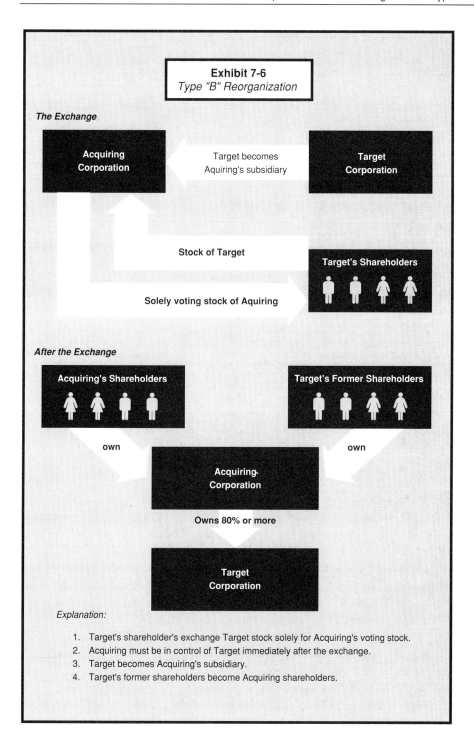

Exhibit 7-6
Type "B" Reorganization

The Exchange

Acquiring Corporation

Target becomes Aquiring's subsidiary

Target Corporation

Stock of Target

Target's Shareholders

Solely voting stock of Aquiring

After the Exchange

Acquiring's Shareholders

Target's Former Shareholders

own

Acquiring Corporation

own

Owns 80% or more

Target Corporation

Explanation:

1. Target's shareholder's exchange Target stock solely for Acquiring's voting stock.
2. Acquiring must be in control of Target immediately after the exchange.
3. Target becomes Acquiring's subsidiary.
4. Target's former shareholders become Acquiring shareholders.

The Regulations sanction what is referred to as a *creeping* "B" reorganization—so called because the requisite control is acquired through a series of acquisitions using solely voting stock. For each separate acquisition to qualify, several requirements must be satisfied.[25]

1. The acquisition must be one of a series of acquisitions that are part of an overall plan to acquire the requisite control.

2. The plan of acquisition must be carried out in a relatively short period of time such as 12 months.

3. The acquisition must be made solely for voting stock.

Prior cash purchases of the target's stock are permissible within this scheme, provided the purchase is a separate transaction and not part of the overall plan.

> **Example 17.**   Acquiring purchased 30% of Target's stock in 1975. Acquiring can acquire the remaining 70% of Target's stock in 1991 in a "B" reorganization as long as only voting stock is used. The prior cash purchase is ignored since it clearly is not part of an expeditious plan to acquire Target's stock.

> **Example 18.**   Same facts as in *Example 17* above except Acquiring purchased the 30% of Target's stock during the last half of 1990. The cash acquisition was made through a tender offer by which Acquiring had hoped to obtain control of Target. Having failed to acquire the necessary 80%, Acquiring then offered its own voting stock for the remaining 70% under a plan of reorganization. Acquiring obtained the remaining stock during the first half of 1991. The stock for stock exchanges qualify as a "B" reorganization. As in the previous example, the prior cash purchase is ignored. Note also that control need not be acquired in the stock exchanges for those exchanges to qualify as a "B" reorganization. Although only 70% of the stock was acquired solely for voting stock, the exchanges still qualify since the acquiring corporation had control after the plan of acquisition was complete. (See *Example 16* above where the same result would occur had the 90% been purchased in a previous transaction.)

Regardless of whether the corporation acquires control in the transaction or already has control, the "B" reorganization has as its end product a parent/subsidiary relationship between the acquiring and target corporation. For instance, in both *Examples 17* and *18*, Target is a subsidiary of Acquiring after the reorganization.

---

[25]   Reg. § 1.368-2(c).

"C" REORGANIZATION

The "C" reorganization is defined as the acquisition of substantially all the assets of a corporation solely for voting stock of the acquiring corporation or its parent.[26] In this reorganization, the target corporation transfers assets to the acquiring corporation in exchange for the acquiring corporation's voting stock and in some circumstances a limited amount of other consideration. The target corporation must liquidate as part of the plan of reorganization unless the IRS waives this requirement.[27] As a result, the shareholders of the target corporation become shareholders in the acquiring corporation. In determining the tax consequences to the liquidating target, the reorganization provisions govern—*not* the liquidation rules of Code §§ 336 and 337.[28] The "C" reorganization is illustrated in Exhibit 7-7.

> **Example 19.** Retail Corp. desires to obtain the operations of one of its suppliers, Manufacturing Corp. Under a plan of reorganization, Retail Corp. issues voting stock, equal to 30% of its total outstanding stock, in exchange for all the assets of Manufacturing Corp. Immediately after the exchange, Manufacturing Corp. liquidates, distributing the stock of Retail Corp. to its shareholders. The exchange qualifies as a C reorganization.

The "C" reorganization is easily distinguished from a "B" reorganization but is sometimes similar to an "A" merger. The "C" reorganization differs from the "B" reorganization in two major aspects. First, the acquiring corporation obtains assets in the "C" reorganization whereas it obtains stock in a "B" reorganization. Second, the target corporation becomes a subsidiary in the "B" reorganization while in a "C" reorganization it is unrelated to the acquiring corporation.

On the other hand, a "C" reorganization closely resembles an "A" merger. The target corporation must liquidate after the exchange, distributing the acquiring corporation's stock and any remaining assets to its shareholders.[29] Therefore, the end result is the same as a merger: the acquiring corporation holds the assets of the target and the target's shareholders become shareholders in the acquiring corporation. Thus, the "C" reorganization is sometimes called the "practical merger." The "C" reorganization permits a business combination where mergers are not practical or allowed under state law. In a "C" reorganization, the acquiring corporation's shareholders need not formally approve of the acquisition. The target's shareholders, however, normally must approve the sale of the assets and the liquidation.

---

[26] § 368(a)(1)(C).

[27] § 368(a)(2)(G).

[28] § 361(b)(1)(A).

[29] § 368(a)(2)(G).

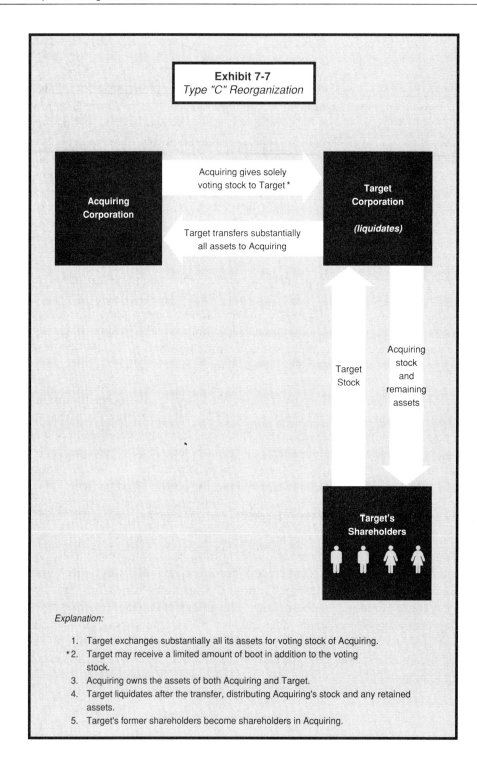

Exhibit 7-7
Type "C" Reorganization

Acquiring gives solely voting stock to Target *

Acquiring Corporation

Target Corporation

(liquidates)

Target transfers substantially all assets to Acquiring

Target Stock

Acquiring stock and remaining assets

Target's Shareholders

Explanation:

1. Target exchanges substantially all its assets for voting stock of Acquiring.
*2. Target may receive a limited amount of boot in addition to the voting stock.
3. Acquiring owns the assets of both Acquiring and Target.
4. Target liquidates after the transfer, distributing Acquiring's stock and any retained assets.
5. Target's former shareholders become shareholders in Acquiring.

As indicated above, the acquiring corporation must obtain substantially all of the target's assets. The phrase "substantially all the assets" is not defined in the Code. For advance ruling purposes, however, the Service requires that the acquiring corporation obtain at least 70 percent of the gross assets *and* 90 percent of the net assets.[30]

> **Example 20.** Target Corporation owns assets with a fair market value of $1 million and a basis of $400,000. Target's liabilities equal $200,000. Acquiring Corporation receives assets with a fair market value of $800,000 and a basis of $250,000 in exchange for its voting stock as part of a plan of reorganization. Since Acquiring Corporation has obtained 80% of the gross assets ($800,000 ÷ $1 million) *and* 100% of the net assets [$800,000 ÷ ($1 million − $200,000)], it satisfies the *substantially all* test.

The type of assets retained by the target corporation is just as important as the amount of assets. The courts generally require that those assets critical to the continuation of the target's business must be transferred. Failure to do so may cause the transaction to fall outside the scope of a "C" reorganization.

The definition of a "C" reorganization also contains a solely-for-voting-stock requirement. In determining whether this requirement is satisfied, liabilities receive special treatment. The assumption of the target corporation's liabilities or the taking of the property subject to a liability—which is normally considered the giving of boot—is disregarded. The amount of the liabilities assumed is immaterial except in the situation described below. Without this rule, the "C" reorganization would rarely be used. Few creditors would allow the transfer of property without the transfer of the related debt for fear that the original debtor will be unable to repay the liability.

> **Example 21.** Same facts as *Example 20* except that Acquiring Corporation assumes the $200,000 of liabilities. The assumption of the liabilities is ignored and Acquiring Corporation is considered to have obtained substantially all of Target's assets for solely voting stock.

In addition to assuming liabilities, the acquiring corporation may transfer a limited amount of boot along with voting stock.[31] The amount of boot is limited to not more than 20 percent of the total consideration. In other words, 80 percent or more of the fair market value of *assets* received by the acquiring corporation must be in exchange for voting stock. For purposes of this test, boot does not include the liabilities assumed by the acquiring corporation unless other property (e.g., cash) is also given. In effect, the amount of boot is limited to 20 percent of the fair market value of the assets transferred reduced by any liabilities assumed or any liabilities to which the transferred

---

[30] Rev. Proc. 77-37, 1977-2 C.B. 568. The same test is applied to triangular mergers.

[31] § 368(a)(2)(B).

property is subject. If the liabilities exceed 20 percent of the value of the assets, only voting stock can be used since these liabilities are ignored if no other boot is transferred.

> **Example 22.** X Corporation transfers all of its assets, with a fair market value of $100,000, to Y Corporation for Y Corporation's voting stock. Y Corporation assumes $30,000 of X Corporation's liabilities. This can qualify as a "C" reorganization since the liabilities are disregarded as long as no boot is transferred.

> **Example 23.** Same facts as *Example 22* except Y Corporation also transfers $1,000 to X Corporation. The total boot is $31,000 ($30,000 liabilities + $1,000 cash). Since the boot exceeds 20% of the fair market value of the assets ($31,000 > 20% × $100,000), this will not qualify as a "C" reorganization.

> **Example 24.** W Corporation desires to acquire the assets of Z Corporation in a "C" reorganization. The assets of Z have a fair market value of $200,000. W will be assuming liabilities of $23,000. The maximum amount of boot that can be transferred in addition to the voting stock is $17,000 [(20% of $200,000 assets) − the $23,000 liabilities assumed].

The "C" reorganization permits the acquiring corporation to restructure the target's operation. Some or all of the assets received can be transferred to a corporation controlled by the acquiring corporation without affecting the "C" reorganization.[32]

> **Example 25.** Retail Corporation acquires all the assets of Manufacturing Corporation in a "C" reorganization. Following the reorganization, Retail transfers the assets received to a newly formed subsidiary, Supply Corp., in a § 351 transaction. The transfer of the assets to Supply Corp. does not affect the "C" reorganization.

> **Example 26.** Same facts as *Example 25* except Manufacturing Corporation also owned some retail outlets in addition to the manufacturing operations. Retail transfers only the manufacturing assets to Supply. The acquisition of Manufacturing still qualifies as a "C" reorganization. Retail was able to restructure Manufacturing so that it is solely a manufacturing company and Retail contains all of the marketing operations.

In lieu of dropping down the assets to a controlled subsidiary, a controlled subsidiary could be used as the acquiring corporation. In such case, the subsidiary may use the voting stock of the corporation that is in control of it (i.e., its parent corporation) in lieu of its own voting stock.[33] The acquiring corporation may not

---

[32] § 368(a)(2)(C).   [33] § 368(a)(1)(C).

use both its own and its parent's voting stock. This rule is identical to the one for a type "B" reorganization.

"D" REORGANIZATION

There are two types of "D" reorganizations.[34] The first is referred to as an *acquisitive "D" reorganization* since it results in the acquisition of target's assets by the acquiring corporation. In this transaction, the acquiring corporation transfers substantially all of its assets to the target corporation in exchange for control of the target corporation.[35] The acquiring corporation then distributes any remaining assets and the target corporation's stock to its shareholders.[36] Although the acquiring corporation does not have to legally liquidate, the distribution of all its assets is a *de facto* liquidation. The shareholders of the acquiring corporation that has been liquidated (either in fact or in effect) become the controlling shareholders of the target corporation. The transaction is illustrated in Exhibit 7-8.

> **Example 27.** Coal Corporation desires to acquire Power Co., its major customer. However, Power Co. must be the surviving corporation because of certain nontransferable licenses. Coal Corp. transfers all its assets to Power Co. in return for 1,000 shares of Power Co., which is 90% of the total issued and outstanding stock of Power Co. Coal Corporation then dissolves by transferring Power Co. stock to its shareholders in return for its own stock. The transaction qualifies as an acquisitive "D" reorganization. Power Co. owns all of the assets it previously owned plus all the assets of Coal Corporation, and Coal Corporation's shareholders receive stock of Power Co. sufficient for control.

It is possible for a transaction to meet the requirements of *both* the "C" reorganization *and* the acquisitive "D" reorganization. In these cases, the transaction is treated as a "D" reorganization.[37]

Divisive "D" Reorganization. The second transaction qualifying as a "D" reorganization is referred to as a *divisive "D" reorganization*. In contrast to the acquisitive "D" where two corporations are combined, the divisive "D" results in the separation of a single corporation into two or more distinct corporations. A corporate division may be called for in a number of instances. For example, the breakup of AT&T into eight separate corporations was mandated by the government under the Federal antitrust laws. On a smaller scale, management might desire to separate a risky business from the rest of the corporation. Divisive "D" reorganizations also are commonly used where shareholders disagree. In this case, the business is split up thus giving each group its own corporation.

---

[34] § 368(a)(1)(D).

[35] §§ 354(b)(1)(A) and 368(a)(1)(D).

[36] § 354(b)(1)(B).

[37] § 368(a)(2)(A).

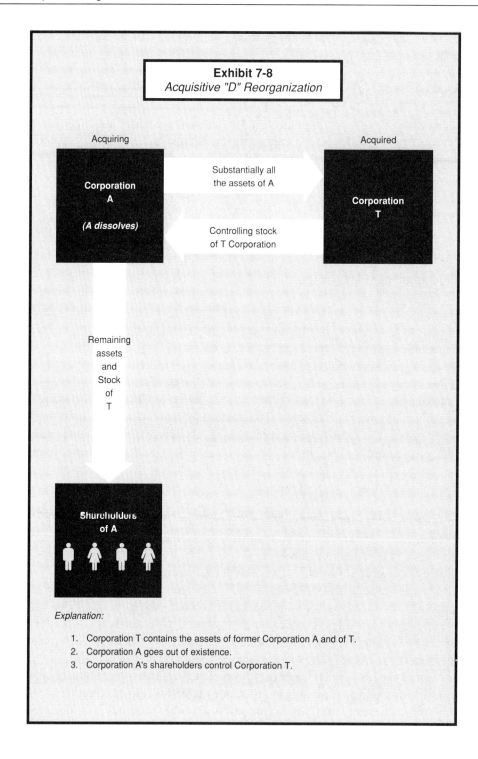

Exhibit 7-8
Acquisitive "D" Reorganization

Explanation:

1. Corporation T contains the assets of former Corporation A and of T.
2. Corporation A goes out of existence.
3. Corporation A's shareholders control Corporation T.

There are two distinct but essential steps in a divisive "D." The first step is the transfer of assets constituting an active business to a corporation in exchange for control of the corporation.[38] In effect, the acquiring corporation creates a subsidiary. The second step is the transfer of all the stock and securities of the controlled corporation to the shareholders of the transferor corporation.[39]

> **Example 28.** Computer Corp. manufactures and sells computers. Over time, Computer has increased the sales of its manufactured components to competitors. On the other hand, sales of its own computers have dropped and its retail outlets have had to stock and sell competing brands. This year management decided to separate the manufacturing and retailing operations. Accordingly, Computer Corp. transferred all of the assets used in the manufacturing operation to a new corporation, Manufacturing, in return for all of its common stock. Computer then distributed the stock of Manufacturing to its shareholders. The transaction is a divisive "D" reorganization. Computer Corp. has been divided into two separate corporations—Computer and Manufacturing. As a result, Computer's shareholders now own shares of both corporations.

The final ownership of the two resulting corporations in a divisive "D" depends on (1) the manner in which the controlled corporation's stock is distributed—pro rata or non-pro rata,[40] and (2) whether the receiving shareholders are required to exchange shares of the original corporation's stock for the shares of the new corporation's stock they receive.[41] The method of distribution and/or exchange produces one of three different types of divisions. These are referred to as the spin-off, the split-off, and the split-up.

Spin-Off. In a *spin-off*, the original corporation transfers some of its assets to a newly formed subsidiary in exchange for all of the subsidiary's stock, which it then distributes to its shareholders (see Exhibit 7-9). The shareholders of the original corporation do not surrender any of their ownership in the original corporation for the subsidiary's stock. Consequently, the shareholders of the original corporation are still shareholders of the original corporation as well as shareholders of the newly formed subsidiary. Note that the entire transaction is virtually identical to a normal dividend distribution. Yet, if all the reorganization requirements are satisfied, the distribution is tax-free to the shareholders.

---

[38] §§ 368(a)(1)(D) and 355(a)(1)(C).

[39] § 355(a)(1)(D)(i). The transferor corporation may keep some stock provided it distributes control to its shareholders and can prove the retention and was not motivated by tax avoidance. § 355(a)(1)(D)(ii).

[40] § 355(a)(2)(A).

[41] § 355(a)(2)(B).

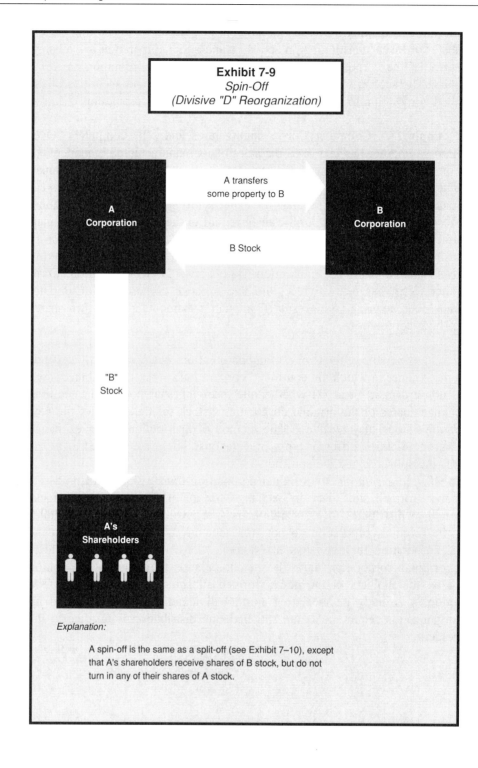

Exhibit 7-9
Spin-Off
(Divisive "D" Reorganization)

A transfers some property to B

A Corporation

B Corporation

B Stock

"B" Stock

A's Shareholders

Explanation:

A spin-off is the same as a split-off (see Exhibit 7–10), except that A's shareholders receive shares of B stock, but do not turn in any of their shares of A stock.

The spin-off transaction is often used when management decides that corporate operations should be divided but the shareholders want to continue an investment in both the original and new corporation.

Example 29. P Corporation, a water company, owns 100% of S Corporation. P established S many years ago to hold a reservoir and the surrounding land for future development. This year P's management determined that it would be in the best interest of P to withdraw from the real estate development business and concentrate on its utility business. Accordingly, P distributed all of its shares in S to its shareholders. The distribution is referred to as a spin-off. Although it is virtually indistinguishable from a dividend distribution, it is a tax-free distribution if the requirements of § 355 are satisfied.

Split-Off. When shareholders prefer different investments in the future operations of the corporation, a *split-off* is used. In a split-off, the original corporation transfers some of its assets to a newly formed subsidiary in exchange for all of the subsidiary's stock, which it then distributes to some or all of its shareholders in exchange for some portion of their original stock. As a result, the two corporations are held by the original shareholders but in a proportion that differs from that which they held in the original corporation. The split-off is presented in Exhibit 7-10.

Example 30. S Corp. is owned equally by B and his three sons: C, D, and E. The corporation has been in the electronics business for a long time and recently has become involved in computers. B died this year and willed equal interests in S Corp. to each of his three sons. Apparently, B had been the glue that held the family business together, for shortly after his death the brothers disagreed. D and E decided that the company should invest more in computers and less in electronics. On the other hand, C is somewhat reluctant about becoming too heavily involved in computers and feels that the corporation's efforts should remain primarily in its traditional business of electronics. As a compromise, the three decide to separate the corporation into two corporations. S Corp. transfers the assets of the computer business to a new corporation, T, in exchange for all of its stock. It subsequently transfers all of the T stock to D and E in exchange for all of their interest in S. As a result, D and E own T Corp. while C owns S Corp. The transaction qualifies as a divisive "D" reorganization.

The sole difference between the spin-off and split-off concerns the shareholder exchange. In a spin-off, shareholders do not surrender any stock in the original corporation for the stock they receive, while in a split-off they do. Consequently, the transaction is much like a redemption. However, like a spin-off, the transaction is nontaxable if all the rules related to reorganizations are followed.

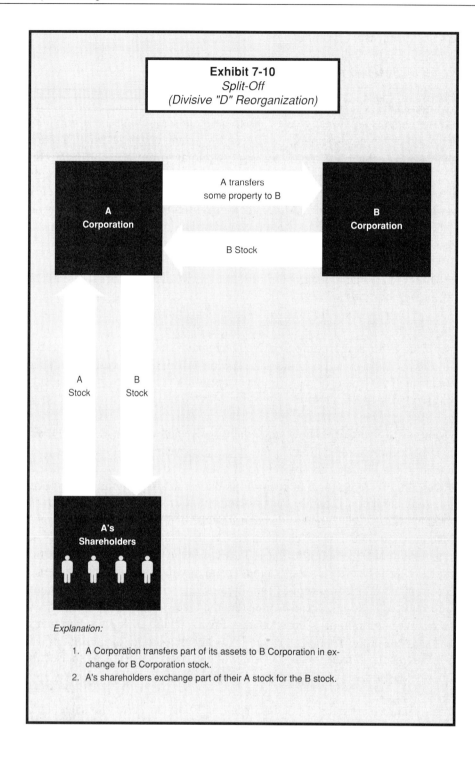

Exhibit 7-10
Split-Off
(Divisive "D" Reorganization)

A transfers some property to B

A Corporation

B Corporation

B Stock

A Stock

B Stock

A's Shareholders

Explanation:

1. A Corporation transfers part of its assets to B Corporation in exchange for B Corporation stock.
2. A's shareholders exchange part of their A stock for the B stock.

Split-Up. A *split-up* varies little from a split-off. In a split-up, the original corporation transfers some of its assets to one newly created subsidiary and the remainder of the assets to another newly created subsidiary. The original corporation then liquidates, distributing the stock of both subsidiaries in exchange for its own stock. The effect of the split-up is to create two new corporations. The dissolution of the original corporation distinguishes this transaction from a split-off and also causes it to be similar to a liquidation. The split-up is illustrated in Exhibit 7-11.

> **Example 31.** Same facts as in *Example 30*. Instead of continuing S Corp. in its present form, C, D, and E decide to set up two new corporations: X Inc. and Y Inc. The assets of the computer business are transferred to X in exchange for all of the X stock while the assets of the electronic business are transferred to Y in exchange for all of the Y stock. In liquidation of S Corp., the X stock is distributed to D and E in exchange for all of their S stock and the Y stock is distributed to C in exchange for all of his S stock. D and E are now shareholders in X while C is the sole shareholder of Y.

Existing Subsidiary. In a divisive "D" reorganization, a corporation transfers assets to one or more newly created subsidiaries and subsequently distributes the stock. In some cases, a corporation simply distributes the stock of an *existing* subsidiary that it may have acquired or formed at another time. In such case, the reorganization provisions of § 368 do not apply. Nevertheless, the distribution is still subject to § 355 and will therefore be nontaxable, assuming the requirements discussed below are met.

Requirements for Divisive "D" Reorganization. As noted above, spin-offs, split-offs, and split-ups must satisfy the requirements imposed by § 355 in order to qualify for favorable treatment as "D" reorganizations.

1. *Distribution of Control*—The original corporation must distribute to its shareholders stock of the newly created subsidiary that constitutes control.

2. *Character of Distribution*—The property distributed by the original corporation must consist solely of stock or securities of the newly created subsidiary. Distributions of other property (including securities in certain circumstances) constitutes boot, and gain must be recognized.

3. *Active Business*—Immediately after the distribution, both the original corporation and the controlled subsidiary must be engaged in the active conduct of a trade or business.

4. *Tax Avoidance Device*—The distribution must not have been a device for bailing out the earnings and profits of either the original corporation or the new subsidiary.

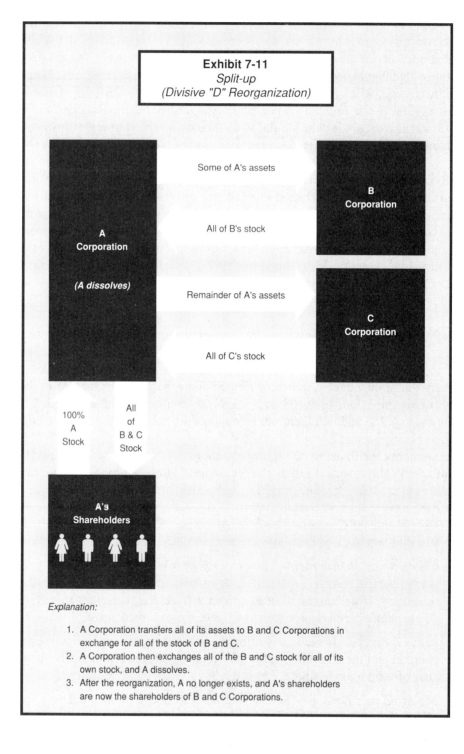

Exhibit 7-11
Split-up
(Divisive "D" Reorganization)

Explanation:

1. A Corporation transfers all of its assets to B and C Corporations in exchange for all of the stock of B and C.
2. A Corporation then exchanges all of the B and C stock for all of its own stock, and A dissolves.
3. After the reorganization, A no longer exists, and A's shareholders are now the shareholders of B and C Corporations.

Distribution Requirement. Nonrecognition is granted only to distributions of stock of a "controlled" corporation. For this purpose, control is present if the distributing parent corporation owns at least 80 percent of the voting power of all classes of the subsidiary's stock entitled to vote and at least 80 percent of the total number of shares of all other classes of stock.[42] Normally, the original corporation is required to distribute all of the stock and securities of the new corporation that it possesses.[43] However, the original corporation may retain some of the stock and securities if it can prove that the retention was not motivated by tax avoidance.[44] As a *minimum*, the original corporation must distribute control of the new corporation (i.e., at least 80% of all stock).

In addition, the distribution must consist solely of stock or securities in order for the shareholders to receive nonrecognition. If the shareholders receive other property such as cash, the distribution may be taxable. The taxation of the distribution depends on whether the division was a spin-off, split-off, or split-up and certain other factors discussed later in this chapter.

Active Business Requirement. The *active business test* requires that both the transferor corporation and the controlled corporation must be engaged in the active conduct of a trade or business immediately after the transfer of assets.[45] These businesses must have been conducted for at least five years prior to the distribution. In addition, neither business could have been acquired within the five-year period in a taxable transaction.[46] These conditions are designed to prevent a corporation from using the "D" reorganization to bail out accumulated cash and other assets in the original corporation at capital gains rates instead of ordinary income rates. Without this rule, the bailout could be accomplished by a "D" reorganization followed by a liquidation or sale of the distributed stock.

> **Example 32.** F Corporation has excess accumulated cash. If it paid a dividend, its shareholders would be required to report ordinary dividend income. Instead, F transfers the cash to Newco, a newly created subsidiary, and distributes Newco stock to its shareholders in what it hopes is a nontaxable "D" reorganization. The shareholders then liquidate Newco and report capital gains on the liquidation. Under the active business test, the original transaction does not qualify as a "D" reorganization because Newco fails to engage in any business after the distribution. Consequently, the shareholders are required to report dividend income on the receipt of Newco stock.

---

[42] § 355(a)(1)(A).

[43] § 355(a)(1)(D)(i).

[44] § 355(a)(1)(D)(ii).

[45] § 355(b)(1)(A).

[46] § 355(b)(2).

Example 33.   Same facts as *Example 32* except F uses the cash to buy an existing business. It transfers the business to Newco and distributes the Newco stock to its shareholders. The shareholders sell the Newco stock and report capital gains. Since the business transferred to Newco was acquired in a taxable transaction (i.e., a purchase), the transaction does not satisfy the active business test and thus is not a valid "D" reorganization. The shareholders must report dividend income on the receipt of Newco stock.

The determination of whether or not a corporation is engaged in an active business is made based on all the facts and circumstances. The minimum requirement for an active business is that the corporate activities include every step in the process of earning income.[47] Ordinarily, this would include collection of income and payment of expenses. In addition, the Regulations indicate that the active conduct of a trade or business does not include either (1) the holding of stock, securities, or other property for investment purposes; or (2) the ownership or operation (including leasing) of real or personal property used in a trade or business unless the owner performs significant services with respect to the operation and management of the property.[48]

Example 34.   L Corporation desires to transfer the land it owns to a new corporation, N, in a "D" reorganization. Some of the land will be held for future appreciation. The remainder would be leased back to L as a parking lot. The assets transferred to N probably would not be considered a trade or business. The investment land lacks the requisite collection of income and payment of expense activities. The leasing activities probably do not contain sufficient services to be considered a business.

As noted above, the active business must have been conducted for at least five years prior to the distribution. It need not be conducted by the original corporation for all of the required five years. In this regard, additions of new products and other similar changes are disregarded provided they do not constitute the acquisition of a new business.[49]

Example 35.   Manufacturing Corporation has been in the business of manufacturing and selling television and stereo equipment for the last 15 years. During the last five years, it discontinued production of black-and-white TVs and started producing miniature portable sets following the construction of a new plant. The changes during the last five years should not prevent Manufacturing from being considered to have been in the business of manufacturing and selling televisions for more than five years.

---

[47]   Reg. § 1.355-3(b)(2)(ii).

[48]   Reg. § 1.355-3(b)(2)(iv)(B).

[49]   Reg. § 1.355-3(b)(3)(ii).

The nebulous features of the active business requirement have led to a significant amount of litigation. Taxpayers have been successful in separating two businesses, dividing one business into two complete businesses,[50] and dividing a single business along functional lines.[51] Whether a particular division qualifies, however, must be determined in light of all the facts and circumstances.

Device Limitation. For a valid "D" reorganization, taxpayers must be able to prove that the transaction was not principally a device for distributing the earnings of the distributing or controlled corporation.[52] Although the device question must be answered based on all the facts and circumstances, there are several factors that indicate that the transaction was used to avoid taxes. For example, subsequent sales of stock by the shareholders, transfer or retention of liquid assets in excess of business needs, and operation of the controlled corporation in a manner similar to that of the pretransfer operation all suggest an improper motive.[53]

> **Example 36.** Bank Corporation has been in existence for 20 years. Six years ago it started performing bookkeeping and accounting work for the public. D, an individual, desires to purchase the bookkeeping and accounting business. Rather than sell the business, Bank distributes the assets to a new corporation, Book, and distributes Book's stock to its shareholders. The shareholders sell half of Book's stock to D. The transaction would probably be considered a device for the distribution of earnings.[54]

> **Example 37.** Same facts as *Example 36* except that Bank transfers cash in excess of Book's needs to Book along with the other assets. The shareholders sell half the stock to E, an individual who expressed interest in Book following the transaction. The fact that excess cash was transferred to Book and the shareholders sold some of the stock, even though not part of the original plan, will probably result in the transaction being considered a device for the distribution of earnings.[55]

The transaction is not considered a device if the distribution to the shareholder would otherwise qualify as a sale under the stock redemption provisions of § 302.[56]

---

[50] *Coady*, 33 T.C. 771 (1960).

[51] *Wilson*, 42 T.C. 914 (1964); *Leslie, Jr.* 40 T.C. 947 (1963).

[52] § 355(a)(1)(B).

[53] Reg. § 1.355-2(c)(2) and (3).

[54] See Reg. § 1.355-2(c)(4), *Example 1.*

[55] See Reg. § 1.355-2(c)(4), *Example 2.*

[56] Reg. § 1.355-2(c)(5).

Example 38. X Corporation transfers an active business to Z Corporation in exchange for all of Z's stock. The Z stock is then distributed to individual J in exchange for all of her X stock. The exchange of Z stock for all of J's stock, standing alone, would be considered a redemption of J's entire interest qualifying for sale treatment under § 302. Therefore, the transaction will not be considered a device for distributing earnings. This *safe harbor* rule favors the split-up over the spin-off and possibly the split-off, which could not meet the conditions of § 302.

"E" REORGANIZATION

The "E" reorganization is defined as a *recapitalization*.[57] Although not defined in the Code, the term recapitalization refers to exchanges of stock and securities by the corporation's shareholders and security holders for new stock and/or securities. In essence, the "E" reorganization permits a corporation to alter the configuration of its capital structure. As such, the "E" reorganization involves only one corporation.

Four exchanges are included under the general heading of recapitalization. They are

1. Stock for Stock

2. Bonds for Stock

3. Bonds for Bonds

4. Stock for Bonds

As a general rule, only the first three exchanges qualify as "E" reorganizations.

Stock for Stock. The exchange of stock in a corporation for other stock in the same corporation qualifies as an "E" reorganization. It is immaterial whether the transaction involves common for common, common for preferred, preferred for common, or preferred for preferred.[58] Also, differences in the voting rights, dividend rates, and preferences on liquidation are ignored.

Example 39. ABC Corporation is equally owned by S and her son. S desires to retire from active involvement in the corporation. She exchanges all of her common stock for nonvoting, nonparticipating, preferred stock. The exchange can qualify as an "E" reorganization.

Example 40. XYZ Corporation has been unable to pay a dividend on its noncumulative, nonvoting, preferred stock. To forestall a fight at the shareholders' meeting, XYZ agrees to exchange one share of participating, cumulative, preferred stock for each share of preferred stock currently outstanding. The exchange can qualify as an "E" reorganization.

---

[57] § 368(a)(1)(E).

[58] Reg. §§ 1.368-2(e)(2) and (3).

Example 41. W Corporation is owned equally by C and his sister K. C and K cannot agree on the future direction of W Corporation. K agrees to exchange all of her W stock for the stock of S, a wholly owned subsidiary of W. This cannot be an "E" reorganization because K is not receiving stock in the same corporation.

Although the "E" reorganization includes exchanges of preferred stock, it does not cover preferred stock with dividends in arrears. The stock received for the dividends will be taxable under the rules of § 305, which makes stock dividends paid on preferred stock taxable.[59]

Bonds for Stock. The exchange of bonds for stock by a security holder qualifies as an "E" reorganization. This provision effectively permits the corporation to pay off its debts with stock.[60] Creditors may be willing to make such an exchange where equity participation appears more profitable. The stock can be either common or preferred. The "E" reorganization does not cover the issuance of stock for accrued interest.

Bonds for Bonds. The exchange of bonds for other bonds of the corporation by a security holder qualifies as an "E" reorganization.[61] However, if the principal amount of the bonds received exceeds the principal amount of the bonds surrendered, gain must be recognized by the bondholder.[62]

Example 42. As part of an "E" reorganization, T exchanges 100 shares of common stock and bonds with a face amount of $1,000 for 50 shares of preferred stock and bonds with a face amount of $1,200. T has received $200 ($1,200 − $1,000) of excess principal on the bonds. He is required to recognize gain on the exchange.

Stock for Bonds. As a general rule, an exchange of stock for bonds by a shareholder does not qualify as an "E" reorganization since the shareholder has upgraded his or her investment position.[63] Even if it did qualify as a reorganization, the bonds received would be treated as "boot." Therefore, the shareholder must recognize income. The income is treated as dividends or capital gains depending on whether the receipt of the bonds was the equivalent of a dividend (e.g., a pro rata distribution).

---

[59]   Reg. § 1.368-2(e)(5).

[60]   Reg. § 1.368-2(e)(1). However, if the value of the stock is less than the principal amount of the debt retired, the corporation must recognize gain [see § 108(e)(1)].

[61]   *Trust of Neustadt v. Comm.*, 42-2 USTC ¶9751, 30 AFTR 320, 131 F.2d 528 (CA-2, 1942).

[62]   § 354(a)(2)(A).

[63]   *Bazley*, 47-1 USTC ¶9288, 35 AFTR 1190, 311 U.S. 737 (USSC, 1947).

"F" REORGANIZATION

An "F" reorganization is defined as "a mere change in identity, form, or place of organization of one corporation, however effected." [64] The "F" reorganization rules normally apply when the corporation changes its name, state of operation, or makes other changes in its corporate charter. In such case, there is a deemed transfer from the old corporation to the new corporation.

> **Example 43.**   The change in name from "American Building Corporation" to "American Corporation" in the corporate charter is an "F" reorganization. There is a deemed transfer from the old corporation (American Building Corporation) to a new corporation (American Corporation).

"G" REORGANIZATION

A "G" reorganization applies to a reorganization as part of bankruptcy. [65] It permits the transfer of some or all the assets of a failing corporation to a new controlled corporation provided the stock and securities of the controlled corporation are distributed to the old corporation's shareholders under the rules for distributions in a "D" reorganization.

JUDICIAL LIMITATIONS

The courts have not felt constrained to grant nonrecognition treatment to a transaction simply because it falls within the definition of a reorganization and can pass the continuity requirements. From almost the beginning, the courts have required corporations and their shareholders to show a business purpose for the reorganization. The earliest and best known case imposing this requirement was *Gregory v. Helvering*. [66] In order to avoid the receipt of dividend income, Gregory had a corporation that she owned undergo what today would meet the definition of a divisive "D" reorganization. According to her instructions, her wholly owned corporation transferred assets to a new corporation in exchange for its stock. The corporation then distributed the shares of stock to Gregory. Shortly after receiving the shares of the new corporation she liquidated it, thereby acquiring its assets at capital-gains rates rather than dividend rates. The Supreme Court acknowledged that the transaction met the literal requirements of a reorganization. However, they refused to grant it nonrecognition treatment on the grounds that it lacked a business purpose other than tax avoidance. Although this case arose prior to the 1954 Code, the courts continue to require a business purpose before a transaction is considered a reorganization.

---

[64]   § 368(a)(1)(F).

[65]   § 368(a)(1)(G).

[66]   35-1 USTC ¶9043, 14 AFTR 1191, 293 U.S. 465 (USSC, 1935).

There is no specific definition of business purpose. The Regulations provide little guidance, indicating only that a transaction that "puts on the form of a reorganization as a disguise for concealing its real character, and the object and accomplishment of which is the consummation of a preconceived plan having no business or corporate purpose, is not a plan of reorganization." Similarly, in § 355, the Regulations provide that "a corporate business purpose is a real and substantial non Federal tax purpose germane to the business."[67] Unfortunately, these statements provide little insight as to what may or may not constitute a business purpose.

PLAN OF REORGANIZATION

The final requirement for a valid reorganization is the existence of a plan of reorganization. This requirement is not contained in § 368, the definitional section, but appears in § 361, the operational section that provides for nonrecognition treatment. The plan must be adopted by each corporation involved in the transaction.[68] However, the fact that the corporations adopt a plan will not result in transactions being classified as reorganizations unless they meet the specific requirements discussed above.[69]

TAX CONSEQUENCES OF REORGANIZATION

The benefits afforded a reorganization are generally limited to "parties to the reorganization." The parties to the reorganization are the acquiring corporation, the target corporation, and any corporation formed during the reorganization.[70] If stock of a corporation that controls the acquiring corporation is used in the exchange, the controlling corporation is also a party to the reorganization. Finally, if the assets acquired from the target are transferred to a subsidiary, the subsidiary is a party to the reorganization.

The shareholders of a party to the reorganization are not parties to the reorganization themselves. Their tax treatment is determined by the property exchanged. Generally, if they exchange stock and/or securities of a party to the reorganization for stock and securities of another party to the reorganization (the same corporation or a different one) the exchange is nontaxable.[71]

The tax treatment of the various participants is discussed below.

---

[67] Reg. § 1.355-2(b).

[68] Reg. § 1.368-3(a).

[69] Reg. § 1.368-2(g).

[70] § 368(b).

[71] § 354(a).

ACQUIRING CORPORATION

Gain or Loss. In a reorganization, the acquiring corporation transfers its stock, securities, and perhaps boot to the target corporation in exchange for its property or stock. Since the acquiring corporation is treated as having issued stock for a contribution of property, it recognizes neither gain nor loss under the general rule allowing nonrecognition of gain on the contribution of property to a corporation.[72] Similarly, the issuance of securities in a reorganization has historically been granted nonrecognition. In contrast, if the acquiring corporation transfers other property or boot, it must recognize gain or loss on the transfer of such boot.[73]

> **Example 44.** In a "C" reorganization, Acquiring Corporation transfers its stock worth $800,000 and land worth $200,000 (basis $50,000) to Target Corporation in exchange for all of its assets and liabilities. Acquiring Corporation must recognize a $150,000 gain on the transfer of the land just as if it had sold the land for cash and transferred such cash to Target Corporation. No gain or loss is recognized on the transfer of the stock.

Distribution of Stock and Securities of a Controlled Corporation. As a general rule, a parent corporation that distributes stock or securities of a subsidiary in a spin-off, split-off, or split-up transaction or any other distribution to which § 355 applies does not recognize gain or loss. However, § 355(d) prescribes special rules to prevent corporate taxpayers from using this provision to convert what is in reality a sale to a nontaxable distribution.

> **Example 45.** P Corporation owns all of the stock of a subsidiary, S. P purchased the stock of S several years ago for $10,000, and it is now worth $100,000. P now wishes to sell S but does not want to recognize any gain. During the year, Buyer purchased 40% of P's stock on the open market for $100,000. Shortly thereafter, as part of a qualifying split-off, P distributed all of its stock in S (worth $100,000) to Buyer in exchange for all of Buyer's P stock (worth $100,000). In effect, P has sold all of the S stock for $100,000. Yet under the general rule, P would not recognize any gain on the transaction.

To ensure that taxpayers cannot disguise sales as nontaxable distributions, Congress adopted a special rule. Section 355(d) generally requires a corporation to recognize gain—but not loss—on the distribution of a subsidiary's stock if, immediately after the distribution, a shareholder holds at least a 50 percent interest in either the subsidiary or the parent that is attributable to stock that was purchased within the five-year period prior to the distribution. Note that the shareholder is not affected by this provision.

---

[72]   § 1032.

[73]   § 361(a) does not apply to the transfer of boot.

Example 46. Same facts as *Example 45* above. P must recognize a gain of $90,000 ($100,000 − $10,000) on the distribution of S stock because Buyer received at least a 50% interest in S (it actually received a 100% interest) as a result of its purchase of P stock during the preceding five years.

Basis of Acquired Property or Stock. When the acquiring corporation obtains the assets of the target corporation, the basis of such assets must be determined. The acquiring corporation's basis in such property is the same as that of the target corporation increased by any gain recognized by the target (normally none, as discussed below).[74] In other words, the basis of the target corporation's assets generally carries over completely intact to the acquiring corporation. These rules apply even if the acquiring corporation receives stock or securities of the target corporation. This calculation is shown in Exhibit 7-12.

Example 47. In a statutory merger (an "A" reorganization), Target Corporation transfers assets worth $500,000 (basis $400,000) in exchange for Acquiring Corporation stock worth $500,000. Acquiring Corporation's basis in the assets received is the same as Target Corporation's basis, $400,000.

Example 48. In a "B" reorganization, Acquiring Corporation transferred stock worth $1 million to T, the sole shareholder of Target Corporation, in exchange for all of his stock. T's basis in his stock was $50,000. Acquiring Corporation's basis in Target Corporation's stock is the same as T's, $50,000.

Exhibit 7-12
*Acquiring Corporation's Basis
for Property Received*

Transferor's basis in property transferred	$xxx,xxx
Plus: Gain recognized by the transferor on the transfer	xx,xxx
Equals: Basis of property to acquiring corporation	$xxx,xxx

---

[74] § 362(b).

As shown in Exhibit 7-12, the basis of the property acquired by the acquiring corporation is the same as the target's basis increased by any gain recognized by the target. In light of changes made by the Tax Reform Act of 1986, the target corporation generally does not recognize gain on the transfer of the property to the acquiring corporation. Consequently, in computing the basis of the assets to the acquiring corporation there will be no gain to consider. In addition, any gain that might be recognized by the target corporation on the transfer to its shareholders, as well as any gain recognized by the shareholders on the receipt of a distribution by the target corporation, does not affect the acquiring corporation's basis in the assets received.

> **Example 49.** In a "C" reorganization, Acquiring Corporation transferred its own stock worth $800,000 and cash of $200,000 to Target Corporation in exchange for all of Target's assets with a basis of $500,000. Target subsequently liquidates as required, distributing the cash and stock to its shareholders. Although Target Corporation's shareholders must recognize gain, the basis of the assets to Acquiring Corporation is limited to $500,000, the basis of the assets in the hands of the Target Corporation. The gain recognized by the shareholders of Target is not added to the basis of the assets.

ACQUIRED (TARGET) CORPORATION

Gain or Loss. In acquisitive reorganizations, the target corporation transfers its assets to the acquiring corporation in exchange for stock, securities, and boot. In such case, the target corporation recognizes no gain or loss on the *receipt* of the stock and securities. In addition, no gain will be recognized on the receipt of boot provided it is distributed to target's shareholders.[75]

> **Example 50.** As part of a "C" reorganization, Target Corporation transfers all of its assets with a basis of $600,000 and a fair market value of $800,000 for stock of the Acquiring Corporation worth $700,000 and cash of $100,000. Target recognizes no gain or loss on the receipt of the stock or cash.

The assumption of the target corporation's liabilities and the transfer of property by the target corporation subject to a liability is not considered the receipt of boot.[76] However, if the principal purpose for the transfer of the liabilities is tax avoidance, the total amount of the liabilities is considered boot.[77] Unlike a corporate formation under § 351, the transfer of liabilities in excess of basis does not produce gain except in the case of a "D" reorganization.[78]

---

[75] § 361(b).

[76] § 357(a).

[77] § 357(b).

[78] § 357(c).

Example 51.   As part of a "C" reorganization, Target Corporation transfers assets with a basis of $800,000 and a fair market value of $1 million. The acquiring corporation gave Target its stock with a fair market value of $900,000 and assumes $100,000 of Target's liabilities. Although Target realizes a $200,000 gain, it does not recognize any gain since liabilities surrendered are not treated as boot. Had the assumption of the liabilities been motivated by tax avoidance, Target would have been treated as having received $100,000 of boot.

Example 52.   Target transfers assets with a basis of $800,000 and a fair market value of $1 million plus a liability of $950,000 to Acquiring Corporation for stock worth $50,000 in a "C" reorganization. Although Target realizes a $200,000 gain ($950,000 + $50,000 − $800,000), none is recognized since liabilities exceeding basis are ignored *except* in a "D" reorganization. Had the transfer been to a controlled corporation in a "D" reorganization, Target would recognize gain of $150,000, the excess of liabilities over basis ($950,000 − $800,000).

Basis.   In most cases, the target corporation has little concern for determining basis since it normally receives stock, securities, or cash which it distributes to its shareholders in liquidation. As explained below, the shareholders who receive such property determine their bases in the property under special rules.

One special situation regarding the target's basis which must be addressed concerns receipts by the target corporation of property *other than* stock, securities, or cash. This particular case requires attention because of the ramifications to the target corporation on a later distribution of such property. When the target receives boot other than cash, the basis of the boot is the same as it would be in the hands of the acquiring corporation, increased by any gain and decreased by any loss recognized by the acquiring corporation on the transfer.[79] As discussed above, the acquiring corporation must recognize gain or loss on the transfer of boot. Consequently, the basis of any boot received by the target is its fair market value.

Example 53.   As part of a "C" reorganization, Acquiring Corporation transferred its own stock worth $900,000 and two parcels of land, one worth $60,000 (basis $10,000) and another worth $40,000 (basis $70,000), to Target Corporation for all of its assets. Acquiring must recognize a $50,000 gain on the transfer of one parcel and a $30,000 loss on the transfer of the other parcel. As a result, Target's basis in the two parcels of land is $60,000 ($10,000 basis + gain of $50,000) and $40,000 ($70,000 basis − loss of $30,000), respectively.

---

[79]   Target is treated *as if* it purchased the boot property.

Liquidation of the Target Corporation. In a "C" or acquisitive "D" reorganization, the target corporation is *required* to liquidate. Accordingly, the target must distribute the stock, securities, and any boot received from the acquiring corporation, as well as any remaining assets to its shareholders. Although the target corporation liquidates, the liquidation rules do not cover this transaction. Instead, Code § 361 prescribes the treatment for the target on the distribution. Under this provision, the target corporation does not recognize any gain or loss on the distribution of the acquiring corporation's stock or securities.[80] However, the Code requires the target to recognize gain on the distribution of any appreciated property.[81] As a practical matter the target recognizes gain only on appreciated property that was not transferred to the acquiring corporation, since the basis of any property received from the acquiring corporation is its fair market value.

> **Example 54.** In a "C" reorganization, Target Corporation transferred all of its assets except land to Acquiring Corporation. The land was worth $300,000 (basis $260,000). The assets transferred were worth $10 million and had a basis of $8 million. In exchange for the assets, Target received stock of the Acquiring Corporation worth $9.7 million, cash of $100,000, and an office building worth $200,000 (basis to Acquiring of $70,000). Acquiring Corporation must recognize gain on the transfer of $130,000. Target's basis in the office building is $200,000 (Acquiring's basis of $70,000 + the gain recognized by Acquiring of $130,000). Target recognizes no gain on the receipt of the stock and other assets. However, it must recognize gain of $40,000 ($300,000 − $260,000) on the distribution of the land that was *not* transferred to Acquiring. Target recognizes no gain on the distribution of the office building since its basis in the building, $200,000, is the same as its value. Note that the effect of the rule requiring the target corporation to recognize gain on the distribution of property operates to cause *only* the gain on retained property to be recognized. This is appropriate since the acquiring corporation previously recognized gain on the transfer of the boot.

SHAREHOLDERS

Gain or Loss. The Code specifically provides nonrecognition for shareholders and security holders if they exchange stock and securities of a party to a reorganization *solely* for stock and securities of another party to the reorganization.[82] The exchange must be pursuant to the plan of reorganization. Subsequent distributions or exchanges that are not part of the plan are not exempt from taxation even if they consist solely of stock and securities of a party to the reorganization.

---

[80]   § 361(c)(1).

[81]   § 361(c)(2).

[82]   § 354(a)(1).

The amount of securities that can be received tax-free is limited to the principal amount of securities surrendered.[83] The fair market value of securities received in excess of the amount surrendered is considered boot.

Example 55. As part of a plan of reorganization, B, an individual, exchanges 100 shares of stock and a security in the principal amount of $1,000 for 300 shares and a security in the principal amount of $1,500. The security received had a fair market value of $1,800 on the date of receipt. B is considered to have received boot of $600 as determined below.

Principal amount of securities received	$1,500
−Principal amount of securities	(1,000)
Excess principal amount received	$500

$$\frac{\text{Excess principal amount}}{\text{Total principal amount}} \times \begin{array}{c}\text{FMV of}\\ \text{Security received}\end{array} = \begin{array}{c}\text{FMV of excess}\\ \text{principal amount}\\ \text{(i.e., boot)}\end{array}$$

$$\frac{\$500}{\$1,500} \times \$1,800 = \$600$$

The solely for stock and securities requirement has been modified to permit a limited amount of boot.[84] The receipt of boot causes the recognition of gain up to the amount of money plus the fair market value of property received. The receipt of boot does not permit the recognition of loss on the transaction, however.[85]

Example 56. As part of a plan of reorganization, A, an individual, received the following in exchange for a share of stock having an adjusted basis to her of $85:

One share of stock worth	$100
Cash	25
Other property worth	50
Total	$175

A's realized gain is $90 ($175 − $85). Total boot received is $75 ($25 + $50). A recognizes income of $75, the lesser of the amount of boot received or the gain realized.

---

[83] § 354(a)(2)(A).

[84] § 356.

[85] § 356(c).

The type of gain recognized is determined by the type of exchange. If the shareholder receives the distribution without having to surrender stock and securities (e.g., a spin-off), then the boot is treated as a dividend.[86] If the shareholder exchanges stock in the transaction and the boot has the effect of a dividend distribution (e.g., a pro rata distribution to all shareholders), the shareholder recognizes dividend income to the extent of his or her ratable share of accumulated earnings and profits.[87] Boot not having the effect of a dividend, or in excess of the shareholder's ratable share of accumulated earnings, is treated as an amount received on the sale of property.

> **Example 57.** Same facts as *Example 56* except A's share of earnings and profit is $30. If the total income is $75, $30 is dividend income and $45 is a capital gain on the exchange of stock.

Recently, the Supreme Court ruled that the determination of dividend equivalency is to be made by treating the boot as having been received in a redemption of the acquired corporation's stock.[88] If the redemption would have produced capital gain under the redemption provisions of § 302, the gain on the reorganization is capital gain.

Basis. In those cases in which the shareholder exchanges stock and securities, the shareholder must calculate the basis of the stock and securities received. The stock and securities have a substituted basis;[89] that is, the basis equals the basis of the stock and securities given up. The basis is increased for gain recognized by the shareholder and decreased for boot received. The basis calculation is shown in Exhibit 7-13.

Exhibit 7-13
*Target Shareholders' Basis
of Stock and Securities Received*

Basis of stock and securities transferred..............	$x,xxx
Plus: Gain recognized.............................	xxx
Dividend income............................	xxx
Minus: Money received	(xxx)
FMV of property received...................	(xxx)
Equals: Basis of stock and securities received.......	$x,xxx

---

[86]   § 356(b).

[87]   § 356(a)(2).

[88]   *Comm. v. Clark,* 89-1 USTC ¶9230, 63 AFTR2d 89-860, 109 S. Ct. 1455 (USSC, 1989).

[89]   § 358(a).

The basis of the boot received is its fair market value.[90] If the taxpayer surrenders both stock and securities for stock and securities, the basis is calculated separately for each exchange.[91]

> **Example 58.** Same facts as *Example 56*. The basis of the stock received is $85 [$85 (basis of stock transferred) + $30 (dividend income) + $45 (gain on exchange) − $25 (cash received) − $50 (other boot received)]. The basis of the boot property is $50.

CARRYOVER OF TAX ATTRIBUTES

From the moment of formation, a corporation begins to accumulate certain tax characteristics. For example, the corporation must select its tax year and method of accounting. Over the years, other characteristics develop. These characteristics include such items as the corporation's accumulated earnings and profits, capital loss carryovers, and net operating loss carryovers. These characteristics are referred to as the corporation's *tax attributes*. In most cases, these tax attributes are carried forward to be used by the corporation. This treatment is much like that given to individual taxpayers. For example, an individual is permitted to carry forward (and carry back) losses to use against other income to mitigate the effects of the annual accounting period requirement. Applying similar logic to corporate taxpayers, it would appear that as long as the *legal identity* of the corporation is maintained, the corporation should be permitted to use the accumulated tax attributes. However, such an approach ignores the fact that a corporation's ownership may change. If the ownership of the corporation should change, the question arises as to whether the tax attributes should be carried over to be used by the corporation under the new ownership, or die with the old ownership. Similarly, if the corporation changes its business, should the attributes arising from the old business be carried over to be used by the new business? The significance of this question becomes apparent when the attribute in question is a *loss carryover*.

> **Example 59.** L Corporation has a large net operating loss carryover, deriving from several years of unprofitable operations. P Corporation is a very profitable corporation that manufactures semiconductors. P currently has plans to manufacture its own line of computers. To this end, P might purchase all of the stock of L, and with the infusion of new assets and

---

[90] § 358(a)(2).   [91] Reg. § 1.358-2(b)(4).

the creation of a new computer manufacturing business, convert L to a profitable corporation. In this case, P would like to see the attributes of L survive the change in ownership so that L's loss carryover can offset current and future profits. Alternatively, P might absorb L in a merger. As in the first situation, P would want L's losses to survive the transfer to offset P's profits. In addition, P would want to inherit L's deficit in E&P (if any) in order to reduce its own E&P and perhaps eliminate any subsequent dividends.

Prior to 1954, there was great controversy over how and when a corporation's tax attributes carried over. This issue was particularly difficult when there was a reorganization such as a merger where the acquiring corporation simply absorbs the target corporation. To eliminate the confusion, Congress established specific rules regarding attribute carryovers in 1954.

CODE § 381: CARRYOVERS IN CERTAIN CORPORATION ACQUISITIONS

The general rules governing the carryover of tax attributes are contained in § 381. This section provides that where a corporation acquires the assets of another corporation in certain tax-free reorganizations and liquidations, selected attributes of the target corporation are carried over to the acquiring corporation. The reorganization transactions in which the tax attributes of the target survive are the "A," "C," acquisitive "D," "F," and "G" reorganizations. In each of these reorganizations, the acquiring corporation obtains the assets of the target corporation and the basis of such assets carries over. Consistent with this approach, the attributes of the target corporation also carry over. An acquiring corporation also inherits the target's attributes when it liquidates the target under the parent-subsidiary liquidation rules of § 332. As may be recalled from Chapter 5, in a § 332 liquidation, no gain or loss is recognized by the parent or subsidiary and the basis of the subsidiary's assets carries over to the parent—thus justifying the carryover of the tax attributes.

The nonqualifying reorganizations in which the attributes *do not* carry over are the "B," divisive "D," and "E." The "B" and "E" reorganizations were omitted since in both cases the corporation continues exactly as before only with changed ownership. There is no need for specific rules for carryovers, since the carryover occurs automatically. The divisive "D" was omitted since the transferor stays in existence and continues an active business. The transferor maintains all carryovers and the controlled corporation is considered a new entity.[92]

---

[92]   Earnings and profits must be allocated between the transferor and controlled corporation under § 312(h).

Following one of the specified reorganizations, § 381 provides for the termination of the tax year of the transferor corporation.[93] The termination occurs on the date the corporation transfers or distributes its assets.[94] Unless the transfer occurs on the last day of the corporation's tax year, this provision results in the corporation having to file a short period tax return.

In addition to providing for the close of the transferor's tax year, § 381 contains a long list of items that carry over or must be considered by the acquiring corporation (see Exhibit 7-14). As can be seen in this exhibit, § 381 allows the carryover of net operating losses and earnings and profits. Without further limitation, these rules would allow a profitable corporation to acquire and use for its benefit the NOLs of a loss corporation as well as any deficit the loss corporation has in E&P (see *Example 59* above). As might be expected, however, Congress took additional steps to prevent possible abuse concerning these particular attributes.

Exhibit 7-14
Tax Attributes

1. Net operating loss carryovers
2. Earnings and profits
3. Capital loss carryovers
4. Method of accounting
5. Inventories
6. Method of computing depreciation allowance
7. Installment method
8. Amortization of bond premium or discount
9. Treatment of certain mining development and exploration expenses
10. Contributions to pension and other benefit plans
11. Recovery of bad debts, prior taxes, or delinquency amounts
12. Involuntary conversions under § 1033
13. Dividend carryover of personal holding company
14. Indebtedness of certain personal holding companies
15. Certain obligations of the transferor corporation
16. Deficiency dividend of personal holding company
17. Percentage depletion on extraction of ores or mining from the waste or residue of prior mining
18. Charitable contribution carryovers
19. Successor insurance companies
20. General business credit
21. Deficiency dividend of regulated investment company
22. Method of computing recovery allowance
23. Minimum tax credit

---

[93] § 381(b)(1). There is an exception for the "F" reorganization. The corporation's tax year does not close.

[94] § 381(b)(2).

EARNINGS AND PROFITS

Section 381(c)(2) is designed to prohibit a profitable corporation from eliminating its own positive balance in E&P by acquiring a loss corporation with a deficit in E&P. In general, the E&P of the target corporation simply carries over and is combined with that of the acquiring corporation. However, a loss corporation's deficit cannot be used to offset any E&P of the profitable corporation existing at the date of the transfer. Rather, such deficit can be used only to offset the E&P arising from the combined corporation's operations after the transfer. Moreover, since dividends are deemed to come first from current E&P, and current E&P is unaffected by any deficit in accumulated E&P, the deficit may provide little or no benefit to the profitable corporation as long as the combined corporations produce current E&P.

> **Example 60.**   Effective December 31, 1991 Profit Corporation with E&P of $100,000 merged with Loss Corporation that had a deficit in E&P of $1.2 million. The $1.2 million deficit of Loss Corporation carries over to Profit Corporation but cannot be used to eliminate Profit's $100,000 of E&P as of December 31.
>
> During 1992, the combined operation generated a profit of $400,000. If the corporation made distributions during 1992, such distributions would be treated as dividends to the extent of current E&P of $400,000. Note that the inherited deficit of Loss Corporation has no effect on the status of the distributions since they are deemed to be dividends to the extent of any current E&P—unaffected by any deficit in accumulated E&P.

> **Example 61.**   Assume the same facts as above except that in 1992, the corporation made no distributions. In 1993 the corporation had no current E&P but distributed $400,000. In this case, only $100,000 of the distribution would be treated as a dividend since the deficit of the Loss Corporation eliminates the $400,000 of post-acquisition E&P. The $100,000 represents the E&P of Profit Corporation accumulated before the acquisition that is unaffected by the deficit of Loss Corporation.

CARRYOVER OF NET OPERATING LOSS

Although all tax attributes are important and should be considered in planning a reorganization, the net operating loss (NOL) undoubtedly draws the most attention. To the extent that the NOL of the target corporation can be used to offset income of the acquiring corporation (e.g., in a merger), it provides needed cash for the business and reduces the actual cost of acquiring the target corporation. This advantage has led to substantial abuse. Indeed, frequent advertisements formerly appeared in *The Wall Street Journal* for corporations indicating that their NOLs made them desirable candidates for acquisition. To limit such abuses, Congress has enacted certain restrictions.

The law provides that the target corporation's NOL can be carried forward and deducted by the acquiring corporation on the return for the first taxable year ending after the date of transfer.[95] However, the actual amount deductible on that first return is limited to

$$\frac{\text{Income of acquiring corporation} \times \text{ Number of days in year after transfer}^{96}}{\text{Number of days in a year}}$$

> **Example 62.**   Target Corporation is merged into Acquiring Corporation in an "A" reorganization on October 31, 1991. Target has an October 31 year-end and an NOL carryover of $365,000. Acquiring Corporation has taxable income before any NOL deduction of $730,000 and a fiscal year ending November 30. On the tax return of Acquiring Corporation for the year ended November 30, 1991, Acquiring can deduct $60,000 of Target's NOL ($730,000 × 30 days in November following merger ÷ 365 days). The remaining $305,000 NOL is carried over to 1992.

Unless the restrictions of § 382 apply (discussed below), there are no special limitations on the NOL carryover for years other than the first year. However, the law does prevent the *carryback* of an NOL generated *after* the reorganization to a tax year of the *transferor* corporation.[97] This prevents a corporation that is suffering losses from acquiring a profitable corporation and using its current loss as an offset against past profits of the target corporation to obtain a refund of prior taxes paid by the target corporation.

> **Example 63.**   Loss Corporation manufactured steel and had been unprofitable for the last several years. During the current year, Loss acquired Profit Corporation, which had taxable income of $10 million for each of the past three years. During the first year of combined operations, the corporation generated a loss of $5 million due to the poor performance of the steel business. None of the $5 million loss can be carried back to a prior year of Profit Corporation to recover taxes paid by Profit Corporation on its taxable income.

Limitation on NOL Carryovers.   The availability of the NOL as a carryover led to many corporate acquisitions motivated by the tax avoidance potential of the carryforward. To prevent the trafficking in losses, Congress enacted § 382, which applies to all acquisitions of corporations with NOLs. The thrust of this provision is that any NOL is in effect the property of the shareholders of the corporation

---

[95]   § 381(c)(1)(A).

[96]   § 381(c)(1)(B).

[97]   § 381(b)(3).

when it incurred the losses. From the view of the architects of § 382, "income generated under different corporate owners which is attributable to capital over and above the capital used in the loss business, is related to a pre-acquisition loss only in the formal sense that it is housed in the same corporate entity."[98] As this statement suggests, the drafters of § 382 were obviously concerned about the possibility that new owners could infuse new capital into the business or divert income-producing opportunities to the corporation and obtain greater utilization of the loss corporation's NOLs than the former owners. Consequently, limitations on the use of a loss carryover are imposed whenever there is a *change of ownership* in the loss corporation such that those shareholders who suffered the economic burden of the corporation's NOLs are no longer in control. Before identifying what changes in ownership trigger the loss limitation, the limitation itself is considered.

Calculation of the Limitation.   Following a significant change of ownership in the loss corporation, the maximum amount of NOL carryover that can be used in any year is limited. The limitation is based on the theory that the loss should be used only to offset income attributable to the loss corporation's assets, and not the income derived from the profitable corporation's business. Section 382 takes an objective approach instead of determining the amount of income that the loss corporation's assets actually generate, thus avoiding the inherent difficulties in making such a determination. The provision assumes that the equity of the loss corporation immediately before the change in ownership is invested in tax-exempt securities that pay interest at a rate prescribed by statute. Thus, the amount of any NOL carryover that can be used when the limitation applies is the product of the fair market value of the corporation's stock before the change and the "long-term tax-exempt rate."[99] Under this approach, the new owners of the corporation obtain the same result as would occur had they invested the amount paid for the loss corporation in tax-exempt securities instead of buying the loss corporation. In making the computation, the value of the loss corporation's stock is normally the price at which the stock changed hands. The long-term tax-exempt rate is generally the highest interest rate on U.S. obligations (e.g., Treasury bonds) with remaining terms exceeding nine years, reduced to reflect difference in rates on taxable and tax-exempt obligations. This rate is to be published monthly by the IRS.

> **Example 64.**   B, an individual, purchased all of the stock of Loss Corporation for $1 million. Loss Corporation had an NOL carryover of $700,000. Since there was a complete change of ownership, the limitation on the NOL carryover applies. In computing the limitation, the value of the loss corporation is assumed to be equal to the amount paid by B, $1 million. Assuming that at the time of the purchase the long-term tax-exempt rate was

---

[98]   Tax Reform Bill of 1986, Senate Finance Committee Report on H.R. 3838, Report 99-313, 99th Congress, 2d Sess., p. 231.

[99]   § 382(b).

6%, the maximum amount of NOL carryover that can be used in any year is $60,000 ($1 million × 6%). Thus, assuming the corporation becomes profitable under the new ownership and generates $100,000 of taxable income, only $40,000 would be taxable since $60,000 of the corporation's NOL can be used. In effect, the new corporation earned $60,000 of taxable income that was not subject to tax, the same as if B had invested $1 million in tax-exempt securities yielding 6%.

Change in Ownership. As noted above, the limitation of § 382 operates only in the taxable year after there has been a substantial change in ownership—a so-called "ownership change." This condition ensures that the new owners cannot benefit from losses that were in fact the economic burden of the previous owners. Generally, the requisite ownership change is deemed to occur whenever there has been more than a 50 percentage point *increase* in ownership by one or more shareholders who own 5 percent of the corporation.[100]

> **Example 65.** Loss Corporation is owned by individual R. During the year, Profit Corporation purchased all of the stock of Loss Corporation from R. The § 382 limitation applies since the ownership of the 5% shareholders has increased by more than 50 percentage points immediately after the change. The same result would occur if three unrelated individuals each purchased 20% of the stock.

The Code indicates that the test to determine whether an ownership change has occurred must be made whenever there is an "owner shift involving a 5 percent shareholder" or an "equity structure shift."[101] An "owner shift involving a 5 percent shareholder" (an *owner shift*) is defined as *any change* in the stock ownership of the corporation that affects the percentage of stock in the corporation owned by any person who is a 5 percent shareholder before or after the change.[102] For example, an owner shift occurs and the test for an ownership change must be made whenever a 5 percent shareholder either sells or buys stock. Similarly, an owner shift occurs if a purchaser not owning 5 percent acquires sufficient stock to meet the 5 percent threshold. Note also that an owner shift could occur even though the shareholder did not buy or sell stock. For example, if an event occurs such as the issuance of stock or a stock redemption that changes a 5 percent shareholder's interest or causes a shareholder to become a 5 percent shareholder, an owner shift has occurred. In effect, § 382 tracks the holdings of 5 percent shareholders to determine whether an ownership change has occurred.

---

[100] § 382(g).

[101] *Ibid.*

[102] § 382(g)(2).

The second event that triggers a test for an ownership change is an *equity structure shift*. An equity structure shift is simply defined as a reorganization other than an "F," divisive "D," or divisive "G" reorganization.[103] Thus, as a practical matter, whenever a reorganization occurs the test for an ownership change must be made.

If either an owner shift or equity structure shift has occurred, the test for an ownership change must be made. The first step in applying this test is identification of the 5 percent shareholders. A 5 percent shareholder is any shareholder holding 5 percent or more of the corporation's stock at any time during the testing period.[104] The testing period is the three-year period ending on the day of the owner shift or equity structure shift. Once all 5 percent shareholders have been identified, their percentage *increase* in ownership for each year during the testing period must be determined. The percentage increase is determined by comparing the shareholder's percentage interest immediately after the owner shift or equity structure shift with the shareholder's lowest percentage interest in the loss corporation during the testing period. The percentage increases of all 5 percent shareholders is then summed to determine if the total increase exceeds 50 percentage points. If the total increase exceeds 50 percent, the § 382 limitation applies.

The following examples illustrate the rules used to determine whether a sufficient change in ownership has occurred.

> **Example 66.**   M owns 10% of Loss Corporation. During the year, M purchased additional stock of Loss Corporation, increasing her ownership to 15%. The purchase constitutes an owner shift since the holdings of a 5% shareholder have changed. Consequently, the test for an ownership change is required. There has been a 50% increase in M's ownership. However, there has been only a 5 *percentage point* increase. Consequently, an ownership change has not occurred.

> **Example 67.**   K owns 15% of Loss Corporation. On February 1, 1992 K purchased additional shares of Loss Corporation's stock to increase her ownership to 45%. The purchase constitutes an owner shift since the holdings of a 5% shareholder have changed. As a result, the test for an ownership change is required. Assuming there have been no other stock transactions since February 2, 1989 (the beginning of the testing period), this is not an ownership change since the 30 percentage point increase did not exceed 50 percentage points.

---

[103]   § 382(g)(3).

[104]   § 382(k)(7).

On June 3, 1993 J, an unrelated party, purchased 25% of Loss Corporation from persons other than K. The purchase constitutes an owner shift since the holdings of J, a 5% shareholder, has occurred. The 5% shareholders during the testing period (6/4/90 to 6/3/93) are J and K. J has a 25 percentage point increase in his holdings and K's holdings have increased 30 percentage points for a total of 55 percentage points. Since the percentage point increase of 55 points exceeds 50, Loss Corporation's ability to use its NOL carryforwards is limited.

Example 68.   R has owned all 1,000 shares of stock of Loss Corporation since its formation several years ago. On May 7, 1991 R sold 400 of his shares to S. On June 3, 1992 the Loss Corporation issued 200 shares to T and U.

The sale on May 7, 1991 is an owner shift involving two 5% shareholders, R and S. There is no ownership change, however, since the increase of the only 5% shareholder whose ownership increased during the testing period (5/6/88 to 5/7/91), S, was only 40 percentage points. R's ownership decrease is ignored.

The issuance of 200 shares to both T and U on June 3, 1992 is an owner shift involving 5% shareholders, T and U (200 ÷ 1,400 = 14.29% each). In addition, the issuance of the shares reduces the interest of R and S to 42.86% (600 ÷ 1,400) and 28.57% (400 ÷ 1,400), respectively. The issuance of these shares causes an ownership change as determined below. Note that the decrease in R's percentage ownership is ignored and does not offset the increases occurring in the other shareholders' interest.

5 Percent Shareholders	Ownership Percentage After	Lowest Percentage Before	Increase
R	42.86%	60%	0 %
S	28.57	0	28.57
T	14.29	0	14.29
U	14.29	0	14.29
			57.15%

In determining whether there is an owner shift involving a 5 percent shareholder, all of the shares not owned by 5 percent shareholders are aggregated and treated as if they were held by a single hypothetical shareholder. In the case of an equity structure shift (i.e., a qualifying reorganization), each group of less than 5 percent shareholders of each corporation is treated as a separate 5 percent shareholder.

Example 69.   Loss Corporation has been a publicly held company since 1983. During the three-year period ending on December 31, 1993, the stock has been actively traded such that there has been a complete change of ownership. However, at no time during this period did any one shareholder own 5% of the stock. Despite the complete turnover in ownership, there has not been an "ownership change" since under the aggregation rule 100% of the stock is deemed to be owned at all times by a single shareholder. Accordingly, this hypothetical shareholder's interest has not changed during the testing period.

Example 70. Loss Corporation has been owned equally by X and Y since its inception in 1981. On July 7 of this year, the corporation issued stock to the public representing 70% of its outstanding stock. No person acquires 5% or more of the stock. Neither X nor Y acquires additional stock so that together they own the remaining 30%. This is an owner shift since the interests of 5% shareholders have been affected (i.e., X, Y, and the hypothetical shareholder). Since all of the shares owned by the less than 5% shareholders are aggregated and treated as owned by a single hypothetical shareholder, this shareholder's ownership has increased by 70 percentage points. Thus, an ownership change has occurred.

Example 71. On June 1, 1991 Loss Corporation was merged into Profit Corporation pursuant to state law. Both corporations were publicly traded corporations and neither had a shareholder owning 5% or more of its stock. As part of the merger, the shareholders of Loss Corporation received 40% of Profit's stock. The merger of Loss Corporation is an equity structure shift since the transaction qualified as a type "A" reorganization. Moreover, an ownership change has occurred since Profit Corporation's shareholders (which are treated as a single 5% shareholder) have *effectively* increased their percentage ownership in the Loss Corporation (although it does not survive) by more than 50 percentage points [from 0 before the reorganization to 60% (100% − 40%) after the reorganization].

Continuity of Business Requirement.   In addition to limiting the use of NOL carryovers where there is a change of ownership in the loss corporation, § 382 may disallow their use entirely. If the loss corporation does not continue its business enterprise for at least two years after there has been an ownership change, none of the NOL carryover can be used.[105] For this purpose, the definition of *business enterprise* is given the same meaning that it has under the continuity of business enterprise doctrine discussed earlier in this chapter. Under this doctrine, the target corporation's historic business must be continued, or alternatively, a significant portion of the target's assets must be used in a business.

Although the above discussion describes the essence of § 382, it should be emphasized that various other complexities of this provision were not considered. As a practical matter, a careful study of § 382 is required if the acquisition of a loss corporation is contemplated.

---

[105]   § 382(c).

BUILT-IN GAINS

Section 382 limits the ability of a profitable corporation to acquire a net operating loss by purchase or reorganization. It does not affect acquisitions by loss corporations, however. As a result, it has been possible for a corporation with an NOL carryover to acquire a corporation with a *built-in gain* (fair market value of assets exceeding basis) and use its NOL to offset the gain on the sale of the acquired corporation's assets. Today, however, this potential is limited by Code § 384.

Two conditions must exist before § 384 will apply. First, there must be a "qualified acquisition." A qualified acquisition is defined as either a stock acquisition or an asset acquisition. In a qualified stock acquisition, the acquiring corporation purchases (or obtains by reorganization) stock of the target sufficient for the acquiring corporation and the target to form an affiliated group (one eligible to file a consolidated return).[106] A qualified asset acquisition is the acquisition of assets in the liquidation of a subsidiary under § 332, or as the result of an "A," "C," or "acquisitive D" reorganization. The second condition that must be present is that either the target or the acquiring corporation must be a "gain corporation." A *gain corporation* is defined as any corporation with a built-in gain. A corporation will meet this condition if the excess of the fair market value of its assets over their adjusted basis exceeds the *lesser* of $10 million *or* 15 percent of the value of the assets.

Following a qualified acquisition, § 384 provides that the NOL carryover cannot offset any recognized built-in gain during the five-year period following the qualified acquisition. As a result, the corporation will pay tax on any recognized gains even though it has unused loss carryovers. It is possible for both §§ 382 and 384 to apply to a reorganization.

SECTION 269

Sections 381 and 382 limit the carryover of certain tax attributes based on objective rules. The IRS can also apply § 269 to prevent tax avoidance. This section provides that if an individual or corporation acquires control of a corporation with the principal purpose of avoiding tax by obtaining a deduction or credit, the Service can disallow the deduction or credit. For purposes of § 269, control is defined as 50 percent or more of the voting power, or 50 percent or more of the fair market value of all the stock. This section is not applied

---

[106] Affiliated groups are discussed in detail in Chapter 8.

unless the *principal purpose* of the acquisition was the avoidance of tax. "Principal purpose" means that the avoidance of tax exceeds any other purpose.[107] Section 269 is very broad in scope and permits the IRS to selectively disallow items. Since it requires a forbidden purpose, the exact extent of its reach is unknown.

> **Example 72.**   G purchases all the stock of Drug Corporation that has an NOL carryover of $300,000. Immediately after purchase, G contributes a profitable hardware business to Drug Corporation. Drug continues to operate both businesses—drugs at a break-even point and hardware profitably. The purchase and transfer will be considered an acquisition for tax avoidance, and the NOL carryover is denied under § 269.[108]

---

[107]   Reg. § 1.269-3(a).

[108]   Adapted from example in Reg. § 1.269-3(b)(1).

PROBLEM MATERIALS

DISCUSSION QUESTIONS

7-1 *Reorganizations in General.* For many, the term *reorganization* brings to mind thoughts of failing businesses and their financial overhaul. For tax purposes, however, the term has a far different meaning.

    a.   Discuss the term *reorganization* and its implications for tax purposes.

    b.   What is the significance of qualifying a transaction as a reorganization?

7-2 *Principles of Reorganizations.* Explain the justification underlying the non-recognition treatment accorded qualifying reorganizations and how, as a practical matter, it has been implemented.

7-3 *Reorganization Situations.* T Corporation has 100 shares of outstanding stock owned by two friends, B and C. The corporation was started by B and C several years ago to publish a computer magazine and has had great success.

    a.   Identify two sets of circumstances where an acquisitive reorganization may be appropriate.

    b.   Identify two sets of circumstances where a divisive reorganization may be appropriate.

7-4 *Control.* Define the term *control* as used in reorganization.

7-5 *"A" Reorganizations.* Define an "A" reorganization.

7-6 *Triangular Mergers.* Describe a triangular merger and explain the circumstances where its use is appropriate.

7-7 *Reverse Triangular Mergers.* Describe a reverse triangular merger and explain the circumstances where its use is appropriate.

7-8 *"B" Reorganizations.* Define a "B" reorganization. What is meant by the term *creeping B* reorganization?

7-9 *"C" Reorganizations.* Define a "C" reorganization.

7-10 *Substantially All Test.* What is the definition of *substantially all the assets* as it applies to a "C" reorganization?

7-11 *Transfer of Liabilities.* What is the effect of the transfer of liabilities in addition to assets in a "C" reorganization?

7-12 *Acquisitive "D" Reorganizations.* Define an acquisitive "D" reorganization.

7-13 *Divisive "D" Reorganizations.* Define a divisive "D" reorganization.

7-14   *Corporate Divisions in General.*   Address the following concerning corporate divisions.

    a.   A corporate division may be necessary for a number of reasons. List several factors that might prompt a corporate division.

    b.   A division can be accomplished through various means: by dividend, redemption, partial liquidation, or under the corporate division rules of § 355. What distinguishes corporate divisions pursuant to § 355 from the other methods?

    c.   Once it is determined that a division will take place, the division can assume three different forms. Identify the three types of corporate divisions, what they resemble, and how they differ.

7-15   *Corporate Divisions: Requirements of § 355.*   List the requirements that must be satisfied under § 355 to secure favorable treatment. Include in your list a brief statement of the purpose of each requirement.

7-16   *Corporate Divisions: Effect on Shareholders.*   Address the following concerning corporate divisions:

    a.   If all of the conditions of § 355 are satisfied, how is the distribution of stock of the controlled corporation treated by the shareholder?

    b.   Explain the concept of boot and the tax consequences to the shareholder if boot is received as part of the corporate division.

    c.   How is the character of any recognized gain determined.

    d.   How are the shareholder's bases determined in the stock, securities, and boot received?

7-17   *Corporate Divisions: Effect on Distributing Corporation.*   Address the following questions concerning corporate divisions.

    a.   Assuming a corporation distributes soley stock or securities of the controlled corporate, how is the distributing corporation's taxable income affected?

    b.   Under what circumstances, if any, does the distributing corporation recognize gain or loss?

7-18   *"E" Reorganizations.*   Describe an "E" reorganization.

7-19   *"F" Reorganizations.*   Describe an "F" reorganization.

7-20   *"G" Reorganizations.*   Describe a "G" reorganization.

7-21   *Acquisitive Reorganizations: Tax Consequences.*   Briefly describe the tax consequences resulting from an acquisitive reorganization for the following:

    a.   Acquiring corporation.

    b.   Target corporation.

    c.   Target corporation's shareholders.

7-22   *Carryover of Tax Attributes.*   Some reorganizations are prompted by the ability to carry over certain tax attributes. Explain.

PROBLEMS

7-23   *Continuity of Interest-Consideration.*   Joan, Jill, and Jane each own 100 percent of the stock of three separate corporations. They combine their separate corporations into a new corporation called Triple J. Under state law the transaction is a consolidation. Joan receives all the common stock of Triple J valued at $300,000. Jill receives all of the nonvoting preferred stock of Triple J valued at $200,000; and Jane receives all the 30-year bonds (value of $100,000) issued by Triple J. Does the transaction qualify as a reorganization?

7-24   *Continuity of Interest-Consideration.*   Retail Corporation is the wholly owned subsidiary of Holding Corporation. On January 2 of this year, Supply Corp. is merged into Retail under state law. Supply's shareholders receive 10 percent of Holding Corporation's common stock (worth $90,000) and $100,000 of Retail's 20-year debenture bonds (worth $100,000) in exchange for all of Supply's common stock. Is this transaction a qualified reorganization?

7-25   *Statutory Merger.*   ACQ Corporation, a widely held conglomerate, has 100,000 shares of a single class of common stock outstanding. Each share is worth $60. ACQ has E&P of $500,000. ACQ plans on merging with T Corporation, which manufactures furniture. T's 1,000 shares are owned equally by A, B, C, D, and E. A and B each paid $100 per share while the other three shareholders paid $150 for their shares. T stock is now worth $120 per share. T has $200,000 of E&P. A and C are also creditors of T. Each paid $50,000 for T's 15-year bonds. The bonds have a $50,000 face value, pay 10 percent interest, and are currently worth $60,000 each. Under the terms of the merger agreement, each T shareholder receives 400 shares of ACQ stock. Each of T's creditors receives 1,000 shares of ACQ stock.

   a.   What gain or loss is realized and recognized by the shareholders and creditors of T?
   b.   What is each shareholder's basis for the stock received?
   c.   What are the tax consequences to ACQ and T?
   d.   Answer questions (a) through (c) above assuming each T shareholder received 350 shares of ACQ and $3,000 cash.

7-26   *"B" Reorganization: Obtaining Control.*   In 1985 Retail Corporation acquired 80 percent of the common stock of Manufacturing Corporation in a qualified "B" reorganization. In 1991 Retail obtains the remaining 20 percent pursuant to a plan of reorganization. Is this a qualified "B" reorganization?

7-27   *"B" Reorganization: Prior Cash Purchase.*   Computer Corp. desires to acquire Component Corp. in a nontaxable "B" reorganization. However, 5 percent of Component's shareholders oppose the transaction. On December 15, 1991 Component redeems the shares of the 5 percent opposing the reorganization for cash. On June 30, 1992 pursuant to a plan of reorganization, Component's shareholders exchange Component common stock for Computer's common stock. Is this a qualified "B" reorganization?

7-28   *"C" Reorganization: Substantially All Test.*   Target Corporation owns assets with a fair market value of $2 million and a basis of $1.6 million. Target's liabilities equal $150,000. Target transfers assets with a fair market value of $1.85 million and a basis of $1.6 million to Acquiring Corporation as part of a reorganization. Target keeps the other assets to pay off its liabilities. Has Acquiring Corporation received substantially all the assets of Target?

7-29   *"C" Reorganization: Computation of Gain/Loss and Basis.*   Target Corporation has assets of $2 million (basis $1.6 million) and liabilities of $150,000. Target transfers all of its assets and liabilities to Acquiring Corporation. Target receives common stock worth $1.5 million and property worth $350,000 with a basis of $100,000 in the exchange. Target subsequently liquidates.

a.   How much gain or loss, if any, must Target recognize?
b.   How much gain or loss, if any, must Acquiring Corporation recognize?
c.   Compute Acquiring Corporation's basis for Target's assets.

7-30   *"B" Reorganization: Computation of Gain/Loss and Basis.*   K owns 1,000 shares of Target Corporation's common stock. She purchased the stock five years ago for $100 per share. K also owns $80,000 of Target's bonds, which she purchased for $80,000. As part of a "B" reorganization, K exchanges her stock and bonds for 500 shares of Acquiring Corporation's common stock with a fair market value of $300 per share plus $100,000 of Acquiring Corporation's bonds with a fair market value of $90,000.

a.   Compute K's realized and recognized gain or loss.
b.   Compute K's basis in the Acquiring Corporation stock and bonds.
c.   Same facts as above except K's share of Target's accumulated earnings and profits is $10,000. Would this change your answer to (a) or (b) above?

7-31   *Corporate Divisions.*   Do the following corporate divisions meet the § 355 requirements relating to the active conduct of a trade or business? If yes, do they qualify as a spin-off, a split-off, or a split-up? Assume all other requirements for a corporate division are met.

   a.   R, Inc. has produced T-shirts for the U.S. and European markets for the past eight years. The officers of R decide to move all European production activities to the East Coast of the United States. In addition, the assets necessary for its European production process will be transferred to E, Inc., a corporation being organized for this purpose. Stock in E, Inc. will be distributed to R, Inc. shareholders. Shareholders will not surrender any of their R shares.

   b.   Although M, Inc. has been an active manufacturer for eight years, it is subject to the alternative minimum tax, primarily because of its substantial investment in equipment. The officers of M propose to transfer all equipment acquired since 1987 to P, Inc., a corporation to be organized for the purpose of owning all equipment to be used by M. After the transfer, M will lease the equipment from P. M will hold 60 percent of P stock and distribute 40 percent to M shareholders. Shareholders will not surrender any of their M shares.

   c.   Twelve years ago, V and W corporations were formed as wholly owned subsidiaries of U, Inc. U has no other assets. Y and Z are equal owners of U, Inc. Y and Z are in complete disagreement about the future of the three corporations. Unable to reconcile these differences, Y and Z agree to have U distribute all its stock in V to Z and all its stock in W to Y. In exchange, Y and Z will surrender all their shares in U, and U will be terminated.

7-32   *Spin-Off: Effect on Shareholder.*   In 1981 RIC Corp. was formed by B, C, D, and E. Each contributed $25,000 for 100 shares of the corporation's stock. The corporation was established to capitalize on the public's increased need for leisure activities. RIC's first transaction in 1981 was to purchase a bowling alley. In anticipation of the exercise craze in the eighties, the corporation purchased all the stock of X Corporation in 1984. X operated a chain of health salons, now aerobic centers. In 1988 RIC purchased all of the stock of Y corporation, which had manufactured a line of health foods since 1966.

   a.   RIC's management currently believes that it has grown too fast and consequently should divest itself of X or Y. Will a spin-off of either subsidiary be nontaxable?

On December 1, 1991 RIC distributed all its X stock pro rata in a transaction that satisfies the requirements of § 355. Immediately after the distribution, the RIC stock and X stock were valued at $240,000 and $40,000, respectively. In addition, RIC distributed X securities pro rata worth $20,000 (face value $22,000). B received X stock valued at $10,000 and X securities worth $5,000. RIC has $90,000 of E&P. X's net worth is $50,000.

   b.   State the amount of realized gain or loss, if either is recognized by B, and its character.

   c.   What is B's basis in his RIC stock and his stock and securities of X?

7-33   *Split-Off: Effect on Shareholder.*   Same facts as in Problem 7-32, except B surrenders all of his stock in RIC for all of the X stock and securities.

     a.   State the amount of gain or loss, if either is recognized by B, and its character.

     b.   What is B's basis in his stock in RIC and his stock and securities of X?

7-34   *Carryover of NOL: Section 382 Limitations.*   Loss Corporation's common stock is owned as follows.

R..............................	45 shares
S..............................	45 shares
T..............................	10 shares

On December 15, 1991 E purchased the stock owned by S and T. He purchased the stock because Loss has a very large NOL carryover.

     a.   Will the NOL carryover be limited by § 382?

     b.   Same facts as above except Loss is merged into Profit Corporation. R, S, and T each receives 1,200 shares of Profit out of the total of 8,000 shares issued and outstanding. Can Profit carry over Loss's NOL without limitation under § 382?

7-35   *Carryover of NOL: Computation.*   Loss Corporation merged into Profit Corporation on December 1, 1991. Loss's NOL is $500,000. Profit Corporation has income before considering Loss's NOL of $182,500 for the year ended December 31, 1991. Compute Profit's taxable income for 1991. (Assume the § 382 limit is greater than the deductible loss.)

7-36   *Section 384 Limitation.*   On December 31, 1991 Profitable Corporation merged into Loss Corporation. Profitable Corporation's only asset is land with a fair market value of $1 million and a basis of $500,000. Loss Corporation has a $5 million NOL carryover from 1990. In 1992, Loss Corporation breaks even on its operations. In addition, Loss Corporation sold the land acquired from Profitable for $1 million. Compute Loss Corporation's taxable income for 1992.

RESEARCH PROBLEMS

7-37 Stable Corporation is an old, established corporation in a mature industry. It has more cash than is needed for its operations. Stable decides to invest its spare cash in corporate stock. After much investigation, Stable purchased 5 percent of Glamour Corporation in February 1990. The purchase was so successful that Stable Corporation acquires an additional 10 percent of Glamour during 1991. In 1991 the IRS audits Stable's 1989 tax return. The agent raises, but does not pursue, an excess accumulated earnings penalty issue. To avoid future problems, Stable decides to diversify. To implement this plan, the corporation tenders its voting stock for the outstanding voting stock of Glamour in a "B" reorganization. The shareholders of Glamour accept the offer and exchange Glamour voting stock for Stable voting stock on January 2, 1992. Will the prior cash purchases of Glamour stock invalidate the "B" reorganization?

7-38 Jim and Jane each own 50% of T Corporation. They disagree on the future direction of the business. To settle the dispute, it is agreed that T Corporation will transfer its retail operations to Newco in exchange for all of its stock. The stock is worth $360,000. T Corporation will exchange the stock of Newco for all the stock of T Corporation owned by Jim. To even up values, T Corporation will also distribute $40,000 cash to Jim. Assuming the transaction qualifies as a "divisive D" reorganization, determine the tax treatment of $40,000 cash distributed to Jim.

LEARNING OBJECTIVES

Upon completion of this chapter you will be able to:

- Discuss the advantages and disadvantages of filing a consolidated return
- Identify who is eligible to file a consolidated return
- Compute consolidated taxable income and tax liability
- Determine the treatment of an intercompany transaction
- Explain the rules limiting the use of one member's losses and credits against the income and tax of other consolidated group members
- Explain how a corporation accounts for its investment in a subsidiary

CHAPTER OUTLINE

Chapter **8**

CONSOLIDATED TAX RETURNS

Although most corporations are required to file their own separate tax returns, certain related corporations (e.g., a parent corporation and its 80% owned subsidiary) are entitled to file a *consolidated tax return*. The consolidated tax return is essentially a method by which to determine the tax liability of a group of affiliated corporations. The tax computation is based on the view that the businesses of the related corporations represent but a single enterprise. Accordingly, it is appropriate to tax the aggregate income of the group rather than the separate income of each corporation. This is not to say, however, that a consolidated return simply reports the sum of each member corporation's taxable income as if the group were one enlarged single corporation. The applicable Treasury Regulations[1] modify the aggregate results by providing special rules requiring the statement of certain items on a consolidated basis (e.g., capital gains) and adjustments for intercompany transactions. The intricacies of these consolidated return rules are the subject of this chapter.

THE HISTORY OF THE CONSOLIDATED RETURN

The origin of the consolidated tax return can be found in the early Regulations concerning the tax imposed on excess profits during World War I. These Regulations authorized the Commissioner of the Internal Revenue Service to prescribe rules necessary to prevent corporations from avoiding the tax by eliminating their "excess profit" by arbitrarily shifting income to another corporation where it would not be considered excessive. As early as 1917, the Commissioner used this power to require the filing of consolidated tax returns by affiliated corporations to limit the benefits of multiple corporations. By 1918, Congress had made the filing of consolidated returns mandatory for affiliated groups for purposes of not only the excess profits tax but also the income tax. In addition, the Commissioner's authority to issue Regulations governing consolidated returns was codified.

---

[1] See generally Reg. §§ 1.1502-11, 12 and 13.

The end of the war produced several changes affecting consolidated returns. The war's end eliminated the need for the excess profits tax and consequently it was repealed. At the same time, the forerunner of § 482 was enacted. This provision permitted the IRS to apportion income, expenses, or credits between two or more organizations that are under common control in order to prevent tax avoidance and clearly reflect income. The repeal of the excess profits tax and the extension of the Commissioner's authority to reallocate income reduced the opportunity for distorting income and thus the need for mandatory consolidated returns for affiliated groups. As a result, in 1921 Congress made the filing of a consolidated return optional.

For the next 14 years, consolidated returns remained optional, although an additional 1 percent tax was imposed on the privilege of filing a consolidated return in 1932. In 1934, influenced by the effects of the Great Depression and the ability of a loss corporation to offset the income of a profitable one, Congress abolished the use of the consolidated tax return.[2] The consolidated tax return soon reappeared with the beginning of World War II as Congress extended corporations the privilege of filing a consolidated return in 1942. This time, however, the cost for filing a consolidated return was increased. Congress imposed a 2 percent penalty on consolidated taxable income—a penalty which was to remain until its repeal in 1964. Since 1942, the filing of a consolidated return has been optional.

Although certain benefits could be gained through filing consolidated returns, for many years affiliated groups often opted to file separate returns to obtain the benefits accorded multiple corporations.

> **Example 1.** P, S, and T are an affiliated group of corporations. Each corporation had taxable income of $50,000 for the year. The group's major competitor, Z Inc., a separate corporation, had taxable income of $150,000. If P, S, and T file their own separate returns reporting $50,000 of taxable income on each return, their combined tax liability will be $22,500 ($7,500 × 3). In contrast, Z's tax liability for its $150,000 of taxable income is $41,750,which is $19,250 greater than the combined liability of P, S, and T. Note that the taxes saved are attributable to the fact that the group's taxable incomes are never taxed at the higher rate (i.e., 34%) or subject to the additional 5% surtax.

In 1969 the benefits of multiple corporations illustrated above were severely curtailed. Under the Tax Reform Act of 1969,[3] affiliated corporations were effectively treated as a single corporation (e.g., in the example above, P, S, and T would be treated like Z) notwithstanding the fact that each corporation filed a separate return.[4] With the elimination of these benefits, there has been increasing interest in the filing of consolidated returns.

---

[2] This election still remained available for certain railroad corporations.

[3] §§ 1561 and 1563.

[4] See discussion on controlled groups in Chapter 1.

THE CONSOLIDATED RETURN REGULATIONS

As previously mentioned, Congress granted the Commissioner (IRS) the authority to promulgate regulations for filing a consolidated tax return. Specifically, Code § 1502 states in part:

> The Secretary shall prescribe such regulations as he may deem necessary in order that the tax liability of any affiliated group of corporations making a consolidated return and of each corporation in the group, both during and after the period of affiliation, may be returned, determined, computed, assessed, collected and adjusted, in such a manner as clearly to reflect the income tax liability and the various factors necessary for the determination of such liability, and in order to prevent avoidance of such tax liability.[5]

It takes little imagination to see that Congress has granted the IRS broad authority to write regulations governing the filing of a consolidated tax return. These Regulations, referred to as legislative regulations,[6] grant a nearly absolute power to the Secretary of the Treasury to prescribe the rules for consolidated tax returns. Although not statutory in form, these regulations have the *force and effect* of law and remain effective unless overturned by the courts or restricted by Congress.

As early as 1928[7] and then again in 1954,[8] Congress contemplated codifying the consolidated return regulations. In 1954 the House Ways and Means Committee wanted the regulations written into the statutes on the grounds that the Regulations had become generally accepted and should be formalized. The Senate Finance Committee, however, rejected this notion.[9] The Senate felt that the detailed consolidated return rules should remain in regulation format. By leaving the Regulations in that form, any rule or tax law change could be readily addressed by the IRS without requiring further action by Congress.[10]

In 1966 the IRS completely overhauled the existing system governing consolidated returns by replacing the old Regulations with a lengthy and intricate set of new Regulations. These "new" Regulations rejected the accounting principles that had served as the basis of the old Regulations and adopted a different approach. The new Regulations remain in effect today and provide the rules for consolidated tax returns, having gone relatively unchanged since their adoption. In fact, the majority of the changes made to the Regulations since 1965 primarily reflect changes passed by Congress that were applicable to all corporations, not just affiliated groups.

---

[5] § 1502.

[6] Legislative Regulations should be contrasted with interpretive Regulations (see Chapter 16 for a discussion).

[7] S. Rept. No. 960, 70th Cong., 1st Session.

[8] H. Rept. No. 1337, 83rd Cong., 2nd Session.

[9] S. Rept. No. 1622, 83rd Cong., 2nd Session.

[10] Whether this logic still applies today with nearly annual tax law changes may be a subject for debate. It often takes years to get Regulations proposed and finalized.

ADVANTAGES AND DISADVANTAGES OF THE CONSOLIDATED TAX RETURN

Although filing a consolidated tax return has advantages, numerous disadvantages exist as well. A review of the various advantages and disadvantages that must be considered before filing a consolidated return is presented below.

ADVANTAGES OF CONSOLIDATED RETURNS

A partial list of the advantages of filing a consolidated income tax return includes the following:

1. Unused losses (both ordinary and capital) and credits of an affiliate may be used to offset the income and tax liability of other affiliated group members in the current year. By utilizing these losses and credits in the current year, the group receives immediate tax benefits and thereby avoids the need for carryovers to recover the benefits. In addition, any excess losses or credits can also be carried back or carried over to subsequent consolidated return years.

2. Intercompany profits on the sale of goods and services may be deferred until later years. This deferral has the added benefits of postponing depreciation recapture as well as investment tax credit recapture.

3. Intercompany dividends between group members are eliminated from income and are not subject to tax.

4. Deductions and credits that are subject to percentage limitations can be determined on a consolidated rather than on a separate company basis. This permits a single corporation subject to such limitations to effectively avoid them.

5. The basis in the stock of a subsidiary is increased by earnings and profits accumulated during consolidated return years. Thus, when a parent corporation disposes of a subsidiary any resulting gains are reduced or losses increased.

DISADVANTAGES OF CONSOLIDATED RETURNS

Some of the more important disadvantages of filing a consolidated return include the following:

1. Electing to file consolidated returns requires compliance with the consolidated return Regulations. This could create additional costs and administrative burdens.

2. The consolidated return election is binding for future years. This election can only be terminated by disbanding the affiliated group or by obtaining permission from the IRS to file separate returns.

3. In the initial consolidated return year, a double counting of inventory profit can occur if any of the group members had intercompany transactions in an affiliated separate return year.

4. Separate return credits and capital losses can be limited by operating losses and capital losses from other members of the group. Thus, the credit and loss carryovers may expire unused due to heavy losses by an affiliated member.

5. A subsidiary member is required to change its tax year to the same year as that of the common parent corporation. This can create a short tax year that is considered a complete tax year for purposes of carrybacks or carryovers in the case of unused losses and credits.

6. Losses of a subsidiary that reduce the tax liability of the group also decrease the parent's tax basis in the subsidiary. This serves to increase a gain or decrease a loss by the parent corporation on the sale of its subsidiary.

7. The rights of minority shareholders must be respected both legally and ethically. As a result, the presence of minority shareholders may create situations that may have adverse effects for the affiliated group.

ELIGIBILITY FOR FILING THE CONSOLIDATED RETURN

Code § 1501 grants an affiliated group the privilege of filing a consolidated tax return on the condition that all eligible members *elect* to do so. If a corporation is a member for a fractional part of a year, the consolidated return must include the income for the short period that the affiliate is a member of the group. As may be expected, these rules are precise and complex.

AFFILIATED GROUPS

The term *affiliated group* refers to one or more chains of includible corporations connected through stock ownership with a common parent corporation.[11] This definition contains two requirements that must be satisfied before the related corporations are treated as an affiliated group. First, the corporation must be an *includible corporation,* and second, the group must pass a *stock ownership test.* If a corporation fails either test, it is not eligible to file a consolidated return with the remaining qualifying corporations.

---

[11] § 1504.

Includible Corporations. The term includible corporation is defined by exception.[12] In other words, an includible corporation is any corporation other than one of the following entities:

1. A corporation exempt from taxation under § 501 (e.g., a non-profit organization)

2. A corporation electing a U.S. Possession tax credit under § 936

3. Certain life or mutual insurance companies not covered by a separate election[13]

4. A foreign corporation[14]

5. A regulated investment company or real estate investment trust

6. A Domestic International Sales Corporation (DISC)

7. An S corporation[15]

Stock Ownership Test. The stock ownership requirements are satisfied when the following tests are met:

1. An includible parent corporation owns directly at least 80 percent of the total voting power *and* 80 percent of the fair market value of the stock of at least one of the other includible corporations.

2. An includible corporation (other than the parent) has at least 80 percent of its voting stock *and* 80 percent of the fair market value of its nonvoting stock owned directly by one or more of the other corporations in the group.

The stock ownership test requires that a group must have a common parent [defined in (1) above] *and* at least one includible subsidiary [defined in (2) above]. If either test is not met, the group is ineligible for filing a consolidated return. When applying the stock ownership tests, nonvoting preferred stock which is not convertible into another class of stock or stock that does not significantly participate in corporate growth is generally ignored.

---

[12] § 1504(b).

[13] Two or more domestic insurance companies can be treated as includible corporations for purposes of filing a consolidated return for the insurance companies alone. See § 1504(c)(1) and Rev. Rul. 77-210, 1977-1 C.B. 267. For years beginning in 1981, insurance companies taxed under §§ 802 or 821, may elect to file consolidated returns with non–life insurance companies, subject to limitations under § 1504(c)(2).

[14] A limited exception exists for wholly owned Canadian or Mexican corporations.

[15] Although S corporations are not specifically excluded under § 1504(b), a provision under § 1361(b)(2)(A) prevents the corporation from becoming a member. A limited exception applies to the affiliated group prohibition where the affiliated corporations do not engage in business or produce gross income. § 1361(c)(6).

Example 2.   Individual A owns 100% of both J and K Corporations. J Corporation owns 60% of T Corporation, the remaining 40% of which is owned by K (see Exhibit 8-1). Neither J nor K qualifies as a parent corporation and consequently the group cannot file a consolidated tax return.[16] It should be noted that neither corporation is owned 80% or more by other corporations, so the second test is failed as well. Had J owned 80% of T, then both tests would have been met for the affiliated group composed of J and T.

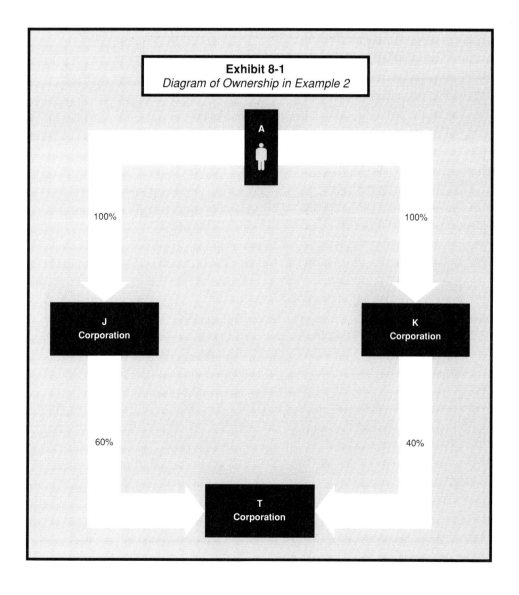

Exhibit 8-1
Diagram of Ownership in Example 2

---

[16] These corporations would fall within the controlled group provisions of §§ 1561 through 1564.

Example 3. P Corporation owns 100% of the stock of both E and F Corporations. E and F each owns 50% of the stock of G Corporation (see Exhibit 8-2). If all corporations are includible corporations, then P, E, F, and G are considered affiliated corporations with P as the parent. G is included in the affiliated group because it is more than 80% owned by other members of the group (E and F). The affiliated group composed of P, E, F, and G is eligible for filing a consolidated tax return.

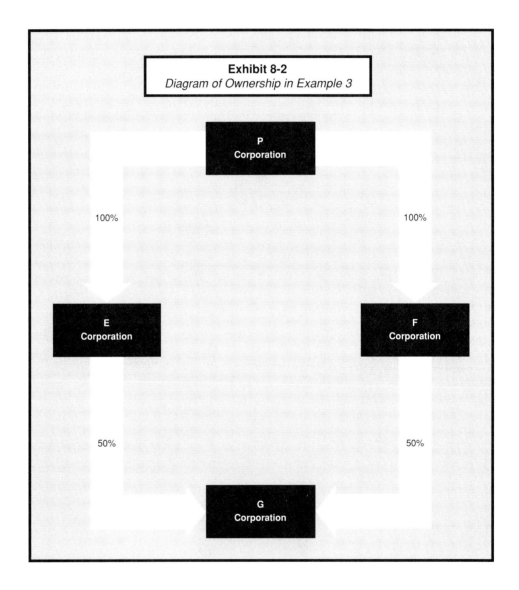

Exhibit 8-2
Diagram of Ownership in Example 3

Example 4.   P Corporation owns 80% of both L and S Corporations. L owns 100% of M Corporation and S owns 80% of both R and S Corporation. R and S own 80% and 20% of T Corporation, respectively (see Exhibit 8-3). If L is a newly formed life insurance company, M a second life insurance company, and S a regulated investment company, two affiliated groups exist. L and M make up an affiliated insurance group with L as the parent. P, S, R, and T make up a second affiliated group with P as the parent. L and M are not includible corporations within the exception of § 1504(c)(2) and S is not includible by definition. Although T is owned 20% by S (not an includible corporation), T is owned 80% by R, an includible corporation, so it is included within the affiliated group. Under a special rule, L and M are eligible to file their own consolidated tax return.

Affiliated Group versus Controlled Group.   An *affiliated group* is treated as a single taxable entity and is eligible to file a consolidated tax return. On the other hand, a *controlled group* is also treated as a single taxable entity, but may not satisfy the definition of affiliated group and thus be denied the privilege of filing a consolidated tax return. The rules defining an affiliated group are quite similar to those defining a parent-subsidiary relationship in a controlled group.[17] Indeed, at first glance these provisions appear to be identical. The fundamental difference, however, rests in the stipulation of "direct" ownership. An affiliated group requires direct ownership, while a parent-subsidiary controlled group does not. An example might best illustrate the differences.

Example 5.   X Corporation owns 70% of both Y and Z Corporations. The remaining 30% of Z is owned by Y and the remaining 30% of Y is owned by Z (see Exhibit 8-4). Under the provisions defining a controlled group, identical ownership is ignored so that X *indirectly* owns 100% of both Y and Z.[18] For purposes of an affiliated group, the 80% *direct* ownership test is not met and thus X, Y, and Z cannot file a consolidated tax return.

---

[17]   See Chapter 1 for a discussion of parent-subsidiary controlled groups.

[18]   See Reg. § 1.1563-1(a)(2) *Example 4* for a more detailed explanation.

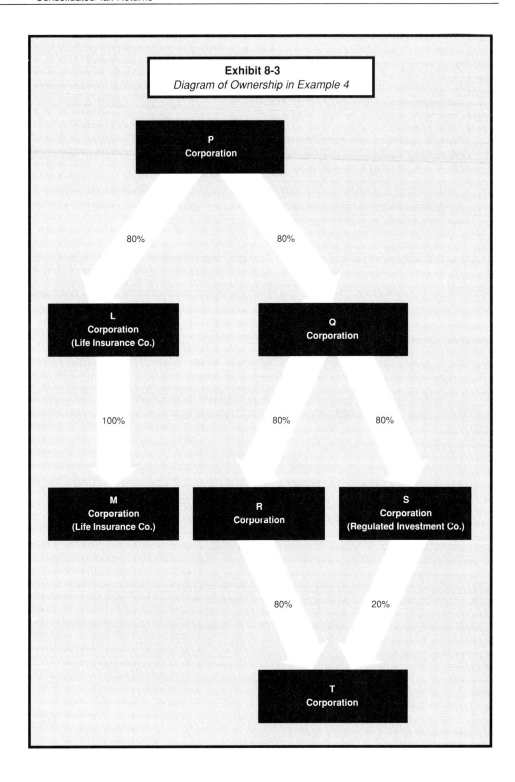

Exhibit 8-3
Diagram of Ownership in Example 4

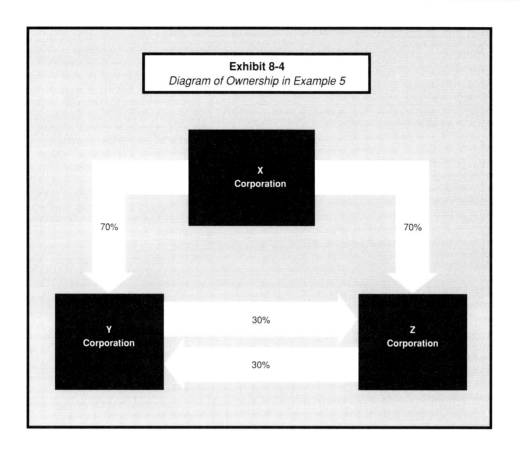

Exhibit 8-4
Diagram of Ownership in Example 5

X Corporation

70%

70%

Y Corporation

Z Corporation

30%

30%

THE ELECTION

If an affiliated group wishes to file a consolidated tax return, Form 1122 (see Exhibit 8-5) must be executed by each subsidiary indicating its consent to file on a consolidated basis. These consent forms must be attached to the initial consolidated tax return, Form 1120. The election must be filed on or before the common parent's due date (including extensions) for filing its tax return. The group can, at any time prior to the extended due date, change its decision and revoke its election to file a consolidated return. Once the extended due date passes, however, the election cannot be withdrawn,[19] and consolidated returns must be filed until the group terminates.

If any member of the group fails to file a consent form or does not join in the filing of a consolidated return, the tax liability of each member is determined as if separate returns were filed.[20] If the common parent can establish to the satisfaction of the Commissioner that the failure of the member to join in the filing was an inadvertent error, the election to file a consolidated tax return remains valid.

---

[19] Reg. § 1.1502-75(a)(1).   [20] Reg. § 1.1502-75(b)(3).

Exhibit 8-5
Consolidated Return Consent Form

Form **1122**
(Rev. December 1983)
Department of the Treasury
Internal Revenue Service

**Authorization and Consent of Subsidiary Corporation
to be Included in a Consolidated Income Tax Return**

(Please type or print)

▶   For the first year a consolidated return is filed, this form must be attached for each subsidiary.

For the calendar year 19____ , or other tax year beginning _____, 19____ and ending _____, 19____

Name	Employer identification number

Number and street

City or town, State, and ZIP code

Name of common parent corporation	Employer identification number

The subsidiary corporation named above authorizes its common parent corporation to include it in a consolidated return for the tax year indicated and for each later year the group must make a consolidated return under the regulations. If the parent corporation does not make a consolidated return on behalf of the subsidiary, the subsidiary authorizes the Commissioner or District Director of Internal Revenue to do so.

The subsidiary consents to be bound by the provisions of the consolidated return regulations.

Signature

Under penalties of perjury, I declare that the subsidiary named above has authorized me to sign this form on its behalf, that I have examined this form, and the information contained herein, and to the best of my knowledge and belief, it is true, correct, and complete.

▶ Signature of officer _____ Date ▶ Title _____

Form **1122** (Rev. 12-83)

DISCONTINUING THE ELECTION

Very often the advantages of filing consolidated returns lose their utility. When this occurs, the group may desire to discontinue its election. However, once a group has elected to file a consolidated return, it is bound by that decision as long as the group remains in existence. A group is generally considered to remain in existence if the common parent has at all times during the tax year at least one subsidiary that was a member of the group at any time during the year.[21]

> **Example 6.**   On January 2, 1990, P, a calendar year corporation, forms a wholly owned subsidiary, S. P and S file a consolidated tax return for 1990 and 1991. If P purchases all the stock of T Corporation on July 1, 1992, and sells all the stock of S on August 1, 1992, P Corporation is still required to file a consolidated return for 1992. In this case, P had at least one subsidiary (either S or T) at all times during the year. If, however, P had sold S and then one month later purchased T, a consolidated tax return could not be filed because there was a time when P had no subsidiary during the year.

---

[21]   Although a group normally terminates when a parent corporation ceases to exist, certain exceptions apply relating to reverse acquisitions, F reorganizations, and downstream mergers.

The election may be discontinued not only by disbanding the group, but also by securing permission of the IRS. Permission is granted only if the group can establish *good cause*. An application must be filed with the IRS at least 90 days before the due date of the tax return (including extensions). An example of a good cause would be a change in the law or regulations that has an adverse effect on the consolidated tax liability.[22] The Regulations also grant the Commissioner discretionary authority to issue blanket permission for all taxpayers to discontinue filing consolidated returns. This authority is generally exercised only when an amendment to the Code or Regulations has an adverse effect on a group or class of corporate taxpayers.[23]

If a corporation is included in a consolidated return and then ceases to be a member of the affiliated group, that corporation (or its successor) cannot return to be reincluded as a member of the affiliated group for a specified period. That period generally ends on the 61st month beginning after the corporation's first taxable year in which it ceased being a member of the group. The Commissioner, however, is authorized to waive application of this rule under conditions it deems appropriate.

DETERMINING THE YEAR INCOME IS REPORTED

According to the Regulations, a consolidated tax return must be filed on the basis of the common parent's tax year.[24] This requires a subsidiary that is not on the same tax year as the parent to make a change in its accounting period to conform to the taxable year of the parent. As a result, the consolidated tax return includes the parent's income for the entire tax year, and the subsidiary's income only for that portion of the year that it was a member of the group.[25] This usually means that a separate return must be filed by the subsidiary for the short period before it joins the group or for the period after it ceases to be a member.[26]

---

[22] Reg. § 1.1502-75(c)(1).

[23] Reg. § 1.1502-75(a)(2).

[24] Reg. § 1.1502-76(a)(1).

[25] Reg. § 1.1502-76(b)(1).

[26] Reg. § 1.1502-76(b)(2).

Example 7. P, S, and T file a consolidated tax return for 1991 on a calendar year basis. If P sells the stock of T to an individual on March 1, 1992, the consolidated tax return for 1992 includes the income of T from January 1 to March 1, 1992. T files a short-period tax return for the remaining 10 months (March through December). If on July 21, 1992, P purchases all the stock of X, a calendar year corporation, the consolidated tax return for 1992 must also include the income or loss for X from July 21 through December 31, 1992. X also must file a short period tax return for the period January 1 through July 20, 1992. If the short period is less than 30 days, an administrative provision, the "30-day rule" (discussed below), allows the subsidiary to waive the requirements for filing a separate return.

Filing a Separate Return. In filing the separate return, the subsidiary's income and deductions must be prorated between the consolidated and separate return years. The allocation can be done according to the permanent records or in proportion to the days of the year that the subsidiary was a member of the group. The due date for the separate return is generally the earlier of the subsidiary's ordinary due date or that of the consolidated tax return.

It should be noted that when a subsidiary files a separate return, the short period is treated as a separate taxable year.[27] This separate year is counted in determining the number of years that a loss or credit carryover can be applied.

The 30-Day Rule. If the conditions of the 30-day rule are satisfied, a tax return for the subsidiary's short year is optional. There are two 30-day rules: one applying when a subsidiary joins the group within the first 30 days of its tax year, the other applying when a subsidiary is a member of the group for less than 30 days.

1. A subsidiary may elect to be included as a member of the group from the beginning of its taxable year if it was acquired within the first 30 days of its taxable year.

2. A subsidiary may elect out of the group for the entire consolidated taxable year if it has been a member of the group for 30 days or less.

Example 8. P and S, affiliated calendar year corporations, have filed consolidated tax returns for the past two years. On January 17, 1992, P purchases all of the outstanding stock of T Corporation, which has been filing a separate tax return on a calendar year since 1988. Because T was purchased within the first 30 days of its tax year, it can elect to have its 1992 income from January 1, 1992 to January 16, 1992, taxed in the consolidated tax return for the calendar year 1992. If T makes no election, it must file a separate tax return for that 16-day period which counts as an entire year for purposes of loss and credit carryovers.

---

[27] Reg. § 1.1502-76(d).

Example 9.   Assume the same facts as in *Example 8*, except that T has been filing tax returns on a September 30 fiscal year. In this case, T is not eligible for the 30-day rule since it was not acquired within the first 30 days of its taxable year. As a result, T must file a separate tax return for the short period October 1, 1991 to January 16, 1992.

Example 10.   Assume the same facts as in *Example 8*, except that T was acquired on December 7, 1992. Since T has been a member of the group for less than 30 days, it can elect to exclude its income from the consolidated return filed for 1992. Making this election would require T to file a separate tax return for all of 1992.

COMPUTATION OF THE CONSOLIDATED TAX LIABILITY: AN OVERVIEW

The consolidated tax return evolved from the premise that the tax liability of a group of related corporations should be based on the results of transactions with parties that are not affiliated with the group. Accordingly, *consolidated taxable income* is generally thought of as simply the combination of the taxable incomes of each individual corporation with transactions between members of the group eliminated. Unfortunately, the actual tax computation is somewhat more complicated. The Regulations specifically provide that consolidated taxable income is the aggregate of (1) the separate taxable incomes of each member of the affiliated group, and (2) those items of income and deduction that must be excluded from the computation of separate taxable income and computed on a consolidated basis. The computation of consolidated taxable income normally involves three steps:

1.   The taxable income of each member corporation is determined as if it filed a separate return.

2.   Certain modifications are made to the taxable incomes computed in step 1 to eliminate (a) transactions between members of the group (e.g., a sale of property from one member to another), and (b) certain items that must be accounted for on a consolidated basis (e.g., capital gains). The result is called *separate taxable income*.

3.   The separate taxable incomes of each member corporation, including the necessary modifications, are combined with those items that must be stated on a consolidated basis to arrive at consolidated taxable income.

Example 11. P Corp. owns 100% of S Inc. P's taxable income during the year was $110,000, including a long-term capital gain of $4,000 and $6,000 of income attributable to a sale of land to S which S treated as a capital expenditure. S had taxable income of $50,000, including a $3,000 short-term capital loss. Consolidated taxable income is the aggregate of the separate taxable income of each corporation and those items which must be reported on a consolidated basis—in this case, the capital gains and losses. The separate taxable income of P is $100,000 ($110,000 total taxable income − $6,000 profit from sales to a member of the group − $4,000 capital gain that must be eliminated and restated on a consolidated basis), and the separate taxable income of S is $53,000 ($50,000 + $3,000 capital loss which must be eliminated and restated on a consolidated basis). The consolidation of each member's capital gains and losses of the group results in a long-term capital gain of $1,000 ($4,000 long-term capital gain of P − $3,000 short-term capital loss of S). Consolidated taxable income is $154,000 ($100,000 + $53,000 + $1,000).

A detailed discussion of the computation of consolidated taxable income follows.

SEPARATE TAXABLE INCOME

The first step in computing consolidated taxable income is to determine the *separate taxable income* of each member of the affiliated group. Separate taxable income is defined as the corporation's taxable income calculated as if it were filing separately except for two modifications. Notwithstanding the two modifications, the calculation of separate taxable income is made applying all of the principles normally encountered when a corporation determines its taxable income. As indicated above, the two modifications required to arrive at separate taxable income concern transactions between members of the affiliated group—so-called intercompany transactions—and certain items which must be computed on a consolidated basis.

Intercompany Transactions. The Regulations identify seven types of *intercompany transactions* which must be accounted for in a particular manner. These are listed below and discussed later in this chapter.

1. Deferred intercompany transactions[28]

2. Intercompany distributions with respect to a member's stock and redemptions of stock, bonds, or other obligations of members of the group[29]

3. Built-in deductions[30]

4. Mine exploration expenditures that are limited by Code § 617(h)[31]

---

[28] Reg. § 1.1502-13.

[29] Reg. § 1.1502-14.

[30] Reg. § 1.1502-15.

[31] Reg. § 1.1502-16.

5. Income or loss from changes in accounting methods[32]

6. Initial inventory adjustments[33]

7. Recapture of excess loss accounts[34]

Single-Entity Modifications. The second modification to separate taxable income concerns certain items which must be recomputed on a consolidated basis (e.g., as if one corporation made all of the charitable contributions). Each of the following items is eliminated in computing separate taxable income.

1. Net operating losses

2. Net capital gains and losses

3. Section 1231 gains and losses

4. Charitable contribution deductions

5. Dividends-received and dividends-paid deductions

CONSOLIDATED ITEMS

Once the separate taxable income of each member corporation is determined, calculations must be made concerning those items which must be treated on a consolidated basis. These items are the same as those that were eliminated from each group member's separate taxable income as noted above (e.g., the member's capital gains and losses and charitable contributions). The various items are combined as if the group were a single corporation. For example, the capital loss of one member offsets the capital gain of another member. In effect, the limitations that normally apply separately to each member are applied to the group as a whole. This can be very advantageous where one member has a net operating loss deduction since the deduction can be used to offset the income of another member thus producing immediate benefits (i.e., the loss does not have to be carried over to a year when the loss corporation has income which may never occur).

The combination of these various items results in the following:

1. The consolidated net operating loss deduction

2. The consolidated capital gain net income

3. The consolidated § 1231 loss

4. The consolidated casualty and theft loss

5. The consolidated charitable contributions deduction

6. The consolidated dividends-received and dividends-paid deduction

---

[32] Reg. § 1.1502-17.

[33] Reg. § 1.1502-18.

[34] Reg. § 1.1502-19.

COMPUTATION OF THE CONSOLIDATED TAX LIABILITY

After the separate taxable income of each member has been determined and the calculations concerning consolidated items have been completed, *consolidated taxable income* may be computed. Consolidated taxable income is determined by combining the separate taxable income of each member with the consolidated items above. This amount is then multiplied by the tax rates normally applying to corporations to determine the group's gross tax. From this amount, the group may deduct any consolidated credits and prepayments to arrive at the net tax liability. The process for computing the consolidated tax liability is presented in Exhibit 8-6 and applied in Exhibits 8-7 and 8-8.

DUAL RESIDENT CORPORATIONS

The Tax Reform Act of 1986 modified Code § 1503(d) to disallow a loss in consolidation for certain "dual resident" corporations. This subsection provides that if a U.S. corporation is subject to a foreign country's tax on worldwide income, any taxable loss it incurs cannot again reduce the taxable income of any other member of a U.S. affiliated group. This provision is effective for taxable years beginning after 1986. Carryforward losses of dual resident corporations incurred prior to 1987 are still available to offset income of other members of U.S. affiliated groups.

INTERCOMPANY TRANSACTIONS

An *intercompany transaction* is defined as a transaction that occurs during a consolidated return year between two or more members of the same affiliated group. However, distributions (dividends, redemptions, or liquidations) between members and dispositions of member obligations (or bad debts with respect to such obligations) are not considered intercompany transactions.[35] If the transaction involves the sale or exchange of property between members or an expenditure that would be capitalized by the acquiring member, it is referred to as a *deferred intercompany transaction* and receives special treatment.[36] Gains or losses on exchanges that are not deferred intercompany transactions are not deferred or eliminated in the consolidation calculation—even though they occur between affiliated members. Deferral or elimination is not necessary since the tax consequences of the transaction for both parties are closed within the same taxable year of both parties. These latter transactions are often referred to as "nondeferred intercompany transactions."

---

[35]   Reg. § 1.1502-13(a)(1)(ii).   [36]   Reg. § 1.1502-13(a)(2).

Exhibit 8-6
The Consolidated Tax Formula

Combine separate taxable incomes to arrive at combined taxable income.

Eliminate:
Intercompany dividends
Disallowed built-in deductions
Net operating loss deductions
Capital gains and losses
Section 1231 gains and losses
Charitable contribution deductions
Dividends-received deductions

Adjust for:
Deferred intercompany gains and losses
Gains and losses on nondividend intercompany distributions
Intercompany profits in inventory
Excess losses of affiliates

Deduct:
Consolidated net operating losses
Consolidated § 1231 losses
Consolidated charitable contributions
Consolidated dividends-received deduction
Consolidated dividends-paid deduction

Add:
Consolidated net capital gains

Equals: Consolidated taxable income

Exhibit 8-7
Example of Computing Consolidated Tax Liability

Descriptions	P	S	T	Combined	Consolidating Adjustments *(see below)		Consolidated
					No.	Amount	
Gross Income:							
Gross receipts	$330,000	$ 80,000	$20,000	$430,000			$430,000
Cost of goods sold	100,000	25,000	5,000	130,000			130,000
Gross profit	$230,000	$55,000	$15,000	$300,000			$300,000
Dividends	50,000	10,000	5,000	65,000	1.	($50,000)	15,000
Other interest	70,000	6,000	2,000	78,000			78,000
Net capital gains	12,000			12,000	2.	(9,000)	3,000
Total income	$362,000	$ 71,000	$22,000	$455,000		($59,000)	$396,000
Deductions:							
Compensation of officers	$ 50,000	$ 25,000	$ 9,600	$ 84,600			$ 84,600
Salaries and wages	120,000	30,000	3,300	153,300			153,300
Repairs	6,000	4,200	1,000	11,200			11,200
Bad debts	3,000	2,000	700	5,700			5,700
Rents	7,200	6,000	3,000	16,200			16,200
Taxes	1,500	1,000	900	3,400			3,400
Interest	1,000	2,200	1,200	4,400			4,400
Contributions	4,000		200	4,200	3.	($ 4,200)	0
Depreciation	56,000	104,800	800	161,600			161,600
Advertising	1,400	2,100	100	3,600			3,600
Other deductions	900	1,000		1,900			1,900
Total deductions	$251,000	$178,300	$20,800	$450,100		($ 4,200)	$445,900
Taxable income (loss) before NOL and special deductions	$111,000	($107,300)	$ 1,200	$ 4,900		($54,800)	($ 49,900)
NOL Deduction		(20,000)		(20,000)	4.	20,000	0
Special Deductions	(50,000)	(8,000)	(4,000)	(62,000)	1.	50,000	(12,000)
Taxable income (loss)	$ 61,000	($135,300)	($ 2,800)	($ 77,100)		$15,200	($ 61,900)

*Explanation:
1. To eliminate intercompany dividends from T to P.
2. To record a separate company capital loss not deductible by S but which may be used to offset P's capital gain.
3. To eliminate the contribution deductions since consolidated taxable income is a loss.
4. To eliminate SRLY NOL by S (explained within).

Exhibit 8-8
U. S. Corporation Income Tax Return

Form **1120**	**U.S. Corporation Income Tax Return**		OMB No. 1545-0123
Department of the Treasury Internal Revenue Service	For calendar year 1990 or tax year beginning _____ 1990, ending _____, 19 ____ ▶ Instructions are separate. See page 1 for Paperwork Reduction Act Notice.		**1990**

Check if a—		Name		**D** Employer identification number
A Consolidated return ☒	Use IRS label. Other- wise, please print or type.	PINC. AND INCLUDIBLE SUBSIDIARIES		76-5432104
B Personal holding co. ☐		Number, street, and room or suite no. (If a P.O. box, see page 2 of Instructions.)		**E** Date incorporated
C Personal service corp.(as defined in Temp. Regs. sec. 1.441-4T—see Instructions) ☐		5757 WESTHEIMER		AUGUST 1, 1986
		City or town, state, and ZIP code		**F** Total assets (see Specific Instructions)
		HOUSTON, TEXAS 77027		$ 592,874

G Check applicable boxes: (1) ☐ Initial return (2) ☐ Final return (3) ☐ Change in address

Income

1a	Gross receipts or sales _____ **b** Less returns and allowances _____ **c** Bal ▶	1c	430,000
2	Cost of goods sold (Schedule A, line 7)	2	130,000
3	Gross profit (line 1c less line 2)	3	300,000
4	Dividends (Schedule C, line 19)	4	15,000
5	Interest	5	78,000
6	Gross rents	6	—
7	Gross royalties	7	
8	Capital gain net income (attach Schedule D (Form 1120))	8	3,000
9	Net gain or (loss) from Form 4797, Part II, line 18 (attach Form 4797)	9	—
10	Other income (see Instructions—attach schedule)	10	
11	**Total income**—Add lines 3 through 10 ▶	11	396,000

Deductions (See Instructions for limitations on deductions.)

12	Compensation of officers (Schedule E, line 4)	12	84,600
13a	Salaries and wages _____ **b** Less jobs credit _____ **c** Balance ▶	13c	153,300
14	Repairs	14	11,200
15	Bad debts	15	5,700
16	Rents	16	16,200
17	Taxes	17	3,400
18	Interest	18	4,400
19	Contributions (**see Instructions for 10% limitation**)	19	—
20	Depreciation (attach Form 4562) 20	161,600	
21	Less depreciation claimed on Schedule A and elsewhere on return . . 21a	—0—	21b 161,600
22	Depletion	22	—
23	Advertising	23	3,600
24	Pension, profit-sharing, etc., plans	24	—
25	Employee benefit programs	25	—
26	Other deductions (attach schedule) ▶	26	1,900
27	**Total deductions**—Add lines 12 through 26. ▶	27	445,900
28	Taxable income before net operating loss deduction and special deductions (line 11 less line 27) .	28	49,900
29	**Less: a** Net operating loss deduction (see Instructions) 29a	—	
	b Special deductions (Schedule C, line 20) 29b	12,000	29c 12,000
30	**Taxable income**—Line 28 less line 29c . (LOSS)	30	(61,900)
31	Total tax (Schedule J, line 10)	31	NONE

Tax and Payments

32	Payments: **a** 1989 overpayment credited to 1990 32a		
	b 1990 estimated tax payments . . 32b	2,000	
	c Less 1990 refund applied for on Form 4466 32c ( ) **d** Bal ▶ 32d		
	e Tax deposited with Form 7004 . . . . 32e		
	f Credit from regulated investment companies (attach Form 2439) . . 32f		
	g Credit for Federal tax on fuels (attach Form 4136). See Instructions . 32g		32h 2,000
33	Enter any **penalty** for underpayment of estimated tax—Check ▶ ☐ if Form 2220 is attached .	33	
34	**Tax due**—If the total of lines 31 and 33 is larger than line 32h, enter amount owed	34	
35	**Overpayment**—If line 32h is larger than the total of lines 31 and 33, enter amount overpaid . .	35	2,000
36	Enter amount of line 35 you want: **Credited to 1991 estimated tax** ▶ _____ **Refunded** ▶	36	NONE

Please Sign Here

Under penalties of perjury, I declare that I have examined this return, including accompanying schedules and statements, and to the best of my knowledge and belief, it is true, correct, and complete. Declaration of preparer (other than taxpayer) is based on all information of which preparer has any knowledge.

▶ *Mary Elizabeth Andrews* | 2/15/91 ▶ PRESIDENT
Signature of officer / Date / Title

Paid Preparer's Use Only

Preparer's signature ▶ *Roy W. Hartman*	Date 2/7/91	Check if self-employed ☐	Preparer's social security number
Firm's name (or yours if self-employed) and address ▶ TAXCO, P.C. 321 MAIN BLVD. HOUSTON, TX		E.I. No. ▶ 74-1897265 ZIP code ▶ 77001	

Example 12.   Corporations P, S, and T form an affiliated group. If T performs maintenance services for P during the year, the income reported by T and the deduction taken by P offset each other in consolidation. In other words, the tax effect of the exchange was closed within the same taxable year for both corporations. This exchange is a nondeferred intercompany transaction and is not eliminated in consolidation.

Example 13.   Assume the same facts as in *Example 12*, except that T makes repairs to equipment instead of performing maintenance. If the repairs are of a material nature that require capitalization, the transaction is a deferred intercompany transaction because T's income will not be offset by P's depreciation deduction in consolidation. In contrast to *Example 12* above, the tax effect of the transaction for both P and T is not closed in the same taxable year. T has income in the current year while P's expense is deducted over several years.

Special Rule for Different Accounting Methods.   A special rule exists for nondeferred intercompany transactions that are not reported by both parties in the same year. The rule states that if an item of income or deduction is taken into account by one member in a consolidated return year and another member takes the corresponding income or deduction in a later year, then both members *must postpone* the income and deduction to the later year.[37]   This is true even if the later year becomes a separate return year. If the item of income or deduction is first taken into account during a separate return before consolidation, this special rule does not apply.

Example 14.   Affiliate S accrues an interest deduction on an obligation to parent P. P maintains its books and records on a cash basis. By definition, this is not an intercompany transaction requiring deferral. However, since S has an opportunity to take an interest deduction before P must recognize the interest income, the special rule for differing accounting methods applies. S is not entitled to the deduction until P properly recognizes the income under its accounting method.

DEFERRED INTERCOMPANY TRANSACTIONS

Intercompany profits and losses on deferred intercompany transactions are deferred by recording them in a suspense account until the occurrence of a specified event. Once the event occurs—referred to as a *restoration event*—the ultimate profit or loss is recognized by the particular member that originally realized it.

The realized gain or loss to be deferred is essentially the net profit or loss on the transaction. In determining the net profit or loss, the cost basis of the property includes both direct and indirect costs. Otherwise, a mismatching of

---

[37]   Reg. § 1.1502-13(b)(2).

indirect expenses and income might occur.[38] Deferral rules also prohibit the selling member from using the installment sales method in determining when gain or loss is to be recognized.[39]

The basis of property acquired in an intercompany transaction includes the deferred gain or loss even though the selling member does not recognize it. The holding period begins on the date of acquisition by the buying member and does not include the holding period of the selling member.[40]

> **Example 15.** Corporations L and K file consolidated returns on a calendar year. On July 21, 1992, L sells an investment asset to K for $40,000. L originally paid $11,000 for the asset in 1988. Due to the deferral rules, L reports no gain and K's basis for the asset is $40,000. If K sells the asset on August 1, 1992 for $46,000 to an unrelated party, L reports a long-term capital gain of $29,000 ($40,000 − $11,000) and K reports a short-term capital gain of $6,000 ($46,000 − $40,000).

Restoration Events. The events that trigger restoration can be classified into two categories: (1) those that require a portion of the deferred gain or loss to be recognized, and (2) those that require recognition of the entire gain or loss. Those in the first category include the following:[41]

1. The depreciation, amortization, or depletion of the property acquired in a deferred intercompany transaction

2. The sale of property on the installment basis to a nonmember where the property sold was acquired in an intercompany transaction

3. The write-down of inventory to market that was acquired in a deferred intercompany transaction

Those events that trigger recognition of any deferred gain or loss in its entirety include:

1. The disposition of property outside of the group (other than an installment sale) where the property was acquired in an intercompany transaction

2. The cessation of the selling or purchasing member's affiliation with the group

3. The filing of a separate return by either the purchasing or selling member of the entire group (e.g., when the IRS grants permission to discontinue filing consolidated returns)

4. The worthlessness or satisfaction of an obligation (other than an obligation of the group) transferred in an intercompany transaction

---

[38] Reg. § 1.1502-13(c)(2).

[39] Reg. § 1.1502-13(c)(1)(ii).

[40] Reg. § 1.1502-13(g).

[41] Reg. § 1.1502-13(d).

If a deferred gain is reported by a selling member because of depreciation, depletion, or amortization taken by the purchasing member, the gain is characterized as ordinary income even though it ordinarily would have been characterized as § 1231 or capital gain. Otherwise, the character of the gain or loss is determined at the time the transaction occurs. The following examples illustrate the deferral accounting system.

Example 16.   Corporations P, S, and T file consolidated returns on a calendar year basis. On January 1, 1990, S, which is in the business of manufacturing machinery, sells a machine to P for $1,000. The cost of the machine is $800. P uses the machine in its trade or business and depreciates the machine using MACRS over a 10-year period. Thus, the annual depreciation for 1990 is $100 ($1,000 × 10%) and $180 ($1,000 × 18%) for 1991. On January 1, 1992, P sells the machine to Z, an individual.

The sale by S to P is a deferred intercompany transaction since the expenditure must be capitalized by P. S defers its $200 gain on the sale ($1,000 − $800) which is characterized as ordinary income. For the years 1990 and 1991, S takes into account $20, and $36 of income, respectively, computed as follows:

$$1990 = \frac{\$200 \text{ deferred}}{\text{gain}} \times \frac{\$100 \text{ depreciation deduction}}{\$1,000 \text{ basis to P subject to depreciation}} = \$20$$

$$1991 = \frac{\$200 \text{ deferred}}{\text{gain}} \times \frac{\$180 \text{ depreciation deduction}}{\$1,000 \text{ basis to P subject to depreciation}} = \$36$$

Upon the sale to Z on January 1, 1992, S takes into account the remaining balance of the deferred gain or $144 [$200 − ($20 + $36)] because the machine is disposed of outside the group.[42]

Example 17.   P and its wholly owned subsidiary, S, file consolidated tax returns on a calendar year basis. On January 10, 1990, S sells land with a basis of $60,000 to P for $100,000. On July 3, 1992, P sells 25% of the outstanding stock of S to Z, an individual. The sale of land from S to P is a deferred intercompany transaction. Thus S defers the $40,000 gain on the sale of land ($100,000 − $60,000). On July 3, 1992, S takes the $40,000 gain into account for 1992 since it ceases to be a member of the affiliated group as of July 3, 1992.

Election to Report Currently.   With the consent of the IRS, a group may elect not to defer gain or loss on *all* deferred intercompany transactions. In such a case, the gain or loss is recognized at the time of the transaction. Once approved, the

---

[42]   Reg. § 1.1502-13(h), *Example 4.*

election is binding to all future consolidated return years unless permission to revoke is given.[43] Such an election may be useful to eliminate laborious book-keeping chores, especially for multiple intercompany transactions or transfers of long-lived assets.

Other Provisions Affecting Deferred Intercompany Transactions. For sales of assets that occur after 1983, special rules exist that may further defer a loss on the sale of those assets beyond the rules found in the consolidated return regulations. In general, the Tax Reform Act of 1984 and temporary regulations attempt to establish a relationship between Code § 267(f) and the rules for controlled groups and consolidated tax returns.[44] If a member of an *affiliated* group ceases to be a member of that group but continues to be a member of a *controlled* group immediately after deconsolidation, temporary regulations under § 267(f), in many instances, override the restoration rules previously discussed for deferred intercompany transactions. In addition, any election "not to defer" a loss is inapplicable and has no effect.[45]

> **Example 18.** P and its wholly owned subsidiary S join in the filing of a consolidated tax return for taxable year 1990 in which P sells property to S for a loss. Due to the deferral requirements, the loss is eliminated in consolidation. On January 1, 1991, all of the stock of S is transferred to P's sole shareholder. Although P and S are no longer affiliated corporations and must file separate tax returns, they remain members of a controlled group and restoration of the loss will not take place.

INVENTORY ADJUSTMENTS

Ordinarily, intercompany sales of inventory are treated like other deferred intercompany transactions and no special attention is necessary. However, a series of complicated adjustments is required where the selling member[46]

1. Is a member of the group filing a consolidated tax return for the current year;

2. Was a member of the group for the immediately preceding tax year;

3. Filed a separate return for that preceding year; and

4. Sold inventory to other member corporations that remained unsold at the end of the separate return year.

The reason a special adjustment must be made can best be explained by the following example.

---

[43] Reg. § 1.1502-13(c)(3).

[44] Reg. §§ 1.267(f)-1T and 1.267(f)-2T.

[45] Reg. § 1.267(f)-2T(c).

[46] Reg. § 1.1502-18(b).

Example 19. During 1991, wholly owned subsidiary S sells to its parent, P, widgets A through E for P's future resale outside of the group. During 1992, S sells to P widgets F through H. For 1991 and 1992, P, using a FIFO basis, sells two widgets (A and B) and three widgets (C, D, and E) outside of the group, respectively. These facts are presented in the following table.

S Corporation			P Corporation		
1991	Cost	Sale to P	1991	Cost	Sales to Nonmembers
Widget A	$100	$150	Widget A	$150	$400
B	125	180	B	180	350
C	135	195	C	195	Ending Inventory
D	145	210	D	210	Ending Inventory
E	150	225	E	225	Ending Inventory
	$655	$960			
1992			1992		
Widget F	$160	$240	Widget C	$195	$400
G	170	260	D	210	400
H	180	280	E	225	400
	$510	$780	F	240	Ending Inventory
			G	260	Ending Inventory
			H	280	Ending Inventory

For the year 1991, if S and P file separate tax returns, S will show a profit of $305 ($960 − $655) and P will show a profit of $420 ($750 − $330). If S and P continue to file separate returns for 1992, S will show a profit of $270 ($780 − $510) and P will show a profit of $570 ($1,200 − $630). If, however, S and P elect to file a consolidated return for 1992, P will still report a profit of $570 for the sales to nonmembers. S, on the other hand, will not report *any* of its $270 profit for the year since all profits on the sales to P (widgets F, G, and H) must be deferred under the intercompany transaction rules. The $270 profit is not reported because (1) 1992 is a consolidated return year, and (2) on a FIFO basis, widgets F, G, and H still remain in P's inventory. S does not have to report any profits on the sale of widgets F, G, and H until a restoration event occurs (e.g., sale to an unrelated party). Note that this deferral occurs only because all four of the conditions noted above have been satisfied.

As the example demonstrates, by electing to file a consolidated return when there is preconsolidation intercompany inventory (e.g., 1992), a dip in reported profits takes place. To address this problem, the Regulations require a special adjustment.

Definitions. In order to calculate the amount of the special inventory adjustment, several terms must be defined.

Intercompany Profit Amount: The intercompany profits attributable to goods that remain in the inventory of group members at the close of the taxable year.[47]

> **Example 20.** Assume the same facts as in *Example 19*. The intercompany profit amount is determined in reference to the intercompany sales from S to P that remained in P's inventory at the end of the year. For 1991 this amounts to $200 (the sum of S's profits on widgets C, D, and E) and for 1992 $270 (the sum of S's profits on widgets F, G, and H).

Initial Inventory Amount: The corporation's intercompany profit amount that existed on the first day of the year for which the group filed its initial consolidated tax return.[48]

> **Example 21.** Assume the same facts as in *Example 19*. The initial inventory amount is $200, representing the intercompany profits of S which are reflected in the opening inventory of P for the first consolidated return year, 1992 (i.e., the closing inventory of P for 1991). The $200 represents the profits in widgets C, D, and E.

Unrecovered Inventory Amount: The lesser of the intercompany profit amount for the current year *or* the initial inventory amount. In a year that a corporation ceases to be a member of a group, its unrecovered inventory amount is considered to be zero.[49]

> **Example 22.** Assume the same facts as in *Example 19*. The unrecovered inventory amount for 1992 is $200. This represents the smaller of the initial inventory amount of $200 (*Example 21*) or the intercompany profit amount for 1992 of $270 (*Example 20*).

Making the Adjustments. As indicated earlier, the primary purpose for making the inventory adjustments is to prevent abnormal distortions of income that would result from filing consolidated returns with preconsolidation intercompany inventory. Thus, the Regulations require that the initial inventory amount must be added to ordinary income of the selling company (S in *Example 19*) in the first year that the inventory is sold outside the group or the selling member leaves the group.[50]

> **Example 23.** Assume the same facts as in *Example 19*. The adjustment for 1992 requires that S recognize the initial inventory amount of $200. Note that this adjustment is required even though S reported the profits in widgets C, D, and E on its separate return in 1991.

---

[47] Reg. § 1.1502-18(a). This definition does not include amounts for which an election not to defer intercompany profits has been made, nor does it include amounts that have been included in income as the result of a restoration event.

[48] Reg. § 1.1502-18(b).

[49] Reg. § 1.1502-18(c).

[50] Reg. § 1.1502-18(b).

It becomes apparent from this example that the inventory adjustment often results in a duplication of profits. In order to compensate for the double counting, a *recovery* of the initial inventory amount occurs when the beginning inventory is disposed of outside of the group. The recovery is in the form of an ordinary deduction and is taken only during a consolidated return year. The deduction is the amount that the current unrecovered inventory amount decreases from that of the previous year.[51] To the extent that the unrecovered inventory amount exceeds that of the preceding year, ordinary income must be recognized.

Example 24. Assume the same facts as in *Example 19*. Although the initial inventory amount (intercompany profits in inventory on first day of consolidated year) of $200 must be included in income in the first year, a deduction is allowed if the intercompany profit drops at the end of the year (see next example). In this case, however, intercompany profits have not dropped but rather increased to $270. No additional income must be reported since the unrecovered inventory amount has not changed [1991 $200 and 1992 $200 (the lesser of $200 initial inventory amount or $270, the intercompany profits amount for 1992)].

Example 25. During 1988, P Corporation forms wholly owned subsidiary S to manufacture its inventory. During 1988, P and S file separate returns, but for the year 1989 elect to file a consolidated tax return. For the years 1988 through 1992 the records indicate the following inventory transactions. In each case, the entire ending inventory is sold in the first few months of the subsequent year.

	1988	1989	1990	1991	1992
Intercompany profit amount in ending inventory P............	$12,000	$8,000	$5,000	$7,000	$14,000

Because P and S filed separate returns for 1988 and have inventory that remained unsold at the end of the year, a special adjustment becomes necessary. The initial inventory amount is $12,000 (the intercompany profit amount for the last separate return year) and must be included as ordinary income in the first consolidated tax return. The unrecovered inventory amount must be computed next. The result for each year is presented below.

	1989	1990	1991	1992
1. Initial inventory amount...................	$12,000	$12,000	$12,000	$12,000
2. Intercompany profit amount..............	8,000	5,000	7,000	14,000
3. Unrecovered inventory amount (smaller of 1. or 2.).....................	8,000	5,000	7,000	12,000

---

[51] In the case of the first consolidated return year, the ordinary deduction is the amount by which the unrecovered inventory amount decreases from the initial inventory amount.

For 1989, the unrecovered inventory amount decreased by $4,000 from the initial inventory amount (which is also the unrecovered inventory amount for the previous year) of $12,000. Thus, a $4,000 ordinary deduction is taken for 1989. Note that the $4,000 deduction is in addition to the $12,000 of income reported as the initial inventory amount. Consequently, the net change in taxable income for 1989 is $8,000 ($12,000 − $4,000). For 1990, consolidated taxable income is reduced by an ordinary deduction of $3,000 (the decrease in the unrecovered inventory amount from $8,000 to $5,000). In 1991 consolidated taxable income includes an additional $2,000 due to the increase in the unrecovered inventory amount ($5,000 to $7,000). In 1992 the increase is $5,000 ($7,000 to $12,000).

For the first separate return year following a consolidated tax return, any unrecovered inventory amount is treated as an ordinary deduction by the seller.[52] This deduction is warranted because it serves to equalize any duplication of profits in the initial consolidated return year.

Example 26. Assume the same facts as in *Example 25* and that on January 1, 1993 P sells all the stock of S to individual A. Since S must now file a separate tax return for 1993, it is entitled to deduct as an ordinary deduction the unrecovered inventory amount of $12,000.[53]

INTERCOMPANY DISTRIBUTIONS

Whether income is recognized on an intercompany distribution depends on the type of distribution that is made. As a general rule, a distribution paid out of earnings and profits (i.e., a dividend) is eliminated from gross income in the consolidated tax return.[54] Because the dividends are eliminated, no dividends-received deduction is available with respect to these dividends.[55] To the extent that a distribution is not a dividend [i.e., a return of capital under §§ 301(c)(2) and (3)], the distributee reduces its basis in the stock of the subsidiary. Contrary to the case under the separate return rules, if the distribution exceeds basis, gain is not recognized. Instead, it is deferred in an account known as an *excess loss account* until the occurrence of some subsequent event such as the sale of a subsidiary's stock. The excess loss account is discussed in detail later in this chapter.

---

[52] Note that any initial inventory amount that has not been included in income because the inventory has not been disposed outside of the group will reduce the final year ordinary deduction.

[53] Recall that according to the definition of the unrecovered inventory amount, in the year a corporation ceases to be a group member, the unrecovered inventory amount is zero. The definition conforms to the practice of taking as an ordinary deduction the decrease in the unrecovered inventory amount, in this case from $12,000 in 1992 to 0 in 1993.

[54] Reg. § 1.1502-14(a).

[55] Reg. § 1.1502-26(b).

Example 27. P and its newly created subsidiary S file a consolidated tax return for 1991. During the year, S distributes $12,000 cash to P. P's basis in its S stock is $7,000 and S has current earnings and profits for its first year of $4,000. For 1990, no gain is recognized. The first $4,000 is treated as a dividend and eliminated in consolidation. The next $7,000 reduces P's basis under § 301(c)(2) to zero. The remaining $1,000 is not taxed as a capital gain but simply increases the excess loss account.

If, as a result of a property distribution, the *distributing* corporation is required to recognize gain or loss, the amount of the gain or loss is to be treated under the intercompany transaction rules. The basis of the property to the distributee is the basis of the property in the hands of the distributing subsidiary increased by any gain recognized on the distribution.

CONSOLIDATED ITEMS

As indicated above, certain items must be eliminated from separate taxable income and accounted for on a consolidated basis. Each of these items is examined below.

THE CONSOLIDATED NET OPERATING LOSS

Perhaps the most important advantage of a consolidated return is that the net operating losses of one group member can be used currently to offset the taxable income of another member. This benefit is often the major reason for electing to file a consolidated return.

To arrive at the consolidated NOL, the first step is to determine each member's separate taxable income or loss. This calculation is made without regard to any NOL *carryovers* or *carrybacks* to the current taxable year. The separate taxable incomes and NOLs are then combined. If the separate NOLs exceed the separate taxable incomes, a consolidated NOL results. Only the consolidated NOL may be carried back or over. In computing the consolidated NOL which is carried over or back, certain items eliminated in computing separate taxable income are taken into account. The items generally restored are the dividends-received deduction, the charitable contribution deduction, the net capital gains or losses, and the § 1231 loss.[56] The consolidated net operating loss can be carried back or carried over subject to certain limitations discussed later in this chapter.

---

[56]   Reg. § 1.1502-21(f).

CONSOLIDATED CAPITAL GAINS AND LOSSES

The Regulations require that capital gains and losses must be computed and reported on a consolidated basis. The first step in the computation is to separate capital gains and losses for each member of the group. The consolidated capital gain net income is then determined by taking into account the following:[57]

1. The aggregate of capital gains and losses from the affiliated members

2. The consolidated § 1231 gains

3. The consolidated net capital loss carryovers

> **Example 28.** Corporations P, S, and T file consolidated tax returns for 1991 and 1992. In 1992 the members had the following capital asset transactions:
>
> 1. P sold to T a § 1231 asset for $12,000 (basis of $8,000).
>
> 2. S sold an asset to an unrelated individual for $1,000. S had purchased the asset from P in 1991 for $3,000. P had deferred a capital gain of $800 on the sale to S.
>
> 3. T sold an asset to an unrelated individual for $15,000 (basis of $7,000).
>
> 4. The group had a consolidated capital loss carryover of $5,000.
>
> The consolidated net capital gain for the group is determined as follows:

P's net capital gain restored into income due to S's disposal	$ 800
T's net capital gain ($15,000 − $7,000)	8,000
S's net capital gain ($1,000 − $3,000)	(2,000)
Capital loss carryover	(5,000)
The $4,000 gain ($12,000 − $8,000) on P's intercompany transaction is not taken into account for this year	0
Consolidated net capital gain	$1,800

Consolidated net capital losses cannot be used to offset consolidated taxable income. An analysis of capital losses and possible limitations is continued in the discussion on loss carryovers later in this chapter.

---

[57] Reg. § 1.1502-22(a)(1).

THE CONSOLIDATED DIVIDENDS-RECEIVED DEDUCTION

The rules for determining the consolidated dividends-received deduction for non-member dividends (intercompany dividends are eliminated) are essentially the same as the computations performed on a separate company basis.[58] The only difference is that the (70 or 80) percent limitation is based on consolidated taxable income excluding the consolidated NOL deduction, the consolidated net capital loss carryback, and the consolidated dividends-paid deduction for certain dividends under § 247.

> **Example 29.** Corporations P, S, T, and U file a consolidated tax return for the year showing consolidated taxable income of $90,000. The companies received dividends during the year from less than 20% owned nonmember domestic corporations as follows:

Corp.	Nonmember Dividends	Separate Taxable Income
P	$ 10,000	$20,000
S	20,000	30,000
T	70,000	40,000
U	0	(10,000)
	$100,000	$80,000

> The dividends-received deduction is limited to the lesser of 70% of $100,000 (the domestic dividends) or 70% of $80,000 (consolidated taxable income) unless a net operating loss is generated for the year. Since an NOL is not created, the dividends-received deduction is limited to $56,000 (70% × $80,000). Notice that on a separate company basis, the aggregate of the dividends-received deductions would produce a $70,000 deduction determined as follows:

Corp.	Deduction	
P	$ 7,000	($10,000 × 70%)
S	14,000	($20,000 × 70%)
T	49,000*	($70,000 × 70%)
	$70,000	

> * This amount is not limited to 70% of $40,000 because the deduction would create a net operating loss.

---

[58] For a discussion, see Chapter 1.

THE CONSOLIDATED CHARITABLE CONTRIBUTION DEDUCTION

The amount that can be deducted as a consolidated charitable contribution is the *lesser* of the following computations.

1. The combined charitable contributions of the individual group members (before limitations) plus any consolidated charitable contribution carryovers to the current year

2. 10 percent of adjusted consolidated taxable income[59]

Adjusted taxable income is consolidated taxable income computed without regard to the dividends-received or the dividends-paid deductions, consolidated loss carryovers, and the consolidated charitable contribution deduction itself.[60]

To the extent that the consolidated charitable contribution exceeds the limitation, the excess amount plus any remaining contributions from separate return years can be carried over to the next year. The five-year carryforward of § 170(d) also applies to the consolidated charitable contribution deduction. If an affiliated corporation ceases to be a member of the group, part of the contribution carryover attributable to the member must be allocated to it. The Regulations prescribe the manner for making this allocation.[61]

THE CONSOLIDATED TAX LIABILITY

For corporations other than insurance companies, the consolidated tax liability consists of one or more of the following taxes:

1. The § 11 corporate income tax on consolidated taxable income

2. The § 541 tax on consolidated undistributed personal holding company income

3. The § 531 tax on consolidated accumulated taxable income

4. The § 58 alternative minimum tax liability on consolidated tax preference items

Instead of the § 11 income tax, the group may elect to use the alternative tax under § 1201 to the extent that consolidated net capital gains exceed consolidated net capital losses, but only for tax years beginning before July 1, 1987. In addition, the group is only entitled to a single graduated tax bracket amount

---

[59] The Regulations still state 5 percent, but the IRS has conformed to the 10 percent amount under Code § 170. Reg. § 1.1502-24(a)(1) and (2).

[60] Reg. § 1.1502-24(c).

[61] Reg. § 1.1502-79(e)(2).

under the controlled group limitations of § 1561(a). For purposes of applying the additional 5 percent surtax on corporations having taxable income in excess of $100,000, the members of the affiliated group are treated as a single corporation.

THE CONSOLIDATED TAX CREDIT

The consolidated tax liability of the group is reduced by any available tax credits also computed on a consolidated basis. Although the Regulations specifically recognize only two credits—the investment tax credit and foreign tax credit— only the investment tax credit is discussed here. An analysis of credit carryovers is reserved for a later portion of this chapter dealing with carryover limitations.

Investment Tax Credit.   The consolidated investment tax credit for purchases before January 1, 1986 is the aggregate of the separate credits earned by each member of the group plus any unused carryovers. In computing the credit for property acquired in an intercompany transaction, the amount of qualified investment is limited to the selling member's basis in the property.[62]

> **Example 30.**   Affiliated member P sells an asset with a cost of $12,000 to affiliated member S for $15,000. Only the original cost of $12,000 is eligible for the investment tax credit to be claimed by S. Note, however, that S's basis in the asset is $15,000.

The ceiling on the amount of consolidated investment tax credits for a taxable year is $25,000 plus 75 percent of the consolidated tax liability in excess of $25,000.[63]

Credit Recapture.   Investment credit must be recaptured whenever property is disposed of outside of the group or ceases to be qualifying property. Any recapture must be added to the consolidated tax liability of the group. If a group member disposes of qualifying property during a separate return year, the member is totally liable for any resulting investment tax credit recapture—regardless of whether the property was placed in service in a consolidated return year.[64]   It should be noted that a sale or exchange between group members is not treated as a disposition for credit recapture purposes. The *purchasing member* must assume liability for the recapture tax in the event separate returns are filed.[65]

> **Example 31.**   Corporations P, S, and T file consolidated tax returns for 1986, a year in which S purchases a machine that qualifies for the investment tax credit. The machine was placed into service and the investment tax credit was taken in 1986. In 1990 P, S, and T continue filing consolidated returns; however, S sells the machine to T. Because this is an intercompany sale, it is not treated as a disposition and recapture is not required.

---

[62]   Reg. § 1.1502-3(a)(2). For purchases after December 31, 1985, the investment tax credit has been repealed.

[63]   Reg. § 1.1502-3(a)(3).

[64]   Reg. § 1.1502-3(f)(1).

[65]   Reg. § 1.1502-3(f)(2).

Example 32. Assume the same facts as in *Example 31*, except that P, S, and T filed separate returns for 1986. The sale from S to T does not trigger recapture because the property remains within the group.

Example 33. Assume the same facts as in *Example 31*, except that T is separated from the group in 1990 and files a separate tax return. If T sells the machine during 1990 to an unrelated individual, it is responsible for the entire investment tax credit recapture on its separate tax return. The holding period of S is used in determining the amount of recapture.

LIMITATIONS AND ADJUSTMENTS DUE TO CONSOLIDATION

One of the attractions of filing a consolidated tax return is the ability of a profitable entity to use the losses and credits of an unprofitable entity. One can only imagine the abuses that would result if some form of limitation were not imposed. As a result, the consolidated return Regulations impose certain restrictions. These involve the following:

1. Separate return limitation years

2. Built-in deductions

3. Consolidated return change in ownership

4. Reverse acquisitions

5. Carryovers and carrybacks to separate return years

In addition to these limitations, the Regulations provide for several other adjustments. These serve to maintain the integrity of a single-entity concept while preventing certain abuses (e.g., the double counting of subsidiary losses) and mitigating the hardships of double taxation when a subsidiary's stock is sold. These include the following:

1. Adjustments for investment in subsidiaries

2. The excess loss account

3. Adjustments for earnings and profits

SEPARATE RETURN LIMITATION YEARS

When a corporation incurs a net operating loss in a separate return year and subsequently carries that loss to a consolidated return year, the Regulations limit the deductible amount of the loss carryover.[66] The limitation is imposed only if the loss year is considered a *separate return limitation year* (SRLY). Generally, this means any loss year for which a separate return was filed, except where the corporation was a member of the group for the entire year or the corporation is the parent in the year to which the loss is being carried. The amount of loss incurred in a SRLY that may be deducted in a consolidated year is limited to the excess of consolidated taxable income (computed without regard to the net operating loss deduction) over consolidated taxable income as reduced by the loss member's income and deductions.[67] In essence, the group's deduction for any member's SRLY losses cannot exceed the member's contribution to consolidated taxable income.[68]

> **Example 34.**   P and S are members of an affiliated group for 1991 and file a consolidated tax return. T Corporation, owned by an individual, incurs a $15,000 net operating loss for 1991. On January 1, 1992, P acquires all the stock of T. In 1992 P, S, and T file a consolidated tax return showing consolidated taxable income of $40,000, of which $6,000 is attributable to the efforts of T. Because of the SRLY rules, only $6,000 of the $15,000 loss is considered a consolidated net operating loss carryover to 1992. The carryover is limited to $40,000 (consolidated taxable income) minus the $34,000 (consolidated taxable income of $40,000 − the loss member's income and deductions of $6,000). The remaining $9,000 ($15,000 − $6,000) may be carried over to 1993 and is subject to the SRLY rules and NOL carryover limitations.

Exceptions to SRLY Rules.   According to the definition of a SRLY noted above, the corporation designated as the common parent for an affiliated group is generally not subject to the SRLY rules since its years are not considered SRLY years. Under this so called *lonely parent rule*, the parent's losses from a "pre" or "post" affiliation year may be used to offset the earnings of other members in a consolidated return year.[69] This exception does not apply if there has been a reverse acquisition[70] or similar merger of a parent into a subsidiary.

---

[66]   Reg. § 1.1502-21.

[67]   Reg. § 1.1502-21(c)(2).

[68]   If there are carryovers from more than one year, they are absorbed in chronological order.

[69]   *F.C. Donovan, Inc. v. U.S.*, 261 F.2d 470 (CA-1, 1958).

[70]   Defined later in this chapter.

Example 35. In 1990, P, a first-year corporation, files a separate return with an operating loss of $12,000. On January 1, 1991, P acquires all the stock of S Corporation. For 1991, P and S file a consolidated tax return reflecting P's taxable income of $5,000 for 1991 and S's taxable income of $24,000. In this case, the SRLY rules are not applicable since P is the common parent. Consequently, all $12,000 of the loss carryover is utilized in 1991.

Example 36. Assume the same facts as in *Example 35*, except that P sells all the S stock on January 1, 1992. If P incurs a $14,000 loss for 1992, the SRLY rules do not restrict P from carrying back the loss from this post-affiliation year to a consolidated return year since P was the parent in the year to which the loss is carried. Therefore, the full amount of the loss can be carried back to 1991 to offset consolidated taxable income without limitation. (Note that the SRLY rules apply to carrybacks as well as carryovers.)

The SRLY rules are also inapplicable for a corporation's separate return year if that corporation was a member of the group for each day of such year.[71] This would occur when the corporation was a member of a group which elected *not* to file on a consolidated basis.[72]

Related Provisions. The SRLY rules are not restricted to net operating losses. The rules also apply to net capital losses, the investment tax credit, and foreign tax credits.

BUILT-IN DEDUCTIONS

The Regulations also impose restrictions on the use of *built-in deductions*.[73] A built-in deduction is a deduction or loss that economically accrues in a separate return year but is recognized in a consolidated return year for tax purposes.

Example 37. S Corporation purchased an investment in 1982 for $22,000. On January 1, 1991, P Corporation purchased all of the stock of S. At that time, S's investment was worth $13,000. If P and S sell the investment in 1991 and file a consolidated tax return for the year, $9,000 ($22,000 − $13,000) is considered a built-in deduction because it economically accrued in years before 1991.

---

[71] Reg. § 1.1502-1(f). See *Braswell Motor Freight Line, Inc. v. U.S.*, 477 F.2d 594 (CA-5, 1973), where a corporation was formed in 1955 and became a member of the group in July of 1957. Although the corporation had no assets or taxable income prior to July 1957, the loss generated in the latter half of the year was subject to the SRLY rules because the corporation was not a member for each day of the year (1957).

[72] Reg. § 1.1502-1(f). The same rule applies to a predecessor of any group member that was a member of the group on each day of the year. A predecessor is a transferor or distributor of assets to the member in a transaction to which § 381(a) applies.

[73] Reg § 1.502-15.

Under the Regulations,[74] a built-in deduction can be deducted in determining consolidated taxable income only to the extent of the acquired member's contribution toward consolidated taxable income. The effect of this limitation is the same as if the loss had occurred in pre-affiliation years subject to the SRLY rules for net operating losses. Deductions and losses not currently used are carried forward indefinitely to succeeding years.[75]

Exceptions.   There are two exceptions to the built-in deduction rule. First, the limitation does not apply to the assets that a group acquires either directly or by acquiring a new member if the acquisition occurred more than 10 years before the first day of the taxable year in which the sale occurs.[76] Second, the limitation does not apply if immediately before the acquisition of the assets, the aggregate adjusted basis of all assets acquired (excluding cash and marketable securities) did not exceed the fair market value of such assets by more than 15 percent.[77] Cash and marketable securities are excluded from the computation in order to prevent avoidance of this rule by making additional cash and security contributions immediately before acquisition.

> **Example 38.**   On May 24, 1981, P acquires all the stock of S Corporation. At the time of the acquisition, S's only assets are land (fair market value of $12,000; basis of $7,000) and machinery (fair market value of $8,000; basis of $15,000). If in a subsequent year the group sells the machinery for $8,000, the built-in deduction rules will not apply since at the time of the original acquisition the aggregate basis of S's assets ($7,000 + $15,000 = $22,000) did not exceed their fair market value ($12,000 + $8,000 = $20,000) by more than 15% ($20,000 × 115% = $23,000).

> **Example 39.**   Assume the same facts as in *Example 38*, except that the only asset of S was the machinery. In this case the basis exceeds the fair market value by 87.5% [($15,000 − $8,000) ÷ $8,000] and the built-in deduction limitation would apply. However, if the group had waited until January 1, 1992 to sell the machinery, the limitation would not apply because the acquisition took place more than 10 years before the year of the sale.

CONSOLIDATED RETURN CHANGE OF OWNERSHIP

If a *consolidated return change of ownership* (CRCO) occurs within or prior to the taxable year, the amount of the consolidated NOL sustained before the change can only be applied against the "post-change" income of the corporations that were members of the group before the change. A CRCO is deemed to occur whenever one or more of the 10 largest shareholders (measured in terms of the fair market value of stock owned) of the common parent owns a percentage (in value) of the parent's outstanding stock that is more than 50 percentage points

---

[74]   Reg. § 1.1502-15(a).

[75]   Reg. § 1.1502-15(a)(1).

[76]   Reg. § 1.1502-15(a)(4)(i)(a).

[77]   Reg. § 1.1502-15(a)(4)(i)(b).

greater than they owned at the beginning of the current or preceding taxable year.[78] The change generally must result from the purchase of stock of the corporation, a redemption (excluding § 303), or a combination of these.[79]

> **Example 40.** T, an individual, owns 40% of Z Corporation. If T purchases an additional 30% of the stock, he experiences a 75% increase in ownership (30 ÷ 40) but only a 30 percentage point change in ownership (70 − 40). The CRCO limitations would not apply.

The CRCO limitation prohibits circumvention of the SRLY rules through use of the lonely parent rule.

> **Example 41.** Corporations P and S, both formed on January 1, 1991, file a consolidated tax return for 1991 reflecting a net operating loss of $500,000, all of which is attributable to P. On January 1, 1992, individual X purchases all the outstanding stock of P Corporation. X subsequently contributes $1 million to P, and P purchases all the stock of T, a very profitable corporation. P, S, and T file a consolidated return for 1992 reflecting consolidated taxable income of $600,000 (before consideration of the $500,000 NOL carryover). The consolidated taxable income attributable to P and S is $350,000. Absent the CRCO limitation, the loss of P could be used in full since the SRLY rules do not apply where the loss corporation is the parent in the year to which the loss is carried (the lonely parent rule). However, because a consolidated return change of ownership took place (X's ownership of P went from 0 to 100% within a two-year period), the NOL carryover from 1991 is limited to the current consolidated taxable income of the old members (P and S) or $350,000.[80] Note that if X had purchased T and T had in turn purchased P and S, the SRLY rules would apply. In effect, X was hoping to circumvent the SRLY rules by making a member of the loss group (P in this case) the parent of the P, S, and T group in order to secure the benefits of the lonely parent rule.

RELATIONSHIP TO § 382

The rules for CRCOs were derived from the early statutory rules of Code § 382 concerning the carryovers of NOLs.[81] The rules under § 382, which were discussed in conjunction with liquidations and reorganizations,[82] may also restrict the use of net operating losses by an affiliated group. The limitations imposed by § 382, however, are far more harsh than those imposed by the consolidated

---

[78] The constructive ownership rules of § 318 apply for this purpose. Reg. § 1.1502-1(g)(2) waives the 50 percent limitation of §§ 318(a)(2)(C) and 318(a)(3)(C).

[79] *Ibid.*

[80] Reg. § 1.1502-21(d)(3)(i).

[81] Reg. § 1.1502-1(g)(1)(i). It should be noted that the Tax Reform Act of 1976 changed the shareholder reference from § 382(a)(2) to § 382(a)(4)(B). The Regulations have not yet reflected this change nor the changes made by the 1986 Act.

[82] See Chapters 5 and 7.

return Regulations. If the taxpayer comes within the purview of § 382, the NOL carryovers can be disallowed in full or limited to a fraction of their total.[83]

> **Example 42.** P, S, and T file a consolidated tax return for calendar year 1990 reflecting a consolidated net operating loss attributable in part to each member. P owns 80% of S's stock, and S owns 80% of T's stock. On January 1, 1991, A purchases 60% of P's stock. During 1991, T's business is discontinued. Because there has been a more than 50 percentage point increase in the ownership of P, the common parent of the group, and since T has not continued in the same trade or business after the increase, under § 382, the portion of the 1990 consolidated NOL attributable to T cannot be included for 1991 or any subsequent years, whether consolidated or separate.[84] If the CRCO rules had applied in lieu of § 382, the group would have been able to carry over its losses and apply them against any future earnings of P, S, or T.

Despite recent changes made by the Tax Reform Act of 1986, Congress intends that the new rules of § 382 should not affect the continued applicability of the Code § 269, CRCO, or SRLY limitations on the use of tax benefits.

REVERSE ACQUISITIONS

In 1966 the Regulations[85] first addressed the problems caused by reverse acquisitions. The problem arose whenever a taxpayer merged a smaller corporation into a larger group and then selected the smaller corporation to be the common parent because of the favorable tax attributes that would survive the merger.[86]

> **Example 43.** Profitable P Corporation plans a merger with loss corporation S. If S merges into P [Type "A" merger under § 368(a)(1)(A)], S's attributes (i.e., NOLs, negative E&P) are limited under § 382. However, should P merge into S, P's attributes disappear and S's attributes survive.

If the transaction qualifies as a reverse acquisition—whether intended or not—the results can have adverse tax consequences to the surviving members.

A reverse acquisition occurs when

1. A common parent ("first corporation"), or subsidiary of the first corporation, acquires (in exchange for stock of the first corporation) either another corporation (second corporation) or group of corporations (second group); and

---

[83] *Ibid.*

[84] Reg. § 1.1502-21(e)(1)(iii). Note that § 382 disallows any use of the NOL because T's business is discontinued. Had T's business been continued, § 382 would limit the amount of the NOL carryover deduction.

See Chapter 7.

[85] Reg. § 1.1502-75(a)(3).

[86] The relative size of the two groups is determined by stock ownership in the surviving common parent.

2. The second corporation's (second group's) shareholders own more than 50 percent of the fair market value of the outstanding stock of the first corporation.

Example 44. R Corporation and its two wholly owned subsidiaries S and T have filed a consolidated tax return for the past five years, showing large consolidated profits each year. R Corporation is owned equally by individuals A, B, and C. N Corporation and its two wholly owned subsidiaries O and P are owned 100% by individual D. The N group has been experiencing consolidated losses each year since its formation three years ago. The ownership of these groups is shown in Exhibit 8-9.

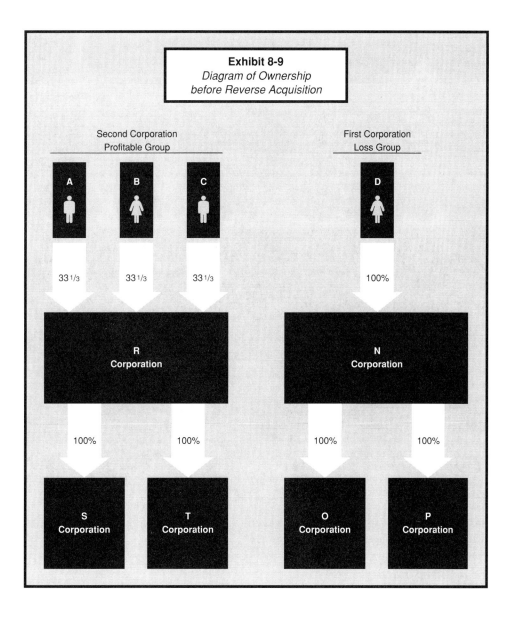

Exhibit 8-9
*Diagram of Ownership
before Reverse Acquisition*

On January 1, 1991 the R group merges into the N group with the R shareholders receiving 90% of the fair market value of the outstanding stock of N. The results of this merger are shown in Exhibit 8-10. Because N ("first corporation") has acquired in exchange for its stock R ("second corporation") and the R shareholders (second corporation's shareholders) own more than 50% of the outstanding stock of N, a reverse acquisition has taken place. In other words, although N survives, R's former shareholders control N.

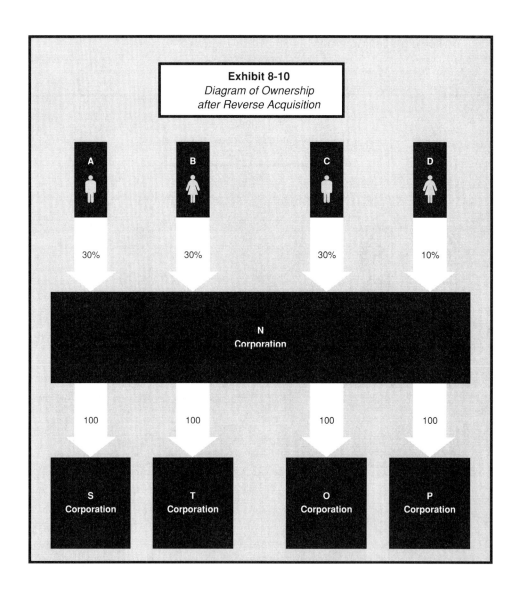

Exhibit 8-10
*Diagram of Ownership
after Reverse Acquisition*

If the rules for a reverse acquisition are met, the Regulations provide the following:[87]

1. The first corporation's group terminates at the date of acquisition (N above).

2. The second corporation's group (R above) is treated as remaining in existence.

3. The first corporation (N) becomes the parent of the continuing group.

When a reverse acquisition has occurred, the taxable years of the first corporation's group (e.g., the loss corporation, N above) ending on or before the acquisition date are subject to the SRLY limitations regardless of the fact that the first corporation becomes the common parent. The taxable years of the second corporation's group generally are not subject to the SRLY rules.[88]

> **Example 45.** Assume the same facts as in *Example 44*. Because the transaction qualifies as a reverse acquisition, corporations N, O, and P ("first group") terminate on the date of the merger. The group (S and T) of which R was the common parent is treated as continuing in existence with N, O, and P being added as members of the group and N taking the place of R as the common parent. The SRLY rules apply to corporations N, O, and P and not to corporations S and T.[89]

A special elective rule exists for groups that have continuously owned at least 25 percent of the fair market value of the stock of the acquired ("second") corporation for five years. The election essentially gives the electing corporation the flexibility of choosing which group survives the acquisition.

---

[87] Reg. § 1.1502-75(d)(3)(i)(b).

[88] Reg. § 1.1502-1(f)(3).

[89] The SRLY rules do not have any effect on profitable corporations.

CARRYBACKS AND CARRYOVERS TO SEPARATE RETURN YEARS

The previous discussion has addressed the carryover of net operating losses from separate return years to consolidated return years. Now consideration must be given to situations where the loss occurs in a consolidated return year and must be carried to a separate return year.

Once a consolidated net operating loss is computed, the rules that apply are similar to those for a single corporation. The consolidated net operating loss is carried back three years and any unused portion (after 1975) is carried over to the 15 succeeding years. Customarily, these NOLs are computed and carried back or forward on a consolidated basis. In certain cases, however, losses, credits, and deductions must be carried to a separate return year. When this is the case, special rules must be followed.

Loss Carrybacks. A consolidated net operating loss must first be apportioned to each member of the group. Once apportioned, the NOL may be carried back and applied against the separate taxable income of the member. The Regulations[90] prescribe that the consolidated NOL is allocated as follows:

$$\frac{\text{Member's separate NOL}}{\substack{\text{Sum of separate NOLs} \\ \text{of all loss members}}} \times \text{Consolidated NOL} = \substack{\text{Member's portion of} \\ \text{consolidated NOL}}$$

Example 46. T, a first-year unaffiliated corporation, had taxable income for 1990 of $350,000. On January 1, 1991, the affiliated group of P and S purchases all the stock of T and files a consolidated return for 1991 showing a consolidated loss of $800,000 computed as follows:

	Consolidated Taxable Income
P	($300,000)
S	400,000
T	(900,000)
Total	($800,000)

T's share of the apportioned consolidated NOL is $600,000 [$800,000 × ($900,000 ÷ [$300,000 + $900,000])] of which $350,000 is carried back to its first year. The remaining $250,000 is carried over to 1992 and may be combined with any of the remaining $200,000 loss attributable to P.

Under § 172(b)(3)(C), a parent can elect to forgo the three-year carryback period. If such an election is made, the loss is carried forward as a consolidated NOL and any refund generated from such loss is paid to the parent. If the election to forgo the carryback is not made, the refund is paid to the affiliated member.[91]

---

[90]   Reg. § 1.1502-79(a)(3).   [91]   Reg. § 1.1502-78(b)(1).

Example 47.   Assume the same facts as in *Example 46*, except that P made an election to forgo the carryback. The entire $800,000 loss is carried over to 1992 and is applied toward any 1992 consolidated taxable income. If P had not made this election, any refund generated from the 1990 carryback would have been paid directly to T.

When a portion of a consolidated net operating loss is attributable to a member which cannot use the loss in a carryback year because the member was not in existence, the other members of the group may be able to utilize the loss if certain conditions are met.[92] The carryback may be used by other members of the group in an equivalent consolidated return year if the corporation unable to use the loss became a member of the group immediately after its organization.

Example 48.   Assume the same facts as in *Example 46*. In addition, assume that P and S had the following consolidated taxable income for earlier years of

1988......................	$250,000
1989......................	975,000
1990......................	100,000

Since T was not a member of the group immediately after its organization, P and S can only carry back its share of the loss, $200,000, to 1988. T may carry back $350,000 of its $600,000 share of the loss to 1990. T's remaining loss of $250,000 carries over to 1992 as a consolidated NOL.

If T had been formed on January 1, 1991 and had become a member of the P and S group immediately after its organization, no carryback period would exist for T. Thus its share of the loss could be used by the other members. Because T would be considered a member of the group for the entire period, its $600,000 share of the loss could be used to offset the remaining $50,000 of consolidated taxable income ($250,000 − $200,000 P carryback) from 1988, and the $550,000 balance could be carried to 1989.

Loss Carryovers.   Under the Regulations,[93] if a corporation ceases to be a member of a group during a consolidated return year, any consolidated net operating loss carryover from a prior taxable year must first be carried to the current consolidated return year. This requirement is observed notwithstanding the fact that all or a portion of the consolidated net operating loss is attributable to the terminating member. Only the portion of the terminating member's loss not absorbed in consolidation can be carried over to the first separate return year.

---

[92]   Reg. § 1.1502-79(a)(2).   [93]   Reg. § 1.1502-79(a)(1)(ii).

Example 49. Assume the same facts as in *Example 46*. Assume further that on June 15, 1992 P sells all the T stock to an outsider. For 1992, P and S file a consolidated return (which includes the income of T for the period January 1 to June 15) while T files a separate return. The 1991 unabsorbed loss carryover attributable to T of $250,000 must be applied first to the 1992 consolidated taxable income. Any unused loss is then applied toward T's 1992 income and any balance is carried forward by T.

INVESTMENT IN SUBSIDIARIES

BASIS ADJUSTMENTS

At the end of each consolidated return year, the parent's basis in the stock of a subsidiary must be adjusted to reflect the economic results of operations. Generally, this requires increasing the parent's basis by any undistributed gains of the subsidiaries and reducing the basis by any losses sustained by the subsidiaries. The purpose of these adjustments is to prevent duplication of gain or loss on a later disposition of the subsidiaries' stock. In theory, following the basis rules is no more difficult than keeping a running checkbook balance. In practice, however, these rules involve a series of intricate net positive and net negative adjustments. These adjustments are made at the end of each taxable year. When one subsidiary owns stock in another subsidiary, the adjustment in the higher-tier subsidiary cannot be made until the adjustment is made for the lower-tier subsidiary. When there is a disposition of the subsidiary's stock, the basis adjustment is made on the date of disposition.[94]

Positive Adjustments. The Regulations prescribe three positive adjustments that increase the basis of the subsidiary's *common* stock. An increase is made for

1. An allocable portion of the subsidiary's undistributed earnings and profits for the taxable year;

2. An allocable portion of any consolidated net operating loss or consolidated net capital loss that is attributable to a subsidiary that could *not* utilize the loss in a carryback to a prior year; and

3. The net positive adjustments that a subsidiary makes in its basis for stock of a lower tier subsidiary.

---

[94]   Reg. § 1.1502-32(a).

Negative Adjustments.   The Regulations prescribe four negative adjustments that decrease the basis of the subsidiary's *common* stock. A decrease must be made for

1. An allocable portion of the subsidiary's deficit in earnings and profits for the taxable year;

2. An allocable portion of a subsidiary's net operating loss or net capital loss that is carried over and absorbed in the current year;

3. Dividends paid by the subsidiary in the current year out of earnings and profits accumulated in a pre-affiliation year or a consolidated return year after December 31, 1965; and

4. The net negative adjustments that a subsidiary makes in its basis for stock of another subsidiary.

> **Example 50.**   On January 1, 1990, P Corporation acquires all the stock of S Corporation for $5,000 and elects to file a consolidated return. On the acquisition date, S had accumulated earnings and profits (E&P) of $1,000 and for 1990 had no E&P. S distributed $300 to P in 1990. In 1991, S had earnings of $700 and an operating loss of $2,300 in 1992. P's basis in S stock as of December 31, 1992 is computed as follows:

Cost	$5,000
1990 distribution of pre-affiliation earnings (3rd negative adjustment)	− 300
Basis (12/31/90)	$4,700
1991 undistributed earnings (1st positive adjustment)	+ 700
Basis (12/31/91)	$5,400
1992 operating loss (1st negative adjustment)	− 2,300
Basis (12/31/92)	$3,100

The results of making positive and negative adjustments can lead to an interesting phenomenon when a corporation disposes of its subsidiary. This phenomenon occurs when a corporation makes basis adjustments in its subsidiary using earnings and profits, but reports taxable income using computations incompatible with earnings and profits calculations. The result is an unintended tax benefit when, for example, a subsidiary uses accelerated depreciation for taxable income purposes but is obligated to use straight-line depreciation in determining its current earnings and profits. This benefit, although unwarranted, was upheld by the Tax Court in *Woods Investment Company*[95] under a literal application of the regulations.

---

[95]   85 T.C. 274 (1986).

Because the required adjustments to basis failed to account for the tax benefits realized by the consolidated group and also failed to require the group to pay tax on the economic profit, Congress effectively overruled the *Woods* decision by adding Code § 1503(e) under the Revenue Act of 1987. Under § 1503(e), gain or loss on the disposition of "intragroup stock" after December 15, 1987 must be determined using earnings and profits without regard to the special adjustments required under §§ 312 (k) and (n) (e.g., depreciation, LIFO recapture, completed-contract method, etc.). In this manner, the outside basis of a subsidiary's stock will reflect the true economic interest in that subsidiary. The term "intragroup stock" includes any property the basis of which is determined by reference to basis of stock in a corporation that was formerly a member of an affiliated group filing consolidated tax returns.

EXCESS LOSS ACCOUNT

When a group files a consolidated tax return, the losses of a subsidiary can exceed the group's investment in that corporation. Instead of denying a deduction for a portion of the losses that exceed basis under the notion that a negative basis is generally not recognized, the Regulations provide for an extension of the basis adjustment rules known as an *excess loss account*.[96] This account serves to maintain a record of these excess deductions until such time when they are recovered.

> **Example 51.** On January 1, 1990, P organized a wholly owned subsidiary, Corporation S. On the same date, S organized a wholly owned subsidiary, Corporation T. P invested $5,000 in S while S invested $3,000 in the stock of T. Consolidated tax returns are filed for the years 1990 through 1992 showing the following separate incomes and losses:

	T	S	P
1990	($2,000)	$1,200	$25,000
1991	(1,800)	300	33,000
1992	(600)	(6,400)	42,000

---

[96]   Reg. § 1.1502-19.

No distributions were made by S or T for any of the years. As of December 31, 1992, the adjusted bases for the stock of S and T are computed as follows:

	S in T		P in S	
1990				
Original basis	$3,000		$5,000	
Loss of T	(2,000)	(1st Neg. Adj.)	(2,000)	(4th Neg. Adj.)
Undistributed earnings of S	0		1,200	(1st Pos. Adj.)
Basis	$1,000		$4,200	
1991				
Loss of T	($1,800)	(1st Neg. Adj.)	($1,800)	(4th Neg. Adj.)
Undistributed earnings of S	0		300	(1st Pos. Adj.)
Basis	0		$2,700	
Excess loss amount	($800)		0	
1992				
Undistributed earnings of T	$ 600	(1st Pos. Adj.)	$ 600	(3rd Pos. Adj.)
Loss of S	0		(6,400)	(1st Neg. Adj.)
Basis	0		0	
Excess loss amount	($200)		($3,100)	

Note that if it had not been for the requirement that P's basis in S must reflect T's operations (4th negative adjustment), P would not have an "excess loss account" with respect to S.

Recovery of Excess Loss Account. The excess loss account generally must be recaptured and included in the investor's income when there is a disposition of the stock outside of the group.[97] On a disposition, gain is always recognized to the extent of the excess loss account.[98]

Dispositions can include a sale, a redemption, or worthlessness of a subsidiary's stock, as well as the termination of a consolidated return.[99] Upon a disposition, the gain to be recognized is generally treated as a capital gain.[100] In the case of an insolvent subsidiary, the excess loss is treated as ordinary income.[101]

---

[97] Reg. § 1.1502-32(e)(2). When an excess loss account has been triggered, any subsequent net positive adjustments must first be applied to reduce the excess loss before any increase can be made to the basis of stock.

[98] Reg. § 1.1502-19(a)(1).

[99] Although a number of exceptions for carryover basis exist (i.e., reorganizations, liquidations, etc.), a discussion of these techniques is beyond the scope of this chapter.

[100] Reg. § 1.1502-19(a)(2).

[101] Reg. § 1.1502-19(a)(1).

Example 52.   Assume the same facts as in *Example 51*, except that on January 1, 1993 S sells all of its stock in T to an unrelated individual. Because at the end of 1992 S has an excess loss account in the T stock of $200, all $200 must be recognized by S as capital gain. This recognition is in addition to any other gain or loss that may be taxable on the sale stock.

Deemed Dividend.   In lieu of making net negative adjustments to the basis of a subsidiary's stock and perhaps creating an excess loss account, the Regulations provide for what is referred to as the *deemed dividend*. Under this technique, the consolidated group may elect to treat the subsidiary as having distributed on the first day of the taxable year all of its accumulated earnings and profits through the end of the prior year.[102] This technique, however, is only available if the subsidiary had pre-1966 earnings or post-1965 earnings from a separate return year during which the subsidiary is a member of the group.[103] The group must elect to make a deemed dividend on or before the parent's due date (including extensions) for filing its return.[104] Once the election is made, each group member that owns stock in the subsidiary is treated as having received an allocable share of the distribution which it immediately contributes back to the subsidiary's capital. The effect of the deemed dividend is eliminated in consolidation and the contribution to capital serves to *increase* the basis of the subsidiary. In essence, the election enables a tax-free step-up in basis, thus reducing the amount of any gain (or increasing the amount of loss) on a subsequent disposition of the stock.

Example 53.   On January 1, 1990, P Corporation purchased 100% of S, a newly formed corporation. For calendar years 1990 and 1991, P and S file separate tax returns in which S had earnings and profits of $20,000 and $35,000, respectively. In 1992 P and S elect to file a consolidated tax return. If P elects to use the deemed-dividend technique, P is treated as if it received a dividend of $55,000 ($20,000 + $35,000). Since P never actually receives the dividend, it is treated as if it received the money and immediately made a corresponding contribution to S's capital, thereby increasing the basis in stock of S. The dividend is never taxed to P because it is eliminated in consolidation on the 1992 tax return.

---

[102]   Reg. § 1.1502-32(f)(2).

[103]   Consequently, a deemed dividend from post-1965 earnings will only be available to subsidiaries of affiliated groups that were eligible to file consolidated returns but chose not to make the election.

[104]   This election was first introduced to aid the affiliated groups filing under the "old" regulations. This election, however, is not limited to these groups and can be extremely useful to step up basis for post-1965 groups that filed separate returns during affiliation years. This election will not be useful to groups filing under the current regulations that did not have separate return affiliation years because the distribution and recontribution effects would cancel under the positive and negative adjustment computation.

LOSS DISALLOWANCE RULE

Beginning in 1990, the Internal Revenue Service adopted controversial *loss disallowance rules* in temporary regulations effective for transactions occurring on or after March 9, 1990.[105] This rule, applicable to any disposition or deconsolidation, serves to deny a deduction for any loss recognized by a member corporation with respect to the stock of a subsidiary. A *disposition* is defined as any event in which gain or loss is recognized in whole or in part. A *deconsolidation* refers to any event that causes a share of stock of a subsidiary to be no longer owned by a member of a consolidated group in which the subsidiary is a member. In order to maintain the integrity of this rule, the temporary regulations also provide for "anti-stuffing" rules that prevent members of the affiliated group from transferring appreciated assets to absorb any losses that would be disallowed in the event of a disposition or deconsolidation.[106]

> **Example 54.** P buys all the stock of T for $100, thus making T a member of the P-T affiliated group. T owns an asset with a basis of $20 and a fair market value of $120. If T sells the asset for its value, $120, P increases its basis to $200 under the investment adjustment system. Five years later if P sells its T stock for $125, the Regulations disallow the $75 loss to P on its disposition of T.

> **Example 55.** P buys all 100 shares of S stock for $100, thus making S a member of the P-S affiliated group. The value of the S stock declines to $50, and P sells 60 shares to an unrelated party for $30. The sale causes a deconsolidation of the remaining 40 shares of S stock. Accordingly, P must reduce the basis of the remaining S stock from $40 to $20 (its current value). In addition, the loss of $30 on the disposition of the 60 shares of S stock is also disallowed to P. If P had attempted to circumvent the loss disallowance rule by transferring appreciated assets to S immediately prior to the sale, the regulations would have triggered the "anti-stuffing rules," requiring a *gain* to be recognized to the extent of the loss disallowance.

---

[105] Reg. § 1.1502-20T(a)(1).

[106] Reg. § 1.1502-20T(d)(1).

EARNINGS AND PROFITS

In order to determine the tax treatment on distributions made by the affiliated group, each member must compute and maintain its own separate E&P account. The computation is similar to the standard rules governing the determination of E&P; however, the following transactions must be taken into account:

1. Gains or losses on intercompany transactions (i.e., the selling member must adjust for intercompany gains and losses for E&P purposes even though the transaction is deferred for taxable income purposes)

2. The initial and recovery inventory adjustment (i.e, these adjustments must be made to the selling member's computation of E&P)

3. Dividend distributions between members (i.e., the distributing corporation must reduce E&P while the distributee increases its E&P)

4. Dispositions of a subsidiary's stock or obligations

5. An allocable share of the consolidated tax liability (i.e., the member's share of the tax liability decreases its E&P)

Earnings and profits are never calculated on a consolidated basis. For years after 1975, each member must reflect its subsidiary's E&P in the computation of its own E&P at the end of each taxable year. The computations are made in a fashion similar to those discussed for basis adjustments in a subsidiary. The higher-tiered corporation makes a series of net negative and net positive adjustments for the lower-tiered subsidiary.[107]

Because the earnings and profits of a subsidiary are directly reflected in a parent's E&P, special computations are not necessary on a later disposition of a subsidiary's stock. Essentially, these adjustments create a situation that is very similar to consolidated E&P without formally requiring an E&P computation on a consolidated basis.

> **Example 56.** P forms S Corporation on January 1, 1991 with a contribution to capital of $1,000. P and S file consolidated returns for 1991 and 1992 with S earning $100 and $300, respectively. In 1992 S distributes $150 in dividends to P. On December 31, 1992 P sells its stock in S for $1,200. As a result of these transactions, P's earnings and profits are increased by $100 and $300 for the 1991 and 1992 earnings. The $150 distribution decreases P's E&P. The disposition of S stock decreases E&P by $50 [$1,200 sales price − ($1,000 contribution + $100 and $300 in earnings − $150 distribution)].

---

[107]   Reg. § 1.1502-33(c)(4)(ii).

The adjustment to E&P to reflect the earnings or loss of subsidiaries is mandatory for years after 1975. For years ending before 1976, adjustments can be made for these earnings only if an election to apply the adjustment rules is made. Once an election is made by the group, it cannot be revoked and remains in effect for all subsequent taxable years.[108]

Allocating Tax Liability. One of the primary adjustments in the computation of earnings and profits concerns the consolidated group's Federal income tax liability. Because taxes paid or accrued decrease the E&P of a member, § 1552 provides methods for allocating the consolidated tax liability to member corporations. The Code and Regulations provide four options for making the allocation. In the event the group fails to elect a specific allocation method, § 1552(b) provides that the tax liability is to be apportioned in the ratio that each member's taxable income bears to consolidated taxable income.

> **Example 57.** Corporation P is the common parent owning all the stock of Corporations S and T. The group files a consolidated tax return for 1991. For the year, the corporations had the following taxable incomes:
>
> | | |
> |---|---:|
> | P | $ 0 |
> | S | 12,000 |
> | T | (2,000) |
> | Total | $10,000 |
>
> The group has not made an election to allocate the tax liability, so the allocation is made under Code § 1552(b). Assume the consolidated tax liability for the year is $1,500 ($10,000 × 15%) all of which is allocable to S (the only profitable company). As a result, S reduces its E&P by $1,500 regardless of which corporation in the group pays the tax liability. If S pays the liability, no further accounting is required. If, however, P pays the tax liability (and this payment is not treated as a loan), P is treated as having made a contribution to S's capital account in the amount of $1,500. On the other hand, if T pays the liability, T is treated as having made a distribution to P, and P, in turn, is treated as having made a contribution to S's capital account. If P is treated as having made a contribution to capital, it increases the basis in its stock.

---

[108] Reg. § 1.1502-33(c)(4)(iii).

OPERATING RULES

The Regulations contain a series of detailed administrative procedures that become operative whenever a group of entities join together to file a consolidated return. Included in these provisions are the following requirements:

1. All group members conform to the same accounting period.

2. The estimated tax payments are to be determined in the aggregate.

3. Each member of the group is liable for the entire tax liability of the group.

4. The parent corporation has the power to act as the agent for the group.

COMMON ACCOUNTING PERIODS

A consolidated tax return must be filed on the basis of the common parent's taxable year. Accordingly, each subsidiary must adopt the parent's annual accounting period for the initial consolidated tax return.[109] The Regulations do not require that a subsidiary obtain advance permission from the Commissioner to change its tax year to conform to the accounting period of the parent.[110] The IRS, however, has ruled that it will allow a parent corporation to change its taxable year to that of its subsidiaries.[111] In such case, a consolidated tax return is permitted for the short taxable year.

ESTIMATED TAX PAYMENTS

If a group files a consolidated tax return for two consecutive years, estimated tax payments must be made on a consolidated basis for each subsequent taxable year until separate returns are filed.[112] If estimated tax payments are made on a consolidated basis but the group files separate returns, the common parent may apportion the estimated payments in any method satisfactory to the Commissioner.[113]

---

[109] Reg. § 1.1502-76(a)(1).

[110] Reg. § 1.442-1(d) states that a Form 1128 need not be filed by a subsidiary.

[111] Rev. Rul. 55-80, 1955-1 C.B. 387.

[112] Reg. § 1.1502-5(a)(1).

[113] Reg. § 1.1502-5(b)(4).

For the first two years that a group files a consolidated return, it may make estimated payments on either a consolidated or separate return basis.[114] If payments are made on a separate company basis, the amounts of any estimated tax payments are aggregated and credited against the consolidated tax liability for the year. As with rules governing the estimated tax payments, any penalties computed under § 6655 (underpayment of estimated taxes) may be determined on a separate or consolidated basis for the first two consolidated return years. This computation is made without regard to whether the estimated taxes were paid on a separate or consolidated basis.

TAX LIABILITY OF THE GROUP

Each member of a consolidated tax return is liable for the entire consolidated tax liability of the group.[115] This liability includes not only taxes but any deficiencies assessed against the group for its consolidated return years. If a subsidiary ceases to be a member of a group before a deficiency is assessed, the IRS may assess the former subsidiary only its allocable share of the deficiency. This allocation is only available, however, if the subsidiary's cessation came from a bona fide sale or exchange of its stock.[116] A tax-sharing agreement entered among the affiliated members is not sufficient to protect any member from imposition of the entire consolidated tax liability.[117] Nevertheless, this agreement may be useful to allow the subsidiary to recover the taxes from the other members.

COMMON PARENT AS AGENT

The common parent corporation is considered to be the sole agent for each subsidiary in the group. Except for minor situations—other than the initial election to be taxed on a consolidated basis—the common parent has full authority to make elections and act for the group. In fact, the Regulations specifically prohibit the subsidiary from exercising these powers.[118] Thus the IRS must deal only with a single corporation, unless, after giving notice to the common parent, it chooses to deal with a specific subsidiary. If the parent corporation contemplates dissolution, it is required to notify the IRS and designate another affiliated member to act as agent in its place. Failure to designate another group member as agent before dissolution allows the remaining members to choose a replacement agent.[119]

---

[114]   Reg. § 1.1502-5(a)(2).

[115]   Reg. § 1.1502-6(a).

[116]   Reg. § 1.1502-6(b).

[117]   Reg. § 1.1502-6(c).

[118]   Reg. § 1.1502-77(a).

[119]   Reg. § 1.1502-77(d).

TAX PLANNING

A number of tax-saving techniques exist for those filing consolidated tax returns. In addition, it should be emphasized that many of the techniques discussed in prior chapters concerning single corporate returns are also available on a consolidated basis. The areas for tax planning discussed below, however, focus on situations involving affiliated groups.

THE DEEMED AND CONSENT DIVIDENDS

The deemed dividend can be one of the most powerful planning tools in the consolidated return area. The deemed-dividend election may be made any year after 1965 by submitting a statement to the Internal Revenue Service center on or before the due date (including extensions) for filing the return. The advantage of making this election is that it increases the parent's basis in a subsidiary by the amount of the earnings and profits accumulated during separate return affiliation years and pre-1966 consolidated return years.

Unless special circumstances dictate (e.g., anticipated tax-free returns of capital), the group should always consider making the election as soon as possible. If the group procrastinates in making the election, the opportunity to increase the parent's basis may be lost. This opportunity can be lost if the group's ownership of the subsidiary falls below 100 percent; if the subsidiary has future deficits that serve to reduce accumulated earnings and profits; or if the laws affecting this provision should be changed.

Application of the deemed-dividend provisions may not always be available to the affiliated group (e.g., because it has less than 100 percent ownership in the subsidiary). If this is the case, the consent-dividend provisions of § 565 may be used to obtain the same effect as the deemed dividend. Under this provision, the consent dividend may apply to a subsidiary that was not wholly owned on every day of the taxable year. In addition, the amount of the E&P to be capitalized by the parent corporation may be selected. Contrasted with a deemed dividend, a consent dividend affects a subsidiary's earnings and profits at the end of the year as opposed to the first day of the taxable year.

ELECTION TO ELIMINATE OR POSTPONE
THE EXCESS LOSS ACCOUNT

Negative adjustments made to the basis of a subsidiary's stock obviously decrease the basis of such stock. As a consequence, an excess loss account can occur even though the group may have sufficient basis in other preferred stock or debt instruments in that particular subsidiary. In order to prevent a lopsided treatment in the event of disposition, the Regulations provide for a special election.[120]

---

[120]   Reg. § 1.1502-32(f).

For years beginning after 1971, if a disposition occurs, an election can be made to reduce the basis of preferred stock or other obligations of that subsidiary held immediately prior to the disposition.[121] If the excess loss account should exceed the basis of these other assets as well, the remaining excess loss account must be included in income.

If the election is made to reduce the basis of other securities, several aspects of the election should be considered. For example, consideration should be given to which stock or obligations will be satisfied in the future, to whether separate returns will be filed in the near future, to future liquidations, and to the extent of any expiring carryovers.

> **Example 58.** On August 15, 1991 P purchases all the common stock of S for $5,000. In addition, P purchases 100 shares of S's preferred stock for $3,200. P and S file a consolidated tax return for 1991 reflecting a $6,300 loss by S. As a result, P must reduce its investment account. Because S's basis is now reduced below zero ($5,000 − $6,300), an excess loss account is created. Thus, if P disposes of S's common stock, a $1,300 capital gain must be recognized. Where the preferred shares have been owned prior to the disposition of S common stock, P can elect to have its basis in the preferred stock reduced to $1,900 ($3,200 − $1,300) instead of reporting the $1,300 capital gain.

THE 30-DAY RULE

If a subsidiary becomes a member of an affiliated group within 30 days after the beginning of its taxable year, it may elect to be a member of a consolidated tax return from the beginning of its tax year. By making this election, the subsidiary does not have to file a short-period tax return. This election may be useful, for example, in situations where a subsidiary has long-term contracts about to mature during the short period. By making the election, the subsidiary may offset that income against any losses of other affiliated members by filing a consolidated tax return for its entire tax year.

The impact of this election should also be considered and addressed whenever a change in ownership of a subsidiary occurs.

---

[121]   Reg. § 1.1502-19(a)(6).

Example 59.   P Corp. has owned 100% of S Inc., an airline company, since 1986. From 1986–1990, S generated substantial losses. In 1991 management was replaced and the corporation reduced its losses. Nevertheless, S estimates that the losses will continue at a rate of $200,000 a month for at least another year. Aware of S's NOL prospects and the increased likelihood of its success, T Corporation wants to acquire S. In this situation, it is imperative that both P and T understand the implications of the 30-day rule when negotiating the terms of the sale. Assuming T acquires S on January 30, 1992, S may elect to be a member of either the P or T group since it is acquired within the first 30 days of its taxable year and it has been a member of the P group for no more than 30 days of its taxable year. If it elects to be a member of the P group, P receives the benefit of S's NOL for the month of January. Alternatively, if S elects to be a member of the T group, T is permitted to use S's loss in its consolidated return. Since T will control S when the election must be made, it also effectively controls the benefits associated with S's NOL. This aspect of the sale should be addressed in the contract and reflected in the price that P receives for its S stock.

PROBLEM MATERIALS

DISCUSSION QUESTIONS

8-1 *Consolidated Regulations.* Describe why Regulations for consolidated tax returns are more authoritative than the Regulations for controlled groups.

8-2 *Choosing to File a Consolidated Return.* Before filing a consolidated return, consideration should be given to both the advantages and disadvantages of such returns. Describe the following:

    a.   Four advantages of filing such returns.
    b.   Four disadvantages of filing a consolidated return.

8-3 *Eligibility to File.* The privilege of filing a consolidated tax return is available only to an affiliated group. Briefly describe the two tests that are necessary to satisfy the requirements of an affiliated group.

8-4 *Includible Corporations.* In each of the following situations, determine whether the corporation is an "includible" corporation.

    a.   John Smith, P.C., an S corporation
    b.   Southwest Pipe, NA., a foreign corporation
    c.   Jet Tool and Die, Inc., an Alaskan Corporation
    d.   AVCO, Inc., a wholly owned finance subsidiary
    e.   Malbert, Inc., a captive insurance company
    f.   A trust taxable as an association

8-5 *Controlled Groups.* Explain how related corporations can be considered a parent-subsidiary controlled group yet not satisfy the requirements to file a consolidated tax return.

8-6 *Election to File Consolidated Returns.* Answer the following questions regarding a corporation's election to file consolidated tax returns.

    a.   At what date must the election be made?
    b.   Can the election be revoked?
    c.   On what form is the election made?
    d.   Describe two situations in which the election can be discontinued.

8-7 *Stock Ownership Test.* Briefly describe the two requirements that must be met in order to satisfy the stock ownership rules.

8-8 *Consolidated Tax Concepts.* Briefly describe the steps necessary to compute consolidated taxable income.

8-9 *Intercompany Transactions.* Distinguish between intercompany transactions and deferred intercompany transactions.

8-10 *Restoration Events.* Describe the two events that trigger the restoration of the deferred intercompany transaction account.

8-11   *Inventory Adjustments.*   Answer the following.

    a.   Under what circumstances must an intercompany adjustment be made?

    b.   Briefly define the following terms.

        1.   Intercompany profit amount
        2.   Initial inventory amount
        3.   Unrecovered inventory amount

8-12   *Investment in Subsidiaries.*   Consider the following:

    a.   Briefly describe why adjustments are made to the basis of the stock of subsidiaries that are held by members of the affiliated group filing a consolidated tax return.

    b.   Identify the three positive adjustments.

    c.   Identify the four negative adjustments.

8-13   *Excess Loss Account.*   Answer the following:

    a.   Define an "Excess Loss Account" and explain why such an account exists.

    b.   Must an "Excess Loss Account" always be used in accounting for investor's investment? Explain.

8-14   *Separate Return Limitation Year.*   Answer the following:

    a.   Define an SRLY and describe situations in which it arises.

    b.   Are there any exceptions to the SRLY limitations?

    c.   What is the "lonely parent rule"?

8-15   *Built-in Deductions.*   Address the following questions:

    a.   When do the restrictions concerning built-in deductions apply?

    b.   Explain when the limited deductions can be utilized.

    c.   Are there any exceptions to the built-in deduction rules? Explain.

8-16   *Consolidated Return Change in Ownership.*   Explain how the CRCO rules are applied and why they exist. Include in your comments their relationship to § 382.

8-17   *Reverse Acquisitions.*   Explain a reverse acquisition and its implications for filing consolidated returns.

8-18   *Operating Rules.*   Answer the following:

    a.   Assuming the parent is on a July 31 year-end and the subsidiary is on a calendar year-end, can a consolidated return be filed?

    b.   In the first consolidated return year, how are estimated tax payments to be made?

    c.   In the third consolidated return year, how are estimated tax payments to be made?

    d.   Who is generally liable for the tax liability of the affiliated group?

    e.   Will a tax-sharing agreement among the members be of any use?

    f.   Under what circumstances may a subsidiary deal with the IRS?

8-19 *Year Income Is Reported.*   On January 18, 1991, P, a calendar year corporation, acquires all the stock of calendar year S corporation.

a.   How may S file for 1991?
b.   Same as above except that P is on an October 31 year-end.
c.   Same as above but S is on an October 31 year-end.
d.   Same as above but S was purchased on December 7, 1991.

PROBLEMS

8-20 *Intercompany Transactions.*   P Corporation, a manufacturer of plumbing equipment, has two subsidiaries: S, a plumbing sales corporation, and T, a plumbing maintenance corporation. P, S, and T file a consolidated return. During 1991, T performs the following for its affiliated members in addition to its services for its customers: (1) July 1, 1991, a $28,750 charge for installation of a water cooling system for P; and (2) October 15, 1991, a $125 charge to repair a cracked water line for S.

a.   How are the services to P reported by T?
b.   How are the services to S reported by T?
c.   If P places the $28,750 charge on account to be paid at a later date, does it matter that P is an accrual basis taxpayer and T is a cash basis taxpayer?

8-21 *Restoration Events.*   Assume the same facts as in Problem 8-20 above. In addition, assume the water cooling system is being depreciated over a ten-year period using the straight-line method. How much income must T report in 1991? In 1992?

8-22 *Inventory Adjustments.*   P is a manufacturing corporation and its subsidiary S is a sales corporation. During 1987 through 1991, P and S have the following intercompany inventory transactions.

	1987	1988	1989	1990	1991
P's intercompany profit in S's inventory...............	$22,000	$26,000	$18,000	$23,000	$20,000

P and S file separate returns for 1987 but file a consolidated return for 1988 through 1991. All the inventory is sold within the first six months on a FIFO basis.

a.   What is the initial inventory amount for 1988?
b.   What is the unrecovered inventory amount for 1988 and which corporation will it affect?
c.   What effect will the transactions have on either corporation from 1989 through 1991?
d.   What difference does it make whether a company is on the FIFO basis or the LIFO basis for inventory adjustments?

8-23   *Consolidated Capital Gains.*   P, S, and T file a consolidated tax return for 1990 and 1991. During 1991, the group had the following capital transactions:

1.   S sold to T land for $35,000 (basis of $12,000).
2.   P sold equipment to its president, Individual X, who owns 40 percent of P's stock, for $11,000 (basis of $20,000). The remainder of P's stock is owned by X's brother.
3.   T sold depreciable equipment for $22,000 which it purchased from P in 1990 for $20,000. The equipment was being depreciated over a five-year period using ACRS.
4.   There is a capital loss carryover from 1990 of $13,000.

Determine the consolidated net capital gain or loss for the year.

8-24   *Separate Return Limitation Years (SRLY).*   On January 1, 1991 affiliated group P, S, and T buys loss corporation X with a net operating loss carryover of $120,000. During 1991, the group has consolidated taxable income as follows:

P	$40,000
S	60,000
T	(20,000)
X	15,000
Consolidated taxable income	$95,000

a.   How much of X's NOL can be utilized in 1991?
b.   How much of the loss can be carried over to 1992?
c.   Suppose that the shareholders of X, instead of selling their stock, purchased all of the stock of S Corporation from the affiliated group. Assuming the same income figures for 1991, what is the amount of X's NOL that can be utilized in 1991?

8-25   *Built-in Deductions.*   P Corporation acquires all the stock of S on January 1, 1991, which has the following assets:

	Fair Market Value	Basis
Cash	$10,000	$10,000
Machinery	8,000	20,000
Land	16,000	14,000
Totals	$34,000	$44,000

a.   If S sells the machinery for $6,000 on May 24, 1991, how much can be deducted in a consolidated tax return if consolidated taxable income is as follows:

P	$17,000
S	4,000
Consolidated taxable income	$21,000

b.   Would your answer to (a) above change if the land was worth $25,000?
c.   Same as (a) above, but S shareholders contribute $30,000 prior to their sale of S stock to P.

8-26 *Consolidated Return Change in Ownership (CRCO).* On January 1, 1991 individual A purchases loss corporation L and its subsidiary M, which has a $40,000 consolidated NOL carryover to 1991. On the same day, A transfers cash to L in exchange for additional L stock, and L, in turn, purchases profitable corporation P.

L, M, and P file a consolidated return for 1991 showing the following:

L	$10,000
M	(8,000)
P	20,000
Consolidated taxable income	$22,000

   a. Ignoring the limitations of § 382, how much of the NOL carryover can be utilized?

   b. How much of the loss is carried over to 1992?

   c. Supposing § 382 is in effect, what is your answer to (b)?

   d. Would it have been better for P to purchase L Corporation?

8-27 *Reverse Acquisition.* Same facts as in Problem 8-26 except that A, instead of purchasing the L stock, purchases the P stock and merges his P Corporation into L, receiving 80 percent of the outstanding stock of L Corporation.

   a. How much of the NOL can be used to offset the consolidated taxable income of $22,000?

   b. How much of the NOL is carried forward to 1992?

   c. Can any of the unused loss be applied to P's prior profitable years?

8-28 *Net Operating Loss Carryovers and Carrybacks.* Corporations P, S, and T file a consolidated tax return for 1991 reflecting separate taxable income in each corporation as follows:

P	($4,000)
S	(8,000)
T	3,000
Consolidated taxable income	($9,000)

   a. How much of the loss is apportioned to P?

   b. How much of the loss is apportioned to S?

   c. How much of the loss is apportioned to T?

   d. Assuming that S was an unaffiliated corporation for 1988 through 1990, determine the amount of its carryback assuming the taxable incomes in each of the following separate return years.

1988	$2,000
1989	3,500
1990	4,000

   e. If P, the parent, makes an election to carry forward the NOL, how much can S carry back to its separate return years?

   f. If the election in (e) above is in effect for 1992 and S is sold on July 1, 1992, what effect will this have on the carryover?

8-29   *Investment in Subsidiaries.*   P, a calendar year corporation, acquires all the stock of S Corporation for $15,000 on January 1, 1991. At the time of the purchase, S has accumulated E&P of $3,000. For 1991, S had earnings (E&P) of $4,000 and made distributions of $2,500 on April 1 and October 1, 1991.

    a.   What is P's basis in S as of December 31, 1991?

    b.   Assume the same facts above but that S acquires T Corporation on July 1, 1992 for $8,000. T has no prior E&P but earns $3,000 for the entire year of 1992. What is S's basis in T if half the earnings are attributable to the consolidated return period?

    c.   Assume the same facts as (b). What is P's basis in S as of December 31, 1992 if S earns $2,300 and makes no distributions during the year?

8-30   *Excess Loss Account.*   On January 1, 1990, P acquires subsidiary S which in turn acquires subsidiary T. P invests $12,000 in S, and S invests $4,000 in T. Consolidated tax returns are filed for 1990 through 1992 reflecting the separate taxable income of each as follows:

	P	S	T
1990.....................	$10,000	($3,000)	($3,500)
1991.....................	15,000	1,600	(2,700)
1992.....................	$20,000	(10,400)	500

    a.   What is P's basis in S for 1990?

    b.   What is S's basis in T for 1990?

    c.   What is P's basis in S for 1992?

    d.   What is S's basis in T for 1992?

    e.   How much gain or loss must S report if it sells all of its stock in T for $6,000 on December 31, 1991? What is the character?

8-31   *Earnings and Profits.*   P Corporation acquires all the stock of corporations S and T on January 1, 1991. P, S, and T file a consolidated tax return for 1991 and 1992. During this two-year period, the corporations had the following earnings (E&P) and made the following distributions:

	Earnings			Distributions		
	P	S	T	P	S	T
1991	$10,000	$50,000	$30,000	$30,000	$12,000	0
1992	12,000	80,000	35,000	40,000	20,000	$5,000

Assume P made distributions to its shareholders of $30,000 and $40,000, respectively, for 1991 and 1992. Determine the taxability of each distribution and the effects it will have on E&P for each year. (Assume no balance in E&P prior to 1991.)

8-32 *Allocating Tax Liability.* For 1991, the affiliated group of P, S, and T files a consolidated tax return reflecting the following taxable incomes and yielding a consolidated tax liability of $3,200.

P...	$ 6,000
S...	18,000
T...	(8,000)
Consolidated taxable income....................	$16,000

    a.   What is P's share of the liability?
    b.   What is S's share of the liability?
    c.   What is T's share of the liability?
    d.   If P pays the entire tax liability, what effect does it have on S and T?

RESEARCH PROBLEMS

8-33 On January 15, 1991 R Corporation purchased all the stock of S and T Corporations. R, S, and T are all calendar year corporations. It was mutually determined and documented in the corporation minutes that an election to file on a consolidated basis would be made for tax year 1991. On February 1, 1992, R inadvertently filed with the Internal Revenue Service a separate tax return for 1991. Realizing the mistake, on February 15, 1992, all three corporations joined in the filing of a consolidated automatic application for extension of time, Form 7004. The extension was granted through September 15, 1992. On September 21, 1992, R, S, and T submitted their 1991 consolidated tax return to the Internal Revenue Service.

    Based upon these facts and circumstances, will R Corporation be able to file a consolidated tax return with its subsidiaries S and T? Does the inadvertent filing of a separate tax return by R have any effect on your answer?

Research aids:

    Reg. § 1.1502-75(a)(1)
    Rev. Rul. 56-67, 1956-1 C.B. 437
    Rev. Rul. 76-393, 1976-2 C.B. 255
    Millette and Associates, Inc. v. Comm., T.C. Memo 1978-180
    Reg. § 1.9100-1

8-34   P Corporation is equally owned by individuals A and B and has been filing a consolidated tax return with its subsidiary S for the past five years. Because of conflicting opinions between A and B on the expansion and administration of P, it is decided that one of the businesses of P and the stock of S should be transferred to A. In accordance with the plan, P transfers assets from one of its businesses to S solely in exchange for additional shares of S stock and immediately thereafter distributes all the stock of S to A. As part of the transaction, A surrenders all of its stock in P. The transaction qualifies as a split-off under §§ 355(a)(1) and 368(a)(1)(D).

    In view of this arrangement, what will the tax consequences be for P if the transfer of assets from P to S included § 38 property?

Research aids:

    Reg. § 1.1502-3(f)(2)(i)
    Reg. § 1.47-3(f)
    Rev. Rul. 82-20, 1982-1 C.B. 6

8-35   P and its wholly owned subsidiaries S, T, and U constitute an affiliated group that has filed consolidated returns for the past five years. Each corporation has been both a "selling member" and a "purchasing member" in a variety of deferred intercompany transactions for which deferred gains currently exist. Because of the prevailing economic climate, P is contemplating the sale of its subsidiaries. If no suitable buyer is found, P may consider liquidating S, T, and U into P. In view of these considerations, what are the "restoration" consequences with respect to the deferred gains that exist among the members? If neither of these alternatives is acceptable, what are the "restoration" consequences if all the members receive permission to discontinue filing a consolidated tax return?

Research aids:

    Reg. § 1.1502-13(f)(1)
    Reg. § 1.1502-75(d)(1)
    Reg. § 1.1502-13(c)(6)

LEARNING OBJECTIVES

Upon completion of this chapter you will be able to:

- Explain the taxation of U.S. citizens' and U.S. residents' foreign source income

- Identify the trade-offs between the foreign tax credit, the foreign tax deduction, and, when applicable, the foreign income exclusions

- Understand the taxation of U.S.–based corporations' foreign source income

- Determine the uses of and tax provisions relating to Foreign Sales Corporations and Controlled Foreign Corporations

- Identify the tax provisions relating to Foreign Personal Holding Companies and Possessions Corporations

- Determine the allocation of income and deductions among affiliated companies

- Understand the tax provisions relating to foreign currency gains and losses

- Explain the U.S. taxation of nonresident aliens

CHAPTER OUTLINE

Chapter 9

INTERNATIONAL TAXATION

INTRODUCTION

All industrial nations reserve the right to tax income earned within their territorial borders. This policy covers income earned by citizens, residents, nonresident aliens, and foreign businesses. In addition, the *Sixteenth Amendment* to the *Constitution of the United States* approaches taxation from a broader jurisdictional principle. It states:

> The Congress shall have the power to lay and collect taxes on income, *from whatever source* derived without apportionment among the several States, and without regard to any census or enumeration. (Emphasis added.)

Consequently, a U.S. citizen's or U.S. resident's *worldwide income* is subject to U.S. taxation. A similar jurisdictional approach has been taken by many industrial nations, including Canada, Japan, and the United Kingdom. Some governments, however, exclude income earned outside their borders from taxation. This type of exclusion applies most often to business entities rather than to individuals. For example, earnings of foreign subsidiaries are excludable income for parent corporations located in France, New Zealand, and Sweden.

With few exceptions, the United States levies taxes on income of U.S. citizens and resident aliens regardless of their place of residence and on income of U.S. corporations regardless of where their activities legally and economically occur. This policy sometimes causes the same income to be taxed at three or more levels. First, foreign-earned income is usually taxed by the host country. Second, most governments withhold taxes on dividend, interest, and royalty payments that leave their countries. Third, the gross income (income before foreign income taxes and withholding taxes are deducted) is taxable in the United States when it is constructively received by a U.S. citizen or corporation. In addition, this income may be subject to state and local income taxes in both the host country and the United States.

TAXATION OF U.S. CITIZENS

Individual U.S. citizens are taxed on their worldwide income. Since most *foreign source* income is also taxed in the foreign country, the Code provides three options that allow individuals to avoid, or at least decrease, the double tax burden.

1. Direct foreign income taxes may be reported as an *itemized deduction*.

2. Instead of a deduction, direct foreign income taxes may be claimed as a *credit* against U.S. income taxes.

3. Qualifying individuals may elect to *exclude* foreign-earned income up to certain statutory amounts.

The first option, an itemized deduction of foreign income taxes, is generally less beneficial than the foreign tax credit. Both the tax credit in option two and the exclusion in option three are subject to limitation. Those limitations applicable to tax credits are based on total foreign source income, while those applicable to exclusions are based on foreign source *earned* income. If the third option is elected, foreign taxes applicable to the amounts excluded cannot be claimed as a tax credit or deduction.

FOREIGN SOURCE INCOME

The source of *earned income* is determined by the place where the work is actually performed.[1] This determination is unaffected by either the location of the employer (or other contractor of services) or the method of payment. For example, salary received by a U.S. citizen for work performed in Germany is foreign source income, even if payment is made by a U.S. corporation to the employee's Indiana bank account. As might be expected, there is an exception to this rule. Treaties generally provide that salaries of U.S. government employees are not foreign source income, even though duties are performed and payments are received in another country.[2]

In addition to salaries, earned income includes professional fees, commissions, and employee benefits.[3] Companies often provide U.S. *expatriates* (U.S. citizens working in a foreign country) with substantial employee benefits. Common examples are extra amounts to cover higher costs of living, housing, home leaves, education for dependents, and income taxes. In some instances, these amounts exceed the employees' base salary and are substantial business costs.

---

[1] § 862(a)(3).

[2] § 911(b)(1)(B)(ii). For example, see the *North Atlantic Treaty Status of Forces Agreement* and the *Treaty of Mutual Co-operation and Security between the United States and Japan*. This is in contrast to some countries that base their sourcing rules on where services are utilized or payment is made.

[3] 911(d)(2)(A).

Proprietors and partners have foreign-earned income to the extent that they perform services for their businesses in another country. As discussed in the partnership chapter (Chapter 10), it is helpful if these amounts are guaranteed payments rather than distributions of profits when a partnership has U.S. source income.[4] If capital is a *material income-producing factor*, earned income is limited to 30 percent of the owner's share of net income.[5]

> **Example 1.** A British partnership has $200,000 of net income in the current year. None of the income is from U.S. sources. J's distributive share is $40,000. He is a U.S. citizen living in London.
>
> 1. If J performs no services for the partnership, he has $40,000 unearned foreign source income.
>
> 2. If J performs services valued at $17,000, and capital is not a material income-producing factor, he has $17,000 earned foreign income and $23,000 unearned foreign income.
>
> 3. If J performs services valued at $17,000, and capital is a material income-producing factor, he has $12,000 (30% of $40,000) earned foreign income and $28,000 unearned foreign income.

The 30 percent limit does not apply to owners of businesses with net losses. When net losses occur, earned income is limited to an owner's share of gross profit from the business. The 30 percent limit also does not apply to incorporated businesses.

Dividends, interest, pensions, annuities, capital gains, gambling winnings, and alimony are considered *unearned income*. Royalties and rents are also unearned income unless services are provided by the recipient. Unearned income usually qualifies as *foreign source* when it is received from a foreign resident or for property used in a foreign country and not effectively connected with U.S. sources. For example, interest is foreign source income even if the income is received in the United States when it is paid by a U.S. citizen who is a resident of a foreign country. In contrast, rents and royalties are foreign source income only if the property is used in a foreign country. Thus, the location of the property, not the residency of the payor, determines the source of rents and royalties.

In general, the source of income from sales of *personal* property (i.e., property other than real estate) is determined by the residency of the seller rather than by where title transfers. Thus, the income is U.S. source when sold by a U.S.

---

[4] § 707(c); Reg. § 1.707-1(c); and *Carey v. U.S.*, 70-1 USTC ¶9455, 25 AFTR2d 70-1395, 427 F.2d 763 (Ct. Cls., 1970) compared with *Foster v. Comm.*, 64-1 USTC ¶9362, 21 AFTR2d 859, 329 F.2d 717 (CA-2, 1964).

[5] § 911(d)(2)(B).

resident and foreign source when sold by a nonresident, regardless of where title transfers.[6] There are, however, several exceptions to this rule. The source of income from the sale of

1. Intangibles contingent on productivity, use, or disposition is generally determined by where the intangible is used, but goodwill is sourced in the country where it was generated.

2. An active affiliated foreign corporation's stock is foreign source if sold in the foreign country where the affiliate had derived more than 50 percent of its gross income in the previous three years.

3. Inventory is generally where title transfers.

4. Depreciable property is based on a recapture rule (i.e., the source of income, to the extent of depreciation expense, is the country where the deduction was claimed, and the source of any remaining income is determined by where title transfers).

5. Personal property other than those listed in 1 through 4 above is foreign if attributable to the seller's foreign office and is subject to a foreign income tax of at least 10 percent.

6. Personal property (other than Subpart F income, discussed later in this chapter) by a nonresident will be U.S. if attributable to a U.S. office (this rule is inapplicable if the property is inventory sold for use outside the United States and a foreign office of the seller materially participated in the sale).

These sourcing rules apply to all sales by foreign persons (other than controlled foreign corporations, discussed later in this chapter).

Very different sourcing rules apply to transportation income from an aircraft or a ship that begins or ends its trip in the United States. These earnings are divided equally between U.S. and foreign source income.[7]

In the past, some taxpayers were able to convert U.S. income to foreign source income by funneling it through a foreign corporation, especially one in a low-tax country. All dividends and interest received by U.S. shareholders from this corporation qualified as foreign source income. But the foreign-source designation is limited when (1) at least 50 percent of the voting power or total stock value of the foreign corporation is owned by U.S. shareholders, and (2) at least 10 percent of the corporation's income is from U.S. sources.[8] When these two requirements are met, a pro rata amount of the dividends and interest received is U.S. source income.[9]

---

[6] § 865(a).

[7] § 863(c)(2).

[8] § 904(g).

[9] § 904(g)(1).

FOREIGN TAX DEDUCTIONS OR CREDITS

Originally, taxes paid to foreign governments were only deductible in the same manner as U.S. state and local taxes.[10] But since 1921, individuals have been able to elect to claim foreign income taxes applicable to U.S. *includible income* as either an itemized deduction or a credit.[11] (See discussion later in this chapter for corporations.) Elections are made annually by filing Form 1116 for the credit or Schedule A for the deduction. Foreign taxes applicable to *excludable* U.S. income do not qualify for either a deduction or a credit.[12]

In most instances, a tax credit provides more benefit than a deduction. However, a deduction may be more advantageous if, when compared to worldwide income, the foreign effective rate of tax is high and foreign income is small.

> **Example 2.** N, a single individual, is a U.S. citizen living and working in Kentucky. She owns common stock in a Canadian corporation. The corporation has no U.S. source income. During the year, she received $850 from the corporation. The dividend was $1,000, less the Canadian dividend withholding of $150. Her U.S. source taxable income is $20,000. N's U.S. tax liability is calculated below using both (A) the foreign tax credit method, and (B) the foreign tax deduction method. The U.S. tax is based on 1991 tax rates. (Assume *all* dollar amounts are expressed in U.S. dollars.)

	(A) Tax Credit	(B) Tax Deduction
U.S. source taxable income..............	$20,000.00	$20,000.00
Foreign source taxable income..........	1,000.00	1,000.00
Foreign tax deduction...................	0	(150.00)
Worldwide taxable income................	$21,000.00	$20,850.00
U.S. tax.................................	$ 3,234.50	$ 3,192.50
Foreign tax credit......................	(150.00)	0
Total U.S. tax...........................	$ 3,084.50	$ 3,192.50

> N saves $108 if she elects the foreign tax credit method.

When the foreign effective rate of tax does not exceed the U.S. effective rate, foreign taxes may be claimed as a credit without limit. However, when the foreign tax rate exceeds the U.S. rate, the foreign tax credit is limited to the U.S.

---

[10] §§ 164(a) and 275(a). "Foreign income taxes" include amounts paid to national and local foreign governments.

[11] §§ 164(a), 901(b) and 903. For a checklist of qualifying taxes in various countries, see

Commerce Clearing House, *Standard Federal Tax Reporter*, Vol. 8 ¶4303.318.

[12] § 911(d)(6).

effective rate.[13]   That is, foreign taxes may be used to offset U.S. taxes up to but not beyond the amount of U.S. taxes attributable to foreign source income. The formula for the limitation is as follows:

$$\text{Foreign tax credit limitation} = \text{U.S. tax} \times \frac{\text{Foreign source taxable income}}{\text{Worldwide taxable income}}$$

Example 3.   Refer to *Example 2*, but assume the Canadian tax was 25% and $250 was withheld from the $1,000 dividend. The foreign tax credit is limited to $154.02 ($3,234.50 × $1,000 ÷ $21,000), and her total U.S. tax is $3,080.48 ($3,234.50 − $154.02). Her excess foreign tax credit is $95.98 ($250 − $154.02). Under the tax deduction method, N's total U.S. tax is $3,164.50 on worldwide taxable income of $20,750 ($21,000 − $250). Thus, she saves $84.02 ($3,164.50 − $3,080.48) in the current year if she elects the foreign tax credit method.

Excess foreign tax credits may be carried to years when the reverse situation exists (i.e., years in which foreign tax credits are *less* than U.S. taxes on foreign source income). The *carryover* of credits is limited to a two-year carryback and a five-year carryforward.[14]   For example, a 1991 excess credit is carried first to 1989. Any part of the credit not used in 1989 is carried to 1990. This process continues into 1992, 1993, 1994, 1995, and finally into 1996. Any 1991 carryover not used before 1997 is lost.

FOREIGN INCOME EXCLUSIONS

The intent of legislation affecting taxation of individuals working abroad is to encourage U.S.-based multinational corporations to employ U.S. expatriates in their foreign operations. One of the expected advantages is that foreign operations managed by U.S. citizens will purchase more goods and services from the United States.

Qualifying individuals (those who meet either the bona fide resident or the physical presence test discussed later) have three separate elections available to them. They may elect to exclude, subject to statutory limitations, their

1.   Foreign-earned income

2.   Employer-provided foreign housing income

3.   Employer-provided housing and meals in company foreign camps

All three elections are made separately, but individuals may not obtain tax benefits from the same income under more than one of the exclusions.

---

[13]   § 904(a).

[14]   § 904(c) and Rev. Rul. 75-268, 1975-2 C.B. 294.

Foreign-Earned Income. The election with the most potential benefit allows qualifying taxpayers to exclude their foreign-earned income from personal services, subject to a $70,000 annual limitation.[15]

> **Example 4.** W, a U.S. citizen, meets the bona fide resident test while employed in Belgium. During the year, she receives a salary of $55,000 and interest income from a Belgian bank of $5,000. W may elect to exclude the $55,000 earned foreign income but not the $5,000 unearned foreign income. If W received additional compensation of $30,000, she may exclude $70,000 but not the remaining $15,000 of compensation ($55,000 + $30,000 − $70,000) nor the $5,000 of interest income.

Limits are applied to each qualifying taxpayer regardless of marital status. Thus, the 1991 limit for either a husband or a wife is $70,000. If a taxpayer does not qualify for the exclusion the entire year, the exclusion is prorated on a daily basis.[16]

> **Example 5.** R, a U.S. citizen, met the physical presence test while employed in Italy through October 31 of the current year. R was employed in the United States the last two months of the year. Thus, she was employed in Italy 304 days and in the United States 61 days. R's salary earned in Italy was $60,000, and her salary earned in the United States was $20,000. R's maximum exclusion is $58,301 [$70,000 × (304 ÷ 365)], which means she has $21,699 ($60,000 − $58,301 + $20,000) includible income for U.S. tax purposes.

Employer-Provided Foreign Housing Income. Many companies provide either housing or cash as a housing allowance for their expatriate employees. Basically, employees living in employer-provided housing must report includible foreign-earned income equal to the company's housing costs. (Note the contrast with legislation for employer-provided housing in the United States.) Individuals, however, are able to elect one of two exclusions applicable to this employee benefit. First, employer-provided housing income qualifies for the annual foreign-earned income exclusion discussed above. Or, individuals may exclude a portion of their employer-provided housing income under a second election available to

---

[15] § 911(b)(2)(A) and Reg. § 1.911-1. [16] § 911(d)(2)(A) and Reg. § 1.911-3(d).

them. This second exclusion is limited to the *housing cost amount*, computed as follows:

1. Qualifying foreign housing expenses, less

2. 16 percent of the GS-14, step 1 salary level of a U.S. government employee (prorated on a daily basis if the taxpayer does not qualify for the exclusion the entire year).[17]

The GS-14, step 1 salary is $52,406 in 1991.

Qualifying foreign housing expenses include all reasonable costs (i.e., not "lavish or extravagant under the circumstances") incurred directly or as a cash allowance to house an employee and also the spouse and all dependents living with the employee.[18] Examples of acceptable expenses are rent or the fair rental value of employer-owned housing, insurance, utilities, repairs, and other costs related to the housing and its furnishings, plus parking fees and local telephone charges. Acceptable expenses do not include capital expenditures, depreciation, domestic help, or expenses that can be claimed as itemized deductions, such as interest and property taxes.[19]

> **Example 6.**   C, a U.S. citizen, meets the bona fide resident test while working in Spain. During the year, he receives a salary of $55,000, employer-provided housing costing $12,000, and other foreign employee allowances of $31,000. As stated above, the GS-14, step 1 salary is $52,406. C's foreign-earned income is $98,000 ($55,000 + $12,000 + $31,000). If he makes both elections, he may exclude $70,000 ($55,000 + $31,000 but limited to the annual exclusion) plus $3,615 [$12,000 − (16% of $52,406 = $8,385)]. Thus, C's includible foreign-earned income is $24,385 ($98,000 − the two exclusions of $70,000 and $3,615).

In most instances, the housing must be near the foreign work place, but there is one exception. If living conditions in the area are dangerous, unhealthy, or otherwise adverse, housing expenses also include money spent to maintain a separate foreign home for the spouse and dependents.[20]

The Code also provides that taxpayers who pay qualifying housing expenses and are not reimbursed by an employer may deduct the expenses *for* A.G.I. This deduction, however, may not exceed the taxpayer's includible foreign-earned income.[21] Any excess expenses may be carried forward one year and deducted to the extent there is taxable foreign-earned income in that year.[22] Regulations extend this provision for a deduction to the self-employed, to employees not re-

---

[17]   § 911(c)(1) and Reg. § 1.911-4.

[18]   § 911(c)(2)(A).

[19]   Reg. § 1.911-4(b).

[20]   § 911(c)(2)(B).

[21]   §§ 911(c)(3)(A) and (B).

[22]   § 911(c)(3)(C) and Reg. § 1.911-4(e)(2).

ceiving employer-provided housing, and to employees with only a portion of their housing costs provided by their employers.[23] According to these regulations, employees may deduct housing expenses they paid (subject to the limitations) that are not attributable to the employer.

Employer Foreign Camps. The third special exclusion is available to employees living in employer-provided camps, generally located in hardship areas. These individuals qualify as living and eating on the business premises at the convenience of their employer. As a result, all of their employer-provided meals and lodging are excludable income.[24]

QUALIFYING INDIVIDUALS

Only individuals whose tax homes are in a foreign country qualify for the foreign-earned income and the housing cost exclusions.[25] In addition, these taxpayers must meet either (1) the bona fide resident or (2) the physical presence test. U.S. citizens may qualify under either test, except that income earned within a country subject to federal travel restrictions (e.g., Cuba, Libya, and Vietnam) does not qualify for either exclusion.[26] U.S. residents who are citizens of another country qualify only under the physical presence test, unless a tax treaty with their country provides otherwise.

The *bona fide resident test* requires that, during an uninterrupted period that includes an entire tax year, individuals must accomplish the following:

1. Maintain bona fide resident status in one or more foreign countries

2. Have foreign-earned income from personal services

3. Receive the foreign income no later than the year following the service

4. Be paid by an entity other than the U.S. government or one of its agencies or instrumentalities

Once the bona fide resident test is met, the entire uninterrupted period of foreign residency qualifies for the exclusion provisions.

Bona fide resident status is not jeopardized if taxpayers continue to own a home in the United States or make brief business or personal trips to the United States.[27] However, there must be a clear intent to return to the foreign tax home or a new one without unreasonable delay. A bona fide foreign resident generally is

---

[23] Reg. §§ 1.911-4(d) and (e).

[24] § 119(c).

[25] §§ 911(d)(1) and (3) and Reg. § 1.911-2(c).

[26] § 911(d)(8) and Rev. Ruls. 72-330, 1972-2 C.B. 444, and 72-598, 1972-2 C.B. 451.

[27] Reg. §§ 1.911-2(b) and (c).

expected to work outside the United States for an extended or indefinite period and establish a permanent family residence in the work area. An intention to return eventually to the United States is not relevant to the test. Residency status is denied those taxpayers who make statements to authorities in the foreign country that they are not residents, and consequently are exempted from being taxed as residents of that country.[28]

Individuals unable to meet the above test may be able to qualify for foreign earned income and employer-provided housing exclusions under the *physical presence test*. In addition to their tax home being in a foreign country, individuals must have been *present* in one or more foreign countries for at least 330 days during any 12 consecutive months.[29]

Taxpayers relying on the physical presence test may be challenged by the IRS on the basis that an assignment of less than one year is *temporary*. At stake is the fact that a foreign residence cannot qualify as a tax when it is temporary. The IRS contends that an assignment of less than one year is temporary when at least two of the three following criteria are met:[30]

1. The taxpayer continues to have work contacts in the U.S. tax home area (e.g., the U.S. employer granted the taxpayer a leave of absence).

2. The taxpayer incurs duplicate living expenses (e.g., both a U.S. and foreign residence are maintained).

3. Either the taxpayer's family occupies the U.S. residence or the taxpayer frequently uses it for lodging.

Anyone expecting to work abroad for more than one year is presumed to have established a foreign tax home. However, this is rebuttable by the IRS if the individual expected the foreign employment to last for less than two years and intended to return to the U.S. tax area when the foreign employment ended.

Unlike the bona fide resident test, exclusions under the physical presence test apply only to those months that fall into one or more of the qualifying 12-month periods. Taxpayers are allowed considerable freedom in selecting the 12 months. They may be any consecutive 12 months, and two periods may overlap.

> **Example 7.** M, a single U.S. citizen, is transferred to Vienna, Austria March 13, 1991 by her company for an indefinite period that is expected to last more than two years. She establishes residency in Vienna, where she remains except for a two-week visit to the United States in August 1991.

---

[28]   § 911(d)(5).

[29]   § 911(d)(1)(B) and Reg. § 1.911-2(d).

[30]   Rev. Rul. 83-82, 1983-1 C.B. 45, and Ltr. Rul. 8452103.

Unexpectedly, M's company transfers her back to the United States May 1, 1992. She prepares her taxes on the calendar year. M does not meet the bona fide resident test because she was not a resident of Austria for an entire tax year. However, she does meet the physical presence test because she was in a foreign country more than 330 days during 12 consecutive months. In fact, she qualifies for the entire 13 months because she has two qualifying 12-month periods, even though they overlap. Her first 12-month period is April 1991 through March 1992 and her second 12-month period is May 1991 through April 1992. As a result, she may elect either or both of the foreign income exclusions for the entire 13 months.

Example 8. Refer to *Example 7*, but assume M was a resident of Vienna from March 31, 1991 until January 10, 1993 and made three additional two-week (14 days each) business trips to the United States. The trips were made during 1992 in January, March, and July. M does not qualify under the physical presence test since she was not present in one or more foreign countries at least 330 days during any 12-month period. However, she qualifies under the bona fide residence test because she was a resident of a foreign country during all of 1992. Since the bona fide resident test is met, M may elect either or both of the foreign income exclusions for the entire period of residency (i.e., from March 31, 1991 until January 10, 1993).

There is one exception to both the bona fide resident and the physical presence tests. If the tests are not met solely because the taxpayer was forced to leave the foreign tax home because of war, civil unrest, or other adverse condition, the minimum time requirement may be waived. Such waivers are granted by the Treasury based on information provided by the State Department.[31]

ELECTIONS TO EXCLUDE

An election under either exclusion provision is applicable for all future taxable years unless revoked by the taxpayer.[32] The election remains in effect but dormant if the taxpayer returns to the United States for an extended period. Although IRS permission to revoke the election is not necessary, it is advisable, because all new elections require IRS consent. If the revocation is made with permission, the IRS may grant the new election regardless of when it is made. Otherwise, a new election is not available for five years.

[31] § 911(d)(4).

[32] § 911(e) and Reg. § 1.911-7(a).

SPECIAL RULES AFFECTING DEDUCTIONS, CREDITS, AND EXCLUSIONS

Taxpayers electing either the annual foreign-earned income exclusion or the housing cost amount exclusion are prevented from obtaining double benefits.[33] First, this means that individuals may not elect two or more exclusions for the same income. For example, individuals may not elect to exclude employer-provided housing under both the housing cost amount and the annual exclusion provisions. In addition, the total amount excluded may not exceed foreign-earned income. Second, the Code provides that a portion of the taxpayers' deductions and credits must be allocated to the excluded foreign-earned income.

Allocations are made in one of two ways. First, all items directly related to any type of income must be allocated to that income. Second, those items not directly related to any type of income are allocated with the following formula: *the deduction to be allocated multiplied by the fraction of excluded foreign-earned income divided by total foreign-earned income.* When the item to be allocated is a credit, the same formula applies except it is based on net amounts. "Net" means that all related deductible expenses are subtracted from both the numerator and the denominator first. Items that may be subject to the formula include moving expenses (to the foreign location and between two foreign countries), unreimbursed employee business expenses, foreign tax credits, child care credits, and the exclusion for meals and lodging provided for the convenience of employers. Generally, expenses incurred in moving back to the United States are deductible against U.S. source income and therefore are not included in the allocation formula. This is true even though employer reimbursement for these moves may qualify as compensation for past services abroad and thus as foreign source income. The result of the allocation requirement is that a portion of the deductions and credits may not be claimed by taxpayers against their includible income. Consequently, the tax benefit of the exclusion is diminished.

Taxpayers who sell their foreign tax homes have a longer period of time to replace the residence in order to defer any gain on it than they do for a U.S. residence.[34] Recall that the period for replacing a U.S. residence is two years. The period for replacing the foreign residence is four years if the taxpayer continues to live outside the United States.

In addition, rules governing foreign moving expenses are more liberal than those covering moves within the United States.[35] The differences include the following:

1. Deductions for temporary living expenses are tripled to 90 days.

2. The limit on expenses for house hunting and temporary living expenses are tripled to $4,500.

---

[33]   § 911(d)(6).

[34]   § 1034(k).

[35]   § 217(h).

3. The limit on house hunting, temporary living, and expenses related to obtaining a new home and disposing of the former home are doubled to $6,000.

4. Moving expenses are extended to include moving household goods to and from storage, and storage costs.

The tax return filing date is two months later for individuals living abroad at the time their return is due.[36] For those electing the calendar year, this means a due date of June 15. Only one taxpayer on a joint return needs to meet the requirements. Although taxpayers are not required to file an extension to obtain the two-month delay, they must attach a statement to the return showing their eligibility. In addition, liberal extensions of time beyond June 15 are granted by the IRS. An automatic extension until August 15 may be obtained by filing Form 4868. An extension beyond August 15 may be requested by filing Form 2688 and showing reasonable cause for the delay. The extensions provide these taxpayers an opportunity to better assess their situations to determine if they will meet the various tests relevant to their foreign tax positions. Any unpaid taxes, of course, are subject to interest. If returns are filed prior to qualifying for the exclusions, computations must be based on the assumption that the tests will *not* be met. Refund claims may be filed when the tests are met.

TAXATION OF U.S.-BASED CORPORATIONS

When a U.S. corporation engages in international operations, new dimensions are added to the already difficult subject of taxation. As might be expected, taxing policies of each country differ in the types of taxes, rate structures, tax bases, and special provisions that are available. Some of these are modified through bilateral treaties negotiated with individual countries. In addition, the U.S. Internal Revenue Code contains numerous options for taxation of a corporation's foreign source income.

A company, for example, may find it beneficial to establish one or more separately taxed entities for its sales to foreign customers. In some instances, it may be to the company's benefit to establish a tax-haven corporation in a country that is a U.S. possession. Or, a company may choose to generate sales through a foreign subsidiary or branch located near the customer. Although numerous factors must be considered when deciding which entity should make the sale to the foreign customer, it is essential that companies adopt a policy of systematic tax planning.

---

[36] Reg. § 1.6081-2.

FOREIGN TAX CREDITS OR DEDUCTIONS

Regardless of the form of operation used, all direct foreign taxes *deemed* paid (or accrued) by the U.S. corporation may be claimed as either a business deduction or a tax credit.[37] These calculations differ for a corporation from those for an individual because of the meaning of the word *deemed*. Qualifying foreign taxes include those payable directly by the U.S. corporation (e.g., foreign withholding taxes on dividends) plus those payable indirectly by it on foreign source income (e.g., foreign income taxes paid by the subsidiary or branch). In order to claim foreign taxes indirectly paid, the U.S. corporation must own at least 10 percent of a foreign corporation's voting stock.[38] The foreign source income is *grossed up* so that the U.S. includible income is the foreign income received *plus all* foreign taxes *deemed* paid by the corporation.[39]

> **Example 9.** U.S. Parent, Inc. has taxable income in the current year from U.S. sources of $500,000. Its wholly owned Canadian subsidiary (which was acquired at the beginning of the year) has foreign source taxable income of $80,000, pays $16,000 in Canadian income taxes (20% tax rate), and has an after-tax income of $64,000 ($80,000 − $16,000) from which a dividend of $32,000 (50% of after-tax income) is declared. Since the dividend is payable to a non-Canadian shareholder, it is subject to a 15% dividend-withholding tax of $4,800 (15% × $32,000). Parent receives $27,200 ($32,000 − $4,800). Foreign taxes deemed paid by Parent total $12,800 ($4,800 + 50% of $16,000). If Parent claims a foreign tax credit for the Canadian taxes, the U.S. income tax liability is $170,800. If Parent claims a foreign tax deduction, its U.S. income tax liability is $179,248.

	Tax Credit	Tax Deduction
Foreign source income..............................	$ 27,200	$ 27,200
Foreign income taxes................................	8,000	8,000
Foreign withholding taxes...........................	4,800	4,800
Grossed-up dividend	$ 40,000	$ 40,000
U.S. source income................................	500,000	500,000
Foreign tax deduction.............................	0	(12,800)
Taxable income	$540,000	$527,200
U.S. tax (34% × T.I.)	$183,600	$179,248
Foreign tax credit...................................	(12,800)	0
U.S. tax liability...................................	$170,800	$179,248

---

[37] §§ 901(b) and 903. For a checklist of qualifying taxes in various countries, see Commerce Clearing House, *Standard Federal Tax Reporter*, Vol. 8, ¶4303.318. Foreign taxes deemed paid computations are *not* available to noncorporate taxpayers.

[38] § 902(a).

[39] § 78 and Reg. § 1.902-1(b)(iii).

In *Example 9*, the foreign subsidiary was acquired in the current year. After the initial year of ownership, the computation of foreign taxes deemed paid is expanded to include taxable income for all years.[40] Thus, the formula for foreign taxes deemed paid is as follows:

$$\frac{\text{Dividend received}}{\text{Accumulated earnings and profits (AE\&P)}} \times \text{Total foreign income taxes}$$

The objective of this legislation is to discourage companies from maximizing foreign tax credits through timing arrangements.

Example 10.   A wholly owned foreign subsidiary has the following information:

	Dividend	E&P	Foreign Income Taxes
1990	$ 0	$100,000	$20,000
1991	44,000	120,000	40,000
Total		$220,000	$60,000

The foreign income taxes deemed paid are $12,000 [($44,000 ÷ $220,000) × $60,000]. Note that if the computation could be based on current year amounts, these taxes deemed paid would be $14,667 [($44,000 ÷ $120,000) × $40,000].

A company with decreasing effective foreign tax rates has the reverse of the situation illustrated in *Example 10*. That is, a higher foreign tax credit is allowed when the effective foreign tax rate is higher for all years than it is for the current year.

The rule governing foreign taxes deemed paid by a U.S. parent corporation extends beyond the wholly owned foreign subsidiary. In addition, if a 10 percent or more owned foreign corporation (first-tier) owns at least 10 percent of another foreign corporation (second-tier), and the second-tier corporation owns at least 10 percent of another foreign corporation (third-tier), a percentage of foreign taxes incurred by all of these corporations may qualify as a foreign tax credit or deduction. However, a first-tier corporation must meet the ownership test before a second-tier corporation can qualify. Similarly, both first- and second-tier corporations must meet the test before a third-tier corporation can qualify. One

---

[40]   §§ 902(a) and 960, effective after 1986. Prior to 1987, dividends were deemed paid first from current year earnings and prof- its and second from accumulated earnings and profits.

further requirement is that the U.S. corporation must own indirectly at least 5 percent of the foreign corporation in order to claim a share of its taxes. As in the 10 percent requirement, the 5 percent ownership test must be met at the first-tier before the second-tier can qualify, and at the first- and second-tier before the third-tier can qualify. In all instances, the ownership interest must be in the form of outstanding voting stock.[41]

Example 11.　X is a U.S. corporation. A, B, and C are foreign corporations. X owns 40% of A (first-tier), A owns 30% of B (second-tier), and B owns 80% of C (third-tier). The 10% test is met at all levels of ownership. In addition, X has an indirect ownership of at least 5% of each tier, determined as follows:

$$\text{X owns } 40\% \times 30\% = 12\% \text{ indirectly of B}$$
$$\text{X owns } 12\% \times 80\% = 9.6\% \text{ indirectly of C}$$

Thus, X may claim a portion of the foreign taxes incurred by A, B, and C. If, however, B owned 35% of C instead of 80% :

$$\text{X owns } 12\% \times 35\% = 4\% \quad \text{indirectly of C}$$

In this situation, X may claim a portion of the foreign taxes incurred by A and B but not by C. If A only owned 8% of B, the 10% test is not met between A and B. This breaks the chain of required ownership and means that foreign taxes paid by B and C are not deemed paid by X.

Examples 9, 10, and *11* deal with a foreign subsidiary. If the foreign operation is a *branch* rather than a subsidiary, however, total foreign source income (or loss) and total foreign taxes for the year are included in the calculations regardless of how much income is received currently by the U.S. corporation. When there is more than one subsidiary and/or branch, foreign source income and foreign taxes from all operations in all countries are totaled and calculations are made in the same manner as illustrated in *Examples 9, 10,* and *11.* This is referred to as the *overall method.*[42] When income is includible from both high and low (compared to the United States) tax rate countries, this approach is particularly beneficial.

There have been exceptions to the overall method for several years. The overall method does not apply to most investment interest, to dividends, nor to foreign trade income of Foreign Sales Corporations (discussed later in this chapter). Separate foreign tax credit (FTC) computations must be made for each of these

---

[41]　§ 902(b).　　　　　　　　　　　　[42]　§ 904(a).

two types of foreign source income. FTC limitations have *five* additional types of foreign source income categories. These foreign income segments or "baskets" are[43]

1. Passive income, which in general includes income that qualifies as foreign personal holding company income under Subpart F (discussed later in this chapter), but not if it (a) is subject to a foreign tax rate greater than the highest U.S. rate (e.g., 34% for corporations and 31% for individuals), (b) is listed in items 2 and 3 below, (c) is from a controlled foreign corporation, (d) is active business rents and royalties from unrelated parties, (e) is from foreign oil and gas extraction, or (f) is interest from financing certain foreign property sales

2. Dividends received from *each* corporation in which the recipient owns between 10 and 50 percent of the voting power or stock value (this limitation is applied on a company by company basis)

3. Interest income subject to a foreign withholding tax or gross income tax of at least 5 percent (referred to as "high withholding tax interest")

4. Income from the active conduct of a banking and financing business, or certain types of income of an insurance company (referred to as "financial services income")

5. Shipping income from leasing, operating, or selling aircraft and vessels used in foreign commerce, and from related services

The object of this separate-category legislation is to segregate income (1) when the foreign tax rate is either very high (e.g., oil extraction income) or very low (e.g., FSC dividends), or (2) when the activity can be transferred to a low tax rate country from the United States (e.g., passive interest). Consequently, expanding the number of categories for applying the FTC limitation is expected to increase unused FTCs among some firms and thus increase U.S income tax collections.

If a foreign source category has a net loss, that loss is allocated among the other categories based on their relative portion of net foreign source income. Any remaining loss reduces U.S. source income. The reverse also is required. That is, a net U.S. loss must be allocated among the foreign source categories in the same manner. There also is a recapture provision. Consequently, any net income in a future year that occurs in a category that suffered a loss in a prior year is allocated among the other categories in the same manner and to the extent that the loss was allocated.[44]

---

[43] § 904(d).   [44] § 904(f)(5).

Tax planning can be very important in obtaining maximum benefits from foreign tax credits. One of the most valuable strategies involves the timing of dividends. If a year-end analysis shows an excess foreign tax credit for the year, it may be useful to have a subsidiary in a low tax rate country declare a dividend. This action gives the U.S. parent corporation access to additional cash without increasing its U.S. tax liability. Similar action is absolutely essential when excess foreign tax credits are about to expire because of the five-year carryforward limitation. The reverse situation is even more rewarding. That is, if U.S. taxes on foreign source income exceed foreign tax credits, a dividend declared by a subsidiary in a high tax rate country results in more cash available in the United States both from the dividend received and from a lower U.S. tax liability.

Example 12. Year-end analysis reveals $100,000 of grossed-up foreign source income, $20,000 of foreign taxes, and $400,000 of U.S. source income. The U.S. effective tax rate of 34% exceeds the foreign effective rate of 20% ($20,000 ÷ $100,000). If a $200,000 grossed-up dividend is made from a subsidiary with qualifying foreign taxes of $82,000, the U.S. tax liability is decreased by $14,000 ($150,000 − $136,000).

	Before Dividend	After Dividend
Foreign source income	$100,000	$300,000
U.S. source income	400,000	400,000
Taxable income	$500,000	$700,000
U.S. tax (34% × T.I.)	$170,000	$238,000
Foreign tax credit	(20,000)	(102,000)
U.S. tax liability	$150,000	$136,000

The limitation on foreign tax credits does not apply since the limit of $102,000 [($300,000 ÷ $700,000) × $238,000] equals total foreign taxes of $102,000 ($20,000 + $82,000).

Similar transactions involving other types of income can achieve the same results, but it generally is simpler to use the dividend approach.

In some instances, it may not be possible for a foreign subsidiary to declare a cash dividend because it does not have enough available cash or because it is politically impossible or undesirable to transfer currency out of the host country. Although seldom used in the past, a *consent dividend* can achieve the same effect as a cash dividend on foreign source income, foreign tax credits, and U.S. tax liabilities even though no asset is transferred.[45] The consent dividend

---

[45] § 565, John L. Kramer and Robert L. Gardner, "Consent Dividends from Foreign Corporations Can Provide Tax Benefits," *The International Tax Journal* 8 (February, 1982), pp. 172–87, and George J. Slezak, "Consent Dividends from Foreign Corporations," *The International Tax Journal* 3 (June 1977), pp. 432–34.

allows a U.S. corporation to elect to be taxed currently on all or part of a foreign subsidiary's income. Generally, no withholding tax is assessed on consent dividends, since no assets leave the foreign country. An added tax planning benefit is that the decision to make a consent dividend is not required until the annual tax return is filed. This, of course, is considerably later than decisions for cash dividends, which must be declared by year-end. Because of the complexity of this strategy, however, a company is advised to obtain, when possible, a prior ruling from the tax authorities of both countries.

DIVIDENDS-RECEIVED DEDUCTION

A U.S. corporation may use the dividends-received deduction for dividends from a foreign corporation's post-1986 E&P. The U.S. corporation must own at least 10 percent of the foreign corporation's voting power *and* stock value. As might be expected, *either* (but not both) the dividend deduction or the FTC can be taken.

ALTERNATE FORMS OF ORGANIZATION

Businesses with transactions outside the United States may use several different types of specialized tax corporations in addition to exporting from the U.S. parent company or operating through a traditional foreign subsidiary or branch. These corporations are the Domestic International Sales Corporation, the Foreign Sales Corporation, the Controlled Foreign Corporation, and the U.S. Possession Corporation. All were created by Congress to provide incentives or disincentives to businesses to act in a particular manner in international transactions. All are products of complicated legislation that must be understood by those involved in foreign trade. Each corporation must be carefully examined, and the one or the combination most appropriate to the operations and desired objectives of the total organization should be selected.

Prior to the creation of special tax corporations, all foreign sales activities of U.S. companies were transacted by exporting products from the United States or selling products through branches or corporate subsidiaries domiciled in foreign countries. The federal income tax treatment is much the same for U.S. domestic sales, for exports from the U.S. parent corporation, and for sales made by foreign branches. That is, all net income or loss from exporting and from foreign branch activities are combined with net income or loss from domestic operations, regardless of whether cash or other assets have been received in the United States. The parent company is then taxed on its consolidated net income from domestic, export, and foreign branch activities. In contrast, net income from foreign incorporated subsidiaries generally is not reported for Federal income taxes until dividends are actually received in the United States. This taxing policy allows companies to defer U.S. taxes on foreign subsidiary net income indefinitely. It also means, however, that net losses from these subsidiaries cannot be used to decrease U.S. taxable income.

TAX INCENTIVES TO EXPORTING

Most industrial nations provide tax incentives to exporters. However, the General Agreement on Tariffs and Trade (GATT) places restrictions on the type of tax incentives they may use. The primary restriction is that GATT members may not exempt exports from direct taxes. As a result, these nations seek other alternatives. In some instances, tax incentives are given to all businesses regardless of the destination of the goods. For example, the United Kingdom has granted businesses special inventory deductions to help offset the effects of inflation and to make exports more competitive worldwide. These same reasons are given by many nations for allowing depreciable assets to be expensed over a period of time considerably shorter than their expected lives. For example, allowances have been made for equipment to be written off in the first year in the United Kingdom and in the first two years in Canada. These special tax provisions for accelerated inventory and depreciation deductions meet GATT requirements since both domestic and export trade are treated identically and the advantages are based on timing differences rather than on exemption from taxes.

Several countries, including members of the European Economic Community, rely extensively on the *value added tax* (VAT) for their revenues. This tax is levied on products at various stages of production. The actual value added to the product (including raw materials, labor, and profit) is determined at each stage and the tax is based on this increase in value. Since the final tax is collected at the products' destination, no VAT is charged on export sales. In contrast, VAT is charged on all domestically sold products regardless of the country of origin. Consequently, the expected effect is that VAT provides an incentive to export and a disincentive to import. VAT is considered an indirect tax, and thus, exempting exports from it does not violate GATT.

THE FOREIGN SALES CORPORATION

Because of the conflict with GATT, Congress created the *Foreign Sales Corporation* (FSC). Since 1984, exporters have been able to utilize either the FSC or the small FSC. A portion of the taxable income of both entities is exempt from U.S. Federal income taxes. However, stringent rules must be met in order to qualify for the exemption.

FSC Requirements. The FSC must meet the following rules:

1. Be created or organized under the laws of a U.S. possession (other than Puerto Rico) or a foreign country that provides for the exchange of information with the United States [in compliance with § 274(h)(6)(C) or by income tax treaty][46]

2. Have no more than 25 shareholders on any day throughout the year (excluding host country directors holding only qualifying shares required by host country law)[47]

3. Have no preferred stock outstanding on any day throughout the year (but presumably may have authorized preferred stock)[48]

4. Maintain permanent books of account at a non–U.S. office (where some business activity for the FSC regularly occurs) plus certain records specified in § 6001 at a U.S. office[49]

5. Have at least one non–U.S. resident (who may be a U.S. citizen) on its board of directors[50]

6. Not be a member of a controlled group that includes a DISC (common ownership needs to exceed only 50% rather than the usual 80%)[51]

7. Make a timely FSC election[52]

8. Adopt the taxable year used by the shareholder with the greatest percentage of voting power[53]

9. Hold all formal directors and shareholders meetings outside the United States and maintain the principal bank account outside the United States (referred to as the foreign management test)[54]

10. Have an economic presence in one or more countries, which includes specified minimum percentages of certain costs to be incurred outside the United States (referred to as the foreign economic process test)[55]

---

[46] § 922(a)(1)(A) and Reg. § 1.922-1(d).

[47] § 922(a)(1)(B) and Reg. § 1.922-1(f).

[48] § 922(a)(1)(C) and Reg. § 1.922-1(g).

[49] § 922(a)(1)(D) and Reg. §§ 1.922-1(h) and (i).

[50] § 922(a)(1)(E) and Reg. § 1.922-1(j).

[51] § 927(d)(4).

[52] § 922(a)(2).

[53] § 441(h)(1).

[54] §§ 924(b)(1) and (c) and Reg. § 1.924(c)-1.

[55] §§ 924(d),(e), and 925(c) and Reg. § 1.924(d)-1.

Exempt Income. A portion of the FSC's *foreign trade income* (FTI) is exempt from the FSC's U.S. Federal income taxes. The amount exempted is dependent on the pricing method selected. If an arm's length price under § 482 (i.e., what an unrelated buyer would pay an unrelated seller) is used, 32 percent of the FTI is excluded by noncorporate shareholders. However, if a statutory price is used, $^{16}/_{23}$ (i.e., almost 70%) is excluded. If the FSC has a corporate shareholder, these rates are reduced by the corporate preference rules to 30 percent and $^{15}/_{23}$ (approximately 65%), respectively.[56] The statutory prices may be used in a related party sale of export property to the FSC, but only if the foreign economic process test above is met by the FSC or its contracting representative.[57] When this occurs, a company may select a transfer price that results in FSC taxable income that does not exceed the greater of the following:

1. 23 percent of the combined taxable income that the related seller and FSC derive from *foreign trade gross receipts* (FTGR)

2. 1.83 percent of FTGR, but limited to twice the amount determined in the combined taxable income method (i.e., 46%)[58]

The limitation on the 1.83 percent method is intended to prevent an FSC from obtaining any tax benefit on a loss transaction. Generally, the 23 percent method provides the greater tax savings of the two statutory methods when the combined profit margin is at least 7.96 percent (1.83 ÷ 0.23).

Example 13. An FSC purchases qualifying export property from a related party and resells it to an unrelated foreign buyer for $1,000. The FSC's direct expenses are $230 and the related party's cost of goods sold is $520, and its selling expenses are $110. The statutory transfer price is determined as follows:

Gross receipts	$1,000
Cost of goods sold	(520)
Combined gross income	$ 480
FSC's direct expenses	(230)
Related party's selling expenses	(110)
Combined taxable income	$ 140

Note that the profit margin is 14% ($140 ÷ $1,000), which means the 23% method will result in greater savings.

---

[56] §§ 291(a)(4), 923(a), and 924(b)(2).   [58] §§ 925(a) and (d).

[57] § 925(c).

	23% Method	1.83% Method
Sales price	$1,000.00	$1,000.00
FSC expenses	(230.00)	(230.00)
FTI (23% × $140)	(32.20)	
FTI (1.83% × $1,000)		(18.30)
Transer price	$ 737.80	$ 751.70

The 23% method would be selected since it results in the greater FTI ($32.20 versus $18.30). The exempt portion of the FTI is $22.40 ($32.20 × $16/23$) for an FSC with only individual shareholders, or $21 ($32.20 × $15/23$) if there is a corporate shareholder. The remaining amount ($32.20 − $22.40 = $9.80 or $32.20 − $21 = $11.20) is taxable to the FSC, and the related party is taxed on $107.80 ($140 − $32.20).

Similar transactions of the FSC may be grouped together. The Senate Finance Committee Report also suggests that special rules should provide that (1) no loss on the sale can be recognized by the related party, (2) marginal costing procedures be available, (3) the pricing method can be selected after the sale is completed, and (4) adjustments to the transfer price should be permitted after the taxable year ends. However, an FSC's exempt income is subject to special limitations if it participates in or cooperates with an international boycott or illegal bribe or makes a payment to a government employee or agent.[59]

The treatment of an FSC's *nonexempt* export income is determined by the transfer pricing method selected. If a statutory method is used, the FSC is taxable on the nonexempt income, based on the rules and rates applicable to U.S. corporations. A special rule also provides that investment income (including carrying charges) is taxed to the FSC at U.S. rates. This provision is designed, in part, to discourage the operation of offshore financing subsidiaries as FSCs. If an arm's length price is used, the FSC is taxable on its nonexempt income, based on the rules and rates applicable to foreign corporations (discussed later in this chapter). The foreign tax credit is not allowed on exempt FTI nor on nonexempt FTI resulting from the use of the statutory pricing methods.

Qualifying Gross Receipts. FTGR includes gross receipts from (1) the sale, exchange, or other disposition of export property; (2) the lease or rental of export property to unrelated parties for use outside the United States; (3) services rendered in connection with items (1) and (2) above; (4) engineering or architectural services for construction projects that are (or are proposed to be) located outside the United States; and (5) managerial services rendered to an unrelated FSC or DISC if at least 50 percent of its gross receipts are from items (1) through (3). FTGR excludes receipts from investments, carrying charges, subsidies, and related parties; receipts for property to be used in the United States; and receipts for half the income from military sales.

---

[59] § 999(b).

FSC E&P. The FSC must establish two E&P accounts; an FTI E&P for *exempt* income to be maintained separately from other E&P. Dividend distributions are deemed to come first from the tax-exempt FTI E&P, and after this balance is exhausted, from other E&P. Although both are includible income, dividends from FTI E&P to a U.S. corporate shareholder qualify for a 100 percent dividend-received deduction, whereas there is no dividend deduction for distributions from other E&P, with two exceptions. After 1986, interest and carrying charges qualify for an 85 percent dividend deduction. (Congress failed to reduce this rate to 80% .) In addition, the 100 percent dividend deduction is allowed for nonexempt amounts if the FSC does not use administrative pricing and the FTI is effectively connected to a U.S. trade or business.[60] The treatment of most tax-exempt income (which does *not* qualify for a dividend-received deduction) can result in some types of FSC income being subject to U.S. corporate tax rates twice. For example, recall that investment income is taxable to the FSC at U.S. corporate rates. Since it is nonexempt income, it will be taxed a second time when distributed to shareholders. Tax planning certainly requires that the FSC avoid this type of income. Noncorporate shareholders are taxed on dividend distributions regardless of whether these come from exempt or nonexempt E&P. In addition, if the statutory pricing rules are used, nonexempt income is treated as U.S. source income, and foreign taxes paid on that income do not qualify for the foreign tax credit.

Qualifying Export Property. Qualifying export property must (1) be tangible property; (2) be manufactured, produced, grown, or extracted in the United States by a non-FSC; (3) have no more than 50 percent of its fair market value attributable to U.S. imports; and (4) primarily be held for sale, lease, or rent in the ordinary course of a trade or business by (or to) an FSC for direct use, consumption, or disposition outside the United States.[61] Export property further *excludes* (1) property leased or rented by an FSC for use by a member of its controlled group; (2) oil, gas, and their primary products; and (3) products prohibited from being exported.

Small FSCs. An FSC may elect to be treated as a small FSC if its controlled group does not include a nonelecting FSC. That is, if the group has more than one FSC, all of them must elect small FSC status.[62] The small FSC's annual tax exemption is limited to the taxable income attributable to no more than $5 million of FTGR. The only advantage of the election is that a small FSC is not required to meet the foreign management and the foreign economic process tests. It must, however, meet the foreign economic process test required by the statutory pricing rules. In many cases, this latter requirement can be achieved by contracting with the FSC's parent corporation that is in compliance with the test.

---

[60]   §§ 245(c) and 927(d)(6).

[61]   § 927(a).

[62]   § 924(b)(2).

FSC Termination. An FSC election is terminated if (1) the FSC revokes the election, or (2) it fails to meet all of the FSC requirements for a period lasting five consecutive years.[63] If one (or more) requirements is violated but not for five consecutive years, the FSC will be treated as a regular foreign corporation for those years when violations occurred.[64]

THE DOMESTIC INTERNATIONAL SALES CORPORATION

The Domestic International Sales Corporation (DISC) is another type of special corporation designed to yield benefits to U.S. businesses involved in exporting. Prior to 1985, extremely favorable income deferral provisions were available to DISCs, but many of these benefits have been eliminated. The form of DISC that now remains, generally called an "interest-charge DISC," is available for certain corporations.[65] Although a limited income deferral provision still exists, interest is due to the government on the tax that would have been due if there were no deferral of income.[66] Shareholders, not the DISC itself, are responsible for any Federal income taxes assessed on DISC income.[67]

Basically, a DISC must be incorporated in the United States, maintain separate accounting records, issue only one class of stock, have a par or stated value for its outstanding stock of at least $2,500 each day of the year, derive at least 95 percent of its gross receipts from exports, have at least 95 percent of its assets be export related, and not be a member of a controlled group that includes an FSC.[68] The DISC is not required to be an active corporation.[69] In fact, most serve as commission DISCs, and rarely buy and sell products. Instead, they receive commissions for acting as export agents. Furthermore, DISCs commonly are wholly owned subsidiaries of U.S. corporations, exist only on paper, have no employees, and do not transact business in their own corporate names.

A DISC may be utilized to defer all of its taxable income attributable to no more than $10 million of qualified export gross receipts (EGR).[70] As stated above, interest is due on the potential tax liability attributable to this deferred income. All DISC income attributable to EGR in excess of $10 million is includible in the shareholders' income currently.[71]

---

[63] § 927(f)(3).

[64] Reg. § 1.927(f)-1(b).

[65] § 992.

[66] § 995(f)(1).

[67] § 995(a).

[68] § 992(a)(1).

[69] Rev. Rul. 72-166, 1972-1 C.B. 220.

[70] §§ 993(a) and 995(b)(1)(E) and (F).

[71] § 995(b).

TAX INCENTIVES FOR FOREIGN OPERATIONS

U.S.-based multinational corporations may defer U.S. taxes on income of their foreign subsidiaries indefinitely. To accomplish this, however, funds of these subsidiaries cannot be received in the United States either directly or indirectly. Thus, if French subsidiary funds are repatriated to the U.S parent and immediately reinvested in a Japanese subsidiary, U.S. taxes must be paid on the French income received. Alternately, if the French subsidiary transfers the funds directly to the Japanese subsidiary, the U.S. tax treatment is the same. That is, the funds are deemed to have gone first to the U.S. parent and taxed as a dividend and then reinvested in the Japanese subsidiary. This deemed dividend approach adds significantly to the cost of using funds generated within an organization for its worldwide operations.

One method used by multinationals in the past to avoid the deemed dividend was to establish a holding company in a country with either low or no taxation on income earned outside its borders. Generally, these holding companies were inactive corporations created for the sole purpose of owning a controlling interest in active corporations throughout the world, including the U.S. parent. Under this organizational arrangement, the French subsidiary funds could be transferred to the Japanese subsidiary with little or no tax consequence. Or, for that matter, funds could be invested in the United States by the holding company without triggering U.S. taxes. In addition, income was shifted to these companies by assigning export, patent, and licensing rights to them. Although use of holding companies in tax-haven countries by U.S. multinationals was curtailed after legislation in 1962 (discussed below), their use by many non–U.S.-based organizations continues to be significant.

Being a tax-haven country is an important business in itself. Countries desiring the designation consciously create attractive tax advantages for multinational operations. In addition, a tax-haven country must have political and economic stability, freely convertible currency, sophisticated banking and financial services, and accessibility to a good, worldwide communications system. Some tax-haven countries have few official restraints and allow considerable anonymity to the business community.

The typical tax-haven country is small, with limited natural resources. The more popular ones have been the Bahamas, Bermuda, Panama, the Netherlands Antilles, Switzerland, Liechtenstein, Luxembourg, Curaçao, the Cayman Islands, Hong Kong, and Liberia. In some instances, the number of corporations organized in these countries rivals the number of people living in them.

THE CONTROLLED FOREIGN CORPORATION

The objective of the Controlled Foreign Corporation (CFC) rules is to prevent corporations from being located in tax-haven countries for the sole purpose of tax avoidance. To accomplish this, the legislation provides that U.S. stockholders be taxed on CFC income when it is earned abroad, regardless of when it is received in the United States. Thus, tax deferral privileges ordinarily granted to foreign corporations are eliminated when CFC requirements are met. Placing tax-haven holding companies at the apex of an organizational structure may now result in a penalty rather than in the tax advantages previously available. Consequently, CFC requirements must be understood in order to avoid the penalties. For this reason, many U.S.-based multinationals reacted to the legislation by eliminating, reducing, or changing the activities of their tax-haven companies.

A foreign corporation may be designated a CFC and its shareholders taxed currently on its *Subpart F income* if it meets a *control test*. The test is met when more than 50 percent of its voting power *or* value of its outstanding stock is controlled directly or indirectly at any time during the year by U.S. stockholders who individually control at least 10 percent of the voting power.[72]

> **Example 14.** If 46% of a foreign corporation's stock is owned by one U.S. shareholder and the remaining 54% is owned equally by six unrelated U.S. shareholders (9% each), it cannot be a CFC. However, if any one of the six shareholders acquires an additional percentage directly or indirectly, the foreign corporation meets the CFC control test. This change in status occurs because the 46% shareholder and the 10% shareholder together meet the 50% and 10% requirements.

Subpart F, commonly referred to as *tainted* income, includes income that frequently had been shielded in the past from U.S. taxation through artificial arrangements with subsidiaries in tax-haven countries. Basically, there are eight types:

1. Income earned from providing insurance protection for U.S. property or residents[73]

2. Income attributable to participation in or cooperation with an international boycott[74]

3. Amounts equal to bribes, kickbacks, and other illegal payments to officials, employees, or agents of a foreign government

4. Passive income such as dividends, interest, rents, royalties, and gains from sale of these passive investment assets[75]

---

[72] §§ 951(b), 957(a), 958(a) and (b).

[73] § 953 and Reg. §§ 1.953-1(a) and 2(a).

[74] § 999.

[75] § 954.

5. Sales commissions, fees, and profits earned as a result of buying and selling goods that are neither produced nor used in the CFC's country, when one of the parties involved in the transaction is related to the CFC

6. Income for management, maintenance, and other services performed outside the CFC's country for the benefit of a related party

7. Income for the use of aircraft or vessels (including activities in space) engaged in foreign commerce

8. Income derived from foreign oil and gas not extracted or consumed in the country in which the CFC is domiciled when the CFC is a member of a related group that has at any time produced at least 1,000 barrels (or the equivalent) of oil or gas per day

The last five types of income are collectively referred to as *foreign base company income*.[76] For foreign tax credit purposes, the first one and possibly all or part of the remaining types of Subpart F income will not qualify as foreign-source income.

The Subpart F provisions contain several exceptions. For example, if foreign base company income is less than the smaller of (1) 5 percent of gross income, or (2) $1 million, none of it is treated as Subpart F income. In contrast, if gross income exceeds 70 percent, all CFC income is Subpart F income.[77] In addition, if the foreign income cannot be repatriated to the United States because it is blocked (such as currency restrictions), it is excluded until the restrictions are removed.[78] Generally, the purpose behind these and other exceptions to Subpart F income is to avoid penalizing foreign corporations with income earned from conducting active businesses. As a result, income of a foreign corporation that is subject to a minimum foreign tax rate is considered not to be organized in order to reduce taxes and is treated as exempt from Subpart F income.[79] To qualify for this exemption, the effective foreign tax rate must exceed 90 percent multiplied by the maximum U.S. corporate rate (e.g., $90\% \times 34\% = 30.6\%$).

U.S. shareholders who own directly or indirectly at least 10 percent of a CFC's voting stock must include in gross income their pro rata share of (1) Subpart F income, (2) all previously excluded Subpart F income no longer meeting exclusion requirements, such as the removal of restrictions on blocked currency, and (3) the increase in CFC earnings that are invested in U.S. property to the extent these earnings would be taxable dividends if distributed to the shareholders. These three types of income are taxable currently, regardless of whether any distributions are received and whether Subpart F income is direct or indirect. When dividends are distributed, however, they are not taxed again.[80] This is

---

[76] §§ 952(a) and 954.

[77] § 954(b)(3).

[78] § 964(b).

[79] § 954(b)(4).

[80] § 951(a).

accomplished by stockholders increasing their adjusted basis in CFC stock when the income is taxed in the United States and decreasing their basis in the stock when these previously taxed earnings are received.[81]

> **Example 15.** U.S Parent owns 700 shares (70% of all stock) of Belgium Corporation. Belgium Corporation owns 100% of Liechtenstein Corporation. Belgium has no Subpart F income but all of Liechtenstein's earnings of $100,000 qualify as Subpart F income. No dividends are paid by any of the corporations. U.S. Parent's tax situation is unaffected by Belgium's earnings since Belgium did not distribute any dividends and has no Subpart F income. Parent's tax situation is affected by Liechtenstein, however, even though Liechtenstein did not distribute any dividends and is not directly owned by Parent. The tax effect occurs because Liechtenstein is a CFC and because Parent owns more than 50% of its stock indirectly. Parent must recognize $70,000 dividend income (70% × 100% × $100,000) and increase its basis for Belgium's stock by $100 per share ($70,000 ÷ 700 shares). Parent also has a deemed foreign tax credit for taxes paid by Liechtenstein.

FOREIGN PERSONAL HOLDING COMPANY

U.S. stockholders may avoid being taxed on all or part of a corporation's undistributed income under the CFC rules but still be taxed under the Foreign Personal Holding Company (FPHC) rules. A foreign corporation qualifies as a FPHC if

1. At least 50 percent of its gross income (or 60% if it was not an FPHC in the previous year) is FPHC income;[82] and

2. More than 50 percent of the voting power *or* value of its outstanding stock was owned at any time during the taxable year directly or indirectly by no more than five U.S. citizens or residents[83]

FPHC income consists of passive income such as dividends, interest, royalties, annuities, net gains from assets that generate either passive income or no current income, net foreign currency gains from transactions in a nonfunctional currency, passive leasing and licensing income, income equivalent to interest, income from estates and trusts, and rents that do not constitute at least 50 percent of the gross income. FPHC income also includes income from personal service contracts and from payments for use of its property by a shareholder who owns directly

---

[81] § 961.

[82] § 552(a)(1) and Reg. § 1.552-2.

[83] §§ 552(a)(2) and 554; Reg. § 1.552-3; and Prop. Reg. § 1.554-2 through 7.

or indirectly at least 25 percent in value of the FPHC's outstanding stock.[84] Undistributed FPHC income is the adjusted taxable income less dividends paid.[85] Adjustments allowed in arriving at adjusted taxable income basically are the same as those allowed a U.S. personal holding company (i.e., those relating to national income taxes, charitable contributions, special deductions, net operating losses, and expenses and depreciation allowable to the FPHC property) but not capital gains. In addition, FPHC income is increased by certain contributions to pension trusts.[86]

FPHC shareholders, much like CFC shareholders, are deemed to have received constructive dividends equal to their interests in undistributed FPHC income. This includible amount increases the shareholders' basis in the stock.[87] When these dividends are distributed, they are not taxed again. Shareholders simply decrease their basis in the stock. The FPHC transfers a like amount from its accumulated earnings and profits to its paid-in or contributed capital.[88] In contrast to the U.S. personal holding company, there is no penalty tax levied on the FPHC (see Chapter 6 for a discussion of the § 541 penalty tax). If income qualifies as includible income for a U.S. shareholder under both the FPHC and the CFC rules, only the CFC rules apply.

THE POSSESSIONS CORPORATION

Unlike the CFC, the Possessions Corporation (PC) is a tax incentive corporation. Its objectives are (1) to encourage U.S. organizations to establish active business operations in countries that are U.S. possessions, and (2) to encourage the repatriation of funds generated by PCs to U.S. stockholders. For purposes of this legislation, U.S. possessions are defined as American Samoa, Guam, Midway Island, Puerto Rico, the Northern Mariana Islands, the Virgin Islands, and Wake Island.[89] A U.S. corporation may elect to be taxed as a PC if during the three preceding years, it earned (1) at least 80 percent of its gross income in a U.S. possession, and (2) at least 75 percent of its gross income from active business operations conducted in a U.S. possession.[90] Once the election is made, it cannot be revoked by the taxpayer for at least 10 years, unless permission is obtained from the Internal Revenue Service. This permission has been available only for hardship cases in which tax avoidance is not a factor. However, permission is not necessary if the former election was made before 1983 and a new election was made before 1988.[91]

---

[84] § 553 and Reg. § 1.553-1.

[85] § 556 and Reg. § 1.561-1.

[86] § 556(b) and Reg. §§ 1.556-2 and 3.

[87] §§ 551(a) and (e), and Reg. § 1.551-5.

[88] § 551(d).

[89] § 936(d)(1) and Reg. § 1.931-1(a)(1). The Virgin Islands were excluded from this list until 1987. However, corporations located in the Virgin Islands have always received tax treatment similar to that of PCs.

[90] § 936(a)(2).

[91] § 936(e) and Prop. Reg. § 1.936-7(c).

A PC's taxable income is computed in the same way as it is for any other U.S. corporation other than a DISC. In arriving at worldwide taxable income, however, taxable possessions income must be calculated separately.[92] This separate computation is necessary because a PC is granted a special tax credit equal to the U.S. tax *attributable* to possessions income.[93] The credit is available regardless of the amount of foreign taxes actually paid on income earned in U.S. possessions.

> **Example 16.** PC has taxable income of $250,000 from Puerto Rican sources and $50,000 from U.S. sources, for a total of $300,000 from all sources. Taxes paid to Puerto Rico total $15,000 and U.S. taxes on $300,000 are $100,250. Computing the special PC tax credit is identical to the method used for determining the foreign tax credit limitation illustrated in *Example 12*. That is, possessions income divided by worldwide income multiplied by the U.S. tax equals either the PC tax credit or the foreign tax credit limitation. In this example, the special PC tax credit is $83,542 [($250,000 ÷ $300,000) × $100,250]. This leaves a U.S. tax liability of $16,708 ($100,250 − $83,542).
>
> Note that the $15,000 in taxes paid to Puerto Rico does not enter into the computation. This is true regardless of the amount of foreign taxes. The special tax credit does not apply to other foreign source income. The regular foreign tax credit computations illustrated in previous examples are used to offset U.S. taxes on a PC's other foreign source income.

In most instances, the PC election results in a significant tax savings. There are situations, however, when the election can be a disadvantage. Since a PC cannot file a consolidated tax return with its U.S. parent or other related corporations, a PC's losses and excess foreign tax credit cannot be used for the benefit of the group. The reverse is also true. That is, losses and excess foreign tax credits of related parties cannot be used to offset PC taxable income or U.S. tax liability. The fact that a PC election must be made for at least 10 years denies it considerable flexibility, and thus, tax benefits can be lost when these situations occur.

Puerto Rico unquestionably is the most popular possession country. This is primarily because of extensive tax exemptions granted by Puerto Rico to businesses.

PCs have extremely low effective tax rates (generally less than 10 percent) because of tax exemptions granted by the possessions and the special tax credit available in the United States. Although there are numerous factors in addition to taxation that must be evaluated, tax advantages available to PCs are sufficient to warrant careful analysis. PC operations in possession countries can take many forms. The more common approaches are either light manufacturing or assembling processes, where a large percentage of the output is sold to U.S. customers. These products, of course, may be distributed worldwide.

---

[92] § 936(d)(2).   [93] § 936(a)(1).

In recent years, some U.S. corporations have transferred their intangible property to a PC. The transfer qualified under § 351 as a tax free exchange. Thus, the U.S. parent created the intangible, deducting all the research and development expenses on its U.S. tax return, and then transferred the intangible to the PC to shelter further revenues. TEFRA curtailed this increasingly popular practice. Basically, the income from intangibles is now classified as U.S. source income rather than possessions country income.[94] This eliminates the special foreign tax credit that is available on qualifying PC income. There are certain exceptions, however. For example, income from intangibles received by PCs with a *significant business presence* (generally measured in terms of local employment) in possessions countries or by PCs that have *manufactured* (or created) the intangibles may qualify as PC income. A complex set of rules and options must also be carefully analyzed by U.S. companies with PCs that receive income attributable to intangible property. Consequently, it will become more difficult for some subsidiaries to meet the required gross income tests.

ALLOCATIONS AFFECTING AFFILIATED COMPANIES

As businesses expand their operations worldwide, more legally separate entities are created. Some of these are in countries where effective tax rates exceed those in the United States and some are in countries with lower effective rates. Although percentages vary among countries, a substantial amount of all international trade occurs between related entities. This trade affects the organizations' total tax liability in some manner. To ensure that multinationals report their share of income from intercompany activities, most industrial nations have legislation that allows tax authorities to adjust income and deductions to reflect taxable income within their borders.

ALLOCATING INCOME AMONG AFFILIATED COMPANIES

Few business decisions have greater impact on the operations of multinational organizations than those involving pricing between affiliated companies located in different countries. Tax laws throughout the world require that transactions between units of the same organization must be at *arm's length*. That is, prices must be based on market values, whether dealing with related or unrelated businesses. The objective of these tax laws is to ensure that all transactions are recorded

---

[94] § 936(h).

as though they occurred between entities that are both legally and economically separate. The difficulty with this premise, of course, is that many multinationals do not operate in this manner. Instead, business decisions often are based on what is best for the organization as a whole. This difference in philosophy between tax authorities and multinationals creates considerable conflict worldwide.

In the United States, the authority to reallocate income and deductions between affiliated companies is provided by § 482 of the Internal Revenue Code. This section deals with five types of transactions: (1) interest on intercompany loans, (2) services performed for a related party, (3) use of tangible property by a related party, (4) intercompany transfers of intangible property, and (5) intercompany sales of tangible property. The Regulations provide quantitative guidelines for determining arm's length values for the first two of these categories when these transactions are not an integral part of either company's business.[95] For example, management services provided by a manufacturing company for its foreign sales subsidiary would not be considered an integral part of either company's business. The Code also prohibits importers from using a transfer price for Federal income taxation that exceeds the comparable U.S. Customs value.[96] In all other situations, qualitative guidelines are provided.[97] As might be expected, these subjective Regulations tend to be vague, and therefore, they allow the Internal Revenue Service and the courts considerable interpretive latitude. Similar legislation exists in most industrial nations.

The problem of intercompany transactions is complicated further by the fact that tax legislation is based on the assumption that these prices often are established to avoid, and possibly evade, taxation. Because of this attitude, § 482 is a preventive measure that can be used by the government but not by taxpayers. Thus, companies have the responsibility of convincing the IRS that pricing policies followed by affiliated companies are the same as those followed by unaffiliated companies. Otherwise, pricing reallocations made by the IRS must be sustained by the courts unless the taxpayer proves them to be unreasonable, arbitrary, or capricious.[98] Proving this may be nearly impossible, especially when the transactions involve unique assets or circumstances where no comparable arm's length price exists. Simply showing that the company's method is based on sound business reasons is inadequate.[99] While such evidence is relevant for disproving fraud charges, shifting income between related parties is subject to § 482 regardless of the motive. This should not, however, prevent multinationals

[95]   Reg. §§ 1.482-2(a), (b), and (c).

[96]   § 1059A.

[97]   Reg. §§ 1.482-2(d) and (e).

[98]   *Eli Lilly and Co. v. U.S.*, 67-1 USTC ¶9248, 19 AFTR 712, 372 F.2d 990 (Ct. Cls., 1967).

[99]   *Your Host, Inc. v. Comm.*, 74-1 USTC ¶9119, 33 AFTR2d 74-385, 489 F.2d 957 (CA-2, 1973), *aff'g* 58 T.C. 10 (1972).

from arranging company activities in order to minimize taxes.[100] Thus, multiple related entities may be formed as long as there is a business purpose for their existence and transactions between them are based on the arm's length standard.

No one group or organization has the authority to establish international standards for taxation. Traditionally, this regulatory authority has been exercised by each nation for transactions affecting businesses operating within its boundaries. In some instances, more than one governmental agency is delegated this authority. For example, transfer prices are of interest to both customs and income tax officials. Laws and taxing objectives differ among countries. Seldom has this been considered a serious problem by most multinationals, especially in countries other than the United States. However, tax practitioners in several countries are reporting both an increasing interest in intercompany transactions and sophistication on the part of government tax auditors. In many instances, these auditors are specialists in international matters and some are consultants with considerable business experience in the industry occasionally even in the company under audit. These and numerous other factors are causing greater interest in the establishment of international standards for taxation.

ALLOCATING DEDUCTIONS AMONG AFFILIATED COMPANIES

In the United States, the authority governing the *allocation of deductions* deemed to benefit affiliated companies is provided by Regulation § 1.861-8. Until 1977, these rules were simple and reallocations were rarely made during tax audits. As a result, if they chose to minimize taxes worldwide, multinationals had considerable latitude in assigning deductions to income from the various affiliated companies. Often, the deductions were simply taken by the corporation directly incurring the expense, usually the U.S. parent. This flexibility was replaced in 1977 by detailed Regulations. Provisions for allocating deductions are now very complex, with numerous examples for various types of deductions.

Under the Regulations, business deductions first must be allocated to each class of gross income. The Code lists 15 different classes of income that are applicable, including business income, rents, interest, and dividends.[101] These allocations are to be made to tax exempt as well as taxable income.[102] The deductions are then apportioned between U.S. source and foreign source income. Although the rules apply to all deductions, those not directly related to

---

[100] *U.S. Steel Corp. v. Comm.*, 80-1 USTC ¶9307, 45 AFTR2d 80-1081, 617 F.2d 942 (CA-2, 1980),*rev'g* 36 TCM 1152, T.C. Memo 1977-290.

[101] § 61 and Reg. § 1.861-8(a)(3).

[102] Reg. § 1.861-8(d)(2).

a specific class of income ordinarily have the most effect on foreign source income. These are primarily interest, research and development, and administrative expenses. If the multinational organization includes specially taxed corporations such as FSCs, DISCs, PCs, and CFCs, apportionments also require separate calculations for each type of specially taxed corporation.[103]

Allocation rules for expenses deemed not directly related to a specific class of income (e.g., interest and administrative costs) require that these expenses be combined and then allocated among the affiliated corporations, according to each one's total asset basis Certain financial institutions are exempt from these rules, and in some instances, taxpayers will be allowed to net interest expense against related interest income.

Even though a multinational's taxable income from all sources usually remains unchanged, many are paying higher taxes as a result of numerous changes in the Regulations. This generally occurs because of the effect these changes have on the foreign tax credit limitation.[104] Recall that *Example 12* illustrated the foreign tax credit limitation as foreign source income divided by worldwide income, with the results multiplied by U.S. taxes before the credit. Thus, a shift in deductions from U.S. source income to foreign source income lowers the foreign tax credit limitation. A shift in deductions may also adversely affect DISC benefits by increasing transfer prices based on the combined taxable income method.[105] The issue is complicated even further if a subsequent tax audit results in a reallocation of income under § 482.

This adjustment may change gross income relationships to the extent that deductions under Regulation § 1.861-8 will need to be recalculated.[106] As a result of the audit, the U.S. parent will pay more U.S. taxes because of the § 482 reallocation and also because of its effect on Regulation § 1.861-8 deductions.

RELIEF FROM DOUBLE TAXATION

Multinational organizations may be assessed income taxes on the same income by two different countries. Although this can occur in several ways, the most common *double taxation* situations result from adjustments made by tax authorities during an audit. In the United States, these basically fall into three categories: (1) reallocation of income or deductions under § 482, (2) reallocation of income or deductions under another Internal Revenue Code section, and (3) a reclassification of foreign source income to U.S. source income.

---

[103] Reg. § 1.861-8(f)(1) and (2).

[104] Reg. § 1.861-8(f)(1)(i).

[105] Reg. § 1.861-8(f)(1)(iii).

[106] Reg. § 1.861-8(f)(4).

Worldwide interest in intercompany transactions by tax authorities causes special concern about the potential for double taxation, especially for U.S.-based multinationals. As a result, the United States has specific procedures governing § 482 audits to ensure the company has an opportunity to avoid double taxation.[107] On first encountering a situation where § 482 is applicable, the Internal Revenue agent must notify the International Examining Group. An International Examiner is assigned to the case if the issues are complex. In the event a § 482 assessment is proposed, the taxpayer must be notified in writing about the adjustment and about any international appeal procedures available for relief from double taxation.

The parent company has several choices when notified of a § 482 adjustment. One, if there is a treaty with the foreign country involved, the parent may seek relief under the treaty's competent authority provision. Two, the parent may request an IRS administrative review of the adjustment. If this is unsuccessful, the company may then seek relief under the competent authority provision. Three, it may pursue the matter in Tax Court, the Court of Claims, or the appropriate District Court at any time. Thus, the taxpayer may turn to the courts as soon as the notice is received, after an unsuccessful administrative review, after an unsuccessful appeal through the competent authority, or during any of these procedures. Four, the parent also may decide at any time to accept the assessment and close the case.

Although no two treaties are identical, most contain a provision establishing a competent authority procedure to help protect taxpayers from double taxation. In the United States, this procedure is administered by the Foreign Operations District (formerly the Office of International Operations). The *competent authority* in each treaty country is responsible for pursuing an equitable solution to the double tax situation. This often includes waiving the statute of limitations when necessary. If an agreement satisfactory to the taxpayer is not reached, there are several possible outcomes. First, the competent authority may instruct the IRS to forgo the § 482 adjustments. Unless otherwise stated, however, this does not preclude the IRS from assessing the same tax under another applicable Code section. Thus, the taxpayer should ensure that the competent authority's instructions include a statement preventing such use of another Code section. Second, the IRS may allow the U.S. parent to treat the income subject to the double tax as an advance to the subsidiary. This allows the amount to be returned tax-free to the U.S. parent.[108] Nevertheless, the foreign country may choose to treat the return of funds as a dividend subject to withholding taxes. Third, some or all of the double tax may be offset by treating the amount in question as foreign source

---

[107]　Rev. Proc. 82-29, 1982-1 C.B. 18.　　　　[108]　Rev. Proc. 65-17, 1965-1 C.B. 833.

income when received in the United States. This results in a higher foreign tax credit limitation. This use of the foreign tax credit is available only to those companies that have sought relief through the competent authority.[109] Fourth, the company still has the option of requesting an IRS administrative review if it has not already done so, or to pursue the matter in U.S. courts.

Several reasons are given for not seeking assistance from the competent authority. Some taxpayers are concerned that the procedure is very time-consuming, taking from one to three years to complete after the authority becomes involved. In order to obtain competent authority help, the company must agree to the adjusted price established by the IRS. Such acceptance may affect future as well as past intercompany transactions and diminish the company's future bargaining ability with tax auditors. In addition, the competent authority acts as the company's advocate, which means the company may be required to share some of its internal documents with them. Not only are companies reluctant to share their documents with an agency of the Treasury Department in general, but there is also the fear that this information will be used to the foreign country's advantage either in audits of other intercompany transactions or in allowing this confidential information to be obtained by competitors. Treaties contain safeguards against this, but there is no guarantee. As a result of these and possibly other reasons, many U.S. companies accept the double taxation without seeking relief through the competent authority.

Competent authority procedures may not be available for double taxation that results from adjustments under Code sections other than § 482.[110] They also are not available when there is no treaty between the United States and the foreign country involved. In these situations, a request for refund may be made directly to the foreign country.[111] It is possible, however, that the request will be refused because the tax authorities believe the original amount is appropriate, because the statute of limitations prevents a review of this situation, or because of political or economic restrictions or conditions In any event, the taxpayer still may seek IRS administrative review and a hearing by the court.

FOREIGN CURRENCY GAINS AND LOSSES

International business is transacted in many currencies, but in most instances U.S. taxable income must be reported in dollars. With some exceptions, the "price" of dollars is determined by supply and demand in an unregulated market.

---

[109] Rev. Rul. 76-508, 1976-2 C.B. 225.

[110] Rev. Proc. 77-16, 1977-1 C.B. 573.

[111] Apparently, the IRS will pay interest on overpayments when the refund is of foreign taxes. Ltr. Rul. 8320004.

Consequently, the exchange rate from a particular currency to dollars may change. These fluctuations produce taxable gains or losses, basically, in four types of situations:

1.   Foreign currency transactions by taxpayers without physical locations in a foreign country

2.   Operations of foreign branches owned by U.S. corporations

3.   Dividend payments by foreign subsidiaries to U.S. corporations

4.   Operations of Controlled Foreign Corporations owned by U.S. taxpayers

Whether exchange gains and losses are ordinary or capital depends on the nature of the transaction. For example, gains and losses that arise in the normal course of business are ordinary.[112] However, those that result from investment or personal transactions produce capital gains or losses.[113]

In the first situation listed above, exchange gains or losses are determined under the *transaction method*. Generally, U.S. taxpayers must use the U.S. dollar for recording international transactions.[114] However, qualifying "§ 988 transactions" may be denominated in another currency. Section 988 applies when the taxpayer (1) is the debtor or creditor of a foreign currency debt, (2) accrues foreign currency receivables or payables for income and expense items, (3) has foreign currency futures and forward contracts (except those qualifying under § 1256, such as hedging, which are beyond the scope of this chapter), *or* (4) disposes of foreign currency. Gains and losses for *each* of these transactions are determined in the foreign currency and then translated into U.S dollars.

The entry for the transaction is recorded at the exchange rate in effect on that date, or, if more than one rate is in use, the one that "properly reflects income" is used.[115] The difference between this amount and the actual amount received (or paid) is the exchange gain or loss.[116] This gain or loss is reported when collection (or payment) is made in the U.S. taxpayer's functional currency, regardless of whether the accrual or the cash basis of accounting is used.[117] Whether the seller or the buyer has an exchange gain or loss depends on which one bore the

---

[112]   *Foundation Co.*, 14 T.C. 1333 (1950), *acq.* 1950-2 C.B. 2.

[113]   Rev. Rul. 74-7, 1974-1 C.B. 198. But, see *National-Standard Co.* 80 T.C. 551 (1983). The Tax Court allowed an ordinary loss when U.S. dollars were used to purchase Belgian francs to repay a Belgian loan originally made in francs. This decision was based on the Court's belief that no sale or exchange occurs with a mere repayment of indebtedness. A full court re-

view of the decision resulted in one strong dissent.

[114]   § 985.

[115]   Rev. Rul. 74-222, 1974-1 C.B. 21.

[116]   *Joyce-Koebel Co.*, 6 BTA 403 (1927), *acq.* VI-2 C.B. 4.

[117]   Rev. Rul. 75-108, 1975-1 C.B. 69.

risk. If the transaction is denominated in the seller's currency, the risk and the resulting gain or loss accrues to the buyer. If the transaction is denominated in the buyer's currency, it is the seller who bears the risk and reports the gain or loss. Thus, a U.S. business that negotiates all foreign sales and purchases in the U.S. dollar has no foreign currency exchange gains or losses.

Example 17. X Corporation sold medical instruments costing $35,000 to a company located in Spain. At the time of sale, the exchange rate was 94 pesetas to $1, and the selling price of the instruments was fixed at 4.7 million pesetas ($50,000). When the payment in pesetas was received, the exchange rate was 96 pesetas to $1, and X converted its 4.7 million pesetas to $48,958. X Corporation reports on the accrual basis and uses the transaction method. X's gross profit on the sale is $15,000 ($50,000 − $35,000). X's ordinary loss from the decrease in value of the dollar in relation to the pesetas is $1,042 ($50,000 − $48,958).

Generally, foreign exchange gains and losses are sourced in the taxpayer's principal country of residence.

Example 18. Refer to *Example 17*, but assume both the sale and the payment are denominated in U.S. dollars. The instruments are sold to the company located in Spain for $50,000 and 30 days later payment of $50,000 is received. X Corporation has no foreign currency exchange gains or losses.

U.S. corporations with foreign branches are subject to the *profit and loss method* for determining their gains and losses. Under this method, all Federal income tax computations must be made in the foreign business's functional currency and then translated into U.S. dollars at the weighted average exchange rate for the taxable year. When distributions are made from this income, any exchange gain or loss (i.e., the difference between the exchange rate at the date of distribution and the weighted average rate used to report post 1986 income) is recognized as ordinary income or loss.[118] However, translated branch losses are deductible by the U.S. taxpayer only to the extent of the U.S. taxpayer's dollar basis in the branch.

Example 19. Y Corporation's newly opened branch in France has net profits of 13,500 francs. The weighted average exchange rate for the year is 2.25 francs to $1. Y received 11,600 francs from the branch on July 15, when the rate was 2.32 francs to $1. Under the profit and loss method, Y Corporation reports $6,000 (13,500 francs ÷ 2.25) ordinary income from branch operations for the year. In addition, Y reports an exchange ordinary loss of $155.56 [(11,600 ÷ 2.32 = $5,000 received) − (11,600 ÷ 2.25 = $5,155.56 taxed)].

[118]   § 987.

When a branch has undistributed income for more than one year, distributions must be prorated among these years. This computation is beyond the scope of the text.

If the U.S. corporation claims a foreign tax credit, net current assets may not be reduced by the branch's accrued foreign tax liabilities.[119] Without this restriction, the U.S. corporation would receive the benefits of both a foreign tax deduction and a foreign tax credit for these accrued taxes.

U.S. corporations report income from foreign corporations (including subsidiaries) only when they receive dividends. The transaction method is applicable. That is, includible dividend income is based on exchange rates in effect when the dividends are received. Subpart F income of the CFC and FPHC income are to be translated in the same manner as income from a branch. Similarly, exchange gains or losses for these two types of income are determined in the same manner as they are for branches and generally are recognized as foreign source ordinary income or loss. In computing FTCs, the foreign income taxes for a branch, a CFC, and a FPHC are translated at the rate used to translate the related includible income.

BLOCKED CURRENCIES

In some instances, taxpayers are unable to convert foreign currencies into U.S. dollars because of exchange restrictions imposed by the issuing government. When this occurs, the currency is referred to as being *blocked*. Generally, taxpayers with income in blocked currencies may elect to defer their U.S. taxes until one of the following occurs:

1. Blockage restrictions are removed.

2. Conversion is made even though the restrictions continue.

3. The blocked currency is used for nondeductible expenditures.

4. The blocked currency is disposed of in some manner, such as by gift, bequest, devise, dividend, or other distribution.

5. A taxpayer who is a resident alien terminates U.S. resident status.[120]

If one of the above occurs such that a portion, but not all, of the income deferral is removed, income is includible on a first-in, first-out basis.[121] That is, regardless of the facts, the first type of income deferred because of blockage is considered to be the first one received.

---

[119]   Rev. Rul. 75-134, 1975-1 C.B. 33.

[120]   Rev. Rul. 74-351, 1974-2 C.B. 144.

[121]   Rev. Rul. 57-379, 1957-2 C.B. 299.

The deferral election for blocked currency generally is not available for income that is includible regardless of whether such income is distributed to the taxpayers. For example, deferral cannot be elected for includible income from a foreign personal holding company[122] or from a foreign partnership.[123] The deferral also is not available when the taxpayer is able to use the funds in the foreign country.[124]

Expenses paid in the blocked currency are deductible only to the extent that the related income is reported.[125] Similar restrictions are placed on deductions for depreciation and on foreign tax credits.

U.S. TAXATION OF ALIENS

Aliens are classified as either nonresidents or residents. *Nonresident aliens* are (1) individuals who are neither residents nor citizens of the United States, and (2) organizations created outside the United States.[126] The tax rate on passive-type investment income paid a nonresident alien, whether an individual or a corporation, is 30 percent of *gross* income.[127] In general, the rate is 31 percent (for individuals, estates or trusts) and 34 percent (for corporate partners) on nonpassive income distributions to foreign owners of U.S. partnerships.[128] However, many treaties establish rates below the 30 and 20 percent levels. For example, the withholding rate on dividends paid to organizations or citizens of Canada, Australia, and Sweden is 15 percent. In contrast, the withholding rate on interest paid to these nonresidents differ: 15 percent for Canada, 10 percent for Australia, and none for Sweden. Interest earned from investment funds on deposit with U.S. banks, savings and loan associations, and insurance companies are exempt from U.S. taxes.[129] In addition, there is no withholding tax for interest on portfolio investment held by nonresident aliens and foreign corporations.[130] Qualifying investments include those issued in the Eurobond market. Finally, if a nonresident alien or a foreign corporation does not engage in business in the United States at any time during the taxable year and its tax liability is fully satisfied by withholding at the source, no tax return is required.[131]

---

[122] *Elder v. Comm.*, 43-2 USTC ¶9519, 31 AFTR 627, 139 F.2d 27 (CA-2, 1943), *rev'g* and *rem'g* 47 BTA 235.

[123] *Max Freudmann*, 10 T.C. 775 (1948), *acq.* 1948-2 C.B. 2.

[124] *Sanford A. Berman*, 45 TCM 1357, T.C. Memo 1983-214.

[125] Rev. Rul. 74-341, 1974-2 C.B. 144.

[126] Reg. §§ 1.871-1 and 2.

[127] §§ 871(a)(1) and 881, and Reg. §§ 1.871-7. In *Barba v. U.S.*, 83-1 USTC ¶9404, 52

AFTR2d 83-5272 (Ct. Cls. 1983), a nonresident alien was taxed on the full amount of his gross receipts from gambling, even though his losses far exceeded his winnings.

[128] §§ 1446 and 6401(b).

[129] § 871(i).

[130] §§ 1441(c)(9) and (10).

[131] Reg. §§ 1.6012-1(b)(2)(i) and 1.6012-2(g)(2)(i).

Example 20. R, a resident and citizen of Japan, receives the following income from U.S. sources in 1991: $1,000 dividend income from a U.S. corporation, $600 interest income on corporate bonds, and $300 interest income on funds deposited in a bank. The U.S.-Japanese treaty establishes a tax rate of 15% on dividends and 10% on taxable interest. These taxes must be withheld by the payors. Thus, R receives the income net of taxes as follows: $850 in dividends ($1,000 − 15% tax of $150); $540 interest ($600 − 10% tax of $60); and $300 of tax-exempt bank interest. R is not required to file a tax return. Note that, because of the treaty, the U.S. tax is the same, regardless of whether R is an individual or a foreign corporation.

Income *effectively connected* with a U.S. trade or business and received by a nonresident alien is subject to the regular U.S. individual or corporate tax rates on *taxable* income.[132] In addition, there is a 30 percent *branch profits* tax on income received by a foreign corporation from its U.S. branch.[133] This tax, however, may be overridden by tax treaty provisions.

Basically, effectively connected income is (1) income earned on assets used or held for use in a trade or business, and (2) income from activities performed within the United States by or for a trade or business. The definition, with some exceptions, includes salaries and other personal service income if material in amount (exceeds $3,000), and the U.S. net income of a trade or business.[134] Special rules apply when the income consists of capital gains.[135]

Taxable income for a nonresident business is much the same as for any similar U.S. business (i.e., effectively connected gross income less related business expenses).[136] However, taxable income for a nonresident individual is effectively connected gross income less (1) the personal exemption amount for the taxpayer (but not the standard deduction), (2) contributions to U.S. charities, (3) casualty and theft losses, and (4) expenses related to the effectively connected gross income, such as travel, entertainment, moving, and state and local income tax expenses.[137] In some instances, treaty provisions extend these deductions. Nonresident aliens may receive both effectively connected income subject to the regular income tax rates and investment income subject to the 30 percent rate.[138]

---

[132] §§ 864(c)(6) and (7), and Reg. §§ 1.864-4 and 1.882.

[133] § 884.

[134] § 864(c), and Reg. § 1.864-2.

[135] § 871(a)(2), and Reg. §§ 1.871-7(d) and 1.882-1(b)(2)(ii).

[136] § 882 and Reg. § 1.882-4(c).

[137] §§ 861(b), 863(a), and 873(b), and Reg. § 1.861-8.

[138] Reg. §§ 1.871-8 and 1.882-1.

Example 21. Refer to *Example 20*, except assume that R also earned and received $20,000 salary from a U.S business while in the United States during June, July, and August. R, a single individual, incurred related business travel expenses of $1,700 and Kentucky state income taxes of $200. R's effectively connected taxable income is $15,950 ($20,000 − $2,150 personal exemption − $1,700 − $200). The tax is calculated on the $15,950, the same as if R were a U.S. citizen or resident. In addition, the payors must withhold the $150 on R's dividends and $60 on R's corporate investment income. Note that R's Japanese source income is not relevant to the U.S. tax calculations.

An exception covers foreign government personnel, teachers, students, and participants in certain exchange or training programs who are temporarily in the United States as nonimmigrants under the Immigration and Nationality Act. These nonresidents are taxed at the regular graduated tax rates on their includible U.S. source income.[139] They are, however, exempt from U.S. taxes on income received from foreign employers.[140]

All aliens are presumed to be nonresidents unless there is evidence to the contrary. Most foreign businesses with physical locations in the United States qualify as residents. An individual is a resident alien if he or she (1) is a lawful permanent resident under the immigration laws of the United States during any part of the calendar year, *or* (2) meets the substantial presence test. This test is met if the individual is present in the United States (1) at least 31 days during the calendar year, and (2) if the number of days present in the current year plus one-third of the days present in the prior year plus one-sixth of the days present in the second prior year equals at least 183 days.[141]

Example 22. T, U, and V are citizens and permanent residents of Austria. They were, however, present in the United States the following number of days:

	T	U	V
1991	25	75	150
1990	330	66	120
1989	300	42	90

T does not meet the substantial presence test in 1991 since his stay in the United States during 1991 was less than 31 days.

---

[139] § 871(c).

[140] § 872(b)(3).

[141] § 7701(b). In addition, under certain circumstances a nonresident may elect to be treated as a resident alien.

U also does not meet the substantial presence test in 1991. Although U was present in the United States the required minimum of 31 days during 1991, the number of days she was present in 1991 plus one-third of the number of days she was present in 1990 plus the number of days she was present in 1989 equals 115 days [75 + ($^1/_3 \times 66 = 33$) + ($^1/_6 \times 42 = 7$) = 115], which is less than the required minimum of 183 days.

V, however, meets both portions of the substantial presence test and qualifies as a U.S. resident alien. First, he was in the United States during 1991 the required 31 days. Second, his 205 days [150 + ($^1/_3 \times 120 = 40$) + ($^1/_6 \times 90 = 15$) = 205] exceeds the required minimum of 183 days.

Resident aliens are taxed in the same manner as U.S. citizens and businesses. That is, they are taxed on their *worldwide income* at the U.S. graduated tax rates applicable to corporations and individuals less foreign tax credits. No distinction is made between investment income and trade or business income.[142]

It is possible for aliens to qualify for nonresident status for part of the year and resident status the remainder (usually in the years of arrival and departure). In such instances, taxable income must be separated and calculated for the two classifications as though the taxpayer had been two separate taxpayers.[143] However, in a year of dual status, some restrictions are placed on an individual's tax return for income received as a resident alien. Nonresident aliens and dual status aliens may not elect to file as a head of household. In addition, married aliens must file separately in the year of dual status. Anyone who is a resident at the end of the year (or is married to such a person) may elect to be taxed as a U.S. resident for the entire year and avoid these restrictions.[144] Although there is some disagreement, the IRS argues dual status taxpayers may not claim the standard deduction.[145] In addition, personal exemptions for the resident alien's dependents and spouse cannot exceed the income received while a resident. This limitation does not, however, apply to individual residents of Canada or Mexico.[146] Similarly, the treaty with Japan allows all personal exemptions.

---

[142] Reg. § 1.871-1(a).

[143] Rev. Rul. 73-578, 1973-2 C.B. 39.

[144] § 6013(g) and Reg. § 1.871-1(a).

[145] § 63(c)(6)(B).

[146] Reg. § 1.873-1(b)(2)(iii).

TAX PLANNING CONSIDERATIONS

Tax planning is essential for many individuals and for all businesses. However, because of the variety of available options and the interrelationships that exist among them, tax planning for those involved in international activities is even more important. The obvious difficulty is that it is impossible to accumulate and evaluate all information relevant to making decisions in an international context. Although minimizing income taxes may not be a primary goal, these taxpayers must develop an international tax strategy.

TAXATION OF U.S. CITIZENS

A U.S. citizen may elect to

1. Report all foreign-earned income and claim the foreign taxes on that income as a credit or an itemized deduction, or

2. Exclude foreign-earned income (up to $70,000 plus the foreign housing expense allowance) and forgo claiming the foreign taxes applicable to this excluded income.

Most U.S expatriates reside in industrial nations such as Canada, the United Kingdom, and West Germany, where effective tax rates exceed those in the United States. It is often better for these taxpayers to select the first option and report all foreign-earned income in order to claim the tax credit. These taxpayers will have no U.S. taxes on this income under either method, but excess foreign tax credits are larger when the exclusion is not elected. Excess credits may be carried back two years and forward five years to reduce total taxes in years when the U.S. effective rate exceeds the foreign rate. Note that if the exclusion is elected, the U.S. effective rate will be lower than it would be if it were not.

In a low tax rate country generally the exclusion should be elected. However, individuals living in such countries must remember that the decision cannot be changed annually. Once the exclusion is elected and then revoked, it is probable that the IRS will not allow its reelection for five years. Consequently, this decision must be made with consideration to future expectations as well as to the present situation.

Taxpayers should determine their taxable income in the foreign country before deciding whether or not to elect the housing expense exclusion. In some countries, employer-provided housing is not taxable. Thus, electing this exclusion would have no effect on foreign tax credits. Other differences between U.S. and foreign tax bases can mean that the country appearing to have the higher effective tax rate may actually have the lower rate. Of course, the higher/lower relationship can change as the countries' tax laws and treaties are revised and as the taxpayers' taxable incomes change. These uncertainties make tax planning difficult but also show the importance of approaching it carefully.

Individuals must be aware of the tax laws of the foreign country in which they will live. One question to be resolved before the move is whether they should establish residency status in that country. As was discussed in this chapter, resident or nonresident status can affect the tax liability significantly in the United States. Similar differences also exist in many other countries.[147]

Individuals who decide to avoid resident status may still be able to qualify for available U.S. exclusions under the physical presence test. Remember, the bona fide resident status is based on a full tax year, whereas physical presence is based on any twelve consecutive months. The shorter the expected length of time of the overseas assignment, the more important the physical presence test becomes. Taxpayers should consider the effect on this test before planning trips to the United States. Shortening the time or delaying the trip by a few days could have a significant tax impact.

A U.S. citizen moving to another country should determine if a treaty exists between that country and the United States. If there is a treaty, the taxpayer is well advised to obtain a copy and study it carefully. Treaties often grant special tax rates and treatment that are considerably more beneficial than those otherwise applicable to the taxpayer. Unfortunately, few tax advisers are aware of specific treaty provisions.

TAXATION OF U.S.-BASED CORPORATIONS

Tax planning for foreign source income requires that the most advantageous method and organizational form be selected for each type of transaction or activity. As long as the effects of taxation differ among the various corporate entities and countries, there is considerable incentive to arrange intercompany transactions with the objective of minimizing the overall tax liability of the company. The international business organization cannot afford to ignore tax consequences or make decisions and then wait until the end of the year to see how costly they were in taxes.

FOREIGN SALES CORPORATION

One of the first decisions to be made in establishing the FSC is deciding where it should be located. Several factors are important. In addition to meeting the basic requirements necessary to the operation of a successful business (e.g., good banking, communication, and transportation facilities; free flow of currencies; simple legal and tax laws with low tax rates; and an adequate supply of any labor needed), the host country must have an agreement to exchange information with the United States. Likely candidates are the U.S. Virgin Islands, Guam, or one of the approximately 35 countries with an income tax treaty containing an

---

[147] For example, see David Wheeler Newman and Samuel Israel, "Planning Opportunities for Expatriates under the Final Section 911 Regulations." *Taxes—The Tax Magazine* 63 (November 1985), pp. 805–12.

information-exchange agreement. Other tax planning strategies might be to avoid using the FSC for sales to third parties resulting in losses; to establish the FSC with individual shareholders rather than a corporate shareholder in closely held operations, because of the limitations on FSCs with corporate shareholders; and to prevent the FSC from receiving investment income, if it does have a corporate shareholder, to avoid the double corporate tax.

CONTROLLED FOREIGN CORPORATION

The intent of the CFC legislation is to penalize inactive corporations located in tax-haven countries. However, it is possible for active corporations to be subjected to these provisions unless their operations are carefully structured. Thus, a crucial tax planning strategy for all foreign corporations is to be fully aware of and alert to the CFC control test, Subpart F income computations, and all available exceptions. Particularly vulnerable to Subpart F are foreign subsidiaries that derive much of their income from providing services or from acting as selling agents for U.S. parent companies.

Strategies for avoiding CFC status can be devised to circumvent the control test. A foreign corporation cannot be a CFC unless 50 percent of its voting power or stock value is controlled directly or indirectly by U.S. stockholders who individually control at least 10 percent of the voting power. To avoid this test, a U.S. parent corporation can "decontrol" its wholly owned foreign subsidiary by distributing at least 50 percent of the subsidiary's stock as a dividend to the parent corporation's shareholders. If the parent's stock is widely held, the 10 percent rule will not be met. Other methods for transferring ownership of the subsidiary's stock also are available.

Decontrol of a foreign subsidiary can be accomplished by issuing preferred voting stock to unrelated non–U.S. persons to the extent that preferred shareholders own 50 percent of total voting stock. The U.S. parent retains 50 percent of the voting power by owning all of the subsidiary's common stock. Preferred stockholders must be free to exercise their voting power. If restrictions are placed on any stockholders, actual ownership will be ignored in favor of effective control.[148]

FOREIGN PERSONAL HOLDING COMPANY

Since Congressional intent for the FPHC provisions is similar to that of the CFC and the domestic PHC, tax planning strategies described for the CFC above and PHC in Chapter 20 generally apply to the FPHC as well.

---

[148] Reg. § 1.957-1(b)(2) But, in July 1982, the IRS replaced its acquiescence with a nonacquiescence on the primary case in this area, *CCA, Inc.*, 64 T.C. 137 (1975), nonacq. The reason given by the Service for this change was that "the Tax Court's finding is clearly erroneous."

POSSESSIONS CORPORATION

It is possible to reduce effective tax rates of the PC further by having it lend funds to the U.S. parent rather than pay dividends. When dividends are paid by a PC operating in Puerto Rico to a U.S. parent corporation, a withholding tax up to 10 percent is collected in Puerto Rico. There is no withholding tax, however, on loans made outside the country, and no Puerto Rican income tax is assessed on the PC's U.S. earned interest. There is an offsetting U.S. tax effect of deductible interest expense for the parent and includible interest income for the PC. The net result is that the U.S. parent has the use of the PC's funds without being assessed the withholding tax. Before making the loan, however, the tax planner must be certain that the U.S. source interest income will not cause the PC to violate either of the gross income requirements of a PC.

U.S. TAXATION OF ALIENS

U.S. taxation of aliens differs significantly, depending on whether an alien is classified as a resident or a nonresident. Since each alien's status is influenced by a number of factors, an individual often can arrange his or her activities in order to qualify for either classification. It is important, however, that these plans be made prior to entering the United States. Although an alien's status can be changed after arrival, this can be difficult and may cause dual status problems in the year of change.

Special rules apply to nonresident aliens present in the United States for their foreign employer no more than ninety days during a tax year. If such an employee's U.S. earned income does not exceed $3,000, it is exempt from U.S. taxes.[149] Similarly, capital gains are exempt for nonresident aliens who are in the United States less than 183 days during a tax year. Most treaties also contain special tax benefits for temporary nonresidents. Knowledge of these rules and a little tax planning can save many aliens both tax dollars and time.

The fact that a tax year may be a fiscal rather than a calendar year allows some taxpayers even greater planning opportunities. For example, a foreign company's employee who is in the United States June through September will exceed the 90-day limit if the calendar year is used but not if a fiscal year ending July 31 is used. With the fiscal year, the alien is in the United States 61 days in each of two years. Of course, if the employee returns to the United States during the second fiscal year for more than 29 days, the limit will be exceeded in the second year.

---

[149]   Reg. § 1.864-2(b).

PROBLEM MATERIALS

DISCUSSION QUESTIONS

9-1 *Basic Concepts.* Determine whether each of the following statements is true or false. If false, rewrite the statement so that it is true. Be prepared to explain each statement.

a. U.S. taxation of foreign source income is based on the jurisdictional principle.

b. A *U.S. taxpayer* may be a U.S. citizen living in Italy, a British citizen living in the United States, a French citizen who has never lived in the United States, or a Japanese company with no branches or subsidiaries in the United States.

c. All industrialized nations tax their citizens on the citizens' worldwide income.

d. A foreign-owned corporation can be a U.S. nonresident alien.

e. A Canadian citizen living in Canada who receives dividend income from a U.S. corporation must file Form 1040 and pay U.S. taxes on the dividend income.

9-2 *Foreign Source Income.* U.S. source income, foreign source income, and foreign source earned income are taxed differently.

a. Explain how the source is determined.

b. List examples of foreign source earned income.

c. Compare foreign source earned income for a U.S. citizen with effectively connected income for a nonresident alien.

9-3 *Foreign Source Earned Income.* I and U organize the IU Computer Software Service as a U.S. partnership. Both partners are U.S. citizens. They expect net income in each of the first three years to exceed $100,000, half from the United States and half from Europe. I will live and manage the activities in the United States and U will live and manage the activities in Europe. They will divide all profits equally.

a. Do either or both partners have foreign source income or foreign-earned income?

b. Advise the partners how the partnership agreement can be written to maximize tax benefits from foreign source income.

9-4 *Foreign Tax Deduction vs Credit.* Is it better to deduct foreign income taxes (rather than take a credit for them) when a U.S. corporation's only foreign operation has a net taxable loss for the year?

a. Assume the foreign business is a branch.

b. Assume the foreign business is a corporation.

9-5 *Foreign Resident Tests.* In order to qualify for certain exclusions, a U.S. citizen must meet either the bona fide resident or the physical presence tests.

    a.   Define both of these tests.

    b.   May a U.S. citizen qualify under either or both tests even though the citizen owns a home in the United States and expects to return to that home permanently at the end of three years?

    c.   May a U.S. citizen who lives in three different countries during a two-year period qualify under either or both tests?

9-6 *Deductions for Foreign Moving Expenses.* Rules for foreign moving expenses differ from those for U.S. moves.

    a.   How do they differ?

    b.   Why do they differ?

9-7 *Foreign Tax Credit—Deemed Paid.* May A Corporation claim a foreign tax credit from foreign taxes paid by D Corporation, even though A does not own any of D's stock?

    a.   Assume A owns 50 percent of B Corporation, B Corporation owns 40 percent of C Corporation, and C corporation owns 60 percent of D corporation.

    b.   Assume the same as (a), except that C Corporation owns 20 percent of D Corporation rather than 60 percent.

9-8 *Congressional Intent.* Complete the statements below by selecting the best answer from the following list:

    A.   Controlled Foreign Corporation

    B.   Domestic International Sales Corporation

    C.   Foreign Branch

    D.   Foreign Corporation

    E.   Foreign Sales Corporation

    F.   Foreign Tax Credit

    G.   Possessions Corporation

    a.   Congressional intent in modifying the _____ legislation was to encourage companies to repatriate earnings to the United States.

    b.   Congressional intent in creating the _____ was to avoid double taxation of foreign source income.

    c.   Congressional intent in creating the _____ was to encourage U.S. organizations to locate manufacturing operations in certain areas specified in the legislation.

    d.   Congressional intent in creating the _____ was to reduce the use of inactive holding companies organized in tax haven countries for the purpose of tax avoidance.

    e.   Congressional intent in creating the _____ was to encourage U.S. exports while avoiding conflict with GATT.

9-9 *Forms of Organization.* AC Corporation intends to sell some of its products to several European customers. What forms of organization should AC use in the following situations and why?

    a.   AC will export its product instead of establishing a foreign manufacturing operation in the first three years. AC expects a profit from these sales.

    b.   AC will establish a foreign manufacturing operation after the first three years. Start-up costs will result in losses for two years, but profits are expected in all future years.

9-10 *Foreign Sales Corporation and Domestic International Sales Corporation.*

    a.   List and discuss the tax advantages available to a U.S. business that establishes an FSC for its exports.

    b.   Under what circumstances should a DISC, rather than a FSC, be used for exports?

9-11 *Possessions Corporation.*

    a.   List and discuss the tax advantages available to a PC.

    b.   May a U.S. parent corporation use a PC as a holding company and avoid Controlled Foreign Corporation status?

9-12 *Code § 482.*

    a.   Why is § 482 important to a U.S.-based multinational corporation?

    b.   Are all transactions between the U.S. parent corporation and its subsidiaries subject to § 482?

    c.   If an IRS audit results in a § 482 shift of income to the U.S. parent corporation, what is the effect on the foreign tax credit?

9-13 *Regulation § 1.861-8.*

    a.   Why is Reg. § 1.861-8 important to a U.S.-based multinational corporation?

    b.   If an IRS audit results in a Reg. § 1.861-8 shift of taxable income to the U.S. parent corporation, what is the effect on the foreign tax credit?

    c.   What is the effect on the U.S. parent corporation and foreign subsidiary if the foreign tax authorities disallow a Reg. § 1.861-8 allocation to the foreign subsidiary?

9-14 *Foreign Currency Gains and Losses.*

    a.   How are foreign currency gains and losses calculated?

    b.   Are foreign currency gains and losses taxable as ordinary or capital?

    c.   What effect does blocked currency have on recognition of foreign currency gains and losses?

9-15 *Resident vs. Nonresident Alien Status.* Aliens subject to U.S. taxation are classified as either residents or nonresidents.

    a.   How does U.S. taxation of residents differ from that of nonresidents?

    b.   What is effectively connected income and how is it taxed to residents and nonresidents?

    c.   How does a foreign taxpayer qualify as a resident?

PROBLEMS

9-16   *Foreign Source Income Exclusions—Partnership.*   K and L form a foreign partnership to provide services to foreign clients interested in establishing businesses in the United States. They expect partnership net income, before payments to partners, to be $100,000 the first year. K and L agree that partner salaries should be $24,000 to K and $36,000 to L. Profits and losses after partners' salaries are shared equally. K will spend all of his time in the United States and L will spend all of his time in Europe. Both K and L are U.S. citizens. Calculate each partner's (1) foreign source partnership income, and (2) foreign source earned income.

     a.   Assume capital is not a material income producing factor.

     b.   Assume capital is a material income producing factor.

9-17   *Foreign Tax Credit—U.S. Citizen.*   T, a U.S. citizen, lives and works in the United States. In 1991, he receives a $35,000 salary from a U.S. company and $2,000 in dividends from a foreign corporation with no U.S. source income. The foreign corporation withheld $600 from the dividend and T received $1,400 cash. T is single, does not itemize deductions, and has no other taxable income and no dependents. Calculate T's U.S. Federal income tax.

9-18   *Foreign Tax Credit- Individual.*   B, a U.S. citizen and resident, was single during 1991 and had the following sources of income.

Salary from a U.S. company..............	$30,000
Dividends from a Mexican Corporation.....	1,000
Interest income from a U.S. bank..........	500

The gross amount of the dividend was $1,000, but the foreign corporation withheld $150 in foreign income taxes. B has $3,200 in itemized deductions for the year (excluding any foreign taxes paid). Calculate B's income tax liability for 1991.

9-19   *Foreign Source Income Exclusions.*   Z, a U.S. citizen, works in France and meets the physical presence test. During 1991, she receives a $62,000 salary while in France for her work there, a $4,000 salary while briefly in the United States for her work here, and a $6,000 dividend while in France from stock she owns in a French company.

     a.   Calculate Z's maximum exclusion.

     b.   If Z receives a $25,000 bonus while in France for her work there, calculate her maximum exclusion.

     c.   Calculate Z's exclusion if she receives the bonus in (b) and her employer provides housing that costs the employer $22,000.

9-20   *Foreign Income Exclusions.*   J worked in Canada from August 1, 1990 through September 30, 1991. During 1991, her salary from work in Canada was $50,000 (in U.S. dollars), and her salary from work in the United States after she returned was $10,000.

    a.   Calculate J's foreign earned income exclusion.

    b.   Assume that a $10,000 allowance for housing is included in J's $50,000 and that the $10,000 meets the rules for qualifying foreign housing expenses. J elects to exclude foreign-earned income, but she does not make the *special* election to exclude employer provided foreign housing income. What is J's foreign earned income exclusion?

    c.   Assume the same facts as in (b) above, except that J elects both the foreign-earned income exclusion and the exclusion for employer-provided foreign housing income. What amounts may be excluded from income? Which election(s) should J make?

9-21   *Bona Fide Resident or Physical Presence Test.*   P, a U.S. citizen, moves to London, England June 1, 1991 and expects to return to the United States December 1, 1992. P is employed by a U.S.-based multinational corporation as an advisor to its British business operations during this period. Every other month, the company requires P to return to the United States for business purposes. Thus, P will be in the United States for seven days every two months, beginning with the last week in July. P's taxable year is the calendar year.

    a.   Does P meet the bona fide resident test for 1991 or 1992?

    b.   Does P meet the physical presence test for 1991 or 1992?

    c.   What recommendations would you make to P that would enhance his situation to exclude foreign source income?

9-22   *Foreign Tax Credit.*   D, Inc. is a domestic corporation that owns 100 percent of F, Inc. Assume F has no Subpart F income so that the Controlled Foreign Corporation rules are not a consideration. F had the following items of income and tax:

	E&P	Foreign Income Taxes
1988	$ 50,000	$12,500
1989	50,000	12,500
1990	40,000	10,000
1991	60,000	15,000
Total	$200,000	$50,000

F pays a $90,000 dividend at the end of 1991. Income taxes of $13,500 were withheld; therefore, D received $76,500. Calculate D's U.S. tax liability on this income before the foreign tax credit limitation. Assume a 34 percent tax rate.

9-23   *Foreign Tax Credit vs. Deduction—Foreign Subsidiary.*   The pretax income earned by a foreign corporation is $30,000. The foreign tax is 30 percent, the dividend withholding tax is 10 percent, and one-third of the after-tax foreign corporate income is remitted to stockholders. U.S. Parent Corporation income before the foreign dividend is $200,000, and it owns 100 percent of the foreign corporation.

     a.   Calculate the U.S. taxes Parent Corporation will pay if the foreign tax is used as a tax credit.

     b.   Calculate the U.S. taxes Parent Corporation will pay if the foreign tax is used as a deduction.

     c.   Calculate the U.S. taxes Parent Corporation will pay if the foreign tax is used as a tax credit but the foreign subsidiary pays a 20 percent foreign tax rate rather than the 30 percent one.

9-24   *Foreign Source Losses—Comparison of Business Organizations.*   During the year, U.S. Parent Corporation had U.S. taxable income of $300,000, and its wholly owned foreign business organization had a taxable loss of $40,000. Calculate U.S. Parent Corporation's worldwide taxable income.

     a.   Assume the business organization is a foreign branch.

     b.   Assume the business organization is a foreign corporation.

9-25   *Ownership Tiers.*   In each of the following independent situations, determine whether the ownership tests are met to allow V, a U.S corporation, to claim foreign taxes paid by F Corporation, S Corporation, and T Corporation.

     a.   V owns 80 percent of F, F owns 20 percent of S, and S owns 40 percent of T.

     b.   V owns 80 percent of F, F owns 50 percent of S, and S owns 8 percent of T.

     c.   V owns 5 percent of F, F owns 100 percent of S, and S owns 80 percent of T.

     d.   V owns 60 percent of F, V and F each own 30 percent of S, and S owns 20 percent of T.

9-26   *Foreign Sales Corporation—Foreign Trade Income.*   An FSC, located in the Virgin Islands, purchased three items of inventory from its U.S.-based parent corporation and resold them to unrelated corporations in Venezuela. Information concerning the inventory sales is

	Item A	Item B	Item C
FSC gross receipts from Venezuela......	$500	$500	$500
FSC direct expenses.....................	75	75	75
Parent arm's length price to FSC.........	495	495	475
Parent cost of goods sold...............	350	250	350
Parent selling expenses.................	25	40	40

Determine the FSC's profit, the transfer price between the parent and FSC, and the exempt FTI for each of the three items.

9-27   *Controlled Foreign Corporation.*   AAA, Inc., a domestic corporation that man-ufactures automobile parts, owns 40 percent of NA, Inc., a Netherland Antilles corporation. The other shareholders of NA are (1) ABC, Inc., a domestic cor-poration, which owns 20 percent, and (2) XYZ, Inc., a foreign corporation, which owns 40 percent. All of NA's current year income ($200,000) consists of sales commissions from buying parts from AAA, Inc. and selling them directly in Mexico. NA made no dividend distributions during the year.

    a.   Is NA a Controlled Foreign Corporation (CFC)?

    b.   How would your answer to (a) above change if ABC, Inc. were a foreign corporation?

    c.   If NA is a CFC, how much income does AAA recognize as a result of NA's activities and what is the effect on AAA's basis in NA's stock?

9-28   *Foreign Source Income—Comparison of Business Organizations.*   During the year, U.S Parent Corporation had U.S. taxable income of $300,000, and its wholly owned subsidiary organization had taxable income of $60,000. Parent Corporation received $20,000 cash from the subsidiary as a partial distribution of the subsidiary's profits for the current year. Calculate U.S. Parent Corporation's worldwide taxable income. Assume all foreign operations have no U.S. source income.

    a.   Assume the subsidiary is a Possessions Corporation.

    b.   Assume the subsidiary is a foreign corporation.

    c.   Assume the subsidiary is a foreign branch.

    d.   Assume the subsidiary is a Controlled Foreign Corporation and all of its income is Subpart F income.

9-29   *Foreign Tax Credit—Comparison of Business Organizations.*   U.S. Parent Cor-poration's taxable income before foreign source income is $100,000. Its wholly owned foreign subsidiary has foreign source taxable income of $80,000, pays a foreign tax of $12,000 (15%), and sends U.S. Parent $17,000 (one-fourth of its $68,000 after tax income). The foreign country collects 10 percent withholding tax on the $17,000 and U.S. Parent receives $15,300. Calculate the U.S. Federal income taxes payable by U.S. Parent.

    a.   Assume the subsidiary is a foreign corporation.

    b.   Assume the subsidiary is a Possessions Corporation.

    c.   Assume the subsidiary is a Controlled Foreign Corporation and all of its income is Subpart F income.

9-30 *Foreign Currency Gains and Losses—Transaction Method.* On December 10, 1991, G, a U.S. corporation on the accrual basis, sells equipment costing $23,000 for $35,000 to a customer in the United Kingdom. Payment is to be made in British pounds, based on the December 10, 1991 exchange rate. The customer sends G 21,000 British pounds in full payment on March 10, 1992. G's wholly owned subsidiary in London has net income for 1991 of 50,000 British pounds. Its sole dividend payment was made on March 10, 1992 and the grossed-up dividend totaled 18,000 British pounds. Exchange rates were as follows:

December 10, 1991	0.60 British pounds for $1
Dedember 31, 1991	0.58 British pounds for $1
Weighted average	0.59 British pounds for $1
March 10,1992	0.57 British pounds for $1

    a.   Calculate the effect on G's 1991 taxable income.
    b.   Calculate the effect on G's 1992 taxable income.

9-31 *Foreign Currency Gains and Losses—Branch.* H Corporation has a new branch operation in Canada. Branch records, stated below in Canadian dollars, reveal the following:

1991 net profits	13,200
Funds sent to H Corporation May 1, 1991	9,100

The Canadian exchange rates per $1 were (1) 0.88 on December 31, 1991; (2) 0.91 on May 1, 1991; (3) 0.95 on December 31, 1991; and (4) 0.93 weighted average for 1991. Calculate H Corporation's Canadian branch income in U.S. dollars for 1991, using the Profit and Loss method.

9-32 *Aliens.* M Corporation, an Italian business, receives the following U.S. source income: (1) $40,000 net income effectively connected with its primary business activities, (2) $2,000 dividends, less $200 U.S. tax withheld, and (3) $400 interest on funds deposited in a bank. M is exempt from the 30 percent branch profits tax by treaty. Calculate M's U.S. Federal income tax.

    a.   M Corporation qualifies as a nonresident alien.
    b.   M Corporation qualifies as a resident alien.

9-33 *Residency.* M is a Mexican citizen living and working in Mexico for a manufacturing company. The company maintains some operations in the United States. M frequently travels to the United States to supervise those operations. During 1991, M worked in the United States from January 3 through January 9 and from June 7 through June 27. In addition, he took a week's vacation in Denver during November. M also states that he was in the United States for 180 days in 1990 and 177 days in 1989. Is M's Mexican salary subject to U.S. taxation?

RESEARCH PROBLEMS

9-34 U.S. Parent Corporation has two wholly owned subsidiaries. One is in West Germany and one is in Romania. The effective income tax rate in Germany is 40 percent, and repatriated earnings are subject to a 15 percent withholding rate. The effective income tax rate in Romania is 20 percent, and repatriated earnings are subject to a 10 percent withholding rate. Presently, the U.S. Parent wishes to receive all its Romanian subsidiary's income in dividends but does not want to receive any of its German income in dividends for at least five years. In order to maximize its foreign tax credits and minimize its U.S. Federal income taxes, U.S. Parent wishes to elect to be taxed on a portion of the German subsidiary's income by using a consent dividend. Since no cash is actually transferred with a consent dividend, it is not subject to the German dividend withholding tax currently. However, it increases U.S. Parent's foreign source income and foreign tax credits (see *Example 12*).

a. How and when does U.S. Parent elect a consent dividend?
b. How is a consent dividend recorded by the subsidiary?
c. What is your advice to the management of U.S. Parent Corporation?

Partial list of research aids:

§ 565
Rev Rul. 78-296, 1978-2 C.B. 183
Letter Rulings 7832023 and 8224113

9-35 L is employed by a small town as a city manager. He is a professional and hopes some day to be the city manager of a large city.

L calls you and requests a meeting. He and T, his wife, will be taking a trip in a few months and are interested in tax planning. The trip will include visits to several cities in Europe and will last six weeks. He has three weeks of paid vacation and three weeks leave of absence without pay. Since his wife is not employed, she can accompany him. In discussing the trip, you learn that L has selected the cities because they interest him professionally. He has made appointments with officials of these cities and hopes to obtain information helpful in his work as a city manager. He believes these contacts eventually will lead to increased trade between these cities and his community. In addition, he admits he and T have always wanted to visit Europe, so the trip will not be all work. He estimates he will spend approximately 20 hours each week in meetings with city officials.

What is your advice to L?

a. What constitutes a business day (activities *and* amount of time spent)? (Be careful, this answer requires some thinking.)

b. How is travel time en route allocated between business and nonbusiness?

c. How are weekends and holidays treated?

d. Prepare a *detailed* list of deductible expenses, assuming L's trip does *not* qualify as primarily business.

e. Prepare a *detailed* list of deductible expenses in addition to those in (d) if L's trip *does* qualify as primarily business. (Use your own knowledge to go beyond the short list you find.)

f. Refer to (d) and (e) and explain how joint expenses are prorated between L and T, assuming his trip qualifies as primarily business and hers does not. Give examples and be specific.

g. Where are deductible expenses reported on the tax return?

PART III

FLOW-THROUGH ENTITIES

CONTENTS

Upon completion of this chapter, you will be able to:

- Define a partnership and a partner for Federal income tax purposes
- Explain the basic tax consequences of forming a new partnership, including
  - Determination of any gain to be recognized by the partners
  - Determination of the basis of the partner's interest in the partnership and the partnership's basis in the property received
  - How partnership liabilities affect a partner's basis
  - The differences in tax treatment for contributions of property compared with contributions of services
- Compute the net operating income or loss for a partnership and the impact of partnership operations on partners' taxable income and self-employment taxes
- Recognize transactions between partners and their partnerships that are subject to special treatment
- Determine the appropriate taxable year for a partnership
- Determine the limitations placed on partnership losses that are recognized by partners
- Explain the advantages and problems involving special allocations available to partnerships

■ CHAPTER OUTLINE ■

Chapter **10**

TAXATION OF PARTNERSHIPS AND PARTNERS

When two or more parties agree to go into business together, they must decide which form of business they should use. Should the business be incorporated or should it operate as a partnership? Although the corporate form is the predominant choice for large businesses, it is not appropriate for all businesses. In many instances, the partnership form is selected. Partnerships are widely used throughout the business world.

In practice, partnerships are found in an assortment of shapes and sizes. For example, two accountants may form a partnership to operate their own accounting firm or a family may organize a partnership to buy land or operate a delicatessen. In contrast, two giant corporations may form a partnership to develop a new product or do research. Partnerships are also used as investment vehicles. For instance, hundreds or thousands of people may invest in partnerships that drill for oil, build office buildings, or make movies. For whatever reason, when two or more parties decide to join together to carry on a business, they often choose to do so as partners in a partnership.

Businesses that are considered to be partnerships under the definition prescribed by the Code are subject to special rules governing partnerships. These rules are contained in Subchapter K of the Code including §§ 701 through 761. As explained below, however, certain partnerships are allowed to elect out of partnership treatment. This chapter first defines a partnership. The remainder of the chapter examines the operation of the special rules applying to partnerships, specifically those rules governing the formation of a partnership and its operations. Chapter 11 examines special problems concerning partnerships and their partners such as family partnerships, distributions, sale of a partnership interest, and retirement of a partner.

DEFINITIONS OF PARTNERSHIP AND PARTNER

The special rules for partnerships and partners generally apply only to those organizations qualifying as partnerships under the Code. Qualification can be crucial because of the distinctive treatment given to partnerships. For example, if an entity that suffers losses is treated as a corporation rather than a partnership, the losses would not flow through and could not be used by the owners. Thus, qualifying as a partnership in this situation is critical. In contrast, consider two individuals who own land together as an investment. These co-owners may simply want to share the expenses and avoid filing a partnership tax return and other recordkeeping required of a partnership. These parties may wish to avoid partnership treatment. Determining whether a partnership exists can be critical for other reasons as well. For example, if co-owners are not partners, each person is allowed to choose his or her own accounting methods (e.g., one owner may use an accelerated depreciation method while the other uses straight-line) and make special elections (e.g., whether to defer gain on an involuntary conversion). As these examples suggest, it is important to understand the definition of a partnership and when the partnership and partners are subject to the special rules of Subchapter K.

WHAT IS A PARTNERSHIP?

The Uniform Partnership Act defines a partnership quite simply as "an association of two or more persons to carry on as co-owners a business for profit."[1] This definition is extended in the Code to include a syndicate, group, pool, joint venture, or other unincorporated organization.[2]

For an organization to qualify as a partnership, there must be at least two partners. Note, however, that there are no restrictions on either the maximum number of partners or on who may own a partnership interest. Individuals, corporations, trusts, estates, and even other partnerships may qualify as partners.

As a practical matter, determining whether an organization qualifies as a partnership for tax purposes is rarely a problem. As long as two or more parties intend to actively participate in a *trade or business for profit as partners*, the activity generally qualifies as a partnership.[3] However, as explained in Chapter 1, unincorporated associations may be treated as corporations (rather than partnerships), if they possess more corporate characteristics than partnership characteristics.[4]

Certain arrangements are not considered to be partnerships. A joint undertaking will not be treated as a partnership if the only joint activity is the sharing of expenses. For example, if two adjacent property owners share the cost of a dam designed to prevent flooding, no partnership exists. Similarly, co-ownership of an apartment building is not a partnership for tax purposes if the co-owners merely rent or lease the property and make repairs. They are not considered partners in this instance because they are not considered to be actively engaged in a trade

---

[1] Uniform Partnership Act, § 6(1).

[2] § 761.

[3] See Reg. §§ 1.761-1(a) and 301.7701-3(a); *Fred P. Fiore*, 39 TCM 64, T.C. Memo 1979-360; and *William N. Gurtman*, 34 TCM 475, T.C. Memo 1975-96.

[4] See Reg. § 301.7701-2(a); *Morrisey v. Comm.*, 36-1 USTC ¶9020, 16 AFTR 1274, 296 U.S. 344 (USSC, 1935); *Phillip G. Larson*, 66 T.C. 159 (1978), *acq.* in 1979-1 C.B. 1; and *Zuchman v. U.S.*, 75-2 USTC ¶9778, 36 AFTR2d 75-6193, 524 F.2d 729 (Ct. Cls., 1975).

or business. If the co-owners of the building provide additional services such as maid service, however, the level of activity may elevate the co-ownership to partnership status. Unfortunately, it is often difficult to determine whether a particular co-ownership is in fact a partnership. Thus, co-owners typically assume they are a partnership and comply with the applicable requirements unless the potential tax costs are high enough to pursue an alternative course.

AVOIDING PARTNERSHIP STATUS

As noted above, not all co-owners of unincorporated activities want to be treated as members of a partnership. The Regulations permit owners of *investment property* to elect that Subchapter K not apply to their ventures if the following requirements are met:[5]

1. They are not actively conducting a trade or business.

2. The activities qualify as investments or production, extraction, or use of property.

3. Taxable income is determinable for each owner without resorting to computations required for a partnership.

4. Each owner retains a separate but undivided ownership interest in the acquisition, operation, and disposition of the property.

Activities meeting the above requirements are treated as *joint tenancies*. In some situations, joint tenancies allow owners to operate with greater simplicity and flexibility than they could by using the partnership form. As a practical matter, it is extremely difficult to determine whether a particular co-ownership meets the requirements of the Regulations. Consequently, the usefulness of this election may be limited.

TYPES OF PARTNERSHIPS

In determining how the special tax rules of Subchapter K apply, the type of partnership and partner can be critical. There are two types of partnerships: general partnerships and limited partnerships. The two differ primarily in the rights and obligations of the partners. The major differences between general and limited partnerships and their partners are summarized below.

1. General partnerships are owned solely by general partners, whereas limited partnerships must have one or more general partners and one or more limited partners.

---

[5] Reg. §§ 1.761-2(a) and (b); and see Rev. Rul. 68-344, 1968-1 C.B. 569. The method of election is described in Reg. § 1.761-2(b)(i).

2. General partners have unlimited liability for partnership debt, whereas limited partners usually are liable only up to the amount of their contribution plus any personally guaranteed debt.

3. General partners participate in the management and control of the partnership, whereas limited partners are not allowed to participate in these activities.

4. General partners are subject to self-employment taxes on partnership earnings, even if they do not perform services for the partnership, whereas limited partners are not.

ENTITY AND AGGREGATE CONCEPTS

Most rules governing the taxation of partnerships are based on either the *aggregate* or the *entity* concept of a partnership.[6] According to the entity concept, partnerships are considered entities distinct and separate from their owners. As such, partnerships may enter into taxable transactions with partners, may own property in their own names, are not legally liable for debts of partners, are required to file annual tax returns (Form 1065) that report the results of operations, and are required to make tax elections for partnership activities that are applicable to all partners. Many other partnership issues are decided according to the aggregate concept, which treats partnerships as conduits, primarily operating for the convenience of the partners. Under this theory, a partnership is viewed as merely a collection of individuals, each owning a direct and undivided interest in partnership assets. For example, this concept provides that partnership revenues, expenses, gains, losses, and credits retain their character and "flow through" to be reported on the partners' own returns. The aggregate concept also prevents the recognition of gain or loss for several types of transactions between partners and partnerships, including the exchange of assets for a capital interest. In some instances, both the entity and aggregate concepts apply to the same transaction. This often occurs when a partner's interest is liquidated, as discussed in Chapter 11.

The inconsistent application of the entity and aggregate concepts significantly complicates taxation of partnerships and partners. Generally, if an individual can determine which concept governs a particular issue the solution is relatively easy. But if it is not clear which concept is applicable to a given situation, the solution is elusive since the two concepts are diametrically opposed. As taxpayers and their advisers seek answers to partnership tax questions, they must first determine whether the entity or the aggregate concept is applicable. Only then can they use their reasoning power to solve the problems and engage in meaningful tax planning.

---

[6] For an interesting historical discussion of the development of this conflict, see Arthur B. Willis, John S. Pennell, and Philip F. Postlewaite, *Partnership Taxation* (Colorado Springs, Co.: Shepard's, Inc.), Chapter 2.

FORMING A PARTNERSHIP

The partnership form of doing business is frequently ignored by many attorneys and accountants. This is partly because they are less comfortable with the rules of Subchapter K than they are with the corporate requirements of Subchapter C and Subchapter S. As a result, many small businesses are operating as corporations when the simplicity and flexibility of a partnership arrangement might serve them better. One of the major reasons given for incorporating is the *limited liability provision*. However, this provision is of little or no benefit to many small businesses since owners often are either required to personally guarantee corporate debts or have most of their capital invested in the business. These incorporated businesses rarely seek outside capital, are frequently subjected to double taxation, and their owners commonly violate the separate entity concept by transacting business for and with the corporation, giving little attention to the legal and tax requirements. The courts are replete with cases where owners have carelessly abused the corporate form and paid a severe penalty for their actions. Many of these activities would have been acceptable with the partnership form.

CONTRIBUTIONS OF PROPERTY

Like any business, a partnership may be formed by contributions of cash, property (i.e., noncash assets), or services in exchange for a *capital interest*. The simplest procedure involves the contribution of cash. There are no current tax consequences involved in this transaction.

When property other than cash is contributed in exchange for a capital interest, the basis of this property to the contributing partner generally differs from its fair market value. Whether this difference results in taxable gain or loss depends on whether the entity or aggregate concept governs. Basically, § 721 applies the aggregate concept to this type of transaction. Therefore, the transfer is considered tax-free and no gain or loss is recognized by either the contributing partner or the partnership.[7] The partner's *initial basis* in the partnership is the total amount of cash plus the adjusted basis of property contributed.[8] This is referred to as a *substituted basis* (i.e., the basis of the transferred property is substituted for the basis of the partner's interest in the partnership). The partner's basis for each asset becomes the partnership's basis for each asset.[9] This is referred to as a *carryover basis* (i.e., the transferring partner's basis is carried over and used as the partnership's basis). There is one exception to this transfer of basis rule. Assets previously held for personal use transfer at the *lower* of market value or

---

[7] § 721 and Reg. § 1.721-1. There is one exception. Gain or loss is recognized if the partnership qualifies as an investment company. § 721(b). In such case, special basis rules apply.

[8] § 722.

[9] § 723.

basis. When an asset's basis exceeds its market value, the transferring partner has a nondeductible personal loss and a basis in the partnership equal to the asset's market value.

When contributing either capital assets or § 1231 assets, the partner's *holding period* for these assets becomes the holding period for the capital interest in the partnership.[10] For all other contributions, the partner's holding period begins with the date the partnership interest is acquired.[11] The partnership's holding period for its contributed assets includes the holding period of the contributing partner.[12]

> **Example 1.**   A contributes $50,000 cash to the AB Partnership and B contributes investment land (a capital asset) with a fair market value of $50,000. B acquired the land three years ago for $30,000. A and B are equal partners. From an economic viewpoint, the AB Partnership has two newly acquired assets each worth $50,000, and B has a realized gain of $20,000. Generally accepted accounting principles also recognize this approach and require that the assets be recorded on the books at their market value of $50,000 each. However, for tax purposes, the transfer of land by B is treated as a tax-free exchange. This results in B's basis in the land being carried over to the partnership causing the partnership's bases in the two assets to be unequal. Cash has a $50,000 basis but land has a $30,000 basis and is treated as held by the partnership for three years. Similarly, A has a $50,000 substituted basis in the partnership, but B has a $30,000 substituted basis in the partnership. A's holding period for his partnership interest is just beginning, but B's holding period is three years.

> **Example 2.**   C contributes proprietorship equipment (a § 1231 asset) with a fair market value of $50,000 to the AB Partnership for a one-third capital interest. The equipment was purchased last year for $70,000 and depreciation of $10,000 was deducted for the proprietorship last year. This transfer also constitutes a tax-free exchange. Therefore, C's $60,000 basis ($70,000 − $10,000) carries over to the partnership as well as her one-year holding period. C's substituted basis in her partnership interest is $60,000 and her holding period is also one year. (Note: the answer is the same regardless of the fair market value of the equipment.)
>
> As noted previously, an exception to this approach would apply if the equipment had been held for personal use. If this is the situation, the partnership's basis for the equipment is $50,000. C has a nondeductible personal loss and her basis in the partnership is $50,000. The holding period also transfers if the equipment qualifies as a capital asset to C. (Note that property held for personal use is not a § 1231 asset.)

---

[10]   § 1223 (1).

[11]   Reg. § 1.1223-1(a).

[12]   § 1223(2) and Reg. § 1.1223-1(b).

The tax-free exchange provisions apply to all *property* contributed, including installment receivables, contracts, accounts receivable, and property created by the contributing party.[13] In contrast, transactions involving (1) the right to use property, such as use through rental or lease agreements, or (2) services performed in exchange for a capital interest, are taxable as ordinary income to the contributing partner.[14] The partnership either has a deductible expense or a capital expenditure, depending on the nature of the services. (Contributions of services are discussed later in this chapter.)

Exhibit 10-1 summarizes the treatment of partnership formations.

EFFECT OF LIABILITIES

One of the most distinctive features of the income taxation of partnerships and their partners involves the treatment of partnership liabilities. Tax rules governing partnership liabilities are found in Code § 752 and are based on the aggregate concept. Under this theory, all partnership debts are the responsibility of the partners. For example, if a partnership borrows $1,000 to purchase an asset, this transaction is treated as if the partners borrowed the money and contributed it to the partnership for purchase of the asset. When the partnership uses its cash to repay the $1,000 debt, this transaction is treated as if the partnership distributed the money to the partners, who then repaid the debt. Following this rationale, a partner's basis in the partnership interest *increases* as his or her share of partnership liabilities increases (because of the *deemed contribution* of money).[15] In addition, the partner's basis *decreases* as his or her share of partnership liabilities decreases (because of the *deemed distribution* of money).[16] Similarly, when a partner assumes a partnership debt, he or she is deemed to have contributed money to the partnership, which then repaid the liability. Also, when a partnership assumes a partner's personal liability, the partnership is deemed to have distributed money with which that partner repaid the debt. If the reduction in the partner's share of liabilities exceeds the partner's basis in the partnership, the excess is a taxable gain (see Chapter 11 for a discussion of cash distributions).

Partner's Share of Partnership Liabilities. Each partner's share of partnership liabilities generally depends on the nature of a specific debt *and* whether the partner is a general or limited partner. All partnership debts are classified as either *recourse* or *nonrecourse*. Classification depends on whether the lender can look to the assets of any partner to satisfy the unpaid portion of the debt in the event the partnership does not have sufficient assets for full repayment. A

---

[13] Property is not defined under § 721 but the definition for § 351 transfers to corporations generally is applied to partnerships. Also see Reg. §§ 1.721-1(a) and 1.453-9(c)(2).

[14] Reg. § 1.721-1(b)(1).

[15] § 752(a).

[16] § 752(b).

Exhibit 10-1
*Summary of Tax Effects
for Partnership Formations*

Transaction	Effect on Partnership	Effect on Partner
1. Contribution of cash or property for a capital interest (no boot received)	Nontaxable; partner's Basis becomes partnership's basis in contributed assets	Nontaxable; partner's basis in contributed assets becomes partner's basis in the partnership
2. Partner assumes partnership liabilities	No effect	Increases partner's basis in partnership, based on P & L ratio
3. Partner's share of liabilities decreases	No effect	Decreases partner's basis in partnership, based on P & L ratio; includible income to the extent this "cash distribution" exceeds the partner's basis in the partnership
4. Special allocations of depreciation, depletion, gain, loss, and income attributable to contributed assets	Required for contributions after 3/84 Optional for contributions before 4/84	Required for contributions after 3/84 Optional for contributions before 4/84
5. Taint on contributed property		
a. Accrued losses on capital assets (for five years)	Capital losses when recognized	Capital losses flow through to the contributing partner
b. Accrued gains on inventory (for five years)	Ordinary gains when recognized	Ordinary gains flow through to the contributing partner
c. Gains or losses on unrealized receivables	Ordinary gains or losses when recognized	Ordinary gains and losses flow through to the contributing partner

Exhibit 10-1 Continued:

Transaction	Effect on Partnership	Effect on Partner
6. Disguised sales– contribution followed by a cash distribution	Transactions are collapsed; may be part purchase	Transactions are collapsed; may be part sale
7. Contributions of services (no boot received)		
a. Unrestricted capital interest received	FMV is either a deductible expense or capitalized, depending on the type of service; other partners sold a portion of their capital interest at the FMV	FMV is includible ordinary income and the basis in the partnership interest
b. Restricted capital interest	Same as above	a. FMV at date restrictions are removed is includible income on that date, or b. May elect that current FMV is includible income currently Amount recognized is the basis in the partnership interest
c. Interest in profits only	Nondeductible distribution of profits	Includible ordinary income (probably as profits are received)

liability is considered to be recourse debt if any partner bears an economic risk of loss in the event the partnership cannot repay the debt. If the lender cannot look beyond the assets of the partnership to satisfy a liability (i.e., no partner is personally liable), the debt is nonrecourse.

Limited partners are not normally responsible for recourse debts in the event the partnership cannot make payment. This responsibility usually rests solely with the general partners. As a result, *general* partners share *recourse* debt based on their respective *loss-sharing ratios*. On the other hand, *nonrecourse* debt is shared by *all* partners based on their respective *profit-sharing ratios* because no individual partner is personally liable for the debt.[17] This sharing arrangement is based on the fact that nonrecourse debt will be paid from the profits of the partnership *and* both general and limited partners will be taxed on their respective shares of profits used for such repayment.

> **Example 3.** G and L each contribute $10,000 to create a partnership in which they will share profits and losses equally. G is the general partner and L is a limited partner. Immediately after its creation, the partnership borrows $150,000 to purchase equipment. Assuming that the $150,000 partnership debt is a nonrecourse liability, each partner's basis in his partnership interest would be determined as follows:

	G	L
Cash contribution	$10,000	$10,000
Plus: Deemed contribution of money under § 752 (50% × $150,000)	75,000	75,000
Basis in partnership interest	$85,000	$85,000

If the debt were classified as a recourse liability, G's basis in the partnership interest would be $160,000 ($10,000 + $150,000), and L's basis would be only $10,000 because a limited partner does not share any of the recourse debt.

Liabilities Transferred to the Partnership.   When property subject to recourse debt is contributed to a partnership, the above rules are applicable *if* full responsibility (and therefore economic risk of loss) for the liability is transferred to the partnership.[18] Full responsibility may not be transferred, for example, when the lender would require a new loan with a higher interest rate. In this type of situation, the contributing partner may continue to be personally liable for this debt and none of it will be shared by any of the other partners.

---

[17]   Reg. § 1.752-1(e).   [18]   Temp. Reg. §§ 1.752-IT(d)(2) and (3).

Example 4.   T transfers property with a fair market value of $25,000, a basis of $10,000, and a *recourse* debt of $4,000 in exchange for a 25% general partnership interest. Because full responsibility for the recourse debt cannot be transferred without cost, T continues to be personally liable for it and is the only partner with an economic risk of loss associated with the debt. Consequently, none of the other partners' bases in the partnership are affected by this liability. T's basis in his partnership interest is determined as follows:[19]

Basis of contributed property................................	$10,000
Plus: Deemed contribution of money	
(increase in share of partnership debt).................	4,000
Less: Deemed distribution of money	
(decrease in share of	
partnership debt or personal debt)	(4,000)
T's basis in partnership interest.............................	$10,000

If the property is encumbered by a nonrecourse debt, the contributing partner is treated as retaining responsibility for any portion of the liability in excess of his or her basis in the property. Any portion of the liability not considered to be retained by the contributing partner is treated as a partnership liability to be shared in all partners' bases.[20]

Example 5.   V transfers property with a fair market value of $25,000, a basis of $10,000, and a *nonrecourse* debt of $4,000 in exchange for a 25% general partnership interest. In this situation, the entire debt is treated as a partnership liability, so all partners will be considered as sharing the debt in accordance with their profit-sharing ratios. V's basis in his partnership interest will be $7,000, computed as follows:[21]

Basis of contributed property................................	$10,000
Plus: Deemed contribution of money	
[share of partnership debt (25% × $4,000)].............	1,000
Less: Deemed distribution of money	
[decrease in personal debt (100% × $4,000)]..........	(4,000)
V's basis in partnership interest	$ 7,000

Note that the basis in the partnership for each of the other partners would be increased by his or her respective share of the deemed contribution of money attributable to the remaining $3,000 of partnership debt.

---

[19]   See Temp. Reg. § 1.752-2T(b), Example 1.   [21]   See Temp. Reg. § 1.752-2T(b), Example 2.

[20]   Temp. Reg. § 1.752-IT(e)(2).

Example 6.   In exchange for a 50% interest in the EZ Partnership, E transfers property that has a fair market value of $27,000 and an adjusted basis of $9,000 and is subject to a nonrecourse debt of $15,000. Z transfers $12,000 cash for the remaining 50% interest. E is treated as retaining responsibility for any portion of the debt in excess of her basis in the property contributed, or $6,000 ($15,000 debt − $9,000 basis). The remaining $9,000 of the nonrecourse debt is treated as a partnership liability. E's basis in her partnership interest is determined as follows:[22]

Basis of contributed property...............................	$ 9,000
Plus: Deemed contribution of money from retained share of nonrecourse debt...............	6,000
Plus: Deemed contribution of money [share of partnership debt (50% × $9,000)].............	4,500
Less: Deemed distribution of money [reduction in personal debt (100% × $15,000)].........	(15,000)
E's basis in partnership interest............................	$ 4,500

Z's basis will be $16,500 [$12,000 cash contributed + $4,500 deemed contribution of money (50% × $9,000 partnership liability)].

Note that the $21,000 sum of the partner's bases in their respective partnership interests ($4,500 + $16,500 = $21,000) equals the partnership's $21,000 total basis in its assets ($12,000 cash + $9,000 carryover basis in property from E).

RECAPTURE PROVISIONS

The contribution of depreciated property in a tax-free exchange for a capital interest does not trigger the §§ 1245 or 1250 depreciation recapture provisions. In such instances, the partner's holding period, basis, and potential recapture of depreciation are transferred to the partnership.[23]

SPECIAL ALLOCATIONS

The nonrecognition principle of § 721 generally is quite beneficial for individuals who wish to exchange property for a partnership interest. Without this special treatment, many taxpayers would be reluctant to contribute appreciated assets to a partnership. Note that any gain or loss realized on the exchange does not escape taxation but is merely postponed. Any gain or loss accruing prior to the contribution of the property is preserved because the partner's basis carries over to the partnership. This basis must be used for depreciation and depletion purposes and for determining gain or loss on a subsequent disposition of the asset.

---

[22]   See Temp. Reg. § 1.752-1T(k), Example 23.

[23]   See §§ 1245(b)(3) and 1250(d)(3) and Reg. §§ 1.1245-2(c)(2) and 1.1250-3(c)(3).

Generally, all items of income, deduction, gain, and loss are allocated to the partners according to their profit and loss ratios (unless the partners have agreed to special allocations, as discussed later in this chapter). Before 1984, taxpayers following this general rule could secure significant tax benefits whenever contributed property had a value that was either greater than or less than its basis. For example, assume P contributes property worth $30,000 (basis $10,000) to a partnership for a 50 percent interest. If the property is later sold for $30,000, the partnership must recognize a $20,000 gain ($30,000 − $10,000 carryover basis). Absent any special rule, only 50 percent of the gain, or $10,000, is allocated to P even though all $20,000 of the gain accrued while in her hands. The remaining $10,000 is allocated to the other partners. Thus, under the normal allocation rule, P has shifted a portion of the precontribution gain and the related tax to the other partners. This may work to P's advantage in one of two ways. If the other partners are family members in a lower tax bracket, P has been able to reduce the tax attributable to a disposition of the property while retaining control of the property through a family partnership. On the other hand, if the partners are unrelated, P has effectively shifted a portion of her tax burden to them.

In 1984 Congress recognized the potential for shifting income (or loss) to achieve tax savings and eliminated the possibility with a *mandatory* special allocation rule. Under this rule, any gain or loss recognized on a disposition of contributed property must be allocated to the contributing partner to the extent of any *precontribution gain or loss* (i.e., the gain or loss that has accrued at the time the property is contributed).[24] The balance of any gain or loss recognized is normally allocated according to the partners' profit- and loss-sharing ratios. In addition, any depreciation of the property must also take into account any difference between the property's value and basis at the time of contribution.[25]

> **Example 7.** This year, T and E formed a partnership with capital interests of 80% and 20%, respectively. E contributed land in exchange for her 20% capital interest. The land had a fair market value of $40,000 and a basis to E of $20,000. Thus, the partnership received an asset with an economic value of $40,000 and a tax basis of $20,000. If the land is later sold for $48,000, the partnership's gain is $28,000 ($48,000 − $20,000). This includes appreciation of $20,000 while owned by E and $8,000 while owned by the partnership. Without the special allocation, E would recognize 20% of the gain, $5,600, and the remaining $22,400 gain would be recognized by T. However, the special allocation rules for precontribution gains and losses require E to recognize $21,600 ($20,000 + 20% of $8,000), and T recognizes $6,400 (80% of $8,000).

---

[24] § 704(c).   [25] Reg. § 1.704-1(c).

Example 8. Refer to *Example 7*. In addition to the land, E contributed a building with a market value of $63,000 to obtain her 20% capital interest. E had purchased the building six years earlier for $90,000 and deducted $36,000 depreciation, based on the straight-line method and a 15-year life ($90,000 ÷ 15 years = $6,000 × 6 years). Thus, the building's basis at contribution was $54,000 ($90,000 − $36,000 accumulated depreciation). The partnership continues to use E's depreciation method. Consequently, annual depreciation is $6,000 ($54,000 ÷ 9 years). T's share of the deduction is $5,600 ($63,000 ÷ 9 years = $7,000 × 80%), and E's share is $400 ($6,000 maximum deduction − $5,600 allocated to T).

Note that T's depreciation deduction is computed as if he had purchased an 80% interest in the building for its fair market value of $63,000. Also note what occurs if depreciation based on market value exceeds actual depreciation. If the building's market value had exceeded $67,500, T could not be allocated his full share. For example, if the building's value had been $72,000, T's share is $6,400 ($72,000 ÷ 9 years = $8,000 × 80%). However, since the partnership's depreciation is $6,000, T cannot be allocated more than $6,000.

Example 9. Refer to *Example 8*. Assume all allocations were properly made to T and the building is sold for $50,000 after it was depreciated seven years as a partnership asset. The building's basis is $12,000 [$90,000 − ($6,000 × 7 = $42,000 + $36,000 prepartnership depreciation = $78,000)] and gain is $38,000 ($50,000 − $12,000). The gain should be allocated as follows:

Partnership	T (80%)	E (20%)	Total
Beginning basis [(1)]	$50,400	$ 3,600	$54,000
Less: Depreciation	(39,200)	(2,800)	(42,000)
Basis when sold	$11,200	$ 800	$12,000
Sale proceeds	$40,000	$10,000	$50,000
Less: Basis	(11,200)	(800)	(12,000)
Section 1231 gain	$28,800	$ 9,200	$38,000

[(1)] $63,000 market value × 80% = $50,400 and $54,000 transfer basis − $50,400 = $3,600

Character of Gain or Loss on Contributed Property. Historically, some taxpayers utilized the partnership rules to convert ordinary income into capital gains or to convert capital losses into ordinary losses. To prevent these conversion possibilities, § 724 creates a special rule governing the character of the gain or loss on the sale of inventory items, capital loss property, and unrealized receivables. These assets are referred to as being *tainted*. To prevent partnerships from avoiding the capital loss and ordinary income classifications, the taint remains with both this property *and* all assets (except corporate stock) received in any future nontaxable exchange for the tainted property.

All gain or loss recognized by the partnership on the sale of property that would be considered inventory to the *contributing* partner is treated as ordinary. Similarly, any loss recognized by the partnership on property that was a capital asset to the contributing partner is treated as a capital loss to the extent of the loss accrued at the time of contribution. The rules for inventory items and capital loss property apply only to dispositions made within *five years* after the date of contribution.[26] Thus, if a partner is patient and can wait more than five years, conversion may still be obtained. In contrast, any gain or loss recognized by the partnership on the disposition of what were unrealized receivables to the contributing partner (e.g., a cash basis taxpayer's rights to receive payments for services) is considered ordinary regardless of when the disposition occurs.[27]

> **Example 10.** On November 1, 1991, D exchanges land held for investment ($7,000 market value, $9,000 basis) and inventory ($4,000 market value, $3,500 basis) for a 20% interest in a partnership. These assets will be used in the partnership business, and therefore qualify as § 1231 assets. Three years later, the partnership sells the land for $6,700 resulting in a loss of $2,300 ($6,700 − $9,000 basis). At the same time, the partnership sells the items previously qualifying as D's inventory for $5,600 resulting in a gain of $2,100 ($5,600 − $3,500 basis). All losses and gains accrued as of November 1, 1991 ($2,000 loss for the property and $500 gain for the inventory) must be allocated to D. The remaining losses ($300 for the property) and gains ($1,600 for the inventory) are divided among the partners according to their profit and loss ratios. Since these assets were sold before the required five-year period elapsed, the character (capital loss for the property and ordinary income for the inventory) is retained. Although these assets were converted by the partnership to business assets, the *entire* gain on the sale of the inventory is ordinary income. In contrast, the capital loss on the sale of the land is limited to the $2,000 precontribution amount. Thus, D has the following gains and losses to report:
>
> | | | |
> |---|---|---|
> | **Land** | Loss to 11/1/91 (100%) | $2,000 capital loss |
> | | Loss after 10/31/91 (20%) | 60 § 1231 loss |
> | **Inventory** | Gain to 11/1/91 (100%) | 500 ordinary income |
> | | Gain after 10/31/91 (20%) | 320 ordinary income |

If the same sales had occurred *more than* five years after the assets had been contributed, the numbers would be the same but all gains and losses would be § 1231 gains and losses. Regardless of the date of sale, the other partners have a $240 ($300 − $60) § 1231 loss on the land since the $2,000 precontribution loss is allocated to D. However, unless the inventory is held for more than five years before its sale, the other partners' share of the gain ($1,600 − $320 = $1,280) will be ordinary income.

---

[26] §§ 724(b) and (c).   [27] § 724(a).

CONTRIBUTION OF SERVICES

When services are contributed to a partnership, the service partner may receive an interest in partnership profits plus any of the following:

1. An unrestricted capital interest
2. A restricted capital interest
3. No capital interest

The amount of income and when it is includible is dependent on which of the three types of partnership interests is received.

An Unrestricted Capital Interest.   If an unrestricted capital interest is received in exchange for services, the fair market value of the interest is includible ordinary income.[28] This amount becomes the service partner's basis in the partnership. The partnership deducts or capitalizes the amount based on the type of services rendered.[29] This is recorded when the partner has includible income. The fact that services were performed in exchange for a partnership interest has no effect on how the amount is recorded by the partnership.

> **Example 11.**   V receives a capital interest in a partnership in exchange for his services. The fair market value of the interest is $15,000. V's services include $10,000 for acquiring land needed for partnership operations and $5,000 for arranging the sale of partnership equipment no longer needed in the business. V has includible ordinary income of $15,000 and a basis in the partnership of $15,000. The partnership capitalizes $10,000 to the land and deducts $5,000 as a selling expense to arrive at the gain or loss on the sale of equipment.

Unless a special allocation is made, as discussed later, all partners will share in any amounts deducted and in any capitalized asset amounts.

A Restricted Capital Interest.   Receipt of a conditional promise of a future capital interest in a partnership, or one subject to substantial risk of forfeiture, may not result in includible income currently. Instead, income is reported when the restrictions are removed or when the capital interest is received.[30] The amount of income to be included is the value of the interest at the time of receipt, determined as if no restriction existed.

---

[28]   Reg. §§ 1.721-1(b)(1) and 1.61-2(d)(1).

[29]   §§ 162 and 263(a)(1).

[30]   § 83(a) covers all property, including a partnership capital interest.

In lieu of reporting the value of the interest as income when received or when the restrictions lapse, a service partner may elect to be taxed currently.[31] In such case, the amount to be included as income is the value of the interest at the time of receipt, determined as if no restriction existed. If the taxpayer elects to include the value of the income currently, no deduction is allowed if the interest is subsequently forfeited.[32] Note that the partnership records the transaction at the same time that the partner includes the value of the partnership interest in income.

> **Example 12.**   T performs services in exchange for a capital interest valued at $25,000. However, the agreement between T and the other partners states that this capital interest is forfeited if T stops performing these services at any time during the next three years. T may choose to recognize the $25,000 (value without the restriction) currently as ordinary income, or recognize the fair market value of the capital interest at the end of the forfeiture period. If T estimates the value of the capital interest at the end of three years to be $45,000, he must decide whether to recognize ordinary income of $25,000 now or of $45,000 three years later. The amount T recognizes becomes his basis in the partnership. Thus, if T decides to recognize $25,000 as ordinary income now and sells his interest for $45,000 at the end of the three years, he has a $20,000 gain on the sale; or if the interest is sold for $22,000, he has a $3,000 recognized loss on the sale. (Whether it is capital or ordinary gain or loss is discussed in Chapter 11.) Alternatively, if T recognizes the $25,000 but forfeits the interest, he has no deduction for the $25,000.

In deciding whether to make the election, a taxpayer should weigh the benefits of conversion of ordinary income to capital gain against the possibility that the tax on the income recognized currently would never be recovered if the interest were forfeited. With the elimination of the capital gains preference and the flattening of the tax rates, however, it appears that deferral of the income would normally be preferable to being taxed currently.

Impact on Partnership and Other Partners.   The contribution of services for a partnership interest affects not only the contributing partner but also the partnership and the remaining partners. Assuming the services are performed for the partnership (rather than for the partners), the effect on the partnership is similar to what occurs when the partnership pays cash for services; that is, the partnership may either deduct or capitalize the expense. The expense is then allocated to the partners. The instant transaction is more complicated, however, because the

---

[31]   § 83(b). The election must be made within 30 days after the capital interest is transferred.

[32]   See last sentence of § 83(b). In addition, the partnership must include in income any amount that was deducted previously. Reg. § 1.83-6(c).

partnership is not paying for the services with cash but with property, specifically an interest in the partnership. This complicates the transaction because taxpayers who pay debts with property are treated as if they sold the property and then used the proceeds to discharge the debt.

Technically, the partnership's transfer of an ownership interest for services is treated as if *three* related transactions occurred. First, the partnership is treated as if it sold an undivided interest in each of its assets and thus must recognize gain or loss equal to the difference between the fair market value of the undivided interest in each asset and a corresponding share of each asset's basis.[33] Second, the partnership is treated as if it used the "proceeds" from this "deemed sale" to pay the service partner.[34] Whether the payment is deductible depends on the nature of the services rendered.[35] The recipient of the ownership interest must recognize ordinary income to the extent of the fair market value of the undivided interest in each of the partnership's assets (net of any liabilities assumed). Third, the recipient is treated as having contributed his or her undivided interest in each of the assets back to the partnership in return for the ownership interest. This "deemed contribution" is a nontaxable transfer under § 721, and the partnership will have a basis equal to the fair market value of the undivided interest in each of its assets deemed recontributed.

All benefits from the second transaction above (i.e., the partnership's deduction or capitalization of the payment to the service partner) *should not* be shared by the service partner. Since the payment was made before the service partner joined the partnership, this allocation may be automatic.[36] However, to ensure this effect, the special allocation rules discussed later should be followed.

Example 13.   In return for services rendered to it by Z, the XY Partnership transfers a one-third ownership interest to Z when it has the following assets:

	Basis	Fair Market Value
Land.................	$15,000	$ 30,000
Building..............	60,000	90,000
	$75,000	$120,000

Assuming no liabilities, the partnership is treated as having sold a one-third interest in the land for $10,000 ($30,000 ÷ 3) and a similar interest in the building for $30,000 ($90,000 ÷ 3). As a result, the partnership must

[33] See *United States v. General Shoe Corp.,* 60-1 USTC ¶9927, 22 AFTR2d 44512, 282 F.2d 9 (CA-6, 1960) and Reg. § 1.83-6(b).

[34] This is a guaranteed payment, as discussed later in this chapter. Reg. § 1.721-1(b)(2).

[35] Jackson E. Cagle, 63 T.C. 86(1974), *aff'd* in 76-2 USTC ¶9672, 38 AFTR2d 76-5834, 539 F.2d 409 (CA-5, 1976).

[36] § 706(c)(2)(B).

recognize a gain of $5,000 [$10,000 deemed sale price − ($15,000 basis ÷ 3 = $5,000)] on the sale of the land, and a gain of $10,000 [$30,000 − ($60,000 basis ÷ 3 = $20,000)] on the building. The character of the gain depends on the character and holding period of the partnership's assets. The partnership is also treated as having made a payment to Z in the amount of $40,000 ($120,000 market value of assets ÷ 3). If the services represent deductible expenses, the partnership is entitled to a $40,000 deduction for the payment. Z has includible compensation of $40,000 and is treated as having contributed the undivided interest in the land and building back to the partnership in return for a one-third ownership interest. Consequently, Z's basis in the ownership interest received is $40,000; and the partnership's basis in its assets are increased as follows:

	2/3 Old Basis	+	Z's 1/3 Interest	=	New Basis
Land..................	$10,000		$10,000		$20,000
Building..............	40,000		30,000		70,000
	$50,000		$40,000		$90,000

Note that the partnership's basis in each of its assets has been increased to reflect the gain recognized as a result of this transaction. Also note that the existing partners must share in the recognition of gain on the deemed sale of partnership assets—but they also will share the benefit of any deduction arising from the payment.

No Capital Interest. If the service partner only receives an interest in future partnership profits and not a capital interest, income may be includible currently. Prior to 1971, the general belief was that none of the income was includible until it was distributable by the partnership to the service partner. Then, in 1971, the Tax Court held that a service partner had includible ordinary income in the year the fair market value of the future interest could be reasonably determined. This decision was upheld on appeal.[37] This particular case may not be representative, however, since it involved several tax-abusive features that may have influenced its outcome. More recent actions indicate that taxpayers may be able to avoid this treatment and have includible income when profits are allocated to them.[38]

---

[37] *Sol Diamond*, 56 T.C. 530 (1971), *aff'd.* in 74-1 USTC ¶9306, 33 AFTR2d 74-852, 492 F.2d 286 (CA-7, 1974).

[38] *Richard O. Wheeler*, 37 TCM 883, T.C. Memo 1978-208 and Ltr. Rul. 7948038. Also see Arthur B. Willis, John S. Pennell, and Philip F. Postlewaite, *Partnership Taxation* (Colorado Springs, Co.: Shepard's, Inc.), Chapter 27; and William S. McKee, William F. Nelson, and Robert L. Whitmire, *Federal Taxation of Partnerships and Partners* (Boston, MA.: Warren, Gorham & Lamont, Inc.), Chapter 5.

COMPARED WITH CORPORATE FORMATION

Many, but not all, of the rules applicable to contributions of assets for a partnership interest also exist under § 351 when assets are exchanged for corporate stock. Three rules discussed in this chapter are different, however, when contributions are made for a partnership interest rather than for corporate stock.

1. The tax-free exchange provisions apply to all partners regardless of their percentage ownership of the partnership, whereas § 351 applies only to contributing shareholders who, as a group, own at least 80 percent of the corporation's stock after the contribution.

2. Special allocations for depreciation, depletion, gains, and losses on contributed property are not available with the corporate form.

3. A partner's basis in the partnership is increased by his or her share of liabilities, whereas liabilities have no effect on a shareholder's basis in stock.

ORGANIZATION COSTS AND SYNDICATION FEES

Both organization costs and syndication fees for a partnership must be capitalized. An election is available at the partnership level to amortize *organization costs* (e.g., legal fees for drafting a partnership agreement) on a straight-line basis over a period of sixty months or longer.[39] In contrast, *syndication fees* paid or accrued to promote or sell a partnership interest may not be amortized at any time.[40] They remain on the books as intangible assets until the partnership is liquidated. Syndication fees generally are not incurred except for widely owned limited partnerships that are established as tax shelters.

OPERATING THE PARTNERSHIP

In contrast with most corporations, trusts, and estates, a partnership is not a taxable entity. Instead, it primarily serves as a *conduit* for accumulating income, expenses, gains, losses, and credits that *flow through* to its owners, based on their capital interests or some other allocation method adopted by them. Following the aggregate concept, all incidence of taxation passes to the partners who must report their share of these items on their own tax returns. In most instances, each item retains its original character. For example, interest on tax-exempt bonds earned by a partnership flows through to owners as tax-exempt income.

---

[39]   § 709(b).   [40]   § 709(a) and Reg. § 1.709-2(b).

Although a partnership does not pay income taxes, it is still required to file a tax return. Form 1065 must be filed for a partnership by the 15th day of the fourth month following the end of its tax year. This means an April 15 due date when a calendar year is selected for the partnership. Because of the flow through concept, the primary purpose of the partnership return is to provide information about the nature and amount of income, expenses, gains, losses, and credits and how they are allocated to each partner.

DETERMINING PARTNERSHIP NET INCOME

Partnership information is divided into two categories: (1) *ordinary income*: includible income and deductible expenses that result in net ordinary income or loss that is not subject to special tax treatment by *any* taxpayer, and (2) *separately stated items:* all other income, expenses, gains, losses, and credits that receive special treatment at the partner level (e.g., capital losses). This division is basic to preparing the partnership tax return. (See Exhibit 10-2 for an illustration of a partially completed Form 1065 and the accompanying Schedules K and K-1. The information is taken from the example in the appendix to Chapter 12—S Corporations.) Classification of an item for reporting purposes is determined at the partnership level.[41] Thus, gain on the sale of business land is § 1231 gain to all partners, even if one of them is a real estate broker, or if one of them held a capital interest in the partnership for less than one year.[42]

A partnership is generally allowed to use either the cash or the accrual method of accounting for determining its income. However, the cash method of accounting *cannot* be used by any partnership that is a tax shelter (discussed in Chapter 11). Similarly, any partnership that has a C corporation as a partner must use the accrual method, unless the partnership (1) is in the farming or timber business, (2) has average annual gross receipts of no more than $5 million for each of the prior three taxable years, or (3) has a corporate partner that is a qualified personal service corporation. A qualified personal service corporation generally is one that provides professional services and is owned substantially (95 percent in value) by employees who perform services in the following fields: law, accounting, health, engineering, architecture, actuarial science, performing arts, or consulting.

---

[41] The DRA of 1984 added an exception to this rule. Capital gain treatment of equity options from dealers does not flow through to limited partners.

[42] Rev. Rul. 67-188, 1967-1 C.B. 216. See *U.S. v. Basye*, 73-1 USTC ¶9250, 31 AFTR2d 73-802, 410 U.S. 441 (USSC, 1973). Also see Rev. Rul. 68-79, 1968-1 C.B. 310.

Exhibit 10-2

Form **1065**	**U.S. Partnership Return of Income**	OMB No. 1545-0099

Department of the Treasury
Internal Revenue Service

For calendar year 1990, or tax year beginning _____, 1990, and ending _____, 19 ____
▶ **See separate instructions.**

19**90**

A Principal business activity
RETAIL

B Principal product or service
CLOTHING

C Business code number
5651

Use IRS label. Otherwise, please print or type.

Name
T COMPANY

Number, street, and room or suite no. (If a P.O. box, see page 9 of the instructions.)
8122 SOUTH S STREET

City or town, state, and ZIP code
NORFOLK, VA 23508

D Employer identification number
88-9138761

E Date business started
1-1-90

F Total assets (see Specific Instructions)
$ 322,000 | 00

		Yes	No

G Check applicable boxes: **(1)** ☒ Initial return **(2)** ☐ Final return
(3) ☐ Change in address **(4)** ☐ Amended return

H Check accounting method: **(1)** ☐ Cash **(2)** ☑ Accrual
(3) ☐ Other (specify) ▶ _____

I Number of partners in this partnership ▶ 2   Yes No

J Is this partnership a limited partnership? . . . . .   ✓

K Are any partners in this partnership also partnerships? .   ✓

L Is this partnership a partner in another partnership? .   ✓

M Is this partnership subject to the consolidated audit procedures of sections 6221 through 6233? If "Yes," see "Designation of Tax Matters Partner" on page 2 . .   ✓

N Does this partnership meet **all** the requirements shown in the instructions for **Question N**? . . . . .   ✓

O Does this partnership have any foreign partners? . . .   ✓

P Is this partnership a publicly traded partnership as defined in section 469(k)(2)? . . . .   ✓

Q Has this partnership filed, or is it required to file, **Form 8264,** Application for Registration of a Tax Shelter? . . .   ✓

R Was there a distribution of property or a transfer (for example, by sale or death) of a partnership interest during the tax year? If "Yes," see the instructions concerning an election to adjust the basis of the partnership's assets under section 754 . . . .   ✓

S At any time during the tax year, did the partnership have an interest in or a signature or other authority over a financial account in a foreign country (such as a bank account, securities account, or other financial account)? (See the instructions for exceptions and filing requirements for form TD F 90-22.1.) If "Yes," enter the name of the foreign country. ▶ _____   ✓

T Was the partnership the grantor of, or transferor to, a foreign trust which existed during the current tax year, whether or not the partnership or any partner has any beneficial interest in it? If "Yes," you may have to file Forms 3520, 3520-A, or 926 . . . .   ✓

Caution: *Include only trade or business income and expenses on lines 1a through 21 below. See the instructions for more information.*

Income

1a Gross receipts or sales	**1a**	470,000		
b Less returns and allowances	**1b**	-0-	**1c**	470,000
2 Cost of goods sold (Schedule A, line 7)			**2**	300,000
3 Gross profit—Subtract line 2 from line 1c			**3**	170,000
4 Ordinary income (loss) from other partnerships and fiduciaries *(attach schedule)*			**4**	
5 Net farm profit (loss) *(attach Schedule F (Form 1040))*			**5**	
6 Net gain (loss) from Form 4797, Part II, line 18			**6**	
7 Other income (loss) (see instructions) *(attach schedule)*			**7**	
8 Total income (loss)—Combine lines 3 through 7			**8**	170,000

Deductions (see instructions for limitations)

9a Salaries and wages (other than to partners)	**9a**	48,000		
b Less jobs credit	**9b**	-0-	**9c**	48,000
10 Guaranteed payments to partners			**10**	24,000
11 Rent			**11**	
12 Interest			**12**	3,300
13 Taxes PROPERTY TAXES = $3,000 ; PAYROLL TAXES = $4,000			**13**	7,000
14 Bad debts			**14**	
15 Repairs			**15**	12,000
16a Depreciation (see instructions)	**16a**	15,000		
b Less depreciation reported on Schedule A and elsewhere on return	**16b**	-0-	**16c**	15,000
17 Depletion **(Do not deduct oil and gas depletion.)**			**17**	
18a Retirement plans, etc.			**18a**	
b Employee benefit programs. LIFE INS.			**18b**	1,400
19 Other deductions *(attach schedule)* UTILITIES TELE. = $2,500 ; OFFICE SUPPLIES = $1,100 ; INSURANCE COSTS = $3,100			**19**	6,700
20 Total deductions—Add lines 9c through 19			**20**	117,400
21 Ordinary income (loss) from trade or business activities—Subtract line 20 from line 8			**21**	52,600

Please Sign Here

Under penalties of perjury, I declare that I have examined this return, including accompanying schedules and statements, and to the best of my knowledge and belief, it is true, correct, and complete. Declaration of preparer (other than general partner) is based on all information of which preparer has any knowledge.

▶ Signature of general partner   ▶ Date

Paid Preparer's Use Only

Preparer's signature ▶	Date	Check if self-employed ▶ ☐	Preparer's social security no.
Firm's name (or yours if self-employed) and address ▶		E.I. No. ▶	
		ZIP code ▶	

For Paperwork Reduction Act Notice, see page 1 of separate instructions.

Form **1065** (1990)

Exhibit 10-2 Continued

Form 1065 (1990)   Page **2**

Schedule A   Cost of Goods Sold

1	Inventory at beginning of year	**1**
2	Purchases less cost of items withdrawn for personal use	**2**
3	Cost of labor	**3**
4a	Additional section 263A costs (see instructions) *(attach schedule)*	**4a**
b	Other costs *(attach schedule)*	**4b**
5	Total—Add lines 1 through 4b	**5**
6	Inventory at end of year	**6**
7	Cost of goods sold—Subtract line 6 from line 5. Enter here and on page 1, line 2	**7** 300,000

8a Check all methods used for valuing closing inventory:

  (i) ☑ Cost   (ii) ☐ Lower of cost or market as described in Regulations section 1.471-4

  (iii) ☐ Writedown of "subnormal" goods as described in Regulations section 1.471-2(c)

  (iv) ☐ Other (specify method used and attach explanation) ▶ -

  b Check this box if the LIFO inventory method was adopted this tax year for any goods *(if checked, attach Form 970)* . . . ▶ ☐

  c Do the rules of section 263A (with respect to property produced or acquired for resale) apply to the partnership? . . ☐ Yes ☑ No

  d Was there any change in determining quantities, cost, or valuations between opening and closing inventory? . . . ☐ Yes ☑ No
  If "Yes," attach explanation.

Schedule L   Balance Sheets

Caution: *Read the instructions for* **Question N** *on page 9 of the instructions before completing Schedules L and M.*

Assets	Beginning of tax year (a)	(b)	End of tax year (c)	(d)
1 Cash				
2a Trade notes and accounts receivable				
b Less allowance for bad debts				
3 Inventories				
4 U.S. government obligations				
5 Tax-exempt securities				
6 Other current assets *(attach schedule)*				
7 Mortgage and real estate loans				
8 Other investments *(attach schedule)*				
9a Buildings and other depreciable assets . . .				
b Less accumulated depreciation				
10a Depletable assets				
b Less accumulated depletion				
11 Land (net of any amortization)				
12a Intangible assets (amortizable only)				
b Less accumulated amortization				
13 Other assets *(attach schedule)*				322,000
14 **Total** assets				
Liabilities and Capital				
15 Accounts payable				
16 Mortgages, notes, bonds payable in less than 1 year				
17 Other current liabilities *(attach schedule)*				
18 All nonrecourse loans				
19 Mortgages, notes, bonds payable in 1 year or more				
20 Other liabilities *(attach schedule)*				
21 Partners' capital accounts				322,000
22 **Total** liabilities and capital				

Schedule M   Reconciliation of Partners' Capital Accounts

(Show reconciliation of each partner's capital account on Schedule K-1 (Form 1065), Item K.)

(a) Partners' capital accounts at beginning of year	(b) Capital contributed during year	(c) Income (loss) from lines 1, 2, 3c, and 4 of Schedule K	(d) Income not included in column (c), plus nontaxable income	(e) Losses not included in column (c), plus unallowable deductions	(f) Withdrawals and distributions	(g) Partners' capital accounts at end of year (combine columns (a) through (f))
		58,900 (a)	0	(7,700 (b))	(19,000 (c))	

Designation of Tax Matters Partner (See instructions.)

Enter below the general partner designated as the tax matters partner (TMP) for the tax year of this return:

Name of designated TMP ▶ _____   Identifying number of TMP ▶ _____

Address of designated TMP ▶ _____

(a) \$52,600 ORD. INC. + \$3,300 INTEREST INC. + \$2,000 DIVIDENDS + \$1,000 NLTCG
   = \$58,900.

(b) \$7,000 CHARITABLE CONT. + \$700 LIFE INS. = \$7,700.

(c) \$12,000 CASH + \$7,000 P/S BASIS IN LAND = \$19,000.

Exhibit 10-2 Continued

Form 1065 (1990)   Page **3**

Schedule K — Partners' Shares of Income, Credits, Deductions, Etc.

	(a) Distributive share items		(b) Total amount
Income (Loss)	**1** Ordinary income (loss) from trade or business activities (page 1, line 21)	**1**	52,600
	2 Net income (loss) from rental real estate activities *(attach Form 8825)*	**2**	
	3a Gross income from other rental activities	3a	
	b Less expenses *(attach schedule)*	3b	
	c Net income (loss) from other rental activities	**3c**	
	4 Portfolio income (loss) (see instructions):		
	a Interest income	**4a**	
	b Dividend income	**4b**	2,000
	c Royalty income	**4c**	
	d Net short-term capital gain (loss) *(attach Schedule D (Form 1065))*	**4d**	
	e Net long-term capital gain (loss) *(attach Schedule D (Form 1065))* $2,200 – $1,200	**4e**	1,000
	f Other portfolio income (loss) *(attach schedule)*	**4f**	
	5 Guaranteed payments to partners	**5**	24,000
	6 Net gain (loss) under section 1231 (other than due to casualty or theft) *(attach Form 4797)*	**6**	
	7 Other income (loss) *(attach schedule)* INTEREST PAID TO T	**7**	3,300
Deductions	**8** Charitable contributions (see instructions) *(attach list)*	**8**	7,000
	9 Section 179 expense deduction *(attach Form 4562)*	**9**	
	10 Deductions related to portfolio income (see instructions) (itemize)	**10**	
	11 Other deductions *(attach schedule)*	**11**	
Invest-ment Interest	**12a** Interest expense on investment debts	**12a**	
	b (1) Investment income included on lines 4a through 4f above	**12b(1)**	
	(2) Investment expenses included on line 10 above	**12b(2)**	
Credits	**13a** Credit for income tax withheld	**13a**	
	b Low-income housing credit (see instructions):		
	(1) From partnerships to which section 42(j)(5) applies for property placed in service before 1990	**13b(1)**	
	(2) Other than on line 13b(1) for property placed in service before 1990	**13b(2)**	
	(3) From partnerships to which section 42(j)(5) applies for property placed in service after 1989	**13b(3)**	
	(4) Other than on line 13b(3) for property placed in service after 1989	**13b(4)**	
	c Qualified rehabilitation expenditures related to rental real estate activities *(attach Form 3468)*	**13c**	
	d Credits (other than credits shown on lines 13b and 13c) related to rental real estate activities (see instructions)	**13d**	
	e Credits related to other rental activities (see instructions)	**13e**	
	14 Other credits (see instructions) REHABILITATION CREDIT	**14**	2,000
Self-Employ-ment	**15a** Net earnings (loss) from self-employment $52,600 + $24,000	**15a**	76,600
	b Gross farming or fishing income	**15b**	
	c Gross nonfarm income	**15c**	
Adjustments and Tax Preference Items	**16a** Accelerated depreciation of real property placed in service before 1987	**16a**	
	b Accelerated depreciation of leased personal property placed in service before 1987	**16b**	
	c Depreciation adjustment on property placed in service after 1986	**16c**	
	d Depletion (other than oil and gas)	**16d**	
	e (1) Gross income from oil, gas, and geothermal properties	**16e(1)**	
	(2) Deductions allocable to oil, gas, and geothermal properties	**16e(2)**	
	f Other adjustments and tax preference items *(attach schedule)*	**16f**	
Foreign Taxes	**17a** Type of income ▶		
	b Foreign country or U.S. possession ▶		
	c Total gross income from sources outside the U.S. *(attach schedule)*	**17c**	
	d Total applicable deductions and losses *(attach schedule)*	**17d**	
	e Total foreign taxes (check one): ▶ ☐ Paid ☐ Accrued	**17e**	
	f Reduction in taxes available for credit *(attach schedule)*	**17f**	
	g Other foreign tax information *(attach schedule)*	**17g**	
Other	**18a** Total expenditures to which a section 59(e) election may apply	**18a**	
	b Type of expenditures ▶		
	19 Other items and amounts required to be reported separately to partners (see instructions) *(attach schedule)*		

		20a Total distributive income/payment items—Combine lines 1 through 7 above		**20a**		

Analysis	**b** Analysis by type of partner:	(a) Corporate	(b) Individual		(c) Partnership	(d) Exempt organization	(e) Nominee/Other
			i. Active	ii. Passive			
	(1) General partners		82,900				
	(2) Limited partners						

Exhibit 10-2 Continued

SCHEDULE K-1 (Form 1065) Department of the Treasury Internal Revenue Service	**Partner's Share of Income, Credits, Deductions, Etc.** ▶ See separate instructions. For calendar year 1990 or tax year beginning ___, 1990, and ending ___, 19 ___	OMB No. 1545-0099 **1990**

Partner's identifying number ▶ 467-63-5052	Partnership's identifying number ▶ 88-9138761
Partner's name, address, and ZIP code	Partnership's name, address, and ZIP code
ADOLPH Z. T. 1291 MAPLE DRIVE NORFOLK, VA 23508	T COMPANY 8122 SOUTH S STREET NORFOLK, VA 23508

A Is this partner a general partner? . . . ☒ Yes ☐ No

B Partner's share of liabilities (see instructions):
Nonrecourse . . . . $ _____
Qualified nonrecourse financing . . $ _____
Other *DATA NOT IN EXAMPLE* . $ __40,000__

C What type of entity is this partner? ▶ _INDIVIDUAL_

D Is this partner a ☐ domestic or a ☐ foreign partner?

E Enter partner's percentage of:
	(i) Before change or termination	(ii) End of year
Profit sharing	_100_ %	_100_ %
Loss sharing *NOT IN EXAMPLE*	_80_ %	_80_ %
Ownership of capital *IN EXAMPLE*	_80_ %	_80_ %

F IRS Center where partnership filed return ▶ _MEMPHIS, TN_

G(1) Tax shelter registration number ▶ _N/A_
(2) Type of tax shelter ▶ _____

H(1) Did the partner's ownership interest in the partnership change after Oct. 22, 1986? . . . . ☐ Yes ☒ No
If "Yes," attach statement. (See Form 1065 Instructions.)
(2) Did the partnership start or acquire a new activity after Oct. 22, 1986? . . . . ☐ Yes ☒ No
If "Yes," attach statement. (See Form 1065 Instructions.)

I Check here if this partnership is a publicly traded partnership as defined in section 469(k)(2) . . . . ☐

J Check applicable boxes: (1) ☐ Final K-1 (2) ☐ Amended K-1

K Reconciliation of partner's capital account:

(a) Capital account at beginning of year	(b) Capital contributed during year	(c) Income (loss) from lines 1, 2, 3, and 4 below	(d) Income not included in column (c), plus nontaxable income	(e) Losses not included in column (c), plus unallowable deductions	(f) Withdrawals and distributions	(g) Capital account at end of year (combine columns (a) through (f))
58,900 (a)	0			(7,700 (b))	(19,000 (c))	

		(a) Distributive share item		(b) Amount	(c) 1040 filers enter the amount in column (b) on:
Income (Loss)	1	Ordinary income (loss) from trade or business activities . . .	1	52,600	} (See Partner's Instructions for Schedule K-1 (Form 1065))
	2	Net income (loss) from rental real estate activities	2		
	3	Net income (loss) from other rental activities	3		
	4	Portfolio income (loss):			
	a	Interest	4a		Sch. B, Part I, line 1
	b	Dividends	4b	2,000	Sch. B, Part II, line 5
	c	Royalties	4c		Sch. E, Part I, line 4
	d	Net short-term capital gain (loss)	4d		Sch. D, line 5, col. (f) or (g)
	e	Net long-term capital gain (loss)	4e	1,000	Sch. D, line 12, col. (f) or (g)
	f	Other portfolio income (loss) (attach schedule)	4f		(Enter on applicable line of your return)
	5	Guaranteed payments to partner	5	24,000	} (See Partner's Instructions for Schedule K-1 (Form 1065))
	6	Net gain (loss) under section 1231 (other than due to casualty or theft)	6		
	7	Other income (loss) (attach schedule) . *INTEREST* . . .	7	3,300	(Enter on applicable line of your return)
Deductions	8	Charitable contributions	8	7,000	Sch. A, line 14 or 15
	9	Section 179 expense deduction (attach schedule)	9		} (See Partner's Instructions for Schedule K-1 (Form 1065))
	10	Deductions related to portfolio income (attach schedule) . . .	10		
	11	Other deductions (attach schedule)	11		
Investment Interest	12a	Interest expense on investment debts	12a		Form 4952, line 1
	b	(1) Investment income included on lines 4a through 4f above .	b(1)		} (See Partner's Instructions for Schedule K-1 (Form 1065))
		(2) Investment expenses included on line 10 above	b(2)		
Credits	13a	Credit for income tax withheld	13a		} (See Partner's Instructions for Schedule K-1 (Form 1065))
	b	Low-income housing credit:			
		(1) From section 42(j)(5) partnerships for property placed in service before 1990	b(1)		
		(2) Other than on line 13b(1) for property placed in service before 1990	b(2)		} Form 8586, line 5
		(3) From section 42(j)(5) partnerships for property placed in service after 1989	b(3)		
		(4) Other than on line 13b(3) for property placed in service after 1989	b(4)		
	c	Qualified rehabilitation expenditures related to rental real estate activities (see instructions) *CREDIT*	13c	2,000	} (See Partner's Instructions for Schedule K-1 (Form 1065))
	d	Credits (other than credits shown on lines 13b and 13c) related to rental real estate activities (see instructions)	13d		
	e	Credits related to other rental activities (see instructions) . . .	13e		
	14	Other credits (see instructions)	14		

For Paperwork Reduction Act Notice, see Form 1065 Instructions.   Schedule K-1 (Form 1065) 1990

(a) $52,600 ORD. INC. + $3,300 INTEREST INC. + $2,000 DIVIDENDS + $1,000 NLTCG = $58,900.

(b) $7,000 CHARITABLE CONT. + $700 LIFE INS. = $7,700.

(c) $12,000 CASH + $7,000 P/S BASIS IN LAND = $19,000.

Section K must be completed before the return is filed.

Exhibit 10-2 Continued

Schedule K-1 (Form 1065) 1990   Page **2**

	(a) Distributive share item		(b) Amount	(c) 1040 filers enter the amount in column (b) on:
Self-em-ployment	**15a** Net earnings (loss) from self-employment	**15a**	76,600	Sch. SE, Section A or B
	b Gross farming or fishing income	**15b**		⎱ (See Partner's Instructions for Schedule K-1 (Form 1065))
	c Gross nonfarm income	**15c**		
Adjustments and Tax Preference Items	**16a** Accelerated depreciation of real property placed in service before 1987	**16a**		
	b Accelerated depreciation of leased personal property placed in service before 1987	**16b**		(See Partner's Instructions for Schedule K-1 (Form 1065) and Form 6251 Instructions)
	c Depreciation adjustment on property placed in service after 1986	**16c**		
	d Depletion (other than oil and gas)	**16d**		
	e (1) Gross income from oil, gas, and geothermal properties . .	**e(1)**		
	(2) Deductions allocable to oil, gas, and geothermal properties .	**e(2)**		
	f Other adjustments and tax preference items *(attach schedule)* .	**16f**		
Foreign Taxes	**17a** Type of income ▶ _____			Form 1116, Check boxes
	b Name of foreign country or U.S. possession ▶ _____			Form 1116, Part I
	c Total gross income from sources outside the U.S. *(attach schedule)*	**17c**		Form 1116, Part I
	d Total applicable deductions and losses *(attach schedule)* . . .	**17d**		Form 1116, Part I
	e Total foreign taxes (check one): ▶ ☐ Paid ☐ Accrued . .	**17e**		Form 1116, Part II
	f Reduction in taxes available for credit *(attach schedule)* . . .	**17f**		Form 1116, Part III
	g Other foreign tax information *(attach schedule)*	**17g**		See Form 1116 Instructions
Other	**18a** Total expenditures to which a section 59(e) election may apply .	**18a**		⎰ (See Partner's Instructions for Schedule K-1 (Form 1065))
	b Type of expenditures ▶ _____			

	(a) Distributive share item	A	B	C	
Recapture of Tax Credits	**19** Recapture of low-income housing credit:				
	a From section 42(j)(5) partnerships			**19a**	⎱ Form 8611, line 8
	b Other than on line 19a			**19b**	
	20 Investment credit properties:	**A**	**B**	**C**	
	a Description of property (State whether recovery or nonrecovery property. If recovery property, state whether regular percentage method or section 48(q) election used.) .				Form 4255, top
	b Date placed in service .				Form 4255, line 2
	c Cost or other basis . .				Form 4255, line 3
	d Class of recovery property or original estimated useful life .				Form 4255, line 4
	e Date item ceased to be investment credit property				Form 4255, line 8
Supplemental Information	**21** Supplemental information required to be reported separately to each partner *(attach additional schedules if more space is needed)*:				
	$700 LIFE INSURANCE				

NET ORDINARY INCOME OR LOSS

All includible income and deductible expenses in determining net *ordinary* income or loss are reported on page 1 of Form 1065. Includible income is listed on lines 1 through 7. In addition to gross receipts from services and gross profit from merchandise sales, ordinary income includes net income or loss from other partnerships and fiduciaries; net income or loss from farming operations; net gains from the recapture provisions of § 1245 and §§ 1250 through 1254; and other income or loss. Deductible expenses are recorded on lines 9 through 19. In general, the list includes employee salaries, rent, interest, taxes, bad debts, repairs, depreciation, depletion, retirement plans, and employee benefit programs. All other deductible ordinary expenses such as utilities, insurance, advertising, and entertainment are accumulated on a separate schedule and reported in total on line 19. Partnership net ordinary income or loss is determined next by subtracting the listed deductible expenses from the includible income. Partners are required to report their share of the net amount. This approach relieves them of the burden of reporting their share of each item affecting partnership ordinary net income or loss.

Page 2 of Form 1065 contains information relating to the cost of goods sold, balance sheet accounts, and a reconciliation of partners' capital accounts. Page 3 (Schedule K) is used to report the partners' shares of income or loss, deductions, credits, self-employment income, tax preferences, investment interest, and foreign taxes. (See Exhibit 10-3 for a summary of the tax effects in this section of the chapter.)

SEPARATELY REPORTED ITEMS

All income, expenses, gains, losses, and credits that *may* be subject to special tax treatment by one or more partners are reported separately on Schedule K, which is filed with Form 1065. These items include rental income and expenses, dividends, portfolio interest, capital gains and losses, § 1231 gains and losses, charitable contributions, qualifying foreign taxes, deductions for the limited expensing election, and any other income, deductions, gains, losses, or credits subject to special tax treatment.[43] These other items include tax credits, itemized deductions attributable to partners, payments to Keogh and Individual Retirement Act plans for partners, and oil and gas depletion. In addition, any specially allocated items such as depreciation and gain or loss on contributed property must be reported separately.

---

[43] § 702(a).

Exhibit 10-3
*Summary of Tax Effects
for Operating the Partnerships*

Transaction	Effect on Partnership	Effect on Partner
1. Net ordinary income	Reported on Form 1065	Distributive share flows through and increases the basis in the partnership; it is includible ordinary income
2. Net ordinary loss	Same as above	Distributive share flows through to the extent of each partner's basis and decreases the basis in the partnership; it is deductible ordinary loss to the extent of the flow through; losses in excess of basis are carried forward until the partner's basis is positive (see Chapter 11 for limitations on deductions)
3. Other income, expenses, gains, losses, and credits	Reported on Schedules K (if more than 10 partners) and K-1	Same as above; character flows through with all items
4. Self-employment income:		
a. General partner	Same as above	Distributive share of ordinary net income (adjusted) plus guaranteed payments
b. Limited partner	Same as above	Guaranteed payment for services performed
5. Partnership elections	All but three must by made by the partnership	Section 703 lists three elections to be made individually by each partner

Each partner's distributive share of partnership ordinary income or loss and other Schedule K items is reported on Schedule K-1. One copy of Schedule K-1 is prepared for each partner and is filed with Form 1065 while another is given to the partner. In this way, the Internal Revenue Service and each partner receive detailed partnership information necessary in determining both the partner's income tax and self-employment tax liability.

SELF-EMPLOYMENT INCOME

Income derived by a partner from a partnership may be considered self-employment income subject to social security taxes. Generally, self-employment income for a partner is composed of the partner's (1) distributive share of partnership ordinary income (Form 1065, page 1) adjusted to eliminate all gains, losses, and *passive* income not earned in the course of the partnership's trade or business, *plus* (2) guaranteed payments (defined later in this chapter).[44] Passive income, gains, and losses generally include interest income (other than that on accounts and notes receivable), dividends, net rents, and net §§ 1245 and 1250 gains. This computation generally is applicable to all partners, regardless of whether any of them perform services for the partnership.[45] However, there are three exceptions. Only *guaranteed payments* for *services performed* are self-employment income for the following:

1. Limited partners[46]

2. Partners who liquidated their ownership interests in a prior year but are being paid from current partnership profits[47]

3. Partners of partnerships that are not engaged in a trade or business[48]

Example 14. The K-10 partnership reports the following information for the year:

Sales...		$200,000
Cost of goods sold...........................		(89,000)
Interest income on trade receivables..........		3,000
Interest income from corporate bonds.........		5,000
Gross rents..................................	$20,000	
Rental expenses.............................	(22,000)	(2,000)
Guaranteed payments to X....................		(17,000)
Other deductions (expenses).................		(30,000)
Net ordinary income........................		$ 70,000
Net capital gain..............................		$ 10,000

The partnership's profits and losses are divided as follows: 40% to X, 35% to Y, and 25% to Z. X and Y are general partners and Z is a limited partner.

---

[44] § 1402 and Reg. § 1.707-1(c). But see Rev. Rul. 64-220, 1964-2 C.B. 335, where guaranteed payments to manage the partnership's rental property were not self-employment income.

[45] *William J. Ellsasser, Est.,* 61 T.C. 241 (1973). The amount from this computation, however, does not necessarily qualify as earned income for Individual Retirement Accounts. §§ 219(f)(1) and 401(c)(2). The same computation is applicable in community property states even though half the partner's distributable share of partnership income may be taxed to his or her spouse.

[46] § 1402(a)(12).

[47] Rev. Rul. 79-34, 1979-1 C.B. 285.

[48] Rev. Ruls. 75-525, 1975-2 C.B. 350, and 79-53, 1979-1 C.B. 286.

The self-employment income of the partnership and X are computed as follows:

Net ordinary income..	$70,000
Adjustments for gain, losses, and passive items:	
Interest income from corporate bonds......................	(5,000)
Net rental loss..	2,000
Partnership self-employment income	$67,000
X's percentage...	× 40%
X's share of partnership self-employment income.............	$26,800
Plus: Guaranteed payments..................................	17,000
X's self-employment income.................................	$43,800

Y's self-employment income is $23,450 ($67,000 × 35%). But Z, the limited partner, has no self-employment income. If X were a limited partner, her self-employment income would be just the guaranteed payments of $17,000.

PARTNERSHIP ELECTIONS

In computing the partnership's income, a number of elections must be made. These include the choice of a taxable year as well as certain accounting methods. With few exceptions, all such elections follow the entity concept and must be made at the partnership level.[49] Consequently, all partners are required to use the same methods for reporting their share of partnership income, deductions, gains, losses, and credits. Uniformity, for example, is required for elections concerning the method of determining inventories and depreciation expense, as well as for determining whether income is reported on the installment basis, and whether certain items are capitalized or expensed. Partners are not, however, required to use these same methods for their other business interests.[50]

TRANSACTIONS BETWEEN A PARTNERSHIP AND ITS PARTNERS

Many types of transactions occur between a partnership and its partners. For example, a partnership and its partners may buy property from each other. A partner may lend money to a partnership or perhaps borrow from it. Similarly, a partner may perform services for a partnership. These services may be performed either in the individual's capacity as a partner (e.g., managing the partnership's business) or as an independent third party (e.g., a partner who has a separate accounting practice might prepare the partnership's monthly financial statements).

---

[49] See § 703(b) for the three elections made by the partners.

[50] Reg. § 1.703-1(b).

In many instances, these transactions are governed by the entity concept and are therefore treated as if they occurred at arm's length between independent parties. However, in other situations, the Code applies the aggregate theory to arrive at a much different result. The treatment of some of the more frequently encountered transactions between a partnership and its partners is considered below. (See Exhibit 10-4 for a summary of the transactions discussed in this section.)

EMPLOYER/EMPLOYEE RELATIONSHIP

If a partner works for his or her partnership, it seems logical that he or she would be treated like any other employee. It also seems logical that the tax benefits extended to shareholders who work for their corporations should be available to partners. However, early court decisions viewed partners differently. These decisions applied the *aggregate theory* and held that a partner could not be an employee of his or her partnership. Thus, partner compensation is not salary and is not subject to withholding taxes.

One of the major disadvantages of the partnership form is that partners who work for their partnerships do not qualify for tax-favored fringe benefits. Recall that an employer can deduct the cost of providing certain benefits to its employees while the employee has no taxable income. These benefits include premiums for accident, health, and group-term life insurance; death benefits; and employer-provided meals and lodging. However, the partnership cannot deduct the cost of providing these to its partners.[51] Instead, the partner, rather than the partnership, is treated as having paid the costs. Of the items listed above, only the health insurance premiums would qualify for deduction by the partner. The partner has a choice: deduct 25 percent of this premium as a self-employed expense or include all of it with his or her itemized medical expenses. (See the discussion in the companion book, *Individual Taxation*.)

In addition, a partner is not entitled to participate with other employees in a qualified pension plan. Instead, each partner may establish his or her own Keogh plan.[52] Although a Keogh plan provides benefits very similar to typical qualified plans, they are not identical. For example, the amount of contributions that can be made is more limited, and loans from the plan are prohibited.[53]

GUARANTEED PAYMENTS

Early court decisions applied the aggregate theory to "salary" payments to a partner and held that a partner could not be an employee of a partnership. The courts viewed the payment of a salary to a partner as simply one step in the division of partnership profits. In effect, the "salary" was simply considered a part of the partner's distributive share of partnership income.

---

[51] See, for example, Reg. § 1.707-1(c), Rev. Ruls. 69-184, 1969-1 C.B. 256, Rev. Rul. 72-596, 1972-2 C.B. 395, and § 119.

[52] §§ 401(a)(10)(A) and (c)(3).

[53] § 401(d).

Exhibit 10-4
*Summary of Tax Effects
for Partner/Partnership Relations*

Transaction	Effect on Partnership	Effect on Partner
1. Partner as an employee	Not applicable—a partner cannot be an employee of a partnership	Not applicable
2. Partner compensation treated as a guaranteed payment	Deductible or capitalized, depending on the type of service performed	Includible ordinary income as of partnership's year end
3. Partner compensation based on partnership profits	Distribution of profits	Same as above
4. Other payments to a partner in a nonpartner status (e.g., interest on debt, rent, and royalty payments)	Deductible when the payment is includible by the partner	Includible as though received from an unrelated party
5. Losses on sales to partnership (partner owns more than 50% of partnership with constructive ownership rules)	FMV is basis; future gain is not recognized to the extent of the partner's disallowed losses	No deduction
6. Capital gain on sales to partnership (partner owns more than 50% of partnership with contructive ownership rules)	Treated as a purchase from a nonpartner	All gain is ordinary income if asset is not a capital or §1231 asset in the hands of the purchaser
7. Sale of depreciable property to partnership (partner owns more than 50% of partnership with contructive ownership rules)	Same as above	Same as above

When Congress rewrote the Code in 1954, however, it recognized that a partner who works for the partnership might be paid a salary much like any other employee without regard to how much income, if any, the partnership might otherwise have. Consequently, it modified the courts' traditional view that a partner's salary was simply a distribution of profits and created unique rules. It is important to recognize that Congress has not gone so far as to treat partners the same as other employees. Instead, it has only created special treatment for compensation to partners that is truly compensation and not a portion of the partner's distributive share. Such amounts are called *guaranteed payments*. A guaranteed payment is specifically defined as an amount paid to a partner that is determined *without regard to the partnership's income*. The treatment of guaranteed payments and the determination of the amount that is considered a guaranteed payment are considered below.

Guaranteed payments to partners may resemble salary payments to other employees and are treated similarly, but not identically. The partnership treats this type of guaranteed payment in the same manner as it would a payment to an independent third party. Therefore, the payment is either deducted in computing the partnership's ordinary income or capitalized (and, if permitted, depreciated or amortized) depending on the nature of the service rendered.[54] The payment is deducted by the partnership in the year that it is paid if the partnership is on the cash method, or in the year that the payment is accrued if the accrual method is used.

Partners who receive guaranteed payments must be concerned with the character of the payments and when they must be reported. A partner treats a guaranteed payment as ordinary income. Although this appears reasonable, recall that the courts once considered such payment as part of the partner's distributive share, causing the partner to receive a greater percentage of the partnership's separately stated items. This is no longer the case, however. Guaranteed payments are always treated as ordinary income.

One of the important distinctions between guaranteed payments and typical salary payments concerns when the partner must include the payment in income. An individual partner who uses the cash method of accounting does not automatically include the payment in the year received. Instead, guaranteed payments are includible in a partner's taxable income as of the end of the tax year in which the partnership either deducts or capitalizes the payments.[55]

---

[54]   See, for example, Rev. Rul. 75-214, 1975-1 C.B. 185, and *Cagle v. Comm.*, 63 T.C. 86 (1974), *aff'd.* in 76-2 USTC ¶9672, 38 AFTR2d 76-5834, 539 F.2d 409 (CA-5, 1976).

[55]   Reg. §§ 1.706-1(a) and 1.707-1(c).

Example 15.   P is an individual taxpayer who reports his income using the cash method and the calendar year. P is a member of the PK partnership, which uses the accrual method of accounting and the calendar year. As of the close of 1991, the partnership owes partner P $30,000, which it subsequently pays on January 15, 1992. The partnership accrues and deducts the payment on its 1991 tax return. Although P does not receive the payment until 1992, he must include the amount in 1991 because that is his tax year in which the partnership year containing the deduction ends.

All compensation that is dependent on the partnership's gross or net income is treated as the partner's distributive share of partnership profits and not a guaranteed payment. Examples include payments that are based on a percentage of net income, or payments that are not made unless the partnership has sufficient net income. These amounts qualify as withdrawals that are not deductible by the partnership but are includible income to the partner as of the partnership's year-end. In most instances, partners' taxable incomes (and their self-employment incomes) are unaffected whether these payments are classified as a guaranteed payment or as distribution of profits.

Example 16.   N receives $20,000 as compensation for services rendered and his distributive share of profits and losses is 40%. Partnership ordinary income before deducting N's compensation is $100,000. If the $20,000 is payable regardless of the partnership's net income, it is a guaranteed payment. If this payment qualifies as a deductible expense, the partnership's ordinary income is $80,000 ($100,000 − $20,000) and N's includible ordinary income is $52,000 ($20,000 + 40% of $80,000).

However, if N's compensation is set at 20% of ordinary income before guaranteed payments are deducted plus a 40% distributive share of remaining partnership profits and losses, the entire $52,000 is a distribution of income since the payments are based on partnership income. In both situations, N has includible ordinary income of $52,000 and the remaining $48,000 is includible ordinary income to the other partner(s).

There are instances when the distinction between a guaranteed payment and a distribution of income does result in a different tax effect on the partners. For example, a guaranteed payment is an ordinary deduction (unless capitalized) that decreases ordinary income or increases (or even creates) ordinary loss of the partnership. A guaranteed payment may result in the compensated partner reporting ordinary income and other partners reporting ordinary losses from the partnership.

Example 17. Assume the same facts as in *Example 16* except the partnership's ordinary income before deducting N's $20,000 compensation is $3,000. If the $20,000 compensation is a deductible guaranteed payment, the partnership has an ordinary loss of $17,000 ($3,000 − $20,000). N has includible ordinary income of $20,000 and ordinary loss of $6,800 (40% of $17,000) for net includible income of $13,200. Other partners report an ordinary loss of $10,200 ($17,000 − $6,800).

In contrast with the above, if N's $20,000 compensation is guaranteed but only up to the amount of partnership net income, N would receive $3,000 and all of it would be a distribution of income. Other partners would have no ordinary gain or loss.

Whether partner compensation is a guaranteed payment or a distribution of ordinary income does not affect the amount or character of partnership items that may be subject to special tax treatment. For example, items such as capital gains and losses, dividends qualifying for the dividends-received deduction, and tax credits are computed without regard to the partnership's ordinary income or loss.[56]

Example 18. A partnership has $5,000 net ordinary income before deducting guaranteed payments of $30,000 paid to H, and a net capital gain of $12,000. H's distributive share is 10%. H's income is determined as follows:

		Partner's Share	
	Partnership	Percent	Amount
Ordinary income *before* guaranteed payments..............	$ 5,000		
Guaranteed payments..................	(30,000)	100%	$30,000
Ordinary loss...........................	$(25,000)	10%	(2,500)
Separately stated items: Capital Gain..........................	$12,000	10%	1,200

Interest payable on a partner's *capital account* (in contrast to a loan from the partner) is treated in a manner similar to compensation for services. Therefore, interest on capital, computed without regard to partnership income (i.e., guaranteed payments), is deductible by the partnership and includible interest income for the partner.[57] In contrast, interest payments based on partnership income are nondeductible by the partnership and includible income to the partner as a distribution of profits, not as interest income. This latter distinction is relevant, for example, in determining the amount of interest income a partner has for the limitation on investment interest expense deductions.

---

[56] Rev. Rul. 69-180, 1969-1 C.B. 183.   [57] § 707(c).

Taxation of interest paid to a partner for loans made to the partnership differs from that of interest paid for use of capital when the partnership adopts the accrual method and the partner uses the cash method. Recall that guaranteed payments are deductible by the partnership and includible by the partner as of the *partnership's year-end* in which the payments were deducted or capitalized. In contrast, interest on debt is deductible by the partnership and includible by the partner when *received* by the partner.[58] This same rule applies to all payments that do not qualify as guaranteed payments.

> **Example 19.** At the end of 1991, an *accrual* basis partnership on the calendar year owes K, a 30% cash basis partner, a guaranteed payment of $4,000 and $1,500 interest on a note. Both amounts are paid January 8, 1992. Partnership net income before these two accruals are considered is $20,000 in 1991 and $30,000 in 1992. The partnership and K apply the partnership's accrual method for the guaranteed payment and report it in 1991. In contrast, they both apply K's cash method for the interest on debt and report it in 1992. Based on these rules, the partnership has net income of $16,000 ($20,000 − $4,000) in 1991 and $28,500 ($30,000 − $1,500) in 1992. K increases includible compensation by $4,000 in 1991 and includible interest by $1,500 in 1992.

TRANSACTIONS IN A NONPARTNER CAPACITY

Most other transactions between a partnership and its partners are governed by the entity concept of partnership taxation. Thus, the effect for all parties is the same as that which would occur in a similar transaction between the partnership and a nonpartner. Two important factors must be present for the entity concept to apply. First, the partner must be participating in the transaction with the partnership in some capacity other than that of a partner (e.g., a partner who is an attorney might perform legal work for the partnership).[59] Second, the price must be based on a fair market value that would be used by two unrelated parties.[60] In all instances, however, the entity concept does not apply to the partnership for accrued expenses to a cash basis partner. Thus, as discussed above for interest, a partnership cannot deduct expenses to a partner until they are reported as income by the partner.

---

[58] §§ 267(a)(2), (c), and (e). This same rule applies to C corporations and their greater than 50 percent shareholders and to S corporations and all of their shareholders, regardless of the ownership interest.

[59] § 707(a). This restriction also is applicable when the business is a corporation under § 267.

[60] § 482.

SALES BETWEEN PARTNER AND PARTNERSHIP

It is not uncommon for partnerships and their partners to buy property from one another. The Code provides special treatment for such sales in *three* situations, effectively applying the aggregate rather than the entity concept to such sales. *First*, losses realized on a sale are disallowed when the partner owns directly or indirectly more than 50 percent of the capital or profits interest in the partnership.[61] In this case, no deduction is allowed for the losses. This is not a deferral; therefore, there is no carryover of basis or holding period. However, if this property is sold later at a gain, the gain is offset by the previously disallowed losses.[62] Similar treatment applies when the sale occurs between two partnerships and the same partners own directly or indirectly more than 50 percent of the capital or profits interest of both partnerships.[63]

> **Example 20.** T sells land to his partnership for $40,000. His basis for the land is $50,000. T owns a 60% capital interest in the partnership. Since he owns more than 50%, his $10,000 loss is disallowed and the partnership's basis for the land is $40,000. If the partnership later sells the land to an unrelated party for $52,000, its gain of $12,000 ($52,000 − $40,000) is reduced by the previously disallowed $10,000 loss, leaving a $2,000 recognized gain. Notice that any sales price between $40,000 and $50,000 would result in no recognized gain or loss. However, a sales price below $40,000 would result in a recognized loss (e.g., a sale for $38,000 results in a $2,000 recognized loss).

> **Example 21.** Assume the same facts as in *Example 20*, except T has a 45% capital interest in the partnership. Since T's capital interest does not exceed 50% , the $10,000 loss is recognized by him. In addition, any future gain on the land must be reported by the partnership without reduction.

A *second* situation in which the aggregate concept applies to sales between a partnership and its partners is when the sale results in capital gain. If the seller owns directly or indirectly more than 50 percent of the capital or profits interest and the property will *not* qualify as a capital asset to the *buyer*, all recognized gain is ordinary income to the seller. This treatment also occurs when a sale is between two partnerships and the same partners meet the 50 percent capital or profits requirement for both partnerships.[64]

---

[61] § 707(b)(1)(A).

[62] § 267(d).

[63] § 707(b)(1)(B). See § 267(c) and Reg. § 1.707-1(b)(3) for the rules governing constructive (indirect) ownership.

[64] § 707(b)(2). A similar provision applies to corporations. See § 1239.

Example 22. M purchased land as an investment in 1970 for $25,000. She sells the land to a partnership for its $100,000 fair market value. The land will be developed, subdivided, and sold in one-acre plots. If M directly or indirectly owns no more than 50% of the partnership's capital or profits, she has a capital gain of $75,000. However, if her interest exceeds 50%, she has ordinary income of $75,000 because the land is not a capital asset in the hands of the partnership.

The *third* situation when the aggregate concept applies occurs with sales of depreciable property between a partnership and its partners. If the partner owns directly or indirectly more than 50 percent of the capital or profits interest, all gain on the depreciable property is ordinary income.[65] This treatment overrides both §§ 1245 and 1250.

REPORTING PARTNERSHIP RESULTS

With few exceptions, partners must report their distributive shares of partnership income, expenses, gains, losses, and credits in their tax year in which or with which the partnership's tax year ends, regardless of when distributions of assets are actually made.[66] This timing requirement, based on the entity concept, makes the selection of a partnership's taxable year an important tax planning issue.

SELECTING A PARTNERSHIP'S TAXABLE YEAR

Generally, it is a tax advantage to defer all includible income as long as possible but to accelerate the deduction of all expenses, losses, and credits. The basic rule, of course, is dependent on the current and future tax positions of the partners. If operations are expected to result in net losses in the early years, the greatest benefit would be achieved by electing a partnership year that coincides with that of the partners. In this way, partners would be able to maximize their distributive shares of partnership losses currently. However, this benefit would be reversed in years when operations result in net income. In these years, the ideal partnership year would end one month after that of the partners.

Example 23. A partnership is organized October 1, 1991. Its net ordinary income for the first 15 months is as follows:

October 1, 1991–December 31,1991	$ 20,000
January 1–31, 1992	10,000
February 1, 1992–December 31,1992	135,000

---

[65] This restriction is also applicable when the business is a corporation. § 1239.

[66] § 706(a).

All partners report on the calendar year. If the partnership's year-end also is December 31, the partners have includible income of $20,000 in 1991 and includible income of $145,000 ($10,000 + $135,000) in 1992. However, if the partnership's year-end is January 31, the partners have no includible income in 1991 and includible income of $30,000 ($20,000 + $10,000) in 1992. Consequently, the income for October 1 through December 31—the deferral period—is shifted to the following year. The $135,000 will be combined with the net income or loss for January 1993 and reported in 1993.

Unfortunately, partners usually do not have the freedom to elect the ideal year-end for their partnerships.

Generally, a partnership can adopt only the taxable year of those owning a *majority interest* in the partnership.[67] For example, assume a fiscal year corporation owns 15 percent of a partnership while the remaining 85 percent is owned by 10 individuals who report on the calendar year. Since individuals using the calendar year own more than 50 percent of the partnership, the partnership must adopt the calendar year. If those having the same taxable year do not own a majority interest, the partnership must adopt the tax year of its *principal* partners—those partners owning at least 5 percent or more of the partnership. If, however, the principal partners have different tax years, the calendar year generally must be used.

A partnership may select another taxable year, subject to IRS approval. The IRS normally gives its approval only if the taxpayer can establish a valid business purpose for the particular taxable year.[68] For example, a summer resort hotel might satisfy this requirement if it establishes that its natural business year ends during September. In addition, the IRS allows a partnership that recognizes 25 percent or more of its gross receipts in the last two months of a twelve-month period for three consecutive years to adopt this twelve-month period as its fiscal year.[69]

Prior to 1987, IRS approval for a fiscal year was easily obtained when no more than three months of income was to be deferred. This option was deleted by the Tax Reform Act of 1986. Consequently, partnerships with these fiscal years generally were required to change their taxable year-ends, beginning in 1987 (e.g., from September 30 to December 31). The Revenue Act of 1987, however, provided a method that allowed these partnerships to continue using their fiscal years. In addition, new partnerships may adopt a fiscal year with a deferral period of no more than three months.[70] Selection of a fiscal year under this exception

---

[67]   § 706(b) and Reg. § 1.706-1(b).

[68]   § 706(b)(1)(C).

[69]   See Rev. Proc. 83-25, 1983-1 C.B. 689.

[70]   § 444(b)(1). Note that a partnership in existence before 1987 may retain its same fiscal year even though the deferral period exceeds three months if the toll charge is paid. § 444(b)(3).

does not come without a cost, however. The election requires that the partnership make *and* maintain a prepaid, non–interest-bearing deposit of the income taxes that otherwise would be deferred by the partners of a fiscal year partnership.[71] The required payment is due on May 15 of each year and is computed at the highest individual taxpayer rate *plus* a toll charge of one percent (e.g., 32% in 1991).[72] If the amount of the required payment for a subsequent year does not change, no payment is required for that year. However, if the amount of the required payment increases, the entity must pay the increase. Conversely, if the amount of the deferred tax decreases relative to that of the prior year, the partnership is entitled to a refund. Under this system, the partnership simply maintains a deferred payment balance with the IRS and adjusts it annually.[73] It also is important to note that the partners do not receive any type of credit for this tax prepayment and no interest is earned on the deposit.

NET LOSSES

The benefit of the aggregate theory is particularly significant when partnership operations result in a net loss. Based on the flow through concept, partners include their distributive shares of the partnership's net loss in their taxable income. However, each partner's deduction of net losses may not exceed that partner's basis in the partnership.[74] Any losses that exceed a partner's basis may be carried forward indefinitely to be deducted by the partner when his or her basis is increased.

> **Example 24.** A partnership has a net loss for 1991 of $50,000. L, a 40% owner, has a basis in the partnership of $17,000. Although L's 40% distributive share of the partnership loss is $20,000, his deduction is limited to his basis of $17,000. He reports the $17,000 loss on his 1991 tax return and carries over the remaining $3,000. His basis in the partnership, reduced by the deducted loss, is $0. If his basis increases to $2,000 at the end of 1992, an additional $2,000 of the 1991 loss is deductible. He reports the $2,000 loss on his 1992 tax return and this reduces his basis in the partnership once again to $0. The remaining loss of $1,000 is carried forward.

---

[71] A transition rule allows the partnership to "build" up the required deposit over the years 1988 to 1991 by paying 25 percent of the 1988 payment, 50 percent of the 1989 payment, 75 percent of the 1990 payment, and 100 percent of the 1991 payment.

[72] § 7519.

[73] § 7519(b). If the required payment for any taxable year is less than $500, the payment need not be made.

[74] § 704(d).

When there is more than one type of partnership loss and the partner's basis is insufficient to absorb all of it, an allocation is made to determine how much of each type of loss is currently deductible by the partner.

> **Example 25.** Refer to *Example 24* except the partnership has an ordinary loss of $40,000 and a capital loss of $10,000. L's 40% share is $16,000 and $4,000, respectively. His current deduction is limited to $13,600 ($16,000 ÷ $20,000 × $17,000) ordinary loss and $3,400 ($17,000 − $13,600) capital loss. The remaining $2,400 ordinary loss and $600 capital loss are carried forward.

The flow through of partnership losses is considered to be the *last* event to occur during a partnership's taxable year. Thus, in determining the partner's basis for loss, the basis is adjusted as follows:

	Beginning basis (including share of partnership liabilities)	$ xx,xxx
+	Contributions of money or other property	x,xxx
+	Increase in share of partnership liabilities	x,xxx
+	Share of partnership's income items	xx,xxx
−	Decrease in share of partnership liabilities	(x,xxx)
−	Distributions of money or other property	(xx,xxx)
−	Share of partnership loss items	(x,xxx)
=	Ending basis in partnership interest	$xxx,xxx

This is generally an advantage to partners whose bases are insufficient to absorb their share of partnership losses. When asset distributions have been made, this rule maximizes the carryover of excess losses. In addition, it provides a tax-planning opportunity for the partners. Year-end actions can be taken to increase a partner's basis. An individual partner may contribute additional assets to the partnership or the partnership may increase its liabilities.[75] It is possible that these year-end actions will be disallowed, however, unless there is a business purpose for them. The reverse actions can be taken to reduce the basis of a partner who wishes to defer the losses to a future year when marginal tax rates are expected to be higher.

> **Example 26.** For the current year, a partnership has a net ordinary loss of $100,000 and a net long-term capital gain of $20,000. D is a 40% owner. Her basis at the beginning of the year was $22,000, including her share of partnership liabilities. She received a cash distribution of $6,000 in June.

---

[75] Reg. § 1.704-1(d).

Year-end partnership liabilities exceed beginning liabilities by $10,000. D's basis before accounting for her share of the partnership's ordinary loss is determined as follows:

	Beginning basis (including share of liabilities)................	$22,000
+	Increase in share of partnership liabilities	
	(40% × $10,000 increase in debts).......................	4,000
+	Share of partnership income items	
	(40% × $20,000 net long-term capital gain)...............	8,000
−	Distribution of money in June	(6,000)
=	D's basis for loss...	$28,000

If no action is taken before the partnership year ends, D's distributive share of the loss is limited to her $28,000 basis, and the remaining $12,000 ($40,000 − $28,000) will be carried forward. However, if she makes a capital contribution that increases her basis by $12,000 before the partnership year ends, her basis becomes $40,000 and she may report her entire share of partnership losses. The same result is achieved if partnership debts are increased an additional $30,000 (40% × $30,000 = $12,000). In contrast, D may reduce her basis and therefore limit her current year deduction of losses by withdrawing assets from the partnership or if partnership liabilities are paid before the year ends.

CLASSIFICATION OF PARTNERSHIP NET LOSSES

Passive Activities. After 1986, income is classified into three categories: (1) active income (e.g., salary and income from activities in which a taxpayer materially participates); (2) portfolio income (e.g., dividends and interest); and (3) passive income (e.g., income from a business in which the individual does not materially participate, such as partnership income to a limited partner).[76] Losses are also assigned to these same three categories to arrive at a net income or loss for each class.

Partnership income or loss can be classified as either active or passive, depending on the owner's involvement. A partner who actively participates in partnership *operations* on a regular, continuous, and substantial basis is deemed to have materially participated and thus has active income or loss from the partnership.[77] Otherwise, the partner has passive income or loss. The passive designation is automatic for a limited partner but is also possible for a general partner.[78] Passive losses are deductible currently only to the extent of a taxpayer's passive income from other activities. (But, see the phase-out and rental real estate exceptions below.) That is, losses from a passive activity organized as a partnership (or S

---

[76] § 469(e).

[77] § 469(h).

[78] § 469(h)(2).

corporation) are deductible against income from other passive activities but not against income from salary, interest, dividends, or active business income. In addition, any portfolio income earned by the passive activity is included with portfolio income and cannot be used to offset any passive loss.[79] Tax credits from the passive activity also are limited to offsetting taxes that are applicable to other passive activities. Disallowed net passive losses and credits are "suspended" and subject to special rules discussed later in this section.[80]

Example 27. M has the following income and loss for the current year:

Salary	$40,000
Dividend income	3,500
Active general partnership interest	4,200
Limited partnership interests in	
B Partnership	(12,000)
Z Partnership	2,000

All partnership interests were acquired after 1986.

M has includible active income of $44,200 ($40,000 + $4,200) and portfolio income of $3,500. Her passive loss of $10,000 ($2,000 − $12,000) is suspended. Therefore, her adjusted gross income is $47,700 ($44,200 + $3,500).

All *suspended* passive losses and credits are carried forward and subjected to the same rules each year.[81] When a taxable disposition of the passive partnership interest is made, all suspended losses (but not credits) are deducted in the following order: (1) any gain from the disposition, (2) any net income from all passive activities, and (3) any other income or gain.[82] Suspended credits are disregarded at the time of the disposition with one exception. If an adjustment to basis was made because of the credit, the taxpayer may elect that the suspended credit be added back to the basis of the property (up to the amount of the original adjustment) before gain or loss on the disposition is computed.[83]

---

[79] § 469(e)(1).

[80] § 469(l). Although limitations on passive losses cover taxable years beginning after 1986, phase-in rules apply to net passive losses for activities owned by a taxpayer before October 22, 1986. Net losses and credits from passive activities acquired in a taxable year beginning prior to that date are allowed as follows: 65 percent for 1987, 40 percent for 1988, 20 percent for 1989, 10 percent for 1990, and zero thereafter.

[81] § 469(b).

[82] § 469(g)(1).

[83] § 469(j)(9).

Rental Real Estate Exception. In recent years, many partnerships have been organized to own real estate for rental, including buildings for commercial as well as residential use. Section 469 also covers these partnerships. As a result, partnership rental activities are considered to be passive for limited partners, regardless of their participation level. However, an individual (and/or spouse) who is a general partner, owns at least 10 percent of the value of the partnership, and actively participates in the real estate rental business may deduct up to $25,000 of the rental loss (and/or credits in amounts equivalent to a deduction) against nonpassive income.[84] Active participation in rental activities is less demanding than material participation required of a partner in other partnerships, as discussed above. In rental real estate partnerships, participation need only be significant (e.g., making management decisions and arranging for services to be performed for the property).

A phase-out schedule for this deduction occurs for individuals with an adjusted gross income exceeding $100,000, computed before the losses are deducted. For every $2 in excess of the $100,000, the $25,000 is reduced by $1.[85] Consequently, no deduction is allowed when adjusted gross income reaches $150,000 [($150,000 − $100,000 = $50,000) ÷ 2 = $25,000].

SPECIAL ALLOCATIONS

Partners' distributive shares of partnership income, gains, losses, deductions, and credits usually are determined by their ownership interests.[86] Earlier in this chapter, however, a deviation from this approach was discussed for special allocations with depreciation, depletion, gains, and losses on property contributed in exchange for a capital interest.[87] Similar allocations may be made for other partnership items, including net income or loss. In order for a special allocation to qualify, it must have *substantial economic effect*.[88] This requirement is designed to prohibit arbitrary allocations of tax benefits without the accompanying economic consequences. As a general rule, the allocation must affect the partners' capital accounts, and consequently, the amount they would receive if the partnership is ever liquidated. The thrust of this rule can be seen in the following example (which is based on the landmark case of *Stanley C. Orrisch*).[89]

---

[84] § 469(i).

[85] § 469(i)(3).

[86] § 704(a).

[87] § 704(c).

[88] § 704(b)(2) and Reg. § 1.704-1(b).

[89] *Stanley C. Orrisch*, 55 T.C. 395 (1971), *aff'd.* in 31 AFTR2d 1069 (CA-9, 1973).

Example 28. Partners C and O each contributed $100,000 to a partnership that purchased a building for $200,000. The partners agreed to allocate all of the depreciation on the property to O. The allocation was acceptable to C since he had no taxable income that could be offset by any depreciation allocated to him. In addition, the partners agreed that on the sale of the property, O would recognize gain equal to any depreciation that had been allocated to him, and the remaining gain would be split equally. For example, if $40,000 depreciation is allocated to O and the partnership sells the property for $250,000, the $90,000 gain ($250,000 − $160,000 basis) would be allocated $65,000 to O ($40,000 depreciation + $25,000 representing 50% of the remaining $50,000 gain) and $25,000 to C. A subsequent distribution of the proceeds according to the partners' capital accounts would result in both receiving $125,000 (O's capital account would be $100,000 − $40,000 + $65,000).

In contrast, if the partnership sells the property for only $160,000 (its adjusted basis), C and O intend to split the proceeds, each receiving $80,000. Thus, O would receive $20,000 more cash than his capital account balance of $60,000 ($100,000 original capital contribution − $40,000 depreciation), and would not bear any economic risk of depreciation previously allocated to him. A special allocation of depreciation with this latter clause could be set aside by the IRS since liquidation proceeds are not required to be distributed in accordance with the partners' capital account balances.

According to the Regulations, an allocation generally has economic effect if four tests are satisfied:[90]

1. The allocation is actually reflected as an appropriate increase or decrease in the partner's capital account.

2. Liquidation proceeds are to be distributed in accordance with the partners' capital account balances.

3. Partners with a deficit in their capital account following the distribution of liquidation proceeds must be required to restore all capital account deficits to the partnership,

4. The shift in tax consequences due to the allocation is not disproportionately large in relation to the shift of economic consequences.

---

[90]   Reg. § 1.704-1(b)(2).

The first three of these tests—concerning the "economic effect" of the allocation—are illustrated in *Example 28* above, when the liquidation of the partnership was not in accordance with the capital accounts. The fourth requirement—the *substantial test*—is considered in the following example.

> **Example 29.** R and S are equal partners. The partnership *expects* to receive $10,000 tax-exempt interest income and other taxable income in excess of $10,000. The partnership agreement states that the $10,000 of tax-exempt income is to be allocated to R while S is to be allocated $10,000 of taxable income. Any remaining income is to be allocated equally between them. The partnership agreement also states that the allocations are to be made to the capital accounts that serve as the basis for distributing liquidating proceeds. Despite the fact that the allocation has economic effect (i.e., the capital accounts are increased), it is not considered substantial because it has no economic consequences since R and S will receive the same amount of income.

The above discussion represents a brief summary of the voluminous regulations that have been issued on the subject of allocations. The regulations establish numerous other conditions that must be observed if a special allocation is to be recognized.

RETROACTIVE ALLOCATIONS

In determining a partner's distributive share of partnership items, consideration must be given to any variation that may occur in the partner's interest during the year. For example, if a partner owns a 20 percent interest for only 30 percent of the year, only 6 percent (20% × 30%) of the various partnership items should be allocated to the partner. This *varying interest rule* must be applied whenever a partner's interest changes (e.g., admission of a new partner or upon a partner's purchase of an additional interest or sale of partnership interest). Note, however, that special allocations can still be made if they have substantial economic effect.

New partners cannot be allocated any partnership items that occurred before they acquired their ownership interests.[91] Despite this basic rule, methods have been devised—primarily by tax shelter promoters—that enable taxpayers to claim a substantial portion of a partnership's net losses even though their capital interests are not purchased until late in the year. One way that this has been achieved is with a cash basis partnership that pays much of its expenses at the end of the year.

---

[91] §§ 706(c)(2)(B) and (d), and *Rodman v. Comm.*, 76-2 USTC ¶9710, 38 AFTR2d 76-5840, 542 F.2d 845 (CA-2, 1976), *rev'g.* and *rem'g.* 32 TCM 1307 T.C. Memo 1973-277 and *Cecil R. Richardson*, 76 T.C. 512 (1981).

Example 30.   A calendar year partnership on the cash basis reports a net loss of $10,000 for the first 11 months of 1991 and an additional net loss of $60,000 for December 1991. G purchases a 10% capital and profits interest December 1, 1991. G's share of the $70,000 loss is $6,000 (10% × $60,000). However, G could be specially allocated up to $60,000 of the loss if the substantial economic effect requirements are met. Under no circumstances may G report any of the loss that occurred before December 1, 1991.

Concerned about cash basis partnerships that delay payment of expenses to attract year-end investors, Congress enacted requirements governing the allocation of certain expenses of cash-basis partnerships that have a change in ownership during the year. Specifically, taxpayers must apply the accrual method to deductible payments made during the taxable year for (1) interest, (2) taxes, (3) use of property, (4) services, and (5) any other item necessary to avoid significant misstatements of income by the partners.[92]

ADJUSTMENTS TO PARTNER'S BASIS

The *partner's basis* in the partnership is referred to repeatedly in this chapter. Numerous examples of items affecting basis are given. The purpose here is to provide a comprehensive summary of items that affect a partner's basis. In all computations of basis, there is one important limitation—basis cannot be negative, not even temporarily.[93]

Generally, basis begins with a partner's contribution of assets or services in exchange for a capital interest. As indicated earlier, a partner's *initial basis* is the total of cash contributed plus the partner's basis for noncash contributions, and less any liabilities transferred to the partnership (subject to certain exceptions discussed earlier).[94] If the partnership interest is received as a gift or inherited, however, the general rules applicable to basis in these situations are used.

As discussed earlier, basis is *increased* by the partner's *share* of partnership liabilities. A general partner's basis includes his or her share of recourse debts (according to the loss sharing ratio) *and* nonrecourse debts (according to the profit sharing ratio.) In contrast, a limited partner's basis usually includes only his

---

[92]   See §§ 706(d)(2) and (3) for greater details.

[93]   §§ 705(a)(2) and 722. Basis also is increased by the amount of recognized gain

when the contribution is to an investment partnership. § 721(b).

[94]   §§ 722 and 752(b).

or her share of nonrecourse debts (according to the profit sharing ratio.)[95] Basis must be adjusted annually to reflect fluctuations that occurred during the year in the partnership's debts and in the partner's share of these debts. Basis also is increased by a partner's distributive share of taxable and tax-exempt partnership income and gains. When partnership net income has been reduced by percentage depletion deducted in excess of the depletable property's basis, this excess is added back to each partner's basis.[96]

A partner's distributive share of losses and expenditures that are neither deductible nor capitalized *reduces* basis. Recall that partnership losses are deductible by each partner only to the extent of that partner's basis.[97] Percentage and cost depletion for oil and gas wells are deductible at the partner level rather than by the partnership. Any of these deductions taken by the partner also reduce basis. However, these deductions may not reduce the partner's basis in the partnership below zero.[98]

Finally, cash distributions, including decreases in partnership liabilities that are deemed to be cash distributions, decrease basis. As will be explained in Chapter 11, a basis reduction is also required when other property is distributed. (For a detailed listing of a partner's basis compared with an S corporation shareholder's basis, see Exhibit 12-2 in Chapter 12.)

> **Example 31.** The TU Partnership owns a shopping center with the following selected account balances for 1991 and 1992.
>
> | | 1990 | 1991 | 1992 |
> | --- | --- | --- | --- |
> | Recourse liabilities .... | $ 70,000 | $ 80,000 | $ 67,000 |
> | Nonrecourse liabilities .... | 418,000 | 400,000 | 430,000 |
> | Net ordinary income (or loss).... | | (40,000) | 8,000 |
> | Tax-exempt interest income...... | | 4,000 | 0 |
> | Section 1231 gains.............. | | 12,000 | 0 |
> | Cash distributions to partners.... | | 14,000 | 16,000 |
>
> Although T and U share profits and losses equally, T is a general partner and U is a limited partner. At the end of 1990, T's basis in the partnership is $200,000 (including liabilities) and U's basis is $130,000 (including liabilities). Bases at the end of 1991 and 1992 are computed as follows:

---

[95] §§ 465 and 752(b). Recall, however, that special rules apply to liabilities created outside the partnership and later transferred to it. Temp. Reg. §§ 1.752-1T and 2T.

[96] § 705(a)(1).

[97] § 705(a)(2).

[98] §§ 613A (c)(7)(D) and 705(a)(3).

	T	U
Basis 12/31/90.....................................	$200,000	$130,000
Increase in recourse debt.........................	+ 10,000	0
Tax-exempt income...............................	+ 2,000	+ 2,000
Section 1231 gains...............................	+ 6,000	+ 6,000
Decrease in nonrecourse debt.....................	− 9,000	− 9,000
Cash distributions................................	− 7,000	− 7,000
Net ordinary loss.................................	− 20,000	− 20,000
Basis 12/31/91	$182,000	$102,000
Increase in nonrecourse debt.....................	+ 15,000	+ 15,000
Net ordinary income.............................	+ 4,000	+ 4,000
Decrease in recourse debt........................	− 13,000	0
Cash distributions................................	− 8,000	− 8,000
Basis 12/31/92.....................................	$180,000	$113,000

When partners cannot practically determine their bases in a partnership, the IRS may allow them to forgo the detailed calculations previously discussed in this chapter.[99] The alternative is to determine their share of the partnership's basis in total assets plus or minus any appropriate adjustments. This method may be used, however, only if the IRS accepts the results as being a reasonable approximation of the basis that would result from the more detailed calculations.[100] It is not to be used as a substitute for acceptable records.[101]

PENALTY ASSESSMENTS AND TAX AUDIT

Substantial penalties may be assessed against the partnership when a complete and timely return is not filed.[102] If reasonable cause is shown, however, the penalties may be waived. Generally, the penalty is $50 per month or fraction of a month (not to exceed $250) multiplied times the number of partners.[103] However, if a "willful failure to file" exists, the more severe penalties that are applicable to all persons may be assessed.[104]

> **Example 32.** A calendar year partnership has 10 partners. The annual return is filed two months and 14 days late. If reasonable cause is not shown, the penalty for late filing is $1,500 ($50 per month or fraction of

---

[99] § 705(b).

[100] Reg. § 1.705-1(b)

[101] *Eugene Coloman*, 33 TCM 411, T.C. Memo 1974-78, *aff'd.* in 76-2 USTC ¶9581, 38 AFTR2d 76-5523, 540 F.2d 427 (CA-9, 1976).

[102] § 6031.

[103] § 6698.

[104] § 7203. See Chapter 17 for a detailed discussion of these penalties.

a month $\times$ 3 = \$150 $\times$ 10 partners). However, if the return is not filed until an IRS audit two years later, the penalty is \$2,500 (\$250 maximum penalty $\times$ 10 partners).

The entity concept applies to a partnership's records. In *Bellis*, the taxpayer claimed Fifth Amendment privileges against self-incrimination and refused to produce certain partnership records in a tax fraud case.[105] The Supreme Court ruled the records were partnership property and applied the entity concept in directing that the records be made available to the Government. The Court did suggest, however, that partnership records might qualify as privileged information under the Fifth Amendment in certain types of organizational structures such as a family partnership or short-term joint venture.[106]

Historically, IRS audits have not been initiated at the partnership level. Instead, the tax treatment of partnership items was determined at the partner level when the returns of individual partners were examined. This approach required separate reviews and proceedings with each partner. Not only was this approach inefficient and costly, but it was possible for different taxpayers to receive conflicting or inconsistent results on the same partnership item. This procedure was ended in 1982. Now, the tax treatment of items is determined at the partnership level and applied uniformly to all partners (with few exceptions).[107] The government is required to notify all partners listed on the return (or on lists provided to the IRS) about any proceedings against the partnership.[108] If there are more than 100 partners, however, notification need not be made to a partner whose profits interest is less than 1 percent. The Code details how the proceedings are to be conducted, who may participate, who may bind the partnership in a settlement agreement, and the judicial review process.[109] For example, a new title, "tax matters partner" (TMP), is created for the partner who represents the other owners in dealing with the IRS. This TMP is assigned the power to bind the other partners in certain situations.

This unified approach to audits requires all partners to report partnership items on their own returns in a manner consistent with the partnership return. If partners deviate from this requirement or if a partnership return is not filed, they must identify the inconsistency in a statement to the Secretary of the Treasury.[110] (Similar rules are applicable to S shareholders.)

---

[105] *Bellis v. Comm.*, 39 AFTR2d 77-815, 417 U.S. 85 (USSC, 1974).

[106] Also see *Comm. v. Slutsky*, 73-1 USTC ¶9186, 31 AFTR2d 73-564, 352 F.Supp. 1105 (DC-NY, 1972), where the Fifth Amendment privilege was extended to a small family partnership.

[107] § 6221.

[108] § 6222.

[109] §§ 6223 through 6231.

[110] § 6222.

The unified audit procedures do not apply to "small" partnerships. A small partnership is defined as one with (1) no more than 10 partners who are either natural persons (excluding nonresident aliens) or estates, *and* with (2) no special allocations of any partnership item.[111] In determining the number of partners, a husband and wife and their estates are counted as one. Based on Congressional intent, the small partnership or a partner can establish that all partners fully reported their shares of partnership items on tax returns filed in a timely manner.[112]

---

[111] § 6231.

[112] Rev. Proc. 84-35, 1984-1, C.B. 509.

TAX PLANNING WITH A PARTNERSHIP

Congressional intent that Subchapter K allow partners considerable flexibility in forming, operating, and liquidating their partnerships also provides numerous tax planning opportunities for partners. Many of these were discussed throughout this chapter. Although tax planning opportunities are too extensive and too personalized to prepare an exhaustive list, some additional ones are mentioned here to encourage the student of taxation to continually analyze tax situations with an eye for tax planning. The thoughtful but imaginative tax adviser who is able to provide clients with planning options that meet their needs is in much demand in today's tax conscious society.

ORGANIZING A PARTNERSHIP

Before a business is organized, all relevant factors should be evaluated to determine the type of organization that best meets the needs of the parties involved. The first step is to prepare a list of these needs and arrange them in their order of importance. For example, questions relevant to determining the owners' needs include the following: (1) Is limited liability important or will the owners be required to guarantee most of the business debt? (2) Will all owners participate in the management of the business? (3) Do the owners desire special allocations of specific business items? (4) Is the business expected to have net profits or net losses in the early years? (5) Do the owners expect to withdraw most of the business profits? (6) Are employee benefits such as deferred compensation plans and health insurance important to one or more of the owners who intend to work in the business? After the owners are satisfied with the list and its order, the tax adviser must evaluate the items in terms of the types of available organizations. This process requires both qualitative and quantitative measures. It should include an analysis of the tax effects on each owner under each type of organization based on projected business activities. Some firms have computer programs to aid in this evaluation. The analysis should be prepared in a form such that the owners can understand the options available to them with minimal explanation. The owners should be given ample opportunity to study the options, ask questions of the tax adviser, and arrive at an informed decision.

After the legal form is selected, the process should be repeated in a similar manner to determine the most desirable operational form. For example, relevant questions include (1) How will profits and losses be split? (2) What assets will each owner contribute and how will they be valued? (3) What are the current and future objectives and goals of the business? (4) What are the responsibilities of each owner? (5) Are any special allocations, guaranteed payments for services, or interest on capital balances desired? (6) What restrictions should be placed on the transfer of an ownership interest? Once the decision process concerning these factors is completed, a detailed agreement should be prepared. The more the owners are involved in the entire process, the greater are their chances for a satisfying business relationship.

The situation of any taxpayer planning to contribute property in exchange for a partnership interest should be evaluated. In some instances, it may be in the individual's best interest to seek an alternate method of obtaining an ownership interest. For example, property with a basis in excess of its market value may provide the owner greater benefits if leased to the partnership. The effects on the other partners and the availability of special allocations discussed in the chapter should also be considered.

OPERATING THE PARTNERSHIP

The flexibility of the partnership allows partners to determine, up until the tax return filing date, how various partnership items will be allocated among them. Thus partners may wait until all the numbers are known before they decide how to allocate partnership profits and losses. Recall, however, that these special allocations must have an economic effect. This is achieved if the allocations affect the capital accounts and the partnership agreement states that liquidation will be based on capital account balances and that partners must restore any capital account deficits.

Year-end tax planning checklists should be developed for all partners and partnerships. This is particularly important for the partner whose basis is low. It might be necessary for this partner to take year-end actions to avoid reporting income when actual and deemed distributions exceed basis. The partnership's year-end planning is dependent on whether it reports on the cash or accrual basis and whether its partners' positions suggest its objectives should be to maximize or minimize net income or net losses.

PROBLEM MATERIALS

DISCUSSION QUESTIONS

10-1 *Aggregate/Conduit versus Entity.*   How does the aggregate/conduit theory differ from the entity theory? Discuss how the transactions below would be treated under (a) the aggregate/conduit theory and (b) the entity theory.

   a.   A contributes appreciated land in exchange for a capital interest.
   b.   B performs services in exchange for a capital interest.
   c.   C contributes a patent with a market value in excess of basis in exchange for a capital interest.
   d.   D, a 40 percent partner, sells equipment to the partnership for a loss.
   e.   E, a 60 percent partner, sells equipment to the partnership for a loss.
   f.   F, a 20 percent partner, performs services and is paid a guaranteed payment by the partnership.

10-2 *Contributions of Property—Basis.*   Generally, a contribution of property in exchange for a partnership interest results in a carryover of basis of the property from the contributing partner to the partnership. Give an example of when the partnership's basis in the property is the property's fair market value.

10-3 *Formation.*   How is the allocation of depreciation, gain, and loss treated for appreciated property contributed to a partnership in the current year?

10-4 *Special Allocations—Contributed Property.*   Explain the Congressional and other equity reasons for the special allocation of precontribution gains and losses on contributed property.

10-5 *Service Partners.*   What is the tax effect on the service partner if a capital interest received is (a) subject to restrictions, or (b) unrestricted?

10-6 *Transfer of Partnership Interest for Services.*   What is the likely effect on an existing partnership and the other partners if a capital interest is transferred to a service partner in return for services rendered to the partnership?

10-7 *Partnership versus Corporation.*   List tax and nontax advantages of the partnership form of business compared with the corporate form.

10-8 *Organization Costs versus Syndication Fees.*   Compare the tax effects of organization costs with syndication fees.

10-9 *Operations.*   Transactions between a partnership and a partner acting in a nonpartner capacity may be treated as though they occurred between the partnership and a nonpartner.

   a.   Give examples of when this occurs.
   b.   Give examples of when this cannot occur.

10-10 *Partner/Employee.*   May a partner be treated as an employee of the partnership? Explain.

10-11 *Timing*. At what point in time does a cash basis partner have includible income or loss for the following?

    a.   Distributive share of partnership net income
    b.   Guaranteed payments for personal services
    c.   Interest income on a loan to the partnership
    d.   Guaranteed payments on a partner's capital account

10-12 *Partnership's Taxable Year*. What choices are available to a partnership when selecting a taxable year? If a partnership elects a fiscal year different from the tax year generally required, what additional requirements are imposed on the partnership?

10-13 *Allocations*. What are the requirements for allocating partnership income, deductions, gains, losses, and credits for contributed property and for other partnership activities?

10-14 *Partner's Basis*. Indicate whether the following (a) increase, (b) decrease, or (c) have no effect on a general partner's basis. Assume all liabilities are recourse liabilities.

    a.   The partnership borrows cash that is to be repaid in two years.
    b.   The partnership earns interest on short-term municipal bonds.
    c.   The partnership has a net loss for the year.
    d.   The partnership has net ordinary income for the year but none of it is distributed to the partners.
    e.   Partnership liabilities total $50,000 at the beginning of the year and $35,000 at the end of the year.

10-15 *Penalties*. Although partners filed their personal tax returns on time, they filed the partnership return two years late. The partners paid a total of $2,000 taxes on partnership income. What are the total penalties and interest amounts that can be assessed if the return was not filed timely due to their ignorance?

10-16 *Audit Requirements*. A 20 percent partner receives a partnership return that he knows contains an error (an understatement of gross income) that is both substantial and intentional on the part of the 80 percent partners. What should he do when filing his personal tax return?

PROBLEMS

10-17   *Formation.*   The A-E Partnership is being formed by five individuals who contribute assets in exchange for a 20 percent capital and profit/loss interest each. Calculate the following: (1) the recognized gain or loss, (2) each partner's basis in the partnership, (3) the partnership's basis for each asset, and (4) the holding period of the partnership interest for the partner and the property for the partnership. Assume all contributed assets will be used in the partnership's trade or business. [Items (a) through (e) are to be treated as a group rather than as independent transactions. Accept all numbers given as correct and do not attempt to verify them.]

   a.   A contributes proprietorship equipment with a fair market value of $10,000. The equipment cost $16,000 when it was purchased four years ago and A deducted $11,000 depreciation as a proprietorship expense during the four years.

   b.   B contributes proprietorship equipment with a market value of $10,000. The equipment cost $20,000 when purchased two years ago and B's basis for the equipment is $12,000.

   c.   C contributes equipment identical to B's equipment. C's equipment also has a market value of $10,000. In fact, C and B purchased their equipment at the same time at the same cost of $20,000. The only difference is that C used the equipment for personal, not business, purposes.

   d.   D contributes land with a market value of $16,000. The land was acquired 10 months ago for $9,000 cash and a $6,000 note payable (recourse debt). The $6,000 note payable is also transferred to the partnership.

   e.   E contributes land with a market value of $18,000. E received the land three years ago as a gift from a relative and has a basis of $5,000. In addition, E transfers an $8,000 mortgage (nonrecourse debt) on the land to the partnership.

10-18   *Contributed Property—Allocations.*   The H and I Equal Partnership was formed at the beginning of the year. H contributed cash of $40,000 and I contributed equipment with a market value of $40,000 and a basis of $25,000. The equipment cost $35,000. I had used the equipment in a proprietorship for three years and did not recapture any depreciation when it was transferred to the partnership. For the sake of simplicity, assume the partnership's depreciation rate for the current year on this equipment is 20 percent. The partnership's net ordinary income, excluding deductions for the equipment, is $60,000.

   a.   Calculate H's distributive share of partnership net ordinary income (after depreciation is deducted).

   b.   H asks you what the tax consequences would have been if the partnership had sold the equipment for $39,000 only five months after I transferred it to the partnership.

10-19 *Sale of Contributed Property.* Z and N are equal partners. Z's interest was obtained by contributing proprietorship assets in a tax-free exchange. One of these assets was used in his proprietorship for one year and in the Z and N partnership for two years. The records show the following:

Asset Cost	Proprietorship Depreciation	Partnership Depreciation	Sale Proceeds
$20,000	$1,600	$8,600	$13,000

The asset's market value at the time of contribution was $19,000, and $4,800 of the $8,600 depreciation was allocated to N and $3,800 to Z. Calculate the amount and type of gain or loss to be reported by Z and N in the year of sale.

10-20 *Sale of Contributed Property—Allocations.* During the current year, X contributed property, which was part of his proprietorship inventory, to the D Partnership in exchange for a one-third interest in partnership profits and losses. At the date of contribution, the property had a basis of $120,000 and a value of $145,000. The property was used in the partnership's business as a nondepreciable § 1231 asset. Two years after its contribution, the partnership sold the property for $160,000.

   a. Calculate the amount and character of the taxable gain recognized on the sale allocable to X.

   b. How would the answer for (a) change if the sale occurred six years rather than two years after contribution?

   c. How would the answer for (a) change if the property had been sold for $100,000 rather than $160,000?

10-21 *Receipt of Partnership Interest for Services.* In return for services rendered to the AX Partnership, T receives a 20 percent unrestricted interest in the partnership with the following assets:

	Basis	Fair Market Value
Inventory	$ 5,000	$ 10,000
Equipment	10,000	15,000
Land	15,000	20,000
Building	40,000	50,000
Totals	$70,000	$95,000

Assuming the partnership has no liabilities and that before T's admission it is owned 60 percent by partner A and 40 percent by partner X, answer the following questions.

   a. How much compensation income must be reported by T?

   b. What is T's basis in the partnership interest received?

   c. What are the tax consequences of this transfer to the AX Partnership? To partners A and X?

   d. What is the partnership's basis in each of its assets following the transfer?

10-22 *Contribution of Services.* The G-H equal partnership was formed several years ago. Since the business has grown so rapidly, the partnership was expanded to include E and F. E and F each obtained a 20 percent profit and capital interest in the partnership in exchange for their services. E's services—the investigation and acquisition of property—have been completed, and he received an unrestricted capital interest at the beginning of the year. F has agreed to serve as a manager of the new operation. Her ownership interest is subject to her continuing as the manager for five consecutive years. At the beginning of the year, the partnership's net assets had a basis of $100,000 and a market value of $300,000. Thus, a 20 percent interest is valued at $60,000. The partners anticipate the business having a value of approximately $500,000 at the end of the five years when the restriction is removed from F's interest. Determine the tax effect on the partnership and each of the four partners for:

a. E's service contribution
b. F's service contribution

10-23 *Net Income and Self-Employment Income.* An accrual basis partnership reports the following information for its calendar year.

Sales...		$500,000
Cost of goods sold		(220,000)
Interest income from tax-exempt bonds.........		22,000
Interest income on trade receivables...........		18,000
Gross rental income...........................	$30,000	
Rental expenses..............................	(26,000)	4,000
Guaranteed payment to W.....................		(24,000)
Interest expense to W on a loan...............		(6,000)
Other deductions (expenses)		(70,000)
Net capital loss...............................		(4,000)

W is a 30 percent, cash basis partner. All but $1/12$ of the guaranteed payment and interest were paid to W during the current year. The $1/12$ was paid the following April 25. W is single and has no other includible income or deductions.

a. Calculate the partnership's net ordinary income.
b. Calculate partner W's AGI.
c. Calculate W's self-employment income assuming she is a general partner.
d. Calculate W's self-employment income assuming she is a limited partner.

10-24 *Taxation of Partners.* An accrual basis partnership has net income of $40,000 before deducting the following amounts due to P, a 20 percent partner: a $12,000 guaranteed payment for services and $5,000 interest on a loan from P. P reports on the cash basis and received no payments or distributions from the partnership during the year. Calculate P's includible income for the current year.

10-25 *Partner's Distributive Shares.*   R is a partner in a three-person partnership, RHS. The partnership agreement states that R is to receive 15 percent of the partnership's net income before deducting any payments to partners. In addition, each partner is allocated one-third of all profits and losses after R receives his compensation. The partnership had $50,000 net income before any payments to partners.

  a.   What is the amount of R's guaranteed payment?
  b.   What is R's total taxable income from RHS?
  c.   What is H's total taxable income from RHS?

10-26 *Payments for Partner Services.*   LLB, a cash basis partnership, has a September 30 taxable year-end. Partner B, a calendar year, cash basis individual, received a guaranteed payment for services rendered to the partnership of $4,500 a month for the partnership's year ending September 30, 1991. The partnership agreed to increase the payment to $6,000 a month for the next fiscal year. On October 12, 1991, B also received a $12,000 payment from the partnership for professional services; B performs such professional services for a variety of clients in his sole proprietorship business. How much income attributable to these payments should B report in 1991?

10-27 *Guaranteed Payments.*   B and G are partners in the DR Partnership. B oversees the daily operations of the business and therefore receives compensation of $50,000, regardless of the amount of the partnership's net income. In addition, his distributive share of profits and losses is 50 percent.

  a.   If the partnership had $75,000 ordinary income before any payments to partners, what are the amount and character of B's total income?
  b.   Same as (a), but assume the partnership had $30,000 ordinary income before payments to partners.
  c.   Same as (a), except assume the partnership had $25,000 ordinary income and $50,000 long-term capital gain before payments to partners.

10-28 *Guaranteed Payments.*   At the end of the current year, the three partners in the ABC partnership had the following preclosing balances in their capital accounts.

Partner A	$ 70,000
Partner B	89,000
Partner C	105,000

The ABC Partnership agreement provides that (1) each partner will receive an annual cash distribution equal to 6 percent of the pre-year-end closing balance in his or her capital account and (2) any remaining income or loss for the year will be allocated equally among the partners. Before accounting for any distributions to the partners, ABC had $54,600 of taxable income for the current year. How much taxable income is allocated to each partner?

10-29 *Transactions.*   V, a 60 percent partner, sells land to the partnership for $8,000. V's basis in the land is $9,000 and his basis in the partnership is $45,000.

    a.   Determine (1) V's recognized gain or loss, (2) V's basis in the partnership, and (3) the partnership's basis in the land after the transaction.

    b.   Determine V's recognized gain or loss (personally and share of partnership's gain or loss) if the partnership sells the land six months later for (1) $7,500, (2) $8,600, or (3) $9,300.

    c.   How would your answers to (a) and (b) differ if V were a 40 percent partner?

10-30 *Operations.*   T is a 30 percent partner who works in the partnership business. Both T and the partnership use the calendar year for tax purposes. The partnership's records for the current year show

Gross profit	$240,000
Guaranteed payments to T	20,000
Keogh contributions for T	7,000
Health insurance premium for T	500
Operating expenses	60,000
Charitable contributions	5,000
Net captial gain	10,000

T is single, has no other income, and has $4,500 personal itemized deductions (including $600 deductible medical expenses). T received the $20,000 guaranteed payments and withdrew an additional $10,000 during the year. T's basis in the partnership was $40,000 at the beginning of the year.

    a.   Calculate the partnership's ordinary income (Form 1065, page 1) for the year.

    b.   Calculate T's taxable income for the year.

    c.   Calculate T's basis in the partnership at the end of the year.

10-31 *Partnership Year-End.*   R, S, and T each owned a retail store as sole proprietors. R and S have a December 31 year-end, and T has a January 31 year-end. In order to take advantage of certain economies of scale, they combined their operations by forming a partnership on December 1, 1991. Each partner has a one-third interest in partnership profits. The partnership's net income was as follows:

December 1 – December 31, 1991	$30,000
January 1 – January 31, 1992	10,000
February 1 – November 30,1992	50,000
December 1 – December 31,1992	25,000

    a.   What tax year(s) may the partnership adopt? Discuss all options.

    b.   Assuming the partnership adopts a December 31 year-end, how much income from the partnership will T report on her tax return for her year ending Janurary 31, 1992?

    c.   Assuming the partnership could adopt a January 31 year-end, how much income from the partnership will R report on his December 31, 1991 tax return? On his December 31, 1992 return?

10-32   *Partnership Net Losses.*   XYZ partnership has three general partners. At the beginning of the year, X had a basis in his partnership interest of $20,000 while Y and Z had a basis of $40,000 each in their partnership interests. X and Y receive 30 percent of partnership income and loss, and Z receives 40 percent. During the year, the partnership incurred a $90,000 ordinary loss.

    a.   How much income or loss will each partner report on his or her individual return and what is each partner's basis in his or her partnership interest at the end of the year? Assume no distributions to or contributions by partners during the year.

    b.   Same as (a) but assume the partnership incurs a $70,000 ordinary loss and a $30,000 capital loss.

10-33   *Basis and Losses.*   A partnership has the following balance sheet information:

Cash....................	$ 30,000	Nonrecourse loans......	$200,000
Land....................	100,000	Recourse loans.........	300,000
Rental buildings.........	500,000	Partners' capital........	130,000

All liabilities were incurred by the partnership. On September 1, W contributes $50,000 cash to the partnership. The agreement states that W is to be allocated 20 percent of all profits and 30 percent of all losses. During the year, the partnership has net ordinary losses of $10,000 each month, and thus, a $120,000 loss for the calendar year.

    a.   Calculate W's basis in the partnership as of September 1, if W is a general partner in a general partnership.

    b.   Calculate W's basis in the partnership as of September 1, if W is a limited partner in a limited partnership.

    c.   If all partners agree, what is the maximum amount of net ordinary loss that can be allocated to W for the year? Explain.

10-34   *Retroactive Allocation.*   A cash basis, calendar year, real estate partnership reported quarterly net losses of $20,000, $24,000, $15,000, and $40,000, respectively. The losses were partly due to $14,000 interest prepaid the fourth quarter for the following January and $18,000 property taxes paid July 1 for the previous year. T sold his entire 20 percent interest to V on June 30. Assume the IRS allows a monthly proration. Calculate the loss to be reported by each of the two partners:

    a.   If no special allocation is made.

    b.   If a special allocation is made to maximize the loss to be reported by V.

10-35   *Basis and Taxation of Partners.*   The TVX Partnership, formed in 1990, owns several office rental buildings. Selected year-end information for its first five years reveals the following:

	1990	1991	1992	1993	1994
Recourse liabilities......	$100,000	$120,000	$130,000	$150,000	$160,000
Nonrecourse liabilities......	500,000	400,000	300,000	250,000	200,000
Net income or (loss)......	(300,000)	(200,000)	(110,000)	(40,000)	70,000
Cash distributed to partners...	50,000	100,000	150,000	100,000	0

All liabilities were incurred by the partnership.

Partner A contributed property with a basis of $50,000 and a market value of $75,000. Nine other partners contributed $75,000 cash each. A is a general partner and the other nine partners are limited partners. They share profits and losses equally, 10 percent each. Prepare a schedule showing (a) the distributive share of profits and losses, and (b) the basis in the partnership each year for the general partner and for one of the limited partners.

10-36   *Allocation of Partnership Liabilities.*   In the current year, individuals M, N, and O form a general partnership, making no initial capital contributions. The three partners share partnership profits and losses in the following manner: 10 percent to M, 45 percent to N, and 45 percent to O. The partnership borrows $50,000 cash on a recourse basis. The partnership also borrows $180,000 on a nonrecourse basis. The nonrecourse debt is secured by investment land purchased by the partnership at a total cost of $200,000 ($20,000 cash plus the $180,000 proceeds of the nonrecourse debt). Calculate the effect of the two partnership liabilities on each partner's basis in the partnership.

10-37   *Penalties.*   The MS Partnership return was filed seven months late due to the illness of the managing partner. During an IRS audit, it was discovered that the partnership had engaged in some improper transactions in order to avoid taxes. Partnership net ordinary income was increased by $50,000 and the partners were assessed $10,750 ($25,000 × 15% marginal rate for M and $25,000 × 28% marginal rate for S) on the understatement. If the assessment is made exactly two years after the return's due date, calculate the total penalty for late filing and the interest for underpayment. Assume the interest rate during the two-year period was an effective rate (after compounding) of 14 percent.

10-38   *Tax Return Problem.*   P and K formed the P&K General Partnership on March 1, 1981 to provide computer consulting services. They share all profits, losses, and capital 60 percent to P and 40 percent to K. The business code and employer identification numbers are 7370 and 24-3897625, respectively. The business office is located at 3010 East Apple Street, Atlanta, Georgia 30304. P and K live nearby at 1521 South Elm Street and 3315 East Apple Street, respectively. Their social security numbers are 403-16-5110 for P and 518-72-9147 for K.

The calendar year, cash basis partnership's December 31, 1990 balance sheet and December 31, 1991 trial balance (both prepared for tax purposes) contain the following information.

	Balance Sheet 12/31/90		Trial Balance 12/31/91	
	Debit	Credit	Debit	Credit
Cash.........................	$ 12,000		$ 22,000	
Note receivable (1)...........	14,000		14,000	
Equipment (2,3)..............	150,000		190,000	
Accumulated depreciation....		$ 38,000		$ 63,500
Recourse notes payable (3,4)		58,000		87,200
Nonrecourse notes payable (4)................		36,000		30,000
P, Capital....................		28,000		28,000
P, Drawing...................			25,400	
K, Capital....................		16,000		16,000
K, Drawing...................			17,000	
Revenues....................				235,000
Interest income (1)...........				1,400
§ 1245 gain..................				3,500
Compensation (5)............			110,000	
Rent expense................			12,000	
Interest expense.............			16,600	
Property and payroll tax expense........			13,800	
Repair expense..............			5,800	
Tax depreciation expense....			29,200	
Health insurance expense (6)			1,600	
Property insurance expense...................			1,500	
Office supplies expense......			3,000	
Utility expense...............			2,200	
Charitable contribution.......			500	
Totals.....................	$176,000	$176,000	$464,600	$464,600

Partnership records also show the following information:

1. The note receivable is from K and is due December 31, 1996. The annual interest rate is 10 percent; K paid $1,400 on December 28, 1991.
2. Equipment was sold May 12, 1991 for $9,800. It was purchased new on May 1, 1989 for $10,000 and its basis when sold was $6,300.
3. New equipment was purchased March 1, 1991 with $5,000 cash and a $45,000 three-year recourse note payable. The first note payment is March 1, 1992.
4. Notes payable are long-term except for $20,000 of the recourse note to be paid next year. All liabilities were created by the partnership.
5. Compensation is composed of guaranteed payments of $30,000 each to P and to K and $50,000 to unrelated employees.
6. Health insurance premiums paid were $400 for P, $400 for K, and $800 for the unrelated employees.

Prepare Form 1065, Schedule K, Schedules L and M (*even though* not required by the IRS instructions to Form 1065), and Schedule K-1 for P. Complete all pages, including responses to all questions. If any necessary information is missing in the problem, assume a logical answer and record it. Do not prepare Schedule K-1 or other required supplemental forms for partner K at this time. Be sure to calculate the self-employment income and record the amounts on Schedules K and K-1.

10-39 *Tax Return Problem.*   During 1990, Lisa Cutter and Jeff McMullen decided they would like to start their own gourmet hamburger business. Lisa and Jeff believed that the public would love the recipes used by Lisa's mom, Tina Wood-brook. They also thought that they had the necessary experience to enter this business, since Jeff currently owned a fast-food franchise businesses while Lisa had experience operating a small bakery. After doing their own market research, they established Slattery's General Partnership. The business address is 5432 Partridge Pl., Tulsa, Oklahoma 74105 and the employer identification number is 88-7654321.

The partnership began modestly. After refurbishing an old gas station that it had purchased, the partnership opened for business on February 25, 1991. Shortly after business began, however, business boomed. By the end of 1991, the company had established two other locations.

Slattery's has three owners whose ownership interests are as follows:

Partner	Interest
Lisa Cutter............	50%
Jeff McMullen.........	20%
Tina Woodbrook.......	30%
Total outstanding....	100%

Slattery's was formed on February 1, 1991. On that date, partners made contributions as follows:

Lisa Cutter contributed $30,000 in cash and 200 shares of MND stock, a publicly held company, which had a fair market value of $20,000. Lisa had purchased the MND stock on October 3, 1986 for $8,000.

Jeff McMullen contributed equipment worth $35,000 and a basis of $28,000.

Tina Woodbrook contributed $30,000 in cash.

Assume 1991 depreciation for tax purposes is $10,560. The partnership is on the accrual basis and has chosen to use the calendar year for tax purposes. Its adjusted trial balance for *financial accounting* purposes reveals the following information:

	Debit	Credit
Cash	$279,800	
Ending inventory	16,000	
Equipment	35,000	
Land	10,000	
Building	15,000	
Improvements to building	55,000	
Accumulated depreciation		$ 9,000
Notes payable		93,000
Accounts payable		40,000
Taxes payable		8,000
Compensation payable		20,000
Capital accounts		100,000
Sales		400,000
Gain on sale of MND stock		18,000
Dividend from MND Corporation		2,000
Cost of goods sold	84,000	
Legal expenses	500	
Accounting expenses	400	
Miscellaneous expenses	2,100	
Premium on key-man life insurance policy	800	
Advertising	8,600	
Utilities	8,000	
Payroll taxes	12,500	
Compensation expenses	120,000	
Insurance	9,000	
Repairs	6,500	
Charitable contributions	17,600	
Depreciation per books	9,000	
Interest expenses	200	

The partnership provided additional information below.

The partnership took a physical count of inventory on December 31, 1991 and determined that ending inventory was $16,000.

On February 9, 1991 the partnership purchased an old gas station for $25,000 to house the restaurant. Of the $25,000 purchase price, $10,000 was allocated to the land while $15,000 was allocated to the building. Prior to opening, the old gas station was renovated. Improvements to the structure were made during February at the cost of $55,000.

The legal costs were for work done by Slattery's attorney in February for drafting the partnership agreement. Accounting fees were paid in May for setting up the books and the accounting system. Miscellaneous expenses included a one-time $100 fee paid in February to operate a business in the State of Oklahoma.

The MND stock was sold for $38,000 on April 3, 1991. Shortly before the sale, MND had declared and paid a dividend. Slattery's received $2,000 on April 1, 1991. MND was incorporated in Delaware.

The partnership purchased refrigeration equipment (7-year property) on February 15, 1991 for $15,000.

Slattery's has elected not to use the limited expensing provisions of Code § 179. In addition, it claimed the maximum depreciation with respect to all other assets. Any other elections required to minimize the partnership's taxable income were made.

Lisa Cutter (Social Security No. 447-52-7943) is the managing partner and spends 90 percent of her working time in the business. She received compensation of $60,000. No other partners recieved compensation. Social security numbers are 306-28-6192 for Jeff and 403-34-6771 for Tina. The key-man life insurance policy covers Lisa's life and the partnership is the beneficiary.

Prepare Form 1065, Schedule K, Schedules L and M (*even though* not required by the IRS instructions to Form 1065), and Schedule K-1 for Lisa. Complete all pages, including responses to all questions. If any necessary information is missing in the problem, assume a logical answer and record it. Do not prepare Schedule K-1 or other required supplemental forms for other partners at this time. Be sure to calculate the self-employment income and record the amounts on Schedules K and K-1.

Note: This problem is based on the tax return problem that appears at the end of Chapters 2 and 12.

LEARNING OBJECTIVES

Upon completion of this chapter you will be able to:

- Explain the unique concepts relevant to family partnerships

- Identify the advantages and problems of limited partnerships and their partners

- Understand the basic principles of tax shelters

- Determine the tax consequences of current and liquidating partnership asset distributions, including

  - Determination of the gain or loss recognized by partners

  - Determination of the basis of each asset and of the partnership interest to the partners

  - Recognition of the impact of § 751 and disproportionate distributions

- Calculate gain or loss on the disposition or retirement of a partnership interest

- Understand the benefits and disadvantages of special partnership optional adjustments to basis

CHAPTER OUTLINE

Chapter 11

SPECIAL PARTNERSHIPS, ASSET DISTRIBUTIONS, AND DISPOSITIONS OF PARTNERSHIP INTERESTS

Chapter 10 emphasized the formation and operation of partnerships. In this chapter, two special types of partnerships—family owned and operated businesses and limited partnerships—are discussed. Both of these partnerships present unique and frequently litigated questions. Consequently, special rules govern their operations.

Distributions of partnership assets also are discussed in this chapter. Some distributions are taxable and some are not. Some taxable distributions result in ordinary gain and some in capital gain or loss. Partners and their tax advisors must be aware of the effect of distributions before the transactions occur.

Finally, the various methods of disposing of a partnership interest are examined. These include sales, retirements, gifts, charitable contributions, incorporations, abandonments, forfeitures, foreclosures, and death of partners. Each disposition affects the parties involved differently.

FAMILY PARTNERSHIPS

Family owned and operated businesses play an important role in our economy and society. Quite often, a partnership is the most suitable form for operating a family business. Members of the same family form partnerships for a variety of reasons. Frequently, there is a sound business purpose and the partnership is operated similar to ones owned by unrelated individuals. That is, each partner contributes property and/or services to the partnership in exchange for a capital interest and participates in the management of the partnership. Generally, these family partnerships are subject to the same tax provisions as other partnerships. However, when the arrangements of family partnerships deviate from that of other partnerships, they may be subject to additional requirements.

TAX SAVINGS POTENTIAL

In some instances, family partnerships are formed primarily for tax reasons. The most common example is the partnership that includes both a parent and one or more otherwise dependent children as partners. The basic tax structure provides considerable incentive when the child is at least 14 years of age.[1]

Although a family may be one economic unit, each member is a separate individual for tax purposes. The tax rate of each person at least 14 years old is determined by his or her taxable income. Consequently, marginal tax rates often are lower for some family members than they are for others. For example, a taxpayer's children who are full-time students usually have little or no taxable income. When a difference in tax rates exists, there may be opportunities for income splitting that reduce the total tax borne by the family unit. Partnerships frequently have been used to obtain these benefits.[2]

A large percentage of the income in our society today is earned by personal service businesses. That is, fees, commissions, or other types of compensation are received for personal services provided by individuals such as entertainers, physicians, beauticians, attorneys, plumbers, consultants, and public accountants. Many of these businesses require minimal capital investment. It has long been held that earned income is taxable to the individual who earns it and cannot be assigned to another.[3] As a result, these businesses seldom provide tax-splitting opportunities through the use of family partnerships.

Another axiom of tax law is that income earned on property is taxable to the owner of such property.[4] This is true even if the property (e.g., a partnership capital interest) is received as a tax-motivated gift from a relative.[5] A capital interest in a partnership is defined as an interest in the assets of the partnership.[6] Thus, when capital is "a material income-producing factor,"[7] a partnership may provide considerable tax savings by splitting income among family members who are partners. The Regulations state that if substantial investments in assets such as inventories, plant, machinery, and equipment are necessary to the business, capital ordinarily will be considered a material income-producing factor.[8] However, when the income of the business consists principally of fees, commissions, or other compensation for personal services, the Regulations state that capital

---

[1]   Recall that after 1986 much of the income-splitting advantages with children under 14 years of age are eliminated.

[2]   However, the child may be subject to self-employment taxes on the partnership income (see Chapter 10).

[3]   *Lucas v. Earl*, 2 USTC ¶496, 8 AFTR 10287, 281 U.S. 111 (USSC, 1930) and *Helvering v. Eubank*, 40-2 USTC ¶9788, 24 AFTR 1063, 311 U.S. 122 (USSC, 1940), *rev'g.* 40-1 USTC ¶9334, 24 AFTR 767, 110 F.2d 737 (CA-2, 1940), *rev'g.* 39 B.T.A. 583 (1939).

[4]   *Helvering v. Horst*, 40-2 USTC ¶9787, 24 AFTR 1058, 311 U.S. 112 (USSC, 1940).

[5]   *Blair*, 37-1 USTC ¶9083, 18 AFTR 1132, 300 U.S. 5 (USSC, 1937).

[6]   Reg. § 1.704-1(e)(1)(v).

[7]   § 704(e)(1).

[8]   Reg. § 1.704-1(e)(1)(iv).

is *not* a material income-producing factor. It should be noted that in this context income refers to *gross income* (i.e., gross receipts less cost of goods sold). Therefore, a partnership may satisfy this test even though it has a net loss for the year.

For nonservice partnerships, investments in many other assets necessary to the business may qualify as well as those listed in the Regulations.[9] For example, working capital often requires a significant investment in assets.[10] In one instance, the court held that a partnership's existing goodwill was an asset for this purpose.[11] However, the Tax Court, in a split decision, ruled that when most of the partnership assets were acquired with debt, contributed capital was not a material income-producing factor.[12] Thus, in this case, capital meant ownership equity rather than debt equity.

The Code does not mention family partnerships when capital is not a material income-producing factor. Most businesses, including those that only provide services, require some capital. In these situations, case law may still allow the family partnership some income-splitting benefits.[13] Alternatively, the family members could own these assets directly or in a second partnership and lease them to the service business.

INCOME ALLOCATION RULES

To prevent abuses of the income-splitting opportunities, Congress established special income allocation rules for family partnerships.[14] The rules apply when an individual (the donee) receives a partnership interest as a gift from a family member (the donor). The same donee/donor relationship can be deemed to exist, however, when the ownership interest is purchased from the family member and even if a fair market price is paid. This occurs if the purchase does not meet the requirements for an arm's length business transaction.[15] For purposes of this statute, family members only include a spouse, ancestors, and lineal descendants and any trusts created for their primary benefit.[16] The donee partner's distributive share of partnership income is subject to two limitations.[17]

---

[9] For example, see *Jeremiah J. O'Donnell, Jr.,* 23 TCM 210, T.C. Memo 1964-38 (1964); and *Jelindo A. Tiberti,* 21 TCM 961, T.C. Memo 1962-174 (1962).

[10] For example, see *Sanford H. Hartman,* 43 T.C. 105 (1964); and *James G. Bennett,* 21 TCM 903, T.C. Memo 1962-163.

[11] *Bateman v. U.S.,* 74-1 USTC ¶9176, 33 AFTR2d, 74-483, 490 F.2d 549 (CA-9, 1973), *aff'g.* 71-2 USTC ¶9546, 28 AFTR2d 71-5306 (D.C. Calif., 1971).

[12] *Carriage Square, Inc.,* 69 T.C. 119 (1977).

[13] *Comm. v. Culbertson,* 49-1 USTC ¶9323, 37 AFTR 1391, 337 U.S. 733 (USSC, 1949), *rev'g.* and *rem'g.* 48-2 USTC ¶9324, 36 AFTR 1168, 168 F.2d 979 (CA-5, 1948), *rev'g.* 6 TCM 692, T.C. Memo 1947-168, on *rem.* 52-1 USTC ¶9233, 41 AFTR 850, 194 F.2d 581 (CA-5, 1952), *rev'g.* 9 TCM 647, T.C. Memo 1950-187.

[14] § 704(e).

[15] § 704(e)(3); Reg. § 1.704-1(e)(3)(ii)(b).

[16] § 704(e)(3); Reg. §§ 1.704- 1(e)(3) and (4).

[17] § 704(e)(2) and Reg. § 1.704-1(e)(3)(i)(b). These two requirements are essentially the same as those added by the Revenue Act of 1951.

1. Reasonable compensation must be allocated to the *donor* partner for all services performed for the partnership. (Note that there is no similar requirement that reasonable compensation be allocated to any other partner, including the donee.)

2. Allocations to the *donee* partner cannot represent a greater return on capital than that allocated to the *donor* partner. (Note that there is no similar requirement that prevents allocating a greater share to any other partner, including the donor, nor even to a donee partner compared with partners other than the donor.)

Unless both requirements are met, partnership income may be reallocated between the donee and the donor, based on these two requirements. These special provisions do not affect the distributive shares of any other partners.

> **Example 1.** A partnership is owned equally by a father and his 15-year-old daughter. Their capital accounts are maintained in the same ratio. The daughter received her ownership interest as a gift from her father. Partnership income of $120,000 for the year is distributed to them equally, $60,000 to each. If the father performed services during the year valued at $20,000, partnership income to the father and daughter may be reallocated by the IRS. The first $20,000 would be allocated to him, and one-half (or $50,000) of the remaining $100,000 would be allocated to each of them. His portion becomes $70,000 ($20,000 + $50,000) and hers becomes $50,000.

> **Example 2.** Assume the same facts as in *Example 1*, except that the partnership is owned equally by a father, his 15-year-old daughter, and a friend. The $120,000 is allocated to them equally, $40,000 to each. If the IRS requires a reallocation, only the father and daughter are affected. Their combined share of $80,000 will be allocated $50,000 to him ($20,000 compensation + one-half of the remaining $60,000) and $30,000 to her (one-half the $60,000). The friend's share remains at $40,000.

Although reasonable compensation is not defined for family partnerships, the definition developed for compensation of corporate employees may be applicable.[18] The partnership requirements do state, however, that compensation must consider (1) the possibility that one partner may have more managerial responsibility than another, and (2) the fact that a general partner has unlimited liability, whereas a limited partner does not.[19]

Presumably, the intent of the allocation provisions is to limit the donees' income to the amount earned on the capital. In reality, this may not occur. Since the full value of the donor partner's services is guaranteed up to the amount of net income, the return on capital may be understated or even nonexistent when the business is unsuccessful and overstated when it is successful.

---

[18] § 162(a)(1). See Chapter 3.   [19] Reg. §§ 1.704-1(e)(3)(i)(c) and (ii)(c).

TESTS OF OWNERSHIP

A legally transferred capital interest between family members may not be recognized as a transfer for tax purposes if the donor retains and exercises *control* over the interest.[20] Retention of control will not disqualify the transfer, however, if it is incidental or if the donor is exercising the control as a trustee, guardian, or custodian of the capital interest for the benefit of the donee. The Regulations list several types of control retained by the donor that indicate whether the transfer of ownership actually occurred. Most of these are derived from prior case law.

1. The donee should have the right to withdraw his or her proportionate share of partnership income.[21] It is not necessary for the funds actually to be withdrawn since income can be retained for reasonable needs of the business. But, if only the donee's and not the donor's share of income is retained, the transfer may be disqualified. The Regulations and the courts have emphasized the importance of actually distributing some current income.[22] These funds must be for the sole use and benefit of the donee. They must not benefit nor be controlled by the donor, nor may they be used to support a donee who is a minor when the donor is obligated to provide that support.

2. The donee should have the right to liquidate or dispose of the capital interest.[23] There should be no restrictions on this right other than those pertaining to reasonable business requirements placed on both the donee and donor. For example, it is acceptable to require a partner to offer the capital interest to the partnership or the partners before transferring it to others. The price should equal the amount available from a third party (i.e., an arm's length or market value price).

3. Rights over assets essential to the business may not be retained by the donor.[24] Any essential assets leased to the partnership by the donor should meet reasonable business terms. If the donor has the right to cancel the lease at will or the lease is for a short period of time, this could jeopardize the partnership's existence. Unfortunately, there is no definition for the terms *essential* or *short* term.

---

[20] Reg. § 1.704-1(e)(2)(i) and *Helvering v. Clifford*, 40-1 USTC ¶9265, 23 AFTR 1077, 309 U.S. 331 (USSC, 1940), *rev'g.* 39-2 USTC ¶9626, 23 AFTR 223, 105 F.2d 586 (CA-8, 1939), *rev'g.* 38 B.T.A. 1532 (1938).

[21] Reg. § 1.704-1(e)(2)(ii)(a).

[22] Reg. § 1.704-1(e)(2)(v). Also see, for example, *Payton v. U.S.*, 70-1 USTC ¶9379, 25 AFTR2d 70-1124, 425 F.2d 1324 (CA-5, 1970), *rev'g.* and *rem'g.* 69-2 USTC ¶9444, 24 AFTR2d 69-5478 (D.C. Tex., 1969), *cert. denied* 400 U.S. 957 (USSC); *Ginsberg v. Comm.*, 74-2 USTC ¶9660, 34 AFTR2d 74-5760, 502 F.2d 965 (CA-6, 1974), *aff'g.* 32 TCM 1019, T.C. Memo 1973-220; and *Acuff v. Comm.*, 62-1, USTC ¶9141, 8 AFTR2d 6000, 296 F.2d 725 (CA-6, 1961), *aff'g.* 35 T.C. 162 (1960).

[23] Reg. § 1.704-1(e)(2)(ii)(b).

[24] Reg. § 1.704-1(e)(2)(ii)(c).

4. The donee should have the right to participate in the management of the partnership.[25] (This right applies only when the donee is a *general* partner.)

5. The donee should be held out publicly as a partner.[26] All written documents should properly reflect the existence of the donee as a partner. This is particularly important when the business was operated previously as a proprietorship.

Although the donor may serve as the trustee, guardian, or custodian for the donee's capital interest, it is more difficult to prove control has been relinquished in this situation than if an unrelated individual who is independent of the donor serves in such capacity. Simply transferring the donee's interest to a trust, corporation, or other partnership is insufficient as long as the donor, in reality, has direct or indirect control over the interest.[27] The appointment of a third party who is *amenable* to the donor's wishes also is suspect. In these instances, other factors are important, such as the written provisions of both the trust and partnership agreements, plus the actions of the third party. The trustee must *actively* represent the interests of the donee before the *fiduciary* responsibility is met.[28] These guidelines pertain to trusts and trustees. However, no rules have been formulated for guardians or custodians. As a result, it might be wise to request a letter ruling when a trust is not used.

It is possible, of course, for the donee partner to exercise control and participate in management. Generally, this is difficult to prove if the donee is a minor or participation is incidental. The Regulations state the participating donee must possess the maturity and experience to properly fulfill the requirement. The Regulations further stress that a donee's "substantial" participation in managing the operations, particularly in major policy decisions, is a strong indication that control over the interest has passed to the donee.[29] Consequently, the implication is that the donee should be involved in top-level management decisions.

Although other partners may choose to avoid management responsibilities of a partnership, this option is not available for the donee's interest. One possible alternative, however, is for the donee to be a *limited* rather than a general part-

---

[25] Reg. § 1.704-1(e)(2)(ii)(d).

[26] Reg. § 1.704-1(e)(2)(iv).

[27] *Comm. v. Sunnen*, 48-1 USTC ¶9230, 36 AFTR 611, 333 U.S. 591 (USSC), *rev'g.* 47-1 USTC ¶9237, 35 AFTR 1217, 161 F.2d 171 (CA-8, 1947), *aff'g.* in part and *rev'g.* in part 6 T.C. 431; and *Krause v. Comm.*, 74-1 USTC ¶9470, 34 AFTR2d 74-5044, 497 F.2d 1109 (CA-6, 1974), *aff'g.* 57 T.C. 890 (1972), 419 U.S. 1108 (USSC) *cert. denied.*

[28] Reg. § 1.704-1(e)(2)(vii). Also see *Jack Smith*, 32 T.C. 1261 (1959) and *Kuney v. U.S.*, 71-2 USTC ¶9646, 28 AFTR2d 71-5714, 448 F.2d 22 (CA-9, 1971), *rev'g.* and *rem'd.* 69-1 USTC ¶9306, 23 AFTR2d 69-1121 (D.C. Wash., 1969), on *rem.* 75-2 USTC ¶9767, 36 AFTR2d 75-6081 (CA-9, 1975), *rev'g.* 29 AFTR2d 72-1046 (D.C. Wash., 1972).

[29] Reg. § 1.704-1(e)(2)(iv).

ner. This form of ownership can be useful for any partner not involved in the partnership's operations.[30] As indicated in Chapter 10, limited partners cannot participate in management. A limited partner is more like an investor who expects a return on the investment through distributions and/or appreciation. Thus, a donor can retain control of partnership operations without violating the limited donee partner's rights of participation in management. In addition, limited donees need not be held out publicly as partners. All other control factors are the same for both types of partners.

LIMITED PARTNERSHIPS

The option for taxpayers to form and operate as limited partnerships has been available for many years. However, their popularity increased significantly during the 1970s and early 1980s. This interest paralleled the growth of syndicated tax shelters. Although the limited partnership form is available to all businesses and can be a distinct advantage in several types of situations, it is most closely identified with tax shelters.

When evaluating whether to establish a general or a limited partnership, there are several important differences to consider. First, limited partnerships must have at least one general partner. Second, all limited partners have limited liability. That is, their potential liability for partnership debts does not extend beyond the assets contributed plus any additional amounts they are obligated by the partnership agreement to contribute. Third, limited partners may not participate in management. A limited partner who participates in management may cause his or her status to be changed to that of a general partner. Fourth, the death, insanity, or retirement of a limited partner does not dissolve the partnership. Fifth, limited partners' interests often are transferable, as are corporate ownership interests. Sixth, limited partners do not have self-employment income from the partnership except to the extent of guaranteed compensation. Seventh, a limited partner's basis is increased by his or her share of nonrecourse but not recourse debt. A holder of *nonrecourse debt* has a claim against specified assets only and not against other partnership assets or any personal assets of a general or limited partner. In contrast, a holder of *recourse debt* has a claim against partnership assets and the personal assets of *general partners* but not limited partners. Recall that partners' shares of partnership liabilities are generally determined by their individual ratios for profits in the case of nonrecourse debt and ratios for losses in the case of recourse debt.[31]

---

[30] Reg. § 1.704-1(e)(2)(ix).

[31] Temp. Reg. §§ 1.752-1T through 4T add an "economic risk of loss analysis" requirement which is beyond the scope of this text.

TAX SHELTERS

Prior to the 1980s, many investors obtained significant tax savings through the use of numerous tax shelter plans available to them. Few of these benefits survived the revisions made to the Code in the late 1980s. Examples of these revisions are the elimination of the special capital gains deduction and the investment tax credit, the deferment of net passive losses until the investment is sold, and lengthened depreciable lives.[32]

Some of the benefits that remain are tax-exempt investments (e.g., certain municipal bonds), tax credits (e.g., rehabilitation investment credit), and percentage depletion in excess of cost depletion. These benefits all decrease the individual's total tax liability permanently. Although few partnerships have significant amounts of tax-exempt income, many do take advantage of tax credits and percentage depletion. Tax credits provide equal tax benefits to all *taxpayers*, and the tax savings from tax-exempt income and excess percentage depletion increase as the marginal tax rate increases.

Example 3. Partnership T has the following year-end information:

	Book Income	Taxable Income
Net income before depletion	$100,000	$100,000
Cost depletion	(10,000)	–
Percentage depletion	–	(40,000)
	$ 90,000	$ 60,000

M and N are equal partners with marginal tax rates of 15% and 28% respectively. Percentage depletion exceeds cost depletion by $30,000 ($40,000 − $10,000). Tax savings provided by this excess for M are $2,250 ($30,000 ÷ 2 = $15,000 × 15%) and for N are $4,200 ($15,000 × 28%).

Although inactive partners cannot deduct their distributive shares of partnership losses, tax savings may be achieved by deferring income. For example, appreciation of partnership assets does not result in includible income to the partners until either the assets or the partnership capital interests are sold. The tax advantage achieved is through the present value of money (i.e., a dollar of taxes deferred may be invested). Thus, any tax payments that can be delayed are equivalent to an interest-free loan from the government. Postponing taxes is not risk free, however. There is no guarantee that the marginal tax rates or the tax law governing the situation will be as predicted: the longer the deferral, the greater the uncertainty.

---

[32] For an in-depth discussion of these and other effects of tax legislation during the 1980s, see the companion book, *Individual Taxation*.

Partners who actively participate (i.e., a regular, continuous, and substantial involvement) in partnership operations may be able to deduct their distributive shares of losses against other business income, including salaries and other active business income. They are subject, however, to the at-risk limitation.

AT-RISK LIMITATION

Recall from Chapter 10 that when a general partnership incurs a net loss, the general partners deduct their share of the losses to the extent of their bases in the partnership. If the share of losses exceeds a partner's basis, the deduction reduces the basis to zero. All remaining losses are carried forward until the basis increases above zero. This effect assumes that all debt is *recourse* debt. The result differs, however, when basis includes *nonrecourse* debt (unless the partnership is engaged in *real estate* activities *and* the debt is from a *qualified* lender, as discussed below). Under § 704(d), the partners' distributive shares of net losses *flow through* to them and reduce their bases as described above. However, *deductions* of these losses are restricted by a § 465 amount that includes only debt on which partners are considered to be "at risk" (i.e., recourse debt). As a result, the partners' *distributive* shares of losses [under § 704(d)] may exceed *deductible* losses (under § 465) for that year. Recall that limited partners' § 704(d) bases do not include a partnership's recourse debt. This debt is also not included in the limited partners' § 465 at-risk amount. In summary, for partnerships not qualifying for the real estate exception:

1. A general partner's § 704(d) basis includes his or her share of both recourse and nonrecourse debt whereas the § 465 at-risk amount includes only his or her share of recourse debt, and

2. A limited partner's § 704(d) basis includes his or her share of nonrecourse debt whereas the § 465 at-risk amount includes no debt.

The at-risk limitation is applied before the § 469 passive loss limitation. Consequently, losses treated as deductible in the following pages are actually deductible only to the extent allowed under the passive loss limitation (as discussed in the companion book, *Individual Taxation*).

At-Risk Rules and Real Estate. The at-risk rules apply to partnership losses that relate to real estate activities *unless* nonrecourse debt is from a qualified lender. Thus, real estate investments are not subject to the at-risk rules to the extent that arm's length third party commercial financing is used, even if the debt is secured solely by real property (i.e., nonrecourse debt).[33] For this exception to the at-risk rules, a qualified lender cannot be (1) related to the taxpayer, (2) the seller or related to the seller, or (3) a recipient of a fee received because of the sale.[34]

---

[33] § 465(b)(6)(C).

[34] In some instances, the taxpayer will be considered at risk on loans from a related party if the loan terms meet the arm's length requirements. The at-risk amount, however, does not include convertible debt.

Example 4.   A general partnership formed by K and L has the following information at the end of the current year:

Nonrecourse loans......................	$100,000
Recourse loans........................	25,000
Net loss...............................	40,000
K, capital (deficit)......................	(3,000)
L, capital..............................	15,000

K and L are equal partners who actively participate in this cattle breeding partnership. The current results to K and L are as follows:

	K		L	
	§ 704(d)	§ 465	§ 704(d)	§ 465
Capital account (deficit)........	$ (3,000)	$ (3,000)	$15,000	$15,000
Nonrecourse loans	50,000	0	50,000	0
Recourse loans..............	12,500	12,500	12,500	12,500
Balance before the loss........	$59,500	$ 9,500	$77,500	$27,500
Net loss......................	(20,000)	(9,500)	(20,000)	(20,000)
Balance after the loss..........	$39,500	$ 0	$57,500	$ 7,500

K's § 704(d) basis is $59,500 [(50% × $100,000 nonrecourse debt) + (50% × $25,000 recourse debt) − $3,000 deficit capital]. K's § 465 at-risk amount is $9,500 [(50% × $25,000 recourse debt) − $3,000 deficit capital]. Therefore, K's $20,000 share of the net loss is distributed to him since it is less than his § 704(d) basis, but only $9,500 is deductible by him since his § 465 at-risk amount cannot absorb more than $9,500. The amounts under §§ 704(d) and 465 are reduced to $39,500 ($59,500 − $20,000) and $0 ($9,500 − $9,500), respectively. The nondeductible $10,500 is *suspended*, to be deducted when K's § 465 amount becomes positive.

L's § 704(d) basis is $77,500 [(50% × $100,000) + (50% × $25,000) + $15,000 capital]. L's § 465 at-risk amount is $27,500. Therefore, L's $20,000 share of the net loss is distributed to her since it is less than her § 704(d) basis, and it is also deductible by her since it is less than her § 465 amount. L's § 704(d) basis becomes $57,500 ($77,500 − $20,000) and her § 465 at-risk amount is $7,500.

Example 5.   Assume the same facts as in *Example 4*, except that the partnership's business is the rental of real estate and that the nonrecourse loans are from *qualified* lenders. As a result, the § 465 limitation on nonrecourse debt is not applicable. The § 704(d) basis is $59,500 for K and $77,500 for L. Both K and L may deduct the $20,000 loss. After the deduction, the § 704(d) basis is $39,500 for K and $57,500 for L.

As *Examples 4* and *5* show, in some instances, real estate partnerships offer significantly higher tax reductions to active partners than any other type of business. (See the companion book, *Individual Taxation*, for limitations on losses for certain real estate activities.)

DAY OF RECKONING

While some partnerships can provide actively participating partners with loss deductions in excess of their actual investment, there is a day of reckoning. The selling price of a partnership interest includes the seller's share of partnership liabilities assumed by the buyer. This same approach to partnership liabilities applies to other dispositions of partnership interests, except on the death of a partner. (The effect of this concept governing dispositions is discussed later in the chapter.) As a result, a partner's gain is increased (or loss reduced) by the amount of net losses previously deducted in excess of the partner's contributed capital.

> **Example 6.** Assume the same facts as in *Example 5* (i.e., a real estate shelter in which L's § 704(d) basis is $57,500, including $62,500 of qualified financing). The following year, L sells her 50% interest for $70,000 cash. The amount realized on the sale is $132,500 ($70,000 + $62,500 debt in basis). The gain is $75,000 ($132,500 − $57,500 basis). Since L's basis included the $62,500 debt, her net loss distributions had exceeded her investment less asset distributions by $5,000 ($62,500 debt − $57,500 basis). This $5,000 added to the $70,000 original investment equals her $75,000 gain.

Note that although losses and asset distributions in excess of investment are taxed when a partner disposes of the net capital interest, the tax benefit from deferral is not lost.

Publicly Traded Partnerships. Partnerships became big business in the 1970s and 1980s. To meet the growing demand of tax-conscious investors, some partnerships are marketed in much the same way as corporations. Purchasing a limited partner capital interest in publicly traded partnerships (PTPs), commonly referred to as master limited partnerships, is similar to purchasing stock in a publicly traded corporation. Prior to the late 1980s, the best of these partnerships provided limited liability to limited partners; tax savings from deductible losses, depletion, and tax credits that exceeded the original investment; and income deferred for many years. In some instances, limited partners received tax-free cash distributions while reporting losses. The worst of these partnerships were shams with assets recorded at values far in excess of market values, questionable nonrecourse debts, and no real economic substance. The sole advantages of these latter PTPs were the tax deductions and credits.

Congress and the IRS used several approaches to curb the tax benefits of limited partnerships. In the past, an effective method was the establishment of "at-risk" rules, discussed earlier in this chapter. However, the Revenue Act of 1987 eliminated most tax benefits previously associated with PTPs.[35] The effective date for these provisions is taxable years beginning after 1987 for new PTPs and after 1997 for PTPs in existence on December 17, 1987. The deferral of the effective date to 1997 is lost if a PTP adds a substantial new line of business to its activities.

A PTP is taxed like a C corporation, unless at least 90 percent of its income is passive income. Passive income includes most interest and dividends, rental income and gains on the disposition of real property, income and gains from certain mineral or natural resource activities, gains from the disposition of capital assets and § 1231 assets held for income production, and income and gains from various types of transactions involving commodities. If a PTP is reclassified as a C corporation, its distributions generally are dividend income. Regardless of whether a PTP meets the 90 percent test, all includible income from the PTP is portfolio income to the owner and, therefore, cannot be used to offset losses from passive activities. It is possible for a PTP to have both portfolio income and losses from business activities. These items cannot be netted. In addition, losses that flow through a PTP to its owners are suspended and deductible solely against income from that particular PTP or when an owner disposes of his or her entire interest in that PTP. Consequently, PTP income is recognized currently and losses are deferred, which is quite different from prior years.

DISTRIBUTIONS OF PARTNERSHIP ASSETS

Distributions of partnership assets are classified as either current or liquidating. Distributions are considered *current*, and thus nonliquidating, when the partners receiving the property retain all or part of their capital interest. Even if a significant percentage of a partner's capital interest in the partnership is liquidated, the distribution still qualifies as current. Therefore, distributions are *liquidating* only when a partner's entire interest in the partnership is relinquished. The tax treatment is identical in many instances for all distributions, whether current or liquidating. However, as is often the case in taxation, exceptions do exist.

CURRENT DISTRIBUTIONS—PROPORTIONATE

Partnerships frequently make current distributions of cash to their owners. A *current distribution* is one that does not liquidate a partner's capital interest nor is a part of a series of distributions that will liquidate the interest. Recall that

---

[35]   § 469(k).

all decreases in a partner's share of partnership liabilities also are treated as though they are distributions of cash.[36] In most instances, cash distributions are nontaxable. There is, however, one exception. At no time may a partner's basis in the partnership be reduced below zero.[37] Consequently, any cash distributed in excess of a partner's basis is taxable income to the partner.[38]

In determining whether cash distributions exceed a partner's basis, all distributions generally are deemed to have been made on the last day of the partnership's taxable year, regardless of when they actually occurred. Thus, a partner has the opportunity to offset the distributions with current year profits, any year-end capital contributions, and increases in partnership liabilities.

> **Example 7.** On January 1 of the current year, A's basis in a calendar year partnership was $30,000 and B's basis was $5,000. Each partner received $20,000 in cash July 2. Partnership taxable income for the year was $24,000. A and B share profits equally. Neither of them made any contributions to the partnership, nor did their share of partnership liabilities change during the year. A's includible income is $12,000 (50% of $24,000) and her basis is $22,000 [($30,000 + $12,000) − $20,000]. B's taxable income is $15,000, composed of $12,000 partnership taxable income and $3,000 gain recognized on the distribution to avoid a negative basis in the partnership [($5,000 + $12,000) − $20,000]. His basis in the partnership is zero [($5,000 + $15,000) − $20,000]. B could have avoided the additional $3,000 taxable income from excess distributions if he had contributed $3,000 to the partnership or if the partnership's debt had increased $6,000 by the end of year. (Note: The answer would have been the same if the $20,000 had been, in part or in total, a reduction in liabilities previously included in the partners' basis.)

Distributions of noncash assets follow the aggregate concept and are tax-free as long as they do not alter the partners' *proportionate interest* in § 751 assets.[39] Section 751 assets consist of *unrealized receivables* and *substantially appreciated inventory*. In many instances, the tax treatment of these distributions is quite similar to the treatment applicable to the reverse situation, when partners contribute property to the partnership for a capital interest. That is, (1) neither the partnership nor the partners recognize gain or loss, (2) the partnership's holding period for capital assets and § 1231 assets carries over to the partners, and (3) the partnership's bases in the assets carry over to the partners.[40]

---

[36] § 752(b).

[37] § 733.

[38] § 731(a)(1).

[39] § 731(a).

[40] § 732(a).

Example 8.   K's basis in the partnership at the end of the year, before distributions are considered, is $60,000. The partnership uses the cash method. Proportionate distributions were made during the year to all partners. K's share was as follows:

	Partnership's Basis	Fair Market Value
Cash...	$ 7,000	$ 7,000
Receivables.................................	0	12,000
Land...	15,000	39,000
Investment stock............................	30,000	32,000
Total assets................................	$52,000	$90,000

The distribution qualifies as a nontaxable transfer. The partnership reduces (debits) K's capital account for $52,000 ($7,000 + $0 + $15,000 + $30,000) and reduces (credits) each of the assets for their respective bases. K's basis in the partnership of $60,000 exceeds the partnership's basis in the assets. Thus, his basis in the assets is (1) $7,000 cash, (2) $0 receivables, (3) $15,000 land, and (4) $30,000 stock. His basis in the partnership is reduced to $8,000 ($60,000 − $52,000).

The tax treatment of property distributions differs from property contributions in one important manner. The partnership's basis in the assets carries over to the distributee partner only to the extent of the partner's basis in the partnership.[41] Thus, when a partner's basis is *less than* that of the property received, the partner's basis must be allocated in the following order:[42]

1.   To all cash received, including cash deemed received when partnership liabilities are decreased

2.   To all assets received that are *not* capital assets or § 1231 assets (generally defined as unrealized receivables and inventory, discussed later in this chapter)

3.   To any capital assets and § 1231 assets received

A second allocation is then required to assign the basis among the assets received in the last two categories. In contrast with the common tax allocation method using relative fair market values, this calculation uses the partnership's *relative bases* for the assets.[43] After all allocations are completed, the partner's basis in the partnership is zero.[44]

---

[41] § 732(a)(2).

[42] Reg. §§ 1.731-1(a)(1)(i) and 1.732-1.

[43] § 732(c).

[44] § 733.

Example 9. Assume the same facts as in *Example 8* (i.e., K's share of the partnership basis is $7,000 cash, $0 receivables, $15,000 land, and $30,000 investment stock), except that K's basis in the partnership is $37,000 (rather than $60,000). Generally, this change has no effect on the partnership but does affect K's situation, since his basis in the partnership is $15,000 less than the partnership's basis in the assets ($37,000 − $52,000).[45] K must allocate his $37,000 basis in the partnership among the assets as follows: (1) $7,000 cash, (2) $0 receivables, (3) $10,000 land [($37,000 basis − $7,000 = $30,000) × ($15,000 ÷ $45,000)], and (4) $20,000 stock (calculated the same as land, except substituting $30,000 for $15,000 in the numerator of the fraction). The $15,000 excess of partnership basis over K's basis is lost to K forever. (Note that fair market values were not used in either example.)

Example 10. Assume the same facts as in *Example 9*, except the land is inventory and the receivables have a $12,000 basis. K must allocate his $37,000 basis in the partnership among the assets as follows: (1) $7,000 cash, (2) $12,000 receivables and $15,000 inventory, and (3) $3,000 stock ($37,000 − $7,000 − $12,000 − $15,000).

When partnership debt is distributed along with the property, all partners' bases are affected. The treatment is similar to that used when a partner contributes debt along with assets to a partnership (see Chapter 10), except in the reverse. First, all partners are treated as though they received a cash distribution equal to their share of the debt and must reduce their bases in the partnership by that amount. Second, the partner assuming the debt is treated as making a capital contribution to the partnership equal to the debt assumed and increases his or her basis in the partnership by that amount.[46] Of course, this partner also must reduce basis for the property received.

Example 11. T receives a current distribution from a 20% owned partnership of equipment with a basis of $12,000 and a liability against it of $4,000. T's basis in the partnership before the distribution is $10,000. T's basis after the distribution is $1,200 [$10,000 − $12,000 − ($4,000 × 20% = $800) + $4,000]. The remaining partners must reduce their bases by a total of $3,200 ($4,000 × 80%).

---

[45] The partnership, however, will be allowed to increase the basis of certain assets it holds by the $15,000 basis lost by K *if* a § 754 election is in effect. See discussion later in this chapter.

[46] § 752(a).

LIQUIDATING DISTRIBUTIONS—PROPORTIONATE

Liquidating distributions that do not alter the partners' proportionate interest in § 751 assets are treated as discussed above for current distributions, with three exceptions. First, when a partner's basis in the partnership *exceeds* the partnership's basis in the distributed assets, the excess must be allocated among the § 1231 and capital assets received. Again, the allocation is determined by the partnership's relative bases in the assets.

> **Example 12.**   Assume the same facts as in *Example 8*, except that this is a liquidating distribution. Recall that K's basis in the partnership is $60,000 and his share of proportionate distributions was
>
> | | Partnership's Basis | Fair Market Value |
> |---|---|---|
> | Cash... | $ 7,000 | $ 7,000 |
> | Receivables.................................. | 0 | 12,000 |
> | Land... | 15,000 | 39,000 |
> | Investment stock............................. | 30,000 | 32,000 |
> | Total assets................................. | $52,000 | $90,000 |
>
> K's $60,000 basis in the partnership is allocated as follows: (1) $7,000 cash, (2) $0 receivables, (3) $17,667 land [($60,000 − $7,000 = $53,000) × ($15,000 ÷ $45,000)], and (4) $35,333 stock (calculated the same as land except substituting $30,000 for $15,000 in the numerator of the fraction).

A second difference in tax treatment of liquidating and nonliquidating distributions occurs when (1) no § 1231 or capital assets are distributed, and (2) a partner's basis in the partnership exceeds the partnership's basis in the distributed assets (including the unrealized receivables and inventory). In a nonliquidating distribution, the difference is simply the partner's remaining basis in the partnership. However, in a liquidating distribution, this difference is treated as a loss since there are no assets to which the basis may be assigned and the partner's interest terminates. Since a partnership interest is considered a capital asset, the loss is a capital loss. Note that when unrealized receivables or inventory are distributed, the basis assigned to these assets cannot exceed the partnership's basis for them.

> **Example 13.**   Assume the same facts as in *Example 12*, except that the land and stock are both inventory items (A and B) that qualify as § 751 assets and that this is a liquidating distribution. K's $60,000 basis in the partnership is allocated as follows: (1) $7,000 cash, (2) $0 receivables, (3) $15,000 inventory A, and (4) $30,000 inventory B. The remaining basis of $8,000 is a capital loss.

A third difference in tax treatment of liquidating and nonliquidating distributions occurs when debt is received. In contrast with current distributions, debt received (whether personal liability is assumed or not) by a partner on liquidation increases the basis of property received (and not the now-eliminated basis in the partnership).[47]

> **Example 14.** T receives a liquidating distribution from a 20% owned partnership of equipment with a basis of $12,000 and a liability against it of $4,000. This is the partnership's sole liability. T's basis in the partnership before the distribution is $10,000. Since this is a liquidating distribution, T's basis in the partnership after the distribution is zero. T's basis in the equipment is $13,200 [$10,000 − ($4,000 × 20% = $800) + $4,000]. Compare this result with *Example 11*, when the facts are identical except they are for a current distribution. In that situation, T's bases are $12,000 in the equipment and $1,200 in the partnership.

When § 751 assets are received as a current or liquidating distribution, the partnership's potential for ordinary gain or loss carries over to the partners.[48] Thus, the collection of unrealized trade receivables by the distributee partners results in ordinary income to them. Similarly, any gain on the sale of inventory is also ordinary income, with one exception. If the inventory is held by a distributee partner for more than five years, the partnership "taint" is eliminated. Whether the gain or loss after five years is capital or ordinary is determined by the character of the assets in the hands of the particular partner.[49] The Code suggests the rules apply only to a *distributee partner*. Consequently, it may be possible to avoid the taint by transferring the inventory in a tax-free gift to a family member or in a tax-free exchange to a corporation. Then, if the property is a capital asset to the new owners, a sale of the property should result in capital gain or loss.

SECTION 751 ASSETS

Section 751 assets, often referred to as "tainted" or "hot" assets, are defined as unrealized receivables and substantially appreciated inventory. *Unrealized receivables* include all amounts due from the sale or exchange of property other than capital assets and from the performance of services that have not been included in income previously.[50] Common examples of unrealized receivables are trade receivables of partnerships reporting on the cash or installment method. Unexpectedly, *unrealized receivables* is also defined to include the recapture provisions of §§ 1245 and 1250 through 1254.[51]

---

[47] § 732(b).

[48] § 735(a).

[49] *Ibid.*

[50] § 751(c).

[51] Reg. § 1.751-1(c)(4). The definition also includes lesser known § 617(f)(2) sales of mining property and § 955(c) sales of stock of a Domestic International Sales Corporation.

The term *inventory* in § 751 is misleading, since it includes most partnership property other than cash. Capital assets and § 1231 assets are excluded from the definition, however, *if* they are also capital assets or § 1231 assets to the partners receiving them.[52] For the inventory to be considered *substantially appreciated*, two tests must be met.[53]

1. The fair market value of the inventory must exceed 120 percent of the partnership's basis in the inventory. In this calculation, the fair market value of inventory refers to its replacement cost, not its resale value.

2. The fair market value of the inventory must exceed 10 percent of the fair market value of all noncash partnership property.

If neither or only one test is met, none of the inventory qualifies as § 751 property.

Example 15.   A partnership has the following assets:

	Partnership's Basis	Fair Market Value
Cash..................................	$ 5,000	$ 5,000
Receivables...........................	30,000	30,000
Inventory.............................	40,000	70,000
Land..................................	60,000	80,000
Section 1231 assets....................	225,000	235,000
Total assets........................	$360,000	$420,000

Assume there is no § 1245 or § 1250 potential depreciation recapture. Both substantially appreciated inventory tests are met *if* the land and § 1231 assets will be capital assets or § 1231 assets to the partner receiving them. Therefore, inventory qualifies as a § 751 asset. In the first test, the fair market value of the inventory items of $100,000 ($30,000 + $70,000) exceeds 120% of their basis, or $84,000 [($30,000 + $40,000 = $70,000) × 120%]. In the second test, the fair market value of the inventory items of $100,000 exceeds 10% of the fair market value of all noncash property, or $41,500 [($420,000 − $5,000 = $415,000) × 10%].

In contrast, if the land and § 1231 assets will *not* be capital assets or § 1231 assets to the partner receiving them, inventory is not substantially appreciated since the first test is not met: $420,000 − $5,000 = $415,000, which does not exceed $360,000 − $5,000 = $355,000 × 120% = $426,000.

---

[52]   § 751(d) and Reg. § 1.751-1(d).   [53]   § 751(d)(1).

Land, building, and equipment are not capital assets or § 1231 assets when they qualify as inventory. Consequently, they are treated as inventory at the partnership level for the two tests if they qualify as inventory at the partner level.

In some situations, the partners can take actions to prevent inventory from qualifying as substantially appreciated. An analysis of the two tests suggests several possibilities. First, current purchases of inventory would increase both the basis and market value of the inventory items by the same amount, thus narrowing the percentage difference between the two numbers in the first test. Second, cash could be temporarily invested in securities. This action increases total noncash property for the 10 percent calculation in the second test. Similarly, a partnership loan could be obtained and temporarily invested in securities. Third, unrealized receivables affect both tests. If some of the receivables can be collected before distribution, the increased ordinary income on their collection may be more than offset if inventory is prevented from being substantially appreciated.

DISPROPORTIONATE DISTRIBUTIONS

As previously discussed, proportionate distributions of partnership property generally do not result in taxable income, regardless of whether they are liquidating or nonliquidating transfers. In contrast, both liquidating and nonliquidating *disproportionate distributions* generally do result in taxable income. The solution is based on the aggregate concept for § 751 assets and the entity concept for all other assets distributed. When a disproportionate distribution occurs, each partner determines the ordinary gain to be reported and the basis in the property received, using the following four steps:

1. Group all assets into two categories: (a) § 751 assets, and (b) non–§ 751 assets (i.e., all other assets).

2. A nontaxable proportionate distribution of each of the two categories of assets is *deemed* to have occurred.

3. Compare the deemed distribution in step 2 with the actual distribution for each of the two categories. If the comparison reveals an inequality, select the category in which the deemed distribution *exceeds* the actual distribution. These excess assets are deemed to have been sold to the partnership for their market values.

   a. The partner recognizes ordinary gain when the excess is for § 751 assets and capital gain when the excess is for non–§ 751 assets.

   b. The partnership records a basis in these deemed purchased assets equal to their market value.

4. Refer to the comparison in step 3 and select the category in which the deemed distribution is less than the actual distribution (i.e., the actual distribution exceeds the deemed distribution). The deemed proceeds paid by the partnership to the partner in step 3 are used by the partner to purchase these excess assets at their market values.

a. The partner records a basis in these deemed purchased assets equal to their market values.

b. The partnership recognizes ordinary gain or capital gain, depending on the nature of the assets deemed sold. This gain is allocated among the other partners (i.e., those partners who did not receive this distribution) according to their post-distribution profit-sharing ratios.

Note that the partner recognizes gain for one of the two categories only and the partnership recognizes gain for the other category. This relationship occurs because a disproportionate distribution means that a partner received more assets from one group than his or her pro rata share, and thus less from the other group.

Example 16. Liquidating Partnership S has the following information:

	Partnership's Basis	Fair Market Value
Inventory..............................	$60,000	$ 90,000
Investment land.......................	24,000	36,000
Capital accounts......................	84,000	126,000

C, a 25% partner, has a basis of $21,000 in the partnership. If he receives 25% of the inventory and of the land, this is a proportionate nontaxable distribution for both him and the partnership. He has received a distribution with a fair market value of $22,500 for inventory (25% of $90,000) and $9,000 for land (25% of $36,000). His basis in the inventory is $15,000 (25% of $60,000) and his basis in the land is $6,000 (25% of $24,000).

Example 17. Assume the same facts as in *Example 16*, except that C receives only land with a value of $31,500 and a basis of $21,000. This is a disproportionate taxable distribution and is subject to the four steps listed above.

1. Inventory is the sole § 751 asset, and investment land is the sole non–§ 751 (or other) asset.

2. C is deemed to have received a proportionate distribution and has

	Basis	FMV
§ 751 assets—inventory................	$15,000	$22,500
Other assets..........................	6,000	9,000

3. C is deemed to have sold all the excess § 751 assets (inventory) deemed received in (2) for their fair market value of $22,500 (25% × $90,000).

Cash..................................	$22,500	
§ 751 assets—inventory.............		$15,000
Gain on sale........................		7,500

Thus, C recognizes an ordinary gain of $7,500 on the deemed sale of this § 751 asset. S records a basis for these deemed purchased assets of $22,500, making its total basis in inventory $67,500 ($22,500 + $60,000 basis before distribution − $15,000 deemed distributed basis). S's basis in the land is $3,000 ($24,000 − $21,000 distributed basis).

4. C is deemed to have used the $22,500 proceeds from the sale of the inventory to purchase the extra amount of land received.

Other assets—land....................	$22,500	
Cash................................		$22,500

As a result of this deemed purchase, C's basis in the land is $28,500 ($22,500 price deemed paid for the extra land + $6,000 basis in his proportionate share of land). S recognizes a capital gain of $7,500 [$22,500 deemed sales price − ($21,000 distributed basis − $6,000 deemed distributed basis)].

There is one exception to the distribution procedure above. If a partner receives property that he or she originally contributed to the partnership, § 751 does not apply to that particular asset.[54]

Example 18. Assume the same facts as in *Example 17*, except that C originally contributed the land to the partnership. Now, § 751 does not apply. C has no gain or loss, and his basis in the land is $21,000 (his basis in the partnership). S simply reduces the basis in the land and C's capital account by $21,000.

Example 19. Assume the same facts as in *Example 17*, except that C receives only inventory with a value of $31,500 and a basis of $21,000. In this situation, C is deemed to have sold his share of the land for $9,000 (25% of $36,000). Thus, he reports capital gain of $3,000 ($9,000 − $6,000 basis). C's basis in the inventory is $24,000 ($9,000 deemed purchase price + $15,000 basis in his share of inventory). Recall that any future

---

[54]   § 751(b)(2)(A).

gain on the inventory is ordinary unless C holds the inventory as a capital asset or a § 1231 asset for more than five years. In such case, the gain would then be capital gain.

S's basis in the land is $27,000 ($9,000 deemed purchase price + $24,000 basis before distribution − $6,000 deemed distributed basis). S's basis in the inventory is $39,000 ($60,000 − $21,000 distributed basis). S recognizes an ordinary gain of $3,000 [$9,000 deemed sales price − ($21,000 distributed basis − $15,000 deemed distributed basis)].

SALES OF PARTNERSHIP CAPITAL INTERESTS

Based on the entity theory, an ownership interest in a partnership is a capital asset. Consequently, in keeping with the general rule, gains and losses on the sale of all or a part of that capital asset should result in a capital gain or loss. It does, with one exception.[55]   Any part of the gain attributable to a selling partner's share of § 751 assets is ordinary gain.[56]   This departure from the common treatment of capital assets follows an aggregate concept argument. That is, if the selling partners had continued their ownership interests, income from these assets would have been ordinary income to them. This one aspect can be a disadvantage of the partnership form when compared with the corporate form. Also recall that losses cannot be recognized on a sale or exchange of any asset between related parties.[57] Thus, any loss realized on the sale of a partnership interest to a relative is not deductible.

ALLOCATION OF SALES PROCEEDS

The tax treatment governing sales of partnership capital interests combines the aggregate and entity theories in a manner similar to that of disproportionate distributions. When the partner sells all or part of the capital interest, two calculations are required.

1. The partner's share of § 751 ordinary gain must be determined as previously discussed.

2. The partner's share of capital gain or loss must be determined. (This computation can also be made by subtracting the partner's basis in the partnership from the amount realized to arrive at the gain or loss on the sale. This gain or loss less the § 751 gain equals the partner's capital gain or loss.)

---

[55]   § 741.

[57]   § 267(b). See Chapter 10.

[56]   § 751(a).

The amount realized on the sale of a partnership interest determined as it is for any other sale. It is the sum of (1) cash, (2) the market value of property received, and (3) the amount of the seller's liabilities assumed by the purchaser.[58] Liabilities in the sale of a partnership interest are composed of the seller's share of partnership debt.[59] Recall from Chapter 10 that a general partner's share of partnership liabilities is based on total debt, whereas a limited partner's share is restricted to nonrecourse debt. The partner's basis also includes this same amount of debt. Thus, it might appear that an identical answer is obtained by eliminating partnership liabilities from the computation. This is correct, with one exception. Liabilities assumed are treated as cash received in the year of sale. This is a significant point *if* the sale is reported on the installment basis.

> **Example 20.** C sells his partnership interest to B for $60,000 when C's basis in the partnership is $51,000. B gives C $10,000 cash and a long-term note for $50,000 and assumes C's partnership liabilities of $15,000. C's gain is $24,000 ($60,000 + $15,000 = $75,000 − $51,000). Assume the partnership has no § 751 assets. If C decides to report the sale on the installment method, he must recognize $8,000 ($10,000 + $15,000 = $25,000 ÷ $75,000 × $24,000) in the year of sale. In contrast, if the $15,000 debt could be excluded from the computations, the gain would remain at $24,000 [$60,000 − ($51,000 − $15,000 = $36,000)], but the gain recognized in the year of sale would be just $4,000 ($10,000 ÷ $60,000 × $24,000).

As illustrated above, the inclusion of debt when computing an installment sale can have a significant effect. If a seller could convince the other partners to pay some of the partnership debt before the sale, it would have a positive effect on the gain recognized in the year of sale.

> **Example 21.** Refer to *Example 20*. Assume the same facts, except that the partnership reduces its debt before the sale. Assume C's share of the reduction is $7,000 and his share of the remaining debt is $8,000. The selling price should not change but the amount received in the year of sale is $18,000 ($10,000 + $8,000) and C's basis is $44,000 ($51,000 − $7,000). Consequently, the recognized gain in the year of sale is $6,352.94 ($18,000 ÷ $68,000 × $24,000).

It is possible for a partner to report both ordinary income and either capital gain or capital loss on the single transaction of selling a capital interest.

---

[58] § 1001(b) and Reg. § 1.1001-2(a)(1).   [59] § 752(d).

Example 22. D sells her 25% partnership interest to E for $20,000 cash. The amount realized is $30,000 ($20,000 cash + 25% × $40,000 liabilities). D's basis is $20,000. The partnership records indicate the following:

	Partnership's Basis	Fair Market Value
Cash...................................	$10,000	$ 10,000
Receivables............................	0	24,000
Section 1231 assets....................	70,000	86,000
Total assets.........................	$80,000	$120,000
Liabilities..............................	$40,000	$ 40,000
Capital accounts.......................	40,000	80,000
Total equities........................	$80,000	$120,000

Assume there is no § 1245 or § 1250 potential depreciation recapture. D has ordinary gain of $6,000 (25% of $24,000 receivables), and the remaining $4,000 gain is capital gain ($30,000 amount realized − $20,000 basis − $6,000 ordinary gain). If D's basis in the partnership is $25,000 rather than $20,000, she still has ordinary gain of $6,000 *but* now has a capital loss of $1,000 ($5,000 gain − $6,000 ordinary gain).

RETIRING A PARTNER'S CAPITAL INTEREST

A partner's interest may be "sold" to the partnership, and thus indirectly to the remaining partners. When the interest is completely liquidated with partnership cash, the recipient is said to be *retiring* from the business. The amount of gain or loss on retirement is determined in the same manner as it is for a sale to another partner or third party. That is, the partner's basis is subtracted from the cash to be received plus the partner's share of partnership liabilities. However, the character of the gain for a retirement may differ from that of a sale. To determine the character of the gain or loss as well as the tax consequences to the partnership, cash payments to a retiring partner are divided into two parts: income payments and property payments.

Income payments generally consist of those payments made for the partner's share of the partnership's *goodwill* and *unrealized receivables.*[60] Partnership agreements, however, may provide that payments for goodwill be treated as property payments. As previously discussed, unrealized receivables encompass several recapture provisions, including those for depreciation under §§ 1245 and 1250. Income payments are ordinary income to the recipient and may be deducted by the partnership. The actual deduction follows the rules for guaranteed payments discussed in Chapter 10. Consequently, if they are determined

---

[60]   § 736(a).

without regard to the partnership's income, they are deductible expenses.[61] If the amount of the payments is restricted or affected in some manner by the partnership's income, they are considered to be distributions of partnership profits, and thus reduce the includible portion for the remaining partners.

Property payments are those made for the partner's interest in all partnership assets other than unrealized receivables (plus goodwill when the partnership agreement specifically provides that it is a property payment).[62] Taxation of these payments follows the rules for liquidating distributions. That is, gain attributable to the retiring partner's share of § 751 assets is ordinary gain and the remainder is capital gain or loss. Since income payments include unrealized receivables, any § 751 gain in property payments would be from substantially appreciated inventory.

Example 23. L, a 25% partner, is retiring from a partnership when its records show the following:

	Partnership's Basis	Fair Market Value	Appreciation Total	Appreciation L's Share
Cash......................	$10,000	$10,000	$ 0	$ 0
Investments...............	4,000	6,800	2,800	700
Section 1231 assets........	6,000	9,600	3,600	900
Unrealized receivables.....	0	8,400	8,400	2,100
Goodwill..................	0	12,000	12,000	3,000
Total....................	$20,000	$46,800	$26,800	$6,700

L receives $11,700 cash from the partnership in retirement of his partnership interest, and has a basis of $5,000. If there is no partnership agreement covering goodwill, L's payments are treated as follows:

	Cash	Basis	Gain
Income payments:			
Unrealized receivables............	$ 2,100	$ 0	$2,100
Goodwill........................	3,000	0	3,000
Subtotal.......................	$ 5,100	$ 0	$5,100
Property payments:			
Cash...........................	$ 2,500	$2,500	$ 0
Investments.....................	1,700	1,000	700
Section 1231 assets.............	2,400	1,500	900
Subtotal.......................	$ 6,600	$5,000	$1,600
Total.........................	$11,700	$5,000	$6,700

---

[61] § 707(c).   [62] § 736(b).

L reports ordinary income of $5,100 and capital gain of $1,600. The partnership has a $5,100 deduction and a $6,600 nondeductible liquidating distribution.

In contrast, if the partnership agreement included goodwill with the property payment, L's ordinary income would be just $2,100 from the unrealized receivables and $4,600 capital gain. This is identical to the effect if L had sold his interest for $11,700. The partnership's deduction also is reduced to $2,100 and the nondeductible distribution is $9,600.

The primary advantage of the partnership retiring a partner's interest, compared with the partners purchasing the interest, is the flexibility allowed for goodwill payments (as illustrated above).

As previously stated, the amount realized includes the retiring partner's share of partnership liabilities, and property payments are ordinary gain to the extent of the partner's share of gain on substantially appreciated inventory.

The total amount of a payment allocated to property cannot exceed the fair market value of the property. Thus, any payment to be made in excess of the property's value is treated as an income payment.

Example 24.   P, a 20% partner, is retiring from a partnership when the records show the following:

	Partnership's Basis	Fair Market Value	Appreciation Total	Appreciation P's Share
Cash......................	$ 5,000	$ 5,000	$ 0	$ 0
Receivables...............	35,000	35,000	0	0
Inventory..................	40,000	70,000	30,000	6,000
Equipment................	220,000	223,000	3,000	600
Section 1245 gain..........	0	7,000	7,000	1,400
Goodwill..................	0	40,000	40,000	8,000
Liabilities..................	(50,000)	(50,000)	0	0
Net assets..............	$250,000	$330,000	$80,000	$16,000

Recall that the § 1245 gain qualifies as an unrealized receivable.

P receives $66,000 cash from the partnership in retirement of her partnership interest and has a basis of $60,000. The amount realized is $76,000 ($66,000 + 20% × $50,000) and P's gain is $16,000 ($76,000 − $60,000). Inventory is substantially appreciated since it meets both tests. If there is no partnership agreement covering goodwill, P's payments are as follows:

	Cash	Basis	Gain
Income payments:			
Unrealized receivables............	$ 1,400	$ 0	$ 1,400
Goodwill.........................	8,000	0	8,000
Subtotal.......................	$9,400	$ 0	$ 9,400
Property payments:			
Cash............................	$ 1,000	$ 1,000	$ 0
Receivables.....................	7,000	7,000	0
Inventory.......................	14,000	8,000	6,000
Section 1231 assets..............	44,600	44,000	600
Subtotal.......................	$66,600	$60,000	$ 6,600
Total........................	$76,000	$60,000	$16,000

P has ordinary income of $15,400 ($9,400 income payments + $6,000 § 751 gain) and capital gain of $600 ($16,000 − $15,400). The partnership has a deduction of $9,400 and a $66,600 nondeductible liquidating distribution.

RETIREMENT WITH INSTALLMENTS

Although all parties might agree that a partnership will retire a partner's interest, it may not be possible or desirable for all the cash to be paid in one lump sum. When payments are fixed in amount but spread over more than one year, each one is allocated between the income and property payments. If there is no agreement to the contrary, a pro rata amount, based on relative total payments, is considered to be a property payment, and the remainder is an income payment. A property payment is treated as a return of the retiring partner's basis in his or her partnership interest until the entire basis is recovered and then as a gain on the deemed sale of the partnership interest. An underpayment in any year reduces the property payment amount first. When this occurs, payments in the next year(s) are considered to be a restoration of this underpayment.

> **Example 25.** Assume the same facts as in *Example 23*, except that $3,900 plus interest will be distributed to L for each of three years. Recall that L's $11,700 amount realized is composed of $5,000 return of basis in his partnership interest, $1,600 capital gain on the deemed sale of the partnership interest, and $5,100 ordinary income. Since property payments are approximately 56.4% ($6,600 ÷ $11,700) of total payments to be made, $2,200 (56.4% × $3,900) is a property payment and reduces L's basis in the partnership interest to $2,800 ($5,000 − $2,200). The remaining $1,700 ($3,900 − $2,200) is an income payment, and L recognizes this $1,700 as ordinary income. If only $3,350 is paid the first year, L still has a $2,200 return of basis but only $1,150 ordinary income ($3,350 − $2,200).

A partner may elect to report the gain from the property payments over the years that the payments are to be received.

Example 26.   Assume the same facts as in *Example 25*, except that L elects to report a pro rata amount of the gain from the property payments. Thus, L recognizes $533 capital gain [($2,200 ÷ $6,600) × $1,600 gain] and reduces his basis in the partnership interest to $3,333 [$5,000 − ($2,200 − $533)]. The income payment and ordinary income are not affected by this election.

Generally, if the agreement for retiring the partner's interest stipulates the allocation and timing of each class of payment, the tax treatment must follow the procedure outlined in the agreement.[63]

Example 27.   Assume the same facts as in *Example 25*, except that the agreement states that the first $6,600, excluding interest, is for property payments. Thus, when the first $3,900 is received, L reduces his basis in the partnership interest to $1,100 ($5,000 − $3,900) and recognizes no capital gain or ordinary income. When the second $3,900 is received, L reduces his basis to zero and recognizes a $1,600 capital gain from the deemed sale of the partnership interest and $1,200 ordinary income ($3,900 − $2,700). The final $3,900 payment is all ordinary income.

Recall that the retiring partner's share of partnership liabilities are deemed to be cash distributions when they are assumed by the other partners. This amount, in addition to cash, can be stipulated in the agreement to be a property payment.

OTHER DISPOSITIONS OF PARTNERSHIP CAPITAL INTERESTS

Partnership capital interests may be disposed of in several ways other than by selling the interest. These include gifts, charitable contributions, incorporations, abandonments, forfeitures, foreclosures, and deaths of partners. The purpose here is to illustrate the special tax effects when Code sections relevant to these topics are applied to transfers of partnership interests.

GIFT OF A PARTNERSHIP INTEREST

A partner may give a capital interest in a partnership to an individual or to a trust that benefits an individual. Rules governing gift taxes payable by the donor and the basis and holding period of the donee are the same whether the transfer is of assets or of a partnership interest.[64] In these instances, the donor's basis in the partnership interest carries over to the donee. Thus, the potential recognition

---

[63]   Reg. § 1.736-1(b)(5)(iii).

[64]   See the discussion relating to gifts in Chapter 13.

of any gain due to appreciation for the partnership interest passes to the donee. This can be quite valuable in a family when the donor's marginal rate exceeds the donee's rate.

Generally, gifts are not subject to *income taxation*. There are some important exceptions, however. For example, if an owner's share of partnership debt exceeds the owner's basis in the partnership, the gift is divided into two portions, one qualifying as a sale and the other as a gift.[65] The sale portion must be determined first. For this calculation, a donor partner's share of partnership debt becomes the amount realized and the debt transferred in excess of basis in the partnership interest is ordinary income to the extent of the § 751 provisions. The *net gift* is the value of the property transferred less the amount realized.

> **Example 28.** L gives his partnership capital interest to his daughter, S. At the time of the transfer, the value of L's share of partnership property is $50,000, his share of partnership debt is $15,000, and his basis in the partnership is $5,000. Since debt exceeds basis, L must report a $10,000 gain ($15,000 amount realized − $5,000 basis in the partnership interest) for income tax purposes. The net gift is $35,000 ($50,000 fair market value − $15,000 amount realized).

Gifts of a partnership interest also may result in income recognition to the donor if the partnership has unrealized trade receivables. In the case of a cash basis partnership, the gift of accounts receivable could be considered a taxable assignment of income, especially if a significant portion has been earned by the donor. In addition, the gift of an interest in a partnership that has installment notes receivable could be considered a taxable disposition of the notes.[66]

CHARITABLE CONTRIBUTION OF A PARTNERSHIP INTEREST

Rules governing contributions of partnership capital interests to charitable organizations are similar to those applicable to non-charitable gifts.[67] That is, the contribution is not subject to any special treatment. However, there are two exceptions for charitable contributions that do not affect other gifts. One applies when debt transferred exceeds the basis of the capital interest transferred. Unlike gifts to individuals, calculations for charitable contributions in these situations require an allocation of the donor partner's basis between the sale portion and the contribution portion of the transfer.[68]

---

[65] Reg. § 1.1001-1(e).

[66] Rev. Rul. 60-352, 1960-2 C.B. 208 takes this position regarding a charitable gift, and this is the result of § 751. However, this position is questionable.

[67] See the discussion relating to gifts in Chapter 13.

[68] Reg. § 1.1011(b).

Example 29.   Assume the same facts as in *Example 28* (i.e., $50,000 market value, $5,000 basis, and $15,000 partnership debt), except that L contributes his interest to a charity. The amount realized on the sale portion is $15,000, the applicable basis is only $1,500 [($15,000 amount deemed realized ÷ $50,000 fair market value) × $5,000 basis], and the reportable gain is $13,500 ($15,000 amount realized − $1,500 basis allocable to the sale portion). The net charitable contribution of $35,000 ($50,000 fair market value − $15,000 sale portion) is subject to the general rules applicable to all charitable contributions of property.

A second exception applies when ordinary income would have been recognized if the partnership interest had been sold at its market value.[69] In this situation, the donor must reduce the charitable deduction by the amount of the potential ordinary income.

Example 30.   G contributes her partnership interest, valued at $43,000, to a charity. If G had sold her interest, she would have recognized $11,000 as ordinary income from § 751 assets. G's charitable deduction is $32,000 ($43,000 − $11,000). Note that G's basis in the partnership interest is not relevant to this situation.

INCORPORATION OF A PARTNERSHIP

Contributions of property in exchange for a partnership interest are discussed at the beginning of this chapter. In addition, there is a brief comparison of these contributions with those made in exchange for corporate stock (see also the discussion in Chapter 2). Recall two major differences:

1.   Contributions of property in exchange for corporate stock under § 351 are tax-free only if the contributors own at least 80 percent of the corporation's stock after the contribution.

2.   A shareholder's basis in stock is unaffected by corporate debt.

When partnership property and debt are exchanged for corporate stock, the 80 percent rule must be met or the transfer is taxable. The transaction is taxable even if the 80 percent rule is met, however, to the extent that any *boot* is received. Boot includes all receipts other than the corporation's stock. In addition, if partnership debt exceeds the partnership's basis in the property, the excess is considered gain from a sale or exchange.[70] The result is the same as discussed previously in connection with gifts of partnership property not qualifying as char-

---

[69]   §§ 170(e). Additional restrictions apply to capital gain property when the contribution is to a private foundation.

[70]   § 357(c).

itable contributions (see *Example 28*). In some instances, the partners may avoid this tax effect by not transferring a portion of the partnership liabilities to the corporation.

The incorporation of a cash basis partnership can result in a shift of income from the partnership that earned the income to the corporation that collected the cash. It is possible that the IRS will use the *assignment of income principle* in these situations to reallocate income or deductions between the partnership and corporation. However, a revenue ruling indicates this argument will not be used when there is no evidence of intentional tax avoidance.[71]

ABANDONMENTS, FORFEITURES, AND FORECLOSURES

The abandonment or forfeiture of a partnership interest and a mortgagee's foreclosure on partnership property are taxable events. If the partner's basis exceeds his or her share of partnership liabilities, the difference is a *capital loss*.[72] In contrast, when the partner's share of partnership liabilities exceeds the basis in the partnership, the same tax consequences as discussed in connection with gifts and incorporation apply. That is, the abandonment, forfeiture, or foreclosure is treated, in part, as a sale. When this occurs, the amount realized is the partner's share of partnership debt, regardless of the market value of the property. In fact, the Supreme Court has held the amount realized was the partner's share of nonrecourse debt, even though the debt exceeded the fair market value of the property.[73]

LIKE-KIND EXCHANGES

Code § 1031 makes it clear that an exchange of partnership *interest* cannot qualify for the like-kind exchange rules under any circumstances. Nevertheless, an exchange of a partnership's *assets* still may qualify for the deferral of realized gain available with the like-kind provisions if all requirements are met. Of course, such exchanges and elections must be made at the partnership level and are applicable to all partners.

---

[71] Rev. Rul. 80-198, 1980-2 C.B. 113.

[72] See § 741 and *Neil J. O'Brien*, 77 T.C. 113 (1981).

[73] *Comm. v. Tufts*, 83-1 USTC ¶9328, 51 AFTR2d 83-1132, 103 U.S. 1826 (USSC, 1983), *rev'g*. 81-2 USTC ¶9574, 48 AFTR2d 81-5660, 651 F.2d 1058 (CA-5, 1981), *rev'g* 70 T.C. 756 (1978) and *Millar v. Comm.*, 78-2 USTC ¶9514, 42 AFTR2d 78-5246, 577 F.2d 212 (CA-3, 1978), *aff'g in part* 67 T.C. 656 (1977).

DEATH OF A PARTNER

There is no taxable gain or loss on the transfer of a partnership interest due to the death of a partner. This is true even if the deceased partner's share of partnership debt exceeds his or her basis in the partnership. In addition, there is no recapture of tax credits. As is the case for all inherited assets, the beneficiary receives the partnership interest with a stepped-up (or stepped-down, as the situation might be) basis.[74]

The transfer of a partnership interest on the death of a partner is not considered to be a sale or exchange. Consequently, the partnership is not terminated if the deceased partner's interest exceeded 50 percent. The partnership also is not terminated if it had been a two-person partnership, as long as the estate or other party shares in the profits and losses.[75] Unless specified in the partnership agreement, the partnership's taxable year does not close for the transfer of the deceased partner's interest to the estate nor to the parties who inherit the interest. The taxable year does close for the seller, however, if the inherited interest is sold or exchanged, and closes for the partnership if more than 50 percent of the partnership's interest is disposed of (other than through death) within a twelve-month period. If the interest is liquidated with partnership distributions, the partnership continues until all distributions are made to the deceased partner's successor.[76]

OPTIONAL ADJUSTMENT TO BASIS

The Internal Revenue Code combines the entity and aggregate concepts in determining the taxability of partnership distributions and sales of partnership capital interests. In some situations, there is no taxable gain or loss to the partners; in some, there is only capital gain or loss; and in others, there is both ordinary gain and either capital gain or loss.

Unless specifically elected otherwise, any gain or loss reported by a partner has no effect on the partnership or on the other partners.[77] This follows the entity concept and is identical to the tax treatment of a corporation and its stockholders. However, because the aggregate or conduit concept is used to calculate net operating income, this applicability of the entity concept can create inequities. These are particularly evident when a capital interest in a partnership with appreciated assets is sold. The selling partner reports gain on the sale, but the purchasing partner must accept the old basis of the assets for purposes of depreciation, amortization, depletion, and gain or loss. This results in the new partner reporting more net income (or less loss) from the partnership. Further confusing the situation, this partner's *outside basis* (basis in the partnership interest) exceeds his or her *inside basis* (basis in the partnership's assets).

---

[74] See the discussion in Chapter 13 regarding transfers of property at death.

[75] Reg. § 1.708-1(b)(1)(i)(a).

[76] See Reg. §§ 1.708-1(b)(1)(i) and 1.736-1(a)(6).

[77] §§ 734(a) and 743(a).

Example 31. A partnership has the following information:

	Partnership's Basis	Fair Market Value
Cash..................................	$10,000	$ 10,000
Section 1231 assets...................	80,000	140,000
Total assets..........................	$90,000	$150,000
Liabilities.............................	$21,000	$ 21,000
Capital accounts......................	69,000	129,000
Total equities........................	$90,000	$150,000

R purchases T's one-third interest in the partnership for $43,000 and assumes responsibility for her share of existing liabilities. T's basis, including partnership liabilities, is $30,000. Recall from the previous discussion that she will report a gain of $20,000 ($43,000 + $7,000 liabilities − $30,000). If $45,000 of the $60,000 difference in § 1231 assets qualifies as potential depreciation recapture, her ordinary income is $15,000 (one-third of $45,000) and her capital gain is $5,000 ($20,000 − $15,000). R's basis in the partnership is his purchase price of $43,000 plus his $7,000 share of the partnership liabilities, for a total outside basis of $50,000. His inside basis is T's inside basis of $30,000 (one-third of $90,000). The difference between R's outside and inside basis is equal to the gain reported by T. R's annual partnership net income will be determined in the same manner as the other partners. That is, depreciation, gain, and loss on § 1231 assets will be calculated on the $80,000 basis.

REQUIRED ELECTION

The inequities encountered by the new partner are quite similar to those that exist when a partner contributes appreciated property in exchange for a capital interest. As discussed in Chapter 10, these inequities can be alleviated with the use of special allocations. However, the Code provides an alternative that is often more attractive in the present type of situation. A partnership may elect that the basis of its property will be adjusted when partners sell a capital interest and when property is distributed to partners.[78] The initial election is included with the annual partnership return.[79] In the case of a sale, the partnership property is adjusted for the difference between the purchasing partner's outside basis and inside basis. The benefit of this adjustment accrues solely to the purchasing partner.[80]

---

[78] §§ 754, 743(a), and 734(a).   [80] § 743(b).

[79] Reg. § 1.754-1.

Example 32.   Assume the same facts as in *Example 31*, except that the partnership has made the adjustment to basis election. This election has no effect on T, the selling partner, or on the other partners. It does affect the partnership's basis in the assets but only with respect to R, the purchasing partner. The partnership's basis in the § 1231 assets is increased by the $20,000 difference between R's outside and inside bases to $100,000. R's inside basis in the partnership is increased by this same $20,000 to $50,000, and now equals his outside basis. For purposes of depreciation, gain, and loss relating to the § 1231 assets, R's share is computed on a basis of $46,667 [($\frac{1}{3}$ of $80,000) + the $20,000 adjustment], while computations for the other partners remain as they were before T's sale to R. That is, they are computed on a basis of $53,333 ($\frac{2}{3}$ of $80,000).

The discussion and examples above pertain to sales when gains result. The reverse occurs when losses result. That is, the basis of the partnership's assets are decreased with respect to the purchasing partner.

The optional adjustment to basis is more complicated when applied to *distributions* to partners.[81] If the election is in effect, the basis in partnership property is *increased* by the following amounts:

1.   All gains recognized by partners receiving the property

2.   The amount that the partnership's basis for distributed property exceeds that property's basis to the partner receiving it

Example 33.   N receives $15,000 cash when her basis in the partnership is $12,000. N recognizes $3,000 gain. If the optional adjustment to basis election is in effect, the basis of partnership assets will be increased by the $3,000.

Example 34.   M receives investment land with a partnership basis of $15,000 when his basis in the partnership is $12,000. M has no recognized gain but his basis in the land is limited to his $12,000 partnership basis. If the optional adjustment to basis election is in effect, the basis of the partnership's remaining assets will be increased by the $3,000.

The amount of the increase to a partnership's basis in property is allocated in two steps. *First*, the allocation is between two classes of property: (1) capital assets and § 1231 assets, and (2) all other property.[82]   *Second*, the allocation is among the properties in each of these two classes.[83]   In the first step, the allocation is based on relative values of net appreciation (total market values less total basis). If either class has a total basis exceeding the total market value, all

---

[81]   §§ 754 and 734.

[82]   § 755(b).

[83]   § 755(c).

of the increase is assigned to the other class. In the second step, the allocation is made only among those assets with a market value in excess of basis. However, the partnership may be able to obtain permission from the IRS to allocate the increase in the second step (but not the first step) among *all* assets, including those with a basis in excess of market value.[84] As a result, some assets would be increased and some decreased such that the net change would be equal to the net appreciation for that class. This produces a more equitable allocation that reflects the relationship existing among the assets.

Example 35. XYZ partnership has the following property after a distribution was made that resulted in a $3,000 recognized gain to the partner:

	Market Value	Basis	Appreciation
Capital and § 1231 assets:			
Land	$34,000	$30,000	$ 4,000
Equipment	20,000	21,000	(1,000)
Goodwill	12,000	0	12,000
Total	$66,000	$51,000	$15,000
Other property:			
Inventory	23,000	20,000	3,000
Total	$89,000	$71,000	$18,000

The $3,000 is allocated in the following manner: (1) $2,500 [($15,000 ÷ $18,000) × $3,000] to capital assets and § 1231 assets, and (2) $500 ($3,000 − $2,500) to other property, in this case inventory. The $2,500 increases the basis of land by $625 [$4,000 ÷ ($4,000 + $12,000) = 0.25 × $2,500], the basis of goodwill by $1,875 ($2,500 − $625), and has no effect on equipment. However, if permission is obtained from the IRS, the $2,500 increases the basis of land by $667 [($4,000 ÷ $15,000) × $2,500] and the basis of goodwill by $2,000 [($12,000 ÷ $15,000) × $2,500] but *decreases* the basis of equipment by $167 [($1,000 ÷ $15,000) × $2,500]. Considering the assets involved, it is unlikely the partnership would desire the permission in this example. This is because the loss of basis in a depreciable asset is offset by increases in nondepreciable assets.

Similar to the above discussion on increases, the bases of partnership assets may be decreased. If the optional adjustment to basis election is in effect *and* this is a *liquidating* distribution, the basis in partnership property is *decreased* by the following amounts:

1. All losses recognized by partners receiving the property

2. The amount that the basis for the distributed property to the partners receiving it exceeds the partnership's basis in that property

---

[84] Reg. § 1.755-1(a)(2).

Example 36.   P receives $12,000 cash to liquidate her capital interest when her basis in the partnership is $15,000. P recognizes a capital loss of $3,000. If the optional adjustment to basis election is in effect, the basis of partnership assets will be decreased by the $3,000.

Example 37.   Q receives investment land with a partnership basis of $12,000 to liquidate his capital interest when his basis in the partnership is $15,000. Q has no recognized loss, but his basis in the land is increased to his $15,000 partnership basis. If the optional adjustment to basis election is in effect, the basis of partnership assets will be decreased by the $3,000.

Example 38.   Refer to *Example 35*. Assume the same numbers but reverse the signs. That is, the $3,000 is a recognized loss and the basis in assets exceeds the market values by $18,000. The calculations are identical to *Example 35*, except each allocation *reduces* the basis in the asset.

There is one instance when a partner is treated as though the optional adjustment to basis is in effect even if it is not. This occurs when property is distributed to a partner who acquired a capital interest within the last two years. The partnership's basis in the property distributed to this partner is adjusted to reflect the purchase price as though the election had been in effect.[85]

If at least 50 percent of the partnership interest is sold or exchanged within 12 months, the optional adjustment to basis election is inapplicable. This is because the partnership terminates and assets are written up or down automatically on the deemed distribution and then these amounts are transferred to the new partnership.

Once the optional adjustment to basis election is made it applies to all sales, distributions, and partner deaths in the year of election and in future years unless the partnership is given permission to revoke the election.[86] If a request for revocation is filed within 30 days after the year-end, it may be retroactively applied to the preceding year. Reasons considered acceptable for approval include a change in the nature of the partnership's business, a substantial increase or change in character of the partnership's assets, or frequent transactions requiring adjustments that result in an administrative burden for the partnership. Approval will not be given when the primary purpose of the revocation is to avoid decreasing the basis of the partnership assets.[87]

---

[85] § 732(d).

[86] § 754.

[87] Reg. § 1.754-2(c).

TAX PLANNING WITH A PARTNERSHIP

Partnerships provide excellent income-splitting opportunities among family members. Children can be employees of their parents' partnership. The amount of salary paid is, of course, dependent on the work performed. Significant tax savings can be achieved through family partnerships. The benefits and difficulties of dependent children as partners were discussed in the chapter. In addition, partnership income may be used to establish an Individual Retirement Account or a Keogh retirement account.

DISPOSING OF PARTNERSHIP INTERESTS

The liquidation of a partnership interest results in ordinary gain under § 751 to the extent of unrealized receivables (including depreciation recapture) and substantially appreciated inventory. In some instances, it may be beneficial for the exiting partner to negotiate an installment sale. This allows the partner to defer recognition of a portion of the gain until proceeds are received. One negative factor, however, is that the partner's share of the partnership debt is included in the amount realized and also in the amount received at the time of sale.

Partners are not taxed when they receive a pro rata distribution of § 751 assets. Thus, tax benefits may be achieved if a partnership makes a pro rata distribution of § 751 assets and of non–§ 751 assets to liquidating partners. This can occur whether the partnership is being liquidated or not. Gain is avoided, however, only as long as the distributed assets are not sold by the partners. The § 751 ordinary income taint is removed from the substantially appreciated inventory after five years but is removed from the unrealized receivables only on the death of the partner. In any case, partners may obtain deferral benefits by disposing of these assets over time or on an installment contract. Capital gains treatment does not adhere to the non–§ 751 assets. Capital gains are available only if these assets continue to qualify for capital gains treatment in the hands of the distributee partner. Although distribution of noncash assets can be complicated, the benefits may warrant the extra planning necessary. In many instances, a partnership can make adjustments that result in inventory being classified as a non–§ 751 asset. This was discussed in the chapter, but it is sufficiently important and overlooked so often that it is worth repeating.

When one or more partners plan to dispose of at least 50 percent of a partnership's capital and profits interest, tax planning can be very important for those partners retaining an interest in the partnership. Under § 708, a partnership terminates for all partners when 50 percent or more of its capital and profits interest is transferred (other than by death of a partner) within a 12-month period. Unless the 50 percent requirement is met, the partnership's year closes for terminating partners but not for continuing partners. Consequently, it is usually in the continuing partners' best interest to avoid a 50 percent transfer within 12 months. It is advisable to include a provision in the partnership agreement to this effect.

PROBLEM MATERIALS

DISCUSSION QUESTIONS

11-1   *Family Partnerships.*   Why are family partnerships subject to special rules? How do the tax effects for a family partnership differ from those of other partnerships?

11-2   *Family Partnerships.*   Why is a service business generally not appropriate for a family partnership? When is it appropriate? Give examples of what qualifies as capital in determining whether it is a material income-producing factor.

11-3   *Family Partnerships.*   When are special partnership allocations required between (a) a donor and a donee and (b) a donor or donee and an unrelated partner? Explain.

11-4   *Limited Partnerships.*   Under what circumstances is a limited partnership more beneficial than a general partnership? Explain.

11-5   *Tax Shelters.*   What are the characteristics and tax benefits of a tax shelter?

11-6   *General Partnerships.*   What are the tax advantages to active partners of a real estate general partnership compared with an oil-drilling general partnership? Explain.

11-7   *Publicly Traded Partnerships (PTPs).*   S has owned a capital interest in a PTP since 1985. Based on the tax provisions passed in 1987, should S be advised to sell this interest? Explain.

11-8   *Distributions—Current.*   Under what circumstances do current nonliquidating partnership distributions to partners result in gain or loss to the partners?

11-9   *Distributions—Liquidating.*   Under what circumstances do liquidating partnership distributions to partners result in gain or loss to the partners?

11-10   *Section 751 Assets.*   What are unrealized receivables? What is the justification for treating a portion of the gain on the sale of a partnership interest as ordinary income?

11-11   *Section 751 Assets.*   What is meant by "tainted" inventory received from a partnership in a current or liquidating distribution? How is the taint removed?

11-12   *Aggregate/Conduit vs. Entity.*   How does the aggregate/conduit theory differ from the entity theory? Discuss how the transactions below would be treated under (a) the aggregate/conduit theory and (b) the entity theory.

    a.   G, a 20 percent partner in a CPA firm, sells the partnership interest to Z.

    b.   H receives a cash distribution that exceeds H's basis in the partnership interest.

    c.   A liquidating partnership distributes the inventory to its owners according to their profit and loss sharing ratios. Neither the basis nor the value of the inventory exceeds any of the partners' bases in the partnership.

11-13 *Selling vs. Retiring a Capital Interest.* What are the possible tax effects for the partner and the partnership when a capital interest is retired by the partnership? How do the tax effects differ when a partnership interest is sold to the other partners directly?

11-14 *Gifts of Capital Interests.* Does a partner have taxable income when giving a partnership interest to (a) a relative or (b) a charity? Does a partner have a deduction for either of these gifts? Explain each answer.

11-15 *Inside vs. Outside Basis.* How can the inside and outside bases of a partner be different? What are the potential inequities of this difference?

PROBLEMS

11-16 *Family Partnerships.* W, A, and E are members of a partnership and share profits and losses equally. Capital is a material income-producing factor for the partnership. Ordinary income for the year is $100,000. Although W is the only partner working in the partnership, no salary is paid or distributed to W. The value of W's work is approximately $30,000. Partners' capital account balances before the current year's income are $50,000 for W and $25,000 each for A and E. Assume you are an IRS agent auditing the partnership return. How much of the $100,000 would you deem taxable to W, to A, and to E, assuming (a) W, A, and E are unrelated, (b) A and E are W's children, 14 and 15 years old, and that a donor/donee relationship exists, or (c) same as b except E is a cousin to W?

11-17 *Sections 704(d) and 465.* A cattle ranch, operated as a partnership, has the following year-end information for a four year period:

	Year 1	Year 2	Year 3	Year 4
Net income (loss)................	($90,000)	($40,000)	$20,000	$40,000
Cash to partners................	0	45,000	30,000	20,000
Recourse debt...................	45,000	42,000	39,000	36,000
Nonrecourse debt...............	80,000	70,000	60,000	50,000

G acquired a 10 percent interest at the beginning of year 1 for $20,000. He has received his 10 percent share of the profits and losses and of the cash during the four years. G is a general partner who actively participates in the partnership business. Calculate his § 704(d) basis and his § 465 at-risk amount at the beginning of years 2 through 5.

11-18 *Sections 704(d) and 465.* Refer to Problem 11-17, but assume the partnership activity is a real estate leasing business. Calculate G's § 704(d) basis and his § 465 at-risk amount at the beginning of years 2 through 5.

11-19   *Current Distributions—Proportionate.*   X is a 50 percent partner in XY, a calendar year partnership. X had a basis in her partnership interest of $10,000 at the beginning of the year. On October 1, she and the other partner withdrew $15,000 each. The partnership's net earnings for the year are $60,000.

    a.   How much gain or loss must X recognize on October 1?

    b.   What is X's taxable income for the year, and what is her basis in her partnership interest at the end of the year?

    c.   How would the answers to (a) and (b) change if partnership earnings had been $6,000 instead of $60,000?

11-20   *Current Distribution—Proportionate.*   B Partnership proposes making a proportionate current distribution to each of its two equal partners of *either* (a) $50,000 cash or (b) partnership inventory ($50,000 market value and $28,000 basis). Prior to any distribution, K's basis in his partnership interest is $40,000. The partnership has no unrealized receivables or substantially appreciated inventory. Based on these facts, what are the tax consequences of the alternative distributions, and what factors should K consider in deciding which alternative to accept?

11-21   *Current Distribution—Proportionate.*   During the current year, partner J received a proportionate distribution from HIJK Partnership, consisting of $13,000 cash and marketable securities (an investment asset to the partnership). The securities had a basis to the partnership of $20,000 and FMV of $33,000. Prior to the distribution, J's basis in his partnership interest was $40,000. The distribution had no effect on J's profit and loss sharing ratio.

    a.   How much gain or loss must J recognize because of this distribution? What basis will J have in the securities? What basis will J have in his partnership interest after the distribution?

    b.   Does the partnership recognize any gain for the distribution of the appreciated securities to J?

    c.   How would the answer to (a) change if J's basis in his interest prior to distribution had been $25,000 rather than $40,000?

11-22   *Current Distribution—Proportionate.*   A partnership makes a current distribution to its owners, based on their capital interests. M receives his 10 percent share of inventory with a basis of $7,000, a market value of $11,000, and a note against it of $3,000.

    a.   Calculate M's gain or loss on the distribution and basis in the partnership after the distribution if his basis in the partnership before the distribution is (1) $15,000, or (2) $4,000.

    b.   Calculate the effect on M's A.G.I. if the $3,000 note is paid by M and the inventory is sold for $12,500 15 months later. M has held the inventory as an investment.

11-23   *Optional Adjustment to Basis—Current Proportionate Distribution.* Refer to Problem 11-22(a). The partnership has a § 754 election in effect. Determine the basis adjustment for the partnership assets.

11-24 *Current Distribution—Proportionate.*   A partnership is curtailing some of its operations and distributing excess assets to its two equal partners. P receives 10 percent of all assets as follows:

	Fair Market Value	Basis
Cash..................................	$4,000	$4,000
Inventory..............................	7,000	5,000
Investment stocks......................	3,000	2,000
Equipment.............................	4,000	6,000

Calculate P's gain or loss, basis in each asset, and basis in the partnership after distribution if P's basis in the partnership before distribution is (a) $20,000, (b) $14,000, or (c) $8,000.

11-25 *Optional Adjustment to Basis—Current Proportionate Distribution.* Refer to Problem 11-24. The partnership has a § 754 election in effect. Determine the basis adjustment for the partnership assets.

11-26 *Liquidating Distribution—Proportionate.*   The FN Partnership is liquidating. Before liquidation, the records show the following:

	Partnership's Basis	Fair Market Value
Cash.....................................	$ 40,000	$ 40,000
Equipment................................	100,000	70,000
Accumulated depreciation	(60,000)	
Capital assets............................	10,000	30,000
Owners capital	90,000	140,000

F, a 50 percent owner, receives one-half of all the assets. F's basis in the partnership is $45,000. Calculate F's ordinary gain and capital gain or loss on the distribution and F's basis for each asset.

11-27 *Liquidating Distribution—Disproportionate.*   Refer to the information in Problem 11-26, but assume that F receives all the equipment (purchased four years ago). Calculate both F's and FN's ordinary gain and capital gain or loss on the distribution and both F's and FN's basis for each asset.

11-28 *Substantially Appreciated Inventory.*   A partnership has the following assets:

	Basis	Fair Market Value
Cash...	$10,000	$10,000
Accounts receivable	15,000	15,000
Inventory.....................................	30,000	38,000
Capital assets................................	40,000	46,000

a.   According to the Regulations, is the inventory substantially appreciated?

b.   How would the answer to (a) change if the inventory had a basis of $25,000 instead of $30,000?

11-29 *Distribution—Disproportionate.* RHS is a cash basis, calendar year partnership. At the beginning of the year, it had the following assets and liabilities:

	Basis	Fair Market Value
Cash	$10,000	$10,000
Accounts receivable	0	15,000
Owners capital	10,000	25,000

R, who was having cash flow problems, wanted to reduce his interest in the partnership. On January 1, he received $8,333 cash, reducing his interest from two-thirds to one-third. How much gain or loss must R and RHS recognize as a result of the transaction?

11-30 *Sale of a Partnership Interest.* Partnership records of a CPA firm show the following:

	Partnership's Basis	Fair Market Value
Cash	$ 8,000	$ 8,000
Accounts receivable	0	40,000
Section 1231 assets	130,000	100,000
Accumulated depreciation	(50,000)	0
	$ 88,000	$148,000
Liabilities	$ 28,000	$ 28,000
Owners' capital	60,000	120,000
	$ 88,000	$148,000

There is potential § 1245 and § 1250 gain of $4,000. M, a 25 percent owner, has a basis in the partnership of $22,000 (including 25% of partnership liabilities). M sells the 25 percent interest to J for $30,000.

a. Calculate M's ordinary gain and capital gain or loss on the sale.
b. How would your answers differ if M's basis in the partnership had been $28,000?

11-31 *Optional Adjustment to Basis—Sale/Purchase.* Refer to Problem 11-30. During the first month after J purchases a 25 percent interest in the partnership, 50 percent of the accounts receivable ($20,000) are collected. Calculate (1) J's distributive share and (2) the other partners' distributive share, of ordinary income or capital gain as a result of this collection under each of the assumptions below:

a. There is no special election under § 754 for partnership assets to be adjusted for the sale in Problem 11-30.
b. There is a special election under § 754 for partnership assets to be adjusted for the sale in Problem 11-30.

11-32 *Sale of a Partnership Interest.*   Q sells her 5 percent partnership interest for $48,000 when her basis is $33,000. In the year of sale, Q receives $8,000 cash and a $40,000 note receivable. In addition, the buyer assumes Q's $12,000 share of partnership liabilities. The partnership has no § 751 assets. Q elects to recognize the gain on the installment basis. She has no other income except salary and interest.

    a.   Calculate the effect on Q's A.G.I. in the year of sale.

    b.   Calculate the effect on Q's A.G.I. in the year following the sale if she receives $5,000 in payment of the note plus $4,000 interest.

11-33 *Sale of a Partnership Interest.*   M is an equal partner in a three-person accrual basis partnership that has the following assets at year-end:

	Basis	Fair Market Value
Cash	$100,000	$100,000
Accounts receivable	100,000	100,000
Land	130,000	160,000
Notes payable	(60,000)	(60,000)
Net Assets	$270,000	$300,000

M sells her entire partnership interest (basis of $110,000) to J for $100,000. Each partner has a capital account with a $90,000 basis and a $100,000 market value.

    a.   Calculate M's ordinary and capital gain on the sale.

    b.   What are J's outside and inside bases in his partnership interest if the partnership does not have a § 754 election in effect?

11-34 *Retiring a Capital Interest.*   A partnership's records show the following:

	Basis	Fair Market Value
Cash	$20,000	$20,000
Unrealized receivables	0	12,000
Section 1231 assets	60,000	60,000
Goodwill	0	16,000

E, a 30 percent partner, is retiring from the business. The agreed price is $32,400 and E's basis in her partnership interest is $24,000. E has no other income except salary and interest. E makes no special elections.

    a.   Determine the amount and character of E's includible income and the effect on partnership net income if the partnership agreement does not mention goodwill.

    b.   Determine the amount and character of E's includible income and the effect on partnership net income if the partnership agreement states goodwill is to be included in the property payments.

    c.   Determine the amount and character of E's includible income and the effect on partnership net income if the partnership agreement does not mention goodwill and the $32,400 will be paid in five equal amounts over five years. E receives $6,480 in the first year.

11-35 *Payments to a Retiring Partner.*   The balance sheet of RST Partnership shows the following:

	Basis	Fair Market Value
Cash...	$ 30,000	$ 30,000
Accounts receivable............................	20,000	20,000
Inventory.......................................	105,000	112,000
§ 1231 assets.................................	94,000	147,000
	$249,000	$309,000
Liabilities.....................................	$ 9,000	$ 9,000
R, capital......................................	80,000	100,000
S, Capital......................................	80,000	100,000
T, Capital......................................	80,000	100,000
	$249,000	$309,000

The § 1231 assets include potential § 1245 gain of $17,000. During the current year, partners S and T agree to liquidate R's interest in the partnership for $115,000, to be paid in annual installments of $23,000 each over a five-year period. The partnership agreement does not specify that any amount of the payment is for partnership goodwill. R's basis in his interest (including his one-third share of partnership liabilities) is $83,000.

a.   What are the tax consequences to R of the series of cash distributions from the partnership?

b.   What are the consequences to the partnership of the liquidating distributions?

11-36 *Section 754 Election and Partnership Distributions.*   Refer to the facts in Problem 11-35. What are the tax consequences to the continuing partnership if a § 754 election is in effect for the year in which R's interest is liquidated?

11-37 *Sale of a Partnership Interest.*   Refer to the facts in Problem 11-35. Assume that U, an unrelated party, will purchase R's interest in RST Partnership for a lump sum payment of $115,000.

a.   What are the tax consequences of the sale to R?

b.   What are U's inside and outside bases in the partnership if no § 754 election is in effect?

11-38 *Consequences of a § 754 Election to a Purchasing Partner.*   Refer to the facts in Problem 11-37. What are the tax consequences to new partner U and to RST Partnership if a § 754 election is in effect for the year in which U purchases R's partnership interest?

11-39 *Disposition of a Capital Interest.*   K owns a 5 percent interest in a partnership. Her interest in the partnership includes $11,000 market value of the assets, $8,000 partnership debt, and $2,000 basis in the partnership. What are the tax consequences to K in each of the following situations? The debts are assumed by the new owner in each case.

a. . K sells the interest for $3,000 cash.

b.   K gives the interest to her son.

c.   K gives the interest to a university.

d.   K dies and leaves the interest to her son.

11-40 *Optional Adjustment to Basis—Current Distribution.* A partnership has the following information after property distributions to partners:

	Basis	Fair Market Value
Cash	$ 8,000	$ 8,000
Receivables	10,000	10,000
Inventory	8,000	28,000
Land	16,000	30,000
Building	94,000	120,000
Equipment	40,000	40,000
Goodwill	0	50,000

Partner distributions resulted in one partner receiving § 1231 property with a partnership basis that exceeded his basis in the partnership by $12,000. The partnership has a § 754 election in effect. Determine the basis of each partnership asset after the adjustments to basis are made.

RESEARCH PROBLEMS

11-41 *Family Partnership.* B operates a proprietorship that manufactures and sells utility tables. Net ordinary income has been increasing approximately 20 percent each year. Last year, net ordinary income was $60,000 on net assets of $225,000. B needs $75,000 to expand the business. Although B's daughter is only 13 years old, she plans to join her father in the business at some point in the future. B is considering forming a partnership with his daughter. His ownership interest would be 75 percent and hers would be 25 percent. If the daughter's interest is held in trust until she reaches 18, can B serve as the trustee without disqualifying the partnership arrangement?

Suggested research materials:

§ 704 and accompanying Regulations
Stern, 15 T.C. 521 (1950)
Bateman v. U.S., 74-1 USTC ¶9176, 33 AFTR2d 74-483, 490 F.2d 549 (CA-9, 1973)
Ginsberg v. Comm., 74-2 USTC ¶9660, 34 AFTR2d 74-5760, 502 F.2d 965 (CA-6, 1974)

11-42 *Corporate Partners.* M and Z are attorneys who wish to combine their proprietorship business activities. They intend to expand their activities and hire six employees. Some problems arise in their negotiations. First, they cannot agree on several tax elections. Second, they want to maximize the tax-deductible retirement contributions for themselves but do not want to include the six employees in the plan, even though this would violate the nondiscriminatory requirements for such plans. They ask you if they can avoid these problems by taking the following actions:

a. Transfer M's proprietorship assets to a newly created professional corporation controlled by M. The corporation will employ M.

b. Transfer Z's proprietorship assets to a newly created professional corporation controlled by Z. The corporation will employ Z.

c. The two newly created corporations form a partnership. The partnership hires the six employees and conducts all of the business activities. The assets remain in the corporations.

LEARNING OBJECTIVES

Upon completion of this chapter you will be able to:

- Identify the requirements necessary to elect S status

- Recognize the actions that terminate S status

- Compute the net operating income or loss for an S corporation and the impact of S corporate operations on shareholders' taxable income

- Recognize transactions between shareholders and their S corporations that are subject to special treatment

- Determine the shareholders' basis in the S corporation stock

- Determine the appropriate taxable year for an S corporation

- Explain the unique concepts relevant to family members

- Calculate gain or loss for the S corporation and its shareholders when asset distributions are made and the S corporation (1) has no AE&P or (2) has AE&P

- Calculate the special taxes on excessive passive income and on built-in gains

- Understand how dispositions of S corporate stock differ from those of C corporate stock

- Compare the four business organizations—proprietorships, partnerships, S corporations, and C corporations (see Appendix)

CHAPTER OUTLINE

Chapter 12

S CORPORATIONS

INTRODUCTION

Congress added Subchapter S to the Internal Revenue Code in 1958, giving birth to a unique tax entity: the S corporation. The S corporation is taxed in a manner very similar to a partnership, while retaining the legal characteristics of a corporation. In providing this distinctive treatment, Congressional intent was to allow small businesses to have "the advantages of the corporate form of organization without being made subject to the possible tax disadvantages of the corporation."[1] As this statement suggests, Congress recognized that many taxpayers who normally would incorporate their businesses to secure limited liability were reluctant to do so because of the possibility of double taxation. Accordingly, one of the major objectives of the Subchapter S legislation was to minimize taxes as a factor in the selection of the form of business organization. To accomplish this objective, a complete set of special rules were designed, most of which are contained in Subchapter S.

Although the treatment of S corporations was intended to be identical to that for partnerships, this goal was not achieved under the 1958 legislation. As originally written, the rules governing S corporations (or Subchapter S corporations as they were initially called) bore little resemblance to partnership rules. Many of these differences were eliminated, however, with the substantial modifications introduced by the Subchapter S Revision Act of 1982. Under the revised rules, Federal income tax treatment of S corporations and their shareholders is similar to that of partnerships and their partners. The S corporation is not subject to the corporate *Federal income tax*. Rather, like a partnership, the S corporation is merely a conduit. The income, deductions, gains, losses, and credits of the S corporation flow through to its shareholders. An S corporation, however, may be subject to a special tax such as the tax on excessive passive income or on built-in gains.

Even though the Federal income tax treatment of an S corporation resembles that of a partnership, the corporation is subject to many rules that apply to regular corporations. For example, since an S corporation is formed in the same manner as a regular corporation, the basic rules governing organization (i.e., the nonrecognition rules contained in § 351 concerning transfers to a controlled

---

[1] S. Rept. No. 1622, 83rd Cong., 2d Sess., 119 (1954).

corporation discussed in Chapter 2) of all corporations also apply to S corporations. Similarly, redemptions of an S corporation's stock, as well as liquidation and reorganization of an S corporation, generally are taxed according to the rules applying to regular corporations. As a practical matter, however, each provision must be closely examined to determine whether special treatment is provided S corporations.

S CORPORATION ELIGIBILITY REQUIREMENTS

The special tax treatment provided for S corporations is available only if the corporation is a *small business corporation*, and all of its shareholders *consent* to the corporation's election to be taxed under Subchapter S. A corporation is considered a small business corporation if it:[2]

1. Is an *eligible domestic* corporation;

2. Does not have more than thirty-five *eligible* shareholders; and

3. Has only *one class of stock* outstanding.

All of these requirements must be met when the election is made and at all times thereafter. Failure at any time to qualify as a small business corporation terminates the election, and as of the date of termination, the corporation is taxed as a regular corporation (hereafter referred to as a C corporation).[3]

The phrase *small business corporation* is clearly a misnomer. As the requirements for this status indicate, the sole restriction on the size of the corporation is the limitation imposed on the *number* of shareholders. Corporations are not denied use of Subchapter S due to the amount of their assets, income, net worth, or any other measure of size. In addition, the S corporation is not required to conduct an active business. Merely holding assets does not bar the corporation from Subchapter S.

ELIGIBLE CORPORATIONS

Subchapter S status is reserved for *eligible domestic corporations*.[4] Thus, foreign corporations do not qualify. In order for a domestic corporation to be eligible, it cannot be a member of an affiliated group. Consequently, an S corporation is prohibited from having an 80 percent owned subsidiary.[5] An important exception,

---

[2] § 1361.

[3] § 1362(d)(2).

[4] § 1361(b); Reg. § 1.1371-1(b) includes any U.S. territory as well as states.

[5] § 1361(b)(2)(A).

however, permits an S corporation to own 80 percent or more of an *inactive* subsidiary.[6] A subsidiary is generally considered inactive if (1) it has not begun business during the parent's taxable year, and (2) it has no gross income during the parent's taxable year.[7] This provision enables an S corporation to establish one or more inactive affiliates that may be used in the future.

> **Example 1.** An S corporation owns and operates a chain of restaurants in Arkansas. The restaurants have been so successful that the corporation is considering expanding to other states. In anticipation of expansion, the corporation established subsidiaries in each of the surrounding states to ensure that the company's name cannot be used by others. Although the corporation is a member of an affiliated group, the S election is not invalidated as long as the subsidiaries are inactive.

Other ineligible corporations include financial institutions, insurance companies, Domestic International Sales Corporations, and corporations electing Code § 936 Puerto Rico and United States Possessions tax credits.[8]

SHAREHOLDER REQUIREMENTS

Subchapter S imposes several restrictions on S corporation shareholders. Not only is the total number of shareholders limited to thirty-five, but certain parties are prohibited from owning stock of the corporation.

Type of Shareholder. The stock of an S corporation may be owned only by individuals who are citizens or resident aliens of the United States, estates, and certain trusts. Nonresident aliens (i.e., generally foreign citizens residing outside the United States), corporations, partnerships, and certain trusts are not allowed to hold stock in an S corporation. This prohibition is directly related to the limitation on the number of shareholders. Absent this prohibition, the thirty-five shareholder restriction could easily be defeated, for example, by allowing a partnership with more than thirty-five partners to own the S corporation stock. A similar result could be obtained if a trust with more than thirty-five beneficiaries were to own the stock. Consequently, acquisition of an S corporation's stock by any one of these parties terminates the election. Rules denying trusts as shareholders have been relaxed over the years. Four types of trusts may be shareholders: (1) grantor and § 678 trusts, (2) qualified Subchapter S trusts (QSSTs), (3) certain testamentary trusts, and (4) voting trusts.[9]

---

[6] § 1361(c)(6).

[7] §§ 1361(c)(6)(A) and (B).

[8] § 1361(b)(2).

[9] § 1361(c)(2). See Chapter 14 for a detailed discussion of trusts.

Number of Shareholders.   As a general rule, a corporation does not qualify as an S corporation if the number of shareholders exceeds 35 at any moment during the taxable year. After being altered several times over the past few years, this limitation on number of shareholders is identical to the private placement exemption of Federal securities laws.[10]

For purposes of counting the number of shareholders in an S corporation, stock owned by a husband and wife is treated as owned by one shareholder. This rule applies whether the stock is owned by the spouses separately or jointly. Consequently, it is possible for an S corporation to have 70 shareholders if all stock is owned by married couples. This treatment is not extended to couples who are divorced but continue to own the stock jointly. Similarly, other persons who are co-owners of the stock but who are not married are counted as separate shareholders.

When a permissible trust is a shareholder of the S corporation, the number of shareholders counted depends on the type of trust. For grantor and § 678 trusts, there is one deemed owner who is considered to be the shareholder. For testamentary trusts, the estate is deemed to be the sole shareholder rather than the beneficiaries. In the case of a QSST, there is one beneficiary who is treated as a shareholder. For a voting trust, each beneficiary is treated as a shareholder. Consequently, all qualifying trusts, *except* voting trusts, represent one shareholder.

When stock is held in the name of a nominee, agent, guardian, or custodian, the beneficial owner of the stock is treated as the shareholder.

> **Example 2.**   XYZ Bank and Trust, a corporation, holds legal title to stock in an S corporation. The corporation holds the stock for the benefit of R, a minor child. In this case, R, the beneficial owner, is treated as the shareholder rather than XYZ. As a result, the S corporation is not denied the benefits of Subchapter S because of a corporate shareholder.

> **Example 3.**   F holds stock in an S corporation as custodian for his two minor children. For purposes of counting shareholders, F is ignored and the children are counted as two separate shareholders.

ONE CLASS OF STOCK

In order to minimize the problems of allocating income of the S corporation among shareholders, the corporation is allowed only one class of stock outstanding. Stock that is authorized but unissued does not invalidate the election. For example, an S corporation may have authorized but unissued preferred stock. Similarly, outstanding stock rights, options, or convertible debentures may be issued without affecting the election.

---

[10]   Offerings of securities to 35 parties or fewer are exempt from registration under Federal securities laws.

Outstanding shares generally must provide identical rights to all shareholders. Differences in rights such as the amount of dividends a shareholder is entitled to or the amount that the shareholder would receive on liquidation are considered as creating a second class of stock, which causes the S election to be terminated. However, differences in *voting rights* are expressly authorized by the Code.[11] This exception enables control of the organization to be exercised in a manner that differs from stock ownership and income allocation.

> **Example 4.** R organized MND, an S corporation. MND issued two classes of common stock to R: class A voting and class B nonvoting stock. The rights represented by the stock are identical except for voting rights, and thus, do not invalidate the S election. Shortly after the organization of the corporation, R gives the class B nonvoting stock to her two children. Although R has shifted income and future appreciation of the stock to her children (assuming certain other requirements are satisfied), she has retained all of the voting control of the corporation.

Debt that does not meet certain rules may be reclassified as stock and thus terminate the S election. Safe-harbor rules provide that *straight debt* is not treated as a second class of stock if[12]

1. The interest rate and interest payment dates are not contingent on either the corporation's profits, management's discretion, or similar factors;

2. The instrument cannot be converted into stock; and

3. The creditor is an individual, estate, or trust that is eligible to hold stock in an S corporation.

Straight debt is defined as any written unconditional promise to pay on demand, or on a specified date, a certain sum of money.

Proposed regulations for § 1361 were issued October 15, 1990 with a *retroactive* effective date, which makes them applicable to all years after 1982. The proposed regulations provide that "non-conforming distributions" to shareholders generally will be treated as a distribution on stock. As a result, stock owned by the shareholders(s) receiving the "non-conforming distribution" will be reclassified as a second class of stock that automatically terminates the S election. Since distributions from S corporate earnings are required to be the same for each share of outstanding stock, a distribution is non-conforming when a stockholder's percentage of the distribution exceeds his or her ownership percentage. Consequently, if an S corporation erroneously paid a shareholder's expense in 1983 (or a later date), the S election was lost at that point and the corporation is

---

[11] § 1361(c)(4).   [12] § 1361(c)(5).

subject to taxation as a C corporation for the remainder of that year and for all future years, or until the S election is reinstated. At this writing, the S Corporation Taxation Committee of the AICPA is drafting comments to be submitted to the IRS requesting that changes be made to the proposed regulations, including a deferral of the effective date.

ELECTION OF S CORPORATION STATUS

A corporation that qualifies as a small business corporation is taxed according to the rules of Subchapter S only if the corporation elects to be an S corporation. This election exempts the business from the corporate income tax and all other Federal income taxes normally imposed on corporations except for (1) the tax on excessive passive investment income, (2) the tax on built-in gains, and (3) the tax from the recapture of investment credits claimed by the corporation prior to the election. In addition, the corporation normally is exempt from the personal holding company tax and the accumulated earnings tax. Although the S corporation generally avoids taxation as a regular corporation, most rules governing regular corporations such as those concerning organization, redemptions, and liquidations apply.

MAKING THE ELECTION: MANNER AND PERIOD OF EFFECT

In order for a corporation to be taxed according to the rules of Subchapter S, an election must be filed on Form 2553. The effective date of the election, as well as the required shareholder consents that must be evidenced on the form, generally depend on when the election is filed.

Current-Year Election.   To be effective for the corporation's current taxable year, the election must be filed by the fifteenth day of the third month of the corporation's taxable year (e.g., March 15 for a calendar year S corporation).[13] In addition, consent to the election must be obtained not only from all shareholders holding stock at the time of election, but also from former shareholders who have held stock during the earlier portion of that taxable year.[14] The consent of former shareholders is required since they will be allocated a share of the income, losses, and other items applicable to the time they held the stock. If only the consent of former shareholders is lacking, the election is effective for the following taxable year. Similarly, if the corporation fails to meet any of the Subchapter S requirements during the pre-election portion of the year, the election is effective for the following taxable year.

---

[13]   §§ 1362(b)(1)(B) and (b)(2).

[14]   §§ 1362(a)(2) and (b)(2)(B)(ii). Although the election must be filed timely, the IRS may grant an extension for filing the consent forms if reasonable cause can be shown. Reg. § 18.1362-2(c).

Example 5.   At the beginning of 1991, D, E, and F owned the stock of GHI Corporation, a calendar year taxpayer. On February 15, 1991, F sold all of her shares in GHI to C. On March 1, 1991, an S corporation election is desired. In order for the election to be effective for 1991, all shareholders on the date of election (C, D, and E), as well as any shareholders in the pre-election portion of the year (F), must consent. Failure to obtain F's consent would cause the election to become effective for 1992.

Election Effective for Subsequent Years.   Elections made after the first two and one-half months of the current taxable year are effective for the following taxable year.[15]   When the election becomes effective in the following taxable year, only shareholders holding stock on the date of election must consent. The consent of shareholders who acquire stock after the election is not required.[16] As noted above, an election made within the first two and one-half months of the year without the consent of former shareholders or without satisfaction of the requirements causes the election to be effective for the following taxable year.

TERMINATION OF THE ELECTION

An election to be taxed as an S corporation is effective until it is terminated. The election may be terminated when the corporation[17]

1.   Revokes the election;

2.   Fails to satisfy the requirements; or

3.   Receives excessive passive income.

Revocation.   The S corporation election may be revoked if shareholders holding a *majority* of the shares of stock (voting and nonvoting) consent.[18]   A revocation filed by the fifteenth day of the third month of the taxable year (e.g., March 15 for a calendar year corporation) normally is effective for the current taxable year.[19]   In contrast, if the revocation is filed after this two and one-half month period has elapsed, it usually becomes effective for the following taxable year.[20]   In both situations, however, a date on or after the date of revocation may be specified for the termination to become effective.[21]

---

[15]   § 1362(b)(3).

[16]   As noted later in the discussion, however, a shareholder owning more than 50 percent of stock may terminate the election.

[17]   § 1362(d).

[18]   § 1362(d)(1)(B).

[19]   § 1362(d)(1)(C)(i).

[20]   § 1362(d)(1)(C)(ii).

[21]   § 1362(d)(1)(D).

Example 6. A calendar year S corporation is owned equally by C, D, and E. On February 12, 1992 C and D consent to revoke the S corporation election. Since C and D own a majority of the outstanding shares of stock, the election is effective beginning on January 1, 1992 unless the revocation specifies February 12, 1992 or some later date.

Example 7. Same as *Example 6* above except the revocation was made on May 3, 1992. The election is effective for the following taxable year beginning January 1, 1993. If the revocation had specified, however, that the termination was to become effective November 2, 1992, the S corporation year would end on November 1, 1992.

As currently designed, the revocation rules allow a new shareholder to terminate the election only if he or she acquires a majority of the shares of stock.

Example 8. An S corporation has 100 shares of outstanding stock, 75 owned by J and 25 owned by B. On June 1 of this year, J sold 60 of her shares to D. Since D owns a majority of the outstanding shares, he may revoke the election.

Failure to Meet the Requirements. If the S corporation fails to satisfy any of the Subchapter S requirements at any time, the election is terminated on the date the disqualifying event occurred.[22] In such case, the corporation is treated as an S corporation for the period ending prior to the date of termination. This often causes the corporation to have two short taxable years: one as an S corporation and one as a C corporation. As a result, income and loss for the entire year must be allocated between the two years. The methods for making these allocations are discussed later in this chapter. The tax returns for both the short S year and short C year must be filed by the *original* due date of the short year C corporate return.[23]

Example 9. C, D, and E own a calendar year S corporation. On June 3 of this year, E sold her stock to a corporation. The S corporation's year ends on June 2. The same result would be obtained if the sale had been to a partnership or to an individual who became the 36th shareholder. The S short year includes January 1 through June 2. The C short year is June 3 through December 31.

S shareholders report their proportionate share of all S short year items in the same manner as they would for a complete year, except computations are made as of the last day the business qualified as an S corporation. The C corporate tax liability, however, must be annualized.[24]

---

[22] § 1362(d)(2).

[23] § 1362(e)(6)(B).

[24] §§ 443(b)(1) and 1362(e)(5)(A).

When termination is *inadvertent*, the Code authorizes the IRS to allow a corporation to continue its S status if the disqualifying action is corrected.[25] It is possible, for example, that if stock is transferred to an ineligible shareholder, the IRS might allow the corporation to correct the violation and continue its S status uninterrupted.

> **Example 10.**   On the advice of his attorney, a majority shareholder transferred his S corporation shares to an ineligible trust. When the shareholder discovered the transfer terminated the S corporation election, the error was corrected. The IRS has ruled, under similar circumstances, that the S election was not lost since termination was inadvertent, it occurred as the result of advice from counsel, and it was corrected as soon as the violation of S status was discovered.[26]

Excessive Passive Income.   Under the passive income test, the election is terminated if the corporation has[27]

1. Passive investment income exceeding 25 percent of its gross receipts for three consecutive years, and

2. C corporation accumulated earnings and profits (AE&P) at the end of each of the three consecutive years.

If both of these conditions are satisfied, the termination becomes effective at the beginning of the first year following the end of the three-year period.[28]

As reflected in the second condition above, the excessive passive income test is reserved *solely* for corporations that were C corporations prior to becoming S corporations. In addition, the test applies to these former C corporations only if they have AE&P from C years. Accordingly, corporations that have never been C corporations as well as corporations that have distributed all AE&P cannot be terminated because of passive investment income.

Passive investment income generally is defined as gross receipts from royalties, rents, dividends, interest (including tax-exempt interest but excluding interest on notes from sales of inventory), annuities, and gains on sales or exchanges of stock or securities.[29]   For this purpose, rents are not considered passive income if significant services are provided (e.g., room rents paid to a hotel).[30]   In computing total gross receipts, costs of goods sold, returns and allowances, deductions, and returns of basis are ignored; receipts from the sale of capital assets are

---

[25]   § 1362(f).

[26]   Rev. Rul. 86-110, 1986-38 I.R.B. 4. Also, see Ltr. Ruls. 8550033 and 8608006.

[27]   § 1362(d)(3).

[28]   § 1362(d)(3)(A)(ii).

[29]   § 1362(d)(3)(D).

[30]   Reg. § 1.1372-4(b)(5)(vi).

included but only to the extent of net gains (i.e., capital gains less capital losses). Consequently, there are no gross receipts when the sale of a capital asset results in a net loss.[31]

> **Example 11.** OBJ, an S corporation, was a C corporation for several years before it elected to be taxed under Subchapter S beginning in 1990. For 1990 and 1991, the corporation had excessive passive income. In addition, at the close of 1990 and 1991, OBJ reported a balance in its AE&P that was attributable to its years as a C corporation. OBJ's income and expenses for 1992 are shown below. No distributions from its AE&P were made during the year. The corporation's passive investment income and total gross receipts, based on its reported items, are determined as follows:

	Reported	Gross Receipts	Passive Income
Sales............................	$200,000	$200,000	$ 0
Cost of goods sold..............	(150,000)	0	0
Interest income..................	30,000	30,000	30,000
Dividends.......................	15,000	15,000	15,000
Rental income (passive).........	40,000	40,000	40,000
Rental expenses.................	(28,000)	0	0
Gain on sale of stock............	15,000	15,000	15,000
Total..........................		$300,000	$100,000

> Because OBJ's passive investment income exceeds 25% of its gross receipts [$100,000 > (25% × $300,000 = $75,000)] for the third consecutive year and it also has a balance of AE&P at the end of each of those years, the election is terminated beginning on January 1, 1993.

Even though a corporation may avoid having its election terminated by failing the excessive passive income test once every three years, a corporation still may be required to pay a tax on its excessive passive investment income. This tax is explained in detail later in this chapter.

ELECTION AFTER TERMINATION

When the election is terminated, whether voluntarily through revocation or involuntarily through failure to satisfy the Subchapter S or passive income requirements, the corporation normally may not make a new election until the fifth taxable year following the year in which the termination became effective.[32] The five-year wait is unnecessary, however, if the IRS consents to an earlier election. Consent usually is given in two instances: (1) when the corporation's ownership

---

[31] §§ 1362(d)(3)(C) and 1222(9).   [32] § 1362(g).

has changed such that more than 50 percent of the stock is owned by persons who did not own the stock at the time of termination, or (2) when the termination was attributable to an event that was not within the control of the corporation or its majority shareholders.[33]

> **Example 12.**   KLZ, an S corporation, was wholly owned by G. The corporation revoked its S election effective on July 17, 1991. KLZ may not make an election until 1996 unless it obtains permission from the IRS. Permission to reelect S status prior to 1996 would be denied since the termination was completely under the control of G. A similar conclusion would be reached if KLZ issued a second class of stock.

> **Example 13.**   Same facts as in *Example 12* above. Assume F purchased all of the corporation's stock in 1992 and desired to reelect S status. Since more than 50 percent of the stock is owned by someone who did not own stock during the year the termination took place, the IRS would probably waive the waiting period.

OPERATING THE S CORPORATION

Federal Income Tax Form 1120S must be filed for an S corporation within two and one-half months following the end of its year. For a calendar year S corporation, the due date is March 15. This requirement coincides with that of the C corporation and is one month less than the period allowed a partnership. However, an automatic six-month extension may be obtained by filing Form 7004. This is the same form and privilege granted C corporations. Since the S corporation is a nontaxable entity that serves as a conduit to its owners, a delayed Form 1120S creates problems for all of its shareholders. These problems occur because the S corporation performs the same role as the partnership. That is, it accumulates income, expenses, gains, losses, and credits that flow through to its owners, based on their ownership interests.[34] Unlike the partnership, there is no provision for special allocations among owners. Thus, the one class of stock requirement means that allocations must be identical for each share of stock outstanding.[35] This can be a significant disadvantage when compared with the more flexible rules governing special allocations for partners.[36]

---

[33]   Reg. § 1.1372-5(a).

[34]   § 1366(a).

[35]   § 1377(a).

[36]   §§ 704(b)(2) and (c).

Consistent with the aggregate concept that is applied to partnerships, all incidence of taxation (with the exceptions discussed later in this chapter) passes to the stockholders who must report their share of the S corporation items on their own tax returns.[37] The character of the items is retained.[38] Consequently, Form 1120S is an information return that summarizes the income, deductions, credits, gains, and losses to be reported by the shareholders.

Also consistent with the partnership provisions, most special elections are made by the S corporation and not by each shareholder. The exceptions to this general approach are the same as those for the partnership and affect few taxpayers.[39]

DETERMINING S CORPORATION NET INCOME

S corporations generally compute net income, gains, and losses in the same manner as a partnership. There are several important differences, however. Three of these are discussed below.

Payments to Shareholder-Employees.   S corporation shareholders who work for the corporation qualify as employees. As a result, salary paid to a shareholder-employee as well as payroll taxes related to the salary are deductible by the S corporation. Recall from Chapter 10 that partnerships can deduct guaranteed payments for compensation paid to partners. However, these payments are not subject to withholding or payroll taxes.[40]   Instead, a partner's compensation is treated as self-employment income.

> **Example 14.**   An owner who works for the business is paid a $20,000 salary during 1991. Net income *before* the salary and any payroll taxes on it is $60,000. If the business is an S or C corporation, the salary is subject to withholding taxes and the corporation must pay FICA and unemployment taxes on it. Corporate taxes are $1,530 FICA (7.65% × $20,000) and $434 unemployment taxes (6.2% on the first $7,000). Corporate net income is $38,036 ($60,000 − $20,000 − $1,530 − $434). If, however, the business is a partnership, there are no payroll taxes for owner compensation and partnership net income is $40,000 ($60,000 − $20,000), which usually qualifies as self-employment income and is subject to that tax at the partner level.

Section 291 Recapture.   Certain S corporations are subject to the special depreciation recapture rules of § 291(a)(1), while a partnership is not.[41]   Recall from Chapter 1 that § 291 reclassifies some of a corporation's § 1231 gains on depreciable realty from capital gain to ordinary income.

---

[37]   § 1363(a).

[38]   § 1366(b).

[39]   § 1363(c).

[40]   Reg. § 1.707-1(c) and Rev. Rul. 69-148, 1969-1 C.B. 256.

[41]   An S corporation that was a C corporation for any of the three immediately preceding taxable years is subject to § 291. See § 1363(b)(4).

Accounting Methods. Certain entities are prohibited from using the cash method of accounting, and consequently are required to use the accrual method. A C corporation normally cannot use the cash method unless its annual gross receipts average $5 million or less or it is a qualified personal service corporation. In contrast, an S corporation or partnership can use the cash method unless the entity is considered a tax shelter [under § 461(i)] or, in the case of a partnership, has a corporate partner. However, even a partnership with a C corporate partner may use the cash method if the corporate partner meets the annual gross receipts test or is a qualified personal service corporation. (Since an S corporation is prohibited from having a C corporation as an owner, the latter restriction is inapplicable to an S corporation.)

The above exceptions should not be considered all inclusive. As will be seen, there are other differences in the taxation of S corporations and partnerships, many of which are significant.

Reporting S Corporation Income. The similarity between the taxation of S corporations and partnerships becomes readily apparent when Forms 1120S and 1065 are compared. (See Exhibit 12-1 for an illustration of Form 1120S. The numbers are taken from the last example in the Appendix to this chapter.) There is one major difference in computing the net ordinary income on page one of the two tax forms, however. Unlike Form 1065, Form 1120S has a section for computing any taxes due on excessive passive investment income and Schedule D built-in gains (both are discussed in a later section of this chapter).

All income, expenses, gains, losses, and credits that may be subject to special treatment by one or more of the shareholders are reported separately on Schedule K, which is filed with Form 1120S.[42] Schedule K-1 is then prepared for the shareholders' use. (See Exhibit 12-1 for an illustration. The numbers are taken from the last example in the Appendix to this chapter.) Again, these schedules are quite similar to the schedules applicable to partnerships and partners. There are three major differences. Two partnership items are not relevant to S corporations. Since S shareholders can be employees of the corporation, the listing of guaranteed payments on the partnership schedule is inapplicable to the S corporation. In addition, the listing for self-employment income on the partnership schedule is omitted from the S corporation schedule. A shareholder does *not* have self-employment income from the business. Neither a shareholder's salary nor any portion of the corporate net income qualifies as self-employment income.[43] Finally, the S corporation schedule includes a section for reporting distributions. These are divided into two categories: (1) distributions from earnings of the S corporation, and (2) if it has been operated as a C corporation in previous years, distributions from earnings of the C corporation. (Distributions are discussed in a later section of this chapter.)

---

[42] § 1366(a)(1)(A).

[43] This is consistent with the C corporation. Note, however, an individual cannot escape FICA taxes completely by receiving "divi-dends" from the corporation. The IRS takes the position that in such case, a portion *or* all of the purported dividends would be compensation subject to withholding and FICA. See Rev. Rul. 74-44, 1974-1 C.B. 287.

Exhibit 12-1

Form **1120S**	**U.S. Income Tax Return for an S Corporation**		OMB No. 1545-0130
Department of the Treasury Internal Revenue Service	For calendar year 1990, or tax year beginning _____, 1990, and ending _____ 19 ____ ▶ See separate instructions.		**1990**

A Date of election as an S corporation **1-1-90**	Use IRS label. Other-wise, please print or type.	Name **T COMPANY**	**C** Employer identification number **88-9138761**
B Business code no. (see Specific Instructions) **5651**		Number, street, and room or suite no. (If a P.O. box, see page 7 of the instructions.) **8122 SOUTH S STREET**	**D** Date incorporated **1-1-90**
		City or town, state, and ZIP code **NORFOLK, VA 23508**	**E** Total assets (see Specific Instructions) $ **322,000**

F Check applicable boxes: (1) ☑ Initial return   (2) ☐ Final return   (3) ☐ Change in address   (4) ☐ Amended return

G Check this box if this is an S corporation subject to the consolidated audit procedures of sections 6241 through 6245 (see instructions before checking this box) . . ▶ ☐

H Enter number of shareholders in the corporation at end of the tax year . . . . ▶

Caution: Include **only** trade or business income and expenses on lines 1a through 21. See the instructions for more information.

Income

1a Gross receipts or sales	470,000	**b** Less returns and allowances –0– c Bal ▶ **1c**	470,000
2 Cost of goods sold (Schedule A, line 7)		**2**	300,000
3 Gross profit (subtract line 2 from line 1c)		**3**	170,000
4 Net gain (loss) from Form 4797, Part II, line 18		**4**	
5 Other income (see instructions) (attach schedule)		**5**	
6 **Total** income (loss)—Combine lines 3 through 5 . . . . . . ▶		**6**	170,000

Deductions (See instructions for limitations.)

7 Compensation of officers		**7**	24,000
8a Salaries and wages	48,000	**b** Less jobs credit –0– c Bal ▶ **8c**	48,000
9 Repairs		**9**	12,000
10 Bad debts		**10**	
11 Rents		**11**	
12 Taxes PROPERTY TAXES = $3,000 ; PAYROLL TAXES = $6,000 . . .		**12**	9,000
13 Interest		**13**	3,300
14a Depreciation (see instructions) **14a** 15,000			
b Depreciation reported on Schedule A and elsewhere on return . . **14b** –0–			
c Subtract line 14b from line 14a		**14c**	15,000
15 Depletion (**Do not deduct oil and gas depletion.** See instructions.) . . .		**15**	
16 Advertising		**16**	
17 Pension, profit-sharing, etc., plans		**17**	
18 Employee benefit programs LIFE INS.		**18**	1,400
19 Other deductions (attach schedule) UTILITIES TELE. = $2,500 ; OFFICE SUPPLIES = $1,100 ; INSURANCE COSTS = $3,100 ▶		**19**	6,700
20 **Total** deductions—Add lines 7 through 19 . . . . ▶		**20**	119,400
21 Ordinary income (loss) from trade or business activities—Subtract line 20 from line 6		**21**	50,600

Tax and Payments

22 **Tax:**			
a Excess net passive income tax (attach schedule) **22a**			
b Tax from Schedule D (Form 1120S) **22b**			
c Add lines 22a and 22b (see instructions for additional taxes)		**22c**	NONE
23 **Payments:**			
a 1990 estimated tax payments **23a**			
b Tax deposited with Form 7004 . . . . **23b**			
c Credit for Federal tax on fuels (attach Form 4136) **23c**			
d Add lines 23a through 23c		**23d**	
24 Enter any **penalty** for underpayment of estimated tax—Check ▶ ☐ if Form 2220 is attached . .		**24**	
25 **Tax due**—If the total of lines 22c and 24 is larger than line 23d, enter amount owed. See instructions for depositary method of payment . . . . ▶		**25**	NONE
26 **Overpayment**—If line 23d is larger than the total of lines 22c and 24, enter amount overpaid ▶		**26**	
27 Enter amount of line 26 you want: **Credited to 1991 estimated tax** ▶ _____ Refunded ▶		**27**	

Please Sign Here — Under penalties of perjury, I declare that I have examined this return, including accompanying schedules and statements, and to the best of my knowledge and belief, it is true, correct, and complete. Declaration of preparer (other than taxpayer) is based on all information of which preparer has any knowledge.

▶ Signature of officer	Date	▶ Title

Paid Preparer's Use Only	Preparer's signature ▶	Date	Check if self-employed ▶ ☐	Preparer's social security number
	Firm's name (or yours if self-employed) and address ▶		E.I. No. ▶ ZIP code ▶	

For Paperwork Reduction Act Notice, see page 1 of separate instructions.   Form **1120S** (1990)

Exhibit 12-1 Continued:

Form 1120S (1990)   Page **2**

Schedule A   **Cost of Goods Sold** (See instructions.)   *(a)*

1	Inventory at beginning of year	1	
2	Purchases	2	
3	Cost of labor	3	
4a	Additional section 263A costs (see instructions) *(attach schedule)*	4a	
b	Other costs *(attach schedule)*	4b	
5	Total—Add lines 1 through 4b	5	
6	Inventory at end of year	6	
7	Cost of goods sold—Subtract line 6 from line 5. Enter here and on line 2, page 1	7	300,000

8a Check all methods used for valuing closing inventory:
(i) ☑ Cost
(ii) ☐ Lower of cost or market as described in Regulations section 1.471-4
(iii) ☐ Writedown of "subnormal" goods as described in Regulations section 1.471-2(c)
(iv) ☐ Other (specify method used and attach explanation) ▶ _____
b Check this box if the LIFO inventory method was adopted this tax year for any goods *(if checked, attach Form 970)* . . . ▶ ☐
c If the LIFO inventory method was used for this tax year, enter percentage (or amounts) of closing inventory computed under LIFO . . . . | 8c | |
d Do the rules of section 263A (with respect to property produced or acquired for resale) apply to the corporation? . . . ☐ Yes ☑ No
e Was there any change in determining quantities, cost, or valuations between opening and closing inventory? . . . . ☐ Yes ☑ No
If "Yes," attach explanation.

Additional Information Required (continued from page 1)

		Yes	No
I	Did you at the end of the tax year own, directly or indirectly, 50% or more of the voting stock of a domestic corporation? For rules of attribution, see section 267(c). If "Yes," attach a schedule showing: **(1)** name, address, and employer identification number; and **(2)** percentage owned.		✓
J	Refer to the list in the instructions and state your principal: **(1)** Business activity ▶ _5651_____ **(2)** Product or service ▶ *CLOTHING-RETAIL*		
K	Were you a member of a controlled group subject to the provisions of section 1561?		✓
L	At any time during the tax year, did you have an interest in or a signature or other authority over a financial account in a foreign country (such as a bank account, securities account, or other financial account)? (See instructions for exceptions and filing requirements for form TD F 90-22.1.)		✓
	If "Yes," enter the name of the foreign country ▶ _____		
M	Were you the grantor of, or transferor to, a foreign trust that existed during the current tax year, whether or not you have any beneficial interest in it? If "Yes," you may have to file Forms 3520, 3520-A, or 926		✓
N	During this tax year did you maintain any part of your accounting/tax records on a computerized system?		✓
O	Check method of accounting: **(1)** ☐ Cash **(2)** ☑ Accrual **(3)** ☐ Other (specify) ▶ _____		
P	Check this box if the S corporation has filed or is required to file **Form 8264,** Application for Registration of a Tax Shelter . . . . ▶ ☐		
Q	Check this box if the corporation issued publicly offered debt instruments with original issue discount . . . . . ▶ ☐		
	If so, the corporation may have to file **Form 8281,** Information Return for Publicly Offered Original Issue Discount Instruments.		
R	If the corporation: **(1)** filed its election to be an S corporation after 1986, **(2)** was a C corporation before it elected to be an S corporation **or** the corporation acquired an asset with a basis determined by reference to its basis (or the basis of any other property) in the hands of a C corporation, and **(3)** has net unrealized built-in gain (defined in section 1374(d)(1)) in excess of the net recognized built-in gain from prior years, enter the net unrealized built-in gain reduced by net recognized built-in gain from prior years (see instructions) . . . . . ▶ $ _____		
S	Check this box if the corporation had subchapter C earnings and profits at the close of the tax year (see instructions) ▶ ☐		

Designation of Tax Matters Person (See instructions.)

Enter below the shareholder designated as the tax matters person (TMP) for the tax year of this return:

Name of designated TMP ▶ _____   Identifying number of TMP ▶ _____

Address of designated TMP ▶ _____

(a) lines 1 through 6 must be completed before the return is filed.

Exhibit 12-1 Continued:

Form 1120S (1990)				Page **3**
Schedule K	**Shareholders' Shares of Income, Credits, Deductions, Etc.**			
	(a) Pro rata share items			(b) Total amount

				(b) Total amount
Income (Loss)	1 Ordinary income (loss) from trade or business activities (page 1, line 21)	**1**		*50,600*
	2 Net income (loss) from rental real estate activities *(attach Form 8825)*	**2**		
	3a Gross income from other rental activities	**3a**		
	b Less expenses *(attach schedule)*	**3b**		
	c Net income (loss) from other rental activities	**3c**		
	4 Portfolio income (loss):			
	a Interest income	**4a**		*3,300*
	b Dividend income	**4b**		*2,000*
	c Royalty income	**4c**		
	d Net short-term capital gain (loss) *(attach Schedule D (Form 1120S))*	**4d**		
	e Net long-term capital gain (loss) *(attach Schedule D (Form 1120S))* *$3,000 + $2,200* *-$1200*	**4e**		*4,000*
	f Other portfolio income (loss) *(attach schedule)*	**4f**		
	5 Net gain (loss) under section 1231 (other than due to casualty or theft) *(attach Form 4797)*	**5**		
	6 Other income (loss) *(attach schedule)*	**6**		
Deductions	7 Charitable contributions (see instructions) *(attach list)*	**7**		*7,000*
	8 Section 179 expense deduction *(attach Form 4562)*	**8**		
	9 Deductions related to portfolio income (loss) (see instructions) (itemize)	**9**		
	10 Other deductions *(attach schedule)*	**10**		
Investment Interest	11a Interest expense on investment debts	**11a**		
	b (1) Investment income included on lines 4a through 4f above	**11b(1)**		
	(2) Investment expenses included on line 9 above	**11b(2)**		
Credits	12a Credit for alcohol used as a fuel *(attach Form 6478)*	**12a**		
	b Low-income housing credit (see instructions):			
	(1) From partnerships to which section 42(j)(5) applies for property placed in service before 1990.	**12b(1)**		
	(2) Other than on line 12b(1) for property placed in service before 1990	**12b(2)**		
	(3) From partnerships to which section 42(j)(5) applies for property placed in service after 1989	**12b(3)**		
	(4) Other than on line 12b(3) for property placed in service after 1989	**12b(4)**		
	c Qualified rehabilitation expenditures related to rental real estate activities *(attach Form 3468)*	**12c**		
	d Credits (other than credits shown on lines 12b and 12c) related to rental real estate activities (see instructions)	**12d**		
	e Credits related to other rental activities (see instructions)	**12e**		
	13 Other credits (see instructions) *REHABILITATION CREDIT*	**13**		*2,000*
Adjustments and Tax Preference Items	14a Accelerated depreciation of real property placed in service before 1987	**14a**		
	b Accelerated depreciation of leased personal property placed in service before 1987	**14b**		
	c Depreciation adjustment on property placed in service after 1986	**14c**		
	d Depletion (other than oil and gas)	**14d**		
	e (1) Gross income from oil, gas, or geothermal properties	**14e(1)**		
	(2) Deductions allocable to oil, gas, or geothermal properties	**14e(2)**		
	f Other adjustments and tax preference items *(attach schedule)*	**14f**		
Foreign Taxes	15a Type of income ▶			
	b Name of foreign country or U.S. possession ▶			
	c Total gross income from sources outside the U.S. *(attach schedule)*	**15c**		
	d Total applicable deductions and losses *(attach schedule)*	**15d**		
	e Total foreign taxes (check one): ▶ ☐ Paid ☐ Accrued	**15e**		
	f Reduction in taxes available for credit *(attach schedule)*	**15f**		
	g Other foreign tax information *(attach schedule)*	**15g**		
Other Items	16a Total expenditures to which a section 59(e) election may apply	**16a**		
	b Type of expenditures ▶			
	17 Total property distributions (including cash) other than dividends reported on line 19 below	**17**		*22,000* (*a*)
	18 Other items and amounts required to be reported separately to shareholders (see instructions) *(attach schedule)*			
	19 Total dividend distributions paid from accumulated earnings and profits	**19**		
	20 Income (loss) (Required only if Schedule M-1 must be completed.)—Combine lines 1 through 6 in column (b). From the result subtract the sum of lines 7 through 11a, 15e, and 16a	**20**		

(*a*) *$12,000 CASH + $10,000 FAIR MKT. VALUE OF LAND = $22,000.*

Exhibit 12-1 Continued:

Form 1120S (1990)   Page **4**

Schedule L Balance Sheets

Assets	Beginning of tax year (a)	(b)	End of tax year (c)	(d)
1 Cash				
2a Trade notes and accounts receivable . . .				
b Less allowance for bad debts				
3 Inventories				
4 U.S. government obligations				
5 Tax-exempt securities				
6 Other current assets (attach schedule) . . .				
7 Loans to shareholders				
8 Mortgage and real estate loans				
9 Other investments (attach schedule) . . .				
10a Buildings and other depreciable assets . .				
b Less accumulated depreciation				
11a Depletable assets				
b Less accumulated depletion				
12 Land (net of any amortization)				
13a Intangible assets (amortizable only) . . .				
b Less accumulated amortization				
14 Other assets (attach schedule)				
15 Total assets				322,000
Liabilities and Shareholders' Equity				
16 Accounts payable				
17 Mortgages, notes, bonds payable in less than 1 year				
18 Other current liabilities (attach schedule) . .				
19 Loans from shareholders				
20 Mortgages, notes, bonds payable in 1 year or more				
21 Other liabilities (attach schedule)				
22 Capital stock				
23 Paid-in or capital surplus				
24 Retained earnings				
25 Less cost of treasury stock	(	)	(	)
26 Total liabilities and shareholders' equity . .				322,000

Schedule M-1 Reconciliation of Income per Books With Income per Return (You are not required to complete this schedule if the total assets on line 15, column (d), of Schedule L are less than $25,000.)

1 Net income per books		5 Income recorded on books this year not included on Schedule K, lines 1 through 6 (itemize):	
2 Income included on Schedule K, lines 1 through 6, not recorded on books this year (itemize): _____		**a** Tax-exempt interest $ _____	
_____		_____	
3 Expenses recorded on books this year not included on Schedule K, lines 1 through 11a, 15e, and 16a (itemize):		6 Deductions included on Schedule K, lines 1 through 11a, 15e, and 16a, not charged against book income this year (itemize):	
a Depreciation $ _____		**a** Depreciation $ _____	
b Travel and entertainment $ _____		_____	
_____		_____	
		7 Total of lines 5 and 6	
4 Total of lines 1 through 3		8 Income (loss) (Schedule K, line 20)—Line 4 less line 7	

Schedule M-2 Analysis of Accumulated Adjustments Account, Other Adjustments Account, and Shareholders' Undistributed Taxable Income Previously Taxed (See instructions.) *(c)*

	(a) Accumulated adjustments account	(b) Other adjustments account	(c) Shareholders' undistributed taxable income previously taxed
1 Balance at beginning of tax year			
2 Ordinary income from page 1, line 21 . . .	50,600		
3 Other additions	9,300 (a)		
4 Loss from page 1, line 21	( )		
5 Other reductions	( )	( )	
6 Combine lines 1 through 5			
7 Distributions other than dividend distributions	29,700 (b)		
8 Balance at end of tax year—subtract line 7 from line 6			

(a) $3,300 INTEREST INC. + $2,000 DIVIDENDS + $4,000 NLTCG = $9,300.

(b) $12,000 CASH + $10,000 FAIR MKT. VALUE LAND + $7,000 CHARITABLE CONTRIBUTION + $700 T'S LIFE INS. = $29,700.

(c) SCHEDULES L AND M MUST BE COMPLETED BEFORE THE RETURN IS FILED.

Exhibit 12-1 Continued:

SCHEDULE K-1 (Form 1120S) Department of the Treasury Internal Revenue Service	Shareholder's Share of Income, Credits, Deductions, Etc. ▶ See separate instructions. For calendar year 1990 or tax year beginning , 1990, and ending , 19	OMB No. 1545-0130 19**90**

Shareholder's identifying number ▶	Corporation's identifying number ▶
Shareholder's name, address, and ZIP code ADOLPH Z. T. 1291 MAPLE DRIVE NORFOLK, VA 23508	Corporation's name, address, and ZIP code T COMPANY 8122 SOUTH S STREET NORFOLK, VA 23508

A Shareholder's percentage of stock ownership for tax year (see Instructions for Schedule K-1) . . . . ▶ 100 %

B Internal Revenue Service Center where corporation filed its return ▶ MEMPHIS, TN

C (1) Tax shelter registration number (see Instructions for Schedule K-1) . . . . ▶

    (2) Type of tax shelter ▶

D If the shareholder acquired corporate stock after 10/22/86, check here ▶ ☐ and enter the shareholder's weighted percentage increase in stock ownership for 1990 (see Instructions for Schedule K-1) . . . . ▶ %

E If any activity for which income or loss is reported on line 1, 2, or 3, was started or acquired by the corporation after 10/22/86, check here ▶ ☐ and enter the date of start up or acquisition in the date space on line 1, 2, or 3 **below.**

F Check applicable boxes: **(1)** ☐ Final K-1   **(2)** ☐ Amended K-1

		(a) Pro rata share items		(b) Amount	(c) Form 1040 filers enter the amount in column (b) on:
Income (Loss)	**1**	Ordinary income (loss) from trade or business activities. If applicable, enter date asked for in item E . . . . . ▶ 1-1-90	1	50,600	
	2	Net income (loss) from rental real estate activities. If applicable, enter date asked for in item E . . . . . ▶	2		See Shareholder's Instructions for Schedule K-1 (Form 1120S).
	3	Net income (loss) from other rental activities. If applicable, enter date asked for in item E . . . . . ▶	3		
	4	Portfolio income (loss):			
	a	Interest	4a	3,300	Sch. B, Part I, line 1
	b	Dividends	4b	2,000	Sch. B, Part II, line 5
	c	Royalties	4c		Sch. E, Part I, line 4
	d	Net short-term capital gain (loss)	4d		Sch. D, line 5, col. (f) or (g)
	e	Net long-term capital gain (loss)	4e	4,000	Sch. D, line 12, col. (f) or (g)
	f	Other portfolio income (loss) *(attach schedule)*	4f		(Enter on applicable line of your return.)
	5	Net gain (loss) under section 1231 (other than due to casualty or theft)	5		See Shareholder's Instructions for Schedule K-1 (Form 1120S)
	6	Other income (loss) *(attach schedule)*	6		(Enter on applicable line of your return.)
Deductions	**7**	Charitable contributions	7	7,000	Sch. A, line 14 or 15
	8	Section 179 expense deduction *(attach schedule)*	8		See Shareholder's Instructions for Schedule K-1 (Form 1120S).
	9	Deductions related to portfolio income (loss) *(attach schedule)* . .	9		
	10	Other deductions *(attach schedule)*	10		
Investment Interest	**11a**	Interest expense on investment debts	11a		Form 4952, line 1
	b	**(1)** Investment income included on lines 4a through 4f above . .	b(1)		See Shareholder's Instructions for Schedule K-1 (Form 1120S)
		(2) Investment expenses included on line 9 above	b(2)		
Credits	**12a**	Credit for alcohol used as fuel	12a		Form 6478, line 10
	b	Low-income housing credit:			
		(1) From section 42(j)(5) partnerships for property placed in service before 1990	b(1)		
		(2) Other than on line 12b(1) for property placed in service before 1990 .	b(2)		Form 8586, line 5
		(3) From section 42(j)(5) partnerships for property placed in service after 1989 .	b(3)		
		(4) Other than on line 12b(3) for property placed in service after 1989	b(4)		
	c	Qualified rehabilitation expenditures related to rental real estate activities (see instructions) CREDIT	12c		
	d	Credits (other than credits shown on lines 12b and 12c) related to rental real estate activities (see instructions)	12d		See Shareholder's Instructions for Schedule K-1 (Form 1120S).
	e	Credits related to other rental activities (see instructions)	12e		
	13	Other credits (see instructions) REHABILITATION CREDIT .	13	2,000	

For Paperwork Reduction Act Notice, see Form 1120S Instructions.   Schedule K-1 (Form 1120S) 1990

ALLOCATIONS TO SHAREHOLDERS

All S corporation items are allocated among the shareholders based on their *ownership percentage* of the outstanding stock on each day of the year.[44] Thus, a shareholder owning 20 percent of the outstanding stock all year is deemed to have received 20 percent of *each item*. The allocation rate can be changed only by increasing or decreasing the percentage of stock ownership. This precludes shareholders from dividing net income or losses in any other manner. Of course, a certain amount of special allocation can be achieved through salaries and other business payments to owners. If there is no change in stock ownership during the year, each item to be allocated is multiplied by the percentage of stock owned by each shareholder. There is *one* exception: actual distributions of assets are assigned to the shareholder who receives them.

> **Example 15.** M owns 100 of an S corporation's 1,000 shares of common stock outstanding. Neither the number of shares outstanding nor the number owned by M has changed during the year. The S corporation items for its calendar year are allocated to M, based on her 10% ownership interest, as follows:
>
> | | Totals Schedule K | M's 10% on Schedule K-1 |
> |---|---|---|
> | Ordinary income (from page 1) | $70,000 | $7,000 |
> | Net capital gain | 2,000 | 200 |
> | Charitable contributions | 4,000 | 400 |
>
> In addition, cash distributions from S earnings are $20 for each 1% stock ownership, paid on the last day of each month. Thus, M received $2,400 ($20 × 12 months × 10 units of 1%).

If the ownership of stock changes during the year, there are two methods for determining the allocations for those shareholders whose interests have changed. These are: (1) the *per day allocation method*, and (2) the *interim closing of books* method. The per day allocation method must be used unless the shareholder completely terminates his or her interest in the S corporation. When an owner's interest is terminated, shareholders may elect to use either method. It should be noted that these same methods apply when the S election is terminated and items must be prorated between the former S corporation and the new C corporation.

---

[44] §§ 1366(a) and 1377(a).

Per-Day Allocation. This method assigns an equal amount of the S items to each day of the year.[45] When a shareholder's interest changes, the shareholder must report a pro rata share of each item for each day that the stock was owned. This computation may be expressed as follows:

$$\frac{\text{Percentage of}}{\text{shares owned}} \times \frac{\text{Percentage of}}{\text{year stock was owned}} = \frac{\text{Portion of}}{\text{item to be reported}}$$

Example 16. Assume the same facts as in *Example 15*, except that M sold all of her shares on August 8. Since the S corporation uses the calendar year, M has held 100 shares for 219 days or 60% of the year (219 ÷ 365). (The day of sale is not an ownership day for M.) Based on the per day allocation method, M's share of the S corporation items is as follows:

	Totals Schedule K	M's 10% on Schedule K-1
Ordinary income (from page 1).................	$70,000	$4,200
Net capital gain...............................	2,000	120
Charitable contributions........................	4,000	240
Total distributions (from S earnings)............	24,000	1,400

The computations for M's share are the totals on Schedule K *multiplied by* her 10% ownership interest *multiplied by* her ownership period of 219 days, or 60% of the year. For example, $70,000 × 10% = $7,000 × 60% = $4,200. M received cash distributions of $1,400 ($20 × 7 months × 10 units).

The per day allocation method also is applicable for a shareholder whose stock interest varies during the year.

Example 17. Assume the same facts as in *Example 16*, except M only sold 20 shares on August 8. Thus, she owned 10% of the business the first 219 days and 8% the remaining 146 days. Based on the per day allocation method, her share of the S corporation items is as follows:

	Totals on Schedule K	M's Share 10%	M's Share 8%	Schedule K-1
Ordinary income (from page 1)................	$70,000	$4,200	$2,240	$6,440
Net capital gain.................	2,000	120	64	184
Charitable contributions.........	4,000	240	128	368
Total distributions (from S earnings).............	24,000	1,400	800	2,200

---

[45] § 1377(a)(1).

The computations for the last 146 days are the totals on Schedule K *multiplied by* her 8% ownership interest *multiplied by* her ownership period of 146 days, or 40% (146 ÷ 365) of the year. For example, $70,000 × 8% = $5,600 × 40% = $2,240. The amount on Schedule K-1 is M's 10% share *plus* her 8% share. For example, $4,200 + $2,240 = $6,440.

Interim Closing of the Books.   As noted above, the per day method must be used unless the shareholder's interest completely terminates. If there is a complete termination of a shareholder's interest, an election may be made to use the interim closing of books method instead of the per day allocation method.[46] This election means the S corporation's taxable year ends when the shareholder's interest is terminated. As a result, the year is divided into two short taxable years and all owners report the actual dollar amounts that were accumulated while they owned their shares. A valid election requires that all parties who owned a share of stock during either part of the year must agree to the election.

Example 18.   Assume the same facts as in *Example 16*, except the interim closing of books method is elected. Since M sells all of her shares on August 8, the S corporation's year ends the day before on August 7. Corporate records show the following amounts for the first 219 days, for the last 146 days, and M's share for the first 219 days.

	First 219 days	*Last 146 days*	*M's 10% on Schedule K-1*
Ordinary income (from page 1)	$15,000	$55,000	$1,500
Net capital gain........................	1,000	1,000	100
Charitable contributions................	0	4,000	0
Total distributions (from S earnings)....	14,000	10,000	1,400

The computations for M's share are the amounts for the first 219 days *multiplied by* her 10% ownership interest.

It is also possible for an S corporation to have an ordinary loss for part of the year and ordinary income for the remaining period.

   The differences in the tax effect of the two methods of dividing S corporation items between exiting shareholders and successor shareholders can be substantial. As a result, the method used could have an impact on the value of the stock being sold or exchanged. All parties involved should be aware of the risks being taken under either method. For example, the exiting shareholder has considerable risk under the per day allocation method. If the S corporation is more profitable than expected in the remaining portion of the year, the former shareholder reports more income than expected while the benefits of these additional profits accrue to the new owner. Of course, the reverse also can be true.

---

[46]   §§ 1377(a)(2) and 302(a)(2)(A)(i).

Although the interim closing of the books method can be elected only when a shareholder's interest is completely terminated, there are other times when it might be preferred to the per day allocation method. For example, it might be desirable when stock is issued to a new shareholder. Fortunately, this may be accomplished through tax planning. First, note that *any* termination of a shareholder's interest qualifies regardless of the number of shares involved. Therefore, when possible, S corporations should have a shareholder who owns just one share of stock. Then, when a complete termination is desired, the interest of this shareholder can be terminated rather easily. To prevent any unexpected results, the shareholder's agreement should clearly define when the interim closing of books method is to be elected.[47]

LOSSES OF THE S CORPORATION

One of the most common reasons a corporation elects Subchapter S status is because of the tax treatment for corporate losses. Recall that the C corporation's benefits are limited to those available from carrying the losses to another year to offset income. Refunds may be obtained to the extent *prior* year income is offset while losses carried to future years reduce the taxes due in those years. Frequently, these carryover benefits provide little or no value to the corporation. For example, many businesses report losses in the first few years, meaning that the carryback privilege would be useless. In addition, many new businesses are never successful. But, even those that are successful receive no tax benefit from their losses currently—generally when the need is the greatest. *Future* tax savings do not provide cash to pay present bills. When the cash for the tax savings is finally received, its purchasing power is diminished because of the time value of money.

The aggregate theory that is applied to S corporations can be a significant advantage when a corporation has a net loss. Based on the flow through concept, shareholders include their distributive shares of the S corporation's losses in their taxable income currently. Thus, the deduction for losses is transferred to the shareholder and generally results in tax savings for the current year. Even if a shareholder is unable to use the loss currently, carryover provisions also apply to an individual's net operating losses (including those from S corporations, partnerships, proprietorships, personal casualties and thefts, and suspended passive business losses—see discussion in Chapter 10). Of course, net capital losses can only be carried forward by individuals.

---

[47]   Lorence L. Bravenec, "The Subchapter S Revision Act of 1982 (Part II)," *The Tax Adviser* 14 (May, 1983), p. 281.

Limitations. Each shareholder's distributive share of net losses may not exceed that shareholder's basis in the corporation. Any losses that exceed a shareholder's basis may be carried forward indefinitely to be used when the shareholder's basis is increased.[48] When basis is insufficient and there is more than one item that reduces basis, the flow through of each item is determined in a pro rata manner. In addition, any items that increase basis flow through to the owner before any items that reduce basis, including distributions on stock.[49]

> **Example 19.** G owns 200 of an S corporation's 1,000 shares of common stock outstanding. Neither the number of shares outstanding nor those owned by G has changed during the year. The S corporation items for its calendar year are allocated to G, based on his 20% ownership interest, as follows:
>
> | | Totals on Schedule K | G's 20% on Schedule K-1 |
> |---|---|---|
> | Ordinary loss (from page 1)............ | ($70,000) | ($14,000) |
> | Net capital loss........................ | (5,000) | (1,000) |
> | Section 1231 gain..................... | 10,000 | 2,000 |
>
> First, G's basis is increased by the $2,000 § 1231 gain. If G's basis in the S corporation after the $2,000 increase is at least $15,000, all of the ordinary loss and capital loss flow through to be reported on his personal return. However, if his basis after the $2,000 increase is $12,000, only $12,000 of the loss is deductible, and it must be prorated. G may report ordinary loss of $11,200 ($14,000 ÷ $15,000 × $12,000 basis) and net capital loss of $800 ($12,000 − $11,200). The remaining ordinary loss of $2,800 and net capital loss of $200 are carried forward to be used at the end of the first year that G's basis increases.

The above allocation of losses is applicable to all losses and separate deductions (e.g., charitable contributions and state income taxes) for owners of both the S corporation and the partnership.

Generally, no carryovers from a C corporation may be used during the years it is taxed as an S corporation (or vice versa). For example, a C corporation with a net operating loss may not use it to offset income in an S year. There is one

---

[48] § 1366(d)(2). Losses may also be subject to limitation under § 465 at-risk rules and § 469 passive activity rules.

[49] § 1366(d)(1).

exception: C corporate NOLs may be used to offset the S corporation's built-in gains (discussed later in this chapter).[50] The S years are counted, however, when determining the expiration period of the carryover. Thus, a carryback of three years means three fiscal or calendar years regardless of whether the corporation was taxed under Subchapter C or S.[51]

RELATIONSHIP BETWEEN AN S CORPORATION AND ITS SHAREHOLDERS

The S corporation is a legal entity, distinctly separate from its owners. As a result, transactions between an S corporation and its shareholders are treated as though occurring between unrelated parties unless otherwise provided. Of course, these transactions must be conducted in an arm's-length manner, based on market values that would be used by unrelated parties.

TRANSACTIONS BETWEEN S CORPORATIONS AND THEIR SHAREHOLDERS

Contributions of property for stock follow the C corporate rules (see Chapter 2). That is, they are nontaxable *only if* the persons involved in the transaction own at least 80 percent of the corporation after the transfer is completed.[52] This generally means a new corporation can be formed with nontaxable exchanges of assets for stock. However, this restriction often results in taxable transfers for similar exchanges when the corporation has been in existence for some time.

Owners may engage in *taxable transactions* with their S corporations. For example, shareholders may lend money, rent property, or sell assets to their S corporations (or vice versa). With few exceptions, owners include the interest income, rent income, or gain or loss from these transactions on their tax returns. Meanwhile, the S corporation is allowed a deduction for the interest, rent, or depreciation expense on assets purchased (if applicable).

> **Example 20.** During the year, K received the following amounts from an S corporation in which she owns 30% of the stock outstanding:
>
> 1. $2,750 interest on a $25,000 loan made to the corporation;
>
> 2. $3,600 rental income from a storage building rented to the corporation; and
>
> 3. $6,300 for special tools sold to the corporation; the tools were acquired for personal use two years ago for $5,800.

---

[50] § 1374(b)(2).

[51] §§ 1371(b) and 1362(e)(6)(A).

[52] § 351. See Chapter 2 for the requirements of tax-free transfers to controlled corporations.

Assume that the S corporation's net ordinary income, excluding the above items, is $40,000, and the depreciation deduction for the tools is $900. Thus, net income for the corporation, after the above three items are considered, is $32,750 ($40,000 − $2,750 − $3,600 − $900). K's income is $2,750 interest, $3,600 rental income, $500 capital gain on sale of a nonbusiness asset ($6,300 − $5,800), and $9,825 ordinary income from the S corporation (30% × $32,750).

There is a restriction, however, on when an S corporation may deduct expenses owed but not paid to a shareholder. An accrual basis business (whether an S corporation or partnership) may not deduct expenses owed to a cash basis owner until the amount is paid.[53]

> **Example 21.**   Assume the same facts as in *Example 20*, except that $2,000 of the $2,750 interest is accrued but not paid at the end of 1990, the S corporation is on the accrual basis, and K is on the cash basis. The interest owed is paid as follows: $600, March 1, 1991; $400, August 10, 1991; $550, October 15, 1991; and $450, January 10, 1992. K reports the interest when received and the S corporation deducts the interest when paid. Assuming both use the calendar year, the amounts are $750 in 1990, $1,550 ($600 + $400 + $550) in 1991, and $450 in 1992.

Two special rules governing related party transactions affect all business forms. Both are discussed in Chapter 10. *First*, realized *losses* on sales between related parties are disallowed.[54] This is not a deferral; therefore, there is no carryover of basis or holding period. However, if this property is later sold at a gain, the gain is offset by the previously disallowed losses.[55] *Second*, recognized gains on sales between related parties of *property* that will be *depreciable* to the new owner are taxed as ordinary income.[56] A related party is defined as one who owns directly or indirectly more than 50 percent of the business when losses are disallowed or when depreciable property is involved. (See the discussion and examples in Chapter 10 regarding these transactions and the definitions of related parties.) A *third* restriction, affecting transactions between partners and their 50 percent owned partnerships, is *not* applicable to either S or C corporations. For these partners, recognized gains on sales of capital assets that will not be capital assets to the partnership are taxed as ordinary income.[57] In contrast, shareholders may sell capital assets to their more than 50 percent owned S or C corporations and the gain is capital, as long as the assets will not be depreciable property to the corporation.

---

[53] §§ 267(a)(2) and 267(e). This same restriction applies to a C corporation if its cash basis shareholders own more than 50 percent of its stock. § 267(b)(10).

[54] §§ 267 and 707(b)(1).

[55] § 267(d).

[56] § 1239.

[57] § 707(b)(2).

DETERMINING SHAREHOLDER BASIS

A shareholder's basis in the S corporation is computed in much the same way as the partner's basis in the partnership.[58] There are three important exceptions, however (see Exhibit 12-2 for a comparison of the partner's basis in the partnership with the shareholder's basis in the S corporation).

First, recall that an S shareholder's contribution of appreciated assets for stock is tax-free with a carryover of basis *only if* the 80 percent of stock ownership rule is met.[59] If it is not met, basis begins with a taxable exchange, and thus is equal to the market value of noncash assets (i.e., basis of the assets plus gain recognized on the contribution).

Second, an S shareholder's basis does *not* include a proportionate share of corporate debt nor does it include any personal guarantees of corporate debt. Instead, it includes all corporate debt owed to this particular shareholder (i.e., this shareholder's receivables from the S corporation).[60] Annual adjustments to basis are required for any increases or decreases in these receivables but no adjustments (nor gain recognition) are required for changes in corporate debt owed to anyone else. To properly apply the rules, shareholders must compute their basis in S stock separately from their basis in the receivables. Most adjustments that affect a shareholder's basis are made to the *stock*. A shareholder's basis in the receivables is adjusted *only* (1) when the actual indebtedness itself changes, (2) when corporate net losses exceed the shareholder's basis in S stock, and (3) to restore any basis reduction due to the flow through of net losses. The third adjustment can be made only with net income and gains earned in subsequent years. The receivable/debt basis is the last to be reduced *but* the first to be restored.

> **Example 22.**   An S corporation incurs a net operating loss of $30,000 in 1991. L, its sole shareholder, has a basis in the stock of $24,000 and a note due him from the corporation totals $10,000. The $30,000 loss flows through to L, first to the extent of his $24,000 stock basis and the remaining $6,000 because of the $10,000 note owed to him. After the appropriate adjustments, his basis is zero for the stock and $4,000 ($10,000 − $6,000) for the note. (If the 1991 loss had been $36,000, only $34,000 would be deductible by L, reducing his basis in both items to zero. The remaining $2,000 loss would be carried forward indefinitely until a positive basis occurs in either item.)

> **Example 23.**   Refer to *Example 22.* The S corporation has net income of $3,000 in 1992 and $8,000 in 1993. L reports the $3,000 in 1992 and increases his basis in the note to $7,000 ($4,000 + $3,000). L reports the $8,000 in 1993 and increases his basis in the note to its face amount of $10,000 ($7,000 + $3,000) and in the stock to $5,000 ($8,000 − $3,000 to the note).

---

[58]   § 1367.

[59]   §§ 351 and 358.

[60]   § 1367(b)(2).

Exhibit 12-2
Adjustments to Ownership Basis
(with emphasis added to highlight differences)

Partner's Basis in the Partnership		Shareholder's Basis in the S Corporation	
	Initial investment		Initial investment
Plus: 1.	Basis of additional capital contributions	**Plus:** 1.	Same as partner
2.	*Share of partnership liabilities* (adjusted annually)	2.	None *except total receivables due from the corporation* (adjusted annually) *can be used for distributions of losses.*
3.	Share of taxable income	3.	Same as partner
4.	Share of separately stated income and gains	4.	Same as partner but also *including gain recognized on distribution of noncash assets*
5.	Share of nontaxable income and gains	5.	Same as partner
6.	Gain recognized by the partner (when cash received exceeds basis)	6.	Same as partner
Less: 1.	Cash distributions received (including *share of decreases in partnership liabilities*)	**Less:** 1.	Cash distributions received (and for distributions of losses and *decreases in debt owed to this shareholder*)
2.	*Basis* of noncash distributions received *(but not to exceed basis)*	2.:	*Market value* of noncash distributions received *(any amount in excess of basis is recognized capital gain)*
3.	Share of net loss (but not to exceed basis)	3.	Same as partner
4.	Share of separately stated expenses and losses (but not to exceed basis)	4.	Same as partner
5.	Share of nondeductible expenses and losses (but not to exceed basis and not a capital expenditure)	5.	Same as partner
6.	Dispositions of ownership interest	6.	Same as partner

After a shareholder's basis in the indebtedness is reduced, repayments of the debt in excess of basis result in includible income. If the debt is a note, bond, or other written debt instrument, the shareholder recognizes capital gain to the extent the payment exceeds basis.[61] If the debt is an *open* account, the shareholder recognizes ordinary income.[62] This ordinary income can be recharacterized as capital gain by converting the open account to a capital contribution; no gain is recognized for this conversion, even if the open account has been reduced by net losses (i.e., its basis is less than its face or market value).[63]

Third, as illustrated later, the distribution of noncash assets (i.e., property) requires the S corporation to recognize gain to the extent that market value exceeds an asset's basis.[64] The basis of the appreciated property to the recipient shareholders is its market value. Thus, a shareholder's basis in the S corporation is increased by his or her proportionate share of the recognized gain and decreased by the market value of assets received. If the market values of these assets exceed the owner's basis in the business, the excess is capital gain from the sale of stock (illustrated later in this chapter with distributions).[65]

OUTSIDE VERSUS INSIDE BASIS

When a shareholder sells his or her interest in the S corporation, any gain or loss reported by the seller has no effect on the business or the purchaser. This can create an inequity for the purchaser, especially if the S corporation has appreciated assets. In this situation, the purchase price is based on the market value of the assets but the new owner must accept the seller's basis in the assets for calculating depreciation, amortization, depletion, and gain or loss. This causes the new owner to report more net income (or less loss) from the S corporation. Further confusing the situation, this shareholder's *outside basis* (basis in the S corporation stock) exceeds his or her *inside basis* (share of the corporation's basis in its net assets). This situation is similar to the one encountered in a partnership.

> **Example 24.** An S corporation (or a partnership) has the following information:
>
> | | Basis | Market Value |
> | --- | --- | --- |
> | Cash | $10,000 | $ 10,000 |
> | Equipment | 80,000 | 140,000 |
> | Capital accounts | $90,000 | $150,000 |

---

[61] § 1232 and Rev. Rul. 64-162, 1964-1 C.B. 304.

[62] Rev. Rul. 68-537, 1968-2 C.B. 372 and *Cornelius v. U.S.*, 74-1 USTC ¶9446, 33 AFTR2d 74-1331, 494 F.2d 465 (CA-5, 1974).

[63] §§ 108(e)(6) and (d)(7)(C).

[64] §§ 311(b) and 336(a).

[65] § 1368(b).

R purchases T's one-third interest for $50,000. If T's basis is $30,000, she will recognize a gain of $20,000 ($50,000 − $30,000). R's basis in the business is his purchase price of $50,000. However, his share of the corporation's (or partnership's) basis in the net assets is $30,000 (one-third of $90,000). R's annual net income will be determined in the same manner as that of the other owners. That is, depreciation, gain, and loss on the equipment will be calculated on the $80,000 basis.

The inequities encountered by the new owner are quite similar to those that exist when an owner contributes appreciated property in a nontaxable exchange for a capital interest. Since there is no provision for correcting these inequities, the new shareholder should be aware of their impact before the transactions are completed. In contrast, recall that there is a special allocation available to partnerships for correcting both types of inequities (see Chapter 10). These two differences can be a significant disadvantage for the S corporation when compared with the partnership form.

SELECTING A TAXABLE YEAR

With few exceptions, owners report their share of S corporation (or partnership) income, deductions, and credits as of the business's year-end regardless of when distributions of assets are actually made.[66] This timing requirement makes the selection of a year-end for the owners and the business an important tax planning decision.

Generally, it is a tax advantage to defer all includible income as long as possible but to accelerate the deduction of all expenses, losses, and credits. The basic rule is, of course, dependent upon the current and future tax positions of the owners. If operations are expected to result in net losses in the early years, the greatest benefit would be achieved by electing a business year that coincides with that of the owners. In this way, owners would be able to recognize their distributive shares of the losses currently. This benefit, of course, would be reversed in years when operations result in net income. When there is net income, the ideal business year would end one month after that of the owners. However, owners do not always have the freedom to elect the ideal year-end for their S corporations.

S corporations, like partnerships, generally are restricted to two types of taxable years.[67] First, an S corporation may use the calendar year.[68] Second, a fiscal year that is a *natural business year* may be used. This second option requires that, during the three previous years, more than 25 percent of the gross business receipts must have been earned the last two months of the selected fiscal year.

---

[66] §§ 706(a) and 1378.

[67] § 1378(b).

[68] § 1378.

Example 25.   An S corporation is organized November 1, 1991. Its net ordinary income for the first 14 months is as follows:

November 1, 1991–December 31, 1991	$ 20,000
January 1, 1992–October 31, 1992....................	200,000
November 1, 1992–December 31, 1992	40,000

All shareholders report on the calendar year. If the S corporation's year-end also is December 31, the owners have includible income of $20,000 in 1991 and $240,000 ($200,000 + $40,000) in 1992. Based on the second option listed above, if the S corporation receives permission for an October 31 year-end, the owners have no includible income in 1991 but have includible income of $220,000 ($20,000 + $200,000) in 1992. The $40,000 will be combined with the net income or loss for the first ten months in 1993 and reported in 1993.

As discussed in Chapter 10, the Revenue Act of 1987 introduced a third option in the selection of a taxable year for a partnership or an S corporation. Either entity may elect to adopt or change its tax year to any fiscal year that does not result in a deferral period longer than three months—or, if less, the deferral period of the year currently in use.[69] Recall, however, that such an election requires that the electing partnership or S corporation make a single tax payment on or before May 15 of each year computed at the highest tax rate imposed on individual taxpayers for the prior year *plus* one percent (e.g., 32 percent if the prior year is 1991) on the prior year's deferred income.[70] In essence, the partnership or S corporation must maintain a non–interest-bearing deposit of the income taxes that would have been deferred without this requirement. Since this option eliminates any tax benefits of income deferral, few S corporations made the election.

S corporations have a fourth year-end option when IRS permission is obtained. Thus, with IRS approval, a fiscal year may be adopted if it is identical to that of owners holding a *majority* of the stock.[71] This option also is available when a majority of the shareholders are currently changing to the same tax year requested or held by the S corporation.

Since restrictions on C corporation year-end choices are much more lenient than those for S corporations, an election by a fiscal year C corporation to become an S corporation also may require a change in the corporate year-end. This new year is applicable to all future years, even if the Subchapter S election is canceled and the business reverts to a C corporation.

---

[69]   § 444. Partnerships and S corporations in existence before 1987 are allowed to continue their fiscal years even if the deferral period exceeds three months.

[70]   § 7519 and Reg § 1.7519-2T(a)(4)(ii).

[71]   Rev. Proc. 87-32, 1987-2 C.B. 396.

FAMILY OWNERSHIP

Many of the benefits available to family businesses from *income splitting* are dependent on which organizational form is selected. Some income splitting, however, may be achieved by employing relatives in the business regardless of the organizational form. For example, owners may hire their children to work for them. All reasonable salaries are deductible business expenses and includible salary income to the children. In addition to the tax benefits, some owners believe this provides personal advantages, including encouraging the children to take an interest in the business at an early age.

In some instances, family businesses are formed primarily for tax reasons. The most common example includes both a parent and one or more otherwise dependent children as owners. The basic tax rate structure provides considerable incentive for this type of arrangement when the child is at least 14 years of age.[72]

Rules similar to those affecting the family partnership (discussed in Chapter 11) are applicable to family S corporations.[73] Thus, if reasonable compensation is not paid for services performed or for the use of capital contributed by a family member, the IRS may reallocate S corporation income or expenses.[74] Unlike the partnership, this rule extends to all family members, including those who are *not* owners and when there is no donee/donor relationship.

> **Example 26.** At the beginning of the year, F made an interest-free loan of $10,000 to an S corporation owned by his daughter. The loan is not repaid by the end of the year. Assume an arm's length interest rate of 12% would have been charged by a commercial lender. The IRS may make an adjustment of $1,200 interest income to F and of $1,200 interest expense to the S corporation. However, the IRS is not compelled to make this adjustment. Note that the IRS has the same options if F is a shareholder along with his daughter in the S corporation.

Two important advantages of using the S corporate form instead of a *general* partnership are that (1) shareholders are not required to participate in management, and (2) corporate stock may have different voting rights. In contrast with the general partnership, the parent can retain management control of an S corporation or a limited partnership without violating other family members' rights of participation. This is an important point since it has been a major problem for many general partnerships.

---

[72] Recall that after 1986 many of the income-splitting advantages with children under 14 years of age are eliminated.

[73] § 1366(e) and Reg. § 1.1373-1(a)(2).

[74] Family member, as defined by the Code, is the same for the partnership and the S corporation. §§ 704(e)(3) and 1366(e).

CURRENT DISTRIBUTIONS OF CORPORATE ASSETS

Rules governing current (i.e., nonliquidating) distributions of S corporate assets are unique although they include some characteristics of partnerships and C corporations. Several factors affect the tax treatment. First, it is relevant if an S corporation has accumulated earnings and profits (AE&P) from previous years when it was operated as a C corporation (see Chapter 3 for a definition of AE&P).[75] Second, there is a difference if distributions include property (i.e., noncash assets). Third, special rules cover distributions made during a qualifying period after the Subchapter S status is terminated (referred to as the post-termination period).

Unlike the partnership, it is not necessary to determine if distributions are proportionate (i.e., representative of § 751 and non–§ 751 assets). Instead, all asset distributions in excess of the S shareholder's basis in the stock are capital gains (unless they qualify under the collapsible corporation provisions discussed in Chapter 3).[76]   The amount of distributions is equal to cash plus the market value of all other assets. Recall that, in all situations other than the allocation of net losses, an S shareholder's basis *excludes* receivables or other obligations of the S corporation. Computations for basis and determination of whether distributions exceed basis occur at the end of the taxable year.

DISTRIBUTIONS IN GENERAL

Distributions from an S corporation generally represent accumulated income that has been previously taxed to the shareholder. Consistent with the principles underlying Subchapter S, this income should not be taxed again when it is distributed. Therefore, distributions normally are considered nontaxable to the extent of the shareholder's basis. For a corporation that has been an S corporation from inception, this will always be the case. However, when a regular C corporation elects S status, distributions may represent earnings and profits that were accumulated during C years and that are taxed again when distributed.

S CORPORATIONS WITH NO AE&P

All cash distributions by S corporations that have no AE&P are nontaxable unless they exceed the shareholder's basis in the stock.[77]   (Property distributions are discussed later in this chapter.)

---

[75] § 312.

[76] §§ 1368(b) and 341.

[77] § 1368(b).

Example 27. D and F have been equal owners of an S corporation for five years. D's basis in the stock is $15,000 and F's basis is $4,000. Corporate net ordinary income for the year totals $10,000 and cash distributions total $22,000. D reports $5,000 (50% × $10,000) ordinary income and has a basis in the stock of $9,000 ($15,000 + $5,000 − $11,000). F reports $5,000 ordinary income and $2,000 capital gain because the $11,000 cash received exceeds her $9,000 basis ($4,000 + $5,000).

When it is known that distributions will exceed a shareholder's basis, the recognition of capital gain can be avoided if the shareholder increases his or her stock basis before the year ends. This may be done by (1) contributing capital to the S corporation, or (2) having debt owed this shareholder converted to capital.

As discussed later in this chapter, realized gains (but not losses) on assets distributed by the S corporation to its shareholders must be recognized by the corporation and passes through to the owners.[78] The basis of the property received by the shareholders is its fair market value (FMV). In addition, unlike the partnership rules, owners must recognize gain when the FMV of the assets received exceeds their basis in the corporate *stock*.[79] This is treated as a partial sale and, consequently, is a capital gain.

Example 28. After using the following equipment for four of its five year ACRS life, an S corporation distributes it to H, its sole owner.

Asset	Cost	Accumulated Depreciation	Basis	Fair Market Value
Equipment	$10,000	$7,900	$2,100	$4,300

Assume H's basis, after all adjustments except the equipment distribution, is $1,800. The S corporation must recognize a § 1245 gain of $2,200 ($4,300 − $2,100). The $2,200 gain flows through to H. H's basis in the equipment is its $4,300 FMV. He must also recognize a $300 capital gain since the $4,300 FMV of the equipment exceeds his $4,000 basis ($1,800 + $2,200).

S CORPORATIONS WITH AE&P

S corporations with accumulated E&P have *three* types of corporate level accounts that determine the treatment of a distribution. The three equity accounts are the Accumulated Adjustments Account, the Accumulated E&P account for S years before 1983, and the Accumulated E&P account for years that the corporation was a regular C corporation.

---

[78] §§ 311(b) and 336(a).   [79] § 1368(b).

Accumulated Adjustments Account.   The *accumulated adjustments account* (AAA) is the initial reference point for determining the source of a distribution and therefore its treatment. The AAA represents post-1982 income of the S corporation that has been taxed to shareholders but has not been distributed. Consequently, distributions from the account are a *nontaxable* return of the shareholder's basis in his or her stock. Distributions from the AAA that exceed the shareholder's stock basis are capital gain.[80]

The AAA is a corporate level equity account that is maintained only if the S corporation has accumulated E&P from years when it was operated as a C corporation.[81] The AAA is the cumulative total of the S corporation's post-1982 income and gains (other than tax-exempt income) as reduced by all expenses and losses (both deductible and nondeductible other than those related to tax-exempt income) and any distributions deemed to have been made from the account. The specific formula for computing the balance in the AAA is shown in Exhibit 12-3. Note that the adjustments to the AAA are identical to those made by shareholders to their basis in their stock with *three* exceptions:[82]

1. Tax-exempt income increases the shareholder's stock basis but has no effect on the AAA.

2. Expenses and losses related to tax-exempt income decrease the shareholder's stock basis but have no effect on the AAA. [However, some nondeductible expenditures reduce the AAA as they do the shareholder's stock basis (e.g., the 20% of meal and entertainment expenses that is not deductible, fines, and penalties).]

3. The various adjustments to the AAA (other than distributions) could create either a positive or negative balance in the AAA account. In contrast, the shareholder's stock basis can never be negative. Note that distributions that decrease the shareholder's stock basis have no effect on the AAA once the AAA's balance is exhausted.

Example 29.   In 1975, T formed ABC Inc. and operated it as a calendar-year C corporation until 1983 when it elected to be treated as an S corporation. T has owned 100% of the stock since the corporation's inception. T's basis in his stock at the beginning of 1991 was $10,000. Other information related to the S corporation for 1991 is shown in the following.

Net ordinary income for 1991	$50,000
Charitable contribution	9,000
Tax-exempt interest income	10,000
Expenses related to tax-exempt interest income	1,000
Disallowed portion of meal expenses	2,000
Cash distributions	20,000
Accumulated adjustments account	10,000

---

[80]   § 1368(b).

[81]   § 1368(c).

[82]   § 1368(e)(1).

Exhibit 12-3
Accumulated Adjustments Account
Computations

Beginning Balance (S years beginning after 1982)

\+ Taxable income (but not tax-exempt income)

\+ Separately stated items of income and gain

− Net loss

− Separately stated expenses and losses

− Nondeductible expenses and losses (other than expenses related to tax-exempt income)

− Cash distributions

− Market value of property distributions

= Accumulated Adjustment Account Balance

The first five items listed above flow through to T. Of these, T must include the $50,000 of ordinary taxable income on his 1991 tax return. In addition, T is allowed to report the $9,000 charitable contribution made by the corporation as an itemized deduction on his return.

T's basis and the balance in the AAA account at the end of the year are computed in the following manner:

	Basis	AAA
Beginning balance	$10,000	$10,000
Net ordinary income for 1991	50,000	50,000
Tax-exempt interest income	10,000	—
Charitable contribution	(9,000)	(9,000)
Disallowed portion of meal expenses	(2,000)	(2,000)
Expenses related to tax-exempt income	(1,000)	—
Cash distribution	(20,000)	(20,000)
Total	$38,000	$29,000

Note that the $9,000 ($38,000 − $29,000) difference between the increase in T's basis in his stock and the corporation's AAA is attributable to the tax-exempt interest income of $10,000 less the $1,000 of expenses related to this income, neither of which affects the AAA.

As noted above, distributions from the AAA are nontaxable to the shareholders unless they exceed the shareholder's stock basis. However, it is rare for shareholders to receive distributions from the AAA that exceed the basis in their stock. Most of the time, the aggregate basis of the shareholders will equal or exceed the AAA (e.g., see *Example 29* above). Nevertheless, the AAA can exceed the shareholder's basis.

Example 30. Same facts as in *Example 29* above. T died on January 1, 1992 and willed all of his stock to his daughter, D. At the time of his death, T's shares were worth $15,000. As a result, D's basis will be $15,000 which is substantially less than the balance in the AAA account of $29,000.

Example 31. Same facts as in *Example 29* above. Due to losses in the stock market, T was forced to sell his shares in ABC. In January 1992, T sold all of his shares to B for $10,000. In this case, B's basis will be less than the $29,000 balance in the AAA. Note that the AAA is a corporate-level account and is unaffected by shareholder transactions.

Previously Taxed Income. The second account from which a distribution may come consists of the AE&P for S years before 1983, commonly referred to as previously taxed income (PTI). As a practical matter, this account may be viewed as the AAA for years prior to 1983. The balance in this account represents taxable income that was earned by the corporation while it was an S corporation prior to 1983 and which has not been distributed to shareholders. Distributions from this account, like those from the AAA, are considered a nontaxable return of the shareholder's basis in his or her stock.

Accumulated E&P of C Years. The third account from which a distribution may come represents earnings and profits accumulated in years when the corporation was a C corporation. Distributions from AE&P are taxable as dividend income.

Other Adjustments Account. Schedule M of Form 1120S creates a fourth classification, entitled *other adjustments account* (OAA). The OAA represents post-1982 tax-exempt income and expenses related to tax-exempt income that do not flow into the AAA. Thus, the OAA is used to show amounts that affect shareholder bases but not the AAA.

Schedule M. Schedule M on page 4 of Form 1120S is a reconciliation of the beginning and ending balances in these corporate accounts: shareholders' undistributed taxable income previously taxed, the AAA, and the OAA.

Example 32. Same facts as in *Example 29* above. The corporation's Schedule M for the year would appear as follows:

Schedule M-2 Analysis of Accumulated Adjustments Account, Other Adjustments Account, and Shareholders' Undistributed Taxable Income Previously Taxed (See instructions.)	(a) Accumulated adjustments account	(b) Other adjustments account	(c) Shareholders' undistributed taxable income previously taxed
1 Balance at beginning of tax year	10,000		
2 Ordinary income from page 1, line 21 . . .	50,000		
3 Other additions		10,000	
4 Loss from page 1, line 21	( )		
5 Other reductions	(11,000 *)(	1,000)	
6 Combine lines 1 through 5	49,000	9,000	
7 Distributions other than dividend distributions	20,000		
8 Balance at end of tax year—subtract line 7 from line 6	29,000	9,000	

* CHARITABLE CONTRIBUTIONS = $9,000 +
  DISALLOWED MEAL EXPENSE = $2,000
  $11,000

Source of Distribution. Cash distributions by S corporations that have AE&P must follow five specific steps:[83]

1. Nontaxable to the extent of AAA (unless they exceed a shareholder's basis in the stock)

2. Nontaxable to the extent of PTI (unless they exceed a shareholder's basis in the stock)

3. Dividend income to the extent of AE&P

4. A return of capital to the extent of the shareholder's basis in the stock (as adjusted by increases or decreases in the OAA)

5. Capital gain for all remaining amounts (including distributions in steps 1 and 2 above in excess of stock basis), determined as though the stock had been sold

All nontaxable distributions (steps 1, 2, and 4 above) decrease a shareholder's basis whereas the taxable ones (steps 3 and 5) do not.

Example 33. J and W have been equal owners of a calendar year S corporation for several years. It has been operated as a C and an S corporation in the past. Balances at the beginning of the year are shown below in the schedule. Operations for the year show $12,000 net ordinary income,

---

[83] § 1368(c).

$2,000 tax-exempt interest income, and $24,000 cash distributions. Based on the five steps listed above, the $24,000 cash distribution offsets (1) all of the $18,000 AAA, (2) all of the $4,000 PTI, and (3) $2,000 ($24,000 − $18,000 − $4,000) of the AE&P. The balances at the end of the year are determined as follows:

	Corporate Accounts				Stock Basis	
	AAA	PTI	AE&P	OAA	J	W
Beginning balances.......	$ 6,000	$4,000	$3,000	$ 0	$10,000	$6,000
Net ordinary income......	12,000				6,000	6,000
Tax-exempt interest income................				2,000	1,000	1,000
Cash distributions:						
Step 1..................	(18,000)				(9,000)	(9,000)
Step 2..................		(4,000)			(2,000)	(2,000)
Step 3.................			(2,000)			
Ending balances..........	0	0	$1,000	$2,000	$ 6,000	$2,000

Both J and W have $6,000 net ordinary income (from S operations) and $1,000 dividend income (from AE&P). Note that J and W recognize dividend income because tax-exempt income does not increase AAA. Also note that there is no longer any need to maintain an account for PTI once the corporation has distributed its PTI.

Example 34. Refer to *Example 33*. Operations for the following year show $10,000 net ordinary income, $600 net capital loss, and $16,000 cash distributions. The balances at the end of this year are determined as follows:

	Corporate Accounts				Stock Basis	
	AAA	AE&P	OAA	Return of Capital	J	W
Beginning balances.......	$ 0	$1,000	$2,000		$6,000	$2,000
Net ordinary income......	10,000				5,000	5,000
Net capital loss..........	(600)				(300)	(300)
Cash distributions:						
Step 1..................	(9,400)				(4,700)	(4,700)
Step 2..................		(1,000)				
Step 3.................			(2,000)		(1,000)	(1,000)
Step 4.................				3,600	(1,800)	(1,000)
Step 5.................						(800)
Ending balances	0	0	0	$3,600	$3,200	0

Both J and W have $5,000 net ordinary income, $300 capital loss, and $500 dividend income. In addition, W has $800 capital gain since the distributions that reduce basis exceed her basis in the stock by $800. Because this S corporation no longer has AE&P, any future distributions will be nontaxable unless they exceed a shareholder's basis in the stock. Also note that the first $2,000 of the $5,600 return of capital distribution was charged to the OAA, reducing its balance to zero.

DISTRIBUTIONS OF PROPERTY

Although most distributions consist solely of cash, an S corporation may distribute property. Rules governing property distributions of an S corporation are a unique blend of both the partnership and C corporation provisions.

An S corporation, like a C corporation, must recognize gain—but not loss—on the distribution of appreciated property. Any gain recognized by the S corporation on the distribution passes through to be reported by the shareholders. In addition, this gain increases each shareholder's stock basis. Upon receipt of the distribution, the shareholder reduces his or her basis by the fair market value of the property received (but not below zero). Any amount in excess of the shareholder's basis is capital gain. The shareholder's basis in the property is its fair market value.

Noncash distributions follow the same five steps as cash distributions except that step 2—PTI—is omitted.[84]

Example 35. Assume the same facts as *Example 33*, except the distribution is of property with a $24,000 market value and a basis of $21,000. Further assume the $3,000 is depreciation recapture and is included in the $12,000 net ordinary income. The balances at the end of the year are determined as follows:

	Corporate Accounts				Stock Basis	
	AAA	PTI	AE&P	OAA	J	W
Beginning balances.......	$ 6,000	$4,000	$3,000	$ 0	$10,000	$6,000
Net ordinary income......	12,000				6,000	6,000
Tax-exempt interest income................				2,000	1,000	1,000
Cash distributions:						
Step 1..................	(18,000)				(9,000)	(9,000)
Step 2..................		0				
Step 3..................			(3,000)			
Step 4..................				(2,000)	(1,500)	(1,500)
Ending balances	0	$4,000	0	0	$ 6,500	$2,500

Both J and W have $6,000 net ordinary income and $1,500 dividend income.

Shareholders may *elect* to omit step 1, distributions from AAA.[85] Although this action may increase includible distributions from AE&P, the advantage is that it accelerates the elimination of AE&P. S corporations with no AE&P avoid several potentially negative rules (such as the tax on excess passive investment income which is discussed in the next section of this chapter). The election requires the consent of all shareholders.

---

[84] Reg. 1.1375-4 (b).   [85] § 1368(e)(3).

Recall that taxation of property distributions for C corporations (see Chapter 3) and partnerships (see Chapter 11) differs from that of S corporations. A comparison of the taxation of property distributions for these three business forms is illustrated in the following example.

Example 36. A business distributes property to its owners with a $15,000 market value and a $9,000 basis. The owners' basis in the business totals $8,000, before the distribution. An S corporation must recognize the $6,000 gain. The character of the gain (i.e., ordinary or capital) is determined in the same manner as any other taxable transaction. This $6,000 gain then flows through to be reported by the owners. The shareholders' basis in the property is $15,000. Since the $15,000 exceeds the shareholders' $14,000 ($8,000 + $6,000) basis in the stock, the $1,000 difference is recognized as a capital gain. The C corporation also recognizes $6,000 gain, which increases its E&P. Assuming the C corporation has at least $15,000 of E&P, its shareholders have $15,000 dividend income, a $15,000 basis in the property, and no change in their stock bases. In contrast, this is a nontaxable distribution for the partnership and the partner. The partnership's $9,000 basis in the property would be the partners' bases except it is limited to the partners' $8,000 bases. A summary of this information follows.

	S Corporation	C Corporation	Partnership
Gain recognized by the business..............	$ 6,000	$ 6,000	$ 0
Business' gain reported by owners............	6,000	0	0
Gain recognized by owners on property received...........................	1,000	15,000	0
Basis in property received.....................	15,000	15,000	8,000
Basis in ownership interest....................	0	14,000	0

POST-TERMINATION DISTRIBUTIONS

When an S corporation election terminates, the business is immediately treated as a C corporation. Without special rules, this treatment could be particularly severe. Recall that distributions for a C corporation are dividends to the extent of E&P.[86] This is true even though the C corporation may have undistributed nontaxable income from S years. In addition, S corporate net losses that did not flow through to a shareholder because his or her basis was zero expire when Subchapter S status is terminated. To alleviate some of the harshness of these rules, a post-termination period is created to allow shareholders to transact certain S corporate activities after the S corporation no longer exists.

---

[86] §§ 301(c)(1) and 316(a).

The post-termination transaction period begins the day after the S corporation's final tax year and ends on whichever occurs *last*:[87]

1. The date one year later

2. The due date, including extensions, for the S corporation's final return

3. The date 120 days after a final court decision, a closing agreement, or some other agreement between the S corporation and the IRS determining that the S corporation terminated in a prior year

During the post-termination period, nontaxable *cash* (but not property) distributions may be made from AAA.[88] If the S corporation had no AE&P but the C corporation has current E&P, the treatment of cash distributions in excess of AAA is uncertain. However, the wording of the Code indirectly suggests that only cash distributions to the extent of AAA qualify for the special post-termination treatment. If this is true, any cash distributions in excess of AAA are dividends from E&P.

NET LOSSES

The post-termination period also can be used by a shareholder to increase his or her basis in *stock* (but not debt/receivables). This allows the flow through of any net loss carryovers that were not available to the shareholder previously because the basis in the S corporation stock plus debt/receivables was zero.[89] *First*, any corporate debt owed the shareholder should be exchanged for stock (but see previous discussion). *Second*, the shareholder should contribute cash or other assets to the C corporation or exchange them for additional stock. It should be noted, however, that gain on any appreciated assets in the exchange may be recognized if the 80 percent ownership rules of § 351 are not met.

TAXES IMPOSED ON THE S CORPORATION

S corporations, like partnerships, normally are considered nontaxable entities. Unlike partnerships, however, S corporations may be required to pay one of the following taxes:

1. Excessive passive investment income tax

2. Tax on built-in gains

3. Investment credit recapture tax

---

[87] § 1377(b).

[88] § 1371(e).

[89] § 1366(d)(3).

TAX ON EXCESSIVE PASSIVE INCOME

When Congress revised Subchapter S in 1982, it was concerned that C corporations with a potential accumulated earnings tax or personal holding company tax, particularly those that are mere holding companies (i.e., those whose principal assets are investment properties such as stocks, securities, and real estate projects), would attempt to escape these penalty taxes by electing to be treated as S corporations. Subchapter S can provide a refuge for these corporations since S corporations normally are exempt from both penalty taxes.[90] To guard against this possibility, two steps were taken. First, as previously explained, when a corporation has AE&P *and* excessive passive income in three consecutive years, the corporation's S election is terminated.[91] Second, an S corporation must pay a special tax on its passive income if it has (1) AE&P at the close of its tax year, *and* (2) passive investment income exceeds 25 percent of its gross receipts that year.[92] Note that similar to the termination provision for excessive passive income (discussed early in this chapter), the tax only applies to corporations that have been operated as C corporations and have AE&P at the end of the taxable year. Consequently, the tax is not imposed on corporations that have distributed all of their AE&P or that have never been C corporations.

The tax on excessive passive income is equal to the maximum corporate rate for the year (34%) multiplied by *excess net passive income* (ENPI). ENPI is computed as follows:

$$ENPI = \frac{Net}{passive} \times \frac{Passive\ investment\ income\ -\ 25\%\ of\ gross\ receipts}{Passive\ investment\ income}$$

In computing the tax, several rules must be observed.

1. For any taxable year, ENPI cannot exceed the corporation's taxable income.[93]

2. Passive investment income is defined the same as it is for the termination provisions of § 1362(d) discussed previously:[94] generally gross receipts from dividends, interest, rents, royalties, and annuities, and gains from sales of capital assets.

---

[90] The accumulated earnings tax and the personal holding company tax do not apply to S corporations because income is not sheltered within the corporate entity but flows through to the shareholders.

[91] § 1362(d)(3).

[92] § 1375(a).

[93] § 1375(b)(1)(B).

[94] §§ 1375(b)(3) and 1362(d)(3)(D)(i).

3. Net passive income is passive investment income reduced by any allowable deductions directly connected with the production of this income. These deductions include such expenses as property taxes and depreciation related to rental property but exclude such deductions as the dividends-received deduction.[95]

The amount of any tax paid reduces the amount of each item of passive investment income that flows through to shareholders. The tax is allocated proportionately based on passive investment income.[96]

> **Example 37.** PTC is owned equally by R and S. At the close of the year, PTC, an S corporation, reports gross receipts of $200,000 and a balance in its AE&P account of $24,000. Gross receipts include $25,000 interest and $50,000 rent. Deductions directly attributable to rents were $30,000, including depreciation, maintenance, insurance, and property taxes. Since the corporation has passive investment income exceeding 25% of its gross receipts [$75,000 > (25% × $200,000 = $50,000)] *and* it has AE&P at the end of the taxable year, the tax on passive income is imposed. Excessive net passive income of $15,000 is computed as follows:
>
> $$(\$75,000 - \$30,000) \times \frac{\$75,000 - (25\% \times \$200,000)}{\$75,000} = \$15,000$$
>
> PTC's excessive passive investment income tax is $5,100 (34% × $15,000). Of this amount, $1,700 ($5,100 × $25,000 ÷ $75,000) is attributed to the interest and the remainder of $3,400 ($5,100 − $1,700) to rent. Since 50% of the passive income flows through to each shareholder, both of them reduce the amount of passive income that they report by their share of the tax, $2,550 (50% × $5,100), or $850 for interest and $1,700 for rent. Thus, each shareholder reports interest of $11,650 ($12,500 − $850) and rent of $23,300 ($25,000 − $1,700) less $15,000 rent expense, or $8,300.

Shareholders of an S corporation that has an ownership in a partnership must be alert to the fact that each partner is deemed to be distributed a percentage of every partnership item, including each item of gross receipts (unless a special allocation is in effect). As a result, the excessive passive investment tax can be triggered by partnership activities.

---

[95] § 1375(b)(2).

[96] § 1366(f)(3).

TAX ON BUILT-IN GAINS

Without special rules, C corporations planning sales or distributions of appreciated property (e.g., as a dividend or in liquidation) could avoid double taxation by electing S status before making the distributions.

> **Example 38.**   R, a regular C corporation, owns land worth $50,000 (basis $10,000). If R Corporation distributes the land to its sole shareholder, D, as a dividend, the corporation recognizes a gain of $40,000 ($50,000 − $10,000) and D recognizes dividend income of $50,000. Therefore, two taxes are imposed. In contrast, compare the result that occurs if R Corporation has S status. R still recognizes a $40,000 gain. However, that gain is not taxed at the corporate level, but flows through to D to be taxed. In addition, D increases his basis in his stock by $40,000. On receipt of the property, D does not report any income but simply reduces the basis in his stock. As a result, there is only a *single tax* if R Corporation has S status.

To eliminate the tax-avoidance possibility of electing S status before the distribution (or a sale), Congress enacted § 1374. This section imposes a special corporate level tax—the *built-in gains tax*—on gains recognized by an S corporation that accrued while it was a C corporation. The built-in gains tax generally applies only to corporations that "convert" from C to S status (i.e., operate as a C corporation and then elect S status) after 1986.[97] The tax applies *only* to gains recognized during the 10-year period following the S election.

Under § 1374, it is presumed that *any* gain recognized on the sale or distribution of any property by a "converted" S corporation is subject to the built-in gains tax. However, the corporation may rebut this presumption and avoid the tax by proving either of the following: (1) the asset sold or distributed was not held on the date that the corporation elected S status; or (2) the gain had not accrued at the time of the election. As a practical matter, this approach requires every C corporation electing S status to have an independent appraisal of its assets in order to rebut the presumption. Note that for purposes of this tax, built-in gains include the unrealized receivables of a cash basis taxpayer as well as any gain on a long-term contract that has not been recognized (e.g., the taxpayer uses the completed contract method of accounting) and any goodwill.

As a general rule, the special tax applies only to S corporations having a *net unrealized built-in gain*. This is defined as the difference between the value and basis of all assets held on the first day the S election is effective. This represents the *maximum* amount that may be subject to the built-in gains tax.

---

[97]   Qualified small corporations electing S status after 1986 are subject to the built-in gains tax only on their ordinary income items.

Example 39. On November 3, 1991, T Corporation made an S election. The election was effective for calendar year 1992. On January 1, 1992, its balance sheet revealed the following assets.

	Adjusted Basis	Fair Market Value	Built-in Gain (Loss)
Inventory	$ 50,000	$ 75,000	$25,000
Land	30,000	70,000	40,000
Stock	20,000	15,000	(5,000)
	$100,000	$160,000	$60,000

T Corporation's net unrealized built-in gain is $60,000. Note that the built-in loss on the stock effectively reduces the taxpayer's future exposure to the built-in gains tax.

Only the *net recognized built-in gain* is subject to tax.[98] This gain is the difference between any built-in gains and built-in losses recognized during the year. In effect, the corporation may offset any built-in gains recognized during the year with built-in losses that are also recognized. Built-in losses include not only accrued losses on property held at the time of conversion but also any amount that is allowable as a deduction and is attributable to pre-S periods (e.g., a cash basis taxpayer's routine payables). In contrast with built-in gains, it is presumed that any loss recognized on the sale of property or any deduction arising from the payment of an expense is *not* a built-in loss. However, the corporation may rebut the presumption by establishing that the fair market value of the property was less than its basis on the first day of the first S year, or that an unrealized payable existed on that date.

Example 40. Refer to the facts in *Example 39*. During 1992, T Corporation sold the inventory and the stock for $77,000 and $15,000, respectively. Although T recognizes a gain of $27,000 ($77,000 − $50,000) on the sale of the inventory, T's built-in gain recognized is limited to the amount accrued on the date of conversion from a C corporation to S status, $25,000. T's net recognized built-in gain that is potentially subject to tax is $20,000 (the built-in gain of $25,000 less the $5,000 built-in loss recognized.)

If T Corporation had sold the land at a gain of $40,000 instead of selling the stock, the total gain for 1992 would have been $67,000 ($40,000 gain from land + $27,000 gain from inventory). However, only $60,000 of this gain would be subject to the § 1374 tax because T's $60,000 net unrealized built-in gain is the maximum amount subject to the tax.

---

[98] § 1374(b). If a C corporation uses the LIFO inventory method, it must recognize the excess of the FIFO inventory value over the LIFO inventory value. This amount recognized by the C corporation will not be included in built-in gains for the S corporation.

The built-in gains tax is computed by multiplying the top tax rate applicable to regular C corporations (i.e., 34%) times the *lesser* of (1) the net built-in gain recognized, or (2) the S corporation's taxable income determined as if the corporation were a C corporation (except a dividends-received deduction is not allowed).[99] The latter amount provides relief for taxpayers who may have large built-in gains during the year but small taxable incomes. The lesser of these two amounts is then reduced by any NOL and capital loss carryforward from C corporate years. In addition, business tax credit carryforwards arising in a C year can be used to reduce the tax.[100] Any net recognized built-in gain not subject to tax because of this limitation is carried over to the following year and treated as if it occurred in that year.[101] The calculation of the tax is summarized below.

	Lesser of built-in gain or taxable income	$x,xxx
−	NOL carryforward from C year	(xxx)
=	Tax base..	$x,xxx
×	Top corporate tax rate.................................	× xx%
=	Potential tax	$x,xxx
−	Business credit carryforward from C year...............	(xxx)
=	Tax..	$x,xxx

Example 41. Refer to the facts in *Example 39*. Assume that T sold the land for $70,000 in 1993, recognizing a $40,000 gain, which is also the total amount of its net realized built-in gain for the year. Also assume that the corporation's taxable income, including this $40,000 gain and a $3,000 NOL carryforward from C years, is $10,000. T's built-in gains tax is computed as follows:

Lesser of:		
Net recognized built-in gains...........................	$40,000	
Taxable income (before NOL)..........................	13,000	
		$13,000
NOL...		(3,000)
Taxable built-in gain.....................................		$10,000
Highest corporate rate....................................		× 34%
Built-in gains tax..		$3,400

Note that the $30,000 of net recognized built-in gain that was not taxed due to the limitation is carried over to the following year and treated as if it were recognized in that year, along with any other built-in gains and losses.

---

[99]   § 1374(b)(1).

[100]   §§ 1374(b)(2) and (3).

[101]   This amount escapes the tax for S corporations electing S status before March 1, 1988.

INVESTMENT CREDIT RECAPTURE

For years beginning after 1983, an S corporation election is treated as a mere change in form of conducting a trade or business.[102] As a result, the electing corporation is not required to recapture unearned investment credits because of the election. When the election is made, however, the S corporation assumes the liability for any recapture tax that may arise for credits claimed during years when the corporation was not an S corporation.[103]

ESTIMATED TAXES

After 1989, S corporations are required to pay estimated taxes for (1) excessive passive investment income taxes (§ 1375), (2) taxes on built-in gains (§ 1374), and (3) investment credit recapture taxes [§ 1371(d)(2)]. The computations of estimated taxes generally follow the rules applicable to C corporations.[104]

DISPOSITION OF OWNERSHIP INTEREST

Based on the entity theory, sales of stock by shareholders of a corporation electing Subchapter S result in capital gain or loss.[105] This, of course, is identical to how stock sales of a nonelecting corporation are treated. However, the amount of the gain or loss will differ since an S shareholder's basis is adjusted for S corporate items whereas a C shareholder's basis is not. All other stock transfers also follow the rules of an exchange or gift of a capital asset.[106] This is a significant advantage for the S (or C) corporate shareholder when compared with the complicated and often unfavorable rules of the partnership. However, recall from the earlier discussion, shareholders who sell or otherwise dispose of their stock must report their share of the S corporation's current year items, based either on the per day allocation method or the interim closing of books method.

As discussed earlier, any debt owed the shareholder with a reduced basis because of net loss flow throughs will result in capital gain when paid if it is a note, bond, or other written debt instrument or ordinary income if it is an open account.[107] Consequently, this is the last chance for a shareholder who is disposing of all the stock to convert the debt to capital and avoid ordinary income when the open accounts are paid.

---

[102]   § 1371(d)(1).

[103]   § 1371(d)(2).

[104]   See § 6655 for estimated taxes applicable to C corporations.

[105]   If certain oil and gas properties are held by the S corporation, a § 751-type (partnership—see Chapter 11) anal-ysis may result in ordinary income; § 1254(b)(2).

[106]   § 1221.

[107]   § 1232; Rev. Ruls. 64-162, 1964-1 C.B. 304 and 68-537, 1968-2 C.B. 372; and *Cornelius v. U.S.*, 74-1 USTC ¶9446, 33 AFTR2d 74-1331, 494 F.2d 465 (CA-5, 1974).

WORTHLESS SECURITIES

S and C shareholders who hold worthless securities, including stock and debt, are subject to the same provisions with one exception. The S corporation's flow through rules apply *before* the deduction for worthless stock or debt. The loss on worthless securities is treated as though it occurred on the last day of the *shareholder's* taxable year (not the S corporation's year) from the sale or exchange of a capital asset. Thus, it is possible for stock to become worthless before corporate activities are completed. In addition, if the S corporation's year ends *after* the stockholder's year ends, worthlessness could occur before the flow through is available. This potential loss of deduction could be a serious disadvantage to shareholders.

The deduction for worthless stock is a capital loss unless the stock qualifies for ordinary loss treatment under § 1244.[108] Bad debts also are capital losses unless the shareholder can establish that they are business bad debts.[109] For example, the debts may have arisen as a result of a business transaction or the shareholder's employment status with the corporation. Business bad debts are ordinary losses.

CORPORATE LIQUIDATION

Generally, provisions governing liquidations and reorganizations for C corporations are applicable to S corporations (see Chapters 5 and 7).

---

[108] Compare §§ 165(g) and 1367(b)(3) with § 1244(a).

[109] Compare §§ 166(a) and (d).

TAX PLANNING

There are numerous tax planning opportunities available to a business regardless of the form of organization selected. Many of these were discussed throughout this and previous chapters. Although tax planning opportunities are too extensive and too personalized to prepare an exhaustive list, a brief comparison of the S corporation, partnership, and C corporation is mentioned here to encourage the student of taxation to continually analyze tax situations with an eye to tax planning. The thoughtful but imaginative tax adviser who is able to provide clients with planning options that meet their needs is in much demand in today's tax-conscious society.

The situation of any taxpayer planning to contribute property in exchange for an ownership interest should be evaluated. In some instances, it may be in the individual's best interest to seek an alternate method of obtaining an ownership interest. For example, property with a basis in excess of its market value may provide the owner greater benefits if leased to the business.

Taxpayers purchasing an interest in a business that owns appreciated assets should be aware that no adjustment to the business's assets can be made except in the partnership, and then only if a special election is in effect. This is particularly relevant to the purchasing partner or S shareholder. When the election cannot be made, the purchase price will exceed the asset bases for purposes of depreciation, depletion, amortization, gains, and losses. Therefore, it is quite possible the purchase price should be adjusted below market value when no election exists. This, of course, is quite important to the seller.

BASIC PRINCIPLES

The S corporation has many of the same advantages and disadvantages as a partnership. Unlike general partners, however, S shareholders have limited liability. This factor often is the major reason for incorporating a business. Some of this protection, however, may be lost if shareholders are required to guarantee corporate liabilities. Regardless of the restrictions, shareholders are protected from a number of debts that are not guaranteed. To achieve this benefit, owners must give up much of the flexibility available to the partnership and are subject to more filing requirements and other formalities.

Two significant advantages of the partnership are not available with any other organizational form. One is the ability to specially allocate partnership items among the partners. This can be particularly useful in alleviating inequities and for tax planning when marginal rates differ among the owners. A second unique attribute of the partnership is the ability to adjust the basis of the assets when a capital interest is sold and when gain is recognized on distribution of partnership assets. An important disadvantage of the partnership is that an owner cannot be an employee. As a result, owner/employee benefits are not deductible by the partnership and the owner has self-employment income. After 1987, owner/employee benefits are nondeductible for an S corporation as well.

In addition to limited liability for its shareholders, the C corporation's major advantage is that it is a separate taxable entity. As a result, owner/employee benefits are deductible expenses. In addition, business income is not taxable to owners until distributed to them. As is often the case, the major advantage also can be a disadvantage. The separate taxable entity concept results in double taxation when corporate profits are distributed to shareholders. It also means that neither losses nor the character of income or deductions flows through to shareholders.

The corporate form may be a disadvantage for businesses with sales of depreciable realty. Section 291(a)(1) serves to reclassify some of a § 1231 gain of C corporations and certain S corporations from capital gain to ordinary income. This section, however, is not applicable to a partnership.

Generally, newly formed businesses provide greater benefits if organized as a partnership or S corporation. This is because operations in the early years often produce net losses. In these two types of businesses, losses are deductible by the owners (subject to the limitation on passive business losses). In contrast, a C corporation's losses must be carried back or forward to offset corporate income in those years. If losses are incurred in the first years, no tax savings will be obtained from these losses until sometime in the future, and then most likely at the lowest corporate rates. Another situation where the flow through concept is important occurs when owners need to have earnings distributed to cover their current living expenses. This, of course, is dependent on the marginal rates of all taxpayers and the percentage and amount of earnings distributed.

Family businesses provide excellent income-splitting opportunities among family members. For example, children can be employees of their parents' businesses. The amount of salary paid is, of course, dependent on the work performed, but significant tax savings can be achieved. The benefits and difficulties of dependent children as general partners were discussed in Chapter 11.

The corporate form often is an advantage for owners who are selling their interests. Stock sales result in capital gains when the business is successful but often qualify for ordinary loss treatment if unsuccessful. The partner may have the opposite effect. That is, gain is ordinary income to the extent of unrealized receivables, substantially appreciated inventory, and depreciation recapture. But sales at amounts below basis are capital losses. This may be an important consideration when establishing a new business or investing in a business for a limited period of time. From this perspective, the S corporation combines the advantage of the flow through concept with the capital gain/ordinary loss benefit when the ownership interest is sold.

APPENDIX: SELECTING A FORM OF DOING BUSINESS

In summary, S corporations and their shareholders are taxed in a manner similar to that of C corporations and their shareholders in the beginning (when the businesses are being formed or stock is being acquired) and in the end (when the businesses are being liquidated or reorganized or the shareholder is disposing of the stock). However, the tax effects while the S corporation is being operated generally conform more closely to those of the partnership. In some instances, S corporation provisions are unique with no counterpart among the C corporation or partnership provisions. Consequently, these three organizational forms offer an important choice to owners of a business. To illustrate some of the differences that should be considered, a comprehensive summary, in a comparative format, is presented in *Example 42* and Exhibit 12-4.

Example 42. T Company, organized January 1, 1990, has the following information for 1991, its second calendar year:

Gross profit	
Sales..	$470,000
Cost of goods sold............................	300,000
Operating Expenses	
Salary (or compensation) to T, the owner	24,000
Salaries to others (2 nonowners)................	48,000
Payroll taxes for T.............................	(1)
Payroll taxes for others........................	4,000 (1)
Employee benefits: (2)	
Life insurance for T...........................	700 (3)
Life insurance for others......................	1,400 (3)
Utilities and telephone..........................	2,500
Office expenses................................	1,100
Insurance......................................	3,100
Interest to T ($300 not paid until 2/1/92)	3,600
Property taxes..................................	3,000
Repairs..	12,000
Depreciation...................................	15,000
Charitable contributions........................	7,000
Other items	
Dividend income (from 25% owned corporation)	2,000
Capital gain (CG)..............................	2,200
Capital loss (CL)..............................	1,200
Rehabilitation investment credit.................	2,000
Cash distributed to owner T.....................	12,000
Land distributed to owner T (basis).............	7,000 (4)

1. Each employee was paid $2,000 per month. FICA is 7.65% × $24,000 = $1,836 and unemployment taxes are 6.2% × $7,000 = $434 for each employee and $2,270 for both taxes. This is rounded to $4,000 to simplify the illustration. If the company is a corporation, payroll taxes for T are $2,000 (rounded). If the company is a proprietorship or partnership, there are no payroll taxes for T. Instead, T is subject to self-employment taxes on his personal tax return.

2. Assume T has agreed to reimburse the business for any expenses that cannot be deducted because he is an owner.

3. Life insurance is group-term life insurance of $50,000 for T and each of the other two employees.

4. Market value of the land distributed is $10,000. It was purchased for the $7,000 on May 2, 1990.

If the business is a proprietorship, T is the owner. For the sake of comparison, assume T is allocated all of the partnership items and is the sole shareholder of the S or C corporation. The Ts (Mr. and Mrs. T) file a joint return, have two exemptions, and $8,000 of personal itemized deductions of interest, taxes, and charitable contributions. They have no other includible income or deductible expenses for the year. On December 31, 1990, T's basis was $100,000.

A. The taxable business income for each of the four organizational forms is computed below.

	Proprietorship	Partnership	S Corporation	C Corporation	
Income					
Sales......................	$470,000	$470,000	$470,000	$470,000	
Cost of goods sold.........	(300,000)	(300,000)	(300,000)	(300,000)	
Gross profit..............	$170,000	$170,000	$170,000	$170,000	
Dividend income...........	0	0	0	2,000	
Net capital gain............	0	0	0	4,000	(1)
Total income.............	$170,000	$170,000	$170,000	$176,000	
Deductions					
Salary (or compensation) to T	0	24,000	24,000	24,000	
Salaries to others..........	48,000	48,000	48,000	48,000	
Payroll taxes for T.........	0	0	2,000	2,000	
Payroll taxes for others	4,000	4,000	4,000	4,000	
Life insurance for T........	0	0	0 (2)	700	
Life insurance for others ...	1,400	1,400	1,400	1,400	
Utilities and telephone	2,500	2,500	2,500	2,500	
Office supplies.............	1,100	1,100	1,100	1,100	
Insurance..................	3,100	3,100	3,100	3,100	
Interest to T...............	0	3,300 (3)	3,300 (3)	3,300 (3)	
Property taxes.............	3,000	3,000	3,000	3,000	
Repairs....................	12,000	12,000	12,000	12,000	
Depreciation...............	15,000	15,000	15,000	15,000	
Charitable contributions....	0	0	0	5,590 (4)	
Dividend deduction	0	0	0	1,600	
Total deductions.........	$ 90,100	$117,400	$119,400	$127,290	
Taxable income..........	$ 79,900	$ 52,600	$ 50,600	$ 48,710	
Tax liability................				$ 7,306 (5)	
Rehabilitation credit........				2,000	
Tax due..................				$ 5,306	

1. The C corporation must recognize the $3,000 ($10,000 − $7,000) § 1231 gain on the land distributed which is treated as capital gain. Thus, $3,000 + $2,200 − $1,200 = $4,000 net capital gain.

2. Since the corporation was formed after 1982 and T owns more than 2% of the stock, the S corporation cannot deduct his employee benefits. Thus, from note 2 on the previous page, this is a loan to T of $700.

3. Accrued expenses to a cash-basis related party are not deductible until paid. The $300 is deductible in 1992.

4. Charitable contributions may not exceed 10% of taxable income computed before the dividends-received deduction, charitable contribution deduction, and net operating and capital loss carrybacks ($48,710 + $5,590 + $1,600 = $55,900 × 10% = $5,590). The $1,410 ($7,000 − $5,590) is carried forward.

5. 15% × $48,710 = $7,306.

B. The Ts' Federal income tax for each of the organizational forms is computed below.

	Proprietorship	Partnership	S Corporation	C Corporation
Net business income.........	$79,000	$52,600	$50,600	$ 0
Business dividend income....	2,000	2,000	2,000	0
Net capital gain..............	1,000 [1]	1,000 [1]	4,000 [1]	0
Salary income...............	0	24,000	24,000	24,000
Interest income..............	0	3,300	3,300	3,300
Cash distribution.............	0	0	0	12,000
Land distribution.............	0	0	0	10,000
Adjusted gross income ..	$82,900	$82,900	$83,900	$49,300
Itemized deductions from the business:				
Charitable contributions....	7,000	7,000	7,000	0
Other itemized deductions[2]..	8,000	8,000	8,000	8,000
Exemptions..................	4,300	4,300	4,300	4,300
Deductions from A.G.I......	19,300	19,300	19,300	12,300
Taxable income............	$63,600	63,600	64,600	$37,000
Federal income tax[3].........	$13,388	$13,388	$13,668	$ 5,940
Self-employment tax[4]	7,687	7,605	0	0
Rehabilitation credit..........	(2,000)	(2,000)	(2,000)	0
Tax due....................	$19,075	$18,993	$11,668	$ 5,940

1. Net capital gains for the proprietor and the partner total $2,200 capital gain − $1,200 capital loss = $1,000. The S corporation must recognize the $3,000 ($10,000 − $7,000) gain on the land distributed. This $3,000 capital gain also flows out to T. Thus, the S shareholder's net capital gains total $1,000 + $3,000 = $4,000.

2. Itemized deductions exceed the standard deduction.

3. 1991 tax rates used: (15% × $34,000 = $5,100) + (28% × remaining taxable income). The surtax is not assessed since taxable income is below the surtax requirement.

4. The self-employment tax for T is [$5,694.58 ($53,400 × 10.664%)] + [$1,992.71 ($79,900 × 2.494%) for the proprietorship and $1,910.40 ($52,600 + $24,000 = $76,600 × 2.494%) for the partnership] = $7,687.29 for the proprietorship and $7,604.98 for the partnership. The 10.664 percent and 2.494 percent are the effective rates for an individual with a 28 percent marginal rate because 50 percent of the self-employment tax is deductible [12.4% − (12.4% × 50% = 6.2% × 28% = 1.736%) = 10.664%] and [2.9% − (2.9% × 50% = 1.45% × 28% = 0.406%) = 2.494%]. The 1991 maximum base is $53,400 and $125,000, respectively, for the two calculations.

C. The combined taxes on income, self-employment, and owner salary for T and each of the organizational forms is computed below.

	Proprietorship	Partnership	S Corporation	C Corporation
Employee taxes on T's salary	$ 0	$ 0	$ 2,000	$ 2,000
FICA taxes paid by T.......	0	0	2,000	2,000
Corporate Federal income tax......................	0	0	0	5,306
T's Federal income and self-employment tax......	19,075	18,993	11,668	5,940
Total tax..................	$19,075	$18,993	$15,668	$15,246

No conclusion should be drawn from this comparison and applied to other situations. For example, the self-employment tax is a substantial cost in the illustration. An owner who has salary income from another source would avoid all or part of the self-employment tax. Different cash and property distributions also would affect the total taxes. In addition, a proprietor and partner would have a $7,000 basis in the land whereas the S and C shareholders would have a $10,000 basis in the land.

D. T's basis in the business or stock for the organizational forms is computed below.

	Partnership	S Corporation	C Corporation
Basis 12/31/90............	$100,000	$100,000	$100,000
Net business income	52,600	50,600	0
Dividend income..........	2,000	2,000	0
Net capital gain.....	1,000	4,000	0
Life insurance.....	(700)	0 [1]	0
Charitable contributions. .	(7,000)	(7,000)	0
Cash distributed..........	(12,000)	(12,000)	0
Property distributed... ...	(7,000)	(10,000)	0
Basis 12/31/91............	$128,900	$127,600	$100,000

The proprietor has a basis in each asset and liability, not in the business itself.

1. T's basis is indirectly reduced by the $700 in premiums since he owes the S corporation this amount.

Exhibit 12-4
Comparative Analysis of Business Forms

Basic Concepts	Items for Comparison	Proprietorship/ Proprietor	Partnership/ Partner	S Corporation/ Shareholder	C Corporation/ Shareholder
	1. What are the restrictions on the number of owners or who may be an owner?	1. One owner who must be an individual	1. None, except there must be at least two owners	1. No more than 35 shareholders (and some states set a minimum number) who must be individuals, estates, or certain trusts	1. None, except some states set a minimum number of shareholders
	2. Are owners liable for business debts that they have not personally guaranteed?	2. Yes.	2. Yes, for general partners but no for limited partners	2. No	2. No
	3. What are the appropriate tax forms and schedules and who files them?	3. Schedules C, SE, and all supporting schedules and forms are filed with proprietor's Form 1040	3. Form 1065 and Schedules K-1 are prepared at the partnership level; partners report their shares on Schedules E, SE, and other supporting schedules and file them with their Form 1040s	3. Same as partnership except Form 1120S and its Schedules K-1 are prepared at the S corporation level	3. Form 1120 and all supporting schedules are filed for the C corporation; shareholders report dividend income on Schedule B and file it with their Form 1040s

Exhibit 12-4 Continued:

Basic Concepts Continued	Items for Comparison	Proprietorship/ Proprietor	Partnership/ Partner	S Corporation/ Shareholder	C Corporation/ Shareholder
	4. Who is the taxpayer?	4. Proprietor	4. Partners (but the partnership may be subject to tax if a year-end different from the partners is used)	4. Shareholders (but the S corporation may be subject to a special tax on certain built-in gains and excess passive investment income or if a year-end different from the share-holders is used)	4. C corporation and shareholders are taxed on dividend income when corporate earnings are distributed
	5. Do owners have self-employment income from the business?	5. Yes, the net income from Schedule C	5. Yes, each *general* partner's share of net ordinary income less passive income from Form 1065 plus his or her guaranteed payments; but for *limited* partners, only their guaranteed payments from services provided to the partnership	5. No	5. No
	6. Must the business's taxable year be the same as the majority owners?	6. Yes	6. Generally, but a different year may be used if the partnership pays a tax on the deferred income	6. Same as partnership	6. No, any generally accepted accounting period may be used

Exhibit 12-4 Continued:

Asset Transfers between Owners and Their Business	Items for Comparison	Proprietorship/ Proprietor	Partnership/ Partner	S Corporation/ Shareholder	C Corporation/ Shareholder
	1. Are contributions of assets for an ownership interest taxable transactions?	1. No, tax-free exchange, all tax attributes transfer to the business except the lower of basis or market value must be used for nonbusiness assets transferred; the term "ownership interest" is not applicable	1. No, same as proprietorship except ownership (capital) interest is applicable	1. No, same as partnership *if* parties to the exchange own more than 80 percent of the corporation after the contribution, but otherwise, a taxable exchange with no carryover of tax attributes	1. Same as S corporation
	2. Are distributions of cash includible income to owners?	2. No.	2. No, except a distribution in excess of the partner's basis in the partnership is treated as a partial sale of the ownership interest	2. No, same as partnership except shareholders' basis for this purpose is their basis in stock and not in corporate debt owed to them	2. Yes, they are nondeductible distributions by the corporation and dividend income to shareholders if from the C corporation's earnings and profits; otherwise it may be same as S corporation in certain situations that are beyond the scope of this chapter

Exhibit 12-4 Continued:

Asset Transfers between Owners and Their Business Continued:	Items for Comparison	Proprietorship/ Proprietor	Partnership/ Partner	S Corporation/ Shareholder	C Corporation/ Shareholder
	3. Do distributions of property result in includible income to either the business or the owners?	3. No, same as contributions except the reverse	3. No, same as proprietorship except the transfer of basis in the assets is limited to the partner's basis in the partnership	3. Yes, S corporation must recognize all realized gain; shareholder receives the assets at their market value with no transfer of tax attributes and any market value in excess of the shareholder's basis in stock (not debt) is treated as a partial sale of the stock	3. Yes, C corporation must recognize realized gain—but not loss—if a nonliquidating distribution; shareholders have dividend income equal to the market value of the assets
	4. May an owner enter into taxable transactions (sales, loans, lease arrangements, etc.) with the business?	4. No	4. Yes, when acting in a nonpartner capacity, but subject to related party restrictions	4. Yes, subject to related party restrictions	4. Same as S corporation
	5. May an accrual basis business deduct accrued expenses to cash basis owners?	5. No, not applicable	5. No, deductible only when paid (except see 6 below)	5. Same as partnership	5. Same as partnership and S corporation

Exhibit 12-4 Continued:

Asset Transfers between Owners and Their Business Continued:	*Items for Comparison*	*Proprietorship/ Proprietor*	*Partnership/ Partner*	*S Corporation/ Shareholder*	*C Corporation/ Shareholder*
	6. Are accrued expenses of the business includible income to cash basis owners? If yes, when?	6. No, not applicable	6. Yes, when received, except guaranteed salary and interest on capital are includible when accrued to a partner whose capital interest exceeds 5 percent	6. Yes, when received	6. Yes, when received
	7. Can owners be employees of the business and be paid salaries subject to employment taxes and withholding?	7. No.	7. No, unless partner's capital interest does not exceed 5 percent	7. Yes	7. Yes
	8. Are fringe benefits for owner/ employees deductible expenses?	8. No	8. No, unless partner's capital interest does not exceed 5 percent	8. No, except for a 2 percent or less shareholder; cost is a debt owed by the shareholder to the S corporation	8. Yes
	9. May the business use the cash method?	9. Yes	9. Yes, unless it qualifies as a tax shelter or has a C corporation as a partner	9. Yes, unless it qualifies as a tax shelter	9. No, unless gross receipts do not exceed $5 million or it qualifies under "type of business" exception

Exhibit 12-4 Continued:

Income, Deductions, and Credits	Items for Comparison	Proprietorship/ Proprietor	Partnership/ Partner	S Corporation/ Shareholder	C Corporation/ Shareholder
	1. Is the business a conduit with the original character of the items flowing through to its owners as of the last day of the business's taxable year?	1. Yes	1. Yes	1. Yes	1. No, the business is an entity and the flow through concept is not applicable
	2. How are capital gains and losses treated?	2. As though received by the proprietor	2. Flow through to each partner	2. Same as partnership	2. Net capital gain includible in corporate taxable income and taxed at regular rates; net capital losses are subject to the carryover rules (back 3 years and forward 5 years) and deductible against capital gains
	3. How is dividend income treated?	3. Includible income as though received by the proprietor	3. Flow through to each partner as dividend income	3. Same as partnership	3. Includible income with a 70 percent dividend deduction (80% if at least 20% of the distributing corporation's stock is owned; 100 % if from an affiliated corporation)

Exhibit 12-4 Continued:

Income, Deductions, and Credits Continued:	Items for Comparison	Proprietorship/ Proprietor	Partnership/ Partner	S Corporation/ Shareholder	C Corporation/ Shareholder
	4. How are charitable contributions treated?	4. An itemized deduction as though contributed by the proprietor	4. Flow through to each partner as an itemized deduction	4. Same as partnership	4. Deductions may not exceed 10 percent of taxable income before certain deductions
	5. Who pays state and local income taxes on the business net income and how are they treated?	5. Proprietor; an itemized deduction as though paid by the proprietor	5. Each partner; an itemized deduction	5. Same as partnership, except some state and local income taxes are assessed on the S corporation and are a deductible expense	5. Deductible expense
	6. How are tax credits treated?	6. As though the credit was earned	6. Qualifying credits flow through to each partner subject to any limitations applicable at the partner level	6. Same as partnership	6. Computed at the corporate level and reduces corporate tax liability
	7. How is net ordinary income treated?	7. Includible with proprietor's A.G.I.	7. Flows through to each partner	7. Same as partnership	7. Included in corporate taxable income
	8. How is net ordinary loss treated?	8. Includible as a reduction of proprietor's A.G.I.	8. Flows through to each partner up to that partner's basis in the partnership; any excess is carried forward	8. Same as partnership	8. Subject to carryover rules (back 3 years and forward 15 years or forward 15 years only) and deductible against net ordinary income

Exhibit 12-4 Continued:

Income, Deductions, and Credits Continued:	Items for Comparison	Proprietorship/ Proprietor	Partnership/ Partner	S Corporation/ Shareholder	C Corporation Shareholder
	9. Is § 291(a)(1) applicable?	9. No	9. No	9. Yes, if C corporation for any of 3 prior tax years	9. Yes
	10. How are items allocated among the owners?	10. Not applicable	10. According to profit and loss ratio or may be specially allocated	10. According to stock ownership ratio	10. Not applicable
	11. Is the basis of business assets adjusted when an ownership interest is sold?	11. Not applicable	11. Yes, if the partners have elected the optional adjustment to basis	11. No	11. No

Basis in the Business	Items for Comparison	Proprietorship/ Proprietor	Partnership/ Partner	S Corporation/ Shareholder	C Corporation Shareholder
	1. Is basis affected by business liabilities?	1. Not applicable	1. Yes, a general partner's basis includes his or her share of partnership liabilities but a limited partner's basis does not	1. No, except a shareholder's basis is increased by the amount of debt owed to him or her for loss flow through	1. No.
	2. Is basis affected by business income, gains, deductions, and losses?	2. Not applicable	2. Yes, all income and gains increase basis and all expenses and losses (that flow through) decrease basis	2. Yes, same as partnership	2. No

Exhibit 12-4 Continued:

Sale of a Business Interest	Items for Comparison	Proprietorship/ Proprietor	Partnership/ Partner	S Corporation/ Shareholder	C Corporation Shareholder
	1. What is the character of gains and losses on the sale of a business interest?	1. Each asset is treated as sold individually and the character of the gain or loss is dependent on that asset	1. Capital gain or loss except ordinary income to the extent of partner's share of unrealized receivables, depreciation recapture, and substantially appreciated inventory	1. Capital gains and losses, except losses may qualify as § 1244 ordinary losses if the corporation meets certain requirements	1. Same as S corporation

Family Ownership	Items for Comparison	Proprietorship/ Proprietor	Partnership/ Partner	S Corporation/ Shareholder	C Corporation Shareholder
	1. Must all owners participate in the management of the business?	1. No	1. Yes, all general partners but limited partners cannot	1. No	1. No
	2. Must a reasonable salary be allocated to family members performing services for the business?	2. No	2. Yes	2. Yes	2. No
	3. May minors be owners of the business?	3. Yes, if they are the sole proprietor	3. Yes	3. Yes	3. Yes

PROBLEM MATERIALS

DISCUSSION QUESTIONS

12-1 *Eligibility Requirements.*   May the following corporations elect Subchapter S? If not, explain why.

    a.   A corporation is 90 percent owned by another corporation. *NO*

    b.   A corporation has 36 shareholders, including Mr. and Mrs. V and Mr. and *yes* Mrs. Z.

    c.   A corporation has 60 percent of its revenues from exports to Europe. *yes*

    d.   A family corporation is owned by a father and his three children. Since *ok* the children are under age 18, their shares are held in a trust fund.

    e.   A corporation has 1,000 shares of common stock outstanding and 500 *OK* shares of authorized but unissued preferred stock.

12-2 *Stock Requirements.*   A mother wishes to establish an S corporation with her two children. However, she is concerned about the one class of stock requirement. She does not want to provide her children with voting control but does *yes* wish to give them 60 percent of the stock. Can she achieve her wishes? Explain.

12-3 *Election.*   F, M, and T are shareholders of a calendar year corporation. On February 15, 1991, they are advised they should elect Subchapter S status. All agree to the election. However, they state that they purchased a 10 percent ownership interest from V on January 4, 1991. V sold his interest because he said he never wanted to have any contact with F, M, or T again. Can they elect Subchapter S for 1991? Explain.   *√ must sign.*

12-4 *Termination of the Election.*   Compare the effects of an intentional revocation, an unintentional violation of the eligibility requirements, and a termination due to the receipt of excessive passive investment income.

12-5 *Termination of the Election.*   A calendar year S corporation unexpectedly receives a government contract on April 3, 1991. The profits from the contract in 1991 will be substantial. The three equal shareholders wish to revoke the election for 1991. Can they? Explain.

12-6 *Passive Investment Income.*   An S corporation with AE&P of $5,000 is expected to receive 30 percent of its gross income from rents but only 18 percent of its net income from these rents. Will the excess passive investment income test be violated? Assume the S corporation's taxable year does not end for seven months and all income is earned equally over the year. Can any action be taken during the next seven months to ensure the test will not be violated?

12-7 *Employee-Owner.*   Which of the three organizational forms—S corporation, C corporation, or partnership—treats owners who work for the business in the following manner?

    a.   The owner's compensation is a deductible business expense.

    b.   The owner's compensation is subject to FICA withholding.

    c.   The employee benefits are deductible expenses.

12-8 *Schedule K-1.* Why must each shareholder of an S corporation be provided with a Schedule K-1?

12-9 *Business Income.* How are each of the following items treated by an S corporation?

a. Dividend income
b. Accrued rental expense to a shareholder
c. Net capital gain
d. Distribution of assets with a market value in excess of basis

12-10 *Family Ownership.* A taxpayer operates a retail store as an S corporation. He has a 16-year-old daughter and a 12-year-old son.

a. Can he employ either or both of them in the business and deduct their salaries?
b. Can they be shareholders in the S corporation?
c. Can a trust be formed to hold the shares of stock owned by a minor child?

12-11 *Stock Basis.* What is outside basis? What is inside basis? Why is it a problem if the outside basis exceeds the inside basis?

12-12 *Property Distributions.* What effect do noncash distributions have on the S corporation and on the shareholder if the S corporation has no AE&P, and:

a. The property's market value exceeds its basis, or
b. The property's basis exceeds its market value?

12-13 *Distributions.* When do cash distributions result in includible income to the S shareholder?

12-14 *Post-Termination Period.* What is a post-termination period? How is it useful?

12-15 *Basic Comparison.* List the tax advantages and the tax disadvantages of an S corporation when compared with:

a. A partnership.
b. A C corporation.

PROBLEMS

12-16 *Termination of Election.* T, the sole shareholder and president of T, Inc., had operated a successful automobile dealership as a regular C corporation for many years. In 1986, however, the corporation elected to be taxed as an S corporation. After T's unexpected heart attack in 1987, the corporation sold most of its assets and retained only a small used car operation. In 1989 and 1990, T, Inc. had paid the tax on excessive passive income and had AE&P (from its C corporation years) at the end of both years. In 1991, the corporation paid no dividends and had the following income and expenses:

Interest income	$50,000
Dividend income	5,000
Gain from prior installment sale	30,000
Used car sales	40,000
Cost of sales	20,000

Is the S election terminated, and if so, when?

12-17 *Consequences of Revocation of an S Election.* In July 1991, the shareholders of S Inc., a calendar year corporation, unanimously vote to revoke their corporation's S election as of August 1, 1991. The corporation's taxable income for January through December 1991 is $432,000, and the shareholders do not elect to perform an interim closing of the corporate books.

a. What tax return(s) must S file for 1991, and what are the due dates of the return(s)?

b. Compute S's corporate taxable income for the 1991 short year for the (1) S corporation and (2) C corporation.

12-18 *Net Income from Operations.* A and B are MDs in the AB partnership. Because of limited liability considerations, their attorney has advised them to incorporate. A typical year for the MDs (who are equal partners) is as follows:

Revenues	$400,000
Operating expenses	190,000
Charitable contributions	10,000
Owner compensation	200,000

a. Calculate AB's ordinary net income if it is taxed as (1) a partnership or (2) an S corporation.

b. Ignoring limited liability considerations, should the partners incorporate and elect S status?

12-19 *Net Income.* A calendar year S corporation, organized in 1988, has the following information for the current taxable year:

Sales..	$180,000
Cost of goods sold..............................	(70,000)
Dividend income................................	5,000
Net capital loss..................................	(4,000)
Salary to Z.......................................	12,000
Life insurance for Z.............................	500
Other operating expenses.......................	40,000
Cash distributions to owners....................	20,000

Assume Z is single and her only other income is $30,000 salary from an unrelated employer. She is a 20 percent owner with a $10,000 basis in the S stock. Calculate the S corporation's net ordinary income and Z's adjusted gross income and ending basis in the S corporation stock.

12-20 *Net Losses.* A calendar year S corporation, organized in 1988, has the following information for the current taxable year:

Sales..	$180,000
Cost of goods sold..............................	(130,000)
Net capital gain.................................	(6,000)
Salary to Z.......................................	18,000
Charitable contributions........................	1,000
Other operating expenses.......................	65,000
Dividend income................................	4,000

Assume Z is single and her only other income is $30,000 salary from an unrelated employer. She is a 40 percent owner with a $10,000 basis in the S stock and no corporate debt owed to her. Calculate the S corporation's net ordinary loss, Z's adjusted gross income, and the character and amount of S corporate items that flow through to her.

12-21 *Allocations.* V owns 500 shares of stock of an S corporation with 2,000 shares outstanding. The calendar year S corporation's records show the following information:

Net ordinary income.............................	$200,000
Net capital loss..................................	(10,000)
Distributions from S earnings....................	30,000

Calculate V's share of the items if on March 15 he sells:

a. 200 of his shares of stock;

b. All 500 shares of his stock and the per day allocation method is used; or

c. All 500 shares of his stock and the interim closing of the books method is used. The records reveal that through March 15, net ordinary income was $60,000, net capital loss was $10,000, and distributions from earnings were $15,000.

12-22 *Basis.* A calendar year business reports the following information as of the end of 1990 and 1991:

	1990	1991
Accounts payable to suppliers..........	$10,000	$11,000
Note payable to City Bank..............	40,000	37,000
Note payable to H......................	12,000	10,000
Cash distributions to owners...........		20,000
Net ordinary income...................		15,000

H, a 30 percent owner, had a basis in the business at the end of 1990 of $9,000. Calculate H's basis at the end of 1991 assuming the business is

a.   A partnership
b.   An S corporation

12-23 *Deductibility of Losses by Shareholders.* B, Inc. was incorporated in 1988, and its shareholders made a valid Subchapter S election for B's first taxable year. At the beginning of 1991, Shareholder Z had a basis of $14,500 in his B stock and held a $10,000 note receivable from B with a $10,000 basis. For 1991, Z was allocated a $32,000 ordinary loss and a $4,000 capital loss from the corporation. B did not make any distributions to its shareholders during the current year.

a.   How much of each allocated loss may Z deduct in 1991?
b.   How much basis will Z have in his B stock and his note receivable at the end of 1991?

12-24 *Basis Adjustments.* Refer to the facts in Problem 12-23 above. In 1992, Z is allocated $7,000 of ordinary income and $5,500 of tax-exempt income from B. B did not make any distributions to its shareholders during the year. What effect will these income allocations have on Z's basis in his B stock and note receivable?

12-25 *Losses and Basis.* J, Inc. is an S corporation that reported the following selected items as of December 31, 1991.

Ordinary loss (from Form 1120S, page 1).........	$30,000
Long-term capital gain...........................	500
Tax-exempt interest income......................	1,000
Notes payable to banks..........................	30,000
(1/1/91 balance = $20,000)	
Notes payable to LJ.............................	5,000
(1/1/91 balance = $0)	

The corporation is owned 60 percent by LJ and 40 percent by RS. At the beginning of the year, they had a basis in their *stock* of $12,000 and $10,000, respectively. How much income or loss will each of the shareholders report for 1991?

12-26 *Basis.* M, a 40 percent owner, has a basis in the S corporate stock of $15,000 and in a note receivable from the S corporation of $8,000. Compute the basis of the stock and the note and the amount of the ordinary loss and income that flow through to M in 1991 and 1992.

a.   The S corporation has a net operating loss of $45,000 in 1991.
b.   The S corporation has a net operating income of $20,000 in 1992.

12-27 *Basis.* A calendar year S corporation has the following information for 1991 and 1992:

	1991	1992
Net ordinary income (or loss)	$(50,000)	$10,000
Dividend income	5,000	2,000

X, an unmarried 60 percent shareholder, has a basis in the stock on January 1, 1991 of $18,000 and a note receivable from the corporation for $12,000. X's only other income is salary from an unrelated business.

a.   Calculate X's basis in the stock and in the note after the above income and loss distributions are recorded for 1991.

b.   Calculate X's basis in the stock and in the note after the above income distributions are recorded for 1992.

c.   Assume the corporation paid the $12,000 note on April 3, 1992. Calculate X's basis in the stock after the above income distributions are recorded for 1992, and calculate the effect on X's adjusted gross income for all 1992 items, including the payment of the note.

12-28 *Inside and Outside Basis.* XYZ is an S corporation owned equally by three shareholders. X has often disagreed with the other shareholders over business matters and now believes he should withdraw from the corporation. X's basis in his stock is $50,000. The corporation's balance sheet appears as follows:

Cash	$100,000
Accounts receivable	50,000
Land	30,000
Equipment (net)	10,000
Accounts payable	30,000
Note payable to X	10,000
Capital accounts	150,000

The equipment's market value is approximately the same as its net book value, but the land is now valued at $60,000. X sells all of his stock to W for $60,000.

a.   How much gain must X recognize?

b.   What is W's "inside" stock basis? What is her "outside" basis?

12-29   *Family Ownership.*   K operates a small retail store as a proprietorship. Annual net ordinary income is expected to be $60,000 next year. The estimated value of her services to the business is $25,000. K's 14-year-old son is interested in the business. She is considering giving him a 30 percent ownership interest in the business. If she does this, she will be paid a salary of $25,000. K files as head of household and does not itemize deductions. Neither she nor her son has any other includible income. Ignore all payroll and self-employment taxes in the following computations.

   a.   Determine next year's tax savings that will be achieved if K establishes an S corporation with her son at the beginning of the year compared with continuing the business as a proprietorship.

   b.   Will K or her son have any includible income if they exchange the appreciated proprietorship assets for the 70 and 30 percent ownership interests, respectively, in the S corporation?

   c.   What advice should you give K on establishing and operating the S corporation?

12-30   *Property Distributions.*   M receives the following equipment from an S corporation as a distribution of profits.

Asset	Cost	Accumulated Depreciation	Basis	Fair Market Value
Equipment	$10,000	$7,900	$2,100	$2,280

The equipment was used in the business for four years of its five-year ACRS life and will be a nonbusiness asset to M. M is a 60 percent owner and has a basis in the stock of $11,000 before the property distribution. Calculate the following amounts.

   a.   The S corporation's recognized gain

   b.   M's basis in the equipment

   c.   The effect on M's basis in the stock

   d.   The effect on M's adjusted gross income

12-31   *Property Distributions.*   Refer to Problem 12-30. Calculate the same amounts if M's basis in the S corporation, before the distribution, is $1,200 instead of the $11,000.

12-32 *Computation of AAA and Basis.*   J formed R Corporation in 1977. The corporation operated as a C corporation from 1977 until 1986, when it elected to be taxed as an S corporation. At the beginning of the current year, J had a basis in his stock of $20,000. The corporation's balance in the AAA at the beginning of the current year was $30,000. R's records for the current year reveal the following information:

Sales	$300,000
Cost of goods sold	120,000
Miscellaneous operating expenses	50,000
Salary to J	40,000
Nondeductible portion of entertainment	4,000
Tax-exempt interest income	13,000
Expenses related to tax-exempt interest income	3,000
Capital gain	7,000
Capital loss	2,000
Charitable contribution	5,000
Cash distribution to J	10,000

Compute J's basis in his stock and the corporation's balance in the AAA as of the end of the taxable year.

12-33 *Cash and Property Distributions.* S, Inc. had previously been a regular C corporation, but elected to be taxed as an S corporation in 1981. It is owned equally by J and G, who have a basis in their stock of $100,000 each at the beginning of the current year. Also at the beginning of the current year, the corporation had the following balances:

Accumulated adjustments account	$50,000
Previously taxed income	40,000
Accumulated earnings and profits	30,000
Other adjustments account	0

During the current year, the corporation had ordinary income of $35,000 and distributed IM stock worth $75,000 to J and cash of $75,000 to G. The stock was purchased four years ago for $50,000.

a.   What are the tax effects of the distribution on the corporation?

b.   What are the consequences to each of the shareholders?

12-34 *Cash Distributions—AE&P.*   A calendar year S corporation has the following balance on January 1, 1991:

Accumulated adjustments account	$13,000
Previously taxed income	2,000
Accumulated earnings and profits	6,000
Other adjustments account	0

The S corporation records show $12,000 net ordinary income, $4,000 tax-exempt income net of related expenses, and $55,000 cash distributions for 1991. Y owns 70 percent of the stock. Her basis in the stock on January 1, 1991 was $7,000, and she has a note receivable from the corporation of $5,000. Y is single, and her only other income is salary from an unrelated business.

a.   Calculate the balances in the corporate accounts as of December 31, 1991.

b.   Calculate the effect on Y's adjusted gross income for 1991.

c.   Calculate the basis in Y's stock and note as of December 31, 1991.

12-35 *Property Distributions—AE&P.* Assume the same facts as in Problem 12-34 except the distribution is stock held more than one year as an investment with a market value of $55,000 and a basis of $53,000.

a. Calculate the balances in the corporate accounts as of December 31, 1991.
b. Calculate the effect on Y's adjusted gross income for 1991.
c. Calculate the basis in Y's stock and note as of December 31, 1991.

12-36 *Distributions from an S Corporation.* D, Inc. was incorporated in 1986, and its shareholders made a valid S election for D's 1989 calendar year. At the end of the current year but before the distribution is considered, D had $19,000 of accumulated earnings and profits from 1986 through 1988, and an accumulated adjustments account of $11,000. D made only one cash distribution of $20,000 during the year, $5,000 of which was paid to shareholder M, who owns 25 percent of D's stock. After all adjustments *except* any required for the distribution, M's basis in his stock was $18,000.

a. What are the tax consequences of the distribution to M, and what is M's basis in his D stock after the distribution?
b. What are the balances in D's accumulated earnings and profits account and accumulated adjustments account after the distribution?

12-37 *Excess Passive Investment Income.* A calendar year S corporation has AE&P of $15,000 from years when it was operated as a C corporation. Its records show the following:

Sales	$100,000
Cost of goods sold	(55,000)
Operating expenses	(15,000)
Dividend income	20,000
Rental income	40,000
Rental expenses	(25,000)

The corporation is owned equally by three brothers. Determine the tax effect on the S corporation and on each brother.

12-38 *Tax on Built-in Gains.* A corporation, organized in 1971, was operated as a C corporation until Subchapter S was elected as of January 1, 1988. Assets held on that date ($80,000 market value and $50,000 basis) are distributed in 1991 when the market value is $90,000. Calculate the 1991 tax on built-in gains if 1991 taxable income, based on computations for a C corporation, is

a. $60,000
b. $20,000

12-39   *Tax on Built-in Gains.*   On February 5, 1991 L Corporation, a cash basis calendar year C corporation, elected S status effective for January 1, 1991. On January 1, L's balance sheet revealed the following assets:

	Adjusted Basis	Fair Market Value
Inventory	$20,000	$85,000
Land	30,000	70,000
Equipment	45,000	15,000

During the year, L sold all of the inventory and the equipment for $90,000 and $12,000, respectively. In addition, during the year the corporation paid $3,000 of routine operating expenses incurred in the previous year. Compute the corporation's built-in gains tax assuming that its taxable income, if it were a C corporation, would have been $100,000 (including the transactions above).

12-40   *Worthless Securities.*   A calendar year S corporation is bankrupt. E, a 60 percent owner for several years, will not receive any assets from the business. His basis in the stock as of January 1, 1991 was $70,000, and he has a note receivable of $25,000 from the corporation. Both are determined to be uncollectible July 1, 1991. The S corporation has a net ordinary loss during 1991 of $30,000; $20,000 before July 1 and $10,000 after July 1. E lent the corporation the $20,000 last year and $5,000 four months ago in an effort to protect his ownership interest in the business. Calculate E's adjusted gross income and capital loss carryovers if his adjusted gross income from other sources totals $120,000.

12-41 *Comprehensive Comparison.* A service business has the following information for the current calendar year:

Revenues from services	$200,000
Operating expenses:	
Depreciation	22,000
Insurance	1,400
Office supplies	1,800
Repairs	2,300
Salary (or compensation) to owners/employee W	25,000
Payroll taxes for W	[1]
Salary to nonowner employees	50,000
Payroll taxes for nonowner employees	4,600
Group-term life insurance premiums:	
For W[2]	750
For nonowner employees	1,320
Utilities and telephone	7,900
Charitable contributions	1,100
Rent expense[3]	4,800
Other items:	
Capital gain	2,000
Capital loss[4]	5,000
Dividend income (from 10% owned corporation)	6,000
Cash distributions to owners	30,000
Rehabilitation credit	3,000

(1) Payroll taxes for W are $2,300 ($25,000 × 7.65% = $1,912.50 FICA + $434 unemployment taxes = $2,346.50, rounded to $2,300 for simplicity) if the business is an S or C corporation.

(2) Assume W has agreed to reimburse the business for any expenses that cannot be deducted because W is an owner.

(3) The rent expense is for a building rented from W. $400 of the rent expenses was accrued at the end of the year but not paid until January of the next year.

(4) There have been no capital gains in prior years.

W is a 90 percent owner and has a basis in the business, before the above information is considered, of $50,000. W has no other includible income, files as married joint, has four exemptions, and has other itemized deductions of $8,500 (including no medical expenses and no miscellaneous deductions).

a. Calculate the net business income for the partnership and the S corporation, and calculate the taxable income and tax liability for the C corporation.

b. Calculate W's Federal income tax liability and self-employment tax liability for each of the three organizational forms.

c. Calculate W's basis in the partnership, S corporation, and C corporation after all information is considered for the year.

12-42 *Tax Return Problem.* Individuals P and K formed P&K Corporation on March 1, 1982 to provide computer consulting services. The company has been an S corporation since its formation, and the stock ownership is divided as follows: 60 percent to P and 40 percent to K. The business code and employer identification numbers are 7389 and 24-3897625, respectively. The business office is located at 3010 East Apple Street, Atlanta, Georgia 30304. P and K live nearby at 1521 South Elm Street and 3315 East Apple Street, respectively. Their social security numbers are 403-16-5110 for P and 518-72-9147 for K.

The calendar year, cash basis corporation's December 31, 1990 balance sheet and December 31, 1991 trial balance contain the following information:

	Balance Sheet 12/31/90		Trial Balance 12/31/91	
	Debit	Credit	Debit	Credit
Cash	$ 12,000		$ 22,000	
Note receivable[1]	14,000		14,000	
Equipment[2,3]	150,000		190,000	
Accumulated depreciation		$ 38,000		$ 63,500
Notes payable[3,4]		94,000		117,200
Capital stock		10,000		10,000
Accumulated adjustments account		34,000		34,000
Cash distributed to P			25,440	
Cash distributed to K			16,960	
Revenues				235,000
Interest income[1]				1,400
§ 1245 gain				3,500
Salary expense[5]			110,000	
Rent expense			12,000	
Interest expense			16,600	
Tax expenses (property and payroll)			13,800	
Repair expense			5,800	
Depreciation expense			29,200	
Health insurance expense[6]			1,600	
Property insurance expense			1,500	
Office supplies expense			3,000	
Utility expense			2,200	
Charitable contributions			500	
Totals	$176,000	$176,000	$464,600	$464,600

(1) The note receivable is from K and is due December 31, 1996. The annual interest rate is 10 percent and K paid $1,400 on December 28, 1991.

(2) Equipment was sold May 12, 1991 for $9,800. It was purchased new on May 1, 1989 for $10,000 and its basis when sold was $6,300.

(3) New equipment was purchased March 1, 1991 with $5,000 cash and a $45,000 three-year note payable. The first note payment is March 1, 1992.

(4) Notes payable are long-term except for $20,000 of the note to be paid next year.

(5) Salary expense is composed of salary of $30,000 each to P and to K and $50,000 to unrelated employees.

(6) Health insurance premiums paid were for the unrelated employees.

Prepare Form 1120S (including Schedules K, L, and M), and Schedule K-1 for shareholder P. Complete all six pages, including responses to all questions. If any necessary information is missing in the problem, assume a logical answer and record it. Do not prepare Schedule K-1 for shareholder K or other required supplemental forms at this time.

Note: This problem is based on the partnership tax return problem that appears at the end of Chapter 10.

12-43 *Tax Return Problem.* During 1990, Lisa Cutter and Jeff McMullen decided they would like to start their own gourmet hamburger business. Lisa and Jeff believed that the public would love the recipes used by Lisa's mom, Tina Woodbrook. They also thought that they had the necessary experience to enter this business, since Jeff currently owned a fast-food franchise business while Lisa had experience operating a small bakery. After doing their own market research, they established Slattery's Inc. and elected to be taxed as an S corporation. The company's address is 5432 Partridge Pl., Tulsa, Oklahoma 74105 and its employer identification number is 88-7654321.

The company started modestly. After refurbishing an old gas station that it had purchased, the company opened for business on February 25, 1991. Shortly after business began, however, business boomed. By the end of 1991, the company had established two other locations.

Slattery's has three shareholders who own stock as follows:

Shareholder	Shares
Lisa Cutter................	500
Jeff McMullen.............	200
Tina Woodbrook..........	300
Total outstanding.......	1,000

Slattery's was formed on February 1, 1991. On that date, shareholders made contributions as follows:

Lisa Cutter contributed $30,000 in cash and 200 shares of MND stock, a publicly held company, which had a fair market value of $20,000. Lisa had purchased the MND stock on October 3, 1986 for $8,000.

Jeff McMullen contributed equipment worth $35,000 and with a basis of $29,000.

Tina Woodbrook contributed $30,000 in cash.

Assume 1991 depreciation for tax purposes is $10,560.

The company is on the accrual basis and has chosen to use the calendar year for tax purposes. Its adjusted trial balance for *financial accounting* purposes reveals the following information:

	Debit	Credit
Cash...................................	$279,800	
Ending inventory.........................	16,000	
Equipment..............................	35,000	
Land...................................	10,000	
Building................................	15,000	
Improvements to building................	55,000	
Accumulated depreciation................		$ 9,000
Notes payable...........................		93,000
Accounts payable........................		40,000
Taxes payable...........................		8,000
Salaries payable.........................		20,000
Capital stock............................		100,000
Sales..................................		400,000
Gain on sale of MND stock...............		18,000
Dividend from MND Corporation...........		2,000
Cost of goods sold.......................	84,000	
Legal expenses..........................	500	
Accounting expenses.....................	400	
Miscellaneous expenses..................	2,100	
Premium on key-man life		
insurance policy	800	
Advertising..............................	8,600	
Utilities................................	8,000	
Payroll taxes............................	12,500	
Salary expenses.........................	120,000	
Insurance...............................	9,000	
Repairs.................................	6,500	
Charitable contributions...................	17,600	
Depreciation per books...................	9,000	
Interest expense.........................	200	

The company has provided additional information below.

The company took a physical count of inventory on December 31, 1991 and determined that ending inventory was $16,000.

On February 9, 1991, the corporation purchased an old gas station for $25,000 to house the restaurant. Of the $25,000 purchase price, $10,000 was allocated to the land while $15,000 was allocated to the building. Prior to opening, the old gas station was renovated. Improvements to the structure were made during February at a cost of $55,000.

The legal costs were for work done by Slattery's attorney in February for drafting the articles of incorporation and by-laws. Accounting fees were paid in May for setting up the books and the accounting system. Miscellaneous expenses included a one-time $100 fee paid in February to the State of Oklahoma to incorporate.

The MND stock was sold for $38,000 on April 3, 1991. Shortly before the sale, MND had declared and paid a dividend. Slattery's received $2,000 on April 1, 1991. MND was incorporated in Delaware.

The corporation purchased refrigeration equipment (7-year property) on February 15, 1991 for $15,000.

Slattery's has elected not to use the limited expensing provisions of Code § 179. In addition, it claimed the maximum depreciation with respect to all other assets. Any other elections required to minimize the corporation's tax liability were made.

Lisa Cutter (Social Security No. 447-52-7943) is president of the corporation and spends 90 percent of her working time in the business. She received a salary of $60,000. No other officers received compensation. Social security numbers are 306-28-6192 for Jeff and 403-34-6771 for Tina. The key-man life insurance policy covers Lisa's life and the corporation is the beneficiary.

Prepare Form 1120S and other appropriate forms and schedules for Slattery's. On separate schedule(s), show all calculations used to determine all reported amounts except those for which the source is obvious or which are shown on a formal schedule to be filed with the return.

Note: This problem is based on the tax return problem that appears at the end of Chapters 2 and 10.

RESEARCH PROBLEMS

12-44 *Incorporating a Proprietorship or Partnership.*   E and F have operated competing businesses for several years. Recently, they agreed to combine their assets and form a corporation. They plan to transfer appreciated property to the newly organized corporation in exchange for stock and notes. The net assets have a market value of $320,000 and a basis to the owners of $175,000. After the exchange, each of them will own stock valued at $100,000 and long-term notes with a face value of $60,000 and an annual interest rate of 10 percent. The term of the notes has not been established yet but E and F are considering making a third of them ($20,000 to E and $20,000 to F) payable at the end of three years, a third payable at the end of five years, and the remainder payable at the end of 10 years. Based on their present plans, will the transfer of appreciated property to the corporation for stock and notes qualify as a nontaxable exchange?

Some suggested research materials:

§ 351 and accompanying Regulations.
Pinellas Ice & Cold Storage Co. v. Comm., 3 USTC ¶1023, 11 AFTR 1112, 287 U.S. 462 (1933).
Camp Wolters Enterprises, Inc., 22 T.C. 737 (1955) *aff'd* in 56-1 USTC ¶9314, 49 AFTR 283, 230 F.2d 555 (CA-5, 1956).
Robert W. Adams, 58 T.C. 41 (1972).

12-45 *Expanding an S Corporation.* L Inc., an S corporation, manufactures computers. Most of its computers are sold through individually owned retail computer stores. This year it decided it wanted to expand its operations into the retail market. To this end, it has decided to acquire Micros Unlimited, which operates a chain of computer retail stores nationwide. According to the proposed plan, L will purchase all of the stock of Micros and then completely liquidate the newly acquired corporation. It will then operate all of the stores of Micro as a separate division of the company. Advise L regarding any problems you foresee in this plan.

Hint: Read the requirements that must be satisfied in order for a corporation to operate as an S corporation.

PART IV

FAMILY TAX PLANNING

CONTENTS

Upon completion of this chapter you will be able to:

- Characterize the types of transfers that are subject to the Federal gift tax

- Compute a donor's total taxable gifts for the current year, including

  - Determination of all available $10,000 exclusions

  - Calculation of any available marital or charitable deduction

- Explain the mechanics of the calculation of the gift tax, including the role of the unified credit

- List the three basic steps involved in the computation of a decedent's taxable estate

- Specify the various types of property interests that must be valued for inclusion in a decedent's gross estate

- Describe any deductions from the gross estate

- Explain the mechanics of the calculation of the estate tax, including the role of the unified credit

- Discuss the purpose of the generation-skipping transfer tax

Chapter **13**

ESTATE AND
GIFT TAXATION

INTRODUCTION

Unlike the Federal income tax, the Federal transfer taxes are not significant revenue producers. For example, in 1988 collection of the Federal transfer taxes represented less than 2 percent of Federal income.[1] Historically, the primary function of these taxes has been to inhibit the accumulation of wealth by family units. Thus, the goal of wealth redistribution underlies the design of the Federal gift, estate, and generation-skipping transfer taxes that are examined in this chapter.

A BRIEF HISTORY

In 1916, Congress enacted the first Federal law designed to tax the transfer of property triggered by the death of an individual. The value of the transfer was measured by the fair market value of the various assets included in the decedent's taxable estate.

Because an individual could avoid the estate tax simply by gifting away his or her property before death, a transfer tax on gifts payable by the donor was deemed necessary to prevent full scale avoidance of the estate tax. The first Federal gift tax was enacted in 1924. Until 1976, the gift tax was computed on the basis of a separate (and less expensive) rate schedule than that of the estate tax. A unique feature of the gift tax is the fact that it is computed on the cumulative amount of gifts made by an individual during his or her lifetime. Because of the progressive transfer tax rates, every gift is more expensive in terms of tax dollars than the last.

Congress enacted several substantial changes in the structure of the transfer tax system in 1976. The first change was the integration of the gift and estate taxes. The two separate rate schedules were replaced by a single, unified transfer tax rate schedule used to compute both the gift and the estate tax. After 1976, a decedent's taxable estate is treated as an individual's *final* taxable gift and is

---

[1] Commissioner of Internal Revenue, *1988 Annual Report*, IRS Publication 55.

taxed on a cumulative basis with actual gifts made during the decedent's life. In addition, a single, *unified* credit was substituted for the $30,000 gift tax exemption and the $60,000 estate tax exemption. The credit is "unified" in the sense that whatever amount is used to offset the gift tax is unavailable to offset the estate tax.

Another change made in 1976 was the introduction of a third Federal transfer tax on generation-skipping transfers. This tax, designed to complement the gift and estate taxes, is quite complex and highly controversial. It is discussed later in this chapter.

The Economic Recovery Tax Act of 1981 (ERTA 1981) continued the restructuring of the transfer tax system begun in 1976. The most important feature of this legislation was the unlimited marital deduction. This deduction makes gifts between spouses completely nontaxable and allows the first spouse to die to leave the family wealth to the surviving spouse at no Federal transfer tax cost. Thus, after 1981, the taxable unit for the imposition of the gift or estate tax is no longer the individual but the marital unit.

PROPERTY INTERESTS

Since the estate and gift taxes concern transfers of property, understanding the two taxes requires an appreciation of the nature of property interests and the different forms of property ownership. In the United States, each of the 50 states has its own system of *property law*—statutory rules that govern an individual's right to own and convey both real and personal property during his or her lifetime. Unfortunately, the specific property laws of each state vary considerably and therefore generalizations about property laws can be dangerous. However, the various state legal systems can be divided into two basic categories: *common law systems* and *community property systems*. The common law system, derived from English laws of property ownership, focuses on individual ownership of assets, regardless of the marital status of the individual. This system has been adopted in 41 states. The community property system is a derivation of Spanish property law and is followed in nine states: Arizona, California, Idaho, Louisiana, Nevada, New Mexico, Texas, Washington, and Wisconsin. Under either system, an individual may own property alone or jointly with another. In addition, an individual may own only a partial interest in the property such as an income interest. The different forms of co-ownership and various types of partial interests are considered below.

FORMS OF CO-OWNERSHIP

The consequences of holding property jointly with another can vary substantially, depending on the type of co-ownership. There are four forms of co-ownership: (1) tenancy in common, (2) joint tenancy, (3) tenancy by the entirety, and (4) community property ownership.

Tenancy in Common. A tenancy in common exists when two or more persons hold title to property, each owning an undivided fractional interest in the whole. The percentage of the property owned by one tenant need not be the same as the other co-tenants but can differ as the co-tenants provide. The most important feature of this type of property interest is that it is treated in virtually all respects like property that is owned outright. Thus, the interest can be sold, gifted, willed, or, when there is no will, passed to the owner's heirs according to the laws of the state. Another important characteristic of a tenancy in common is the *right of partition*. This right permits co-owners who disagree over something concerning the property to go to court to secure a division of the property among the owners. In some cases, however, a physical division is impossible (e.g., 50 acres of land where each acre's value is dependent on the whole), and consequently, the property must be sold with the proceeds split between the owners.

Joint Tenancy. Under a joint tenancy arrangement, two or more persons hold title to property, each owning the same fractional interest in the property. Joint tenancy normally implies the right of survivorship (joint tenancy with right of survivorship, or JTWROS). This means that upon the death of one joint tenant, the property automatically passes to the surviving joint tenants. Consequently, the disposition of the property is not controlled by the decedent's will. Like tenants in common, joint tenants have the right to sever their interest in the property. This is a particularly valuable right since the tenant may wish to disinherit the other joint tenants.

Tenancy by the Entirety. A tenancy by the entirety is a JTWROS between husband and wife. The critical difference between a tenancy by the entirety and a JTWROS is that in most states a spouse cannot sever his or her interest without the consent of the other spouse. In addition, in some states the husband has full control over the property while alive and is entitled to all the income from it.

Community Property. In a community property system, married individuals own an equal, undivided interest in all wealth acquired during the course of the marriage, regardless of which spouse made any individual contribution to the marital wealth. In addition to a half interest in such "community property," a spouse may also own property in an individual capacity as "separate property." Generally, assets acquired prior to marriage and assets received by gift or inheritance are separate property. However, in all nine community property states there exists a strong legal presumption that all property possessed during marriage is community, and that presumption can only be overcome by convincing proof of the property's separate nature.

Marital Property. Before leaving the subject of joint ownership, the concept of marital property deserves attention. Except in community property states, it is a common mistake to assume that all property acquired during marriage is jointly held. State laws vary widely on this issue. In some states, only property specifically titled as JTWROS is treated as jointly held. In these and other states, it is not unusual that property acquired during marriage belongs to the husband regardless of whose earnings were used to acquire the property. In other states, each spouse is deemed to own that which can be traced to his or her own earnings. Because of the problems with marital property, transfers of such property should be evaluated carefully to ensure that the rights of either spouse are not violated.

PROPERTY INTERESTS: LIFE ESTATES, REVERSIONS, AND REMAINDERS

Persons who own property outright have virtually unlimited rights with respect to their property. They can sell it, mortgage it, or transfer it as they wish. In addition, they can divide the ownership of the property in any number of ways. In this regard, it is not uncommon for property owners to transfer ownership in property to someone temporarily. During the period of temporary ownership, the beneficiary could have the right to use, possess, and benefit from the income of the property. Assuming that the beneficiary's interest is limited to the income from the property, he or she would be treated as having an *income interest*. The time to which the beneficiary is entitled to the income from the property could be specified in any terms, such as common measures of time: days, weeks, months, or years. Alternatively, the time period could be determined by reference to the occurrence of a specific event. For example, when an individual has an income interest for life, the interest is referred to as a *life estate*. In this case, the person entitled to the life estate is called the *life tenant*.

The owner of property has the right to provide for one or more temporary interests, subject only to the *rule against perpetuities*. This rule requires that the property pass outright to an individual within a certain time period after the transfer. Normally, ownership of the property must vest at a date no later than 21 years after the death of persons alive at the time the interest is created. After any temporary interests have been designated, the owner has the right to provide for the outright transfer of the property. If the owner specifies that the property should be returned to the owner or his or her estate, the interest following the temporary interest is referred to as a *reversionary interest*. If the property passes to someone other than the owner, the interest is called a *remainder interest*. The holder of the remainder interest is the *remainderman*.

Life estates, remainders, and reversions are property interests which can be transferred, sold, and willed (except for life estates) like other types of property. These interests can also be reached by creditors in satisfaction of their claims. However, a person can establish a trust with so-called *spendthrift* provisions, which prohibit the beneficiary from assigning or selling his or her interest (e.g., a life estate) or using the assets to satisfy creditors.

THE GIFT TAX

The statutory provisions regarding the Federal gift tax are contained in §§ 2501 through 2524 of the Internal Revenue Code. These rules provide the basis for the gift tax formula found in Exhibit 13-1. The various elements of this formula are discussed below.

Exhibit 13-1
Computation of Federal Gift Tax Liability

Fair market value of all gifts made in the current year..................................		$xxx,xxx
Less the sum of		
Annual exclusions ($10,000 per donee)....................................	$xx,xxx	
Marital deduction...............................	xx,xxx	
Charitable deduction	x,xxx −	xx,xxx
Taxable gifts for current year........................		$xxx,xxx
Plus: All taxable gifts made in prior years.................................		+ xx,xxx
Taxable transfers to date.............................		$xxx,xxx
Tentative tax on total transfers to date		$ xx,xxx
Less the sum of		
Gift taxes computed at current rates on prior years' taxable gifts..............	$ x,xxx	
Unified transfer tax credit.......................	x,xxx −	xx,xxx
Gift tax due on current gifts..........................		$ xx,xxx

---

TRANSFERS SUBJECT TO TAX

Section 2511 states that the gift tax shall apply to transfers in trust or otherwise, whether the gift is direct or indirect, real or personal, tangible or intangible. The gift tax is imposed only on transfers of property; gratuitous transfers of services are not subject to tax.[2] The types of property interests to which the gift tax applies are virtually unlimited. The tax applies to transfers of such common items as money, cars, stocks, bonds, jewelry, works of art, houses, and every other type of item normally considered property. It should be emphasized that no property is specifically excluded from the gift tax. For example, the transfer of municipal bonds is subject to the gift tax, even though the income from the bonds is tax free.

The gift tax reaches transfers of partial interests as well. One example is a transfer of property in trust where the income interest is given to someone—the income beneficiary—for his or her life, while the trust property or remainder interest is given to another person—the remainderman—upon the income beneficiary's death. In this case, the donor would be treated as having made two separate gifts, a gift of the income interest and a gift of the remainder interest.

---

[2] Rev. Rul. 56-472, 1956-2 C.B. 21.

The application of the gift tax to both direct and indirect gifts ensures that the tax reaches all transfers regardless of the method of transfer. Direct gifts encompass the common types of outright transfers (e.g., father transfers bonds to daughter, or grandmother gives cash to grandson). On the other hand, indirect gifts are represented primarily by transfers to trusts and other entities. When a transfer is made to a trust, it is considered a gift to the beneficiaries of the trust. Similarly, a transfer to a corporation or partnership is considered a gift to the shareholders or partners. However, if the donor owns an interest in a partnership or corporation, he or she is not treated as making a gift to the extent it would be a gift to himself or herself. An individual may also be treated as making a gift if he or she refuses to accept property and the property passes to another person on account of the refusal.

Most taxpayers understand that the gift tax is imposed on transfers of property motivated by affection and generosity. However, the tax may also be imposed on a transfer of property not intended as a gift within the commonly accepted definition of the word. The tax is intended to apply to any transfer of wealth by an individual that reduces his or her potential taxable estate. Therefore, § 2512 provides that any transfer of property, in return for which the transferor receives *less than adequate or full consideration* in money or money's worth, is a transfer subject to the gift tax.

Adequate Consideration. Revenue Ruling 79-384 provides an excellent example of a transfer for insufficient consideration.[3] The taxpayer in the ruling was a father, who had made an oral promise to his son to pay him $10,000 upon the son's graduation from college. The son graduated but the father refused to pay him the promised amount. The son then successfully sued the father, who was forced to transfer the $10,000. The IRS ruled that the father had received no consideration in money or money's worth for the transfer and therefore had made a taxable gift to his son.

Revenue Ruling 79-384 illustrates two important concepts. First, *donative intent* on the part of a transferor of property is not necessary to classify the transfer as a taxable gift.[4] Second, anything received by the transferor in exchange for the property must be subject to valuation in monetary terms if it is to be consideration within the meaning of § 2512.[5] The father did receive the satisfaction resulting from his son's graduation, and this consideration was sufficient to create an enforceable oral contract between father and son. However, because the consideration could not be objectively valued in dollar terms it was irrelevant for tax purposes.

---

[3] 1979-2 C.B. 12.

[4] Reg. § 25.2511-1(g)(1).

[5] Reg. § 25.2512-8.

The question of sufficiency of consideration normally arises when transfers of assets are made between family members or related parties. When properties are transferred or exchanged in a bona fide business transaction, the Regulations specify that sufficiency of consideration will be presumed because of the arm's-length negotiation between the parties.[6]

Transfers of wealth to dependent family members that represent support are not taxable gifts. The distinction between support payments and gifts is far from clear, particularly when the transferor is not legally obligated to make the payments. Section 2503(e) specifies that amounts paid on behalf of any individual for tuition to an educational organization or for medical care shall not be considered taxable gifts to such individual.

Payments that a divorced taxpayer is legally required to make for the *support* of his or her former spouse are not taxable gifts.[7] However, Regulation § 25.2512-8 specifies that payments made prior to or after marriage in return for the recipient's relinquishment of his or her *marital property rights* are transfers for insufficient consideration and subject to the gift tax. Section 2516 provides an exception to this rule. If a transfer of property is made under the terms of a written agreement between spouses and the transfer is (1) in settlement of the spouse's marital property rights, or (2) to provide a reasonable allowance for support of any minor children of the marriage, no taxable gift will occur. For the exception to apply, divorce must occur within the three-year period beginning on the date one year before such agreement is entered into.

Retained Interest. The final criterion of a taxable transfer is that the transfer must be complete. A transfer is considered complete only if the donor has surrendered all control over the property. For this reason, when the donor alone retains the right to revoke the transfer, the transfer is incomplete and the gift tax does not apply. Similarly, the donor must not be able to redirect ownership of the property in the future; nonetheless, to have a completed gift it is not necessary that the donees have received the property or that the specific donees even be identified.[8]

> **Example 1.** Donor D transfers $1 million into an irrevocable trust with an independent trustee. The trustee has the right to pay the income of the trust to beneficiaries A, B, or C *or* to accumulate the income. After 15 years, the trust will terminate and all accumulated income and principle will be divided among the surviving beneficiaries. Because D has parted with all control over the $1 million, it is a completed gift, even though neither A, B, or C has received or is guaranteed any specified portion of the money.

---

[6] *Ibid.*

[7] Rev. Rul. 68-379, 1968-2 C.B. 414.

[8] Reg. § 25.2511-2(a).

VALUATION AND BASIS

The value of a transfer subject to the Federal gift tax is measured by the fair market value of the property transferred less the value of any consideration received by the transferor. Determining fair market value can be the most difficult aspect of computing a gift tax due. Fair market value is defined in the Regulations as "the price at which such property would change hands between a willing buyer and a willing seller, neither being under any compulsion to buy or to sell, and both having reasonable knowledge of relevant facts."[9]

The determination of an asset's fair market value must be made on the basis of all relevant facts and circumstances. The Regulations under § 2512 are quite detailed and extremely useful in that they prescribe methods for valuation of a variety of assets.

> **Example 2.** Donor S transfers 10 shares of the publicly traded common stock of XYZ Corporation on June 8, 1991. On that date, the highest quoted selling price of the stock was $53 per share. The lowest quoted selling price was $48 per share. Regulation § 25.2512-2(b)(1) specifies that the fair market value of the XYZ stock on June 8, 1990 shall be the mean between the highest and lowest quoted selling price [($53 + $48) ÷ 2], or $50.50 per share.

The valuation of a gift of a partial interest in property is a particularly difficult matter. As part of the Revenue Reconciliation Act of 1990, Congress enacted a set of complex valuation rules that may apply if a donor gives away part of his or her interest in property while retaining an interest in the same property. The general effect of these new rules is to assign a zero value to the donor's retained interest unless such interest is "qualified" by meeting a strict set of statutory requirements. Note that when a retained interest is not a qualified interest, the value of the gifted interest equals the entire value of the property.

> **Example 3.** In the current year Donor D transfers property worth $100,000 into a trust, retaining the right to receive all the income generated by the property for the next 20 years. At the end of the 20-year period, the trust property will be distributed to D's children. Clearly the discounted present value of the children's right to receive the property in 20 years is substantially less than $100,000. However, under the new § 2702 valuation rules, a retained income interest is not a qualified interest, so the value of D's gift to his children upon formation of the trust is $100,000.

The basis of an asset in the hands of a donee is calculated under the rules of § 1015. Generally, the basis of property received as a gift is the basis of the

---

[9]   Reg. § 25.2512-1.

asset in the hands of the donor, increased by the amount of any gift tax paid attributable to the excess of fair market value over the donor's basis at the date of gift. This general rule applies only if the asset is sold at a gain by the donee. If the carryover basis rule would result in a realized loss upon subsequent sale, the basis of the asset will be considered the *lesser* of the carryover basis (donor's basis) *or* the asset's fair market value at date of gift. If the asset is sold at a price greater than the fair market value at date of gift but less than its carryover basis, no gain or loss is recognized.

THE GIFT TAX EXCLUSION

When computing taxable gifts made during a current year, a donor may exclude the first $10,000 of gifts made to any donee. This is an *annual exclusion*, subject to the single requirement that a gift eligible for the exclusion must be a gift of a *present* or *current interest* in property.[10] Regulation § 25.2503-3(b) defines a present interest as one that gives the donee "an unrestricted right to the imme-diate use, possession, or enjoyment of property or the income from property." Therefore, the $10,000 annual exclusion is not available for a gift that can only be enjoyed by the donee at some future date, even if the donee does receive a current ownership interest in the gift.

> **Example 4.**   Donor D gifts real estate to donees M and N. M is given *a life estate* (the right to the income from the property for as long as M lives). N receives *the remainder interest* (complete ownership of the property upon the death of M). Although both M and N have received legal property interests, D may claim only one exclusion for his gift to M. The gift to N is a gift of a future rather than a current interest.

Securing the obvious tax benefit of the $10,000 annual exclusion can be difficult if the gift in question is made to a minor or an incapacitated donee. In such cases the donor may be reluctant to give an unrestricted current interest in the donated property. A complete discussion of strategies for making gifts to minors or incapacitated donees is included in Chapter 15.

GIFT SPLITTING

Because of the progressivity of the gift tax and the availability of the annual $10,000 exclusion, gift taxes on a transfer can be minimized by increasing the number of donors. A gift made by a married individual residing in a community property state may have two donors (husband and wife) because of state property law. Property laws in the forty-one non–community property states do not produce this *two donor* result. To compensate for this difference, § 2513 provides a *gift splitting* election to a married donor.

---

[10]   § 2503(b).

If a donor makes the proper election on his or her current gift tax return, one-half of all gifts made during the year will be considered to have been made by the donor's spouse. Both spouses must consent to gift splitting for the election to be valid. Since evidence of the spouse's consent is necessary when gift splitting is used, a gift tax return must be filed.

> **Example 5.**   In the current year, husband H makes two gifts of $100,000 each to his son and daughter. His wife, W, makes a gift of $5,000 to their daughter. H and W elect gift splitting on their current gift tax returns. As a result, H will report a gift to the daughter of $52,500 and a gift to the son of $50,000, and will claim two $10,000 gift tax exclusions. W will report exactly the same gifts and claim two $10,000 exclusions.
>
> Without gift splitting, H would still be entitled to $20,000 of exclusions, but W could only claim an exclusion of $5,000 for her gift to the daughter.

GIFTS TO POLITICAL AND CHARITABLE ORGANIZATIONS

Code § 2501(a)(5) excludes gifts of money or other property to a political organization from the statutory definition of taxable transfers. If a gratuitous donation is made to a qualified charitable organization, § 2522 provides a deduction for such gift from the donor's taxable gifts for the calendar year. Thus, transfers made without sufficient consideration to qualifying political or charitable groups are not subject to the Federal gift tax.

THE GIFT TAX MARITAL DEDUCTION

Because of the 1981 changes in § 2523, gifts to spouses made after December 31, 1981 are fully deductible by the donor. The marital deduction is permitted only if certain requirements are satisfied. A full discussion of these requirements is considered in conjunction with the discussion of the marital deduction for estate tax purposes.

The gift tax marital deduction allows an individual to make tax-free transfers of wealth to his or her spouse. This opportunity to equalize the wealth owned by husband and wife plays an essential role in family tax planning, a role that will be discussed in Chapter 15.

COMPUTATION AND FILING

Unlike the income tax, which is computed on annual taxable income, the Federal gift tax is *computed cumulatively* on taxable gifts made during a donor's lifetime. This is done by adding taxable gifts for the current year to all taxable gifts made in prior years, calculating the gross tax on the sum of cumulative gifts, and subtracting the amount of gift tax calculated on prior years' gifts.[11]

---

[11]   § 2502(a). The amount of gift tax calculated on prior years' gifts is based on current gift tax rates, *regardless* of the rates in effect when the gifts were actually made.

The transfer tax rate schedule in effect for 1984 through 1992 is reproduced in Exhibit 13-2. Exhibit 13-3 contains the transfer tax rate schedule applicable to transfers made after December 31, 1992. Note that the only difference in these two rate structures is at the highest transfer tax rates of 50 and 55 percent.

Exhibit 13-2
Unified Transfer Tax Rate Schedule

For Gifts Made and for Deaths before 1993

If the amount with respect to which the tentative tax to be computed is	*The tentative tax is*
Not over $10,000	18 percent of such amount
Over $10,000 but not over $20,000	$1,800 plus 20 percent of the excess of such amount over $10,000
Over $20,000 but not over $40,000	$3,800 plus 22 percent of the excess of such amount over $20,000
Over $40,000 but not over $60,000	$8,200 plus 24 percent of the excess of such amount over $40,000
Over $60,000 but not over $80,000	$13,000 plus 26 percent of the excess of such amount over $60,000
Over $80,000 but not over $100,000	$18,200 plus 28 percent of the excess of such amount over $80,000
Over $100,000 but not over $150,000	$23,800 plus 30 percent of the excess of such amount over $100,000
Over $150,000 but not over $250,000	$38,800 plus 32 percent of the excess of such amount over $150,000
Over $250,000 but not over $500,000	$70,800 plus 34 percent of the excess of such amount over $250,000
Over $500,000 but not over $750,000	$155,800 plus 37 percent of the excess of such amount over $500,000
Over $750,000 but not over $1,000,000	$248,300 plus 39 percent of the excess of such amount over $750,000
Over $1,000,000 but not over $1,250,000	$345,800 plus 41 percent of the excess of such amount over $1,000,000
Over $1,250,000 but not over $1,500,000	$448,300 plus 43 percent of the excess of such amount over $1,250,000
Over $1,500,000 but not over $2,000,000	$555,800 plus 45 percent of the excess of such amount over $1,500,000
Over $2,000,000 but not over $2,500,000	$780,800 plus 49 percent of the excess of such amount over $2,000,000
Over $2,500,000 but not over $3,000,000	$1,025,800 plus 53 percent of the excess of such amount over $2,500,000
Over $3,000,000	$1,290,800 plus 55 percent of the excess of such amount over $3,000,000

Exhibit 13-3
Unified Transfer Tax Rate Schedule

For Gifts Made and for Deaths after 1992

If the amount with respect to which the tentative tax to be computed is	The tentative tax is
Not over $10,000	18 percent of such amount
Over $10,000 but not over $20,000	$1,800 plus 20 percent of the excess of such amount over $10,000
Over $20,000 but not over $40,000	$3,800 plus 22 percent of the excess of such amount over $20,000
Over $40,000 but not over $60,000	$8,200 plus 24 percent of the excess of such amount over $40,000
Over $60,000 but not over $80,000	$13,000 plus 26 percent of the excess of such amount over $60,000
Over $80,000 but not over $100,000	$18,200 plus 28 percent of the excess of such amount over $80,000
Over $100,000 but not over $150,000	$23,800 plus 30 percent of the excess of such amount over $100,000
Over $150,000 but not over $250,000	$38,800 plus 32 percent of the excess of such amount over $150,000
Over $250,000 but not over $500,000	$70,800 plus 34 percent of the excess of such amount over $250,000
Over $500,000 but not over $750,000	$155,800 plus 37 percent of the excess of such amount over $500,000
Over $750,000 but not over $1,000,000	$248,300 plus 39 percent of the excess of such amount over $750,000
Over $1,000,000 but not over $1,250,000	$345,800 plus 41 percent of the excess of such amount over $1,000,000
Over $1,250,000 but not over $1,500,000	$448,300 plus 43 percent of the excess of such amount over $1,250,000
Over $1,500,000 but not over $2,000,000	$555,800 plus 45 percent of the excess of such amount over $1,500,000
Over $2,000,000 but not over $2,500,000	$780,800 plus 49 percent of the excess of such amount over $2,000,000
Over $2,500,000	$1,025,800 plus 50 percent of the excess of such amount over $2,500,000

Example 6. In 1987, X made his first taxable gift of $100,000. Tax (before credits) on this amount was $23,800. X made a second taxable gift of $85,000 in 1991. The tax (before credits) on the second gift is $26,200, computed as follows:

1987 taxable gift	$100,000
1991 taxable gift	+ 85,000
Cumulative gifts	$185,000
Tax on $185,000	$ 50,000
Less: Tax on 1987 taxable gift	− 23,800
Tax on 1991 gift	$ 26,200

This cumulative system of gift taxation *and* the progressive rate schedule of § 2001 cause a higher tax on the 1991 gift, even though the 1991 gift was $15,000 *less* than the 1987 gift.

A 5 percent surtax applies to any amount of a donor's taxable gifts or a decedent's taxable estate exceeding $10 million, but not in excess of $21,040,000 ($18,340,000 for transfers made after 1992). The purpose of the surtax is to gradually eliminate the tax benefit of both the progressive transfer tax rate structure *and* the unified credit of §§ 2505 and 2010.

Example 7. In 1991, Z makes his first taxable gift of $14 million. Tax before credits on this amount is $7,540,800, computed as follows:

55% on amount of gift in excess of $3,000,000	$6,050,000
Plus: Tax on first $3,000,000 of the gift	1,290,800
Plus: 5% surtax on amount of gift in excess of $10,000,000	200,000
Total tax before credits	$7,540,800

Unified Credit. Only a single credit is available to offset the Federal gift tax—the unified credit authorized by § 2505. The amount of this lifetime credit is currently $192,800. This amount of credit offsets the tax on $600,000 of taxable transfers. Thus, an individual may make substantial transfers of wealth before any tax liability is incurred. The unified credit must be used when available—a taxpayer may not decide to postpone use of the credit if he or she makes a taxable gift during the current year.[12]

---

[12] Rev. Rul. 79-398, 1979-2 C.B. 338.

Example 8. In 1987, Y made her first taxable gift of $350,000. The tax calculated on this gift is $104,800, and Y must use $104,800 of her available unified credit so that the actual gift tax due is reduced to zero. In 1991, Y makes her second taxable gift of $650,000. The tax on this gift is $153,000, computed as follows:

Taxable gift for 1991		$ 650,000
Plus: 1987 taxable gift		+ 350,000
Taxable transfers to date		$1,000,000
Tentative tax on total transfers		
to date (see Exhibit 13-2)		$ 345,800
Less: Gift taxes calculated on 1987 gift		− 104,800
Tentative tax on 1991 gift		$ 241,000
Less: Remaining unified transfer		
tax credit:		
Total credit available for 1991	$192,800	
Less: Unified transfer tax		
credit used		
in 1987	− 104,800	− 88,000
Gift tax due on 1991 gift		$ 153,000

Filing Requirements. The Federal gift tax return, Form 709, is filed annually on a calendar year basis. The due date of the return is the April 15th after the close of the taxable year. If a calendar year taxpayer obtains any extension to file his or her Federal income tax return, such extension automatically applies to any gift tax return due. If the donor dies during a taxable year for which a gift tax return is due, the gift tax return must be filed by the due date (nine months after death) plus any extensions of the donor's Federal estate tax return.[13]

THE OVERLAP BETWEEN THE GIFT AND ESTATE TAXES

A beginning student of the Federal transfer tax system might reasonably assume that an inter vivos (during life) transfer of property that is considered complete and therefore subject to the gift tax would also be considered complete for estate tax purposes, so that the transferred property would not be included in the decedent's taxable estate. This, however, is not the case. The gift tax and the estate tax are not mutually exclusive; property gifted away in earlier years can be included in the donor's taxable estate. The relationship between the two taxes is illustrated in the following diagram:

---

[13] § 6075(b).

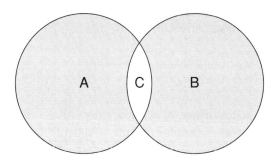

Circle A represents property transferred by the decedent during his or her lifetime and subject to the gift tax. Circle B represents the decedent's taxable estate. Overlap area C represents property already subject to a gift tax that is nevertheless included in the donor/decedent's taxable estate.

Examples of transfers that fall into the overlap area above will be presented later in the chapter. At this point, however, it is important to note that any gift tax paid on a transfer which is considered incomplete for estate tax purposes reduces the amount of estate tax payable.[14]

TRANSFERS OF PROPERTY AT DEATH

ROLE OF A WILL

Each of the 50 states gives its citizens the right to transfer the ownership of their property at death by means of a valid will. State law provides various formal requirements for valid wills, and as a result great care must be taken that a will is drafted in strict accordance with such requirements. There are few restrictions on the right of an individual to dispose of property at death in any manner he or she chooses. The most common restriction is the right under state law of a surviving spouse to receive a specified statutory share of the deceased individual's wealth. The statutory share rules effectively prevent an individual from completely disinheriting a surviving spouse.[15]

INTESTACY

When a person dies with no will or an invalid will, the transfer of his or her wealth is determined under the intestacy laws of the deceased's state of residence. Again, the particulars of the intestacy laws of each state are different. As a general rule, property will pass in order in prescribed shares to a decedent's surviving

---

[14] § 2001(b)(2).

[15] Modern statutory share laws have their origins in the English common law property concepts of the "dower" rights of a widow and the "curtesy" rights of a widower.

spouse, children and lineal descendants, parents and lineal ascendants, collateral relatives, and finally, if no relatives of any degree can be located, to the state of residence itself.

PROBATE

Probate is the legal process whereby a decedent's will is established as genuine and valid, and during which creditors of the decedent may submit their claims for payment from the estate. A decedent's probate estate consists of property interests owned at death that will pass under the terms of a decedent's will (or under the laws of intestacy if no valid will exists). It is extremely important for an individual engaged in estate planning to be aware of any property interests that he or she owns but which will *not* be included in the probate estate at death. A major example of such a property interest is a joint tenancy with right of survivorship (JTWROS). As previously explained, upon the death of one of the joint tenants, ownership of the asset automatically shifts to the surviving joint tenant or tenants. This is true *regardless* of the provisions of the deceased joint tenant's will. Similarly, survivor benefits, such as those from a life insurance policy or an annuity, or payments from pension and profit sharing plans, pass directly to the beneficiary and are not controlled by the will.

It should be apparent that those individuals who have amassed any amount of wealth and who wish to control the disposition of that wealth at death should have a validly executed will. However, there are compelling reasons why *every* responsible adult should have a will. When an individual dies intestate (without a valid will), the resulting legal and administrative complications can cause unnecessary hardship and confusion for the surviving family. Finally, one of the most critical functions of a will is to name a guardian for the decedent's minor children; failure to have a will to do so can result in years of family discord and distress.

THE TAXABLE ESTATE

Code §§ 2001 through 2056 contain the statutory rules providing for the imposition of a tax on the transfer of the taxable estate of every decedent who is a citizen or resident of the United States. Sections 2101 through 2108 provide for an estate tax on the value of assets located within the United States owned by a nonresident alien decedent. Discussion of this latter tax is beyond the scope of an introductory text.

Computation of a decedent's taxable estate involves three basic steps:

1. Identification and valuation of assets includible in the gross estate

2. Identification of deductible claims against the gross estate and deductible expenses of estate administration

3. Identification of any deductible bequests out of the gross estate

THE GROSS ESTATE CONCEPT

Section 2031 broadly states that "the value of the gross estate of the decedent shall be determined by including to the extent provided for in this part the value at the time of his death of all property, real or personal, tangible or intangible, wherever situated." The Regulations under this section make it clear that property located in a foreign country is included in this definition.[16]

Sections 2033 through 2044 identify the various types of property that are includible in a decedent's gross estate. Section 2033 is the most commonly applied of these Code sections. It requires the inclusion of any property interest owned by the decedent at date of death. The property interests specified in § 2033 correspond to the legal concept of a decedent's *probate estate*, property interests that will pass to the beneficiaries under the terms of the decedent's will.[17] If the decedent dies without a valid will, these interests will be distributed to the decedent's heirs under the state intestacy laws.

All individuals are, in a sense, on the accrual method of accounting for estate tax purposes. Any legal claim to or interest in an asset that exists at death is includible in the gross estate. For example, a cash basis taxpayer who performed substantial services and was to be paid $20,000 would not report the fee as income until collected. However, if death occurred before collection, the decedent is considered to have owned a $20,000 asset, the right to the fee, which would be includible in his or her gross estate.

The concept of the gross estate is much broader than the legal probate estate. Exhibit 13-4 lists the various types of property interests and assets includible in the gross estate and the statutory authority for each inclusion. These various inclusions are discussed in more detail later in the chapter.

Although the estate tax reaches virtually all types of property interests, it does not extend to property in which the decedent had a life estate created by another. Section 2033 does not require inclusion of such property, since the decedent's only interest in the property terminated upon death.

> **Example 9.** Upon W's death, she transferred stock worth $300,000 in trust, giving her son a life estate and the remainder to her grandson. When the son subsequently dies, his estate does not include the stock, since his interest terminates at his death and he is not transferring the property to the grandson.

The above example illustrates why the life estate is one of the most important devices used in estate planning. Note that the son is entitled to use the property for his life, yet the property escapes taxation in his estate. The 1976 Tax Reform Act addressed this problem in one respect with the generation-skipping transfer tax, discussed later in this chapter. These changes, however, have not eliminated all of the benefits of using the life estate.

---

[16]   Reg. § 20.2031-1(a).   [17]   Reg. § 20.2031-1(a)(1).

Exhibit 13-4
*Property Included in
the Gross Estate*

Property	*Statutory Authority*
Any property interest owned by the decedent at death	Section 2033

Includes
  cash
  stocks, bonds, other investments securities
  personal assets
  personal residence
  collectibles (antiques, etc.)
  investment real estate
  business interests (sole proprietorship, partnership interest)	

Certain gifts made within three years of death (limited application after 1981)	Section 2035
Assets transferred during life in which the decedent retained an income interest or control over the enjoyment of the assets or the income therefrom	Section 2036
Assets transferred during life in which the decedent retained more than a 5 percent reversionary interest and possession of which could only be obtained by surviving the decedent	Section 2037
Assets transferred during life if, at death, the decedent possessed the right to alter, amend, revoke, or terminate the terms of the transfer	Section 2038
Certain survivor benefits and annuities	Section 2039
Joint tenancies with right of survivorship	Section 2040
Assets over which the decedent held a *general* power of appointment	Section 2041

Insurance proceeds on the decedent's life if
 	
  (1) payable to the decedent's estate; *or*
  (2) the decedent possessed any incident of ownership in the policy at death.
	Section 2042

Assets in a QTIP trust in which the decedent had the income interest	Section 2044

VALUATION OF GROSS ESTATE AND BASIS

Once an asset is identified as part of the gross estate, its fair market value at date of death must be determined. Practically, valuation of assets is the most difficult and subjective problem in computing a decedent's gross estate. Many assets, such as capital stock in a closely held corporation, have no readily ascertainable fair market value. Fortunately the estate tax Regulations, like their gift tax counterparts, provide detailed guidelines to the valuation of many types of assets.[18]

In the 41 common law states, a surviving spouse may have a legally enforceable claim against assets owned by a decedent that cannot be defeated by the terms of the decedent's will. Section 2034 states that the value of property included in the decedent's gross estate is not diminished by such a claim. In the nine community property states, most property owned by a married individual is community property in which both spouses have equal interests. Only one-half the value of such community property is included in a decedent's gross estate.

Although the gross estate is normally valued as of the decedent's date of death, § 2032 allows the executor to elect an alternative valuation date of six months after death. If the election is made, the alternative valuation date must be used for every asset in the gross estate. If an asset is disposed of within six months of death, its value at date of disposition is used. This choice of two possible dates for valuation gives the executor some flexibility in minimizing the value of the gross estate and any estate tax liability.

For income tax purposes, the basis of property in the hands of a person acquiring the property from a decedent is the property's fair market value at date of death or on the alternate valuation date under Code § 2032.[19] Under § 1223(11), assets acquired from a decedent are presumed to have a holding period in excess of six months. In the case of community property, the adjustment to fair market value is available for the *entire property* rather than just the one-half interest that is included in the gross estate of the decedent spouse.[20]

In situations in which the Federal estate tax to be imposed on a particular estate is minimal, an executor might actually elect the alternate valuation date in order to increase the valuation of assets included in the gross estate, thus achieving maximum step-up in the basis of the assets for income tax purposes. Section 2032(c) eliminates this particular tax planning option by providing that no § 2032 election may be made unless such election will decrease the value of the gross estate *and* the amount of the Federal estate tax imposed.

---

[18] See Reg. § 20.2031.

[19] § 1014(a). This rule does not apply to items of property that constitute income in respect of a decedent. § 1014(c). For a com-

plete discussion of income in respect of a decedent, see Chapter 14.

[20] § 1014(b)(6).

SPECIAL USE VALUATION: § 2032A

The requirement that property in a decedent's gross estate be valued at fair market value can create hardship if a principal estate asset is real property used in a family business. The value of such real property as it is used in the business may be considerably less than its potential selling price on the open market. As a result, an estate might be forced to sell the real estate and terminate the family business in order to pay the Federal estate tax.

Section 2032A allows that qualifying real estate used in a closely held business may be valued based on its business usage rather than market value. The requirements for qualification under this section are formidable. For example, the fair market value of the real estate in question and any related personal property must equal or exceed 50 percent of the gross estate (within certain adjustments) before the special use valuation of Code § 2032A may be elected. In addition, the real estate alone must comprise 25 percent of the adjusted gross estate. During at least five of the eight years preceding the decedent's death, the real estate must have been used by the decedent or the decedent's family for farming purposes or in a trade or business. If these requirements are satisfied, the maximum reduction from fair market value of qualifying real estate is $750,000.

> **Example 10.**   Decedent F owned a large farm south of a major urban center. As farming property, F's real estate was worth $4 million; however, developers wanting to acquire the real estate for future use as commercial and residential property had offered F $7 million for the real estate. If all the qualifications of § 2032A can be met, F's real property would be valued at $6.25 million in his gross estate, and would take an income tax basis of $6.25 million.

The estate tax savings offered by the election of qualified-use valuation is conditional upon the continued use of the qualified real property in the family farm or other business. If the heirs of the decedent dispose of the real property or discontinue its qualified use within 10 years of the decedent's death, Code § 2032A(c) requires that the heirs repay the estate tax saved by the original use of the § 2032A election.

GROSS ESTATE INCLUSIONS

The Federal estate tax is not a property tax levied on the value of property owned at death. Instead, it is a transfer tax levied on the value of any shift in a property interest that occurs because of a decedent's death. As a result, a decedent's gross estate may include assets not owned by a decedent at death, the transfer of which is not controlled by the terms of the decedent's will.

INSURANCE ON THE LIFE OF THE DECEDENT

The proceeds of an insurance policy on the life of a decedent do not come into existence until the death of the insured and are paid to the beneficiaries specified in the insurance contract, not the beneficiaries named in the decedent's will. However, § 2042 provides that such proceeds shall be included in the decedent's gross estate if either of the following is true:

1. The decedent's estate is the beneficiary,

2. The decedent, at his or her death, possessed any incident of ownership in the life insurance policy, alone or in conjunction with any other person.

The term *incident of ownership* implies any economic interest in the policy and is broadly interpreted by the IRS. The Regulations under § 2042 list the power to change the policy's beneficiary, the right to cancel or assign the policy, and the right to borrow against the policy as incidents of ownership.[21]

> **Example 11.** In 1982, T purchased an insurance policy on his own life. Under the terms of the policy, beneficiary B would receive $150,000 upon T's death. In 1983, T transferred the ownership of the policy to his wife, W, retaining none of the incidents of ownership in the policy. In 1991, T died. The $150,000 paid to B is not includible in T's gross estate. Had T retained the right to change the beneficiary, however, the proceeds would have been included in his gross estate.

Note in *Example 11* that if W had predeceased her husband, the fair market value of the insurance policy (approximately its cash surrender value, if any) would be includible in W's gross estate under § 2033 as an asset owned at death.

SURVIVOR BENEFITS

Section 2039 requires that the value of an annuity or any payment receivable by a beneficiary by reason of surviving a decedent be included in the decedent's gross estate. This rule only applies to the extent that the value of the annuity or payment is attributable to contributions made by the decedent or the decedent's employer. A second condition for applicability is that the payment or annuity be payable to the decedent or that the decedent possess the right to payment at death. For example, social security death benefits paid to a decedent's family are not covered by § 2039 because the decedent had no right to the payments during his or her lifetime.

The value of an annuity includible under § 2039 is the replacement cost to the beneficiary of a comparable commercial annuity.[22]

---

[21]   Reg. § 20.2042-1(c)(2).   [22]   Reg. § 20.2031-8(a).

Example 12.   H purchased a self and survivor annuity contract that was to pay him $1,500 a month for his life and, upon his death, $1,000 a month to his widow, W. At the date of H's death, W would have to pay $24,000 to purchase a $1,000 a month lifetime annuity for herself. Under § 2039, the value of the annuity received by W, $24,000, is includible in H's gross estate.

JOINT INTERESTS

Nonspousal Joint Tenancies.   As discussed earlier in the chapter, a joint tenancy with right of survivorship is a form of equal co-ownership of an asset that causes full ownership of the asset to vest automatically in the survivor when the first joint tenant dies. The decedent's will cannot change this result; property owned in joint tenancy is not included in a decedent's probate estate. Some portion of the value of this property may be includible in the decedent's gross estate, however. Under § 2040, it is necessary to determine the proportion of the decedent's original contribution toward the acquisition of the asset. This same proportion of the value of the asset at date of death must be included in the decedent's gross estate.

Example 13.   Brothers A and B decided to purchase a tract of real estate as equal joint tenants with right of survivorship. A contributed $40,000 and B contributed $10,000 toward the $50,000 purchase price. At A's death, the real estate was worth $150,000. A's gross estate must include $120,000, 80% [$40,000 ÷ ($40,000 + $10,000)] of the real estate's value. If B had died before A, only $30,000, 20% of the real estate's value, would be includible in B's gross estate.

Note in *Example 13* that in the year the real estate was acquired, A made a taxable gift to B of $15,000, the difference between half the value of the asset when purchased, $25,000, and B's $10,000 contribution. In spite of this completed gift, a portion of the property is taxed in A's gross estate under the authority of § 2040 if he dies before B.

Spousal Joint Tenancies.   If a husband and wife own property as joint tenants with right of survivorship, § 2040(b) contains a rule that requires 50 percent of the value of the property to be included in the gross estate of the first spouse to die, regardless of the original contribution of that spouse.

GENERAL POWERS OF APPOINTMENT

A *power of appointment* is a right to dispose of property that the holder of the power does not legally own. It is normally created by the will of a decedent in conjunction with a transfer of property in trust. Typically, the decedent's will provides for the transfer of property in trust, giving an individual a life estate and a power to appoint the remainder interest during his or her life or at death through a will. By so doing, the decedent transfers the ability to control the property's disposition to the holder of the power, even though the holder does not own the property. In effect, a power of appointment gives a person the right to fill in the blanks of another person's will.

A power of appointment may be *specific*, meaning that the holder of the power may only give the property to members of a specified eligible group of recipients which does *not* include the holder. Alternatively, the power may be *general*, so that the holder may appoint the property to himself or herself, or his or her creditors, estate, or creditors of that estate. The terms of the power should specify to whom ownership of the property will go if the holder deliberately or inadvertantly fails to exercise the power.

A *general power of appointment* over property is tantamount to actual ownership of the property. If the holder appoints the property to another person, the exercise is treated as a taxable gift per § 2514.[23] Section 2041 provides that if a decedent holds a general power over property at his or her death, the value of the property must be included in the gross estate.

> **Example 14.**   Individual I has the right to appoint ownership of certain real estate to any of I's children or grandchildren. He may exercise the right during life or by will. Upon I's death, his will appoints the property to his daughter, D. Because I held only a *specific power*, the value of the appointed property is *not* included in D's gross estate.

> **Example 15.**   Individual M has the right to appoint ownership of certain real estate to *himself* or any of his brothers and sisters. He may exercise the right during life or by will. However, M dies without exercising the power. The terms of the power provide that if the power is not exercised the property shall go to M's uncle. Because M possessed a *general power* of appointment, the date of death value of the property must be included in M's gross estate.

Nontaxable Powers.   As indicated above, a specific power of appointment over property will not result in inclusion of the property in the holder's gross estate. There are other situations where a power does not cause taxation. If the holder's power to appoint property for his or her benefit is limited to an *ascertainable standard*, it is not a general power of appointment and inclusion is not required. A power is considered limited to a standard if appointments of property may be made solely for the holder's health, education, maintenance, or support in his or her accustomed manner of living. The language used to describe the scope of the holder's power is extremely important. For example, a power is not considered limited if it permits appointments for the holder's comfort, happiness, or well-being.

---

[23]   If the holder of a general power releases the power or allows it to lapse, the transfer of ownership is still considered a taxable gift made by the holder. See §§ 2514(b) and (e).

Example 16. H's will provided for the transfer of $600,000 in trust, giving his wife a life estate and a power to appoint the property to herself for her support. Upon the wife's death, nothing is included in her gross estate since she does not have a general power of appointment. The power does not cause inclusion since it is limited to an ascertainable standard.

TRANSFERS TAKING EFFECT AT DEATH

Taxpayers who are reluctant to give away property during life but who also want to minimize the tax burden on their estate have designed a variety of inter vivos gifts with "strings attached." Such gifts are subject to a condition or restriction that enables the donor to continue to benefit from or enjoy the property until death. Such a transfer may be complete for gift tax purposes. Nevertheless, for estate tax purposes it may be classified as a transfer taking effect at death, with the result that the date of death value of the property is includible in the donor's gross estate.

Code §§ 2036, 2037, and 2038 govern transfers taking effect at death. Because these three sections were added to the Code at different times, there is a confusing amount of overlap in their coverage. The sections' requirements are very complex and difficult to apply. However, a brief description of each section can give the beginning tax student an idea of their general functions.

One important rule to remember is that all three sections can only require the inclusion in a decedent's gross estate of property that was originally owned by the decedent. A second rule is that the sections are inapplicable if the transfer of the property by the decedent was for sufficient consideration.

Code § 2036. This section requires that the value of any property given away by the decedent, but to which the decedent retained the right to the property's income or the right to designate who may possess or enjoy the property, shall be included in the decedent's gross estate. Section 2036 also specifies that the retention of the voting rights of shares of stock in a controlled corporation represents a retention of enjoyment.[24]

Example 17. In 1987, F made a completed gift of rental property to his son, S, subject to the condition that F was to receive the net rent from the property for the rest of his life. Upon F's death in 1991, the date of death value of the rent property must be included in F's gross estate, even though S is the owner of the property.

---

[24] § 2036(b)(2) defines a controlled corporation as a corporation in which the decedent controlled (directly or indirectly) at least 20 percent of the voting power of all classes of stock.

Example 18. In 1991, M transferred assets into an irrevocable trust for the sole benefit of her grandchildren. Under the terms of the trust instrument, M reserved the right to designate which of the grandchildren should receive the annual income of the trust. Because M retained the right to designate the persons who shall possess the income from the trust assets, the value of the trust assets will be included in M's gross estate upon her death.

The IRS is very aggressive in applying § 2036. For example, in a situation in which a parent gifts a family residence to a child but continues to occupy the residence rent free, the parent is considered to have retained a beneficial interest in the residence, with the result that the value of the residence will be includible in the parent's gross estate.[25]

Code § 2037. This statute requires inclusion in a decedent's gross estate of the value of previously transferred property if two conditions are met:

1. Possession or enjoyment of the property can only be obtained by surviving the decedent,

2. The decedent owns a reversionary interest in the property, the value of which exceeds 5 percent of the value of the property. The value of the reversion is computed as of the moment immediately before death, based on actuarial tables.[26]

Regulation § 20.2037-1(e) gives the following example of the application of Code § 2037.

Example 19. The decedent transferred property in trust, with the income payable to his wife for life and with the remainder payable to the decedent or, if he is not living at his wife's death, to his daughter or her estate. The daughter cannot obtain possession or enjoyment of the property without surviving the decedent. Therefore, if the decedent's reversionary interest immediately before death exceeded 5% of the value of the property, the value of the property less the value of the wife's outstanding life estate is includible in the decedent's gross estate.

Note in *Example 19* that the decedent's reversionary interest was extinguished at death and did not constitute an interest in property that would be transferred under the terms of the decedent's will. However, it is the event of the decedent's death that completes the transfer of the remainder interest in the trust to the daughter or her estate.

---

[25] Rev. Rul. 70-155, 1970-1 C.B. 189; and *Estate of Linderme*, 52 T.C. 305 (1966).

[26] Reg. § 20.2037-1(c)(3).

Code § 2038. If, on the date of death, the decedent had the power to alter, amend, or revoke the enjoyment of any property previously given away by the decedent, § 2038 requires that the date of death value of the property be included in the decedent's gross estate. Obviously, a revocable transfer falls within § 2038. However, the scope of the section is broad enough to apply to much less obvious types of powers.

> **Example 20.**   Individual Z creates an irrevocable trust for the benefit of her children and names the trust department of a national bank as trustee. The only right retained by Z allows her to replace the trustee with a different trust department. Upon Z's death, Revenue Ruling 79-353 [27] states that Code § 2038 applies and the value of the trust corpus must be included in Z's gross estate.

GIFTS IN CONTEMPLATION OF DEATH

For many years, Code § 2035 required that the date of death value of any gift made by the decedent during the three years prior to death, plus the amount of any gift tax paid on such gifts, be included in the decedent's gross estate. In 1981, Congress drastically altered this section so that it currently applies only to gifts of interests described in the sections governing transfers taking effect at death (§§ 2036, 2037, and 2038) and § 2042, relating to gifts of life insurance. In addition, § 2035 applies for determining the applicability of provisions such as § 2032A, concerning special use valuation (e.g., any property given away within three years of death is added back to the gross estate in applying the 50 and 25% tests). Notwithstanding the limited application of the general rule, § 2035(c) continues to require the inclusion in the gross estate of any gift tax paid within three years of death.

> **Example 21.**   Refer to the facts in *Example 17*. Assume that in 1990, one year prior to his death, F made a gift of his retained income interest in the rental property to his granddaughter, D. Section 2035 applies to the transfer of the income interest, with the result that the date of death value of the rental property and any gift tax paid on the 1990 gift are included in F's gross estate.

TRANSFERS FOR INSUFFICIENT CONSIDERATION

A transfer for which the donor received consideration less than the value of the transferred property is vulnerable to the application of §§ 2035, 2036, 2037, or 2038 upon the donor's death. However, § 2043 does allow the estate an offset for the consideration received.[28]

---

[27]   1979-2 C.B. 325.   [28]   See Reg. § 20.2043-1(a).

Example 22. Individual A transferred her 100 shares of stock in Famco Corporation to her daughter, D, subject to the condition that A would retain the voting rights in the shares. At date of transfer, the fair market value of the stock was $500,000, and D paid A only $300,000 cash in exchange. The transfer constituted a taxable gift of $200,000. Upon A's death, the value of the stock, $1.2 million, is includible in A's gross estate under § 2036. However, A's estate may reduce this value by $300,000, the amount of the consideration received by A.

The § 2043 consideration offset equals the value of the consideration at date of receipt. Therefore, in *Example 22* only 40 percent ($200,000 ÷ $500,000) of the value of the property was transferred without consideration, but 75 percent [($1.2 million − $300,000) ÷ $1.2 million] of the date of death value of the property must be included in the gross estate.

DEDUCTIONS FROM THE GROSS ESTATE

Not all of the value of a decedent's gross estate will be available for transfer to estate beneficiaries or other individuals. Some of the value must first be used to pay off debts of the decedent and other claims against the estate. The second step in computing an individual's taxable estate is to identify the debts and claims that are deductible against the gross estate.

CODE §§ 2053 AND 2054

Section 2053 authorizes deductions for unpaid mortgages or liens on property included in the gross estate and for personal debts of the decedent. In computing these deductions, a decedent is on the accrual basis, so that liabilities accrued at death but not yet paid are deductible for estate tax purposes.[29]

Also deductible are the decedent's funeral expenses and administrative expenses of the estate. Administrative expenses include legal, accounting, and other professional fees and expenses of selling estate assets to provide necessary funds. In addition, expenses incurred in preserving the estate, including the costs of maintaining and storing property (e.g., utility bills on the decedent's home) are deductible. These expenses can only be taken as an estate tax deduction if they are not also claimed as income tax deductions by the estate.[30]

Losses incurred during the settlement of an estate that are caused by casualty or theft and are not compensated for by insurance are deductible under § 2054. If deducted on the estate tax return, a loss may not be deducted again on the estate's income tax return.[31]

---

[29] Reg. § 20.2053-4.

[30] § 642(g).

[31] *Ibid.*

The gross estate less §§ 2053 and 2054 deductions represents the net estate available for transfer to beneficiaries or other individuals. Dispositions of the net estate to a qualified charity or the decedent's surviving spouse can result in further deductions on the estate tax return.

CHARITABLE CONTRIBUTIONS

An estate may deduct the value of any transfer of assets to a qualified charitable organization under § 2055. Qualifying organizations are specifically defined in the statute. If an individual is willing to leave his or her entire estate for public, charitable, or religious use, there will be no taxable estate.

For a charitable contribution to be deductible, it must consist of the decedent's entire interest in the underlying property. For example, if a decedent bequeaths a life interest in real estate to his son and the remainder interest in the property to charity, the value of the remainder interest is not deductible. Alternatively, if the decedent bequeaths the interest in the real estate to a charity for a term of years (e.g., 20 years), and the remainder to his son, the value of the income interest is not deductible. However, this restriction does not apply if the transfer is in a specific statutory form: a *charitable lead trust*, where an income interest is given to the charity, or a *charitable remainder trust*, where a remainder interest is given to the charity.[32]   A detailed description of such trusts is beyond the scope of this text, but they do allow a decedent to create both a charitable and a noncharitable interest in the same property and secure a deduction for the charitable interest. The restriction also is inapplicable to a charitable contribution of a remainder interest in a personal residence or farm and to certain contributions for conservation purposes.[33]

If an individual taxpayer is considering making bequests to charity upon his or her death, his or her tax adviser should certainly explore the possibility of having the individual make such charitable contributions during his or her life. Such inter vivos contributions would serve a dual purpose: The donated assets would be removed from the individual's potential taxable estate, and the donation would create a deduction for income tax purposes.

THE MARITAL DEDUCTION

Code § 2056 provides an unlimited deduction for the value of property passing to a surviving spouse. If a married taxpayer, no matter how wealthy, is willing to leave all his or her property to the surviving spouse, no transfer tax will be imposed on the estate.[34] Only upon the subsequent death of the spouse will the couple's wealth be subject to taxation. Planning for maximizing the benefit of the unlimited marital deduction is discussed in Chapter 15.

---

[32]   § 2055(e)(2).

[33]   *Ibid.*

[34]   No marital deduction is allowed for the value of property passing to a surviving spouse who is not a U.S. citizen unless the property is placed in a "qualified domestic trust." §§ 2056(d) and 2056A.

In certain instances, interests transferred to the surviving spouse are not deductible—so-called *nondeductible terminable interests*. If a decedent leaves an interest in property to his or her spouse that can or will terminate at a future date *and* if after termination another person receives an interest in the property from the decedent, the value of the interest passing to the spouse is ineligible for the marital deduction.[35] Absent this rule, the interest would escape taxation entirely, since it terminates prior to or with the death of the surviving spouse and thus is not included in his or her gross estate.

> **Example 23.** Decedent M leaves a life estate in real property to his surviving spouse, S, with the remainder after S's death left to M's granddaughter. The interest passing to S is a terminable interest ineligible for the marital deduction.

The property need not pass directly to the surviving spouse to qualify for the marital deduction. Section 2056(b)(5) generally allows the deduction if the surviving spouse is entitled to annual payments of all of the income from the property for life and has a general power of appointment over the property exercisable during life or at death. In this case, the entire value of the property will be included in the estate of the surviving spouse because of his or her general power of appointment.

Under § 2056(b)(7), a marital deduction is also available for the value of *qualifying terminable interest property* left to a surviving spouse. Qualifying terminable interest property is property from which the entire income must be paid to the spouse at least annually. During the spouse's lifetime, no one else must be able to receive any interest in the property. Upon the spouse's death, the property may pass to anyone. If the executor elects, the entire value of the property is deductible on the decedent's estate tax return.

Section 2044 requires that when the surviving spouse dies, the entire value of the qualifying terminable interest property at that time must be included in the spouse's gross estate. If the surviving spouse gives away the income interest during life, § 2519 requires that the gift will consist of the entire value of the property. The rationale for this exception, along with the planning opportunities it creates, are discussed in Chapter 15.

COMPUTATION OF THE ESTATE TAX

Once the value of the taxable estate has been determined, the first step in computing the estate tax liability is to add the taxable estate to the amount of the decedent's *adjusted taxable gifts*. Adjusted taxable gifts are defined in Code § 2001(b) as the total amount of taxable gifts (after any available exclusion or

---

[35] § 2056(b).

deduction) made after December 31, 1976 *other than* gifts includible in the gross estate of the decedent.

The transfer tax rates of § 2001(c) are then applied to the sum of the taxable estate plus adjusted taxable gifts. The tentative tax calculated is then reduced by any gift taxes payable at current rates for gifts made after December 31, 1976. The result is the amount of Federal estate tax liability *before* credits.[36]

ESTATE TAX CREDITS

The major credit available to reduce the Federal estate tax is the unified credit of Code § 2010. This credit is identical in amount to the § 2505 unified gift tax credit described earlier. The § 2010 credit may be used by the estate of every decedent, regardless of prior usage of the gift tax credit. However, the mechanics of the estate tax calculation ensure that the decedent's estate benefits from the credit only to the extent that it was not used to offset any gift tax during his or her lifetime. It is important to understand that the two credits combined will shelter a maximum of $600,000 of transfers from the imposition of any Federal transfer tax.

All other estate tax credits have a single underlying purpose—to reduce or eliminate the effect of multiple taxation of a single estate. Sections 2011 and 2014 provide a credit against the Federal estate tax for the death taxes imposed by the state in which the decedent resided or by a foreign government. Section 2012 authorizes a credit for pre-1977 gift taxes paid by the decedent on property that must be included in the gross estate and therefore is subject to the estate tax.

If two family members die within a short period of time, the same property may be included in both taxable estates and be subject to two rounds of estate taxation in rapid succession. Section 2013 provides a credit to the estate of the second decedent to mitigate this excessive taxation. The credit generally is computed as a percentage of the amount of tax attributable to the inclusion of property in the estate of the first decedent. The percentage is based on the number of years between the two deaths as follows:

0–2 years	100%
3–4 years	80%
5–6 years	60%
7–8 years	40%
9–10 years	20%

---

[36] Estates of decedents dying after December 31, 1986 will be liable for an additional amount of estate tax equal to 15 percent of the decedent's "excess retirement accumulation" per § 4981A(d).

If the second decedent outlived the first by more than 10 years, no § 2013 credit is allowed.

> **Example 24.** Individual A died in March 1989. Under the terms of his will, A left $1 million in assets to his younger sister, B. B died unexpectedly in December 1991 and the assets inherited from A were included in B's taxable estate. The amount of tax paid by A's estate that is attributable to the assets is calculated at $100,000. The § 2013 credit available to B's estate is $80,000 (80% × $100,000).

The formula for computing the estate tax is presented in Exhibit 13-5.

Exhibit 13-5
Estate Tax Formula

Gross estate (§§ 2031 through 2046)........		$x,xxx,xxx
Less the sum of		
Expenses, indebtedness,		
and taxes (§ 2053)..................	$ xx,xxx	
Losses (§ 2054)......................	x,xxx	
Charitable bequests (§ 2055)..........	xx,xxx	
Marital deduction (§ 2056).............	xxx,xxx	− xxx,xxx
Taxable estate(§ 2051).....................		$ xxx,xxx
Plus: Taxable gifts made after		
December 31,1976 [§ 2001(b)]...		+ xx,xxx
Total taxable transfers......................		$ xxx,xxx
Tentative tax on total transfers (§ 2001).....		$ xxx,xxx
Less the sum of		
Gift taxes paid on post-1976		
taxable gifts (§ 2001).................	$ x,xxx	
Unified transfer tax credit (§ 2010)......	xx,xxx	
Other tax credits (§§ 2011 through 2016)	x,xxx	− xx,xxx
Estate tax liability..........................		$ xx,xxx

A COMPREHENSIVE EXAMPLE

The following example will illustrate the complete computation of the Federal estate tax.

In 1987, taxpayer M makes his first taxable gift to his son S. The fair market value of the property transferred is $200,000. The gift tax is computed as follows:

Value of gift	$200,000
Less: Annual exclusion	− 10,000
Taxable gift	$190,000
Gift tax before credits	$ 51,600
Less: Unified credit	− 51,600
Gift tax liability for 1987	$ 0

In 1988, M makes gifts to son S and daughter D. The value of each transfer is $250,000.

Value of gifts	$500,000
Less: Annual exclusions	− 20,000
Taxable gifts for 1988	$480,000
Plus: 1987 taxable gift	+ 190,000
Taxable transfers to date	$670,000
Tentative tax on total transfers to date	$218,700
Less: Tax on 1987 gift	− 51,600
Less: 1988 Unified credit	
($192,800 − $51,600)	− 141,200
1988 gift tax liability	$ 25,900

M dies in 1991, leaving a taxable estate valued at $1.6 million. The estate tax is computed as follows:

Taxable estate		$1,600,000
Plus: Taxable gifts made in prior years		+ 670,000
Total taxable transfers		$2,270,000
Tentative tax on total transfers		$ 913,100
Less the sum of		
Gift taxes paid on post-1976		
taxable gifts (on 1988 gift)	$ 25,900	
Unified credit	192,800	− 218,700
Estate tax liability		$ 694,400

PAYMENT OF THE ESTATE TAX

The Federal estate tax return, Form 706, is due nine months after the date of the decedent's death, and any tax liability shown is payable with the return. However, Congress appreciates the fact that the payment of the estate tax is often unforeseen, and has provided for a variety of relief measures for the estate with a substantial tax liability and insufficient liquidity to pay the tax nine months after death.

Section 6161 authorizes the Secretary of the Treasury to extend the time of payment of the estate tax for up to 10 years past the normal due date. To obtain an extension, the executor must show reasonable cause for the delay in payment. For example, the fact that the executor of an estate requires additional time to sell a particularly illiquid asset to generate the cash with which to pay the estate tax might be accepted as reasonable cause for an extension of the payment date for the estate tax.

Section 6166 allows an estate to pay a portion of its estate tax liability in installments if a substantial portion of the estate consists of the decedent's interest in a closely held business.[37] An estate is eligible if more than 35 percent of the *adjusted gross estate* (gross estate less §§ 2053 and 2054 deductions for debts of the decedent, funeral and administrative expenses, and losses) consists of the value of such an interest. The percentage of the estate tax liability that can be deferred is based on the ratio of the value of the closely held business to the value of the adjusted gross estate.

If a decedent owned an interest in more than one closely held business, the values of the interests can be combined to meet the 35 percent *if* the decedent's interest represents 20 percent or more of the total value of the business.

Example 25.   The taxable estate of decedent X is composed of the following:

		Value
Sole proprietorship		$ 400,000
40% interest in closely held		
corporation		500,000
Other assets		1,400,000
Gross estate		$2,300,000
Less sum of		
Code §§ 2053 and 2054 deductions	$300,000	
Code § 2055 charitable deduction	500,000	– 800,000
Taxable estate		$1,500,000

The decedent owned 100% of the value of the sole proprietorship and 40% of the value of the closely held corporation. The combined values of these interests, $900,000, represents 45% of the adjusted gross estate of $2,000,000. Therefore, the executor may elect to defer payment on 45% of the estate tax liability.

---

[37] § 6166(b) provides specific definition of the phrase "interest in a closely held business."

The tax deferred under § 6166 is payable in 10 equal annual installments. The first installment is payable five years and nine months after death. The IRS does charge the estate interest on the unpaid balance for the entire 15-year period.[38] If the estate disposes of 50 percent or more of the value of the qualifying closely held interest, any outstanding amount of deferred estate tax must be paid immediately.

THE GENERATION-SKIPPING TRANSFER TAX

As part of the Tax Reform Act of 1976, Congress added a third type of transfer tax to the Internal Revenue Code. The *generation-skipping transfer tax* (GSTT) was designed to "plug a loophole" in the coverage of the gift and estate taxes. The original version of the GSTT was intimidatingly complex, and was criticized by tax practitioners from the moment of enactment.

The Tax Reform Act of 1986 retroactively repealed the 1976 version of the GSTT and replaced it with a new tax applicable to testamentary transfers occurring after the date of enactment and to inter vivos transfers made after September 25, 1985. Any tax actually paid under the 1976 GSTT is fully refundable. Only time will tell if the new version of the GSTT is any more workable than the old version.

A traditional generation-skipping transfer involves at least three generations of taxpayers. For example, Grandfather G could create a trust, income payable to Son S for S's life with the trust assets passing to Grandson GS upon S's death. G would pay a gift tax upon the transfer of assets into trust. However, upon S's death his income interest terminates and S, according to § 2035, is not considered to own a property interest in the trust assets at the time of his death. Although the enjoyment of the trust assets is transferred from the second generation (S) to the third generation (GS), neither the Federal gift or estate tax is imposed on the value of the transfer. In addition to this type of generation-skipping transfer, which benefits at least two generations of taxpayers, the 1986 version of the GSTT also applies to certain "direct skips," outright transfers of wealth for the sole benefit of a person at least two generations younger than the transferor.[39]

Generally, the value of property transferred in a taxable generation-skipping transaction is subject to a flat-rate tax of 55 percent until 1992, and 50 percent for subsequent taxable years.[40] However, each transferor is allowed a lifetime exemption of $1 million for generation-skipping transfers of any type.[41]

---

[38] See § 6601(j) for applicable interest rate.

[39] § 2612.

[40] § 2641.

[41] § 2631.

TAX PLANNING CONSIDERATIONS

The statutory rules of Federal gift, estate, and generation-skipping taxes have been examined in this chapter. Any individual taxpayer who desires to maximize the accumulated wealth available to family members will want to minimize the burden of these three transfer taxes. Tax planning for transfer taxes would be incomplete, however, without consideration of any interrelated Federal income taxes. Many gifts are made by transfers to a trust, and the income taxation of the trust entity and its beneficiaries may have a significant impact upon the original tax minimization plan. For this reason, the Federal income taxation of trusts, estates, and beneficiaries is discussed in the next chapter (Chapter 14). The tax planning considerations for transfer taxes and any attendant income taxes are incorporated in Chapter 15, *Family Tax Planning*.

PROBLEM MATERIALS

DISCUSSION QUESTIONS

13-1 *Interrelation of Federal Estate and Gift Taxes.* Discuss the various reasons why the Federal gift and estate taxes can be considered as a single, unified transfer tax.

13-2 *Entity for Transfer Tax Purposes.* Why can the married couple rather than each individual spouse be considered the taxable entity for transfer tax purposes?

13-3 *What Constitutes a Gift?* Businessperson B offers X $40,000 for an asset owned by X. Although X knows the asset is worth $60,000, he is in desperate need of cash and agrees to sell. Has X made a $20,000 taxable gift to B? Explain.

13-4 *Adequate Consideration.* During the current year, K offered to pay $50,000 to his only son, S, if S would agree to live in the same town as K for the rest of K's life. K is very elderly and frail and desires to have a relative close at hand in case of emergency. Does the $50,000 payment constitute a taxable gift made by K?

13-5 *When Is a Gift Complete?* Wealthy Grandmother G wants to provide financial support for her Grandson GS. She opens a joint checking account with $20,000 of cash. At any time, G or GS may withdraw funds from this account. Has G made a completed gift to GS by opening this account? At what point is the gift complete?

13-6 *Cumulative Nature of Transfer Taxes.* The Federal income tax is computed on an annual basis. How does this contrast to the computation of the Federal gift tax?

13-7 *Purpose of Unified Transfer Tax Rates.* A decedent's taxable estate can be considered the last taxable gift the decedent makes. Why?

13-8 *Incomplete Transfers.* The Federal gift tax and estate tax are not mutually exclusive. Give examples of transfers that may be treated as taxable gifts but that do not remove the transferred assets from the donor's gross estate.

13-9 *Computation of Taxable Estate.* What are the three steps involved in computing the taxable estate of a decedent?

13-10 *Probate Estate vs. Gross Estate.* How can the value of a decedent's probate estate differ from the value of his or her gross estate for tax purposes?

13-11 *Special Use Valuation of § 2032A.* The gross estate of decedent F consists of a very successful farming operation located 80 miles east of an expanding metropolitan area. The estate includes 2,000 acres of real estate worth $400,000 as agricultural land. However, a real estate developer is willing to pay $1.5 million for the property because of its potential for suburban development. Discuss the utility of § 2032A to F's estate.

13-12 *Powers of Appointment.* What are some *nontax* reasons for the creation of a power of appointment? What is the difference between a specific and a general power?

13-13 *Gifts in Contemplation of Death.* Discuss the scope of § 2035 concerning gifts made within three years of death after the enactment of ERTA 1981.

13-14 *Estate Tax Credits.* With the exception of the unified credit of § 2010, what is the basic purpose of the various estate tax credits?

13-15 *Due Date of Estate Tax Return and Payment.* Why is the tax law particularly lenient in authorizing extensions for payment of the Federal estate tax?

13-16 *Unified Transfer Tax Credit.* Section 2010 appears to allow a second $192,800 credit against the Federal estate tax (in addition to the credit allowed for gift tax purposes under § 2505). Is this the case?

13-17 *Generation-Skipping Transfers.* Decedent T's will created a trust, the income from which is payable to T's invalid daughter D for her life. Upon D's death, the trust assets will be paid to T's two sons (D's brothers) in equal shares. Has T made a generation-skipping transfer? Explain.

PROBLEMS

13-18 *Gift Splitting.* During the current year, Mr. and Mrs. Z make the following cash gifts to their adult children:

Mr. Z:	
to son M	$30,000
to daughter N	8,000
Total	$38,000
Mrs. Z:	
to son M	$ 2,000
to daughter N	12,000
to daughter O	18,000
Total	$32,000

   a. Assume Mr. and Mrs. Z do *not* elect to split their gifts per § 2513. Compute the total taxable gifts after exclusions for each.

   b. How does the amount of taxable gifts change if Mr. and Mrs. Z *elect* to split their gifts?

13-19 *Computing Gift Tax Liability.* B, a single individual, made a cash gift of $200,000 to his niece C in 1988. In the current year, B gives C an additional $200,000 and nephew D $450,000. Compute B's gift tax liability for the current year.

13-20 *Computing Taxable Gifts.* C, a single individual, makes the following transfers during the current year.

	Fair Market Value
Cash to sister D	$13,000
Real estate:	
Life estate to brother B	28,000
Remainder to nephew N	21,000
Cash to First Baptist Church	25,000

What is the total amount of taxable gifts C must report?

13-21 *Computing Taxable Gifts.* During the current year, L, a widower, makes the following transfers:

	Fair Market Value
Tuition payment to State College for nephew N, age 32	$ 6,000
New automobile to nephew N	9,000
Cash to a local qualified political committee	15,000

What is the total amount of taxable gifts L must report?

13-22 *Computing Taxable Gifts.* During the current year, Z, a widow, makes the following transfers:

	Fair Market Value
Real estate located in France to son J	$500,000
City of Philadelphia municipal bonds to daughter K	120,000
Payment to local hospital for medical expenses of brother-in-law M	18,000

What is the total amount of taxable gifts Z must report?

13-23 *Basis of Gifted Assets.* During the current year, L received a gift of land from his grandmother. The land had a basis to the grandmother of $100,000 and a fair market value of $250,000 on the date of the gift. A gift tax of $30,000 was paid on the transfer.

    a.   If L subsequently sells the land for $300,000, how much gain or loss will he recognize?

    b.   What would be the amount of L's recognized gain or loss on the sale if the land had a tax basis of $325,000 (rather than $100,000) to the grandmother?

13-24 *Marital Deduction.*   F died during the current year, leaving a gross estate valued at $5 million. F's will specifically provided that *no* amount of her wealth was to be left to her estranged husband, G. However, under applicable state law, G is legally entitled to $1 million of his deceased wife's assets. How does the payment of $1 million affect the value of

a.   F's *gross* estate,
b.   F's *taxable* estate?

13-25 *Gross Estate Inclusions.*   Q was a cash basis taxpayer who died in the current year. On the date of Q's death, he owned corporate bonds, principal amount of $50,000, with accrued interest of $3,950. On the date of death, the bonds were selling on the open market for $54,000. Six months later the market price of the bonds had dropped to $51,500; there was $3,200 of accrued interest on the bonds as of this date. Neither market price includes any payment for accrued interest.

a.   Assuming the executor of Q's estate does not elect the alternate valuation date, what amounts should be included in Q's gross estate because of his ownership of the bonds?

b.   Assuming the executor does elect the alternate valuation date, what amounts should be included in Q's gross estate?

13-26 *Interests in Trusts Included in Gross Estate.* M's mother left property in trust (Trust A), with the income payable to M for M's lifetime and the remainder to M's daughter. At M's death, Trust A was worth $6.5 million. M's grandfather created a trust (Trust B), with the income payable to M's father for his lifetime. Upon the father's death, the remainder in Trust B was payable to M or M's estate. At M's death, his 82-year-old father was still living and Trust B was worth $2.1 million. Assuming a 9.8% interest rate, what are the values of the inclusions in M's gross estate attributable to M's interests in Trust A and Trust B? (See Table A, contained in Appendix A.)

13-27 *Computing Gross Estate.*   Upon A's death, certain assets were valued as follows:

	Fair Market Value
Probate estate	$ 750,000
Insurance proceeds on a policy on A's life. The policy has always been owned by A's niece, the beneficiary	150,000
Corpus of Trust A. A possessed the right to give the ownership of the corpus to herself or any of her family. In her will she left the corpus to cousin K	15,000,000

Based on these facts, what is the value of A's gross estate?

13-28   *Computing Gross Estate.*   Upon G's death, the following assets were valued:

	Fair Market Value
Probate estate	$ 350,000
Social security benefits payable to G's widow	38,000
Annuity payable to G's widow out of G's employer's pension plan	20,000

Corpus of revocable trust created by
    G for the benefit of his children 10
    years prior to death. Upon G's death,
    the trust becomes irrevocable ....
	1,000,000

What is the value of G's gross estate?

13-29   *Gifts Included in Gross Estate.*   Donor D, age 66, makes a gift in trust for his grandchildren K and L. Under the terms of the trust instrument, D will receive the income from the trust for the rest of his life. Upon his death, the trust assets will be distributed equally between K and L.

a.   D's assets transferred into trust are worth $1 million. Assuming that D's income interest is not a "qualified interest" within the meaning of § 2702(b), what is the amount of the taxable gift to K and L?

b.   Upon the date of D's death, at age 77, the value of the trust assets is $2.5 million. What amount, if any, is included in D's gross estate?

13-30   *Gifts in Contemplation of Death.*   In 1990, S made a taxable gift of marketable securities to his nephew and paid a gift tax of $14,250. In 1991, S gave an income interest in trust property to the same nephew and paid a gift tax of $5,000. S originally created the trust in 1978, retaining the income interest for life and giving the remainder to another family member. S died in 1992 when the marketable securities were worth $300,000 and the trust property was worth $972,000. Based on these facts, what amounts, if any, are included in S's gross estate?

13-31   *Gifts Included in Gross Estate.*   In 1975, F transferred real estate into a trust, the income from which was payable to M during her lifetime. Upon M's death, the trust property will be distributed in equal portions among M's children. However, the trust instrument gives F the right to change the remainder beneficiaries at any time. F dies in the current year without ever having changed the original trust provisions. At date of death, the trust property is worth $3.9 million and M is 60 years old. Assuming a 10% interest rate, determine the amount, if any, to be included in F's gross estate. (See Table A, contained in Appendix A.)

13-32   *Including Insurance in Gross Estate.*   Decedent R left a probate estate of $3,000,000. Two years prior to his death, R gave all incidents of ownership in an insurance policy on his own life to his daughter S, the policy beneficiary. Because the policy had a substantial cash surrender value, R paid a gift tax of $77,000 on the transfer. Upon death, the insurance policy paid $5,000,000 to S. What is the value of R's gross estate?

13-33   *Joint Tenancy.*   In 1985, individual Q pays $500,000 for an asset and takes title with his brother R as joint tenants with right of survivorship. R makes no contribution toward the purchase price. In the current year, when the asset is worth $1.2 million, Q dies and ownership of the asset vests solely in R.

    a.   What are the gift tax consequences of the creation of the joint tenancy?

    b.   How much of the date of death value of the asset must be included in Q's gross estate?

    c.   How much would be included in the gross estate of R if R, rather than Q, died in the current year?

13-34   *Computing Taxable Estate.*   Decedent T left a gross estate for tax purposes of $1.1 million. T had personal debts of $60,000 and his estate incurred funeral expenses of $12,000 and legal and accounting fees of $35,000. T's will provided for $100,000 bequest to the American Cancer Society, with all other assets passing to his grandchildren. Compute T's taxable estate.

13-35   *Sections 2053 and 2054 Expenses.*   Decedent D died on July 1 of the current year. D owned a sailboat valued at $85,000 as of the date of death. However, on December 1 of the current year, the boat was destroyed in a storm, and the estate was unable to collect any insurance to compensate for the loss. In December, the executor of D's estate received a $2,200 bill from the company that had stored the sailboat from January 1 through December 1 of the current year.

    a.   If the executor does not elect the alternate valuation date, will the $85,000 value of the boat be included in D's gross estate? D's taxable estate?

    b.   May any portion of the $2,200 storage fee be deducted on D's Federal estate tax return? On the first income tax return filed by the estate?

13-36   *Marital Deduction Assets.*   J, who was employed by Gamma Inc. at the date of his death, had been an active participant in Gamma's qualified retirement plan. Under the terms of the plan, J's widow will receive an annuity of $1,500 per month for the next 20 years. The replacement value of the annuity is $145,000. In his will, J left his interest in a patent worth $50,000 to his widow; the patent will expire in 8 years. To what extent will these transfers qualify for a marital deduction from J's gross estate?

13-37   *Qualified Terminable Interest Trust.*   Under the will of decedent H, all his assets (fair market value of $10 million) are to be put into trust. His widow, W, age 64, will be paid all the income from the trust every quarter for the rest of her life. Upon W's death, all the assets in the trust will be distributed to the couple's children and grandchildren. During W's life, no part of the trust corpus can be distributed to anyone but W.

    a.   What amount of marital deduction is available on H's estate tax return?

    b.   W dies eight years after H and under the terms of H's will the trust assets are distributed. What percentage, if any, of the value of these assets must be included in W's gross estate?

13-38 *Deferring Estate Tax Payments.*   Decedent X has the following taxable estate:

Sole proprietorship		$ 900,000
Ten percent interest in a		
closely held corporation		100,000
Other assets		600,000
Gross estate		$1,600,000
Less sum of		
§§ 2053 and 2054 deduction	$400,000	
§ 2056 marital deduction	200,000	− 600,000
Taxable estate		$1,000,000

Assume the estate tax liability on this estate is $300,000.

a.   How much of the liability may be deferred under § 6166?

b.   If X died in November 1991, when is the first installment payment of tax due?

13-39 *Computing Estate Tax Liability.*   Decedent Z dies in the current year and leaves a taxable estate of $1.4 million. During his life, Z made the following unrestricted gifts:

	Fair Market Value
1988: Gift of 2,000 shares of Acme stock to son S	$900,000
1989: Gift of cash to daughter D	600,000
1989: Gift of cash to wife W	700,000

Compute Z's estate tax liability after utilization of the available unified credit.

13-40 *Gifts Included in Gross Estate.*   In 1967, P transferred $500,000 of assets into an irrevocable trust for the exclusive benefit of his children. Under the terms of the trust agreement, annual income must be distributed among the children according to P's direction. When the youngest child attains the age of 25 years, the trust corpus will be distributed equally among the living children. P dies in the current year while the trust is still in existence and the corpus has a fair market value of $3,200,000. How much, if any, of the corpus must be included in P's gross estate?

13-41 *Powers of Appointment.*   In 1980, donor D transferred $100,000 of assets into an irrevocable trust for the exclusive benefit of her minor grandchildren. Under the terms of the trust agreement, the grandchildren will receive the annual income from the trust, and when the youngest grandchild attains the age of 21, the trust corpus will be divided among the living grandchildren as S, D's only child, so directs. S dies in the current year while the trust is still in existence and the corpus has a fair market value of $400,000. S's valid will directs that the corpus of the trust will go entirely to grandchild Q. How much, if any, of the corpus must be included in S's gross estate?

RESEARCH PROBLEMS

13-42   In 1974, JW gifted 30 percent of her stock in W Corporation to her favorite nephew, N. Although she retained a 50 percent interest in W Corporation and her husband owned the remaining 20 percent of the outstanding stock, JW was concerned that the family might eventually lose control of the firm. To reassure JW, the three stockholders agreed to restrict transferability of their stock by signing an agreement that any shareholder wishing to dispose of W Corporation stock must offer the stock to the corporation for a formula price based on the average net earnings per share for the three previous years. The corporation would then be obligated to purchase the stock at the formula price. At the time the buy-sell agreement was entered into, this formula resulted in a price very close to the stock's actual fair market value.

JW died in the current year at a time when the value of her W Corporation stock was substantially depreciated because of certain unfavorable local economic conditions. Several independent appraisals of the stock valued JW's 50 percent interest at $650,000. However, the formula under the 1974 buy-sell agreement resulted in a value of only $150,000 for the decedent's 50 percent interest. What is the correct value of the 50 percent interest in the corporation for estate tax purposes?

Some suggested research materials:

Rev. Rul. 59-60, 1959-1 C.B. 237.
Estate of Littick, 31 T.C. 181 (1958), *acq.* 1959-2 C.B. 5.
Code § 2703 (enacted by the Revenue Reconciliation Act of 1990).

13-43   In 1979, Mr. and Mrs. B (residents of a common law state) created two trusts for the benefit of their children. Mr. B transferred $600,000 of his own property into trust, giving the income interest to his wife for her life, and the remainder interest to the children. Mrs. B transferred $640,000 of her own property into trust, giving the income interest to her husband for his life, and the remainder interest to the children. In the current year, Mrs. B dies. How much, if any, of the current value of the corpus of the 1979 trust created by Mrs. B will be included in her gross estate?

Some suggested research materials:

United States v. Estate of Grace, 69-1 USTC ¶12,609,
23 AFTR2d 69-1954, 395 U.S. 316 (USSC, 1969).

LEARNING OBJECTIVES

Upon completion of this chapter you will be able to:

- Compute fiduciary accounting income and determine the required allocation of such income among the various beneficiaries of the fiduciary

- Identify the special rules that apply to the computation of fiduciary taxable income

- Explain the concept of income and deductions in respect of a decedent

- Compute both the taxable and nontaxable components of a fiduciary's distributable net income

- Describe the defining characteristics of a simple and a complex trust, including

    - The computation of the deduction for distributions to beneficiaries for both types of trusts

    - The distinction between tier one and tier two distributions from a complex trust

- Determine the tax consequences of fiduciary distributions to the recipient beneficiaries

CHAPTER OUTLINE

Chapter **14**

INCOME TAXATION OF ESTATES AND TRUSTS

INTRODUCTION

Trusts and estates are taxable entities subject to a specialized set of tax rules contained in Subchapter J of the Internal Revenue Code (§§ 641 through 692). The income taxation of trusts and estates (commonly referred to as fiduciary taxpayers) and their beneficiaries is the subject of this chapter. Grantor trusts, a type of trust not recognized as a taxable entity and therefore not subject to the rules of Subchapter J, are discussed in Chapter 15.

THE FUNCTION OF ESTATES AND TRUSTS

ESTATES

An estate as a legal entity comes into existence upon the death of an individual. During the period of time in which the decedent's legal affairs are being settled, assets owned by the decedent are managed by an executor or administrator of the estate. Once all legal requirements have been satisfied, the estate terminates and ownership of all estate assets passes to the decedent's beneficiaries or heirs.

During its existence, the decedent's estate is a taxable entity that files a tax return and pays Federal income taxes on any income earned.[1] Normally an estate is a transitional entity that bridges the brief gap in time between the death of an individual taxpayer and the distribution of that individual's wealth to other taxpayers. However, estates as taxpayers may continue in existence for many years if the correct distribution of a decedent's wealth is in question. If the administration of a decedent's estate is unreasonably prolonged, the IRS may treat the estate as terminated for tax purposes after a reasonable amount of time for settlement of the decedent's affairs has elapsed.[2]

---

[1]   § 641(a)(3).

[2]   Reg. § 1.641(b)-3(a).

TRUSTS

A trust is a legal arrangement in which an individual, the *grantor*, transfers legal ownership of assets to one party, the *trustee*, and the legal right to enjoy and benefit from those assets to a second party, the *beneficiary* (or beneficiaries). Such an arrangement is usually designed for the protection of the beneficiary. Often trust beneficiaries are minor children or family members incapable of competently managing the assets themselves.

The terms of the trust, the duties of the trustee, and the rights of the various beneficiaries are specified in a legal document, the *trust instrument*. The assets put into trust are referred to as the trust *corpus*.

The role of the trustee is that of a fiduciary; he or she is required to act in the best interests of the trust beneficiaries rather than for his or her own interests. The position of trustee is usually filled by the professional trust department of a bank or a competent friend or family member. Professional trustees receive an annual fee to compensate them for services rendered.

The purpose of a trust is to protect and conserve trust assets for the sole benefit of the trust beneficiaries, not to operate a trade or business. A trust that becomes involved in an active, profit-making business activity runs the risk of being classified as an *association* for Federal tax purposes, with the unfavorable result that it will be taxed as a corporation rather than under the rules of Subchapter J.[3]

TRUST BENEFICIARIES

An individual who desires to establish a trust has virtually unlimited discretion as to the identity of the trust beneficiaries and the nature of the interest in the trust given to each beneficiary. For example, assume grantor A creates a trust consisting of $1 million of assets. A could specify in the trust instrument that individual B is to receive all the income of the trust for B's life, and upon B's death the assets in the trust are to be distributed to individual C. In this example, both B and C are trust beneficiaries. B owns an *income interest* in the trust, while C owns a *remainder interest* (the right to the trust corpus at some future date).

A grantor can give trust beneficiaries any mix of rights to trust income or corpus (trust assets) that will best accomplish the goals of the trust. In the previous example, if grantor A decided that the trust income might be insufficient to provide for B, the trust document could specify that B also will receive a certain amount of trust corpus every year. Alternatively, if A believed that B might not need all the trust income annually, the trust document could provide that the trustee could accumulate income to distribute to B at some later point. As the student can see, a trust can be a wonderfully flexible arrangement for providing for the needs of specific beneficiaries.

---

[3] See *Morrissey v. Comm.*, 36-1 USTC ¶9020,
16 AFTR 1274, 296 U.S. 344 (USSC, 1936),
for this result.

FIDUCIARY ACCOUNTING INCOME

The income of an estate or trust for legal and accounting purposes is determined by reference to the governing instrument (the decedent's valid will or trust instrument) and applicable state law. In many cases such fiduciary accounting income is different from the concept of taxable income as defined in the Internal Revenue Code. The administrator or trustee will always refer to fiduciary accounting income rather than taxable income in carrying out his or her duties.

One major difference between fiduciary accounting income and taxable income is the classification of fiduciary capital gains. Typically, capital gains represent an increase in the value of the corpus of the fiduciary and are not available for distribution to income beneficiaries. Of course, for Federal tax purposes capital gains represent taxable income. Similarly, stock dividends are often regarded as an increase in corpus rather than trust income, even though the dividend may be taxable income under the Internal Revenue Code.

Trustee fees are generally deductible for tax purposes. However, for fiduciary accounting purposes such fees may be charged *either* to trust income or to trust corpus.

The following items of trust receipts and disbursements illustrate the concept of fiduciary accounting income:

Receipts:

Dividends	$10,000
Interest from municipal bonds	12,000
Long-term capital gain allocable to corpus under state law	6,500
Stock dividend allocable to corpus under the trust instrument	4,000
Total receipts	$32,500

Disbursements:

Trustee fee (half allocable to trust income; half allocable to corpus under the trust instrument)	$ 3,000

Based on the above, the accounting income of the trust would be $20,500, computed as follows:

Dividends	$10,000
Interest from municipal bonds	12,000
	$22,000
Less: One-half of the trustee fee ($3,000 ÷ 2)	(1,500)
Trust accounting income	$20,500

If the trustee of this particular trust was required to distribute the entire amount of trust income to a particular group of beneficiaries, the trustee would make a payment of $20,500. Note that this amount bears little relationship to the *taxable income* generated by the trust's activities.

INCOME TAXATION OF FIDUCIARIES

For Federal tax purposes, fiduciaries are taxable entities.[4] Every estate that has annual gross income of $600 or more and every trust that has either annual gross income of $600 or more *or* any taxable trust income must file an income tax return. Furthermore, if a fiduciary has a beneficiary who is a nonresident alien, that fiduciary must file a return regardless of the amount of its gross or taxable income for the year.[5]

Form 1041, the fiduciary income tax return, must be filed by the 15th day of the fourth month following the close of the fiduciary's taxable year (see Appendix B for sample Form 1041). An estate may adopt a calendar or any fiscal taxable year. However, the taxable year of a trust must be a calendar year.[6] In the case of an estate, the first taxable year begins on the day following the date of death of the decedent.[7] In the case of a trust, the date of creation as specified in the controlling trust instrument marks the beginning of the first taxable year.

Fiduciaries generally must make quarterly estimated tax payments in the same manner as individuals. However, no estimated taxes must be paid by an estate or a grantor trust to which the residual of the grantor's estate is distributed for any taxable year ending within the two years following the decedent's death.[8] A trustee may *elect* to treat any portion of an excess estimated tax payment made by a trust as a payment of estimated tax made by a beneficiary. If the election is made, the payment is considered as having been distributed to the beneficiary on the last day of the trust's taxable year and then remitted to the government as estimated tax paid by the beneficiary on January 15th of the following year.[9]

> **Example 1.** On April 15, 1991, Trust T made an estimated tax payment of $14,000. However, later in the year, the trustee decided to distribute all 1991 trust income to beneficiary B. Because Trust T will have no 1991 tax liability, the trustee may elect to treat the $14,000 payment as a cash distribution made to beneficiary B on December 31, 1991. Beneficiary B will report the $14,000 as part of his 1991 estimated tax payment made on January 15, 1992.

Section 641(b) provides that "the taxable income of an estate or trust shall be computed in the same manner as in the case of an individual, except as otherwise provided in this part." Thus many of the rules governing the taxation of individuals apply to fiduciaries. Before examining the specific rules unique to fiduciary income taxation, it will be useful to look at the basic formula for computing fiduciary taxable income.

---

[4] See §§ 7701(a)(6) and 641(a).

[5] § 6012(a)(3), (4), and (5).

[6] § 645. This requirement does not apply to tax-exempt and charitable trusts.

[7] See Reg. §§ 1.443-1(a)(2), and 1.461-1(b).

[8] § 6654(l).

[9] § 643(g).

Step One: Compute fiduciary accounting income and identify any receipts and disbursements allocated to corpus (under either the trust instrument or state law).

Step Two: Compute fiduciary taxable income *before* the deduction for distributions to beneficiaries authorized by Code §§ 651 and 661.

Step Three: Compute the deduction for distributions to beneficiaries. This step will require a computation of fiduciary "distributable net income" (DNI).

Step Four: Subtract the deduction for distributions to arrive at *fiduciary taxable income.*

Step One, the computation of fiduciary accounting income, was discussed earlier. Detailed discussions of Steps Two and Three constitute most of the remainder of this chapter.

FIDUCIARY TAXABLE INCOME

Unless otherwise modified, the fiduciary computes its taxable income in a manner identical to that of an individual taxpayer. The principal difference is the deduction granted for distributions made to beneficiaries, explained later in this chapter. In addition, § 642 contains a number of special provisions that must be followed in computing fiduciary taxable income and the final tax. These unique aspects of estate and trust taxation are considered below.

FIDUCIARY TAX RATES

The tax rates for estates and trusts for 1991 are shown in Exhibit 14-1. Note that there is very little progressivity in the fiduciary rate schedule; taxable income in excess of $10,350 is taxed at the highest 31 percent rate. However, under § 1(j), any component of fiduciary taxable income consisting of net long-term capital gain is taxed at a maximum 28 percent rate.

Exhibit 14-1
Income Tax Rates for Estates and Trusts

For Taxable Years Beginning after 1990

If taxable income is		The tax is	Of the amount
Over—	But not over—		over—
$ 0	$ 3,450	15%	$ 0
3,450	10,350	$ 517.50 + 28%	3,450
10,350	—	2,449.50 + 31%	10,350

Example 2. Estate E has taxable income for calendar year 1991 of $70,000, $20,000 of which is net long-term capital gain. E's tax liability for the year is $14,741 ($2,449.50 + 31% of the excess of $50,000 over $10,350) *plus* $5,600 (28% of the $20,000 capital gain), for a total liability of $20,341.

In determining their final tax liability, fiduciaries are subject to the alternative minimum tax provisions.[10] Generally, the alternative minimum tax is computed with any items of tax preference allocated between the fiduciary and the beneficiaries.

STANDARD DEDUCTION AND PERSONAL EXEMPTION

Unlike individual taxpayers, fiduciaries are not entitled to a standard deduction.[11] However, a fiduciary, like an individual taxpayer, is entitled to a personal exemption. The amount of the exemption depends on the type of fiduciary. The personal exemption for an estate is $600. The exemption for a trust that is required by the trust instrument to distribute all trust income currently is $300. The exemption for any trust not subject to this requirement is $100.[12]

LIMITATIONS ON DEDUCTIBILITY OF FIDUCIARY EXPENSES

Because fiduciaries generally do not engage in the conduct of a business, the gross income of a fiduciary usually consists of investment income items such as dividends, interest, rents, and royalties. Fiduciary expenses are normally deductible under the authority of § 212, which provides for the deduction of ordinary and necessary expenses paid for the management, conservation, or maintenance of property held for the production of income.

Before specific fiduciary expenses can be deducted, they must be allocated among the various income items received by the fiduciary. Expenses directly attributable to taxable fiduciary income are fully deductible. For example, rent expenses are directly attributable to rent income and are deductible by the fiduciary. However, expenses that cannot be *directly connected* with any specific type of income must be allocated proportionately to each item of distributable income. Any amount of expenses allocated to distributable tax-exempt income is not deductible by the fiduciary.[13]

Example 3. During the year, Estate E receives $9,000 of tax-exempt interest and $36,000 of taxable interest, and recognizes a $10,000 capital gain allocable to corpus. The estate pays $3,000 of administrative fees that are not directly attributable to any item of income. Those fees must be proportionally allocated to the various items of *distributable* income; therefore,

---

[10]   § 59(c).

[11]   § 63(c)(6)(D).

[12]   § 642(b).

[13]   Reg. § 1.652(b)-3(b).

20% of the fee ($9,000 tax-exempt income ÷ $45,000 total distributable income) must be allocated to tax-exempt income, and only $2,400 ($3,000 × 80%) of the fee is deductible by the estate.

Section 642(g) provides a second major limitation on the deductibility of fiduciary expenses. If an administrative expense is claimed as a deduction on the estate tax return of a decedent, it may not also be claimed as a deduction on an income tax return of the decedent's estate or subsequent trust. However, administrative expenses that could be deducted for either estate tax or income tax purposes can be divided between the two returns in whatever portions achieve maximum tax benefit.[14]

Section 67(a) limits certain miscellaneous itemized deductions, including the § 212 deduction for investment expenses. Such itemized deductions are allowed only to the extent they exceed 2 percent of adjusted gross income. Section 67(e) provides that the deduction for expenses paid or incurred in connection with the administration of a fiduciary that would have been avoided if the property were not held by the fiduciary shall be allowable in computing the adjusted gross income of the fiduciary. In other words, fiduciary expenses such as trustee fees which are incurred only because of the choice of the trust form are not considered itemized deductions subject to the 2 percent floor. The § 68 overall limitation on itemized deductions, enacted by the Revenue Reconciliation Act of 1990, is *not* applicable to fiduciaries.

CHARITABLE CONTRIBUTIONS

Section 642(c) authorizes an unlimited charitable deduction for any amount of gross income paid by a fiduciary to a qualified charitable organization. Fiduciaries are given a great deal of flexibility as to the timing of charitable contributions; if a contribution is paid after the close of one taxable year but before the close of the next taxable year, the fiduciary may elect to deduct the payment in the earlier year.[15]

If a fiduciary receives tax-exempt income that is available for charitable distribution, its deduction for any charitable contribution made normally must be reduced by that portion of the contribution attributable to tax-exempt income.[16]

Example 4. During the current year, Trust T receives $30,000 of tax-exempt interest, $25,000 of taxable interest, and $45,000 of taxable dividends. The trust makes a charitable contribution of $20,000 during the year. Because 30% of the trust's income available for distribution is nontaxable, 30% of the charitable distribution is nondeductible and the trust's deduction for charitable contributions is limited to $14,000.

---

[14] Reg. § 1.642(g)-2.

[15] § 642(c)(1). See Reg. § 1.642(c)-1(b) for the time and manner in which such an election is to be made.

[16] Reg. § 1.642(c)-3(b).

DEPRECIATION, DEPLETION, AND AMORTIZATION

The total allowable amount of depreciation, depletion, and amortization that may be deducted by the fiduciary (or passed through to the beneficiaries) is determined in the normal manner. However, a fiduciary is not entitled to expense any portion of the cost of eligible property under § 179.

Deductions for depreciation and depletion available to a fiduciary depend upon the terms of the controlling will or trust instrument. If the controlling instrument authorizes a reserve for depreciation or depletion, any *allowable* (deductible) tax depreciation or depletion will be deductible by the fiduciary to the extent of the specified reserve. If the allowable tax depreciation or depletion exceeds the reserve, the excess deduction is allocated between the fiduciary and beneficiaries based upon the amount of fiduciary income allocable to each.[17]

> **Example 5.** Trust R owns rental property with a basis of $300,000. The trust instrument authorizes the trustee to maintain an annual depreciation reserve of $15,000 (5% of the cost of the property). For tax purposes, however, the current year's depreciation deduction is $22,000. The trust instrument provides that one-half of annual trust income including rents will be distributed to the trust beneficiaries. For the current year, the trust is entitled to a depreciation deduction of $18,500 (5% of $300,000 + one-half the tax depreciation in excess of $15,000).

Note that if the controlling instrument is silent, depreciation and depletion deductions are simply allocated between fiduciary and beneficiaries on the basis of fiduciary income allocable to each. If a fiduciary is entitled to statutory amortization, the amortization deduction also will be apportioned among fiduciary and beneficiaries on the basis of income allocable to each.[18]

FIDUCIARY LOSSES

Because the function of a trust generally is to conserve and protect existing wealth rather than to engage in potentially risky business activities, it is unusual for a trust to incur a net operating loss. It is not unusual, however, for an estate that includes a business interest owned by a decedent to incur this type of loss. In any case, if a net operating loss does occur, a fiduciary may carry the loss back 3 years and forward for 15.[19] Capital losses incurred by a fiduciary are deductible against capital gains; a maximum of $3,000 of net capital loss may be deducted against other sources of income.[20] Nondeductible net capital losses are carried forward to subsequent taxable years of the fiduciary.[21]

---

[17] Reg. § 1.167(h)-1; Reg. § 1.611-1(c)(4).

[18] Reg. § 1.642(f)-1.

[19] § 172(b)(1).

[20] § 1211(b).

[21] § 1212(b).

Fiduciaries are also subject to the limitations imposed on passive activity losses and credits by § 469.[22] Therefore, a fiduciary may only deduct current losses from passive activities against current income from passive activities. Any nondeductible loss is suspended and carried forward to subsequent taxable years. If an interest in a passive activity is distributed by a fiduciary to a beneficiary, any suspended loss of the activity is added to the tax basis of the distributed interest.[23]

Unlike the net losses of a partnership or an S corporation, fiduciary losses do not flow through to beneficiaries. An exception to this rule applies for the year in which a trust or estate terminates. If the terminating fiduciary has net operating losses, capital loss carryforwards, or current year deductions in excess of current gross income, § 642(h) provides that such unused losses and excess deductions become available to the beneficiaries succeeding to the property of the fiduciary.

Casualty losses of a fiduciary are subject to the rules pertaining to individual taxpayers. For casualty losses, the limitation of the deduction to that amount in excess of 10 percent of adjusted gross income applies, although the concept of adjusted gross income is normally not associated with trusts or estates.[24] In addition, § 642(g) prohibits the deduction by a fiduciary of any loss that has already been claimed as a deduction on an estate tax return.

INCOME AND DEDUCTIONS IN RESPECT OF A DECEDENT

The death of an individual taxpayer can create a peculiar timing problem involving the reporting of income items earned or deductible expenses incurred by the taxpayer prior to death. For example, if a cash basis individual had performed all the services required to earn a $5,000 consulting fee but had not collected the fee before death, by whom shall the $5,000 of *income in respect of a decedent* (IRD) be reported? The individual taxpayer who earned the income never received payment, but the recipient of the money, the individual's estate, is not the taxpayer who earned it. Section 691(a) gives a statutory solution to this puzzling question by providing that any income of an individual not properly includible in the taxable period prior to the individual's death will be included in the gross income of the recipient of the income, typically the estate of the decedent or a beneficiary of the estate. Common IRD items include unpaid salary or commissions, rent income or interest accrued but unpaid at death, and the amount of a § 453 installment obligation that would have been recognized as income if payment had been received by the decedent prior to death.

Certain expenses incurred by a decedent but not properly deductible on the decedent's final return because of nonpayment are afforded similar statutory treatment. Under § 691(b), these *deductions in respect of a decedent* (DRD) are

---

[22] § 469(a)(2)(A).

[23] § 469(j)(12).

[24] See Form 4684 and its instructions for this computation.

deducted by the taxpayer who is legally required to make payment. Allowable DRD items include business and income-producing expenses, interest, taxes, and depletion.

ESTATE TAX TREATMENT AND THE § 691(c) DEDUCTION

Items of IRD and DRD represent assets and liabilities of the deceased taxpayer. As such, these items will be included on the decedent's estate tax return. Because IRD and DRD also have future income tax consequences, special provisions in the tax law apply to these items. First, even though the right to IRD is an asset acquired from a decedent, the basis of an IRD item does not become the item's fair market value at date of death. Instead, under § 1014(c), the basis of the item to the decedent carries over to the new owner. This special rule preserves the potential income that must be recognized when the IRD item is eventually collected. The character of IRD also is determined by reference to the decedent taxpayer.

Secondly, items of DRD that are deducted as § 2053 expenses on an estate tax return are *not* subject to the rule prohibiting a deduction on a subsequent income tax return.[25] Finally, a taxpayer who recognizes an item of IRD as income may be entitled to an income tax deduction [authorized by § 691(c)] for the amount of the Federal estate tax imposed on the value of the item. The deduction is a percentage of the estate tax attributable to the total *net* IRD included in an estate based on the ratio of the recognized IRD item to all IRD items. Estate tax attributable to net IRD is the excess of the actual tax over the tax computed without including the IRD in the taxable estate.

> **Example 6.** Taxpayer T's estate tax return included total IRD items valued at $145,000. DRD items totaled $20,000. If the *net* IRD of $125,000 had not been included in T's estate, the Federal estate tax liability would have decreased by $22,000. During the current year, the estate of T collected half ($72,500) of all IRD items and included this amount in estate gross income. T's estate is entitled to a § 691(c) deduction of $11,000.

THE DISTRIBUTION DEDUCTION AND THE TAXATION OF BENEFICIARIES

The central concept of Subchapter J is that income recognized by a fiduciary will be taxed *either* to the fiduciary itself or to the beneficiaries of the fiduciary. The determination of the amount of income taxable to each depends upon the amount of annual distributions from the fiduciary to the beneficiary. Conceptually, distributions to beneficiaries represent a flow-through of trust income that will be

---

[25] § 642(g).

taxed to the beneficiary. Under §§ 651 and 661, the amount of the distribution will then be available as a *deduction* to the fiduciary, reducing the taxable income the fiduciary must report. Income that flows through the fiduciary to a beneficiary retains its original character; therefore, the fiduciary acts as a *conduit,* similar to a partnership in this respect.[26]

All distributions made from a fiduciary are considered to be distributions of fiduciary income to the extent thereof. Distributions of income can be made in both cash and property. However, § 663(a)(1) provides that specific gifts or bequests properly distributed from a fiduciary to a beneficiary under the terms of the governing instrument do not represent distributions of income. Correspondingly, the fiduciary does not recognize gain or loss upon the distribution of a specific property bequest.

> **Example 7.** During the current year, the Estate of Z recognized $30,000 of income, all of which is taxable. During the year, the executor of the estate distributed a pearl necklace to beneficiary B. The necklace had a fair market value of $6,000. If the will of decedent Z specifically provided for the distribution of the necklace to B, no estate income will be taxed to her. Alternatively, if there were no such specific bequest and B received the necklace as part of her general interest in estate assets, she will have received an income distribution.

The amount of income associated with a property distribution from a fiduciary depends upon the tax treatment of the distribution *elected* by the fiduciary. § 643(e)(3) provides an election under which the fiduciary recognizes gain or loss on the distribution of appreciated or depreciated property as if the property had been sold at its fair market value. In this case, the amount of fiduciary income carried by the property distribution and the basis of the property in the hands of the beneficiary equals the property's fair market value. If the election is not made, the distribution of property produces no gain or loss to the fiduciary, and the amount of fiduciary income carried by the distribution is the lesser of the basis of such property in the hands of the fiduciary or the property's fair market value.[27] In the case where the election is not made, the basis of the property in the hands of the fiduciary will carry over as the basis of the property in the hands of the beneficiary.[28]

> **Example 8.** During the current year, Trust T distributes property to beneficiary B. The distribution is not a specific gift of property. On the date of distribution, the property has a basis to the trust of $10,000 and a fair market value of $17,000. If the trust so elects, it will recognize a $7,000 gain on the distribution, and B will be considered to have received a $17,000 income distribution and will have a $17,000 basis in the property. If the

---

[26] §§ 652(b) and 662(b).

[27] § 643(e)(2).

[28] § 643(e)(1).

trustee does not make the election, it will not recognize any gain upon distribution of the property. B will be considered to have received only a $10,000 income distribution and will have only a $10,000 basis in the property.

When a beneficiary is entitled to a specific gift or bequest of a sum of money (a pecuniary gift or bequest), and the fiduciary distributes property in satisfaction of such gift or bequest, any appreciation or depreciation in the property is recognized as a gain or loss to the fiduciary.[29]

> **Example 9.**   Under the terms of E's will, beneficiary M is to receive the sum of $60,000. E's executor distributes 600 shares of corporate stock to M to satisfy this pecuniary bequest. At the time of distribution, the stock has a fair market value of $100 a share and a basis to E's estate of $75 a share. Upon distribution, the estate must recognize a capital gain of $15,000 (600 shares × $25 per share appreciation). Note that because this distribution represents a specific bequest, it is not an income distribution to M and the § 643(e)(3) election is inapplicable. The basis of the stock to M will be its fair market value.

In any case in which the distribution of depreciated property by a trust to a beneficiary results in the recognition of loss, § 267 disallows any deduction of the loss by the trust. However, § 267 does not disallow such losses recognized by an estate.

THE ROLE OF DISTRIBUTABLE NET INCOME

To calculate the distribution deduction available to a fiduciary and the amount of fiduciary income taxable to beneficiaries, it is first necessary to calculate the *distributable net income* (DNI) of the fiduciary. DNI represents the net income of a fiduciary available for distribution to income beneficiaries.

DNI has several important characteristics. First, it does not include taxable income that is unavailable for distribution to income beneficiaries. For example, in most states capital gains realized upon the sale of fiduciary assets are considered to represent a part of *trust corpus* and are not considered *fiduciary income*. Such capital gains, while taxable, are not included in DNI. Secondly, DNI may include nontaxable income that is available for distribution to income beneficiaries.

At this point, it would appear that the amount of DNI is the same amount as fiduciary accounting income. However, there is an important difference between the two concepts. All expenses that are deductible *for tax purposes* by the fiduciary enter into the DNI calculation, even if some of these expenses are chargeable to corpus and not deducted in computing fiduciary accounting income.

---

[29]   Reg. § 1.661(a)-2(f)(1).

A beneficiary who receives a distribution from a fiduciary with both taxable and nontaxable DNI is considered to have received a proportionate share of each.[30]

> **Example 10.** Trust A has DNI of $80,000, $30,000 of which is nontaxable. During the year, beneficiary X receives a distribution of $16,000. This distribution consists of $10,000 of taxable DNI [$16,000 distribution × ($50,000 taxable DNI ÷ $80,000 total DNI)] and $6,000 of nontaxable DNI.

The amount of a fiduciary's *taxable* DNI represents *both* the maximum income that may be taxed to beneficiaries and the maximum deduction for distributions available to the fiduciary in computing its own taxable income.[31] Therefore, computing DNI is crucial to the correct computation of the taxable incomes of both beneficiary and fiduciary. Note that in *Example 10* Trust A is entitled to a deduction for distributions to beneficiaries of $10,000.

THE COMPUTATION OF DNI

Section 643 defines DNI as fiduciary taxable income before any deduction for distributions to beneficiaries, adjusted as follows:

1. No deduction for a personal exemption is allowed.

2. No deduction against ordinary income for net capital losses is allowed.

3. Taxable income allocable to corpus and not available for distribution to income beneficiaries is excluded.

4. Tax-exempt interest reduced by expenses allocable thereto is included.

> **Example 11.** A trust that is not required to distribute all income currently has the following items of income and expense during the current year:

Tax exempt interest	$10,000
Dividends	5,000
Rents	20,000
Long-term capital gains allocable to corpus	8,000
Rent expense	6,700
Trustee fee allocable to income	3,500

---

[30] Reg. § 1.662(b)-1.   [31] §§ 651(b) and 661(c).

The trust's taxable income before any deduction for distributions to beneficiaries is $23,700, computed as follows:

Dividends		$ 5,000
Rents		20,000
Capital gain		8,000
		$33,000
Less: Rent expense	$6,700	
Trustee fee allocable to *taxable* trust income*	2,500	
Exemption	100	(9,300)
Taxable income before distribution deduction		$23,700

$$\text{*\$3,500 fee} \times \frac{\$25,000 \text{ taxable trust income}}{\$35,000 \text{ total trust income}}$$

The trust's DNI is $24,800, computed as follows:

Trust taxable income before distribution deduction	$23,700
Add back exemption	100
	$23,800
Exclude: Nondistributable capital gain	(8,000)
Include: *Net* tax exempt interest ($10,000 total − $1,000 allocable to trustee fee)**	9,000
Distributable net income (DNI)	$24,800

$$\text{**\$3,500 fee} \times \frac{\$10,000 \text{ tax-exempt income}}{\$35,000 \text{ total trust income}}$$

SIMPLE TRUSTS

Section 651 defines a *simple trust* as one that satisfies these conditions:

1. Distributes all trust income currently

2. Does not take a deduction for a charitable contribution for the current year

3. Does not make any current distributions out of trust corpus

Because of the requirement that a simple trust distribute all trust income to its beneficiaries, all taxable DNI of a simple trust is taxed to the beneficiaries, based upon the relative income distributable to each.

Example 12. Trust S is required to distribute 40% of trust income to beneficiary A and 60% of trust income to B. The trust's DNI for the current year is $100,000, of which $20,000 is nontaxable. For the current year, beneficiary A must report $32,000 of trust income (40% of *taxable* DNI) and B must report $48,000 of trust income (60% of *taxable* DNI). Trust S's deduction for distributions to beneficiaries is $80,000.

In *Example 12,* the tax results would not change if the trustee had failed to make actual distributions to the beneficiaries. In the case of a simple trust, the taxability of income to beneficiaries is not dependent upon cash flow from the trust.[32]

COMPLEX TRUSTS AND ESTATES

Any trust that does not meet all three requirements of a simple trust is categorized as a *complex trust.* The categorization of a trust may vary from year to year. For example, if a trustee is required to distribute all trust income currently but also has the discretion to make distributions out of trust corpus, the trust will be *simple* in any year in which corpus is not distributed, but *complex* in any year in which corpus is distributed.

Computing the taxable income of complex trusts and estates generally is more difficult than computing the taxable income of a simple trust. Complex trusts and estates potentially may distribute amounts of cash and property that are less than or in excess of DNI.

If distributions to beneficiaries are less than or equal to DNI, each beneficiary is required to report the amount of the distribution representing *taxable DNI* in his or her gross income. Taxable DNI remaining in the fiduciary is taxed to the fiduciary.

> **Example 13.** In the current year, Trust C has DNI of $50,000, of which $20,000 is nontaxable. During the year, the trustee makes a $5,000 distribution to both beneficiary M and beneficiary N. M and N will each report $3,000 of income from Trust C [$5,000 distribution × ($30,000 taxable DNI ÷ $50,000 total DNI)]. Trust C is allowed a $6,000 deduction for distributions to beneficiaries.[33] As a result, $24,000 of taxable DNI will be reported by (and taxed to) Trust C.

When distributions to beneficiaries exceed DNI, the entire taxable portion of DNI will be reported as income by the beneficiaries. However, it may be necessary to allocate DNI among a number of beneficiaries who have received distributions during the taxable year. To make the proper allocation, distributions to beneficiaries must be categorized as *tier one* or *tier two* distributions. A tier one distribution is any distribution of fiduciary income *required to be paid currently.* A tier two distribution is any other distribution properly made to a beneficiary.[34]

Fiduciary DNI is first allocated proportionally to any first-tier distributions; if any DNI remains, it is then allocated proportionally to second-tier distributions.[35]

---

[32] § 652(a).

[33] § 661(c).

[34] §§ 662(a)(1) and (2).

[35] § 662(a)(2). For purposes of determining DNI available for first-tier distribution only, no charitable contribution deduction is allowed.

Example 14. In the current year, Trust F has DNI of $90,000, all of which is taxable. Under the terms of the trust instrument, the trustee is required to make a $50,000 distribution of income to beneficiary A. The trustee also has discretion to distribute additional amounts of income or corpus to beneficiaries A, B, or C. During the current year, the trustee distributes $60,000 to A, $25,000 to B, and $25,000 to C. The first $50,000 of DNI is allocated to A because of the $50,000 *first-tier distribution* A received. The remaining $40,000 of DNI is allocated proportionally to the *second-tier distributions* received by A, B, and C. This allocation is $6,666, $16,667 and $16,667, respectively.

Note that all Trust F's DNI is allocated and taxed to the three beneficiaries; none is taxed to the trust. Beneficiary A received $60,000 from the trust, of which $56,666 is taxable ($50,000 first-tier distribution + $6,666 second-tier distribution). B and C each received $25,000, of which $16,667 is taxable. Trust F's deduction for distributions to beneficiaries is limited to $90,000, its taxable DNI for the year.

REPORTING REQUIREMENTS FOR BENEFICIARIES

A beneficiary who receives a distribution from a fiduciary will receive a summary of the tax consequences of the distribution in the form of a Schedule K-1 from the executor or trustee. The K-1 will tell the beneficiary the amounts and character of the various items of income that constitute the taxable portion of the distribution.

A beneficiary also may be entitled to depreciation or depletion deductions and various tax credits because of distributions of fiduciary income. Such items are also reflected on the Schedule K-1.

If the taxable year of a beneficiary is different from that of the fiduciary, the amount of fiduciary income taxable to the beneficiary is included in the beneficiary's tax year within which the fiduciary's year ends.[36]

Example 15. For tax purposes, Estate E is on a fiscal year ending January 31. During its fiscal year ending January 31, 1991, but prior to December 31, 1990, the estate made cash distributions to beneficiary Z, a calendar year taxpayer. Because of these distributions, Z must report income of $8,000. However, this income will be reported on Z's 1991 individual tax return.

THE SEPARATE SHARE RULE

In certain circumstances, the rules governing the taxation of beneficiaries of a complex trust can lead to an inequitable result. Assume a grantor created a single trust with two beneficiaries, A and B. The grantor intended that each beneficiary

---

[36] §§ 652(c) and 662(c).

have an equal interest in trust income and corpus. The trustee has considerable discretion as to the timing of distributions of income and corpus. Consider a year in which beneficiary A was in exceptional need of funds and, as a result, the trustee distributed $15,000 to A as A's half of trust income for the year *plus* $10,000 out of A's half of trust corpus. Because B had no need of current funds, the trustee distributed neither income nor corpus to B.

If the trust's DNI was $30,000 for the year, the normal rules of Subchapter J would dictate that A would have to report and pay tax on $25,000 of trust income. However, the clear intent of the grantor is that A only be responsible for half of trust income and no more. To reflect such intent, § 663(c) provides the following rule: If a single trust contains substantially separate and independent shares for different beneficiaries, the trust shall be treated as separate trusts for purposes of determining DNI. Therefore, using this separate share rule, beneficiary A's *separate trust* would have DNI of only $15,000, the maximum amount taxable to A in the year of distribution. This rule is inapplicable to estates.

A COMPREHENSIVE EXAMPLE

The AB Trust is a calendar year taxpayer. In the current year, the trust books show the following:

Gross rental income	$25,000
Taxable interest income	10,000
Tax-exempt interest income	15,000
Long-term capital gain	8,000
Trustee fee	6,000
Rent expenses	3,000
Contribution to charity	1,500
Distributions to	
Beneficiary A	20,000
Beneficiary B	20,000

Under the terms of the trust instrument the capital gain and one-third of the trustee fee are allocable to corpus. The trustee is required to maintain a reserve for depreciation on the rental property equal to one-tenth of annual gross rental income. (For tax purposes, assume actual tax depreciation is $1,300.) The trustee is required to make an annual distribution to beneficiary A of $12,000 and has the discretion to make additional distributions to A or beneficiary B.

Based on these facts, the computation of the income taxable to the trust and the beneficiaries is as follows:

Step One: Compute fiduciary accounting income.

Gross rental income	$25,000
Taxable interest income	10,000
Tax-exempt interest income	15,000
	$50,000
Trustee fee charged against income	(4,000)
Rent expenses	(3,000)
Depreciation ($1/10 \times$ $25,000)	(2,500)
Fiduciary accounting income	$40,500

Step Two: Compute fiduciary taxable income before the § 661 deduction for distributions to beneficiaries.

Gross rental income	$25,000
Taxable interest income	10,000
Long-term capital gain	8,000
	$43,000
Deductible trustee fee	(4,200)*
Deductible rent expense	(3,000)
Deductible depreciation allocable to fiduciary	(1,300)
Deductible charitable contribution	(1,050)*
Exemption	(100)
Taxable income before §661 deduction	$33,350

* $35,000 ÷ $50,000 of gross fiduciary accounting income is taxable; thus, only 70% of both the $6,000 trustee fee and $1,500 charitable contribution is deductible.

Step Three: Compute DNI and the § 661 deduction for distributions to beneficiaries.

Taxable income from Step Two	$33,350
Add back:	
Exemption	100
Net tax-exempt income	12,750*
Subtract:	
Capital gain allocable to corpus	(8,000)
Distributable net income (DNI)	$38,200

* $15,000 tax-exempt interest less 30% of the $6,000 trustee fee and $1,500 charitable contribution.

Because distributions to beneficiaries exceeded DNI, the trust will deduct the entire amount of taxable DNI, $25,450 ($38,200 − $12,750).

Step Four: Subtract the § 661 deduction for distributions to beneficiaries.

Taxable income before deduction	$33,350
Section 661 deduction	(25,450)
Trust taxable income	$ 7,900

Tax Consequences to Beneficiaries: The $40,000 cash distribution to beneficiaries exceeds the total DNI of $38,200; thus, the entire amount of DNI must be allocated to the beneficiaries.

Total DNI...	$38,200
Allocation to first-tier	
distribution to Beneficiary A..................................	(12,000)
DNI available for allocation to	
second-tier distributions......................................	26,200

	Second-tier Distributions	DNI Allocation
Beneficiary A.......................	$ 8,000 (29%)	$ 7,483
Beneficiary B......................	20,000 (71%)	18,717
Total..............................	$28,000(100%)	$26,200

The composition of DNI is as follows:

	Rent	Taxable Interest	Tax-exempt Interest	Total
Gross receipts..........	$25,000	$10,000	$15,000	$50,000
Rent expense..........	(3,000)			(3,000)
Depreciation............	(1,300)			(1,300)
Trustee fee*............		(4,200)	(1,800)	(6,000)
Charitable				
contribution**.........	(750)	(300)	(450)	(1,500)
Total...................	$19,950	$ 5,500	$12,750	$38,200

* The trustee fee allocable to taxable income may be arbitrarily allocated to **any** item of taxable income. Reg. § 1.652(b)-3(b).
** In the absence of a specific provision in the trust instrument, the charitable contribution is allocated proportionally to each class of income. Reg. $ 1.642(c)-3(b)(2).

Each beneficiary should report the following:

	Rent	Taxable Interest	Tax-exempt Interest	Total DNI Allocated
Beneficiary A...........	$10,175*	$2,805	$ 6,503	$19,483
Beneficiary B...........	9,775	2,695	6,247	18,717
Total...................	$19,950	$5,500	$12,750	$38,200

* Beneficiary A's proportionate share of DNI ($12,000 first-tier distribution + $7,483 second-tier distribution = $19,483 ÷ $38,200 total DNI) multiplied times $19,950 total rent income included in DNI equals Beneficiary A's share of rent income. This same procedure is used to determine each beneficiary's share of all other items.

A completed Form 1041 for the AB Trust and a Schedule K-1 for Beneficiary A are shown on the following pages.

Form **1041** Department of the Treasury—Internal Revenue Service **U.S. Fiduciary Income Tax Return** 19**90**

For the calendar year 1990 or fiscal year beginning _____ , 1990, and ending _____ , 19 ____ OMB No. 1545-0092

Check applicable boxes:
- ☐ Decedent's estate
- ☐ Simple trust
- ☐ Complex trust
- ☐ Grantor type trust
- ☐ Bankruptcy estate
- ☐ Family estate trust
- ☐ Pooled income fund

Number of Schedules K-1 attached (see instructions) . . ▶ _____

Name of estate or trust (grantor type trust, see instructions)
A B TRUST

Name and title of fiduciary

Number, street, and room or suite no. (If a P.O. box, see page 5 of Instructions.)

City, state, and ZIP code

Employer identification number

Date entity created

Nonexempt charitable and split-interest trusts, check applicable boxes (see instructions):
- ☐ Described in section 4947(a)(1)
- ☐ Not a private foundation
- ☐ Described in section 4947(a)(2)

Check applicable boxes: ☐ First return ☐ Final return ☐ Amended return
Change in Fiduciary's ▶ ☐ Name or ☐ Address

Income

1	Interest income	1	10,000
2	Dividends	2	
3	Income (or losses) from partnerships, other estates, or other trusts (see instructions)	3	
4	Net rental and royalty income (or loss) (attach Schedule E (Form 1040))	4	20,700
5	Net business and farm income (or loss) (attach Schedules C and F (Form 1040))	5	
6	Capital gain (or loss) (attach Schedule D (Form 1041))	6	8,000
7	Ordinary gain (or loss) (attach Form 4797)	7	
8	Other income (state nature of income) _____	8	
9	**Total income** (combine lines 1 through 8)	9	38,700

Deductions

10	Interest	10			
11	Taxes	11			
12	Fiduciary fees	12	4,200		
13	Charitable deduction (from Schedule A, line 6)	13	1,050		
14	Attorney, accountant, and return preparer fees	14			
15a	Other deductions NOT subject to the 2% floor (attach schedule)	15a			
b	Allowable miscellaneous itemized deductions subject to the 2% floor	15b			
c	Add lines 15a and 15b		15c		
16	**Total** (add lines 10 through 15c)			16	5,250
17	Adjusted total income (or loss) (subtract line 16 from line 9). Enter here and on Schedule B, line 1 ▶			17	33,450
18	Income distribution deduction (from Schedule B, line 17) (see instructions) (attach Schedules K-1 (Form 1041))			18	25,450
19	Estate tax deduction (including certain generation-skipping transfer taxes) (attach computation)			19	
20	Exemption			20	100
21	**Total deductions** (add lines 18 through 20) ▶			21	25,550
22	Taxable income of fiduciary (subtract line 21 from line 17)			22	7,900
23	**Total tax** (from Schedule G, line 7) ▶			23	1,504

Tax and Payments (Please attach check or money order here)

24a	Payments: 1990 estimated tax payments and amount applied from 1989 return	24a	
b	Treated as credited to beneficiaries	24b	
c	Subtract line 24b from line 24a	24c	
d	Tax paid with extension of time to file: ☐ Form 2758 ☐ Form 8736 ☐ Form 8800	24d	
e	Federal income tax withheld	24e	
	Credits: f Form 2439 _____; g Form 4136 _____; h Other _____; Total ▶	24i	
25	**Total** payments (add lines 24c through 24e, and 24i) ▶	25	
26	**Penalty** for underpayment of estimated tax (see instructions)	26	
27	If the total of lines 23 and 26 is larger than line 25, enter **TAX DUE**	27	1,504
28	If line 25 is larger than the total of lines 23 and 26, enter **OVERPAYMENT**	28	
29	Amount of line 28 to be: **a** Credited to 1991 estimated tax ▶ _____; **b** Refunded ▶	29	

Please Sign Here

Under penalties of perjury, I declare that I have examined this return, including accompanying schedules and statements, and to the best of my knowledge and belief, it is true, correct, and complete. Declaration of preparer (other than fiduciary) is based on all information of which preparer has any knowledge.

▶ _____ ▶ _____
Signature of fiduciary or officer representing fiduciary   Date   EIN of fiduciary (see instructions)

Paid Preparer's Use Only

Preparer's signature ▶	Date	Check if self-employed ▶ ☐ Preparer's social security no.
Firm's name (or yours if self-employed) and address ▶		E.I. No. ▶
		ZIP code ▶

For Paperwork Reduction Act Notice, see page 1 of the separate Instructions.   Form **1041** (1990)

Form 1041 (1990)   Page **2**

Schedule A — Charitable Deduction—Do not complete for a simple trust or a pooled income fund.

1	Amounts paid or permanently set aside for charitable purposes from current year's gross income . . .	1	1,500	
2	Tax-exempt interest allocable to charitable distribution (see instructions)	2	450	
3	Subtract line 2 from line 1	3	1,050	
4	Enter the net short-term capital gain and the net long-term capital gain of the current tax year allocable to corpus paid or permanently set aside for charitable purposes (see instructions)	4		
5	Amounts paid or permanently set aside for charitable purposes from gross income of a prior year (see instructions)	5		
6	**Total** (add lines 3 through 5). Enter here and on page 1, line 13	6	1,050	

Schedule B — Income Distribution Deduction (see instructions)

1	Adjusted total income (from page 1, line 17) (see instructions)	1	33,450	
2	Adjusted tax-exempt interest (see instructions)	2	12,750	
3	Net gain shown on Schedule D (Form 1041), line 17, column (a). (If net loss, enter zero.)	3		
4	Enter amount from Schedule A, line 4	4		
5	Long-term capital gain included on Schedule A, line 1	5		
6	Short-term capital gain included on Schedule A, line 1	6		
7	If the amount on page 1, line 6, is a capital loss, enter here as a positive figure	7		
8	If the amount on page 1, line 6, is a capital gain, enter here as a negative figure	8	(8,000)	
9	Distributable net income (combine lines 1 through 8)	9	38,200	
10	Amount of income for the tax year determined under the governing instrument (accounting income)	10	40,500	
11	Amount of income required to be distributed currently (see instructions)	11	12,000	
12	Other amounts paid, credited, or otherwise required to be distributed (see instructions)	12	28,000	
13	Total distributions (add lines 11 and 12). (If greater than line 10, see instructions.)	13	40,000	
14	Enter the amount of tax-exempt income included on line 13	14	12,750	
15	Tentative income distribution deduction (subtract line 14 from line 13)	15	27,250	
16	Tentative income distribution deduction (subtract line 2 from line 9)	16	25,450	
17	Income distribution deduction. Enter the smaller of line 15 or line 16 here and on page 1, line 18 . . .	17	25,450	

Schedule G — Tax Computation (see instructions)

1	Tax: **a** Tax rate schedule.... 1,504 ....; **b** Other taxes................. ; . . . . Total ▶	1c	1,504	
2a	Foreign tax credit (attach Form 1116)	2a		
b	Credit for fuel produced from a nonconventional source.	2b		
c	General business credit. Check if from: ☐ Form 3800 or ☐ Form (specify) ▶	2c		
d	Credit for prior year minimum tax (attach Form 8801)	2d		
3	**Total** credits (add lines 2a through 2d) . . . . ▶	3		
4	Subtract line 3 from line 1c	4	1,504	
5	Recapture taxes. Check if from: ☐ Form 4255 ☐ Form 8611	5		
6	Alternative minimum tax (attach Form 8656)	6		
7	**Total** tax (add lines 4 through 6). Enter here and on page 1, line 23 . . . . ▶	7	1,504	

Other Information (see instructions)

		Yes	No
1	Did the estate or trust receive tax-exempt income? (If "Yes," attach a computation of the allocation of expenses.) . . . Enter the amount of tax-exempt interest income and exempt-interest dividends ▶ $ 15,000	✓	
2	Did the estate or trust have any passive activity losses? (If "Yes," enter these losses on **Form 8582**, Passive Activity Loss Limitations, to figure the allowable loss.)		✓
3	Did the estate or trust receive all or any part of the earnings (salary, wages, and other compensation) of any individual by reason of a contract assignment or similar arrangement?		✓
4	At any time during the tax year, did the estate or trust have an interest in or a signature or other authority over a financial account in a foreign country (such as a bank account, securities account, or other financial account)? (See the instructions for exceptions and filing requirements for Form TD F 90-22.1.) . . . . If "Yes," enter the name of the foreign country ▶		✓
5	Was the estate or trust the grantor of, or transferor to, a foreign trust which existed during the current tax year, whether or not the estate or trust has any beneficial interest in it? (If "Yes," you may have to file Form 3520, 3520-A, or 926.) .		✓
6	Check this box if this entity has filed or is required to file **Form 8264**, Application for Registration of a Tax Shelter . ▶ ☐		
7	Check this box if this entity is a complex trust making the section 663(b) election . . . . ▶ ☐		
8	Check this box to make a section 643(e)(3) election (attach Schedule D (Form 1041)) . . . . ▶ ☐		
9	Check this box if the decedent's estate has been open for more than 2 years . . . . ▶ ☐		
10	Check this box if the trust is a participant in a Common Trust Fund that was required to adopt a calendar year . . ▶ ☐		

SCHEDULE D
(Form 1041)
Department of the Treasury
Internal Revenue Service

Capital Gains and Losses
▶ File with Form 1041. See the separate Form 1041 instructions.

OMB No. 1545-0092

19**90**

Name of estate or trust   *A B TRUST*

Employer identification number

Do not report **section 644 gains** on Schedule D (See Form 1041 instructions for line 1b, Schedule G.)

Part I   Short-Term Capital Gains and Losses—Assets Held One Year or Less

(a) Description of property (Example, 100 shares 7% preferred of "Z" Co.)	(b) Date acquired (mo., day, yr.)	(c) Date sold (mo., day, yr.)	(d) Gross sales price	(e) Cost or other basis, as adjusted, plus expense of sale (see instructions)	(f) Gain (or loss) (col. (d) less col. (e))
1					

2 Short-term capital gain from installment sales from Form 6252	2	
3 Net short-term gain (or loss) from partnerships, S corporations, and other fiduciaries	3	
4 Net gain (or loss) (combine lines 1 through 3)	4	
5 Short-term capital loss carryover (see instructions)	5 (	)
6 Net short-term gain (or loss) (combine lines 4 and 5). Enter here and on line 15 below . . . . . . ▶	6	

Part II   Long-Term Capital Gains and Losses—Assets Held More Than One Year

(a)	(b)	(c)	(d)	(e)	(f)
7					8,000

8 Long-term capital gain from installment sales from Form 6252	8	
9 Net long-term gain (or loss) from partnerships, S corporations, and other fiduciaries	9	
10 Capital gain distributions	10	
11 Enter gain, if applicable, from Form 4797	11	
12 Net gain (or loss) (combine lines 7 through 11)	12	8,000
13 Long-term capital loss carryover (see instructions)	13 (	)
14 Net long-term gain (or loss) (combine lines 12 and 13). Enter here and on line 16 below . . . . . ▶	14	8,000

Part III   Summary of Parts I and II

		(a) Beneficiaries	(b) Fiduciary	(c) Total
15 Net short-term gain (or loss) from line 6, above	15			
16 Net long-term gain (or loss) from line 14, above	16		8,000	8,000
17 Total net gain (or loss) (combine lines 15 and 16) . . . . ▶	17		8,000	8,000

If line 17, column (c), is a net gain, enter the gain on Form 1041, line 6, and DO NOT complete Parts IV and V. If line 17, column (c), is a net loss, complete Parts IV and V, as necessary.

For Paperwork Reduction Act Notice, see page 1 of the Instructions for Form 1041.

Schedule D (Form 1041) 1990

SCHEDULE K-1 (Form 1041)	Beneficiary's Share of Income, Deductions, Credits, Etc.—1990	OMB No. 1545-0092
Department of the Treasury Internal Revenue Service	for the calendar year 1990, or fiscal year beginning ...., 1990, ending ...., 19 ..... Complete a separate Schedule K-1 for each beneficiary.	19**90**

Name of estate or trust		☐ Amended K-1 ☐ Final K-1

Beneficiary's identifying number ▶	Estate's or trust's employer identification number ▶
Beneficiary's name, address, and ZIP code	Fiduciary's name, address, and ZIP code
BENEFICIARY A	*A B TRUST*

Reminder: *If you received a short year 1987 Schedule K-1 that was from a trust required to adopt a calendar year, be sure to include one-fourth of those amounts reported as income, in addition to the items reported on this Schedule K-1, on the appropriate lines of your 1990 Form 1040 and related schedules.*

(a) Allocable share item	(b) Amount	(c) Calendar year 1990 Form 1040 filers enter the amounts in column (b) on:
1 Interest	2,805	Schedule B, Part I, line 1
2 Dividends		Schedule B, Part II, line 5
3a Net short-term capital gain		Schedule D, line 5, column (g)
b Net long-term capital gain		Schedule D, line 12, column (g)
4a Other taxable income: (itemize)		Schedule E, Part III
(1) Rental, rental real estate, and business income from activities acquired before 10/23/86		
(2) Rental, rental real estate, and business income from activities acquired after 10/22/86	10,175	
(3) Other passive income		
b Depreciation, including cost recovery (itemize):		
(1) Attributable to line 4a(1)		
(2) Attributable to line 4a(2)		
(3) Attributable to line 4a(3)		
c Depletion (itemize):		
(1) Attributable to line 4a(1)		
(2) Attributable to line 4a(2)		
(3) Attributable to line 4a(3)		
d Amortization (itemize):		
(1) Attributable to line 4a(1)		
(2) Attributable to line 4a(2)		
(3) Attributable to line 4a(3)		
5 Income for minimum tax purposes	12,980	
6 Income for regular tax purposes (add lines 1 through 4a) . .	12,980	
7 Adjustment for minimum tax purposes (subtract line 6 from line 5)		Form 6251, line 4t
8 Estate tax deduction (including certain generation-skipping transfer taxes) (attach computation)		Schedule A, line 26
9 Excess deductions on termination (attach computation) . .		Schedule A, line 21
10 Foreign taxes (list on a separate sheet)		Form 1116 or Schedule A (Form 1040), line 7
11 Tax preference items (itemize):		
a Accelerated depreciation		(Include on the applicable)
b Depletion		(line of Form 6251)
c Amortization		
12 Other (itemize):		
a Trust payments of estimated taxes credited to you . . .	6,503	Form 1040, line 56
b Tax-exempt interest		Form 1040, line 8b
c Short-term capital loss carryover		Schedule D, line 6, column (f)
d Long-term capital loss carryover		Schedule D, line 15, column (f)
e		(Include on the applicable line)
f		(of appropriate tax form)
g		

For Paperwork Reduction Act Notice, see page 1 of the Instructions for Form 1041.   Schedule K-1 (Form 1041) 1990

SPECIALIZED TRUST PROBLEMS

A complete discussion of the taxation of fiduciaries should include the following specialized problem areas:

1. The § 644 special tax on certain trusts;

2. Accumulation distributions; and

3. The sixty-five day rule.

While a technical exploration of these complex areas is beyond the scope of this text, the following paragraphs will provide a conceptual introduction to the areas.

SPECIAL TAX COMPUTATION—CODE § 644

An individual planning to sell an appreciated asset might be tempted to utilize an existing trust or to create a new trust for the purpose of reducing the tax bill upon sale. Because trusts are taxable entities, a transfer of the appreciated asset to the trust prior to sale would appear to cause the gain on sale to be taxed to the trust. If the marginal tax rate of the trust was lower than that of the individual transferor, a net tax savings would be achieved.

To discourage this assignment of income scheme, Congress enacted § 644. This statute provides that if an appreciated asset is transferred into trust *and* the trust sells or exchanges the asset *within two years* of the transfer, the trust's tax on the gain recognized is computed in an unusual way. The amount of the gain not in excess of the amount of the appreciation in the asset at date of transfer to the trust is taxed as if the transferor rather than the trust made the sale.[37] Although the gain is taxed to the trust, the tax is computed based on the marginal rate of the transferor.

> **Example 16.** In 1990, individual X transfers real property (basis $100,000, fair market value $250,000) into a family trust. X pays no gift tax on the transfer. In 1991, the trust sells the real property for $330,000. The tax on $150,000 of the gain recognized upon sale will be computed as if such gain were included in X's 1991 taxable income. The tax on the remaining $80,000 of recognized gain is taxed under normal Subchapter J rules. The entire tax is paid by the trust.

In a tax regime in which there is only minimal progressivity, there is scant potential for the type of abuse that § 644 was designed to prevent. Since 1986, the tax rates imposed on the income of a trust have been higher than those imposed on the income of an individual. As a result, the deliberate assignment of income to a trust from an individual offers no opportunity for tax savings, and § 644 has little current vitality.

---

[37] § 644(a)(2).

ACCUMULATION DISTRIBUTIONS

The trustee of a complex trust may have the discretion whether or not to distribute trust income to trust beneficiaries. In a year in which the marginal tax rate of the beneficiaries is higher than that of the trust (an historic rather than a current possibility), and the beneficiaries are not in immediate need of trust funds, the trustee might be tempted to accumulate income in the trust so that it would be taxed at the cheaper trust rates. Then in a later year, the accumulated income, net of taxes, could be distributed as nontaxable corpus to the beneficiaries.

Congress decided to curb this abuse of the complex trust in 1969 and enacted what are now §§ 665 through 668 of Subchapter J. These sections, referred to as the *throwback rules*, are very complex and require a series of intricate computations. However, the theory underlying this part of the tax law is not difficult to understand.

If a complex trust fails to distribute all of its DNI for one or a series of taxable years and instead pays tax at the trust level on the DNI, the accumulated DNI after taxes is referred to as *undistributed net income* (UNI).[38] In a subsequent tax year in which the trust distributes amounts to beneficiaries in excess of its current DNI, such excess is deemed to be a distribution of any trust UNI.[39] The amount of distributed UNI *plus* the taxes originally paid by the trust attributable to the UNI is taxed as an *accumulation distribution* to the recipient beneficiary.[40]

The tax rate imposed on an accumulation distribution is computed under a complex averaging formula that uses three earlier tax years of the recipient beneficiary as a base. If the tax liability computed by use of this formula is greater than the tax already paid by the trust, the beneficiary must pay the excess in the year the distribution is received. If the formula results in a tax liability less than the taxes already paid, *no refund* is available to the beneficiary.[41]

Accumulation distributions are reported by a trust on Schedule J, Form 1041. This form is reproduced in Appendix B.

The accumulation distribution rules do not apply to simple trusts and estates. Also, income accumulated by a trust on behalf of a beneficiary who has not yet attained the age of twenty-one is not subject to the throwback rules.[42]

---

[38] § 665(a).

[39] § 665(b).

[40] § 667(a).

[41] § 666(e).

[42] § 665(b).

THE SIXTY-FIVE DAY RULE

Many trustees want to avoid accumulating DNI at the trust level because of the complexity of the throwback rules and the expense of compliance. Because DNI is often not calculated until after the close of the trust's taxable year, a trustee may not know the amount of current distributions necessary to avoid accumulation. To alleviate this timing problem, § 663(b) provides that a trustee *may elect* that any distribution made within the first 65 days of a taxable year will be considered paid to the beneficiary on the last day of the preceding taxable year.[43] This rule allows a trustee to make distributions after the close of a year to eliminate any accumulations of DNI for that year.

---

[43]   See Reg. § 1.663(b)-2 for the manner and
time for making such an election.

TAX PLANNING CONSIDERATIONS

The tax planning considerations for the use of trusts are discussed in Chapter 15, *Family Tax Planning*.

PROBLEM MATERIALS

DISCUSSION QUESTIONS

14-1 *Trusts and Estates as Conduits.*   What does it mean to describe a fiduciary as a *conduit* of income? To what extent does a fiduciary operate as a conduit?

14-2 *Purpose of Trusts.*   Trusts are usually created for nonbusiness purposes. Give some examples of situations in which a trust could be useful.

14-3 *Trust as a Separate Legal Entity.*   A trust cannot exist if the only trustee is also sole beneficiary. Why not?

14-4 *Trust Expenses Allocable to Corpus.*   For what reason might the grantor of a trust stipulate that some amount of trust expenses be paid out of trust corpus rather than trust income?

14-5 *Use of Fiduciaries to Defer Income Taxation.*   Although a trust must adopt a calendar year for tax purposes, an estate may adopt any fiscal year, as well as a calendar year, for reporting taxable income. Why is Congress willing to allow an estate more flexibility in the choice of taxable year?

14-6 *Trust Accounting Income vs. Taxable Income.*   Even though a trustee may be required to distribute all trust income currently, the trust may still have to report taxable income. Explain.

14-7 *Deductibility of Administrative Expenses.*   Explain any options available to the executor of an estate with regard to the deductibility of administrative expenses incurred by the estate.

14-8 *Capital Loss Deductions.*   To what extent may a fiduciary deduct any excess of capital losses over capital gains for a taxable year?

14-9 *Operating Losses of a Fiduciary.*   How does the tax treatment of operating loss incurred by a fiduciary differ from the treatment of such losses by a partnership or an S corporation?

14-10 *Purpose of DNI.*   Discuss the function of DNI from the point of view of the fiduciary and the point of view of beneficiaries who receive distributions from the fiduciary.

14-11 *Taxable vs. Nontaxable DNI.*   Why is it important to correctly identify any nontaxable component of DNI?

14-12 *Charitable Deductions.*   Enumerate the differences in the charitable deduction allowable to a fiduciary and the charitable deduction allowable to an individual.

14-13 *Timing Distributions from an Estate.*   Why might a beneficiary of an estate prefer *not* to receive an early distribution of property from the estate?

14-14 *Simple vs. Complex Trusts.*   All trusts are complex in the year of termination. Why?

14-15 *Trust Reserves for Depreciation.* Discuss the reason why a grantor of a trust would require the trustee to maintain a certain reserve for depreciation of trust assets.

14-16 *Purpose of Accumulation Distribution Tax.* It has been stated that Congress intended that *all* ordinary income earned by trust be taxed to trust beneficiaries. Discuss. (Review the rules on the taxation of accumulation distributions.)

14-17 *Accumulations for Minors and the Throwback Rules.* What reasons can you identify for the exclusion of accumulations of income for minor beneficiaries from the "throwback" rules?

PROBLEMS

14-18 *Computation of Fiduciary Accounting Income.* Under the terms of the trust instrument, the annual fiduciary accounting income of Trust MNO must be distributed in equal amounts to individual beneficiaries M, N, and O. The trust instrument also provides that capital gains or losses realized on the sale of trust assets are allocated to corpus, and that 40 percent of the annual trustee fee is to be allocated to corpus. For the current year, the records of the trust show the following:

Dividend income	$38,000
Tax-exempt interest income	18,900
Taxable interest income	12,400
Capital loss on sale of securities	(2,500)
Trustee fee	5,000

Based on these facts, determine the required distribution to each of the three trust beneficiaries.

14-19 *Tax Consequences of Property Distributions.* During the taxable year, beneficiary M receives 100 shares of Acme common stock from Trust T. The basis of the stock is $70 per share to the trust, and its fair market value at date of distribution is $110 per share. The trust's DNI for the year is $60,000, all of which is taxable. There were no other distributions made or required to be made by the trust.

a. Assume the stock distribution was in satisfaction of an $11,000 pecuniary bequest to M. What is the tax result to M? To Trust T? What basis will M have in the Acme shares?

b. Assume the distribution did not represent a specific bequest to M, and that Trust T did not make a § 643(e)(3) election. What is the tax result to M? To Trust T? What basis will M have in the Acme shares?

c. Assume now that Trust T did make a § 643(e)(3) election with regards to the distribution of the Acme shares. What is the tax result to M? To Trust T? What basis will M have in the Acme shares?

14-20 *Trust's Depreciation Deduction.* Under the terms of the trust instrument, Trustee K is required to maintain a reserve for depreciation equal to $3,000 per year. All trust income, including rents from depreciable trust property, must be distributed currently to trust beneficiaries.

    a.   Assume allowable depreciation for tax purposes is $2,000. What is the amount of the depreciation deduction available to the trust? To the trust beneficiaries?

    b.   Assume allowable depreciation for tax purposes is $7,000. What is the amount of the depreciation deduction available to the trust? To the trust beneficiaries?

14-21 *Trust Losses.* Complex Trust Z has the following receipts and disbursements for the current year:

Receipts:	
Rents	$ 62,000
Proceeds from sale of securities	
(basis of securities = $55,000)	48,000
Dividends	12,000
Total receipts...	$120,000
Disbursements:	
Rent expenses...	$ 70,000
Trustee fee (100 percent	
allocable to income)...................................	4,000
Total disbursements.....................................	$ 74,000

The trustee made no distributions to any beneficiaries during the current year. Based on these facts, compute trust taxable income for the current year.

14-22 *Deductibility of Funeral and Administrative Expenses.* Decedent L died on May 12 of the current year, and her executor elected a calendar taxable year for L's estate. Prior to December 31, L's estate paid $4,800 of funeral expenses, $19,900 of legal and accounting fees attributable to the administration of the estate, and a $6,100 executor's fee. Before consideration of any of these expenses, L's estate has taxable income of $60,000 for the period May 13 to December 31. Decedent L's taxable estate for Federal estate tax purposes is estimated at $1,700,000.

    a.   To what extent are the above expenses deductible on L's estate tax return (Form 706) or on the estate's income tax return (Form 1041) for the current year? On which return would the deductions yield the greater tax benefit?

    b.   Assume that L was married at the time of her death and that all the property included in her gross estate was left to her surviving spouse. Does this fact change your answer to (a)?

14-23 *Amount of Distribution Taxable to Beneficiary.* During the current year, Trust H has DNI of $50,000, of which $30,000 is nontaxable. The trustee made a $10,000 cash distribution to beneficiary P during the year; no other distributions were made.

    a.   How much taxable income must P report?

    b.   What deduction for distributions to beneficiaries may Trust H claim?

14-24 *Deductibility of Trust Expenses.*   Trust A has the following receipts and disbursements for the current year:

Receipts:	
Nontaxable interest	$ 40,000
Taxable interest	30,000
Rents	30,000
Total receipts	$100,000

Disbursements:	
Charitable donation	$ 10,000
Rent expense	6,500
Trustee fee	5,000
Total disbursements	$ 21,500

a. What is Trust A's deduction for charitable contributions for the current year?
b. How much of the trustee fee is deductible?
c. How much of the rent expense is deductible?

14-25 *Computation of DNI and Trust's Tax Liability.*   Trust M has the following receipts and disbursements for the current year:

Receipts:	
Nontaxable interest	$ 4,000
Taxable interest	25,000
Rents	11,000
Long-term capital gain allocable to corpus	9,000
Total receipts	$49,000

Disbursements:	
Rent expense	$ 2,400
Trustee fee	1,000
Total disbursements	$ 3,400

The trustee is required to distribute all trust income to beneficiary N on a quarterly basis.

a. Compute Trust M's DNI for the current year.
b. Compute Trust M's taxable income for the current year.
c. Compute Trust M's tax liability for the current year.

14-26   *Taxation of Trust and Beneficiaries.*   Trust B has the following receipts and disbursements for the current year:

Receipts:

Nontaxable interest......................................	$10,000
Dividends...	10,000
Rents..	30,000
Long-term capital gain allocable	
to corpus...	15,000
Total receipts...	$65,000

Disbursements:

Rent expense..	$ 7,500
Trustee fee..	5,000
Total disbursements....................................	$12,500

During the year, the trustee distributes $20,000 to beneficiary C and $10,000 to beneficiary D. None of these distributions is subject to the throwback rule. The trust and both beneficiaries are calendar year taxpayers.

a.   Compute Trust B's DNI for the current year.
b.   Compute Trust B's taxable income for the current year.
c.   How much taxable income must each beneficiary report for the current year?

14-27   *Distributions from Complex Trusts.*   Under the terms of the trust instrument, the trustee of Trust EFG is required to make an annual distribution of 50 percent of trust accounting income to beneficiary E. The trustee can make additional discretionary distributions out of trust income or corpus to beneficiaries E, F, or G. During the current year, the trust accounting income of $85,000 equaled taxable DNI.

a.   Assume that the trustee made current distributions of $60,000 to E and $10,000 to G. How much taxable income must each beneficiary report for the current year? What is the amount of the trust's deduction for distributions to beneficiaries?

b.   Assume that the trustee made current distributions of $80,000 to E and $40,000 to G. How much taxable income must each beneficiary report for the current year? What is the amount of the trust's deduction for distributions to beneficiaries?

14-28   *First- and Second-Tier Distributions.*   For the current year, Trust R has DNI of $100,000, of which $25,000 is nontaxable. The trustee is required to make an annual distribution of $60,000 to beneficiary S. Also during the year, the trustee made discretionary distributions of $40,000 to beneficiary T and $30,000 to beneficiary U. None of these distributions is subject to the throwback rules. How much taxable income must each beneficiary report?

14-29 *Accumulation Distribution.* In 1989 and 1990, complex Trust C had taxable DNI of $18,000 and $28,500, respectively. No distributions were made to beneficiaries in either year and the trust paid income taxes totaling $13,041 for the two years. In 1991, trust DNI was $33,000 and the trustee distributed $100,000 to beneficiary W.

    a. What is the amount of the accumulation distribution received by W in 1991?

    b. Explain how such distribution is taxed.

14-30 *Special Tax Computation of § 644.* In 1990, individual J transferred land into existing trust H. The beneficiaries of the trust are all members of J's family. At date of transfer, the basis of the land to J was $50,000 and its fair market value was $125,000. The trust sold the land in 1991 for $150,000. Explain how the $100,000 gain on the sale is taxed.

14-31 *Income in Respect of a Decedent.* Individual K is a self-employed business consultant. In the current year, K performed services for a client and billed the client for $14,500. Unfortunately, K died on October 10 of the current year, before he received payment for his services. A check for $14,500 was received by K's executor on November 18. At the date of K's death, he owed a local attorney $1,600 for legal advice concerning a child custody suit in which K was involved. K's executor paid this bill on December 15.

    a. Assuming that K was a cash basis taxpayer, describe the tax consequences of the $14,500 receipt and the $1,600 payment by K's executor.

    b. How would your answer change if K had been an accrual basis taxpayer?

14-32 *Income in Respect of a Decedent.* Early in 1991, Z (an unmarried cash basis taxpayer) sold investment land with a basis of $50,000 for $200,000. In payment, Z received an installment note for $200,000, payable over the next ten years. Z died on December 1, 1991. As of the date of death, Z had received no principal payments on the note. Accrued interest on the note as of December 1, 1991 was $18,000, although the first interest payment was not due until early in 1992.

    a. Assuming that no election is made to avoid installment sale treatment, how much of the $150,000 gain realized by Z will be included on her final income tax return? How much of the accrued interest income will be included?

    b. In 1992, the estate of Z collects the first annual interest payment on the note of $19,700, and the first principal payment of $20,000. What are the income tax consequences to the estate of these collections?

    c. Assume that the amount of estate tax attributable to the inclusion of the IRD represented by the installment note and the accrued interest in Z's taxable estate is $10,000, and that there are no other IRD or DRD items on the estate tax return. Compute the § 691(c) deduction available on the estate's 1992 income tax return.

TAX RETURN PROBLEM

14-33   The MKJ trust is a calendar year, cash basis taxpayer. For 1990, the trust's
books and records reflect these transactions:

Income:		
Dividends...		$ 30,000
Gross rents..		25,000
Interest:		
Bonds of the City of New York........................	$25,000	
U.S. government bonds..............................	20,000	45,000
Capital gains:		
General Motors stock received from		
estate of MKJ:		
Sales price—December 2, 1990...................	48,000	
Less: Basis (FMV on date of death)...............	(30,000)	18,000
Total income...		$118,000
Expenses:		
Trustee commissions		
(allocable to income).............................		$ 4,000
Legal fee...		28,800
Contribution-American Cancer Society		
(paid out of corpus)................................		12,000
Depreciation—rental property.........................		2,000
Real estate tax—rental property......................		4,000
Repairs and maintenance—rental property............		4,200
Total expenses...		$ 55,000
Net income for 1990...................................		$ 63,000

The legal fee was a legitimate trust expense, allocated by the trustee to the
various income classes as follows:

Dividends..	$ 9,400
Taxable interest...	6,600
Tax-exempt interest.......................................	6,000
Rents...	6,800
Total legal fee..	$28,800

The propriety of this allocation is *not* in question. Under the terms of the trust
instrument, the $2 000 depreciation reserve equals the available tax depreciation
deduction for the year. The trust instrument also specifies that all capital gains
are allocable to corpus and that the trustee has discretion as to the amount of
trust income distributed to BTJ, the sole trust beneficiary. During 1990, the
trustee distributes $24,000 of income to BTJ.

Required:
Complete Form 1041 and Schedule D for the MKJ trust. **Note:** If the student
is required to complete a Schedule K-1 for beneficiary BTJ, he or she should
refer to Reg. §§ 1.661(b)-1, 1.661(c)-2, and 1.661(c)-4, and the comprehensive example in this chapter in order to determine the character of any income
distributed to the beneficiary.

RESEARCH PROBLEM

14-34   In 1987 N transferred $600,000 of assets into an irrevocable trust for the benefit of her mother, M. The independent trustee, T, is required to distribute annually all income to M. The trust instrument also provides that any capital gains or losses realized upon the sale of trust assets are to be allocated to trust corpus. In 1988 and 1990, the trustee sold trust assets and distributed an amount equal to the capital gain realized to M, in addition to the required distribution of trust income. During the current year, T sold certain trust securities and realized a net gain of $25,000. The trust also earned $10,000 of other income. During the year, $35,000 was distributed to M. Should the DNI of the trust for the current year include the $25,000 capital gain?

Suggested research materials:

§ 643 and accompanying Regulations
Rev. Rul. 68-392, 1968-2 C.B. 284

LEARNING OBJECTIVES

Upon completion of this chapter you will be able to:

- Explain the concept of income shifting and the judicial constraints on this tax planning technique

- Describe the marriage penalty and the singles penalty and identify the taxpayer situations in which either might occur

- Identify different planning techniques that achieve tax savings by the shifting of income among family members

- Characterize a regular corporation, an S corporation, and a partnership in terms of their viability as intrafamily income-shifting devices

- Explain how the "kiddie tax" is computed on the unearned income of a minor child

- Understand the role of a trust as a vehicle for intrafamily income shifting

- Distinguish between a grantor trust and a taxable trust

- Specify the tax advantages of *inter vivos* gifts as compared to testamentary transfers of wealth

- Explain the potential tax advantages and disadvantages of the estate tax marital deduction

CHAPTER OUTLINE

Chapter 15

FAMILY TAX PLANNING

INTRODUCTION

Under the United States system of taxation, individuals are viewed as the basic unit of taxation. However, most individuals who are members of a nuclear family tend to regard the family as the economic and financial unit. For example, the individual wage earner with a spouse and three children must budget his or her income according to the needs of five people rather than one individual. Similarly, the family that includes a teenager who has received a college scholarship may perceive the scholarship as a financial benefit to all its members.

The concept of family tax planning is a product of this family-oriented economic perspective. Such planning has as its goal the minimization of taxes paid by the family unit as opposed to the separate taxes paid by individual members. Minimization of the total annual income tax bill of a family results in greater consumable income to the family unit. Minimization of transfer taxes on shifts of wealth among family members increases the total wealth that can be enjoyed by the family as a whole.

Before beginning a study of family tax planning, it is important to remember that such planning is only one aspect of the larger issue of family financial planning. Nontax considerations may often be more important to a family than the tax consequences of a course of action. For example, a family that faces the possibility of large medical expenses might be more concerned with their short-term liquidity needs than minimization of their current tax bill. A competent tax adviser must always be sensitive to the family's nontax goals and desires before he or she can design a tax plan that is truly in the family's best interests.

FAMILY INCOME SHIFTING

A general premise in tax planning holds that, given a single amount of income, two taxpayers are always better than one. This premise results from the progressive structure of the United States income tax. As one taxpayer earns an increasing amount of income, the income is taxed at an increasing marginal rate. If the income can be diverted to a second taxpayer with less income of his or her own, the diverted amount will be taxed at a lower marginal rate. The reductions in the individual tax rates enacted as part of the Tax Reform Act of 1986 substantially decrease the progressivity of the income tax. However, even under a progressive tax structure consisting only of three rates (15%, 28%, and 31%), opportunities for tax savings through family income shifting still exist.

A family unit composed of several individuals theoretically represents a single economic unit which nonetheless is composed of separate taxpayers. A shift of income from one of these taxpayers to another has no effect economically. However, if the shift moves the income from a high tax bracket to a low tax bracket, the family has enjoyed a tax savings. A simple example can illustrate this basic point.

> **Example 1.**   Family F is composed of a father and his 15-year-old daughter. The father earns taxable income of $50,000 a year, an amount that represents total family income. During the summer, the daughter needs $5,000 for various personal expenses. To earn the money, she agrees to work for her father for a $5,000 salary, payment of which represents a deductible expense to him. The tax bill on the father's $45,000 income is $6,736 (1990 head-of-household rates, $4,750 standard deduction, two $2,050 exemptions). The tax bill on the daughter's $5,000 income is $263 (1990 single rates, $3,250 standard deduction, no exemption). The total family tax bill is $6,999. If the father had simply agreed to pay the daughter's personal expenses rather than shifting income to her, the family tax bill based on $50,000 of taxable income would be $8,136.

The tax savings in the above example is attributable to two factors. First, the daughter as a taxpayer with earned income is entitled to a $3,250 standard deduction, which shelters $3,250 of the income shifted to her from any taxation at all.[1] Second, the income taxable to the daughter is subject to a 15 percent tax rate; if this income had been taxed on the father's return, it would have been subject to a 28 percent tax rate.

The fact that the daughter is a taxpayer does not prevent the father from qualifying as a head of household for filing purposes. However, because the daughter is claimed as a dependent on her father's return, she is not entitled to a personal exemption on her own return.[2]

JUDICIAL CONSTRAINTS ON INCOME SHIFTING

The Federal courts have consistently recognized that the United States system of taxation cannot tolerate arbitrary shifting of income from one family member to another. The decisions in a number of historic cases have established clear judicial doctrine that limits the assignment of income from one taxpayer to another.

---

[1]   § 63(c)(5).   [2]   § 151(d)(2).

The 1930 Supreme Court case of *Lucas v. Earl*[3] involved a husband and wife who entered into a contract providing that the earnings of either spouse should be considered as owned equally by each. The contract was signed in 1901, twelve years before the first Federal income tax law was written, and was legally binding upon the spouses under California law.

The taxpayers contended that because of the contract certain attorney fees earned by Mr. Earl should be taxed in equal portions to Mr. and Mrs. Earl. However, the Supreme Court agreed with the government's argument that the intent of the Federal income tax law was to tax income to the individual who earns it, an intent that cannot be avoided by anticipatory arrangements to assign the income to a different taxpayer. The decision of the Court ended with the memorable statement that the tax law must disregard arrangements "by which the fruits are attributed to a different tree from that on which they grew."[4]

The Supreme Court followed the same logic in its 1940 decision in *Helvering v. Horst*.[5] This case involved a father who owned corporate coupon bonds and who detached the negotiable interest coupons from the bonds shortly before their due date. The father then gifted the coupons to his son, who collected the interest upon maturity and reported the income on his tax return for the year.

The Court's decision focused on the fact that ownership of the corporate bonds themselves created the right to the interest payments. Because the father owned the bonds, he alone had the right to and control over the interest income. In exercising his control by gifting the interest coupons to his child, the father realized the economic benefit of the income represented by the coupons and therefore was the individual taxable on the income.

These two cases illustrate the two basic premises of the assignment of income doctrine. Earned income must be taxed to the individual who performs the service for which the income is paid. Investment income must be taxed to the owner of the investment capital that generated the income. All legitimate efforts to shift income from one individual to another must take into account these judicial constraints.

JOINT FILING AND THE SINGLES PENALTY

The most obvious candidates for intrafamily income shifting are a husband and wife, one of whom has a much larger income than the other. However, since 1948 married couples have been allowed to file a joint income tax return, which reports the total income earned by the couple and taxes the income on the basis of one progressive rate schedule.[6]

---

[3] 2 USTC ¶496, 8 AFTR 10287, 281 U.S. 111 (USSC, 1930).

[4] *Ibid.,* 281 U.S. 115.

[5] 40-2 USTC ¶9787, 24 AFTR 1058, 311 U.S. 112 (USSC, 1940).

[6] § 6013. Married individuals may choose to file separate returns, but they must use the rate schedule of § 1(d), which simply halves the tax brackets of the married filing jointly rate schedule of § 1(a). As a general rule, separate filing results in a greater tax than joint filing and such filing status is elected only for nontax reasons.

Joint filing originally was intended as a benefit to married couples. Prior to 1969, the joint filing tax rates were designed to tax one-half of total marital income at the tax rates applicable to single individuals. The resultant tax was then doubled to produce the married couple's tax liability. This perfect split and the corresponding tax savings were perceived as inequitable by unmarried taxpayers, who felt they were paying an unjustifiable "singles penalty."

To illustrate, consider the situation of a single taxpayer with taxable income of $24,000. In 1965 this taxpayer owed $8,030 of income tax, with the last dollar of income taxed at a 50 percent marginal tax rate. A married couple with the same 1965 taxable income owed only $5,660 and faced a marginal tax rate of only 32 percent.

THE MARRIAGE PENALTY

In 1969 Congress attempted to alleviate the singles penalty by enacting a new (and lower) rate schedule for single taxpayers.[7] While this action did reduce (but not eliminate) the singles penalty, it also created a marriage penalty for certain individuals. To illustrate both types of penalties, consider taxpayers J and S and the following situations.

Initially, assume J is single and has a taxable income (after a $3,250 standard deduction and $2,050 personal exemption) of $30,000. His 1990 tax liability as a single taxpayer is $5,872. If J marries S during the year and S has no taxable income of her own, the couple may file a joint tax return reflecting a $5,450 standard deduction and two exemptions totaling $4,100. Their 1990 tax liability as a married couple will be only $3,863. In this situation, marriage has saved J $2,009 of tax and a *singles penalty* can be said to exist.

Now assume that S also earns a salary that results in $30,000 of taxable income to her as a single taxpayer. If she and J remain single, each will pay a tax of $5,872, for a total tax bill of $11,744. However, if they choose to marry, their combined taxable income will increase to $61,050 because of the loss of $1,050 of standard deduction. Their tax liability as a married couple is $12,876, and J and S are paying a *marriage penalty* of $1,132.

Generally, a singles penalty may occur when *one* income can be taxed at married, rather than single, rates. A marriage penalty may occur when *two* incomes are combined and taxed at married, rather than singles, rates. Today, two-income families have become the rule rather than the exception, and the marriage penalty has received considerable publicity. Because marital status is determined as of the last day of the taxable year,[8] couples have attempted to avoid the marriage penalty by obtaining a technically legal divorce shortly before year end. When

---

[7] Act. § 803(a), P.L. 91-172, Dec. 30, 1969.   [8] § 7703(a).

a couple has immediately remarried and the only purpose of the divorce was to enable the husband and wife to file as single taxpayers, the IRS and the courts have had little trouble in concluding that the divorce was a sham transaction and therefore ineffective for tax purposes.[9]

INCOME SHIFTING TO CHILDREN AND OTHER FAMILY MEMBERS

Because a married couple is considered one rather than two taxpayers for Federal tax purposes, intrafamily income shifting usually involves a transfer of income from parents to children (or, less commonly, other family members) who are considered taxpayers in their own right.

The fact that children are taxpayers separate and distinct from their parents is recognized by § 73, which states "amounts received in respect of the services of a child shall be included in his gross income and not in the gross income of the parent, even though such amounts are not received by the child." The Regulations elaborate by stating that the statutory rule applies even if state law entitles the parent to the earnings of a minor child.[10]

Because children typically will have little or no income of their own, a shift of family income to such children can cause the income to be taxed at a lower marginal rate. The income shifted from parent to child also represents wealth that is owned by the child rather than the parent. Thus, the future taxable estate of the parent will not include the accumulated income that is already in the hands of younger-generation family members.

INCOME-SHIFTING TECHNIQUES

The next section of this chapter explores a variety of techniques whereby income can be successfully shifted to family members in a lower marginal tax bracket. The circumstances of each particular family situation will dictate the specific technique to be used.

FAMILY MEMBERS AS EMPLOYEES

The first technique for intrafamily income shifting is for a low-bracket family member to become an employee of a family business. This technique does not involve the transfer of a capital interest in the business, so the family member who owns the business does not dilute his or her ownership by this technique.

In the simplest case in which the family business is a sole proprietorship, any family members who become employees must actually perform services the value

---

[9]   Rev. Rul. 76-255, 1976-2 C.B. 40; and *Boyter v. Comm.*, 82-1 USTC ¶9117, 49 AFTR2d 451, 668 F.2d 1382 (CA-4, 1981).

[10]   Reg. § 1.73-1(a).

of which equates to the amount of compensation received. This requirement implies that the employee is both capable and qualified for his or her job and devotes an appropriate amount of time to the performance of services.

> **Example 2.** F owns a plumbing contracting business as a sole proprietorship. During the current year, F employs his son S as an apprentice plumber for an hourly wage of $10. The total amount paid to S for the year is $9,000.

If the father can prove to the satisfaction of the IRS that his son performed services worth $10 per hour and that the son actually worked 900 hours during the year, the father may deduct the $9,000 as wage expense on his tax return and the son will report $9,000 of compensation income on his own return.

If, on the other hand, the IRS concludes that the son was not a legitimate employee of his father's business, the transfer of $9,000 to the son would be recharacterized as a gift. As a result, the father would lose the business deduction, and no income shift from father to son would occur.

Obviously, the legitimacy of the employment relationship between father and son can only be determined by an examination of all relevant facts and circumstances. Facts to be considered would include the age of the son, his prior work experience and technical training, and his actual participation on contracted jobs requiring an apprentice plumber.

When a family member is an employee of a family business, any required payroll taxes on his or her compensation must be paid. However, compensation paid to an employer's children under the age of 18 is not subject to Federal payroll tax.[11]

FAMILY EMPLOYEES OF PARTNERSHIPS AND CORPORATIONS

If a family member wants to work as an employee of a family business that is in partnership or corporate form, the requirement that the value of his or her services equate to the amount of compensation received does not change. If the employment relationship is valid, the partnership or corporation may deduct the compensation paid to the family member. If the family member is not performing services that justify the salary he or she is drawing from the business, the IRS may recharacterize the payment.

In the case of a partnership, the payment may be recharacterized as a constructive cash withdrawal by one or more partners followed by a constructive gift of the cash to the pseudo-employee.

---

[11] §§ 3121(b)(3)(A) and 3306(c)(5).

Example 3.   Brothers X, Y, and Z are equal partners in Partnership XYZ. The partnership hires S, the sister of the partners, to act as secretary-treasurer for the business. S's salary is $20,000 per year. Assume that S has no business or clerical training and performs only minimal services for the business on a very sporadic basis. As a result, the IRS disallows a deduction to the partnership for all but $5,000 of the payment to the sister. The nondeductible $15,000 will be treated as a withdrawal by the partners that was transferred as a gift to the sister.

Constructive cash withdrawals from a partnership could have adverse tax consequences to the partners. If the withdrawal exceeds a partner's basis in his or her partnership interest, the excess constitutes capital gain to the partner.[12] Similarly, a constructive gift to a family member could result in an unexpected gift tax liability.

When the employer is a family corporation and a salary or wage paid to a nonshareholder family member is disallowed, the tax results can be extremely detrimental. Not only does the corporation lose a deduction, but the payment could be recharacterized as a constructive dividend to the family members who are shareholders, followed by a constructive gift to the family member who actually received the funds.[13]   Thus, the corporate shareholders would have dividend income without any corresponding cash, and a potential gift tax liability.

The lesson to be learned from the preceding discussion should be clear. If an intrafamily income shift is to be accomplished by hiring a family member as an employee of a family business, the family member must perform as a legitimate employee. If the employment relationship has no substance, the unintended tax consequences to the family could be costly indeed.

FAMILY MEMBERS AS OWNERS OF THE FAMILY BUSINESS

A second technique for intrafamily income shifting is to make a low-bracket family taxpayer a part owner of the family business. By virtue of his or her equity or capital interest, the family member is then entitled to a portion of the income generated by the business. This is a more extreme technique in that it involves an actual transfer of a valuable asset. Moreover, the disposition of a partial ownership interest may cause dilution of the original owner's control of the business. These and other negative aspects of this technique will be discussed in greater detail later in the chapter.

The gratuitous transfer of an equity interest in a business will constitute a taxable gift to the original owner.

---

[12]   § 731(a).

[13]   *Duffey v. Lethert,* 63-1 USTC ¶9442, 11 AFTR2d 1317 (D.Ct. Minn., 1963).

Example 4. M runs a very successful business as a sole proprietorship. She wants to bring her son S into the business as an equal general partner. Under the terms of a legally binding partnership agreement, she contributes her business, valued at $1 million, to the partnership. Although the son will have a 50% capital interest in the partnership, he contributes nothing. As a result, M has made a $500,000 taxable gift to S.

Of course, if the transfer of the equity interest is accomplished by sale rather than gift, no initial gift tax liability will result. But in a typical family situation, the equity interest is being transferred to a family member without significant income or wealth, so that family member lacks the funds to purchase the interest. Also, the income tax consequences of a sale could be more expensive than gift tax consequences, depending upon the facts and circumstances. The prudent tax adviser should explore both possible methods of transfer when designing a particular plan.

FAMILY PARTNERSHIPS

A family partnership can be used as a vehicle for the co-ownership of a single business by a number of family members. As a partner, each family member will report his or her allocable share of partnership income (or loss) on his or her individual tax return.[14] Therefore, through use of a partnership, business income can be shifted to family members with relatively low marginal tax brackets.

If the family partnership is primarily a service business, only a family member who performs services can receive an allocation of partnership income. In such service partnerships the physical assets of the business (the capital of the partnership) are not a major factor of income production. Rather, it is the individual efforts and talents of the partners that produce partnership income. An attempt to allow a family member who cannot perform the appropriate services to participate in partnership income is an unwarranted assignment of earned income.

If the family partnership is one in which capital is a major income-producing factor, the mere ownership of a capital interest will entitle a family member to participate in partnership income. The determination of whether or not capital is a material income-producing factor is made by reference to the facts of each situation. However, capital is ordinarily a material income-producing factor if the operation of the business requires substantial inventories or investment in plant, machinery, or equipment.[15]

Section 704(e)(1) specifies that a family member will be recognized as a legitimate partner if he or she owns a capital interest in a partnership in which capital is a material income-producing factor. This is true even if the family member received his or her interest as a gift. However, § 704(e)(2) limits the amount of partnership income that can be shifted to such a donee partner. Under this statute, the income allocated to the partner cannot be proportionally greater than his or her interest in partnership capital.

---

[14]   § 702(a).   [15]   Reg. § 1.704-1(e)(1)(iv).

Example 5. Grandfather F is a 50% partner in Magnum Partnership. At the beginning of the current year, F gives his grandson G a 20% capital interest in Magnum (leaving F with a 30% interest). For the current year Magnum has taxable income of $120,000. The *maximum* amount allocable to G is $24,000 (20% × $120,000). If F wanted to increase the dollar amount of partnership income shifted to G, he must give G a greater equity interest in the partnership.

Section 704(e)(2) contains a second restriction on income allocation. A donor partner who gifts a capital interest must receive reasonable compensation for any services he or she renders to the partnership before any income can be allocated to the donee partner.

Example 6. Refer to the facts in *Example 5*. During the current year, F performs services for Magnum worth $15,000 but for which he receives no compensation. Half of the $120,000 partnership income is still allocable to F and G with respect to their combined 50% capital interests; however, the maximum amount allocable to G decreases to $ 18,000 [($60,000 − $15,000 allocated to F as compensation for services) × 40%].

Note that in the above example, Grandfather F might be willing to forgo any compensation for the services performed for Magnum in order to increase the amount of partnership income shifted to his grandson. Unfortunately, § 704(e)(2) effectively curtails this type of indirect assignment of earned income.

Family members are not able to avoid the dual limitations of § 704(e) by arranging a transfer of a capital interest to a lower-bracket family member by sale rather than by gift. Under § 704(e)(3), a capital interest in a partnership purchased by one member of a family from another is considered to be created by gift from the seller. In this context the term *family* includes an individual's spouse, ancestors, lineal descendants, and certain family trusts.

REGULAR CORPORATIONS

Family businesses are frequently owned as closely held corporations. There are a number of business reasons why the corporate form is popular. For example, shareholders in a corporation have limited liability so that creditors of the corporation cannot force the shareholders to pay the debts of the corporation out of the shareholders' personal assets. There are also tax benefits to the corporate form of business. The owners of the business can function as employees of the corporate entity. As employees, they may participate in a wide variety of tax-favored employee benefit plans, such as employer-sponsored medical reimbursement plans. If the family business were in sole proprietorship or partnership form, the owners of the business would be self-employed and ineligible to participate in such employee benefit plans.

The corporate form of business must be regarded as a mixed blessing from a tax point of view. The incorporation of a family business does result in the creation of a new taxable entity, separate and distinct from its owners. Business income has been shifted to the corporate taxpayer, and because corporate tax rates are progressive, a net tax savings to the business can be the result.[16]

> **Example 7.** Individual T owns a sole proprietorship that produces $100,000 of net income before taxes. Ignoring the availability of any deductions or exemptions, T's 1990 tax on this income is $24,862 (Schedule Y). If T incorporates the business and draws a salary of $50,000, he will pay an individual tax of only $9,782. The corporation also will have income of $50,000 ($100,000 net income − $50,000 salary to T). The corporate tax on $50,000 is $7,500. Therefore, the *total* tax on the business income has decreased to $17,282 ($9,782 + $7,500).

The tax savings to T's business ($7,580) achieved by incorporation is certainly dramatic. However, the potential problem created by the incorporation of T's business is that the after-tax earnings of the business are now in the corporation rather than in T's pocket. If T needs or wants more than $40,218 ($50,000 salary − $9,782 tax liability) of after-tax personal income, he may certainly have his corporation pay out some of its after-tax earnings to him as a dividend. But any dividends paid must be included in T's gross income and taxed at the individual level.

This double taxation of corporate earnings paid to shareholders as dividends can quickly offset the tax savings resulting from using a corporation as a separate entity. Therefore, shareholders in closely held corporations usually become very adept in drawing business income out of their corporations as deductible business expenses rather than nondeductible dividends.

Shareholders who are also employees will usually try to maximize the amount of compensation they receive from the corporation. Section 162(a)(1) authorizes the corporation to deduct a *reasonable* allowance for salaries or other compensation paid. If the IRS determines that the compensation paid to an owner employee is unjustifiably high and therefore *unreasonable,* the excessive compensation can be reclassified as a dividend. As a result, the corporation loses the deduction for the excessive compensation, and to a corresponding extent, business earnings are taxed twice.

---

[16]   Because of the 5 percent surtax on taxable income between $100,000 and $335,000, corporations with taxable income in excess of $335,000 face a flat 34 percent tax rate rather than a progressive rate. Qualified personal service corporations pay a flat 34 percent of their total taxable income. § 11(b)(2).

Other types of deductible payments from corporations to shareholders include rents paid for corporate use of shareholder assets and interest on loans made to the corporation by shareholders. The arrangements between corporation and shareholder that give rise to such rent or interest payments will be subject to careful scrutiny by the IRS. If an arrangement lacks substance and is deemed to be a device to camouflage the payments of dividends to shareholders, the corporate deduction for the payments will be disallowed.

Because it is a taxpayer in its own right, a regular corporation cannot be effectively used to shift business income to low-bracket family members. If such family members are made shareholders in the corporation and have no other relationship to the corporate business (employee, creditor, etc.), the only way to allocate business earnings to them is by paying dividends on their stock. As previously discussed, dividend payments are usually considered prohibitively costly from a tax standpoint.

Closely held regular corporations do have tremendous utility in other areas of tax planning. However, for purposes of intrafamily income shifting, the S corporation is a highly preferable alternative to a regular corporation.

S CORPORATIONS

The complex set of statutory provisions that govern the tax treatment of S corporations is explained in Chapter 12. For family tax planning purposes, the most important characteristic of an S corporation is that the corporate income escapes taxation at the corporate level and is taxed to the corporation's shareholders. This characteristic makes an S corporation a very useful mechanism for intrafamily income shifting.

Section 1366(a) provides that the taxable income of an S corporation is allocated to the shareholders on a pro rata basis. Thus, any individual who is a shareholder will report a proportionate share of the corporate business income on his or her personal tax return for the year with or within which the S corporation's taxable year ends.

> **Example 8.** Individual M owns a sole proprietorship with an annual net income before taxes of $200,000. Ignoring the availability of any itemized deductions or exemptions, M's personal tax on this income is $56,000 (Schedule Y). If at the beginning of 1990 M incorporates the business, gives each of his four unmarried children 20 percent of the stock, and has the shareholders elect S status for the corporation, the corporate income of $200,000 will be taxed in equal amounts to the five shareholders. Ignoring other deductions or exemptions, the 1990 tax bill on the business income will be $41,670 [$6,982 from Schedule Y + (4 × $8,672 from Schedule X)].

A shareholder who is also an employee of a family-owned S corporation will not be able to divert corporate income to other shareholders by forgoing any compensation for services rendered to the corporation. Code § 1366(e) provides that if such a shareholder employee does not receive reasonable compensation from the S corporation, the IRS may reallocate corporate income to the shareholder employee so as to accurately reflect the value of his or her services.

Because shareholders of an S corporation are taxed on all the taxable income earned by the corporation, subsequent cash withdrawals of this income by shareholders are tax free.[17] However, the technical requirements for cash withdrawals from an S corporation are dangerously complicated. Because of the complexity of these requirements and many other tax aspects of S corporations, family tax plans involving their use should be carefully designed and monitored by the family tax adviser.

NEGATIVE ASPECTS OF OWNERSHIP TRANSFERS

A high-bracket taxpayer who desires to shift income to low-bracket family members by making such members co-owners of the taxpayer's business must reconcile himself or herself to several facts First, the transfer of the equity interest in the business must be complete and legally binding so that the recipient of the interest has "dominion and control" over his or her new asset. A *paper* transfer by which the transferor creates only the illusion that a family member has been given an equity interest in a business will be treated as a sham transaction, ineffective for income shifting purposes.[18]

As a general rule, the recipient of an ownership interest in a family business is free to dispose of the interest, just as he or she is free to dispose of any asset he or she owns. If the recipient is a responsible individual and supportive of the family tax planning goals, his or her legal right to assign the interest may not be a problem. But if the recipient is a spendthrift in constant need of ready cash, he or she may sell the interest to a third party, thereby completely subverting the family tax plan.

One popular technique that can prevent an unexpected and undesired disposition of an interest in a family business is a buy-sell agreement. A taxpayer can transfer an equity interest to a low-bracket family member on the condition that should the family member desire to sell the interest he or she must first offer the interest to its original owner at an independently determined market value. Such an agreement is in no way economically detrimental to the family member, yet affords a measure of protection for both the original owner and the family tax plan.

---

[17]   § 1368(b).   [18]   For example, see Reg. § 1.704-1(e)(2).

A related aspect of the requirement that the taxpayer must legally surrender the ownership of the business interest transferred is that the transfer is irrevocable. Ownership of the interest cannot be regained if future events cause the original tax plan to become undesirable. For example, an estrangement between family members could convert a highly satisfactory intrafamily income shifting plan into a bitterly resented trap. A father who has an ill-favored son as an employee can always fire him. It is another matter entirely if the son is a 40 percent shareholder in the father's corporation.

A change in economic circumstances could also cause a taxpayer to regret a transfer of a business interest. Consider a situation in which a formerly high-income taxpayer suffers a severe financial downturn. A tax plan that is shifting income *away* from such a taxpayer could suddenly become an economic disaster.

PRESERVATION OF CONTROL OF THE BUSINESS

A taxpayer who is contemplating transferring an ownership interest in a business to one or more family members should also consider any resultant dilution of his or her control of the business. The taxpayer may be willing to part with an equity interest in order to shift business income to low-bracket family members, but may be very reluctant to allow such family members to participate in the management of the business.

A limited partnership can be used to bring family members into a business without allowing them a voice in management. A family member who owns a capital interest as a limited partner in a partnership may be allocated a share of business income, subject to the family partnership rules, and yet be precluded from participating in management of the business.

If the family business is in corporate form, various classes of stock with differing characteristics can be issued. For example, nonvoting stock can be given to family members without any dilution of the original owner's voting power, and hence control, over the business. If the original owner does not want to draw any dividends out of the corporate business but is willing to have dividends paid to low-bracket family members, nonvoting preferred stock can be issued to such family members.

Unfortunately, this flexibility in designing a corporate capital structure that maximizes income-shifting potential while minimizing loss of control is not available to S corporations. To qualify for S status a corporation may have only one class of stock outstanding.[19] Thus, all outstanding shares of stock in an S corporation must be identical with respect to the rights they convey in the profits and assets of the corporation. However, shares of stock in S corporations may have different *voting rights* without violating the single class of stock requirement.[20]

---

[19]   § 1361(b)(1)(D).   [20]   § 1361(c)(4).

SHIFTS OF INVESTMENT INCOME

In many ways the shifting of investment income to family members is simpler than the shifting of business income. Questions of forms of co-ownership and control are not as difficult to resolve if the income-producing asset to be transferred is in the form of an investment security rather than a business interest.

The simplest means to shift investment income from one taxpayer to another is an outright gift of the investment asset. Even gifts to minors who are under legal disabilities with regard to property ownership can be accomplished under state Uniform Gifts to Minors Acts. By using a custodian to hold the property for the benefit of a minor, the donor has shifted the investment income to the minor's tax return.[21]

Although gifting of investment property is a relatively simple technique, the donor must be aware that the transfer must be complete. The asset (and the wealth it represents) is irrevocably out of the donor's hands. If the donor attempts to retain an interest in or control over the asset, the gift may be deemed incomplete and the attempted income shift ineffectual.

If a donee receives an unrestricted right to a valuable investment asset, there is always the worry that he or she will mismanage it, or worse, assign it to a third party against the wishes of the donor. Because of these negative aspects of outright gifts, the private trust has become a very popular vehicle for the transfer of investment assets, especially when minor children are involved. A subsequent section of the chapter explores the use of trusts in family tax planning.

TAXATION OF UNEARNED INCOME OF MINOR CHILDREN

The Tax Reform Act of 1986 significantly limited the ability of parents to shift investment income to their children. Section 1(i) provides that any *net unearned income* of a minor child in excess of a $500 base is taxed at the marginal rate applicable to the income of the child's parents.[22] A minor child is one who has not obtained the age of 14 by the close of the taxable year and who has at least one living parent on that date.

Net unearned income is generally defined as passive investment income such as interest and dividends, reduced by the $500 standard deduction available against unearned income of a dependent.[23] The amount of net unearned income for any taxable year may not exceed the child's taxable income for the year. The *source* of the unearned income is irrelevant for purposes of this so-called "kiddie tax."

---

[21] Rev. Rul. 56-484, 1956-2 C.B. 23. However, income earned by the custodian account used for the support of the minor will be taxed to the person legally responsible for such support (i.e., the parent).

[22] In the case of parents who are not married, the child's tax is computed with reference to the tax rate of the custodial parent. If the parents file separate tax returns, the tax rate of the parent with the *greater* taxable income is used. § 1(i)(5).

[23] § 63(c)(5).

Example 9. In 1989 grandchild G, age 10, received a gift of investment securities from her grandparents. G's current year dividend income from the securities totaled $7,189. G had no other income or deductions for the year. G's parents claimed G as a dependent and reported taxable income of $215,000 on their joint return. G's taxable income is $6,689 ($7,189 gross income − a $500 standard deduction) and her net unearned income to be taxed at her parents' rates is $6,189 ($7,189 − the $500 base − a $500 standard deduction). If this income had been included on G's parents' return, it would have been taxed at a marginal rate of 31% and the resulting tax liability would have been $1,919. Therefore, G's tax liability is 15% of $500 (G's taxable income − her net unearned income) plus $1,919, a total of $1,994.

In certain cases parents may elect to include a dependent's unearned income on their return, rather than filing a separate return and making the "kiddie tax" calculation.

THE TRUST AS A TAX PLANNING VEHICLE

As discussed in Chapter 14, a private trust is a legal arrangement whereby the ownership and control of property is vested in a trustee while the beneficial interest in the property is given to one or more beneficiaries. The trustee has a fiduciary responsibility to manage the property for the sole benefit of the beneficiaries.

ADVANTAGES OF THE TRUST FORM

The use of a trust has many nontax advantages. If an individual desires to make a gift of property to a donee who is not capable of owning or managing the property, the gift can be made in trust so that a competent trustee can be selected to manage the property free from interference from the donee-beneficiary.

The trust form of property ownership is very convenient in that it allows the legal title to property to be held by a single person (the trustee) while allowing the beneficial enjoyment of the property to be shared by a number of beneficiaries. If legal ownership of the property were fragmented among the various beneficiaries, they would all have to jointly participate in management decisions regarding the property. This cumbersome and oftentimes impractical co-ownership situation is avoided when a trustee is given sole management authority over the property.

If a donor would like to give property to several donees so that the donees have sequential rather than concurrent rights in the property, the trust form for the gift is commonly the solution.

Example 10. Individual K owns a valuable tract of income-producing real estate. She would like ownership of the real estate to ultimately pass to her three minor grandchildren. She also would like to give her invalid brother an interest in the real estate so as to provide him with a future source of income. K can transfer the real estate into trust, giving her brother an income interest for a designated time period. Upon termination of the time period, ownership of the real estate will go to K's grandchildren.

TAX CONSEQUENCES OF TRANSFERS INTO TRUST

The use of the trust form can have distinct income tax advantages to a family because both the trust itself and any beneficiaries who receive income from the trust are taxpayers in their own right.

Example 11. F, a high-bracket taxpayer, transfers income-producing assets into a trust of which his four grandchildren are discretionary income beneficiaries. In the current year, the trust assets generate $100,000 of income of which the trustee distributes $24,000 to each child. The $100,000 of investment income will be taxed to five relatively low-bracket taxpayers, the four grandchildren and the trust itself.

It is important to remember that unearned income *distributed* from a trust to a beneficiary who is under the age of 14 is subject to the rule of § 1(i). The income will be taxed at the marginal rate applicable to the beneficiary's parents, even if the parents did not create the trust.

The accumulation distribution rules of §§ 665 through 668 severely limit arbitrary shifting of income between a trust and its beneficiaries. Under these rules, income that is accumulated by (and therefore taxed to) a trust and then distributed in a later year to a beneficiary will be taxed to the beneficiary in the year of distribution. This tax is computed by a complex set of rules intended to simulate the tax the beneficiary would have paid if the trust income had originally been distributed rather than accumulated.[24]

The purpose of the accumulation distribution rules is to prevent a trust from being used as a tax shelter in a year in which the trust's marginal tax rate is less than that of the income beneficiaries. However, the rules do not apply to accumulations of income made before the appropriate income beneficiary reaches the age of 21.[25]

---

[24] See Chapter 14 for a discussion of these "throwback" rules.

[25] § 665(b)(2).

GIFT-LEASEBACKS

A popular and controversial method for family income shifting through use of a trust involves a technique known as a gift-leaseback. Typically, a taxpayer who owns assets that he or she uses in a trade or business transfers the assets as a gift in trust for the benefit of the taxpayer's children (or other low-bracket family members). The independent trustee then leases the assets back to the taxpayer for their fair rental value. The rent paid by the taxpayer to the trust is deducted as a § 162 ordinary and necessary business expense and becomes income to the taxpayer's children because of their status as trust beneficiaries.

The IRS has refused to recognize the validity of gift-leaseback arrangements and has consistently disallowed the rent deduction to the transferor of the business assets under the theory that the entire transaction has no business purpose. However, if the trust owning the leased assets has an independent trustee and the leaseback arrangement is in written form and requires payment to the trust of a reasonable rent, the Tax Court and the Second, Third, Seventh, Eighth, and Ninth Circuits have allowed the transferor to deduct the rent paid.[26] To date, the Fourth and Fifth Circuits have supported the government's position that gift-leaseback transactions are shams to be disregarded for tax purposes.[27] Given this split between the appellate courts, the future of gift-leasebacks as income-shifting devices will probably be determined by the Supreme Court.

GIFT TAX CONSIDERATIONS

The obvious income tax advantage of a family trust, such as the one described in *Example 11* above, can be offset if the original gift of property into the trust is subject to a substantial gift tax. Thus, the first step in designing a family trust is the minimization of any front-end gift tax. If the fair market value of the transferred property is less than the taxable amount sheltered by the unified credit of § 2505, no gift tax will be paid. However, the reader should bear in mind that the use of the credit against inter vivos gifts reduces the future shelter available on the donor's estate tax return.

An essential element in the minimization of any gift tax for transfers into trust is securing the $10,000 annual exclusion (§ 2503) for the amount transferred to each beneficiary-donee. This can be difficult when certain of the donees are given only a prospective or future interest in the trust property.

---

[26] See *May v. Comm.*, 76 T.C. 7(1981), *aff'd.* 84-1 USTC ¶9166, 53 AFTR2d 84-626 (CA-9, 1984).

[27] See *Mathews v. Comm.*, 75-2 USTC ¶9734, 36 AFTR2d 75-5965, 520 F.2d 323 (CA-5, 1975).

Example 12. Donor Z transfers $100,000 into trust. The independent trustee has the discretion to distribute income currently among Z's five children, or she may accumulate it for future distribution. Upon trust termination, the trust assets will be divided equally among the children. Because the five donees have only future interests in the $100,000, Z may not claim any exclusions in computing the amount of the taxable gift.[28]

SECTION 2503(c) AND CRUMMEY TRUSTS

One method of securing the exclusion for transfers into trust is to rely on the *safe harbor* rules of § 2503(c). Under this subsection a transfer into trust will not be considered a gift of a future interest if

1. The property and income therefrom may be expended for the benefit of the donee-beneficiary before he or she reaches age 21; and

2. If any property or income is not so expended, it will pass to the donee-beneficiary at age 21 or be payable to his or her estate if he or she dies before that age.

One drawback to the "§ 2503(c) trust" is that the trust assets generally must go to the beneficiaries at age 21. Many parent-donors would prefer to postpone trust termination until their children-donees attain a more mature age. This goal can be accomplished through the use of a *Crummey trust*.[29]

A Crummey trust is one in which the beneficiaries are directly given only a future right to trust income or corpus. The term of the trust may extend well beyond the time when the beneficiaries reach age 21. However, the trust instrument contains a clause (the Crummey clause) which authorizes any beneficiary or his or her legal representative to make a current withdrawal of any current addition to the trust of up to $10,000. The withdrawal right is made noncumulative from year to year. As long as the beneficiary is given notification of this right within a reasonable period before it lapses for the year, the donor will be entitled to an exclusion for the current transfers into trust.[30] It should be noted that most donors anticipate that their donees will never exercise their withdrawal right; the Crummey clause is included in the trust instrument for the *sole purpose* of securing the $10,000 exclusion for gift tax purposes.

---

[28] Reg. § 25.2503-3(c), Ex. 3.

[29] The amusing designation comes from the court case which established the validity of the technique—*Crummey v. Comm.,* 68-2 USTC ¶12, 541, 22 AFTR2d 6023, 397 F.2d

82 (CA-9, 1968). The IRS *acquiesced* to this decision in Rev. Rul. 73-405, 1973-2 C.B. 321.

[30] Rev. Rul. 81-7, 1981-1 C.B. 27.

GRANTOR TRUSTS

In certain cases a taxpayer may desire to transfer property into trust but does not want to surrender complete control over the property. Alternatively, the taxpayer may want to dispose of the property (and the right to income from the property) for only a limited period of time. Prior to the enactment of the 1954 Internal Revenue Code there was no statutory guidance as to when the retention of powers over a trust by the grantor (transferor) would prevent the trust from being recognized as a separate taxable entity. Nor was there statutory guidance as to the tax status of a reversionary trust, the corpus of which reverted to the grantor after a specified length of time.

The judicial attitude toward these *grantor* trusts was reflected in the Supreme Court decision of *Helvering v. Clifford*.[31] This case involved a taxpayer who transferred securities into trust for the exclusive benefit of his wife. The trust was to last for five years, during which time the taxpayer as trustee would manage the trust corpus as well as decide how much, if any, of the trust income was to be paid to his wife. Upon trust termination, corpus was to return to the taxpayer while any accumulated income was to go to the wife.

In reaching its decision, the Court noted the lack of a precise standard or guide supplied by statute or regulations. As a result, the Court turned to a subjective evaluation of all the facts and circumstances of this particular short-term trust arrangement and held that "the short duration of the trust, the fact that the wife was the beneficiary, and the retention of control over the corpus by respondent all lead irresistably to the conclusion that the respondent continued to be the owner."[32] As a result, the trust income was held to be taxable to the grantor rather than the trust or its beneficiary.

The authors of the 1954 Internal Revenue Code recognized that the uncertainty regarding the tax treatment of grantor trusts was undesirable and supplanted the subjective *Clifford* approach with a series of code sections (§§ 671 through 679) containing more objective rules as to the taxability of such trusts. The basic operative rule is contained in § 671—if §§ 673 through 679 specify that the grantor (or another person) shall be treated as the owner of any portion of a trust, the income, deductions, or credits attributable to that portion of the trust shall be reported on the grantor's (or other person's) tax return. If §§ 673 through 679 are inapplicable, the trust shall be treated as a separate taxable entity under the normal rules of Subchapter J (see Chapter 14).

---

[31] 40-1 USTC ¶9265, 23 AFTR 1077, 309 U.S. 331 (1940).

[32] *Ibid.*, 309 U.S. 332.

REVERSIONARY TRUSTS

Section 673 provides that the grantor shall be treated as the owner of any portion of a trust in which he or she has a reversionary interest, if upon creation of the trust the value of the reversion exceeds 5 percent of the value of the assets subject to reversion.[33]

Example 13. In the current year, grantor G transfers assets worth $500,000 into trust. Niece N, age 20, will receive the income from the trust for 15 years, after which the trust will terminate and the assets returned to G. On the date the trust is created, the reversion is properly valued at $121,000. Because the reversion is worth more than 5% of $500,000, the income will be taxed to G, even though it will be distributed to N.

Example 14. If in the previous example, N had been given the income from the trust for her life, the proper value of G's reversion would only be $13,000. Because this reversionary interest is worth only 2.6% of the value of the trust assets, the trust is not a grantor trust and the income will be taxed to N.

In the case of a trust in which a lineal descendant of the grantor (child, grandchild, etc.) is the income beneficiary, and the grantor owns a reversionary interest that takes effect only upon the death of the beneficiary prior to the age of 21, the trust *will not* be considered a grantor trust.[34]

INTEREST-FREE LOANS

Through use of a reversionary trust, a taxpayer may divert income to low bracket family members only if he or she is willing to part with control of the trust corpus for a significant period of time. For many years the use of an interest-free demand loan between family members seemed to provide an alternative to a reversionary trust. A taxpayer could loan a sum of money to a family member on a demand basis and the money could be invested to earn income for that family member. Because the loan was interest-free, the creditor-taxpayer had no income from the temporary shift of wealth and could call the loan (demand payment) at any time.

---

[33] The Tax Reform Act of 1986 repealed the popular Clifford trust device, whereby the transfer of assets into a reversionary trust which lasted at least 10 years resulted in an income shift to the beneficiaries. How-

ever, Clifford trusts in existence on or before March 1, 1986 will not be considered grantor trusts under the new law.

[34] § 673(b).

The IRS was understandably hostile to such loans and argued that the creditor was making a gift of the use of the money to the borrower and that the amount of the gift equaled the interest that the creditor would have charged an unrelated borrower. On February 22, 1984 the Supreme Court agreed with the IRS position in *Dickman v. Commissioner.*[35]

Before the ink on the *Dickman* decision had dried, Congress addressed the problem by enacting Code § 7872, concerning below-interest and no-interest loans. The thrust of this provision is to impute interest income to the creditor-donor and correspondingly allow an interest deduction for the borrower-donee. Therefore, the creditor-donor is effectively treated as having received interest income and then gifting such income to the borrower. The deemed transfer is subject to the gift tax to the extent the interest exceeds the annual exclusion. As a result, interest-free loans are no longer an effective device for shifting income.

> **Example 15.** On January 1 of the current year, father F lent $175,000 to his daughter, S. The loan was interest-free and F may demand repayment at any time. The current interest rate as determined by the IRS is 10% per annum. On December 31 of the current year, S is considered to have paid $17,500 of deductible interest to F, and F is considered to have received $17,500 of taxable interest income from S. On the same date, F is considered to have made a $17,500 gift to S which is eligible for the $10,000 annual gift tax exclusion.

POWER TO CONTROL BENEFICIAL ENJOYMENT

Section 674(a) contains the general rule that a grantor shall be treated as the owner of any portion of a trust of which the grantor, a nonadverse party, or both, controls the beneficial enjoyment. However, if the exercise of such control requires the approval or consent of an *adverse party,* the general rule shall not apply. An adverse party is defined in § 672(a) as any person who has a substantial beneficial interest in the trust that would be adversely affected by the exercise of the control held by the grantor.

> **Example 16.** F transfers income-producing property into trust with City Bank as independent trustee. F's two children are named as trust beneficiaries. However, F retains the unrestricted right to designate which of the children is to receive annual distributions of trust income. This is a grantor trust with the result that all trust income is taxed to F.

---

[35] 84-1 USTC ¶13, 560, 53 AFTR2d 84-1608, 104 S.Ct. 1086 (USSC, 1984).

Example 17.   Refer to the facts in *Example 16*. Assume that the trust instrument provides that the trust income will be paid out on an annual basis in equal portions to F's two children. However, F retains the right to adjust the amount of the income distributions at any time with the consent of the older child C. Because C is an adverse party with respect to the one-half of the income to which he is entitled, only the other half of the income is considered subject to F's control. As a result, only half the trust property is deemed owned by F and only half the trust income is taxable directly to him.[36]

The general rule of § 674(a) is subject to numerous exceptions contained in §§ 674(b), (c), and (d). Any tax adviser attempting to avoid the grantor trust rules should be aware of these exceptions. For example, § 674(c) provides that the power to distribute income within a class of beneficiaries will not cause the grantor trust rules to apply if the power is solely exercisable by an independent trustee.

Example 18.   M transfers income-producing property into trust and names Midtown Bank as independent trustee. The trustee has the right to *sprinkle* (distribute) the annual income of the trust among M's three children in any proportion the trustee deems appropriate. Even though the power to control the enjoyment of the income is held by a nonadverse party, such party is independent of the grantor and the trust is not a grantor trust.

OTHER GRANTOR TRUSTS

Section 675 provides that the grantor shall be treated as the owner of any portion of a trust in respect of which he or she holds certain administrative or management powers.

Example 19.   T transfers 60% of the common stock in his closely held corporation into trust with City National Bank as independent trustee. All income of the trust must be paid to T's only grandchild. However, T retains the right to vote the transferred shares. Because T has retained an administrative power specified in § 675(4), he will be taxed on the income generated by the corporate stock.

If a grantor, a nonadverse party, or both have the right to revest in the grantor the ownership of any portion of trust property, § 676 provides that such portion of the trust is considered to be owned by the grantor. Therefore, revocable trusts are grantor trusts for income tax purposes.

---

[36]   Reg. § 1.672(a)-1(b).

Under § 677, a grantor also is treated as owner of any portion of a trust the income of which *may be* distributed to the grantor or spouse without the approval of any adverse party. This rule also applies if trust income may be used to pay premiums for insurance on the life of the grantor and spouse. This provision is inapplicable if the beneficiary of the policy is a charitable organization.

> **Example 20.** Individual J transfers income-producing assets into trust and designates Second National Bank as independent trustee. Under the terms of the trust instrument, the trustee may distribute trust income to either J's spouse or J's brother. In the current year the trustee distributes all trust income to J's brother. Since a nonadverse party (the trustee) could have distributed the trust income to J's spouse, this is a grantor trust and all income is taxed to J.

If trust income may be expended to discharge a legal obligation of the grantor, § 677 applies,[37] subject to two important exceptions. Section 682 creates an exception for *alimony trusts*. In certain divorce situations an individual who is required to pay alimony may fund a reversionary trust, the income from which will be paid to the grantor's former spouse in satisfaction of the alimony obligation. Under § 682, the recipient of the trust income rather than the grantor will be taxed on the income regardless of the applicability of any other of the grantor trust rules.

As a second exception, § 677(b) specifies that if trust income may be distributed for the support or maintenance of a beneficiary (other than the grantor's spouse) whom the grantor is legally obligated to support, such a provision by itself will not cause the trust to be a grantor trust. However, to the extent trust income is actually distributed for such purposes, it will be taxed to the grantor.

The final type of trust that is not recognized as a separate taxable entity is described in § 678. Under this provision, a person *other than* the grantor may be treated as the owner of a portion of a trust if such person has an unrestricted right to vest trust corpus or income in himself or herself. Section 678 shall not apply to the situation in which a person, in the capacity of trustee, has the right to distribute trust income to a beneficiary whom the person is legally obligated to support. Only to the extent that trust income is actually so expended will the income be taxed to the person.

> **Example 21.** Grantor G creates a trust with an independent corporate trustee and names his children and grandchildren as beneficiaries. The trust instrument also provides that G's sister S has the unrestricted right to withdraw up to one-third of trust corpus at any time. S is considered the owner of one-third of the trust and will be taxed on one-third of the income, regardless of the fact that such income is not distributable to her.

---

[37] Reg. § 1.677(a)-1(d).

GRANTOR TRUSTS AND THE TRANSFER TAX RULES

As a general rule, a transfer of assets into trust that is incomplete for income tax purposes, so that the grantor is taxed on trust income, is also incomplete for gift and estate tax purposes.

> **Example 22.** M transfers income-producing properties into a trust but retains the right to designate which of the specified trust beneficiaries will receive a distribution of trust income. The arrangement is a grantor trust per § 674. Under the gift tax Regulations, M has not made a completed gift of the income interest in the trust, and per § 2036 the value of the trust corpus will be included in M's gross estate upon his death.

However, it should be emphasized that the general rule doesn't always hold.

> **Example 23.** Grantor G transfers assets into a reversionary trust that will last only eight years. During the existence of the trust, all income must be paid to G's cousin, C. For income tax purposes, this is a grantor trust and all trust income is taxable to G. However, for gift tax purposes G has made a completed gift of the income interest to C.

TRANSFER TAX PLANNING

The first part of this chapter dealt with a variety of techniques to shift income within a family group and thereby minimize the family's income tax burden. The second part of the chapter focuses on family tax planning techniques designed to reduce any transfer tax liability on intrafamily shifts of wealth. At this point, the student should be cautioned against thinking of income tax planning and transfer tax planning as two separate areas; both types of planning should be considered as highly interrelated aspects of a single integrated family tax plan.

A second aspect of transfer tax planning of which any tax adviser should be aware is that a client's nontax estate planning goals may conflict with an optimal tax-oriented estate plan. From a client's point of view, an orderly disposition of wealth that benefits the heirs in the precise manner that the client desires may be the primary planning objective, regardless of the tax cost. A client planning for his or her own death may be most concerned with his or her own emotional and psychological needs as well as those of other family members. Minimization of the Federal estate tax levied on the estate simply may not be a central concern. A tax adviser who fails to appreciate the client's priorities and who designs an estate plan that fails to reflect the client's nontax needs is not acting in the best interest of that client.

TAX PLANNING WITH INTRAFAMILY GIFTS

Before enactment of the Tax Reform Act of 1976, the Federal transfer tax savings associated with gifting assets to family members during the donor's life rather than transferring the assets at death were obvious. The gift tax rates were only 75 percent of the estate tax rates, and because of the progressive nature of both rate schedules, inter vivos gifts could shift an individual's wealth out of a high marginal estate tax bracket into a lower marginal gift tax bracket.

The Tax Reform Act of 1976 integrated the gift and estate taxes by providing a single rate schedule for both taxes and by including in the estate tax base the amount of post 1976 gifts made by a decedent.[38] Thus, any inter vivos gift made by a decedent after 1976 has the effect of boosting his or her taxable estate into a higher tax bracket.

> **Example 24.**   In 1987, D makes a taxable gift of $400,000, her only taxable inter vivos transfer. D dies in the current year, leaving a taxable estate of $1,500,000. The base for computing D's estate tax is $1.9 million, her taxable estate plus the $400,000 taxable gift.

Because of the integration of the gift and estate taxes, the tax benefit of inter vivos giving has been reduced but certainly not eliminated. The following advantages of making gifts have survived the integration process.

1.   All appreciation in value of the transferred property that occurs after the date of gift escapes taxation in the donor's gross estate. Refer to *Example 24.* If the value of the gifted asset increased from $400,000 in 1987 to $700,000 in the current year, the $300,000 appreciation is not taxed in D's estate. It should be noted that inter vivos transfers of appreciating assets do have a potentially serious negative income tax consequence. The basis of such assets to the donee will be a carryover basis from the donor, increased by the amount of any gift tax paid attributable to the difference between the value of the gift and the donor's tax basis.[39] If the donor retained the property until death, the basis of the property would be stepped up to its fair market value at date of death.[40] Thus, a transfer of the asset during life rather than at death preserves rather than eliminates pre-death appreciation in the value of the asset that will be subject to income taxation on subsequent sale.

---

[38]   § 2001(b).

[39]   § 1015.

[40]   § 1014.

2. Future income generated by property that the donor has transferred will be accumulated by younger generation family members rather than in the estate of the donor.

3. The availability of the annual $10,000 exclusion allows a donor to give away a substantial amount of wealth completely tax free.

4. All other factors being equal, it is cheaper to pay a gift tax rather than an estate tax. This is true because the dollars used to pay a gift tax are never themselves subject to a Federal transfer tax. However, dollars used to pay an estate tax have been included in the taxable estate and are subject to the estate tax.

"FREEZING" THE VALUE OF ASSETS IN THE GROSS ESTATE

A long-range plan of inter vivos giving from older generation to younger generation family members is a basic component of most family tax plans. However, elderly individuals can be very reluctant about making substantial gifts of their wealth, even when they fully understand the tax advantages in doing so. Psychologically it is difficult to part with wealth that is the result of a lifetime of endeavor. Elderly individuals often fear that gifts of property might leave them without sufficient income or capital to provide for their future comfort and security. They may even worry that their children and grandchildren might "desert" them if the offspring were given the family wealth too soon.

For these and many other reasons it may be difficult for the tax adviser to persuade an older client to transfer existing wealth during his or her lifetime. However, the same client may be much more amenable to simply "freezing" the value of his or her current estate, so that future accumulations of wealth are somehow transferred to younger members of the family and therefore not subject to estate tax upon the client's death.

One of the simplest techniques for freezing the value of an asset in a taxpayer's estate is for the taxpayer to sell the asset to a younger generation family member.

> **Example 25.** Grandfather G owns several acres of undeveloped real estate with a current value of $1 million. The land is located near a rapidly growing metropolitan area and its value is expected to triple over the next decade. If G sells the real estate to his granddaughter D for $1 million cash, the value of his current estate is unchanged. However, the future increase in the value of the land has been removed from G's estate and will belong to D.

An attractive variation of the selling technique illustrated in *Example 25* is an installment sale to the granddaughter. If D does not have $1 million of cash readily available (a most realistic assumption), G could simply accept his granddaughter's bona fide installment note as payment for the land. If the note is to be paid off over 20 years, G could use the installment sale method of reporting any taxable gain on the sale. If G had no need for cash during the term of the note, he could forgive his granddaughter's note payments and interest as they become due. Such forgiveness of indebtedness would not change the income tax consequences of the installment sale to G and would represent a gift to D eligible for the annual $10,000 exclusion.[41]

SELECTED DISPOSITIONS OF ASSETS AT DEATH

Only two types of gratuitous dispositions of assets at death give rise to a deduction for purposes of computing the taxable estate. The first type is a disposition of assets to a qualified charity. Section 2055 authorizes an *unlimited* charitable deduction for the value of such dispositions. If a wealthy taxpayer desires to transfer a portion of his or her estate to a qualified charity under the terms of a will, he or she may do so at no transfer tax cost. However, from a tax planning perspective it is preferable for the taxpayer to make a charitable donation during life rather than at death. Not only will the donated property be removed from the donor's potential estate, but the donation will give rise to an income tax deduction under § 170.

The second type of disposition that can result in a reduction of the transferor's gross estate is a bequest to a surviving spouse. Under § 2056(a) the value of any qualifying interest in property included in a decedent's gross estate that passes to the decedent's surviving spouse constitutes a deduction (the *marital deduction*) from the gross estate. Thus, if a decedent leaves his or her entire estate to the surviving spouse, the taxable estate of the decedent will be zero.

At first glance, it would appear that all of a decedent's property should be left to his or her spouse to avoid estate taxes. However, using the marital deduction to reduce a decedent's taxable estate to zero could result in a waste of the decedent's unified credit under § 2010. Moreover, all of the property would be taxed as part of the surviving spouse's estate to the extent it is not consumed or given away. For these reasons, an effective estate plan will attempt to leave a *taxable estate* exactly equal to the tax shelter provided by this credit.

TAX ADVANTAGES OF THE UNLIMITED MARITAL DEDUCTION

The unlimited marital deduction permits a deferral of any estate tax on the wealth accumulated by a married couple until the death of the second spouse. This deferral can be highly advantageous even if the bequest to the surviving spouse causes the wealth to be subsequently taxed at a higher marginal tax rate.

---

[41]   See Rev. Rul. 77-299, 1977-2 C.B. 343 for the IRS's negative reaction to this tax plan.

To illustrate, assume that W has a net estate of $1.4 million. W's will provides that all her wealth in excess of the amount sheltered by the available § 2010 credit shall pass to her husband, H. W dies in 1991, when the credit will shelter a taxable estate of $600,000; therefore, $800,000 of her estate is transferred to her husband and becomes a marital deduction against W's gross estate. No estate tax is due upon W's death. If H has $2 million of wealth in addition to his $800,000 inheritance from W, and if he outlives his wife by five years, the estate tax upon his death will be $983,000 (the § 2001 tax on $2.8 million less the unified credit of $192,800).[42]

If W had not left any of her estate to H, the estate tax payable on her death would have been $320,000, computed at a marginal rate of 43 percent. However, because of the marital bequest, her estate was "stacked" on that of her surviving spouse. As a result, the actual tax on her estate was $395,000 computed at a marginal rate of 50 percent.[43] But the actual tax payment was deferred for five years. Using a conservative discount rate of 8 percent, the present value of a $395,000 tax paid at the end of five years is only $268,995. Thus, the use of the unlimited marital deduction saved the family of H and W approximately $51,000 in estate taxes.[44]

In addition to the deferral of tax available through use of the unlimited marital deduction, the postponement of tax until the death of the second spouse increases the length of time during which estate planning objectives can be accomplished. The surviving spouse can continue or even accelerate a program of inter vivos giving to younger generation family members. Deferral also provides the surviving spouse with the opportunity to seek advice about areas of estate planning neglected before the death of the first spouse.

QUALIFYING TERMINAL INTEREST PROPERTY

Section 2056(b) denies a marital deduction for an interest in property that passes to a surviving spouse if the interest will terminate at some future date and if after termination someone other than the surviving spouse will receive an interest in the property. This restriction was designed to ensure that assets escaping taxation in the estate of the first spouse by virtue of a marital deduction do, in fact, become the property of the surviving spouse includible in that spouse's taxable estate.

---

[42] For simplicity's sake, this example assumes no appreciation in assets between the two deaths.

[43] $395,000 is the difference between $983,000 (the tax on H's estate including his inheritance from W) and $588,000 (the tax on H's estate without an inheritance from W).

[44] $320,000 (current tax on W's estate without a marital deduction) minus $268,995 (present value of actual tax of $395,000 to be paid at the end of five years assuming an 8% discount rate).

Prior to the enactment of the Economic Recovery Tax Act of 1981 (ERTA 1981), a wealthy taxpayer desiring to secure the tax savings offered by the use of the marital deduction had to be willing to entrust to his or her surviving spouse the ultimate disposition of the assets passing to that spouse. Because of § 2056(b), the surviving spouse had to receive control over the transferred assets sufficient to pull the assets into that spouse's gross estate. This generally required an outright transfer of the property to the surviving spouse, or transfer in trust giving the spouse a general power of appointment. In certain situations wealthy taxpayers were reluctant to accept this condition. For example, a taxpayer with children from a previous marriage might be concerned that his surviving second wife might not leave the marital deduction assets to these children upon her death. As a result, the taxpayer might not take advantage of the marital deduction in order to leave his wealth directly to his children.

To increase the utility of the marital deduction, Congress added § 2056(b)(7) to the law as part of ERTA 1981. This paragraph allows a marital deduction equal to the value of *qualifying terminable interest property*. Such property is defined as property in which the surviving spouse is entitled to all the income, payable at least annually for life. During the life of the spouse, no one may have a power to appoint any part of the property to any one other than the spouse.

> **Example 26.** Under the will of X, $1 million worth of assets are transferred into trust. X's surviving spouse, S, must be paid the entire trust income on a quarterly basis. During S's life, no person has any power of appointment over trust corpus, and upon S's death, trust corpus will be divided equally among X's living grandchildren. Because the assets are qualifying terminable interest property, X's estate may claim a marital deduction of $1 million.

Upon the death of the surviving spouse, the entire date of death value of the qualifying terminable interest property must be included in the surviving spouse's gross estate per § 2044. Thus, even though the property is passing to a recipient chosen by the first spouse to die, it is taxed in the estate of the second spouse.[45]

LIQUIDITY PLANNING

The Federal estate tax is literally a once-in-a-lifetime event. Because taxpayers do not have to pay the tax on a regular recurring basis, many individuals give little thought to the eventual need for cash to pay the tax.

---

[45] If the surviving spouse gives away the income interest in the qualifying terminable interest property during life, § 2519 requires that the entire value of the property constitute a taxable gift. When either § 2044 or § 2519 applies, § 2207(A) allows the estate or donor to recover an appropriate amount of transfer tax from the party receiving the actual property.

When an individual dies leaving a large estate but little cash with which to pay death taxes and other expenses, serious problems can result. The family may be forced to sell assets at distress prices just to obtain cash. In a severe situation, a decedent's carefully designed dispositive plan may be shattered because of the failure to anticipate the liquidity needs of the estate.

One of the functions of a competent tax adviser is to foresee any liquidity problem of his or her client's potential estate and to suggest appropriate remedies. The remainder of this chapter covers some of the common solutions to the problem of a cash poor estate.

SOURCE OF FUNDS

An excellent source of funds with which to pay an estate tax is insurance on the life of the potential decedent. For a relatively small cash outlay, a taxpayer can purchase enough insurance coverage to meet all the liquidity needs of his or her estate. It is absolutely vital that the insured individual does not possess any incidents of ownership in the policies and that his or her estate is not the beneficiary of the policies. If these two rules are observed, the policy proceeds will not be included in the insured's estate and needlessly subjected to the estate tax.[46]

A second source of funds is any family business in which the decedent owned an interest. Under the terms of a binding buy-sell agreement, the business could use its cash to liquidate the decedent's interest. If the business is in corporate form, a redemption of the decedent's interest under § 303 can be a highly beneficial method of securing funds. If the fairly straightforward requirements of § 303 are met, the corporation can purchase its own stock from the decedent's estate without danger of the payment being taxed as a dividend. Because the estate's basis in the stock has been stepped up to its fair market value at date of death, the estate normally will realize little or no taxable gain on sale. The amount of the corporate distribution protected by § 303 cannot exceed the amount of death taxes and funeral and administrative expenses payable by the estate.[47]

In order for a redemption of stock to qualify under § 303, the value of the stock must exceed 35 percent of the value of the gross estate less § 2053 and § 2054 expenses.[48] Careful pre-death planning may be necessary to meet this requirement.

> **Example 27.** C owns a 100% interest in F Corporation, a highly profitable business with substantial cash flow. However, the value of the F stock is only 29% of the value of C's projected estate. As C's tax adviser, you could recommend that C (1) gift away other assets to reduce the estate, or (2) transfer assets into F Corporation as a contribution to capital in order to increase the stock's value.

---

[46]   § 2042.

[47]   § 303(a).

[48]   § 303(b)(2)(A).

FLOWER BONDS

Certain issues of Treasury bonds known as *flower bonds* may be used to pay the Federal estate tax at their par value plus accrued interest.[49] Because these bonds have very low interest rates, they are obtainable on the open market at a price well below their par value. Thus, an estate can satisfy its Federal tax liability with bonds that cost much less than the amount of that liability. The bonds must be included in the decedent's estate at their par, rather than market value.[50]

PLANNING FOR DEFERRED PAYMENT OF THE ESTATE TAX

Under § 6166, an estate may be entitled to pay its Federal estate tax liability on an installment basis over a 15-year period. This provision can be a blessing for an illiquid estate. However, only estates that meet the requirements of § 6166 may use the installment method of payment. As a result, pre-death planning should be undertaken to ensure qualification.

Basically, only an amount of estate tax attributable to a decedent's interest in a closely held business may be deferred.[51] In addition, the value of the closely held business must exceed 35 percent of the gross estate minus Code § 2053 and § 2054 deductions. If a deferral of estate tax is desirable in a specific situation, the tax adviser should make certain that such requirements are met on a prospective basis.

CONCLUSION

This chapter has introduced the reader to one of the most fascinating and satisfying areas of tax practice—family tax planning. Such planning involves arrangements whereby family income can be shifted to low-bracket members so as to reduce the income taxes paid by the family unit. The use of trusts also has been discussed, and grantor trusts whose income is taxed not to the trust or its beneficiaries but to the grantor have been described.

Transfer tax planning techniques for reducing the family transfer tax burden have been introduced. Such techniques include long-range programs of inter vivos giving, asset freezes, selective use of the marital deduction, and liquidity planning. The family tax planner should never lose sight of the basic premise of family tax planning: only a plan that meets the subjective nontax goals and desires of a family as well as the objective goal of tax minimization is a truly well-designed plan.

---

[49] § 6312 provided the authorization for such usage. However, the section was repealed with respect to bonds issued after March 3, 1971. Bonds issued before this date and still outstanding continue to be eligible for payment of the estate tax.

[50] Rev. Rul. 69-489, 1969-2 C.B. 172.

[51] § 6166(a)(2).

PROBLEM MATERIALS

DISCUSSION QUESTIONS

15-1 *Assignment of Income Doctrine.* Explain the assignment of income doctrine as it relates to earned income. How does the doctrine apply to investment income?

15-2 *Income Shifting.* Assignment of income from one taxpayer to another can result in a tax savings only in a tax system with a progressive rate structure. Discuss.

15-3 *Family Employees.* List some of the factors the IRS might consider in determining whether a particular family member is a bona fide employee of a family business.

15-4 *Shareholder/Employee.* Discuss the tax consequences if the IRS determines that a family member is receiving an amount of unreasonable compensation from a family-owned corporation if that family member is a shareholder. What if the family member is not a shareholder?

15-5 *Gift of Business Interest.* An individual who transfers an equity interest in his or her business to a family member may be accomplishing an income shift to that family member. What are some nontax risks associated with such an equity transfer?

15-6 *Buy-Sell Arrangements.* How may a buy-sell agreement be utilized when an intrafamily transfer of an equity interest in a business is contemplated?

15-7 *Regular Corporation vs. S Corporation.* As a general rule, a regular corporation is an inappropriate vehicle by which to shift business income to low-bracket family members. Discuss.

15-8 *Limitation on Using S Corporations.* An S corporation may have only a single class of common stock outstanding. How does this fact limit the utility of the S corporation in many family tax plans?

15-9 *Use of Grantor Trusts.* Grantor trusts are ineffective as devices for shifting income to trust beneficiaries. However, such trusts may be very useful in achieving nontax family planning goals. Explain.

15-10 *Crummey Trusts.* What is a Crummey trust and why might a grantor prefer a Crummey trust to a § 2503(c) trust?

15-11 *Reversionary Trusts and Interest-Free Loans.* Can a trust in which the grantor has the right to receive his or her property back after a specified period of time be considered a valid trust for tax purposes so that the income is taxed to the beneficiaries rather than the grantor? Can an interest-free demand loan achieve an income shift from the lender to the debtor?

15-12 *Inter Vivos Gifts.* Why are inter vivos gifts beneficial from a transfer tax planning viewpoint?

15-13 *Limitations of Inter Vivos Gifts.*   For what reasons might an elderly taxpayer be reluctant to make inter vivos gifts?

15-14 *Estate Freezes.*   Define an "asset freeze" as the term relates to estate planning.

15-15 *Current vs. Testamentary Contributions.*   Is it preferable to make a charitable contribution during a taxpayer's life or at his or her death under the terms of his or her will?

15-16 *Marital Deduction.*   Discuss the tax benefits associated with the unlimited marital deduction of § 2056.

15-17 *Limiting Estate Taxes.*   Why is it generally inadvisable for a taxpayer to plan to reduce his or her taxable estate to zero? What can be considered an "optimal" size for a decedent's taxable estate?

15-18 *Qualifying Terminable Interests.*   In what circumstances would a taxpayer desire to make a bequest to a surviving spouse in the form of qualifying terminable interest property? What are the tax consequences of such a bequest?

PROBLEMS

15-19 *Using Family Employees.*   F runs a carpet installation and cleaning business as a sole proprietorship. In the current year, the business generates $83,000 of net income.

   a.   Assume F is married, has three children (all under the age of 19), does not have any other source of taxable income and does not itemize deductions. What is his current year tax liability?

   b.   Assume F can use all three children in his business as legitimate part-time employees. He pays each child $6,000 per year, but continues to provide more than one-half of their support. Compute the family's total tax bill for the current year.

15-20 *Sole Proprietorship vs. Corporation.*   Single individual K owns a sole proprietorship that is K's only source of income. In the current year, the business has net income of $130,000.

   a.   If K does not itemize deductions, what is her current year tax liability?

   b.   If K incorporates the business on January 1 and pays herself a $40,000 salary (and no dividends), by how much will she have reduced the tax bill on her business income? (Assume the corporation will not be a personal service corporation.)

15-21 *Sole Proprietorship vs. Corporation.*   Mr. and Mrs. C own their own business, which they currently operate as a sole proprietorship. Annual income from the business averages $400,000. Mr. and Mrs. C are considering incorporating the business. They estimate that each of them could draw a reasonable annual salary of $75,000. In order to maintain their current standard of living, they would also have to draw an additional $50,000 cash out of the business annually in the form of dividends. Based on these facts, compute the income tax savings or cost that would result from the incorporation. In making your calculation, ignore any deductions or exemptions available on the C's joint return.

15-22 *Singles Penalty.* Single taxpayer S has current year taxable income of $35,000 (after all available deductions and exemptions). His fiance F has a taxable income of $6,000. Should F and S marry before or after December 31? Support your conclusion with calculations.

15-23 *Marriage Penalty.* Taxpayers H and W are married and file a joint return. Both are professionals and earn salaries of $28,000 and $39,000, respectively. Assuming H and W have no other income, and do not itemize deductions, compute any *marriage penalty* they will pay.

15-24 *Married vs. Head-of-Household.* Refer to the facts in Problem 15-23. Assume H and W are not married and H has a child by a previous marriage that entitles him to file as a head-of-household. If H and W marry, will the marriage penalty they incur be more or less than in Problem 15-23?

15-25 *Unearned Income of a Minor Child.* In the current year, taxpayer M receives $12,000 of interest income and earns a salary of $2,500 from a summer job. M has no other income or deductions. M is 13 years old and is claimed as a dependent on his parents' jointly filed tax return. His parents report taxable income of $200,000. Based on these facts, compute M's income tax liability.

15-26 *Sheltering Unearned Income of a Minor Child.* Taxpayer P made a gift of investment securities to his 13-year-old dependent daughter, D, under the Uniform Gift to Minors Act. The securities generate annual dividend income of $4,000. P is considering a second gift to D that would generate an additional $3,000 of investment income annually. Calculate the amount of tax savings to the family if P could employ D in his business and pay her an annual salary of $3,000, rather than making the second gift. In making your calculation, assume P is in a 31 percent tax bracket.

15-27 *Family Partnerships.* F owns a 70 percent interest in Mako Partnership, in which capital is a material income producing factor. On January 1 of the current year, F gives his son S a 35 percent interest in Mako (leaving F with a 35% interest). For the current year, Mako has taxable income of $200,000.

a. Assume F does not perform any services for Mako. What is the maximum amount of partnership income allocable to S?
b. Assume F performs services for Mako for which he normally would receive $30,000. However, F has not charged the partnership for his services. Based on these facts, what is the maximum amount of partnership income allocable to S in the current year?

15-28 *Gift of S Corporation Stock.* Grandfather G owns all 100 shares of the outstanding stock of Sigma, Inc., a calendar year S corporation. On January 1 of the current year, G gives 10 shares of Sigma stock to each of his four minor grandchildren under the Uniform Gift to Minors Act. For the current year, Sigma reports taxable income of $70,000. To whom is this income taxed?

15-29 *Gift-Leaseback.* Taxpayer B owns land used in his sole proprietorship with a tax basis of $75,000 and a fair market value of $100,000. B gives this land to an irrevocable simple trust for the equal benefit of his three children (ages 14, 16, and 19) and leases back the land from the trust for a fair market rental of $9,000 per year.

    a.   Assuming that all three children are B's dependents and have no other source of income, calculate the tax savings to the family of this gift-leaseback arrangement. In making your calculation, assume B is in a 31 percent tax bracket.

    b.   What are the gift and estate tax consequences of this transaction to B and his family? Assume that B has made no prior taxable gifts and that he is married.

15-30 *Use of Trusts.* Grandfather Z is in the habit of giving his 15-year-old grandchild, A, $10,000 annually as a gift. Z's taxable income is consistently over $200,000 per year, and A has no income. If Z creates a valid trust with investment assets just sufficient to yield $12,000 of income a year and specifies in the trust instrument that A is to receive the trust income annually, what will be the net tax savings to the family? (For purposes of this problem, *ignore* the fact that A may be claimed as a dependent on the return of another taxpayer.)

15-31 *Reversionary Trusts.* Grantor G transfers $100,000 of assets into a trust that will last for 10 years, after which time the assets will revert to G or his estate. During the trust's existence all income must be paid to beneficiary M on a current basis. For the current year, ordinary trust income is $18,000 and the trust recognizes a capital gain of $3,000. To whom are these amounts taxed?

15-32 *Reversionary Trusts.* Refer to the facts in Problem 15-31. Assume that under the terms of the trust agreement the trust will last for M's lifetime. Upon M's death, the trust corpus will revert to G or his estate. On the date the trust is created, M is 25 years old. For the current year, ordinary trust income is $18,000 and the trust recognizes a capital gain of $3,000. To whom are these amounts taxed?

15-33 *Irrevocable Trusts.* F transfers assets into an irrevocable trust and designates First City Bank as independent trustee. F retains no control over the trust assets. The trustee may distribute income to either of F's two adult brothers or to S, F's minor son whom F is legally obligated to support. During the year, the trustee distributed all of the trust income to one of F's brothers. To whom will the income be taxed?

15-34 *Irrevocable Trusts.* M transfers assets into an irrevocable trust and appoints National Bank independent trustee. M retains no control over trust assets. Under the terms of the trust agreement, M's sister N is given the right to determine which of M's three children will receive trust income for the year. N herself is not a trust beneficiary. During the year, N directs that trust income be divided equally between M's three children. To whom will the income be taxed?

15-35 *Irrevocable Trusts.* Grantor B transfers assets into an irrevocable trust and designates Union State Bank independent trustee. B retains no control over trust assets. Under the terms of the trust instrument the trustee must use trust income to pay the annual insurance premium on a policy on B's life. Any remaining income must be distributed to B's grandson, GS. For the current year, trust income totals $60,000, of which $9,000 is used to pay the required insurance premium. To whom will the income be taxed?

15-36 *Grantor Trusts.* Although T is not a beneficiary of the ABC Trust, T does have the right under the terms of the trust instrument to appoint up to 10 percent of the trust assets to himself or any member of his family. T has never exercised this right. For the current year, the trust income of $80,000 is distributed to the income beneficiaries of the trust.

a.   To whom will the income be taxed?
b.   If T dies before exercising his right to appoint trust corpus, will the possession of the right have any estate tax consequences?

15-37 *Gift Splitting.* Every year D gives each of her nine grandchildren $15,000 in cash to be used toward their education.

a.   If D is unmarried, what is the amount of her annual taxable gift?
b.   If D is married and she and her husband elect to "gift split," what is the amount of her annual taxable gift?

15-38 *Terminable Interest Trusts.* Taxpayer Q dies in the current year and leaves a net estate of $3 million. Under the terms of his will, $2.4 million of the estate will be put into trust. Q's widow W will be paid trust income annually and during W's life no person has the right to appoint any of the trust corpus. Upon W's death, the trust corpus will be divided among Q's offspring from a previous marriage. The remaining $600,000 of Q's estate is to be paid to unrelated friends named in Q's will.

a.   What is the amount of Q's taxable estate?
b.   What is the estate tax liability on Q's taxable estate? (Q made no taxable gifts during his lifetime.)
c.   W outlives Q by only eight years. If the value of the corpus of the trust created for W's benefit by Q is $6.3 million at the date of W's death, what amount must be included in W's gross estate?

15-39 *Inter Vivos Gifts.*   Decedent T died in the current year and left the following taxable estate:

	Fair Market Value
Investment real estate............................	$1,000,000
Cash and securities..............................	3,500,000
Gross estate.....................................	$4,500,000
Less: §2053 and §2054 expenses..............	(500,000)
Taxable estate...................................	$4,000,000

After payment of all death taxes, the estate will be divided equally among T's five surviving married children.

a.   If T has never made any inter vivos gifts, compute the estate's Federal estate tax liability (before credit for any state death tax paid).

b.   How much tax could have been saved if T had made cash gifts equal to the maximum annual exclusion under § 2503 to each of his children and their spouses in each of the 10 years preceding his death?

15-40 *Liquidity Planning.*   Decedent D left the following taxable estate:

	Fair Market Value
Life insurance proceeds from policy on D's life (D owned the policy at his death)...........	$ 500,000
Real estate......................................	1,300,000
Stock in Acme Corporation (100% owned by D)...................................	650,000
Gross estate.....................................	$2,450,000
Less: §2053 and §2054 expenses..............	(450,000)
Taxable estate...................................	$2,000,000

a.   If D has never made any inter vivos gifts and dies in the current year, what is the estate's Federal estate tax liability (before credit for any state death tax paid)?

b.   How much tax could have been avoided if D had *not* been the owner of the life insurance policy?

c.   Can the Acme stock qualify for a § 303 redemption? What if the life insurance proceeds were not included in the gross estate?

RESEARCH PROBLEMS

15-41   In 1986, P, a resident of St. Louis, Missouri, created an irrevocable trust for the benefit of his teenage son, S, and his brother, B. The independent trustee, T, has discretionary power to use the trust income for the "payment of tuition, books, and room and board at any institution of higher learning that S chooses to attend." After an 11-year period, the trust will terminate with any accumulated income payable to S and the trust corpus payable to B. In the current year, S received an income distribution of $7,000 from the trust, which he used to attend a state-supported school, the University of Missouri. To whom will the $7,000 of trust income be taxed?

Some suggested research aids:

> § 677 and accompanying regulations
> *Morrill, Jr. v. United States,* 64-1 USTC ¶9463, 13 AFTR2d 1334, 228
>   F.Supp. 734 (D. Ct. Maine, 1964).
> *Braun, Jr.,* 48 TCM 210, T.C. Memo 1984-285.

15-42   Decedent D died on January 19, 1990. Under the terms of D's will, D's sister S, age 57, is to receive $500,000 as a specific bequest. The remainder of D's estate will be distributed to D's various grandchildren. On June 8, 1991, S decides to join a religious community and take a vow of poverty. She makes written notification to the executor of D's estate that she will not accept her bequest from her late sister, and that the $500,000 should be added to the amount to be distributed to the grandchildren. What are the transfer tax consequences of S's action?

Suggested research aid:

> § 2518

PART **V**

TAX RESEARCH AND TAX PRACTICE

CONTENTS

LEARNING OBJECTIVES

Upon completion of this chapter you will be able to:

- Describe the process in which Federal tax law is enacted and subsequently modified or evaluated by the judiciary

- Interpret citations to various statutory, administrative, and judicial sources of the tax law

- Identify the source of various administrative and judicial tax authorities

- Locate most statutory, administrative, and judicial authorities

- Evaluate the relative strength of various tax authorities

- Understand the importance of communicating the results of tax research

CHAPTER OUTLINE

Chapter 16

SOURCES AND APPLICATIONS OF FEDERAL TAX LAW

Mastery of taxation requires an understanding of how and where the rules of taxation originate. What might be called the "body of tax law" consists not only of the legislative provisions enacted by Congress, but also court decisions and administrative (Treasury Department) releases that explain and interpret the statutory provisions. In the aggregate, the statutes, court decisions, and administrative releases constitute the *legal authority* that provides the consequences given a particular set of facts. The tax treatment of any particular transaction normally must be based on some supporting authority. The tax rules contained in each of the earlier chapters all have their origin in some authoritative pronouncement.

This chapter introduces the sources of tax law and explains how these and other information relating to taxes may be accessed and used in solving a particular tax question. This process of obtaining information and synthesizing it to answer a specific tax problem is referred to as *tax research*. The importance of tax research cannot be overemphasized. The vast body of tax law and its everchanging nature place a premium on knowing how to use research materials.

AUTHORITATIVE SOURCES OF TAX LAW

Sources of tax law can be classified into two broad categories: (1) the law, and (2) official interpretations of the law. The law consists primarily of the Constitution, the Acts of Congress, and tax treaties. In general, these sources are referred to as the *statutory* law. Most statutory law is written in general terms for a typical situation. Since general rules, no matter how carefully drafted, cannot be written to cover variations on the normal scheme, interpretation is usually required. The task of interpreting the statute is one of the principal duties of the Internal Revenue Service (IRS) as representative of the Secretary of the Treasury. The IRS annually produces thousands of releases that explain and clarify the law. To no one's surprise, however, taxpayers and the government do not always agree on how a particular law should be interpreted. In situations where the taxpayer or the government decides to litigate the question, the courts, as final arbiters, are given the opportunity to interpret the law. These judicial interpretations, administrative interpretations, and the statutory law are considered in detail below.

STATUTORY LAW

The Constitution of the United States provides the Federal government with the power to tax. Disputes concerning the constitutionality of an income tax levied on taxpayers without apportionment among the states were resolved in 1913 with passage of the Sixteenth Amendment. Between 1913 and 1939, Congress enacted revenue acts that amounted to a complete rewrite of all tax law to date, including the desired changes. In 1939, due primarily to the increasing complexity of the earlier process, Congress codified all Federal tax laws into Title 26 of the *United States Code,* which was then called the *Internal Revenue Code of 1939.* Significant changes in the Federal tax laws were made during World War II and the post-war period of the late 1940s. Each change resulted in amendments to the 1939 Code. By 1954, the codification process had to be repeated in order to organize all additions to the law and to eliminate obsolete provisions. The product of this effort was the *Internal Revenue Code of 1954.* After 1954, Congress took great care to ensure that each new amendment to the 1954 Code was incorporated within its organizational structure with appropriate cross-references to any prior provisions affected by a new law. Among the changes incorporated into the 1954 Code in this manner were the Economic Tax Recovery Act (ERTA) of 1981, the Tax Equity and Fiscal Responsibility Act (TEFRA) of 1982, and the Deficit Reduction Act (DRA) of 1984. In 1986, Congress again made substantial revision in the tax law. Consistent with this massive redesign of the 1954 Code, Congress changed the title to the *Internal Revenue Code of 1986.* Like the 1954 Code, the 1986 Code is subject to revisions introduced by a new law. Recent changes incorporated into the 1986 Code were the Revenue Act of 1987, the Technical and Miscellaneous Revenue Act (TAMRA) of 1988, the Revenue Reconciliation Act of 1989, and the Revenue Reconciliation Act of 1990.

The legislative provisions contained in the Code are by far the most important component of tax law. Although procedure necessary to enact a law is generally well known, it is necessary to review this process with a special emphasis on taxation. From a tax perspective, the *intention* of Congress in producing the legislation is extremely important since the primary purpose of tax research is to interpret the legislative intent of Congress.

THE MAKING OF A TAX LAW

Article I, Section 7, Clause 1 of the Constitution provides that the House of Representatives of the U.S. Congress has the basic responsibility for initiating revenue bills.[1] The Ways and Means Committee of the House of Representatives must consider any tax bill before it is presented for vote by the full House of Representatives. On bills of major public interest, the Ways and Means Committee holds public hearings where interested organizations may send representatives

---

[1]   Tax bills do not originate in the Senate, except when they are attached to other bills.

to express their views about the bill. The first witness at such hearings is usually the Secretary of the Treasury, representing the President of the United States. In many cases, proposals for new tax legislation or changes in existing legislation come from the President as a part of his political or economic programs.

After the public hearings have been held, the Ways and Means Committee usually goes into closed session, where the Committee prepares the tax bill for consideration by the entire House. The members of the Committee receive invaluable assistance from their highly skilled staff, which includes economists, accountants, and lawyers. The product of this session is a proposed bill that is submitted to the entire House for debate and vote.

After a bill has been approved by the entire House, it is sent to the Senate and assigned to the Senate Finance Committee. The Senate Finance Committee may also hold hearings on the bill before its consideration by the full Senate. The Senate's bill generally differs from the House's bill. In these situations, both versions are sent to the Joint Conference Committee on Taxation, which is composed of members selected from the House Ways and Means Committee and from the Senate Finance Committee. The objective of this Joint Committee is to produce a compromise bill acceptable to both sides. On occasion, when compromise cannot be achieved by the Joint Committee or the compromise bill is unacceptable to the House or the Senate, the bill "dies." If, however, compromise is reached and the Senate and House approve the compromise bill, it is then referred to the President for his approval or veto. If the President vetoes the bill, the legislation is "killed" unless two-thirds of both the House and the Senate vote to override the veto. If the veto is overridden, the legislation becomes law.

It should be noted that at each stage of the process, information is produced that may be useful in assessing the intent of Congress. One of the better sources of Congressional intent is a report issued by the House Ways and Means Committee. This report contains the bill as well as a general explanation. This explanation usually provides the historical background of the proposed legislation along with the reasons for enactment. The Senate Finance Committee also issues a report similar to that of the House. Because the Senate often makes changes in the House version of the bill, the Senate's report is also an important source. Additionally, the Joint Conference Committee on Taxation issues its own report, which is sometimes helpful. Two other sources of intent are the records of the debates on the bill and publications of the initial hearings.

The following diagram illustrates the normal flow of a bill through the legislative process and the documents that are generated in this process.

Committee reports and debates appear in several publications. Committee reports are officially published in pamphlet form by the U.S. Government Printing Office as the bill proceeds through Congress. The enacted bill is published in the *Internal Revenue Bulletin* and the *Internal Revenue Cumulative Bulletin*. The debates are published in the *Congressional Record*. In addition to these official government publications, several commercial publishers make this information available to subscribers.

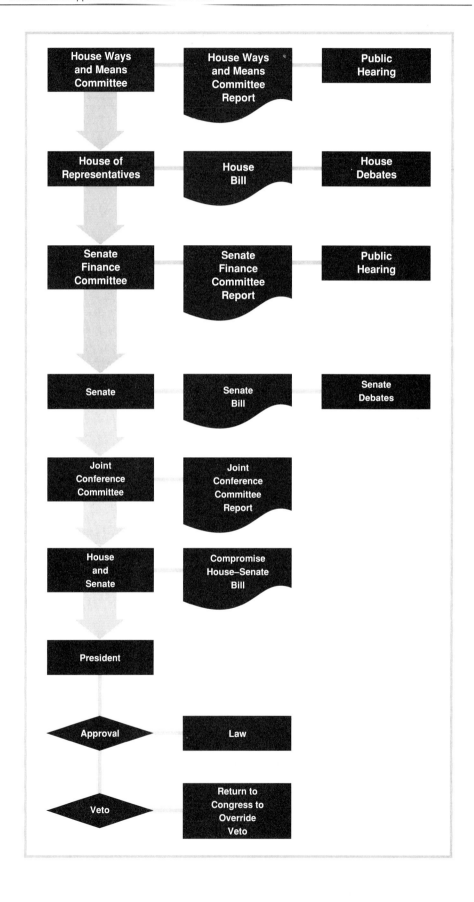

ORGANIZATION OF THE CODE

Once a tax bill becomes tax law, it is incorporated into the existing structure of the *Internal Revenue Code*.[2] The ability to use the Internal Revenue Code is essential for all individuals who have any involvement with the tax laws. It is normally the starting point for research. The following format is the basic organization of the Code.

Title 26 of the United States Code (referred to as the Internal Revenue Code)

   Subtitle A—Income Taxes

      Chapter 1—Normal Taxes and Surtaxes

         Subchapter A—Determination of Tax Liability

            Part I—Tax on Individuals

               Sections 1 through 5

When working with the tax law, it is often necessary to make reference to or *cite* a particular source with respect to the Code. The *section* of the Code is the source normally cited. A complete citation for a section of the Code would be too cumbersome. For instance, a formal citation for Section 1 of the Code would be "Subtitle A, Chapter 1, Subchapter A, Part I, Section 1." In most cases, citation of the section alone is sufficient. Sections are numbered consecutively throughout the Code so that each section number is used only once. Currently the numbers run from Section 1 through Section 9602. Not all section numbers are used, so that additional ones may be added by Congress in the future without the need for renumbering.[3]

Citation of a particular Code section in tax literature ordinarily does not require the prefix "Internal Revenue Code" because it is generally understood that, unless otherwise stated, references to section numbers concern the Internal Revenue Code of 1986 as amended. However, since most Code sections are divided into subparts, reference to a specific subpart requires more than just its section number. Section 170(a)(2)(B) serves as an example.

---

[2] All future use of the term Code or Internal Revenue Code refers to the *Internal Revenue Code of 1986*.

[3] It is interesting to note that when it adopted the 1954 Code, Congress deliberately left section numbers unassigned to provide room for future additions. Recently, however, Congress has been forced to distinguish new sections by alphabetical letters following a particular section number. See, for example, Sections 280, 280A, 280B, and 280C of the 1986 Code.

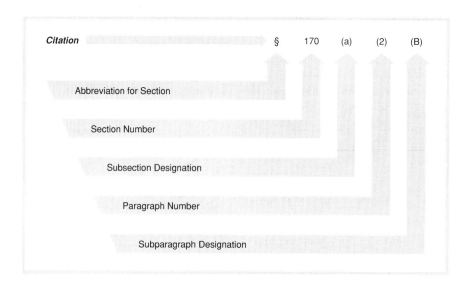

All footnote references used throughout this text are made in the form given above. In most cases, the "§" or "§§" symbols are used in place of the terms "section" or "sections," respectively.

Single-volume or double-volume editions of the Internal Revenue Code are published after every major change in the law. Commerce Clearing House, Inc. (CCH), Prentice Hall (PH), and the Research Institute of America (RIA) all publish these editions. Additionally, the Code is included in each of the major tax services that are discussed in a later section of this chapter.

TAX TREATIES

The laws contained in tax treaties represent the third and final component of the statutory law. Tax treaties (also referred to as tax conventions) are agreements between the United States and other countries that provide rules governing the taxation of residents of one country by another. For example, the tax treaty between the United States and France indicates how the French government taxes U.S. citizens residing in France and vice versa. Tax treaties, as law, have the same authority as those laws contained in the Code. In fact, treaty provisions normally take precedence over those contained in the Code. For example, § 7852(d) specifically provides that none of the Code's provisions apply in any case when such provisions are contrary to any treaty obligation. For this reason, persons involved with an international tax question must be aware of tax treaties and recognize that the Code may be superseded by a tax treaty. International taxation and tax treaties are considered in detail in Chapter 9.

ADMINISTRATIVE INTERPRETATIONS

After Congress has enacted a tax law, the Executive branch of the Federal government has the responsibility for enforcing it. In the process of enforcing the law, the Treasury interprets, clarifies, defines, and analyzes the Code in order to apply Congressional intention of the law to the specific facts of a taxpayer's situation. This process results in numerous administrative releases including the following:

1. Regulations

2. Revenue rulings and letter rulings

3. Revenue procedures

4. Technical advice memoranda

REGULATIONS

Congress has authorized the Secretary of the Treasury to prescribe and issue all rules and regulations needed for enforcement of the Code.[4] The Secretary, however, usually delegates the power to write the regulations to the Commissioner of the Internal Revenue Service. Normally, regulations are first published in proposed form—*proposed regulations*—in the Federal Register. Upon publication, interested parties have 30 days for comment. At the end of 30 days, the Treasury responds in light of the comments in any of three ways: it may (1) withdraw the proposed regulation; (2) amend it; or (3) leave it unchanged. In the latter two cases, the Treasury normally issues the regulation in its final form as a *Treasury decision* (often referred to as TDs) and it is published in the Federal Register. Thereafter, the new regulation is included in Title 26 of the *Code of Federal Regulations*.

The primary purpose of the regulations is to explain and interpret particular Code sections. Although regulations have not been issued for all Code sections, they have been issued for the great majority. In those cases where regulations exist, they are an important authoritative source on which one can usually rely. Regulations can be classified into three groups: (1) legislative; (2) interpretive; and (3) procedural.

Legislative Regulations. Occasionally, Congress will give specific authorization to the Secretary of the Treasury to issue regulations on a particular Code section. For example, under § 1502, the Secretary is charged with prescribing the regulations for the filing of a consolidated return by an affiliated group of corporations. There are virtually no Code sections governing consolidated returns, and

---

[4] § 7805(a).

the regulations in effect serve in lieu of the Code. In this case and others where it occurs, the regulation has the force and effect of a law, with the result that a court reviewing the regulation usually will not substitute its judgment for that of the Treasury Department unless the Treasury has clearly abused its discretion.[5]

Interpretative Regulations.   Interpretative regulations explain the meaning of a Code section and commit the Treasury and the Internal Revenue Service to a particular position relative to the Code section in question. This type of regulation is binding on the IRS but not on the courts, although it is "a body of experience and informed judgment to which courts and litigants may properly resort for guidance."[6]   Interpretive regulations have considerable authority and normally are invalidated only if they are inconsistent with the Code or are unreasonable.

Procedural Regulations.   Procedural regulations cover such areas as the information a taxpayer must supply to the IRS and the internal management and conduct of the IRS in certain matters. Those regulations affecting vital interests of the taxpayers are generally binding on the IRS, and those regulations stating the taxpayer's obligation to file particular forms or other types of information are given the effect of law.

Citation for Regulations.   Regulations are arranged in the same sequence as the Code sections they interpret. Thus, a regulation begins with a number that designates the type of tax or administrative, definitional, or procedural matter and is followed by the applicable Code section number. For example, Treasury Regulation Section 1.614-3(f)(5) serves as an illustration of how regulations are cited throughout this text.

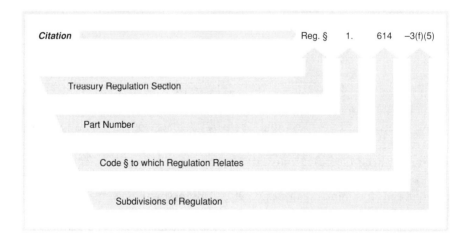

| Citation | | | | Reg. § | 1. | 614 | -3(f)(5) |

Treasury Regulation Section

Part Number

Code § to which Regulation Relates

Subdivisions of Regulation

---

[5] *Anderson, Clayton & Co. v. U.S.,* 77-2 USTC ¶9727, 40 AFTR2d 77-6102, 562 F.2d 972 (CA-5, 1977), *Cert. den.* at 436 U.S. 944 (USSC, 1978).

[6] *Skidmore v. Swift and Co.,* 323 U.S. 134 (USSC, 1944).

The part number of a Treasury regulation is used to identify the general area covered by the regulation as follows.

Part Number	Law Subject
1	Income Tax
20	Estate Tax
25	Gift Tax
31	Employment Tax
48–49	Excise Tax

The various subdivisions of a regulation are not necessarily related to a specific subdivision of the Code.

Sometimes the Treasury issues temporary regulations when it is necessary to meet a compelling need. For example, temporary regulations are often issued shortly after enactment of a major change in the tax law. These temporary regulations have the same binding effect as final regulations until they are withdrawn or replaced. Such regulations are cited as Temp. Reg. §.

Temporary regulations should not be confused with proposed regulations. The latter have no force or effect.[7] Nevertheless, proposed regulations provide insight into how the IRS currently interprets a particular Code section. For this reason, they should not be ignored.

REVENUE RULINGS

Revenue rulings also are official interpretations of the Federal tax laws and are issued by the National Office of the IRS. Revenue rulings do not have quite the authority of regulations, however. Regulations are a direct extension of the law-making powers of Congress, whereas revenue rulings are an application of the administrative powers of the Internal Revenue Service. In contrast to rulings, regulations are usually issued only after public hearings and must be approved by the Secretary of the Treasury.

Unlike regulations, revenue rulings are limited to a given set of facts. Taxpayers may rely on revenue rulings in determining the tax consequences of their transactions; however, taxpayers must determine for themselves if the facts of their cases are substantially the same as those set forth in the revenue ruling.

Revenue rulings are published in the weekly issues of the *Internal Revenue Bulletin*. The information contained in the *Internal Revenue Bulletins* (including, among other things, revenue rulings) is accumulated and usually published semiannually in the *Cumulative Bulletin*. The *Cumulative Bulletin* reorganizes the material according to Code section. Citations for the *Internal Revenue Bulletin* and the *Cumulative Bulletin* are illustrated on the following page.

---

[7] Federal law (i.e., the Administrative Procedure Act) requires any federal agency, including the Internal Revenue Service, that wishes to adopt a substantive rule to publish the rule in proposed form in order to give interested persons an opportunity to comment. Proposed regulations are issued in compliance with this directive.

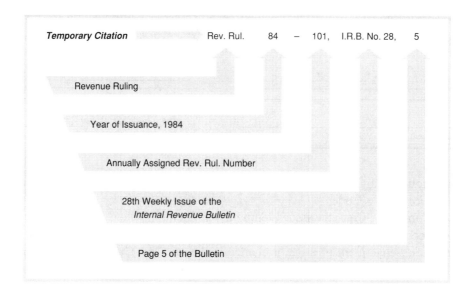

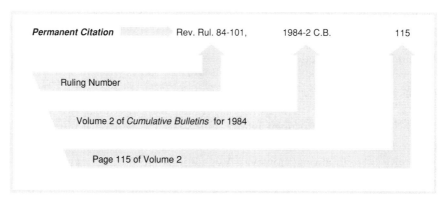

REVENUE PROCEDURES

Revenue procedures are statements reflecting the internal management practices of the IRS that affect the rights and duties of taxpayers. Occasionally they are also used to announce procedures to guide individuals in dealing with the IRS or to make public something the IRS believes should be brought to the attention of taxpayers. Revenue procedures are published in the weekly *Internal Revenue Bulletins* and bound in the *Cumulative Bulletin* along with revenue rulings issued in the same year. The citation system for revenue procedures is the same as for revenue rulings except that the prefix "Rev. Proc." is substituted for "Rev. Rul."

LETTER RULINGS

Taxpayers who are in doubt about the tax consequences of a contemplated transaction may ask the National Office of the IRS for a ruling on the tax question involved. Generally, the IRS has discretion about whether to rule or not and has issued guidelines describing circumstances under which it will issue a ruling on a question posed by a taxpayer.[8] Unlike revenue rulings, letter rulings (or private rulings) apply *only* to the particular taxpayers asking for the ruling and are not applicable to all taxpayers. For those requesting a ruling, the response might provide insurance against surprises because, as a practical matter, a favorable ruling should preclude any controversies with the IRS on a subsequent audit. During the process of obtaining a ruling, the IRS may recommend changes in a proposed transaction to assist the taxpayers in achieving the result they wish. Since 1976, the IRS has made individual rulings publicly available after deleting information that tends to identify the taxpayer. Such rulings appear in digests by the leading tax commentators and by publishers such as CCH and PH.

TECHNICAL ADVICE MEMORANDA

Either a taxpayer or an IRS district's Appeals Division may request advice from the National Office of the IRS about the Code, Regulations, and statutes and their impact on a specific set of facts. Generally, such requests take place during an audit or during the appeals process of the audit, and give both the taxpayer and the revenue agent an opportunity to resolve a dispute over a technical question. If the National Office renders advice favorable to the taxpayer, normally it must be applied. However, if the advice is against the taxpayer, the taxpayer does not lose his or her right to further pursue the issue in question with the IRS.

Citations for letter rulings and technical advice follow a multi-digit file number system. IRS Letter Ruling 9042002 serves as an example.

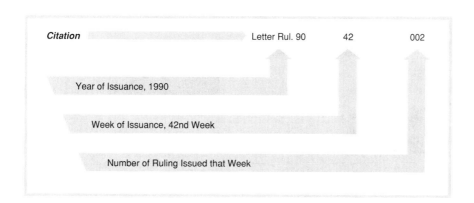

Citation	Letter Rul. 90	42	002
Year of Issuance, 1990			
Week of Issuance, 42nd Week			
Number of Ruling Issued that Week			

JUDICIAL INTERPRETATIONS

The Congress passes the tax law and the Executive branch of the Federal government enforces and interprets it, but under the American system of checks and balances, it is the Judiciary branch that ultimately determines whether the

---

[8] See Rev. Proc. 82-22, 1982-1 C.B. 469 for a description of the areas in which the IRS has refused to issue advanced rulings. Note, also, that the IRS is required to charge taxpayers a fee for letter rulings, opinion letters, determination letters, and similar requests. The fees range from $50 to $1,000. See § 6591.

Executive branch's interpretation is correct. This provides yet another source of tax law—court decisions. It is therefore absolutely essential for the student of tax as well as the tax practitioner to have a grasp of the judicial system of the United States and how tax cases move through this system.

Before litigating a case in court, the taxpayer must have exhausted the administrative remedies available to him or her within the Internal Revenue Service. If the taxpayer has not exhausted his or her administrative remedies, a court will deny a hearing because the claim filed in the court is premature.

All litigation begins in what are referred to as *courts of original jurisdiction,* or *trial courts,* which "try" the case. There are three trial courts: (1) the Tax Court; (2) the U.S. District Court; and (3) the U.S. Claims Court. Note that the taxpayer may select any one (and only one) of these three courts to hear the case. If the taxpayer or government disagrees with the decision by the trial court, it has the right to appeal to either the U.S. Court of Appeals or the U.S. Court of Appeals for the Federal Circuit, whichever is appropriate in the particular case. If a litigating party is dissatisfied with the decision by the appellate court, it may ask for review by the Supreme Court, but this is rarely granted. The judicial system is illustrated and discussed below.

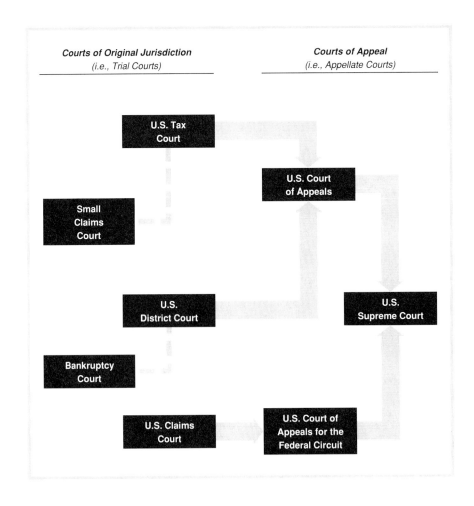

TRIAL COURTS

U.S. Tax Court. The Tax Court, as its name suggests, specializes in tax matters and hears no other types of cases. The judges on the court are especially skilled in taxation. Usually, prior to being selected as a judge by the President, the individual was a practitioner or IRS official who was noted for his or her expertise. This Court is composed of 19 judges who "ride circuit" throughout the United States (i.e., they travel and hear cases in various parts of the country). Occasionally, the full Tax Court hears a case, but most cases are heard by a single judge who submits his or her opinion to the chief judge, who then decides whether the full court should review the decision.

Besides its expertise in tax matters, two other characteristics of the Tax Court should be noted. Perhaps the most important feature of the Tax Court is that the taxpayer does not pay the alleged tax deficiency before bringing his or her action before the court. The second facet of the Tax Court that bears mentioning is that a trial by jury is not available.

U.S. District Courts. For purposes of the Federal judicial system, the United States is divided into 11 geographic areas called circuits which are subdivided into districts. For example, the second circuit, which is composed of Vermont, Connecticut, and New York, contains the District Court for the Southern District of New York, which covers parts of New York City. Other districts may include very large areas, such as the District Court for the State of Arizona, which covers the entire state. A taxpayer may take a case into the District Court for the district in which he or she resides, but only after the disputed tax deficiency has been paid. The taxpayer then sues the IRS for a refund of the disputed amount. The District Court is a court of general jurisdiction and hears many types of cases in addition to tax cases. This is the only court in which the taxpayer may obtain a jury trial. The jury decides matters of fact but not matters of law. However, even in issues of fact, the judge may, and occasionally does, disregard the jury's decision.

U.S. Claims Court. The United States Claims Court was established on October 1, 1982. Prior to that time it was called the "U.S. Court of Claims." The U.S. Claims Court hears cases involving certain claims against the Federal government, including tax refunds. This Court is made up of 16 judges and usually meets in Washington, D.C. A taxpayer must pay the disputed tax deficiency before bringing an action in this court, and may not obtain a jury trial. Appeals from the U.S. Claims Court are taken to the U.S. Court of Appeals for the Federal Circuit, an appellate court created at the same time as the U.S. Claims Court.

The following chart illustrates the position of the taxpayer in bringing an action in these courts.

	U.S. Tax Court	U.S. District Court	U.S. Claims Court
Jurisdiction	Nationwide	Specific district in which court is sitting	Nationwide
Subject Matter	Tax cases only	Many different types of cases, both criminal and civil	Claims against the Federal government, including tax refunds
Payment of Contested Amount	Taxpayer does not pay deficiency, but files suit against IRS Commissioner to stop collection of tax	Taxpayer pays alleged deficiency and then files suit against the U.S. government for refund	Taxpayer pays alleged deficiency and then files suit against the U.S. government for refund
Availability of jury trial	No	Yes	No
Appeal taken to	U.S. Court of Appeals	U.S. Court of Appeals	U.S. Court of Appeals for the federal Circuit
Number of Courts	1	95	1
Number of Judges Per Court	19	1	16

Small Claims Cases. When the amount of a tax assessment is relatively small, the taxpayer may elect to submit the case to the division of the Tax Court hearing small claims cases. If the amount of tax at issue is $10,000 per year or less, the taxpayer can obtain a decision with a minimum of formality, delay, and expense; but the taxpayer loses the right to appeal the decision. The Small Claims Court is administered by the chief judge of the Tax Court, who is authorized to assign small claims cases to special trial judges. These cases receive priority on the trial calendars, and relatively informal rules are followed whenever possible. The special trial judges' opinions are not published on these cases, and the decisions are not reviewed by any other court or treated as precedents in any other case.

Bankruptcy Court. Under limited circumstances, it is possible for the bankruptcy court to have jurisdiction over tax matters. The filing of a bankruptcy petition prevents creditors, including the IRS, from taking action against a taxpayer, including the filing of a proceeding before the Tax Court if a notice of deficiency is sent after the filing of a petition in bankruptcy. In such cases, a tax claim may be determined by the bankruptcy court.

APPELLATE COURTS

U.S. Courts of Appeals. The appropriate appellate court depends on which trial court hears the case. Taxpayer or government appeals from the District Courts and the Tax Court are taken to the U.S. Court of Appeals that has jurisdiction over the court in which the taxpayer lives. Appeals from the U.S. Claims Court are taken to the U.S. Court of Appeals for the Federal Circuit, which has the same powers and jurisdictions as any of the other Courts of Appeals except that it only hears specialized appeals. Courts of Appeals are national courts of appellate jurisdiction. With the exceptions of the Court of Appeals for the Federal Circuit and the Court of Appeals for the District of Columbia, these appellate courts are assigned various geographic areas of jurisdiction as follows:

Court of Appeals for the Federal Circuit (CA-FC)	*District of Columbia Circuit (CA-DC)*	*First Circuit (CA-1)*	
U.S. Claims Court	District of Columbia	Maine Massachusetts New Hampshire Puerto Rico Rhode Island	

Second Circuit (CA-2)	*Third Circuit (CA-3)*	*Fourth Circuit (CA-4)*	*Fifth Circuit (CA-5)*
Connecticut New York Vermont	Delaware New Jersey Pennsylvania Virgin Islands	Maryland N. Carolina S. Carolina Virginia W. Virginia	Canal Zone Louisiana Mississippi Texas

Sixth Circuit (CA-6)	*Seventh Circuit (CA-7)*	*Eighth Circuit (CA-8)*	*Ninth Circuit (CA-9)*
Kentucky Michigan Ohio Tennessee	Illinois Indiana Wisconsin	Arkansas Iowa Minnesota Missouri Nebraska N. Dakota S. Dakota	Alaska Arizona California Guam Hawaii Idaho Montana Nevada Oregon Washington

Tenth Circuit (CA-10)	*Eleventh Circuit (CA-11)*	
Colorado New Mexico Kansas Oklahoma Utah Wyoming	Alabama Florida Georgia	

Taxpayers may appeal to the Courts of Appeal as a matter of right, and the Courts must hear their cases. Very often, however, the expense of such an appeal deters many from proceeding with an appeal. Appellate courts review the record of the trial court to determine whether the lower court completed its responsibility of fact finding and applied the proper law in arriving at its decision.

District Courts must follow the decision of the Appeals Court for the circuit in which they are located. For instance, the District Court in the Eastern District of Missouri must follow the decision of the Eighth Circuit Court of Appeals because Missouri is in the Eighth Circuit. If the Eighth Circuit has not rendered a decision on the particular issue involved, then the District Court may make its own decision or follow the decision in another Circuit.

The Tax Court is a national court with jurisdiction throughout the entire country. Prior to 1970, the Tax Court considered itself independent and indicated that it would not be bound by the decisions of the Circuit Court to which its decision would be appealed. In *Golsen,*[9] however, the Tax Court reversed its position. Under the *Golsen rule,* the Tax Court now follows the decisions of the Circuit Court to which a particular case would be appealed. Even if the Tax Court disagrees with a Circuit Court's view, it will decide based upon the Circuit Court's view. On the other hand, if a similar case arises in the jurisdiction of another Circuit Court that has not yet ruled on the same issue, the Tax Court will follow its own view, despite its earlier decision following a contrary Circuit Court decision.

U.S. Courts of Appeals generally sit in panels of three judges, although the entire court may sit in particularly important cases. They may reach a decision that affirms the lower court or that reverses the lower court. Additionally, the Appellate Court could send the case back to the lower court (remand the case) for another trial or for rehearing on another point not previously covered. It is possible for the Appellate Court to affirm the decision of the lower court on one particular issue and reverse it on another.

Generally, only one judge writes a decision for the Appeals Court, although in some cases no decision is written and an order is simply made. Such an order might hold that the lower court is sustained, or that the lower court's decision is reversed as being inconsistent with one of the Appellate Court's decisions. Sometimes other judges (besides the one assigned to write the opinion) will write additional opinions agreeing with (concurring opinion) or disagreeing with (dissenting opinion) the majority opinion. These opinions often contain valuable insights into the law controlling the case, and often set the ground for a change in the court's opinion at a later date.

U.S. Supreme Court.   The Supreme Court of the United States is the highest court of the land. No one has a *right* to be heard by this Court. It only accepts cases it wishes to hear, and generally those involve issues that the Court feels are of national importance. The Supreme Court generally hears very few tax cases. Consequently, taxpayers desiring a review of their trial court decision find it solely at the Court of Appeals. Technically, cases are submitted to the Supreme

---

[9]   *Jack E. Golsen,* 54 T.C. 742 (1970).

Court through a request process known as the "Writ of Certiorari." If the Supreme Court decides to hear the case, it grants the Writ of Certiorari; if it decides not to hear the case, it denies the Writ of Certiorari. It is important to note that there is another path to review by the U.S. Supreme Court—*by appeal*—as opposed to by Writ of Certiorari. This "review by appeal" may be available when a U.S. Court of Appeals has held that a state statute is in conflict with the laws or treaties of the United States. The "review by appeal" may also be available when the highest court in a state has decided a case on grounds that a Federal statute or treaty is invalid, or when the state court has held a state statute valid despite the claim of the losing party that the statute is in conflict with the U.S. Constitution or a Federal law. Review by the U.S. Supreme Court is still discretionary, but a Writ of Certiorari is not involved.

The Supreme Court, like the Courts of Appeals, does not conduct another trial. Its responsibility is to review the record and determine whether or not the trial court correctly applied the law in deciding the case. The Supreme Court also reviews the decision of the Court of Appeals to determine if the court used the correct reasoning.

In general, the Supreme Court only hears cases when one or more of the following conditions apply:

1. When the Court of Appeals has not used accepted or usual methods of judicial procedure or has sanctioned an unusual method by the trial court

2. When a Court of Appeals has settled an important question of Federal law and the Supreme Court feels such an important question should have one more review by the most prestigious court of the nation

3. When a decision of a Court of Appeals is in apparent conflict with a decision of the Supreme Court

4. When two or more Courts of Appeals are in conflict on an issue

5. When the Supreme Court has already decided an issue but feels that the issue should be looked at again, possibly to reverse its previous decision

CASE CITATION

Tax Court Decisions. Prior to 1943, the Tax Court was called the Board of Tax Appeals. The decisions of the Board of Tax Appeals were published as the *United States Board of Tax Appeals Reports* (BTA). Board of Tax Appeals cases are cited as follows:

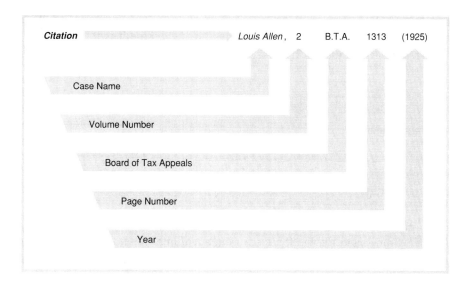

The Tax Court renders two different types of decisions with two different citation systems: regular decisions and memorandum decisions.

Tax Court *regular* decisions deal with new issues that the court has not yet resolved. In contrast, decisions that deal only with the application of already established principles of law are called *memorandum* decisions. The United States government publishes regular decisions in *United States Tax Court Reports* (T.C.). Tax Court regular decisions are cited as follows:

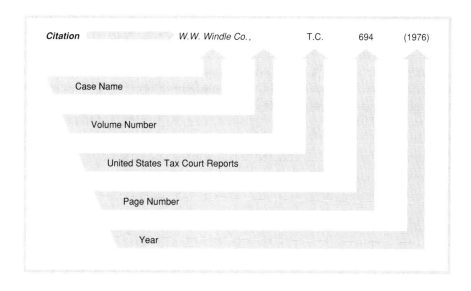

Like revenue rulings and the *Cumulative Bulletins*, there is a time lag between the date a Tax Court regular decision is issued and the date it is bound in a *U.S. Tax Court Report* volume. In this case, the citation appears as follows:

Temporary Citation:

W.W. Windle Co., 65 T.C. _____, No. 79 (1976).

Here the page is left out, but the citation tells the reader that this is the 79th regular decision issued by the Tax Court since Volume 64 ended. When the new volume (65th) of the Tax Court Report is issued, then the permanent citation may be substituted for the old one. Both CCH and PH have tax services that allow the researcher to find these temporary citations.

The IRS has adopted the practice of announcing its acquiescence or nonacquiescence to the regular decisions of the Tax Court that are adverse to the position taken by the government.[10] That is, the Service announces whether it agrees with the Tax Court or not. The IRS does not follow this practice for the decisions of the other courts, or even for memorandum decisions of the Tax court, although it occasionally announces that it will or will not follow a decision of another Federal court with a similar set of facts. The IRS may withdraw its acquiescence or nonacquiescence at any time and may do so even retroactively. Acquiescences and nonacquiescences are published in the weekly *Internal Revenue Bulletins* and the *Cumulative Bulletins*.

Although the U.S. government publishes the Tax Court's regular decisions, it does not publish memorandum decisions. However, both CCH and PH publish them. CCH publishes the memorandum decisions under the title *Tax Court Memorandum Decisions* (TCM), while PH publishes these decisions as *Prentice Hall TC Memorandum Decisions* (T.C. Memo). In citing Tax Court memorandum decisions, some authors prefer to use both the PH and the CCH citations for their cases.

In an effort to provide the reader the greatest latitude of research sources, this dual citation policy has been adopted for this text. The case of *Jerome Prizant* serves as an example of the dual citation of Tax Court memorandum decisions.

---

[10]   The IRS' acquiescence is symbolized by "A" or "Acq." and its nonacquiescence by "NA" or "Nonacq."

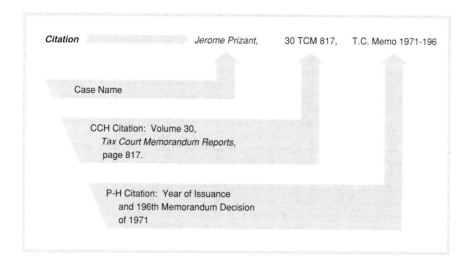

Citation → Jerome Prizant, 30 TCM 817, T.C. Memo 1971-196

Case Name

CCH Citation: Volume 30,
   Tax Court Memorandum Reports,
      page 817.

P-H Citation: Year of Issuance
      and 196th Memorandum Decision
         of 1971

Citations for U.S. District Court, Court of Appeals, and Claims Court. Commerce Clearing House, Prentice Hall, and West Publishing Company all publish decisions of the District Courts, Courts of Appeals, and the Claims Court. When available, all three citations of a case are provided in this text.[11] CCH publishes the decisions of these courts in its *U.S. Tax Cases* (USTC—not to be confused with the U.S. Tax Court Reports) volumes, and PH offers these decisions in its *American Federal Tax Reports* (AFTR) series. West Publishing Company reports these decisions in either its *Federal Supplement Series* (F. Supp.—District Court decisions), or its *Federal Second Series* (F.2d—Claims Court and Courts of Appeals decisions).

The citation of the U.S. District Court decision of *Cam F. Dowell, Jr. v. U.S.* is illustrated for each of the three publishing companies as follows:

[11] When all three publishers do not print the case, only the citations to the cases published are provided.

CCH Citation:

Cam F. Dowell, Jr. v. U.S., 74-1 USTC ¶9243, (D.Ct. Tx., 1974).

Interpretation: This case is reported in the first volume of the *U.S. Tax Cases,* published by CCH for calendar year 1974 (74-1), located at paragraph (¶) 9243, and is a decision rendered in 1974 by a U.S. District Court located in Texas (Tx).

PH Citation:

Cam. F. Dowell, Jr. v. U.S., 33 AFTR2d 74-739, (D.Ct Tx., 1974).

Interpretation: Reported in the 33rd volume of the second series of the *American Federal Tax Reports* (AFTR2d), published by PH for 1974, and located at page 739.

West Citation:

Cam F. Dowell, Jr. v. U.S., 370 F.Supp. 69 (D.Ct. Tx., 1974).

Interpretation: Located in the 370th volume of the *Federal Supplement Series* (F.Supp), published by West Publishing Company, and located at page 69.

The multiple citation of the U.S. District Court case illustrated above appears as follows:

Cam F. Dowell, Jr. v. U.S., 74-1 USTC ¶9243, 33 AFTR2d 74-739, 370 F.Supp. 69 (D.Ct. Tx., 1974).

Decisions of the Claims Court (Ct. Cls.), the Courts of Appeals (e.g., CA-1, CA-2, etc.), and the Supreme Court (USSC) are published by CCH and PH in the same reporting source as District Court decisions (i.e., USTCs and AFTRs). Claims Court and Court of Appeals decisions are reported by West Publishing Company in its *Federal Second Series* (F.2d). Supreme Court decisions are published by West Publishing Company in its *Supreme Court Reports* (S.Ct.), and the U.S. Government Printing Office publishes Supreme Court decisions in its *Supreme Court Reports* (U.S.).

An example of the multiple citation of a Court of Appeals decision follows:

Citation:

Millar v. Comm., 78-2 USTC ¶9514, 42 AFTR2d 78-5246, 577 F.2d 212 (CA-3, 1978).

A multiple citation of a Supreme Court decision would appear as follows:

Citation:

Fausner v. Comm., 73-2 USTC ¶9515, 32 AFTR2d 73-5202, 413 U.S. 838 (USSC, 1973).

Note that in each of the citations above, the designation "Commissioner of the Internal Revenue Service" is simply abbreviated to "Comm." In some instances, the IRS or U.S. is substituted for Comm., and older cases used the Commissioner's name. For example, in *Gregory v. Helvering,* 293 U.S. 465 (USSC, 1935), Mr. Helvering was the Commissioner of the Internal Revenue Service at the time the case was brought to the Court. Also note that the citation contains a reference to the Appellate Court rendering the decision (i.e., CA-3, or USSC) and the year of issuance.

Exhibits 16-1 and 16-2 summarize the sources of case citations from various reporter services.

Exhibit 16-1
Reporters of Tax Court Decisions

Reporter	Abbr.	Type	Publisher
Tax Court Reports	TC	Regular	Government Printing Office
Tax Court Memorandum Decisions	TCM	Memorandum	Commerce Clearing House
Tax Court Memorandum Decisions	PH TC Memo	Memorandum	Prentice Hall, Inc.

Exhibit 16-2
Reporters of Decisions Other Than Tax Court

Reporter	*Abbr.*	*Courts Reported*	*Publisher*
Supreme Court Reports	U.S.	Supreme Court	Government Printing Office
Supreme Court Reporter	S. Ct.	Supreme Court	West Publishing
Federal Supplement	F. Supp.	District Courts	West Publishing
Federal Reporter	F. F. 2d	Cts. of Appeal and Claims Ct.	West Publishing
American Federal	AFTR	District Courts	Prentice Hall, Inc.
Tax Reports	AFTR 2d	Claims Court, Cts. of Appeal, and Supreme Ct.	Prentice Hall, Inc.
United States Tax	USTC	Same as AFTR and AFTR2d	Commerce Clearing House

SECONDARY SOURCES

The importance of understanding the sources discussed thus far stems from their role in the taxation process. As mentioned earlier, the statutory law and its official interpretations constitute the legal authorities that set forth the tax consequences for a particular set of facts. These legal authorities, sometimes referred to as *primary authorities,* must be distinguished from so-called *secondary sources* or *secondary authorities*. The secondary sources of tax information consist mainly of books, periodicals, articles, newsletters, and editorial judgments in tax services. When working with the tax law, it must be recognized that secondary sources are unofficial interpretations—mere opinions—that have no legal authority.

Although secondary sources should not be used as the supporting authority for a particular tax treatment (except as a supplement to primary authority or in cases where primary authority is absent), they are an indispensable aid when seeking an understanding of the tax law. Several of these secondary materials are discussed briefly below.

TAX SERVICES

"Tax service" is the name given to a set of books that contains a vast quantity of tax-related information. In general, a tax service is a compilation of the following: the Code, regulations, court decisions, IRS releases, and explanations of these primary authorities by the editors. As the listing of contents suggests, a tax service is invaluable since it contains, all in one place, a wealth of tax information, including both primary and secondary sources. Moreover, these materials are updated constantly to reflect current developments—an extremely important feature given the dynamic nature of tax law. The major tax services are

Publisher	Name of Publication
Commerce Clearing House	*Standard Federal Tax Reporter—Income Taxes*
Prentice Hall	*Federal Taxes—Series D*, including *Citator*
The Bureau of National Affairs, Inc.	*Tax Management Portfolios—U.S. Income*
Research Institute of America	*Federal Tax Coordinator—2nd Series*
Mertens	*Law of Federal Income Taxation*

The widespread use of computers also has found its way into tax research. For example, *LEXIS* is a computerized data base that a user can access through his or her personal computer. The *LEXIS* data base contains almost all information available in an extensive tax library. Suppliers of tax services are currently making their own computer-based system available to their customers, or are in the process of perfecting such a system. Undoubtedly computers will be basic to tax research in the future, particularly within the large law and accounting firms that have enough work to make the use of such a system economical.

Commerce Clearing House, Prentice Hall, and other publishers issue weekly summaries of important cases and other tax developments that many practitioners and scholars find helpful in keeping current with developments in the tax field. The Bureau of National Affairs publishes the *Daily Tax Bulletin,* a comprehensive daily journal of late-breaking tax news that often reprints entire cases or regulations of particular importance. *Tax Notes,* published by Tax Analysts, is a weekly publication addressing legislative and judicial developments in the tax field. *Tax Notes* is particularly helpful in following the progress of tax legislation through the legislative process.

TAX PERIODICALS

In addition to these services, there are a number of quality publications (usually published monthly) that contain articles on a variety of important tax topics. These publications are very helpful when new tax acts are passed, because they often contain clear, concise summaries of the new law in a readable format. In addition, they serve to convey new planning opportunities and relay the latest IRS and judicial developments in many important sub-specialities of the tax profession. Some of the leading periodicals include the following:

Estate Planning	*Taxation for Lawyers*
Journal of Corporate Taxation	*Taxes—The Tax Magazine*
Journal of Real Estate Taxation	*The International Tax Journal*
Journal of Taxation	*The Review of Taxation of Individuals*
Journal of the American Taxation Association	*The Tax Adviser*
Tax Law Journal	*The Tax Executive*
Tax Law Review	*The Tax Lawyer*
Taxation for Accountants	*Trusts and Estates*

In addition to these publications, many law journals contain excellent articles on tax subjects.

Several indexes exist that may be used to locate a journal article. Through the use of a subject index, author index, and in some instances a Code section index, articles dealing with a particular topic may be found. Three of these indexes are

Title	Publisher
Index to Federal Tax Articles	Warren, Gorham and Lamont
Federal Tax Articles	Commerce Clearing House
The Accountant's Index	American Institute of Certified Public Accountants

In addition, the PH tax service contains a section entitled "Index to Tax Articles."

TAX RESEARCH

Having introduced the sources of tax law, the remainder of this chapter is devoted to working with the law—or more specifically, the art of tax research. Tax research may be defined as the process used to ascertain the optimal answer to a question with tax implications. Although there is no perfect technique for researching a question, the following approach normally is used:

1. Obtain all of the facts

2. Diagnose the problem from the facts

3. Locate the authorities

4. Evaluate the authorities

5. Derive the solution and possible alternative solutions

6. Communicate the answer

Each of these steps is discussed below.

OBTAINING THE FACTS

Before discussing the importance of obtaining all the facts, the distinction between closed-fact research and open or controlled-fact research should be noted. If the research relates to a problem with transactions that are complete, it is referred to as closed-fact research and normally falls within the realm of tax practice known as tax compliance. On the other hand, if the research relates to contemplated transactions, it is called controlled or open-fact research and is an integral part of tax planning.

In researching a closed-fact problem, the first step is gathering all of the facts. Unfortunately, it is difficult to obtain all relevant facts upon first inquiry. This is true because it is essentially impossible to understand the law so thoroughly that all of the proper questions can be asked before the research task begins. After the general area of the problem is identified and research has begun, it usually becomes apparent that more facts must be obtained before an answer can be derived. Consequently, additional inquiries must be made until all facts necessary for a solution are acquired.

DIAGNOSING THE ISSUE

Once the initial set of facts is gathered, the tax issue or question must be identified. Most tax problems involve very basic questions such as these:

1. Does the taxpayer have gross income that must be recognized?

2. Is the taxpayer entitled to a deduction?

3.   Is the taxpayer entitled to a credit?

4.   In what period is the gross income, deduction, or credit reported?

5.   What amount of gross income, deduction, or credit must be reported?

As research progresses, however, such fundamental questions can be answered only after more specific issues have been resolved.

> **Example 1.**   R's employer owns a home in which R lives. The basic question that must be asked is whether the home constitutes income to R. After consulting the various tax sources, it can be determined that § 61 requires virtually all benefits to be included in income unless another provision specifically grants an exclusion. In this case, § 119 allows a taxpayer to exclude the value of employer-provided housing if the housing is on the employer's premises, the lodging is furnished for the convenience of the employer, and the employee is required by the employer to accept the housing. Due to the additional research, three more specific questions must be asked:
>
> 1.   Is the home on the employer's premises?
>
> 2.   Is the home provided for the employer's convenience?
>
> 3.   Is R required to live in the home?

As the above example suggests, diagnosing the problem requires a continuing refinement of the questions until the critical issue is identified. The refinement that occurs results from the awareness that is gained through reading and rereading the primary and secondary authorities.

> **Example 2.**   Assume the same facts in *Example 1*. After determining that one of the issues concerns whether R's home is on the business premises, a second inquiry is made of R concerning the location of his residence. (Note that as the research progresses, additional facts must be gathered.) According to R, the house is located in a suburb, 25 miles from his employer's downtown office. However, the house is owned by the employer, and hence R suggests that he lives on the employer's premises. He also explains that he often brings work home and frequently entertains clients in his home. Having uncovered this information, the primary authorities are

reexamined. Upon review, it is determined that in *Charles N. Anderson,*[12] the court indicated that an employee would be considered on the business premises if the employee performed a significant portion of his duties at the place of lodging. Again the question must be refined to ask: Do R's work and entertainment activities in the home constitute a significant portion of his duties?

LOCATING THE AUTHORITIES

Identification of the critical issue presented by any tax question begins by first locating, then reading and studying the appropriate authority. Locating the authority is ordinarily done using a tax service. With the issue stated in general terms, the subject is found in the index volume and the location is determined. At this point, the appropriate Code sections, regulations, and editorial commentary may be perused to determine their applicability to the question.

> **Example 3.**   In the case of R above, the problem stated in general terms concerns income. Using an index, the key word, *income,* could be located and a reference to information concerning the income aspects of lodging would be given.

Once information relating to the issue is identified, the authoritative materials must be read. That is, the appropriate Code sections, regulations, rulings, and cases must be examined and studied to determine how they relate to the question. As suggested above, this process normally results in refinement of the question, which in turn may require acquisition of additional facts.

EVALUATING THE AUTHORITY

After the various authorities have been identified and it has been *verified* that they are applicable, their value must be appraised. This evaluation process, as will become clear below, primarily involves appraisal of court decisions and revenue rulings.

The Code.   The Internal Revenue Code is the final authority on most tax issues since it is the Federal tax law as passed by Congress. Only the courts can offset this authority by declaring part of the law unconstitutional, and this happens rarely. Most of the time, however, the Code itself is only of partial help. It is written in a style that is not always easy to understand, and it contains no examples of its application. Accordingly, to the extent the Code can be understood as clearly applicable, no stronger authority exists, except possibly a treaty. But in most cases, the Code cannot be used without further support.

[12]   67-1 USTC ¶9136, 19 AFTR2d 318, 371 F.2d 59 (CA-6, 1966).

Treasury Regulations. As previously discussed, the regulations are used to expand and explain the Code. Because Congress has given its authority to make laws to the Executive branch's administrative agency—the Treasury—the regulations that are produced are a very strong source of authority, although not as strong as the Code itself. Normally, the major concern with regulations is whether they are consistent with the Code. If the regulations are inconsistent, the Court will not hesitate to invalidate them.

Judicial Authority. The value of a court decision depends on numerous factors. On appraising a decision, the most crucial determination concerns whether the outcome is consistent with other decisions on the same issue. In other words, consideration must be given to how other decisions have evaluated the one in question. An invaluable tool in determining the validity of a case is a *citator*. A tax citator is a volume containing an alphabetical listing of virtually all tax cases. After the name of each case, there is a record of other decisions that have cited (in the text of their facts and opinions) the first case.

> **Example 4.** Assume the same facts as in *Example 2*. Examination of the *Anderson* case in a citator reveals that it has been cited by courts in other decisions numerous times. For example, two cases in which the *Anderson* decision was discussed are *U.S. Jr. Chamber of Commerce*[13] and *Jan J. Wexler*.[14]

It is important to note that tax citators often use abbreviations for subsequent case history. For example, the abbreviations *aff'g* and *aff'd* mean "affirming" and "affirmed" and indicate that an appeals court has upheld the decision in question. Similarly, *rev'g* and *rev'd* mean "reversing" and "reversed" and indicate that a trial court's decision was overturned. Finally, *rem'g* and *rem'd* mean "remanding" and "remanded" and indicate that the case has been sent back to a lower court for reconsideration.

The validity of a particular decision may be assessed by examining how the subsequent cases viewed the cited decision. For example, subsequent cases may have agreed or disagreed with the decision in question, or distinguished the facts of the cited case from those examined in a later case.

Another important factor that must be considered in evaluating a court decision is the level of the court that issued it. Decisions issued by trial courts have less value than those issued by appellate courts. And, of course, decisions of the Supreme Court are the ultimate authority.

A court decision's value rises appreciably if the IRS agrees with its result. As discussed earlier, the IRS usually indicates whether it acquiesces or does not acquiesce to regular Tax Court decisions. The position of the Service may also be published in a revenue ruling.

---

[13]   64-2 USTC ¶9637, 14 AFTR2d 5223, 334 F.2d 660 (Ct. Cls., 1964).

[14]   75-1 USTC ¶9235, 35 AFTR2d 75-550, 507 F.2d 842 (CA-6, 1975).

Rulings. The significance of revenue rulings lies in the fact that they reflect current IRS policy. Since agents of the IRS are usually reluctant to vary from that policy, revenue rulings carry considerable weight.

Revenue rulings are often evaluated in court decisions. Thus, a tax service should be used to determine whether relevant rulings have been considered in any decisions. By examining the Court's view of the ruling, possible flaws may be discovered.

Private letter rulings issued to the taxpayer must be followed for that taxpayer by the IRS as long as the transaction is carried out in the manner initially approved. Variation from the facts on which the ruling was based permits the Service to revise its position. With its enactment of the Revenue Reconciliation Act of 1989, Congress has established that all taxpayers can rely on letter rulings even though they are issued to specific taxpayers.

DERIVING THE SOLUTION

Once all the relevant authorities have been evaluated, a conclusion must be drawn. Before deriving the final answer or answers, however, an important caveat is warranted: the researcher must ensure that the research reflects all current developments. The new matters section of a tax service can aid in this regard. The new matters section updates the textual discussion with any late-breaking developments. For instance, the section will contain any new cases, regulations, or pronouncements of the Internal Revenue Service that may bear on the discussion of the topic covered in the main text.

After the current validity of the research is verified, the questions that have been formulated must be answered. In some cases the answers are clear; all too often, however, they are not. In such cases, it seems that from a practical viewpoint the issue should always be resolved in the taxpayer's favor, since the probability that a particular return will be subject to audit is very low. This decision also depends on several other factors, such as a taxpayer's personal attitudes, the amount of the tax at issue, and whether the tax return contains other items that might be at risk. Prior to enactment of the Tax Equity and Fiscal Responsibility Act (TEFRA), this was often the result. Under the rules enacted by TEFRA, however, the taxpayer may be subject to a penalty. This penalty is levied if there is a substantial understatement of tax attributable to a particular treatment for which the taxpayer does not have substantial authority.[15] (No penalty is imposed if the treatment is disclosed on the return.) Although the criterion of substantial authority has yet to be defined, the standard probably

---

[15] § 6661.

lies somewhere between "reasonable support" and "more likely than not." In any event, it is clear that taxpayers must be concerned with their conclusion and its supporting authority more than ever before.[16]

COMMUNICATING THE FINDINGS

The final product of the research effort is a memorandum recording the research and a letter to the interested parties. Although many formats are suitable for the memorandum, one technique typically used is structured as follows:

1. Description of the facts

2. Statement of the issues or questions researched

3. Report of the conclusions (brief answers to the research questions)

4. Discussion of the rationale and authorities that support the conclusions

5. Summary of the authorities consulted in the research

A good tax memorandum is essential. If the research findings are not communicated intelligently and effectively, the entire research effort is wasted.

---

[16] It should be noted that the Internal Revenue Code contains penalties for improper conduct by tax return preparers as well. These penalties run the gamut from offenses such as failing to furnish a completed copy of a return to the taxpayer to penalties for negligence and fraud. These penalties are discussed in Chapter 17.

PROBLEM MATERIALS

DISCUSSION QUESTIONS

16-1   *Making a New Tax Law.*   Describe the Congressional process of making a tax bill into final law.

16-2   *Legislative vs. Interpretative Regulations.*   Explain the difference between a legislative Treasury Regulation and an interpretative Regulation.

16-3   *Proposed vs. Final Regulations.*   Distinguish between proposed and final Regulations. How would either type of Regulation involving Code § 704 be cited?

16-4   *Revenue Rulings and Revenue Procedures.*   Distinguish between a Revenue Ruling and a Revenue Procedure. Where can either be found in printed form?

16-5   *Private vs. Published Rulings.*   Distinguish between a private letter ruling and a Revenue Ruling. Under what circumstances would a taxpayer prefer to rely on either of these sources?

16-6   *Technical Advice Memoranda.*   What are Technical Advice Memoranda? Under what circumstances are they issued?

16-7   *Trial Courts.*   Describe the trial courts that hear tax cases. What are the advantages or disadvantages of litigating a tax issue in each of these courts?

16-8   *The Appeals Process.*   A taxpayer living in Indiana has exhausted her appeals within the IRS. If she chooses to litigate her case, trace the appeals process assuming she begins her effort in each of the following trial courts:

a.   The U.S. Claims Court
b.   The U.S. District Court
c.   The U.S. Tax Court
d.   The Small Claims Division of the U.S. Tax Court

16-9   *Tax Court Decisions.*   Distinguish between a Regular Tax court decision and a Memorandum decision.

16-10   *Authority of Tax Law Sources.*   Assuming that you have discovered favorable support for your position taken in a controversy with an IRS agent in each of the sources listed below, indicate how you would use these authoritative sources in your discussion with the agent.

a.   A decision of the U.S. District Court having jurisdiction over your case if litigated
b.   Treasury Regulation
c.   The Internal Revenue Code
d.   A decision of the Supreme Court
e.   A decision of the Small Claims Court
f.   A decision of the U.S. Tax Court
g.   A private letter ruling issued to another taxpayer
h.   A Revenue Ruling
i.   A tax article in a leading periodical

16-11   *Tax Services.*   What materials are generally found in leading tax services? Which does your library have?

PROBLEMS

16-12   *Interpreting Citations.*   Interpret each of the following citations:

a.   Reg. § 1.721-1(a).
b.   Rev. Rul. 60-314, 1960-2 C.B. 48.
c.   Rev. Proc. 81-54, 1981-2 C.B. 44.
d.   Rev. Rul. 90-104, I.R.B. 1990-52, 5.
e.   § 351.

16-13   *Citation Abbreviations.*   Explain each of the abbreviations below.

a.   B.T.A.
b.   Acq.
c.   D. Ct.
d.   CA-9
e.   F. Supp.
f.   NA.
g.   Ct. Cls.
h.   USTC
i.   AFTR
j.   *Cert. Den.*
k.   *aff'g* and *aff'd*
l.   *rev'g* and *rev'd*
m.   *rem'g* and *rem'd*

16-14   *Interpreting Citations.*   Identify the publisher and interpret each of the following citations:

a.   41 TCM 289.
b.   93 S. Ct. 2820 (USSC, 1973).
c.   71-1 USTC ¶9241 (CA-2, 1971).
d.   236 F. Supp. 761 (D. Ct. Va., 1974).
e.   T.C. Memo 1977-20.
f.   48 T.C. 430 (1967).
g.   6 AFTR2d 5095 (CA-2, 1960).
h.   589 F.2d 446 (CA-9, 1979).
i.   277 U.S. 508 (USSC, 1928).

16-15   *Citation Form.*   Record the following information in its proper citation form.

a.   Part 7, subdivision (a)(2) of the income tax Regulation under Code § 165
b.   The 34th Revenue Ruling issued March 2, 1987, and printed on pages 101 and 102 of the appropriate document
c.   The 113th letter ruling issued the last week of 1986

16-16 *Citation Form.* Record the following information in its proper citation form.

    a.   A 1982 U.S. Tax Court case in which Roger A. Schubel sued the IRS Commissioner for a refund, published in volume 77 on pages 701 through 715 as a regular decision

    b.   A 1974 U.S. Tax Court case in which H. N. Schilling, Jr. sued the IRS Commissioner for a refund, published by (1) Commerce Clearing House in volume 33 on pages 1097 through 1110 and (2) Prentice Hall as its 246th decision that year

    c.   A 1966 Court of Appeals case in which Boris Nodiak sued the IRS Commissioner in the second Circuit for a refund, published by (1) Commerce Clearing House in volume 1 of that year at paragraph 9262, (2) Prentice-Hall in volume 17 on pages 396 through 402, and (3) West Publishing Company in volume 356 on pages 911 through 919.

RESEARCH PROBLEMS

16-17 *Using a Citator.* Use either the Commerce Clearing House or Prentice-Hall Citator in your library and locate *Richard L. Kroll, Exec. v. U.S.*

    a.   Which Court of Appeals Circuit heard this case?

    b.   Was this case heard by the Supreme Court?

    c.   James B. and Doris F. Wallach are included in the listing below the citation for Kroll. In what court was the Wallach case heard?

16-18. *Using a Citator.* Using any available citator, locate the case of *Corn Products v. Comm.*, 350 U.S. 46. What effect did the decision in *Arkansas Best v. Comm.* (58 AFTR2d 86-5748, 800 F.2d 219) have on the precedential value of the *Corn Products* case?

16-19. *Locating Court Cases.* Locate the case of *Robert Autrey, Jr. v. United States*, 89-2 USTC ¶9659, and answer the following questions.

    a.   What court decided the case on appeal?

    b.   What court originally tried the case?

    c.   Was the trial court's decision upheld or reversed?

16-20 *Locating Court Cases.* Locate the case of *Estate of James C. Freeman*, 67 T.C. 202, and answer the following questions.

    a.   What court tried the case?

    b.   Identify the various types of precedential authority the judge used in framing his opinion.

16-21 *Locating Court Cases.* Locate the cited court cases and answer the questions below.

    a.   *Stanley A. and Lorriee M. Golantly,* 72 T. C. 411 (1979). Did the taxpayers win their case?

    b.   *Hamilton D. Hill,* 41 TCM 700, T.C. Memo ¶71,127 (1971). Who was the presiding judge?

    c.   *Patterson (Jefferson) v. Comm.,* 72-1 USTC ¶9528, 29 AFTR2d 1181 (Ct. Cls., 1972). What was the issue being questioned in this case?

16-22   *Completing Citations.*   To the extent the materials are available to you, complete the following citations:

a.   Rev. Rul. 85-153, _____ C.B._____.

b.   *Lawrence W. McCoy,* _____ T.C. _____ (1962).

c.   *Reginald Turner,* _____, TCM _____, T.C. Memo 1954-38.

d.   *RCA Corp. v. U.S.,* _____ USTC _____ (CA-2, 1981).

e.   *RCA Corp. v. U.S.,* _____ AFTR2d _____ (CA-2, 1981).

f.   *RCA Corp. v. U.S.,* _____ F.2d _____ (CA-2, 1981).

g.   *Comm. v. Wilcox,* _____ S. Ct. _____ (USSC, 1946).

h.   _____, 79-1 USTC ¶9139 (USSC, 1979).

i.   _____, 34 T.C. 842 (1960).

j   *A. V. Johnson,* 23 TCM 2003, T.C. Memo _____.

k.   *Samuel B. Levin v. Comm.,* 43 AFTR2d 79-1057(_____).

16-23   *Examination of Tax Sources.*   For each of the tax sources listed below, identify at least one of the tax issues involved. In addition, if the source has a temporary citation, provide its permanent citation (if available).

a.   *Battelstein Investment Co. v. U.S.,* 71-1 USTC ¶9227, 27 AFTR2d 71-713, 442 F.2d 87 (CA-5, 1971).

b.   *Joel Kerns,* 47 TCM, _____ T.C. Memo 1984-22.

c.   *Patterson v. U.S.,* 84-1 USTC ¶9315 (CA-6, 1984).

d.   *William Sennett,* 80 T.C. 825 (1983).

e.   *Thompson Engineering Co., Inc.,* 80 T.C. 672 (1983).

f.   *Towne Square, Inc.,* 45 TCM 478, T.C. Memo 1983-10.

g.   Rev. Rul. 85-13, I.R.B. No. 7, 28.

h.   Rev. Proc. 85-49, I.R.B. No. 40, 26.

i.   *William F. Sutton, et al. v. Comm.,* 84 T.C. _____ No. 17.

j.   Rev. Rul. 86-103, I.R.B. No. 36, 13.

k.   *Hughes Properties, Inc.,* 86-1 USTC ¶9440, 58 AFTR2d 86-5015, _____ U.S. _____ (USSC, 1986).

l.   Rev. Rul. 87-105, I.R.B. No. 43, 13.

16-24   *Office in the Home.*   T comes to you for advice regarding the deductibility of expenses for maintaining an office in his home. T is currently employed as an Executive Vice President for Zandy Corporation. He has found it impossible to complete his job responsibilities during the normal forty-hour weekly period. Although the office building in which he works is open nights and weekends, the heating and air conditioning systems are shut down at night (from 6 p.m.) and during the entire weekend. As a result, T has begun taking work home with him on a regular basis. The work is generally done in the den of T's home. Although T's employer does not require him to work at home, T is convinced that he would be fired if his work assignments were not completed on a timely basis. Given these facts, what would you advise T about taking a home-office deduction?

Partial list of research aids:

§ 280A
Reg. § 1.280A
M.G. Hill, 43 TCM 832, T.C. Memo 1982-143

16-25 *Journal Articles.* Refer to Problem 16-24 above. Consult an index to periodicals (e.g., AICPA's *Accountants Index*; Warren, Gorham, and Lamont's *Index to Federal Tax Articles*; or CCH's *Federal Tax Articles*) and locate a journal article on the topic of tax deductions for an office in the home. Copy the article. Record the citation for the article (i.e., author's name, article title, journal name, publication date, and first and last pages of the article) at the top of your paper. Prepare a two-page summary of the article, including all relevant issues, research sources, and conclusions. Staple your two-page summary to the article. The grade for this exercise will be based on the relevance of your article to the topic, the accuracy and quality of your summary, and the quality of your written communication skills.

16-26 *Deductible Medical Expenses.* B suffers from a severe form of degenerative arthritis. Her doctor strongly recommended that she swim for at least one hour per day in order to stretch and exercise her leg and arm muscles. There are no swimming pools nearby, so B spent $15,000 to have a swimming pool installed in her back yard. This expenditure increased the fair market value of her house by $5,000. B consults you about whether she can deduct the cost of the swimming pool on her individual tax return. What do you recommend?

> **Hint:** You should approach this problem by using the tax service volumes of either Prentice Hall, Commerce Clearing House, or Research Institute of America. Prentice Hall and Commerce Clearing House are organized according to Code Sections, so you should start with Code § 213. You will find the Code Sections on the back binding of the volumes. Research Institute of America has a very extensive index, so look under the term "medical expenses."

16-27 *Deductible Educational Expenses.* T is a CPA with a large accounting firm in Houston, Texas. He has been assigned to the international taxation group of his firm's tax department. As a result of this assignment, T enrolls in an international tax law course at the University of Houston Law School. The authorities of the University require T to enroll as a regular law student; and, theoretically, if he continues to attend courses, T will graduate with a law degree. Will T be able to deduct his tuition for the international tax law course as a business expense?

> **Hint:** Go to either the Prentice Hall or Commerce Clearing House tax service and use it to find the analysis of Code § 162. When you have found the discussion of § 162, find that part of the subsection dealing with educational deductions. Read the appropriate Regulations and then note the authorities listed after the Regulations. Read over the summaries provided and then choose those you think have the most relevance to the question asked above. Read these cases and other listed authorities, and formulate a written response to the question asked in light of these cases and other authorities. Finally, for the authorities you choose, go to the Prentice Hall or Commerce Clearing House Citator and use it to ensure that your authorities are current.

LEARNING OBJECTIVES

Upon completion of this chapter you will be able to:

- Identify the conditions that might be likely to result in an IRS audit

- Explain IRS audit procedures, including the procedure for proposed audit adjustments

- Explain the procedure for appealing an adverse audit outcome

- Understand and be able to determine the statute of limitations for assessments, collections, and refund claims

- Determine when delinquency, accuracy-related, fraud, and information reporting penalties apply to taxpayers, and be able to compute them

- Identify situations when interest applies to a payment due to the IRS or a refund due from the IRS, and the rates applicable

- Explain the rules for practice before the IRS

- Identify the penalties that may apply to a tax return preparer

- Understand the AICPA's Statements on Responsibilities in Tax Practice

CHAPTER OUTLINE

Chapter **17**

TAX PRACTICE
AND PROCEDURE

With this chapter, the emphasis switches from issues of substantive tax law (i.e., the various rules that must be applied to determine the tax) to the procedural problems of complying with these laws. While considerations such as filing a tax return, paying the tax, and resolving disputes might seem mundane, they are a critical part of the taxation process. Indeed, if there were no provisions concerning compliance, revenues would go uncollected. The procedural aspect of taxation is the subject of this chapter.

THE COMPLIANCE PROCESS IN GENERAL

The Federal tax system relies heavily on the concepts of *voluntary compliance* and *self-assessment* in order to collect tax revenues. Voluntary compliance implies that the taxpayer is responsible for reporting the appropriate tax liability to the Federal government, paying the tax, and otherwise complying with current tax laws. This is typically accomplished when the taxpayer properly reports all taxable items, deductions, and credits on a Federal tax return that is filed on or before the due date. Self-assessment is reflected in the burden imposed on the taxpayer to compute taxable income and the tax liability for that income by applying current law to the relevant facts for the tax year. The IRS does not determine tax liability, but instead relies on the taxpayer to compute, report, and pay the proper amount of tax.

The principles underlying the Federal tax assessment collection process differ markedly from those found in other systems of taxation. For example, contrast the Federal method with the assessment technique and *involuntary* taxpayer compliance found in a sales tax system. Under the sales tax system, a purchaser of goods pays the sales tax to the merchant that is responsible for assessing and collecting the tax at the time of the transaction. Also, compare the Federal method to that used for obtaining local property taxes. Under most property tax systems, a field employee assesses the value of the property, after which the appropriate governing body sends a tax bill to the property owner.

To maintain the integrity of the self-assessment system, Congress has charged the Secretary of the Treasury with the responsibility of administering and enforcing the Internal Revenue Code. With this responsibility, Congress also has given the Secretary the authority to prescribe the rules and Regulations necessary for enforcing the tax laws. The Secretary, in turn, has delegated this rule-making authority to the Commissioner of the Internal Revenue Service. Thus, it is the duty of the IRS to ensure compliance with the tax laws. The organizational structure of the IRS is shown in Exhibit 17-1.

ADMINISTRATIVE REVIEW: THE AUDIT PROCESS

The IRS enforces the Federal tax law primarily through a systematic review of tax returns that have been filed. The review process begins when a tax return is filed. Every return is scanned for math and clerical errors as well as exclusions, deductions, and credits obviously claimed in error. This process includes matching information contained on such forms as the 1099 and the W-2 with amounts reported by the taxpayer. If any additional liability results from this review, the IRS Service Center issues an assessment for the correct amount of tax along with a brief statement explaining why the tax return was in error and a calculation of the additional amount owed. Alternatively, if a refund is owed to the taxpayer, it is issued. Typically, a taxpayer can resolve any questions concerning these adjustments by telephone or written correspondence with the IRS. This level of review is applied to *all* tax returns, as opposed to a more rigorous examination reserved only for selected tax returns.

Selection of Returns for Audit. Prior to selecting returns for audit, all returns are classified by type (e.g., individual, corporate, and partnership). Individual returns are then grouped in audit classes according to their adjusted gross incomes while corporate returns are divided into audit classes by gross assets. The selection of returns from each class is done primarily through the use of the Discriminant Function System (DIF) developed from data obtained in audits made in connection with the Taxpayer Compliance Measurement Program (TCMP). In contrast to most audits, a TCMP audit (which involves random selection of returns from the various groups of taxpayers) requires a detailed review of every item on the return in order to determine the degree of taxpayer compliance. Using the information compiled from TCMP audits, formulas are constructed that score returns as to their likelihood for containing significant tax error. Those returns with the highest score in each class are then scrutinized by the Examination (Audit) Division of the IRS to decide which returns it will audit, the type of audit to be performed, and how extensive the audit will be. The factors that determine whether a return will or will not be audited have not been publicly disclosed by the IRS. Many factors may be gleaned from experience, however, including the following:

1. Exceeding "normal" ranges for itemized deductions at various income levels

2. Previous audits that resulted in a deficiency assessment against the taxpayer

Exhibit 17-1
IRS Organization Chart

Department of the Treasury

Commissioner
Senior Deputy Commissioner

Assistants to the Commissioner[1]

Assistants to the Senior Deputy Commissioner

- - - (Appeals) - - -

- - - (Technical & Legal Services) - - -

Assistant Commissioner
(Inspection)

Divisions:
- Internal Audit Division
- Internal Security Division

Chief Counsel
Deputy Chief Counsel

- Associate Chief Counsel (Finance and Management)
  - General Legal Services
  - Office of Information Systems
  - Office of Planning & Finance
  - Office of Human Resources
- Associate Chief Counsel (Technical)
  - Financial Institutions & Products
  - Corporate
  - Passthroughs & Special Industries

- Income Tax & Accounting
- Employee Benefits & Exempt Organizations
- Associate Chief Counsel (International)
  - Technical
  - Litigation & Field Advice
- Associate Chief Counsel (Litigation)
  - Criminal Tax
  - Disclosure Litigation
  - General Litigation
  - Tax Litigation

- National Director of Appeals
  - Office of Training & Quality Programs
  - Office of Field Services
  - Office of Large Case Programs
  - Office of TEFRA & Tax Shelter Programs
  - Office of Information Management Services
  - Office of AES
  - Office of Appraisal Services

Regional Counsel (7)
Deputy Regional Counsel
- Criminal Tax
- General Litigation
- Tax Litigation

Assistant Regional Counsel
- General Legal Services

Regional Director of Appeals

District Counsel

Regional Inspectors(7)
Assistant Regional Inspectors
- Internal Audit
- Internal Security

Regional Commissioners (7)

Assistant Regional Commissioners
- Resources Management
- Criminal Investigation
- Examination
- Data Processing
- Collection

Service Center Directors (10)

Divisions:
- Compliance
- Resources Management
- Computer Services & Accounting
- Processing
- Tax Accounts
- Quality Assurance & Management Support

District Directors (63)

Divisions:
- Collection
- Criminal Investigation
- Examination
- Employee Plans & Exempt Organizations
- Resources Management
- Taxpayer Service

*Not same in all districts

Deputy Commissioner (Operations)

Chief Information Officer

Deputy Commissioner (Planning & Resources)

Assistant Commissioner (Criminal Investigation)
- Office of Enforcement
- Office of Planning & Development
- Automated Criminal Investigation Project Office

Assistant Commissioner (Examination)
- Office of Examination Programs
- Office of Examination Planning and Research
- Office of Disclosure
- Office of Examination Quality and Customer Advocacy
- Office of Examination Automation
- Office of matrix Projects

Assistant Commissioner (Collection)
- Office of Planning & Management
- Office of Field Operations
- Office of Evaluation & Research
- Office of Continuous Quality Improvement
- Office of the Integrated Collection System Project
- Office of the Connectivity Project

Assistant Commissioner (Employee Plans & Exempt Organizations)
- Exempt Organizations Technical Division
- Employee Plans Technical and Actuarial Division
- Employee Plans & Exempt Organizations Operations Division
- Office of Planning
- Office of Program Development and Quality

Assistant Commissioner (Returns Processing)
- Office of Legislative and Management Support
- Office of Information Systems and Resources
- Returns Processing and Accounting Division
- Statistics o' Income Division
- Office of Electronic Filing Systems
- Office of Integrated Management Systems

Assistant Commissioner (Taxpayer Services)
- Taxpayer Service Division
- Tax Forms and Publications Division
- Automated Taxpayer Service System Project Office

Assistant Commissioner (Finance)/Controller

Assistant Commissioner (Planning & Research)
- Finance Division
- Planning Division
- Research Division

Assistant Commissioner (Human Resources, Management & Support)
- Human Resources Division
- National Office Resources Management Division
- Facilities & Information Management Support Division
- Contracts & Acquisitions Division
- Director of Practice

Assistant Commissioner (International)
- Office of Resources Management
- Office of Taxpayer Service and Compliance
- Office of Tax Administration Advisory Services
- Office of International Programs

Assistant Chief Information Officer (Information Systems Development)
- Systems Acquisition Division
- Systems Design Division
- Systems Integration Division
- Project Management Division

Assistant Chief Information Officer (Information Systems Management)
- Planning, Budgeting and Review Staff
- Office of Information Systems Management
- Compliance Systems Division
- Tax Systems Division
- Quality Assurance Division
- Telecommunications Division
- Detroit Computing Center
- Martinsburg Computing Center

1. Public Affairs, Legislative Liaison, Taxpayer Ombudsman, Equal Opportunity, Quality, Assistants to the Commissioner, Legislative Affairs Division

3. Activity in sensitive areas, such as oil and gas, equipment leasing, real estate ventures, and other tax shelters

4. Taking a deduction that may be easily abused, such as home office expenses, casualty and theft losses, and business use of automobiles

5. Activity in a cash-transaction business where the opportunity for abuse is high and the ability to trace cash is low

6. A discrepancy between informational returns (e.g., Form 1099 and Form 1065–Schedule K1) and the income shown on the taxpayer's return

7. Self-employed persons, especially those in typically high-income businesses

8. Individuals with high gross income

9. Information from all other sources, including but not limited to informants, financial statements, and public records.

Examples of these possibilities are illustrated below.

Example 1.   Taxpayer A has gross income of $15,000 and claims a $10,000 deduction for interest. A may expect to be audited due to the large amount of interest deduction claimed relative to her total gross income.

Example 2.   Taxpayer B's individual income tax return has been audited for each of the last five years. Each year's audit has resulted in a deficiency. B files Form 1040 for the current year in good form. B's current year return may be audited based on the record from prior years.

Example 3.   Taxpayer C reports a net operating loss from participating as a limited partner in the XYZ Oil and Gas Partnership. C may be audited due to activity in the sensitive area of oil and gas.

Example 4.   Taxpayer D files Form 1040 and claims a casualty loss deduction for the theft of $2,000 in cash. D may be audited due to the potential for abuse in deducting a casualty loss.

Example 5.   Taxpayer E reports only $5,000 of gross income on Form 1040 for the entire year. E states on the return that his occupation is that of a magazine salesman. E may be audited since this is typically an occupation in which many transactions are paid for in cash.

Time Limit on Audits.   In order for an assessment to be enforceable, it must be made within the statute of limitations. Accordingly, an audit generally must be performed within three years from the due date of the tax return.[1]   There are

---

[1]   § 6501 and Reg. § 301.6501.

circumstances and exceptions which shorten, lengthen, or suspend the period of the statute of limitations as discussed later in this chapter.

The IRS attempts to complete audits of income tax returns within 27 months of whichever comes later—the dates that they are due or are filed. The issuance of a refund check for overpayment of taxes is absolutely no indication of whether or not the IRS will audit this particular return.

Conduct of the Audit. The Examination Division of the Internal Revenue Service conducts all examinations of tax returns. The audit is usually performed in the district where the tax return was originally filed. When the taxpayer has moved to another district, when it is discovered that the records to be examined are located in another district, or when it is determined that the audit could be performed more conveniently and swiftly in another district, then the Examination Division of that other district will conduct the audit.[2]

Auditing is conducted either in the local IRS office or in the field. Typically, only individual taxpayers are audited in the IRS office, as this imposes the burden of transporting financial data on the taxpayers most likely to have few records. In an office audit situation, the IRS usually sends an information guide instructing the taxpayer about which records are to be brought to the office. Although some individuals are audited extensively, most are required only to substantiate amounts for selected income, deductions, or credits by showing cancelled checks, receipts, or other supporting evidence. Sometimes an audit is conducted entirely through written correspondence (called a correspondence audit). If the taxpayer is requested to appear in the IRS office, he or she may go alone, or may be accompanied by an attorney, a certified public accountant, an individual enrolled to practice before the IRS, or even an unenrolled but qualified individual. If the taxpayer chooses not to appear personally, any of the individuals named above may represent the taxpayer—provided that such individual has a written power of attorney (Form 2848) executed by the taxpayer.[3]

The field audit is conducted by revenue agents (rather than office auditors). Although the IRS's preferred audit location is the taxpayer's business, the audit may be performed in the taxpayer's home, or in the office of the taxpayer's representative. Field audits are typically conducted on businesses (e.g., large sole proprietorships, corporations, or partnerships), thus alleviating the burden of transporting to an IRS office the often voluminous records maintained by the business enterprise. A field audit of a business usually extends widely in scope, involving examination of many items and possibly several years of activity. The audit often begins with a conference between the IRS field agent and the taxpayer and the taxpayer's representative. At this time, the IRS must provide the taxpayer with an explanation of the audit process and the taxpayer's rights in the audit

---

[2] Statement of Procedural Rules, Reg.   [3] § 7521(c).
§ 601.105(k).

process.[4] The IRS may not require the taxpayer to accompany the representative unless an administrative summons is issued to the taxpayer.[5] However, the IRS may notify the taxpayer directly if it is believed that the representative is causing an unreasonable delay or hindering the IRS audit.

During the initial conference, the IRS agent scrutinizes the taxpayer's records and requests explanation and substantiation of various items that he or she found to be questionable. IRS agents have the power to summon the taxpayer's records and to compel witnesses to testify.[6] Several meetings between the IRS agent conducting the audit and the taxpayer or the taxpayer's representative may take place. At such meetings, the IRS may ask for additional explanation and substantiation for items already being examined, and very possibly, the IRS may decide that it wants to expand the scope of the audit to examine additional items. The taxpayer and the IRS are allowed to make audio recordings of any interview as long as advance notice is given.[7] In addition, if at any time during the interview, the taxpayer clearly states to the IRS representative conducting the interview that he or she wishes to consult with an attorney, CPA, or any other person qualified to represent the taxpayer, then the interview shall be suspended.[8]

Proposed Audit Adjustments. In either type of audit, if the IRS does not agree with the return as filed, it may propose that adjustments be made to the tax liability. The IRS may find that the taxpayer overstated the tax liability on the return and has overpaid the actual tax bill for the period under audit. More likely, due to the Discriminant Function System, the IRS will propose that the tax liability be adjusted upward for the period audited, indicating that the taxpayer owes additional tax.[9]

The IRS findings (i.e., an overpayment, an underpayment, or no change in the tax liability for the period audited) are set out in a report called "Income Tax Examination Changes" after the audit is finished. The report explains the adjustments proposed by the IRS in terms of the dollar amounts and the issues which underlie the suggested changes The report may be reviewed by the auditor's supervisor and subsequently by a member of the review staff of the IRS's Examination Division. Normally, these reviewers may agree with the report as is, but they may ask for more information from the taxpayers or even bring up new issues that relate to the audit.

Issues that may arise during the audit may be questions of fact, questions of law, or mixed questions of fact and law. A question of fact involves a dispute over whether something did or did not occur. For example, whether or not a business expense for office rent was actually incurred and the amount of the expense are facts that may be questioned. A question of law involves a dispute

---

4   § 7521(b)(1).

5   § 7521(c).

6   § 7602.

7   § 7521(a).

8   § 7521(b)(2).

9   § 6211.

over the interpretation of a law and its application in the taxpayer's situation. For example, whether the taxpayer is permitted to deduct a particular expense under some Code provision is a question of law. A mixed question of fact and law involves a dispute over how the law applies in a situation where the facts are ambiguous or subject to different interpretations. For instance, the IRS may question whether a company has paid its president reasonable compensation. Whether the compensation paid to the president (and principal shareholder) is to be treated as dividends or as salary may depend on the facts, such as the intentions of the parties, the amount paid, the amount of services rendered, or the value of the services. Resolution of the issue also depends on the law, which in this type of case specifies various factors that may or may not have importance in the situation, depending on how the law is interpreted. For instance, the law may be interpreted so that the value of the services rendered is of paramount importance. Alternatively, the law may be interpreted to place the highest emphasis on the amount of services rendered and little importance on the value. Clearly, the mixed questions of fact and law are the most troublesome issues raised by an audit.

A taxpayer and an IRS agent may settle any type of question by reaching an agreement on the issues raised in the audit. Questions of fact are usually the easiest to resolve as they most often deal with matters that may be traced to tangible evidence; these questions become more difficult where the subject under scrutiny is less tangible, such as the taxpayer's intent at a given time. In resolving a question of law, the IRS must follow its current policy as established by Regulations, Rulings, and other releases. The IRS may not take a position that differs from its announced policy even though the IRS has a high probability of prevailing if the issue should be tried in court. This also is true in resolving a mixed question of fact and law.

Closing the Audit. After the audit has been completed, a taxpayer that agrees with the proposed adjustments is asked to sign either the Report of Individual Income Tax Changes (issued in an office audit), the Revenue Agent's Report [issued in a field audit and generally known as the RAR (see Exhibit 17-2)], or Form 870, Waiver of Restrictions on Assessment and Collection of Deficiency in Tax [most commonly used for situations involving partial agreements (see Exhibit 17-3)]. By signing these forms, the taxpayer waives the right to pursue the appeal process within the IRS and also waives the right to petition the Tax Court for relief. However, anyone who signs one of the above forms may pay the deficiency and, if he or she chooses, sue for a refund of the deficiency in U.S. District Court or U.S. Claims Court. This path may bypass the IRS Appeals Division and procedure and take the taxpayer directly to court. The IRS encourages its personnel to try to settle issues at the audit level, and at least arrive at partial agreements to lighten the workload of the Appeals Division and the Tax Court.[10] If the taxpayer and the IRS are unable to agree on one or more issues, the taxpayer may keep the case open by refusing to sign one of the above

---

[10]   Rev. Rul. 266, 1953-2 C.B. 450.

Exhibit 17-2
Revenue Agent's Report (RAR)

Page ____ of ____ Pages

Form **4549** (Rev. June 1988)	Department of the Treasury – Internal Revenue Service **Income Tax Examination Changes**	Return Form No.

Name and Address of Taxpayers	S.S. or E.I. Number	Filing Status

	Person With Whom Examination Changes Were Discussed	Name and Title

	Year:	Year:	Year:
1. Adjustments to Income			
a.			
b.			
c.			
d.			
e.			
f.			
g.			
2. Total Adjustments			
3. Adjusted Gross or Taxable Income Shown on Return or as Previously Adjusted			
4. Corrected Adjusted Gross or Taxable Income			
5. Tax			
6. Alternative Tax, if Applicable (From Page _____)			
7. Corrected Tax Liability (Lesser of line 5 or 6)			
8. Less Credits (Specify) a.			
b.			
c.			
9. Balance (Line 7 less total of lines 8a through 8c)			
10. Plus a. Tax from Recomputing Prior Year Investment Credit			
b. Self-Employment Tax			
c.			
11. Total Corrected Income Tax Liability (Line 9 plus total of lines 10a through 10c)			
12. Total Tax Shown on Return or as Previously Adjusted			
13. Deficiency – Increase in Tax or (Overassessment–Decrease in Tax) (Line 11 adjusted by Line 12)			
14. Adjustments to Prepayment credits			
15. Balance due or (Overpayment) (Line 13 adjusted by Line 14) Not Including Interest			
16. Penalties, If Any (See explanation)			

Other Information: (See notices on the back of this form.)

Examiner's Signature	District	Date

Consent to Assessment and Collection — I do not wish to exercise my appeal rights with the Internal Revenue Service or to contest in the United States Tax Court the findings in this report. Therefore, I give my consent to the immediate assessment and collection of any increase in tax and penalties, and accept any decrease in tax and penalties above, plus any interest as provided by law. It is understood that this report is subject to acceptance by the District Director.

NOTE: If a joint return was filed, both taxpayers must sign.	Signature of Taxpayer	Date	Signature of Taxpayer	Date
By		Title		Date

Form **4549** (Rev. 6-88)

Exhibit 17-3
Form 870

Form **870** (Rev. February 1986)	Department of the Treasury — Internal Revenue Service **Waiver of Restrictions on Assessment and Collection of Deficiency in Tax and Acceptance of Overassessment**	Date received by Internal Revenue Service

Names and address of taxpayers *(Number, street, city or town, State, ZIP code)*

Social security or employer identification number

Increase (Decrease) in Tax and Penalties

Tax year ended	Tax	Penalties			
	$	$	$	$	$
	$	$	$	$	$
	$	$	$	$	$
	$	$	$	$	$
	$	$	$	$	$
	$	$	$	$	$
	$	$	$	$	$

(For instructions, see back of form)

Consent to Assessment and Collection

I consent to the immediate assessment and collection of any deficiencies *(increase in tax and penalties)* and accept any overassessment *(decrease in tax and penalties)* shown above, plus any interest provided by law. I understand that by signing this waiver, I will not be able to contest these years in the United States Tax Court, unless additional deficiencies are determined for these years.

Signatures		Date
		Date
By	Title	Date

Form **870** (Rev. 2-86)

forms. By not signing and by doing nothing further, the taxpayer will receive a letter explaining the appeal process. The taxpayer must then be ready to pursue the appeal process to avoid having the proposed deficiency assessed.

The signing of a Report of Individual Income Tax Examination Changes, an RAR, or Form 870 at the audit level does *not* bar the IRS from opening new issues, requesting more information, and assessing more deficiencies (although this is somewhat unlikely), even after the taxpayer has paid the deficiency already assessed. Similarly, the taxpayer does not lose the right to use the IRS Appeals Division for any *additional* issues or deficiencies raised by the IRS after an agreement has been signed. Thus, a signed agreement does nothing to bind either the IRS or the taxpayer from seeking further relief; it merely precludes the taxpayer from seeking a settlement in the IRS Appeals Division on issues and deficiencies already in question that are covered in the agreement. The signing of Form 870 stops the running of interest on the deficiency 30 days after the form is filed.

APPEALS PROCEDURE

A taxpayer who does not agree with the outcome of an audit may choose to challenge the findings by appealing the case to a higher level of the IRS. (Contrast this with the taxpayer who pays the deficiency and signs one of the forms discussed above, then requests a refund from the IRS with the intention of bringing suit for such refund in U.S. District Court or U.S. Claims Court if the refund claim is denied. Such a taxpayer typically seeks to avoid the appellate procedure within the IRS.) The taxpayer who pursues an appeal within the IRS starts the process by refusing to sign an agreement. The IRS then sends the taxpayer a copy of the Revenue Agent's Report, a Form 870, and a so-called *30-day letter* (see Exhibit 17-4) which instructs the taxpayer to make use of the appellate procedure in the IRS. The letter typically urges the taxpayer to respond within 30 days by either agreeing to the RAR and signing either the RAR or Form 870, or requesting an appellate conference. The letter also explains that if there is no response, a "90-day letter" (discussed below) containing a statutory notice of deficiency will be issued.

Written Protest. If the taxpayer wants a conference with the IRS Appeals Division, a written protest for appeal must be filed with a request for an appellate conference. The protest is required in all cases except (1) where the deficiency is no greater than $2,500 for each tax period audited, or (2) the deficiency was assessed in an office or correspondence audit.

The protest must contain a statement that supports the taxpayer's position with regard to questions of fact as well as a statement and analysis of the law upon which the taxpayer is relying. The protest also must list the specific adjustments proposed by the audit that the taxpayer wishes to challenge.

Exhibit 17-4
30-Day Letter

Internal Revenue Service   Department of the Treasury
District Director

Date: In Reply Refer to:

                                                Person to Contact:

                                                Contact Telephone Number:

                                                Tax Year Ended and Deficiency/
                                                   Overassessment:

Dear

    We are enclosing a report proposing adjustments to the amount of your tax for the year(s) shown above. Please read the report, decide whether you agree or disagree with us, and respond within 30 days from the date of this letter. [Our report may not reflect the results of examinations of flow-through entities (partnerships, S corporations, trusts, etc.) in which you may have an interest.]

    IF YOU AGREE, you should:

1. Sign and date the enclosed agreement form.

2. Return the signed agreement form to us in the enclosed envelope.

3. Enclose payment of the tax and interest if additional tax is due, if you wish to stop the further running of interest. (The person whose name and telephone number appear above will be able to tell you how much interest is due to the date you intend to make payment. See the enclosed Publication 5 for additional payment information.)

    After we receive your signed agreement form, we will close your case and bill you for any unpaid tax or interest.

    IF YOU DO NOT AGREE and wish a conference with the Regional Office of Appeals, you MUST LET US KNOW within 30 days.

1. If the proposed change to your tax is $2,500 OR LESS for any tax period, you may call the person whose name and telephone number appear above; he or she will arrange for your case to be forwarded to Appeals. Or, you may send us your request by checking the appropriate section at the end of this letter; an additional copy of this letter is provided for this purpose. Mail this to us in the enclosed envelope.

2. If the proposed change to your tax is more than $2,500 but is $10,000 or less for any tax period, you must provide us with a BRIEF written statement of the disputed issues. This should be shown in the area found at the end of this letter; an additional copy of this letter is provided for this purpose. Mail this to us in the enclosed envelope.

3. If the proposed change to your tax is MORE THAN $10,000 for any tax period, we will require a written protest. Follow the instructions in the enclosed Publication 5. Mail the protest to us in the enclosed envelope.

(over)

                                                Letter 950(DO) (Rev. 11–87)

The Appellate Conference.   The IRS does not allow the taxpayer an appellate conference as a matter of right. Rather, it offers the process as a privilege for a taxpayer who wishes to dispose of a case at an administrative level (i.e., within the IRS, before reaching the trial court). The taxpayer who refuses to comply with tax laws on the basis of moral or political reasons normally is not granted an appellate conference.

The purpose of an appeals conference is to review the findings of the audit and the issues raised in hopes of arriving at a resolution of the case. The conference itself takes place in an informal manner. Usually, only the taxpayer's representative attends the conference as the taxpayer's lack of technical understanding may hinder the proceedings. As a practical matter, the taxpayer's representative often requests that the taxpayer not attend the conference. The IRS agents that performed the audit typically are not present; instead, the IRS is represented by officers of the Appeals Division. Witnesses are seldom asked to testify as their sworn affidavits usually suffice.

A taxpayer should not pursue an appellate review of an IRS audit without an understanding of the risk involved. The personnel at this level usually have more experience than the agents who conducted the audit, and are likely to construct more sophisticated arguments against the taxpayer and possibly raise new issues. Also, the taxpayer must take into account the costs of professional services necessary to appeal a case. The research for and the drafting of a written protest, along with professional fees for representation at the appellate conference, may involve considerable expense. These costs should be balanced against the amount of the disputed deficiency weighted by the probability of a favorable outcome.

During the appellate conference, the taxpayer or his or her representative meets with members of the IRS Appeals Division. In an effort to settle the case, the IRS may agree to resolve an issue in favor of the taxpayer in exchange for a reciprocal agreement by the taxpayer to resolve one or more other issues in favor of the IRS. This practice may occur only with issues raised at the audit level, and not with new issues that might be raised at the appellate level. The Appeals Division may not raise new issues at the appellate level unless the grounds of a new issue have significant tax impact.[11]

The Appeals Division has authority to settle all cases without regard to the amount of tax involved. One of the many factors considered by the Appeals Division is whether or not there exists a *hazard of litigation*. This term has not been clearly defined but obviously relates to the probability that the taxpayer will continue to pursue the case to the trial court level or beyond, as well as being related to the taxpayer's chances of winning there. The primary objective of the Appeals Division is to settle cases and keep them from going to court. As a result, the Appeals Division may offer to accept only a percentage of the

---

[11]   Statement of Procedural Rules, Reg. § 601.106(d)(1).

deficiency proposed by the IRS. Each item might be adjusted and settled in such a manner. For example, if a question exists as to the deductibility of an item, the IRS may settle for one-half of the tax deficiency related to that item. However, this should not be construed as meaning that the Appeals Division will automatically concede issues or cases involving a low tax liability.

Settlement with Appeals Division. At any stage in the appellate process, the taxpayer may be requested to sign Form 870-AD (Appellate Division), Offer of Waiver of Restrictions on Assessment and Collection of Deficiency, in order to settle the case. This form is similar to Form 870 inasmuch as it sets forth the concessions arrived at between the IRS and the taxpayer. However, the two forms differ in one important respect. As a general rule, signing Form 870 does not preclude the IRS from further audits. In contrast, acceptance of the Form 870-AD by the IRS means that the case *will not* be reopened in the absence of fraud, misrepresentation of material fact, significant error in mathematical calculation, or other administrative malfeasance. Most practitioners regard the agreement delineated on the Form 870-AD as a binding one. The issue of whether or not either party may reopen the case after the agreement is executed has not been resolved.[12]

Unlike Form 870, filing Form 870-AD does not stop the running of interest until the offer is accepted by the IRS. Also, if Form 870-AD is signed, the IRS may make a valid assessment without issuing the customary 90-day letter containing a notice of deficiency which is otherwise required.

THE 90-DAY LETTER: NOTICE OF DEFICIENCY

As suggested above, the IRS is normally prohibited from assessing and collecting the tax until 90 days after the taxpayer has been notified of the tax deficiency. The required statutory notice of deficiency, commonly referred to as the 90-day letter (see Exhibit 17-5), may be issued at various times during the review process. The letter is usually sent following the rejection or denial of the taxpayer's appeal. A taxpayer who fails to settle a case with the IRS Appeals Division receives the letter shortly after an IRS regional counsel has reviewed the case. The 90-day letter is also sent to taxpayers that do not respond to the 30-day letter. In addition, the taxpayer may request issuance of the 90-day letter since a petition to the Tax Court cannot be filed until statutory notice of the deficiency has been received. It should be noted that issuance of the 90-day letter *suspends* the running of the statute of limitations.

---

[12] See *W.R. Lowe*, 63-2 USTC ¶9778, 12 AFTR2d 5951, 223 F. Supp. 948 (1963); but cf. *W.A. Morse*, 59-1 USTC ¶9359, 6 AFTR2d 5353, 183 F. Supp. 847 (1959).

Exhibit 17-5
90-Day Letter

Internal Revenue Service
District Director

Department of the Treasury

Date:

Social Security or
   Employer Identification Number:

Tax Year Ended and Deficiency:

Person to Contact:

Contact Telephone Number:

We have determined that there is a deficiency (increase) in your income tax as shown above. This letter is a NOTICE OF DEFICIENCY sent to you as required by law. The enclosed statement shows how we figured the deficiency.

If you want to contest this deficiency in court before making any payment, you have 90 days from the above mailing date of this letter (150 days if addressed to you outside of the United States) to file a petition with the United States Tax Court for a redetermination of the deficiency. To secure the petition form, write to United States Tax Court, 400 Second Street, NW., Washington, D.C. 20217. The completed petition form, together with a copy of this letter must be returned to the same address and received within 90 days from the above mailing date (150 days if addressed to you outside of the United States).

The time in which you must file a petition with the Court (90 or 150 days as the case may be) is fixed by law and the Court cannot consider your case if your petition is filed late. If this letter is addressed to both a husband and wife, and both want to petition the Tax Court, both must sign the petition or each must file a separate, signed petition.

If you dispute not more than $10,000 for any one tax year, a simplified procedure is provided by the Tax Court for small tax cases. You can get information about this procedure, as well as a petition form you can use, by writing to the Clerk of the United States Tax Court at 400 Second Street, NW., Washington, D.C. 20217. You should do this promptly if you intend to file a petition with the Tax Court.

You may represent yourself before the Tax Court, or you may be represented by anyone admitted to practice before the Court. If you decide not to file a petition with the Tax Court, we would appreciate it if you would sign and return the enclosed waiver form. This will permit us to assess the deficiency quickly and will limit the accumulation of interest. The enclosed envelope is for your convenience. If you decide not to sign and return the statement and you do not timely petition the Tax Court, the law requires us to assess and bill you for the deficiency after 90 days from the above mailing date of this letter (150 days if this letter is addressed to you outside the United States).

(over)

Letter 531(DO) (Rev. 1-87)

Assessment. Before the tax can be collected, it must be assessed. Assessment is the act of recording the amount of tax due on the books of the government.[13] As noted above, the IRS generally cannot make an assessment of a deficiency until a 90-day letter has been mailed to the taxpayer and the 90 days of notice have elapsed. In addition, the IRS cannot assess a deficiency where the taxpayer has filed a petition with the Tax Court until the court's decision has become final.[14]

Assessments of tax shown on a return, math errors, credits taken in error, and delinquency penalties not related to a deficiency do not require the 90-day letter of statutory notice. It is required, however, for all deficiencies, penalties for fraud and negligence, and delinquency penalties related to deficiencies.

BEYOND APPELLATE CONFERENCE PROCEDURES

After the appellate conference and related negotiations have been completed, an office of the Appeals Division reviews the case. When a settlement was reached in the appellate conference but not approved by the reviewing officer, the taxpayer is granted a conference with the reviewing officer.[15] If the reviewer approves the appellate conference findings, he or she forwards them to the District Director where the case originated.

In cases where a settlement is not reached at the appellate conference or the post-conference review, the Appeals Division sends a 90-day letter to the taxpayer stating that an assessment will be made if he or she does not pay the deficiency or petition the Tax Court within 90 days. Generally, this notice marks the end of the administrative appeals process and availability of any remedies at the administrative level. Consequently, the taxpayer must either pay the deficiency and sue to recover it in District Court or the Claims Court, or he or she must file a petition for a determination of the case by the Tax Court. In the latter event, the taxpayer need not pay the deficiency before filing a claim for relief.

ADDITIONAL SETTLEMENT TECHNIQUES

As mentioned above, the taxpayer may be requested to settle the dispute during the audit by signing Form 870, or during the appellate process by signing Form 870-AD. By entering into this type of agreement, the parties avoid the statutory requirement that a notice of deficiency (i.e., a 90-day letter) be sent and that 90 days expire before an assessment is made. Other commonly used settlement methods include closing agreements, offers in compromise, and agreements to extend the statute of limitations for assessment.

---

[13] § 6213.

[14] § 6213. Also, see § 7481 for the date that a Tax Court decision becomes final.

[15] Statement of Procedural Rules, Reg. § 601.106(f)(3).

Closing Agreements.   A written closing agreement can be entered into by any authorized officer or employee of the IRS.[16] A closing agreement may be made at any time before the case has been heard by the Tax Court. Such agreements are considered binding in the absence of fraud, misrepresentation, or substantial error.

Offers in Compromise.   Except in criminal cases involving drugs, an authorized officer or employee of the IRS may enter an agreement to settle a case for a lower amount of tax plus penalties and interest. A compromise agreement settles the taxpayer's entire liability. It occurs when there is doubt about the liability because of the uncertainty surrounding questions of fact or law, or about the collectibility of the amount owed.[17] A compromise is usually offered after a deficiency has been assessed and the tax liability has become fixed. A compromise agreement is binding on the IRS and the taxpayer.[18]

Extensions of Limitation Period.   An audit or an appellate review often requires more time to finish than that remaining in the limitations period. In unusual circumstances only, the IRS asks the taxpayer to agree to an extension of the limitations period.[19] This agreement must be written and it may be entered into only by a District Director or a Regional Officer of the IRS. The taxpayer does not have to enter into the Agreement, but it is unwise to refuse to do so. Such a refusal prompts the IRS to prematurely stop negotiations and assess a deficiency against the taxpayer. This precludes further dealings with the IRS until the taxpayer files a petition with the Tax Court or pays the assessment and files a claim for a refund. An extension is executed on Form 872 or Form 872-A. The agreement extends the limitations period either to a specific date, or until a written notification is made by one party to the other declaring the end of the additional period. In either case, the termination of the agreement becomes effective only after the passage of an additional period of 90 days (i.e., the length of time needed for the statutory notice of deficiency) plus an extra 60 days.[20]

> **Example 6.**   Individual taxpayer A enters into an agreement with the IRS to extend the statute of limitations for 1988. The limitations period normally expires April 15, 1992, but due to unusual circumstances, A has agreed to keep the period open until June 30, 1992. The running of the period of limitation for assessment is suspended from April 15, 1992 to November 27, 1992. Ninety days for the statutory notice of assessment plus 60 extra days are added to the specified date of June 30, 1992.

---

[16]   Reg. § 301.7121-1. Also, see Rev. Proc. 68-16, 1968-1 C.B. 770.

[17]   Reg. § 301.7122-1(a).

[18]   *Alamo Foods Co.*, 1 USTC ¶207, 6 AFTR 6464, 16 F.2d 694 (CA-5, 1927), cert. den., 274 U.S. 741.

[19]   Rev. Proc. 57-6, 1957-1 C.B. 729.

[20]   § 6503(a)(1).

Example 7. Individual taxpayer B enters into an agreement with the IRS to extend the limitations period for 1988. The limitations period normally expires on April 15, 1992, but due to unusual circumstances, B has agreed to keep the period open until one party notifies the other in writing that the extension is terminated. On July 31, 1992, B notifies the IRS in writing that the extension period is over. The running of the period of limitation for assessment is suspended from April 15, 1992 to December 28, 1992. Ninety days for the statutory notice of assessment plus 60 extra days are added to the notice date of July 31, 1992.

EXHAUSTING THE ADMINISTRATIVE REMEDIES

As mentioned above, the taxpayer may at any time during the audit and appellate process request a 90-day letter from the IRS, pay the assessed deficiency, and file a claim for refund in District Court or Claims Court. Before filing suit in either of these courts, however, the taxpayer must first exhaust his or her administrative remedies making a formal, written request for a refund from the IRS. The taxpayer's request for refund is considered by the District Director for the district that conducted the audit. If the request is rejected, a 30-day letter is sent to the taxpayer explaining the appellate procedure. The taxpayer must follow the same appellate procedure with the Appeals Division of the IRS as is followed by a taxpayer who has not yet paid a deficiency. The difference is that this taxpayer, by virtue of having already paid the deficiency, must file a suit for refund in the District Court or Claims Court, and may not go to the Tax Court for relief.

THE STATUTE OF LIMITATIONS

The Internal Revenue Code contains several statutes of limitation. These statutes provide that after a certain event has occurred, legal action related to the event may not be brought if a specified amount of time has passed. The statute of limitations establishes an absolute defense against any legal action brought after its expiration. In deciding the type of events that should have a limitations period and the length of that period, many factors must be considered. These factors include the significance of the event, its seriousness in nature as well as its magnitude. Also important is the availability of records, witnesses, or other evidence related to the event and the difficulty of obtaining them due to the passage of time. Other considerations involve the overall harm to the legal system that might occur if legal action is barred, including the detriment to the party that has suffered from the event as opposed to the burden imposed on the judicial system by allowing legal action to be brought on events of the more distant past. Finally, it is desirable to have events beyond a certain point of time in the past considered legally settled. This affords peace of mind to the parties involved inasmuch as the event can no longer be the cause for legal action. This too must be balanced against the harm suffered by any party in deciding whether or not to bar legal action and after what length of time.

ASSESSMENTS

General Rule. The general period of limitations for tax assessment is three years from the date the return is filed or the date the return is due, whichever is later.[21] Several exceptions to this rule exist, however.

> **Example 8.** Taxpayer A files a tax return in good form on April 1, 1992 for 1991. The statute of limitations expires April 15, 1995, three years from the later of the date the return is due (April 15, 1992) or the date it was filed.

> **Example 9.** Taxpayer E files an income tax return for 1991 in good form on April 10, 1992. On April 1, 1993, Taxpayer E files a Form 1040X to amend the 1991 tax return. The statute of limitations remains unchanged and expires on April 15, 1995, three years from the later of the date the return is due (April 15, 1992) or the date the return is actually filed.

Fraudulent Return. There is no statute of limitations barring assessment where the taxpayer has filed a false or fraudulent return with intent to evade taxes. Similarly, where the taxpayer makes a willful attempt to defeat or evade taxes other than income, estate, and gift taxes there is no limitation period for assessment.

> **Example 10.** Taxpayer C, a waitress, files a tax return for 1991, intentionally omitting $3,000 of cash she received in tips from taxable income. She hopes to evade the tax on the $3,000. No statute of limitations applies.

No Return. Where the taxpayer files no tax return, assessment may be made or a court action begun at any time.[22]

Substantial Omission of Income. If the taxpayer omits gross income from the return in an amount greater than 25 percent of the gross income shown on the return, the limitations period is extended to six years.[23] The limitations period also is extended to six years where a personal holding company files a return without including a schedule that itemizes income and lists major stockholders.[24]

Prompt Assessments. A request for prompt assessment of tax liability for a decedent, a decedent's estate, or a corporation in dissolution may be requested. If it is granted, the usual three-year period is shortened to 18 months from the time the request for a prompt assessment is made.[25]

---

[21] § 6501(a).

[22] § 6501(c) and Reg. § 301.6501(c)-1.

[23] § 6501(e) and Reg. § 301.6501(e)-1.

[24] § 6501(f) and Reg. § 301.6501(f)-1.

[25] Reg. § 301.6501(d)-1.

Carryback and Carryovers.   If the taxpayer wishes to carry back a net operating loss or a capital loss to an earlier year, the assessment period begins with the due date of the return for the year in which the loss occurred, instead of the carryback year.[26] The period for assessment on the years that generate net operating losses and capital losses is not extended by carrying forward such items.[27]

> **Example 11.**   Corporation Y, a calendar year taxpayer, has filed an income tax return for 1991 which shows a net operating loss. The corporation carries the net operating loss back to 1988, the third tax year preceding 1991, and then, if there is still an unused loss, to 1989, the second tax year preceding 1991. The statute of limitations ends for these carryback years in three years from the later of the date that the 1991 return is due (March 15, 1992) or the date the 1991 return is actually filed. Assuming the 1991 return is filed on March 3, 1992, the statute of limitations runs out on March 15, 1995 for all three returns.

Amended Returns.   Normally, an amended return does not change the length of the limitations period. However, the statute of limitations period is extended by 60 days where an amended return is filed and the normal assessment period would expire in less than 60 days from the date of filing the amended return.

> **Example 12.**   Taxpayer F files an income tax return for 1991 in good form on April 10, 1992. On April 1, 1995, Taxpayer F files a Form 1040X to amend the 1991 tax return. The statute of limitations expires 60 days after Taxpayer F files the Form 1040X, since less than 60 days remain in the original limitations period when the amended return is filed.

Suspension of Assessment Period.   The running of the limitations period for assessing tax is suspended when a statutory notice of deficiency (i.e., a 90-day letter) is mailed to the taxpayer or after the taxpayer has filed a petition with the Tax Court.[28] When the statutory notice of deficiency is sent to the taxpayer, the statute of limitations stops running for the 90 days of the notice period and for 60 days thereafter. When a case is pending before the Tax Court, the statute of limitations on assessment is suspended from running until the Tax Court's decision becomes final and for 60 days thereafter. This suspension of the limitations period gives the IRS the additional time it might need to make an assessment, since it may not make an assessment during the statutory notice period or while a petition is before the Tax Court.

---

[26]   §§ 6501(h) and (j) and Reg. §§ 301.6501(h)-1 and 301.6501(j)-1.

[27]   Reg. § 301.6501(j)-1.

[28]   § 6503(a)(1).

Example 13.   Taxpayer G files an income tax return for 1991 on April 1, 1992. After an audit of this return and appeal to the IRS, a 90-day letter is sent to the taxpayer on March 1, 1995. The statute of limitations expires on July 28, 1995. The limitations period would have expired on April 15, 1995, but the 90-day letter suspends the limitations period for the 90 days following the date of the notice plus an extra 60 days.

COLLECTIONS

After an assessment has been made in a proper and timely manner, the IRS must begin proceedings to collect the tax within six years of the assessment.[29] During this time, the IRS must either levy against the taxpayer's property or initiate court proceedings to recover the tax assessed. The limitations period for tax collection may be extended by written agreement between the taxpayer and the IRS. Such an agreement may allow the taxpayer additional time needed to pay off taxes, and thus prevent a levy against the taxpayer's property.

REFUND CLAIMS

The taxpayer must file a timely and valid claim in order to receive a refund for an overpayment of tax. Refunds are properly filed by individuals on Form 1040X, Individual Amended Income Tax Return, and by corporations on Form 1120X, Corporate Amended Income Tax Return.[30] Other taxpayers make refunds by filing Form 843. The rules applying to refund claims are stated below.

1.   The refund claim must be filed within three years from the date on which the tax return to which it relates was filed, or within two years of the actual payment of the tax.[31]

2.   If no tax return is filed, the refund claim must be filed within two years of the date the tax was paid.

3.   Where a return is filed and tax is paid, the amount of the refund may not exceed the tax paid within the three-year period.

4.   Where a refund is claimed after three years from the date the return is filed (or was due), but within two years of the payment of the tax, the refund amount may not exceed the amount paid during the last two years.

It should be noted that estimated income tax payments and income tax withholdings on wages are deemed to be paid on the due date of the return to which they relate.

---

[29]   § 6502(a) and Reg. § 301.6502-1(a).

[30]   Reg. § 301.6402-3.

[31]   § 6511(a) and Reg. § 301.6511(a)-1.

Example 14.   Taxpayer A files an individual income tax return for 1991 on April 15, 1992. All of A's income tax withholding and estimated income tax payments totalling $10,000 are deemed paid April 15, 1992. On April 1, 1995, A files a refund claim for $2,000 of tax by filing Form 1040X, Amended Individual Income Tax Return. A may receive the entire $2,000 since the refund is based on a valid claim filed within three years of the date the return was filed.

Example 15.   Taxpayer B files an individual income tax return for 1991 on April 15, 1992. B has paid $9,000 of her $10,000 stated tax liability in withholding and estimated tax payments by April 15, 1992. B pays the remaining $1,000 of tax due on April 15, 1994. On April 1, 1996, B claims a refund of $2,000 by filing Form 1040X, Amended Individual Income Tax Return. B may receive only $1,000, the amount she has paid during the past two years. Since three years have passed since B filed her income tax return for 1991 (on April 15, 1992), B cannot claim a refund under the three-year rule. B may claim a refund only for an amount equal to the tax paid in the past two years under the two-year rule.

Mitigation Provisions.   Provisions exist to "mitigate" or reduce the effect of the statute of limitations in cases where a rigid imposition of the rule would work an unfair hardship on the IRS or the taxpayer.[32] According to these rules, where the statute of limitations has expired, adjustments may be made on a return that relates to the expired period for specified reasons. These reasons often involve cases where an item of income, deduction, or credit has been erroneously claimed in a "closed" year and the proper period for the taxpayer to claim this item is in a subsequent "open" year. Other applicable situations occur when the taxpayer has claimed an item of income, deduction, or credit that rightfully belongs to a related taxpayer.[33] In these instances, the statute of limitations is not observed so that the taxpayer is not allowed a double benefit from claiming a specific item of deduction or credit in a closed year and then again in an open year. Conversely, a taxpayer is spared the double burden of having to include an income item in both a closed year and again in an open year. Also, if a taxpayer improperly claims an item of income, deduction, or credit that belongs to a related taxpayer, the statute of limitations will not be observed, so the item may be reallocated. The purpose of the mitigations rule is to prevent the IRS or the taxpayer from maintaining *inconsistent* positions from which either would inequitably benefit, where such inconsistent positions could otherwise not be challenged due to the expiration of the limitations period.

---

[32]   §§ 1311 through 1314 and Reg. §§ 1.1311(a)-1 through 1.1311(c)-1.

[33]   *Ibid.*

Example 16. Taxpayer H files an income tax return for 1991 that claims a deduction for the cost of repairing a building used for business. In 1992 H decides that it is more appropriate to treat the cost of the building repair as a capital expenditure and depreciate it. A depreciation deduction is taken for a portion of the cost of the repair in 1992 and subsequent years. In 1996, although the statute of limitations has expired on the 1991 return, the IRS may adjust that return and disallow the deduction for the entire cost of the repair. This prevents a double benefit for the taxpayer that has deducted the entire cost once, and now seeks to depreciate the cost over the life of the asset.

Example 17. Taxpayer J incorrectly includes in his own income the $3,500 that his minor son has earned on his summer job during 1991. The IRS audits the son in 1996 and determines that he should have filed a return reporting the $3,500 for the year 1991. The son files the 1991 return late and pays tax on the $3,500 income, plus penalty and interest. Taxpayer J may claim a refund for the tax paid (plus interest) on the $3,500 erroneously reported for 1991 even though the statute of limitations otherwise treats this year as closed. This allows the allocation of the $3,500 income away from the father to the son despite the expiration of the limitations period.

PENALTIES

To encourage taxpayers to comply with the Federal tax laws, Congress has enacted numerous penalties. These penalties cover a variety of violations, such as failure to file and pay taxes on a timely basis, negligence in preparing the tax return, and outright fraud. The penalties are usually monetary in nature. However, where the taxpayer goes beyond these civil offenses and purposefully attempts to evade tax, criminal penalties—including jail sentences—may result.

Penalties are referred to by the Internal Revenue Code as "additions to the tax," "additional amounts," and "assessable penalties."[34] All such amounts are treated as additional "tax," to be assessed, collected, and paid in the same manner as regular taxes.[35] Thus, assessment procedures, restrictions on assessment, and the statute of limitations for assessment and collection apply to penalties. Some penalties are computed in the same manner as interest; nevertheless, such penalties are nondeductible since they are considered additional Federal taxes.

---

[34] See §§ 6651 through 6665, §§ 6671 through 6724.

[35] § 6659, and specifically, Reg. § 301.6659-1(a).

The Revenue Reconciliation Act of 1989 restructured and modified the civil tax penalty provisions of the Internal Revenue Code. In general, the changes apply to returns due and actions taken after December 31, 1989. The civil tax penalties are now categorized into four major groups:

1. Delinquency penalties

2. Accuracy-related and fraud penalties

3. Information reporting penalties

4. Protestor, promoter, and preparer penalties

Each of these penalties is discussed below.

DELINQUENCY PENALTIES

For whatever reason, taxpayers may be inclined to postpone the inevitable; that is, the filing of a tax return and the payment of taxes. For those taxpayers who are delinquent in such duties, two penalties exist—the failure-to-file penalty and the failure-to-pay penalty. Both penalties play an integral part in the efficient operation of the Federal tax system.

Failure to File.   A penalty is imposed on a taxpayer for failure to file a tax return by the due date.[36] The penalty is 5 percent of the net tax due for each month or part thereof that the return is late. The net tax due is the amount of tax shown on the return less any amount that is paid by the later of (1) the due date of the return, or (2) the month the penalty is assessed. The total penalty for failure to file may not exceed 25 percent of the net tax due.

The failure-to-file penalty does not apply in several instances. It does not apply where the taxpayer has obtained a proper extension (i.e., a timely filed extension request accompanied by 100% of the estimated tax due), and the return is filed within the extended period. Note, however, that individuals who obtain an extension and properly file their return within the extended period may still be subject to the failure-to-pay penalty discussed below. The failure-to-file penalty also is waived where the failure to file is attributable to reasonable cause (e.g., insufficient postage and other reasons as discussed below).

To encourage taxpayers who owe small amounts of tax to file a tax return, a minimum failure-to-file penalty is imposed. The minimum penalty is the lesser of (1) $100, or (2) 100 percent of the amount of the net tax due. The minimum penalty applies when the return is filed more than 60 days late (e.g., filed after June 14 for the calendar year taxpayer). This penalty is also waived if the failure to file is attributable to reasonable cause.

---

[36]   § 6651(a) and Reg. § 301.6651-1(a).

Example 18. S, a calendar year taxpayer, computed his tax for 1991 and determined that he would receive a refund of $150. He did not file his return claiming his refund until August 3, 1992. No penalty is assessed since the penalty is based on the net amount due, which was zero. Had S owed $150, the normal failure-to-file penalty would have been only $30 (5% × 4 months × $150). However, the minimum penalty of $100 would apply if S had owed $150 since the return was filed more than 60 days late (the lesser of $150 tax due or $100).

Example 19. R, a calendar year taxpayer, determined that her tax liability before prepayments for 1991 was $10,000. Estimated tax payments and withholding during the year totaled $7,000. When April 15, 1992 arrived, R had no money to pay the $3,000 in tax due so she postponed filing until August 3, 1992. The failure-to-file penalty is $600 ($3,000 × 5% × 4 months).

Failure to Pay. When a taxpayer fails to pay the tax owed at the time it is due, a penalty is imposed.[37] The penalty normally is one-half of one percent of the net tax due for each month that the tax is unpaid. In certain situations, however, the rate of penalty is increased to one percent per month. The increased penalty applies if the IRS notifies the taxpayer of its intent to levy on the taxpayer's assets (usually the *fourth* notice sent to the taxpayer requesting payment) or gives notice and demand for payment because the collection of the tax is in jeopardy.

The total penalty for failure to pay the tax when due may not exceed 25 percent of the net tax due. For example, a taxpayer that owes $1,000 on a 1991 tax return that remains unpaid until the year 2004 pays a failure to pay penalty of a maximum of $250. Note that in light of the penalty rate, 0.5 percent per month, 50 months—or more than four years—must pass before the maximum penalty applies. However, other penalties may also be imposed on the taxpayer when there is such a long delinquency, and in addition, interest on the amount owed is charged.

In the case of an individual, the failure-to-pay penalty does not apply if the taxpayer obtains an automatic extension and pays 90 percent of the total tax liability due (before any prepayments or withholding) by the original filing date. In such case, the taxpayer simply remits the balance due with the tax return. If the taxpayer fails to pay 90 percent of the tax by the original due date, the failure-to-pay penalty is imposed and applies on the net tax due. If the taxpayer does pay 90 percent of the tax by the original due date but fails to pay the balance by the extended due date, the failure-to-pay penalty applies on the net tax due.

---

[37] *Ibid.*

When taxpayers fail to file a return, it is not uncommon to find that they also have not paid the tax they owe. In such case, the taxpayer is subject to both the failure-to-file and failure-to-pay penalties. However, to mitigate the harsh effect of this double penalty, the failure-to-file penalty is reduced by the failure-to-pay penalty for any month both penalties apply.[38]

Example 20. Same facts as in *Example 19* above. The failure-to-file and failure-to-pay penalties would be computed as follows:

Failure to pay (0.005 × 4 × $3,000)		$ 60
Gross failure to file (0.05 × 4 × $3,000)	$600	
Reduction for failure to pay........................	− 60	
Failure to file...................................		+ 540
Total failure to file and pay penalties		$600

In effect, a taxpayer who fails to file and pay the balance of the tax owed must pay a penalty of 5 percent a month (4.5% failure-to-file penalty plus 0.5% failure-to-pay penalty). As previously stated, each penalty independently may not exceed a maximum of 25 percent. It also should be noted that in addition to failure-to-file and failure-to-pay penalties, the taxpayer must pay interest on the amount of unpaid taxes starting on the due date of the return. In such case, the taxpayer, in all likelihood, also would be subject to the penalty for failure to pay estimated taxes—in essence, interest starting prior to the due date of the return.[39] Interest and the penalty for underpayment of taxes are discussed below. It should be noted, however, that none of these penalties are imposed if the civil fraud penalty is assessed.

Reasonable Cause. When a taxpayer shows that failure to file a tax return or to pay a tax is due to reasonable cause, no penalty is assessed. The concept of reasonable cause—as it applies to delinquency penalties—is not clearly defined by the Internal Revenue Code or the Regulations. The standard enunciated is that of "ordinary business care and prudence."[40] This obviously allows the IRS and the courts wide latitude in applying these penalties. The taxpayer carries the burden of proving reasonable cause to the District Director by showing that despite the exercise of ordinary business care and prudence, the return could not be filed or the tax paid when due.[41] Reasonable cause includes death or serious illness of the taxpayer,[42] natural disasters or other casualties that destroy the

[38] § 6651(c)(1).

[39] § 6651(d).

[40] § 6651(a) and Reg. § 301.6651-1(c).

[41] *Ibid.*

[42] *Gladys Forbes Est.*, 12 TCM 176 (1953), and *Ward v. Comm.*, 58-2 USTC ¶9922 (D.Ct. Tenn., 1958).

taxpayer's records or assets, unavoidable absence of the taxpayer, and reliance on the advice of an attorney.[43] Reasonable cause does not include reliance on the advice of an accountant,[44] ignorance[45] or forgetfulness[46] of the taxpayer, or nonincapacitating illness.[47] In determining whether there is reasonable cause to abate a penalty, all the facts and circumstances for each case are considered. In addition, the IRS *must* abate any penalties or additions to tax that are a result of the taxpayer's reliance on IRS written advice, when the advice was in response to a specific written request of the taxpayer and the taxpayer provided the IRS with adequate and accurate information.[48]

FAILURE TO PAY ESTIMATED INCOME TAX

Under the "pay-as-you-go" system for collection of taxes, taxpayers are effectively required to estimate their tax for the taxable year and pay the estimated amount in installments during the year. For individuals, these payments normally are made either through the withholding system for salaries and wages or by direct payments of estimated taxes by the taxpayer. For corporate taxpayers, only the latter option is available. A penalty is imposed on anyone who fails to make adequate payments of the estimated taxes. Penalties for individuals, corporations, trusts, and estates are examined below.

Individuals. The *required installment* of tax due from an individual must be paid on April 15, June 15, September 15, and January 15 of the following year. The required installment is 25 percent of the *required annual payment*, which is the lesser of the following:

1. 90 percent of the tax shown on the return before any prepayments

2. 100 percent of the tax shown on the return of the individual for the preceding taxable year

3. The *annualized income installment*[49]

For purposes of these rules, the tax on the return includes the alternative minimum tax as well as any self-employment taxes that may be due.

---

[43] *Tennyson, Jr. v. Comm.*, 76-1 USTC ¶9264 (D.Ct. Ark., 1976).

[44] *Inter-American Life Ins. Co.*, 56 T.C. 497, *aff'd.* (CA-9,1973) 73-1 USTC ¶9127, 31 AFTR2d 73-412, 469 F.2d 697 (CA-9, 1973).

[45] *Stonegate of Blacksburg, Inc.*, 33 TCM 956, T.C. Memo 1974-213.

[46] *Christie Coal and Coke Co., Inc.*, 28 TCM 498, T.C. Memo 1978-404.

[47] *H.W. Pinkham*, 17 TCM 1071, T.C. Memo 1958-216.

[48] § 6404(f).

[49] § 6654.

The effect of these rules is to allow a taxpayer to avoid penalty if quarterly installments are made of either 22.5 percent of the current year's tax or 25 percent of last year's tax. The latter provision permits the taxpayer to base the installment on the prior year's tax even if the tax in such year was zero. However, it should be noted that the required installment cannot be based on the prior year's tax if the preceding year was not a taxable year of 12 months or the individual did not file a return for such year. The annualized income installment is discussed below.

If the taxpayer fails to pay the required installment—in effect 25 percent of the lowest of the three amounts above—a penalty is imposed on the *amount of the underpayment* The underpayment for any required installment is computed as follows:

$$
\begin{array}{ll}
& \underline{\text{Required installment}} \\
- & \underline{\text{Installments paid to that due date including withholding}} \\
= & \underline{\text{Amount of the underpayment}}
\end{array}
$$

The penalty assessed on the underpayment is computed in the same manner as interest, but because it is a penalty the amount paid is not deductible. The penalty is computed as follows:

$$
\begin{array}{ll}
& \underline{\text{Amount of underpayment for period}} \\
\times & \underline{\text{Annual interest rate}} \\
\times & \underline{\text{Period outstanding}} \\
= & \underline{\text{Penalty on underpayment for period}}
\end{array}
$$

The annual interest rate to be applied is the "average predominant prime rate quoted by commercial banks to large business" as determined by the members of the Federal Reserve System. The rate for January 1 through June 30 is the average rate charged for the six-month period running from April 1 through September 30 of the prior year.[50] Similarly, the rate from July 1 through December 31 is the average rate charged for the six-month period running from September 30 of the prior year to March 31 of the current year. The period of time for computing interest begins on the due date of the installment and runs to the earlier of the date the payment is made or the due date of the return (e.g., April 15). For this purpose, withholding is deemed to occur ratably throughout the year regardless of when it was actually made. Payments not made by the due date of the return become subject to the failure-to-pay penalty.

> **Example 21.** During 1991, P, a single taxpayer, paid $750 of estimated tax each installment due date. His employer withheld $1,000 during the year. His tax return, filed April 15, 1992, showed a total tax before prepayments of $15,000. T's tax liability for 1990 was $8,000. The required

---

[50] § 6621.

installment is $2,000 [the *lesser* of $2,000 ($8,000 × 100% × 25%) or $3,375 ($15,000 × 90% × 25%)]. The underpayments and the penalty, assuming a 10% interest rate, are computed as follows:

	4/15/91	6/15/91	9/15/91	1/15/92	Total
Installment required: (25% × $8,000)...	$2,000	$2,000	$2,000	$2,000	$8,000
Less: Amounts paid:					
Estimate..........	− 750	− 750	− 750	− 750	−3,000
Withholding (ratably).........	− 250	− 250	− 250	− 250	−1,000
Underpayment amount...........	$1,000	$1,000	$1,000	$1,000	$4,000
Days outstanding ÷ 365.............	× 365/365	× 304/365	× 212/365	× 90/365	
Rate................	× 10%	× 10%	× 10%	× 10%	
Nondeductible penalty...........	$ 100	$ 83	$ 58	$ 25	$ 266

Example 22.   Same facts as *Example 21* above except P's tax liability for 1990 was $2,800. Since P's installment for each period exceeds $700 (25% of last year's tax of $2,800) no penalty is assessed.

The annualized income installment is determined in two steps. First, the taxpayer must compute the total tax that would be due if income actually received through the month ending before the due date of the installment were annualized. The required installment is 22.5, 45, 67.5, and 90 percent of the annualized tax for each installment, respectively.

Example 23.   Assume the same facts as in *Example 21* above except that P's income and itemized deductions through March consisted of wages of $6,000, self-employment income from commissions of $1,000, and $891.50 of itemized deductions. P's annualized tax for the first period is computed as follows:

Wages..	$ 6,000
+ Self-employment income..................................	+ 1,000
− Self-employment tax deduction: ($1,000 × 92.35% = $923.50 × 15.3% = $141 ÷ 2)....	− 71
= Actual adjusted gross income	$6,929
Annualized adjusted gross income ($6,929 × 4)...	$27,716
− Annualized itemized deductions ($891.50 × 4).............	− 3,566
− Exemption..	− 2,150
= Annualized taxable income................................	$22,000
Tax on annualized income (rounded)........................	$ 3,515
+ Self-employment tax ($1,000 × 92.35% = $923.50 × 15.3% = $141.29 × 4).......................	+ 565
Total tax...	$ 4,080

P's annualized income installment for the first period is $918 ($4,080 × 22.5%). Since this amount is less than the required installment based on last year's tax, P can avoid penalty by paying $918 as determined above.

No underpayment penalty is imposed where the balance of tax after reduction for withholding is $500 or less. In addition, the IRS may waive the underpayment penalty in the event of a casualty or unusual circumstances where it might be incquitable to impose the additional tax. The IRS also may waive the penalty for retired taxpayers who are age 62 or disabled where the underpayment was due to reasonable cause rather than willful neglect.

Corporations. A corporate taxpayer generally avoids penalty for failure to pay estimated taxes if 90 percent of the tax is paid during the year. Specifically, the corporate taxpayer must pay $1/4$ of this amount—22.5 percent of the tax shown on the return—on the fifteenth day of the fourth, sixth, ninth, and twelfth months of the taxable year (April 15, June 15, September 15, and December 15 assuming a calendar year taxpayer).[51] In addition, the penalty is not imposed where the installment for any period is

1. At least 25 percent of the tax shown on the prior year's return; or

2. Equal to or exceeds 90 percent of the tax due for each quarter based on annualized taxable income.

No penalty is imposed on a corporate taxpayer if its tax for any year is less than $500. In addition, the exception related to the prior year (1 above) is available to so-called *large corporations* (i.e., a corporation having taxable income exceeding $1 million in any of the three preceding taxable years) for the first quarter only.

Trusts and Estates. Like individuals and corporations, trusts and estates are required to pay estimated taxes. An estate, however, need not make estimated tax payments for the first two years of its existence. The penalties for trusts and estates are computed in the same manner as individuals.

ACCURACY-RELATED PENALTIES

The Revenue Reconciliation Act of 1989 consolidated several existing penalties into an "accuracy-related" category.[52] The 20 percent accuracy-related penalty now applies to the portion of the tax underpayment that is attributable to negligence or disregard of the rules or regulations, substantial understatement of income tax, substantial valuation misstatement for income tax purposes, substantial

---

[51] § 6655.   [52] § 6662.

overstatement of pension liabilities, or substantial estate or gift valuation understatement. Only one accuracy-related penalty may be imposed on any specific underpayment of tax. The accuracy-related penalty may be imposed in conjunction with the delinquency penalties when the situation so warrants. However, it may not be imposed when a fraud penalty is assessed.[53]

Interest on the accuracy-related penalty runs from the due date of the return (including extensions) until the date the penalty is paid.[54] The accuracy-related penalty as it applies to negligence and to the substantial understatement of income tax is discussed here.

Negligence. The accuracy-related penalty may be imposed for underpayment of taxes due to negligence or disregard of the rules and regulations.[55] The penalty is 20 percent of the portion of the underpayment that is attributable to negligence or disregard of the rules or regulations. "Negligence" includes any failure to make a reasonable attempt to comply with the tax laws, and "disregard" includes any careless, reckless, or intentional disregard.[56]

> **Example 24.** J filed her 1990 return on April 15, 1991. On August 16, 1994, the IRS assessed an additional $10,000 of tax attributable to her failure to report income. The accuracy-related penalty attributable to negligence is $2,000 ($10,000 × 20%). Also, interest is due on both the additional tax and the penalty.

Negligence is often found where the taxpayer fails to report income (e.g., cash receipts), or claims substantial amounts of deductions that are not substantiated (e.g., travel and entertainment) or that are not authorized by the Code. A taxpayer is automatically considered negligent for failure to report *any* type of income for which there was an information return (e.g., Form 1099) filed by the payer. In this case, only the portion of the underpayment of the tax related to the information return is used in computing the negligence penalty.[57]

Negligence also has been found where the taxpayer was lax in keeping books and records,[58] where the taxpayer signed erroneous returns prepared by an accountant without checking them,[59] where the taxpayer lost or failed to keep records,[60] and where the taxpayer filed incomplete tax returns.[61] Where the tax-

---

[53] § 6662(b).

[54] § 6601(e)(2)(B).

[55] § 6662(b)(1).

[56] § 6662(c).

[57] § 6662(a) and (b).

[58] *H.S. Glazer,* 40 TCM 1065, T.C. Memo 1980-37; and *H.G. Sealy,* 39 TCM 827, T.C. Memo 1980-7.

[59] *Mackay,* 11 B.T.A. 569 (1928), Acq.

[60] *Estella Collins,* 9 TCM 14 (1950), and *W.R. McKinley,* 37 TCM 1769, T.C. Memo 1978-428.

[61] *G.C. Lamb,* 32 TCM 305, T.C. Memo 1973-71.

payer had an honest misunderstanding of the facts or the law similar to what an ordinary reasonable person might have, the negligence penalty was not applied.[62] The penalty also was avoided where the taxpayer relied on an accountant's advice regarding an item of a controversial nature.[63]

Substantial Understatement of Income Tax. The accuracy-related penalty may be imposed for underpayment of taxes due to any substantial understatement of income tax.[64] This portion of the accuracy-related penalty is designed to deter taxpayers from taking unreasonable or insupportable positions on their tax returns with the hope that they will never be audited. The penalty is 20 percent of the portion of the underpayment that is attributable to the substantial understatement of income tax. The tax liability is considered to be substantially understated when the amount of the understatement is more than the greater of (1) 10 percent of the correct tax, or (2) $5,000.[65] The penalty may be totally or partially waived by the IRS when the taxpayer has substantial authority for the position taken on the return or the item is disclosed on the return.

Reasonable Cause. The accuracy-related penalty may be waived either totally or partially if the taxpayer can show that he or she had reasonable support *and* acted in good faith with respect to the position taken on the return.[66]

FRAUD PENALTIES

Civil Fraud Penalty. A penalty equal to 75 percent of the amount of underpayment attributable to fraud is imposed when the taxpayer is found to have been fraudulent. However, if the IRS establishes that any portion of an underpayment is attributable to fraud, then the penalty applies to the *entire* underpayment, except for any portion that the taxpayer establishes is *not* attributable to fraud.[67]

As mentioned above, when the fraud penalty is assessed, no accuracy-related penalty is assessed on the same portion of the underpayment.[68] However, if the failure to file a return is shown to be fraudulent, then the failure-to-file penalty is tripled.[69] The same reasonable cause exception that applies to the accuracy-related penalty applies to the civil fraud penalty.[70]

[62] *C.B. Baker*, 40 TCM 983, T.C. Memo 1980-319; and *E.G. Harris*, 36 TCM 1426, T.C. Memo 1977-385.

[63] *R. Wolman*, 34 TCM 1143, T.C. Memo 1975-266.

[64] § 6662(b)(2).

[65] § 6662(d)(1)(A).

[66] § 6664(c)(1).

[67] § 6663.

[68] § 6662(b).

[69] § 6651(f).

[70] § 6664(c)(1).

The IRS carries the burden to prove fraud against a taxpayer by a preponderance of the evidence.[71] Civil fraud has not been clearly defined, but requires more than negligent acts or omissions by the taxpayer. In determining the presence of fraud, all facts and circumstances of the case are considered. Fraud has been found where the taxpayer made misleading statements during the course of an examination,[72] where the taxpayer changed a book entry to understate income,[73] where the taxpayer treated personal expenses as business expenses,[74] and where the taxpayer concealed income by having other persons report the income.[75] Fraud was not found where the taxpayer failed to report a large amount of gross income because of an error and where no intent to commit fraud existed,[76] where the taxpayer with little business knowledge signed false returns prepared by his partner,[77] and where the taxpayer claimed a deduction that he or she honestly but erroneously believed to be permitted.[78] Before assessing the fraud penalty, the courts must find an "intent to defraud." This intent may be evidenced by an actual desire by the taxpayer to commit fraud or by the taxpayer's reckless disregard of the facts and circumstances.

Criminal Fraud Penalties.   The law imposes not only civil penalties for fraud, but also criminal penalties.[79] A civil fraud offense must be proven by a preponderance of the evidence, and the penalty is based on the amount of tax or interest owed. In contrast, a criminal penalty must be proven beyond a reasonable doubt, and the penalty is measured by the severity of the fraud as opposed to the amount of tax underpaid. The penalties imposed for criminal fraud are the most severe imposed by the Code.

---

[71] See § 7454(a). Fraud is not presumed, and a finding of fraud by the IRS does not create a presumption that the taxpayer committed fraud. The IRS must prove taxpayer fraud in all cases where it is alleged. See *A. Windsberg*, 37 TCM 455, T.C. Memo 1978-1.

[72] *Herrald, Inc.*, 35 TCM 1129, T.C. Memo 1976-258.

[73] *K Haddad*, 19 TCM 599, T.C. Memo 1960-112.

[74] *Hicks Co., Inc.* 73-1 USTC ¶9109, 31 AFTR2d 73-382, 470 F.2d 870 (CA-1, 1973).

[75] *A.S. Hershenson*, 21 TCM 1204, T.C. Memo 1962-228.

[76] *U.S. v. Bank of Powers*, 39-2 USTC ¶9665, 26 AFTR 1115 (D.Ct. Ore., 1939), appeal dismissed, 23 AFTR 839, 106 F.2d 1019 (1939).

[77] *F.A. Herman*, 18 TCM 569, T.C. Memo 1959-129.

[78] *M. Bailey*, 29 TCM 272, T.C. Memo 1970-64, *aff'd. per curiam*, 71-1 USTC ¶9359, 27 AFTR2d 71-1210, 439 F.2d 723 (CA-6, 1971), cert. den., 404 U.S. 867.

[79] § 7201, et. seq.

Exhibit 17-6
Criminal Offenses and Penalties

Offense	Maximum Penalty	Source
1. Willful attempt to evade or defeat any tax	$100,000 fine[a] or five years imprisonment or both	§ 7201
2. Willful failure to collect or truthfully account for and pay over any tax	$10,000 fine or five years imprisonment or both	§ 7202
3. Willful failure to pay a tax or an estimated tax, to make a required return, to keep required records or to supply required information	$25,000 fine[b] or one year imprisonment or both	§ 7203
4. Willfully furnishing an employee with a false statement regarding tax withholdings on wages	$1,000 fine or one year imprisonment or both	§ 7204
5. Making a declaration under penalty of perjury not believed by the maker to be true, preparing or assisting in preparation of fraudulent returns or other documents, or concealing goods or property in respect of any tax	$100,000 fine[a] or three years imprisonment or both	§ 7206

[a] In the case of a corporate taxpayer, no imprisonment and a $500,000 fine
[b] In the case of a corporate taxpayer, no imprisonment and a $100,000 fine

---

A criminal offense of fraud requires that the taxpayer *willfully* attempt to evade or defeat the tax.[80] A taxpayer may be convicted of a misdemeanor or a felony and may be subject to fines or imprisonment or both, depending on the degree of fraud. The most common offenses and highest penalties appear in Exhibit 17-6. The opinion of the IRS weighs heavily in the decision of whether to prosecute a taxpayer for criminal fraud, and if so, how much penalty to seek. The decision to prosecute is ultimately made by the Department of Justice.

A criminal penalty may be imposed for *willful* failure to pay an estimated tax, as shown in Exhibit 17-6.[81] As with other criminal offenses, the penalty is not based on the amount of tax owed, but on the severity of the offense.

---

[80] Ibid.

[81] § 7203.

INFORMATION REPORTING PENALTIES

To ensure taxpayers are reporting all of the income they receive, Congress requires those who make certain payments to taxpayers to file information returns such as the well-known Forms W-2 and 1099. This information is then matched against what taxpayers actually show on their returns to determine if all income has been properly reported. Consistent with its goal to match all taxpayer returns and information returns, Congress imposes a penalty for failure to file information returns as well as a penalty for failure to provide copies of such returns to the persons to whom they relate. For many years, the penalty for failure to file information returns was quite modest, $1 per return up to $1,000, and did little to encourage taxpayers to comply. In fact, in 1979 it was estimated that fewer than 60 percent of the required information returns for nonemployee compensation were filed. Over the past several years, this penalty has increased significantly. The penalty is currently $50 for each failure to file correct information returns ($250,000 annual maximum),[82] $50 for each failure to furnish a correct information return to a taxpayer ($100,000 annual maximum),[83] and $50 for each failure to comply with any other information reporting requirements ($100,000 annual maximum).[84] Each of these penalties also requires that the information returns be filed with the IRS or furnished to the taxpayer on or before the required date. If the failure to file or failure to furnish a correct information return is due to the taxpayer's intentional disregard, then the penalty is $100 per failure (with no maximum penalty).[85] Information returns include such forms as those for interest (Form 1099-INT), dividends (Form 1099-DIV), wage payments (Form W-2), withholding of tax on interest and dividends, compensation for services and direct sales, rental and other business payments in excess of $600, and other items peculiar to specialized industries.[86] Criminal penalties also apply for the *willful* failure to file informational returns or the *willful* making of falsified statements regarding wage withholdings, as described in Exhibit 17-6.[87]

A penalty of $50 per partner is imposed for every month that a partnership return is not filed.[88] This penalty is assessed against the partnership itself, but the individual partners are ultimately liable for the penalty to the extent they are responsible for partnership debts.

---

[82] § 6721(a)(1).

[83] § 6722(a).

[84] § 6723.

[85] §§ 6721(e) and 6722(c).

[86] § 6724(d).

[87] See §§ 7203 and 7204 for criminal penalties regarding informational returns.

[88] § 6698.

A heavier penalty applies to taxpayers for making statements that result in reduced withholdings on wages when no reasonable basis for such statement exists.[89] The penalty imposed is $500 for each statement in civil cases. Where such a statement is *willfully* made, a criminal penalty of $1,000 (or one year imprisonment, or both) per occurrence also may be imposed.[90] The goal of this penalty is to encourage taxpayer compliance with the wage-withholding system. The penalty is applied to an understatement by the taxpayer of wages upon which withholding is based, or an overstatement of the amount of itemized deductions a taxpayer is entitled to take for the purpose of claiming exemptions on withholding. Such a misstatement might be made in the taxpayer's Form W-4, Employee's Withholding Allowance Certificate, which is typically executed when an employee is hired.

OTHER PENALTIES

Frivolous Return Penalty. In recent years, high rates, complexity, and overall dissatisfaction with the system have spawned a growing number of taxpayers who resent the payment of taxes. Taxpayers who actively engage in protest activities might claim 99 dependents, attach statements to their return indicating that they will not pay because the tax is unconstitutional, or submit forms that are illegible and cannot be processed. A penalty now exists for taxpayers who maintain a frivolous position on a return. A civil penalty of $500 may be imposed on any taxpayer that files a return with insufficient data to determine the correctness of the tax liability or a return that obviously has a substantially incorrect tax liability.[91] It must be shown that the taxpayer has the intent to assume a frivolous position or to delay or impede the administration of the income tax laws.[92] Imposition of this penalty does not preclude the levy of any other penalty that otherwise applies.

Aiding and Abetting Penalty. When a person aids or abets the preparation of a false document, a civil penalty of $1,000 may be imposed on that person for each document or return that contains an understatement of tax liability.[93] Only one penalty may be imposed on a person for each taxable event or taxable period relating to the understatement of a tax liability. Thus, if a person aids only one taxpayer in understating the tax liability in a return or a document, only one penalty may be imposed on that person for each taxable event or taxable period involved, regardless of how many understated returns or documents were prepared. More than one penalty may be imposed on a person when there is

---

[89] § 6682 and Reg. § 301.6682-1.

[90] § 7205.

[91] § 6702.

[92] *Ibid.*

[93] § 6701.

more than one taxable event involved, the understatement occurs in more than one period, or the tax liability of more than one taxpayer is understated. This penalty may be supplemented by criminal penalties for *willful* attempts to prepare or assist in preparation of fraudulent returns, as shown in Exhibit 17-6, or any other penalty except the return preparer penalty.

INTERACTION OF CIVIL PENALTIES

As mentioned previously, it is possible for certain civil penalties to be imposed on the same amount of tax underpayment as other civil penalties. However, in some situations Congress has specifically limited the multiple application of penalties. The interaction of the delinquency, accuracy-related, fraud, and several other civil penalties is shown in Exhibit 17-7.

PREPARER PENALTIES

The preparer of income tax returns is subject to several penalties regarding various acts or omissions that may occur in the preparation of a tax return or in tax practice. These penalties are discussed in greater detail in the "Tax Practice" section of this chapter.

DEPENDENTS' IDENTIFICATION NUMBERS

The IRS has long been plagued by taxpayers who claim exemptions for persons who do not exist. To deter taxpayers from making such claims, the law requires that the taxpayer who claims an exemption for a dependent who is at least one year old during the tax year *must* report the dependent's taxpayer identification number on his or her return.[94] Normally, such number is the dependent's Social Security number or other taxpayer identification number obtained from the IRS. Failure to report such number (or correct number) results in an automatic penalty of $5 per number.[95]

INTEREST

The Federal government generally charges a taxpayer interest whenever the assessed tax is not paid in a timely manner. Although the interest charge obviously compensates the government for use of funds rightfully theirs, it serves what perhaps is a more important purpose. The interest charge eliminates some of the incentive for the taxpayer either to delay payment of taxes or to avoid payment of taxes by taking aggressive positions on returns.

---

[94]　§ 6109(e).　　　　　　　　　　　[95]　§ 6676(e).

Exhibit 17-7
Interaction of Civil Penalties

Penalty	Source	Penalty Based Upon:	Interaction with Other Penalties
Delinquency penalties			Can be imposed in conjunction with other types of penalties
Failure-to-file	§ 6651(a)	Net amount of tax due (generally, the rate is 5% per month or portion of a month; maximum 25%)	Reduced by failure-to-pay penalty when failure-to-file and failure-to-pay penalties run concurrently
Failure-to-pay	§ 6651(a)	Net amount of tax due (generally, the rate is 1/2% per month or portion of a month; maximum 25%	
Estimated tax penalty	§ 6654	Amount of the underpayment for the period of the underpayment (in general, 90% of the total tax is required to be paid in installments during the year; the penalty rate varies, similar to the interest rate)	
Accuracy-related penalties	§ 6662	Amount of the underpayment attributable to the particular accuracy-related penalty (generally, rate is 20%)	Only one accuracy-related penalty may be imposed on any specific underpayment of tax; can be imposed in conjunction with delinquency penalties; and cannot be imposed in same portion of underpayment on which fraud penalty is imposed
Negligence or disregard of rules or regulations			
Substantial understatement of tax			
Substantial valuation misstatement of income tax			
Substantial overstatement of pension liabilities			
Substantial estate or gift tax valuation understatement			
Civil fraud penalty	§ 6663	Amount of the underpayment attributable to fraud (generally, rate is 75%)	When fraud penalty is assessed, no accuracy-related penalties may be assessed on the same portion of the underpayment
Frivolous return penalty	§ 6702	Flat penalty of $500	Can be imposed in conjunction with any other penalties
Aiding & abetting penalty	§ 6701	Flat penalty of $1,000; $10,000 if related to the tax liability of a corporation	May be supplemented by criminal penalties for willful attempts to prepare or assist in preparation of fraudulent return(s), OR any other penalty EXCEPT the return preparer penalty

To provide equitable treatment between the government and taxpayers, the Code also provides for interest when there has been an overpayment of tax. Thus, taxpayers that have paid more tax than the amount owed for a given period are compensated.

Differential Rate of Interest.   Historically, the interest rate charged on underpayments has been substantially less than the market rate of interest. For example, during 1980 the tax interest rate was 12 percent while the average prime rate was 15.27 percent. In 1981 Congress believed that this disparity between tax and market rates of interest was leading to the increasing number and amount of delinquent accounts. For this reason, action has been taken over the years to bring tax interest rates more in line with commercial practices.[96] Prior to the Tax Reform Act of 1986, the rate of interest charged on underpayments as well as overpayments of tax was the same, generally the prime rate. However, in 1986 Congress took a hint from commercial lenders and noted that financial institutions seldom borrow and lend money at the same rate. Moreover, Congress wanted to ensure that its practices did not encourage taxpayers to delay paying taxes as long as possible to take advantage of an excessively low rate, or overpay to take advantage of an excessively high rate. Based on this view, Congress created a one percent differential between these two rates.

The interest rate charged on underpayments is three points *over* the Federal short-term rate, while the rate paid on overpayments is two points over such rate.[97] These rates are updated and published for each calendar quarter. The rate is based on the average market yield of short-term government obligations. This new approach, coupled with the fact that the deduction for interest on tax deficiencies will no longer be available after 1990, should foster earlier payment of potential tax deficiencies.

Underpayments.   Interest is charged on the amount of unpaid taxes, including deficiencies and penalties, from the payment due date to the date of receipt by the IRS.[98] The due date for payment is considered to be the last date prescribed for payment of the tax without regard for any extension of time,[99] March 15 and April 15 for calendar year corporations and individuals, respectively.

Interest on a deficiency or other tax underpayment is computed and charged until the time of notice and demand for payment. The notice and demand for taxes to be paid is not the "90-day letter," but rather it is a formal written demand by the IRS for payment, made within 60 days after an assessment of tax.[100] If a taxpayer does not pay the amount due within 10 days after the date of the

---

[96]   § 6621 and Reg. § 301.6621-1.

[97]   § 6621(a)(1). For example, the interest rates in effect at the time of this writing are (1) 11 percent for underpayments, and (2) 10 percent for overpayments.

[98]   § 6601(a) and Reg. § 301.6601-1.

[99]   § 6601(b)(1) and Reg. § 301.6601-1.

[100]   §§ 6601(e)(1) and 6303 and Reg. § 301.6303-1.

notice, then interest is computed and charged until the actual payment is made. However, if the taxpayer pays the amount due within 10 days of the date of the notice and demand, then no interest is charged after the date of the notice.[101]

No interest is charged on penalties if they are paid within 10 days of notice and demand. If not paid by that time, interest is imposed only from the date of notice and demand.[102]

Prior to 1983, interest was not charged on the portion of an amount owed that represented interest. Since 1982, however, interest is compounded daily under specific statutory direction.[103] As a result, the extra burden of "interest on interest" will apply until the amount owed is paid.[104]

Form 870 and Interest. As described in an earlier section, Form 870 (Waiver of Restrictions on Assessment and Collection of Deficiency in Tax) operates as an agreement between the taxpayer and the IRS to settle a dispute over a proposed deficiency. If the taxpayer signs Form 870, interest stops accruing on the deficiency 30 days after the form is filed.[105] At any time after Form 870 is filed, the IRS may send a notice for the amount of tax deficiency plus penalties and interest. If this notice is sent more than 30 days after Form 870 is filed, no interest accrues from the end of the 30-day period until the date of the notice.[106]

Overpayments. An overpayment of tax refunded 45 days within the later of the date the return is filed or the due date of the return does not accrue interest.[107] When an overpayment arises because of a carryback (e.g., carryback of a net operating loss, capital loss, or credit), interest begins to accrue on the later of the due date of the return in which the carryback arose or the date that the claim for the refund is filed. However, the 45-day rule still applies in this case and the interest is not paid on such overpayment if the refund is made within 45 days of the appropriate date.[108]

When a refund is claimed on an overpayment, interest accrues from the date of the overpayment to a date not more than 30 days before the refund check is issued.[109] A taxpayer may request that the overpayment be credited to a subsequent tax period liability, instead of taking payment in a check. In such event, the interest runs from the date of the overpayment to the due date of the amount against which the credit is taken.[110]

---

[101] § 6601(e) and Reg. § 301.6601-1.

[102] *Ibid.*

[103] § 6622.

[104] *Ibid.*

[105] § 6601(c) and Reg. § 301.6601-1.

[106] *Ibid.*

[107] §§ 6611(a) and (e), and Reg. § 301.6611-1.

[108] § 6611(f) and Reg. § 301.6611-1

[109] § 6611(b) and Reg. § 301.6611-1.

[110] *Ibid.*

TAX PRACTICE

Individuals involved in preparing tax returns, representing taxpayers in tax matters before the IRS, and providing other tax-related services must be aware of the various rules governing their conduct. Failure to follow these rules may result in penalty or loss of the right to engage in tax practice. The rules governing tax practice are contained primarily in *Treasury Circular Number 230* and various provisions of the Code. In addition, CPAs and attorneys engaged in tax practice also must follow the rules of conduct imposed by their professional organizations, the American Institute of Certified Public Accountants (AICPA) and the American Bar Association.

PRACTICE BEFORE THE IRS: TREASURY CIRCULAR 230

Circular 230 prescribes the standards that an individual must satisfy to be eligible to practice before the IRS. *Practice before the IRS* does not include the preparation of a tax return, the appearance as a witness for the taxpayer, or the furnishing of information at the request of the Service. Rather, the term *practice* comprehends all matters connected with presentations made to the Service regarding the client's rights, privileges, or liabilities under the law. In essence, satisfying the requirements of Circular 230 enables the practitioner to represent a client before the Service. As suggested above, however, individuals who merely prepare returns or give advice related to tax matters are not subject to the rules of Circular 230. As explained within, various provisions of the Code control the conduct of these persons.

Circular 230 identifies three categories of individuals that may practice before the IRS: attorneys, Certified Public Accountants, and enrolled agents. An enrolled agent is an individual who passes a written examination administered by the IRS, if the individual has not engaged in conduct that would justify suspension or disbarment of an attorney or CPA, or an enrolled agent.[111] An individual that is not enrolled or otherwise admitted to practice before the IRS may practice in the following circumstances.

1. An individual may represent himself or herself, his or her employer, a partnership of which he or she is a member or full-time employee, or may represent without compensation a member of his or her immediate family.

2. A corporation, trust, estate, association, or organized group may be represented by its officers or regular full-time employees.

---

[111]   31 C.F.R. § 10.3-4 (1986). This citation refers to Title 31 of the Code of Federal Regulations, Part 10, Sections 3 and 4.

3. Trusts, receiverships, guardianships, or estates may be represented by their trustees, receivers, guardians, administrators, executors, or their regular full-time employees.

4. Any governmental unit, agency, or authority may be represented by an officer or regular employee in the course of his or her official duties.

5. Enrollment is not required for representation outside of the United States before personnel of the IRS.

6. A person who is not under disbarment or suspension from practice before the IRS or other practice of his or her profession and who signs a return for a taxpayer may appear without enrollment as the taxpayer's representative.[112]

Circular 230 also provides rules that set forth a standard of conduct for professionals who practice before the IRS. The following are duties and restrictions relating to the practice of attorneys, CPAs, or enrolled agents.

1. No practitioner shall neglect or refuse to submit records or information promptly in any matter before the IRS, upon proper and lawful request by an officer or employee of the IRS, unless the individual refusing to submit the records or information believes in good faith or on reasonable grounds that the records or information is privileged or that the request for the same is of doubtful legality.[113]

2. A practitioner that practices before the IRS must, when requested, provide information about a violation of the Regulations concerning practice by any person and must also testify about such information in a disbarment or suspension proceeding, unless he or she believes in good faith and on reasonable grounds that such information is privileged or that the request is of doubtful legality.[114]

3. A practitioner must advise a client of any noncompliance, error, or omission he or she knows of with respect to any return or document that the client is required to file.[115]

---

[112] 31 C.F.R. § 10.7 (1986).

[113] C.F.R. § 10.20(a)(1986). *U.S. v. Arthur Young & Co.*, 84-1 USTC ¶9305, 53 AFTR2d 84-866, 104 S. Ct. 1495 (USSC, 1984), where the U.S. Supreme Court held that accountant client privilege does not bar enforcement of an IRS summons for the workpapers prepared by an independent CPA during an audit of its client's finances.

[114] 31 C.F.R. § 10.20(b)(1986).

[115] 31 C.F.R. § 10.21 (1986).

4. A practitioner must exercise due diligence

    a. In preparing, assisting in preparation, approving, and filing of documents relating to the IRS;

    b. In determining the correctness of oral and written representation that he or she makes to the IRS; and

    c. In determining the correctness of oral and written representations that he or she makes to clients regarding matters relating to the IRS.[116]

5. No practitioner may unreasonably delay the disposition of any matter before the IRS.[117]

6. No practitioner may charge a client an unconscionable fee for representation.[118]

7. No practitioner may represent conflicting interests in his or her practice except by express consent of the interested parties after full disclosure is made.[119]

8. No practitioner may engage in the practice of using a form of public communication that contains a false, fraudulent, misleading, deceptive, unduly influencing, coercive, or unfair statement of claim. This includes, but is not limited to, statements pertaining to the quality of services rendered unless the statement can be verified by facts, claims of special expertise, and statements or suggestions that the ingenuity or prior record of the practitioner, rather than the merit of the matter, are principal factors likely to determine the result of the matter.

9. No practitioner may engage in direct or indirect, uninvited solicitation of employment regarding tax matters. Solicitation includes, but is not limited to, in-person contacts, telephone communications, and personal mailings designed specifically for the recipient. Solicitation does not include seeking new business from an existing or former client in a related matter, or solicitation by mailings where the contents are designed for the general public.[120]

TAX RETURN PREPARATION

No laws or regulations preclude any individual from becoming a tax return preparer, regardless of the individual's educational background, degree of competence, or experience. An *income tax return preparer* is defined as a person that prepares for compensation, or employs a person to prepare for compensation, any

---

[116] 31 C.F.R. § 10.22 (1986).

[117] 31 C.F.R. § 10.23 (1986).

[118] 31 C.F.R. § 10.28 (1986).

[119] 31 C.F.R. § 10.29 (1986).

[120] 31 C.F.R. § 10.30 (1986).

return or claim for refund regarding income tax. This includes the preparation of a substantial portion of the return or refund claim.[121] Various rules require certain items to be disclosed and impose an ethical standard on income tax return preparers. Many penalties may be imposed by the IRS for noncompliance by preparers, in addition to the power of the IRS to obtain injunctive relief in court to stop a preparer from performing certain unauthorized acts.[122] The penalties include the following:

1. $1,000 per return or claim for refund where the preparer willfully attempts to understate the liability of the taxpayer or where the preparer understates the taxpayer's liability by reckless or intentional disregard of the rules or regulations[123]

2. $250 per return or claim for refund where the preparer understates the liability of the taxpayer and the understatement is due to an unrealistic undisclosed or frivolous position of which the preparer knew (or reasonably should have known).[124] If there was reasonable cause for the understatement and the preparer acted in good faith, the penalty may be waived

3. $500 per occurrence if the preparer endorses or otherwise negotiates a check made in respect of income taxes and issued to the taxpayer[125]

4. $50 per occurrence if the preparer fails to furnish a copy of the return to the taxpayer, unless it is shown that such failure is due to reasonable cause and not willful neglect[126]

5. $50 per occurrence if the preparer fails to sign a return, where the preparer is required by regulation to sign the return, unless it is shown that such failure is due to reasonable cause and not willful neglect[127]

6. $50 per occurrence if the preparer fails to furnish an identifying number where the preparer is also required to sign the return, unless it is shown that such failure is due to reasonable cause and not willful neglect[128]

7. $50 per occurrence if the preparer fails to maintain a copy of a return, or retain a record of the return available for inspection, unless it is shown that such failure is due to reasonable cause and not willful neglect[129]

[121] § 7701(a)(36). Reg. § 301.7701-15 defines more clearly the terms "income tax return preparer," "substantial portion," and "return and claim for refund."

[122] § 7407(a).

[123] § 6694(b).

[124] § 6694(a).

[125] § 6695(f) and Reg. § 1.6695-(f).

[126] § 6695(a) and Reg. § 1.6695-1(a).

[127] § 6695(b) and Reg. § 1.6695-1(b).

[128] § 6695(c) and Reg. § 1.6695-1(c).

[129] § 6695(d) and Reg. § 1.6695-1(d).

8. $50 per occurrence where a preparer fails to make available and maintain a list of the preparer's employees during a return period, plus $50 for each failure to record a required item in the record, unless it is shown that such failure is due to reasonable cause and not willful neglect[130]

9. $250 per occurrence where a preparer either discloses information connected to the preparation of a tax return or uses the information for anything other than the preparation of a tax return.[131]

A noteworthy civil penalty imposed by statute allows the taxpayer to bring a civil action (i.e., a law suit) against the United States or a return preparer where a Federal government employee or the return preparer knowingly or negligently discloses unauthorized information regarding the taxpayer or the taxpayer's return.[132] The law provides that if such unauthorized disclosure occurs, the culpable party must pay the litigation costs plus the greater of (a) $1,000, or (b) actual or punitive damages. Unauthorized disclosures include acts whereby a Federal employee or a return preparer discloses a return or return information obtained in the preparation, review, or administration of the return to parties outside those designated as authorized.[133] Examples of authorized parties include

1. Persons designated by the taxpayer to receive return information

2. State tax officials

3. Persons having a material interest, such as a taxpayer's spouse regarding an individual return, a partner regarding a partnership return, or a shareholder or officer regarding a corporation return

4. Committees of Congress or the President of the United States

5. Federal officers and employees involved in tax administration

6. Certain nontax administration personnel of the Federal government, including criminal investigators, the Department of Commerce, and the Federal Trade Commission[134]

Statutes of this type which provide for civil actions and impose punitive damages are indeed rare. This indicates a special concern by the Federal government to curb abuse in this area and tighten confidentiality surrounding this information.

---

[130] § 6695(e) and Reg. § 1.6695-1(e).

[131] § 6713.

[132] § 7431.

[133] Confidentiality and disclosure of returns and return information is covered by § 6103.

[134] Ibid.

The above penalties are intended to regulate the practices of income tax return preparers for compensation. These penalties are civil in nature. Criminal penalties include the following:

1. $10,000 or three years imprisonment, or both, for willfully making fraudulent understatements where the preparer aids or assists in the preparation of the return or document[135]

2. $10,000 or one year imprisonment, or both, for willful disclosure of a fraudulent document by the preparer to the IRS[136]

3. $1,000 or one year imprisonment, or both, for improper disclosure by a preparer of information used in preparation of a return[137]

It is evident that criminal transgressions involve more severe penalties than civil infractions. In any event, all penalties indicate a desire by the Federal government and the IRS to motivate those in a position of trust (i.e., preparers) to exercise a high standard of care, and to sanction certain failures to maintain that standard.

CODES OF PROFESSIONAL CONDUCT

In addition to the rules of practice prescribed by the Code and Treasury Circular 230, CPAs and attorneys involved in tax practice must also abide by the additional rules of conduct imposed by their organizations—the American Institute of Certified Public Accountants and the American Bar Association. Each of these professional organizations has a code of professional ethics for its members. Failure to comply with the applicable rules may result in the member's suspension or expulsion from the organization.

Ethical codes for attorneys and CPAs have a great deal in common with the rules set forth in Circular 230 of the IRS. A professional code is written more broadly and does not necessarily cover the same material as Circular 230. Where the ethical code and Circular 230 coincide on subject matter, the professional must follow the rule that imposes the higher standard.

AICPA Statements on Responsibilities in Tax Practice. The general rules of conduct prescribed by the AICPA concern such matters as independence, integrity and objectivity, advertising, contingent fees, and responsibilities of the accountant when undertaking an engagement—but none that relate specifically to tax practice. Acknowledging that individuals engaged in tax practice have ethical concerns beyond those covered in the general rules of conduct, the AICPA began issuing *Statements on Responsibilities in Tax Practice* in 1964.

---

[135] § 7206.

[136] § 7207.

[137] § 7216.

In 1988, the AICPA issued revised Statements on Responsibilities in Tax Practice in response to changes in the tax laws and the increasing importance of tax practice to CPAs. The new statements are advisory in nature, and are intended to provide guidance and clarification as to the accountant's responsibilities in various aspects of tax practice.[138] The eight statements are summarized below:

1. The CPA should not recommend to a client that a position be taken or prepare a return with a position taken unless the CPA has a *good faith belief* that the position has a realistic possibility of being sustained administratively or judicially on its merits if challenged. Even if the CPA feels that the position does not meet the good faith belief standard, the position may be taken on a return as long as it is not frivolous and is adequately disclosed. The client should be advised of potential penalties and whether the opportunity to avoid the penalties exists through disclosure. The CPA should not recommend a position that exploits the audit selection process or has no merits. The CPA has both the right and the responsibility to be an advocate for the client if the above standards are met.[139]

2. When there are questions on a return that have not been answered, the CPA should make a reasonable effort to obtain appropriate answers from the client and provide the answers to the questions on the return. The significance of the question in terms of the information's effect on taxable income or loss and tax liability may be considered in determining whether the answer to a question may be omitted. However, omission of an answer is not justified simply because the answer may prove to be disadvantageous to the client.[140]

3. The CPA ordinarily may rely on information provided by the client or a third party in preparing a return and is not required to examine or review documents or other evidence supporting client information in order to sign the return. The CPA should encourage the client to provide supporting data where appropriate. When preparing the current return, the CPA should make use of returns from prior years wherever feasible. The CPA cannot ignore the implications of information furnished or information known by the CPA, and is required to make reasonable inquiries where information as presented appears to be incomplete or incorrect.[141]

---

[138] American Institute of Certified Public Accountants, Statements on Responsibilities in Tax Practice (1988 revision), Introduction.

[139] *Ibid*, No. 1

[140] *Ibid*, No. 2

[141] *Ibid*, No. 3

4. A CPA may prepare returns involving the use of estimates if such use is generally acceptable and does not conflict with the Internal Revenue Code, or if under the circumstances, exact data cannot be obtained in a practical manner. When estimates are used, they should be presented in such a manner as to avoid the implication of greater accuracy than that which exists. The CPA should be satisfied that estimated amounts are not unreasonable under the circumstances.[142]

5. A CPA may recommend a tax return position that differs from the way an item was previously treated in an IRS examination, IRS appeals conference, or a court decision for that taxpayer, unless the taxpayer is bound to a specific treatment for the item in the later year (such as by a formal closing agreement). The CPA should still follow the *good faith belief* standard in recommending tax return positions, discussed above.[143]

6. A CPA should advise the client promptly upon learning of an error in a previously filed return, or upon learning of a client's failure to file a required return. The advice of the CPA may be oral, and should include a recommendation of the measures to be taken. The CPA is not obliged to inform the IRS and may not do so without the permission of the client, except where required by law. If the error in a prior year might cause a material understatement of tax liability, the CPA may not be able to prepare the current year return. This is especially the case where an error in a prior year has carryover potential.[144]

7. When the CPA represents a client in an administrative proceeding regarding a return with an error known to the CPA that has resulted or may result in more than an insignificant effect on the client's tax liability, the CPA should request permission from the client to disclose the error to the IRS. Absent such permission, the CPA should consider withdrawing from the engagement.[145]

---

[142] *Ibid*, No. 4

[143] *Ibid*, No. 5

[144] *Ibid*, No. 6

[145] *Ibid*, No. 7

8. In providing tax advice to a client, the CPA must use judgment to ensure that the advice reflects professional competence and appropriately serves the client's needs. No standard format or guidelines can be established to cover all situations and circumstances involving written or oral advice. The CPA may communicate with the client when subsequent developments affect advice previously provided with respect to significant matters. However, the CPA cannot be expected to have assumed responsibility for initiating such communication except while assisting the client in implementing procedures or plans associated with the advice provided. The CPA may undertake this obligation by specific agreement with his or her client.[146]

The CPA must look to the ethical standards of the accounting profession as a guideline for the level of performance and standard of care required in tax practice today. The *good faith belief* standard discussed in Statement No. 1 above relates to all advice provided by the CPA to the client on tax return positions. This applies not only as a general rule, but also specifically to the above Statements.

---

[146] *Ibid*, No. 8

PROBLEM MATERIALS

DISCUSSION QUESTIONS

17-1 *Self-Assessment and Voluntary Compliance.*   The Federal income tax system is based on the concepts of self-assessment and voluntary compliance. Describe how these concepts arc applied in the Federal income tax system and discuss how they do or do not appear in other tax systems.

17-2 *Selection of Returns for Audit.*   It is known that many factors are considered by the IRS in deciding whether or not to select a return for audit. List five or more factors and briefly discuss why each factor has importance in the return selection process.

17-3 *Return Selection and Audits.*   Individual taxpayer X's income tax return has been selected for audit because the amount of mortgage interest and contributions deducted by X appear excessive in light of X's gross income. Corporate taxpayer A's income tax return has been selected for audit by use of the Taxpayer Compliance Measurement Program (TCMP).

    a. Where will each audit most likely be conducted?
    b. How extensive will each audit probably be? Why?
    c. Who will conduct each audit?

17-4 *Items Indicating Significant Tax Error.*   Listed below are several items which might appear on a return. Each item may or may not suggest that a significant tax error on the return is probable. Evaluate each item as to whether it invites (or does not invite) closer scrutiny by the IRS.

    a. An individual taxpayer files Form 1040 but does not include Schedule B, Interest and Dividend Incomes. The taxpayer reports interest income of $425 on the Form 1040. (Form 1040 instructs the taxpayer to attach Schedule B if interest income equals or exceeds $400.)
    b. Same as (a) except the individual reports interest income of $10,000 on Form 1040.
    c. A self-employed taxpayer shows on her return gross income in the amount of $500,000 and taxable income of $50,000.
    d. A medical doctor reports gross income of $2,500 for a taxable year.
    e. A real estate broker who works out of his home deducts a home office expense, indicating that the percentage used to arrive at the deduction is based on the use of one room in the house out of seven rooms. The taxpayer also claims exemptions for cleven children.
    f. A taxpayer who works as a neighborhood ice cream salesperson reports gross income of $5,000 for the tax year.
    g. An individual taxpayer with gross income of $20,000, all from earnings as a factory worker, claims deductions in the amount of $7,000 for mortgage interest, $4,000 for real property taxes, and $2,000 for contributions on Schedule A, Itemized Deductions.

h.   A taxpayer claims, in each respective year, a $12,000 casualty loss deduction for cash stolen in 1989, a $5,000 casualty loss deduction for a diamond necklace stolen in a burglary in 1990, and a $7,000 casualty loss deduction for bearer bonds lost in a fire in 1991.

i.   A taxpayer who was audited three years ago, where the audit resulted in a tax deficiency of $200, files a return with no exceptional characteristics.

j.   Same as (i) except the prior audit resulted in a tax deficiency of $50,000.

17-5   *Refund or Balance Due Upon Filing.*   Many taxpayers believe that receipt of a refund check after the filing of Form 1040 for a year signifies that the IRS does not intend to audit the taxpayer. Conversely, many taxpayers believe that paying a balance due (owed when the Form 1040 is filed) calls attention from the IRS to the return, making an audit more likely. Comment on the validity of these ideas and discuss why a refund or a balance due does or does not play a role in whether a return is examined.

17-6   *Types of Audits.*   The IRS distinguishes between audits that are performed in the field and those that are performed in the IRS office. Describe what types of taxpayers are most likely to be involved in each kind of audit and give reasons why. Also state which type of audit is usually the most extensive and why the different types of audits may differ in scope.

17-7   *Substantiation of Items on Returns.*   The IRS requires that the taxpayer show evidence during an audit of a return for various items being examined.

a.   What types of supporting evidence are considered valuable for substantiating items of income or deductions?

b.   What kinds of problems might arise during an audit that could prompt the IRS to disagree with the amounts of the income or the amounts of the deductions claimed on the return?

c.   What types of problems might arise during an audit that would prompt the IRS to broaden the scope of the audit and call additional items into question?

17-8   *The Revenue Agent's Report.*   At the end of the audit, the IRS makes proposals for adjustment (or no adjustment) of the tax liability for the return examined. The findings of the IRS in the audit, the proposals for adjustment, and the reasons for the proposed adjustments are set out by the IRS in the Revenue Agent's Report. Briefly discuss the importance of this report. State what purposes this report might fulfill from a practical standpoint in terms of the taxpayer audit and appeal process.

17-9   *Form 870.*   After the audit is completed, the IRS and the taxpayer may agree on the proposed adjustments by signing Form 870. Briefly discuss the effects of signing this form and why it is important.

17-10   *Form 870 versus Form 870-AD.*   Compare and contrast Form 870, which may be used after the audit, with Form 870-AD, which is used after the appeal. Specifically consider the following points:

a.   Setting forth the concessions arrived at between the IRS and the taxpayer;

b.   The running of interest on a proposed deficiency;

c.   Further audits concerning the same tax period; and

d.   The degree to which each form is considered to be a binding agreement.

17-11 *Written Protest.* In what circumstances and in what specific conditions is a taxpayer required to file a written protest?

17-12 *30-Day Letter.* Briefly summarize what information is contained in a 30-day letter and describe the circumstances warranting its issue.

17-13 *Appellate Review.* Describe what risks the taxpayer takes by pursuing an appellate review of a case. Against what possible benefits should the taxpayer balance such risks in order to decide whether to proceed further?

17-14 *Appellate Conference.* Briefly summarize what happens during an appellate conference, including what parties usually attend and why.

17-15 *Hazards of Litigation.* The term "hazards of litigation" is rather ill-defined. Try to clarify the meaning of this term and describe the role that the concept plays in the appellate review process.

17-16 *The 90-Day Letter.* Why is the 90-day letter referred to as the statutory notice of deficiency? When will this letter be sent to the taxpayer and what is its effect?

17-17 *Assessment.* The term "assessment" signifies an important event. What is this event and what is its importance?

17-18 *Settlement Authority.* During the various stages of a case, from the audit through appellate review and to the trial court, different IRS officials have the authority to settle the case. Describe what officials have authority to settle the case at the various stages.

17-19 *Additional Settlement Techniques.* The items listed below are settlement techniques used as alternatives to the signing of Form 870 or Form 870-AD. State when each of the following techniques might be used and comment on its effect.

a.   Closing agreements
b.   Offers in compromise
c.   Extensions of limitations period

17-20 *Proposed Deficiency: Alternatives.* The IRS proposes a deficiency of $10,000 for the 1991 tax return of individual T.

a.   If T agrees with the proposed deficiency, what must he do and what are the ramifications of his actions?
b.   If T disagrees with the proposed deficiency, what steps must he take to pursue the matter further within the IRS?

17-21 *Purpose of Limitations Period.* A statute that limits the amount of time in which a legal action may be brought typically seeks to strike a balance between several conflicting interests. State the nature of the conflicting interests and describe how a limitations period operates to achieve a balance.

17-22   *Limitations Periods.* The statute of limitations varies in length depending on the circumstances of the case. In each of the examples below, state the length of the limitations period and give reasons why the period is greater than (or less than) the general three-year period.

a.   The taxpayer files a tax return which omits 10 percent of the taxpayer's gross income. The taxpayer knows of the omission and hopes that it will not be discovered.

b.   The taxpayer has income of $1,000 and files no return for the period.

c.   Same as (b) only the taxpayer has income of $100,000.

d.   The taxpayer has income of $100,000 but reports only $75,000 as gross income on the tax return for the period.

e.   Same as (d) only the taxpayer reports $70,000 as gross income on the tax return for the period.

f.   The taxpayer is a decedent's estate, and the executor has requested that a prompt assessment of taxes be made.

g.   A corporate taxpayer files a return on March 3, 1992 which shows a net operating loss of $10,000 for 1991. The taxpayer carries the loss back and applies it to the third taxable year preceding the year of the loss.

h.   The taxpayer files an amended return while only 75 days remain in the three-year period from the date the original return was due (or filed, if later).

i.   Same as (h) only there are 50 days remaining in the original three-year limitation period.

j.   A 90-day letter has been mailed to the taxpayer for a certain tax year.

17-23   *Collections.* A separate statute of limitations applies to collections. When does this limitations period begin and what is its length? Discuss why the period may be extended.

17-24   *Refund Claims.* The rules that define the limitations periods for refund claims are often referred to as the "two-year or three-year" rules. Discuss why the rules are called this and briefly describe the rules.

17-25   *Mitigation Provisions.* The law provides that in certain circumstances the statute of limitations will not bar the taxpayer or the IRS from adjusting a return for a year otherwise considered closed by virtue of the limitations period. Describe in what circumstances the finality of the statute of limitations will be mitigated and why this rule serves a useful purpose.

17-26   *Failure-to-Pay Penalty.* The penalty for failure to pay is computed on a certain amount of tax. Describe this base amount and state how large this penalty can become. Include in the description the time periods for the penalty and what happens after the penalty reaches its maximum.

17-27   *Failure-to-File Penalty.* The penalty for failure to file a tax return accumulates much faster than does the penalty for failure to pay. Describe the failure-to-file penalty and give reasons for why it builds so much faster than the failure-to-pay penalty.

17-28   *Delinquency Penalties.* The delinquency penalties include the failure-to-pay and the failure-to-file penalties. Briefly discuss what these two penalties have in common and the special relationship between them.

17-29 *Underpayment Penalty for Estimated Taxes.* What fundamental premises of the Federal tax system compel the need for this penalty? The rate of the penalty is indexed directly to the same provisions that fix the rate of interest used by the IRS. Briefly describe the penalty and give reasons why (or why not) the rate used to compute the penalty is appropriate.

17-30 *Accuracy-Related Penalty: Negligence.* Describe the circumstances relating to the acts or omissions of a taxpayer in which a penalty for negligence may be imposed. Briefly outline a standard for the taxpayer to follow to avoid this penalty.

17-31 *Accuracy-Related Penalty: Substantial Understatement.* The law imposes a penalty on substantial understatements of the tax liability shown on a return. Describe the rules relating to this penalty and the conditions in which it is *not* applied despite an understatement.

17-32 *Civil Fraud Penalty.* A penalty is imposed equal to 75 percent of the tax underpayment where fraud is involved. Describe the circumstances in which fraud may be found and state which party carries the burden of proof.

17-33 *Accuracy-Related and Fraud Penalties.* Contrast the accuracy-related penalty for negligence with the civil fraud penalty. Contrast the circumstances in which each one applies. Briefly state whether both penalties may be imposed concurrently and give reasons why this should or should not be allowed.

17-34 *Criminal Penalties.* Several criminal penalties apply in addition to the civil penalties in various circumstances. Contrast and compare the criminal penalty with the civil penalty, especially with regard to the standard of proof required and the manner in which the amount of the penalty is determined. Describe these criminal penalties and the acts to which they pertain. Should criminal penalties be involved every time a civil penalty applies?

17-35 *Frivolous Return Penalty.* Describe the typical circumstances in which the frivolous return penalty is imposed. State whether or not other penalties may be imposed in addition to this penalty and give reasons why this is (or is not) a good policy.

17-36 *Interest and Penalties.* Taxpayer B, an individual, filed for an extension, paying 90 percent of the tax that he believed he owed. Answer the following questions:

    a.   Assuming that B's final tax liability was $10,000 and he owes $2,000 of additional tax, will he owe any interest or other penalties? Explain.

    b.   Assuming that B is entitled to a refund of $1,000, is he entitled to any interest? Explain.

17-37 *Interest as an Inducement to Pay.* The Code has many penalty provisions which the IRS may invoke where a taxpayer has not paid all of the taxes owed. Discuss the purpose of interest in light of the fact that there are so many penalties available, and compare the role of interest with that of penalties.

17-38 *Interest and Accrual Dates.* Describe upon what amounts the interest is charged and when it begins and stops accruing. State how interest is compounded and whether or not the Code allows for interest to be charged on interest.

17-39 *Tax Practitioner Guidelines.* The IRS has several guidelines pertaining to what individuals it will allow to practice before it. Describe the professional qualifications these guidelines require, and discuss why (or why not) this type of policy is beneficial. Include in the discussion what parties are benefited and how.

17-40 *Nonprofessional Tax Practitioners.* The law allows individuals other than attorneys and CPAs to practice before the IRS. What standards are set for enrolled agents admitted to practice? Discuss the importance of allowing individuals not in an organized profession to practice before the IRS.

17-41 *Other Individuals Allowed to Practice.* In various circumstances, an individual may practice before the IRS to a limited degree without being an attorney, accountant, or enrolled agent. Briefly describe four situations in which this may occur and discuss the reasons why this is (or is not) a good rule in each instance.

17-42 *Tax Return Preparer.* In order to become an income tax return preparer, an individual need not meet any educational or professional requirements. Describe what an individual must do to be considered an income tax return preparer. Discuss how this differs from qualification for practice before the IRS.

17-43 *Penalties for Income Tax Return Preparers.* The law imposes several penalties on the income tax return preparer for various acts and omissions. Describe five such acts or omissions and the related penalties. For each one, discuss the purpose for the rule and give reasons why (or why not) the purpose is an important one in tax practice. Generally, discuss why there are so many rules pertaining to the income tax return preparer.

17-44 *Criminal Penalties Relating to Return Preparation.* In addition to the civil penalties, the law imposes criminal penalties on certain acts relating to tax return preparation. How do these penalties differ from the civil penalties in nature? Discuss whether the criminal penalties seem fair, given their maximum limits. State why or why not.

17-45 *"Tax Specialist" Representations.* The tax practice law and most professional ethical codes expressly prohibit a professional from making representations of special knowledge regarding tax matters. Discuss the reasons for such a rule and consider the rule in light of the lack of such a constraint on the nonprofessional tax practitioner or the income tax return preparer. Also discuss the fairness of the rule in comparison to the IRS rules that allow for the designation of personnel as revenue agents or revenue officers. Consider any unfair advantages that might be created by this scheme.

17-46 *Ethics and Statements on Responsibilities in Tax Practice.* The AICPA guidelines, set forth in the *Statements on Responsibilities in Tax Practice*, address in a general manner a set of situations typically encountered by the CPA. Focusing on one Statement, create a hypothetical example and make specific assertions about what the Statement requires, given the set of hypothetical facts. Discuss how well the Statement delineates the action to be taken in a factual situation from a practical standpoint.

17-47 *Professional Conduct.* The large amount of malpractice litigation in the accounting world relating to tax practice suggests that the professional standard of conduct in this area is still rather ill-defined. Discuss how a professional tax practitioner might ascertain a standard which, if properly followed, would provide greater security from findings of malpractice. Include in the discussion the sources to which the professional must look in order to find such a standard. Also evaluate the costs to the profession and to the public involved in the evolution of a standard.

PROBLEMS

17-48 *Interest.* The rate of interest used by the IRS has some special characteristics and applications.

   a.   How frequently is the interest compounded?

   b.   May the IRS charge interest on interest?

   c.   How much interest may be charged on a penalty paid within 10 days of the date it is assessed?

   d.   What happens to the accrual of interest on a tax deficiency when the taxpayer signs Form 870? Form 870-AD?

   e.   When does interest begin to run on the tax overpayment if a taxpayer files a Form 1040 that requests a refund?

   f.   When does interest begin to run on the tax overpayment if a taxpayer files a claim for a refund?

17-49 *Statute of Limitations.* The limitations period varies from case to case, depending on the circumstances. In each situation described below, state when the statute of limitations expires.

   a.   Calendar year taxpayer A files a 1991 individual income tax return on March 31, 1992.

   b.   Same facts as (a) except the return is for a corporation.

   c.   Taxpayer B files a 1991 return on April 1, 1992, which shows $15,000 of gross income. B actually has gross income of $16,000 but hopes to not pay tax on $1,000 by not reporting it.

   d.   Taxpayer C files a 1991 income tax return on March 1, 1992 which shows $7,500 of gross income. C actually has gross income of $10,000 but has inadvertently omitted $2,500 from the return.

   e.   Same as (d) except C reports $7,200 on the return, inadvertently omitting $2,800.

   f.   Taxpayer D has income of $25,000 for 1991 and files no returns.

   g.   Taxpayer E is an estate for an individual who died on December 31, 1991. The estate tax return is filed March 15, 1992. On April 1, 1992, the executor of Taxpayer E files a request for a prompt assessment.

   h.   Taxpayer F files a 1991 income tax return on April 10, 1992. On April 1, 1993, F files an amended return for the 1991 tax return.

   i.   Same as (h) except F files the amended return on April 1, 1995.

17-50 *Penalties.*   Compute the penalties in the following situations.

    a.   Taxpayer A files a 1991 income tax return on April 15, 1992, showing a tax liability of $10,000 and a balance due of $1,000. A does not pay the $1,000 until June 30, 1992.

    b.   Same as (a) except A does not pay the $1,000 balance due until April 1, 1995.

    c.   Taxpayer B filed no 1991 income tax return until July 31, 1992. The return shows a tax liability of $5,000 with a balance due of $100. B pays the $100 on April 15, 1992, without the return.

    d.   Same as (c) except B does not pay the balance due until the return is filed.

    e.   Taxpayer C files a 1991 income tax return on April 1, 1992, negligently reporting $1,000 less than C's actual tax liability.

    f.   Taxpayer D files a 1991 income tax return on April 15, 1992, which fraudulently reports $500 less than D's actual tax liability.

17-51 *The Decision to Appeal.*   Taxpayer Z disagrees with the findings of an audit which rest on the controversy of a single issue. The prepared IRS adjustment is a $20,000 deficiency. Z has retained counsel to take the appeal from start to finish for $6,500. Z's personal expenses to proceed with the audit, including time lost at work, amount to an estimated $1,500. Indicate whether Z should proceed with the appeal or pay the proposed deficiency (disregarding any penalties and interest) in each of the following circumstances.

    a.   The probability of winning the appeal for Z is 50 percent.

    b.   The probability of winning the appeal for Z is 40 percent.

    c.   The probability of winning the appeal for Z is 30 percent.

17-52 *Estimated Taxes: Individual.*   In 1991 R's gross tax liability before prepayments is $20,000. His gross tax liability in 1990 was $12,000.

    a.   What is the lowest required installment that R can make for 1991 and avoid penalty? (Ignore the annualized income installment.)

During 1991, R (a single taxpayer) paid estimated taxes of $1,000 on each due date. In addition, R's employer withheld a total of $3,000 during the year. R filed and paid the balance of his liability on April 15, 1992. Assume the applicable interest rate charged on underpayments for 1991 is 10 percent.

    b.   Compute R's penalty, if any, for failure to pay estimated taxes. Compute the penalty with respect to the first installment only.

    c.   Briefly explain the "annualized income installment" and its function.

17-53 *Estimated Taxes: Corporation.*   During 1991, K Corp. had taxable income of $500,000. Its taxable income for 1990 was $100,000.

    a.   What is the minimum installment of estimated taxes that K must make to avoid penalty? Assume the corporation has never had taxable income greater than $500,000.

    b.   Same as (a) except the corporation's taxable income in 1990 was $1.5 million.

17-54   *Ethics.*   The CPA encounters various situations that fall under ethical rules that prescribe or proscribe certain acts. Comment on the following situations and state what the CPA should do in each case.

a.   A CPA receives no compensation for preparing the income tax return of a neighbor. The neighbor requests that the CPA sign the preparer's declaration.

b.   A CPA prepares a Form 1120 for a corporation, but is unable to show a breakdown of the compensation of officers due to lack of information.

c.   A CPA assists a corporate client through an audit of a return in which it is found that an officer has received unreasonable compensation. No prospective statements are made by the IRS that specifically deal with future years. The CPA is currently assisting the client in the preparation of a current income tax return for a period when the same officer received the same compensation for the same amount of work.

d.   A CPA has knowledge of an error in the ending inventory of a prior year. The CPA is asked to prepare the return for the current year.

e.   A CPA is asked to prepare a return where the client has provided information indicating that the client pays several thousands of dollars in office rent. The CPA knows the client actually owns the office which it claims to be renting.

f.   A CPA takes a position contrary to an Income Tax Regulation (i.e., a Treasury Regulation) with reasonable support for the position.

g.   A CPA takes a position contrary to a specific section of the Internal Revenue Code with reasonable support for the position.

RESEARCH PROBLEMS

17-55   Q filed a fraudulent income tax return for 1984. In 1986, Q realized the error of his ways and filed a nonfraudulent amended income tax return for the 1984 tax year, and paid the additional taxes due. In 1991, the IRS assessed the 75 percent civil fraud penalty under § 6663 on Q's 1984 tax. Q asserts that the normal 3-year statute of limitations expired in 1989, since he filed a nonfraudulent amended return in 1986. The position of the IRS is that there is no statute of limitations due to fraud. Which party is likely to prevail? Why?

Research aid:

Reg. § 301.6501(a)-1(b).

17-56 On April 10, 1991, N realized that she would not be able to file her 1990 tax return by April 15,1991. She phoned her accountant and told him that she was delayed but expected a very large refund. The accountant informed her that she would not be penalized since no tax was due. When N finished her tax return, she found that $4,000 additional tax was due. She filed her 1990 return and paid the $4,000 additional tax in July 1991. The IRS assessed failure-to-file and failure-to-pay penalties. N agrees that she owes the penalty for failure to pay, but does not feel that she should be penalized for failure to file since she relied on the advice of her accountant. Should N be penalized for failure to file? Why or why not?

Research aid:

§ 6651(a).

Appendix **A**

ESTATE AND GIFT TAX VALUATION TABLES

Table A

Single Life Remainder Factors
Various Interest Rates
(See Notes to Table A)

Age	9.8%	10.0%	10.2%	Age	9.8%	10.0%	10.2%
0	.01954	.01922	.01891	25	.02902	.02784	.02673
1	.00834	.00801	.00770	26	.03052	.02928	.02811
2	.00819	.00784	.00751	27	.03219	.03088	.02965
3	.00832	.00795	.00760	28	.03403	.03264	.03134
4	.00862	.00822	.00786	29	.03604	.03458	.03322
5	.00904	.00862	.00824	30	.03825	.03671	.03527
6	.00954	.00910	.00869	31	.04067	.03905	.03753
7	.01013	.00966	.00923	32	.04329	.04160	.04000
8	.01081	.01031	.00986	33	.04616	.04438	.04269
9	.01159	.01107	.01059	34	.04926	.04738	.04561
10	.01249	.01194	.01142	35	.05260	.05063	.04877
11	.01351	.01293	.01239	36	.05617	.05411	.05215
12	.01463	.01402	.01345	37	.05999	.05783	.05578
13	.01582	.01517	.01457	38	.06407	.06180	.05965
14	.01698	.01630	.01567	39	.06841	.06604	.06379
15	.01810	.01738	.01672	40	.07303	.07055	.06820
16	.01917	.01842	.01772	41	.07794	.07535	.07288
17	.02018	.01940	.01866	42	.08312	.08041	.07784
18	.02118	.02035	.01958	43	.08858	.08576	.08308
19	.02218	.02131	.02050	44	.09434	.09141	.08861
20	.02320	.02229	.02143	45	.10042	.09736	.09445
21	.02424	.02328	.02238	46	.10680	.10363	.10060
22	.02532	.02430	.02336	47	.11352	.11022	.10707
23	.02644	.02538	.02438	48	.12055	.11713	.11386
24	.02767	.02655	.02550	49	.12787	.12433	.12094

(Continued)

Table A *(Continued)*

Age	9.8%	10.0%	10.2%	Age	9.8%	10.0%	10.2%
50	.13548	.13182	.12831	80	.53248	.52705	.52171
51	.14342	.13963	.13600	81	.55035	.54499	.53974
52	.15172	.14780	.14405	82	.56796	.56270	.55753
53	.16038	.15635	.15247	83	.58523	.58007	.57500
54	.16940	.16524	.16124	84	.60218	.59713	.59216
55	.17878	.17450	.17039	85	.61886	.61392	.60906
56	.18854	.18414	.17991	86	.63511	.63030	.62555
57	.19870	.19419	.18984	87	.65071	.64602	.64139
58	.20927	.20464	.20018	88	.66574	.66117	.65666
59	.22024	.21551	.21093	89	.68045	.67601	.67163
60	.23158	.22674	.22206	90	.69502	.69071	.68646
61	.24325	.23831	.23353	91	.70921	.70504	.70093
62	.25524	.25020	.24532	92	.72267	.71864	.71466
63	.26754	.26240	.25742	93	.73524	.73135	.72750
64	.28016	.27493	.26987	94	.74680	.74303	.73931
65	.29317	.28787	.28271	95	.75727	.75362	.75001
66	.30663	.30124	.29601	96	.76657	.76303	.75953
67	.32053	.31508	.30978	97	.77504	.77160	.76819
68	.33488	.32937	.32401	98	.78267	.77931	.77599
69	.34961	.34405	.33863	99	.78971	.78644	.78319
70	.36468	.35907	.35361	100	.79624	.79304	.78987
71	.38000	.37436	.36886	101	.80245	.79932	.79622
72	.39558	.38991	.38439	102	.80892	.80586	.80283
73	.41143	.40575	.40021	103	.81577	.81279	.80983
74	.42763	.42195	.41639	104	.82338	.82048	.81760
75	.44424	.43856	.43301	105	.83282	.83003	.82726
76	.46129	.45563	.45009	106	.84659	.84397	.84137
77	.47873	.47311	.46761	107	.86676	.86443	.86211
78	.49652	.49094	.48548	108	.90020	.89840	.89600
79	.51488	.50897	.50356	109	.95537	.95455	.95372

Notes to Table A:

1. These single life remainder factors are excerpts from Notice 89-60, 1989-22 I.R.B. (May 30, 1989). The IRS released tables for various interest rates beginning at 8.2 percent and incrementing by 0.2 percent up to 12.0 percent. Only three different rates are illustrated here.

2. These single life remainder factors can be used to determine the appropriate income factor for valuation of an income interest by using the following formula:

$$\text{Income factor} = 1.000000 - \text{Remainder factor}$$

Table B

Term Certain Remainder Factors
Various Interest Rates

Number of Years	9.8%	10.0%	10.2%	Number of Years	9.8%	10.0%	10.2%
1	.910747	.909091	.907441	31	.055122	.052099	.049246
2	.829460	.826446	.823449	32	.050202	.047362	.044688
3	.755428	.751315	.747232	33	.045722	.043057	.040552
4	.688003	.683013	.678069	34	.041641	.039143	.036798
5	.626597	.620921	.615307	35	.037924	.035584	.033392
6	.570671	.564474	.558355	36	.034539	.032349	.030301
7	.519737	.513158	.506674	37	.031457	.029408	.027497
8	.473349	.466507	.459777	38	.028649	.026735	.024952
9	.431101	.424098	.417221	39	.026092	.024304	.022642
10	.392624	.385543	.378603	40	.023763	.022095	.020546
11	.357581	.350494	.343560	41	.021642	.020086	.018645
12	.325666	.318631	.311760	42	.019711	.018260	.016919
13	.296599	.289664	.282904	43	.017951	.016600	.015353
14	.270127	.263331	.256719	44	.016349	.015091	.013932
15	.246017	.239392	.232957	45	.014890	.013719	.012642
16	.224059	.217629	.211395	46	.013561	.012472	.011472
17	.204061	.197845	.191828	47	.012351	.011338	.010410
18	.185848	.179859	.174073	48	.011248	.010307	.009447
19	.169260	.163508	.157961	49	.010244	.009370	.008572
20	.154153	.148644	.143340	50	.009330	.008519	.007779
21	.140395	.135131	.130073	51	.008497	.007744	.007059
22	.127864	.122846	.118033	52	.007739	.007040	.006406
23	.116452	.111678	.107108	53	.007048	.006400	.005813
24	.106058	.101562	.097195	54	.006419	.005818	.005275
25	.096592	.092296	.088198	55	.005846	.005289	.004786
26	.087971	.083905	.080035	56	.005324	.004809	.004343
27	.080119	.076278	.072627	57	.004849	.004371	.003941
28	.072968	.069343	.065905	58	.004416	.003974	.003577
29	.066456	.063039	.059804	59	.004022	.003613	.003246
30	.060524	.057309	.054269	60	.003663	.003284	.002945

Note: Like Table A, this table contains excerpts from Notice 89-60, but only 3 different interest rates are illustrated. The Table B from Notice 89-60 contains factors for 8.2 percent through 12.0 percent.

Appendix B

TAX FORMS

B-1   U.S. Corporation Income Tax Return

Form **1120**	**U.S. Corporation Income Tax Return**	OMB No. 1545-0123

Department of the Treasury
Internal Revenue Service

For calendar year 1990 or tax year beginning _____, 1990, ending _____, 19 ____

▶ Instructions are separate. See page 1 for Paperwork Reduction Act Notice.

19 90

Check if a—
A Consolidated return ☐
B Personal holding co. ☐
C Personal service corp.(as defined in Temp. Regs. sec. 1.441-4T—see Instructions) ☐

Use IRS label. Otherwise, please print or type.

Name

Number, street, and room or suite no. (If a P.O. box, see page 2 of Instructions.)

City or town, state, and ZIP code

D Employer identification number

E Date incorporated

F Total assets (see Specific Instructions)

$

G Check applicable boxes: (1) ☐ Initial return   (2) ☐ Final return   (3) ☐ Change in address

Income

1a	Gross receipts or sales	**b** Less returns and allowances	c Bal ▶ 1c
2	Cost of goods sold (Schedule A, line 7).		2
3	Gross profit (line 1c less line 2)		3
4	Dividends (Schedule C, line 19)		4
5	Interest		5
6	Gross rents		6
7	Gross royalties		7
8	Capital gain net income (attach Schedule D (Form 1120))		8
9	Net gain or (loss) from Form 4797, Part II, line 18 (attach Form 4797)		9
10	Other income (see Instructions—attach schedule).		10
11	**Total income**—Add lines 3 through 10 ▶		11

Deductions (See Instructions for limitations on deductions.)

12	Compensation of officers (Schedule E, line 4)		12
13a	Salaries and wages	**b** Less jobs credit	c Balance ▶ 13c
14	Repairs		14
15	Bad debts		15
16	Rents		16
17	Taxes		17
18	Interest		18
19	Contributions (**see Instructions for 10% limitation**)		19
20	Depreciation (attach Form 4562)	20	
21	Less depreciation claimed on Schedule A and elsewhere on return	21a	21b
22	Depletion		22
23	Advertising		23
24	Pension, profit-sharing, etc., plans		24
25	Employee benefit programs		25
26	Other deductions (attach schedule)		26
27	**Total deductions**—Add lines 12 through 26. ▶		27
28	Taxable income before net operating loss deduction and special deductions (line 11 less line 27)		28
29	**Less: a** Net operating loss deduction (see Instructions)	29a	
	b Special deductions (Schedule C, line 20)	29b	29c

Tax and Payments

30	**Taxable income**—Line 28 less line 29c		30
31	**Total tax** (Schedule J, line 10)		31
32	**Payments: a** 1989 overpayment credited to 1990	32a	
	b 1990 estimated tax payments	32b	
	c Less 1990 refund applied for on Form 4466	32c ( ) **d** Bal ▶ 32d	
	e Tax deposited with Form 7004	32e	
	f Credit from regulated investment companies (attach Form 2439)	32f	
	g Credit for Federal tax on fuels (attach Form 4136). See Instructions	32g	32h
33	Enter any **penalty** for underpayment of estimated tax—Check ▶ ☐ if Form 2220 is attached		33
34	**Tax due**—If the total of lines 31 and 33 is larger than line 32h, enter amount owed		34
35	**Overpayment**—If line 32h is larger than the total of lines 31 and 33, enter amount overpaid		35
36	Enter amount of line 35 you want: **Credited to 1991 estimated tax** ▶ **Refunded** ▶		36

Please Sign Here

Under penalties of perjury, I declare that I have examined this return, including accompanying schedules and statements, and to the best of my knowledge and belief, it is true, correct, and complete. Declaration of preparer (other than taxpayer) is based on all information of which preparer has any knowledge.

▶ Signature of officer   Date   ▶ Title

Paid Preparer's Use Only

Preparer's signature ▶	Date	Check if self-employed ☐	Preparer's social security number
Firm's name (or yours if self-employed) and address ▶		E.I. No. ▶	
		ZIP code ▶	

Form 1120 (1990)   Page **2**

Schedule A Cost of Goods Sold (See Instructions for line 2, page 1.)

1	Inventory at beginning of year	**1**
2	Purchases	**2**
3	Cost of labor	**3**
4a	Additional section 263A costs (see Instructions—attach schedule)	**4a**
b	Other costs (attach schedule)	**4b**
5	**Total**—Add lines 1 through 4b	**5**
6	Inventory at end of year	**6**
7	**Cost of goods sold**—Line 5 less line 6. Enter here and on line 2, page 1.	**7**

8a Check all methods used for valuing closing inventory:
    (i) ☐ Cost **(ii)** ☐ Lower of cost or market as described in Regulations section 1.471-4 (see Instructions)
    (iii) ☐ Writedown of "subnormal" goods as described in Regulations section 1.471-2(c) (see Instructions)
    (iv) ☐ Other (Specify method used and attach explanation.) ▶ _____ ☐
  b Check if the LIFO inventory method was adopted this tax year for any goods (if checked, attach Form 970) . . . . . . ☐
  c If the LIFO inventory method was used for this tax year, enter percentage (or amounts) of
    closing inventory computed under LIFO **8c**
  d Do the rules of section 263A (with respect to property produced or acquired for resale) apply to the corporation? . . ☐ Yes ☐ No
  e Was there any change in determining quantities, cost, or valuations between opening and closing inventory? If "Yes,"
    attach explanation . . . . ☐ Yes ☐ No

Schedule C Dividends and Special Deductions (See Instructions.)

	(a) Dividends received	(b) %	(c) Special deductions: (a) × (b)
1 Dividends from less-than-20%-owned domestic corporations that are subject to the 70% deduction (other than debt-financed stock)		70	
2 Dividends from 20%-or-more-owned domestic corporations that are subject to the 80% deduction (other than debt-financed stock)		80	
3 Dividends on debt-financed stock of domestic and foreign corporations (section 246A)		see Instructions	
4 Dividends on certain preferred stock of less-than-20%-owned public utilities . . .		41.176	
5 Dividends on certain preferred stock of 20%-or-more-owned public utilities . . .		47.059	
6 Dividends from less-than-20%-owned foreign corporations and certain FSCs that are subject to the 70% deduction		70	
7 Dividends from 20%-or-more-owned foreign corporations and certain FSCs that are subject to the 80% deduction		80	
8 Dividends from wholly owned foreign subsidiaries subject to the 100% deduction (section 245(b))		100	
9 **Total**—Add lines 1 through 8. See Instructions for limitation			
10 Dividends from domestic corporations received by a small business investment company operating under the Small Business Investment Act of 1958		100	
11 Dividends from certain FSCs that are subject to the 100% deduction (section 245(c)(1))		100	
12 Dividends from affiliated group members subject to the 100% deduction (section 243(a)(3))		100	
13 Other dividends from foreign corporations not included on lines 3, 6, 7, 8, or 11			
14 Income from controlled foreign corporations under subpart F (attach Forms 5471)			
15 Foreign dividend gross-up (section 78)			
16 IC-DISC and former DISC dividends not included on lines 1, 2, or 3 (section 246(d))			
17 Other dividends			
18 Deduction for dividends paid on certain preferred stock of public utilities (see Instructions)			
19 **Total dividends**—Add lines 1 through 17. Enter here and on line 4, page 1. ▶			

20 **Total deductions**—Add lines 9, 10, 11, 12, and 18. Enter here and on line 29b, page 1 . . . . ▶

Schedule E Compensation of Officers (See Instructions for line 12, page 1.)
Complete Schedule E only if total receipts (line 1a, plus lines 4 through 10, of page 1, Form 1120) are $500,000 or more.

(a) Name of officer	(b) Social security number	(c) Percent of time devoted to business	Percent of corporation stock owned		(f) Amount of compensation
			(d) Common	(e) Preferred	
1		%	%	%	
		%	%	%	
		%	%	%	
		%	%	%	
		%	%	%	

2 Total compensation of officers . . . .
3 **Less:** Compensation of officers claimed on Schedule A and elsewhere on return . . . . (   )
4 Compensation of officers deducted on line 12, page 1 . . . .

Form 1120 (1990)   Page **3**

Schedule J	Tax Computation

1 Check if you are a member of a controlled group (see sections 1561 and 1563) . . . . . . ▶ ☐

2 If the box on line 1 is checked:

  a Enter your share of the $50,000 and $25,000 taxable income bracket amounts (in that order):

    (i) |$_____| **(ii)** |$_____|

  b Enter your share of the additional 5% tax (not to exceed $11,750) ▶ |$_____|

3 Income tax (see Instructions to figure the tax). Check this box if the corporation is a qualified personal service corporation (see Instructions on page 12). ▶ ☐ . . . . | **3** |

4a Foreign tax credit (attach Form 1118) . . . . | **4a** |

  b Possessions tax credit (attach Form 5735) . . . . | **4b** |

  c Orphan drug credit (attach Form 6765) . . . . | **4c** |

  d Credit for fuel produced from a nonconventional source (see Instructions) . . . . | **4d** |

  e General business credit. Enter here and check which forms are attached:

    ☐ Form 3800 ☐ Form 3468 ☐ Form 5884

    ☐ Form 6478 ☐ Form 6765 ☐ Form 8586 . . . . . . | **4e** |

  f Credit for prior year minimum tax (attach Form 8801) . . . . . | **4f** |

5 **Total**—Add lines 4a through 4f . . . . | **5** |

6 Line 3 less line 5 . . . . | **6** |

7 Personal holding company tax (attach Schedule PH (Form 1120)) . . . . | **7** |

8 Recapture taxes. Check if from: ☐ Form 4255 ☐ Form 8611 . . . . | **8** |

9a Alternative minimum tax (attach Form 4626). See Instructions . . . . | **9a** |

  b Environmental tax (attach Form 4626) . . . . | **9b** |

10 **Total tax**—Add lines 6 through 9b. Enter here and on line 31, page 1 . . . . | **10** |

Additional Information (See General Instruction F.)   **Yes No**

H Refer to the list in the Instructions and state the principal:

  (1) Business activity code no. ▶ _____

  (2) Business activity ▶ _____

  (3) Product or service ▶ _____

I **(1)** Did the corporation at the end of the tax year own, directly or indirectly, 50% or more of the voting stock of a domestic corporation? (For rules of attribution, see section 267(c).) . .

    If "Yes," attach a schedule showing: (a) name, address, and identifying number; (b) percentage owned; and (c) taxable income or (loss) before NOL and special deductions of such corporation for the tax year ending with or within your tax year.

  (2) Did any individual, partnership, corporation, estate, or trust at the end of the tax year own, directly or indirectly, 50% or more of the corporation's voting stock? (For rules of attribution, see section 267(c).) If "Yes," complete (a) through (c) . . . .

    (a) Attach a schedule showing name, address, and identifying number.

    (b) Enter percentage owned ▶ _____

    (c) Was the owner of such voting stock a foreign person? (See Instructions.) **Note:** *If "Yes," the corporation may have to file Form 5472* . . . .

    If "Yes," enter owner's country ▶ _____

J Was the corporation a U.S. shareholder of any controlled foreign corporation? (See sections 951 and 957.) . . . .

  If "Yes," attach Form 5471 for each such corporation.

K At any time during the tax year, did the corporation have an interest in or a signature or other authority over a financial account in a foreign country (such as a bank account, securities account, or other financial account)? . . . .

  (See General Instruction F and filing requirements for form TD F 90-22.1.)

  If "Yes," enter name of foreign country ▶ _____

L Was the corporation the grantor of, or transferor to, a foreign trust that existed during the current tax year, whether or not the corporation has any beneficial interest in it? . . . . . .

  If "Yes," the corporation may have to file Forms 3520, 3520-A, or 926.

M During this tax year, did the corporation pay dividends (other than stock dividends and distributions in exchange for stock) in excess of the corporation's current and accumulated earnings and profits? (See sections 301 and 316.) . . . .

  If "Yes," file Form 5452. If this is a consolidated return, answer here for parent corporation and on **Form 851**, Affiliations Schedule, for each subsidiary.

N During this tax year, did the corporation maintain any part of its accounting/tax records on a computerized system? . . . . .

O Check method of accounting:

  (1) ☐ Cash

  (2) ☐ Accrual

  (3) ☐ Other (specify) ▶ _____

P Check this box if the corporation issued publicly offered debt instruments with original issue discount . . . . . . ☐

  If so, the corporation may have to file Form 8281.

Q Enter the amount of tax-exempt interest received or accrued during the tax year ▶ |$_____|

R Enter the number of shareholders at the end of the tax year if there were 35 or fewer shareholders ▶

Form 1120 (1990)   Page **4**

Schedule L — Balance Sheets

Assets	Beginning of tax year		End of tax year	
	(a)	(b)	(c)	(d)
1 Cash				
2a Trade notes and accounts receivable				
b Less allowance for bad debts	( )		( )	
3 Inventories				
4 U.S. government obligations				
5 Tax-exempt securities (see Instructions)				
6 Other current assets (attach schedule)				
7 Loans to stockholders				
8 Mortgage and real estate loans				
9 Other investments (attach schedule)				
10a Buildings and other depreciable assets				
b Less accumulated depreciation	( )		( )	
11a Depletable assets				
b Less accumulated depletion	( )		( )	
12 Land (net of any amortization)				
13a Intangible assets (amortizable only)				
b Less accumulated amortization	( )		( )	
14 Other assets (attach schedule)				
15 Total assets				
Liabilities and Stockholders' Equity				
16 Accounts payable				
17 Mortgages, notes, bonds payable in less than 1 year				
18 Other current liabilities (attach schedule)				
19 Loans from stockholders				
20 Mortgages, notes, bonds payable in 1 year or more				
21 Other liabilities (attach schedule)				
22 Capital stock: a Preferred stock				
b Common stock				
23 Paid-in or capital surplus				
24 Retained earnings—Appropriated (attach schedule)				
25 Retained earnings—Unappropriated				
26 Less cost of treasury stock		( )		( )
27 Total liabilities and stockholders' equity				

Schedule M-1 — Reconciliation of Income per Books With Income per Return (This schedule does not have to be completed if the total assets on line 15, column (d), of Schedule L are less than $25,000.)

1 Net income per books		7 Income recorded on books this year not included on this return (itemize):	
2 Federal income tax		a Tax-exempt interest $ _____	
3 Excess of capital losses over capital gains		_____	
4 Income subject to tax not recorded on books this year (itemize): _____		_____	
_____		8 Deductions on this return not charged against book income this year (itemize):	
5 Expenses recorded on books this year not deducted on this return (itemize):		a Depreciation . . . $ _____	
a Depreciation . . . $ _____		b Contributions carryover $ _____	
b Contributions carryover $ _____		_____	
c Travel and entertainment . $ _____		_____	
_____		9 Total of lines 7 and 8	
6 Total of lines 1 through 5		10 Income (line 28, page 1)—line 6 less line 9	

Schedule M-2 — Analysis of Unappropriated Retained Earnings per Books (line 25, Schedule L) (This schedule does not have to be completed if the total assets on line 15, column (d), of Schedule L are less than $25,000.)

1 Balance at beginning of year		5 Distributions: a Cash	
2 Net income per books		b Stock	
3 Other increases (itemize): _____		c Property	
_____		6 Other decreases (itemize): _____	
_____		_____	
		7 Total of lines 5 and 6	
4 Total of lines 1, 2, and 3		8 Balance at end of year (line 4 less line 7)	

SCHEDULE PH
(Form 1120)

Department of the Treasury
Internal Revenue Service

U.S. Personal Holding Company Tax

▶ See separate instructions. Attach to tax return.

OMB No. 1545-0123

1990

Name | Employer identification number

Part I—Undistributed Personal Holding Company Income

Additions

1	Taxable income before net operating loss deduction and special deductions. Enter amount from line 28, Form 1120. See instructions	1
2	Contributions deducted in figuring line 1. Enter amount from line 19, Form 1120	2
3	Excess expenses and depreciation under section 545(b)(6). Enter amount from line 2, Schedule A. See instructions	3
4	Total. Add lines 1 through 3	4

Deductions

5	Federal and foreign income, war profits, and excess profits taxes not deducted in figuring line 1. See instructions (attach schedule)	5
6	Contributions deductible under section 545(b)(2). See instructions for limitation	6
7	Net operating loss for the preceding tax year deductible under section 545(b)(4). See instructions.	7
8a	Net capital gain. Enter amount from Schedule D (Form 1120), line 10. Foreign corporations see instructions	8a
b	**Less:** Income tax on this net capital gain (see section 545(b)(5)). Attach computation	8b	8c
9	Amounts used or irrevocably set aside to pay or retire qualified indebtedness. See instructions .	9
10	Deduction for dividends paid (other than dividends paid after the end of the tax year). Enter amount from line 5, Schedule B.	10
11	Total. Add lines 5 through 10	11
12	Subtract line 11 from line 4	12
13	Dividends paid after the end of the tax year (other than deficiency dividends defined in section 547(d)) but not more than the smaller of line 12 or 20% of line 1, Schedule B. See instructions .	13
14	**Undistributed personal holding company income.** Subtract line 13 from line 12. Foreign corporations see instructions.	14

Part II—Information Required Under Section 6501(f). If the information on personal holding company income **and** stock ownership is not submitted with the corporation's return, the limitation period for assessment and collection of personal holding company tax is 6 years.

Personal Holding Company Income (See instructions.)

15	Dividends	15
16a	Interest	16a
b	**Less:** Amounts excluded under section 543(a)(1)(A), 543(a)(1)(B), 543(a)(1)(D), or 543(b)(2)(C). Attach schedule	16b	16c
17	Royalties (other than mineral, oil, gas, or copyright royalties)	17
18	Annuities	18
19a	Rents	19a
b	**Less:** Adjustments described in section 543(b)(2)(A) (attach schedule)	19b	19c
20a	Mineral, oil, and gas royalties	20a
b	**Less:** Adjustments described in section 543(b)(2)(B)(attach schedule)	20b	20c
21	Copyright royalties	21
22	Produced film rents	22
23	Compensation received for use of corporation property by 25% shareholder	23
24	Amounts received under personal service contracts and from their sale	24
25	Amounts includible in taxable income from estates and trusts	25
26	**Personal holding company income.** Add amounts in right column for lines 15 through 25	26

Part III—Tax on Undistributed Personal Holding Company Income

27	**Personal holding company tax.** Enter 28% of line 14 here and on line 7, Schedule J (Form 1120), or on the proper line of the appropriate tax return	27

For Paperwork Reduction Act Notice, see page 1 of the Instructions for Forms 1120 and 1120-A.   Schedule PH (Form 1120) 1990

Schedule PH (Form 1120) 1990   Page **2**

Stock Ownership   Enter the names and addresses of the individuals who together owned directly or indirectly at any time during the last half of the tax year more than 50% in value of the outstanding stock of the corporation.

(a) Name	(b) Address	Highest percentage of shares owned during last half of tax year	
		(c) Preferred	(d) Common
		%	%
		%	%
		%	%
		%	%
		%	%

Schedule A   Excess of Expenses and Depreciation Over Income From Property Not Allowable Under Section 545(b)(6). See instructions for Part I, line 3.

(a) Kind of property	(b) Date acquired	(c) Cost or other basis	(d) Depreciation	(e) Repairs, insurance, and other expenses (section 162) (attach schedule)	(f) Total of columns (d) and (e)	(g) Income from rent or other compensation	(h) Excess (col. (f) less col. (g))
1							

2 Total excess of expenses and depreciation over rent or other compensation. Enter here and on line 3, Part I.
   Note: *Attach a statement showing the names and addresses of persons from whom rent or other compensation was received for the use of, or the right to use, each property.*

Schedule B   Deduction for Dividends Paid (Determined Under Section 562)

1	Taxable dividends paid. Do not include dividends considered as paid in the preceding tax year under section 563, or deficiency dividends as defined in section 547	**1**	
2	Consent dividends. Attach Forms 972 and 973	**2**	
3	Taxable distributions. Add lines 1 and 2	**3**	
4	Dividend carryover from first and second preceding tax years. Attach computation	**4**	
5	Deduction for dividends paid. Add lines 3 and 4 and enter the result here and on line 10, Part I . . .	**5**	

B-2 U.S. Income Tax Return for an S Corporation

Form **1120S**	**U.S. Income Tax Return for an S Corporation**	OMB No. 1545-0130

Department of the Treasury
Internal Revenue Service

For calendar year 1990, or tax year beginning _____, 1990, and ending _____, 19 ___.
▶ **See separate instructions.**

19 90

A Date of election as an S corporation	Use IRS label. Other-wise, please print or type.	Name		C Employer identification number
B Business code no. (see Specific Instructions)		Number, street, and room or suite no. (If a P.O. box, see page 7 of the instructions.)		D Date incorporated
		City or town, state, and ZIP code		E Total assets (see Specific Instructions) $

F Check applicable boxes:　(1) ☐ Initial return　　(2) ☐ Final return　　(3) ☐ Change in address　　(4) ☐ Amended return

G Check this box if this is an S corporation subject to the consolidated audit procedures of sections 6241 through 6245 (see instructions before checking this box) . . ▶ ☐

H Enter number of shareholders in the corporation at end of the tax year . . . . ▶

Caution: *Include **only** trade or business income and expenses on lines 1a through 21. See the instructions for more information.*

Income

1a	Gross receipts or sales [＿＿＿＿] **b** Less returns and allowances [＿＿＿＿] **c** Bal ▶	1c	
2	Cost of goods sold (Schedule A, line 7)	2	
3	Gross profit (subtract line 2 from line 1c)	3	
4	Net gain (loss) from Form 4797, Part II, line 18	4	
5	Other income (see instructions) *(attach schedule)*	5	
6	**Total** income (loss)—Combine lines 3 through 5 . . . . ▶	6	

Deductions (See instructions for limitations.)

7	Compensation of officers	7	
8a	Salaries and wages [＿＿＿＿] **b** Less jobs credit [＿＿＿＿] **c** Bal ▶	8c	
9	Repairs	9	
10	Bad debts	10	
11	Rents	11	
12	Taxes	12	
13	Interest	13	
14a	Depreciation (see instructions) . . . . . 14a [＿＿＿]		
b	Depreciation reported on Schedule A and elsewhere on return . . 14b [＿＿＿]		
c	Subtract line 14b from line 14a	14c	
15	Depletion (**Do not deduct oil and gas depletion.** See instructions.)	15	
16	Advertising	16	
17	Pension, profit-sharing, etc., plans	17	
18	Employee benefit programs	18	
19	Other deductions *(attach schedule)*	19	
20	**Total** deductions—Add lines 7 through 19 . . . . ▶	20	
21	Ordinary income (loss) from trade or business activities—Subtract line 20 from line 6	21	

Tax and Payments

22	**Tax:**		
a	Excess net passive income tax *(attach schedule)* . . . . . 22a [＿＿＿]		
b	Tax from Schedule D (Form 1120S) . . . . 22b [＿＿＿]		
c	Add lines 22a and 22b (see instructions for additional taxes)	22c	
23	**Payments:**		
a	1990 estimated tax payments . . . . 23a [＿＿＿]		
b	Tax deposited with Form 7004 . . . . 23b [＿＿＿]		
c	Credit for Federal tax on fuels *(attach Form 4136)* . . . . . 23c [＿＿＿]		
d	Add lines 23a through 23c	23d	
24	Enter any **penalty** for underpayment of estimated tax—Check ▶ ☐ if Form 2220 is attached .	24	
25	Tax due—If the total of lines 22c and 24 is larger than line 23d, enter amount owed. See instructions for depositary method of payment . . . . ▶	25	
26	**Overpayment**—If line 23d is larger than the total of lines 22c and 24, enter amount overpaid ▶	26	
27	Enter amount of line 26 you want: **Credited to 1991 estimated tax** ▶ [＿＿＿] Refunded ▶	27	

Please Sign Here

Under penalties of perjury, I declare that I have examined this return, including accompanying schedules and statements, and to the best of my knowledge and belief, it is true, correct, and complete. Declaration of preparer (other than taxpayer) is based on all information of which preparer has any knowledge.

▶ _____　_____　▶ _____
　Signature of officer　　Date　　Title

Paid Preparer's Use Only

Preparer's signature ▶	Date	Check if self-employed ▶ ☐	Preparer's social security number
Firm's name (or yours if self-employed) and address ▶		E.I. No. ▶	
		ZIP code ▶	

For Paperwork Reduction Act Notice, see page 1 of separate instructions.

Form **1120S** (1990)

Form 1120S (1990)   Page **2**

Schedule A   **Cost of Goods Sold** (See instructions.)

1 Inventory at beginning of year	1	
2 Purchases	2	
3 Cost of labor	3	
4a Additional section 263A costs (see instructions) *(attach schedule)*	4a	
b Other costs *(attach schedule)*	4b	
5 Total—Add lines 1 through 4b	5	
6 Inventory at end of year	6	
7 Cost of goods sold—Subtract line 6 from line 5. Enter here and on line 2, page 1	7	

8a Check all methods used for valuing closing inventory:
    (i) ☐ Cost
    (ii) ☐ Lower of cost or market as described in Regulations section 1.471-4
    (iii) ☐ Writedown of ''subnormal'' goods as described in Regulations section 1.471-2(c)
    (iv) ☐ Other (specify method used and attach explanation) ▶ ....
  b Check this box if the LIFO inventory method was adopted this tax year for any goods *(if checked, attach Form 970)* . . . ▶ ☐
  c If the LIFO inventory method was used for this tax year, enter percentage (or amounts) of closing
    inventory computed under LIFO **8c**
  d Do the rules of section 263A (with respect to property produced or acquired for resale) apply to the corporation? . . ☐ Yes ☐ No
  e Was there any change in determining quantities, cost, or valuations between opening and closing inventory? . . . . ☐ Yes ☐ No
    If ''Yes,'' attach explanation.

Additional Information Required (continued from page 1)

	Yes	No
I Did you at the end of the tax year own, directly or indirectly, 50% or more of the voting stock of a domestic corporation? For rules of attribution, see section 267(c). If ''Yes,'' attach a schedule showing: **(1)** name, address, and employer identification number; and **(2)** percentage owned.		
J Refer to the list in the instructions and state your principal:		
(1) Business activity ▶ .... **(2)** Product or service ▶		
K Were you a member of a controlled group subject to the provisions of section 1561?		
L At any time during the tax year, did you have an interest in or a signature or other authority over a financial account in a foreign country (such as a bank account, securities account, or other financial account)? (See instructions for exceptions and filing requirements for form TD F 90-22.1.)		
If ''Yes,'' enter the name of the foreign country ▶		
M Were you the grantor of, or transferor to, a foreign trust that existed during the current tax year, whether or not you have any beneficial interest in it? If ''Yes,'' you may have to file Forms 3520, 3520-A, or 926		
N During this tax year did you maintain any part of your accounting/tax records on a computerized system?		
O Check method of accounting: **(1)** ☐ Cash **(2)** ☐ Accrual **(3)** ☐ Other (specify) ▶		
P Check this box if the S corporation has filed or is required to file **Form 8264,** Application for Registration of a Tax Shelter . . . . ▶ ☐		
Q Check this box if the corporation issued publicly offered debt instruments with original issue discount . . . . ▶ ☐		
If so, the corporation may have to file **Form 8281,** Information Return for Publicly Offered Original Issue Discount Instruments.		
R If the corporation: **(1)** filed its election to be an S corporation after 1986, **(2)** was a C corporation before it elected to be an S corporation **or** the corporation acquired an asset with a basis determined by reference to its basis (or the basis of any other property) in the hands of a C corporation, and **(3)** has net unrealized built-in gain (defined in section 1374(d)(1)) in excess of the net recognized built-in gain from prior years, enter the net unrealized built-in gain reduced by net recognized built-in gain from prior years (see instructions) . . . . . ▶ $		
S Check this box if the corporation had subchapter C earnings and profits at the close of the tax year (see instructions) ▶ ☐		

Designation of Tax Matters Person (See instructions.)

Enter below the shareholder designated as the tax matters person (TMP) for the tax year of this return:

Name of
designated TMP ▶ _____   Identifying
number of TMP ▶ _____

Address of
designated TMP ▶ _____

Form 1120S (1990)

Page **3**

Schedule K — Shareholders' Shares of Income, Credits, Deductions, Etc.

	(a) Pro rata share items		(b) Total amount
Income (Loss)	**1** Ordinary income (loss) from trade or business activities (page 1, line 21)	**1**	
	2 Net income (loss) from rental real estate activities *(attach Form 8825)*	**2**	
	3a Gross income from other rental activities **3a**		
	b Less expenses *(attach schedule)* **3b**		
	c Net income (loss) from other rental activities	**3c**	
	4 Portfolio income (loss):		
	a Interest income	**4a**	
	b Dividend income	**4b**	
	c Royalty income	**4c**	
	d Net short-term capital gain (loss) *(attach Schedule D (Form 1120S))*	**4d**	
	e Net long-term capital gain (loss) *(attach Schedule D (Form 1120S))*	**4e**	
	f Other portfolio income (loss) *(attach schedule)*	**4f**	
	5 Net gain (loss) under section 1231 (other than due to casualty or theft) *(attach Form 4797)*	**5**	
	6 Other income (loss) *(attach schedule)*	**6**	
Deductions	**7** Charitable contributions (see instructions) *(attach list)*	**7**	
	8 Section 179 expense deduction *(attach Form 4562)*	**8**	
	9 Deductions related to portfolio income (loss) (see instructions) (itemize)	**9**	
	10 Other deductions *(attach schedule)*	**10**	
Investment Interest	**11a** Interest expense on investment debts	**11a**	
	b (1) Investment income included on lines 4a through 4f above	**11b(1)**	
	(2) Investment expenses included on line 9 above	**11b(2)**	
Credits	**12a** Credit for alcohol used as a fuel *(attach Form 6478)*	**12a**	
	b Low-income housing credit (see instructions):		
	(1) From partnerships to which section 42(j)(5) applies for property placed in service before 1990.	**12b(1)**	
	(2) Other than on line 12b(1) for property placed in service before 1990	**12b(2)**	
	(3) From partnerships to which section 42(j)(5) applies for property placed in service after 1989	**12b(3)**	
	(4) Other than on line 12b(3) for property placed in service after 1989 . .	**12b(4)**	
	c Qualified rehabilitation expenditures related to rental real estate activities *(attach Form 3468)*	**12c**	
	d Credits (other than credits shown on lines 12b and 12c) related to rental real estate activities (see instructions)	**12d**	
	e Credits related to other rental activities (see instructions)	**12e**	
	13 Other credits (see instructions)	**13**	
Adjustments and Tax Preference Items	**14a** Accelerated depreciation of real property placed in service before 1987	**14a**	
	b Accelerated depreciation of leased personal property placed in service before 1987 . . .	**14b**	
	c Depreciation adjustment on property placed in service after 1986	**14c**	
	d Depletion (other than oil and gas)	**14d**	
	e (1) Gross income from oil, gas, or geothermal properties	**14e(1)**	
	(2) Deductions allocable to oil, gas, or geothermal properties	**14e(2)**	
	f Other adjustments and tax preference items *(attach schedule)*	**14f**	
Foreign Taxes	**15a** Type of income ▶		
	b Name of foreign country or U.S. possession ▶		
	c Total gross income from sources outside the U.S. *(attach schedule)*	**15c**	
	d Total applicable deductions and losses *(attach schedule)*	**15d**	
	e Total foreign taxes (check one): ▶ ☐ Paid ☐ Accrued	**15e**	
	f Reduction in taxes available for credit *(attach schedule)*	**15f**	
	g Other foreign tax information *(attach schedule)*	**15g**	
Other Items	**16a** Total expenditures to which a section 59(e) election may apply	**16a**	
	b Type of expenditures ▶		
	17 Total property distributions (including cash) other than dividends reported on line 19 below	**17**	
	18 Other items and amounts required to be reported separately to shareholders (see instructions) *(attach schedule)*		
	19 Total dividend distributions paid from accumulated earnings and profits	**19**	
	20 Income (loss) (Required only if Schedule M-1 must be completed.)—Combine lines 1 through 6 in column (b). From the result subtract the sum of lines 7 through 11a, 15e, and 16a	**20**	

Form 1120S (1990)

Schedule L   Balance Sheets

Assets	Beginning of tax year (a)	(b)	End of tax year (c)	(d)
1 Cash				
2a Trade notes and accounts receivable				
b Less allowance for bad debts				
3 Inventories				
4 U.S. government obligations				
5 Tax-exempt securities				
6 Other current assets (attach schedule)				
7 Loans to shareholders				
8 Mortgage and real estate loans				
9 Other investments (attach schedule)				
10a Buildings and other depreciable assets				
b Less accumulated depreciation				
11a Depletable assets				
b Less accumulated depletion				
12 Land (net of any amortization)				
13a Intangible assets (amortizable only)				
b Less accumulated amortization				
14 Other assets (attach schedule)				
15 Total assets				
Liabilities and Shareholders' Equity				
16 Accounts payable				
17 Mortgages, notes, bonds payable in less than 1 year				
18 Other current liabilities (attach schedule)				
19 Loans from shareholders				
20 Mortgages, notes, bonds payable in 1 year or more				
21 Other liabilities (attach schedule)				
22 Capital stock				
23 Paid-in or capital surplus				
24 Retained earnings				
25 Less cost of treasury stock		( )		( )
26 Total liabilities and shareholders' equity				

Schedule M-1   Reconciliation of Income per Books With Income per Return (You are not required to complete this schedule if the total assets on line 15, column (d), of Schedule L are less than $25,000.)

1 Net income per books		5 Income recorded on books this year not included on Schedule K, lines 1 through 6 (itemize):	
2 Income included on Schedule K, lines 1 through 6, not recorded on books this year (itemize):		a Tax-exempt interest $...............	
....		....	
3 Expenses recorded on books this year not included on Schedule K, lines 1 through 11a, 15e, and 16a (itemize):		6 Deductions included on Schedule K, lines 1 through 11a, 15e, and 16a, not charged against book income this year (itemize):	
a Depreciation $.......................		a Depreciation $.....................	
b Travel and entertainment $................		....	
....		7 Total of lines 5 and 6	
4 Total of lines 1 through 3		8 Income (loss) (Schedule K, line 20)—Line 4 less line 7	

Schedule M-2   Analysis of Accumulated Adjustments Account, Other Adjustments Account, and Shareholders' Undistributed Taxable Income Previously Taxed (See instructions.)

	(a) Accumulated adjustments account	(b) Other adjustments account	(c) Shareholders' undistributed taxable income previously taxed
1 Balance at beginning of tax year			
2 Ordinary income from page 1, line 21			
3 Other additions			
4 Loss from page 1, line 21	( )		
5 Other reductions	( )	( )	
6 Combine lines 1 through 5			
7 Distributions other than dividend distributions			
8 Balance at end of tax year—subtract line 7 from line 6			

SCHEDULE K-1
(Form 1120S)
Department of the Treasury
Internal Revenue Service

Shareholder's Share of Income, Credits, Deductions, Etc.
▶ See separate instructions.
For calendar year 1990 or tax year
beginning _____ , 1990, and ending _____ , 19 __

OMB No. 1545-0130

19**90**

Shareholder's identifying number ▶

Corporation's identifying number ▶

Shareholder's name, address, and ZIP code

Corporation's name, address, and ZIP code

A Shareholder's percentage of stock ownership for tax year (see Instructions for Schedule K-1) . . . . ▶ _____ %

B Internal Revenue Service Center where corporation filed its return ▶ ....

C **(1)** Tax shelter registration number (see Instructions for Schedule K-1) . . . . ▶ ....

(2) Type of tax shelter ▶ ....

D If the shareholder acquired corporate stock after 10/22/86, check here ▶ ☐ and enter the shareholder's weighted percentage increase in stock ownership for 1990 (see Instructions for Schedule K-1) . . . . ▶ _____ %

E If any activity for which income or loss is reported on line 1, 2, or 3, was started or acquired by the corporation after 10/22/86, check here ▶ ☐ and enter the date of start up or acquisition in the date space on line 1, 2, or 3 **below.**

F Check applicable boxes: **(1)** ☐ Final K-1   **(2)** ☐ Amended K-1

	(a) Pro rata share items		(b) Amount	(c) Form 1040 filers enter the amount in column (b) on:
Income (Loss)	**1** Ordinary income (loss) from trade or business activities. If applicable, enter date asked for in item E . . . . . ▶ _____	**1**		See Shareholder's Instructions for Schedule K-1 (Form 1120S).
	2 Net income (loss) from rental real estate activities. If applicable, enter date asked for in item E . . . . . ▶ _____	**2**		
	3 Net income (loss) from other rental activities. If applicable, enter date asked for in item E . . . . . ▶ _____	**3**		
	4 Portfolio income (loss):			
	a Interest	**4a**		Sch. B, Part I, line 1
	b Dividends	**4b**		Sch. B, Part II, line 5
	c Royalties	**4c**		Sch. E, Part I, line 4
	d Net short-term capital gain (loss)	**4d**		Sch. D, line 5, col. (f) or (g)
	e Net long-term capital gain (loss)	**4e**		Sch. D, line 12, col. (f) or (g)
	f Other portfolio income (loss) *(attach schedule)*	**4f**		(Enter on applicable line of your return.)
	5 Net gain (loss) under section 1231 (other than due to casualty or theft)	**5**		See Shareholder's Instructions for Schedule K-1 (Form 1120S)
	6 Other income (loss) *(attach schedule)*	**6**		(Enter on applicable line of your return.)
Deductions	**7** Charitable contributions	**7**		Sch. A, line 14 or 15
	8 Section 179 expense deduction *(attach schedule)*	**8**		See Shareholder's Instructions for Schedule K-1 (Form 1120S).
	9 Deductions related to portfolio income (loss) *(attach schedule)* .	**9**		
	10 Other deductions *(attach schedule)*	**10**		
Investment Interest	**11a** Interest expense on investment debts	**11a**		Form 4952, line 1
	b (1) Investment income included on lines 4a through 4f above .	**b(1)**		See Shareholder's Instructions for Schedule K-1 (Form 1120S)
	(2) Investment expenses included on line 9 above	**b(2)**		
Credits	**12a** Credit for alcohol used as fuel	**12a**		Form 6478, line 10
	b Low-income housing credit:			
	(1) From section 42(j)(5) partnerships for property placed in service before 1990	**b(1)**		Form 8586, line 5
	(2) Other than on line 12b(1) for property placed in service before 1990 .	**b(2)**		
	(3) From section 42(j)(5) partnerships for property placed in service after 1989 .	**b(3)**		
	(4) Other than on line 12b(3) for property placed in service after 1989	**b(4)**		
	c Qualified rehabilitation expenditures related to rental real estate activities (see instructions)	**12c**		See Shareholder's Instructions for Schedule K-1 (Form 1120S).
	d Credits (other than credits shown on lines 12b and 12c) related to rental real estate activities (see instructions)	**12d**		
	e Credits related to other rental activities (see instructions) . . .	**12e**		
	13 Other credits (see instructions)	**13**		

For Paperwork Reduction Act Notice, see Form 1120S Instructions.   Schedule K-1 (Form 1120S) 1990

Schedule K-1 (Form 1120S) (1990)   Page **2**

(a) Pro rata share items		(b) Amount	(c) Form 1040 filers enter the amount in column (b) on:
Adjustments and Tax Preference Items	**14a** Accelerated depreciation of real property placed in service before 1987	14a	See Shareholder's Instructions for Schedule K-1 (Form 1120S) and Form 6251 Instructions.
	b Accelerated depreciation of leased personal property placed in service before 1987.	14b	
	c Depreciation adjustment on property placed in service after 1986 .	14c	
	d Depletion (other than oil and gas)	14d	
	e (1) Gross income from oil, gas, or geothermal properties	e(1)	
	(2) Deductions allocable to oil, gas, or geothermal properties . .	e(2)	
	f Other adjustments and tax preference items *(attach schedule)* . .	14f	
Foreign Taxes	**15a** Type of income ▶		Form 1116, Check boxes
	b Name of foreign country or U.S. possession ▶		Form 1116, Part I
	c Total gross income from sources outside the U.S. *(attach schedule)*	15c	Form 1116, Part I
	d Total applicable deductions and losses *(attach schedule)*	15d	Form 1116, Part I
	e Total foreign taxes (check one): ▶ ☐ Paid ☐ Accrued . . .	15e	Form 1116, Part II
	f Reduction in taxes available for credit *(attach schedule)*	15f	Form 1116, Part III
	g Other foreign tax information *(attach schedule)*	15g	See Form 1116 Instructions
Other Items	**16a** Total expenditures to which a section 59(e) election may apply . .	16a	See Shareholder's Instructions for Schedule K-1 (Form 1120S).
	b Type of expenditures ▶		
	17 Property distributions (including cash) other than dividend distributions reported to you on Form 1099-DIV.	17	
	18 Amount of loan repayments for "Loans from Shareholders". . .	18	

	19	Recapture of low-income housing credit:			
		a From section 42(j)(5) partnerships	19a	} Form 8611, line 8
		b Other than on line 19a	19b	

		A	**B**	**C**	
Recapture of Tax Credits	**20** Investment credit properties:				
	a Description of property (State whether recovery or non-recovery property. If recovery property, state whether regular percentage method or section 48(q) election is used.)				Form 4255, top
	b Date placed in service .				Form 4255, line 2
	c Cost or other basis . .				Form 4255, line 3
	d Class of recovery property or original estimated useful life .				Form 4255, line 4
	e Date item ceased to be investment credit property				Form 4255, line 8

21 Supplemental information required to be reported separately to each shareholder *(attach additional schedules if more space is needed):*

Supplemental Information

....
....
....
....
....
....
....
....
....
....
....

B-3   U.S. Partnership Return of Income

Form **1065** Department of the Treasury Internal Revenue Service	**U.S. Partnership Return of Income** For calendar year 1990, or tax year beginning _____ , 1990, and ending _____ 19 ____ ▶ **See separate instructions.**	OMB No. 1545-0099 19**90**

A Principal business activity	Use IRS label. Otherwise, please print or type.	Name	D Employer identification number
B Principal product or service		Number, street, and room or suite no. (If a P.O. box, see page 9 of the instructions.)	E Date business started
C Business code number		City or town, state, and ZIP code	F Total assets (see Specific Instructions) $

			Yes	No
G Check applicable boxes: **(1)** ☐ Initial return **(2)** ☐ Final return **(3)** ☐ Change in address **(4)** ☐ Amended return		Q Has this partnership filed, or is it required to file, **Form 8264,** Application for Registration of a Tax Shelter? . . .		
H Check accounting method: (1) ☐ Cash (2) ☐ Accrual (3) ☐ Other (specify) ▶ _____		R Was there a distribution of property or a transfer (for example, by sale or death) of a partnership interest during the tax year? If "Yes," see the instructions concerning an election to adjust the basis of the partnership's assets under section 754		
	Yes	No		
I Number of partners in this partnership ▶ _____				
J Is this partnership a limited partnership?				
K Are any partners in this partnership also partnerships? . .			S At any time during the tax year, did the partnership have an interest in or a signature or other authority over a financial account in a foreign country (such as a bank account, securities account, or other financial account)? (See the instructions for exceptions and filing requirements for form TD F 90-22.1.) If "Yes," enter the name of the foreign country. ▶ _____		
L Is this partnership a partner in another partnership? . .					
M Is this partnership subject to the consolidated audit procedures of sections 6221 through 6233? If "Yes," see "Designation of Tax Matters Partner" on page 2					
N Does this partnership meet **all** the requirements shown in the instructions for **Question N?**			T Was the partnership the grantor of, or transferor to, a foreign trust which existed during the current tax year, whether or not the partnership or any partner has any beneficial interest in it? If "Yes," you may have to file Forms 3520, 3520-A, or 926		
O Does this partnership have any foreign partners? . . .					
P Is this partnership a publicly traded partnership as defined in section 469(k)(2)?					

Caution: *Include* **only** *trade or business income and expenses on lines 1a through 21 below. See the instructions for more information.*

Income	**1a** Gross receipts or sales	1a		
	b Less returns and allowances	1b	1c	
	2 Cost of goods sold (Schedule A, line 7)		2	
	3 Gross profit—Subtract line 2 from line 1c		3	
	4 Ordinary income (loss) from other partnerships and fiduciaries *(attach schedule)*		4	
	5 Net farm profit (loss) *(attach Schedule F (Form 1040))*		5	
	6 Net gain (loss) from Form 4797, Part II, line 18		6	
	7 Other income (loss) (see instructions) *(attach schedule)*		7	
	8 Total income (loss)—Combine lines 3 through 7		8	

Deductions (see instructions for limitations)	**9a** Salaries and wages (other than to partners)	9a		
	b Less jobs credit	9b	9c	
	10 Guaranteed payments to partners		10	
	11 Rent		11	
	12 Interest		12	
	13 Taxes		13	
	14 Bad debts		14	
	15 Repairs		15	
	16a Depreciation (see instructions)	16a	16c	
	b Less depreciation reported on Schedule A and elsewhere on return	16b		
	17 Depletion **(Do not deduct oil and gas depletion.)**		17	
	18a Retirement plans, etc.		18a	
	b Employee benefit programs		18b	
	19 Other deductions *(attach schedule)*		19	
	20 Total deductions—Add lines 9c through 19		20	
	21 Ordinary income (loss) from trade or business activities—Subtract line 20 from line 8		21	

Please Sign Here	Under penalties of perjury, I declare that I have examined this return, including accompanying schedules and statements, and to the best of my knowledge and belief, it is true, correct, and complete. Declaration of preparer (other than general partner) is based on all information of which preparer has any knowledge	
	▶ _____ Signature of general partner	▶ _____ Date

Paid Preparer's Use Only	Preparer's signature ▶	Date	Check if self-employed ▶ ☐	Preparer's social security no.
	Firm's name (or yours if self-employed) and address ▶		E.I. No. ▶	
			ZIP code ▶	

For Paperwork Reduction Act Notice, see page 1 of separate instructions.   Form **1065** (1990)

Form 1065 (1990)   Page **2**

Schedule A   Cost of Goods Sold

1 Inventory at beginning of year	**1**	
2 Purchases less cost of items withdrawn for personal use	**2**	
3 Cost of labor	**3**	
4a Additional section 263A costs (see instructions) *(attach schedule)*	**4a**	
b Other costs *(attach schedule)*	**4b**	
5 Total—Add lines 1 through 4b	**5**	
6 Inventory at end of year	**6**	
7 Cost of goods sold—Subtract line 6 from line 5. Enter here and on page 1, line 2	**7**	

8a Check all methods used for valuing closing inventory:

    (i) ☐ Cost   (ii) ☐ Lower of cost or market as described in Regulations section 1.471-4

    (iii) ☐ Writedown of "subnormal" goods as described in Regulations section 1.471-2(c)

    (iv) ☐ Other (specify method used and attach explanation) ▶ ....

  b Check this box if the LIFO inventory method was adopted this tax year for any goods *(if checked, attach Form 970)* . . . . . ▶ ☐

  c Do the rules of section 263A (with respect to property produced or acquired for resale) apply to the partnership? . . ☐ **Yes** ☐ **No**

  d Was there any change in determining quantities, cost, or valuations between opening and closing inventory? . . . ☐ **Yes** ☐ **No**
    If "Yes," attach explanation.

Schedule L   Balance Sheets

Caution: *Read the instructions for* **Question N** *on page 9 of the instructions before completing Schedules L and M.*

Assets	Beginning of tax year		End of tax year	
	(a)	(b)	(c)	(d)
1 Cash				
2a Trade notes and accounts receivable				
b Less allowance for bad debts				
3 Inventories				
4 U.S. government obligations				
5 Tax-exempt securities				
6 Other current assets *(attach schedule)*				
7 Mortgage and real estate loans				
8 Other investments *(attach schedule)*				
9a Buildings and other depreciable assets				
b Less accumulated depreciation				
10a Depletable assets				
b Less accumulated depletion				
11 Land (net of any amortization)				
12a Intangible assets (amortizable only)				
b Less accumulated amortization				
13 Other assets *(attach schedule)*				
14 Total assets				
Liabilities and Capital				
15 Accounts payable				
16 Mortgages, notes, bonds payable in less than 1 year				
17 Other current liabilities *(attach schedule)*				
18 All nonrecourse loans				
19 Mortgages, notes, bonds payable in 1 year or more				
20 Other liabilities *(attach schedule)*				
21 Partners' capital accounts				
22 Total liabilities and capital				

Schedule M   Reconciliation of Partners' Capital Accounts
(Show reconciliation of each partner's capital account on Schedule K-1 (Form 1065), Item K.)

(a) Partners' capital accounts at beginning of year	(b) Capital contributed during year	(c) Income (loss) from lines 1, 2, 3c, and 4 of Schedule K	(d) Income not included in column (c), plus nontaxable income	(e) Losses not included in column (c), plus unallowable deductions	(f) Withdrawals and distributions	(g) Partners' capital accounts at end of year (combine columns (a) through (f))
				( )	( )	

Designation of Tax Matters Partner (See instructions.)

Enter below the general partner designated as the tax matters partner (TMP) for the tax year of this return:

Name of designated TMP ▶ _____   Identifying number of TMP ▶ _____

Address of designated TMP ▶ _____

Form 1065 (1990)   Page **3**

Schedule K	**Partners' Shares of Income, Credits, Deductions, Etc.**	
	(a) Distributive share items	**(b) Total amount**

Income (Loss)	**1** Ordinary income (loss) from trade or business activities (page 1, line 21)	**1**	
	2 Net income (loss) from rental real estate activities *(attach Form 8825)*	**2**	
	3a Gross income from other rental activities	**3a**	
	b Less expenses *(attach schedule)*	**3b**	
	c Net income (loss) from other rental activities	**3c**	
	4 Portfolio income (loss) (see instructions):		
	a Interest income	**4a**	
	b Dividend income	**4b**	
	c Royalty income	**4c**	
	d Net short-term capital gain (loss) *(attach Schedule D (Form 1065))*	**4d**	
	e Net long-term capital gain (loss) *(attach Schedule D (Form 1065))*	**4e**	
	f Other portfolio income (loss) *(attach schedule)*	**4f**	
	5 Guaranteed payments to partners	**5**	
	6 Net gain (loss) under section 1231 (other than due to casualty or theft) *(attach Form 4797)*	**6**	
	7 Other income (loss) *(attach schedule)*	**7**	
Deduc-tions	**8** Charitable contributions (see instructions) *(attach list)*	**8**	
	9 Section 179 expense deduction *(attach Form 4562)*	**9**	
	10 Deductions related to portfolio income (see instructions) (itemize)	**10**	
	11 Other deductions *(attach schedule)*	**11**	
Invest-ment Interest	**12a** Interest expense on investment debts	**12a**	
	b (1) Investment income included on lines 4a through 4f above	**12b(1)**	
	(2) Investment expenses included on line 10 above	**12b(2)**	
Credits	**13a** Credit for income tax withheld	**13a**	
	b Low-income housing credit (see instructions):		
	(1) From partnerships to which section 42(j)(5) applies for property placed in service before 1990	**13b(1)**	
	(2) Other than on line 13b(1) for property placed in service before 1990	**13b(2)**	
	(3) From partnerships to which section 42(j)(5) applies for property placed in service after 1989	**13b(3)**	
	(4) Other than on line 13b(3) for property placed in service after 1989	**13b(4)**	
	c Qualified rehabilitation expenditures related to rental real estate activities *(attach Form 3468)*	**13c**	
	d Credits (other than credits shown on lines 13b and 13c) related to rental real estate activities (see instructions)	**13d**	
	e Credits related to other rental activities (see instructions)	**13e**	
	14 Other credits (see instructions)	**14**	
Self-Employ-ment	**15a** Net earnings (loss) from self-employment	**15a**	
	b Gross farming or fishing income	**15b**	
	c Gross nonfarm income	**15c**	
Adjustments and Tax Preference Items	**16a** Accelerated depreciation of real property placed in service before 1987	**16a**	
	b Accelerated depreciation of leased personal property placed in service before 1987 . . .	**16b**	
	c Depreciation adjustment on property placed in service after 1986	**16c**	
	d Depletion (other than oil and gas)	**16d**	
	e (1) Gross income from oil, gas, and geothermal properties	**16e(1)**	
	(2) Deductions allocable to oil, gas, and geothermal properties	**16e(2)**	
	f Other adjustments and tax preference items *(attach schedule)*	**16f**	
Foreign Taxes	**17a** Type of income ▶ --		
	b Foreign country or U.S. possession ▶ -------------------------------		
	c Total gross income from sources outside the U.S. *(attach schedule)*	**17c**	
	d Total applicable deductions and losses *(attach schedule)*	**17d**	
	e Total foreign taxes (check one): ▶ ☐ Paid ☐ Accrued	**17e**	
	f Reduction in taxes available for credit *(attach schedule)*	**17f**	
	g Other foreign tax information *(attach schedule)*	**17g**	
Other	**18a** Total expenditures to which a section 59(e) election may apply	**18a**	
	b Type of expenditures ▶ --		
	19 Other items and amounts required to be reported separately to partners (see instructions) *(attach schedule)*		
Analysis	**20a** Total distributive income/payment items—Combine lines 1 through 7 above	**20a**	

b Analysis by type of partner:	**(a)** Corporate	**(b)** Individual		**(c)** Partnership	**(d)** Exempt organization	**(e)** Nominee Other
		i. Active	ii. Passive			
(1) General partners						
(2) Limited partners						

SCHEDULE K-1
(Form 1065)
Department of the Treasury
Internal Revenue Service

Partner's Share of Income, Credits, Deductions, Etc.
▶ See separate instructions.
For calendar year 1990 or tax year
beginning _____, 1990, and ending _____, 19___

OMB No. 1545-0099

1990

Partner's identifying number ▶ _____ | Partnership's identifying number ▶ _____

Partner's name, address, and ZIP code | Partnership's name, address, and ZIP code

A Is this partner a general partner? . . . ☐ Yes ☐ No
B Partner's share of liabilities (see instructions):
Nonrecourse . . . . $ _____
Qualified nonrecourse financing . . $ _____
Other . . . . $ _____
C What type of entity is this partner? ▶ _____
D Is this partner a ☐ domestic or a ☐ foreign partner?

E Enter partner's percentage of:

	(i) Before change or termination	(ii) End of year
Profit sharing	_____%	_____%
Loss sharing	_____%	_____%
Ownership of capital . . .	_____%	_____%

F IRS Center where partnership filed return ▶ _____
G(1) Tax shelter registration number ▶ _____
(2) Type of tax shelter ▶ _____
H(1) Did the partner's ownership interest in the partnership change after Oct. 22, 1986? . . . . ☐ Yes ☐ No
If "Yes," attach statement. (See Form 1065 Instructions.)
(2) Did the partnership start or acquire a new activity after Oct. 22, 1986? . . . . ☐ Yes ☐ No
If "Yes," attach statement. (See Form 1065 Instructions.)
I Check here if this partnership is a publicly traded partnership as defined in section 469(k)(2) . . . . ☐
J Check applicable boxes: (1) ☐ Final K-1 (2) ☐ Amended K-1

K Reconciliation of partner's capital account:

(a) Capital account at beginning of year	(b) Capital contributed during year	(c) Income (loss) from lines 1, 2, 3, and 4 below	(d) Income not included in column (c), plus nontaxable income	(e) Losses not included in column (c), plus unallowable deductions	(f) Withdrawals and distributions	(g) Capital account at end of year (combine columns (a) through (f))
				( )	( )	

		(a) Distributive share item		(b) Amount	(c) 1040 filers enter the amount in column (b) on:
Income (Loss)	1	Ordinary income (loss) from trade or business activities . . .	1		(See Partner's Instructions for Schedule K-1 (Form 1065))
	2	Net income (loss) from rental real estate activities	2		
	3	Net income (loss) from other rental activities	3		
	4	Portfolio income (loss):			
	a	Interest	4a		Sch. B, Part I, line 1
	b	Dividends	4b		Sch. B, Part II, line 5
	c	Royalties	4c		Sch. E, Part I, line 4
	d	Net short-term capital gain (loss)	4d		Sch. D, line 5, col. (f) or (g)
	e	Net long-term capital gain (loss)	4e		Sch. D, line 12, col. (f) or (g)
	f	Other portfolio income (loss) (attach schedule)	4f		(Enter on applicable line of your return)
	5	Guaranteed payments to partner	5		(See Partner's Instructions for Schedule K-1 (Form 1065))
	6	Net gain (loss) under section 1231 (other than due to casualty or theft)	6		
	7	Other income (loss) (attach schedule)	7		(Enter on applicable line of your return)
Deductions	8	Charitable contributions	8		Sch. A, line 14 or 15
	9	Section 179 expense deduction (attach schedule)	9		(See Partner's Instructions for Schedule K-1 (Form 1065))
	10	Deductions related to portfolio income (attach schedule) . . .	10		
	11	Other deductions (attach schedule)	11		
Investment Interest	12a	Interest expense on investment debts	12a		Form 4952, line 1
	b	(1) Investment income included on lines 4a through 4f above .	b(1)		(See Partner's Instructions for Schedule K-1 (Form 1065))
		(2) Investment expenses included on line 10 above	b(2)		
Credits	13a	Credit for income tax withheld	13a		(See Partner's Instructions for Schedule K-1 (Form 1065))
	b	Low income housing credit:			
		(1) From section 42(j)(5) partnerships for property placed in service before 1990	b(1)		Form 8586, line 5
		(2) Other than on line 13b(1) for property placed in service before 1990	b(2)		
		(3) From section 42(j)(5) partnerships for property placed in service after 1989	b(3)		
		(4) Other than on line 13b(3) for property placed in service after 1989	b(4)		
	c	Qualified rehabilitation expenditures related to rental real estate activities (see instructions)	13c		(See Partner's Instructions for Schedule K-1 (Form 1065))
	d	Credits (other than credits shown on lines 13b and 13c) related to rental real estate activities (see instructions)	13d		
	e	Credits related to other rental activities (see instructions) . . .	13e		
	14	Other credits (see instructions)	14		

For Paperwork Reduction Act Notice, see Form 1065 Instructions.

Schedule K-1 (Form 1065) 1990

Schedule K-1 (Form 1065) 1990   Page **2**

	(a) Distributive share item		(b) Amount	(c) 1040 filers enter the amount in column (b) on:
Self-employment	**15a** Net earnings (loss) from self-employment	**15a**		Sch. SE, Section A or B
	b Gross farming or fishing income	**15b**		(See Partner's Instructions for)
	c Gross nonfarm income	**15c**		(Schedule K-1 (Form 1065))
Adjustments and Tax Preference Items	**16a** Accelerated depreciation of real property placed in service before 1987	**16a**		
	b Accelerated depreciation of leased personal property placed in service before 1987	**16b**		(See Partner's Instructions for Schedule K-1 (Form 1065) and Form 6251 Instructions)
	c Depreciation adjustment on property placed in service after 1986	**16c**		
	d Depletion (other than oil and gas)	**16d**		
	e (1) Gross income from oil, gas, and geothermal properties . .	**e(1)**		
	(2) Deductions allocable to oil, gas, and geothermal properties .	**e(2)**		
	f Other adjustments and tax preference items (attach schedule) .	**16f**		
Foreign Taxes	**17a** Type of income ▶ _____			Form 1116, Check boxes
	b Name of foreign country or U.S. possession ▶ _____			Form 1116, Part I
	c Total gross income from sources outside the U.S. (attach schedule)	**17c**		Form 1116, Part I
	d Total applicable deductions and losses (attach schedule) . . .	**17d**		Form 1116, Part I
	e Total foreign taxes (check one): ▶ ☐ Paid ☐ Accrued . .	**17e**		Form 1116, Part II
	f Reduction in taxes available for credit (attach schedule) . . .	**17f**		Form 1116, Part III
	g Other foreign tax information (attach schedule)	**17g**		See Form 1116 Instructions
Other	**18a** Total expenditures to which a section 59(e) election may apply .	**18a**		(See Partner's Instructions for Schedule K-1 (Form 1065))
	b Type of expenditures ▶ _____			
Recapture of Tax Credits	**19** Recapture of low-income housing credit:			
	a From section 42(j)(5) partnerships	**19a**		} Form 8611, line 8
	b Other than on line 19a	**19b**		

	20 Investment credit properties:	A	B	C	
	a Description of property (State whether recovery or nonrecovery property. If recovery property, state whether regular percentage method or section 48(q) election used.) .				
					Form 4255, top
	b Date placed in service .				Form 4255, line 2
	c Cost or other basis . .				Form 4255, line 3
	d Class of recovery property or original estimated useful life .				Form 4255, line 4
	e Date item ceased to be investment credit property				Form 4255, line 8

Supplemental Information

21 Supplemental information required to be reported separately to each partner (attach additional schedules if more space is needed):

_____

_____

_____

_____

_____

_____

_____

B-4   U.S. Fiduciary Income Tax Return

Form 1041 Department of the Treasury—Internal Revenue Service
U.S. Fiduciary Income Tax Return 1990

| For the calendar year 1990 or fiscal year beginning , 1990, and ending , 19 | OMB No. 1545-0092 |

Check applicable boxes:
- ☐ Decedent's estate
- ☐ Simple trust
- ☐ Complex trust
- ☐ Grantor type trust
- ☐ Bankruptcy estate
- ☐ Family estate trust
- ☐ Pooled income fund

Name of estate or trust (grantor type trust, see instructions) | Employer identification number

Name and title of fiduciary | Date entity created

Number, street, and room or suite no. (If a P.O. box, see page 5 of Instructions.)

City, state, and ZIP code

Nonexempt charitable and split-interest trusts, check applicable boxes (see instructions):
- ☐ Described in section 4947(a)(1)
- ☐ Not a private foundation
- ☐ Described in section 4947(a)(2)

Number of Schedules K-1 attached (see instructions) . . ▶

Check applicable boxes:
☐ First return   ☐ Final return   ☐ Amended return
Change in Fiduciary's ▶   ☐ Name or   ☐ Address

Income

1	Interest income	1
2	Dividends	2
3	Income (or losses) from partnerships, other estates, or other trusts (see instructions)	3
4	Net rental and royalty income (or loss) (attach Schedule E (Form 1040))	4
5	Net business and farm income (or loss) (attach Schedules C and F (Form 1040))	5
6	Capital gain (or loss) (attach Schedule D (Form 1041))	6
7	Ordinary gain (or loss) (attach Form 4797)	7
8	Other income (state nature of income)	8
9	**Total** income (combine lines 1 through 8) ▶	9

Deductions

10	Interest	10	
11	Taxes	11	
12	Fiduciary fees	12	
13	Charitable deduction (from Schedule A, line 6)	13	
14	Attorney, accountant, and return preparer fees	14	
15a	Other deductions NOT subject to the 2% floor (attach schedule)	15a	
b	Allowable miscellaneous itemized deductions subject to the 2% floor	15b	
c	Add lines 15a and 15b	15c	
16	**Total** (add lines 10 through 15c)	16	
17	Adjusted total income (or loss) (subtract line 16 from line 9). Enter here and on Schedule B, line 1 . ▶	17	
18	Income distribution deduction (from Schedule B, line 17) (see instructions) (attach Schedules K-1 (Form 1041))	18	
19	Estate tax deduction (including certain generation-skipping transfer taxes) (attach computation)	19	
20	Exemption	20	
21	**Total deductions** (add lines 18 through 20) ▶	21	

Tax and Payments

22	Taxable income of fiduciary (subtract line 21 from line 17)	22
23	**Total tax** (from Schedule G, line 7) ▶	23
24a	Payments: 1990 estimated tax payments and amount applied from 1989 return	24a
b	Treated as credited to beneficiaries	24b
c	Subtract line 24b from line 24a	24c
d	Tax paid with extension of time to file: ☐ Form 2758 ☐ Form 8736 ☐ Form 8800	24d
e	Federal income tax withheld	24e
	Credits: f Form 2439 ....; g Form 4136 ....; h Other ....; Total ▶	24i
25	**Total** payments (add lines 24c through 24e, and 24i) ▶	25
26	**Penalty** for underpayment of estimated tax (see instructions)	26
27	If the total of lines 23 and 26 is larger than line 25, enter **TAX DUE**	27
28	If line 25 is larger than the total of lines 23 and 26, enter **OVERPAYMENT**	28
29	Amount of line 28 to be: a **Credited to 1991 estimated tax** ▶ .... b **Refunded** ▶	29

Please Sign Here

Under penalties of perjury, I declare that I have examined this return, including accompanying schedules and statements, and to the best of my knowledge and belief, it is true, correct, and complete. Declaration of preparer (other than fiduciary) is based on all information of which preparer has any knowledge.

▶ Signature of fiduciary or officer representing fiduciary | Date | ▶ | EIN of fiduciary (see instructions)

Paid Preparer's Use Only

Preparer's signature ▶	Date	Check if self-employed ▶ ☐	Preparer's social security no.
Firm's name (or yours if self-employed) and address ▶		E.I. No. ▶	
		ZIP code ▶	

For Paperwork Reduction Act Notice, see page 1 of the separate Instructions.   Form **1041** (1990)

Form 1041 (1990)   Page 2

Schedule A   Charitable Deduction—Do not complete for a simple trust or a pooled income fund.

1	Amounts paid or permanently set aside for charitable purposes from current year's gross income	1
2	Tax-exempt interest allocable to charitable distribution (see instructions)	2
3	Subtract line 2 from line 1	3
4	Enter the net short-term capital gain and the net long-term capital gain of the current tax year allocable to corpus paid or permanently set aside for charitable purposes (see instructions)	4
5	Amounts paid or permanently set aside for charitable purposes from gross income of a prior year (see instructions)	5
6	**Total** (add lines 3 through 5). Enter here and on page 1, line 13	6

Schedule B   Income Distribution Deduction (see instructions)

1	Adjusted total income (from page 1, line 17) (see instructions)	1
2	Adjusted tax-exempt interest (see instructions)	2
3	Net gain shown on Schedule D (Form 1041), line 17, column (a). (If net loss, enter zero.)	3
4	Enter amount from Schedule A, line 4	4
5	Long-term capital gain included on Schedule A, line 1	5
6	Short-term capital gain included on Schedule A, line 1	6
7	If the amount on page 1, line 6, is a capital loss, enter here as a positive figure	7
8	If the amount on page 1, line 6, is a capital gain, enter here as a negative figure	8
9	Distributable net income (combine lines 1 through 8)	9
10	Amount of income for the tax year determined under the governing instrument (accounting income) **10**	
11	Amount of income required to be distributed currently (see instructions)	11
12	Other amounts paid, credited, or otherwise required to be distributed (see instructions)	12
13	Total distributions (add lines 11 and 12). (If greater than line 10, see instructions.)	13
14	Enter the amount of tax-exempt income included on line 13	14
15	Tentative income distribution deduction (subtract line 14 from line 13)	15
16	Tentative income distribution deduction (subtract line 2 from line 9)	16
17	Income distribution deduction. Enter the smaller of line 15 or line 16 here and on page 1, line 18	17

Schedule G   Tax Computation (see instructions)

1	Tax: **a** Tax rate schedule.......................; **b** Other taxes...................; . Total ▶		1c
2a	Foreign tax credit (attach Form 1116)	2a	
b	Credit for fuel produced from a nonconventional source.	2b	
c	General business credit. Check if from: □ Form 3800 or □ Form (specify) ▶	2c	
d	Credit for prior year minimum tax (attach Form 8801)	2d	
3	**Total** credits (add lines 2a through 2d) ▶		3
4	Subtract line 3 from line 1c		4
5	Recapture taxes. Check if from: □ Form 4255 □ Form 8611		5
6	Alternative minimum tax (attach Form 8656)		6
7	**Total** tax (add lines 4 through 6). Enter here and on page 1, line 23 ▶		7

Other Information (see instructions)

		Yes	No
1	Did the estate or trust receive tax-exempt income? (If "Yes," attach a computation of the allocation of expenses.) Enter the amount of tax-exempt interest income and exempt-interest dividends ▶ $		
2	Did the estate or trust have any passive activity losses? (If "Yes," enter these losses on **Form 8582**, Passive Activity Loss Limitations, to figure the allowable loss.)		
3	Did the estate or trust receive all or any part of the earnings (salary, wages, and other compensation) of any individual by reason of a contract assignment or similar arrangement?		
4	At any time during the tax year, did the estate or trust have an interest in or a signature or other authority over a financial account in a foreign country (such as a bank account, securities account, or other financial account)? (See the instructions for exceptions and filing requirements for Form TD F 90-22.1.) If "Yes," enter the name of the foreign country ▶		
5	Was the estate or trust the grantor of, or transferor to, a foreign trust which existed during the current tax year, whether or not the estate or trust has any beneficial interest in it? (If "Yes," you may have to file Form 3520, 3520-A, or 926.)		
6	Check this box if this entity has filed or is required to file **Form 8264**, Application for Registration of a Tax Shelter . ▶ □		
7	Check this box if this entity is a complex trust making the section 663(b) election ▶ □		
8	Check this box to make a section 643(e)(3) election (attach Schedule D (Form 1041)) ▶ □		
9	Check this box if the decedent's estate has been open for more than 2 years ▶ □		
10	Check this box if the trust is a participant in a Common Trust Fund that was required to adopt a calendar year . ▶ □		

SCHEDULE K-1 (Form 1041)

Department of the Treasury
Internal Revenue Service

Beneficiary's Share of Income, Deductions, Credits, Etc.—1990

for the calendar year 1990, or fiscal year
beginning ...., 1990, ending ...., 19 .....
Complete a separate Schedule K-1 for each beneficiary.

OMB No. 1545-0092

19 90

Name of estate or trust

☐ Amended K-1
☐ Final K-1

Beneficiary's identifying number ▶

Estate's or trust's employer identification number ▶

Beneficiary's name, address, and ZIP code

Fiduciary's name, address, and ZIP code

Reminder: *If you received a short year 1987 Schedule K-1 that was from a trust required to adopt a calendar year, be sure to include one-fourth of those amounts reported as income, in addition to the items reported on this Schedule K-1, on the appropriate lines of your 1990 Form 1040 and related schedules.*

(a) Allocable share item	(b) Amount	(c) Calendar year 1990 Form 1040 filers enter the amounts in column (b) on:
1　Interest		Schedule B, Part I, line 1
2　Dividends		Schedule B, Part II, line 5
3a　Net short-term capital gain		Schedule D, line 5, column (g)
b　Net long-term capital gain		Schedule D, line 12, column (g)
4a　Other taxable income: (itemize)		Schedule E, Part III
(1) Rental, rental real estate, and business income from activities acquired before 10/23/86		
(2) Rental, rental real estate, and business income from activities acquired after 10/22/86		
(3) Other passive income		
b　Depreciation, including cost recovery (itemize):		
(1) Attributable to line 4a(1)		
(2) Attributable to line 4a(2)		
(3) Attributable to line 4a(3)		
c　Depletion (itemize):		
(1) Attributable to line 4a(1)		
(2) Attributable to line 4a(2)		
(3) Attributable to line 4a(3)		
d　Amortization (itemize):		
(1) Attributable to line 4a(1)		
(2) Attributable to line 4a(2)		
(3) Attributable to line 4a(3)		
5　Income for minimum tax purposes		
6　Income for regular tax purposes (add lines 1 through 4a)		
7　Adjustment for minimum tax purposes (subtract line 6 from line 5)		Form 6251, line 4t
8　Estate tax deduction (including certain generation-skipping transfer taxes) (attach computation)		Schedule A, line 26
9　Excess deductions on termination (attach computation)		Schedule A, line 21
10　Foreign taxes (list on a separate sheet)		Form 1116 or Schedule A (Form 1040), line 7
11　Tax preference items (itemize):		
a　Accelerated depreciation		(Include on the applicable line of Form 6251)
b　Depletion		
c　Amortization		
12　Other (itemize):		
a　Trust payments of estimated taxes credited to you		Form 1040, line 56
b　Tax-exempt interest		Form 1040, line 8b
c　Short-term capital loss carryover		Schedule D, line 6, column (f)
d　Long-term capital loss carryover		Schedule D, line 15, column (f)
e		(Include on the applicable line of appropriate tax form)
f		
g		

For Paperwork Reduction Act Notice, see page 1 of the Instructions for Form 1041.　　　　Schedule K-1 (Form 1041) 1990

SCHEDULE J
(Form 1041)

Department of the Treasury
Internal Revenue Service

Trust Allocation of an Accumulation Distribution
(Under Code Section 665)

▶ File with Form 1041.
▶ See the separate Form 1041 instructions.

OMB No. 1545-0092

1990

Name of trust

Employer identification number

Part I **Accumulation Distribution in 1990**

For definitions and special rules, see the regulations under sections 665-668 of the Internal Revenue Code.
See the Form 4970 instructions for certain income that minors may exclude and special rules for multiple trusts.

1 Enter amount from Schedule B (Form 1041), line 12, for 1990	1
2 Enter amount from Schedule B (Form 1041), line 9, for 1990	2
3 Enter amount from Schedule B (Form 1041), line 11, for 1990	3
4 Subtract line 3 from line 2. If line 3 is more than line 2, enter zero	4
5 Accumulation distribution for 1990. (Subtract line 4 from line 1.)	5

Part II **Ordinary Income Accumulation Distribution (Enter the applicable throwback years below.)**

If the distribution is thrown back to more than five years (starting with the earliest applicable tax year beginning after December 31, 1968), attach additional schedules. (If the trust was a simple trust, see Regulations section 1.665(e)-1A(b).)

		Throwback year ending 19	Throwback year ending 19	Throwback year ending 19	Throwback year ending 19	Throwback year ending 19 ....
6 Distributable net income (see instructions)	6					
7 Distributions (see instructions) .	7					
8 Undistributed net income (subtract line 7 from line 6) . . .	8					
9 Enter amount from page 2, line 25 or line 31, as applicable . .	9					
10 Subtract line 9 from line 8 . .	10					
11 Enter amount of prior accumulation distributions thrown back to any of these years	11					
12 Subtract line 11 from line 10 .	12					
13 Allocate the amount on line 5 to the earliest applicable year first. Do not allocate an amount greater than line 12 for the same year (see instructions) . .	13					
14 Divide line 13 by line 10 and multiply result by amount on line 9	14					
15 Add lines 13 and 14	15					
16 Tax-exempt interest included on line 13 (see instructions) . . .	16					
17 Subtract line 16 from line 15 .	17					

For Paperwork Reduction Act Notice, see page 1 of the Instructions for Form 1041.

Schedule J (Form 1041) 1990

Schedule J (Form 1041) 1990   Page **2**

Part III Taxes Imposed on Undistributed Net Income (Enter the applicable throwback years below.)

If more than five throwback years are involved, attach additional schedules. If the trust received an accumulation distribution from another trust, see the regulations under sections 665-668 of the Internal Revenue Code.

If the trust elected the alternative tax on capital gains, **OMIT** lines 18 through 25 **AND** complete lines 26 through 31.	Throwback year ending 19	Throwback year ending 19	Throwback year ending 19	Throwback year ending 19	Throwback year ending 19 ......
(The alternative tax on capital gains was repealed for tax years beginning after December 31, 1978.)					
18 Tax (see instructions) . .					
19 Net short-term gain (see instructions)					
20 Net long-term gain (see instructions)					
21 Total net capital gain (add lines 19 and 20)					
22 Taxable income (see instructions)					
23 Enter percent (divide line 21 by line 22, but not more than 100%)	%	%	%	%	%
24 Multiply amount on line 18 by the percentage on line 23 . .					
25 Tax on undistributed net income. (Subtract line 24 from line 18. Enter here and on page 1, line 9.) . . .					
Complete lines 26 through 31 only if the trust elected the alternative tax on long-term capital gain.					
26 Tax on income other than long-term capital gain (see instructions).					
27 Net short-term gain (see instructions)					
28 Taxable income less section 1202 deduction (see instructions)					
29 Enter percent (divide line 27 by line 28, but not more than 100%)	%	%	%	%	%
30 Multiply amount on line 26 by the percentage on line 29 . .					
31 Tax on undistributed net income. (Subtract line 30 from line 26. Enter here and on page 1, line 9.) . . .					

Part IV Allocation to Beneficiary

Complete Part IV for each beneficiary. If the accumulation distribution is allocated to more than one beneficiary, attach an additional Schedule J with Part IV completed for each additional beneficiary. If more than five throwback years are involved, attach additional schedules.

Beneficiary's name		Identifying number		
Beneficiary's address (number and street including apartment number or rural route)		Enter amount from line 13 allocated to this beneficiary **(a)**	Enter amount from line 14 allocated to this beneficiary **(b)**	Enter amount from line 16 allocated to this beneficiary **(c)**
City, state, and ZIP code				
32 Throwback year 19	32			
33 Throwback year 19	33			
34 Throwback year 19	34			
35 Throwback year 19	35			
36 Throwback year 19	36			
37 Total (add lines 32 through 36)	37			

B-5   Amended Tax Return Form

Form **1120X** (Rev. June 1988) Department of the Treasury Internal Revenue Service	**Amended U.S. Corporation Income Tax Return**	OMB No. 1545-0132 Expires 6-30-91

| | | **For tax year ending in** ▶ _ _ _ _ _ _ _ _ _ _ (Enter month and year) |

Please Type or Print

Name		Employer identification number
Number and street (or P.O. box number if mail is not delivered to street address)		
City or town, state, and ZIP code		Telephone number (optional) ( )

Enter name and address used on original return (if same as above, write "Same")

Internal Revenue Service Center where original return was filed ▶

Fill in Applicable Items and Use Part II To Explain Any Changes

Part I Income and Deductions	(a) As originally reported or as adjusted (See Specific Instructions)	(b) Net change (Increase or Decrease— explain in Part II)	(c) Correct amount
1 Total income (line 11 of Form 1120 or 1120-A)			
2 Total deductions (total of lines 27 and 29c, Form 1120, or lines 23 and 25c, Form 1120-A)			
3 Taxable income (subtract line 2 from line 1)			
4 Tax (line 31, Form 1120, or line 27, Form 1120-A)			

Payments and Credits

5a Estimated tax payments (include overpayment in prior year allowed as a credit)			
b Amount of refund applied for on Form 4466			
c Subtract line 5b from line 5a			
6 Tax deposited with Form 7004 (automatic extension of time to file).			
7 Credit from regulated investment companies			
8 Credit for Federal tax on fuels			
9 Other payment or refundable credit (specify) ▶ _			
10 Tax deposited or paid with (or after) the filing of the original return			
11 Total of lines 5c through 10, column (c)			
12 Overpayment, if any, as shown on original return or as later adjusted			
13 Subtract line 12 from line 11			

Tax Due or Refund

14 Tax due (subtract line 13 from line 4, column (c)). Make check payable to Internal Revenue Service (see instructions). . . . . ▶	
15 Refund (subtract line 4, column (c), from line 13)	

Please Sign Here

Under penalties of perjury, I declare that I have filed an original return and that I have examined this amended return, including accompanying schedules and statements, and to the best of my knowledge and belief, this amended return is true, correct, and complete. Declaration of preparer (other than taxpayer) is based on all information of which preparer has any knowledge.

Signature of officer	Date	Title

Paid Preparer's Use Only	Preparer's signature ▶	Date	Check if self-employed ▶ ☐	Preparer's social security no.
	Firm's name (or yours if self-employed) and address ▶		E.I. No. ▶	
			ZIP code ▶	

For Paperwork Reduction Act Notice, see instructions on back.

Form **1120X** (Rev. 6-88)

Form 1120X (Rev. 6-88)   Page **2**

Part II Explanation of Changes to Income, Deductions, Credits, Etc. Enter the line reference from page 1 for which a change is reported, and give the reason for each change. Show any computation in detail. Attach any schedules needed.

Check here ▶ ☐ if the change is due to a net operating loss carryback, a capital loss carryback, a general business credit carryback, or for tax years beginning before 1986, a research credit carryback.

General Instructions

(Section references are to the Internal Revenue Code.)

Paperwork Reduction Act Notice.—We ask for this information to carry out the Internal Revenue laws of the United States. The information is used to ensure that taxpayers are complying with these laws and to allow us to figure and collect the correct amount of tax. You are required to give us this information.

Purpose of Form.—Use Form 1120X to correct **Form 1120**, U.S. Corporation Income Tax Return, or **Form 1120-A**, U.S. Corporation Short-Form Income Tax Return, as you originally filed it or as it was later adjusted by an amended return, claim for refund, or an examination. Please note that it often takes 3 to 4 months to process Form 1120X.

Do not use this form to apply for a tentative refund or a quick refund of estimated tax.

● For a quick refund of estimated tax, file **Form 4466**, Corporation Application for Quick Refund of Overpayment of Estimated Tax. File Form 4466 only within 2½ months after the end of the tax year and before the corporation files its tax return.

● For a tentative refund due to the carryback of a net operating loss, a net capital loss, unused credits, or overpaid tax resulting from a claim-of-right adjustment under section 1341(b)(1), file **Form 1139**, Corporation Application for Tentative Refund. You may use Form 1139 only if one year or less has passed since the tax year in which the carryback or adjustment occurred. For additional information on net operating losses and a worksheet to help figure the corporation's net operating loss deduction in a carryback year, see **Publication 536**, Net Operating Losses.

When To File.—File Form 1120X only after the corporation has filed its original return. Generally, Form 1120X must be filed within 3 years after the date the original return was due or 3 years after the date the corporation filed it, whichever was later. A Form 1120X based on a net operating loss carryback, a capital loss carryback, a general business credit carryback, or for tax years beginning before 1986, a research credit carryback, generally must be filed within 3 years after the due date of the return for the tax year of the net operating loss, capital loss, or unused credit. Other claims for refund must be filed within 3 years after the date the original return

was due, 3 years after the date the corporation filed it, or 2 years after the date the tax was paid, whichever is later.

What To Attach.—If you are amending your return to include any item (loss, credit, deduction, other tax benefit, or income) relating to a tax shelter required to be registered, you must attach **Form 8271**, Investor Reporting of Tax Shelter Registration Number.

Information on Income, Deductions, Tax Computation, etc.—Refer to the instructions for the Form 1120 and related schedules and forms, for the year being amended, concerning the taxability of certain types of income, the allowability of certain expenses as deductions from income, computation of tax, etc.

Note: *Deductions for such items as charitable contributions and dividends received may have to be refigured due to changes made to items of income or expense.*

Where To File.—Mail this form to the Internal Revenue Service Center where the corporation filed its original return.

Specific Instructions

Tax Year.—In the space above the employer identification number, enter the ending month and year of the calendar or fiscal year for the tax return you are amending.

Column (a)

Enter the amounts from your return as originally filed or as you later amended it. If your return was changed or audited by IRS, enter the amounts as adjusted.

Column (b)

Enter the net increase or net decrease for each line you are changing. Bracket all decreases. Explain the increase or decrease in Part II. If the change involves an item of income, deduction, or credit that the corporation income tax return or its instructions requires the corporation to support with a schedule, statement, or form, attach the appropriate schedule, statement, or form to Form 1120X.

Column (c)

Lines 1 and 2.—Add the increase in column (b) to the amount in column (a) or subtract the column (b) decrease from column (a). Report the result in column (c). For any item not changed, enter the amount from column (a) in column (c).

Line 4.—Figure the new amount of tax using the taxable income on line 3, column (c). Use Schedule J, Form 1120, or Part I, Form 1120-A, of the original return to make the necessary tax computation.

Line 6.—If you are amending a tax year prior to 1983 for which you filed Form 7005, include on line 6 the amount you deposited with Form 7005.

Line 12—Overpayment.—Enter the amount of overpayment received (or expected to be received) or the amount to be credited to estimated tax, as shown on the original return. That amount must be considered in preparing Form 1120X since any refund due from the original return will be refunded separately (or credited to estimated tax) from any additional refund claimed on Form 1120X.

Line 14—Tax due.—Make the check payable to "Internal Revenue Service" for the amount shown on line 14 and attach it to this form. Do not use the depositary method of payment.

Line 15—Refund.—If the corporation is entitled to a refund larger than the amount claimed on the original return, line 15 will show only the additional amount of refund. This additional amount will be refunded separately from the amount claimed on the original return.

Signature.—The return must be signed and dated by the president, vice president, treasurer, assistant treasurer, chief accounting officer, or any other corporate officer (such as tax officer) authorized to sign. A receiver, trustee, or assignee must sign and date any return required to be filed on behalf of a corporation.

Preparer.—If a corporate officer filled in Form 1120X, the Paid Preparer's space should remain blank. If someone prepares Form 1120X and does not charge the corporation, that person should not sign the return. Certain others who prepare Form 1120X should not sign. See the Form 1120 instructions and **Publication 1045**, Information for Tax Practitioners, for more information on preparers and their responsibilities.

Note: *IRS will figure any interest due and will either include it in the refund or bill the corporation for the interest.*

★ U.S.GPO:1988-0-205-236

B-6   Application for Extension of Time to File Income Tax Return

Form **7004**
(Rev. September 1989)
Department of the Treasury
Internal Revenue Service

**Application for Automatic Extension of Time
To File Corporation Income Tax Return**

OMB No. 1545-0233
Expires 8-31-92

Name of corporation

Employer identification number

Number and street (or P.O. box number if mail is not delivered to street address)

City or town, state, and ZIP code

Check type of return to be filed:

☐ Form 1120   ☐ Form 1120F   ☐ Form 1120L   ☐ Form 1120-POL   ☐ Form 1120S
☐ Form 1120-A   ☐ Form 1120-FSC   ☐ Form 1120-ND   ☐ Form 1120-REIT   ☐ Form 990-C
☐ Form 1120-DF   ☐ Form 1120-H   ☐ Form 1120-PC   ☐ Form 1120-RIC   ☐ Form 990-T

Form 1120F filers: Check here ► ☐ if you do not have an office or place of business in the U.S.

1a I request an automatic 6-month extension of time until ...., 19 ....., to file the income tax return of the
corporation named above for ► ☐ calendar year 19 ....., or ► ☐ tax year beginning ...., 19 .....,
and ending ...., 19 ......
b If this tax year is for less than 12 months, check reason:
☐ Initial return   ☐ Final return   ☐ Change in accounting period   ☐ Consolidated return to be filed

2   If this application also covers subsidiaries to be included in a consolidated return, complete the following:

Name and address of each member of the affiliated group	Employer identification number	Tax period

3 Tentative tax (see instructions) . . . . | **3** |
4 **Credits:**
a Overpayment credited from prior year . . | **4a** |
b Estimated tax payments for the tax year | **4b** |
c Less refund for the tax year applied
for on Form 4466 . . . . | **4c** | ( ) | Bal ► | **4d** |
e Credit from regulated investment companies . . . . | **4e** |
f Credit for Federal tax on fuels . . . . | **4f** |

5 Total—Add lines 4d through 4f . . . . | **5** |
6 **Balance due**—Line 3 less line 5. **Deposit this amount with a Federal Tax Deposit (FTD) Coupon**
(see instructions) . . . . | **6** |

Signature.—Under penalties of perjury, I declare that I have been authorized by the above-named corporation to make this application, and to the best of my knowledge and belief, the statements made are true, correct, and complete.

....
(Signature of officer or agent)   (Title)   (Date)

Form **7004** (Rev. 9-89)

B-7 Underpayment of Estimated Tax

Form **2220**	**Underpayment of Estimated Tax by Corporations**	OMB No. 1545-0142
Department of the Treasury Internal Revenue Service	▶ See separate Instructions. ▶ Attach to your tax return.	19**90**

Name		Employer identification number

Note: *In most cases, IRS can figure the penalty and the corporation will not have to complete this form. See the separate Instructions for more information.*

Part I   **Figuring The Underpayment**

1 Total tax (see Instructions)	**1**	
2a Personal holding company tax included on line 1 (Schedule PH (Form 1120), line 27) .	**2a**	
b Credit for Federal tax on fuels (see Instructions)	**2b**	
c Total—Add lines 2a and 2b	**2c**	
3 Subtract line 2c from line 1. If the result is less than $500, **do not** complete or file this form. The corporation does not owe the penalty	**3**	
4a Enter 90% of line 3	**4a**	
b Enter the tax shown on the corporation's 1989 tax return. **(Caution:** *See Instructions before completing this line.)*	**4b**	
c **Estimated tax.** Enter the **smaller** of line 4a or line 4b	**4c**	

		(a)	(b)	(c)	(d)
5	**Installment due dates.** Enter in columns (a) through (d) the 15th day of the 4th, 6th, 9th, and 12th months of the corporation's tax year . . . . ▶				
6	**Required installments.** Enter 25% of line 4c in columns (a) through (d) unless **a** or **b** below applies to the corporation:				
a	If the corporation uses the annualized income installment method and/or the adjusted seasonal installment method, complete the worksheet in the Instructions and enter the amounts from line 45 in each column of line 6. Also check this box ▶ ☐ and attach a copy of the worksheet.				
b	If the corporation is a "large corporation," check this box ▶ ☐ and see the Instructions for the amount to enter in each column of line 6				
	Complete lines 7 through 14 for one column before completing the next column.				
7	Amount paid or credited for each period. (See Instructions.) (For column (a) only, enter the amount from line 7 on line 11.)				
8	Enter amount, if any, from line 14 of previous column . .				
9	Add lines 7 and 8				
10	Add amounts on lines 12 and 13 of the previous column and enter the result				
11	Subtract line 10 from line 9. If less than zero, enter **zero.** (For column (a) only, enter the amount from line 7.)				
12	Remaining underpayment from previous period. If the amount on line 11 is zero, subtract line 9 from line 10 and enter the result. Otherwise, enter zero				
13	**UNDERPAYMENT.** If line 11 is less than or equal to line 6, subtract line 11 from line 6 and enter the result. Then go to line 7 of the next column. Otherwise, go to line 14 . . .				
14	**OVERPAYMENT.** If line 6 is less than line 11, subtract line 6 from line 11 and enter the result. Then go to line 7 of the next column				

Go to Part II on the back to figure the penalty.

For Paperwork Reduction Act Notice, see page 1 of the separate Instructions.   Form **2220** (1990)

Form 2220 (1990)   Page **2**

Part II Figuring the Penalty

		(a)	(b)	(c)	(d)
15	Enter the date of payment or the 15th day of the 3rd month after the close of the tax year, whichever is earlier. *(Form 990-PF and Form 990-T filers:* Use 5th month instead of 3rd month.)				
16	Number of days from due date of installment on line 5 to the date shown on line 15				
17	Number of days on line 16 after 4/15/90 and before 4/1/91 .				
18	Number of days on line 16 after 3/31/91 and before 7/1/91 .				
19	Number of days on line 16 after 6/30/91 and before 10/1/91				
20	Number of days on line 16 after 9/30/91 and before 1/1/92 .				
21	Number of days on line 16 after 12/31/91 and before 2/16/92 . .				
22	$\frac{\text{Number of days on line 17}}{365} \times 11\% \times$ the underpayment on line 13 . .				
23	$\frac{\text{Number of days on line 18}}{365} \times$ *% $\times$ the underpayment on line 13 . .				
24	$\frac{\text{Number of days on line 19}}{365} \times$ *% $\times$ the underpayment on line 13 . .				
25	$\frac{\text{Number of days on line 20}}{365} \times$ *% $\times$ the underpayment on line 13 . .				
26	$\frac{\text{Number of days on line 21}}{366} \times$ *% $\times$ the underpayment on line 13 . .				
27	Add lines 22 through 26				

28 **PENALTY.** Add columns (a) through (d), line 27. Enter here and on line 33, Form 1120; line 29, Form 1120-A; or comparable line for other income tax returns **28**

*If the corporation's tax year ends after December 31, 1990, see the Instructions for lines 23 through 26.

Department of the Treasury
Internal Revenue Service

Instructions for Form 2220

Underpayment of Estimated Tax by Corporations

(Section references are to the Internal Revenue Code unless otherwise noted.)

Paperwork Reduction Act Notice

We ask for the information on this form to carry out the Internal Revenue laws of the United States. You are required to give us this information. We need it to ensure that you are complying with these laws and to allow us to figure and collect the right amount of tax.

The time needed to complete and file this form will vary depending on individual circumstances. The estimated average time is:

Form	Recordkeeping	Learning about the law or the form	Preparing the form	Copying, assembling, and sending the form to IRS
2220	18 hrs., 11 min.	1 hr., 32 min.	3 hrs., 46 min.	32 min.
Worksheet, Pt. I	11 hrs., 43 min.	6 min.	17 min.	...
Worksheet, Pt. II	24 hrs., 23 min.	...	24 min.	...
Worksheet, Pt. III	5 hrs., 16 min.	...	5 min.	...

If you have comments concerning the accuracy of these time estimates or suggestions for making this form more simple, we would be happy to hear from you. You can write to both the IRS and the Office of Management and Budget at the addresses listed in the instructions for the tax return with which this form is filed. **DO NOT** send the tax form to either of these offices. Instead, see the instructions in your income tax return for information on where to file.

Purpose of Form

Corporations (including S corporations), tax-exempt organizations subject to the unrelated business income tax, and private foundations use Form 2220 to determine whether they are subject to the penalty for underpayment of estimated tax and, if so, the amount of the penalty.

Who Must Pay the Underpayment Penalty

If the corporation did not pay enough estimated tax by any due date for paying estimated tax, it may be charged a penalty. This is true even if the corporation is due a refund when its return is filed. The penalty is figured separately for each installment due date. Therefore, the corporation may owe a penalty for an earlier installment due date, even if it paid enough tax later to make up the underpayment.

Generally, a corporation is subject to the penalty if its tax liability is $500 or more and it did not timely pay the lesser of 90% of its tax liability for 1990, or 100% of its tax liability for 1989 (if it filed a 1989 return showing at least some amount of tax and the return covered a full 12 months). However, a "large corporation" (defined in the instructions for line 6b) may base only its first required installment on 100% of the prior year's tax liability. A corporation may be able to reduce or eliminate the penalty by using the annualized income installment method or the adjusted seasonal installment method.

IRS May Be Able To Figure the Penalty for the Corporation

Generally, the corporation does not have to file this form because IRS can figure the amount of any penalty and bill the corporation. However, complete and attach this form if:

a. The annualized income installment method and/or the adjusted seasonal installment method is used (see the instructions for line 6),

b. The corporation is a "large corporation" computing its first required installment based on the prior year's tax, or

c. An insurance company requests a waiver of the penalty as discussed in the instructions for line 13 under **Waiver of Penalty for Insurance Companies.**

How To Use This Form

Complete Part I of Form 2220 to determine the underpayment for any of the four installment due dates. If there is an underpayment on line 13 (column (a), (b), (c), or (d)), go to Part II to figure the penalty. Attach Form 2220 to the income tax return and check the box on line 33, page 1, of Form 1120; line 29 of Form 1120-A; or the comparable line of any other income tax return the corporation is required to file (e.g., Form 990-C, 1120L, 1120S, etc.).

Part I. Figuring The Underpayment

Complete lines 1 through 14 in Part I. Follow the instructions below.

Line 1.—Enter the tax from line 31, Form 1120; line 27, Form 1120-A; or the comparable line for other income tax returns (except as noted below).

Interest due under the look-back method for completed long-term contracts is not treated as an increase in tax for purposes of computing the estimated tax penalty. Do not include on line 1 any interest due under the look-back method included in tax on the corporation's income tax return. Instead, write on the dotted line to the left of the entry space, "From Form 8697" and the amount of interest due in brackets.

Filers of Forms 990-PF, 990-T, 1120L, 1120-PC, 1120-REIT, 1120-RIC, and 1120S: See the instructions for the appropriate tax return for the definition of tax for purposes of the estimated tax provisions.

Line 2b.— Enter the amount of the credit(s) from line 32g, Form 1120; line 28g, Form 1120-A; or the comparable line for other income tax returns.

Line 4b.—All filers other than S corporations.—Figure the corporation's 1989 tax in the same manner as the amount on line 3 of this form was determined, using the taxes and credits from its 1989 tax return. Skip line 4b and enter the amount from line 4a on line 4c if either of the following apply: **(1)** the corporation did not file a tax return for 1989 that showed at least some amount of tax; **or (2)** the corporation had a 1989 tax year of less than 12 months.

S corporations.—Enter on line 4b the sum of: (i) 90% of the sum of the investment credit recapture tax and the built-in gains tax (or the tax on certain capital gains) shown on the return for the 1990 tax year, and (ii) 100% of any excess net passive income tax shown on the S corporation's return for the 1989 tax year. If the 1989 tax year was for less than 12 months, do not complete this line. Instead, enter the amount from line 4a on line 4c.

Line 6.— (a) Annualized Income Installment Method or Adjusted Seasonal Installment Method: If the corporation's income varied during the year because, for example, it operated its business on a seasonal basis, it may be able to lower the amount of one or more required installments by using the annualized income installment method or the adjusted seasonal installment method. For example, a ski shop, which receives most of its income during the winter months, may benefit from using one or both of these methods in figuring its required installments. The annualized income installment or adjusted seasonal installment may be less than the required installment under the regular method for one or more due dates, thereby reducing or eliminating the penalty for those due dates.

To use one or both of these methods to figure one or more required installments, use the worksheet on pages 3 and 4 of these instructions. If the worksheet is used for any payment due date, it must be used for **all** payment due dates. To arrive at the amount of each required installment, the worksheet automatically selects the smallest of: (a) the annualized income installment, (b) the adjusted seasonal installment (if applicable), or (c) the regular installment under section 6655(d) (increased by any reduction recapture under section 6655(e)(1)(B)).

If the corporation is using only the annualized income installment method, it must complete Parts I and III of the worksheet. If it is using only the adjusted seasonal installment method, it must complete Parts II and III of the worksheet. If the corporation is using both methods, it must complete the entire worksheet. Enter in each column on line 6 of Form 2220 the amounts from the corresponding column of line 45 of the worksheet. Also attach a copy of the worksheet to Form 2220 and check the box on line 6a.

(b) "Large corporations": A "large corporation" is a corporation (other than an S corporation) that had, or its predecessor had, taxable income of $1 million or more for any of the 3 tax years immediately preceding the tax year involved. For this purpose, taxable income is modified to exclude net operating loss or capital loss carrybacks or carryovers. Members of a controlled group, as defined in section 1563, must divide the $1 million amount among themselves in accordance with rules similar to those in section 1561.

If the annualized income installment method or adjusted seasonal installment method is not used, follow the instructions below to figure the amount to enter on line 6. Also check the box on line 6b. (If the corporation is using the annualized income installment method and/or the adjusted seasonal installment method, these instructions apply to line 41 of the worksheet.)

If line 4a is less than line 4b: Enter 25% of line 4a in columns (a) through (d) on line 6. *If line 4b is less than line 4a:* Enter 25% of line 4b in column (a) on line 6. In column (b), determine the amount to enter by: (i) subtracting line 4b from line 4a, (ii) adding the result to the amount on line 4a, and (iii) multiplying the total by 25%. In columns (c) and (d), enter 25% of line 4a.

Line 7.—In column (a), enter the estimated tax payments deposited by the 15th day of the 4th month of the corporation's tax year; in column (b), enter payments made after the 15th day of the 4th month through the 15th day of the 6th month of the tax year; in column (c), enter payments made after the 15th day of the 6th month through the 15th day of the 9th month of the tax year; and, in column (d), enter payments made after the 15th day of the 9th month through the 15th day of the 12th month of the tax year.

Include in the estimated tax payments any overpayment of tax from the corporation's 1989 return that was credited to the corporation's 1990 estimated tax.

Line 13.—If line 13 shows an underpayment, complete Part II to figure the penalty.

Waiver of Penalty for Insurance Companies.—The Revenue Reconciliation Act of 1990 (Act) changed the way an insurance company handles the amortization of policy acquisition expenses and the treatment of salvage. No penalty will be imposed on any underpayment of estimated tax attributable to the changes made by the Act to IRC sections 807(e), 832(b)(4), 832(b)(5), and 848, for any period before March 16, 1991. Accordingly, for any installment due date before March 16, 1991, if an insurance company has an underpayment on line 13 which is due to changes made by the Act, the penalty for that underpayment will be waived.

To claim the waiver, affected companies should compute the penalty by refiguring Form 2220 through line 27 on the basis of the law in effect before the changes were made and write the word "WAIVER" on the

Page 2

bottom margin of page 1. Also write "Waiver-$(amount)" on the dotted line to the left of line 28. Subtract the waiver amount from the total of columns (a) through (d), line 27, to arrive at the amount to be entered on line 28. Attach an explanation showing your computation of the amount of the penalty to be waived.

Part II. Figuring The Penalty

Complete lines 15 through 28 to determine the amount of the penalty. The penalty is figured for the period of underpayment determined under section 6655 at a rate determined under section 6621. For underpayments paid after March 31, 1991, see the instructions for lines 23 through 26.

Line 15.—A payment of estimated tax is applied against underpayments of required installments in the order that installments are required to be paid, regardless of which installment the payment pertains to. For example, a corporation has an underpayment for the April 15 installment of $1,000. The June 15 installment requires a payment of $2,500. On June 10, the corporation deposits $2,500 to cover the June 15 installment. However, $1,000 of this payment is considered to be for the April 15 installment. The penalty for the April 15 installment is figured to June 10 (56 days). The underpayment for the June 15 installment will then be $1,500.

If the corporation has made more than one payment for a required installment, attach a separate computation for each payment.

Line 23.—For underpayments paid after March 31, 1991, and before July 1, 1991, use the interest rate that the IRS will determine in January 1991.

Line 24.—For underpayments paid after June 30, 1991, and before October 1, 1991, use the interest rate that the IRS will determine in April 1991.

Line 25.—For underpayments paid after September 30, 1991, and before January 1, 1992, use the interest rate that the IRS will determine in July 1991.

Line 26.—For underpayments paid after December 31, 1991, use the interest rate that the IRS will determine in October 1991.

Instructions for Worksheet

Part I—Annualized Income Installment Method

Line 4.—*Filers of Forms 990-PF and 990-T:* The period to be used to figure taxable income for each column is as follows: Column (a), first 2 months; column (b), first 4 months; column (c), first 7 months; and column (d), first 10 months.

Line 5.—*Filers of Forms 990-PF and 990-T:* The annualization amount to be used in each column is as follows: Column (a), 6; column (b), 3; column (c), 1.71429; and column (d), 1.2.

Line 9.—Enter the taxes the corporation owed because of events that occurred during the months shown in the column headings used to figure annualized taxable income. Include the same taxes used to figure line 1 of Form 2220, but do not include the personal holding company tax.

Figure the alternative minimum tax and environmental tax on **Form 4626,**

Alternative Minimum Tax–Corporations. Figure alternative minimum taxable income and modified alternative minimum taxable income based on the corporation's income and deductions during the months shown in the column headings used to figure annualized taxable income. Multiply the alternative minimum taxable income and modified alternative minimum taxable income by the annualization amounts used to figure annualized taxable income (on line 2 or line 5) before subtracting the exemption amounts (see sections 55(d) and 59A(a)(2)).

Line 11.—Enter the credits allowed due to events that occurred during the months shown in the column headings used to figure annualized taxable income.

Line 15.—Before completing line 15 in columns (b) through (d), complete line 16; Part II (if applicable); and lines 40 through 45, in each of the preceding columns. For example, complete line 16, lines 17 through 39 (if using the adjusted seasonal installment method), and lines 40 through 45, in column (a) before completing line 15 in column (b).

Part II—Adjusted Seasonal Installment Method

Do **not** complete this part unless the corporation's base period percentage for any six consecutive months of the tax year equals or exceeds 70%. The term "base period percentage" for any period of six consecutive months is the average of the three percentages figured by dividing the taxable income for the corresponding six consecutive month period in each of the 3 preceding tax years by the taxable income for each of their respective tax years.

Example: An amusement park that has a calendar year as its tax year receives the largest part of its taxable income during the six-month period from May through October. To compute its base period percentage for the period May through October 1990, it must figure its taxable income for the period May through October in each of the years: 1987, 1988, and 1989. The taxable income for each May-through-October period is then divided by the total taxable income for the tax year in which the period is included, resulting in the following quotients: .69 for May through October 1987, .74 for May through October 1988, and .67 for May through October 1989. Since the average of .69, .74, and .67 is equal to .70, the base period percentage for May through October 1990 is 70%. Therefore, the amusement park qualifies for the adjusted seasonal installment method.

Line 33.—Enter the taxes the corporation owed because of events that occurred during the months shown in the column headings above line 17. Include the same taxes used to figure line 1 of Form 2220, but do not include the personal holding company tax.

Figure the alternative minimum tax and environmental tax on Form 4626. Figure alternative minimum taxable income and modified alternative minimum taxable income based on the corporation's income and deductions during the months shown in the column headings above line 17. Divide the alternative minimum taxable income and modified alternative minimum taxable income by the amounts shown on line 24 before subtracting the exemption amounts (see sections 55(d) and 59A(a)(2)). For columns (a) through (c) only, multiply the alternative minimum tax and environmental tax so determined by the amounts shown on line 31.

Line 35.—Enter the credits allowed due to events that occurred during the months shown in the column headings above line 17.

Line 38.—Before completing line 38 in columns (b) through (d), complete lines 39 through 45 in each of the preceding columns. For example, complete lines 39 through 45 in column (a) before completing line 38 in column (b).

Worksheet to Figure Required Installments Using the Annualized Income or Adjusted Seasonal Installment Methods Under Section 6655(e)

Note to Form 1120S filers.—*For purposes of lines 1, 4, 17, 18, and 19, below, "taxable income" refers to excess net passive income or the amount on which tax is imposed under section 1374(a) (or the corresponding provisions of prior law), whichever applies.*

Part I Annualized Income Installment Method		(a)	(b)	(c)	(d)
			Period		
			First 3 months	First 6 months	First 9 months
(1) Enter taxable income for each period.	1				
(2) Annualization amounts.	2		4	2	1.33333
(3) Multiply line 1 by line 2.	3				
Form 990-PF and Form 990-T filers: *Do not use the periods shown directly above line 4 or the annualization amounts shown on line 5 when figuring lines 4 and 6. Instead, see the Instructions for Worksheet lines 4 and 5.*			Period		
		First 3 months	First 5 months	First 8 months	First 11 months
(4) Enter taxable income for each period.	4				
(5) Annualization amounts.	5	4	2.4	1.5	1.09091
(6) Multiply line 4 by line 5.	6				
(7) Annualized taxable income. In column (a), enter the amount from line 6, column (a). In columns (b), (c), and (d), enter the **smaller** of the amounts in each column on line 3 or line 6.	7				
(8) Figure tax on the amount in each column on line 7 using the Instructions for Form 1120, Schedule J, line 3 (or the comparable line of the tax return).	8				
(9) Enter other taxes for each payment period (see Instructions).	9				
(10) Total tax. Add lines 8 and 9.	10				
(11) For each period, enter the same type of credits as allowed on Form 2220, lines 1 and 2b (see Instructions).	11				
(12) Total tax after credits. Subtract line 11 from line 10. If less than zero, enter zero.	12				
(13) Applicable percentage.	13	22.5%	45%	67.5%	90%
(14) Multiply line 12 by line 13.	14				
(15) Enter the combined amounts of line 45 from all preceding columns (see Instructions).	15				
(16) Subtract line 15 from line 14. If less than zero, enter zero.	16				

Part II Adjusted Seasonal Installment Method (Caution: *Use this method only if the base period percentage for any 6 consecutive months is at least 70%. See the Instructions for more information.*)

		(a)	(b)	(c)	(d)
			Period		
		First 3 months	First 5 months	First 8 months	First 11 months
(17) Enter taxable income for the following periods:					
a Tax year beginning in 1987	17a				
b Tax year beginning in 1988	17b				
c Tax year beginning in 1989	17c				
(18) Enter taxable income for each period for the tax year beginning in 1990.	18				

Page 3

		(a)	(b)	(c)	(d)
				Period	
		First 4 months	First 6 months	First 9 months	Entire year
(19)	Enter taxable income for the following periods: **a** Tax year beginning in 1987	19a				
	b Tax year beginning in 1988	19b				
	c Tax year beginning in 1989	19c				
(20)	Divide the amount in each column on line 17a by the amount in column (d) on line 19a.	20				
(21)	Divide the amount in each column on line 17b by the amount in column (d) on line 19b.	21				
(22)	Divide the amount in each column on line 17c by the amount in column (d) on line 19c.	22				
(23)	Add lines 20 through 22.	23				
(24)	Base period percentage for months before filing month. Divide line 23 by 3.	24				
(25)	Divide line 18 by line 24.	25				
(26)	Figure tax on the amount on line 25 using the Instructions for Form 1120, Schedule J, line 3 (or the comparable line of the return).	26				
(27)	Divide the amount in columns (a) through (c) on line 19a by the amount in column (d) on line 19a.	27				
(28)	Divide the amount in columns (a) through (c) on line 19b by the amount in column (d) on line 19b.	28				
(29)	Divide the amount in columns (a) through (c) on line 19c by the amount in column (d) on line 19c.	29				
(30)	Add lines 27 through 29.	30				
(31)	Base period percentage for months through and including the filing month. Divide line 30 by 3.	31				
(32)	Multiply the amount in columns (a) through (c) of line 26 by the percentage in the corresponding column of line 31. In column (d), enter the amount from line 26, column (d).	32				
(33)	Enter other taxes for each payment period (see Instructions).	33				
(34)	Total tax. Add lines 32 and 33.	34				
(35)	For each period, enter the same type of credits as allowed on Form 2220, lines 1 and 2b (see Instructions).	35				
(36)	Total tax after credits. Subtract line 35 from line 34. If less than zero, enter zero.	36				
(37)	Multiply line 36 by 90%.	37				
(38)	Enter the total of amounts in all preceding columns of line 45.	38				
(39)	Subtract line 38 from line 37. If less than zero, enter zero.	39				

Part III   Required Installments

		1st installment	2nd installment	3rd installment	4th installment
(40)	If only one of the above parts was completed, enter the amounts in each column from line 16 or line 39. (If both parts were completed, enter the lesser of the amounts in each column from line 16 or line 39.)	40				
(41)	Divide line 4c, Form 2220, by 4 and enter the result in each column. (**Note:** *"large corporations" see line 6(b) Instructions on page 2 for the amount to enter.*)	41				
(42)	Enter the amount from line 44 for the preceding column.	42				
(43)	Add lines 41 and 42 and enter the total.	43				
(44)	If line 43 is more than line 40, subtract line 40 from line 43. Otherwise, enter zero.	44				
(45)	**Required installments.**—Enter the lesser of line 40 or line 43 here and on Form 2220, line 6.	45				

Page 4

B-8 Computation of Minimum Tax

Form **4626**	**Alternative Minimum Tax—Corporations**	OMB No. 1545-0175

Form **4626**

Department of the Treasury
Internal Revenue Service

Alternative Minimum Tax—Corporations
(including environmental tax)
▶ See separate instructions.
▶ Attach to your tax return.

OMB No. 1545-0175

19**90**

Name | Employer identification number

1	Taxable income or (loss) before net operating loss deduction. (**Important:** See instructions if you are subject to the environmental tax.)	**1**	
2	**Adjustments:**		
a	Depreciation of tangible property placed in service after 1986	**2a**	
b	Amortization of certified pollution control facilities placed in service after 1986	**2b**	
c	Amortization of mining exploration and development costs paid or incurred after 1986	**2c**	
d	Amortization of circulation expenditures paid or incurred after 1986 (personal holding companies only)	**2d**	
e	Basis adjustments in determining gain or loss from sale or exchange of property	**2e**	
f	Long-term contracts entered into after February 28, 1986	**2f**	
g	Installment sales of certain property	**2g**	
h	Merchant marine capital construction funds	**2h**	
i	Section 833(b) deduction (Blue Cross, Blue Shield, and similar type organizations only)	**2i**	
j	Tax shelter farm activities (personal service corporations only)	**2j**	
k	Passive activities (closely held corporations and personal service corporations only)	**2k**	
l	Certain loss limitations	**2l**	
m	Other adjustments	**2m**	
n	Combine lines 2a through 2m		**2n**
3	**Tax preference items:**		
a	Depletion	**3a**	
b	Tax-exempt interest from private activity bonds issued after August 7, 1986	**3b**	
c	Appreciated property charitable deduction	**3c**	
d	Intangible drilling costs	**3d**	
e	Reserves for losses on bad debts of financial institutions	**3e**	
f	Accelerated depreciation of real property placed in service before 1987	**3f**	
g	Accelerated depreciation of leased personal property placed in service before 1987 (personal holding companies only)	**3g**	
h	Amortization of certified pollution control facilities placed in service before 1987	**3h**	
i	Add lines 3a through 3h		**3i**
4	Pre-adjustment AMTI. Combine lines 1, 2n, and 3i		**4**
5	**Adjusted current earnings adjustment:**		
a	Enter your adjusted current earnings	**5a**	
b	Subtract line 4 from line 5a (even if one or both of these figures is a negative number). Enter zero if the result is zero or less (see instructions for examples)	**5b**	
c	Multiply line 5b by 75%		**5c**
6	Combine lines 4 and 5c. If zero or less, stop here (you are not subject to the alternative minimum tax)		**6**
7	Alternative tax net operating loss deduction. (Do not enter more than 90% of line 6.)		**7**
8	Alternative minimum taxable income (subtract line 7 from line 6)		**8**
9	**Exemption phase-out computation (members of a controlled group, see instructions for lines 9a through 9c):**		
a	Tentative exemption amount. Enter $40,000	**9a**	
b	Enter $150,000	**9b**	
c	Subtract line 9b from line 8. If zero or less, enter zero	**9c**	
d	Multiply line 9c by 25%	**9d**	
e	Exemption. Subtract line 9d from line 9a. If zero or less, enter zero		**9e**
10	Subtract line 9e from line 8. If zero or less, enter zero		**10**
11	Multiply line 10 by 20%		**11**
12	Alternative minimum tax foreign tax credit (see instructions for limitation)		**12**
13	Tentative minimum tax (subtract line 12 from line 11)		**13**
14	Regular tax liability before all credits except the foreign tax credit and possessions tax credit		**14**
15	**Alternative minimum tax**—Subtract line 14 from line 13. If the result is zero or less, enter zero. Also enter the result on line 9a, Schedule J, Form 1120, or on the comparable line of other income tax returns		**15**
16	**Environmental tax**—Subtract $2,000,000 from line 6 (computed without regard to your environmental tax deduction), and multiply the result, if any, by 0.12% (.0012). Enter on line 9b, Schedule J, Form 1120, or on the comparable line of other income tax returns (members of a controlled group, see instructions)		**16**

For Paperwork Reduction Act Notice, see separate instructions.   Form **4626** (1990)

90  **Department of the Treasury**
Internal Revenue Service

Instructions for Form 4626

Alternative Minimum Tax—Corporations

(Section references are to the Internal Revenue Code unless otherwise noted.)

General Instructions

Paperwork Reduction Act Notice.—We ask for the information on this form to carry out the Internal Revenue laws of the United States. You are required to give us this information. We need it to ensure that you are complying with these laws and to allow us to figure and collect the right amount of tax.

The time needed to complete and file this form will vary depending on individual circumstances. The estimated average time is:

Recordkeeping . . . . . . 10 hrs., 31 min.

Learning about the law
or the form . . . . 11 hrs., 49 min.

Preparing and sending the
form to IRS . . . . 12 hrs., 31 min.

If you have comments concerning the accuracy of these time estimates or suggestions for making this form more simple, we would be happy to hear from you. You can write to both the IRS and the Office of Management and Budget at the addresses listed in the instructions for the tax return with which this form is filed.

Changes you should note:

(1) Lines 5 through 5c were modified to reflect the change from the book income adjustment to the adjusted current earnings adjustment.

(2) Line 14 of the 1989 Form 4626, which was entitled "general business credit allowed against alternative minimum tax," was deleted. This amount is now requested as a "write-in" entry on the dotted line to the left of the entry space on line 9a, Schedule J, Form 1120 (or on the comparable line of other income tax returns).

Who Must File.—You must file this form if your taxable income or (loss) before the net operating loss **(NOL)** deduction when combined with your adjustments and tax preference items (including the adjusted current earnings adjustment) totals more than the lesser of: (a) $40,000, or (b) your allowable exemption amount.

Short Period Return.—If this is a short period return, use the formula in section 443(d) to determine your alternative minimum taxable income **(AMTI)** and your alternative minimum tax **(AMT)**.

Apportionment of Differently Treated Items in Case of Certain Entities.—If you are preparing Form 4626 for a regulated investment company, real estate investment trust, or a common trust fund, see section 59(d).

Credit for Prior Year Minimum Tax.—See **Form 8801**, Credit for Prior Year Minimum Tax, for details concerning the computation of the credit.

Line-by-Line Instructions

Line 1.—Enter your taxable income or (loss) before the NOL deduction. For example, if you file Form 1120, subtract line 29b from line 28.

Important: *If you are subject to the environmental tax, you will generally need to figure that tax on line 16 before completing line 1 (see instructions for line 16).*

Line 2a—Depreciation of tangible property placed in service after 1986 (or after 7/31/86 if you made the transitional election under section 203(a)(1)(B) of the Tax Reform Act of 1986).

Caution: *If you have a depreciation adjustment attributable to a passive activity or a tax shelter farm activity, do not include that adjustment on line 2a. Instead, include the adjustment on line 2j or 2k.*

The depreciation expense allowable for regular tax purposes under section 167 with respect to any tangible property placed in service after 1986 must be recomputed for AMT purposes under the alternative depreciation system **(ADS)** described in section 168(g) as follows:

(1) For any real property described in section 1250(c) (generally nonresidential real and residential rental), use the straight line method over 40 years using the same mid-month convention you used for regular tax purposes;

(2) For any tangible property (other than the real property described in (1) above) with respect to which depreciation for regular tax purposes is determined using the straight line method, recompute your depreciation expense using the straight line method over the property's "class life" using the same convention you used for regular tax purposes;

(3) For all tangible property other than property described in (1) or (2) above, use the 150% declining balance method, switching to the straight line method the first tax year it gives a larger deduction, over the property's class life. Use the same convention you used for regular tax purposes.

In applying the above rules:

(1) The "class life" to be used for AMT purposes has a different meaning than the recovery period used for regular tax purposes (although these periods could possibly be the same in some instances). The class lives you need to use for AMT purposes can be found in Rev. Proc. 87-56, 1987-2 C.B. 674, or in **Publication 534**, Depreciation. Use 12 years for any tangible personal property that does not have an assigned class life;

(2) See Rev. Proc. 87-57, 1987-2 C.B. 687, for optional tables (14 through 18) that can be used in computing depreciation for AMT purposes. (These optional tables have been reproduced in Publication 534.);

(3) Do not make an adjustment for:
(a) property for which you made a section 168(g)(7) election (to use the ADS of section 168(g)) for regular tax purposes, **(b)** property expensed under section 179 for regular tax purposes, or **(c)** property described in sections 168(f)(1) through (4); and

(4) You must take into consideration the transitional rules (described in section 56(a)(1)(C)) and the normalization rules (described in section 56(a)(1)(D)).

Subtract your recomputed AMT expense from the depreciation expense you claimed for regular tax purposes and enter the result on line 2a. If the total recomputed AMT expense exceeds the depreciation expense you claimed for regular tax purposes, enter the difference as a negative amount.

Note: *Depreciation that is capitalized to inventory under the uniform capitalization rules must be refigured using the rules described above.*

Line 2b—Amortization of certified pollution control facilities placed in service after 1986.—The amortization deduction you claimed for regular tax purposes is not allowed for AMT purposes.

For AMT purposes, you must use the ADS described in section 168(g). As such, use the straight line method over the facility's class life (which may be found in Rev. Proc. 87-56 or in Publication 534). **Note:** *Section 168(g) applies to 100% of the asset's amortizable basis. Do not reduce your AMT basis by the 20% section 291 adjustment that applied for regular tax purposes.*

Subtract your recomputed AMT expense from the expense you claimed for regular tax purposes and enter the result on line 2b. If your recomputed AMT expense is greater than the expense you claimed for regular tax purposes, enter the difference as a negative amount.

Line 2c—Amortization of mining exploration and development costs paid or incurred after 1986.—If, for regular tax purposes, you elected the optional 10-year writeoff under section 59(e) for all assets in this category, skip this line (no adjustment is necessary).

The deduction you claimed for regular tax purposes under sections 616(a) and 617(a) is not allowed for AMT purposes. Instead, you must capitalize such costs and amortize them ratably over a 10-year period beginning with the tax year in which you made them. **Note:** *The 10-year amortization applies to 100% of the mining development and exploration costs paid or incurred during the tax year. Do not reduce your AMT basis by the 30% section 291 adjustment that applied for regular tax purposes.*

Subtract your recomputed AMT expense from the expense you claimed for regular tax purposes and enter the result on line 2c. If your recomputed AMT expense is greater than the expense you claimed for regular tax purposes, enter the difference as a negative amount. See section 56(a)(2)(B) if you had a loss with respect to any mine or other natural deposit (other than an oil, gas, or geothermal well).

Line 2d—Amortization of circulation expenditures paid or incurred after 1986 (personal holding companies only).—If, for regular tax purposes, you elected the optional 3-year writeoff under section 59(e) for all of these expenditures, skip this line (no adjustment is necessary).

The deduction you claimed for regular tax purposes (under section 173) for these expenditures incurred after 1986 is not allowed for AMT purposes. Instead, you must capitalize these expenditures and amortize them ratably over a 3-year period beginning with the tax year in which you made them.

Subtract your recomputed AMT expense from the expense you claimed for regular tax purposes and enter the result on line 2d. If your recomputed AMT expense is greater than the expense you claimed for regular tax purposes, enter the difference as a negative amount. See section 56(b)(2)(B) if you had a loss with respect to circulation expenditures deducted under section 173.

Line 2e—Basis adjustments in determining gain or loss from sale or exchange of property.—If, during the tax year, you disposed of property for which you are making (or have previously made) any of the adjustments described in lines 2a through 2d above, you must recompute the property's adjusted basis for AMT purposes. You must then recompute the property's gain or loss.

For AMT purposes, the property's adjusted basis is its cost less all applicable depreciation or amortization deductions allowed during the current tax year and previous tax years for AMT purposes. This recomputed basis is subtracted from the sales price to arrive at gain or loss for AMT purposes.

Note: *You may also have gains or losses from lines 2j, 2k, and 2l that must be taken into consideration on line 2e. For example, if for regular tax purposes, you report a loss from the disposition of an asset used in a passive activity, you include the loss in your computations for line 2j to determine whether any passive activity loss is limited for AMT purposes. You then include the portion of the AMT passive activity loss allowed* that pertains to the disposition of the asset on line 2e in determining your AMT basis adjustment. In this respect, it may be helpful to refigure Form 8810 and related worksheets and Schedule D (Form 1120), Form 4684 (Section B), or Form 4797 for AMT purposes.

Enter the difference between the gain or loss reported on your tax return for regular tax purposes and your recomputed gain or loss for AMT purposes. If the gain recomputed for AMT purposes is less than the gain computed for regular tax purposes OR if the loss recomputed for AMT purposes is more than the loss computed for regular tax purposes OR if you recomputed a loss for AMT purposes and computed a gain for regular tax purposes, enter the difference as a negative amount.

Line 2f—Long-term contracts entered into after February 28, 1986.—For AMT purposes, you must use the percentage of completion method rules described in section 460(b) to determine the taxable income from any "long-term contract" (defined in section 460(f)) you entered into after 2/28/86. However, this rule does not apply to: **(1)** any "home construction contract" (as defined in section 460(e)(6)) you entered into after 6/20/88 with respect to which you meet the "small" home construction contract requirements of section 460(e)(1)(B) or **(2) any** home construction contract you entered into in a tax year beginning after 9/30/90, regardless of whether you meet the "small" home construction contract requirements of section 460(e)(1)(B).

Note: In the case of a contract described in section 460(e)(1), the percentage of the contract completed is to be determined using the simplified procedures for allocating costs outlined in section 460(b)(4).

Subtract the income you reported for regular tax purposes from the income you recomputed for AMT purposes and enter the difference on line 2f. If the recomputed AMT income is less than the income you reported for regular tax purposes, enter the difference as a negative amount.

Line 2g—Installment sales of certain property.—With respect to any disposition of inventory (as defined in section 1221(1)) after 3/1/86, the installment method of accounting cannot be used in determining income for AMT purposes (except for certain dispositions of timeshares or residential lots for which you elected to pay interest under section 453(l)(2)(B)). Application of rules in computing adjustment:

(1) Dealer dispositions: For dealer dispositions occurring after 3/1/86 but before 1/1/88, you will have adjustments if you used the installment method for regular tax purposes but were required for AMT purposes to report the entire gain in the year of disposition. In such cases, enter the income you reported for regular tax purposes for the current year with respect to those dispositions on line 2g as a negative amount.

For dealer dispositions occurring after 1987, generally no adjustments are necessary since the installment method of accounting generally cannot be used for either regular tax purposes or for AMT purposes.

(2) Nondealer dispositions: For nondealer dispositions occurring after 3/1/86 but before the first day of your tax year that began in 1987, you will have adjustments if you used the installment method for regular tax purposes but were required for AMT purposes to report the entire gain in the year of disposition. In such cases, enter the income you reported for regular tax purposes for the current year with respect to those dispositions on line 2g as a negative amount.

For nondealer dispositions occurring on or after the first day of your tax year that began in 1987, generally no adjustments are necessary since you are allowed to use the installment method of accounting for both regular tax purposes and AMT purposes.

Line 2h—Merchant marine capital construction funds.—Amounts deposited in these funds (established under section 607 of the Merchant Marine Act of 1936) after 1986 are not deductible

Page 2

for AMT purposes. Furthermore, earnings on these funds are not excludable from gross income for AMT purposes. Therefore, if you deducted these amounts or excluded them from income for regular tax purposes, you must add them back on line 2h. See section 56(c)(2) for more information.

Line 2i—Section 833(b) deduction (Blue Cross, Blue Shield, and similar type organizations only).—This deduction is not allowed for AMT purposes. Therefore, if you took this deduction for regular tax purposes, you must add it back on line 2i.

Line 2j—Tax shelter farm activities (personal service corporations only).—Complete line 2j only if you have a gain or loss from a tax shelter farm activity (as defined in section 58(a)(2)) that is **not** a passive activity. If the tax shelter farm activity **is** a passive activity, you must include the gain or loss in your computations for line 2k below.

Recompute all gains and losses you reported for regular tax purposes from tax shelter farm activities by taking into account your AMT adjustments and tax preference items.

Important: To avoid duplication, any AMT adjustment or tax preference item taken into account on line 2j must not be included in the amounts to be entered on any other line of this form.

Determine your tax shelter farm activity gain or loss for AMT purposes using the same rules you used for regular tax purposes with the following modification: No recomputed loss is allowed, except to the extent the personal service corporation is insolvent (see section 58(c)(1)). Furthermore, a recomputed loss may not be used in the current tax year to offset gains from other tax shelter farm activities. Instead, any recomputed loss must be suspended and carried forward indefinitely until: **(1)** you have a gain in a subsequent tax year from that same tax shelter farm activity, OR **(2)** the activity is disposed of.

Note: The amount of any tax shelter farm activity loss that is not deductible (and is therefore carried forward) for AMT purposes is likely to differ from the amount (if any) that is carried forward for regular tax purposes. Therefore, it is essential that you retain adequate records for both AMT purposes and regular tax purposes.

Enter on line 2j the difference between the gain or loss you recomputed for AMT purposes and the gain or loss you reported for regular tax purposes. If you reported a loss for AMT purposes and a gain for regular tax purposes OR if you recomputed a loss for AMT purposes that exceeds the loss you reported for regular tax purposes OR if you reported a gain for regular tax purposes that exceeds the gain you recomputed for AMT purposes, enter the difference as a negative amount.

Line 2k—Passive activities (closely held corporations and personal service corporations only).—Recompute all passive activity gains and losses you reported for regular tax purposes by taking into account your AMT adjustments, tax preference items, and AMT prior year unallowed losses.

Important: To avoid duplication, any AMT adjustment or tax preference item must not be included in the amounts to be entered on any other line of this form.

Determine your passive activity gain or loss for AMT purposes using the same rules you used for regular tax purposes with the following modifications: **(1)** Do not use the phase-in of disallowance rules of section 469(m); and **(2)** If the corporation is insolvent, see section 58(c)(1).

Disallowed losses of a personal service corporation are suspended until the corporation has income from that (or any other) passive activity or until the passive activity is disposed of (i.e., its passive losses cannot offset "net active income" (defined in section 469(e)(2)(B)) or "portfolio income"). Disallowed losses of a closely held corporation that is not a personal service corporation are treated the same except that, in addition, they may be used to offset "net active income."

Note: The amount of any passive activity loss that is not deductible (and is therefore carried forward) for AMT purposes is likely to differ from the amount (if any) that is carried forward for regular tax purposes. Therefore, it is essential that you retain adequate records for both AMT purposes and regular tax purposes.

Enter on line 2k the difference between the gain or loss you recomputed for AMT purposes and the gain or loss you reported for regular tax purposes. If you reported a loss for AMT purposes and a gain for regular tax purposes OR if you recomputed a loss for AMT purposes that exceeds the loss you reported for regular tax purposes OR if you reported a gain for regular tax purposes that exceeds the gain you recomputed for AMT purposes, enter the difference as a negative amount.

Tax shelter farm activities that are passive activities.—Recompute all gains and losses you reported for regular tax purposes by taking into account your AMT adjustments, tax preference items, and AMT prior year unallowed losses.

Important: To avoid duplication, any AMT adjustment or tax preference item taken into account here must not be included in the amounts to be entered on any other line of this form. These recomputed gains and losses should enter into the determination of your passive activity gain or loss for AMT purposes described above. Use the same rules outlined above, with the following additional modification: Recomputed gains from tax shelter farm activities that are passive activities may be used to offset recomputed losses from other passive activities; however, recomputed losses from tax shelter farm activities that are passive activities may not be used to offset recomputed gains from other passive activities. (Recomputed losses from tax shelter farm activities that are passive activities are disallowed and must be suspended and carried forward as explained in the instructions for line 2j.)

Line 2l—Certain loss limitations.—Recompute gains and losses you reported for regular tax purposes from at-risk activities and partnerships by taking into account your AMT adjustments and tax preference items. If you have recomputed losses that must (in accordance with section 59(h)) be limited for AMT purposes by section 465 or by section 704(d) OR if, for regular tax purposes, you reported losses from at-risk activities or partnerships that were limited by those sections, compute the difference between the loss limited for AMT purposes and the loss limited for regular tax purposes with respect to each applicable at-risk activity or partnership. If the loss limited for regular tax purposes exceeds the loss limited for AMT purposes, enter the difference as a negative amount.

Line 2m—Other adjustments.—Include on this line:

(1) Income eligible for the possessions tax credit—The corporation's AMTI is not to include any income (from the sources described in section 936(a)(1)) that is eligible for the possessions tax credit of section 936. Therefore, if you included this type of income in your taxable income for regular tax purposes, enter the amount on line 2m as a negative amount.

(2) Income with respect to the alcohol fuel credit—The corporation's AMTI is not to include any amount with respect to the alcohol fuel credit that was included in your gross income in accordance with section 87. Therefore, if you included this type of income in your income for regular tax purposes, enter the amount on line 2m as a negative amount.

(3) Income as a beneficiary of an estate or trust—If the corporation is a beneficiary, enter the amount from Schedule K-1 (Form 1041), line 7.

Line 3a—Depletion.—In the case of mines, wells, and other natural deposits, enter the amount by which your depletion deduction under section 611 exceeds the adjusted basis of the property at the end of your tax year. In computing the year-end adjusted basis, use the rules of section 1016; however, do not reduce basis by the current year's depletion deduction.

Figure the excess separately for each property. If the depletion deduction for any property does not exceed the property's year-end adjusted basis, the shortfall is not to be considered on line 3a. (In other words, do not use a shortfall for one property to offset the excess of depletion deduction over adjusted basis for any other property.)

Note: *In the case of iron ore and coal (including lignite), the section 291 adjustment is to be applied before figuring this tax preference item.*

Line 3b—Tax-exempt interest from private activity bonds issued after August 7, 1986.—Enter the interest you earned on "specified private activity bonds" reduced by any deduction that would have been allowable if the interest were includible in gross income for regular tax purposes. Generally, the term "specified private activity bonds" means any private activity bond (as defined in section 141) issued after 8/7/86. See section 57(a)(5) for exceptions and for more information.

Line 3c—Appreciated property charitable deduction.—Enter the amount by which your contribution deduction allowable under section 170 would be reduced if all capital gain and section 1231 property were taken into account at its adjusted basis (rather than its fair market value).

Line 3d—Intangible drilling costs.—*If, for regular tax purposes, you elected the optional 60-month writeoff under section 59(e) for all assets in this category, skip this line (no adjustment is necessary).*

Intangible drilling costs **(IDCs)** from oil, gas, and geothermal properties are a tax preference item to the extent that "excess IDCs" exceed 65% of the "net income" from the properties. The tax preference item is computed separately for geothermal deposits, and for oil and gas properties that are not geothermal deposits.

"Excess IDCs" are the excess of: **(1)** the amount of IDCs you paid or incurred with respect to oil, gas, or geothermal properties that you elected to expense for regular tax purposes under section 263(c) (not including any section 263(c) deduction for nonproductive wells) reduced by the section 291 adjustment for integrated oil companies; over **(2)** the amount that would have been allowed had you amortized that amount over a 120-month period starting with the month the well was placed in production. **Note:** *If you prefer not to use the 120-month period, you can elect to use any method that is permissible in determining cost depletion.*

"Net income" is the gross income you received or accrued from all oil, gas, and geothermal wells less the deductions allocable to these properties (reduced by the excess IDCs).

Line 3e—Reserves for losses on bad debts of financial institutions.—Enter the excess of: **(1)** the deduction allowable for a reasonable addition to a reserve for bad debts of a financial institution to which section 593 applies (reduced by the section 291 adjustment) over **(2)** the amount that would have been allowable had the financial institution maintained its bad debt reserve for all tax years on the basis of actual experience.

Line 3f—Accelerated depreciation of real property placed in service before 1987.—Enter the excess of the depreciation claimed for the property for regular tax purposes over the depreciation allowable for AMT purposes as refigured using the straight line method. Figure this amount separately for each property and include only positive adjustments on line 3f. For 15-, 18-, or 19-year real property, use the straight line method over 15, 18, or 19 years, respectively. For low-income housing property, use the straight line method over 15 years.

Line 3g—Accelerated depreciation of leased personal property placed in service before 1987 (personal holding companies only).—For leased personal property, other than recovery property, enter the excess of the depreciation claimed for the property for regular tax purposes over the depreciation allowable for AMT purposes

as refigured using the straight line method. Figure this amount separately for each property and include only positive adjustments on line 3g.

For leased recovery property, other than 15-, 18-, or 19-year real property, or low-income housing, enter the amount by which your depreciation deduction determined for regular tax purposes is more than the deduction allowable for AMT purposes using the straight line method over the following recovery period:

3-year property	5 years
5-year property	8 years
10-year property	15 years
15-year public utility property	22 years

Line 3h—Amortization of certified pollution control facilities placed in service before 1987.—If, for regular tax purposes, you made an election under section 169 to amortize the basis of a certified pollution control facility over a 60-month period, your tax preference with respect to each such facility is computed as follows:

(1) Reduce the current year amortization deduction by the 20% section 291 adjustment;

(2) Reduce the result in (1) above by the deduction you would have been allowed under section 167; and

(3) Multiply the result in (2) above by 59 5/6 %. Include only positive adjustments on line 3h.

Line 5a—Adjusted current earnings.—*If you are preparing Form 4626 for a regulated investment company or a real estate investment trust, skip lines 5a through 5c (they do not apply).*

If you are preparing Form 4626 for an affiliated group that has filed a consolidated tax return for the current tax year under the rules of section 1501, you must determine adjusted current earnings (ACE) on a consolidated basis.

Your ACE is your line 4 pre-adjustment AMTI, with the following additional adjustments:

(1) ACE depreciation adjustment. This adjustment is computed in the following two steps:

(a) Add back all current year depreciation expense you deducted for AMT purposes in arriving at your line 4 pre-adjustment AMTI.

(b) Subtract your current year ACE depreciation expense, which is computed as follows: For each asset, compute your current year depreciation expense for ACE purposes based on the method of depreciation described after the appropriate classification (see (i) through (iv) below) for such asset:

(i) Property placed in service after 1989. Depreciate the basis of such property using the ADS described in section 168(g).

(ii) Property placed in service in a tax year beginning before 1990 to which the modified accelerated cost recovery system **(MACRS)** applies (i.e., generally property placed in service in tax years beginning after 1986 and before 1990). Depreciate the adjusted basis of such property (which, for these purposes, is the adjusted basis of such property for AMT purposes as of the close of the last tax year beginning before 1990) using the straight line method over the remainder of the recovery period applicable to such property under the ADS of section 168(g). In doing so, use the applicable convention that would have applied to the property under section 168(g).

(iii) Property placed in service in a tax year beginning before 1990 to which the original accelerated cost recovery system **(ACRS)** applies (i.e., generally property placed in service in tax years beginning after 1980 and before 1987). Depreciate the adjusted basis of such property (which, for these purposes, is the adjusted basis of such property for regular tax purposes as of the close of the last tax year beginning before 1990) using the straight line method over the remainder of the recovery period applicable to such property under the ADS of section 168(g). In doing so, use the convention that would have applied to the property under section 168(g).

(iv) Property placed in service before 1981 and property described in sections 168(f)(1) through (4). Use the depreciation expense you claimed for regular tax purposes.

(2) Adjustments based on general rules for computing earnings and profits **(E & P)**:

(a) Any income item that is not "taken into account" (defined below) in determining your line 4 pre-adjustment AMTI but that is "taken into account" in determining your E&P must be included in determining your ACE. Any such income item may be reduced by all items that relate to such income item and that would be deductible in computing your pre-adjustment AMTI if the income items to which they relate were included in your pre-adjustment AMTI for the tax year. Examples of adjustments for such income items include: **(i)** interest income from tax-exempt obligations excluded under section 103 less any costs incurred in carrying such tax-exempt obligations; and **(ii)** proceeds of life insurance contracts excluded under section 101 less the basis in the contract for purposes of ACE.

Note: *Do not make an adjustment for any income from discharge of indebtedness excluded from gross income under section 108 (or any corresponding provision of prior law repealed by the Bankruptcy Tax Act of 1980).*

An income item is considered "taken into account" without regard to the timing of its inclusion in your pre-adjustment AMTI or your E&P. Therefore, only income items that are "permanently excluded" from your pre-adjustment AMTI are included in your ACE. An income item will not be considered "taken into account" merely because the proceeds from that item might eventually be reflected in your pre-adjustment AMTI (for example, that of a shareholder) on the liquidation or disposal of a business.

Adjustment for buildup in life insurance contracts. Include in your ACE the income on life insurance contracts (as determined under section 7702(g)) for the tax year less the portion of any premium that is attributable to insurance coverage.

(b) Generally, no deduction is allowed in computing your ACE for items not "taken into account" (defined below) for purposes of computing your E&P for the tax year. Therefore, these amounts increase your ACE to the extent they are deductible in computing your line 4 pre-adjustment AMTI (i.e., they would be positive adjustments to your line 4 pre-adjustment AMTI in arriving at your ACE). However, there are exceptions. Do not add back: **(i)** any deduction allowable under section 243 or 245 for any dividend that qualifies for a 100% dividends-received deduction under section 243(a), 245(b), or 245(c); and **(ii)** any dividend received from a "20-percent owned corporation" (as defined in section 243(c)(2)), but only to the extent such dividend is attributable to income of the paying corporation that is subject to federal income tax. Also see sections 56(g)(4)(C)(iii) and (iv) for special rules for dividends from section 936 companies and certain dividends received by certain cooperatives.

An item is considered "taken into account" without regard to the timing of its deductibility in computing your line 4 pre-adjustment AMTI or your E&P. Therefore, only deduction items that are "permanently disallowed" in computing your E&P are disallowed in computing your ACE.

(c) Generally, no deduction is allowed for an item in computing your ACE if the item is not deductible in computing your line 4 pre-adjustment AMTI (even if the item is deductible for purposes of computing your E&P). The only exceptions to this general rule are the related reductions to an income item described in the second sentence of item (2)(a) above. Deductions that are not allowed in computing your ACE include: **(i)** capital losses in excess of capital gains; **(ii)** bribes, fines, and penalties disallowed under section 162; **(iii)** charitable

Page 3

contributions in excess of the limitations of section 170; **(iv)** expenditures for meals and entertainment in excess of the limitations of section 274; **(v)** Federal taxes disallowed under section 275; and **(vi)** golden parachute payments in excess of the limitation of section 280G. **Note:** *No adjustment is necessary for these items since they were not allowed in computing your line 4 pre-adjustment AMTI.*

(3) Other adjustments based on specific rules for computing E&P.

(a) Intangible drilling costs. For purposes of computing your ACE, determine your deduction for intangible drilling costs (as defined in section 263(c)) in the manner provided in section 312(n)(2)(A).

(b) Certain amortization provisions do not apply. For purposes of computing your ACE, section 173 (relating to circulation expenditures) and section 248 (relating to organizational expenditures) do not apply to amounts paid or incurred in tax years beginning after 1989.

(c) LIFO inventory adjustments. The adjustments provided in section 312(n)(4) apply in computing your ACE.

(d) Installment sales. For any installment sale in a tax year beginning after 1989, you generally cannot use the installment method for purposes of computing your ACE. However, the installment method may be used with respect to the applicable percentage (as determined under section 453A) of the gain from any installment sale to which section 453A(a)(1) applies.

(4) Disallowance of loss on exchange of debt pools. For purposes of computing your ACE, you may not recognize any loss on the exchange of any pool of debt obligations for another pool of debt obligations having substantially the same effective interest rates and maturities.

(5) Acquisition expenses of certain life insurance companies. For purposes of computing your ACE, acquisition expenses of life insurance companies (other than "small insurance companies," defined below) must be capitalized and amortized in accordance with the treatment generally required under generally accepted accounting principles (and in such a manner as if this rule applied to all applicable tax years).

A "small insurance company" is any insurance company that meets the requirements of section 806(a)(3), except that section 806(c)(2) does not apply.

Note: *This adjustment was repealed by the Revenue Reconciliation Act of 1990; however, it applies in full to tax years beginning after December 31, 1989 but before September 30, 1990, and in part to tax years that include September 30, 1990 (see section 11301(d)(2)(B) for a special proration rule for tax years that include September 30, 1990).*

See new section 848(i) for a special rule for the treatment of qualified foreign contracts under the ACE adjustment.

(6) Depletion. For purposes of computing your ACE, the allowance for depletion with respect to any property placed in service in a tax year beginning after 1989 must be determined under the cost depletion method of section 611.

(7) Treatment of certain ownership changes. If a corporation undergoes an ownership change (within the meaning of section 382) in a tax year beginning after 1989, and such corporation has a net unrealized built-in loss (within the meaning of section 382(h)), then the adjusted basis of each asset of such corporation (immediately after the ownership change) must be adjusted to its proportionate share (determined on the basis of respective fair market values) of the fair market value of the assets of such corporation (determined under section 382(h)) immediately before the ownership change. For purposes of determining whether you have a built-in loss, you must use the aggregate adjusted basis of your assets that is used in computing your ACE. **Note:** *These new adjusted bases must be subsequently*

used for all ACE calculations (such as depreciation and gain or loss on disposition of an asset).

Line 5b.—*If you are preparing Form 4626 for an affiliated group that has filed a consolidated tax return for the current tax year under the rules of section 1501, you must figure line 5b on a consolidated basis.*

The following examples illustrate the calculation to be performed on line 5b.

Example 1: Corporation C determines its line 5a ACE to be $25,000. If its line 4 pre-adjustment AMTI were $10,000, it would enter the $15,000 difference on line 5b. If its line 4 amount were instead $30,000, it would enter zero on line 5b since the difference is less than zero. Finally, if its line 4 amount were a negative $100,000, it would enter the difference of $125,000 on line 5b.

Example 2: Corporation D determines its line 5a ACE to be a negative $25,000. If its line 4 pre-adjustment AMTI were a negative $30,000, it would enter the difference of $5,000 on line 5b.

Line 7—Alternative tax net operating loss deduction.— Your alternative tax net operating loss deduction (**ATNOLD**) is the NOL you determined for regular tax purposes under section 172, except that:

(1) In the case of a loss year beginning after 1986, the NOL you determined for regular tax purposes from such year must be: **(a)** reduced by the positive AMT adjustments provided in sections 56 and 58, and **(b)** reduced by the tax preference items you determined under section 57 (but only to the extent they increased the NOL you determined for regular tax purposes).

(2) In applying the rules outlined in section 172(b)(2) (regarding the determination of the amount of carrybacks and carryovers), you must use the modification to those rules described in section 56(d)(1)(B)(ii).

(3) If, for any tax year beginning before 1987, you had minimum tax that was deferred under section 56(b) (as in effect before the enactment of the Tax Reform Act of 1986) and that deferred tax has not been paid, the amount of NOL carryovers that you may carry over to this year for AMT purposes must be reduced by your tax preference items that gave rise to the deferred add-on minimum tax. (Section 701(f)(2)(B) of the Tax Reform Act of 1986.)

(4) Your ATNOLD is limited to 90% of your AMTI computed without regard to your ATNOLD. Therefore, enter on line 7 the smaller of the ATNOLD or 90% of the amount on line 6.

Note: *The amount of any NOL that is not deductible for AMT purposes may be carried back or carried over in accordance with the rules outlined in section 172(b). The amount carried back or carried over for AMT purposes is likely to differ from the amount (if any) that is carried back or carried over for regular tax purposes; therefore, it is essential that you retain adequate records for both AMT purposes and regular tax purposes.*

Line 9a. Tentative exemption amount .—All members of a controlled group of corporations are limited to one $40,000 exemption, which must be divided equally among the members (unless all of the members consent to an unequal allocation). If you are preparing Form 4626 for a member of a controlled group, enter such member's share of the $40,000 exemption on line 9a.

Lines 9b and 9c.—In computing the reduction of the tentative exemption amount, the line 8 AMTI of all members of a controlled group of corporations must be taken into account and the decrease of the tentative exemption amount must be divided equally among the members (unless all of the members consent to an unequal allocation). If you are preparing Form 4626 for a member of a controlled group, enter such member's share of the $150,000 floor on line 9b, and subtract that line 9b amount from such member's share of the combined line 8 AMTI of all members of the controlled group of corporations and enter the difference on line 9c. See section 1561 for additional information.

Line 12—Alternative minimum tax foreign tax credit.—Refigure the foreign tax credit you claimed for regular tax purposes as follows:

(1) For each separate limitation, recompute both the numerator (foreign source taxable income) and the denominator (worldwide taxable income) of the limitation fraction by taking into account your AMT adjustments and tax preference items;

(2) Substitute line 11 of Form 4626 for the "total U.S. income tax against which the credit is allowed";

(3) For each separate limitation, multiply the fraction in (1) above by the amount in (2) above to determine your recomputed limitation;

(4) For each separate limitation, take the lesser of the total foreign taxes paid with respect to that separate limitation and the recomputed limitation from (3) above; and

(5) Add the credits you recomputed for each separate limitation and enter the result on line 12.

Note: *For purposes of determining whether any income is high-taxed in applying the separate income category limitations for the AMT foreign tax credit, the AMT rate is to be used instead of the regular rate.*

Your AMT foreign tax credit is subject to a 90% limit (i.e., the credit cannot be more than the amount on line 11 less 10% of the amount that would be on that line if Form 4626 were recomputed using zero on line 7). For tax years beginning after March 31, 1990, the 90% limit does not apply to certain corporations that meet the requirements of section 59(a)(2)(C). For tax years that include March 31, 1990, these corporations should see section 7612 of the Revenue Act of 1989 for a special proration rule.

Note: *With respect to any separate limitation, any AMT foreign tax credit you cannot claim (because of the limitation fraction or the 90% limit discussed above) may be carried back or carried over in accordance with the rules outlined in section 904(c). However, foreign taxes paid or accrued in a tax year beginning after 1986 that were carried back (for regular tax purposes) to offset tax in a tax year beginning before 1987 may not be used in computing the AMT foreign tax credit for the current tax year.*

Note also: *The amount of any foreign tax credit that you cannot claim (and is therefore carried back or carried over) for AMT purposes is likely to differ from the amount (if any) that is carried back or carried over for regular tax purposes. Therefore, it is essential that you retain adequate records for both AMT purposes and regular tax purposes.*

Line 14.—Enter your regular tax liability for the tax year (as defined in section 26(b)) less your foreign tax credit and your possessions tax credit. Be sure to **include** any tax on accumulation distribution of trusts you computed on Form 4970. **Do not include** any recapture of investment credit you computed on Form 4255 or any recapture of low-income housing credit you computed on Form 8611. If you file Form 1120, this is line 3, Schedule J, minus the sum of lines 4a and 4b, Schedule J.

Line 16—Environmental tax.—*If you are preparing Form 4626 for a regulated investment company or a real estate investment trust, skip line 16 (it does not apply).*

Compute your environmental tax as follows:

(1) Complete line 1 of Form 4626 without taking into account any environmental tax deduction.

(2) Complete lines 2a through 6 of Form 4626.

(3) Skip lines 7 through 15 and compute your environmental tax on line 16 of Form 4626.

Note: *If you are completing line 16 for a member of a controlled group of corporations, all members of the controlled group are limited to one $2,000,000 exemption, which must be divided equally among the members (unless all of the members consent to an unequal allocation). See section 1561 for additional information.*

Then compute your AMT as follows: Complete line 1 of Form 4626 taking into account any deduction you are allowed with respect to the environmental tax. Then complete lines 2a through 15 of Form 4626.

Page 4

B-9   Forms for Tax Credits

Form **1116**

Department of the Treasury
Internal Revenue Service

Foreign Tax Credit

Individual, Fiduciary, or Nonresident Alien Individual
► Attach to Form 1040, 1040NR, 1041, or 990-T.
► See separate Instructions.

OMB No. 1545-0121

1990

Attachment
Sequence No. 19

Name

Identifying number as shown on page 1 of your tax return

Use a separate Form 1116 for each category of income listed below. Check only **one** box. Before you check a box, read **Categories of Income** on page 2 of the Instructions. This form is being completed for credit for taxes on:

☐ Passive income
☐ High withholding tax interest
☐ Financial services income

☐ Shipping income
☐ Dividends from a DISC or former DISC
☐ Certain distributions from a foreign sales corporation (FSC) or former FSC

☐ Lump-sum distributions (see Instructions before completing form)
☐ General limitation income—all other income from sources outside the United States (including income from sources within U.S. possessions)

Resident of (name of country) ►

Note: If you paid taxes to one foreign country or U.S. possession, use column A in Part I and line A in Part II. If you paid taxes to **more than one** foreign country or U.S. possession, use a separate column and line for each country or possession.

Part I   Taxable Income or Loss From Sources Outside the United States for Separate Category Checked Above

	Foreign Country or U.S. Possession			Total
	A	B	C	(Add Cols. A, B, and C)
Enter the name of the foreign country or U.S. possession ►				
1 Gross income from sources within country shown above and of the type checked above. (See Instructions.):				

Applicable deductions and losses (See Instructions.):

2 Expenses directly allocable to the income on line 1 (attach schedule)				
3 Pro rata share of other deductions not directly allocable:				
a Certain itemized deductions or standard deduction. (See Instructions.)				
b Other deductions (attach schedule)				
c Add lines 3a and 3b				
d Total foreign source income. (See Instructions.)				
e Gross income from all sources. (See Instructions.)				
f Divide line 3d by line 3e				
g Multiply line 3c by line 3f				
4 Pro rata share of interest expense. (See Instructions.):				
a Home mortgage and personal interest from line 7 of the worksheet on page 3 of the Instructions				
b Other interest				
5 Losses from foreign sources				

6 Add lines 2, 3g, 4a, 4b, and 5   6

7 Subtract line 6 from line 1. Enter the result here and on line 14   ►   7

Part II   Foreign Taxes Paid or Accrued (See Instructions.)

Country	Credit is claimed for taxes (you must check one):	Foreign taxes paid or accrued								
		In foreign currency				In U.S. dollars				
	☐ Paid ☐ Accrued	Taxes withheld at source on:			(d) Other foreign taxes paid or accrued	Taxes withheld at source on:			(h) Other foreign taxes paid or accrued	(i) Total foreign taxes paid or accrued (add cols (e) through (h))
	Date paid or accrued	(a) Dividends	(b) Rents and royalties	(c) Interest		(e) Dividends	(f) Rents and royalties	(g) Interest		
A										
B										
C										

8 Add lines A through C, column (i). Enter the total here and on line 9   ►   8

For Paperwork Reduction Act Notice, see page 1 of separate Instructions.

Form **1116** (1990)

Form 1116 (1990)   Page 2

Part III   Figuring the Credit

9	Enter amount from line 8. This is the total foreign taxes paid or accrued for the category of income checked above Part I	9
10	Carryback or carryover (attach detailed computation)	10
11	Add lines 9 and 10	11
12	Reduction in foreign taxes. (See Instructions.)	12
13	Subtract line 12 from line 11. This is the total amount of foreign taxes available for credit	13
14	Enter amount from line 7. This is your taxable income or (loss) from sources outside the United States (before adjustments) for the category of income checked above Part I. (See Instructions.)	14
15	Adjustments to line 14. (See Instructions.)	15
16	Combine the amounts on lines 14 and 15. This is your net foreign source taxable income. (If the result is zero or less, you have no foreign tax credit for the type of income you checked on page 1. Skip lines 17 through 21.)	16
17	**Individuals:** Enter amount from Form 1040, line 35. If you are a nonresident alien, enter amount from Form 1040NR, line 33. **Estates and trusts:** Enter your taxable income without the deduction for your exemption	17
18	Divide line 16 by line 17. (If line 16 is more than line 17, enter the figure "1.")	18
19	**Individuals:** Enter amount from Form 1040, line 40, **less** any amounts on Form 1040, lines 41 and 42. If you are a nonresident alien, enter amount from Form 1040NR, line 38, **less** any amount on Form 1040NR, line 39. **Estates and trusts:** Enter amount from Form 1041, Schedule G, line 1c, or Form 990-T, line 8	19
20	Multiply line 19 by line 18. (Maximum amount of credit)	20
21	Enter the amount from line 13 or line 20, whichever is smaller. (If this is the only Form 1116 you are completing, skip lines 22 through 29 and enter this amount on line 30. Otherwise, complete the appropriate lines in Part IV.) . . . . ▶	21

Part IV   Summary of Credits From Separate Parts III (See Instructions.)

22	Credit for taxes on passive income	22
23	Credit for taxes on high withholding tax interest	23
24	Credit for taxes on financial services income	24
25	Credit for taxes on shipping income	25
26	Credit for taxes on dividends from a DISC or former DISC	26
27	Credit for taxes on certain distributions from a FSC or former FSC . .	27
28	Credit for taxes on lump-sum distributions	28
29	Credit for taxes on general limitation income (all other income from sources outside the U.S.)	29
30	Add lines 22 through 29	30
31	Reduction of credit for international boycott operations. (See "Reduction of Credit for International Boycott Operations" in instructions for line 12.)	31
32	Subtract line 31 from line 30. This is your foreign tax credit. Enter here and on Form 1040, line 43; Form 1040NR, line 40; Form 1041, Schedule G, line 2a; or Form 990-T, line 9a . . . . . . ▶	32

Form **3800**	**General Business Credit**	OMB No. 1545-0895
Department of the Treasury Internal Revenue Service	▶ Attach to your tax return. ▶ See separate Instructions.	19**90** Attachment Sequence No. **22**
Name(s) as shown on return		Identifying number

Part I — Tentative Credit

1	Current year investment credit (Form 3468, Part I)	**1**	
2	Current year jobs credit (Form 5884, Part I)	**2**	
3	Current year credit for alcohol used as fuel (Form 6478)	**3**	
4	Current year credit for increasing research activities (Form 6765, Part III)	**4**	
5	Current year low-income housing credit (Form 8586, Part I)	**5**	
6	Current year disabled access credit (Form 8826, Part I).	**6**	
7	**Current year general business credit**—Add lines 1 through 6	**7**	
8	Passive activity credits included on lines 1 through 6 (see Instructions)	**8**	
9	Subtract line 8 from line 7	**9**	
10	Passive activity credits allowed in 1990 (see Instructions)	**10**	
11	Carryforward of general business credit, WIN credit or ESOP credit to 1990 (see Instructions). . .	**11**	
12	Carryback of general business credit to 1990	**12**	
13	Tentative general business credit—Add lines 9 through 12	**13**	

Part II — General Business Credit Limitation Based on Amount of Tax

14a	Individuals—Enter amount from Form 1040, line 40			
b	Corporations—Enter amount from Form 1120, Schedule J, line 3 (or Form 1120-A, Part I, line 1)	}	**14**	
c	Other filers—Enter regular tax before credits from your return			
15	Credits that reduce regular tax before the general business credit—			
a	Credit for child and dependent care expense (Form 2441) . . .	**15a**		
b	Credit for the elderly or the disabled (Schedule R, Form 1040) . . .	**15b**		
c	Foreign tax credit (Form 1116 or Form 1118).	**15c**		
d	Possessions tax credit (Form 5735)	**15d**		
e	Mortgage interest credit (Form 8396)	**15e**		
f	Credit for fuel from a nonconventional source.	**15f**		
g	Orphan drug credit (Form 6765)	**15g**		
h	Total credits that reduce regular tax before the general business credit. Add lines 15a through 15g and enter here		**15h**	
16	Net regular tax—Subtract line 15h from line 14		**16**	
17	Tentative minimum tax:			
a	Individuals—Enter amount from Form 6251, line 17			
b	Corporations—Enter amount from Form 4626, line 13.	}	**17**	
c	Estates and Trusts—Enter amount from Form 8656, line 37			
18	Net income tax:			
a	Individuals—Add line 16 above and line 19 of Form 6251. Enter the total			
b	Corporations—Add line 16 above and line 15 of Form 4626. Enter the total	}	**18**	
c	Other filers—See Instructions			
19	If line 16 is more than $25,000, enter 25% of the excess		**19**	
20	Subtract line 17 or line 19, whichever is greater, from line 18. Enter the result. If less than zero, enter zero		**20**	
21	**General business credit**—Enter the smaller of line 13 or line 20. Also enter this amount on Form 1040, line 44; Form 1120, Schedule J, line 4e; Form 1120-A, Part I, line 2a; or on the appropriate line of your return. (Individuals, estates, and trusts, see instructions if the credit for increasing research activities is claimed. C corporations, see instructions for Schedule A if the investment credit is claimed or if the corporation has undergone a post-1986 "ownership change.")		**21**	

For Paperwork Reduction Act Notice, see page 1 of the separate Instructions to this form.   Form **3800** (1990)

Form 3800 (1990)   Page **2**

| **Schedule A** | **Additional General Business Credit Allowed By Section 38(c)(2)—Only Applicable to C Corporations** |

1   Enter the portion of the credit shown on line 13, page 1, that is attributable to the regular investment credit under section 46 . . . . **1**

2   Tentative minimum tax (from line 17, page 1) **2**

3   Multiply line 2 by 25% (.25) **3**

4   Enter the amount from line 20, page 1. . . . . **4**

5   Enter the portion of the credit shown on line 13, page 1, that is NOT attributable to the regular investment credit under section 46 . . . **5**

6   Subtract line 5 from line 4 (if less than zero, enter zero) **6**

7   Subtract line 6 from line 1 (if less than zero, enter zero) **7**

8   For purposes of this line only, recompute the amount on line 11, Form 4626, by using zero on line 7, Form 4626, and enter the result here . **8**

9   Multiply line 8 by 10% (.10) **9**

10 Net income tax (from line 18, page 1) **10**

11 General business credit (from line 21, page 1) **11**

12 Subtract line 11 from line 10. . . . . **12**

13 Subtract line 9 from line 12 . . . . **13**

14 Enter the smallest of line 3, line 7, or line 13. . . . . **14**

15 Subtract line 14 from line 2 . . . . **15**

16 Enter the greater of line 15, above, or line 19, page 1 . . . . **16**

17 Subtract line 16 from line 10. DO NOT enter more than the amount on line 13, page 1. . . . . . **17**

18 Enter the lesser of line 17, above, or line 16, page 1. Enter this amount also on line 21, page 1, instead of the amount previously computed on that line. Write "Sec. 38(c)(2)" in the margin next to your entry on line 21, page 1 . . . . **18**

19 If line 17 is greater than line 18, enter the excess here (see Instructions) **19**

B-10   Other Tax Forms

Form **4562** Department of the Treasury Internal Revenue Service	**Depreciation and Amortization** (Including Information on Listed Property) ▶ See separate instructions. ▶ Attach this form to your return.	OMB No. 1545-0172 **1990** Attachment Sequence No. **67**
Name(s) shown on return		**Identifying number**

Business or activity to which this form relates

Part I   Election To Expense Certain Tangible Property (Section 179) (Note: *If you have any "Listed Property," also complete Part V.*)

1 Maximum dollar limitation (see instructions)	**1**	$10,000
2 Total cost of section 179 property placed in service during the tax year (see instructions)	**2**	
3 Threshold cost of section 179 property before reduction in limitation	**3**	$200,000
4 Reduction in limitation—Subtract line 3 from line 2, but do not enter less than -0-	**4**	
5 Dollar limitation for tax year—Subtract line 4 from line 1, but do not enter less than -0-	**5**	

(a) Description of property	(b) Cost	(c) Elected cost	
6			

7 Listed property—Enter amount from line 26	**7**		
8 Total elected cost of section 179 property—Add amounts in column (c), lines 6 and 7	**8**	
9 Tentative deduction—Enter the lesser of line 5 or line 8	**9**	
10 Carryover of disallowed deduction from 1989 (see instructions)	**10**	
11 Taxable income limitation—Enter the lesser of taxable income or line 5 (see instructions)	**11**	
12 Section 179 expense deduction—Add lines 9 and 10, but do not enter more than line 11	**12**	
13 Carryover of disallowed deduction to 1991—Add lines 9 and 10, less line 12 ▶	**13**		

Note: *Do not use Part II or Part III below for automobiles, certain other vehicles, cellular telephones, computers, or property used for entertainment, recreation, or amusement (listed property). Instead, use Part V for listed property.*

Part II   MACRS Depreciation For Assets Placed in Service ONLY During Your 1990 Tax Year (Do Not Include Listed Property)

(a) Classification of property	(b) Mo. and yr. placed in service	(c) Basis for depreciation (Business use only—see instructions)	(d) Recovery period	(e) Convention	(f) Method	(g) Depreciation deduction
14 General Depreciation System (GDS) (see instructions):						
a 3-year property						
b 5-year property						
c 7-year property						
d 10-year property						
e 15-year property						
f 20-year property						
g Residential rental property			27.5 yrs.	MM	S/L	
			27.5 yrs.	MM	S/L	
h Nonresidential real property			31.5 yrs.	MM	S/L	
			31.5 yrs.	MM	S/L	
15 Alternative Depreciation System (ADS) (see instructions):						
a Class life					S/L	
b 12-year			12 yrs.		S/L	
c 40-year			40 yrs.	MM	S/L	

Part III   Other Depreciation (Do Not Include Listed Property)

16 GDS and ADS deductions for assets placed in service in tax years beginning before 1990 (see instructions).	**16**	
17 Property subject to section 168(f)(1) election (see instructions)	**17**	
18 ACRS and other depreciation (see instructions)	**18**	

Part IV   Summary

19 Listed property—Enter amount from line 25	**19**	
20 Total—Add deductions on line 12, lines 14 and 15 in column (g), and lines 16 through 19. Enter here and on the appropriate lines of your return. (Partnerships and S corporations—see instructions) . .	**20**	
21 For assets shown above and placed in service during the current year, enter the portion of the basis attributable to section 263A costs (see instructions).	**21**	

For Paperwork Reduction Act Notice, see page 1 of the separate instructions.   Form **4562** (1990)

Form 4562 (1990) Page **2**

Part V Listed Property.—Automobiles, Certain Other Vehicles, Cellular Telephones, Computers, and Property Used for Entertainment, Recreation, or Amusement

If you are using the standard mileage rate or deducting vehicle lease expense, complete columns (a) through (c) of Section A, all of Section B, and Section C if applicable.

Section A.—Depreciation (Caution: *See instructions for limitations for automobiles.*)

22a Do you have evidence to support the business use claimed? ☐ Yes ☐ No | 22b If "Yes," is the evidence written? ☐ Yes ☐ No

(a) Type of property (list vehicles first)	(b) Date placed in service	(c) Business use percentage	(d) Cost or other basis	(e) Basis for depreciation (business use only)	(f) Recovery period	(g) Method/ Convention	(h) Depreciation deduction	(i) Elected section 179 cost
23 Property used more than 50% in a trade or business:								
		%						
		%						
		%						
24 Property used 50% or less in a trade or business:								
		%				S/L –		
		%				S/L –		
		%				S/L –		

25 Add amounts in column (h). Enter the total here and on line 19, page 1 . . . . **25**

26 Add amounts in column (i). Enter the total here and on line 7, page 1 . . . . **26**

Section B.—Information Regarding Use of Vehicles—*If you deduct expenses for vehicles:*

● Always complete this section for vehicles used by a sole proprietor, partner, or other "more than 5% owner," or related person.

● If you provided vehicles to your employees, first answer the questions in Section C to see if you meet an exception to completing this section for those vehicles.

	(a) Vehicle 1		(b) Vehicle 2		(c) Vehicle 3		(d) Vehicle 4		(e) Vehicle 5		(f) Vehicle 6	
27 Total business miles driven during the year (DO NOT include commuting miles) . .												
28 Total commuting miles driven during the year												
29 Total other personal (noncommuting) miles driven												
30 Total miles driven during the year—Add lines 27 through 29												
	Yes	No	Yes	No	Yes	No	Yes	No	Yes	No	Yes	No
31 Was the vehicle available for personal use during off-duty hours?												
32 Was the vehicle used primarily by a more than 5% owner or related person? . . .												
33 Is another vehicle available for personal use?												

Section C.—Questions for Employers Who Provide Vehicles for Use by Their Employees

(Answer these questions to determine if you meet an exception to completing Section B. **Note:** *Section B must always be completed for vehicles used by sole proprietors, partners, or other more than 5% owners or related persons.)*

	Yes	No
34 Do you maintain a written policy statement that prohibits all personal use of vehicles, including commuting, by your employees?		
35 Do you maintain a written policy statement that prohibits personal use of vehicles, except commuting, by your employees? (See instructions for vehicles used by corporate officers, directors, or 1% or more owners.)		
36 Do you treat all use of vehicles by employees as personal use?		
37 Do you provide more than five vehicles to your employees and retain the information received from your employees concerning the use of the vehicles?		
38 Do you meet the requirements concerning qualified automobile demonstration use (see instructions)?		

Note: *If your answer to 34, 35, 36, 37, or 38 is "Yes," you need not complete Section B for the covered vehicles.*

Part VI Amortization

(a) Description of costs	(b) Date amortization begins	(c) Amortizable amount	(d) Code section	(e) Amortization period or percentage	(f) Amortization for this year
39 Amortization of costs that begins during your 1990 tax year:					

40 Amortization of costs that began before 1990 . . . . **40**

41 Total. Enter here and on "Other Deductions" or "Other Expenses" line of your return **41**

Form **4797**

Department of the Treasury
Internal Revenue Service

Sales of Business Property

(Also, Involuntary Conversions and Recapture Amounts Under Sections 179 and 280F)

▶ Attach to your tax return. ▶ See separate Instructions.

OMB No. 1545-0184

1990

Attachment Sequence No. **27**

Name(s) shown on return

Identifying number

Part I   Sales or Exchanges of Property Used in a Trade or Business and Involuntary Conversions From Other Than Casualty and Theft—Property Held More Than 1 Year

1 Enter here the gross proceeds from the sale or exchange of real estate reported to you for 1990 on Form(s) 1099-S (or a substitute statement) that you will be including on line 2, 10, or 20 . . . . **1**

(a) Description of property	(b) Date acquired (mo., day, yr.)	(c) Date sold (mo., day, yr.)	(d) Gross sales price	(e) Depreciation allowed or allowable since acquisition	(f) Cost or other basis, plus improvements and expense of sale	(g) LOSS ((f) minus the sum of (d) and (e))	(h) GAIN ((d) plus (e) minus (f))
2							

3 Gain, if any, from Form 4684, Section B, line 21 . . . .

4 Section 1231 gain from installment sales from Form 6252, line 22 or 30 . . . .

5 Gain, if any, from line 32, from other than casualty and theft . . . .

6 Add lines 2 through 5 in columns (g) and (h) . . . . (   )

7 Combine columns (g) and (h) of line 6. Enter gain or (loss) here, and on the appropriate line as follows: . . . . . .

    Partnerships.—Enter the gain or (loss) on Form 1065, Schedule K, line 6. Skip lines 8, 9, 11, and 12 below.

    S corporations.—Report the gain or (loss) following the instructions for Form 1120S, Schedule K, lines 5 and 6. Skip lines 8, 9, 11, and 12 below, unless line 7 is a gain and the S corporation is subject to the capital gains tax.

    All others.—If line 7 is zero or a loss, enter the amount on line 11 below and skip lines 8 and 9. If line 7 is a gain and you did not have any prior year section 1231 losses, or they were recaptured in an earlier year, enter the gain as a long-term capital gain on Schedule D and skip lines 8, 9, and 12 below.

8 Nonrecaptured net section 1231 losses from prior years (see Instructions) . . . .

9 Subtract line 8 from line 7. If zero or less, enter -0-. Also enter on the appropriate line as follows (see instructions): . . . . .

    S corporations.—Enter this amount (if greater than zero) on Form 1120S, Schedule D, line 7, and skip lines 11 and 12 below.

    All others.—If line 9 is zero, enter the amount from line 7 on line 12 below. If line 9 is more than zero, enter the amount from line 8 on line 12 below, and enter the amount from line 9 as a long-term capital gain on Schedule D.

Part II   Ordinary Gains and Losses

10 Ordinary gains and losses not included on lines 11 through 16 (include property held 1 year or less):

11 Loss, if any, from line 7 . . . .

12 Gain, if any, from line 7, or amount from line 8 if applicable . . . .

13 Gain, if any, from line 31 . . . .

14 Net gain or (loss) from Form 4684, Section B, lines 13 and 20a . . . .

15 Ordinary gain from installment sales from Form 6252, line 21 or 29 . . . .

16 Recapture of section 179 deduction for partners and S corporation shareholders from property dispositions by partnerships and S corporations (see Instructions) . . . .

17 Add lines 10 through 16 in columns (g) and (h) . . . . (   )

18 Combine columns (g) and (h) of line 17. Enter gain or (loss) here, and on the appropriate line as follows: . . . .

  a   For all except individual returns: Enter the gain or (loss) from line 18 on the return being filed.

  b   For individual returns:

    (1) If the loss on line 11 includes a loss from Form 4684, Section B, Part II, column (b)(ii), enter that part of the loss here and on line 21 of Schedule A (Form 1040). Identify as from "Form 4797, line 18b(1)". See Instructions . . . .

    (2) Redetermine the gain or (loss) on line 18, excluding the loss, if any, on line 18b(1). Enter here and on Form 1040, line 15

For Paperwork Reduction Act Notice, see page 1 of separate Instructions.

Form **4797** (1990)

Form 4797 (1990)

Part III   Gain From Disposition of Property Under Sections 1245, 1250, 1252, 1254, and 1255

19	Description of section 1245, 1250, 1252, 1254, and 1255 property:	Date acquired (mo., day, yr.)	Date sold (mo., day, yr.)
A			
B			
C			
D			

	Relate lines 19A through 19D to these columns ▶	Property A	Property B	Property C	Property D
20	Gross sales price (**Note:** See line 1 before completing.)				
21	Cost or other basis plus expense of sale				
22	Depreciation (or depletion) allowed or allowable				
23	Adjusted basis. Subtract line 22 from line 21				
24	Total gain. Subtract line 23 from line 20				
25	**If section 1245 property:**				
a	Depreciation allowed or allowable from line 22				
b	Enter the **smaller** of line 24 or 25a				
26	**If section 1250 property:** If straight line depreciation was used, enter zero on line 26g unless you are a corporation subject to section 291.				
a	Additional depreciation after 12/31/75 (see Instructions)				
b	Applicable percentage multiplied by the **smaller** of line 24 or line 26a (see Instructions)				
c	Subtract line 26a from line 24. If line 24 is not more than line 26a, skip lines 26d and 26e				
d	Additional depreciation after 12/31/69 and before 1/1/76				
e	Applicable percentage multiplied by the **smaller** of line 26c or 26d (see Instructions)				
f	Section 291 amount (corporations only)				
g	Add lines 26b, 26e, and 26f				
27	**If section 1252 property:** Skip this section if you did not dispose of farmland or if you are a partnership.				
a	Soil, water, and land clearing expenses				
b	Line 27a multiplied by applicable percentage (see Instructions)				
c	Enter the **smaller** of line 24 or 27b				
28	**If section 1254 property:**				
a	Intangible drilling and development costs, expenditures for development of mines and other natural deposits, and mining exploration costs (see Instructions)				
b	Enter the **smaller** of line 24 or 28a				
29	**If section 1255 property:**				
a	Applicable percentage of payments excluded from income under section 126 (see Instructions)				
b	Enter the **smaller** of line 24 or 29a				

Summary of Part III Gains (Complete property columns A through D, through line 29b before going to line 30.)

30	Total gains for all properties. Add columns A through D, line 24	
31	Add columns A through D, lines 25b, 26g, 27c, 28b, and 29b. Enter here and on line 13. (See the Instructions for Part IV if this is an installment sale.)	
32	Subtract line 31 from line 30. Enter the portion from casualty and theft on Form 4684, Section B, line 15. Enter the portion from other than casualty and theft on Form 4797, line 5	

Part IV   Election Not to Use the Installment Method (Complete this part only if you elect out of the installment method and report a note or other obligation at less than full face value.)

33	Check here if you elect out of the installment method	▶ ☐
34	Enter the face amount of the note or other obligation	▶ $
35	Enter the percentage of valuation of the note or other obligation	▶ %

Part V   Recapture Amounts Under Sections 179 and 280F When Business Use Drops to 50% or Less (See Instructions for Part V.)

		(a) Section 179	(b) Section 280F
36	Section 179 expense deduction or section 280F recovery deductions		
37	Depreciation or recovery deductions (see Instructions)		
38	Recapture amount. Subtract line 37 from line 36. (See Instructions for where to report.)		

Form **4970**

Department of the Treasury
Internal Revenue Service

Tax on Accumulation Distribution of Trusts

▶ Attach to beneficiary's tax return.
▶ See instructions on back.

OMB No. 1545-0192

19**90**

Attachment
Sequence No. **73**

Name(s) as shown on return

Social security number

Name and address of trust

Employer identifying number

Type of trust:
☐ Domestic ☐ Foreign

Beneficiary's date of birth

Enter number of trusts from which you received
accumulation distributions in this tax year. . . . ▶

Part I Average Income and Determination of Computation Years

1	Amount of current distribution that is considered distributed in earlier tax years. (From Schedule J (Form 1041), line 37, column (a)).	1
2	Distributions of income accumulated before you were born or reached age 21	2
3	Subtract line 2 from line 1	3
4	Taxes imposed on the trust on amounts from line 3. (From Schedule J (Form 1041), line 37, column (b))	4
5	Total (add lines 3 and 4).	5
6	Tax-exempt interest included on line 5. (From Schedule J (Form 1041), line 37, column (c)). . . .	6
7	Taxable part of line 5 (subtract line 6 from line 5)	7
8	Number of trust's earlier tax years in which amounts on line 7 are considered distributed	8
9	Average annual amount considered distributed (divide line 3 by line 8). . . . . [9]	
10	Multiply line 9 by .25 . . . . [10]	
11	Number of earlier tax years to be taken into account (see instructions).	11
12	Average amount for recomputing tax (divide line 7 by line 11). Enter here and in each column on line 15 . .	12

13	Enter your taxable income before this distribution for the 5 immediately preceding tax years	1989	1988	1987	1986	1985

Part II Computation of Tax Attributable to the Accumulation Distribution

			(a) 19....	(b) 19....	(c) 19....
14	Enter the amounts from line 13, eliminating the highest and lowest taxable income years.	14			
15	Enter amount from line 12 in each column.	15			
16	Recomputed taxable income (add lines 14 and 15)	16			
17	Income tax on amounts on line 16	17			
18	Income tax before credits on line 14 income	18			
19	Additional tax before credits (subtract line 18 from line 17) . . .	19			
20	Tax credit adjustment	20			
21	Subtract line 20 from line 19	21			
22	Minimum and alternative minimum tax adjustments	22			
23	Combine lines 21 and 22	23			

24	Add columns (a), (b), and (c), line 23	24
25	Divide the amount on line 24 by three	25
26	Multiply the amount on line 25 by the number of years on line 11	26
27	Enter the amount from line 4	27
28	Partial tax (subtract line 27 from line 26) (If line 27 is more than line 26, enter zero.)	28
29	Interest charge on accumulation distribution from foreign trusts	29
30	Add lines 28 and 29	30

For Paperwork Reduction Act Notice, see back of form.

Form **4970** (1990)

General Instructions

(Section references are to the Internal Revenue Code.)

Paperwork Reduction Act Notice.— We ask for the information on this form to carry out the Internal Revenue laws of the United States. You are required to give us the information. We need it to ensure that taxpayers are complying with these laws and to allow us to figure and collect the right amount of tax

The time needed to complete and file this form will vary depending on individual circumstances. The estimated average time is:

Recordkeeping . . . . 1 hr., 12 mins.

**Learning about the
law or the form** . . . . . . 16 mins.

Preparing the form . . . 1 hr., 30 mins.

**Copying, assembling,
and sending the form to
the IRS** . . . . 20 mins.

If you have comments concerning the accuracy of these time estimates or suggestions for making this form more simple, we would be happy to hear from you. You can write to both the IRS and the Office of Management and Budget at the addresses listed in the instructions of the tax return with which this form is filed.

Purpose of Form.—If you are the beneficiary of a trust that accumulated its income , instead of distributing it currently, use Form 4970 to figure the partial tax under section 667. The fiduciary notifies the beneficiary of an "accumulation distribution" by completing Part IV of Schedule J (Form 1041).

Thus, if you received a distribution for this tax year from a trust that accumulated its income, instead of distributing it each year (and the trust paid taxes on that income), you must complete Form 4970 to compute any additional tax liability. The trustee must give you a completed Part IV of Schedule J (Form 1041) so you can complete this form.

If you received accumulation distributions from more than one trust during the current tax year, prepare a separate Form 4970 for each trust from which you received an accumulation distribution. You can arrange the distributions in any order you want them considered to have been made.

Definitions

Undistributed net income (UNI).— Undistributed net income is the distributable net income (DNI) of the trust for any tax year less: (1) the amount of income required to be distributed currently and any other amounts properly paid or credited or required to be distributed to beneficiaries in the tax year; and (2) the taxes imposed on the trust attributable to such DNI.

Accumulation distribution.—An accumulation distribution is the amount by which amounts properly paid, credited, or required to be distributed currently for the tax year exceed the DNI of the trust reduced by the amount of income required to be distributed currently.

Generally, except for tax-exempt interest, the distribution loses its character upon distribution to the beneficiary. See section 667(d) for special rules for foreign trusts.

Line-by-Line Instructions

Line 1.—For a nonresident alien or foreign corporation, include only your share of the accumulation distribution that is attributable to U.S. sources or is effectively connected with a trade or business carried on in the U.S.

Line 2.—Enter any amount from line 1 that represents UNI of a domestic trust considered to have been distributed before you were born or reached age 21. However, if the multiple trust rule applies, see the instructions for line 4.

Line 4—Multiple Trust Rule.—If you received accumulation distributions from two or more other trusts that were considered to have been made in any of the earlier tax years in which the current accumulation distribution is considered to have been made, do not include on line 4 those accumulation distributions from column (a), Part IV of the current accumulation distribution considered to have been distributed in the same earlier tax year(s).

For this special rule only count as trusts those trusts for which the sum of this accumulation distribution and any earlier accumulation distributions from the trust, which are considered under section 666(a) to have been distributed in the same earlier tax year, is $1,000 or more.

If the trust is a foreign trust, see section 665(d).

Line 8.—You can determine the number of years which the UNI is deemed to have been distributed by counting the "throwback years" for which there are entries on lines 32 through 36 of Part IV of Schedule J (Form 1041).These throwback rules apply even if you would not have been entitled to receive a distribution in the earlier tax year if the distribution had actually been made then. **Note:** *There can be more than five "throwback years."*

Line 11.—From the number of years entered on line 8, subtract any year in which the distribution from column (a), Part IV of Schedule J (Form 1041) is less than the amount on line 10 of Form 4970. If the distribution for each throwback year is more than line 10, then enter the same number on line 11 as you entered on line 8.

Line 13.—Enter your taxable incomes for years 1985–1989, even if less than five years of the trust had accumulated income after the beneficiary became 21. Use the taxable income as reported, amended by you, or as changed by IRS. Include in the taxable income amounts considered distributed as a result of prior accumulation distributions whether from the same or another trust, and whether made in an earlier year or the current year.

If you are not an individual, and your taxable income as adjusted is less than zero, enter zero.

If you are an individual, and your taxable income as adjusted for 1985–1986 is less than your zero bracket amount, enter your zero bracket amount. For 1987-1989, enter the amount of your taxable income, but not less than zero.

Line 17.—Figure the income tax (not including any minimum tax or alternative minimum tax) on the income on line 16 using the tax rates in effect for your particular earlier tax year shown in each of the three columns. You may use the Tax Rate Schedules, etc., as applicable. You can get the Tax Rate Schedules and earlier year forms from many IRS offices.

Line 18.—Enter your income tax (not including any minimum tax or alternative minimum tax) as originally reported, corrected, or amended, before reduction for any credits for your particular earlier year shown in each of the three columns.

Line 20.—Nonrefundable credits that are limited to tax liability, such as the general business credit, may be changed because of an accumulation distribution. If the total allowable credits for any of the three computation years increases, enter the increase on line 20. However, do not treat as an increase the part of the credit that was allowable as a carryback or carryforward credit in the current or any preceding year other than the computation year.

To refigure these credits, you must consider changes to the tax before credits for each of the three computation years due to previous accumulation distributions.

If the accumulation distribution is from a domestic trust that paid foreign income taxes, the limitation on the foreign tax credit under section 904 is applied separately to the distribution. If the distribution is from a foreign trust, see sections 667(d) and 904(f)(4) for special rules.

Attach the proper form for any credit you refigure. The amount determined for items on this line is limited to tax law provisions in effect for those years involved.

Line 22.—Use and attach a separate **Form 4626, Form 6251,** or **Form 8656** to recompute the minimum and alternative minimum tax for each earlier year and show any change in those taxes in the bottom margin of the forms. Enter the adjustments on this line.

Line 28.—For estate taxes and generation-skipping transfer taxes, reduce the partial tax by the estate tax or generation-skipping transfer tax attributable to the accumulation distribution. See section 667(b)(6) for the computation.

Line 29.—For an accumulation distribution from a foreign trust, an interest charge must be added to the partial tax. This interest charge is not deductible under any section and is figured as follows:

(1) Figure 6% of line 28.

(2) Total the number of years from the year(s) of allocation to the year of distribution (including the year of allocation, but not the year of distribution).

(3) Divide the number in step (2) by the total years of allocation (line 8).

(4) Multiply the answer in step (1) by the decimal in step (3).

(5) Subtract line 28 from line 1. This is the maximum interest.

(6) Enter on line 29 the amount from step (4) or step (5), whichever is less.

If this form is not being used for distributions from a foreign trust, enter zero on line 29.

Line 30—*Individuals.*—Enter the amount from this line on line 39, Form 1040.

Estates and Trusts.—Include the amount on line 1b, Schedule G, Form 1041.

Other filers.—Add the result to the total tax liability before credits on your income tax return for the year of the accumulation distribution. Attach this form to that return.

Appendix C

TABLE OF CASES CITED

Appendix **D**

TABLE OF CODE SECTIONS CITED

Appendix **E**

TABLE OF
PROPOSED AND TEMPORARY
REGULATIONS CITED

Proposed Regulations

Temporary Regulations

Appendix F

TABLE OF REVENUE PROCEDURES AND REVENUE RULINGS CITED

Revenue Procedures

Rev. Proc.	Page
57-6	17-16
65-17	9-36
68-16	17-16
77-16	9-37
77-37	2-9, 7-4, 7-14, 7-16, 7-25
82-22	16-11
82-29	9-36
83-25	10-39
83-59	2-15
84-35	10-51
87-32	12-30
87-57	3-11, 3-12

Revenue Rulings

Rev. Rul.	Page
217	2-6
266	17-7
54-230	3-13
55-80	8-54
56-472	13-5
56-484	15-14
57-379	9-40
59-259	7-6
60-352	11-29
64-162	12-28, 12-47
64-220	10-29
67-188	10-21
68-55	2-11
68-79	10-21
68-344	10-3

Rev. Rul.	Page
68-348	5-4
68-379	13-7
68-537	12-28, 12-47
69-148	12-12
69-180	10-35
69-184	10-31
69-440	3-35
69-489	15-31
70-104	4-14
70-155	13-25
72-48	5-26
72-330	9-9
72-596	10-31
72-598	9-9
73-305	6-5
73-405	15-18
73-578	9-44
74-7	9-38
74-44	12-13
74-222	9-38
74-296	4-16
74-341	9-41
74-351	9-40
75-67	6-34
75-108	9-38
75-134	9-40
75-214	10-33
75-249	6-34
75-250	6-34
75-268	9-6
75-290	6-34
75-502	4-11
75-525	10-29

Letter Rulings

Appendix G

GLOSSARY OF TAX TERMS

—A—

A. (see Acquiescence).

Accelerated Cost Recovery System (ACRS). An alternate form of depreciation enacted by the Economic Recovery Tax Act of 1981 and significantly modified by the Tax Reform Act of 1986. The cost of a qualifying asset is recovered over a set period of time. Salvage value is ignored. § 168.

Accelerated Depreciation. Various depreciation methods which produce larger depreciation deductions in the earlier years of an asset's life than straight-line depreciation. Examples: double-declining balance method (200% declining balance) and sum-of-the-years'-digits method. § 167 (*see also* Depreciation).

Accounting Method. A method by which an entity's income and expenses are determined. The primary accounting methods used are the accrual method and the cash method. Other accounting methods include the installment method; the percentage of completion method (for construction); and various methods for valuing inventories, such as FIFO and LIFO. §§ 446 and 447 (*see also* the specific accounting methods).

Accounting Period. A period of time used by a taxpayer in determining his or her income, expenses, and tax liability. An accounting period is generally a year for tax purposes, either a calendar year, a fiscal year, or a 52-53 week year. §§ 441 and 443.

Accrual Method of Accounting. The method of accounting which reflects the income earned and the expenses incurred during a given tax period. However, unearned income of an accrual basis taxpayer must generally be included in an entity's income in the year in which it is received, even if it is not actually earned by the entity until a later tax period. § 446.

Accumulated Adjustment Account (AAA). A summary of all includable income and gains, expenses, and losses of an S Corporation for taxable years after 1982, except those that relate to excludable income, distributions, and redemptions of an S Corporation. Distributions from the AAA are not taxable to the shareholders. §§ 1368(c)(1) and (e)(1).

Accumulated Earnings Credit. A reduction in arriving at a corporation's accumulated taxable income (in computing the Accumulated Earnings Tax). Its purpose is to avoid penalizing a corporation for retaining sufficient earnings and profits to meet the reasonable needs of the business. § 535(c).

Accumulated Earnings Tax.   A penalty tax on the unreasonable accumulation of earnings and profits by a corporation. It is intended to encourage the distribution of earnings and profits of a corporation to its shareholders. §§ 531-537.

Accumulated Taxable Income.   The amount on which the accumulated earnings tax is imposed. §§ 531 and 535.

Accuracy-related Penalty.   Any of the group of penalties that includes negligence or disregard of rules or regulations, substantial understatement of income tax, substantial valuation misstatement for income tax purposes, substantial overstatement of pension liabilities, and substantial estate or gift valuation understatement. § 6662.

Acquiescence.   The public endorsement of a regular Tax Court decision by the Commissioner of the Internal Revenue Service. When the Commissioner acquiesces to a regular Tax Court decision, the IRS generally will not dispute the result in cases involving substantially similar facts (*see also* Nonacquiescence).

Ad Valorem Tax.   A tax based on the value of property.

Adjusted Basis.   The basis (i.e., cost or other basis) of property plus capital improvements minus depreciation allowed or allowable. See § 1016 for other adjustments to basis. § 1016 (*see also* Basis).

Adjusted Gross Income.   A term used with reference to individual taxpayers. Adjusted gross income consists of an individual's gross income less certain deductions and business expenses. § 62.

Adjusted Ordinary Gross Income (AOGI).   A term used in relation to personal holding companies. Adjusted ordinary gross income is determined by subtracting certain expenses related to rents and mineral, oil, and gas royalties, and certain interest expense from ordinary gross income. § 543(b)(2).

Administrator.   A person appointed by the court to administrate the estate of a deceased person. If named to perform these duties by the decedent's will, this person is called an executor (executrix).

AFTR (American Federal Tax Reports).   Published by Prentice-Hall, these volumes contain the Federal tax decisions issued by the U.S. District Courts, U.S. Claims Court, U.S. Circuit Courts of Appeal, and the U.S. Supreme Court (*see also* AFTR2d).

AFTR2d (American Federal Tax Reports, Second Series).   The second series of the American Federal Tax Reports. These volumes contain the Federal tax decisions issued by the U.S. District Courts, U.S. Claims Court, U.S. Circuit Courts of Appeal, and the U.S. Supreme Court (*see also* AFTR).

Alternate Valuation Date.   The property contained in a decedent's gross estate must be valued at either the decedent's date of death or the alternate valuation date. The alternate valuation date is six months after the decedent's date of death, or, if the property is disposed of prior to that date, the particular property disposed of is valued as of the date of its disposition. § 2032.

Alternative Minimum Tax.   A tax imposed on taxpayers only if it exceeds the "regular" tax of the taxpayer. Regular taxable income is adjusted by certain timing differences, then increased by tax preferences to arrive at alternative minimum taxable income.

Amortization. The systematic write-off (deduction) of the cost or other basis of an intangible asset over its estimated useful life. The concept is similar to depreciation (used for tangible assets) and depletion (used for natural resources) (*see also* Goodwill and Intangible Asset).

Amount Realized. Any money received, plus the fair market value of any other property or services received, plus any liabilities discharged on the sale or other disposition of property. The determination of the amount realized is the first step in determining realized gain or loss. § 1001(b).

Annual Exclusion. The amount each year that a donor may exclude from Federal gift tax for each donee. Currently, the annual exclusion is $10,000 per donee per year. The annual exclusion does not generally apply to gifts of future interests. § 2503(b).

Annuity. A fixed amount of money payable to a person at specific intervals for either a specific period of time or for life.

Appellate Court. A court to which other court decisions are appealed. The appellate courts for Federal tax purposes include the Courts of Appeals and the Supreme Court.

Arm's Length Transaction. A transaction entered into by unrelated parties, each acting in their own best interest. It is presumed that in an arm's length transaction the prices used are the fair market values of the properties or services being transferred in the transaction.

Articles of Incorporation. The basic instrument filed with the appropriate state agency when a business is incorporated.

Assessment of Tax. The imposition of an additional tax liability by the Internal Revenue Service (i.e., as the result of an audit).

Assignment of Income. A situation in which a taxpayer assigns income or income-producing property to another person or entity in an attempt to avoid paying taxes on that income. An assignment of income or income-producing property is generally not recognized for tax purposes, and the income is taxable to the assignor.

Association. An entity which possesses a majority of the following characteristics: associates; profit motive; continuity of life; centralized management; limited liability; free transferability of interests. Associations are taxed as corporations. § § 7701(a)(3). Reg. § 301.7701-2.

At-Risk Limitation. A provision which limits a deduction for losses to the amounts "at risk." A taxpayer is generally not "at risk" in situations where nonrecourse debt is used. § 465.

Attribution. (*see* Constructive Ownership).

Audit. The examination of a taxpayer's return or other taxable transactions by the Internal Revenue Service in order to determine the correct tax liability. Types of audits include correspondence audits, office audits, and field audits (*see also* Correspondence Audit, Field Audit, and Office Audit).

—B—

Bad Debt.   An uncollectible debt. A bad debt may be classified either as a business bad debt or a nonbusiness bad debt. A business bad debt is one which arose in the course of the taxpayer's business (with a business purpose). Nonbusiness bad debts are treated as short-item capital losses rather than as ordinary losses. § 166.

Bargain Sale, Rental, or Purchase.   A sale, rental, or purchase of property for less than its fair market value. The difference between the sale, rental, or purchase price and the property's fair market value may have its own tax consequences, such as a constructive dividend or a gift.

Bartering.   The exchange of goods and services without using money.

Basis.   The starting point in determining the gain or loss from the sale or other disposition of an asset, or the depreciation (or depletion or amortization) on an asset. For example, if an asset is purchased for cash, the basis of that asset is the cash paid. §§ 1012, 1014, 1015, 334, 358, 362.

Beneficiary.   Someone who will benefit from an act of another, such as the beneficiary of a life insurance contract, the beneficiary of a trust (i.e., income beneficiary), or the beneficiary of an estate.

Bequest.   A testamentary transfer (by will) of personal property (personalty).

Board of Tax Appeals (B.T.A.).   The predecessor of the United States Tax Court, in existence from 1924 to 1942.

Bona Fide.   Real; in good faith.

Boot.   Cash or property that is not included in the definition of a particular type of nontaxable exchange [see §§ 351(b) and 1031(b)]. In these nontaxable exchanges, a taxpayer who receives boot must recognize gain to the extent of the boot received or the realized gain, whichever is less.

Brother-Sister Corporations.   A controlled group of two or more corporations owned (in certain amounts) by five or fewer individuals, estates, or trusts. § 1563(a)(2).

Burden of Proof.   The weight of evidence in a legal case or in a tax proceeding. Generally, the burden of proof is on the taxpayer in a tax case. However, the burden of proof is on the government in fraud cases. § 7454.

Business Purpose.   An actual business reason for following a course of action. Tax avoidance alone is not considered to be a business purpose. In areas such as corporate formation and corporate reorganizations, business purpose is especially important.

—C—

Capital Asset.   All property held by a taxpayer (e.g., house, car, clothing) except for certain assets that are specifically excluded from the definition of a capital asset, such as inventory or depreciable and real property used in a trade or business.

Capital Contribution. Cash, services, or property contributed by a partner to a partnership or by a shareholder to a corporation. Capital contributions are not income to the recipient partnership or corporation. §§ 721 and 118.

Capital Expenditure. Any amount paid for new buildings or for permanent improvements; any expenditures which add to the value or prolong the life of property or adapt the property to a new or different use. Capital expenditures should be added to the basis of the property improved. § 263.

Capital Gain. A gain from the sale or other disposition of a capital asset. § 1222.

Capital Loss. A loss from the sale or other disposition of a capital asset. § 1222.

Cash Method of Accounting. The method of accounting which reflects the income received (or constructively received) and the expenses paid during a given period. However, prepaid expenses of a cash basis taxpayer that benefit more than one year may be required to be deducted only in the periods benefitted (e.g., a premium for a three-year insurance policy may have to be spread over three years).

CCH. (*see* Commerce Clearing House).

C Corporation. A so-called regular corporation that is a separate tax-paying entity and subject to the tax rules contained in Subchapter C of the Internal Revenue Code (as opposed to an S corporation that is subject to the tax rules of Subchapter S of the Code).

Certiorari. A Writ of Certiorari is the form used to appeal a lower court (U.S. Court of Appeals) decision to the Supreme Court. The Supreme Court then decides, by reviewing the Writ of Certiorari, whether it will accept the appeal or not. The Supreme Court generally does not accept the appeal unless a constitutional issue is involved or the lower courts are in conflict. If the Supreme Court refuses to accept the appeal, then the certiorari is denied (cert. den.).

Claim of Right Doctrine. If a taxpayer has an unrestricted claim to income, the income is included in that taxpayer's income when it is received or constructively received, even if there is a possibility that all or part of the income may have to be returned to another party.

Closely-Held Corporation. A corporation whose voting stock is owned by one or a few shareholders, and is operated by this person or closely-knit group.

Collapsible Corporation. A corporation which liquidates before it has realized a substantial portion of its income. Shareholders treat the gain on these liquidating distributions as ordinary income (rather than dividend income or capital gains). § 341.

Commerce Clearing House. A publisher of tax materials, including a multivolume tax service, volumes which contain the Federal courts' decisions on tax matters (USTC), and the Tax Court regular (T.C.) and memorandum (TCM) decisions.

Community Property. Property that is owned together by husband and wife, where each has an undivided one-half interest in the property due to their marital status. The nine community property states are: Arizona, California, Idaho, Louisiana, Nevada, New Mexico, Texas, Washington, and Wisconsin.

Complex Trust. Any trust that does not meet the requirements of a simple trust. For example, a trust will be considered to be a complex trust if it does not distribute the trust income currently, it takes a deduction for a charitable contribution for the current year, or if it distributes any of the trust corpus currently. § 661.

Condemnation. The taking of private property for a public use by a public authority. The public authority compensates the owner of the property taken in a condemnation. An exercise of the power of eminent domain (*see also* Involuntary Conversion).

Conduit Principle. The provisions in the tax law which allow specific tax characteristics to be passed through certain entities to the owners of the entity without losing their identity. For example, the short-item capital gains of a partnership would be passed through to the partners and retain their character as short-item capital gains on the tax returns of the partners. This principle applies in varying degrees to partnerships, S corporations, estates, and trusts.

Consent Dividend. A term used in relation to the accumulated earnings tax and the personal holding company tax. A consent dividend occurs when the shareholders consent to treat a certain amount as a taxable dividend on their tax returns even though there is no distribution of cash or property. The purpose of this is to obtain a dividends-paid deduction. § 565.

Consolidated Return. A method used to determine the tax liability of a group of affiliated corporations. The aggregate income (with certain adjustments) of the group is viewed as the income of a single enterprise. § 1501.

Consolidation. The statutory combination of two or more corporations in a *new* corporation. § 368(a)(1)(A).

Constructive Dividends. The constructive receipt of a dividend. Even though a taxable benefit was not designated as a dividend by the distributing corporation, a shareholder may be designated by the IRS as having received a dividend if the benefit has the appearance of a dividend. For example, if a shareholder uses corporate property for personal purposes rent-free, he or she will have a constructive dividend equal to the fair rental value of the corporate property.

Constructive Ownership. In certain situations the tax law attributes the ownership of stock to persons "related" to the person or entity that actually owns the stock. The related party is said to constructively own the stock of that person. For example, under § 267(c) a father is considered to constructively own all stock actually owned by his son. §§ 267, 318 and 544(a).

Constructive Receipt. When income is available to a taxpayer, even though it is not actually received by the taxpayer, the amount is considered to be constructively received by the taxpayer and should be included in income (e.g., accrued interest on a savings account). However, if there are restrictions on the availability of the income, it is generally not considered to be constructively received until the restrictions are removed (e.g., interest on a six-month certificate of deposit is not constructively received until the end of the six-month period, if early withdrawal would result in loss of interest or principal).

Contributions to the Capital of a Corporation. (*see* Capital Contributions).

Controlled Foreign Corporation. A foreign corporation in which more than 50 percent of its voting power is controlled directly or indirectly at any time during the year by U.S. stockholders who individually control at least 10 percent of the voting power. U.S. shareholders are taxed on their share of the income as it is earned, rather than when it is distributed. §§ 951-964.

Corpus. The principal of a trust, as opposed to the income of the trust. Also called the *res* of the trust.

Correspondence Audit. An IRS audit conducted through the mail. Generally, verification or substantiation for specified items are requested by the IRS, and the taxpayer mails the requested information to the IRS (*see also* Field Audit and Office Audit).

Cost Depletion. (*see* Depletion).

Court of Appeals. The U.S. Federal court system has 13 circuit Courts of Appeals which consider cases appealed from the U.S. Claims Court, the U.S. Tax Court, and the U.S. District Courts. A writ of certiorari is used to appeal a case from a Court of Appeals to the U.S. Supreme Court (*see also* Appellate Court).

Creditor. A person or entity to whom money is owed. The person or entity who owes the money is called the debtor.

—D—

Death Tax. A tax imposed on property upon the death of the owner, such as an estate tax or inheritance tax.

Debtor. A person or entity who owes money to another. The person or entity to whom the money is owed is called the creditor.

Decedent. A deceased person.

Deductions in Respect of a Decedent (DRD). Certain expenses that are incurred by a decedent but are not properly deductible on the decedent's final return because of nonpayment. Deductions in respect of a decedent are deducted by the taxpayer who is legally required to make payment. § 691(b).

Deficiency. An additional tax liability owed to the IRS by a taxpayer. A deficiency is generally proposed by the IRS through the use of a Revenue Agent's Report.

Deficit. A negative balance in retained earnings, or in earnings and profits.

Dependent. A person who derives his or her primary support from another. In order for a taxpayer to claim a dependency exemption for a person, there are five tests which must be met: support test, gross income test, citizenship or residency test, relationship or member of household test, and joint return test. § 152.

Depletion. As natural resources are extracted and sold, the cost or other basis of the resource is recovered by the use of depletion. Depletion may be either cost or percentage (statutory) depletion. Cost depletion has to do with the recovery of the cost of natural resources based on the units of the resource sold. Percentage depletion uses percentages given in the Internal Revenue Code multiplied by the gross income from the interest, subject to limitations. §§ 613 and 613A.

Depreciation.   The systematic write-off of the basis of a tangible asset over the asset's estimated useful life. Depreciation is intended to reflect the wear, tear, and obsolescence of the asset (*see also* Amortization and Depletion).

Depreciation Recapture.   The situation in which all or part of the realized gain from the sale or other disposition of depreciable business property could be treated as ordinary income. See text for discussion of §§ 291, 1245, and 1250.

Determination Letter.   A written statement regarding the tax consequences of a transaction issued by an IRS District Director in response to a written inquiry by a taxpayer that applies to a particular set of facts. Determination letters are frequently used to state whether a pension or profit-sharing plan is qualified or not, to determine the tax-exempt status of non-profit organizations, and to clarify employee status.

Discretionary Trust.   A trust in which the trustee or another party has the right to determine whether to accumulate or distribute the trust income currently, and/or which beneficiary is to receive the trust income.

Discriminant Function System (DIF).   The computerized system used by the Internal Revenue Service in identifying and selecting returns for examination. This system uses secret mathematical formulas to select those returns which have a probability of tax errors.

Dissent.   A disagreement with the majority opinion. The term is generally used to mean the explicit disagreement of one or more judges in a court with the majority decision on a particular case.

Distributable Net Income (DNI).   The net income of a fiduciary that is available for distribution to income beneficiaries. DNI is computed by adjusting an estate's or trust's taxable income by certain modifications. § 643(a).

Distribution in Kind.   A distribution of property as it is. For example, rather than selling property and distributing the proceeds to the shareholders, the property itself is distributed to the shareholders.

District Court.   A trial court in which Federal tax matters can be litigated; the only trial court in which a jury trial can be obtained.

Dividend.   A payment by a corporation to its shareholders authorized by the corporation's board of directors to be distributed pro rata among the outstanding shares. However, a constructive dividend does not need to be authorized by the shareholders (*see also* Constructive Dividend).

Dividends-Paid Deduction.   A deduction allowed in determining the amount that is subject to the accumulated earnings tax and the personal holding company tax. §§ 561-565.

Dividends-Received Deduction.   A deduction available to corporations on dividends received from a domestic corporation. The dividends-received deduction is generally 70 percent of the dividends received. If the recipient corporation owns 20 percent or more of the stock of the paying corporation, an 80 percent deduction is allowed. The dividends-received deduction is 100 percent of the dividends received from another member of an affiliated group, if an election is made. §§ 243-246.

Domestic Corporation.   A corporation which is created or organized in the United States or under the law of the United States or of any state. § 7701(a)(4).

Domestic International Sales Corporation (DISC).   A U.S. corporation which derives most of its income from exports. A portion of the income taxes on a DISC's income is deferred as long as the DISC requirements are met. §§ 991-997.

Donee.   The person or entity to whom a gift is made.

Donor.   The person or entity who makes a gift.

Double Taxation.   The situation where income is taxed twice. For example, a regular corporation pays tax on its taxable income, and then, when this income is distributed to the corporation's shareholders, the shareholders are taxed on the dividend income.

—E—

Earned Income.   Income from personal services. § 911(d)(2).

Earnings and Profits.   The measure of a corporation's ability to pay dividends to its shareholders. Distributions made by a corporation to its shareholders are dividends to the extent of the corporation's earnings and profits. §§ 312 and 316.

Eminent Domain.   (*see* Condemnation).

Employee.   A person in the service of another, where the employer has the power to specify how the work is to be performed (*see also* Independent Contractor).

Encumbrance.   A liability.

Entity.   For tax purposes, an organization that is considered to have a separate existence, such as a partnership, corporation, estate, or trust.

Escrow.   Cash or other property that is held by a third party as security for an obligation.

Estate.   All of the property owned by a decedent at the time of his or her death.

Estate Tax.   A tax imposed on the transfer of a decedent's taxable estate. The estate, not the heirs, is liable for the estate tax. §§ 2001-2209 (*see also* Inheritance Tax).

Estoppel.   A bar or impediment preventing a party from asserting a fact or a claim in court that is inconsistent with a position he or she had previously taken.

Excise Tax.   A tax imposed on the sale, manufacture, or use of a commodity or on the conduct of an occupation or activity. Considered to include every Internal Revenue Tax except the income tax.

Executor.   A person appointed in a will to carry out the provisions in the will and to administer the estate of the decedent. (Feminine of executor is executrix.)

Exempt Organization.   An organization (such as a charitable organization) that is exempt from Federal income taxes. §§ 501-528.

Exemption.   A deduction allowed in computing taxable income. Personal exemptions are available for the taxpayer and his or her spouse. Dependency exemptions are available for the taxpayer's dependents. §§ 151-154 (*see also* Dependent).

Expatriate (U.S.).   U.S. citizen working in a foreign country.

—F—

F.2d (Federal Reporter, Second Series).   Volumes in which the decisions of the U.S. Claims Court and the U.S. Courts of Appeals are published.

F. Supp. (Federal Supplement).   Volumes in which the decisions of the U.S. District Courts are published.

Fair Market Value.   The amount which a willing buyer would pay a willing seller in an arm's length transaction.

Fed. (Federal Reporter).   Volumes in which the decisions of the U.S. Claims Court and the U.S. Courts of Appeals are published.

FICA (Federal Insurance Contributions Act).   The law dealing with social security taxes and benefits. §§ 3101-3126.

Fiduciary.   A person or institution who holds and manages property for another, such as a guardian, trustee, executor, or administrator. § 7701(a)(6).

Field Audit.   An audit conducted by the IRS at the taxpayer's place of business or at the place of business of the taxpayer's representative. Field audits are generally conducted by Revenue Agents (*see also* Correspondence Audit and Office Audit).

FIFO (First-in, First-out).   A method of determining the cost of an inventory. The first inventory units acquired are considered to be the first sold. Therefore, the cost of the inventory would consist of the most recently acquired inventory.

Filing Status.   The filing status of an individual taxpayer determines the tax rates that are applicable to that taxpayer. The filing statuses include: Single, Head of Household, Married Filing Jointly, Married Filing Separately, Surviving Spouse (Qualifying Widow or Widower).

Fiscal Year.   A period of 12 consecutive months, other than a calendar year, used as the accounting period of a business. § 7701(a)(24).

Foreign Corporation.   A corporation which is not organized under U.S. laws. Other than a domestic corporation. § 7701(a)(5).

Foreign Personal Holding Company (FPHC).   A foreign corporation in which five or fewer U.S. citizens or residents owned more than 50 percent of the value of its outstanding stock during the taxable year and at least 50 percent of its gross income (or 60 percent if it was not an FPHC in the previous year) is foreign personal holding company income. §§ 551-558.

Foreign Sales Corporation (FSC).   A corporation created or organized under the laws of a U.S. possession (other than Puerto Rico) or certain foreign countries, has no more than 25 shareholders at any time, has no outstanding preferred stock, maintains a set of records at an office outside the United States and certain records inside the United States, has at least one non-U.S. resident member of the board of directors, is not a member of a controlled group which has a DISC as a member, makes a timely FSC election, and meets foreign management and foreign economic process tests. §§ 921-927.

Foreign Source Income.   Income derived from sources outside the United States. The source of earned income is determined by the place where the work is actually performed. Unearned income usually qualifies as foreign source income when it is received from a foreign resident or for property used in a foreign country and not effectively connected with U.S. sources.

Foreign Tax Credit.   A credit available against taxes for foreign income taxes paid or deemed paid. A deduction may be taken for these foreign taxes as an alternative to the foreign tax credit. §§ 27 and 901-905.

Fraud.   A willful intent to evade tax. For tax purposes, fraud is divided into civil fraud and criminal fraud. The IRS has the burden of proof of proving fraud. Civil fraud has a penalty of 75 percent of the underpayment [§ 6653(b)]. Criminal fraud requires a greater degree of willful intent to evade tax (§§ 7201-7207).

Freedom of Information Act.   The means by which the public may obtain information held by Federal agencies.

Fringe Benefits.   Benefits received by an employee in addition to his or her salary or wages, such as insurance and recreational facilities.

FUTA (Federal Unemployment Tax Act).   A tax imposed on the employer on the wages of the employees. A credit is generally given for amounts contributed to state unemployment tax funds. §§ 3301-3311.

Future Interest.   An interest in which the possession or enjoyment of which will come into being at some point in the future. The annual exclusion for gifts only applies to gifts of present interests, as opposed to future interests.

—G—

General Partner.   A partner who is jointly and severally liable for the debts of the partnerships. A general partner has no limited liability (*see* Limited Partner).

Generation-Skipping Tax.   A transfer tax imposed on a certain type of transfer involving a trust and at least three generations of taxpayers. The transfer generally skips a generation younger than the original transferor. The transfer therefore results in the avoidance of one generation's estate tax on the transferred property. §§ 2601-2622.

Gift.   A transfer of property or money made without adequate valuable or legal consideration.

Gift-Splitting.   A tax provision which allows a married person who makes a gift of his or her property, to elect, with the consent of his or her spouse, to treat the gift as being made one-half by each the taxpayer and his or her spouse. The effect of gift-splitting is to take advantage of the annual gift tax exclusions for both the taxpayer and his or her spouse. § 2513.

Gift Tax.   A tax imposed on the donor of a gift. The tax applies to transfers in trust or otherwise, whether the gift is direct or indirect, real or personal, tangible or intangible. §§ 2501-2524.

Goodwill.   An intangible asset which has an indefinite useful life, arising from the difference between the purchase price and the value of the assets of an acquired business. Goodwill is not amortizable since it has no ascertainable life. § 263(b).

Grantor.   The person who creates a trust.

Grantor Trust.   A trust in which the transferor (grantor) of the trust does not surrender complete control over the property. Generally, the income from a grantor trust is taxable to the grantor rather than to the person who receives the income. §§ 671-677.

Gross Estate.   The value of all property, real or personal, tangible or intangible, owned by a decedent at the time of his or her death. §§ 2031-2046.

Gross Income.   Income that is subject to Federal income tax. All income from whatever source derived, unless it is specifically excluded from income (e.g., interest on state and local bonds). § 61.

Guaranteed Payment.   A payment made by a partnership to a partner for services or the use of capital, without regard to the income of the partnership. The payment generally is deductible by the partnership and taxable to the partner. § 707(c).

—H—

Half-Year Convention.   When using ACRS, personalty placed in service at any time during the year is treated as placed in service in the middle of the year, and personalty disposed of or retired at any time during the year is treated as disposed of in the middle of the year. However, if more than 40 percent of all personalty placed in service during the year is placed in service during the last three months of the year, the mid-quarter convention applies. § 168(d)(4)(A).

Heir.   One who inherits property from a decedent.

Hobby.   An activity not engaged in for profit. § 183.

Holding Period.   The period of time that property is held. Holding period is used to determine whether a gain or loss is short-item or long-term. §§ 1222 and 1223.

H.R. 10 Plans.   (*see* Keogh Plans).

—I—

Incident of Ownership.   Any economic interest in a life insurance policy, such as the power to change the policy's beneficiary, the right to cancel or assign the policy, and the right to borrow against the policy. § 2042(2).

Income Beneficiary.   The person or entity that is entitled to receive the income from property. Generally used in reference to trusts.

Income in Respect of a Decedent (IRD).   Income that had been earned by a decedent at the time of his or her death, but is not included on the final tax return because of the decedent's method of accounting. Income in respect of a decedent is included in the decedent's gross estate and also on the tax return of the person who receives the income. § 691.

Independent Contractor.   One who contracts to do a job according to his or her own methods and skills. The employer has control over the independent contractor only as to the final result of his or her work (*see also* Employee).

Indirect Method.   A method used by the IRS in order to determine whether a taxpayer's income is correctly reported, when adequate records do not exist. Indirect methods include the Source and Applications of Funds Method and the Net Worth Method.

Information Return.   A return which must be filed with the Internal Revenue Service even though no tax is imposed, such as a partnership return (Form 1065), Form W-2, and Form 1099.

Inheritance Tax.   A tax imposed on the privilege of receiving property of a decedent. The tax is imposed on the heir.

Installment Method.   A method of accounting under which a taxpayer spreads the recognition of his or her gain ratably over time as the payments are received. §§ 453, 453A and 453B.

Intangible Asset.   A nonphysical asset, such as goodwill, copyrights, franchises, or trademarks.

Inter Vivos Transfer.   A property transfer during the life of the owner.

Intercompany Transaction.   A transaction that occurs during a consolidated return year between two or more members of the same affiliated group.

Internal Revenue Service.   Part of the Treasury Department, it is responsible for administering and enforcing the Federal tax laws.

Intestate.   No will existing at the time of death.

Investment Tax Credit.   A credit against tax that was allowed for investing in depreciable tangible personalty before 1986. The credit was equal to 10 percent of the qualified investment. §§ 38 and 46-48.

Investment Tax Credit Recapture.   When property, on which an investment credit has been taken, is disposed of prior to the full time period required under the law to earn the credit, then the amount of unearned credit must be added back to the taxpayer's tax liability—this is called recapture of the investment tax credit. § 47.

Involuntary Conversion.   The complete or partial destruction, theft, seizure, requisition, or condemnation of property. § 1033.

Itemized Deductions.   Certain expenditures of a personal nature which are specifically allowed to be deductible from an individual taxpayer's adjusted gross income. Itemized deductions (e.g., medical expenses, charitable contributions, interest, taxes, moving expenses, and miscellaneous itemized deductions) are deductible if they exceed the taxpayer's standard deduction.

—J—

Jeopardy Assessment. If the IRS has reason to believe that the collection or assessment of a tax would be jeopardized by delay, the IRS may assess and collect the tax immediately. §§ 6861-6864.

Joint and Several Liability. The creditor has the ability to sue one or more of the parties who have a liability, or all of the liable persons together. General partners are jointly and severally liable for the debts of the partnership. Also, if a husband and wife file a joint return, they are jointly and severally liable to the IRS for the taxes due.

Joint Tenancy. Property held by two or more owners, where each has an undivided interest in the property. Joint tenancy includes the right of survivorship, which means that upon the death of an owner, his or her share passes to the surviving owner(s).

Joint Venture. A joining together of two or more persons in order to undertake a specific business project. A joint venture is not a continuing relationship like a partnership, but may be treated as a partnership for Federal income tax purposes. § 761(a).

—K—

Keogh Plans. A retirement plan available for self-employed taxpayers. § 401.

"Kiddie" Tax. Unearned income of a child under age 14 is taxed at the child's parent's marginal tax rate. § 1(i).

—L—

Leaseback. A transaction in which a taxpayer sells property and then leases back the property.

Lessee. A person or entity who rents or leases property from another.

Lessor. A person or entity who rents or leases property to another.

Life Estate. A trust or legal arrangement by which a certain person (life tenant) is entitled to receive the income from designated property for his or her life.

Life Insurance. A form of insurance which will pay the beneficiary of the policy a fixed amount upon the death of the insured person.

LIFO (Last-in, First-out). A method of determining the cost of an inventory. The last inventory units acquired are considered to be the first sold. Therefore, the cost of the inventory would consist of the earliest acquired inventory.

Like-Kind Exchange. The exchange of property held for productive use in a trade or business or for investment (but not inventory, stock, bonds, or notes) for property that is also held for productive use or for investment (i.e., realty for realty; personalty for personalty). No gain or loss is generally recognized by either party unless boot (other than qualifying property) is involved in the transaction. § 1031.

Limited Liability. The situation in which the liability of an owner in an organization for the organization's debts is limited to the owner's investment in the organization. Examples of taxpayers which have limited liability are corporate shareholders and the limited partners in a limited partnership.

Limited Partner. A partner whose liability for partnership debts is limited to his or her investment in the partnership. A limited partner may take no active part in the management of the partnership according to the Uniform Limited Partnership Act (*see* General Partner).

Limited Partnership. A partnership with *one* or more general partners *and* one or more limited partners. The limited partners are liable only up to the amount of their contribution plus any personally guaranteed debt. Limited partners cannot participate in the management or control of the partnership.

Liquidation. The cessation of all or part of a corporation's operations or the corporate form of business and the distribution of the corporate assets to the shareholders. §§ 331–337.

Lump Sum Distribution. Payment at one time of an entire amount due, or the entire proceeds of a pension or profit-sharing plan, rather than installments payments.

—M—

Majority. Of legal age (*see* Minor).

Marital Deduction. Upon the transfer of property from one spouse to another, either by gift or at death, the Internal Revenue Code allows a transfer tax deduction for the amount transferred.

Market Value. (*see* Fair Market Value).

Material Participation. Occurs when a taxpayer is involved in the operations of an activity on a regular, continuous, and substantial basis. § 469(h).

Mid-Month Convention. When using ACRS, realty placed in service at any time during a month is treated as placed in service in the middle of the month, and realty disposed of or retired at any time during a month is treated as disposed of in the middle of the month. § 168(d)(4)(B).

Mid-Quarter Convention. Use for all personalty placed in service during the year if more than 40 percent of all personalty placed in service during the year is placed in service during the last three months of the year. § 168(d)(4)(C).

Merger. The absorption of one corporation (target corporation) by another corporation (acquiring corporation). The target corporation transfers its assets to the acquiring corporation in return for stock or securities of the acquiring corporation. Then the target corporation dissolves by exchanging the acquiring corporation's stock for its own stock held by its shareholders.

Minimum Tax. (*see* Alternative Minimum Tax).

Minor. A person who has not yet reached the age of legal majority. In most states, a minor is a person under 18 years of age.

Mortgagee.   The person or entity that holds the mortgage; the lender; the creditor.

Mortgagor.   The person or entity that is mortgaging the property; the debtor.

—N—

NA.   (*see* Nonacquiescence).

Negligence Penalty.   An accuracy-related penalty imposed by the IRS on taxpayers who are negligent or disregard the rules or regulations (but are not fraudulent), in the determination of their tax liability. § 6662.

Net Operating Loss (NOL).   The amount by which deductions exceed a taxpayer's gross income. § 172.

Net Worth Method.   An indirect method of determining a taxpayer's income used by the IRS when adequate records do not exist. The net worth of the taxpayer is determined for the end of each year in question and adjustments are made to the increase in net worth from year to year for nontaxable sources of income and nondeductible expenditures. This method is often used when a possibility of fraud exists.

Ninety-day Letter.   (*see* Statutory Notice of Deficiency).

Nonacquiescence.   The public announcement that the Commissioner of the Internal Revenue Service disagrees with a regular Tax Court decision. When the Commissioner nonacquiesces to a regular Tax Court decision, the IRS generally will litigate cases involving similar facts (*see also* Acquiescence).

Nonresident Alien.   A person who is not a resident or a citizen of the United States.

—O—

Office Audit.   An audit conducted by the Internal Revenue Service on IRS premises. The person conducting the audit is generally referred to as an Office Auditor (*see also* Correspondence Audit and Field Audit).

Office Auditor.   An IRS employee who conducts primarily office audits, as opposed to a Revenue Agent, who conducts primarily field audits (*see also* Revenue Agent).

Ordinary Gross Income.   A term used in relation to personal holding companies. Ordinary gross income is determined by subtracting capital gains and § 1231 gains from gross income. § 543(b)(1).

—P—

Partial Liquidation.   A distribution which is not essentially equivalent to a dividend, or a distribution which is attributable to the termination one of two or more businesses (which have been active businesses for at least five years). § 302(e).

Partner.   (*see* General Partner and Limited Partner).

Partnership. A syndicate, group, pool, joint venture, or other unincorporated organization, through or by means of which any business, financial operation, or venture is carried on, and which is not a trust, estate, or corporation. §§ 761(a) and 7701(a)(2).

Passive Activity. Any activity which involves the conduct of any trade or business in which the taxpayer does not materially participate. Losses from passive activities generally are deductible only to the extent of passive activity income. § 469.

Passive Investment Income. A term used in relation to S corporations. Passive investment income is generally defined as gross receipts derived from royalties, rents, dividends, interest, annuities, and gains on sales or exchanges of stock or securities. § 1362(d)(3)(D).

Pecuniary Bequest. Monetary bequest (*see also* Bequest).

Percentage Depletion. (*see* Depletion).

Percentage of Completion Method of Accounting. A method of accounting which may be used on certain long-item contracts in which the income is reported as the contract reaches various stages of completion.

Personal Holding Company. A corporation in which five or fewer individuals owned more than 50 percent of the value of its stock at any time during the last half of the taxable year and at least 60 percent of the corporation's adjusted ordinary gross income consists of personal holding company income. § 542.

Personal Property. All property that is not realty; Personalty. This term is also often used to mean personal use property (*see also* Personal Use Property and Personalty).

Personal Use Property. Any property used for personal, rather than business purposes. Distinguished from "personal property."

Personalty. All property that is not realty (e.g., automobiles, trucks, machinery and equipment).

P.H. (*see* Prentice Hall).

Portfolio Income. Interest and dividends. Portfolio income, plus annuities and royalties, are not considered to be income from a passive activity for purposes of the passive activity loss limitations. § 469(e).

Power of Appointment. A right to dispose of property that the holder of the power does not legally own.

Preferred Stock Bailout. A scheme by which shareholders receive a nontaxable preferred stock dividend, sell this preferred stock to a third party, and report the gain as a long-item capital gain. This scheme, therefore, converts what would be ordinary dividend income to capital gain. Section 306 was created to prohibit use of this scheme.

Prentice Hall. A publisher of tax materials, including a multi-volume tax service and volumes which contain the Federal courts' decisions on tax matters (AFTR, AFTR2d.).

Present Interest. An interest in which the donee has the present right to use, possess, or enjoy the donated property. The annual exclusion is available for gifts of present interests, but not for gifts of future interests (*see also* Future Interest).

Previously Taxed Income (PTI). A term used to refer to the accumulated earnings and profits for the period that a Subchapter S election was in effect prior to 1983. Distributions from PTI are not taxable to the shareholders.

Private Letter Ruling. A written statement from the IRS to a taxpayer in response to a request by the taxpayer for the tax consequences of a specific set of facts. The taxpayer who receives the Private Letter Ruling is the only taxpayer that may rely on that specific ruling in case of litigation.

Probate. The court-directed administration of a decedent's estate.

Prop. Reg. (Proposed Regulation). Treasury (IRS) Regulations are generally issued first in a proposed form in order to obtain input from various sources before the regulations are changed (if necessary) and issued in final form.

Pro Rata. Proportionately.

—Q—

Qualified Pension or Profit-Sharing Plan. A pension or profit-sharing plan sponsored by an employer that meets the requirements set forth by Congress in Code § 401. §§ 401-404.

Qualified Terminable Interest Property (QTIP). Property which passes from the decedent in which the surviving spouse has a qualifying income interest for life. An election to treat the property as qualified terminable interest property has been made. § 2056(b).

—R—

RAR. (*see* Revenue Agent's Report).

Real Property. (*see* Realty).

Realized Gain or Loss. The difference between the amount realized from the sale or other disposition of an asset and the adjusted basis of the asset. § 1001.

Realty. Real estate; land, including any objects attached thereto which are not readily movable (e.g., buildings, sidewalks, trees, and fences).

Reasonable Needs of the Business. In relation to the accumulated earnings tax, a corporation may accumulate sufficient earnings and profits to meet its reasonable business needs. Examples of reasonable needs of the business include working capital needs, amounts needed for bona fide business expansion, and amounts needed for redemptions for death taxes. § 537.

Recapture. The recovery of the tax benefit from a previously taken deduction or credit. The recapture of a deduction results in its inclusion in income, and the recapture of a credit results in its inclusion in tax (*see also* Depreciation Recapture and Investment Credit Recapture).

Recognized Gain or Loss.   The amount of the realized gain or loss that is subject to income tax. § 1001.

Redemption.   The acquisition by a corporation of its own stock from a shareholder in exchange for property. § 317(b).

Reg. (Regulation—Treasury Department Regulation).   (*see also* Regulations).

Regulations (Treasury Department Regulations).   Interpretations of the Internal Revenue Code by the Internal Revenue Service.

Related Party.   A person or entity that is related to another under the various code provisions for constructive ownership. §§ 267, 318 and 544(a).

Remainder Interest.   Property that passes to a remainderman after the life estate or other income interest expires on the property.

Remainderman.   The person entitled to the remainder interest.

Remand.   The sending back of a case by an appellate court to a lower court for further action by the lower court. The abbreviation for "remanding" is "rem'g."

Reorganization.   The combination, division, or restructuring of a corporation or corporations.

Resident Alien.   A person who is not a citizen of the United States, who is a resident of the United States, or who meets the substantial presence test. § 7701(b).

Revenue Agent.   An employee of the Internal Revenue Service who performs primarily field audits.

Revenue Agent's Report (RAR).   The report issued by a Revenue Agent in which adjustments to a taxpayer's tax liability are proposed. (IRS Form 4549; Form 1902 is used for office audits.)

Revenue Officer.   An employee of the Internal Revenue Service whose primary duty is the collection of Tax. (As opposed to a Revenue Agent who audits returns.)

Revenue Procedure.   A procedure published by the Internal Revenue Service outlining various processes and methods of handling various matters of tax practice and administration. Revenue Procedures are published first in the Internal Revenue Bulletin and then compiled annually in the Cumulative Bulletin.

Revenue Ruling.   A published interpretation by the Internal Revenue Service of the tax law as applied to specific situations. Revenue Rulings are published first in the Internal Revenue Bulletin and then compiled annually in the Cumulative Bulletin.

Reversed (Rev'd.).   The reverse of a lower court's decision by a higher court.

Reversing (Rev'g.).   The reversing of a lower court's decision by a higher court.

Revocable Transfer.   A transfer which may be revoked by the transferor. In other words, the transferor keeps the right to recover the transferred property.

Rev. Proc. (*see* Revenue Procedure).

Rev. Rul. (*see* Revenue Ruling).

Right of Survivorship. (*see* Joint Tenancy).

Royalty. Compensation for the use of property, such as natural resources or copyrighted material.

—S—

S Corporation. A corporation which qualifies as a small business corporation and elects to have §§ 1361-1379 apply. Once a Subchapter S election is made, the corporation is treated similar to a partnership for tax purposes. An S corporation uses Form 1120S to report its income and expenses. (*see* C Corporation).

Section 38 Property. Property subject to the investment tax credit (*see also* Investment Tax Credit).

Section 751 Assets. Unrealized receivables and appreciated inventory items of a partnership. A disproportionate distribution of § 751 assets generally results in taxable income to the partners.

Section 1231 Property. Depreciable property and real estate used in a trade or business held for more than one year. Section 1231 Property may also include timber, coal, domestic iron ore, livestock, and unharvested crops.

Section 1244 Stock. Stock of a small business corporation issued pursuant to § 1244. A loss on § 1244 stock is treated as an ordinary loss (rather than a capital loss) within limitations. § 1244.

Section 1245 Property. Property which is subject to depreciation recapture under § 1245.

Section 1250 Property. Property which is subject to depreciation recapture under § 1250.

Securities. Evidences of debt or of property, such as stock, bonds, and notes.

Separate Property. Property that belongs separately to only one spouse (as contrasted with community property in a community property state). In a community property state, a spouse's separate property generally includes property acquired by the spouse prior to marriage, or property acquired after marriage by gift or inheritance.

Severance Tax. At the time they are severed or removed from the earth, a tax on minerals or timber.

Sham Transaction. A transaction with no substance or bona fide business purpose that may be ignored for tax purposes.

Simple Trust. A trust that is required to distribute all of its income currently and does not pay, set aside, or use any funds for charitable purposes. § 651(a).

Small Business Corporation.   There are two separate definitions of a small business corporation, one relating to S corporations, and one relating to § 1244. If small business corporation status is met under § 1361(b), then a corporation may elect Subchapter S. If small business corporation status is met under § 1244(c)(3), then losses on § 1244 stock may be deducted as ordinary (rather than capital) losses, within limitations.

Special Use Valuation.   A special method for valuing real estate for estate tax purposes. The special use valuation allows that qualifying real estate used in a closely held business may be valued based on its business usage rather than market value. § 2032A.

Specific Bequest.   A bequest made by a testator in his or her will giving an heir a particular piece of property or money.

Spin-off.   A type of divisive corporate reorganization in which the original corporation transfers some of its assets to a newly formed subsidiary in exchange for all of the subsidiary's stock which it then distributes to its shareholders. The shareholders of the original corporation do not surrender any of their ownership in the original corporation for the subsidiary's stock.

Split-off.   A type of divisive corporate reorganization in which the original corporation transfers some of its assets to a newly formed subsidiary in exchange for all of the subidiary's stock which it then distributes to some or all of its shareholders in exchange for some portion of their stock.

Split-up.   A type of divisive corporate reorganization in which the original corporation transfers some of its assets to one newly created subsidiary and the remainder of the assets to another newly created subsidiary. The original corporation then liquidates, distributing the stock of both subsidiaries in exchange for its own stock.

Standard Deduction.   A deduction that is available to most individual taxpayers. The standard deduction or total itemized deductions, whichever is larger, is subtracted in computing taxable income. §§ 63(c) and (f).

Statute of Limitations.   Law provisions which limit the period of time in which action may be taken after an event occurs. The limitations on the IRS for assessments and collections are included in §§ 6501-6504, and the limitations on taxpayers for credits or refunds are included in §§ 6511-6515.

Statutory Depletion.   (*see* Depletion).

Stock Option.   A right to purchase a specified amount of stock for a specified price at a given time or times.

Subchapter S.   Sections 1361-1379 of the Internal Revenue Code (*see also* S Corporation).

Substance vs. Form.   The essence of a transaction as opposed to the structure or form that the transaction takes. For example, a transaction may formally meet the requirements for a specific type of tax treatment, but if what the transaction is actually accomplishing is different from the form of the transaction, the form may be ignored.

Surtax. An additional tax imposed on corporations with taxable income in excess of $100,000. The surtax is 5 percent of the corporation's taxable income in excess of $100,000 up to a maximum surtax of $11,750. § 11(b).

—T—

Tangible Property. Property which may be touched (e.g., machinery, automobile, desk) as opposed to intangibles which may not be touched (e.g., goodwill, copyrights, patents).

Tax Avoidance. Using the tax laws to avoid paying taxes or to reduce one's tax liability (*see also* Tax Evasion).

Tax Benefit Rule. The doctrine by which the amount of income that a taxpayer must include in income when the taxpayer has recovered an amount previously deducted is limited to the amount of the previous deduction which produced a tax benefit.

Tax Court (United States Tax Court). One of the three trial courts which hears cases dealing with Federal tax matters. A taxpayer need not pay his or her tax deficiency in advance if he or she decides to litigate the case in Tax Court (as opposed to the District Court or Claims Court).

Tax Credits. An amount that is deducted directly from a taxpayer's tax liability, as opposed to a deduction which reduces taxable income.

Tax Evasion. The illegal evasion of the tax laws. § 7201 (*see also* Tax Avoidance).

Tax Preference Items. Those items specifically designated in § 57 which may be subject to a special tax on tax preference items (*see also* Alternative Minimum Tax).

Tax Shelter. A device or scheme used by taxpayers either to reduce taxes or defer the payment of taxes.

Taxable Estate. Gross estate reduced by the expenses, indebtedness, taxes, losses, and charitable contributions of the estate, and by the marital deduction. § 2051.

Taxable Gifts. The total amount of gifts made during the calendar year, reduced by charitable gifts and the marital deduction. § 2503.

T.C. (Tax Court: United States Tax Court). This abbreviation is also used to cite the Tax Court's Regular Decisions (*see also* Tax Court and T.C. Memo).

T.C. Memo. The term used to cite the Tax Court's Memorandum Decisions (*see also* Tax Court and T.C.).

Tenancy by the Entirety. A form of ownership between a husband and wife where each has an undivided interest in the property, with the right of survivorship.

Tenancy in Common. A form of joint ownership where each owner has an undivided interest in the property, with no right of survivorship.

Testator. A person who makes or has made a will; one who dies and has left a will.

Thin Corporation.   A corporation in which the amount of debt owed by the corporation is high in relationship to the amount of equity in the corporation. § 385.

Treasury Regulations.   (*see* Regulations).

Trial Court.   The first court to consider a case, as opposed to an appellate court.

Trust.   A right in property that is held by one person or entity for the benefit of another. §§ 641-683.

—U—

Unearned Income.   Income that is not earned or is not yet earned. The term is used to refer to both prepaid (not yet earned) income and to passive (not earned) income.

Unearned Income of a Minor Child.   (*see* "Kiddie" tax).

Unified Transfer Tax.   The Federal tax that applies to both estates and gifts after 1976.

Unified Transfer Tax Credit.   A credit against the unified transfer tax which allows a taxpayer to make a certain amount of gifts and/or have a certain size estate without incurring any Federal estate or gift tax.

Uniform Gift to Minors Act.   An Act that provides a way to transfer property to minors. A custodian manages the property on behalf of the minor, and the custodianship terminates when the minor achieves majority.

USSC (U.S. Supreme Court).   This abbreviation is used to cite U.S. Supreme Court cases.

U.S. Tax Court.   (*see* Tax Court).

USTC (U.S. Tax Cases).   Published by Commerce Clearing House. These volumes contain all the Federal tax related decisions of the U.S. District Courts, the U.S. Claims Court, the U.S. Courts of Appeals, and the U.S. Supreme Court.

—V—

Valuation.   (*see* Fair Market Value).

Vested.   Fixed or settled; having the right to absolute ownership, even if ownership will not come into being until some time in the future.

Appendix **H**

MODIFIED ACRS AND ORIGINAL ACRS TABLES

MODIFIED ACRS TABLES

ORIGINAL ACRS TABLES

Modified ACRS Accelerated Depreciation Percentages
Using the Half-Year Convention
for 3-, 5-, 7-, 10-, 15-, and 20-Year Property
Placed in Service after December 31, 1986

Recovery Year	Property Class					
	3-Year	*5-Year*	*7-Year*	*10-Year*	*15-Year*	*20-Year*
1	33.33	20.00	14.29	10.00	5.00	3.750
2	44.45	32.00	24.49	18.00	9.50	7.219
3	14.81	19.20	17.49	14.40	8.55	6.677
4	7.41	11.52	12.49	11.52	7.70	6.177
5		11.52	8.93	9.22	6.93	5.713
6		5.76	8.92	7.37	6.23	5.285
7			8.93	6.55	5.90	4.888
8			4.46	6.55	5.90	4.522
9				6.56	5.91	4.462
10				6.55	5.90	4.461
11				3.28	5.91	4.462
12					5.90	4.461
13					5.91	4.462
14					5.90	4.461
15					5.91	4.462
16					2.95	4.461
17						4.462
18						4.461
19						4.462
20						4.461
21						2.231

Source: Rev. Proc. 87-57, Table 1.

Modified ACRS Depreciation Rates
for Residential Real Property
Placed in Service after December 31, 1986

Recovery Year	Month Placed in Service					
	1	2	3	4	5	6
1	3.485	3.182	2.879	2.576	2.273	1.970
2	3.636	3.636	3.636	3.636	3.636	3.636
3	3.636	3.636	3.636	3.636	3.636	3.636
4	3.636	3.636	3.636	3.636	3.636	3.636
5	3.636	3.636	3.636	3.636	3.636	3.636
6	3.636	3.636	3.636	3.636	3.636	3.636
7	3.636	3.636	3.636	3.636	3.636	3.636
8	3.636	3.636	3.636	3.636	3.636	3.636
9	3.636	3.636	3.636	3.636	3.636	3.636
10	3.637	3.637	3.637	3.637	3.637	3.637
11	3.636	3.636	3.636	3.636	3.636	3.636
12	3.637	3.637	3.637	3.637	3.637	3.637
13	3.636	3.636	3.636	3.636	3.636	3.636
14	3.637	3.637	3.637	3.637	3.637	3.637
15	3.636	3.636	3.636	3.636	3.636	3.636
16	3.637	3.637	3.637	3.637	3.637	3.637
17	3.636	3.636	3.636	3.636	3.636	3.636
18	3.637	3.637	3.637	3.637	3.637	3.637
19	3.636	3.636	3.636	3.636	3.636	3.636
20	3.637	3.637	3.637	3.637	3.637	3.636
21	3.636	3.636	3.636	3.636	3.636	3.636
22	3.637	3.637	3.637	3.637	3.637	3.637
23	3.636	3.636	3.636	3.636	3.636	3.636
24	3.637	3.637	3.637	3.637	3.637	3.637
25	3.636	3.636	3.636	3.636	3.636	3.636
26	3.637	3.637	3.637	3.637	3.637	3.637
27	3.636	3.636	3.636	3.636	3.636	3.636
28	1.970	2.273	2.576	2.879	3.182	3.485
29	0.000	0.000	0.000	0.000	0.000	0.000

Recovery	Month Placed in Service					
Year	7	8	9	10	11	12
1	1.667	1.364	1.061	0.758	0.455	0.152
2	3.636	3.636	3.636	3.636	3.636	3.636
3	3.636	3.636	3.636	3.636	3.636	3.636
4	3.636	3.636	3.636	3.636	3.636	3.636
5	3.636	3.636	3.636	3.636	3.636	3.636
6	3.636	3.636	3.636	3.636	3.636	3.636
7	3.636	3.636	3.636	3.636	3.636	3.636
8	3.636	3.636	3.636	3.636	3.636	3.636
9	3.636	3.636	3.636	3.636	3.636	3.636
10	3.636	3.636	3.636	3.636	3.636	3.636
11	3.637	3.637	3.637	3.637	3.637	3.637
12	3.636	3.636	3.636	3.636	3.636	3.636
13	3.637	3.637	3.637	3.637	3.637	3.637
14	3.636	3.636	3.636	3.636	3.636	3.636
15	3.637	3.637	3.637	3.637	3.637	3.637
16	3.636	3.636	3.636	3.636	3.636	3.636
17	3.637	3.637	3.637	3.637	3.637	3.637
18	3.636	3.636	3.636	3.636	3.636	3.636
19	3.637	3.637	3.637	3.637	3.637	3.637
20	3.636	3.636	3.636	3.636	3.636	3.636
21	3.637	3.637	3.637	3.637	3.637	3.637
22	3.636	3.636	3.636	3.636	3.636	3.636
23	3.637	3.637	3.637	3.637	3.637	3.637
24	3.636	3.636	3.636	3.636	3.636	3.636
25	3.637	3.637	3.637	3.637	3.637	3.637
26	3.636	3.636	3.636	3.636	3.636	3.636
27	3.637	3.637	3.637	3.637	3.637	3.637
28	3.636	3.636	3.636	3.636	3.636	3.636
29	0.152	0.455	0.758	1.061	1.364	1.667

Source: Rev. Proc. 87-57, Table 7.

Modified ACRS Depreciation Percentages
for Nonresidential Real Property
Placed in Service after December 31, 1986

Recovery Year	Month Placed in Service					
	1	*2*	*3*	*4*	*5*	*6*
1	3.042	2.778	2.513	2.249	1.984	1.720
2	3.175	3.175	3.175	3.175	3.175	3.175
3	3.175	3.175	3.175	3.175	3.175	3.175
4	3.175	3.175	3.175	3.175	3.175	3.175
5	3.175	3.175	3.175	3.175	3.175	3.175
6	3.175	3.175	3.175	3.175	3.175	3.175
7	3.175	3.175	3.175	3.175	3.175	3.175
8	3.175	3.174	3.175	3.174	3.175	3.174
9	3.174	3.175	3.174	3.175	3.174	3.175
10	3.175	3.174	3.175	3.174	3.175	3.174
11	3.174	3.175	3.174	3.175	3.174	3.175
12	3.175	3.174	3.175	3.174	3.175	3.174
13	3.174	3.175	3.174	3.175	3.174	3.175
14	3.175	3.174	3.175	3.174	3.175	3.174
15	3.174	3.175	3.174	3.175	3.174	3.175
16	3.175	3.174	3.175	3.174	3.175	3.174
17	3.174	3.175	3.174	3.175	3.174	3.175
18	3.175	3.174	3.175	3.174	3.175	3.174
19	3.174	3.175	3.174	3.175	3.174	3.175
20	3.175	3.174	3.175	3.174	3.175	3.174
21	3.174	3.175	3.174	3.175	3.174	3.175
22	3.175	3.174	3.175	3.174	3.175	3.174
23	3.174	3.175	3.174	3.175	3.174	3.175
24	3.175	3.174	3.175	3.174	3.175	3.174
25	3.174	3.175	3.174	3.175	3.174	3.175
26	3.175	3.174	3.175	3.174	3.175	3.174
27	3.174	3.175	3.174	3.175	3.174	3.175
28	3.175	3.174	3.175	3.174	3.175	3.174
29	3.174	3.175	3.174	3.175	3.174	3.175
30	3.175	3.174	3.175	3.174	3.175	3.174
31	3.174	3.175	3.174	3.175	3.174	3.175
32	1.720	1.984	2.249	2.513	2.778	3.042
33	0.000	0.000	0.000	0.000	0.000	0.000

Recovery Year	Month Placed in Service					
	7	8	9	10	11	12
1	1.455	1.190	0.926	0.661	0.397	0.132
2	3.175	3.175	3.175	3.175	3.175	3.175
3	3.175	3.175	3.175	3.175	3.175	3.175
4	3.175	3.175	3.175	3.175	3.175	3.175
5	3.175	3.175	3.175	3.175	3.175	3.175
6	3.175	3.175	3.175	3.175	3.175	3.175
7	3.175	3.175	3.175	3.175	3.175	3.175
8	3.175	3.175	3.175	3.175	3.175	3.175
9	3.174	3.175	3.175	3.175	3.174	3.175
10	3.175	3.174	3.175	3.174	3.175	3.174
11	3.174	3.175	3.174	3.175	3.174	3.175
12	3.175	3.174	3.175	3.174	3.175	3.174
13	3.174	3.175	3.174	3.175	3.174	3.175
14	3.175	3.174	3.175	3.174	3.175	3.174
15	3.174	3.175	3.174	3.175	3.174	3.175
16	3.175	3.174	3.175	3.174	3.175	3.174
17	3.174	3.175	3.174	3.175	3.174	3.175
18	3.175	3.174	3.175	3.174	3.175	3.174
19	3.174	3.175	3.174	3.175	3.174	3.175
20	3.175	3.174	3.175	3.174	3.175	3.174
21	3.174	3.175	3.174	3.175	3.174	3.175
22	3.175	3.174	3.175	3.174	3.175	3.174
23	3.174	3.175	3.174	3.175	3.174	3.175
24	3.175	3.174	3.175	3.174	3.175	3.174
25	3.174	3.175	3.174	3.175	3.174	3.175
26	3.175	3.174	3.175	3.174	3.175	3.174
27	3.174	3.175	3.174	3.175	3.174	3.175
28	3.175	3.174	3.175	3.174	3.175	3.174
29	3.174	3.175	3.174	3.175	3.174	3.175
30	3.175	3.174	3.175	3.174	3.175	3.174
31	3.174	3.175	3.174	3.175	3.174	3.175
32	3.175	3.174	3.175	3.174	3.175	3.174
33	0.132	0.397	0.661	0.926	1.190	1.455

Source: Rev. Proc. 87-57, Table 7.

Modified ACRS Accelerated Depreciation Percentages
Using the Mid-Month Convention
for 3-, 5-, 7-, 10-, 15-, and 20-Year Property
Placed in Service after December 31, 1986

3-Year Property:

Recovery Year	Quarter Placed in Service			
	1	2	3	4
1	58.33	41.67	25.00	8.33
2	27.78	38.89	50.00	61.11
3	12.35	14.14	16.67	20.37
4	1.54	5.30	8.33	10.19

5-Year Property:

	1	2	3	4
1	35.00	25.00	15.00	5.00
2	26.00	30.00	34.00	38.00
3	15.60	18.00	20.40	22.80
4	11.01	11.37	12.24	13.68
5	11.01	11.37	11.30	10.94
6	1.38	4.26	7.06	9.58

7-Year Property:

	1	2	3	4
1	25.00	17.85	10.71	3.57
2	21.43	23.47	25.51	27.55
3	15.31	16.76	18.22	19.68
4	10.93	11.37	13.02	14.06
5	8.75	8.87	9.30	10.04
6	8.74	8.87	8.85	8.73
7	8.75	8.87	8.86	8.73
8	1.09	3.33	5.53	7.64

10-Year Property:

	1	2	3	4
1	17.50	12.50	7.50	2.50
2	16.50	17.50	18.50	19.50
3	13.20	14.00	14.80	15.60
4	10.56	11.20	11.84	12.48
5	8.45	8.96	9.47	9.98
6	6.76	7.17	7.58	7.99
7	6.55	6.55	6.55	6.55
8	6.55	6.55	6.55	6.55
9	6.56	6.56	6.56	6.56
10	0.82	6.55	6.55	6.55
11		2.46	4.10	5.74

Recovery	Quarter Placed in Service			
Year	1	2	3	4

15-Year Property:

1	8.75	6.25	3.75	1.25
2	9.13	9.38	9.63	9.88
3	8.21	8.44	8.66	8.89
4	7.39	7.59	7.80	8.00
5	6.65	6.83	7.02	7.20
6	5.99	6.15	6.31	6.48
7	5.90	5.91	5.90	5.90
8	5.91	5.90	5.90	5.90
9	5.90	5.91	5.91	5.90
10	5.91	5.90	5.90	5.91
11	5.90	5.91	5.91	5.90
12	5.91	5.90	5.90	5.91
13	5.90	5.91	5.91	5.90
14	5.91	5.90	5.90	5.91
15	5.90	5.91	5.91	5.90
16	.74	2.21	3.69	5.17

20-Year Property:

1	6.563	4.688	2.813	0.938
2	7.000	7.148	7.289	7.430
3	6.482	6.612	6.742	6.872
4	5.996	6.116	6.237	6.357
5	5.546	5.658	5.769	5.880
6	5.130	5.233	5.336	5.439
7	4.746	4.841	4.936	5.031
8	4.459	4.478	4.566	4.654
9	4.459	4.463	4.460	4.458
10	4.459	4.463	4.460	4.458
11	4.459	4.463	4.460	4.458
12	4.460	4.463	4.460	4.458
13	4.459	4.463	4.461	4.458
14	4.460	4.463	4.460	4.458
15	4.459	4.462	4.461	4.458
16	4.460	4.463	4.460	4.458
17	4.459	4.462	4.461	4.458
18	4.460	4.463	4.460	4.459
19	4.459	4.462	4.461	4.458
20	4.460	4.463	4.460	4.459
21	.557	1.673	2.788	3.901

Source: Rev. Proc. 87-57.

Alternative Depreciation System
Recovery Periods

General Rule: Recovery period is the property's class life unless:

1. There is no class life (see below), or
2. A special class life has been designated (see below).

Type of Property	*Recovery Period*
Personal property with no class life	12 years
Nonresidential real property with no class life	40 years
Residential rental property with no class life	40 years
Cars, light general purpose trucks, certain technological equipment, and semiconductor manufacturing equipment	5 years
Computer-based telephone central office switching equipment	9.5 years
Railroad track	10 years
Single purpose agricultural or horticultural structures	15 years
Municipal waste water treatment plants, telephone distribution plants	24 years
Low-income housing financed by tax-exempt bonds	27.5 years
Municipal sewers	50 years

Modified ACRS and ADS Straight-Line Depreciation Percentages
Using the Half-Year Convention
for 3-, 5-, 7-, 10-, 15-, and 20-Year Property
Placed in Service after December 31, 1986

Recovery Year	Property Class					
	3-Year	5-Year	7-Year	10-Year	15-Year	20-Year
1	16.67	10.00	7.14	5.00	3.33	2.50
2	33.33	20.00	14.29	10.00	6.67	5.00
3	33.33	20.00	14.29	10.00	6.67	5.00
4	16.67	20.00	14.28	10.00	6.67	5.00
5		20.00	14.29	10.00	6.67	5.00
6		10.00	14.28	10.00	6.67	5.00
7			14.29	10.00	6.67	5.00
8			7.14	10.00	6.66	5.00
9				10.00	6.67	5.00
10				10.00	6.66	5.00
11				5.00	6.67	5.00
12					6.66	5.00
13					6.67	5.00
14					6.66	5.00
15					6.67	5.00
16					3.33	5.00
17						5.00
18						5.00
19						5.00
20						5.00
21						2.50

Source: Rev. Proc. 87-57.

ADS Straight-Line Depreciation Percentages
Real Property
Using the Mid-Month Convention
for Property Placed in Service after December 31, 1986

Month Placed In Service	Recovery Year		
	1	2-40	41
1	2.396	2.500	0.104
2	2.188	2.500	0.312
3	1.979	2.500	0.521
4	1.771	2.500	0.729
5	1.563	2.500	0.937
6	1.354	2.500	1.146
7	1.146	2.500	1.354
8	0.938	2.500	1.562
9	0.729	2.500	1.771
10	0.521	2.500	1.979
11	0.313	2.500	2.187
12	0.104	2.500	2.396

Source: Rev. Proc. 87-57, Table 13.

Original ACRS
Accelerated Recovery Percentages
for 3-, 5-, 10-, and 15-Year Public Utility Property

Personalty Placed in Service after 1980 and before 1987

Recovery Year	Property Class			
	3-Year	5-Year	10-Year	15-Year Public Utility
1	25%	15%	8%	5%
2	38	22	14	10
3	37	21	12	9
4		21	10	8
5		21	10	7
6			10	7
7			9	6
8			9	6
9			9	6
10			9	6
11				6
12				6
13				6
14				6
15				6

Original ACRS
Accelerated Recovery Percentages
for 15-Year Realty

Placed in Service after 1980 and before March 16, 1984

Recovery Year	Month Placed in Service											
	1	2	3	4	5	6	7	8	9	10	11	12
1	12	11	10	9	8	7	6	5	4	3	2	1
2	10	10	11	11	11	11	11	11	11	11	11	12
3	9	9	9	9	10	10	10	10	10	10	10	10
4	8	8	8	8	8	8	9	9	9	9	9	9
5	7	7	7	7	7	7	8	8	8	8	8	8
6	6	6	6	6	7	7	7	7	7	7	7	7
7	6	6	6	6	6	6	6	6	6	6	6	6
8	6	6	6	6	6	6	5	6	6	6	6	6
9	6	6	6	6	5	6	5	5	5	6	6	6
10	5	6	6	6	5	5	5	5	5	5	6	5
11	5	5	5	5	5	5	5	5	5	5	5	5
12	5	5	5	5	5	5	5	5	5	5	5	5
13	5	5	5	5	5	5	5	5	5	5	5	5
14	5	5	5	5	5	5	5	5	5	5	5	5
15	5	5	5	5	5	5	5	5	5	5	5	5
16			1	1	2	2	3	3	4	4	4	5

Original ACRS
Accelerated Recovery Percentages
for Low-Income Housing

Placed in Service after 1980 and before March 16, 1984

Recovery Year	Month Placed in Service											
	1	2	3	4	5	6	7	8	9	10	11	12
1	13	12	11	10	9	8	7	6	4	3	2	1
2	12	12	12	12	12	12	12	13	13	13	13	13
3	10	10	10	10	11	11	11	11	11	11	11	11
4	9	9	9	9	9	9	9	9	10	10	10	10
5	8	8	8	8	8	8	8	8	8	8	8	9
6	7	7	7	7	7	7	7	7	7	7	7	7
7	6	6	6	6	6	6	6	6	6	6	6	6
8	5	5	5	5	5	5	5	5	5	5	6	6
9	5	5	5	5	5	5	5	5	5	5	5	5
10	5	5	5	5	5	5	5	5	5	5	5	5
11	4	5	5	5	5	5	5	5	5	5	5	5
12	4	4	4	5	4	5	5	5	5	5	5	5
13	4	4	4	4	4	4	5	4	5	5	5	5
14	4	4	4	4	4	4	4	4	4	5	4	4
15	4	4	4	4	4	4	4	4	4	4	4	4
16			1	1	2	2	2	3	3	3	4	4

Original ACRS
Accelerated Recovery Percentages
for 18-Year Realty

Realty Placed in Service after March 15, 1984 and before May 9, 1985

Recovery Year	Month Placed in Service											
	1	2	3	4	5	6	7	8	9	10	11	12

The applicable percentage is:

	1	2	3	4	5	6	7	8	9	10	11	12
1	9	9	8	7	6	5	4	4	3	2	1	0.4
2	9	9	9	9	9	9	9	9	9	10	10	10.0
3	8	8	8	8	8	8	8	8	9	9	9	9.0
4	7	7	7	7	7	8	8	8	8	8	8	8.0
5	7	7	7	7	7	7	7	7	7	7	7	7.0
6	6	6	6	6	6	6	6	6	6	6	6	6.0
7	5	5	5	5	6	6	6	6	6	6	6	6.0
8	5	5	5	5	5	5	5	5	5	5	5	5.0
9	5	5	5	5	5	5	5	5	5	5	5	5.0
10	5	5	5	5	5	5	5	5	5	5	5	5.0
11	5	5	5	5	5	5	5	5	5	5	5	5.0
12	5	5	5	5	5	5	5	5	5	5	5	5.0
13	4	4	4	5	4	4	5	4	4	4	5	5.0
14	4	4	4	4	4	4	4	4	4	4	4	4.0
15	4	4	4	4	4	4	4	4	4	4	4	4.0
16	4	4	4	4	4	4	4	4	4	4	4	4.0
17	4	4	4	4	4	4	4	4	4	4	4	4.0
18	4	3	4	4	4	4	4	4	4	4	4	4.0
19		1	1	1	2	2	2	3	3	3	3	3.6

Original ACRS
Accelerated Cost Recovery Percentages
for 19-Year Real Property

Realty Placed in Service after May 8, 1985 and before 1987

Recovery Year	Month Placed in Service											
	1	2	3	4	5	6	7	8	9	10	11	12
The applicable percentage is:												
1	8.8	8.1	7.3	6.5	5.8	5.0	4.2	3.5	2.7	1.9	1.1	0.4
2	8.4	8.5	8.5	8.6	8.7	8.8	8.8	8.9	9.0	9.0	9.1	9.2
3	7.6	7.7	7.7	7.8	7.9	7.9	8.0	8.1	8.1	8.2	8.3	8.3
4	6.9	7.0	7.0	7.1	7.1	7.2	7.3	7.3	7.4	7.4	7.5	7.6
5	6.3	6.3	6.4	6.4	6.5	6.5	6.6	6.6	6.7	6.8	6.8	6.9
6	5.7	5.7	5.8	5.9	5.9	5.9	6.0	6.0	6.1	6.1	6.2	6.2
7	5.2	5.2	5.3	5.3	5.3	5.4	5.4	5.5	5.5	5.6	5.6	5.6
8	4.7	4.7	4.8	4.8	4.8	4.9	4.9	5.0	5.0	5.1	5.1	5.1
9	4.2	4.3	4.3	4.4	4.4	4.5	4.5	4.5	4.5	4.6	4.6	4.7
10	4.2	4.2	4.2	4.2	4.2	4.2	4.2	4.2	4.2	4.2	4.2	4.2
11	4.2	4.2	4.2	4.2	4.2	4.2	4.2	4.2	4.2	4.2	4.2	4.2
12	4.2	4.2	4.2	4.2	4.2	4.2	4.2	4.2	4.2	4.2	4.2	4.2
13	4.2	4.2	4.2	4.2	4.2	4.2	4.2	4.2	4.2	4.2	4.2	4.2
14	4.2	4.2	4.2	4.2	4.2	4.2	4.2	4.2	4.2	4.2	4.2	4.2
15	4.2	4.2	4.2	4.2	4.2	4.2	4.2	4.2	4.2	4.2	4.2	4.2
16	4.2	4.2	4.2	4.2	4.2	4.2	4.2	4.2	4.2	4.2	4.2	4.2
17	4.2	4.2	4.2	4.2	4.2	4.2	4.2	4.2	4.2	4.2	4.2	4.2
18	4.2	4.2	4.2	4.2	4.2	4.2	4.2	4.2	4.2	4.2	4.2	4.2
19	4.2	4.2	4.2	4.2	4.2	4.2	4.2	4.2	4.2	4.2	4.2	4.2
20	0.2	0.5	0.9	1.2	1.6	1.9	2.3	2.6	3.0	3.3	3.7	4.0

Original ACRS
Straight-Line Recovery Percentages
for 3-, 5-, 10-, and 15-Year Public Utility Property

Personalty Placed in Service before 1987

Recovery Year	Optional Recovery Period in Years							
	3	5	10	12	15	25	35	45
The applicable percentage is:								
1	17	10	5	4	3	2	1	1.1
2	33	20	10	9	7	4	3	2.3
3	33	20	10	9	7	4	3	2.3
4	17	20	10	9	7	4	3	2.3
5		20	10	9	7	4	3	2.3
6		10	10	8	7	4	3	2.3
7			10	8	7	4	3	2.3
8			10	8	7	4	3	2.3
9			10	8	7	4	3	2.3
10			10	8	7	4	3	2.3
11			5	8	7	4	3	2.3
12				8	6	4	3	2.2
13				4	6	4	3	2.2
14					6	4	3	2.2
15					6	4	3	2.2
16					3	4	3	2.2
17						4	3	2.2
18						4	3	2.2
19						4	3	2.2
20						4	3	2.2
21						4	3	2.2
22						4	3	2.2
23						4	3	2.2
24						4	3	2.2
25						4	3	2.2
26						2	3	2.2
27							3	2.2
28							3	2.2
29							3	2.2
30							3	2.2
31							3	2.2
32							2	2.2
33							2	2.2
34							2	2.2
35							2	2.2
36							1	2.2
37								2.2
38								2.2
39								2.2
40								2.2
41								2.2
42								2.2
43								2.2
44								2.2
45								2.2
46								1.1

Original ACRS
Straight-Line Recovery Percentages
for 18-Year Realty

Realty Placed in Service after March 15, 1984 and before May 9, 1985

Recovery Year	Month Placed in Service					
	1-2	3-4	5-7	8-9	10-11	12
	The applicable percentage is:					
1	5	4	3	2	1	0.2
2	6	6	6	6	6	6.0
3	6	6	6	6	6	6.0
4	6	6	6	6	6	6.0
5	6	6	6	6	6	6.0
6	6	6	6	6	6	6.0
7	6	6	6	6	6	6.0
8	6	6	6	6	6	6.0
9	6	6	6	6	6	6.0
10	6	6	6	6	6	6.0
11	5	5	5	5	5	5.8
12	5	5	5	5	5	5.0
13	5	5	5	5	5	5.0
14	5	5	5	5	5	5.0
15	5	5	5	5	5	5.0
16	5	5	5	5	5	5.0
17	5	5	5	5	5	5.0
18	5	5	5	5	5	5.0
19	1	2	3	4	5	5.0

Original ACRS
Straight-Line Recovery Percentages
for 19-Year Realty

Realty Placed in Service after May 8, 1985 and before 1987

Recovery Year	Month Placed in Service											
	1	2	3	4	5	6	7	8	9	10	11	12
The applicable percentage is:												
1	5.0	4.6	4.2	3.7	3.3	2.9	2.4	2.0	1.5	1.1	.7	.2
2	5.3	5.3	5.3	5.3	5.3	5.3	5.3	5.3	5.3	5.3	5.3	5.3
3	5.3	5.3	5.3	5.3	5.3	5.3	5.3	5.3	5.3	5.3	5.3	5.3
4	5.3	5.3	5.3	5.3	5.3	5.3	5.3	5.3	5.3	5.3	5.3	5.3
5	5.3	5.3	5.3	5.3	5.3	5.3	5.3	5.3	5.3	5.3	5.3	5.3
6	5.3	5.3	5.3	5.3	5.3	5.3	5.3	5.3	5.3	5.3	5.3	5.3
7	5.3	5.3	5.3	5.3	5.3	5.3	5.3	5.3	5.3	5.3	5.3	5.3
8	5.3	5.3	5.3	5.3	5.3	5.3	5.3	5.3	5.3	5.3	5.3	5.3
9	5.3	5.3	5.3	5.3	5.3	5.3	5.3	5.3	5.3	5.3	5.3	5.3
10	5.3	5.3	5.3	5.3	5.3	5.3	5.3	5.3	5.3	5.3	5.3	5.3
11	5.3	5.3	5.3	5.3	5.3	5.3	5.3	5.3	5.3	5.3	5.3	5.3
12	5.3	5.3	5.3	5.3	5.3	5.3	5.3	5.3	5.3	5.3	5.3	5.3
13	5.3	5.3	5.3	5.3	5.3	5.3	5.3	5.3	5.3	5.3	5.3	5.3
14	5.2	5.2	5.2	5.2	5.2	5.2	5.2	5.2	5.2	5.2	5.2	5.2
15	5.2	5.2	5.2	5.2	5.2	5.2	5.2	5.2	5.2	5.2	5.2	5.2
16	5.2	5.2	5.2	5.2	5.2	5.2	5.2	5.2	5.2	5.2	5.2	5.2
17	5.2	5.2	5.2	5.2	5.2	5.2	5.2	5.2	5.2	5.2	5.2	5.2
18	5.2	5.2	5.2	5.2	5.2	5.2	5.2	5.2	5.2	5.2	5.2	5.2
19	5.2	5.2	5.2	5.2	5.2	5.2	5.2	5.2	5.2	5.2	5.2	5.2
20	.2	.6	1.0	1.5	1.9	2.3	2.8	3.2	3.7	4.1	4.5	5.0

INDEX

— F —

— Q —

— T —

1991 Tax Rate Schedules for Individuals

Caution: The Internal Revenue Service has not yet issued its Tax Tables for 1991. In prior years, taxpayers were required to use the Tax Tables—instead of these Tax Rate Schedules—to compute their tax, if taxable income was less than $50,000.

Schedule X—Single

If taxable income is:		The tax is:	Of the amount over—
Over—	But not over—		
$ 0	$20,350	15%	$ 0
20,350	49,300	$ 3,052.50 + 28%	20,350
49,300	...	11,158.50 + 31%	49,300

Schedule Y-1—Married filing jointly or Qualifying widow(er)

If taxable income is:		The tax is:	Of the amount over—
Over—	But not over—		
$ 0	$34,000	15%	$ 0
34,000	82,150	$ 5,100.00 + 28%	34,000
82,150	...	18,582.00 + 31%	82,150

Schedule Y-2—Married filing separately

If taxable income is:		The tax is:	Of the amount over—
Over—	But not over—		
$ 0	$17,000	15%	$ 0
17,000	41,075	$ 2,550.00 + 28%	17,000
41,075	...	9,291.00 + 31%	41,075

Schedule Z—Head of household

If taxable income is:		The tax is:	Of the amount over—
Over—	But not over—		
$ 0	$27,300	15%	$ 0
27,300	70,450	$ 4,095.00 + 28%	27,300
70,450	...	16,177.00 + 31%	70,450